Visual C++™ Developer's Guide

Visual C++™ Developer's Guide

Nabajyoti Barkakati and Peter D. Hipson

A Division of Prentice Hall Computer Publishing
201 West 103rd Street, Indianapolis, IN 46290

This book is dedicated to:

My wife Leha, and daughters Ivy, Emily, and Ashley—Naba
My first grandson, Jerasak Mann Theplama—Peter

FIRST EDITION

International Standard Book Number: 0-672-30370-1

Library of Congress Catalog Card Number: 93-73967

96 95 94 4 3 2

Interpretation of the printing code: the rightmost double-digit number is the year of the book's printing; the rightmost single-digit, the number of the book's printing. For example, a printing code of 93-1 shows that the first printing of the book occurred in 1993.

Trademarks

Composed in AGaramond and MCPdigital by Prentice Hall Computer Publishing

Printed in the United States of America

Publisher
Richard K. Swadley

Associate Publisher
Jordan Gold

Acquisitions Manager
Stacy Hiquet

Managing Editor
Grant Fairchild

Acquisitions Editor
Greg Croy

Development Editor
Phillip W. Paxton

Production Editor
Sandy Doell

Copy Editors
Anne Clark
Mary Inderstrodt

Editorial Coordinator
Bill Whitmer

Editorial Assistants
Sharon Cox
Molly Carmody

Technical Reviewer
Bob Zigon

Marketing Manager
Greg Wiegand

Cover Designer
Katherine Hanley

Director of Production and Manufacturing
Jeff Valler

Imprint Manager
Kelli Widdifield

Book Designer
Michele Laseau

Production Analyst
Mary Beth Wakefield

Proofreading/Indexing Coordinator
Joelynn Gifford

Graphics Image Specialists
Teresa Forrester
Tim Montgomery
Dennis Sheehan
Susan Vandewalle

Production
Nick Anderson
Amanda Byus
Lisa Daugherty
Mitzi Foster Gianakos
Dennis Clay Hager
Carla Hall
Betty Kish
Linda Koopman
Sean Medlock
Mike Mucha
Juli Pavey
Angela M. Pozdol
Linda Quigley
Michelle M. Self
Tonya R. Simpson
Dennis Wesner
Donna Winter
Barbara Webster
Alyssa Yesh

Indexers
Jeanne Clark
Michael Hughes
Joy Dean Lee
Suzanne Snyder

Overview

Contents

Part III Learning C++

Part IV Applying OOP Techniques in C++

Part VIII Process Control and Memory Management Functions

Preface

Until recently, C was the language of choice for most programmers developing DOS applications or creating Windows programs. C has its limitations however, and recently C++ has begun to gain a large and loyal following as the successor to standard C programming. Much of C++'s popularity comes from its support of object-oriented programming (OOP), which has become the new wave in programming techniques. Because C++ was developed from C, most C++ compilers (including Visual C++) also compile C code—making the transition from C to C++ easier.

The combination of C++ and the Microsoft Foundation Class library (Version 2.0 is included with Visual C++) gives you a set of powerful tools to create applications for both the DOS environment and Windows. With OOP you are able to organize your code into modules based on real-world objects. Although you can apply OOP techniques with any language (even native C), C++ includes the necessary language constructs that make it easier to implement OOP techniques. The class and function libraries that compose the MFC libraries are needed because C++ provides only a small set of keywords for controlling program execution and defining new data types; all other tasks such as input and output, string manipulations, and mathematical computations are relegated to the library of functions.

To fully utilize the power and flexibility of the Visual C++ environment, you must become familiar with three distinct subjects: C++, OOP concepts and techniques, and the tools and libraries that are part of Visual C++. Further, to create complete applications, you must gain some experience in the synergistic use of OOP, C++, and the libraries. Although many books are published on these topics, most suffer from one or more drawbacks:

- Books that cover object-oriented design principals do not pay much attention to C++.
- Books designed to teach C++ do not adequately describe how to implement OPP techniques in C++.
- Books designed as reference guides to the Microsoft C library do not cover C++ and OOP.
- The documentation that is included with Visual C++ has all the information you need—many, many thousands of pages—but is too extensive to be an easy-to-use tutorial and reference.

Due to these shortcomings, there is a definite need for a comprehensive source of information for all three topics: C++, OOP, and the Visual C++ class and function libraries. *Visual C++ Developer's Guide* is intended to answer the needs of intermediate to advanced programmers who are learning C++ and OOP in order to develop DOS or Windows applications using Visual C++. This book will help to teach C++ and OOP, and at the same time, serve as a reference guide to the function and class libraries that are part of Visual C++. Because C++ and OOP are likely to be new to many C programmers, this book includes in-depth tutorials that will gently introduce C++ and the use of OOP concepts with C++ programs.

Visual C++ Developer's Guide features the following:

- A description of the Visual Workbench, which is the primary Windows-based interface between Visual C++ and the programmer.
- A quick overview of ANSI Standard C.
- Extensive tutorials on the basic concepts of object-oriented programming.
- A discussion of data abstraction, inheritance, and polymorphism.
- A step-by-step introduction of the features of C++, such as classes and virtual functions that support OOP.
- A discussion of how C++ differs from ANSI Standard C.
- Detailed examples showing how to use OOP techniques.
- A description of the different approaches to building a library of reusable classes in C++.
- Detailed coverage of the Microsoft Foundation Class (MFC) libraries.
- Reference entries for the class and function libraries that are part of Visual C++.
- A disk with the source code for the example programs that are part of this book.
- Real-world examples of C++ and OOP techniques in both DOS and Windows applications.

Visual C++ Developer's Guide uses short, simple example programs to help illustrate the syntactical details of OOP techniques. Features of C++ are always presented in the context of an OOP concept that the feature supports.

The *Visual C++ Developer's Guide* also includes coverage of the class and function libraries that are necessary for building real-world applications. Specifically, the book covers application development for both the DOS and Windows environments using the MFC libraries—a collection of over 100 classes designed to make Windows programming easier. The last part of this book serves as a complete reference for the standard C runtime and the MFC libraries that are part of Visual C++.

To make it easier for you, all the example programs can be found on the source code diskette that is found inside the back cover.

It's easy to be overwhelmed with the new syntax of C++ and the details of how everything fits together in a program that uses object-oriented design techniques. For those programmers who are unfamiliar with programming under Windows, there is also the problem of the extensive Windows interface. With a grasp of the fundamentals of OOP, however, and with the help of the MFC and C function libraries, you will find it relatively easy to employ OOP techniques in your applications. We sincerely hope that *Visual C++ Developer's Guide* gets you started on your way to harnessing the full power of object-oriented techniques, C++, and the Visual C++ libraries.

Acknowledgments

Many thanks to Phil Paxton, Greg Croy, Joe Wikert, and Stacy Hiquet for their support and suggestions in the writing of this book.

Thanks to Microsoft Corporation for providing beta copies of the product.

And a very special thanks to our families—they are the ones who made it possible for us to write this book.

Introduction

Ladies and Gentlemen. May I draw your attention to the center ring, where I'm very proud to introduce the *Visual C++ Developer's Guide.*

No—no, not that kind of introduction! OK, I think I've got it. Let me try again…

This book was written to assist the reader in becoming more proficient in writing programs in the C++ language.

The Visual C++ Developer's Guide is an intermediate to advanced book that introduces you to the basic concepts of object-oriented programming (OOP) and shows you how to apply OOP techniques when programming in C++. This book is also a comprehensive reference to Visual C++, Microsoft's latest C/C++ compiler.

The C++ programming language is, in the world of computer languages, rather new.

First developed by Dennis Ritchie at Bell Laboratories, the C language was introduced in 1972, and ran on a DEC PDP-11. The ANSI standard for C, which replaced the standard written by Kernighan and Ritchie in 1978, is only a few years old. C was developed as the language UNIX would be written in, in a very good attempt to create an operating system that could be ported to different CPU types with a minimum of effort. Because UNIX, written in C, needed only to be recompiled to convert from one CPU to another, it was felt that UNIX would become very popular. Generally, however, UNIX hasn't become the leading operating system, but C has become one of the most used computer languages.

C's structure is similar to PL/I, a popular language on IBM's mainframe computers. It is also similar in structure to FORTRAN, Pascal and BASIC. C is a simple language with a very small group of keywords and no support for such things as I/O or advanced math. All the power of C comes from the simplicity of the language and the use of a standard library of functions.

What You Will Need

To get the best value out of Visual C++ and this book, you will need access to a computer with considerable power. The authors suggest that your computer be an 80486 with a clock speed of at least 25 MHz (though a faster 80386 can perform well), more than 100M of free hard disk space (prior to installing Visual C++, which will take as much as 70M). Of course, Windows 3 (or later) is also needed to run Visual C++.

The example programs in this book were all compiled on the author's system, a 486DX2/50 with 16M of RAM, 1024 × 768, 256 color display, and 2.2 gigabytes of hard disk, running Windows for Workgroups and DOS 6. The compiler was run with the Visual Workbench, but I tried the DOS command line version of the compiler (in a Windows DOS box) and it ran well.

Who This Book Is For

This book is intended for both the intermediate and advanced programmer who already has some experience in writing C and/or C++ applications, or perhaps the programmer who is very experienced with a similar language, such as PL/I or Pascal, and who is working at improving his or her programming skills.

Regardless of whether you are an intermediate programmer or a more experienced one, you probably want to improve your skills. This book is intended to make improving your skills as easy as possible, perhaps even fun!

What This Book Is About

This book focuses on the basic concepts of OOP, how OOP helps you handle changes in software requirements easily, and how C++ supports OOP. The Visual C++ Developer's Guide also covers programming with the IO stream I/O library and shows how to call C functions from C++, organize C++ class libraries, and use the Microsoft Foundation Class libraries. After you master the basics of OOP, C++, and the C++ class libraries, the *Visual C++ Developer's Guide* moves on to the subject of developing more realistic applications. Though many programmers are moving to the Windows operating environment, there is still a demand for DOS applications, and this book gives examples of both DOS applications and Windows-based programs.

This book has several purposes: First, it introduces you to the more advanced parts of the C++ language and OOP techniques. More than a few things are covered in this book that I doubt you'll see elsewhere, perhaps including some of my most embarrassing moments.

This book is both tutorial and reference. To look up items in the book, use the index and the Table of Contents.

What This Book Will Do For You

Perhaps this book will make you popular. Maybe it won't. If you improve your C++ programming skills, then I really suspect you'll be more popular because there seems always to be a demand for *good* C++ programmers. OK, there is a demand for people who are good at many things, but C++ programmers are more and more in demand, and for quite some time will seem to be scarce.

The first part of this book, as a learning tool, is basically tutorial. At the end of each chapter you'll find a summary of what is covered in that chapter. This book is divided into eight parts, plus a bibliography.

Part I, "Getting Started with Microsoft Visual C++," includes the first four chapters, which cover installing Visual C++, getting started with the Visual Workbench, ANSI Standard C, and the Microsoft extensions to Standard C.

Part II, "Learning Object-Oriented Programming," introduces Object-Oriented Programming. The first chapter in this part introduces the basics of OOP, and the second chapter shows C++ and OOP techniques.

Part III, "Learning C++," teaches the C++ programming language from the perspective of OOP. The seven chapters in this part show how to use OOP techniques.

Part IV, "Applying OOP Techniques in C++," introduces you to building and using libraries of OOP functions. The final chapter in this part shows how to use AppWizard to build an OOP Windows application.

Part V, "Microsoft Foundation Class Library," is a reference that covers the Microsoft Foundation Class library. This part is subdivided into two chapters, the first a reference to the general programming MFC objects, and the second chapter a reference to Windows MFC objects.

Part VI, "Functions for File Handling and I/O," is a reference that covers the various I/O and file-handling functions.

Part VII, "Data Processing Functions," is a reference that covers the data processing functions.

Part VIII, "Process Control and Memory Management Functions," is a reference that covers process control and memory allocation functions.

The final part of the book is a bibliography that introduces many other sources of information that will prove to be of value to you, the C++ programmer.

Each of the chapters in this book is divided into related sections. In this book each section can be used by itself. Many of the sections contain example programs, and in many chapters a single example program is used to demonstrate several of the chapter's topics.

Wherever possible, the chapters are organized to allow you to start at the beginning of the chapter and continue to the end. The need to look ahead is, we hope, minimized. Those chapters that have reference sections (Chapters 19 through 32) are arranged with a tutorial section, followed by the actual reference.

How to Use This Book

How you use this book depends on how proficient you are in programming with C++. If you are an experienced C++ programmer, you will probably not have to spend as much time with the first part of this book.

If you are a newer C++ programmer, I'd suggest that you spend a day or so (if necessary, the next few weeks) learning the ins and outs of C++ programming. Use all the example programs in this book, and any other programs that you can find, such as the MFC example programs provided with the compiler. Practice makes perfect. As your C programming skills grow, you'll have moments of enlightenment, where you'll have a flash of understanding and see the bigger picture: what objects are, what a derived class is, or perhaps the difference between and `char`, `char&`, and `char*`. If you don't understand something at first, re-read the section, play with the example program, change the example program and see what your changes do. Don't be afraid of C++ programming: It may be different in how it works, but it's not too difficult.

You can expect to make slow progress at first—I was an excellent PL/I programmer, with many years of graphics programming experience, and when I heard that it'd take me a year or so to become proficient in C, I scoffed. After about a year, much of it learning, I realized that I did understand C programming and that it wasn't so bad or difficult. One high point in a C programmer's learning curve is when the concept of pointers and indirection is clear. Another is when you understand the concepts of static and automatic variables. Yet another is the understanding of when a function can modify a variable and when it can't. I don't know when I considered myself an acceptable C programmer, but if you are producing usable applications in two to four months, you are doing well. You shouldn't be discouraged if you don't seem to understand everything in the first few weeks—that's what this book is for: to make you a better C programmer!

A note on my programming environment: I use a "no-name" 386/33, with 160M of local hard disk. It's networked (using LanManager and Ethernet) with several other computers, all of which sit on a table beside my desk. The server has 220M of disk, giving me a total of almost 400M of disk space. I have in front of me four monitors and keyboards, connected to three computers and a graphics terminal. If I were to do it all over, I'd have only a 486 (or a 586), and not bother with all that other hardware, but I don't have that choice. I also have a slew of printers, including a laser printer, three daisy wheel printers, a thermal printer, a high speed (1000 LPM) line printer, and two color ink jet printers. I mainly use only the laser printer. I just can't bring myself to get rid of the others, and sometimes they are handy to have around.

If I were to recommend a platform to develop C software then I'd recommend at least a 386/25, preferably a 386/33 or a 486 system. A 286 will not do because you cannot run Visual C++ on anything less than a 386. CPU speed is important because both the compiler and the linker are noticeably slow when you don't have a fast CPU. There's nothing like compiling 200,000 lines of C code in just a few seconds. I'd suggest that you have at least a 100M hard disk (I used 80M for three years, and got to be an expert on how to live with too small a hard disk). My latest hard disk, a 1050M IDE drive, really performs (less than seven millisecond seek time, 512K on-drive cache, and more). That drive cost less than the first hard drive, an incredibly slow 5M drive that I bought about ten years ago for $1950! Of course, I thought I'd never, ever fill that drive! Things change. Usually for the better.

Since Visual C++ arrived it has become my favorite development system for both Windows applications and DOS programs as well. Visual C++ is powerful and easy to use, and it supports C++, ANSI C, and Microsoft's extensions. The Visual Workbench, Visual C++'s integrated debugging environment, makes the edit/compile/debug cycle easy to handle.

Conventions Used in This Book

There are a number of conventions in this book, and if you understand them, they will make using the book easier. These conventions include:

- All program listings and code fragments are in a `monospaced` font. This allows you to quickly find the actual C/C++ code, and be able to count space characters, and so forth.
- Something that must be substituted (such as a filename, variable, or a value) will be in *`monospaced italic`*.
- To highlight important keywords in a chapter's text **`monospaced bold`** will be used.
- In listings generated using AppWizard, changes made to the generated code are also shown in **`monospaced bold`**.
- Index items, important topics, keywords, and so forth are in ***bold italic***. This will enable you to find a given index reference on a page.
- When a listing's title shows a filename in uppercase, then that listing will be found on the sample source diskette with that name. If no filename is given or it is in lowercase, then it may not be a separate source file on the diskette. Generally, the text indicates which file a nontrivial code fragment is from.

Command Syntax

Throughout this book, you will often see descriptions of commands with arguments shown in square brackets (`[...]`) or angle brackets (`<...>`). The arguments enclosed in `[...]` are optional, the ones inside `<...>` are required. Also, arguments shown in *`italic monospace`* font are place holders; you must enter a specific value when actually using the command. For instance, in the command

```
CL <filename>
```

`<filename>` is a place holder. On the other hand, CL must be entered exactly as shown because it appears in regular monospace font.

A Note on Practicing C

There really is only one way to learn. You can read, attend lectures, or discuss a subject, but until you start practicing and using it, you aren't learning. Practice is it: the best tool you can use to learn. (If you are reading this in a bookstore, this book is one of the best practice tools you can buy!)

Don't be afraid to practice with the programs provided in this book. Practice doesn't mean copying the programs from the diskette, compiling, running the program, and feeling as if you've learned something. The only things that process will teach you is how to copy files and use Visual C++'s compiler, something which isn't that difficult. You need to practice, practice, and practice some more. Take the example programs and change them, expand them, and enhance them. Make the example programs do things they weren't intended to do, and learn from your mistakes.

One point to always remember: Because C is a language that can do many powerful things and because many of us are programming on PC's using DOS or Windows, be very careful. It's very easy to "trash" the disk.

How to Contact the Authors

You can contact either of the authors if you have any questions or comments.

To reach Naba Barkakati, please use one of the following methods:

- Write to: LNB Software Inc., 7 Welland Court, North Potomac, MD 20878
- If you have access to an Internet node, send e-mail to

  `naba@grebyn.com`

- If you are a CompuServe user, specify the following in the ***SEND TO:*** address:

  `>INTERNET:naba@grebyn.com`

- From MCI mail, specify the following when sending mail:

  ```
  EMS: INTERNET
  MBX: naba@grebyn.com
  ```

To reach Peter D. Hipson, please use one of the following methods:

- Write to Peter D. Hipson, P.O. Box 88, West Peterborough, NH 03468-0088
- If you are a CompuServe user, specify the following in the ***SEND TO:*** address:

  `>70444,52`
- If you have a fax machine, you can send your fax to the number below. If you can accept a faxed reply, be sure to include your fax number.

  (603) 532-7669

Please do not telephone either of the authors, even if you should find their phone numbers. When you write, if you enclose a SASE, we promise to send a prompt reply. The other methods of contacting the authors should also get you a prompt reply as well!

Of course, if you find fault with this book, please let us know. It is our goal to write books that are useful and valuable. If you wish to criticize the book, send your critiques to Peter Hipson, who is currently accepting blame for whatever *The Visual C++ Developer's Guide*'s shortcomings are.

A Note on Practicing C++

Good luck improving your C++ programming skills. Have fun writing your software, and remember Peter's golden rule:

Always back up your disk frequently!

I

Getting Started with Microsoft Visual C++

1

The Microsoft Visual C++ Environment

This book's major goal is to help you, the C programmer, learn the basic concepts of Windows programming, object-oriented programming (OOP), and C++ programming using the Microsoft Visual C++ compiler. At the same time, this book serves as a reference guide to the C++ classes (the Microsoft Foundation Classes, V2.0) and the C function libraries that accompany Microsoft Visual C++. However, before you get into OOP, C++, and the Microsoft Visual C++ libraries, you need to know what tools Microsoft Visual C++ offers to help you carry out the essential programming tasks of editing, compiling, linking, and debugging. To help familiarize you with the Microsoft Visual C++ environment, this chapter provides an overview of the Microsoft Visual C++ product, including what components it contains and how to set up and use it on a PC running Windows. Visual C++ is primarily a Windows application. Although you can compile under a DOS window, the best programmer's interface with Visual C++ is the Visual Workbench.

Visual C++ comes in two versions:

- The professional version, which includes a more advanced optimizing compiler, more extensive documentation, and the ability to create DOS-based applications.
- The personal version, which is available at a slightly lower cost, doesn't have as advanced a compiler, has fewer manuals, and will not enable you to create DOS-based applications.

Throughout this book we'll be using the professional version of the compiler—the difference in price compared to the reduction in compiler features doesn't really make the personal version a good buy.

This chapter also introduces the interactive development environment called Visual Workbench, and includes a short look at CL, the DOS command-line interface to the compiler and linker. Chapter 2, "Program Development Tools in Visual C++," further describes the rest of the program development tools—such as LIB, LINK, NMAKE, and CV—that help you manage the "edit-compile-link-debug" cycle of building applications. Of course, with the Visual Workbench, you won't have to concern yourself as much about the mechanics of actually creating an executable program. The Visual Workbench does most of the work for you.

Chapter 3 "An Overview of ANSI Standard C," and Chapter 4 "Microsoft Visual C++ Extensions to Standard C," summarize the features of the C programming language. Although this book assumes that you already know C, you may want an overview of the C language as a refresher, especially to review the features of ANSI Standard C and the extensions to the language that are specific to Microsoft C. One book that might help you with both C and C++ Programming is *Advanced C*, from Sams Publishing. Another reason for reviewing ANSI C is the similarity in syntax between ANSI C and Microsoft C. You'll find an overview of ANSI C in Chapter 3, and Chapter 4 describes how Microsoft augments ANSI C with certain keywords necessary to fully utilize the capabilities of the Intel 80x86 microprocessors used in MS-DOS PCs.

A Quick Tour of Microsoft Visual C++

Microsoft Visual C++ is many products in one. Included with the product are a number of manuals. There are three flavors of Visual C++—Standard version, Professional version, and the C7 update. With each of these flavors, the documentation supplied with Visual C++ varies.

The Professional version, the premium product, has more features and functionality than the Standard version. The Professional version is supplied with the following manuals:

Presenting Visual C++
Visual Workbench User's Guide
App Studio User's Guide
C++ Tutorial
Class Library User's Guide
Programming Techniques
Programming Tools for Windows
CodeView Debugger User's Guide
Command-Line Utilities User's Guide
Source Profiler User's Guide
Class Library Reference
C Language Reference
C++ Language Reference
Run-Time Library Reference
iostream Class Library Reference
Comprehensive Index
MFC Quick Reference
Windows 3.1 SDK: Getting Started
Windows 3.1 SDK: Programmer's Reference, Volume 1: Overview
Windows 3.1 SDK: Programmer's Reference, Volume 2: Functions
Windows 3.1 SDK: Programmer's Reference, Volume 3: Messages, Structures, and Macros
Windows 3.1 SDK: Programmer's Reference, Volume 4: Resources

The Standard version, a less-featured version of Visual C++ (aimed at the occasional software writer, and not really intended for the professional developer) has only a limited number of manuals:

Presenting Visual C++
Visual Workbench User's Guide
App Studio User's Guide
C++ Tutorial
Class Library User's Guide
Programming Techniques

Class Library Reference
MFC Quick Reference Card

The C7 update, built around the Professional version of Visual C++, is available to registered users of Microsoft C7.0. The update version has the following manuals:

Presenting Visual C++
Visual Workbench User's Guide
App Studio User's Guide
Class Library User's Guide
Class Library Reference
MFC Quick Reference Card
C/C++ Version 7.0 Update

Purchasers of Visual C++ also can purchase additional SDK books. These manuals include:

Getting Started
Programming Tools
Guide To Programming
Multimedia Programmer's Reference
Multimedia Programmer's Guide
Windows For Pen Computing Programmer's Reference
The Windows Interface: An Application Design Guide
The Win32 Application Programming Interface: An Overview

An order form is included with Visual C++ and can be used to order these books.

Microsoft also is including a copy of Phar Lap's 286/DOS-Extender Lite, a product that allows DOS programs to access up to 2M of extended memory.

Visual C++ provides a complete Windows programming environment for C and C++, and contains all the supporting tools and libraries necessary to write Microsoft Windows and DOS applications. As a programmer, you primarily will use the following tools:

- The Visual Workbench, used for editing source files, interfacing with many of the supplied utilities, including C and C++ compiler. The Visual Workbench allows you to build applications, and debug them, without ever leaving the Visual Workbench. Normally, the Visual Workbench will help you in using other development tools—for example, running the compiler, linker, and resource compiler to create the executable application for you.

- Application Wizard, often called AppWizard, a program developer used to create initial Windows applications.

- Class Wizard, a utility for managing C++ classes (in programs developed using Application Wizard).
- Application Studio, often called App Studio, a program for editing a Windows application's resources, such as menus, dialog boxes, bitmaps, icons, and cursors.
- LINK, the DOS-based linker for combining one or more object modules into an executable file.
- LIB, the DOS-based library manager for managing collections of object modules in a single file.
- NMAKE, the DOS-based make utility for automating program development.
- CV and CVW, the CodeView debuggers, for DOS and for Windows, respectively.

There are a few more utilities (all DOS-based) that you may not normally use, but are handy when you need their functionality. These utilities include:

- EXEHDR, a utility for displaying and modifying information contained in the header portion of an .EXE file.
- CVPACK, for compressing the size of executable files that contain information needed by the CodeView debugger.
- HELPMAKE, a utility for converting text files (of special format) into databases that are used by a number of Microsoft applications, such as the Visual Workbench, for displaying on-line help.
- IMPLIB, the import librarian for creating a special type of library, called an *import library*, from one or more dynamic link libraries. Import libraries are used in Microsoft Windows programs.
- MSD, the Microsoft Diagnostics tool that enables you to see important information about your PC's hardware and software configuration.

In addition, Microsoft Visual C++ includes a number of Windows-based utilities. These Windows utilities include:

- SPY, a program that allows you to examine messages, and message parameters, being sent to a window (including an application's main window).
- DDESPY, a program that allows you to see the DDE exchange between a DDE server and a client application.

- HEAPWALKER, a utility that lets you examine Windows memory to see what memory objects exist, what memory objects each running application has allocated, and how Windows memory is being utilized.
- STRESSAPP, a program that allows you to force Windows to allocate resources until there are no more resources left for your application. This allows you to see what happens to your application when certain resources are no longer available.
- ZOOMIN, a small application that allows you zoom into a small part of the screen.
- DEBUGWIN, a utility that allows you to see the messages that the debugging version of Windows produces. (Normally you'd need a terminal attached to COM1: to see the debugging messages.)
- MFC TRACE OPTIONS, a utility that allows you to set the debug options that MFC uses.
- HOTSPOT EDITOR, a program you can use to create and edit *hypergraphics*—bitmaps that have one or more spots at which the user can cause an action to take place.

How you use Microsoft Visual C++ depends on your needs. You can compile and link your program using one of the following approaches:

- Accessing the compiler and linker from the Visual Workbench, using the Project, Build and Project, Rebuild All menu selections.
- Running the compiler and linker from the DOS command line.
- Using NMAKE to automate the compiling and linking process.

Using Visual Workbench is the most efficient method to develop applications using Visual C++. Running the compiler under DOS is possible. However, it's not efficient—you must run an editor to edit the source code, then compile (and link) the source code.

Generally, you'll find the Visual Workbench's editor an effective programming tool. The editor can, to a limited extent, be configured to your liking. Using Visual Workbench's tool bar, you can interactively access the compiler and linker. The Visual Workbench is a Windows application with a rather standard Windows MDI user interface. With Windows running in enhanced mode (80386 protected mode) you can run and debug applications using the debugger, which is an integral part of the Visual Workbench. The Visual Workbench enables you to go through the entire cycle—developing and editing the source file; creating the Windows resources; compiling, linking, and running the program; and debugging, all without ever leaving the Visual Workbench.

For a large software project involving many source modules, using the Visual Workbench is a must. The Visual Workbench will create a project file (similar to NMAKE's .MAK files), which contains all the directives needed for the Visual Workbench to compile and link necessary modules. With a project file, after you edit one or more source files, selecting the Visual Workbench's Project Build icon will compile all affected files—for example, changing a header file requires compiling all source files that include the altered header file. (A *button* appears as text within angle brackets.)

As you'll learn from the description of the Visual Workbench in this chapter, the project file describes the interdependence of source, object, and executable files. The Visual Workbench uses the knowledge of the interdependency to compile the appropriate files and build a new executable program.

You specify various options for the compiler and linker, both when a project is first created and after it has been created, using the Options menu. Later in this chapter, summary descriptions demonstrate how to set the compiler and linker options from the Visual Workbench. At the end of this chapter there's a tutorial in creating a simple Visual Workbench project. But first, the next section briefly describes how to set up Microsoft Visual C++. Following that section, you'll find an overview of the Visual Workbench and CL, the command-line interface to the compiler and linker. Many other tools included with Microsoft Visual C++ are described in Chapter 2, "Program Development Tools in Visual C++."

Microsoft Visual C++ Requires Windows

Microsoft Visual C++ requires Microsoft Windows running in Enhanced Mode, and an 80386 or 80486 system with an absolute minimum of four megabytes of memory to run. The compiler is a 32-bit Windows/DOS application that runs in the protected mode of the Intel 80386 and 80486 microprocessors.

Although the Microsoft Visual C++ compiler, linker, and other program-generation utilities will run in a DOS window, once you start using the Visual Workbench it's unlikely that you'll be using the compiler as a DOS application very often.

Setting Up Microsoft Visual C++

Installing Microsoft Visual C++ is straightforward with the SETUP program included with the product. SETUP decompresses files from the distribution disks and copies them to specific directories on your hard disk. You have the option of indicating the drive and the directory in which you want Microsoft Visual C++ installed. After starting Windows, the basic steps to install Visual C++ are as follows:

1. Insert the first install disk (disk #1) into the appropriate disk drive—a: or b:—depending on the disk size and your system's configuration.

2. From the Program Manager, select File, Run. Enter the following program name (using the correct drive letter) in the Command Line edit box:

   ```
   A: SETUP
   ```

3. Once SETUP starts (see Figure 1.1), read and respond to the screens that are displayed. Help is available at any time by pressing the on-screen `Help` button (see Figure 1.2). By responding to the questions presented in SETUP's screens, you'll accomplish the following:

   Select the drive and directory in which you want to install Microsoft Visual C++. Take note of how much disk space Visual C++ requires. In the default installation, expect to use about 52 megabytes of disk space. If you install any of the optional parts of Visual C++, you can expect to use even more disk space.

   Select the *memory models* (see Figure 1.3) for which you want the libraries installed. If you aren't familiar with memory models, you can make a safe choice by installing libraries for all memory models except for the Compact model (which usually isn't used by inexperienced programmers).

   Decide whether you want sample programs copied to your hard disk. In general, looking up these samples can provide valuable insight into various programming techniques.

Microsoft Visual C++ also suggests changing the CONFIG.SYS file. At the beginning of the install, it is suggested that you have the `BUFFERS` parameter set to at least 30. In addition, the setup program suggests that you run disk-caching software (such as SmartDrv), with caching (read only) set `on` for the floppy disk from which you're installing. (Face it: when a product comes on twenty-plus diskettes, anything you can do to speed up the process is going to be welcome. The difference between having caching on and `off` can be an install time of twenty minutes or an install time of three or four hours. I don't know about you, but I've got better things to do with my time....)

After you've set the configuration you want (if you agree with the default configuration options SETUP presents), you must select the Continue button. This tells SETUP to install the compiler and build the libraries for the memory models you've selected. SETUP also creates a program group (see Figure 1.4) from which you can select Visual C++'s utilities. There will be icons (in the Visual C++ Program Manager's Group) to enable you to use each of the help files that come with Visual C++.

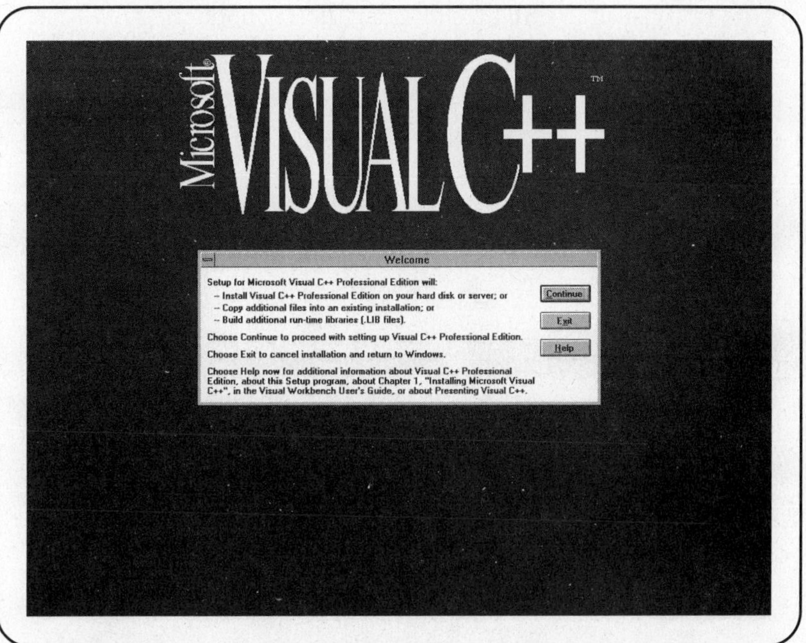

Figure 1.1. Visual C++ SETUP program, opening screen.

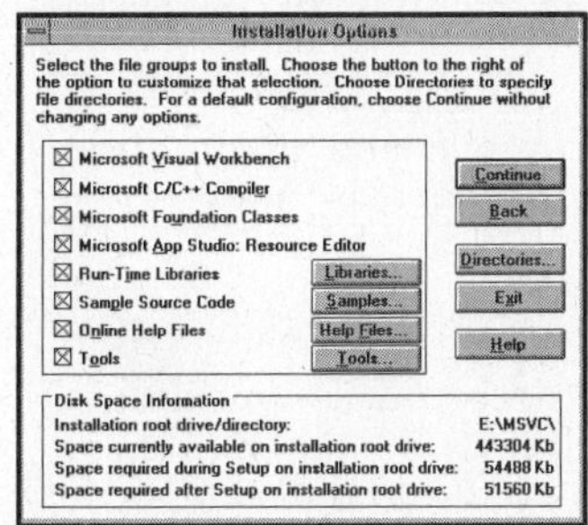

Figure 1.2. Visual C++ SETUP program, initial options.

Figure 1.3. Visual C++ SETUP program, library options.

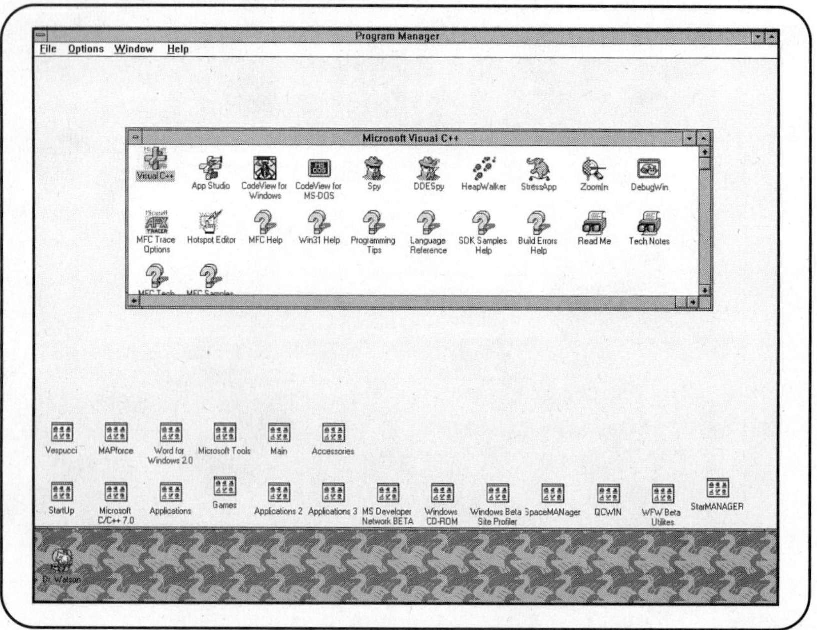

Figure 1.4. The Visual C++ Program Manager Group.

To be able to run the compiler and other utilities from the DOS command line, you must use the batch file MSVCVARS.BAT. This file is created by SETUP, which adds definitions for the necessary environment variables to MSVCVARS.BAT. You can run this batch file from a DOS window. MCVCVARS.BAT will set the necessary environment variables for you. If you desire, you can include this file in your AUTOEXEC by either directly including the lines from the file, or by calling it. If you include MSVCVARS.BAT to your autoexec, be sure to add it after the environment variables are set.

The MSVCVARS.BAT file (from my installation; yours may vary slightly) contains the following commands:

```
@echo off
set TOOLROOTDIR=D:\MSVC
set PATH=D:\MSVC\BIN;%PATH%
set INCLUDE=D:\MSVC\INCLUDE;D:\MSVC\MFC\INCLUDE;%INCLUDE%
set LIB=D:\MSVC\LIB;D:\MSVC\MFC\LIB;%LIB%
```

From your experience with MS-DOS, you already know that an environment variable, such as `PATH`, basically is a name for an arbitrary string and is defined using the `SET` command. Entering `SET` at the DOS prompt displays the current settings of the environment variables, while

```
SET PATH=C:\;C:\dos6
```

defines `PATH` as the string `C:\;C:\dos6`, thus replacing its previous definition. Here are the environment variables that SETUP defines:

`TOOLROOTDIR` — A single directory where the Visual C++ tools (found in subdirectories) are found. For example:

```
SET TOOLROOTDIR=D:\MSVC
```

`PATH` — The locations that DOS is to search when a command not found in DOS's internal command list is entered.

```
SET PATH=D:\MSVC\BIN;%PATH%
```

Notice how the original path is appended to the end of the new path variable by using the `%PATH%` environment variable.

`INCLUDE` — List of semicolon-separated directory names in which the C and C++ include files (usually files with .H extension) are located. For example:

```
setINCLUDE=D:\MSVC\INCLUDE;D:\MSVC\MFC\INCLUDE;%INCLUDE%
```

Notice how the original include path is appended to the end of the new include path variable by using the `%INCLUDE%` environment variable.

`LIB` — List of semicolon-separated directory names in which the libraries are located. For example:

```
LIB=D:\MSVC\LIB;D:\MSVC\MFC\LIB;%LIB%
```

Notice how the original lib path is appended to the end of the new library-path variable by using the `%LIB%` environment variable.

The Microsoft Visual C++ tools use these environment variables to locate files that are used.

Building DOS MFC Libraries

Even with the great number of diskettes that Visual C++ comes on, not all parts of the compiler's libraries are supplied on the installation diskettes. One part that is missing is the Microsoft Foundation Classes (MFC) real mode (DOS) libraries.

This shortcoming is easy to take care of. Microsoft provides an excellent make file to enable you to build (or rebuild) any of the MFC libraries. In addition, it's possible (but definitely not recommended) to modify the original MFC source, and rebuild the libraries to include your own changes. However, you should carefully consider two things before making any changes. First, what possible side effects these changes will have. Second, what you will do to implement your changes when it comes time to install the next new Microsoft version of the MFC libraries.

To create the new MFC DOS libraries, first open a DOS window. Then follow these steps:

1. Using the MSVCVARS.BAT file (if you have not added a call to MSVCVARS in your AUTOEXEC) set up the environment for the DOS command-line version of the compiler.
2. Change to the directory (MSVC\MFC\SRC) that contains the MFC source files.
3. Read the file README.TXT, which contains detailed instructions on the process of building the make files.
4. Build each of the libraries needed. I suggest you either build all memory models for which you have run-time libraries installed, or simply build all the MFC libraries. You'll need to build both a release version and a debug version of each memory model.

As an example, the command to build the MFC DOS medium memory model, debug version, of the library is:

```
NMAKE DEBUG=1 TARGET=R MODEL=M
```

Once you've built the MFC DOS libraries you can create DOS projects that use the MFC libraries

Using the Visual Workbench

When you have successfully installed Microsoft Visual C++, you can try out the C and C++ compiler from the Visual Workbench, an all-in-one C and C++ programming environment. The Visual Workbench is a rather standard Windows MDI application, and if you're familiar with the usage of MDI applications you'll have few problems with this product. Using the Visual Workbench, you can

- Edit one or more source files
- Browse (edit in read-only mode) source files
- Build an executable file by compiling source files and linking one or more object files
- Run the newly built program
- Use the built-in debugger to find any programming errors

Additionally, the Visual Workbench offers a voluminous amount of on-line help. In fact, the best way to learn the Visual Workbench is to start using it and browsing through the on-line help. For your convenience, though, the next few sections briefly summarize some of the significant options offered in the Visual Workbench's menus—especially the options that are important for C and C++ programming.

You can customize the Visual Workbench's on-screen colors and its ability to color according to C/C++ syntax and keywords. The Visual Workbench is not extended or customized as easily as was the old Programmer's Workbench. Unfortunately, the Visual Workbench's editor doesn't have as much flexibility as many programmers would like. I'm sure that, with future releases of the product, we'll see a more flexible and powerful editor that we can reconfigure and for which we can write macros. What you see described here is the default configuration of the Visual Workbench—except for screen colors. We changed some of the colors to ensure that the black-and-white prints appearing in this book are more legible.

Getting Started with the Visual Workbench

You can start the Visual Workbench only from Microsoft Windows. To start the Visual Workbench, simply select the proper icon from the Visual C++ program group (as shown in Figure 1.4).

Selecting the Visual C++ icon brings up the Visual Workbench (Figure 1.5). What appears on-screen depends on your last session with the Visual Workbench. If when you last closed the Visual Workbench you had a project open, the Visual Workbench automatically starts with that project.

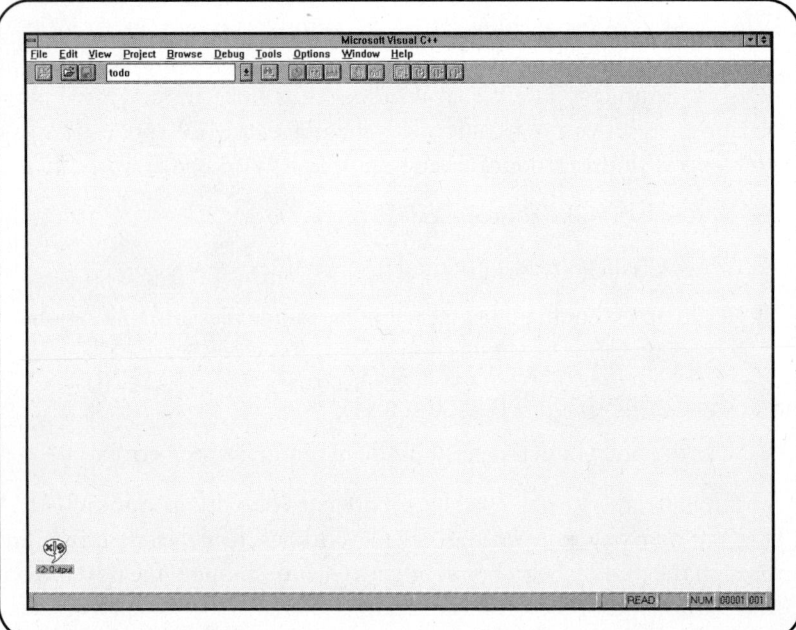

Figure 1.5. The Visual C++ Visual Workbench.

Exiting the Visual Workbench

As with most other Windows applications, to exit the Visual Workbench, press Alt+F4. An alternative exit sequence is to bring up the File menu using the mouse or by pressing Alt+F, and then select the Exit option (using the mouse or pressing the X key).

At startup, the Visual Workbench reads certain initial settings from a file named MSVC.INI (found in the Windows base directory) and automatically reloads the project that was loaded when the Visual Workbench last was used. You can modify many of the defaults used by the Visual Workbench by editing this file. Unlike many .INI files, many of the statements in MSVC.INI can be changed only by editing the file. You should make it a habit not to modify an .INI file while the application is running, however—many applications, as they exit, rewrite the .INI file, and you could lose any changes you have made. When modifying the MSVC.INI file, make sure to keep a copy handy—just in case you make an error in editing.

Command Syntax

Throughout this book, you'll often see descriptions of commands with arguments shown in square brackets (`[...]`) or angular brackets (<...>). The arguments enclosed in `[...]` are optional, the ones inside <...> are required. Also, arguments shown in *`italic monospace`* font are place holders; you must enter a specific value when actually using the command. For instance, in the command

```
CL <filename>
```

`<filename>` is a place holder. On the other hand, `CL` must be entered exactly as shown because it appears in regular monospace font.

Command-Line Options for the Visual Workbench

The Visual Workbench allows you to select a few options when started. These options are needed only when you're having problems with the Visual Workbench (usually, when you compile). To understand how the Visual Workbench runs the compiler, and what the Visual Workbench must do to interface with the compiler, you need to know that the actual compiler (and linker and resource compiler) are not Windows applications. Rather, they are DOS (32-bit) applications linked to the Visual Workbench using a program called WinTee.

WinTee is a small utility that is run when the Visual Workbench starts the compiler. This program takes the output from the compiler and sends it to the Visual

Workbench. This output information (such as error messages) then is displayed in the Visual Workbench Output window.

Because of this rather complex method of running the compiler, there sometimes are problems. To help eliminate these problems, the Visual Workbench has a number of options, listed in Table 1.1, below.

Table 1.1. The Visual Workbench options.

Option	Description
`/V`	Using the `/V` option tells WinTee to run with an icon. Its default mode is to be invisible. You then can open WinTee's icon and see the messages from the compiler as they're being sent to the Visual Workbench.
`/C`	Using `/C` tells the Visual Workbench to have Windows compact memory prior to running any of the Visual C++ tools. This is useful on systems where memory is very low. However, this option will slow down builds.
`/M`	Using the `/M` option tells the Visual Workbench to start the WinTee utility each time it's needed, and to have WinTee end when it is done with a task. The default mode is to start it the first time it is needed and leave it running, which does use memory.
`/Wn`	The `/Wn` option sets the number of seconds (*n*) that WinTee uses to time-out. This option is useful in some cases where slow drives (or systems) are present.
`/R`	Runs WinTeer (which is less efficient than WinTee) rather than WinTee. This may solve some problems which other options don't fix.

Getting Help in the Visual Workbench

The Visual Workbench has so many features that it's going to take several chapters to document all of them. AppWizard will be covered in Chapter 18, "Using AppWizard to Create C++ Windows Applications." Other parts of the Visual Workbench will be covered throughout the book. The Visual Workbench does offer extensive on-line help, however, so you need only know how to navigate the help system. Once you discover how to get help in the Visual Workbench, you can learn the Visual Workbench's features as you need them.

There are three ways you can get help in the Visual Workbench:

- Select the Help menu item either by clicking it with the mouse or by pressing Alt+H and then Enter.
- Place the cursor on a keyword (or a compiler error number) and press F1 to get help for that keyword (or error number).
- Press Shift+F1 to call help in the context-sensitive mode.

Keypress Notations

In the Microsoft Visual C++ documentation and in this book, you often will see references to key combinations such as Alt+S, Shift+F1, and Ctrl+F4. This notation means that you have to press two keys simultaneously. Thus, for Alt+F, keep the Alt key pressed down while you press the F key. Similarly, to get Ctrl+F4, keep the Ctrl (Control) key pressed down and press the F4 key. Notice that Alt+F is the same as Alt+f; you don't need to press the Shift key for an uppercase F when you want the Alt+F key combination.

Figure 1.6 shows the result of pressing Alt+H, then Enter, to go to the Visual C++ help system. As you can see, with the help system you get a table of contents. If you have a topic you want to search for, you can call up the Search menu by pressing Alt+S.

You can select any of the topics listed in the contents screen of the help system simply by selecting the small green button located to the left of the table of contents item in which you're interested.

For example, if you select the topic Wizards to create applications for Windows, you get the screen shown in Figure 1.7.

Wizards are Microsoft's tools to help you build Windows applications. As you can see, this is a list of various Wizard topics. From this screen, you can get more help on any of the topics that have a click button to their right. If you were to select the keyword `Modify code and resources`, a multipage description of how to modify code and resources with Class Wizard appears (Figure 1.8). In addition to these (though not shown in the figure), there's a button that brings up a sample of the code which does what the help document describes. As you can see, the Visual Workbench's on-line help system includes detailed information on almost all aspects of Microsoft Visual C++.

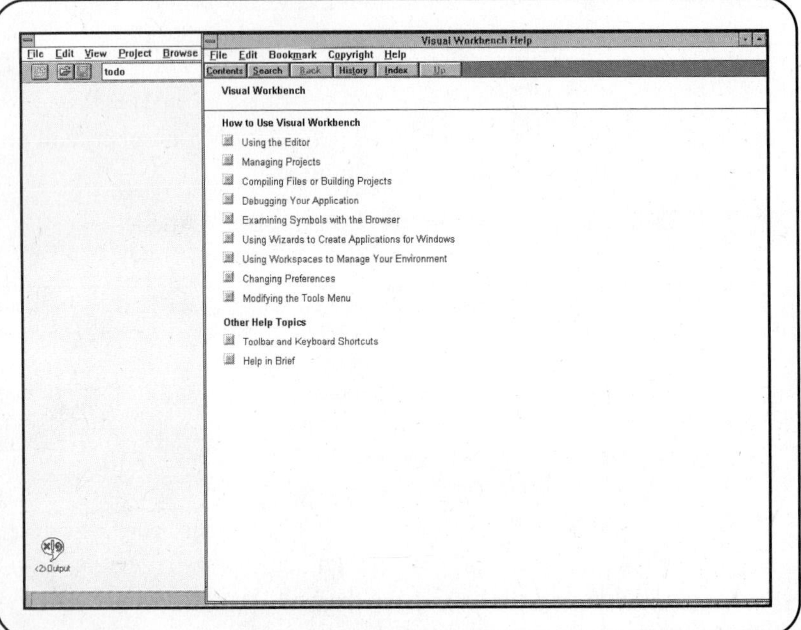

Figure 1.6. The Visual C++ Main Help Window.

Using the Visual Workbench Menus

Because the Visual Workbench is a Windows application, almost all your interaction with it occurs through menus and the toolbar. As you can see in Figure 1.9, the main menu options appear on a menu bar at the top of the Visual Workbench's display. Below the menu bar is the Visual Workbench tool bar. The bottom of the Visual Workbench is a message area and a status bar. The Visual Workbench treats the rest of the display as a *desktop* on which you can open multiple, overlapping windows.

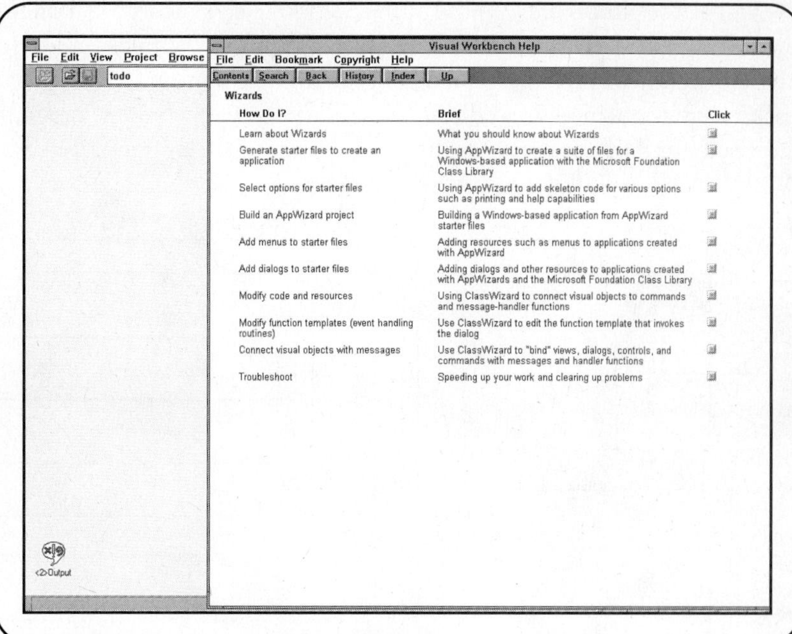

Figure 1.7. Selecting Wizards from the Help table of contents.

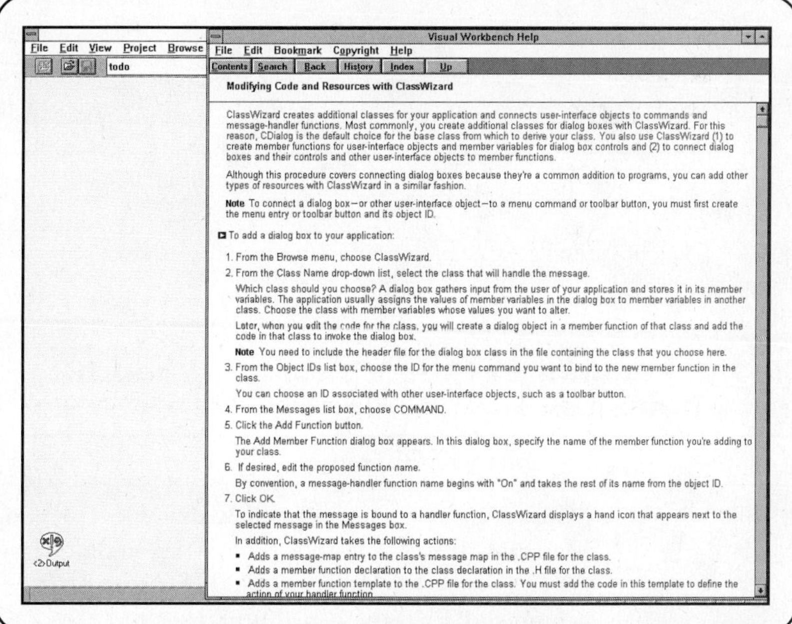

Figure 1.8. The Modifying Code and Resources with Class Wizard Help topic.

As you can see in Figure 1.9, the Visual Workbench's menu bar has ten items: File, Edit, View, Project, Browse, Debug, Tools, Options, Window, and Help. Each of these items leads to a pop-up menu. Through these pop-up menus, you can perform tasks such as opening and editing files, compiling and linking programs, running programs, and (if necessary) debugging programs. The options offered in the Visual Workbench's pull-down menus are summarized in Table 1.2.

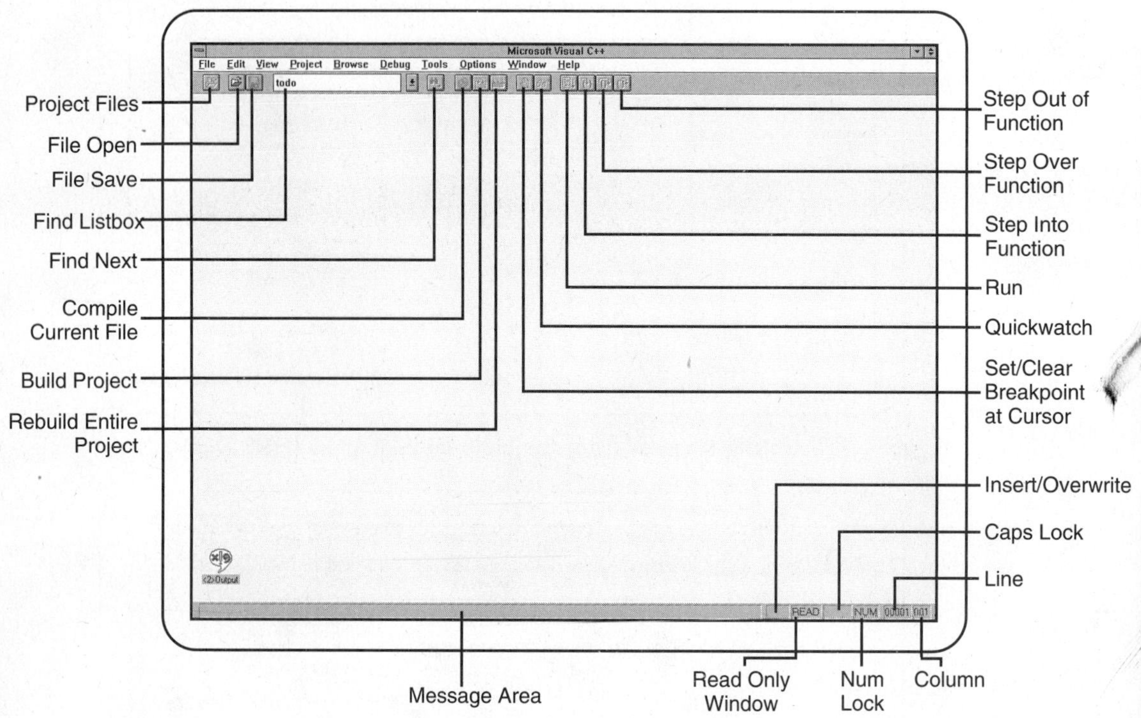

Figure 1.9. The Visual Workbench main window.

Table 1.2. Summary of the Visual Workbench's pull-down menus.

Title	Summary of Options
File	Creates a new file or opens an existing file for editing. Closes and saves files. Finds one or more files on disk. Starts a DOS session from which you can return by entering the EXIT command. Exits the Visual Workbench.

Title	Summary of Options
Edit	Cuts, copies, and pastes text; undoes and redoes the last editing command. Search, Replace, and Find are part of the Edit menu item.
View	Finds and replaces a text string or pattern. Marks a location in the file and moves to a marked location.
Project	Sets up and edits a *project* (a list of modules and their interdependencies). Compiles a C or C++ source file. Builds an executable program. Locates a source line with errors in case building an executable file fails.
Browse	Locates definitions of functions and variables. Views which functions call other functions. Views the C++ class hierarchy and runs Class Wizard.
Debug	Controls the debugging (go, stop, step over, and so on).
Tools	Runs whatever tools currently are defined. The default tools are App Studio and Codeview. You may add other tools (Windows applications, such as Spy, HeapWalker, and Stress) as desired.
Options	Customizes the look and behavior of the Visual Workbench (colors, directories, tools, and fonts). Specifies C and C++ compiler options. Specifies options for LINK and the Resource compiler.
Window	Manages the windows in the Visual Workbench's desktop. Allows movement between windows.
Help	Allows entry into the help system, including help on major topics. Displays the Visual Workbench's version number and copyright notice.

Menu Selections with the Mouse

Mouse Actions

You can perform a number of actions with the mouse. Here are the six basic actions with which you can interact with the Visual Workbench (and other Windows applications):

- *Press* a mouse button by holding the button down without moving the mouse.
- *Release* a mouse button that you have previously held down. This usually initiates some action.
- *Click* a mouse button by quickly pressing and releasing it.
- *Double-click* a mouse button by clicking it twice in rapid succession without moving the mouse.
- *Drag* the mouse cursor by pressing a mouse button and moving the mouse while keeping the button pressed.
- *Move* the mouse cursor by moving the mouse without pressing any button

In response to certain menu selections, the Visual Workbench displays dialog boxes. A *dialog box* is a window through which the Visual Workbench solicits input from (or sometimes provides information to) the user. Usually, the dialog box has check boxes in which you indicate your choices, lists from which you pick a selection, and text-entry fields where you enter text.

When interacting with a dialog box using a mouse, you just move the mouse cursor to an item and click the left button. Clicking a check box turns on a selection. If you click a text-entry area such as a box for entering a filename, you'll see another cursor in that area waiting for you to enter the requested information.

Menu Selections with the Keyboard

While I don't recommend trying to use either Windows or the Visual Workbench without a mouse, it can be done. Generally, there are going to be applications (such as App Studio) which require a mouse. However, there are times when you're using the keyboard and it's just plain inconvenient to reach over to use the mouse. You can access most of the Visual Workbench's functions from the keyboard. Here's a brief description of how to access the Visual Workbench's menus using the keyboard.

Press the Alt key to activate the menu bar. As you can see, one letter of each item is underscored. Also, notice that the File menu is highlighted. This is because File is the current choice; if you press Enter (or the down arrow), the File pull-down menu appears.

You can activate the pull-down menu for a specific option in one of two ways:

- Use the left and right arrow keys to select a main menu option, then press Enter.
- Press the underlined character of the main menu option you want, displaying the pull-down menu for that option.

Once a pull-down menu is displayed, you can use the left and right arrows to switch to other pull-down menus. Within a pull-down menu, use the up and down arrows to indicate the selection. As you press the up or down arrow, the selected item will be highlighted. Press the Enter key to activate the selection. If you do not want to make a selection from a pull-down menu, press the Alt key again, or press the Esc key to get out of the pull-down menu system.

A faster way to access menu items is to press the Alt key and the underlined letter of one of the items on the menu bar. For example, to get the Help menu, simultaneously press the Alt key and H—this commonly is written as Alt+H. Once the Help menu appears, notice the underlined character in many of the items in the menu. This character is called a *hot key* or *mnemonic key.* Press the underlined character to activate that item. For instance, when the Help menu is up, press A to activate the About... menu item.

Next to some menu items, notice the names of keystrokes. In the Files menu, for example, Ctrl+N is next to the New option. These are the *shortcut keys* or *accelerator keys*—pressing these key combinations activates that menu option even when the pull-down menu is not displayed. Thus, pressing Ctrl+N always brings up the File Open dialog box. Table 1.3 summarizes the purposes of several shortcut keys and a number of other keys in the Visual Workbench. Notice that some keystrokes are listed two or more times—the correct function is dependent on the mode in which the Visual Workbench is working.

Table 1.3. Shortcut keys in the Visual Workbench.

Keystroke	Function
Alt	Selects/deselects the main menu
Alt+F5	Ends the debugging session
Alt+F8	Rebuilds the project, compiling all the files
Alt+F9	Toggles hexadecimal display
Alt+X	Expands an entire graph
Backspace	Deletes one character to the left
Ctrl+]	Finds matching brace
Ctrl+A	Redoes the last undo
Ctrl+Alt+T	Toggles display of tab symbols
Ctrl+B	Opens the Breakpoints dialog box
Ctrl+C, Ctrl+Insert	Copies selected text to the Clipboard, without deleting it
Ctrl+<down arrow>	Scrolls down one line at a time
Ctrl+End	Moves to the end of the file
Ctrl+Enter	Moves to the first nonblank character of the next line
Ctrl+F	Displays a Find dialog box
Ctrl+F3	Finds the selected text
Ctrl+F4	Closes the active window
Ctrl+F6	Switches to the next document window
Ctrl+F7	Toggles mixed mode
Ctrl+F8	Compiles the active source file

Keystroke	Function
Ctrl+F9	Opens a Modify Variable dialog box
Ctrl+Home	Moves to the beginning of the file
Ctrl+K	Opens the Call Stack dialog box
Ctrl+<left arrow>	Moves one word to the left
Ctrl+number pad's *	Returns to the original symbol location
Ctrl+number pad's +	Jumps to the next reference in the browse list
Ctrl+number pad's -	Jumps to the previous reference in the browse list
Ctrl+O	Opens a Toolbar file
Ctrl+P	Same as pressing the Project Files Toolbar button
Ctrl+<right arrow>	Moves one word to the right
Ctrl+S	Saves a Toolbar button
Ctrl+T	Deletes to the end of the word
Ctrl+Tab	Switches to the previously active window
Ctrl+<up arrow>	Scrolls up one line at a time
Ctrl+V, Shift+Insert	Inserts the contents of the Clipboard at the current cursor position
Ctrl+X, Shift+Delete	Copies selected text to the Clipboard, deleting it from the current window
Ctrl+Y	Copies the current line to the Clipboard, deleting it
Ctrl+Z, Alt+Backspace	Undoes the last edit or change, with the number of undoes limited by the size of the undo buffer
Delete	Deletes one character to the right
<down arrow>	Moves one line down
End	Moves to the end of the line
End, then Enter	Inserts one blank line below the current cursor position
F2	Finds the next bookmark

continues

Table 1.3. continued

Keystroke	Function
F3	Repeats the last find
F4	Finds the next error
F5	Same as selecting Debug, Go from the menu
F5	Continues execution from the current statement
F6	Cycles forward through all open windows
F7	Executes the program to insertion-point position
F8	Executes the next statement, tracing the flow into function calls
F9	Toggles the Breakpoints button
F10	Single-steps, stepping around function calls
F11	Jumps to the definition of a selected symbol
Home	Moves to the first nonblank character of the current line
Home, then Home	Moves to column 1 of the current line
Home, then Enter	Inserts one blank line above the current cursor position
Insert	Toggles keyboard insert mode on or off
<left arrow>	Moves one character to the left
number pad's *	Expands all nodes in a branch
number pad's +, or number pad's Enter, or Shift+Plus	Expands active node one level
number pad's -	Collapses active node one level
Page Down	Moves down one page at a time
Page Up	Moves up one page at a time
Return	In the Find dialog box; searches forward
<right arrow>	Moves one character right

Keystroke	Function
Shift+Ctrl+End	Selects to the end of file
Shift+Ctrl+F6	Switches to the previous document window
Shift+Ctrl+Home	Moves to the beginning of the file
Shift+Ctrl+<left arrow>	Selects the word to the left
Shift+Ctrl+<right arrow>	Selects the word to the right
Shift+<down arrow>	Selects the current line
Shift+End	Selects to the end of the line
Shift+F2	Finds the previous bookmark
Shift+F3	Opens the Find dialog box
Shift+F4	Finds the previous error
Shift+F5	Starts program execution from the beginning
Shift+F6	Cycles backward through all open windows
Shift+F7	Same as pressing the Step Out button
Shift+F7	Executes program out of current function and stops on the first line after the function call
Shift+F8	Builds the project using dependency rules
Shift+F9	Opens a QuickWatch dialog box
Shift+F11	Jumps to the first reference of the selected symbol
Shift+Home	Selects to the beginning of the line
Shift+<left arrow>	Selects the character to the left
Shift+Page Down	Selects one screen down
Shift+Page Up	Selects one screen up
Shift+Return	In the Find dialog box; searches backward
Shift+<right arrow>	Selects the character to the right
Shift+<up arrow>	Selects the line above
Tab	Inserts a tab
<up arrow>	Moves one line up

When a menu option ends in an ellipsis (...), selecting the menu option causes the Visual Workbench to display a dialog box in which you must enter information. In such dialog boxes, you can either use the mouse, or keystrokes (generally, the Alt key plus the underlined character of the dialog item you wish to modify) to navigate through the options. You can discard a dialog box and throw away things you have changed—or end just about any dialog or menu selection in the Visual Workbench—by pressing the Esc key. (You can always think of Esc as the 'panic out' key.) Pressing the Tab key moves the cursor from one group of options to another, while Shift+Tab moves the cursor from option to option in the reverse order. Once the cursor is at the item you want, you can select it by pressing space.

For example, if you select the Colors... option from the Visual Workbench's Options menu (press Alt+O and then press C), the Visual Workbench displays the dialog box shown in Figure 1.10. Initially, the cursor is in the list labeled Color: (on the left side of the window). Within this list, you can select an item by using the up and down arrows. Pressing the Tab key moves the cursor to the next list (the one labeled Foreground:). The last line of the dialog box shows three buttons labeled `OK`, `Cancel`, and `Help`. (A *button* appears as text within angle brackets.) You can get to these options by repeatedly pressing the Tab key. Navigating through a dialog box is tedious without a mouse, but it can be done.

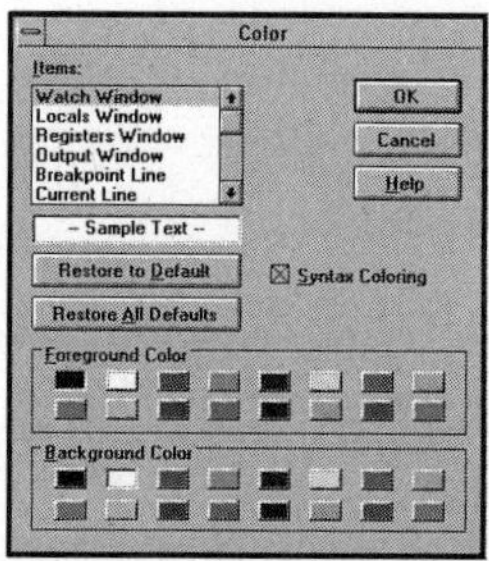

Figure 1.10. The Colors dialog box in the Visual Workbench.

Editing a Program

One of the first steps in writing a simple program is to prepare the source file. The Visual Workbench includes a text editor you can use to prepare the source files for your program. By default, the Visual Workbench's editor uses commands similar to those used in many other Windows editors.

To create a new source file, start by selecting the New option from the File menu. This creates a window named `Untitled.1`. You can immediately start entering text in this window. To save the text in a file, select Save As... from the File menu. The Visual Workbench displays a dialog box and prompts you for the name of the file. When you select the `OK` button in the dialog box, the Visual Workbench saves the text in the specified file.

To edit an existing source file, select Open... from the File menu. The Visual Workbench displays a dialog box with the list of files in the current directory (see Figure 1.11). You can either:

- Type the name of a file in the text-entry area labeled File Name:
- Pick a file from the filename list (by double clicking with the mouse)

You can change the directory or drive by making a selection from the list of drives and directories. Selecting a directory brings up the list of files in that directory in the filename list. After selecting a file, select the `OK` button to load the file.

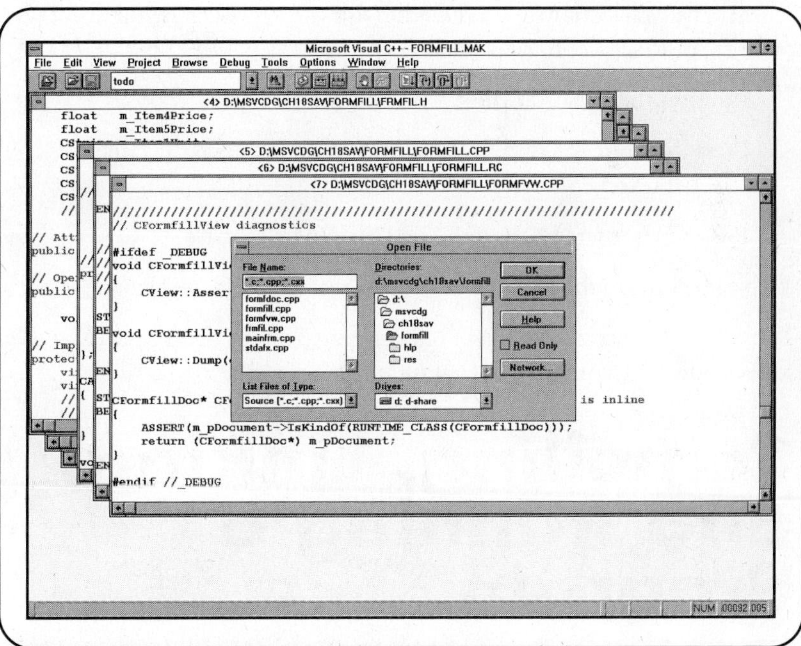

Figure 1.11. The Open File dialog box in the Visual Workbench.

Editing a file is straightforward with a mouse:

1. Move the mouse cursor to the desired position.
2. Click the left mouse button.
3. Begin typing the new text.

To select text for cut-and-paste operations:

1. Press the left mouse button at the starting location.
2. Drag the mouse cursor to the end of the text you want to select.

You then can select Copy or Cut from the Edit menu. Your selection goes into an internal buffer called a *clipboard*. Later, you can paste this text anywhere in the file (or in another file) by using the Paste option from the Edit menu. Do remember that there is only one clipboard in Windows, so be careful not to overwrite the text you have saved in the clipboard with something else—you get no warning when whatever is in the clipboard is going to be overwritten.

As with menu selections, you can edit with the keyboard if you don't want to use the mouse. For example, to select text:

1. Position the cursor at the start of the selection.
2. Press the Shift key and use the arrow keys to move the cursor to the end of the selected text.
3. Press Ctrl+Insert to copy the text into the clipboard.

To paste, position the cursor where you want to insert the text and press Shift+Insert.

Table 1.3 summarizes the basic editing functions in the Visual Workbench and describes how to accomplish these tasks with keystrokes.

Compiling, Linking, and Running a Program

Once the source files are ready, you must compile and link the source files to create an executable program. In the Visual Workbench, the way to build a program is to define a project. To do this, follow these steps:

1. Start by selecting New... from the Project menu. This brings up the New Project dialog box (see Figure 1.12).

2. Enter a name up to eight characters long for the project.
3. Select the type of executable file you want to build (such as DOS EXE or DOS COM). The Visual Workbench appends a .MAK extension to the name and treats that file as the project.

You then see the Project, Edit dialog box, shown in Figure 1.13, where you can edit the project by specifying the Project C (or C++) source files. You also can specify object, library, definition, and resource files in the Project, Edit dialog box.

Editing the project involves adding or deleting names of source files from the project. Later, should you desire to add new source files to your project, select Project, Edit to see the Project, Edit dialog box again.

Once you define a project, you can build the executable program either by selecting Rebuild All from the Project menu or the Visual Workbench's tool bar (see Figure 1.9). The Visual Workbench will invoke CL, the program that compiles and links, with the appropriate options. When the Visual Workbench completes building the executable file, a dialog box appears (see Figure 1.14) giving you an opportunity to examine any errors or warnings generated during the compile and link operations.

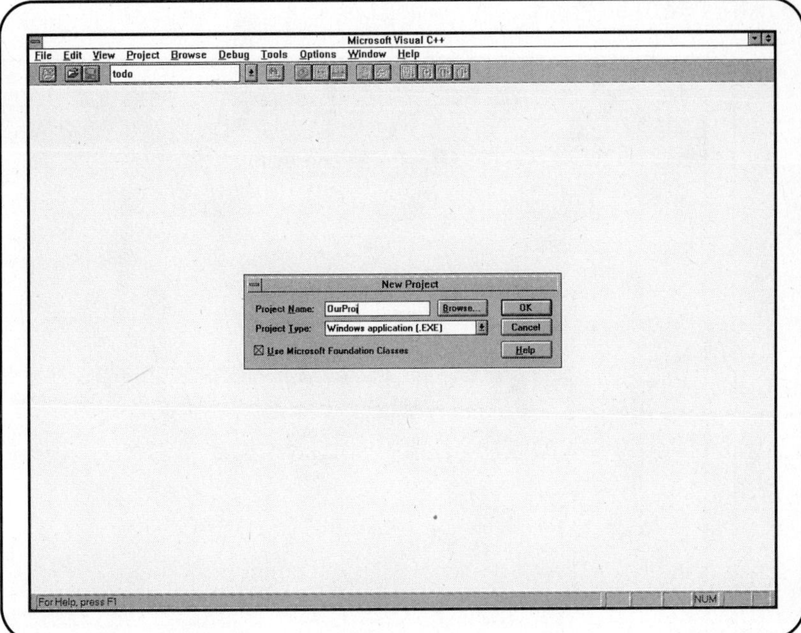

Figure 1.12. The Project, New dialog box.

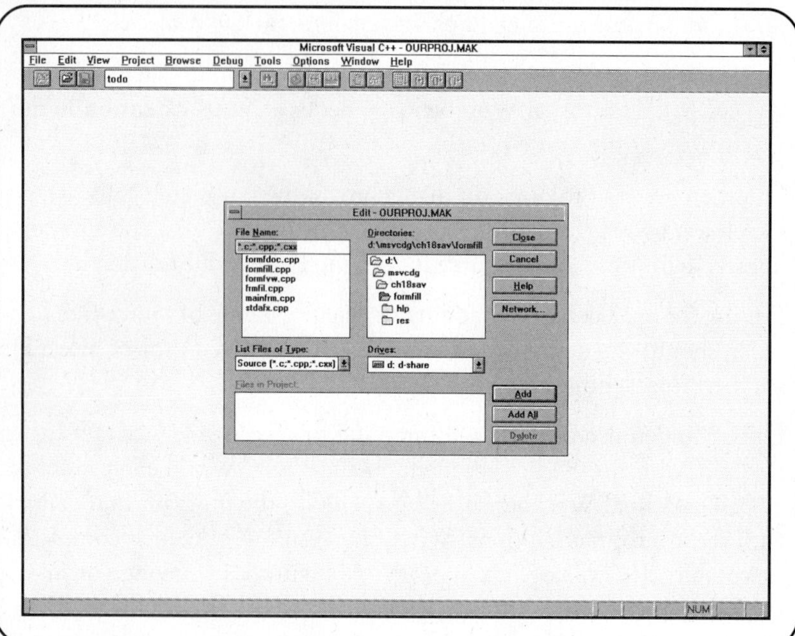

Figure 1.13. The Project, Edit dialog box.

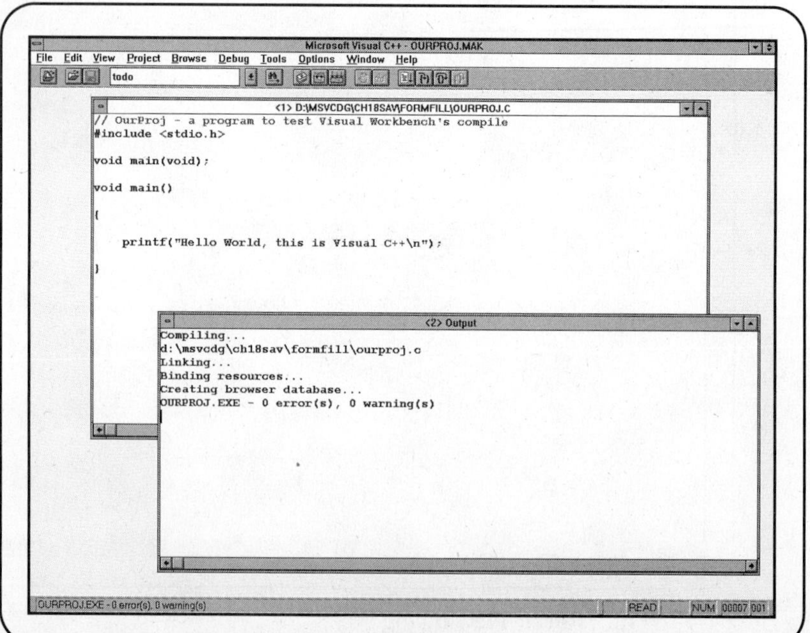

Figure 1.14. The successful building of OurProj—a 'hello' program.

Once the executable file is successfully built, you can run it by selecting the Go option from the Debug menu.

Browsing

A useful feature of the Visual Workbench, Browse enables you to see how your program is organized. You can see information such as the order in which functions call each other; where a function, variable, or class is defined; and the hierarchy of classes in C++ programs. The Browse functions are accessible through the Browse menu, but you must open the database used by Browse before you can access these functions.

Select the Browse menu item, then choose Select Open fn.BSC. When the file to be browsed is opened, you are presented with a new window, called Browse. In this window, which actually is built using a form entry format, you can select whatever objects (or object types) you need information on. (See Chapter 18, "Using AppWizard to Create C++ Windows Applications.")

As an example, select the Call Graph... option from the Query type listbox (see Figure 1.15). From the Symbol list, select `*` (shorthand for all). Browse then presents a list of browseable objects from which you can select the object that interests you. Selecting `CFormfillView::CFormfillView()` lists the object's hierarchical tree, as shown in Figure 1.15, below.

Setting Project Options

So far you've seen how to compile and link using the default settings of the compiler and the linker. These settings include items such as the memory model (described more fully in Chapter 4, "Microsoft Visual C++ Extensions to Standard C"), the processor for which object code is generated (8086, 80186, 80286, or 80386), the levels of optimization, and whether information is generated for source-level debugging by CodeView. (This chapter presents more about debugging in a moment.) This section tells you how to set options used by the linker and resource compiler.

To set these options, select the Project Options item from the Options menu. This action displays a dialog box, from which you can specify:

- The type of program this project is (such as a Windows .EXE, a DOS real-mode application, a QuickWin program, a DLL, and so on)

- Whether you're creating a debugging version of the project (which creates an executable program with debugging information in it) or a release version (which creates a smaller, more compact, version without debugging information)

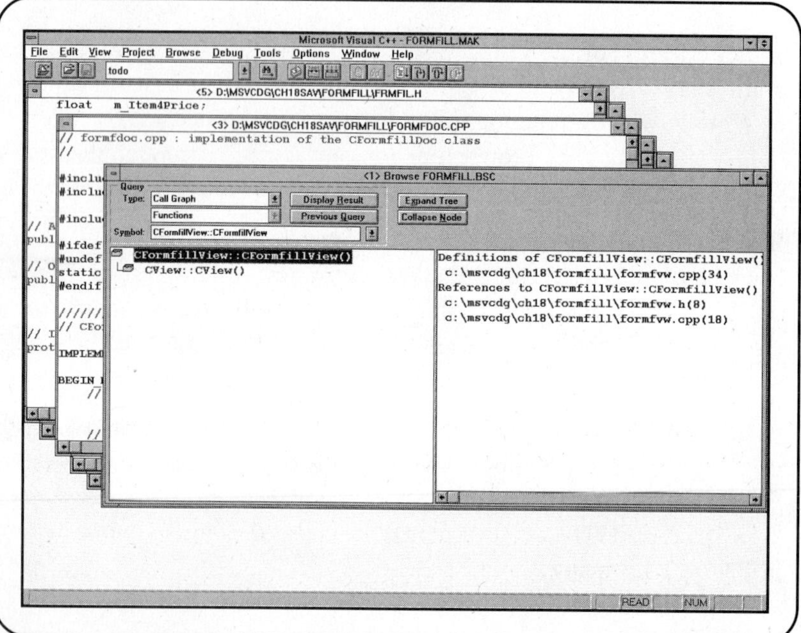

Figure 1.15. The Browse window.

In addition, you can change the options for the compiler, linker, and resource compiler by selecting the correct button in the Customize Build Options group box.

Figure 1.16 shows the Visual C++ Compiler Options dialog box. This box is dynamic, in that the information contained in the Category Settings section changes when the Category list item selection changes. This attribute makes this one dialog box the equivalent to twelve separate dialog boxes. In addition, you can choose whether an option applies to only the debug version, the release version, or to both versions.

The Linker Options... dialog box (Figure 1.17) works much like the Compiler Options... dialog box. The main difference is that the linker has fewer options, which are grouped into five different groups. Again, like the compiler options, the linker options can affect either the debugging version of your project, the release version, or both versions.

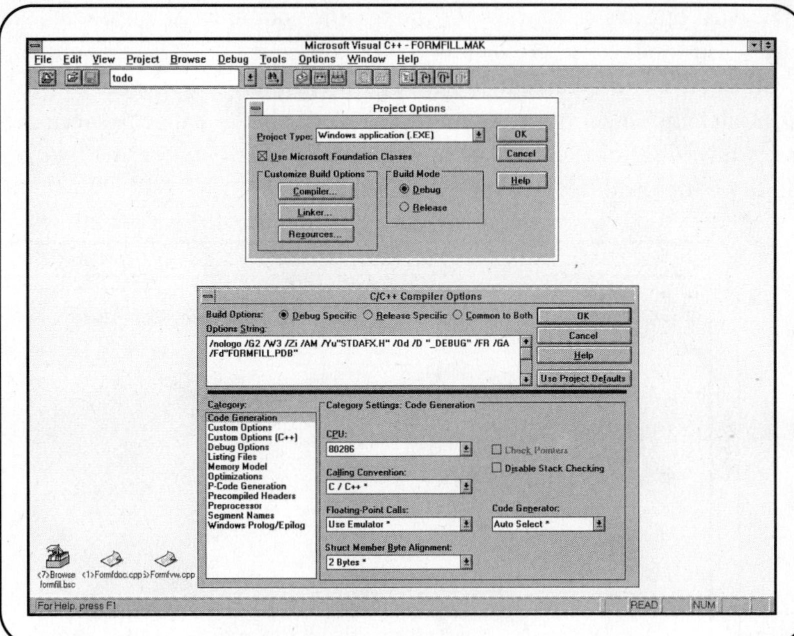

Figure 1.16. Project options, Compiler options.

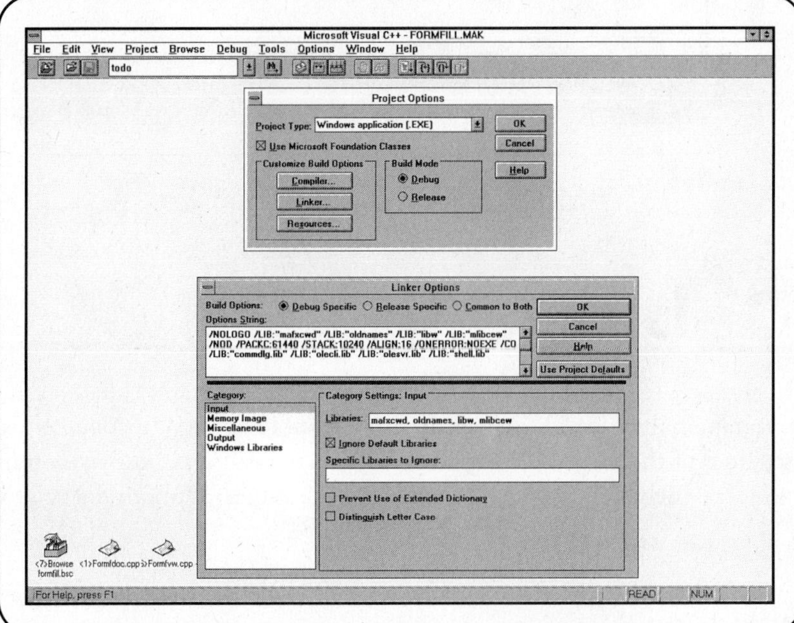

Figure 1.17. Project options, Linker options.

The final options category is for the resource compiler (Figure 1.18). Because only protected-mode projects (Windows programs and DLLs) have resources, this button is not active if the current project is a DOS (real mode) application. Unlike the compiler and linker options, resource options don't change between the debug and release versions of the project. The only difference between the two versions is the ability to define different symbols for each version.

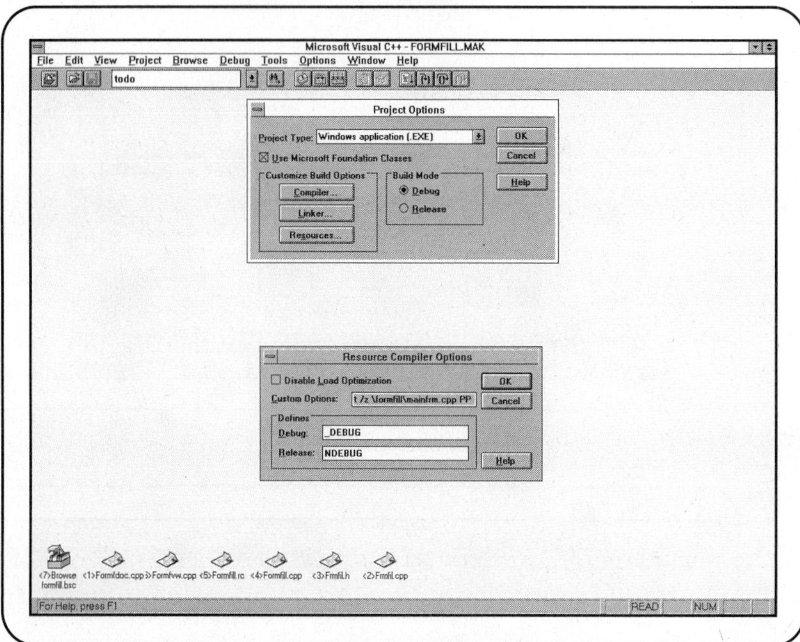

Figure 1.18. Project options, Resource Compiler options.

Debugging

In addition to compiling, linking, and running a program, you also can debug your program in the Visual Workbench. If you want to debug at the source-code level—to see lines of the source file as you step through your program—you must build the project in debug mode. (See Figure 1.16, the Project Options dialog box.)

Disappearing Bugs

Generally, you'll find that most projects already are being built in the debug version. This is normal, because the debug version is the default for a new project. One important note: don't forget to change the build mode to release mode when you're done debugging. A debug version of a project has a much, much larger executable file. In addition you must test the application as a release mode application—sometimes there are bugs that manifest themselves only when the release mode has been selected. Bummer... that makes it much more difficult to find these bugs—creating a debugging version of the project causes the bugs to disappear!

The Visual Workbench has its own debugger built in. Generally, you'll find this debugger to be more than adequate for most applications. You can, however, invoke the CodeView debugger by selecting Codeview from the Tools menu item. Consult Chapter 2, "Program Development Tools in Visual C++," for more information on CodeView.

Now you can debug the program by selecting Go from the Debug menu. When you do, the Visual Workbench runs the application, and you see the application running in a normal manner. It's now possible to select break points, watch variable values, view registers, and so on using the Visual Workbench's debugger.

Using CL

Although the Visual Workbench's interactive environment is convenient, sometimes you may prefer to invoke the compiler and linker directly from the DOS command line; for example, if you have an existing project that's not compatible with the Visual Workbench. NMAKE is much more flexible in what it will accept for its input file compared with what the Visual Workbench will accept as a project file.

The CL.EXE program provides a command-line interface to the Microsoft Visual C++ compiler and linker, and works almost exactly like the Microsoft C 7.0 CL command does. The main difference is the addition of some new compiler options that C 7.0 doesn't offer.

Compiling and Linking with CL

Using CL to compile and link a program with one or only a few source files is simple. You can compile and link the C++ source files FORMFILL.CPP and FORMPACK.CPP (see Chapter 17, "Building MS-DOS Applications in C++") and create the executable program named FORMFILL.EXE by issuing the following command at the MS-DOS prompt:

```
CL FORMFILL.CPP FORMPACK.CPP
```

This command runs the C++ compiler with the default settings, links the resulting object files, and creates an executable program named FORMFILL.EXE.

CL determines how to process a file based on the filename extension. Table 1.4 lists the extensions CL understands.

Table 1.4. Interpretation of file extensions by CL.

Extension	How CL Processes a File
.C	C source file. Compile using C compiler.
.CPP or .CXX	C++ source file. Compile using C++ compiler.
.ASM	Assembly language file. Assemble using the Microsoft Macro Assembler (MASM), which must be already installed.
.OBJ	Object file. Pass to linker for use during linking.
.LIB	Library file. Pass to linker for use in linking.
.DEF	Module definition file (used in Microsoft Windows programs). Pass name to linker.
Other extensions	Object file. Pass name to linker.

However, more often than not, you'll want to use CL with certain options. Each option is a combination of letters and numbers, preceded by a slash (/), which instructs CL to take some specific action. For instance, you may want to use a large memory model, generate code for an 80386 processor, disable optimizations (because you want to debug), and include information for the CodeView debugger. To do this, you have to run CL with the command

```
CL /AL /G3 /Od /Zi FORMFILL.CPP FORMPACK.CPP
```

where `/AL` selects the large memory model, `/G3` generates 80386 code, `/Od` disables optimizations, and `/Zi` ensures inclusion of information needed for source-level debugging with the CodeView debugger.

Options are case-sensitive

All CL options except `/HELP` are case-sensitive. At the DOS command line, type `CL /HELP` to view detailed list of the options that CL supports.

Using the *CL* Environment Variable

If you run CL to compile and link several times, you may find it tedious to type the long command line every time. Besides, you can enter a maximum of 128 characters at the DOS prompt, and a long list of CL options can exceed the 128-character limit. One way to avoid both the repetitive typing and the character limit is to define an environment variable named `CL`, and set it to the list of options you want. Thus, if you set the environment variable **`CL`** as

```
SET CL=/AL /G3 /Od /Zi
```

and run CL with the command

```
CL /I. FORMFILL.CPP FORMPACK.CPP
```

it would be the equivalent of typing

```
CL /AL /G3 /Od /Zi /I. FORMFILL.CPP FORMPACK.CPP
```

This way, you get all the options that were already set in the CL environment variable followed by anything else that you entered when invoking CL from the command line. The `/I.` option indicates that CL should search the current directory for include files.

Environment Variables and CL

CL uses the settings of the environment variables `INCLUDE` to locate the header files and `LIB` to locate the libraries during linking. If you get an error message that says some include files were not found, check the setting of the `INCLUDE` variable. (To see all the environment variables, type `SET` at the DOS prompt.) In particular, if you are including header files from your current working directory, make sure one of the directories listed in `INCLUDE` is the current directory (indicated by a single period). For example, if Microsoft Visual C++ is installed in C:\MSVC, the definition of `INCLUDE` should be as follows:

```
SET INCLUDE=D:\MSVC\INCLUDE;.
```

CL Options

CL accepts more than 130 command-line options in order to offer you, the programmer, complete control over building an executable program. Of course, you don't need to explicitly specify every option when using CL; the options have default settings adequate for most programming tasks. However, if you ever need them, the options are there.

To familiarize yourself with the kinds of operations that the command-line options control, Table 1.5 summarizes the commonly used CL options according to category. Table 1.6 provides a complete alphabetical listing of all the options that CL accepts. Note that a number of options are meant for future versions of the compiler—most notably, the options that generate 32-bit code for 80386 and 80486 processors.

Notice that within the list of options items, angular brackets (<...>) signify required parameters, while those in square brackets (`[...]`) denote optional parameters. Items in italics are place holders for parameters that you must supply.

Table 1.5. Summary, by category, of commonly used CL options.

Category	Options
Memory models	/AS small model (default); /AC compact model /AM medium model /AL large model /AH huge model /AT tiny model (to create .COM files)
Floating-point library	/FPa uses the alternate math library /FPc uses the floating-point emulator library /FPc87 uses the math coprocessor library /FPi uses inline 8087 code with the emulator (default) /FPi87 uses inline 8087 instructions
Optimization	/O enables optimization (same as /Ot) /O1 Minimizes space /O2 Maximizes speed /Oa ignores aliasing /Od disables optimizations /Oe enables registers allocations /Of Toggles p-code quoting /Og enables global optimization /Oi enables intrinsic functions /Ol enables loop optimizations /On disables "unsafe" optimizations /Op enables precision optimizations /Or disables inline return /Os optimizes for space /Ot optimizes for speed (default) /Ow assumes aliasing in function calls only /Ox enables maximum optimization (same as /Ob1cegilnot /Gs)
Preprocessor	/C retains comments /D<*name*>[=*text*] defines a macro /E sends preprocessor output to stdout

continues

Table 1.5. continued

Category	Options
	/EP same as /E, but does not add #line directives to output /I<name> searches a specified directory when including files /P sends preprocessor output to file /U<name> removes a predefined macro /u removes all predefined macros /X ignores standard directories when searching for include files
Code generation	/G0 generates 8086 instructions (default) /G1 generates 80186 instructions /G2 generates 80286 instructions /G3 generates 80386 instructions /Gm places strings in a constant segment /Gc generates Pascal-style function calls /Gr generates _fastcall type calls /Gs does not generate calls to function that checks for stack overflow /Gt[*number*] sets the data size threshold for separate segments /Gw generates the Windows entry
Output files	/Fa[*file*] names an assembly listing file /Fc[*file*] names a mixed source/object listing file /Fe<*file*> names an executable file /Fl[*file*] names an object listing file /Fm[*file*] names a map file /Fo<*file*> names an object file /Fr[*file*] names a source information file for the Browser /FR[*file*] names an extended source information file for Browse /Fs[*file*] names a source listing file
Language extensions	/Za disables Microsoft-specific extensions /Zd embeds line-number information /Ze enables Microsoft-specific extensions (default)

Category	Options
	/Zg generates function declarations (prototypes) /Zi generates symbolic debugging information /Zl removes default library information /Zp[*n*] packs structures on the *n*-byte boundary (*n* = 1, 2, or 4) /Zs performs a syntax check only
Listings	/Sl<*columns*> sets line width /Sp<*lines*> sets page length /St<*string*> sets title string /Ss<*string*> sets subtitle string
Miscellaneous	/c Do a compile only, do not link /H<*number*> external name length /J default char type is unsigned /f uses the fast compile feature /Tc<*file*> assumes the file is C source file /Tp<*file*> assumes the file is C++ source file /V<*string*> embeds the version string in the object file /W<*n*> sets the warning level (n = 0, 1, 2, 3, 4 or X)
Assembly language	/MA<*MASM switch*> passes options to MASM /Ta<*file*> assembles a file without .ASM /Fx[*file*] name for MASM's cross-reference file
Linking	/F <*hex number*> sets tack size (in bytes) /Lr links real-mode executable files /link [*linker options and libraries*] /ML links C runtime as part of DLL /MD uses C runtime as DLL

Table 1.6. Alphabetical summary of commonly used CL options.

Option	Interpretation by CL
/A<*string*>	Uses the custom memory model specified by <*string*>, where <*string*> consists of three letters, one from each

continues

Table 1.6. continued

Option	Interpretation by CL
	of the following groups (see Chapter 2, "Program Development Tools in Visual C++," for more details):
	Code size: `s` or `l`
	Data size: `n`, `f`, or `h`
	Segment order: `d`, `u`, or `w`
`/AC`	Uses the compact memory model (same as option `/Asfd`).
`/AH`	Uses the huge memory model (same as option `/Alhd`).
`/AL`	Uses the large memory model (same as option `/Alfd`).
`/AM`	Uses the medium memory model (same as option `/Alnd`).
`/AS`	Uses the small memory model (same as option `/Asnd`). This is the default setting.
`/AT`	Uses the tiny memory model (for creating .COM files).
`/batch`	Operates in batch mode (terminates compilation in case of an error).
`/Bm` *<Kbytes>*	Uses the specified number of kilobytes during the second pass of the compiler. The default is 2K or 2,048 bytes.
`/C`	Preserves comments during preprocessing. Valid only with options `/E`, `/P`, or `/EP`.
`/c`	Compiles without linking.
`/D`*<name>*`[=`*text*`]`	Defines the specified macro.
`/E`	Preserves `#line` directives in listings of preprocessed files.
`/EP`	Does not include `#line` directives in listings of preprocessed files.

Option	Interpretation by CL
/f	Invokes fast compilation by turning off all default optimizations. This is equivalent to the /qc option in the earlier versions of Microsoft C.
/F <*hexnum*>	Sets the program's stack size to the number of bytes specified by the hexadecimal number <*hexnum*>. The default stack size is 2,048 bytes.
/f-	Selects the optimizing compiler.
/Fa[*file*]	Uses a specified name for the assembly listing file. If a name is missing, this option uses the source filename with an .ASM extension.
/Fc[*file*]	Uses a specified name for the combined source and assembly listing file. If a name is missing, this option uses the source filename with a .COD extension.
/Fd[*file*]	Uses a specified name for the .PDB file.
/Fe<*file*>	Uses a specified name for the executable file.
/Fl[*file*]	Uses a specified name for object code listing file. If a name is missing, this option uses the source filename with a .COD extension.
/Fm[*file*]	Uses a specified name for the linker map file. If a name is missing, this option uses the source filename with a .MAP extension.
/Fo<*file*>	Uses a specified name for the object file. In the absence of this option, the compiler uses the source file's name with an .OBJ extension.
/Fp<*file*>	Uses a specified name for the precompiled header file. The default uses the source file's name with a .PCH extension.
/FPa	Generates calls to an alternate math library for floating-point arithmetic.
/FPc	Generates calls to a floating-point emulator library for floating-point arithmetic.

continues

Table 1.6. continued

Option	Interpretation by CL
`/FPc87`	Generates calls to an 80x87 library. Requires a math coprocessor at runtime.
`/FPi`	Generates inline code to use the emulator library. The code is such that the program can use an 80x87, if one is found at runtime. This is the default option for floating-point math.
`/FPi87`	Generates inline 80x87 instructions that require an 80x87 math coprocessor at runtime.
`/FR[`*`file`*`]`	Uses a specified name for the extended source information file for the Browser (that is, a Browse information file with local symbols). The default is the source filename with an .SBR extension.
`/Fr[`*`file`*`]`	Uses a specified name for the source information file for the Browser (that is, a Browse information file without any local symbols).
`/Fs[`*`file`*`]`	Uses a specified name for the source listing file. If a name is missing, this option uses the source filename with an .LST extension.
`/G0`	Generates 8086 instructions (this is the default).
`/G1`	Generates 80186 instructions.
`/G2`	Generates 80286 instructions.
`/G3`	Generates 80386 instructions.
`/GA`	Optimizes the entry and exit code for all far functions qualified by the `_export` keyword (see Chapter 4, "Microsoft Visual C++ Extensions to Standard C," for details). Used in Windows programs.
`/Gc`	Uses Pascal/FORTRAN naming and function calling conventions.
`/GD`	Optimizes the entry and exit code for all far functions qualified by the `_export` keyword (see Chapter 4, "Microsoft Visual C++ Extensions to Standard C," for

Option	Interpretation by CL
	details). Used in Windows dynamic link libraries (DLLs).
`/Gd`	Uses C naming and function calling conventions. This option is on by default.
`/Ge`	Embeds calls to a stack-checking function that tests for stack overflow. This option is turned on by default.
`/GE`<*string*>	Customizes the entry and exit code in Windows programs (see on-line help for further information).
`/Gf`	Enables string pooling (only one copy of identical strings is kept in memory).
`/Gn`	Optimizes p-code by removing certain code sequences. See Microsoft Visual C++ manuals for more information on p-code.
`/Gp`<*number*>	Uses <*number*> of entry tables, at most, for p-code.
`/Gq`	Generates real-mode Windows entry and exit code. Provided for functional compatibility with the `/GW` option in Microsoft C 6.0.
`/Gr`	Uses fastcall calling convention, whereby function arguments are passed in registers.
`/Gs`	Does not include calls to stack-checking functions.
`/Gt`<*number*>	Places each data item exceeding the specified number of bytes in its own segment. The default value is 256 bytes.
`/GW`	Generates entry and exit codes for a real-mode Windows application. Use only for functions not marked `_export`.
`/Gw`	Generates entry and exit codes for a real-mode Windows application. Use for functions marked `_export`.
`/Gx`	Allocates uninitialized and extern data as near data (see Chapter 4, "Microsoft Visual C++ Extensions to Standard C," for an explanation of near data).

continues

Table 1.6. continued

Option	Interpretation by CL
`/Gx-`	Allocates uninitialized and extern data as far data (see Chapter 4, "Microsoft Visual C++ Extensions to Standard C," for an explanation of far data).
`/Gy`	Enables linking on a function-by-function basis instead of at a module level.
`/H<number>`	Assumes that external names are, at most, `<number>` characters long.
`/HELP`	Lists the compiler options, pausing after each full screen.
`/I<path>`	Searches a specified directory when attempting to find include files.
`/J`	Changes the default type of a `char` data type from signed to unsigned.
`/Ld`	Selects a dynamically linked library.
`/link <options>`	Provides the specified options to the linker.
`/Ln`	Does not link standard startup code from CRT.LIB. Use this with the `/AT` option to link in your own startup code.
`/Lr`	Links to create real-mode executable files. This option is on by default.
`/Lw`	Selects a statistically linked library.
`/MA<option>`	Passes the specified options to the Microsoft Macro Assembler (MASM).
`/Mq`	Compiles as a QuickWin application that has a limited Windows-based user interface.
`/ND<name>`	Uses a specified name for the data segment.
`/NM<name>`	Uses a specified name for code segment. This option has been retained for compatibility with earlier versions of Microsoft C.

Option	Interpretation by CL
/nologo	Does not display the sign-on banner.
/NQ<*name*>	Combines the p-code temporary segments.
/NT<*name*>	Uses a specified name for a code segment.
/NV<*name*>	Uses a specified name for a far virtual table segment (used in C++).
/O	Enables optimization (the same as specifying /Ot).
/O1	Minimizes the size of the executable program.
/O2	Maximizes the performance of the executable program.
/Oa	Assumes no *aliasing*; aliasing occurs when the same memory location is accessed using more than one name (for example, through two pointers).
/Ob<*n*>	Controls the inline expansion of functions. Notice that <*n*> is a single digit from 0 to 2. /Od0 disables inline expansion. /Od1 uses inline expansions for only those functions that you explicitly mark as candidates for inline expansion. /Od2 allows the compiler to generate inline expansions at its discretion.
/Oc	Enables local common sub-expression optimization.
/Od	Disables all optimizations.
/Oe	Enables global register allocation.
/Of[-]	Turns on or off p-code quoting (see on-line help for more information on p-code).
/Og	Enables global common sub-expression optimization.
/Oi	Generates intrinsic (inline) functions.
/Ol	Enables loop code optimization.
/On	Disables loop code optimization.
/Oo[-]	Turns on or off optimizations that occur after code has been generated.

continues

Table 1.6. continued

Option	Interpretation by CL
`/Op[-]`	Improves consistency of tests for equality and inequality of floating-point values.
`/Oq`	Enables maximum p-code optimization.
`/Or`	Uses a common exit sequence for all return statements in a function.
`/Os`	Optimizes for space.
`/Ot`	Optimizes for time.
`/Ov[-]`	Toggles frame sorting of p-code (see on-line help for details).
`/OV`*<n>*	Limits the size of inline functions.
`/Ow`	Assumes that aliasing can occur only across function calls. Aliasing occurs when the same memory location is accessed using more than one name (for example, through two pointers).
`/Ox`	Uses maximum optimization.
`/Oz`	Enables extra loop and global optimization.
`/P`	Writes the preprocessor output to a file (the default filename is the same as the source file's name but with an .I extension).
`/Sl`*<number>*	Uses the specified number of characters as the width of lines in the source listing (from 79 to 132). The default is 79.
`/Sp`*<number>*	Uses the specified number of lines as the size of page in the source listing (from 15 to 255). The default is 63.
`/Ss`*<string>*	Uses a specified string as the subtitle in the source listing.
`/St`*<string>*	Uses a specified string as the title in the source listing.
`/Ta`*<file>*	Assumes that the specified file is an assembly language source file regardless of its extension.

Option	Interpretation by CL
/Tc<*file*>	Assumes that the specified file is a C source file regardless of its extension.
/Tp<*file*>	Assumes that the specified file is a C++ source file regardless of its extension.
/u	Undefines all preprocessor macros.
/U<*name*>	Undefines the specified preprocessor macro.
/V<*string*>	Embeds the specified string in the object code. You can place a version number in the object file using this option.
/Vd{0¦1}	Enables or disables vtordisp.
/Vm<*x*>}	Controls how pointers to members are defined.
/w	Disables all warnings.
/W<*number*>	Sets the warning level to the specified <number>, an integer from 0 to 5. Warning level 0 means no warning messages are generated; at level 5 the compiler treats all warnings as fatal errors. Default is 1.
/WX	Same as /W5; treats all warnings as fatal.
/X	Does not search standard directories for include files.
/Yc	Generates a precompiled header file.
/Yd	Places information for the debugger in the precompiled header file.
/YX	Automatic precompiled headers.
/Yu	Uses the precompiled header file for faster compilation.
/Z7	Generates Microsoft C7 compatible CodeView information.
/Za	Disables Microsoft-specific extensions (Chapter 2,"Program Development Tools in Visual C++," describes these extensions).

continues

Table 1.6. continued

Option	Interpretation by CL
/Zd	Embeds line number information in the object file to support debugging.
/Ze	Enables Microsoft-specific extensions.
/Zg	Generates a prototype declaration for each function.
/Zi	Embeds detailed information in the object files to enable debugging with CodeView.
/Zl	Does not embed names of default libraries in the object file.
/Zn	Does not use the SBRPACK utility to reduce the size of .SBR files generated by the /FR or /Fr options.
/Zp<*number*>	Packs structures on multiples of <*number*> bytes where <*number*> is 1, 2, or 4.
/Zr	Checks for null or out-of-range pointers in programs being compiled with the /f option.
/Zs	Checks syntax only without generating any object or executable file.

A Visual Workbench Session

A quick tour of the Visual Workbench wouldn't be complete without creating an elementary application. Let's take it step-by-step.

1. First, create a simple program. Since we're trying to keep things easy here, let's use the classic Hello program:

```
#include <stdio.h>

int main()

{
```

```
    printf("Hello from Visual C++\n");

    return(0);

}
```

2. After writing the program, save the file. Selecting the Save As... menu item under files produces a dialog box prompt for a filename. Let's call this program HELLO.C.
3. Once the source file(s) have been saved, it's time to create the project. Select Project, New... and provide a project name (don't forget to make sure that you save the project in the correct directory). Specify that this project is to be a DOS Executable program.
4. When Visual Workbench prompts for the files that are part of this project, select HELLO.C (which you saved in step 2, above).
5. After selecting the project's files, select Close from the Project Edit dialog box.
6. Select Project, Build All. Because this project is simple, we can go ahead and accept whatever options that Visual Workbench provides for a DOS program.
7. Assuming you didn't make any typing mistakes, your program should compile and link correctly, with no errors. If you get a linker error stating that the MAFXCRD or MAFXCR library wasn't found, you forgot to build the MFC DOS versions of the libraries. A successful compile and link will produce the following in the output window:

```
Compiling...
d:\msvcdg\test.c
Linking...
Creating browser database...
TEST.EXE - 0 error(s), 0 warning(s)
```

8. Run the program (just to convince you that all went as expected). The program's output will be:

```
DOS6 6.0 (MICKEY): 19:54:35 D:\MSVCDG
hello
Hello from Visual C++

DOS6 6.0 (MICKEY): 19:54:37 D:\MSVCDG
```

For additional practice, try creating a new project using the same source file (HELLO.C), and creating a QuickWin program. Hint: the only change is in the third step above.

Summary

Microsoft Visual C++ is a combination of program development tools and utilities. Its most visible component is the Visual Workbench, which is the main interface between you—the programmer—and Visual C++. This chapter briefly described how to use the Visual Workbench, summarized the Visual Workbench's features, and pointed out that the best way to learn about all of Microsoft Visual C++'s tools is through the extensive on-line help provided by the Visual Workbench. The last part of this chapter described CL, the command-line interface to the Visual C++ compiler and linker.

Although you can perform all the edit/compile/link/debug chores from the Visual Workbench, it's helpful to be familiar with individual program-development tools. That way, you can set up makefiles that invoke these tools, and access such makefiles using NMAKE, should you find it necessary.

2

Program Development Tools in Visual C++

Chapter 1, "The Microsoft Visual C++ Environment," provided you with an overview of the Microsoft Visual C++ programming environment—the tools it offers and how the Visual C++ compiler typically is used. Chapter 1 also describes Visual Workbench—the easiest way to interface with Visual C++—and CL, the command-line version of the compiler. This chapter describes how to use a number of other program development tools: LINK, LIB, NMAKE, and CODEVIEW. (Notice that CL also invokes LINK to create executable programs. However, Chapter 1 did not show LINK's options.)

- LINK is a tool that combines a number of object modules and libraries to create an executable file (either an .EXE or a .COM file).
- LIB enables you to store many object modules in a single library file (a .LIB file).

- NMAKE automates the use of the compiler, linker, and the other tools.
- CV is the CodeView debugger that enables you to find errors in your programs.

For each of these tools, this chapter presents a short description of how to use the tool and lists the options offered by the tool. In all cases, these options can be selected from the Visual Workbench's project options.

Nothing in this chapter should be considered to indicate that you must use any of the utilities described. Virtually all program development can (and should) be done using the Visual Workbench. All of the tools described here are available (and often are used automatically, without interaction on your part) from the Visual Workbench. Occasionally, however, it's necessary to use the command-line versions of these utilities—and so, they're described here. Because these tools aren't often used directly under Visual C++, we don't cover them in great detail.

Getting Help

You can use the on-line help facility in Visual Workbench or select the appropriate help file (select the icon from the Visual C++ program group in Windows Program Manager) to find out more about program-development tools. To get help on most program-development tools in Microsoft Visual C++, use the command-line option `/?` (or `/HELP`) to see a short list of all the command-line options the tool accepts. Thus, if you want to learn more about NMAKE, enter

```
NMAKE /HELP
```

at the DOS command prompt. This will display a list of valid options for NMAKE.

Some tools, such as CODEVIEW, stand alone and provide help through menus in their user interface.

LINK, the Linker

The job of LINK, the Microsoft linker, is to combine one or more object files (.OBJ) and libraries (.LIB files) into an executable file (.EXE). The linker is necessary because MS-DOS cannot execute .OBJ files, even if there is only a single source file for a program. The resulting .OBJ file must be converted to an .EXE format before MS-DOS can load it into memory and run it. LINK performs this conversion from .OBJ format to .EXE.

Usually, the linker is called by the Visual Workbench; if you are using the command line compiler (CL), the compiler will call the linker. Because the Visual Workbench is so powerful, it's unlikely that you'll have many opportunities to use the linker directly.

Additionally, when a software project is broken down into a number of modules or source files, one source file might call functions that are defined in another file. When the compiler translates each source file into an object file, it embeds information about external functions and variables referenced in that source file. The linker then blends all the object files and ensures that all external functions and variables are found and referenced correctly in the executable program it generates. LINK can also search through libraries (.LIB files) to resolve these references to external functions and variables.

Using LINK

Most of the time you'll invoke LINK indirectly through the Visual Workbench or CL, but LINK often is invoked directly in *makefiles* (described later in this chapter). Source files are first compiled into object files and then LINK is invoked to link the object files together with the required libraries. You can invoke LINK in three different ways.

- Enter the command

  ```
  LINK
  ```

  without any options. When you press Enter, LINK runs in interactive mode, prompting for names of object files and libraries. Here's an example of the dialog:

  ```
  Object Modules [.obj]: iotest.obj /farcall
  Run File [iotest.exe]: iotest.exe /noi
  List File [nul.map]:
  Libraries [.lib]:
  Definitions File [nul.def]: ;
  ```

  The strings `/farcall` and `/noi` are command-line options for LINK—you can embed them as you respond to the prompts.

- Enter the LINK command with options and filenames on the command line. The syntax is

  ```
  LINK [opt] <objfiles>,[exefile],[mapfile],[libs],[deffile] [;]
  ```

  where [opt] refers to one or more optional LINK options (listed later in Table 2.1) and <objfiles> denotes the required object filenames. The other fields in the command are optional except for the separating commas—they are required. You can, however, enter a semicolon anywhere after the names of the object files to end the command line. In this case, LINK uses default values for the remaining filenames.

- Place all LINK options and filenames in a text file and invoke LINK as follows:

  ```
  LINK @<response-file>
  ```

  where <response-file> is the name of the file containing the input commands meant for LINK. Notice that LINK does not assume any specific filename extension for the response file; you should provide the complete filename for the response file.

The simplest way to link a few object files is to invoke LINK as follows:

```
LINK windraw shapes winview;
```

In this case, LINK will look for the files WINDRAW.OBJ, SHAPES.OBJ, and WINVIEW.OBJ and automatically search certain default libraries to complete the linking process and create an executable file named WINDRAW.EXE.

Filenames for LINK

In the example showing LINK's interactive mode prompts, you may have noticed several types of files that LINK uses or generates. LINK's command syntax also shows these filenames:

```
LINK [opt] <objfiles>,[exefile],[mapfile],[libs],[deffile] [;]
```

You already know about the <objfiles> field, which contains the names of the object files that LINK combines to create the executable file.

The <exefile> field refers to the name of the executable file. If you do not specify a name, LINK takes the name of the first object file, changes the extension to .EXE, and uses that as the name of the executable file.

The `<mapfile>` field in the LINK command line refers to the name of the map file created by LINK. The map file usually contains a list of segments and a list of all global variables and functions, but you can use the `/MAP:FULL` option to generate more information about each object file. If you don't provide the name of the map file, LINK does not create it. However, if you specify the `/MAP` option, LINK creates a map file even if you do not explicitly provide a map filename. LINK derives the default name for the map file from the name of the first object file by changing the extension to .MAP.

The `<libs>` field in the LINK command is a list of library files (.LIB) that should be searched to locate external functions and variables. Even if you do not specify library files explicitly, the object files created by the Microsoft Visual C++ Compiler contain embedded information about the standard libraries that LINK should search.

The `<deffile>` field denotes the name of a module definition file—something LINK needs when creating Windows applications or Dynamic Link Libraries (DLLs). You'll see an example of the definition file in Chapter 17, "Building Microsoft Windows Applications in C++," when we discuss how to build a Windows application using Microsoft Visual C++ .

Overlays

When you write MS-DOS applications, you should be aware of the 640K limit on memory accessible under DOS. *Overlays* provide one way to squeeze a large application into a fixed amount of memory. The idea is simple: suppose you have an application that performs one of two tasks—we'll call them tasks A and B—but never both tasks at the same time. You organize your application into three modules (files):

- MAIN.C, which contains your application's main function and the definitions of functions and variables used for both tasks A and B. The main function also calls functions from the other two modules.
- TASK_A.C, which contains the functions needed to perform task A. Functions in TASK_A.C can call those in MAIN.C, but do not call any function from the module TASK_B.C.
- TASK_B.C, which contains the functions needed to perform task B. Functions from TASK_B.C do not call any function or refer to any variable defined in TASK_A.C.

This type of organization is ideal for overlays. Basically, when you run the application, you want DOS to load into memory only the code belonging to module MAIN.

Then, when the application performs task A, the TASK_A module is loaded into memory. Afterwards, when the application performs task B, the TASK_B module is loaded at the same location in memory where TASK_A resides—that is, TASK_B is overlaid on top of TASK_A. Thus, at any time, only MAIN and either TASK_A or TASK_B remain in memory. Instead of requiring memory to load all three modules at once, your application can get by with a smaller amount of memory.

Old-Style Overlays

LINK can embed information in an executable file to ensure the loading of modules on the fly (provided you specify the organization of the overlaid modules to LINK). In the example, each of the modules (MAIN, TASK_A, and TASK_B) is an overlay, with the MAIN module serving as the *root overlay*—the one that has to stay in memory throughout the execution of your program. Once you compile these three source modules and create the object files MAIN.OBJ, TASK_A.OBJ, and TASK_B.OBJ, you can create an old-style overlay program with the following command:

```
LINK /OLD MAIN + (TASK_A + TASK_B);
```

Notice the `/OLD` flag, which ensures that LINK incorporates the Microsoft Overlay Manager.

New Overlays with MOVE

With Visual C++, Microsoft has introduced a new way of creating DOS programs with overlays—they call it the *Microsoft Overlay Virtual Environment* (MOVE). MOVE is a dynamic-overlay manager for use in creating DOS programs with overlays. Microsoft warns that old-style overlays that use the static overlay manager may not be supported in the future.

MOVE offers several advantages over the static overlay manager:

- MOVE allows up to 2,047 overlays; the static manager allows only 255 overlays.
- MOVE allows more than one overlay in memory at the same time; the old scheme allows only one overlay at a time.
- MOVE allows inter-overlay function calls through pointers to functions; the old static overlay manager does not allow this type of function call between overlays.

- MOVE has a scheme for *caching* (temporarily storing) overlays in conventional, expanded, or extended memory; the static overlay manager must reload each overlay from the .EXE file on the disk.

To build an overlay program using MOVE, you must create a text file known as a *module-definition file* (a .DEF file) that describes the overlays. The linker uses the module-definition file to determine the memory layout of the code and data of the overlay program. Normally, you don't need a module-definition file to link an MS-DOS program, but the linker needs a module-definition file when linking an overlaid DOS program.

To see how to build an overlay program that uses MOVE, consider the example from the previous section. In that example, an application contains three modules: MAIN.C, TASK_A.C, and TASK_B.C. Suppose you want to build an overlay program, MAIN.EXE, with three overlays: the code from MAIN.C in the root overlay and the code from TASK_A.C and TASK_B.C in two separate overlays. Here are the steps to build the program.

1. Compile MAIN.C, TASK_A.C, and TASK_B.C with the `/AL` or `/AM` option. This ensures that the object code from each module resides in a segment with a unique name (in this case the names are MAIN_TEXT, TASK_A_TEXT, and TASK_B_TEXT).

2. Use a text editor to create a file named MAIN.DEF with the following lines in it:

   ```
   SEGMENTS TASK_A-TEXT OVL:1

   SEGMENTS TASK_B-TEXT OVL:2
   ```

   This specifies that you want the TASK_A_TEXT segment in overlay number 1 and the TASK_B_TEXT segment in overlay number 2. Use any overlay number from 1 to 65535. Overlay number 0 refers to the root overlay.

3. Build the overlaid executable file, MAIN.EXE, with the following LINK command:

   ```
   LINK main TASK_a TASK_b, main, , , main.def
   ```

LINK Options

LINK accepts a number of options. When you compile and link using CL, you can pass these options to LINK through CL's `/link` option. Table 2.1 lists LINK's command-line options and their meanings (the portion of the option shown in square brackets is optional).

> **Shortening LINK Command-Line Options**
>
> LINK's command-line options have long descriptive names, but all you have to type are the first two or three characters. The optional portion of the option is listed within square brackets ([...]) in Table 2.1.

Table 2.1. LINK options.

Option	Interpretation by LINK
/?	Displays the list of command-line options.
/A[LIGNMENT]:<*size*>	Aligns the segments in the executable file at the boundaries specified by <*size*>, which is in bytes. LINK does not use this option for DOS programs. The default is to align along 512-byte boundaries. Windows programs require alignment at 16-byte boundaries.
/B[ATCH]	Suppresses the prompts for directory names when libraries or object files are not found. This option is useful in batch files or makefiles meant for NMAKE.
/CO[DEVIEW]	Generates an executable file with embedded information that will be used by the Microsoft CodeView debugger CV.
/CP[ARMAXALLOC]:<*num*>	Sets to <*num*> the maximum number of 16-byte paragraphs needed by a program. Valid range for <*num*> is from 1 to 65,535. LINK uses this option only for DOS programs. LINK normally sets the number of paragraphs to 65,535; because this is

Option	Interpretation by LINK
	more than the limit of DOS' memory, DOS ends up allocating the largest contiguous block of free memory to the program.
`/DO[SSEG]`	Orders segments according to the DOS segment-ordering convention, proceeding from low to high addresses. All segments of class `CODE` come first. The segments not in `DGROUP` come next, followed by the segments belonging to the `DGROUP` group of segments. By default, LINK orders segments this way when it links programs that link with the C and C++ libraries. Notice that the `/DOSSEG` option also inserts 16 null bytes at the beginning of the _TEXT segment, if the _TEXT segment exists in the program.
`/DS[ALLOCATE]`	Loads data starting at the high end of the data segment. This option is meant for assembly language programs that are linked as DOS .EXE files.
`/DY[NAMIC][:`*num*`]`	Creates a DOS executable file that contains overlays. The optional number *num* specifies the maximum number of inter-overlay calls. The default value is 256.
`/E[XEPACK]`	Removes a series of repeated null characters and optimizes to reduce the size of the executable file. Notice that CodeView cannot debug packed executable files.
`/F[ARCALLTRANSLATION]`	Translates far calls within the same segment into near calls to improve efficiency. This option is turned off by default.
`/HE[LP]`	Displays the list of valid options.

continues

Table 2.1. continued

Option	Interpretation by LINK
/HI[GH]	Places information in the executable file that causes DOS to load the program as high as possible in memory. This option is used with /DSALLOC in assembly language programs that are linked as a DOS .EXE file.
/INF[ORMATION]	Displays information about the linking process as LINK builds the executable file.
/LI[NENUMBERS]	Adds the line number of the source files to the map file. The object file must have been compiled with either the /Zd or /Zi option. Specifying one of these options creates a map file (with .MAP extension).
/M[AP][:*code*]	Creates a map file (.MAP extension) with a list of segments and a list of all global symbols in the program. The *code* parameter can be either the FULL or 0 keyword. With FULL, LINK includes information about each object file's contribution to each segment, whereas /M:0 restricts the map file to a list of segments and globals.
/NOD[EFAULTLIBRARYSEARCH]	Does not search default libraries (the library names are embedded in the object files). If you want to stop LINK from searching for a specific default library only, use the option /NOD:<*libname*>, where <*libname*> is the default library LINK should ignore.
/NOE[XTDICTIONARY]	Does not search extended dictionaries—lists symbols and their locations in libraries created by LIB. You should use /NOE when you are redefining a function that already exists in a standard library.

Option	Interpretation by LINK
/NOF[ARCALLTRANSLATION]	Disables the /FARCALL option. By default, /NOFARCALL is turned on—that is, /FARCALL is not active.
/NOG[ROUPASSOCIATION]	Ignores group associations when assigning addresses to data and code in the executable file. This option is included for compatibility with older versions of Microsoft compilers and linkers.
/NOI[GNORECASE]	Does not ignore case in symbols. This option is turned off by default—LINK normally ignores case when looking for global variables and functions.
/NOL[OGO]	Does not display the copyright notice at start-up. This option works only if it's the first option in the command line.
/NON[ULLSDOSSEG]	Produces the same effect as the /DOSSEG option, except that /NON does not insert the 16 null bytes at the start of the _TEXT segment.
/NOP[ACKCODE]	Turns off the /PACK option—that is, code-segment packing is disabled.
/NOPACKF[UNCTIONS]	Retains code belonging to unreferenced packaged functions in the executable file. Packaged functions are generated by compiling C or C++ source files with the /Gy option.
/OL[DOVERLAY]	Uses the old-style static overlay manager to create an overlaid DOS program. The new overlay system is known as Microsoft Overlaid Virtual Environment (MOVE).
/ON[ERROR]:N[OEXE]	Does not overwrite the existing .EXE file if an error occurs during the linking process.

continues

Table 2.1. continued

Option	Interpretation by LINK
/O[VERLAYINTERRUPT]:<*n*>	Uses <*n*> as the interrupt number for loading overlays. The default interrupt number is 63 (Hex 3F); you can specify any number from 1 to 255.
/PACKC[ODE][:<*num*>]	Packs adjacent code segments into 64K blocks. The optional numeric parameter specifies the maximum size of a packed code segment. The default is 36 bytes less than 64K (65,536 – 36 = 65,500 bytes). By default, LINK packs code segments.
/PACKD[ATA][:<*num*>]	Combines adjacent data segments into the same physical segment. The optional <*num*> parameter specifies the maximum size of a packed data segment. The default value is 64K, or 65,536 bytes.
/PACKF[UNCTIONS]	Removes code belonging to unreferenced packaged functions from the executable file. Packaged functions are generated by compiling C or C++ source files with the /Gy option.
/PAU[SE]	Pauses before writing the executable file to disk. This option is retained for compatibility with old systems without hard disks. The pause allows the user to swap disks so the executable file can be written on a disk with enough free space.
/PM[TYPE]:<*type*>	Creates an executable file of the specified <*type*>. The <*type*> is one of the following strings: PM for Windows applications VIO for character-mode applications that can run inside a window in Windows

Option	Interpretation by LINK
	`NOVIO` for character-mode applications that have to run in full-screen mode under Windows
`/Q[UICKLIBRARY]`	Builds a quick library (.QLB extension) instead of an .EXE file. Quick libraries can be used by Microsoft QuickBasic and early versions Microsoft QuickC. They are a variant of DLLs in the sense that applications use quick libraries to access the code in the library at runtime.
`/r`	Does not use extended memory under DOS; completes the linking process using conventional memory. This option is case-sensitive and must appear first on the command line.
/SE[GMENTS][:<*n*>]	Sets the maximum number of segments in the program to <*n*>, where <*n*> is any number from 1 to 16,384. By default, LINK allows up to 128 segments in a program.
/ST[ACK]:<*n*>	Sets the stack size to <*n*> bytes, where <*n*> is any positive, even number from 0 to 65,536. The default stack size is 2,048 bytes.
`/T[INY]`	Creates a .COM file instead of an .EXE file.
`/W[ARNFIXUP]`	Issues a "fix-up warning" whenever a fix-up value is determined using displacement from the beginning of a group of segments. The *fix-up value* is information that the linker needs to *resolve* (fix up) addresses of external functions and variables referenced in the object files.

LIB, the Library Manager

LIB, the Microsoft Library Manager, organizes one or more object modules into a single library file (with a .LIB extension). Instead of keeping a large number of object files and providing their names to the linker, you can use LIB to keep all object files in a single library file and make the linker search the library file for any required object files. Use LIB to create a new library and modify an existing library file.

As with LINK, the Visual Workbench can create libraries directly. You normally wouldn't need to use the command line version of LIB.

Using LIB

Like LINK, you can invoke LIB in three ways:

- Enter `LIB` at the DOS command prompt. This will start LIB in the interactive mode, where it prompts for input. The following is a sample interaction showing the addition of an object module (iostat.obj) to a library (diskio.lib):

  ```
  Library name: diskio.lib
  Operations: +iostat.obj
  List file: diskio.lis
  Output library: diskio1.lib
  ```

- Enter a complete `LIB` command at the DOS prompt. The full syntax is

  ```
  LIB <library> [options] [commands] [,listfile][,newlibrary] [;]
  ```

  where *<library>* is the name of the library file (.LIB extension) being created or modified and *[options]* denotes one or more LIB options (listed in Table 2.2). The *[commands]* field indicates what operations, if any, LIB should perform on *<library>*. If you do not specify any commands, LIB checks that the specified library is a valid one and exits. If you provide a filename in the *[listfile]* field, LIB places an alphabetic list of symbols and modules in that file. The *[newlibrary]* field indicates the name of the library where LIB places the results of the operations it performs on *<library>*—LIB does not alter the original library; it copies the original library to *<newlibrary>* and makes the modifications on the new library. If you omit the *<newlibrary>* field, LIB copies the original library to a file with the same name but with a .BAK extension, and then modifies the original library. If you omit the optional fields, you must either provide the separating commas indicated in the syntax or enter a semicolon to end the command line.

- Place all LIB options and filenames in a text file and invoke LIB as follows:

  ```
  LIB @<response_file>
  ```

  where *<response_file>* is the name of the file containing the input commands meant for LIB. Notice that LIB does not assume any specific filename extension for the response file; you should provide the complete filename for the response file.

The simplest example of using LIB is to create a new library. To create a library named TXTWIN.LIB, enter the following command:

```
LIB TXTWIN;
```

LIB assumes the extension .LIB and creates an empty library file named TXTWIN.LIB. Now you can add object files to this library. For instance, to add the modules TVIDEO.OBJ and TWINDOW.OBJ to the library TXTWIN.LIB, you would enter

```
LIB TXTWIN +TVIDEO +TWINDOW;
```

The plus signs (+) preceding the names of the object modules are commands to LIB to add those modules to the specified library (TXTWIN.LIB). LIB automatically selects the filename extensions. Later, if you want to remove the TWINDOW module from the TXTWIN library, enter this:

```
LIB TXTWIN -TWINDOW;
```

LIB Options and Commands

The command line for LIB has the following syntax:

```
LIB <library> [options] [commands] [,listfile][,newlibrary] [;]
```

Here, the `[options]` field can be any one of the options listed in Table 2.2. You can view this list by entering **LIB /?** at the command prompt. Also, the **LIB /HELP** command will bring up Microsoft QuickHelp with help on LIB.

Table 2.2. Options for LIB.

Option	Interpretation by LIB
`/?`	Displays list of LIB options.
`/HELP`	Runs Microsoft QuickHelp and displays on-line help for LIB.
`/I[GNORECASE]`	Ignores case when comparing symbols. This is the default.
`/NOE[XTDICTIONARY]`	Does not build an extended dictionary of cross references between modules.
`/NOI[GNORECASE]`	Does not ignore case when comparing symbols. Libraries for C and C++ are built with the `/NOI` option.
`/NOL[OGO]`	Does not display the copyright message at start-up.
`/P[AGESIZE]:`*<n>*	Sets the page size to *<n>* bytes. The page size refers to the alignment modules within the library files—modules start at locations that are multiples of the page size from the beginning of the file. The default page size is 16; you can specify any value that is an integer power of 2 and is from 16 to 32,768.

You specify the operations to be performed on a library in the `[`*`commands`*`]` field in the LIB command line. Table 2.3 lists the operations that LIB supports.

Table 2.3. Commands supported by LIB.

Command	Action by LIB
`+`*<name>*	Adds the object file or library specified by *<name>*. If *<name>* has no extension, LIB assumes that *<name>* refers to an .OBJ file. In this case *<name>* can be a library that explicitly indicates the .LIB extension. For example, to add the contents of the CHART.LIB library to GRAPH.LIB, you would enter `LIB GRAPH +CHART.LIB;`

Command	Action by LIB
`-<name>`	Deletes the module specified by `<name>`.
`-+<name>`	Replaces the specified object file (deletes the module from the library and then adds the new object file).
`*<name>`	Extracts the specified module into an object file with the same name. The module still remains in the library.
`-*<name>`	Extracts the specified module and then deletes it from the library.

NMAKE, the Program Maintenance Utility

Microsoft NMAKE is a program maintenance utility patterned after the UNIX MAKE utility. The following sections provide an overview of NMAKE. You should consult the online help or the *Microsoft Visual C++ Environment and Tools Manual* for a detailed description of NMAKE.

You can pass a Visual Workbench project file (which also will have the extension .MAK) to NMAKE.

Generally, NMAKE is most valuable in creating a project that has it's own makefile—where you don't want to go to the bother of creating a new Visual Workbench project.

The Makefile

NMAKE works by reading and interpreting a *makefile*—a text file that you must prepare according to a specified syntax. By default, NMAKE expects the makefile to be named MAKEFILE, literally. In fact, if you invoke NMAKE by entering

```
NMAKE
```

at the DOS prompt, NMAKE will search for a text file named MAKEFILE. If the file exists, NMAKE will interpret its contents and act upon the commands contained in that file.

The makefile describes how NMAKE should maintain your program—how it should create the object files and which object files should be linked to create the executable program.

For a program that consists of several source and header files, the makefile indicates which items will be created by NMAKE—these usually are the .OBJ and .EXE files—and how these files depend on other files. For instance, suppose you had a C++ source file named FORM.CPP containing the following statement:

```
#include "form.h"    // Include header file
```

FORM.OBJ clearly depends on the source file FORM.CPP and the header file FORM.H. In addition to these dependencies, you must also specify how NMAKE should convert the FORM.CPP file into FORM.OBJ. In this case, suppose you want NMAKE to use CL with the options `/c /AL /Zi /Od`. This fact can be expressed by the following lines in the makefile:

```
# This is a comment in the makefile
# The following lines indicate how FORM.OBJ depends
# on FORM.CPP and FORM.H and how to build FORM.OBJ.

FORM.OBJ: FORM.CPP FORM.H
          CL /c /AL /Zi /Od FORM.CPP
```

Here, FORM.OBJ is the *target* and FORM.CPP and FORM.H are the *dependent files.* The line following the dependency indicates how to build the target from its dependents.

The biggest benefit of using NMAKE is that it avoids unnecessary compilations. After all, you could invoke CL in a DOS batch file to compile and link all the modules in your program, but the batch file will compile everything even if the compilations are unnecessary. NMAKE, on the other hand, only builds a target if one or more of its dependents has changed since the last time the target was built. It verifies this by examining the time of last modification stamped on the files.

One curious aspect of NMAKE is that it treats the target as the name of a goal to be achieved—the target does not have to be a file. For example, you can have a target such as

```
clean:
        erase form.exe
        erase form.obj
```

which specifies an abstract target named clean that does not depend on anything. This dependency statement says that to make clean, NMAKE should invoke two commands: `erase form.exe` and `erase form.obj`. Thus, the net effect of creating the target named clean is to delete the files FORM.EXE and FORM.OBJ.

Macros

In addition to the basic service of building targets from dependents, NMAKE provides many nice features that make it easy for you to express the dependencies and rules for building a target from its dependents. For example, if you need to compile a large number of C++ files with the same CL options, it would be tedious to type the options for each file. You can avoid this by defining a symbol, or *macro*, in NMAKE as follows:

```
# Define macros for standard options for CL
CLFLAGS=/c /AL /Zi /Od
# Define macro used to invoke CL
CL=cl $(CLFLAGS)
# Now define the rule for building FORM.OBJ
FORM.OBJ: FORM.CPP FORM.H
          $(CL) FORM.CPP
```

Notice how the CL options are defined as a macro named `CLFLAGS`. This symbol is used to define another macro named `CL` that uses `CLFLAGS`. To use a macro elsewhere in the makefile, follow a `$` with the macro within parentheses. For instance, NMAKE replaces all occurrences of `$(CLFLAGS)` with the definition of the macro `CLFLAGS`.

NMAKE has a number of predefined macros, as well as some macros with special meanings (these are listed in Table 2.4). You can see a list of all NMAKE macros by entering the `/P` option when you run NMAKE. When you see the list of predefined macros that NMAKE displays, you'll notice that NMAKE considers all environment variables to be predefined macros.

Table 2.4. Some predefined macros in NMAKE.

Macro	Meaning
`$*`	Name of the target file without the extension.
`$@`	Complete name of the target.
`$**`	All names appearing in the list of dependents.

continues

Table 2.4. continued

Macro	Meaning
`$<`	Name of a dependent file that is out of date with respect to the target.
`$?`	All dependent files that are out of date with respect to the target.
`$(CC)`	Command used to invoke the C compiler; by default, `CC = CL`.
`$(CFLAGS)`	Undefined, but used by NMAKE when invoking `$(CC)`—the C compiler. Thus, you can pass options to the C compiler by defining the `CFLAGS` macro.
`$(CPP)`	Command used to invoke the C++ compiler; by default, `$(CPP) = CL`.
`$(CPPFLAGS)`	Undefined, but used by NMAKE when invoking `$(CPP)`—the C++ compiler. Thus, you can pass options to the C++ compiler by defining the `CPPFLAGS` macro.

Inference Rules

NMAKE also supports the definition of rules—known as *inference rules*—that define how a file with one extension is created from a file with another extension. Consider, for example, the rule for generating an object file (.OBJ file) from a C++ source (.CPP) file. Because this involves running CL with a specified set of options, this is a good candidate for an inference rule. You have only to define an inference rule once in a makefile. For example, to instruct NMAKE to build an .OBJ file from a .CPP file by using CL with the `/c` option, you would write the following inference rule:

```
# Inference rule to make .OBJ file from .CPP file
.CPP.OBJ:
        $(CPP) /c $<
```

This rule utilizes the macro CPP, which is predefined in NMAKE as CL. Notice the use of another macro, `$<`, in this rule—you could also write this as `$(<)`. As you can see from Table 2.4, this predefined macro represents the name of a dependent file that is out of date with respect to the target.

To help you set up makefiles, NMAKE already defines a number of inference rules, including the one that builds .OBJ files from .CPP files.

A Sample Makefile

You can easily write a makefile if you use NMAKE's predefined macros and its built-in inference rules. Consider, for example, a makefile that creates the executable WINDRAW.EXE from three C++ source files (WINDRAW.CPP, SHAPES.CPP, and WINVIEW.CPP) and a header file (WINDRAW.H). Assume that each source file includes the header file. Given this, NMAKE will create WINDRAW.EXE if you use the following makefile with NMAKE:

```
#################################################################
#  Sample makefile for Microsoft NMAKE
#  Comments start with '#'
#
#  Macro to define memory model

MODEL=S

# Define flags for the C++ compiler

CPPFLAGS=/A$(MODEL) /Od /Zi

# Define the target "all" — the first target (NMAKE builds this)
# one by default).

all: windraw.exe

# Compile the files

windraw.obj: windraw.cpp windraw.h

winview.obj: winview.cpp windraw.h

shapes.obj: shapes.cpp windraw.h

# Invoke LINK to create the executable with support for debugging

windraw.exe:  windraw.obj shapes.obj winview.obj
     LINK /CO $**, $@;
```

Notice that this makefile mostly relies on NMAKE's built-in inference rules. The conversion of .CPP files to .OBJ files uses the built-in rule. The flags to the C++ compiler are passed by defining the macro CPPFLAGS. The target named `all` is defined as the first target for a reason: if you invoke NMAKE specifying no targets on the command line (see the syntax presented in the next section), it builds the first target it finds. By defining the first target as WINDRAW.EXE, you can ensure that NMAKE builds this executable file even if you do not explicitly specify it as a target. UNIX programmers traditionally use `all` as the name for the first target, but the target's name is immaterial—all that matters is that it is the first target in the makefile.

Running NMAKE

You may run NMAKE in either of two ways:

- From the DOS command prompt, invoke NMAKE using the following syntax:

  ```
  NMAKE [options] [/f makefile] [/x errfile] [macrodefs] [targets]
  ```

  where `[options]` is one or more option(s) from Table 2.5, `[macrodefs]` is a macro definition of the form `MACRO=STRING` that is passed to NMAKE, and `[targets]` is the name of one or more targets (or a pseudotarget) from the makefile you want built. The `/f` and `/x` options are explicitly shown because these options require you to provide filenames—you must provide the name of a makefile for the `/f` option and the name of a file to log errors for the `/x` option.

- Place all NMAKE options and filenames in a text file and invoke NMAKE as follows:

  ```
  NMAKE @<command_file>
  ```

  where <command_file> is the name of the file containing the command-line input meant for NMAKE. Notice that NMAKE does not assume a specific filename extension for the command file; you should provide the complete filename for the command file.

If you save the sample makefile from the previous section in a file named MAKEFILE, all you have to do is type `NMAKE` and press Enter to build the target—in this case, WINDRAW.EXE. However, if the makefile has a different name—WINDRAW.MAK, for example—you must use a command-line option to indicate this to NMAKE as follows:

```
NMAKE /f windraw.mak
```

In fact, NMAKE accepts many more options on the command line. Table 2.5 shows a list of NMAKE's options.

Table 2.5. Options for NMAKE.

Option	Interpretation by NMAKE
/A	Builds all targets in the makefile, including those with dependents that are not out of date with respect to the target.
/B	Builds a target even if the time stamps of the target and dependents are equal.
/C	Suppresses nonfatal errors or warning messages.
/D	Displays the time stamp of each file.
/E	Overrides macro definitions in the makefile with definitions of environment variables of the same name.
/F<*file*>	Designates <*file*> as the name of the makefile.
/HELP	Displays on-line help on NMAKE by invoking Microsoft QuickHelp.
/I	Ignores exit codes from commands listed in the makefile.
/K	Continues to build unrelated targets even if an error occurs when building one of the targets.
/M	Does not swap to expanded or extended memory; instead, it swaps to disk only.
/N	Displays but does not execute the makefile's commands. Use this option to find out what a makefile might cause NMAKE to do before actually doing it.
/NOLOG	Suppresses the NMAKE copyright message.
/P	Displays all macro definitions and inference rules.
/Q	Checks time stamps for specified targets but does not build a target. This command is useful when NMAKE is invoked from a batch file.
/R	Ignores predefined macros and inference rules.
/S	Suppresses the display of commands listed in the makefile. With this option, NMAKE silently performs its job.

continues

Table 2.5. continued

Option	Interpretation by NMAKE
`/T`	Changes the time stamp of the specified targets, but does not build the target.
`/V`	Inherits macros when NMAKE is recursively called.
`/X<file>`	Sends all error messages to the file named `<file>`.
`/?`	Displays a brief summary of NMAKE's command-line syntax and its list of options.

CodeView, the CodeView Debugger

When you debug a program in Visual Workbench, Visual Workbench invokes its own debugger. Regardless of how powerful the Visual Workbench debugger is, there are times when only CodeView (CV) will do the necessary debugging. One example of this is debugging in assembly language. Because Visual Workbench's debugger is a C/C++ source level debugger only, you cannot get a disassembled listing, nor can you debug at the assembly level.

You can run CV from the DOS command line. However, it's best to simply select it from the option in Visual Workbench's Tools menu. There actually are two versions of CodeView: one designed to debug standard DOS applications, and another version (CVW) which has been enhanced to debug Windows-based applications.

CV also is a source-level debugger—which means that, if you write a C or C++ program, and compile and link it with the appropriate options, you'll be able to trace the program's execution under CV one source line at a time. The ability to view the source code as you debug the program is helpful in tracking down the cause of errors. In fact, you'll often notice the erroneous statement as soon as the program fails under CV.

CV provides a full-screen interface. You interact with CV through pull-down menus and by entering commands in a special command window. The following sections briefly describe CV.

> **CodeView's Interface Is Similar to Visual Workbench's**
>
> Interacting with CodeView's full-screen interface is similar to the way you work with Visual Workbench. Consult Chapter 1, "The Microsoft Visual C++ Environment," for a description of Visual Workbench.

Using CodeView

You can start CodeView either by selecting the CodeView: option from the Tools menu in Visual Workbench or by running CV.EXE, the CV executable file, from the DOS command line. The command-line syntax for CV is

```
cv [options] <file> [arguments]
```

where `<file>` is the name of the executable file (with the extension .EXE by default) to be loaded for debugging and `[options]` is one or more of the CV options listed in Table 2.6. The `[arguments]` are passed to the program being debugged as its command-line arguments.

Table 2.6. Options for CodeView.

Option	Interpretation by CV
`/2`	Uses two monitors for debugging. The current default monitor shows the program's output, and the CV display appears on the other monitor. This is useful for debugging graphics programs.
`/25`	Uses the 25-line display mode (this is the default).
`/43`	Uses the 43-line display mode on EGA or VGA systems.
`/50`	Uses the 50-line display mode on a VGA system.
`/B`	Displays in black and white even if a color display is available.
`/C<commands>`	Executes the CV commands in `<commands>` as soon as CV runs. Table 2.7 lists the commands that you can type into

continues

Table 2.6. continued

Option	Interpretation by CV
	CV's command window. The /C option is equivalent to starting CV and typing the specified <*commands*> in the command window.
/D[*buffersize*]	Uses a disk buffer of a specified size to overlay portions of CV executable file. The [*buffersize*] argument is a numeric value from 16 to 128—it is interpreted as the size of the disk buffer in kilobytes. The default buffer is 64K.
/E	Uses expanded memory accessible via a driver as specified by the Lotus/Intel/Microsoft Expanded Memory Specification 4.0 (LIM EMS 4.0).
/F	Uses "screen flipping." In this case, CV uses multiple video pages to enable you to switch between the CV screen and a screen showing the program's output. This option is not available on the monochrome display adapter.
/I[*n*]	Enables or disables IBM PC-style interrupt handling. This is automatically enabled if CodeView determines that your computer is fully IBM-compatible. The optional parameter [*n*] is either 0 or 1. The /I0 option tells CV to handle Intel 8259 interrupts, while /I1 tells CV to ignore these interrupts.
/M	Does not use a mouse even if one is available. Useful for debugging programs that use the mouse.
/N[*n*]	Enables or disables IBM PC-style nonmaskable interrupt handling. The optional parameter [*n*] is either 0 or 1. The /N0 option tells CV to handle Intel 8259 nonmaskable interrupts (NMI), while the /N1 option tells CV to ignore NMI.
/R	Uses the debugging registers in an 80386 or 80486 system. The *debugging registers* are special-purpose internal registers in Intel 80386 and 80486 processors that can hold up to four breakpoints during debugging.

Option	Interpretation by CV
/S	Uses screen swapping. CV uses a memory buffer to save the screen's contents while you watch the output of your program.
/TSF	Toggles the `Statefileread` flag in the `[CodeView]` section of the TOOLS.INI file. This flag controls whether CV reads the current states from the CURRENT.STS file and the colors from the CLRFILE.CV4 file.
/X	Enables the use of extended memory—the memory above 1 megabyte that is accessible to an Intel 80286, 80386, or 80486 processor. This option is not necessary anymore because CV automatically uses extended memory if an extended memory driver (XMS) is installed in your system.

CodeView Start-Up

If you want to use CodeView to debug the C++ program named SHAPETST.EXE that appears in Chapter 6, "C++ and Object-Oriented Programming," you can select the CodeView: option from the Tools menu after building the executable file with support for debugging (see Chapter 1 for a discussion of these options in Visual Workbench). Otherwise, you can type

```
cv shapetst
```

at the DOS prompt. Figure 2.1 shows the initial screen displayed by CV. Notice that the CV start-up screen has, like Visual Workbench, a main menu bar. The menu bar enables your interaction with CV through the pull-down menus that appear when you select items from the menu bar.

This screen also has three windows:

- A *local* window, at the top. In the local window, CV displays the values of local variables as it executes the program step-by-step.
- A *source* window, in the middle. CV uses the source window to display the source code and uses the command window for you to enter commands.

- A *command* window, at the bottom. Notice the greater-than sign prompt (>) in the command window.

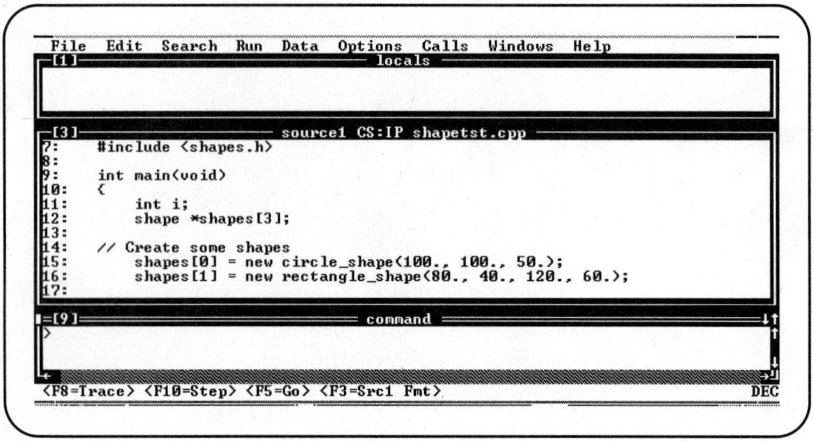

```
File  Edit  Search  Run  Data  Options  Calls  Windows  Help
[1]                         locals

[3]              source1 CS:IP shapetst.cpp
7:      #include <shapes.h>
8:
9:      int main(void)
10:     {
11:         int i;
12:         shape *shapes[3];
13:
14:     // Create some shapes
15:         shapes[0] = new circle_shape(100., 100., 50.);
16:         shapes[1] = new rectangle_shape(80., 40., 120., 60.);
17:
[9]                         command
>

<F8=Trace> <F10=Step> <F5=Go> <F3=Src1 Fmt>                          DEC
```

Figure 2.1. Initial screen in CodeView.

Debugging the Program

Usually, you'll run your program under CV once you find that the program isn't working correctly. Your first goal should be to locate the offending code that's causing the program to fail. You can gather this information in several ways.

For some errors, such as dividing by zero, you can load the program into CV and press the F5 function key to let CV begin executing the program. When the error occurs, CV will stop and the source window will display the line where the error occurred.

However, for many errors you must step through your program one statement at a time. CV tells you how to do this with a message on the status line—the last line in the CV start-up screen (see Figure 2.1). This line shows the meaning of a number of function keys. The comment `<F8=Trace>` means that you can step through the program one line at a time by stepping into each function as your program calls it. Pressing F10 works similarly, but it steps over function calls—that is, it treats each function call as a single step. Table 2.7 lists a number of keys you can use to navigate through CV's user interface and control how CV steps through your program.

Table 2.7. Shortcut keys in CodeView.

Keystroke	Interpretation by CV
Alt+*n*	Makes the specified window visible and sends all keypresses to that window. Here, *n* is a number from 0 to 9 denoting the following windows: 0 Help; 1 Locals 2 Watch; 3 Source 1 4 Source 2; 5 Memory 1 6 Memory 2; 7 Register 8 8087; 9 Command
Alt+F4	Exits CV.
Alt+F5	Arranges windows.
Alt+C	Displays the **C**alls menu.
Alt+D	Displays the **D**ata menu.
Alt+E	Displays the **E**dit menu.
Alt+F	Displays the **F**ile menu.
Alt+H	Displays the **H**elp menu.
Alt+O	Displays the **O**ptions menu.
Alt+R	Displays the **R**un menu.
Alt+S	Displays the **S**earch menu.
Alt+W	Displays the **W**indows menu.
Ctrl+F4	Closes the window.
Ctrl+F5	Restores the window to normal size.
Ctrl+F7	Moves the window.
Ctrl+F8	Resizes the window.
Ctrl+F9	Reduces (minimizes) the window to an icon.
Ctrl+F10	Makes the window as large as possible (maximizes).

continues

Table 2.7. continued

Keystroke	Interpretation by CV
Ctrl+U	Displays a dialog window through which the programmer can delete a *watch expression*—an expression with a value that is continually displayed by CodeView.
Ctrl+W	Displays a dialog window where the programmer can enter a watch expression.
F1	Displays context-sensitive help in a window. The information displayed is determined by the word on which the cursor rests.
F2	Displays the CPU registers in a window on the right side of the screen. If the window is already displayed, pressing F2 closes the window.
F3	Cycles through the following display formats for the source window: source code, assemble code, or both.
F4	Displays the output screen.
F5	Executes up to the next breakpoint or to the end of the program if there are no breakpoints.
F6	Moves the cursor to the next window (used to move from one window to another).
F7	Executes up to the line on which the cursor rests.
F8	Executes the next statement, stepping into procedure calls.
F9	Sets or clears a breakpoint on the line containing the cursor.
F10	Executes the next statement, stepping over procedure calls.
Up arrow	Moves the cursor up one line.
Down arrow	Moves the cursor down one line.
PgUp	Scrolls up one page.
PgDn	Scrolls down one page.
Home	Jumps to the beginning of the buffer associated with the current window.

Keystroke	Interpretation by CV
End	Jumps to the end of the buffer associated with the current window.
Shift+F1	Displays the table of contents of on-line help information.
Shift+F5	Arranges the windows in a nonoverlapping manner.
Shift+F6	Moves the cursor to the previous window (used to move from one window to another).
Shift+F9	Displays the QuickWatch dialog box.

Breakpoints, Watches, and Commands

A smart way to locate errors with CV is to set a *breakpoint* at a statement near the suspect code and press the F5 key to begin executing the program. CV will stop (or "break") when it reaches a breakpoint. The easiest way to set a breakpoint is through a command that you enter at the prompt in the command window. For example, to set a breakpoint on line number 15, you would enter

```
bp .15
```

in the command window. Notice that the line with the breakpoint is highlighted in Figure 2.2.

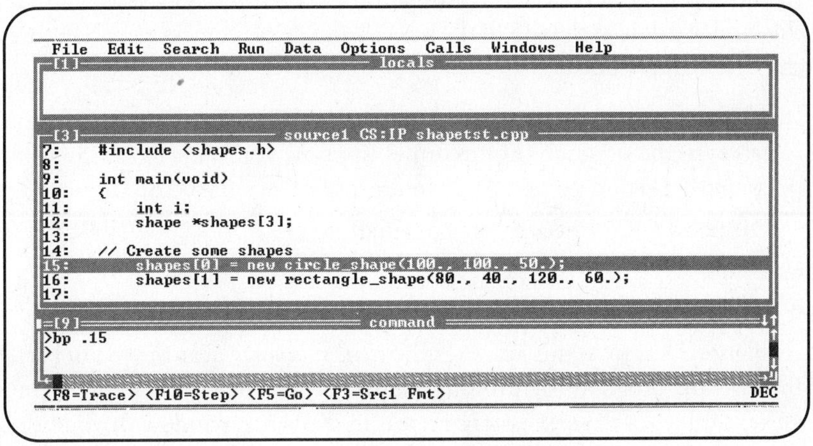

```
 File  Edit  Search  Run  Data  Options  Calls  Windows  Help
-[1]-------------------------- locals ---------------------------

-[3]------------------ source1 CS:IP shapetst.cpp ---------------
7:     #include <shapes.h>
8:
9:     int main(void)
10:    {
11:        int i;
12:        shape *shapes[3];
13:
14:    // Create some shapes
15:        shapes[0] = new circle_shape(100., 100., 50.);
16:        shapes[1] = new rectangle_shape(80., 40., 120., 60.);
17:
-[9]-------------------------- command --------------------------
>bp .15
>
<F8=Trace> <F10=Step> <F5=Go> <F3=Src1 Fmt>                   DEC
```

Figure 2.2. Setting a breakpoint using the CV command bp.

When you want to enter a command, the cursor must be in the command window. If the cursor is not in the command window, press the F6 function key repeatedly until the cursor moves to the command window.

Once the breakpoint is set, you can run the program up to the breakpoint by entering a `G` in the command window (see Figure 2.3). You can get the same effect by pressing the F5 key. A third way is to use the `E` command, which steps through the program at slow speed and stops at the breakpoint.

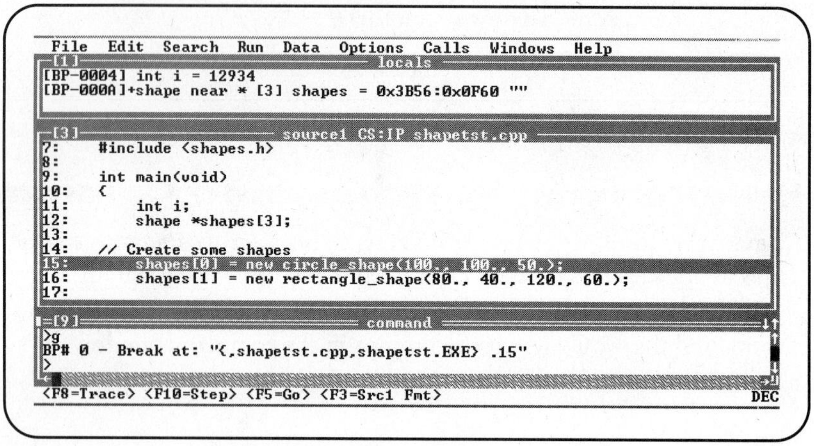

```
 File  Edit  Search  Run  Data  Options  Calls  Windows  Help
[1]                          locals
[BP-0004] int i = 12934
[BP-000A]+shape near * [3] shapes = 0x3B56:0x0F60 ""

[3]                   source1 CS:IP shapetst.cpp
7:     #include <shapes.h>
8:
9:     int main(void)
10:    {
11:        int i;
12:        shape *shapes[3];
13:
14:    // Create some shapes
15:        shapes[0] = new circle_shape(100., 100., 50.);
16:        shapes[1] = new rectangle_shape(80., 40., 120., 60.);
17:

[9]                          command
>g
BP# 0 - Break at: "{,shapetst.cpp,shapetst.EXE} .15"
>
<F8=Trace> <F10=Step> <F5=Go> <F3=Src1 Fmt>                      DEC
```

Figure 2.3. Executing a program up to a breakpoint.

As shown in Figure 2.3, as the program runs, CV displays values of local variables in the local window at the top of the screen, and displays messages about breakpoints in the command window.

In addition to breakpoints, you can watch the value of any expression involving variables in the program. For example, suppose you want to see the value of the expressions `2*i+1` and `shapes[0]` as your program executes. You can set up these watch expressions by entering the following commands in the command window:

```
w? 2*i+1
w? shapes[0]
```

As Figure 2.4 shows, this activates the *watch window* near the menu bar. As you step through the program (by pressing the F10 key or by entering the `P` command), the current values of the expressions appear in the watch window. If you need to, use the mouse or the options in the Window menu to resize the watch window.

The CV commands provide a powerful way to control the debugging session. As you can see from the summary of CV commands in Table 2.8, you can do almost anything through the commands. For example, you can even exit CV by typing `Q` in the command window.

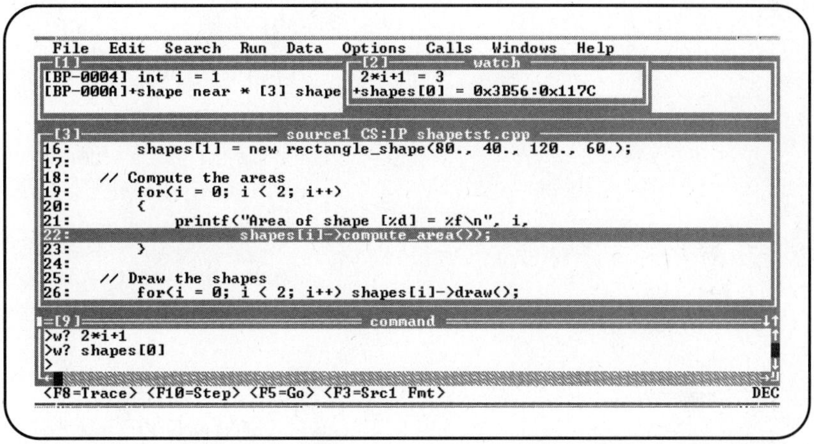

```
 File  Edit  Search  Run  Data  Options  Calls  Windows  Help
[1]                                     [2]          watch
[BP-0004] int i = 1                      2*i+1 = 3
[BP-000A]+shape near * [3] shape        +shapes[0] = 0x3B56:0x117C

[3]                 source1 CS:IP shapetst.cpp
        shapes[1] = new rectangle_shape(80., 40., 120., 60.);

    // Compute the areas
        for(i = 0; i < 2; i++)
        {
            printf("Area of shape [%d] = %f\n", i,
                   shapes[i]->compute_area());
        }

    // Draw the shapes
        for(i = 0; i < 2; i++) shapes[i]->draw();
[9]                              command
>w? 2*i+1
>w? shapes[0]
>
<F8=Trace> <F10=Step> <F5=Go> <F3=Src1 Fmt>                          DEC
```

Figure 2.4. Watching an expression in CodeView.

Table 2.8. Summary of CodeView commands.

Command	Interpretation by CV
`<` *`file¦device`*	Reads all subsequent command input from the specified device or file.
`>` *`file¦device`*	Writes all subsequent command output to the specified device or file. A `T` in front of the `>` indicates that output should also appear on the CV screen. Use `>>` to append output to an existing file.
`=` *`device`*	Redirects input and output to the specified *`device`*. For example,

continues

Table 2.8. continued

Command	Interpretation by CV
	= CON directs CV to use the command window for input and output.
`* comment`	Interprets the rest of the line as a comment.
`:`	Pauses for half a second before continuing the execution of commands from a file.
`"`	Pauses the execution of commands being read from a file and waits for a keypress.
`!DOScommand`	Runs a new copy of COMMAND.COM and executes the command *DOScommand*. If no command is given, the DOS prompt appears and you can interact with DOS. Enter EXIT to return to CV.
`# number`	Sets tabs to all *number* spaces. The valid range of *number* is from 1 to 19.
`.`	Displays the current source line in the center of the source window.
`/ text`	Searches for a string or an expression in the source file.
`7`	Displays the contents of the math coprocessor registers.
`? expression[, format]`	Evaluates the expression and displays the result in the specified format. For example, to see the variable `status` in hexadecimal, enter `>? status, x`. You also can

Command	Interpretation by CV
	set the value of a variable with this command. For example, to set status to `0x3fab` (in C-style hexadecimal notation), enter `>? status=0x3fab`.
`?? symbol`	Opens the QuickWatch dialog box and displays the value of *symbol*. You can view structures and arrays in the QuickWatch dialog box.
`@`	Redraws the screen.
`\`	Switches to the output screen.
`A address`	Assembles machine instructions at the specified address. If no address is given, instructions are assembled at the current instruction pointer, `CS:IP` (`CS` is the code segment register, and `IP` is the instruction pointer).
`BC [*¦list]`	Clears the specified breakpoints. An asterisk (`*`) clears all breakpoints. The list of breakpoints is a set of numbers indicating specific breakpoints.
`BD [*¦list]`	Disables the specified breakpoints.
`BE [*¦list]`	Enables the specified breakpoints.
`BL`	Lists the current breakpoints.
`BP`	Sets a breakpoint at the current instruction. Enter `HBP` to see detailed syntax.
`D [address¦range]`	Displays the contents of the memory specified by *range* or

continues

Table 2.8. continued

Command	Interpretation by CV
	`address`. If no argument is given, the option displays 128 bytes from the last address used with the `D` command. The address can be of the form `ds:0000`, expressed in terms of the contents of the data segment register and an offset.
`DA [`*address*`¦`*range*`]`	Displays bytes in ASCII format.
`DB [`*address*`¦`*range*`]`	Displays bytes in hexadecimal.
`DD [`*address*`¦`*range*`]`	Displays double words in hexadecimal.
`DI [`*address*`¦`*range*`]`	Displays integers in decimal.
`DIU [`*address*`¦`*range*`]`	Displays unsigned integers in decimal.
`DIX [`*address*`¦`*range*`]`	Displays unsigned integers in hexadecimal.
`DL [`*address*`¦`*range*`]`	Displays long integers in decimal.
`DLU [`*address*`¦`*range*`]`	Displays long unsigned integers in decimal.
`DLX [`*address*`¦`*range*`]`	Displays long unsigned integers in hexadecimal.
`DR [`*address*`¦`*range*`]`	Displays short real numbers: 4-byte floating-point values (C's `float` variables).
`DRL [`*address*`¦`*range*`]`	Displays long real numbers: 8-byte floating-point values (C's `double` variables).
`DRT [`*address*`¦`*range*`]`	Displays 10-byte real numbers.
`DW [`*address*`¦`*range*`]`	Displays words (2-byte) in hexadecimal.

Command	Interpretation by CV
`E`	Animates a program (traces through one step at a time with a pause between each step). Set the speed of animation with the `TF`, `TM`, and `TS` commands.
`G [`*`breakpoint`*`]`	Executes up to the specified breakpoint. If you do not specify a breakpoint, CV executes up to the first one. If you have not yet set up a breakpoint, CV runs the program until it ends.
`H[`*`command`*`]`	Displays help information on the specified *`command`*. For example, to see the syntax of the command to set breakpoints (`BP`), enter `> hbp`.
`I` *`port_address`*	Reads a byte from the specified I/O port address (a 16-bit address).
`K`	Displays the names of functions that have been called thus far. The output appears in the command window.
`L`	Restarts the program from the beginning.
`MC` *`range address`*	Compares the block of memory specified by *`range`* to a similar sized block that starts at *`address`*. The *`range`* is specified by two addresses or by an address followed by an `L` and the number of bytes.
`MD`*`format`* `[`*`range`*`¦`*`address`*`]`	Displays the block of memory specified by a *`range`* or an *`address`*. The *`format`* field is one or two characters that denotes the format

continues

Table 2.8. continued

Command	Interpretation by CV
	in which CodeView displays the memory dump. Valid characters for *format* are: A, B, C, I, IU, IX, L, LU, LX, R, RL, and RT.

ME *address* [*list of values*]	Enters a specified *list of values* into memory starting at *address*. If you do not specify the *list of values*, CodeView displays the current value and waits for you to enter a new value. For example
	`> me ds:100 "IVY " "EMILY " "ASHLEY"`
	loads the three strings into the memory starting at the address DS:100. After this command, you can verify the contents at that area of memory with the MDA command as follows:
	`>mda ds:100 L 0x10`
	`35EA:0064  IVY EMILY ASHLEY`

MF *range list*	Fills the block of memory specified by *range* with the *list* of bytes.
MM *range address*	Copies the block of memory specified by *range* to a similar sized block that starts at *address*.
MS *range list*	Searches the block of memory specified by *range* for occurrences of the values specified in *list*.
N *number*	Changes the current radix to *number*. The radix determines how input values are interpreted and how numerical values are displayed by CV. The radix can be 8 (octal),

Command	Interpretation by CV
	10 (decimal), or 16 (hexadecimal). The default radix is 10.
`O port data_byte`	Sends a byte of data to the specified I/O port address. When `O` is used without parameters, CV displays the current options (the ones appearing in the Options menu).
`OA [+¦-], OB [+¦-], OC [+¦-], OF [+¦-], OH [+¦-], OL [+¦-], ON [+¦-], OS [+¦-], O3 [+¦-], OV [+¦-]`	If there are no parameters, `OA`, `OB`, `OC`, `OF`, `OH`, `OL`, `ON`, `OS`, `O3`, and `OV`, respectively, direct CV to display the current status of the following options: `Status Bar`, `Bytes Coded`, `Case Sense`, `Flip/Swap`, `Horizontal Scroll Bar`, `Show Symbol Address`, `Native Mode`, `Symbols`, `386`, and `Vertical Scroll Bar`. A + following the command turns the option on; a - turns it off.
`P [count]`	Executes the current statement, stepping over function calls. The optional *count* indicates the number of times CodeView repeats this command.
`Q`	Exits CodeView and returns to DOS.
`R [register] [value]`	Displays the contents of a *register* and enables the user to change it to *value*. If you do not specify a

continues

Table 2.8. continued

Command	Interpretation by CV
	register, CodeView displays the current contents of all registers.
`S+`	Displays source code only.
`S-`	Displays the unassembled machine instructions only.
`S&`	Displays source code and the unassembled code.
`T [`*`count`*`]`	Executes the current statement, stepping into procedure calls. The optional *`count`* field indicates how many times CV repeats this command.
`TF`	Sets the trace speed to fast (no wait between steps).
`TM`	Sets the trace speed to medium (0.25 seconds between steps).
`TS`	Sets the trace speed to slow (0.5 second between steps).
`U [`*`range`*`]`	Disassembles the contents of memory locations in the specified range.
`USE [`*`language`*`]`	Uses the syntax of the specified language (which can be BASIC, C, CPP, FORTRAN, or Auto). If you do not specify any language, the `USE` command displays the current selection from the **L**anguage... item of the **O**ptions menu.
`VM`*`format`*	Views the memory in the specified format. The *`format`* field can be up to two characters that denotes the format in which CV displays the

Command	Interpretation by CV
	memory. Valid characters for `format` are: `A`, `B`, `C`, `I`, `IU`, `IX`, `L`, `LU`, `LX`, `R`, `RL`, and `RT`.
`VS[num] [format] [line]`	Views lines from a source file. The *num* field indicates a source window that can be either 1 or 2. The *format* field is `+`, `-`, or `&` to display source lines, assembly code, or mixed source and assembly, respectively. The *line* field indicates a line in the source file (for example, `.15` means line number 15).
`W`	Lists the current watch expressions and their values.
`WC [*¦number]`	Deletes the specified watch expression (or deletes all if the command is `WC *`).
`W? expression[, format]`	Displays the value of expression as program executes.
`WP? expression`	Stops the program's execution when the expression becomes true (nonzero). This is known as a *watchpoint*.
`Xscope [context][symbol]`	Displays the names and addresses of symbols in a module identified by the context. Enter `HX` to see description of syntax. Use the command `X*` to see all symbols in the current module.
`Y[* or number]`	Deletes the specified watch expression. Use `Y*` to delete all watch expressions. To delete a

continues

Table 2.8. continued

Command	Interpretation by CV
	specific watch expression by number, first enter `W` to see a list of all watch expressions and pick the number from that list.

Summary

In addition to the C and C++ compilers, Microsoft Visual C++ includes a large assortment of programming tools and utilities. This chapter provided an overview of the following (DOS-based) program development tools: LINK, the linker; LIB, the library manager; the NMAKE program maintenance utility; and CV, the CodeView debugger. By reading this chapter, you have gained an understanding of how to use each of these tools for program development. You should consult the extensive on-line help in Visual Workbench, and the printed documentation provided with Visual C++, for detailed information on these tools as well as others not described in this chapter.

An Overview of ANSI Standard C

In late 1989, the C programming language went through a significant transition. That's when the American National Standards Institute (ANSI) adopted a standard for C, referred to as the ANSI X3.159 1989, which defines not only the C language but also the standard header files, standard libraries, and the behavior of the C preprocessor. Prior to the ANSI standard, the C language as defined by Kernighan and Ritchie's 1978 book was the de facto standard—one that often goes by the name K&R C. As for the library, the de facto standard was the C library in UNIX. ANSI C changes this by clearly specifying all aspects of C: the language, the preprocessor, and the library.

One goal of this book is to provide you with complete details of the C++ programming language—explaining its syntax and showing how to use its features to write object-oriented programs. However, before getting into C++ in earnest, you should become familiar with the ANSI standard for the C programming language, because certain seemingly new features of C++ are already in ANSI C. Because C++ existed and continued to evolve as C was being standardized during the period from 1983 through 1989, many features that appeared in C++ also found their way into ANSI C. Therefore, if you know ANSI C, you'll find many C++ constructs familiar. This chapter briefly describes ANSI C.

The Structure of a C Program

As Figure 3.1 shows, a typical C program is organized into one or more *source files*, or *modules*. Each file has a similar structure with comments, preprocessor directives, declarations of variables and functions, and their definitions. You usually will place each group of related variables and functions in a single source file.

Some files are simply a set of declarations that are used in other files through the `#include` directive of the C preprocessor. These files are usually referred to as *header files* and have names ending with the .h extension. In Figure 3.1, the file, shapes.h, is a header file that declares common data structures and functions for the program. Another file, shapes.c, defines the functions. A third file, shapetst.c, implements the main function—the function in which the execution of a C program begins. These files with names ending in .c are the source files where you define the functions needed by your program. Although Figure 3.1 shows only one function in each source file, in typical programs there are many functions in a source file.

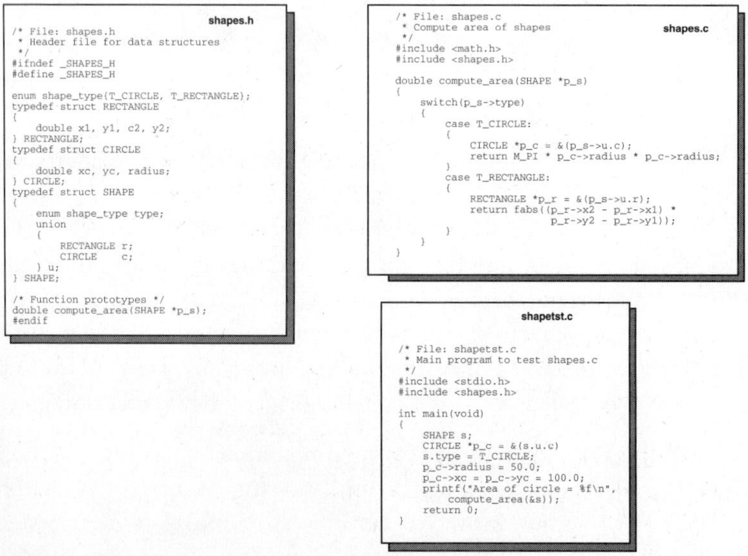

shapes.h

```
/* File: shapes.h
 * Header file for data structures
 */
#ifndef _SHAPES_H
#define _SHAPES_H

enum shape_type{T_CIRCLE, T_RECTANGLE};
typedef struct RECTANGLE
{
    double x1, y1, c2, y2;
} RECTANGLE;
typedef struct CIRCLE
{
    double xc, yc, radius;
} CIRCLE;
typedef struct SHAPE
{
    enum shape_type type;
    union
    {
        RECTANGLE r;
        CIRCLE    c;
    } u;
} SHAPE;

/* Function prototypes */
double compute_area(SHAPE *p_s);
#endif
```

shapes.c

```
/* File: shapes.c
 * Compute area of shapes
 */
#include <math.h>
#include <shapes.h>

double compute_area(SHAPE *p_s)
{
    switch(p_s->type)
    {
        case T_CIRCLE:
        {
            CIRCLE *p_c = &(p_s->u.c);
            return M_PI * p_c->radius * p_c->radius;
        }
        case T_RECTANGLE:
        {
            RECTANGLE *p_r = &(p_s->u.r);
            return fabs((p_r->x2 - p_r->x1) *
                         p_r->y2 - p_r->y1));
        }
    }
}
```

shapetst.c

```
/* File: shapetst.c
 * Main program to test shapes.c
 */
#include <stdio.h>
#include <shapes.h>

int main(void)
{
    SHAPE s;
    CIRCLE *p_c = &(s.u.c)
    s.type = T_CIRCLE;
    p_c->radius = 50.0;
    p_c->xc = p_c->yc = 100.0;
    printf("Area of circle = %f\n",
        compute_area(&s));
    return 0;
}
```

Figure 3.1. Source files of a C program.

You must compile and link the source files to create an executable program. The exact steps for building programs from C source files depends on the compiler and the operating system. You can find this information in your compiler's documentation.

Declaration Versus Definition

A *declaration* determines how the program interprets a symbol. A *definition*, on the other hand, actually creates a variable or a function. Definitions cause the compiler to set aside storage for data or code, but declarations do not. For example,

```
int x, y, z;
```

is a definition of three integer variables, but

```
extern int x, y, z;
```

is a declaration indicating that the three integer variables are defined in another source file.

Within each source file, the components of the program are laid out in a standard manner. As Figure 3.2 shows, the typical components of a C source file are as follows:

1. The file starts with some comments that describe the purpose of the module and that provide some other pertinent information, such as the name of the author and revision dates. In ANSI C, comments start with `/*` and end with `*/`.

2. Commands for the preprocessor, known as *preprocessor directives*, follow the comments. The first few directives typically are for including header files and defining constants.

3. Declarations of variables and functions that are visible throughout the file come next. In other words, the names of these variables and functions may be used in any of the functions in this file. Here, you also define variables needed within the file. Use the `static` keyword as a prefix when you want to confine the visibility of the variables and functions to this module only. On the other hand, the `extern` keyword indicates that the items you declare are defined in another file.

4. The rest of the file includes definitions of functions. Inside a function's body, you can define variables that are local to the function and that exist only while the function's code is being executed.

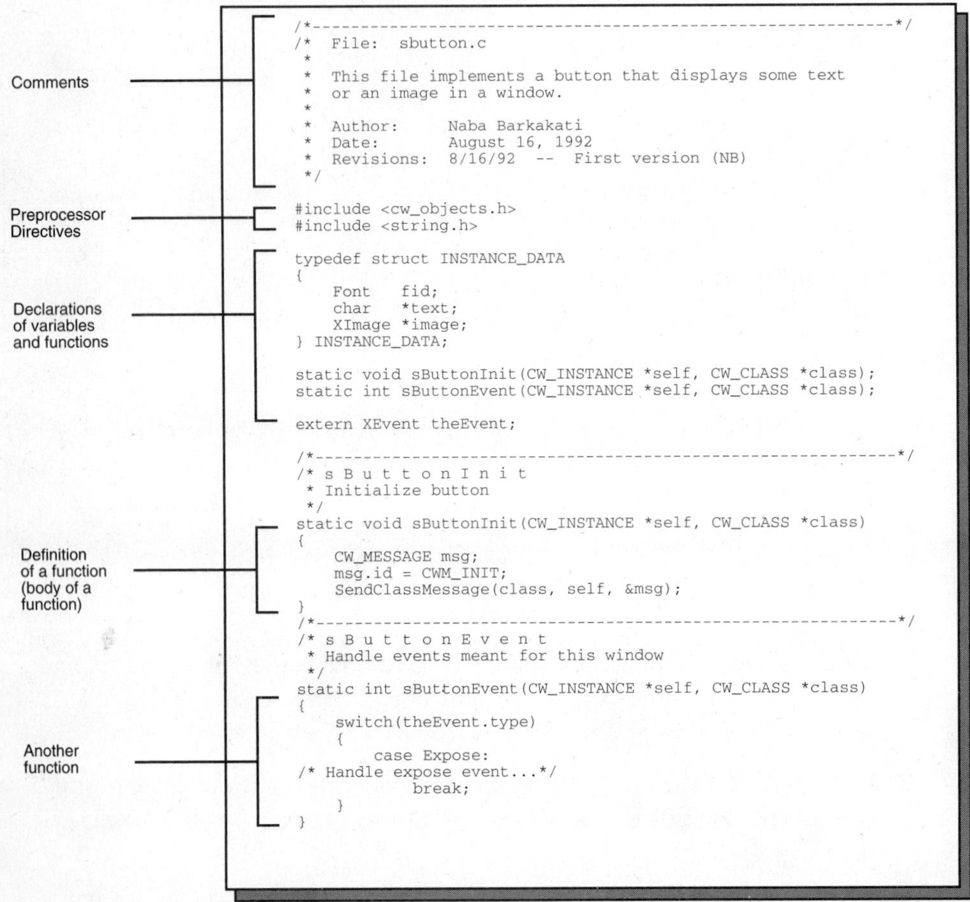


```
/*----------------------------------------------------------*/
/*  File:  sbutton.c
 *
 *  This file implements a button that displays some text
 *  or an image in a window.
 *
 *  Author:     Naba Barkakati
 *  Date:       August 16, 1992
 *  Revisions:  8/16/92  --  First version (NB)
 */

#include <cw_objects.h>
#include <string.h>

typedef struct INSTANCE_DATA
{
    Font   fid;
    char   *text;
    XImage *image;
} INSTANCE_DATA;

static void sButtonInit(CW_INSTANCE *self, CW_CLASS *class);
static int sButtonEvent(CW_INSTANCE *self, CW_CLASS *class);

extern XEvent theEvent;

/*-----------------------------------------------------------*/
/* s B u t t o n I n i t
 * Initialize button
 */
static void sButtonInit(CW_INSTANCE *self, CW_CLASS *class)
{
    CW_MESSAGE msg;
    msg.id = CWM_INIT;
    SendClassMessage(class, self, &msg);
}
/*-----------------------------------------------------------*/
/* s B u t t o n E v e n t
 * Handle events meant for this window
 */
static int sButtonEvent(CW_INSTANCE *self, CW_CLASS *class)
{
    switch(theEvent.type)
    {
        case Expose:
/* Handle expose event...*/
            break;
    }
}
```

Figure 3.2. Layout of a typical C source file.

ANSI C Keywords

Here's a list of all the ANSI C keywords:

`auto`	`double`	`int`	`struct`
`break`	`else`	`long`	`switch`
`case`	`enum`	`register`	`typedef`
`char`	`extern`	`return`	`union`
`const`	`float`	`short`	`unsigned`
`continue`	`for`	`signed`	`void`
`default`	`goto`	`sizeof`	`volatile`
`do`	`if`	`static`	`while`

The keywords `const`, `enum`, `void`, and `volatile` are new in ANSI C.

ANSI C Escape Sequences and Trigraphs

In C, you can insert nonprintable characters, such as a tab, in strings by using an *escape sequence*—a sequence of characters that starts with a backslash (`\`). For example, a tab and a newline character are represented by `\t` and `\n`. ANSI C has enlarged the set of escape sequences. Table 3.1 lists the escape sequences supported in ANSI C.

Table 3.1. ANSI C escape sequences.

Sequence	Name	Interpretation or Action
`\a`	Alert	Rings bell
`\b`	Backspace	Moves backward one space

continues

Table 3.1. continued

Sequence	Name	Interpretation or Action
`\f`	Form feed	Moves to the beginning of the next page
`\n`	Newline	Moves to the beginning of the next line
`\r`	Carriage return	Moves to the beginning of the current line
`\t`	Horizontal tab	Moves to the next tab position on this line
`\v`	Vertical tab	Moves to the next vertical tab position
`\\`	Backslash	\
`\'`	Single quote	‘
`\"`	Double quote	“
`\?`	Question mark	?
`\<octal digits>`	Octal constant	Depends on the printer or terminal
`\x<hexadecimal digits>`	Hexadecimal	Depends on the printer or terminal

ANSI C also introduces the concept of *trigraph sequences*, enabling programmers to enter certain important characters from their keyboard, even if their keyboards do not have that feature—for instance, non-English keyboards may not have some characters that English keyboards have. Each three-character trigraph sequence begins with a pair of question marks (`??`) followed by a third character. For example, if a keyboard does not have a backslash (`\`), a programmer can use the trigraph `??/` to enter it in a C program. Table 3.2 lists the nine trigraph sequences available in ANSI C.

Table 3.2. ANSI C trigraph sequences.

Trigraph	Translation
??(	[
??/	\
??)	]
??'	^
??<	{
??!	|
??>	}
??-	~
??=	#

Preprocessor Directives

Preprocessing refers to the first step in translating, or *compiling*, an ANSI C file into machine instructions. Traditionally, the C preprocessor has been used for this task. Although the ANSI standard does not require a separate preprocessor, most C compilers provide a distinct preprocessor.

The preprocessor processes the source file and acts on the commands, called *preprocessor directives*, embedded in the program. These directives begin with the pound sign (#). Usually, the compiler automatically invokes the preprocessor before beginning compilation. However, most compilers give you the option of invoking the preprocessor alone. You can utilize three major capabilities of the preprocessor to make your programs modular, more readable, and easier to customize:

- You can use the `#include` directive to insert the contents of a file into your program. With this, you can place common declarations in one location and use them in all source files through file inclusion. The result is a reduced risk of mismatches between declarations of variables and functions in separate program modules.

- Through the #define directive, you can define macros that enable you to replace one string with another. You can use the #define directive to give meaningful names to numeric constants, thus improving the readability of your source files.
- With directives such as #if, #ifdef, #else, and #endif, you can compile only selected portions of your program. You can use this feature to write source files with code for two or more systems, but compile only those parts that apply to the computer system on which you compile the program. With this strategy you can maintain multiple versions of a program using a single set of source files.

Including Files

You can write modular programs by exploiting the #include directive. This is possible because the C preprocessor enables you to keep commonly used declarations in a single file that you can insert in other source files as needed. ANSI C supports three forms of the #include directive. As a C programmer, you should be familiar with the first two forms:

```
#include <stdio.h>
#include "winobj.h"
```

Use the first form of #include to read the contents of a file—in this case, the standard C header file stdio.h from the default location where all the header files reside. You can use the second form, which displays the filename within double quotation marks, when the file being included (winobj.h) is in the current directory. The exact conventions for locating the file being included depend on the compiler.

ANSI C provides a third way of specifying the name of the file in the #include directive. You can now specify the name of the file through a macro. The following example illustrates how this might be done:

```
/* The following was introduced in ANSI C */

#ifdef WINDOWS
    #define  SYSTEM_DEFINES  "windef.h"
#else
    #define  SYSTEM_DEFINES  "dosdef.h"
#endif

#include SYSTEM_DEFINES
```

This example uses the `#ifdef` and `#define` directives (described in the section titled "Conditional Directives") to set the symbol `SYSTEM_DEFINES` to the name of the file to be included, depending on the definition of the symbol `WINDOWS`.

Defining Macros

By defining a macro, you can define a symbol (a *token*) to be equal to some C code. You then can use that symbol wherever you want to use that code in your program. When the source file is preprocessed, every occurrence of a macro's name is replaced with its definition. A common use of this feature is to define a symbolic name for a numerical constant and then use the symbol instead of the numbers in your program. This improves the readability of the source code, because with a descriptive name you're not left guessing why a particular number is being used in the program. You can define such macros in a straightforward manner using the `#define` directive, as follows:

```
#define PI          3.14159
#define GRAV_ACC    9.80665
#define BUFSIZE     512
```

Once these symbols are defined, you can use `PI`, `GRAV_ACC`, and `BUFSIZE` instead of the numerical constants throughout the source file.

The capabilities of macros, however, go well beyond replacing a symbol for a constant. A macro can accept a parameter and replace each occurrence of that parameter with the provided value when the macro is used in a program. Thus, the code that results from the expansion of a macro can change depending on the parameter you use when running the macro. For example, here is a macro that accepts a parameter and expands to an expression designed to calculate the square of the parameter:

```
#define square(x) ((x)*(x))
```

If you use `square(z)` in your program, it becomes `((z)*(z))` after the source file is preprocessed. This macro is essentially equivalent to a function that computes the square of its arguments, except that you don't call a function—the expression generated by the macro is placed directly in the source file.

Side Effects of Macros

When the preprocessor expands a macro, it replaces each parameter with the one you provide when using the macro. If you're not careful when you define the macro, you may end up with code that does something completely different from what you intended. For example, if you define square(x) as x*x, a macro invocation of the form square(a+b) would expand to a+b*a+b, which certainly is not the square of a+b. However, with square(x) defined as ((x)*(x)), square(a+b) results in ((a+b)*(a+b)), which gives you the correct result. So, as a general rule, you should use parentheses liberally when defining a macro with parameters.

An interesting new feature of the ANSI C preprocessor is the *token-pasting* operator, denoted by a pair of pound signs (##). With this operator, you can append one token to another and create a third valid token. The following scenario provides an example of where you might use this. Suppose you have two types of data files, and an integer at the beginning of each file identifies each type. File type 1 uses the hexadecimal constant `0x4d4d`, while type 2 uses `0x4949` in the first two bytes. To read these files in your program, you want to refer to the type with a macro of the form `Type(n)` where *n* is either `1` or `2`. Here's how you can use the token-pasting operator `##` to define the `Type(n)` macro:

```
#define TYPE1    0x4d4d
#define TYPE2    0x4949
#define Type(n) TYPE##n
```

With this definition, when the preprocessor expands the macro `Type(2)`, it replaces *n* with `2` and generates the string `TYPE##2`, which upon interpretation of the token-pasting operator, becomes the token `TYPE2`. The preprocessor finds that `TYPE2` is defined as `0x4949` and uses that as the replacement for the macro `Type(2)`.

Another new feature of the ANSI C preprocessor is the *string-izing* operator, which creates a string out of any parameter with a `#` prefix by putting that parameter in quotes. Suppose you want to print the value of certain variables in your program. Instead of calling the `printf` function directly, you can define a utility macro that will do the work for you. Here's how you might write the macro:

```
#define Trace(x)       printf(#x" = %d\n", x)
```

Then, to print the value of a variable named current_index (for instance), you can write:

```
Trace(current_index);
```

When the preprocessor expands this, it generates the statement:

```
printf("current_index"" = %d\n", current_index);
```

At this point, another new feature of ANSI C becomes relevant: ANSI C stipulates that adjacent strings will be concatenated. Applying this rule, the macro expansion becomes:

```
printf("current_index = %d\n", current_index);
```

This is exactly what you would write to print the value of the current_index variable.

Conditional Directives

You can use the *conditional directives*, such as #if, #ifdef, #ifndef, #else, #elif, and #endif, to control which parts of a source file are compiled and under what conditions. With this feature, you maintain a single set of source files that can be selectively compiled with different compilers and in different environments. Another common use is to insert printf statements for debugging that are compiled only if a symbol named DEBUG is defined. Conditional directives start with either #if, #ifdef, or #ifndef and may be followed by any number of #elif directives (or none at all). Next comes an optional #else, followed by an #endif directive that marks the end of that conditional block. Here are some common ways of using conditional directives. To include a header file only once, you can use the following:

```
#ifndef _ _PROJECT_H
#define _ _PROJECT_H
/*  Declarations to be included once */
/* ... */

#endif
```

The following prints a diagnostic message during debugging (when the symbol DEBUG is defined):

```
#ifdef DEBUG
    printf("In read_file: bytes_read = %d\n", bytes_read);
#endif
```

The following example shows how you can include a different header file depending on the version number of the software. To selectively include a header file, you can use the following:

```
#if CPU_TYPE == 8086
    #include <real_mode.h>
#elif CPU_TYPE == 80386
    #include <prot_mode.h>
#else
    #error Unknown CPU type.
#endif
```

The `#error` directive is used to display error messages during preprocessing.

Other Directives

Several other preprocessor directives perform miscellaneous tasks. For example, you can use the `#undef` directive to remove the current definition of a symbol. The `#pragma` directive is another special-purpose directive that you can use to convey information to the C compiler. You can use pragmas to access special features of a compiler, and, as such, they vary from one compiler to another. (See Chapter 4, "Microsoft Visual C++ Extensions to Standard C," for more information on pragmas.)

ANSI standard C compilers maintain several predefined macros (see Table 3.3). Of these, the macros `__FILE__` and `__LINE__` refer to the current source filename and the current line number being processed. You can use the `#line` directive to change these. For example, to set `__FILE__` to `"file_io.c"` and `__LINE__` to `100`, you would type:

```
#line 100 "file_io.c"
```

Table 3.3. Predefined macros in ANSI C.

Macro	Definition
`__DATE__`	This is a string containing the date on which you invoke the C compiler. The date is in the form `MMM DD YYYY` (for example, `Oct 26 1992`).
`__FILE__`	This expands to a string containing the name of the source file.
`__LINE__`	This is a decimal integer with a value that is the line number within the current source file.

Macro	Definition
`__STDC__`	This macro expands to the decimal constant `1` to indicate that the C compiler conforms to the ANSI standard.
`__TIME__`	This string displays the time at which you started compiling the source file. The time is in the form `HH:MM:SS` (for example, `21:59:45`).

Additionally, Microsoft Visual C++ defines the macro `__cplusplus`, defined when (and only when) a C++ source module is being compiled.

Declaration and Definition of Variables

In C, you must either define or declare all variables and functions before you use them. The definition of a variable specifies three things:

- Its *visibility*, which indicates exactly where the variable can be used: is it defined for the whole file or only in a function?
- Its *lifetime*, which determines whether the variable exists temporarily (for example, a local variable in a function) or permanently (as long as the program is running).
- Its *type* and, where allowed, its *initial value*. For example, an integer variable `x` initialized to `1` is defined as:

```
int  x = 1;
```

If a variable you're using is defined in another source file, declare the variable with an `extern` keyword, like this:

```
extern int message_count;
```

You must define this variable without the `extern` qualifier in at least one source file. When the program is built, the linker resolves all references to the `message_count` variable and ensures that they all use the same variable.

Basic Types

C has four basic data types:

- char and int are for storing characters and integers.
- float and double are for floating-point numbers.

The ANSI standard specifies only the minimum range of values that each type must be able to represent. The exact number of bytes used to store each data type may vary from one compiler to another. For example, ANSI C requires that the size of an int be at least two bytes, which is what most MS-DOS C compilers provide. Most UNIX C compilers, on the other hand, use four bytes for an int. Most systems use a single byte for a char. Common sizes for float and double are four and eight bytes, respectively. You can define variables for these basic data types in a straightforward manner:

```
char   c;
int    i, j, bufsize;
float  volts;
double mean, variance;
```

With C, you can expand the basic data types into a much larger set by using the long, short, and unsigned qualifiers as prefixes. The long and short qualifiers are size modifiers. For example, in ANSI C a long int is at least four bytes long, whereas a short int has a minimum size of only two bytes. The size of an int is system-dependent, but it will definitely be, at least, as large as a short.

The unsigned qualifier is reserved for int and char types only. Normally, each of these types hold negative as well as positive values. This is the default signed form of these data types. You can use the unsigned qualifier when you want the variable to hold positive values only. Here are some examples of using the short, long, and unsigned qualifiers:

```
unsigned char  mode_select, printer_status;
short          record_number; /* Same as "short int"          */
long           offset;        /* Same as "long int"           */
unsigned       i, j, msg_id;  /* Same as "unsigned int"       */
unsigned short width, height; /* Same as "unsigned short int" */
unsigned long  file_pos;      /* Same as "unsigned long int"  */
long double    result;
```

Notice that when the short, long, and unsigned qualifiers are used with int types, you can drop the int from the declaration. Also, ANSI C enables you to extend the double data type with a long prefix.

The exact sizes of the various data types and the ranges of values they can store depend on the C compiler. ANSI C requires that these limits be defined in the header files, limits.h and float.h. You can examine these files in your system to determine the sizes of the basic data types that your C compiler supports.

Enumerations

ANSI C introduces the `enum` data type, which you can use to define your own *enumerated list*—a fixed set of named integer constants. For example, you can declare a Boolean data type named `BOOLEAN` using `enum`, as follows:

```
/* Declare an enumerated type named BOOLEAN */
    enum BOOLEAN {false = 0, true = 1, stop = 0, go = 1,
                  off = 0, on = 1};

/* Define a BOOLEAN called "status" and initialize it */
    enum BOOLEAN status = stop;
```

This example first declares `BOOLEAN` to be an enumerated type. The list within the braces shows the *enumeration constants* that are valid values of an `enum BOOLEAN` variable. You can initialize each constant to a value of your choice, and several constants can use the same value. In this example, the constants `false`, `stop`, and `off` are set to `0`, while `true`, `go`, and `on` are initialized to `1`. The example then defines an enumerated `BOOLEAN` variable named `status`, which initially is set to the constant `stop`.

Structures, Unions, and Bit Fields

In C, you use `struct` to group related data items together, and refer to that group by a name. For example, the declaration of a structure to hold variables of a queue might look like this:

```
/* Declare a structure */
struct QUEUE
{
    int  count;     /* Number of items in queue    */
    int  front;     /* Index of first item in queue */
    int  rear;      /* Index of last item in queue  */
    int  elemsize;  /* Size of each element of data */
```

```
    int  maxsize;    /* Maximum capacity of queue    */
    char *data;      /* Pointer to queued data       */
};

/* Define two queues */
struct QUEUE rcv_q, xmit_q;
```

The elements inside the `QUEUE` structure are called its *members*. You can access these members by using the *member selection operator* (`.`). For instance, `rcv_q.count` refers to the `count` member of the `rcv_q` structure.

A `union` is like a `struct` except that, instead of grouping related data items together as a `struct` does, a `union` allocates storage for several data items starting at the same location. Thus, all members of a `union` share the same storage location. You can use unions to view the same data item in different ways. Suppose you're using a compiler that supports 4-byte `longs`, and you want to access the 4 individual bytes of a `long` integer. Here's a `union` that lets you accomplish this:

```
union
{
    long  file_type;
    char  bytes[4];
} header_id;
```

With this definition, `header_id.file_type` refers to the `long` integer, while `header_id.bytes[0]` is the first byte of that `long` integer.

In C, you also can define structures that contain groups of bits that are packed into an `int`. These *bit fields* are useful for manipulating selected bits of an integer, and often are used when accessing hardware devices such as disk drive controllers and serial ports. Think of a bit field as a structure with bits as members. The declaration of a bit field is like that for any other structure, except for the syntax used to indicate the size of each group of bits. For example, the text display memory in the IBM PC uses a 16-bit cell for each character: the least-significant 8 bits for the character's ASCII code and the other 8 bits for attributes such as foreground and background colors. A 16-bit bit field describing this layout might be as follows:

```
struct TEXT_CELL
{
    unsigned  c:8, fg_color:4, bg_color:3, blink_on:1;
};
```

This bit field definition assumes that the compiler packs the bit fields from the least significant bit to the most significant bit. The exact order of the bits in a bit field depends on the compiler.

Arrays

An *array* is a collection of one or more identical data items. You can declare arrays of any type of data, including structures and types defined by typedef. For example, to define an array of 80 characters, you would write the following:

```
char    string[80];
```

The characters in the string array occupy successive storage locations, beginning with location 0. Thus, in this example, string[0] refers to the first character in this array, while string[79] refers to the last one. You can define arrays of other data types and structures similarly:

```
struct Customer                   /* Declare a structure        */
{
    int  id;
    char first_name[40];
    char last_name[40];
};

struct Customer customers[100]; /* Define array of structures */
int             index[64];      /* An array of 64 integers    */
```

You also can define multidimensional arrays. For example, to represent an 80-column by 25-line text display, you can use a two-dimensional array, as follows:

```
unsigned char text_screen[25][80];
```

Each item of text_screen is an array of 80 unsigned chars, and text_screen contains 25 such arrays. In other words, the two-dimensional array is stored by laying out one row after another in memory. You can use expressions such as text_screen[0][0] to refer to the first character in the first row and text_screen[24][79] to refer to the last character of the last row of the display screen. Higher-dimensional arrays are defined similarly:

```
float coords[3][2][5];
```

This example defines coords as a three-dimensional array of three data items: each item is an array of two arrays, each of which, in turn, is an array of five float variables. Thus, you interpret a multidimensional array as an "array of arrays."

Pointers

A *pointer* is a variable that can hold the address of any type of data except a bit field. For example, if p_i is a pointer to an integer variable, you can define and use it as follows:

```
/* Define an int pointer and an integer */
   int *p_i, count;

/* Set pointer to the address of the integer "count" */
    p_i = &count;
```

In this case, the compiler will allocate storage for an int variable count and a pointer to an integer p_i. The number of bytes necessary to represent a pointer depends on the underlying system's addressing scheme. You should not use a pointer until it contains the address of a valid object. The example shows p_i being initialized to the address of the integer variable count using the & operator, which provides the address of a variable. Once p_i is initialized, you can refer to the value of count with the expression *p_i, which is read as "the contents of the object with its address in p_i."

Pointers are useful in many situations; an important one is the dynamic allocation of memory. The standard C libraries include functions such as malloc and calloc, which you can call to allocate storage for arrays of objects. After allocating memory, these functions return the starting address of the block of memory. Because this address is the only way to reach that memory, you must store it in a variable capable of holding an address—a pointer.

Suppose you allocated memory for an array of 50 integers and saved the returned address in p_i. Now you can treat this block of memory as an array of 50 integers with the name p_i. Thus, you can refer to the last element in the array as p_i[49], which is equivalent to *(p_i + 49). Similarly, ANSI C treats the name of an array as a pointer to the first element of the array. The difference between the name of an array and a pointer variable is that the name of the array is a constant without the explicit storage necessary to hold the address of the array's first element, while the pointer is an actual storage location capable of holding the address of any data.

In addition to storing the address of dynamically allocated memory, pointers commonly are used as arguments to functions. When a C function is called, all of its arguments are *passed by value*—that is, the function gets a copy of each argument, not the original variables appearing in the argument list of the function call. Thus, a C function cannot alter the value of its arguments. Pointers provide a way out. To change the value of a variable in a function, you can pass it a pointer to the variable and the function can alter the value through the pointer.

Type Definitions

Through the typedef keyword, C provides you with a convenient way of assigning a new name to an existing data type. You can use the typedef facility to give meaningful names to data types used in a particular application. For example, a graphics application might declare a data type named Point as follows:

```
/* Declare a Point data type */
    typedef struct Point
    {
        short x;
        short y;
    } Point;

/* Declare PointPtr to be pointer to Point types */
    typedef Point *P_PointPtr;

/* Define some instances of these types and initialize them */
    Point     a = {0, 0};
    PointPtr  p_a = &a;
```

As shown by the Point and PointPtr types, you can use typedef to declare complex data types conveniently.

Type Qualifiers: *const* and *volatile*

ANSI C introduces two new keywords, const and volatile, which you can use as qualifiers in a declaration. The const qualifier in a declaration tells the compiler that the particular data object must not be modified by the program. This means that the compiler must not generate code that might alter the contents of the location where that data item is stored. On the other hand, volatile specifies that the value of a variable may be changed by factors beyond the program's control. You can use both keywords on a single data item to mean that, while the item must not be modified by your program, it may be altered by some other process. The const and volatile keywords always qualify the item that immediately follows them. The information provided by the const and the volatile qualifiers is supposed to help the compiler optimize the code it generates. For example, suppose the variable block_size is declared and initialized as follows:

```
const int block_size = 512;
```

In this case, the compiler need not generate code to load the value of `block_size` from memory. Instead, it can use the value `512` wherever your program uses `block_size`. Now suppose you added `volatile` to the declaration and changed the declaration to:

```
volatile const int block_size = 512;
```

This says that the contents of `block_size` may be changed by some external process. Therefore, the compiler cannot optimize away any reference to `block_size`. You may need to use such declarations when referring to an I/O port or video memory, because these locations can be changed by factors beyond your program's control.

Expressions

An *expression* is a combination of variables, function calls, and operators that results in a single value. For example, here is an expression with a value that is the number of bytes needed to store the null-terminated string `str` (an array of `char`s with a zero byte at the end):

```
(strlen(str) * sizeof(char) + 1)
```

This expression involves a function call, `strlen(str)`, and the multiplication (*), addition (+), and `sizeof` operators.

ANSI C has a large number of operators that are an important part of expressions. Table 3.4 provides a summary of the operators in ANSI C.

Table 3.4. Summary of ANSI C operators.

Name of Operator	Syntax	Result
ARITHMETIC OPERATORS		
Addition	`x+y`	Adds `x` and `y`.
Subtraction	`x-y`	Subtracts `y` from `x`.
Multiplication	`x*y`	Multiplies `x` and `y`.
Division	`x/y`	Divides `x` by `y`.
Remainder	`x%y`	Computes the remainder that results from dividing `x` by `y`.
Preincrement	`++x`	Increments `x` before use.

Name of Operator	Syntax	Result
Postincrement	x++	Increments x after use.
Predecrement	--x	Decrements x before use.
Postdecrement	x--	Decrements x after use.
Minus	-x	Negates the value of x.
Plus	+x	Maintains the value of x unchanged.
RELATIONAL AND LOGICAL OPERATORS		
Greater than	x>y	Value is 1 if x exceeds y; otherwise, value is 0.
Greater than or equal to	x>=y	Value is 1 if x exceeds or equals y; otherwise, value is 0.
Less than	x<y	Value is 1 if y exceeds x; otherwise, value is 0.
Less than or equal to	x<=y	Value is 1 if y exceeds or equals x; otherwise, value is 0.
Equal to	x==y	Value is 1 if x equals y; otherwise, value is 0.
Not equal to	x!=y	Value is 1 if x and y are unequal; otherwise, value is 0.
Logical NOT	!x	Value is 1 if x is 0; otherwise, value is 0.
Logical AND	x&&y	Value is 0 if either x or y is 0.
Logical OR	x¦¦y	Value is 0 if both x and y are 0.
ASSIGNMENT OPERATORS		
Assignment	x=y	Places the value of y into x.
Compound assignment	x O=y	Equivalent to x = x O y, where O is one of the following operators: +, -, *, /, %, <<, >>, &, ^, or ¦.

continues

Table 3.4. continued

Name of Operator	Syntax	Result
DATA ACCESS AND SIZE OPERATORS		
Subscript	`x[y]`	Selects the yth element of array x.
Member selection	`x.y`	Selects member y of structure (or union) x.
Member selection	`x->y`	Selects the member named y from a structure or union with x as its address.
Indirection	`*x`	Contents of the location with x as its address.
Address of	`&x`	Address of the data object named x.
Size of	`sizeof(x)`	Size (in bytes) of the data object named x.
BITWISE OPERATORS		
Bitwise NOT	`~x`	Changes all 1s to 0s and 0s to 1s.
Bitwise AND	`x&y`	Result is the bitwise AND of x and y.
Bitwise OR	`x¦y`	Result is the bitwise OR of x and y.
Bitwise exclusive OR	`x^y`	Result contains 1s where corresponding bits of x and y differ.
Left shift	`x<<y`	Shifts the bits of x to the left by y bit positions. Fills 0s in the vacated bit positions.
Right shift	`x>>y`	Shifts the bits of x to the right by y bit positions. Fills 0s in the vacated bit positions.

Name of Operator	Syntax	Result
MISCELLANEOUS OPERATORS		
Function call	`x(y)`	Result is the value returned (if any) by function `x`, which is called with argument `y`.
Type cast	`(type)x`	Converts the value of `x` to the `type` named in parentheses.
Conditional	`z?x:y`	If `z` is not `0`, evaluates `x`; otherwise, evaluates `y`.
Comma	`x,y`	Evaluates `x` first and then `y`.

Operator Precedence

Typical C expressions consist of several operands and operators. When writing complicated expressions, you must be aware of the order in which the compiler evaluates the operators. For example, a program uses an array of pointers to integers defined as follows:

```
typedef int *IntPtr;   /* Use typedef to simplify declarations */
IntPtr  iptr[10];      /* An array of 10 pointers to int       */
```

Now, suppose that you encounter the expression `*iptr[4]`. Does this refer to the value of the `int` with the address in `iptr[4]`, or is this the fifth element from the location with the address in `iptr`? In other words, is the compiler going to evaluate the subscript operator (`[]`) before the indirection operator (`*`), or is it the other way around? To answer questions such as these, you need to know the *precedence*, or order in which the program applies the operators.

Table 3.5 summarizes ANSI C's precedence rules. The table shows the operators in order of decreasing precedence. The operators with highest precedence—those that are applied first—are shown first. The table also shows the *associativity* of the operators—this is the order in which operators at the same level are evaluated.

Table 3.5. Precedence and associativity of ANSI C operators.

Operator Group	Operator Name	Notation	Associativity
Postfix	Subscript	x[y]	Left to right
	Function call	x(y)	
	Member selection	x.y	
	Member selection	x->y	
	Postincrement	x++	
	Postdecrement	x—	
Unary	Preincrement	++x	Right to left
	Predecrement	—x	
	Address of	&x	
	Indirection	*x	
	Plus	+x	
	Minus	-x	
	Bitwise NOT	~x	
	Logical NOT	!x	
	Sizeof	sizeof x	
	Type cast	(type)x	
Multiplicative	Multiply	x*y	Left to right
	Divide	x/y	
	Remainder	x%y	
Additive	Add	x+y	Left to right
	Subtract	x-y	
Shift	Left shift	x<<y	Left to right
	Right shift	x>>y	
Relational	Greater than	x>y	Left to right
	Greater than or equal to	x>=y	
	Less than	x<y	
	Less than or equal to	x<=y	
Equality	Equal to	x==y	Left to right
	Not equal to	x!=y	
Bitwise AND	Bitwise AND	x&y	Left to right

Operator Group	Operator Name	Notation	Associativity
Bitwise XOR	Bitwise exclusive OR	`x^y`	Left to right
Bitwise OR	Bitwise OR	`x¦y`	Left to right
Logical AND	Logical AND	`x&&y`	Left to right
Logical OR	Logical OR	`x¦¦y`	Left to right
Conditional	Conditional	`z?x:y`	Right to left
Assignment	Assignment	`x=y`	Right to left
	Multiply assign	`x *= y`	
	Divide assign	`x /= y`	
	Remainder assign	`x %= y`	
	Add assign	`x += y`	
	Subtract assign	`x -= y`	
	Left shift assign	`x <<= y`	
	Right shift assign	`x >>= y`	
	Bitwise AND assign	`x &= y`	
	Bitwise XOR assign	`x ^= y`	
	Bitwise OR assign	`x ¦= y`	
Comma	Comma	`x,y`	Left to right

Getting back to the question of interpreting `*iptr[4]`, a quick look at Table 3.5 tells you that the `[]` operator has precedence over the `*` operator. Thus, when the compiler processes the expression `*iptr[4]`, it evaluates `iptr[4]` first, and then it applies the indirection operator, resulting in the value of the `int` with the address in `iptr[4]`.

Statements

You use statements to represent the actions C functions will perform and to control the flow of execution in the C program. A *statement* consists of keywords, expressions, and other statements. Each statement ends with a semicolon.

A special type of statement, the *compound statement*, is a group of statements enclosed in a pair of braces (`{...}`). The body of a function is a compound statement. Also known as *blocks*, such compound statements can contain local variables.

The following alphabetically arranged sections describe the types of statements available in ANSI C.

The *break* Statement

You use the `break` statement to jump to the statement following the innermost `do`, `for`, `switch`, or `while` statement. It also is used to exit from a `switch` statement. Here's an example that uses `break` to exit a `for` loop:

```
for(i = 0; i < ncommands; i++)
{
    if(strcmp(input, commands[i]) == 0) break;
}
```

The *case* Statement

The `case` statement marks labels in a `switch` statement. Here's an example:

```
switch (interrupt_id)
{
    case XMIT_RDY:
        transmit();
        break;

    case RCV_RDY:
        receive();
        break;
}
```

Compound Statement or Block

A *compound statement*, or *block*, is a group of declarations followed by statements, all enclosed in a pair of braces (`{...}`). The body of a function and the block of code following an `if` statement are some examples of compound statements. In the following example, the declarations and statements within the braces constitute a compound statement:

```
if(theEvent.xexpose.count == 0)
{
    int i;
/* Clear the window and draw the figures
 * in the "figures" array
 */
    XClearWindow(theDisplay, dWin);
```

```
        if(numfigures > 0)
            for(i=0; i<numfigures; i++)
                draw_figure(theDisplay, dWin,
                            theGC, i);
}
```

The *continue* Statement

The continue statement begins the next iteration of the innermost do, for, or while statement in which it appears. You can use continue when you want to skip the execution of the loop. For example, to add the numbers from 1 to 10, excluding 5, you can use a for loop that skips the body when the loop index (i) is 5:

```
for(i=0, sum=0; i <= 10, i++)
{
    if(i == 5) continue;    /* Exclude 5 */
    sum += i;
}
```

The *default* Label

You use default as the label in a switch statement to mark code that will execute when none of the case labels match the switch expression.

The *do* Statement

The do statement, together with while, forms iterative loops of the kind

```
do
  statement
  while(expression);
```

where the statement (usually a compound statement) executes until the expression in the while statement evaluates to 0. The expression is evaluated after each execution of the statement. Thus, a do-while block always executes at least once. For example, to add the numbers from 1 to 10, you can use the following do statement:

```
i = 1;
sum = 0;
do
{
    sum += i;
```

```
    i++;
}
while(i <= 10);
```

Expression Statements

Expression statements are evaluated for their side effects. Some typical uses of expression statements include calling a function, incrementing a variable, and assigning a value to a variable. Here are some examples:

```
printf("Hello, World!\n");
i++;
num_bytes = length * sizeof(char);
```

The *for* Statement

Use the `for` statement to execute a statement any number of times based on the value of an expression. The syntax is as follows:

```
for (expr_1; expr_2; expr_3) statement
```

where the `expr_1` is evaluated once at the beginning of the loop, and the statement is executed until the expression `expr_2` evaluates to 0. The third expression, `expr_3`, is evaluated after each execution of the statement. The expressions, `expr_2` and `expr_3`, are optional. Here's an example that uses a `for` loop to add the numbers from 1 to 10:

```
for(i=0, sum=0; i <= 10; sum += i, i++);
```

In this example, the actual work of adding the numbers is done in the third expression, and the statement controlled by the `for` loop is a null statement (a lone ;).

The *goto* Statement

The `goto` statement transfers control to a statement label. Here's an example that prompts the user for a value and repeats the request if the value is not acceptable:

```
ReEnter:
    printf("Enter offset: ");
    scanf(" %d", &offset);
    if(offset < 0 || offset > MAX_OFFSET)
    {
        printf("Bad offset: %d Please reenter:\n",
               offset);
        goto ReEnter;
    }
```

The *if* Statement

You can use the if statement to test an expression and execute a statement only when the expression is not zero. An if statement takes the following form:

```
if ( expression )  statement
```

The statement following the if is executed only if the expression in parentheses evaluates to a nonzero value. That statement usually is a compound statement. Here's an example:

```
if(mem_left < threshold)
{
     Message("Low on memory! Close some windows.\n");
}
```

The *if-else* Statement

The if-else statement is a form of the if statement together with an else clause. The statement has the syntax

```
if ( expression )
     statement_1
else
     statement_2
```

where statement_1 is executed if the expression within the parentheses is not zero. Otherwise, statement_2 is executed. Here is an example that uses if and else to pick the smaller of two variables.

```
if ( a <= b)
     smaller = a;
else
     smaller = b;
```

The *Null* Statement

The null statement, represented by a solitary semicolon, does nothing. Use null statements in loops when all processing is done in the loop expressions rather than in the body of the loop. For example, to locate the zero byte marking the end of a string, you might use the following:

```
char str[80] = "Test";
int i;

for (i=0; str[i] != '\0'; i++)
                                        ;  /* Null statement */
```

The *return* Statement

The `return` statement stops executing the current function and returns control to the calling function. The syntax is

```
return expression;
```

where the value of the expression is returned as the value of the function.

The *switch* Statement

The `switch` statement performs a multiple branch, depending on the value of an expression. It has the following syntax:

```
switch (expression)
{
     case value1:
          statement_1
          break;
     case value2:
          statement_2
          break;
             .
             .
             .
     default:
          statement_default
}
```

If the expression being tested by `switch` evaluates to `value1`, `statement_1` is executed. If the expression is equal to `value2`, `statement_2` is executed. The value is compared with each `case` label, and the statement following the matching label is executed. If the value does not match any of the `case` labels, the block `statement_default` following the `default` label is executed. Each statement ends with a `break` statement that separates the code of one `case` label from another. Here is a `switch` statement that calls different routines depending on the value of an integer variable named `cmd`:

```
switch (cmd)
{
     case 'q':
          quit_app(0);

          case 'c':
          connect();
          break;

     case 's':
          set_params();
          break;

     case '?':
     case 'H':
          print_help();
          break;

     default:
          printf("Unknown command!\n");
}
```

The *while* Statement

The `while` statement is used in the form

```
while (expression) statement
```

where the statement is executed until the expression evaluates to 0. A `while` statement evaluates the expression before each execution of the statement. Thus, a `while` loop executes the statement zero or more times. Here is a `while` statement for copying one array to another:

```
i = length;
while (i >= 0)  /* Copy one array to another */
{
     array2[i] = array1[i];
     i—;
}
```

Functions

Functions are the building blocks of C programs. A *function* is a collection of declarations and statements. Each C program has at least one function: the `main` function. This is the function where the execution of a C program begins. The ANSI C library also is composed mostly of functions, although it contains quite a few macros.

Function Prototypes

In ANSI C, you must declare a function before using it. The function declaration tells the compiler what type of value the function returns and the number and type of arguments it takes. Most C programmers are used to declaring functions only when they return something other than an `int` because that is how Kernighan and Ritchie's definition of C works. For example, in the old UNIX C library, the memory allocation function, `calloc`, would return a pointer to a `char` (as you will see soon, the ANSI C version of `malloc` returns a `void` pointer). Thus, an old-style C program that uses `calloc` includes the declaration:

```
char *calloc();
```

You can continue to use this in ANSI C, but you also can declare a function as a complete *function prototype*, showing the return type as well as a list of arguments. The `calloc` function in the ANSI C library returns a `void` pointer and accepts two arguments, each of type `size_t`, which is an unsigned integer type of sufficient size to hold the value of the `sizeof` operator. Thus, the ANSI C prototype for `calloc` is

```
void *calloc(size_t, size_t);
```

This shows the type of each argument in the argument list. You also can include an identifier for each argument and write the prototype as follows:

```
void *calloc(size_t num_elements, size_t elem_size);
```

In this case, the prototype looks exactly like the first line in the definition of the function, except that you stop short of defining the function and end the line with a semicolon. With well-chosen names for arguments, this form of prototype can provide a lot of information about the function's use. For example, one look at the prototype of `calloc` should tell you that its first argument is the number of elements to allocate, and the second one is the size of each element.

Prototypes also help the compiler check function arguments and generate code that may use a faster mechanism for passing arguments. From the prototype, the compiler can determine the exact number and type of arguments to expect. Therefore, the prototype enables the compiler to catch any mistakes you might make when calling a function, such as passing the wrong number of arguments (when the function takes a fixed number of arguments) or passing a wrong type of argument to a function.

The *void* Type

What do you do when a function doesn't return anything or accept any parameters? To handle these cases, ANSI C provides the `void` type, which is useful for declaring functions that return nothing and for describing pointers that can point to any type of data. For example, you can use the `void` return type to declare a function such as `exit` that does not return anything:

```
void exit(int status);
```

On the other hand, if a function doesn't accept any formal parameters, its list of arguments is represented by a `void`:

```
FILE *tmpfile(void);
```

The `void` pointer is useful for functions that work with blocks of memory. For example, when you request a certain number of bytes from the memory allocation routine, `malloc`, you can use these locations to store any data that fits the space. In this case, the address of the first location of the allocated block of memory is returned as a `void` pointer. Thus, the prototype of `malloc` is

```
void *malloc(size_t numbytes);
```

Functions with a Variable Number of Arguments

If a function accepts a variable number of arguments, you can indicate this by using an ellipsis (`...`) in place of the argument list; however, you must provide at least one argument before the ellipsis. A good example of such functions is the `printf` family of functions, defined in the header file stdio.h. The prototypes of these functions are as follows:

```
int fprintf(FILE *stream, const char *format, ...);
int printf(const char *format, ...);
int sprintf(char *buffer, const char *format, ...);
```

As you can see, after a list of required arguments, the variable number of arguments is indicated by an ellipsis.

The ANSI C Library

The ANSI standard for C defines all aspects of C: the language, the preprocessor, and the library. The prototypes of the functions in the library, as well as all necessary data structures and preprocessor constants, are defined in a set of standard header files. Table 3.6 lists the standard header files, including a summary of their contents.

Table 3.6. Standard header files in ANSI C.

Header File	Purpose
assert.h	Defines the `assert` macro. Used for program diagnostics.
ctype.h	Declares functions for classifying and converting characters.
errno.h	Defines macros for error conditions, `EDOM` and `ERANGE`, and the integer variable `errno` where library functions return an error code.
float.h	Defines a range of values that can be stored in floating-point types.
limits.h	Defines the limiting values of all integer data types.
locale.h	Declares the `lconv` structure and the functions necessary for customizing a C program to a particular locale.
math.h	Declares math functions and the `HUGE_VAL` macro.
setjmp.h	Defines the `setjmp` and `longjmp` functions that can transfer control from one function to another without relying on normal function calls and returns. Also defines the `jmp_buf` data type used by `setjmp` and `longjmp`.
signal.h	Defines symbols and routines necessary for handling exceptional conditions.
stdarg.h	Defines macros that provide access to the unnamed arguments in a function that accepts a varying number of arguments.

Header File	Purpose
stddef.h	Defines the standard data types `ptrdiff_t`, `size_t`, and `wchar_t`; the symbol `NULL`; and the macro `offsetof`.
stdio.h	Declares the functions and data types necessary for input and output operations. Defines macros such as `BUFSIZ`, `EOF`, `NULL`, `SEEK_CUR`, `SEEK_END`, and `SEEK_SET`.
stdlib.h	Declares many utility functions, such as the string conversion routines, random number generator, memory allocation routines, and process control routines (such as `abort`, `exit`, and `system`).
string.h	Declares the string manipulation routines such as `strcmp` and `strcpy`.
time.h	Defines data types and declares functions that manipulate time. Defines the types `clock_t` and `time_t` and the `tm` data structure.

Summary

One quick way to grasp C++'s seemingly new syntax is to learn ANSI standard C, because many features of C++ have been incorporated into ANSI standard C (officially known as ANSI X3.159 1989). For instance, function prototypes, as well as `void` and `enum` types, appear in both ANSI C and C++. Because many syntactical details of C++ are similar to those of ANSI C, a knowledge of ANSI C is helpful when you write programs in C++. This chapter provided a quick overview of ANSI C.

4

Microsoft Visual C++ Extensions to Standard C

As its title indicates, Chapter 3 provided an "Overview of ANSI Standard C." Microsoft Visual C++, however, adds a number of keywords, global variables, and predefined macros to support the unique needs of the Intel 80x86 microprocessor family and the MS-DOS operating system. In particular, the unique memory-addressing scheme of the Intel 80x86 microprocessors has resulted in a number of *memory models* that specify how a program's code and data are organized in memory. In addition to the compiler options summarized in Chapter 1, "The Microsoft Visual C++ Programming Environment," Microsoft Visual C++ also includes many keywords and compiler directives (called *pragmas*) to support these memory models. This chapter describes the keywords, pragmas, and preprocessor macros unique to Microsoft Visual C++. Other compiler-specific information, such as limits on the values of various data types, also is described in this chapter.

This chapter describes the keywords, pragmas, and preprocessor macros that are unique to the Microsoft Visual C++ compiler and not part of ANSI standard C. The C++ language itself can be thought of as an extension of ANSI standard C, but C++ is not covered in this chapter. Chapters 5 through 13 teach C++ from the viewpoint of object-oriented programming.

Keywords Unique to Microsoft Visual C++

In Chapter 3, you saw the reserved keywords of ANSI C. The ANSI standard requires that compiler-specific reserved words start with two leading underscores. Microsoft Visual C++ follows this rule and defines 20 additional reserved words, each with two leading underscores. Table 4.1 summarizes these Microsoft-specific reserved words. The sections following this table briefly describe some of these keywords.

Table 4.1. Microsoft-specific keywords and special-meaning items.

Keyword	Purpose
`__asm`	Used to insert assembly language code in a C or C++ source file.
`__based`	Used as an address qualifier when declaring a data item or a function to indicate that the address of that item is the 16-bit offset within a specified base segment.
`__cdecl`	Used to indicate that the function or variable that follows uses the C naming and calling conventions (during function calls, arguments are pushed on the stack from right to left; names are case-sensitive and an underscore prefix is added to each name).
`__emit`	Used to embed machine code within a program.

Keyword	Purpose
`__export`	Indicates that a function or data item is exported from a dynamic link library (DLL).
`__far`	An address qualifier indicating that full 32-bit segment:offset addressing is used for a function or a variable.
`__fastcall`	Indicates that a function uses a calling convention that passes arguments in the registers for faster function calls.
`__fortran`	Used to indicate that a function or variable uses the FORTRAN and Pascal naming and calling conventions (during function calls, arguments are pushed on the stack from left to right and names are converted to all uppercase).
`__huge`	Used to indicate that a data item must be addressed using a 32-bit segment:offset address and that it may exceed 64K in size.
`__inline`	Causes the compiler to insert a copy of a function's body wherever the function is called (such functions are called *inline functions* and are used in both C and C++).
`__interrupt`	Indicates that a function is an interrupt handler, thus forcing the compiler to generate appropriate entry and exit codes to meet the requirements of an interrupt handler.
`__loadds`	Used to force the compiler to load the data segment register (the DS register) with a specified value before calling a function. The previous value of DS is restored just before the function returns.
`__near`	An addressing modifier indicating that a function or data item should be accessed using its 16-bit offset address only.

continues

Table 4.1. continued

Keyword	Purpose
`__pascal`	Used to indicate that a function or variable uses the FORTRAN and Pascal naming and calling conventions.
`__saveregs`	Forces the compiler to generate code to save and restore all CPU registers when entering and exiting a function.
`__self`	Name of the segment where a based pointer is stored.
`__segment`	Microsoft-specific data type used to declare a variable capable of holding a 16-bit segment address.
`__setenvp`	If your application doesn't need to access variables in the environment, you can provide a function called `__setenvp` in the same file as your main function, and make your executable file smaller.
`__setargv`	Special function (`setargv.obj`) that expands filenames that are entered in the MS-DOS format (such as `*.dat`) and passes the expanded list to the application. This function is much more powerful than the standard version, which simply passes the filename without expansion to the application. In addition, should you not need to process any command-line arguments, you can provide a function called `__setargv` in the same file as your main function—which will make your executable file smaller.
`__set_new_handler`	You can use the `__set_new_handler` function to take control when a new C++ operator fails to allocate memory.
`__segname`	Used to specify the name of a segment.

Keywords to Support Memory Models

C programmers who work on UNIX systems generally need not think about the memory-addressing scheme of their underlying system's central processing unit (CPU). On Intel 80x86 microprocessor-based MS-DOS PCs, the memory-addressing scheme is not so transparent to programmers—at least not if you want to write realistic applications that manipulate large amounts of textual or graphical information.

Intel 80x86 Processors

The term Intel 80x86 processors refers to the entire family of Intel microprocessors including the 8088, 8086, 80186, 80286, 80386, 80386SX, and 80486. It's common to use the term 80x86 to refer to these binary-compatible microprocessors that power most MS-DOS PCs. Individual models often are referred to by their last three digits, such as 186, 286, 386, or 486. The 8086, 186, and 286 are 16-bit microprocessors, meaning that they can handle units of data as large as 16 bits. The 8088, used in the original IBM PC and XT, is like the 8086, but its data path to the outside world is only 8 bits wide—that is, the 8088 can retrieve only 8 bits of information at a time. The more modern 386 and 486 are 32-bit processors that can process 32-bit data internally and access memory in 32-bit units. The 386SX is a version of the 386 that can process 32-bit data internally, but it can only retrieve information from memory in 16-bit units.

Segment:Offset Addressing in 80x86 Processors

The memory-addressing scheme used by the 80x86 microprocessors brings up the concept of *segments*. Under the MS-DOS operating system, all 80x86 processors—including the 80386 and 80486 that are capable of 32-bit processing—run in *real mode*. In real mode, all 80x86 processors behave like the 8086; they use 16-bit internal registers and can address up to a megabyte of physical memory using a 20-bit value as the address of any 8-bit byte in memory.

The concept of segments arises because a single 16-bit register cannot hold the entire 20-bit physical address. Intel's solution is to break down each memory address into two parts, a segment address and an offset, each a 16-bit value. The *segment address* is simply the address of the first byte of a block of memory located anywhere in the 1M addressable locations. The *offset address* is the location of a byte with respect to the beginning of the segment—the first byte in the segment is at offset 0, the second at offset 1, and so on. With this segment:offset-addressing scheme, two registers—one containing the segment address and the other the offset—can hold the address of any byte in physical memory.

Because a 16-bit number can hold values from 0 to 65,535, the offset can be up to 65,536 or 64K in size. Also, a 16-bit segment address can represent as many as 65,536 segments. However, this does not mean that the MS-DOS PC can access 65,536 segments that are each 64K in size. With the segment:offset-addressing scheme, Intel also stipulates that you should compute the 20-bit physical address by applying the following formula:

```
20-bit physical address = (16-bit segment address) _ 16 + (16-bit offset
address)
```

Thus, the processor still is limited to the amount of physical memory that it can access using a 20-bit address.

The advantage of segmented memory addressing is that if all of a program's data fits into a single segment (which can be up to 64K in size), the 80x86 processor can set up the segment address in a register and access any data item using only a 16-bit offset. This results in a speedier program because the processor doesn't need to manipulate the segment portion of the address.

The 640K Barrier Under MS-DOS

Although Intel 80x86 processors operating in real mode can address up to 1M or 1,024K of physical memory, 384K of addressable space above the lower 640K is normally reserved for adapter ROMs (read-only memory), video buffers, and other hardware. That is why only 640K of memory is available under MS-DOS.

Standard Memory Models

Because of the 80x86 processor's segmented memory addressing, the Microsoft Visual C++ compiler organizes code and data into one or more segments. To begin with, Microsoft Visual C++ gives you six predefined memory segmentation schemes, called *memory models*. Table 4.2 summarizes these memory models.

Table 4.2. Standard memory models in Microsoft Visual C++.

Model	Description
Tiny	All code and data must fit in a single, 64K segment. Use the Tiny model to build .COM files. Use CL's `/AT` command-line option to select the Tiny model.
Small	Program size is limited to one segment of code and one segment of data. The compiler assumes the Small memory model by default. You can explicitly specify the Small memory model with the `/AS` option.
Medium	Program size is limited to only one segment of data, but many segments of code. All data addresses are 16-bit offsets, but code uses explicit segment and offset addresses. The `/AM` compiler option selects the Medium memory model.
Compact	The program can contain several data segments, but only one code segment. All the program's data objects have full segment:offset addresses, whereas code addresses are offset only. Use the `/AC` compiler option to select the Compact model.
Large	The program can contain multiple segments of data and code. The total size of a program is limited only by the available memory under MS-DOS, but a single data item can be no larger than 64K. The `/AL` compiler option selects the Large memory model.
Huge	This is similar to the Large model, but you can have arrays that exceed the 64K segment limit. Each element of the array is still subject to the 64K size limit. For arrays up to 128K in size, an element can be any size up to 64K. If the array size exceeds 128K, the size of each element must be a power of 2 and less than 64K. In the Huge model, address arithmetic is performed in such a way that arrays can span multiple segments. Use the `/AH` compiler option to specify the Huge model.

Custom Memory Models

In addition to the six predefined memory models shown in Table 4.2, you can construct custom memory models through the `/Axyz` compiler option, where *x*, *y*, and *z* indicate the addressing conventions for three specific items:

- The first letter (*x*) indicates how functions are addressed. It can be one of the following:

  `s` indicates near functions (16-bit offset addresses only)

  `l` indicates far functions (32-bit segment:offset addresses)

- The second letter (*y*) indicates how data are addressed. It can be one of the following:

  `n` indicates near data (16-bit offset addresses only)

  `f` indicates far data (32-bit segment:offset addresses)

  `h` indicates huge data (segment:offset addressing and greater than 64K)

- The third letter (*z*) indicates how the stack and data segments are set up. It can be one of the following:

  `d` The SS register is the same as DS. The stack is in the data segment.

  `u` SS is not the same as DS. DS is reloaded on function entry.

  `w` SS is not the same as DS. DS is not reloaded on function entry.

In fact, five of the six standard memory models can be specified by the following custom equivalents:

Option for the Custom Model	Option for the Standard Model
/AS	/Asnd
/AM	/Alnd
/AC	/Asfd
/AL	/Alfd
/AH	/Alhd

For most projects, you may not need to customize memory models to this extent. Instead, you may only want to mix an occasional far data item with an otherwise small model program. The next section describes how to do this.

Near, Far, and Huge

It's common practice among MS-DOS programmers to use the terms *near* and *far* as adjectives that specify the addressing requirements for a function or a data. A near address is a 16-bit offset, whereas a far address requires the full 32-bit segment:offset address. The keywords `__near` and `__far` are used as qualifiers to indicate near and far addressing, respectively.

In a similar vein, the term huge array refers to an array that can exceed the 64K segment limit and is declared with the `__huge` keyword. A based pointer or based variable refers to such items declared with the `__based` keyword.

Overriding Default Addressing Conventions

What if you wanted a small memory program for efficiency, but needed a single large array? Do you use the Medium model because your program has more than 64K of data? The answer is no. Microsoft Visual C++ provides several keywords that you can use to declare explicitly the addressing convention for each individual variable or function. For instance, to declare a single far data item, you need only add a `__far` prefix to the variable's name.

Microsoft Visual C++ supports the following four keywords:

- `__near`
- `__far`
- `__huge`
- `__based`

These keywords are used to indicate the addressing requirements of data and functions. You can use these four keywords to mix data items and function calls with an addressing convention that differs from the defaults used by the selected standard memory model. Table 4.3 summarizes the use of these keywords.

Table 4.3. The `__near`, `__far`, `__huge`, and `__based` keywords.

Keyword	Description
`__near`	Both data and functions that are qualified with a `__near` keyword are accessed with 16-bit addresses. Pointers are 16-bit values and all address arithmetic is performed assuming 16-bit values.
`__far`	Data can be anywhere in memory, but a single data item cannot exceed 64K in size and must not cross any segment boundary. Both function and data are accessed through full 32-bit segment:offset addresses. All pointers are 32-bit values. However, pointer arithmetic is performed with the 16-bit offsets only because no data item is expected to extend beyond the boundary of a segment.
`__huge`	You can declare huge data only; the `__huge` keyword is not applicable to functions. Data can be anywhere in memory and individual arrays can exceed 64K in size. Data is accessed with 32-bit segment:offset addresses. Pointers to data are 32 bits, and all pointer arithmetic is done using the full 32-bit addresses.
`__based`	A function or data item qualified with the `__based` keyword is addressed through its 16-bit offset in a specified segment. In other words, the `__based` keyword forces the compiler to place that function or data item in a specific segment. The compiler uses the 16-bit offset when performing address arithmetic for based variables.

Other Special Keywords

As you can see from Table 4.1, there are many more Microsoft-specific keywords supported by Microsoft Visual C++. These keywords serve a number of purposes from embedding assembly language statements in a C or C++ program to controlling events that occur when entering or leaving a function. The following sections describe some of these keywords.

Embedding Assembly Language Code in C and C++

The __asm keyword enables you to place assembly language statements directly inside a C or C++ program. You can place a single line of assembly language in your program by prefixing the statement with the __asm keyword, like this:

```
// Assembly language statements—one per line
    __asm mov ah, 02h
    __asm mov dl, 7
    __asm int 21h
```

If you prefer, you can place both statements on a single line:

```
// Multiple __asm statements on a single line
    __asm mov ah, 02h  __asm mov dl, 7  __asm int 21h
```

You also can embed a block of assembly language statements by enclosing them inside a pair of braces ({...}) and prefixing the block with the __asm keyword. For example, the preceding statements could be written as follows:

```
__asm    // An __asm block
{
    mov ah, 01h
    mov dl, 7
    int 21h
}
```

Certain restrictions apply regarding the type of assembly language statements you can place inside a C or C++ source file:

- First, the inline assembler recognizes only a subset of the directives available under the Microsoft Macro Assembler (MASM). You can use the EVEN and ALIGN directives. Among the MASM operators, you can use LENGTH, TYPE, and SIZE with C or C++ arrays, and SEG and OFFSET with C or C++ variables. You can reference C and C++ symbols including constants, macros, variables, and function names inside __asm blocks.
- Second, the processor instructions you embed in the program must permanently alter the registers used in function calls. If you use an __asm block within a function, you must ensure that the values of the DI, SI, DS, SS, SP,

and BP registers are preserved. On the other hand, you can change the AX, BX, CX, DX, and ES registers any way you like. Similarly, if you alter the direction flag using the `STD` or `CLD` instructions, you should restore the flag to its original value before returning from the function.

If you want to return a value from a function using `__asm` blocks, you must follow certain conventions:

- If the return value is a `char`, `int`, or a `near` pointer, place the return value in the AX register before returning.
- If the return value is a `long` or a `far` pointer, place the high word (the most-significant 16 bits) in DX and the low word in AX.
- To return a value larger than 32 bits, store the value in memory and return a pointer to the value through DX and AX.

The __emit Keyword

Use the `__emit` keyword for embedding literal bytes into the object code generated by the compiler. You can use `__emit` inside an `__asm` block to mimic MASM's DB directive. Using `__emit`, you can define a single byte at the current location in the current code segment. One reason for using the `__emit` keyword is to embed special instructions that the inline assembler cannot generate. For instance, you could embed 80386-specific instructions, which the inline assembler does not accept. The syntax for using the `__emit` keyword is

```
__asm __emit <value>
```

where *<value>* is an 8-bit quantity. For example, to embed a 0x66 (in C's notation for hexadecimal values), you would write:

```
__asm __emit 0x66
```

The __interrupt Keyword

The `__interrupt` keyword enables you to declare a function as an interrupt handler. (Interrupt handlers are described in Chapter 32, "DOS and BIOS Calls.") When the compiler translates a function with the `__interrupt` qualifier, the compiler generates code to save all CPU registers (except SS) on the stack before entering the function, and restores all registers when exiting the function. Additionally, as per normal operation for interrupt handlers, the compiler generates an `IRET` instruction to return from the function.

An interrupt handler must be a far function. If you're using the small or compact memory models, you must declare the interrupt handler with the `__far` keyword. Here is a sample declaration using the `__interrupt` keyword:

```
void __interrupt __far int_handler(unsigned _es, unsigned _ds,
                                   unsigned _di, unsigned _si,
                                   unsigned _bp, unsigned _sp,
                                   unsigned _bx, unsigned _dx,
                                   unsigned _cx, unsigned _ax,
                                   unsigned _ip, unsigned _cs,
                                   unsigned _flags )
{
// Code goes here. Refer to registers by the names shown in
// the argument list. Use __asm to embed assembly language
// statements in the interrupt handler.

// ...
}
```

Inside the interrupt handler, you can access the registers by the names shown in the argument list. You can use whatever names you care to for the arguments. To avoid confusion, you may wish to declare them consistently, as shown in the preceding example: use the same names as the real registers, but place underscores in front of them. If you alter the contents of a register inside the interrupt handler, that register will contain the changed value when the interrupt handler returns.

All the precautions that apply to assembly language interrupt handlers also apply to those written in C. Remember that on entry to the interrupt handler, the interrupt enable flag is cleared (set to zero). All further interrupts consequently are disabled. Because most devices (such as the keyboard and the time-of-day timer) rely on interrupts, you should immediately call the `_enable` function (described in Chapter 32) to enable the interrupts. Once you have enabled the interrupts, keep in mind that another interrupt may occur at any time. Make sure that your interrupt handler function can itself be interrupted without problems. To ensure this, avoid calling any C library function that relies on DOS calls (through INT 21H) or BIOS functions. These include the I/O and graphics functions.

Predefined Global Variables and Preprocessor Macros

Microsoft Visual C++ includes a number of predefined global variables in the C library. These variables contain important information, such as the DOS version number, the current operating system (DOS or Windows), and a pointer to the environment variables. You can refer to these global variables if you include the header file where they are declared. These global variables are automatically initialized when your program starts up. Table 4.4 lists the predefined global variables in Microsoft Visual C++.

Table 4.4. Predefined global variables in Microsoft Visual C++.

Name	Type, Declaration, and Purpose
`_amblksiz`	Type: `unsigned` Declared in: malloc.h. This variable controls how memory is obtained from the operating system for eventual allocation by the library functions `malloc` and `calloc`. The memory allocation functions request memory from DOS in chunks of the size specified by the value of the `_amblksize` variable. The default value is 8,192 bytes (or 8K). The huge array allocation function, `halloc`, does not use this variable.
`_cpumode`	Type: `unsigned char` Declared in: stdlib.h. This variable is set to a value that indicates the mode in which the processor is running. The value can be one of two defined constants, `_REAL_MODE` or `_PROT_MODE`, which are also defined in stdlib.h.
`_daylight`	Type: `int` Declared in: time.h. This variable has a nonzero value if a daylight saving time zone is specified in the `TZ` environment variable; otherwise,

Name	Type, Declaration, and Purpose
	the variable has a zero value. Use this variable when converting local time to Greenwich Mean Time (also known as Universal Coordinated Time or by its French acronym, UTC).
`_doserrno`	Type: `int` Declared in: stdlib.h. This variable contains the MS-DOS error code returned by the last MS-DOS system call.
`_environ`	Type: `char *_environ[];` Declared in: stdlib.h. This is an array of pointers to the strings that constitute the environment of the current program. You can directly access the environment variables through this array. The library functions `getenv` and `_putenv` use the `_environ` array.
`errno`	Type: `int` Declared in: stdlib.h. This variable is set to an error code corresponding to the last error.
`_fmode`	Type: `int` Declared in: stdlib.h. This variable controls the default file translation mode. The default value is 0, which means files are translated in the text mode.
`_osmajor`	Type: `unsigned char` Declared in: stdlib.h. This is the major version number of the operating system. For example, if you have MS-DOS 5.0, `_osmajor` is 5.
`_osminor`	Type: `unsigned char` Declared in: stdlib.h. This is the minor version number of the operating system. For MS-DOS 5.0, `_osminor` is 0; for MS-DOS 3.3, `_osminor` is 30 (decimal).

continues

Table 4.4. continued

Name	Type, Declaration, and Purpose
`_osmode`	Type: `unsigned char` Declared in: stdlib.h. This variable contains a constant that indicates what operating system is currently running. The value can be one of the defined constants, `_DOS_MODE` or `_WIN_MODE`, which respectively indicate that either MS-DOS or Windows is the current operating system.
`_osversion`	Type: `unsigned` Declared in: dos.h. This 2-byte value contains the complete version number of the underlying operating system. The least-significant byte contains the major version number and the most-significant byte (the "high" byte) contains the minor version number. Thus, for MS-DOS 3.1, `_osversion` is 0x0a03 (in hexadecimal); for DOS 5.0, `_osversion` is 5.
`_pgmptr`	Type: `extern char __far *_pgmptr;` Declared in: stdio.h. The `_pgmptr` variable is automatically initialized at startup to point to the drive, path, and filename of the program.
`_psp`	Type: `unsigned` Declared in: stdlib.h. This variable contains the segment address of the program segment prefix (PSP) of the program. The PSP contains information about the process, such as the command-line arguments, a pointer to the environment block, and the return address. The PSP begins at offset 0 of the segment address contained in `_psp`.
`sys_errlist`	Type: `char *sys_errlist[];` Declared in: stdlib.h. This variable comprises an array of strings, each corresponding to a system error message.
`sys_nerr`	Type: `int` Declared in: stdlib.h. This variable consists of the total number of strings in the `sys_errlist` array.

Name	Type, Declaration, and Purpose
`_timezone`	Type: `long` Declared in: time.h. This variable contains the difference in seconds between Greenwich Mean Time and the local time.
`_tzname`	Type: `char *tzname[2];` Declared in: time.h. This is an array of two null-terminated strings with `tzname[0]` set to the three-letter time zone name (for example, EST or PST), and `tzname[1]` set to the name of the daylight saving time zone (see Chapter 28, "Date and Time Management," for details).

The Microsoft Visual C++ preprocessor also defines a number of macros (symbols) that you can use in your source files without defining them. As explained in Chapter 3, ANSI C also contains a number of preprocessor macros that are predefined. In addition to these ANSI-standard preprocessor macros, Microsoft Visual C++ defines the additional macros listed in Table 4.5. You can use these macros to conditionally compile sections of code based on conditions, such as the processor type and the memory model being used.

Table 4.5. Microsoft-specific predefined preprocessor macros in Microsoft Visual C++.

Symbol	Purpose
`_CHAR_UNSIGNED`	Defined when the `/J` option is used. When this macro is defined, the default type of `char` is assumed to be `unsigned`.
`_FAST`	Defined when the fast compile option `/f` is specified.
`_M_I86`	Identifies the machine for which the compiler is generating code as a member of the Intel 80x86 family. The `M_I86` macro has the same meaning as `_M_I86` and is retained for compatibility with earlier versions of Microsoft C when the `/Ze` compiler option is used.

continues

Table 4.5. continued

Symbol	Purpose
`_M_I8086`	Identifies the machine for which the compiler is generating code as an Intel 8086. The `M_I8086` macro has the same meaning as `_M_I8086` and is retained for compatibility with earlier versions of Microsoft C when the `/Ze` compiler option is used. This macro is defined when the compiler option `/G0` is used.
`_M_I286`	Identifies the machine for which the compiler is generating code as an Intel 80286. The `M_I286` macro has the same meaning as `_M_I286` and is retained for compatibility with earlier versions of Microsoft C when the `/Ze` compiler option is used. This macro is defined when the `/G1` or `/G2` compiler options are used.
`_M_I86xM`	Identifies the memory model. The letter represented by `x` depends on the memory model: `_M_I86TM` for Tiny, `_M_I86SM` for Small, `_M_I86CM` for Compact, `_M_I86MM` for Medium, `_M_I86LM` for Large, and `_M_I86HM` for Huge. The same set of symbols without the leading underscores also are defined for compatibility with older versions of Microsoft C when the `/Ze` compiler option is used.
`_MSC_VER`	Defined as the version of the Microsoft Visual C++ compiler. For Microsoft Visual C++, `_MSC_VER` is defined as 700.
`_MSDOS`	Defined when the operating system is MS-DOS. The `MSDOS` symbol, with the same meaning as `_MSDOS`, is also defined when the `/Ze` compiler option is used.
`_PCODE`	Defined when the compiler is translating to p-code. This macro is defined when the `/Oq` option is selected.

Symbol	Purpose
`_WINDLL`	Defined when the file is being compiled as a Windows protected-mode DLL by selecting the `/GD` compiler option.
`_WINDOWS`	Defined when code generation for Windows protected mode is selected with `/GA`, `/Gn`, `/GW`, `/Mq`, or `/GD`.

Pragmas

You can use the `#pragma` preprocessor directive to instruct the C compiler to turn on or off specific features. Pragmas vary from one compiler to another. The following is a list of pragmas supported by the Microsoft Visual C++ compiler:

- `#pragma alloc_text(segname, function1, function2, ...)`

  Instructs the compiler to place the far functions `function1`, `function2`, and so on, in the code segment named `segname`. Although the `alloc_text` pragma is retained for compatibility with older versions of Microsoft C, the preferred method of locating a function in a specific segment is through the `_based` keyword.

- `#pragma auto_inline(on)` or `#pragma auto_inline(off)`

  Turns on or off the inline expansion of functions. If you do not provide a value in the parentheses, the inline expansion is turned on.

- `#pragma check_pointer(on)` or `#pragma check_pointer(off)`

  Turns on or off pointer-checking. Also see compiler option `/Zr` in Chapter 1.

- `#pragma check_stack(on)` or `#pragma check_stack(off)`

  Turns on or off the generation of stack checking code. Also see compiler option `/Gs` in Chapter 1.

- `#pragma comment(comment_type, comment_string, ...)`

  Places a specified comment record in an object file. You should use this pragma only if you know Microsoft's object file format and understand what comment records signify. Please consult the online help in the C/C++ compiler for more information.

- `#pragma function(func1, func2, ...)`

  Instructs the compiler to generate function calls instead of using the intrinsic forms of the functions named `func1`, `func2`, and so on.

- `#pragma inline_depth(level)`, where `level` is a number from 0 to 255

  Controls the number of times inline expansion can occur when an inline function is called recursively.

- `#pragma inline_recursion(on)` or `#pragma inline_recursion(off)`

  Turns on or off recursive expansion of inline functions.

- `#pragma intrinsic(func1, func2,...)`

  Instructs the compiler to use the intrinsic forms of the functions named `func1`, `func2`, and so on. Using the intrinsic form, a function implies inline placement of the function's code. This results in faster execution because you do not incur the overhead of a function call. This is also controlled by the `/Oi` option.

- `#pragma linesize(nchar)`where `nchar` is a number from 79 to 132.

  Specifies the number of characters per line in source listings generated by the compiler.

- `#pragma loop_opt(on)` or `#pragma loop_opt(off)`

  Turns on or off loop optimization. This also is controlled by the compiler options `/Ol` and `/Ox`.

- `#pragma message(message_string)`

  Directs the compiler to display the message string during the compiling process.

- `#pragma optimize("optimization_flags", on)` or `#pragma optimize ("optimization_flags", off)`

  Turns on or off the specified optimization flags. This pragma must appear outside a function.

- `#pragma pack(1)` or `#pragma pack(2)` or `#pragma pack(4)`

  Packs structures for alignment at multiples of a specified number of bytes. This also is selected by compiler option `/Zp`.

- `#pragma page(count)`, where `count` is an optional value from 1 to 127

  Instructs the compiler to skip the specified number of pages in the source listing.

- `#pragma pagesize(lines)`, where `lines` is a number from 15 to 255

  Specifies the number of lines per page in source listings generated by the compiler.

- `#pragma skip(lines)`, where `lines` is a number from 1 to 127

  Directs the compiler to insert the specified number of blank lines in the listing.

- `#pragma subtitle("a subtitle goes here")`

  Specifies the subtitle that appears below the title on each page of the listing.

- `#pragma title("this is the title")`

  Specifies the title that appears in the upper-left corner of each page of the listing.

Size and Capacity of Basic Data Types

The size and numerical limits of several standard C data types depend on the compiler. Following the ANSI standard requirement, Microsoft Visual C++ provides the numerical limits of integer and floating-point variables in the header files limits.h and float.h. Table 4.6 provides a combined listing of the size and numerical limits of the standard C data types.

Table 4.6. Sizes and numerical limits of basic data types in Microsoft Visual C++.

Type Name	Storage Size in Bytes	Range of Values
`char`	1	–128 to 127
`int`	2	–32,768 to 32,767
`short`	2	–32,768 to 32,767
`long`	4	–2,147,483,648 to 2,147,483,647

continues

Table 4.6. continued

Type Name	Storage Size in Bytes	Range of Values
`unsigned char`	1	0 to 255
`unsigned`	2	0 to 65,535
`unsigned short`	2	0 to 65,535
`unsigned long`	4	0 to 4,294,967,295
`enum`	2	–32,768 to 32,767
`float`	4	Approximately 1.2E –38 to 3.4E+38 with 7-digit precision
`double`	8	Approximately 2.2E –308 to 1.8E+308 with 15-digit precision
`long double`	10	Approximately 3.4E –4932 to 1.2E+4932 with 19-digit precision

Knowing the size and numerical limits of the data types can help you decide the type of variable you want for a specific purpose. For example, instead of using a 2-byte `int` for a variable with values between 0 and 255, you can use an `unsigned char`. Similarly, 4-byte `float` variables might be sufficient where you might otherwise use an 8-byte `double` variable.

Note also that the size of the `int` data type can be a problem for C or C++ code that might otherwise be portable. Although `int` is a 2-byte data type in all MS-DOS systems, on almost all other systems, an `int` occupies 4 bytes and is the same as a `long`. This size difference can create subtle problems when you move Microsoft Visual C++ code to other systems. One way to minimize these problems is to use `short` where you need 2-byte storage and `long` where you need a 4-byte data type.

Summary

To fully support MS-DOS and Microsoft Windows environments, Microsoft Visual C++ includes a number of reserved keywords in addition to those required by ANSI standard C. Many of these keywords are necessary to support the segmented memory-addressing scheme used by the Intel 80x86 microprocessors in MS-DOS systems. The segmented memory architecture also brings up the concept of memory models—a number of standard ways to organize segments of code and data. Microsoft Visual C++ supports six standard memory models: Tiny, Small, Medium, Compact, Large, and Huge—each of which is activated by a specific compiler option. Additionally, you can mix and match data and functions that require addressing conventions other than those supported by the currently selected memory model.

This chapter also described a number of predefined global variables, preprocessor macros, and compiler directives or pragmas that let your programs take full advantage of the capabilities of Microsoft Visual C++.

Learning Object-Oriented Programming

Basics of Object-Oriented Programming

Part I was an overview of the tools that Microsoft Visual C++ provides for writing programs in C and C++. Part II covers object-oriented programming (OOP).

Object-oriented programming isn't new; its underlying concepts—*data abstraction, inheritance,* and *polymorphism*—have been around for quite some time (for example, in languages such as Simula67 and SmallTalk). What is new is the increasing interest in OOP among programmers in general, and C programmers in particular. One of the reasons for this growing appeal is the popularity of the C++ programming language, which improves C (the current language of choice among software developers) by introducing several new programming constructs that directly support object-oriented techniques. If you program in C, you will find it reasonably easy to learn the syntax of C++. However, you'll need to reorient your thinking if you want to use object-oriented techniques in your programs.

The best way to learn C++ is to understand the basic concepts of OOP and see how C++ supports OOP. This book uses this approach, explaining OOP through examples and, at the same time, teaching the C++ programming language—explaining its features and their relationship to OOP. This chapter begins by explaining the basic terminology of OOP. Examples show how you can apply object-oriented techniques in C. Chapter 6, "C++ and Object-Oriented Programming," furnishes you with an overview of C++ with an emphasis on OOP. Chapter 6 also revisits the examples of Chapter 5 rewritten in C++. Seeing the examples again illustrates how an object-oriented programming language such as C++ makes it easy to apply object-oriented methods.

To best utilize Visual C++, the Visual Workbench, and Windows, all the example programs in this chapter are QuickWin programs. To conserve space on the source code diskette, none of the programs are provided in executable format. You can create the executable programs from the files contained on the source code diskette. To create the executable files, use the files from the source code diskette, load the project into the Visual Workbench, and select the toolbar button `re-build all`.

What is Object-Oriented Programming?

The term *object-oriented programming* (OOP) is widely used, but experts do not agree on its exact definition. However, most of them agree that OOP involves defining *abstract data types* (ADTs), which represent complex real-world or abstract objects, and organizing your program around these ADTs with an eye toward exploiting their common features. The term *data abstraction* refers to the process of defining ADTs, whereas *inheritance* and *polymorphism* refer to the mechanisms that enable you to take advantage of the common characteristics of the ADTs (the *objects* in OOP). These terms are explored in this chapter.

The term *abstract data type* refers to a programmer-defined data type together with a set of operations that can be performed on that data. It is called *abstract* to distinguish it from the fundamental, *built-in* C data types, such as `int`, `char`, and `double`. In C, you can define an ADT by using `typedef` and `struct` and implementing the operations with a set of functions. As you soon will learn, C++ has much better facilities for defining and using ADTs.

Before jumping into OOP, take note of two points:

- First, OOP is only a method of designing and implementing software. The use of object-oriented techniques adds nothing to your finished software product that the user can see. As a programmer implementing the software, however, you can gain significant advantages through the use of object-oriented methods—especially in large software projects. You can manage complexity better with OOP than with approaches that force you to map the problem to fit the features of the language. Using OOP, you can take advantage of the modularity of objects to implement your program in relatively independent units that are easier to maintain and extend. Therefore, OOP lets you stay close to the conceptual, higher-level model of the real-world problem you're trying to solve. You also can share code among objects through inheritance.
- Second, OOP has nothing to do with any programming language, although a programming language that supports OOP makes it easier to implement object-oriented techniques. As you will see shortly, with some discipline you can use objects even in C programs.

Procedure-Oriented Programming

Before you get into OOP, take a look at conventional, procedure-oriented programming in a language such as C. In the procedure-oriented approach, you view a problem as a sequence of things to do. You organize the related data items into C structures (`structs`) and write the necessary functions (procedures) to manipulate the data. In the process, you complete the sequence of tasks that solves your problem.

Although the data may be organized into structures, the primary focus is on the *functions.* Each C function transforms data in some way. For example, one function may calculate the average value of a set of numbers, another may compute the square root of a number, and another may print a string. You don't need to look far to find examples of this kind of programming—C function libraries are implemented this way. Each function in a library performs a well-defined operation on its input arguments and returns the transformed data as a return value. Arguments may be pointers to data that the function directly alters, or the function may display graphics on a video monitor.

An Example in C

For a better understanding of procedure-oriented programming, suppose that you want to write a computer program that works with geometric shapes such as rectangles and circles. The program should be able to draw any shape and compute its area. This section takes a conventional approach to writing such a program.

As shown in Figure 5.1, you can break down the tasks of the program into two procedures: one to draw a shape and the other to compute its area. Call each function with a single argument: a pointer to a data structure that contains a shape's pertinent information, such as the coordinates of a circle's center and its radius.

Figure 5.1 also shows a new data structure, called `SHAPE`. It's easy to define an appropriate data structure for each geometric shape, but functions need a pointer to a single data structure. How do you reconcile these different structures into one, single structure?

A common technique is to combine the different structures into one using a C `union`, with an additional integer flag to indicate the shape being handled by the new data structure at any given moment. A data type results, `SHAPE`, which is graphically illustrated in Figure 5.1. In keeping with common C coding style, you should define these data types in a header file, CSHAPES.H, as shown in Listing 5.1.

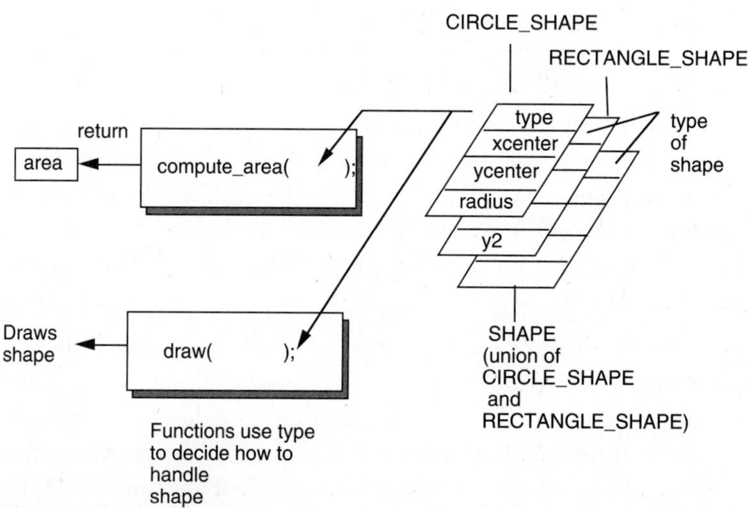

Figure 5.1. C data and procedures for handling geometric shapes.

Listing 5.1. CSHAPES.H. Definition of data types for shapes.

```
/*-------------------------------------------------------------*/
/*  File:  cshapes.h
```

```
 *
 *  Defines data types for manipulating geometric shapes
 *  in C
 */
#ifndef CSHAPES_H     /* Used to avoid including file twice */
#define CSHAPES_H

#include <math.h>     /* For declaration of fabs            */

#define M_PI        3.14159265358979323846 /* Value of "Pi" */

#define T_CIRCLE    1
#define T_RECTANGLE 2

/* Define each individual shape's data structure. */

typedef struct CIRCLE_SHAPE
{
    short   type;    /* Type of shape (T_CIRCLE)     */
    double  x, y;    /* Coordinates of center        */
    double  radius;  /* Radius of circle             */
} CIRCLE_SHAPE;

typedef struct RECTANGLE_SHAPE
{
    short   type;    /* Type of shape (T_RECTANGLE)  */
    double  x1, y1;  /* Coordinates of the corners   */
    double  x2, y2;
} RECTANGLE_SHAPE;

/* Now define a union of the two structures */

typedef union SHAPE
{
    short           type;       /* type of shape     */
    CIRCLE_SHAPE    circle;     /* data for circle   */
    RECTANGLE_SHAPE rectangle;  /* data for rectangle*/
} SHAPE;

/* Function prototypes */
```

continues

Listing 5.1. continued

```
double compute_area(SHAPE *p_shape);
void   draw(SHAPE *p_shape);

#endif  /* #ifndef CSHAPES_H  */
```

The data structure for each shape is, essentially, a block of memory. Because the members of a C union all share the same block of memory, you need a way to determine which member is valid at any time. This example does so by declaring the very first field in the union `SHAPE` as a short integer, which denotes the type of the shape. Knowing the type, you can access the right structure in `SHAPE` to extract information about the shape. The code in Listing 5.2 shows how the structures in the `SHAPE` union are used.

After the data structures are defined, you can start writing the functions that operate on the data. In fact, as required by ANSI standard C, the CSHAPES.H header file already includes the *prototypes* for the functions `compute_area` and `draw_shape`. Listing 5.2 shows the implementation of these functions. The functions are straightforward: a `switch` statement is used to handle each shape individually.

Listing 5.2. CSHAPES.C. Functions for geometric shapes.

```
/*-------------------------------------------------------------*/
/*  File: cshapes.c
 *
 *  C functions to operate on geometric shapes.
 */
#include <stdio.h>
#include "cshapes.h"

/*-------------------------------------------------------------*/
/*  c o m p u t e _ a r e a
 *
 *  Compute the area of the shape and return the area.
 */
double compute_area(SHAPE *p_shape)
{
    double area;

/* Handle each shape according to its type */
```

```
    switch(p_shape->type)
    {
        case T_CIRCLE:
            area = M_PI * p_shape->circle.radius
                        * p_shape->circle.radius;
            break;

        case T_RECTANGLE:
            area = fabs(
               (p_shape->rectangle.x2 - p_shape->rectangle.x1) *
               (p_shape->rectangle.y2 - p_shape->rectangle.y1));
            break;

        default:  printf("Unknown shape in 'compute_area'!\n");
    }
    return area;
}
/*-----------------------------------------------------------------*/
/*  d r a w
 *
 *  "Draw" a shape (print information about shape)
 */
void draw(SHAPE *p_shape)
{
/* Handle each shape according to its type */
    printf("Draw: ");
    switch(p_shape->type)
    {
        case T_CIRCLE:
            printf("Circle of radius %f at (%f, %f)\n",
                    p_shape->circle.radius,
                    p_shape->circle.x, p_shape->circle.y);
            break;

        case T_RECTANGLE:
            printf("Rectangle with corners:"
                   " (%f, %f) at (%f, %f)\n",
                    p_shape->rectangle.x1,
                    p_shape->rectangle.y1,
                    p_shape->rectangle.x2,
                    p_shape->rectangle.y2);
            break;
```

continues

Listing 5.2. continued

```
        default:  printf("Unknown shape in 'draw'!\n");
    }
}
```

To keep the program simple, this example does not proceed with the steps that actually display the shapes on a particular graphics device. Instead, the `draw` function simply prints the name, location, and size of the shape. The `compute_area` function uses a standard formula to compute the area and return the result.

You can test these functions with the simple program STEST1.C, shown in Listing 5.3. This program defines an array of two shapes and initializes them. It then computes the area of each shape and "draws" it. In a more realistic implementation, you might include utility functions such as `create_circle` and `create_rectangle` to dynamically allocate and initialize a `SHAPE` union and return a pointer to it.

Listing 5.3. STEST1.C. Program to test shape-handling functions.

```
/*-----------------------------------------------------------------*/
/*  File:  stest1.c
 *
 *  Program to test shape-handling functions of Listing 5.2.
 *  Compile and link with the file shown in Listing 5.1
 */
#include <stdio.h>
#include "cshapes.h"

int main()
{
    int i;
    SHAPE s[2];

/* Initialize the shapes */

/* A 40x20 rectangle with lower left corner at (80,30) */
    s[0].type = T_RECTANGLE;
    s[0].rectangle.x1 = 80.0;
    s[0].rectangle.y1 = 30.0;
```

```
    s[0].rectangle.x2 = 120.0;
    s[0].rectangle.y2 = 50.0;

/* A circle at (200.0, 100.0) of radius 50.0 units */
    s[1].type = T_CIRCLE;
    s[1].circle.x = 200.0;
    s[1].circle.y = 100.0;
    s[1].circle.radius = 50.0;

/* Compute the areas... */
    for(i = 0; i < 2; i++)
        printf("Area of shape[%d] = %f\n", i,
                                    compute_area(&s[i]));

/* Draw the shapes... */
    for(i = 0; i < 2; i++) draw(&s[i]);
    return 0;
}
```

Build the STEST1.C program by compiling and linking the files shown in Listings 5.2 and 5.3. Use these steps:

1. In the Visual Workbench, create a new project and add the files STEST1.C and CSHAPES.C to the project.
2. Perform the actual compile and link by selecting Rebuild All from the toolbar to create the executable file STEST1.EXE. (For more information on the Visual Workbench, consult Chapter 1.)

When you run STEST1.C, it produces the following output:

```
Area of shape[0] = 800.000000
Area of shape[1] = 7853.981634
Draw: Rectangle with corners: (80.000000, 30.000000) at (120.000000,
50.000000)
Draw: Circle of radius 50.000000 at (200.000000, 100.000000)
```

Even though this example is somewhat contrived, it does embody the general style of procedure-oriented programming in C. Programmers design data structures first, and then write procedures to manipulate the data. The usual practice is to handle different types of related data (such as the geometric shapes circle and rectangle) with `switch` statements.

Adding a New Shape

Some problems do exist with conventional procedure-oriented programming. Consider what happens when you want your program to handle another type of geometric shape—say, a triangle. To do this, you must follow these steps:

1. Define a data structure for triangles. If you choose to represent the triangle by the coordinates of its vertices, you might add the following structure to the CSHAPES.H file (Listing 5.1):

```
#define T_TRIANGLE  3

typedef struct TRIANGLE_SHAPE
{
    short   type;    /* Type of shape (T_TRIANGLE)    */
    double  x1, y1;  /* Coordinates of the corners    */
    double  x2, y2;
    double  x3, y3;
} TRIANGLE_SHAPE;
```

2. Add a new member to the `SHAPE` union to reflect the addition of the new shape:

```
typedef union SHAPE
{
    short           type;       /* type of shape     */
    CIRCLE_SHAPE    circle;     /* data for circle   */
    RECTANGLE_SHAPE rectangle;  /* data for rectangle*/
    TRIANGLE_SHAPE  triangle;   /* data for triangle */
} SHAPE;
```

3. In the CSHAPES.C file (Listing 5.2), add code in the functions `compute_area` and `draw` to handle triangles. Specifically, add additional case statements in the `switch` statement for each function, as in the following example:

```
/*  In the compute_area function  */

 double compute_area(SHAPE *p_shape)
{
    double area;

/* Handle each shape according to its type */
    switch(p_shape->type)
    {
          .
          .
```

```
        case T_TRIANGLE:
        {
            double x21, y21, x31, y31;

            x21 =  p_shape->triangle.x2 - p_shape->triangle.x1;
            y21 =  p_shape->triangle.y2 - p_shape->triangle.y1;
            x31 =  p_shape->triangle.x3 - p_shape->triangle.x1;
            y31 =  p_shape->triangle.y3 - p_shape->triangle.y1;

            area = fabs(y21 * x31 - x21 * y31) / 2.0;
        }

       break;
        .
        .
    }

/*-------------------------------------------------------------*/
/* In function: draw() */
void draw(SHAPE *p_shape)
{
    printf("Draw: ");
    switch(p_shape->type)
    {
        .
        .
        case T_TRIANGLE:
            printf("Triangle with vertices: "
                   "(%f, %f) (%f, %f) (%f, %f)\n",
                    p_shape->triangle.x1, p_shape->triangle.y1,
                    p_shape->triangle.x2, p_shape->triangle.y2,
                    p_shape->triangle.x3, p_shape->triangle.y3);
            break;
        .
        .
    }
}
```

4. Test operations on the triangle shape. For example, you can define a triangle shape and use the shape as follows:

```
    SHAPE s;
    s.type = T_TRIANGLE;
```

```
        s.triangle.x1 = 100.0;
        s.triangle.y1 = 100.0;
        s.triangle.x2 = 200.0;
        s.triangle.y2 = 100.0;
        s.triangle.x3 = 150.0;
        s.triangle.y3 = 50.0;
    /* Compute the area... */
        printf("Area of triangle = %f\n", compute_area(&s));

    /* Draw the triangle... */
        draw(&s);
```

This exercise illustrates the types of changes you must make when a new data type—a new *object*—is added to an existing program written in conventional, procedure-oriented style. Notice that you have to edit working code—the `switch` statements in the `compute_area` and `draw` functions—when you want to handle triangles in addition to the rectangles and circles that the program was originally designed to accept. If this were a realistic program with many files, a change such as this would require you to edit `switch` statements in most of the files.

As you see next, the object-oriented approach avoids this problem by keeping data structures together with the functions that operate on them. This effectively localizes the changes that become necessary when you decide to add a new object to your program. This is one of the benefits of OOP.

Object-Oriented Programming Terminology

As mentioned earlier, there are three basic underlying concepts in OOP:

- Data Abstraction
- Inheritance
- Polymorphism

Individually, these concepts have been known and used before, but their use as the foundation of OOP is new.

Data Abstraction

To understand data abstraction, consider the file I/O routines in the C runtime library. With these routines, you can view the file as a stream of bytes, and perform various operations on this stream by calling the file I/O routines. For example, you can call `fopen` to open a file, `fgetc` to read a character from it, `fputc` to write a character to it, and `fclose` to close it. This abstract model of a file is implemented by defining a data type named `FILE` to hold all relevant information about a file. The C constructs `struct` and `typedef` are used to define `FILE`. The definition of `FILE` is in the header file STDIO.H. You can think of this definition of `FILE`, together with the functions that operate on it, as a new data type, just like C's `int` or `char`.

You don't have to know the C data structure that defines the `FILE` data type to use `FILE`. In fact, while the underlying data structure of `FILE` can vary from one system to another, the C file I/O routines work in the same manner on all systems. This is possible because you never access the members of the `FILE` data structure directly. Instead, you rely on the functions and macros that essentially hide the inner details of `FILE`. This is known as *data hiding.*

Data abstraction is the process of defining a data type, often called an *abstract data type* (ADT), using data hiding. The definition of an ADT specifies not only the internal representation of the ADT's data, but the functions that other program modules will use to manipulate the ADT. Data hiding ensures that you can alter the internal structure of the ADT without breaking the programs that call functions operating on that ADT. Thus, C's `FILE` data type, shown in Figure 5.2, is an example of an ADT.

Objects, Classes, and Methods

In OOP, you create an *object* from an ADT. Essentially, an ADT is a collection of variables and the functions necessary to operate on those variables. The variables represent the information contained in the object, while the functions define the operations that can be performed on that object. You can think of the ADT as a template from which specific instances of objects can be created as needed.

The term *class* is often used for this template; consequently, "class" is synonymous with "ADT." In fact, C++ provides the `class` declaration precisely for defining an ADT—the template from which objects are created. The ADT is a template for objects in the sense that creating an object involves setting aside a block of memory for the variables of that object.

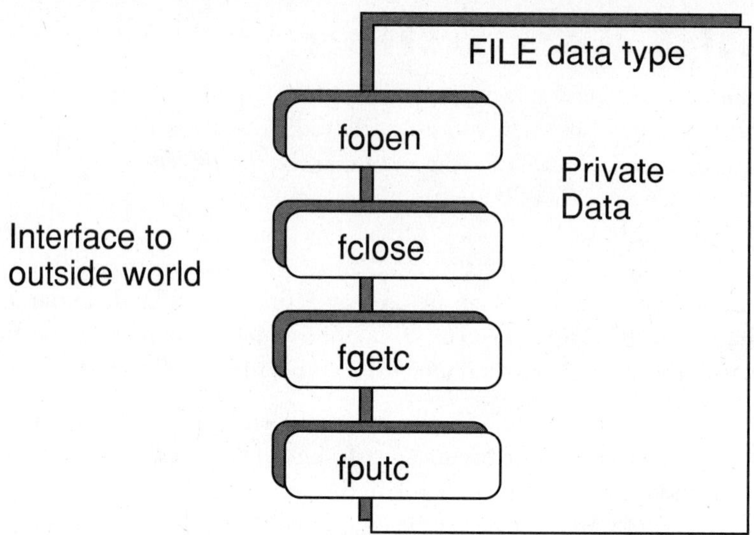

Figure 5.2. C's `FILE` type as an example of an ADT.

The functions that operate on an object are known as *methods*. This term comes from the object-oriented language SmallTalk. Methods define the behavior of an object. In C++, methods are called the *member functions* of the class.

Another common OOP concept also originated in SmallTalk: the idea of *sending a message* to an object, directing the object to perform an operation by invoking one of the methods. In C++, you do this by calling the appropriate member function of the object. For objects implemented in C, you can send a message by calling a function that accepts a pointer to a data structure representing the ADT's internal structure. Of course, the function must be capable of handling the operation you want. For instance, C's file I/O routines accept a pointer to the `FILE` structure as an argument. The file I/O routines then use that pointer to identify the file on which the I/O operation is to be performed.

Inheritance

Data abstraction does not cover an important characteristic of objects: real-world objects do not exist in isolation. Each object is related to one or more other objects. In fact, you can often describe a new kind of object by pointing out how the new object's characteristics and behavior differ from that of a class of objects that already exists. This is what you do when you describe an object with a sentence such as "B is just like A, except that B has...and B does...." Here, you're defining objects of type B in terms of those of type A.

This notion of defining a new object in terms of an old one is an integral part of OOP. The term *inheritance* is used for this concept because you can think of one class of objects inheriting the data and behavior from another class. Inheritance imposes a hierarchical relationship on classes, where a child class inherits from its parent. In C++ terminology, the parent class is the *base class*, and the child class is the *derived class*.

Multiple Inheritance

A real-world object often exhibits characteristics that it inherits from more than one type of object. For example, you could classify a lion as a carnivore on the basis of its eating habits, or as a mammal on the basis of its biological class. When modeling a corporation, you may want to describe a technical manager as someone who is an engineer as well as a manager. An example from the programming world is a full-screen text editor. It displays a block of text on-screen, and also stores the text in an internal buffer so that you can perform operations (such as inserting a character, deleting a character, and so on). Thus, you may want to say that a text editor inherits its behavior from two classes: a text buffer class, and a text display class that, for instance, manages an 80-character by 25-line text display area.

These examples illustrate *multiple inheritance*—the idea that a class can be derived from more than one base class. Many object-oriented programming languages do not support multiple inheritance, but C++ does.

Polymorphism

In a literal sense, *polymorphism* means the quality of having more than one form. In the context of OOP, polymorphism means that a single operation can behave differently in different objects. In other words, different objects can react differently to the same message.

For example, consider the operation of addition. For two numbers, addition should generate the sum. In a programming language that supports OOP, you should be able to express the operation of addition with a single operator: a plus sign (+). When this is supported, you can use the expression `x+y` to denote the sum of `x` and `y` for many different types of `x` and `y`: integers, floating-point numbers, and complex numbers, to name a few. You even can define the + operation to mean the concatenation of two strings.

Similarly, suppose a number of geometric shapes all respond to the message `draw`. Each object reacts to this message by displaying its shape on a display screen. Obviously, the actual mechanism for displaying the object differs from one shape to another, but all shapes perform this task in response to the same message.

Polymorphism helps by enabling you to simplify the syntax that performs the same operation on a collection of objects. For example, by exploiting polymorphism, you can compute the area of each geometric shape in an array of shapes with a simple loop such as this one:

```
/* Assume "shapes" is an array of shapes (rectangles, circles,
 * etc.) and "compute_area" is a function that computes the
 * area of a shape.
 */
for (i = 0; i < number_of_shapes; i++)
    area_of_shape = shapes[i].compute_area();
```

The program can do this because, regardless of the exact geometric shape, each object supports the `compute_area` function and computes the area in a way appropriate for that shape.

Object-Oriented Programming in C

Once you know the basic concepts of OOP, it isn't difficult to implement them in a C program, provided you have somehow identified the objects and what they do. Deciding how to organize your software around objects—physical or abstract—falls under the topic of object-oriented analysis and design. The remainder of this chapter uses geometric shapes as an example, and shows one way to handle these shapes using object-oriented techniques.

Defining Objects in C

To illustrate the use of OOP techniques in C, consider the example of the geometric shapes introduced earlier in this chapter to explain procedural programming. The task is to write a computer program that handles geometric shapes such as rectangles and circles. The program should draw any shape and compute its area.

To implement the program using objects, you should first work out the details of how to support message-handling and inheritance. Figure 5.3 gives an overview of the data structures you can use to implement the objects.

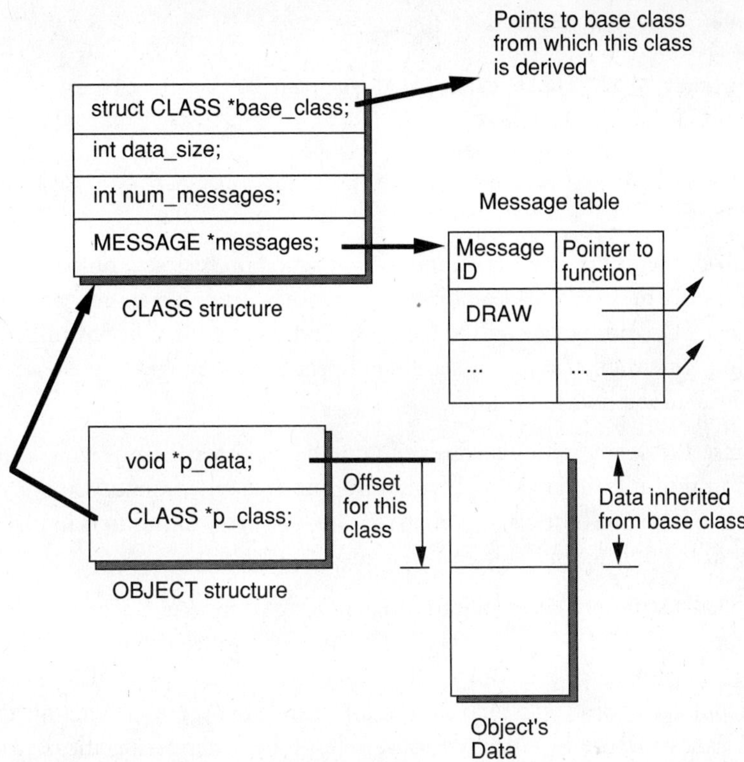

Figure 5.3. Data structures for OOP in C.

An easy way to handle messages is to assign each message an *identifier* (ID). You can associate each message ID with the pointer to a function that handles the message. To maintain this association, you can use a data structure such as the MESSAGE structure shown below:

```
typedef struct MESSAGE
{
   int  message_id;            /* Message identifier        */
   int  (*message_handler)(); /* Function to handle message */
} MESSAGE;
```

With this definition of MESSAGE, a program can handle messages for a class by maintaining an array of MESSAGE structures. (You can think of this as a table of messages.) To exploit inheritance, each class data structure needs a pointer to the base class. This pointer will be NULL when a class is not derived from another class. Thus, a possible declaration of the CLASS data structure is as follows:

```
typedef struct CLASS
{
    struct CLASS *base_class;   /* Pointer to "base" class */
    int          data_size;     /* Size of instance's data */
    int          num_messages; /* Number of messages      */
    MESSAGE      *messages;     /* Table of messages       */
} CLASS;
```

Later on, you'll see a utility function that sends messages to objects. That function handles the messages by searching the `messages` array for an entry with a matching message ID, and by calling the function with the pointer stored in that entry. You can implement inheritance by sending unprocessed messages to the base class through the `base_class` pointer.

Because the `CLASS` structure has only one base class, this implementation does not support multiple inheritance. If you want multiple inheritance, you must make room for more than one base class, perhaps through an array of pointers in place of the lone `base_class` pointer in the `CLASS` structure.

The `CLASS` structure can facilitate the handling of messages sent to an object, but it cannot accommodate the object's data. This is because each object has its own data. In other words, a single copy of the class structure can serve all the objects of that class, but each object must have room for its own data. You can handle this by defining a data structure specifically meant to hold the instance-specific data of an object, as follows:

```
typedef struct OBJECT
{
    void   *p_data;  /* Data for an instance of the object */
    CLASS  *p_class; /* Pointer to the class structure     */
} OBJECT;
```

As you can see, this `OBJECT` data structure holds a pointer to its data and a pointer to its class so that messages can be processed by consulting the message table in the class. The function responsible for creating an object also allocates room for the object's data and saves the pointer in the `p_data` field of the `OBJECT` structure. The `data_size` variable in the `CLASS` structure represents the number of bytes of memory needed for an object's data.

The file SHAPEOBJ.H, shown in Listing 5.4, declares the data structures and functions necessary to this scheme of implementing objects in C.

Listing 5.4. SHAPEOBJ.H. Definition of shapes in an example of OOP in C.

```
/*  File:  shapeobj.h
 *
 *  Header file with definitions of shapes for
 *  an example of object-oriented programming in C.
 *
 */

#if !defined(SHAPEOBJ_H)
#define SHAPEOBJ_H

#include <stdio.h>
#include <stdlib.h>    /* For mem. alloc routines         */
#include <stdarg.h>    /* For variable no. of arguments */
#include <math.h>      /* For declaration of fabs       */

#define M_PI        3.14159265358979323846 /* Value of "Pi" */

typedef struct MESSAGE
{
    int  message_id;            /* Message identifier         */
    int  (*message_handler)(); /* Function to handle message */
} MESSAGE;

typedef struct CLASS
{
    struct CLASS *base_class;  /* Pointer to "base" class */
    int          data_size;    /* Size of instance's data */
    int          num_messages; /* Number of messages      */
    MESSAGE      *messages;    /* Table of messages       */
} CLASS;

typedef struct OBJECT
{
    void   *p_data;  /* Data for an instance of the object */
    CLASS  *p_class; /* Pointer to the class structure     */
} OBJECT;

/* Define some messages */
#define  ALLOCATE_DATA 1
```

continues

Listing 5.4. continued

```
#define  DRAW          2
#define  COMPUTE_AREA  3

/* Functions to create objects */

OBJECT *new_circle(double x, double y, double radius);
OBJECT *new_rectangle(double x1, double y1,
                      double x2, double y2);

/* Utility functions to handle messages */

int send_message(OBJECT *p_obj, int msgid, ...);
int class_message(CLASS *p_class, OBJECT *p_obj, int msgid,
                  va_list argp);
void *allocate_memory(size_t bytes);
int  get_offset(CLASS *p_class);

#endif /* #if !defined(SHAPEOBJ_H) */
```

Implementing Geometrical Shapes

To illustrate the use of these structures, you can implement two shapes: a circle and a rectangle. Because each shape must draw itself and compute its area, move these functions to a common base class called `generic_shape`. Figure 5.4 shows the inheritance hierarchy of shapes.

The AnyShape program, shown in listings 5.5, 5.6, and 5.7 show the implementation of the generic shape, the circle, and the rectangle. When you study the listings you notice that each file includes a `CLASS` structure, properly initialized with a message table, a pointer to the base class (if any), and the size of the data structure for each instance of that class. The circle and rectangle classes include functions you can call to create an instance of each.

For example, to create a circle, call the `new_circle` function (see Listing 5.6) with the coordinates of the center and radius as arguments. This function allocates an `OBJECT` structure, sends a message to the base class for allocating the instance data, and returns a pointer to the newly allocated `OBJECT` structure.

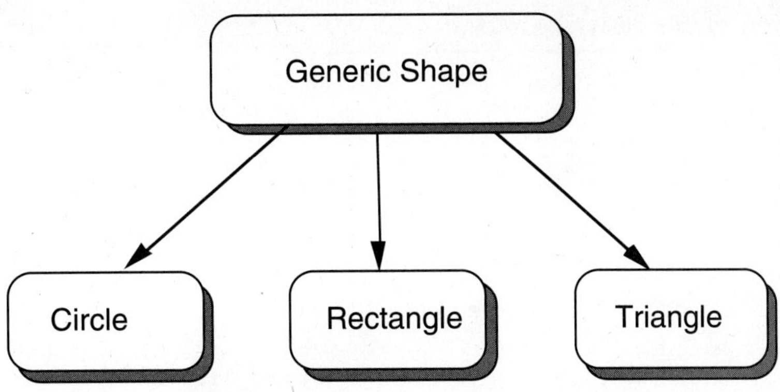

Figure 5.4. Inheritance hierarchy of geometric shapes.

Listing 5.5. ANYSHAPE.C. Implementation of a generic shape class.

```
/*  File:  anyshape.c
 *
 *  This is the generic "shape" class.
 *  Data and functions common to all shapes appear here.
 *
 */
#include "shapeobj.h"

static int allocate_data(OBJECT *p_obj, va_list argp);

static MESSAGE messages[] =
{
    ALLOCATE_DATA,  allocate_data
};

/* The "class" data structure */

CLASS generic_shape =
{
    NULL,                               /* No base class     */
    0,                                  /* No common data    */
```

continues

Listing 5.5. continued

```
    sizeof(messages)/sizeof(MESSAGE), /* How many messages */
    messages                          /* Message table     */
};

/*-----------------------------------------------------------------*/
/*  a l l o c a t e _ d a t a
 *
 *  Allocate memory for an object's data.
 */
static int allocate_data(OBJECT *p_obj, va_list argp)
{
    CLASS  *p_class;
    int    size = 0;

/* Determine sum of instance data sizes for each class in the
 * hierarchy of this object
 */
    for(p_class = p_obj->p_class, size = 0;
        p_class != NULL; p_class = p_class->base_class)
            size += p_class->data_size;

/* Allocate the necessary number of bytes */
    p_obj->p_data = allocate_memory(size);

    return 1;
}
```

Listing 5.6. O_CIRCLE.C. Implementation of the circle class.

```
/*  File:  o_circle.c
 *
 *  This is the circle class of shapes.
 */

#include "shapeobj.h"

typedef double *P_DOUBLE;
```

```
typedef struct CIRCLE_DATA
{
    double  x, y;     /* Coordinates of center */
    double  radius;   /* Radius of circle      */
} CIRCLE_DATA;

extern CLASS generic_shape; /* The base class */

static int compute_area(OBJECT *p_obj, va_list argp);
static int draw(OBJECT *p_obj, va_list argp);

static MESSAGE messages[] =
{
    COMPUTE_AREA,  compute_area,
    DRAW,          draw
};

/* The "class" data structure */

CLASS circle_class =
{
    &generic_shape,                    /* Ptr to base class  */
    sizeof(CIRCLE_DATA),               /* Data for circles   */
    sizeof(messages)/sizeof(MESSAGE), /* Number of messages */
    messages                           /* The message table  */
};

static int circle_offset = -1;  /* Offset to circle's data   */
/*-------------------------------------------------------------*/
/*  n e w _ c i r c l e
 *
 *  Create an instance of a circle and initialize it
 */
OBJECT *new_circle(double x, double y, double radius)
{
    OBJECT   *p_obj;
    CIRCLE_DATA *p_data;

    p_obj = (OBJECT *) allocate_memory(sizeof(OBJECT));
    p_obj->p_class = &circle_class;
```

continues

Listing 5.6. continued

```
/* Send message to allocate memory for data */
    send_message(p_obj, ALLOCATE_DATA, 0);

/* Get offset to circle-specific data */
    if(circle_offset < 0)
        circle_offset = get_offset(&circle_class);
    p_data = (CIRCLE_DATA *)((char *)p_obj->p_data +
                                  circle_offset);
    p_data->x = x;
    p_data->y = y;
    p_data->radius = radius;

    return(p_obj);
}
/*-------------------------------------------------------------*/
/*  c o m p u t e _ a r e a
 *
 *  Compute area of circle. Arguments expected:
 *      pointer to a double where answer is returned.
 */
static int compute_area(OBJECT *p_obj, va_list argp)
{
    int           status = 0;
    double        *p_area;
    CIRCLE_DATA   *p_data;

/* Set up the pointer to circle's data */
    p_data = (CIRCLE_DATA *)((char *)p_obj->p_data +
                             circle_offset);
/* Get pointer to double where answer is to be returned */
    p_area = va_arg(argp, P_DOUBLE);
    if(p_area != NULL)
    {
        *p_area = M_PI * p_data->radius * p_data->radius;
        status = 1;
    }
    return(status);
}
/*-------------------------------------------------------------*/
/*  d r a w
 *
```

```
 *  Draw the circle (for now, just print a message).
 *  Does not expect any arguments
 */
static int draw(OBJECT *p_obj, va_list argp)
{
    CIRCLE_DATA   *p_data;

/* Set up the pointer to circle's data */
    p_data = (CIRCLE_DATA *)((char *)p_obj->p_data +
                             circle_offset);
    printf("Draw: Circle of radius %f at (%f, %f)\n",
            p_data->radius, p_data->x, p_data->y);

    return 1;
}
```

Listing 5.7. O_RECT.C. Implementation of the rectangle class.

```
/*  File:  o_rect.c
 *
 *  This is the rectangle class of shapes.
 */

#include <shapeobj.h>

typedef double *P_DOUBLE;

typedef struct RECTANGLE_DATA
{
    double  x1, y1;  /* Coordinates of the corners   */
    double  x2, y2;
} RECTANGLE_DATA;

extern CLASS generic_shape; /* The base class */

static int compute_area(OBJECT *p_obj, va_list argp);
static int draw(OBJECT *p_obj, va_list argp);

static MESSAGE messages[] =
{
```

continues

Listing 5.7. continued

```
    COMPUTE_AREA,  compute_area,
    DRAW,          draw
};

/* The "class" data structure */

CLASS rectangle_class =
{
    &generic_shape,                   /* Ptr to base class  */
    sizeof(RECTANGLE_DATA),           /* Data for rectangles*/
    sizeof(messages)/sizeof(MESSAGE), /* Number of messages */
    messages                          /* The message table  */
};

static int rectangle_offset = -1; /* Offset to rectangle's data*/
/*-------------------------------------------------------------*/
/*  n e w _ r e c t a n g l e
 *
 *  Create an instance of a rectangle and initialize it
 */
OBJECT *new_rectangle(double x1, double y1, double x2, double y2)
{
    OBJECT   *p_obj;
    RECTANGLE_DATA *p_data;

    p_obj = (OBJECT *) allocate_memory(sizeof(OBJECT));
    p_obj->p_class = &rectangle_class;

/* Send message to allocate memory for data */
    send_message(p_obj, ALLOCATE_DATA, 0);

/* Get offset to rectangle-specific data */
    if(rectangle_offset < 0)
        rectangle_offset = get_offset(&rectangle_class);
    p_data = (RECTANGLE_DATA *)((char *)p_obj->p_data +
                                     rectangle_offset);
    p_data->x1 = x1;
    p_data->y1 = y1;
    p_data->x2 = x2;
    p_data->y2 = y2;
```

```
    return(p_obj);
}
/*-------------------------------------------------------------*/
/*  c o m p u t e _ a r e a
 *
 *  Compute area of a rectangle. Arguments expected:
 *      pointer to a double where answer is returned.
 */
static int compute_area(OBJECT *p_obj, va_list argp)
{
    int             status = 0;
    double          *p_area;
    RECTANGLE_DATA   *p_data;

/* Set up the pointer to rectangle's data */
    p_data = (RECTANGLE_DATA *)((char *)p_obj->p_data +
                              rectangle_offset);
/* Get pointer to double where answer is to be returned */
    p_area = va_arg(argp, P_DOUBLE);
    if(p_area != NULL)
    {
        *p_area = fabs((p_data->x2 - p_data->x1) *
                       (p_data->y2 - p_data->y1));
        status = 1;
    }
    return(status);
}
/*-------------------------------------------------------------*/
/*  d r a w
 *
 *  Draw the rectangle (for now, just print a message).
 *  Does not expect any arguments
 */
static int draw(OBJECT *p_obj, va_list argp)
{
    RECTANGLE_DATA   *p_data;

/* Set up the pointer to rectangle's data */
    p_data = (RECTANGLE_DATA *)((char *)p_obj->p_data +
                              rectangle_offset);
    printf("Draw: Rectangle with corners: "
```

continues

Listing 5.7. continued

```
            "(%f, %f) at (%f, %f)\n",
             p_data->x1, p_data->y1,
             p_data->x2, p_data->y2);
    return 1;
}
```

Allocating An Object's Data

When developing a framework for OOP in C, one tricky problem involves the allocation of an object's data. Suppose you're allocating the data structure for an object with a class that inherits data from a base class. In the current implementation, the data for both the base class and the derived class is laid out in a single block with one following the other. Each class can access its data, provided it knows the offset for the start of its data in this block of memory. Figure 5.5 illustrates the layout of data for a derived class and a base class.

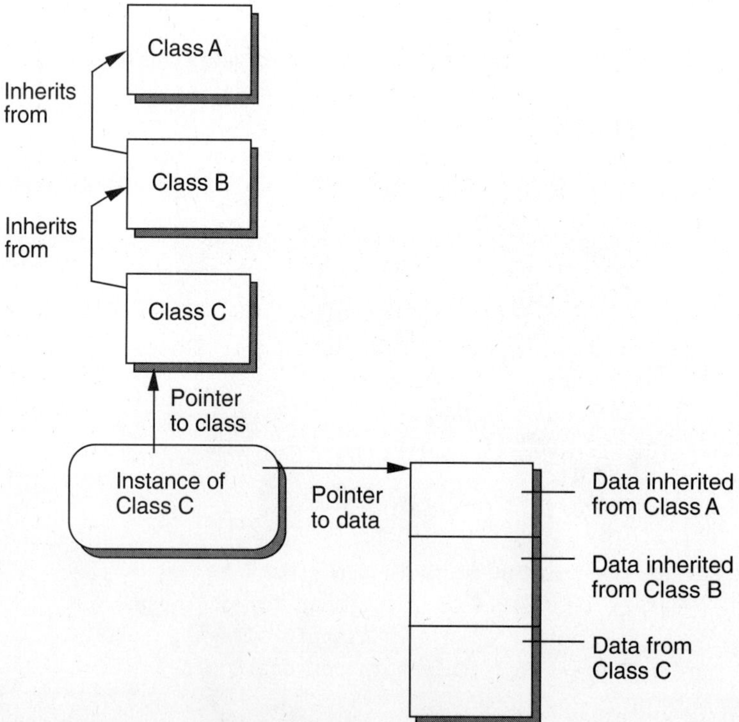

Figure 5.5. Layout of an object's data.

For the geometric shapes addressed in this chapter, the `allocate_data` function handles the allocation of the data block in the generic shape class (see Listing 5.5). This function figures the amount of storage needed by adding the sizes of data blocks for all classes in the hierarchy, and then allocates the data. When an object needs to access its data (for instance, in the `new_circle` function of Listing 5.6), it obtains the offset to its data structure by calling a utility function named `get_offset`.

Utility Functions

Because C does not directly support sending messages to objects, you must devise your own means of doing so. For the messaging scheme used in our approach, you can accomplish this by writing a set of utility functions that invoke the appropriate function in response to a message. Listing 5.8 presents the file OOPUTIL.C, which defines a number of utility functions to help implement OOP in C. You may want to study the `send_message` function to see how messages are dispatched to an object's class, and how any message not handled by a class is passed up the class hierarchy.

Listing 5.8. OOPUTIL.C. Utility functions for OOP in C.

```
/*-------------------------------------------------------------*/
/*  File: ooputil.c
 *
 *  Utility routines for example of OOP in C
 *
 */

#include "shapeobj.h"

/*-------------------------------------------------------------*/
/*  s e n d _ m e s s a g e
 *
 *  Process message sent to an object by passing it to its class
 */
int send_message(OBJECT *p_obj, int msgid, ...)
{
    int      status;
    va_list argp;
    va_start(argp, msgid);
    status = class_message(p_obj->p_class, p_obj, msgid, argp);
```

continues

Listing 5.8. continued

```
    va_end(argp);
    return(status);
}
/*--------------------------------------------------------------*/
/*  c l a s s _ m e s s a g e
 *
 *  Search through the message table for a specific message
 *  and call the "message handler" if found
 */
int class_message(CLASS *p_class, OBJECT *p_obj, int msgid,
                  va_list argp)
{
    int i, status;

    if(p_class == NULL) return 0;

    if(p_class->messages != NULL)
    {
        for(i = 0; i < p_class->num_messages; i++)
            if(p_class->messages[i].message_id == msgid)
            {
                return ((*p_class->messages[i].message_handler)
                                                 (p_obj, argp));
            }
/* If the message is not handled, send it to the base class */
        status = class_message(p_class->base_class, p_obj,
                               msgid, argp);
    }
    return(status);
}
/*--------------------------------------------------------------*/
/*  a l l o c a t e _ m e m o r y
 *
 *  Allocate memory. Check for failure to allocate.
 */
void *allocate_memory(size_t numbytes)
{
    void *ptr;
    if((ptr = calloc(1, numbytes)) == NULL)
    {
```

```
        fprintf(stderr, "Error allocating %d bytes of memory."
            "Exiting...", numbytes);
        exit(1);
    }
    return(ptr);
}
/*-------------------------------------------------------------*/
/*  g e t _ o f f s e t
 *
 *  An instance's data is the concatenation of data of
 *  all classes in its hierarchy. This function computes
 *  the offset to the beginning of data for a specific class.
 */
int  get_offset(CLASS *p_class)
{
    int size = 0;
/* Traverse the class hierarchy up to the "root" class and add
 * up the sizes of data belonging to each class
 */
    for(p_class = p_class->base_class;
        p_class != NULL;
        p_class = p_class->base_class) size += p_class->data_size;

    return size;
}
```

Using the Shapes

Once the framework for C-based OOP is in place, you can easily create shapes and use them. For example, to create a circle with a radius of 50 centered at the point (100,100), use the following:

```
    OBJECT *circle1;

/* Create a circle at (100, 100) with radius = 50 */
    circle1 = new_circle(100.0, 100.0, 50.0);
```

You can compute the area of this circle by sending it a COMPUTE_AREA message and passing it the arguments expected by this message, as follows:

```
double area;
send_message(circle1, COMPUTE_AREA, &area);
printf("Area of circle = %f\n", area);
```

The file STESTOBJ.C, in Listing 5.9, shows an example that uses the circle and rectangle shapes. To build the executable file for this example, compile and link the following files:

- STESTOBJ.C (Listing 5.9)
- OOPUTIL.C (Listing 5.8)
- ANYSHAPE.C (Listing 5.5)
- O_CIRCLE.C (Listing 5.6)
- O_RECT.C (Listing 5.7)

Create a Visual Workbench project with these files. Make the executable file a QuickWin program (if you desire, you can make it a DOS application). Of course, the sample code diskette contains the necessary project file, already created for you.

Listing 5.9. STESTOBJ.C. Main function for testing the shape objects.

```
/*-------------------------------------------------------------*/
/*  File:  stestobj.c
 *
 *  Test C-based OOP implementation of geometric shapes.
 */

#include <shapeobj.h>

int main(void)
{
    int    i;
    double area;
    OBJECT *shapes[3];

/* Create some shapes */
    shapes[0] = new_circle(100.0, 100.0, 50.0);
    shapes[1] = new_rectangle(100., 150., 200., 100.);

/* Compute the area of the shapes */
    for(i = 0; i < 2; i++)
    {
     send_message(shapes[i], COMPUTE_AREA, &area);
        printf("Area of shape [%d] = %f\n", i, area);
    }
```

```
/* "Draw" the shapes */
    for(i = 0; i < 2; i++)
        send_message(shapes[i], DRAW);

    return 0;
}
```

Adding a New Shape Object

Earlier, this chapter discussed a procedural implementation of the geometric shapes and showed the steps needed to handle a new shape, such as a triangle. To see how OOP helps reduce the ripple effect of change, consider the addition of a triangle shape to the collection of shape objects. Here's what you do:

Prepare a new file—call it O_TRIANG.C—that defines the data and functions for the triangle shape. Listing 5.10 shows a sample implementation of O_TRIANG.C.

Listing 5.10. O_TRIANG.C. Implementation of a triangle shape.

```
/*-------------------------------------------------------------*/
/*  File:  o_triang.c
 *
 *  This is the triangle class of shapes
 */

#include <shapeobj.h>

typedef double *P_DOUBLE;

typedef struct TRIANGLE_DATA
{
    double  x1, y1;  /* Coordinates of the corners   */
    double  x2, y2;
    double  x3, y3;
} TRIANGLE_DATA;

extern CLASS generic_shape; /* The base class */
```

continues

Listing 5.10. continued

```
static int compute_area(OBJECT *p_obj, va_list argp);
static int draw(OBJECT *p_obj, va_list argp);

static MESSAGE messages[] =
{
    COMPUTE_AREA,  compute_area,
    DRAW,          draw
};

/* The "class" data structure */

CLASS triangle_class =
{
    &generic_shape,                     /* Ptr to base class   */
    sizeof(TRIANGLE_DATA),              /* Data for triangles */
    sizeof(messages)/sizeof(MESSAGE),  /* Number of messages */
    messages                            /* The message table   */
};

static int triangle_offset = -1;  /* Offset to triangle's data */
/*-------------------------------------------------------------*/
/*  n e w _ t r i a n g l e
 *
 *  Create an instance of a triangle and initialize it
 */
OBJECT *new_triangle(double x1, double y1, double x2, double y2,
                     double x3, double y3)
{
    OBJECT   *p_obj;
    TRIANGLE_DATA *p_data;

    p_obj = (OBJECT *) allocate_memory(sizeof(OBJECT));
    p_obj->p_class = &triangle_class;

/* Send a message to allocate memory for data */
    send_message(p_obj, ALLOCATE_DATA, 0);

/* Get the offset to triangle-specific data */
    if(triangle_offset < 0)
        triangle_offset = get_offset(&triangle_class);
```

```
    p_data = (TRIANGLE_DATA *)((char *)p_obj->p_data +
                                        triangle_offset);

    p_data->x1 = x1;
    p_data->y1 = y1;
    p_data->x2 = x2;
    p_data->y2 = y2;
    p_data->x3 = x3;
    p_data->y3 = y3;

    return(p_obj);
}
/*-------------------------------------------------------------*/
/*  c o m p u t e _ a r e a
 *
 *  Compute the area of triangle. Arguments expected:
 *      pointer to a double where answer is returned.
 */
static int compute_area(OBJECT *p_obj, va_list argp)
{
    int            status = 0;
    double         *p_area;
    TRIANGLE_DATA   *p_data;

/* Set up the pointer to triangle's data */
    p_data = (TRIANGLE_DATA *)((char *)p_obj->p_data +
                                triangle_offset);
/* Get the pointer to double where answer will be returned */
    p_area = va_arg(argp, P_DOUBLE);
    if(p_area != NULL)
    {
        double x21, y21, x31, y31;

          x21 =  p_data->x2 - p_data->x1;
          y21 =  p_data->y2 - p_data->y1;
          x31 =  p_data->x3 - p_data->x1;
          y31 =  p_data->y3 - p_data->y1;

        *p_area = fabs(y21 * x31 - x21 * y31) / 2.0;
        status = 1;
    }
    return(status);
```

continues

Listing 5.10. continued

```
}
/*-------------------------------------------------------------*/
/*  d r a w
 *
 *  Draw the triangle (for now, just print a message).
 *  Does not expect any arguments
 */
static int draw(OBJECT *p_obj, va_list argp)
{
    TRIANGLE_DATA   *p_data;

/* Set up the pointer to triangle's data */
    p_data = (TRIANGLE_DATA *)((char *)p_obj->p_data +
                              triangle_offset);
    printf("Draw: Triangle with vertices: "
                 "(%f, %f) (%f, %f) (%f, %f)\n",
                  p_data->x1, p_data->y1,
                  p_data->x2, p_data->y2,
                  p_data->x3, p_data->y3);
    return 1;
}
```

That's it! All you do is write a single module implementing the new object. Once you have done this, you can use the new shape in your programs (of course, you have to compile O_TRIANG.C and link with it to build the program). For example, you can create a triangle, compute its area, and draw it as follows:

```
    OBJECT *t;
    double area;

/* Create a triangle */
    t = new_triangle(100.,100., 200.,100., 150.,50.);

/* Compute its area */
    send_message(t, COMPUTE_AREA, &area);
        printf("Area of triangle = %f\n", area);
    }

/* "Draw" the triangle */
    send_message(t, DRAW);
```

Clearly, OOP techniques make it easy to add new capabilities to the program because you don't need to modify existing code, only those new modules with code necessary to support the new objects.

Problems with OOP in C

Although you can define data structures to implement objects in C, several problems occur when implementing OOP in C.

- As a basic tenet of OOP, you must access and manipulate the object's data by calling the functions provided by that object. This ensures that the internal implementation details of the object stay hidden from the outside world, thus enabling you to change these details without affecting other parts of the program. While object-oriented languages enforce this principle of data hiding, implementing object-oriented techniques in a C program requires discipline on your part because C allows code to directly accesses members of an object's data structure.
- You are responsible for ensuring that the data structures of an object are laid out properly to support data inheritance from base classes. You must write utility functions to allow an object to access its data properly.
- You must devise a scheme to invoke methods of objects in response to messages. Inheritance of behavior also requires support functions for properly dispatching messages.

In spite of these problems, the modularity and localization of change afforded by OOP is worth the trouble, even if you write your object-oriented programs in C. Of course, as you see in Chapter 6, "C++ and Object-Oriented Programming," OOP becomes much easier if you use a programming language such as C++, which supports the basic necessities of object-orientation: data abstraction, inheritance, and polymorphism.

Summary

Object-oriented programming, or OOP for short, relies on three basic concepts: data abstraction, inheritance, and polymorphism.

Data abstraction is the capability of defining *abstract data types*, or ADTs (essentially, user-defined data types), which encapsulate some data and a set of well-defined operations. Such user-defined data types can represent objects in software. The term *class* refers to the template from which specific instances of objects are created. Objects perform specific actions in response to messages (which function calls may implement).

Inheritance is the mechanism that allows one object to behave like another, except for some modifications. Inheritance implies a hierarchy of classes with derived classes inheriting behavior from base classes. In the context of software, inheritance promotes the sharing of code and data among classes.

Polymorphism occurs when different objects react differently to the same message. In particular, OOP is a new way of organizing your program using a collection of objects with classes that are organized in a predefined hierarchy with a view to sharing code and data through inheritance.

A comparison of two implementations of an example—one using a procedural approach and the other using OOP—shows that object-based organization enhances the modularity of the program by placing related data and functions in the same module. Therefore, an object-based program can accommodate changes more easily than a procedural program. Although you can implement object-oriented techniques in a procedural programming language, such as C, you can do this more easily when the language has features that support OOP.

C++ and Object-Oriented Programming

Chapter 5, "Basics of Object-Oriented Programming," provided an overview of object-oriented programming (OOP) terminology and demonstrated how to implement the object-oriented techniques in a procedure-oriented language such as C. However, the example shown in Chapter 5 clearly illustrates several problems with using OOP in C:

- The language does not enforce information hiding.
- The programmer must implement message passing.
- The programmer must devise clever schemes to implement inheritance.

Consider, for instance, C's `FILE` data type. Although you can think of it as an object, the file I/O functions are not closely tied to the `FILE` data type. Also, the internal details of the `FILE` data type aren't really hidden because C has no way to prevent you from accessing the members of the `FILE` data structure. When writing object-oriented software in C, you can achieve information hiding only through self-discipline—you and others working on the software must agree not to directly access the contents of data structures that should be hidden.

Basically, although it's possible to use OOP techniques in C, the lack of built-in support for OOP requires extra work to enforce the principles of data abstraction and to set up the mechanisms for inheritance and polymorphism. C++, on the other hand, was designed with OOP in mind. C++ was built by adding certain features to C that ease the task of implementing objects. This chapter describes these features and illustrates the ease of using OOP in C++ by reimplementing the first chapter's example of geometric shapes.

This chapter does not feature a complete description of all the C++ features. Instead, it provides an overview of the features necessary for object-oriented programming. In particular, this chapter does not delve into the syntactical details of C++. Part III, "Learning C++," covers all aspects of C++ in detail. Of course, you can supplement this book's coverage of C++ and OOP by consulting one or more of the references listed at the end of this book.

A Brief History of C++

C++ was developed in the early 1980s by Bjarne Stroustrup of AT&T Bell Laboratories. He created C++ while adding features to C to support efficient, event-driven simulation programs. His inspiration came from the language Simula67, which supported the concept of a class. AT&T made many improvements to this initial language before releasing it commercially in 1985. C++ has continued to evolve since then, with AT&T controlling the releases.

In the beginning, AT&T supplied a translator, called *cfront*, for converting C++ programs into C. These programs then were compiled using a C compiler. By the time Release 1.2 of AT&T's C++ came out, C++ compilers were becoming available for PCs and workstations. AT&T released C++ 2.0 in 1989 and followed it promptly with Release 2.1. Microsoft Visual C++ conforms to the specifications of AT&T C++ Release 2.1.

The X3J16 committee of the American National Standards Institute (ANSI) currently is in the process of drafting a standard specification for the C++ programming language based on the following documents:

- The ANSI C standard (ANSI X3.159-1989—Programming Language C).
- The AT&T *C++ Language System Release 2.1 Reference Manual* (also available as *The Annotated C++Reference Manual* by Margaret A. Ellis and Bjarne Stroustrup, published by Addison-Wesley in 1990).

Object-Oriented Programming in C++

Chapter 5 mentioned three basic concepts that underlie OOP: *data abstraction, inheritance*, and *polymorphism.* To review, here's how these concepts help OOP:

- *Data abstraction* helps you tie data and functions together, which effectively defines a new data type with its own set of operations. Such a data type is called an *abstract data type* (ADT), also referred to as a *class.*
- *Inheritance* helps you organize the classes in a hierarchy so that you can place common data and functions in a base class from which other classes can inherit them.
- *Polymorphism* helps you keep your programs conceptually simple by enabling you to call the same function to perform similar tasks in all classes of a hierarchy.

C++ includes features that support these concepts, shown graphically in Figure 6.1.

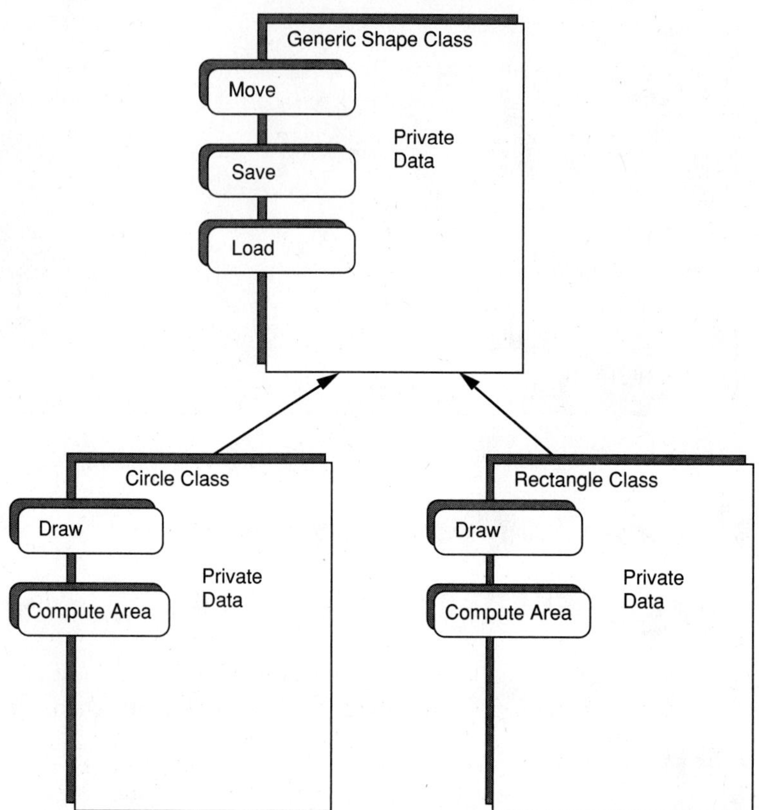

Figure 6.1. Data abstraction, inheritance, and polymorphism in OOP.

Data Abstraction in C++

In C, an abstract data type, such as `FILE`, is declared with a construct such as this:

```
typedef struct
{
    char     *buf;     /* Buffer for file I/O         */
    unsigned flags;    /* Flags to indicate status    */
      .                /* Other internal variables    */
      .
} FILE;                /* This is the FILE data type */
```

The operations on `FILE` are separate functions, each of which takes a pointer to a `FILE` structure as an argument. C++ introduces the class construct to augment C's `struct`.

Using class, you could define the File data type, equivalent to C's FILE, as shown in Listing 6.1.

Listing 6.1. FILE.H. A data type for file I/O.

```
/*  File: file.h
 *
 *  A File class for file I/O
 */
#if !defined(FILE_H)
#define FILE_H

#include <stdio.h>   // For C File I/O function declarations

class File
{
    FILE     *fp;    // C stream
//  ...              // Other internal variables

public:
    File(const char *name,                // Constructor
         const char *open_mode);
    ~File();                              // Destructor
    size_t read(const size_t howmany,     // Read from file
                const size_t elem_size,   //   into buffer
                void *buffer);
    size_t write(const size_t howmany,    // Write buffer to
                 const size_t elem_size,  //  file
                 const void *buffer);
};                                        // Note the semicolon
#endif
```

C++ Comments

C++ recognizes standard C comments, which start with the /* characters and end after the */ characters. Additionally, C++ treats as a comment everything following the // characters up to the end of the line. You can use the C format for comments spanning multiple lines, and the new style is convenient for single-line comments.

The Meaning of `const`

The `const` keyword prefixing the name of a variable indicates that the variable is a constant and must not be modified by the program. Similarly, if a function's argument is a pointer and that pointer is declared as a `const`, the function cannot modify the contents of the location referenced by that pointer.

As a C programmer (especially if you know ANSI C), you should find most of Listing 6.1 familiar. Don't be concerned, however, if you understand little of this; the rest of this chapter explains much of it. Also, Part III of this book covers the C++ features again, in detail. In particular, Chapter 7, "C++ and ANSI Standard C," provides an overview of ANSI C and compares it with C++.

Listing 6.1 assumes that the `File` class will provide a higher-level abstraction for file I/O, but that it will use C's file I/O functions for the actual work. That is why a pointer to a `FILE` exists in the class. As you'll see, the constructor of the `File` class sets up this `FILE` pointer when an instance of the `File` class is created.

If you examine the declaration of the `File` class in Listing 6.1, you can see that it looks very similar to C's `struct`, except for the ANSI C-style declaration of several functions following the `public:` keyword. These functions, called *member functions,* operate on the data items being encapsulated in the class. The data items in the class declaration are called *member variables.*

The `public:` keyword is significant because all member functions and variables appearing after the keyword are accessible to other parts of the program. The initial members of the class—those that appear before the `public:` keyword—are considered private. Such `private` variables and functions are not accessible to any function other than those declared within the class. The C++ compiler enforces this rule and displays an error message if any outside function refers to the `private` members of any class.

When you define a class in C++, you're defining a new, possibly complex, data type. The compiler hides the internal details of this data type from the outside world. The only way the outside functions can access the data is through the public member functions. Therefore, the `class` construct enables you to implement data abstraction and promotes modularity.

`class` Versus `struct`

C++ continues to support ANSI C's `struct` keyword. In fact, C++ expands the definition of `struct` by allowing the inclusion of member functions. In C++, the only difference between a `class` and a `struct` is that the `struct`'s contents are always public.

Defining the Member Functions for File

When declaring a class, you declare its member functions—but you don't define them. Typically, you define the member functions in a separate file. That way, you can think of the header file with the class declaration as a specification of the *interface* to the class, while the file containing function definitions is the *implementation* of the class. Ideally, if the interface is defined clearly enough, programmers using the class don't need to know the details of the implementation. For the `File` class, plan to call standard C file I/O functions to implement the member functions. You can do this in a straightforward manner, as shown in Listing 6.2.

It's common for the class definition file (which typically is a header file) and the file where the class functions are defined to share the same name, with the file's extension being the distinguishing feature.

The C++ Filename Extension

This book uses .CPP as the filename extension for C++ source files. Header files have the .H extension, as they do in C. Microsoft Visual C++ accepts both .CPP and .CXX as extensions for C++ source files.

Listing 6.2. FILE.CPP (first part). Definition of member functions of the `File` class.

```
/*-------------------------------------------------------------*/
/*  File:  file.cpp
 *
```

continues

Listing 6.2. continued

```
 *  Illustrates data encapsulation in C++
 */
#include "file.h"
/*-------------------------------------------------------------*/
// Constructor — opens a file
File::File(const char *name, const char *open_mode)
{
    fp = fopen(name, open_mode);
}
/*-------------------------------------------------------------*/
// Destructor — closes a file
File::~File()
{
    if(fp != NULL) fclose(fp);
}
/*-------------------------------------------------------------*/
size_t File::read(const size_t howmany,    // Read from file
                  const size_t elem_size,   //   into buffer
                  void *buffer)
{
    if(fp != NULL)
        return(fread(buffer, elem_size, howmany, fp));
    else
        return 0;
}
/*-------------------------------------------------------------*/
size_t File::write(const size_t howmany,   // Write buffer to
                   const size_t elem_size,  //  file
                   const void *buffer)
{
    if(fp != NULL)
        return(fwrite(buffer, elem_size, howmany, fp));
    else
        return 0;
}
```

You do need to be aware of one operator—the *scope resolution operator*, denoted by a pair of colons (`::`). When defining the member functions, use the scope resolution operator to indicate the class with which the function is associated. Therefore, the notation `File::read` identifies `read` as a member function of the `File` class. You also can use the scope resolution operator without a class name to indicate a globally defined function or variable. For example, the following code illustrates how you can differentiate between a globally defined `int` variable and a local one with the same name:

```
int AllDone;       //Variable visible throughout file

void AnyFunction(void)
{
    int AllDone;  // Local variable with same name
    AllDone = 1;  // Refers to local variable

    if(::AllDone) // This refers to the global "AllDone"
        DoSomething();
}
```

The same approach can be used to call a global function in a member function of the same name.

Constructors and Destructors

Notice that the `File` class contains a member function named `File` and another named `~File`. The two member functions are called the *constructor* and the *destructor* of the class, respectively. The C++ compiler calls a constructor, if one is defined, whenever an instance of a class is created. You can use the constructor to handle any specific requirements for initializing objects of a class. For example, if an object needs extra storage, you can allocate memory in the constructor. In the `File` class, the constructor calls `fopen` to open the file. Notice that the constructor function always has the same name as the class.

You also can define a *destructor* function for a class, if any need exists to clean up after an object is destroyed (for example, if you want to free memory allocated in the constructor). The C++ compiler calls the destructor function of a class whenever it needs to destroy an instance of that class. The destructor has the same name as the class except for a tilde (~) prefix. Therefore, the destructor function for the `File` class is `~File()`. Notice that, in the `File` class, you simply close the file that the constructor opened.

Using the File Class

You can define an instance of the `File` class and access its member functions just as you would define a C `struct`. For example, to define an instance of the `File` class named `f1` and call its `read` function, you would write the following:

```
// Open file named "test.dat" for reading
File   f1("test.dat", "rb");
char   buffer[128];
size_t bytes_read;
//...
bytes_read = f1.read(128, sizeof(char), buffer);
```

For a more meaningful example, consider the small program shown in Listing 6.3. It uses the `File` class to copy the contents of one file to another by reading from one and writing to the other.

Listing 6.3. FILE.CPP (second part). Program to copy from one file to another.

```
/*-------------------------------------------------------------*/
/*  Main function to copy file "test.dat" to "copy.out"
 */
void main(void)
{
// Open files...
    File f1("test.dat", "rb");
    File f2("copy.out", "wb");

    char   buffer[512];
    size_t count;

// Read a chunk from one file and write it to the other...
    while((count = f1.read(512, sizeof(char), buffer)) != 0)
    {
        f2.write(count, sizeof(char), buffer);
    }
}
```

Inheritance in C++ Classes

When declaring a class, you also can indicate whether it inherits from any other classes. On the first line of the `class` declaration, place a colon (:) followed by a list of base classes from which this class inherits.

For example, suppose you want to declare the `circle_shape` class, which is derived from a generic `shape` class. In this case, the first line of the declaration of the `circle_shape` class looks like this:

```
class circle_shape: public shape
{

// Declare member variables and member functions...

}
```

Here, the `shape` class is the *base class* and `circle_shape` is the *derived class.* The `public:` keyword preceding `shape` signifies that any public member variables and functions of `shape` will be accessible to the `circle_shape` class.

Polymorphism and Dynamic Binding

C++ provides a way to override a function defined in a base class with a function defined in a derived class. Another feature of C++ is that you can use pointers to a base class to refer to objects of a derived class. With these two features you can implement polymorphic behavior in C++ classes.

Suppose you have a base class called `shape`. This class encapsulates data and functions common to other classes of shapes, such as `circle_shape` and `rectangle_shape`, which are derived from the `shape` class. One of the functions is `draw`, which draws the shape. Because each shape is drawn differently, the base class defines the `draw` function with the `virtual` keyword:

```
class shape
{
public:
    virtual void draw(void) const{ }
// Other member functions...
};
```

The `virtual` keyword tells the C++ compiler that the `draw` function defined in the base class should be used only if the derived classes do not define it. In this case, the base class defines `draw` as a "do nothing" function.

In a derived class, you can override this definition by supplying a function with the same name, like this:

```
class circle_shape: public shape
{
// Private data...
public:
// Other member functions...
    virtual void draw(void) const;
};
```

Later, you must actually define the `draw` function for the `circle_shape` class. You can do the same for the `rectangle_shape` class. Once you do this, you can apply the same member function to instances of different classes, and the C++ compiler will generate a call to the correct draw function:

```
// Create instances of circle_shape and rectangle_shape
circle_shape c1(100.,100.,50.);
rectangle_shape r1(10.,20.,30.,40.);

c1.draw();    // "draw" from "circle_shape" class is called
r1.draw();    // "draw" from "rectangle_shape" class is called
```

Although this is polymorphic behavior, it's not an interesting example because both the C++ compiler and you can determine, by studying the code, exactly which function should be called. In fact, this case is referred to as the *static binding* of virtual functions, because the compiler can determine the function to be called at compile time.

The more interesting case is that of *dynamic binding*, which happens when a virtual function is invoked through a pointer to an object and the type of the object is not known during compilation. This is possible because C++ enables you to use a pointer to a base class when referring to an instance of a derived class. For example, suppose you want to create a number of shapes, store them in an array, and draw them. Here's how you might do it:

```
    int i;
    shape *shapes[2];    // Array of pointers to base class

// Create some shapes and save the pointers
    shapes[0] = new circle_shape(100., 100., 50.);
    shapes[1] = new rectangle_shape(80., 40., 120., 60.);

// Draw the shapes
    for(i = 0; i < 2; i++) shapes[i]->draw();
```

Notice how you can loop through the pointers to the shapes and call the `draw` member function of each object. Because `draw` is a `virtual` function, the actual `draw` function called at runtime depends on the type of shape that the `shapes[i]` pointer references. If `shapes[i]` points to an instance of `circle_shape`, the `circle_shape::draw()` function is called. On the other hand, if `shapes[i]` points to an instance of `rectangle_shape`, the `draw` function of `rectangle_shape` is called. At runtime, the pointers in the `shapes` array can point to any instance of the classes derived from the `shape` base class. The actual function being called varies according to the pointer's type determined at runtime. That's why this style of virtual function call is called *dynamic binding*.

Geometric Shapes in C++

To illustrate how C++'s object-oriented features help you write object-oriented programs, consider the examples of geometric shapes from Chapter 5, "Basics of Object-Oriented Programming," (Listings 5.5, 5.6, and 5.7) which presented a C-based implementation of shape objects. In this section, that example is rewritten in C++. Notice that the code is much more compact: you no longer need additional C utility routines to support the implementation of objects.

Adding Libraries for the Linker

When creating a QuickWin program, you need to add two libraries to the linker's list of libraries to use. To do this, in the Visual Workbench, select Options, Project, Linker, and add the following libraries to the project:

1. `SHELL`
2. `COMMDLG`

These libraries are needed to eliminate undefined references created by the Microsoft Foundation Class library.

The Shape Classes

The first step in implementing the geometric shapes in C++ is to define the classes. As in the C version of the program (see Chapter 5), you start with an abstract base class, called `shape`. This class is abstract because you never create an instance of this class. You use it to encapsulate data and functions common to all derived classes, thus promoting inheritance and polymorphism (through the `virtual` keyword, explained later). As shown in Figure 6.2, all other shapes are derived from this base class. The SHAPES.H file, shown in Listing 6.4, contains the actual declaration of the classes.

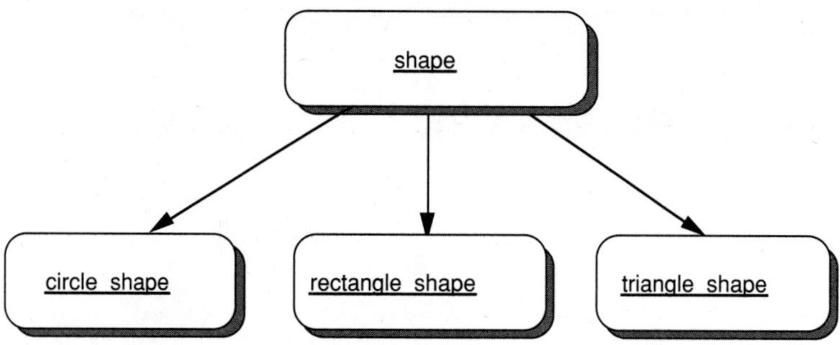

Figure 6.2. A class hierarchy for geometric shapes.

Listing 6.4. SHAPES.H. Classes of geometric shapes in C++.

```
/*-------------------------------------------------------------*/
/*  File:  shapes.h
 *
 *  C++ header file with definitions of geometrical shapes
 */

#if !defined(SHAPES_H)
#define SHAPES_H

#include <stdio.h>
#include <math.h>

#define M_PI 3.141592653589793  //Value of "Pi"

// Define an abstract shape class "abstract" because you
// do not create any instances of this class. It's there
```

```
// to encapsulate common data and functions that will be
// shared by all shapes

class shape
{
// In this case, you do not have any data,
// only member functions
public:
    virtual double compute_area(void) const
    {
        printf("Not implemented\n");
        return 0.0;
    }
    virtual void draw(void) const{ }
};

// Define the "circle" class

class circle_shape: public shape
{
private:
    double x, y;   // Coordinates of center
    double radius; // Radius of circle
public:
    circle_shape(double x, double y, double radius);
    virtual double compute_area(void) const;
    virtual void draw(void) const;
};

// Define the "rectangle" class

class rectangle_shape: public shape
{
private:
    double x1, y1;  // Coordinates of opposite corners
    double x2, y2;
public:
    rectangle_shape(double x1, double y1, double x2, double y2);
    double compute_area(void) const;
    void draw(void) const;
};

#endif  // #if !defined(SHAPES_H)
```

The SHAPES.H header file declares the member functions of the classes, but usually the definitions are placed in separate modules. For smaller functions, you can define a function directly in the body of the class, as you did for the compute_area function in the shape class.

> **const Member Functions**
>
> Use the const keyword after the arguments in the declaration of a member function if that member function does not modify any member variable. This tells the compiler that it can safely apply this member function to a const instance of this class. For example, the following is permissible because compute_area is a const member function:
>
> ```
> // Define a const circle
>    const circle_shape c1(100.0, 100.0, 50.0);
>    double area = c1.compute_area();
> ```

Circle and Rectangle Classes

Listings 6.5 and 6.6 show the implementation of the circle_shape and rectangle_shape classes, respectively. You implement each class in its own file, just as you would for a larger project. You implement a class by defining its member functions. In this example, each class has two member functions: draw and compute_area. The definition of each member function resembles a standard C function, except for the scope resolution operator (::), which indicates the class to which that function belongs. For example, the compute_area function of the circle_shape class is defined as follows:

```
double circle_shape::compute_area(void) const
{
    return (M_PI * radius * radius);
}
```

Listing 6.5. CIRCLE.CPP.
C++ implementation of the circle_shape class.

```
/*-------------------------------------------------------------*/
/*  File:  circle.cpp
 *
```

```
 *  Definition of the "circle" class of shapes in C++
 */

#include "shapes.h"
/*-------------------------------------------------------------*/
circle_shape::circle_shape(double xc, double yc, double r)
{
    x = xc;
    y = yc;
    radius = r;
}
/*-------------------------------------------------------------*/
double circle_shape::compute_area(void) const
{
    return (M_PI * radius * radius);
}
/*-------------------------------------------------------------*/
void circle_shape::draw(void) const
{
    printf("Draw: Circle of radius %f centered at (%f, %f)\n",
            radius, x, y);
}
```

Listing 6.6. RECT.CPP. C++ implementation of the `rectangle_shape` class.

```
/*-------------------------------------------------------------*/
/*  File:  rect.cpp
 *
 *  Definition of the "rectangle" class of shapes in C++
 */

#include "shapes.h"

rectangle_shape::rectangle_shape(double xul, double yul,
                                 double xlr, double ylr)
{
    x1 = xul;
    y1 = yul;
```

continues

Listing 6.6. continued

```
    x2 = xlr;
    y2 = ylr;
}
/*-------------------------------------------------------------*/
double rectangle_shape::compute_area(void) const
{
    return fabs( (x1-x2) * (y1-y2) );
}
/*-------------------------------------------------------------*/
void rectangle_shape::draw(void) const
{
    printf("Draw: Rectangle with corners (%f, %f) (%f, %f)\n",
            x1, y1, x2, y2);
}
```

Using the Shape Classes

Listing 6.7 shows a sample C++ program, SHAPETST.CPP, which creates instances of circle and rectangle shapes and tests their member functions. To build the executable file of this program, compile and link the following files in this order:

1. SHAPETST.CPP (Listing 6.7)
2. CIRCLE.CPP (Listing 6.5)
3. RECT.CPP (Listing 6.6)

Each of these files needs the SHAPES.H header file shown in Listing 6.4.

**Listing 6.7. SHAPETST.CPP.
A C++ program to test the shape classes.**

```
/*-------------------------------------------------------------*/
/*  File:  shapetst.cpp
 *
 *  Program to test the "shape" classes
 */

#include <shapes.h>
```

```
int main(void)
{
    int i;
    shape *shapes[3];

// Create some shapes
    shapes[0] = new circle_shape(100., 100., 50.);
    shapes[1] = new rectangle_shape(80., 40., 120., 60.);

// Compute the areas
    for(i = 0; i < 2; i++)
    {
        printf("Area of shape [%d] = %f\n", i,
               shapes[i]->compute_area());
    }

// Draw the shapes
    for(i = 0; i < 2; i++) shapes[i]->draw();

// Destroy the shapes
    delete shapes[0];
    delete shapes[1];

    return 0;
}
```

This sample program uses dynamic binding of the `virtual` function by storing pointers to different types of shapes in an array and invoking the member functions of the appropriate class through the pointer. This is a good example of how dynamic binding and polymorphism are used in C++ programs.

Adding a New Shape Class

How would you add a new shape, such as a triangle, to the classes that already exist? With an object-oriented program, it's easy to accomplish this. Here are the steps:

1. Insert the declaration of a `triangle_shape` class at the end of the SHAPES.H header file (Listing 6.4). Here is the definition:

```
// Define the "triangle" class

class triangle_shape: public shape
{
private:
    double x1, y1;  // Coordinates of the corners
    double x2, y2;
    double x3, y3;
public:
    triangle_shape(double x1, double y1,
                   double x2, double y2,
                   double x3, double y3);
    double compute_area(void) const;
    void draw(void) const;
};
```

2. Define the member functions of the `triangle_shape` class in a separate file. Listing 6.8 shows the file TRIANGLE.CPP, which defines the functions.

Once you complete these two steps, you can begin using the `triangle_shape` class in your program. However, you do need to rebuild your project with the TRIANGLE.CPP file (Listing 6.8). For example, you can write code such as this:

```
    int i;
    shape *shapes[3];

// Create some shapes
    shapes[0] = new circle_shape(100., 100., 50.);
    shapes[1] = new rectangle_shape(80., 40., 120., 60.);
    shapes[2] = new triangle_shape(100.,100., 200.,100.,150.,50.);

// Compute the areas
    for(i = 0; i < 3; i++)
    {
        printf("Area of shape [%d] = %f\n", i,
               shapes[i]->compute_area());
    }
```

Listing 6.8. TRIANGLE.CPP.
C++ implementation of the `triangle_shape` class.

```
/*-------------------------------------------------------------*/
/*  File:  triangle.cpp
 *
```

```
 *  Definition of the "triangle" class of shapes in C++
 */

#include "shapes.h"

/*-------------------------------------------------------------*/
triangle_shape::triangle_shape(double xa, double ya,
                       double xb, double yb, double xc, double yc)
{
    x1 = xa;
    y1 = ya;
    x2 = xb;
    y2 = yb;
    x3 = xc;
    y3 = yc;
}
/*-------------------------------------------------------------*/
double triangle_shape::compute_area(void) const
{
    double area, x21, y21, x31, y31;
    x21 =  x2 - x1;
    y21 =  y2 - y1;
    x31 =  x3 - x1;
    y31 =  y3 - y1;
    area = fabs(y21 * x31 - x21 * y31) / 2.0;
    return (area);
}
/*-------------------------------------------------------------*/
void triangle_shape::draw(void) const
{
    printf("Draw: Triangle with corners at\n"
           "      (%f, %f) (%f, %f) (%f, %f)\n",
            x1, y1, x2, y2, x3, y3);
}
```

Creating Objects at Runtime

One important feature of C++ is the ability to create instances of a class at runtime. In C, you use memory allocation routines such as `calloc` or `malloc` to dynamically allocate data. These functions return a pointer to the allocated data. When you no longer need the data, you can reclaim the memory by calling `free` with the pointer as the argument. C++ provides the operators `new` and `delete` to create and destroy objects, respectively.

Listing 6.7 illustrates how to use the `new` operator to create the geometric shapes and how to use `delete` to destroy them. Like `calloc` or `malloc`, `new` also returns a pointer to the newly created instance of the class. Unlike `malloc`, which returns a generic pointer (`void *`) that you must cast to the type of your data, `new` returns a pointer to the correct data type. Additionally, `new` automatically calls the constructor of the class to initialize the new instance.

Summary

Object-oriented programming is easier to practice if the programming language supports the basic necessities of OOP: data abstraction, inheritance, and polymorphism. C++ was developed from C by adding precisely the kind of features that support OOP.

C++ provides the `class` construct to define abstract data types, supplies the `virtual` keyword to permit polymorphic functions, and includes the syntax necessary to indicate the inheritance relationship between a derived class and one or more base classes.

C++'s `class` construct is similar to C's `struct`, but it has many more features. In particular, with `class` you can define the operations on the object—instances of a class—by member functions and operators. A C++ program manipulates objects by calling the member functions only. This enhances the modularity of programs because you are free to change the internal representation of objects without affecting other parts of a program.

III

Learning C++

7

C++ and ANSI Standard C

In Chapter 6, "C++ and Object-Oriented Programming," you encountered a small but important subset of C++ features that specifically supports object-oriented programming. C++ possesses many more features that may not directly support OOP but, nevertheless, are needed to write complete programs. Many of these features match what is in ANSI C, but some small differences exist between the two.

This chapter describes some major features of C++ and demonstrates how C++ differs from ANSI C. If you're accustomed to ANSI standard C, knowing the differences between C++ and ANSI C can help you avoid potential problems when writing C++ programs. Consult Chapter 4, "Microsoft Visual C++ Extensions to Standard C," for an overview of ANSI standard C.

Features of C++

The following sections provide a quick overview of C++ features that differ from those in ANSI C. The coverage of the topics in the following sections is sparse because these topics are covered in more detail in Chapters 8 through 12.

New Features for Functions in C++

As with C, C++ programs contain functions. C++ introduces several new requirements that make functions efficient and safe to use. One helpful change is the use of *prototypes* for functions. Although you can use prototypes in ANSI C, they're not mandatory; you can either use a prototype or define the function before it's called. In C++, you must declare a function before using it.

Default Arguments

As an additional improvement to functions in C++, you can specify the default values for arguments when you provide a prototype for a function. For example, if you're defining a function, named `create_window`, that sets up a window (a rectangular region) in a graphics display and fills it with a background color, you may opt to specify default values for the window's location, size, and background color, as follows:

```
// A function with default argument values
// Assume that window is a user-defined type

Window create_window(int x = 0, int y = 0, int width = 100,
                     int height = 50, int bgpixel = 0);
```

When `create_window` is declared in this way, you can use any of the following calls to create new windows:

```
Window w;

// The following is same as: create_window(0, 0, 100, 50, 0);
w = create_window();

// This is same as: create_window(100, 0, 100, 50, 0);
w = create_window(100);

// Equivalent to create_window(30, 20, 100, 50, 0);
w = create_window(30, 20);
```

As you can see from these examples, it's impossible to give a nondefault value for the `height` argument without specifying the values for `x`, `y`, and `width`, because `height` follows them and the compiler can match arguments only by position. In other words, the first argument you specify in a call to `create_window` always matches `x`, the second one matches `y`, and so on. Therefore, the only arguments you can leave unspecified are trailing arguments.

Overloaded Function Names

In C++ you can have several functions with the same name as long as their argument lists differ. When this happens, the function's name is *overloaded.* You can use overloading to give a meaningful name to related functions that perform the same task.

For example, if you're evaluating the absolute value of numbers, the ANSI C library includes three functions for this purpose: `abs` for `int` arguments, `labs` for `long`, and `fabs` for the absolute value of a `double`. In C++, you can use the `abs` name for all three versions and declare them as follows:

```
int    abs(int x);
long   abs(long x);
double abs(double x);
```

After you declare these functions, you can use them as follows:

```
int i, diff = -2;
long offset;
double x;

i = abs(diff);            // abs(int)    called
offset = abs(-21956L);    // abs(long)   called
x = abs(-3.55);           // abs(double) called
```

The C++ compiler selects the correct function by comparing the types of arguments in the call with those specified in the function's declaration.

When you overload functions in C++, you must ensure that the number and type of arguments of all overloaded versions are different. C++ does not permit overloading for functions that differ only in the type of return value. Thus, you cannot overload functions such as `double compute(int)` and `float compute(int)`, because their argument lists are identical.

Inline Functions

Inline functions are like preprocessor macros because the compiler substitutes the entire function body for each inline function call. The inline functions are provided to support efficient implementation of OOP techniques in C++. Because the OOP approach requires the extensive use of member functions, the overhead of function calls can hurt the performance of a program. For smaller functions, you can use the `inline` specifier to avoid the overhead of function calls.

On the surface, inline functions look like preprocessor macros—but the two differ in a crucial aspect. Unlike macros, the compiler treats inline functions as true functions. To see how this can be an important factor, consider the following example.

Suppose you define a macro named `multiply`, as follows:

```
#define multiply(x,y) (x*y)
```

If you use this macro like this:

```
x = multiply(4+1,6);  // you want the product of 4+1 and 6
```

by straightforward substitution of the `multiply` macro, the preprocessor transforms the left side of this statement into the following code:

```
x = (4+1*6);
```

This evaluates to 10 instead of 30, the desired result of multiplying (4+1) and 6. Of course, you know that the solution is to use parentheses around the macro arguments, but consider what happens when you define an inline function exactly as you defined the macro:

```
#include <stdio.h>

// Define inline function to multiply two integers.

inline int multiply(int x, int y)
{
    return(x * y);
}

// An overloaded version that multiplies two doubles

inline double multiply(double x, double y)
{
    return(x * y);
}

main()
{
    printf("Product of 5 and 6 = %d\n", multiply(4+1,6));
    printf("Product of 3.1 and 10.0 = %f\n",
```

```
        multiply(3.0+.1, 10.0));
}
```

When you compile and run this program, it correctly produces the following output:

```
Product of 5 and 6 = 30
Product of 3.1 and 10.0 = 31.000000
```

As you can see from this example, inline functions don't produce the kinds of errors that plague ill-defined macros. Because inline functions behave like true functions, you can overload them and rely on the compiler to use the correct function-based argument types. However, because the body of an inline function is duplicated wherever that function is called, you should use inline functions only when the functions are small in size.

Friend Functions

C++ introduces another new keyword to help you implement OOP techniques efficiently: the `friend` specifier.

The rules of data encapsulation in a class are such that only member functions can access the private data of a class. Of course, a class can provide special member functions that can return the values of its private variables, but this approach may be too inefficient in some cases.

In such instances, you may want to allow a function outside the class to directly access data that is private to the class. You can do this by declaring that outside function within the class with the `friend` access specifier. For example, suppose you want to define the nonmember function `add` to add two complex numbers. The following program illustrates how you might use `friend` functions to accomplish this. Note that this is a simplistic definition of a complex class; it's intended to show you how `friend` functions work.

```
#include <stdio.h>

class complex
{
    float real, imag;
public:
    friend complex add(complex a, complex b);
    friend void print(complex a);
    complex() { real = imag = 0.0;}
    complex(float a, float b) { real = a; imag = b;}
};
```

```
complex add(complex a, complex b)
{
    complex z;
    z.real = a.real + b.real;
    z.imag = a.imag + b.imag;
    return z;
}

void print(complex a)
{
    printf(" (%f + i %f)\n", a.real, a.imag);
}

main()
{
    complex a, b, c;
    a = complex(1.5, 2.1);
    b = complex(1.1, 1.4);

    printf("Sum of ");
    print(a);
    printf("and");
    print(b);

    c = add(a,b);

    printf(" = ");
    print(c);
}
```

This program uses the `friend` function `add` to add two complex numbers and the `friend` function `print` to display the results. When you execute this program, it generates this result:

```
Sum of  (1.500000 + i 2.100000)
and (1.100000 + i 1.400000)
 =  (2.600000 + i 3.500000)
```

Reference Types as Arguments

Unfortunately, the `add` function has a drawback stemming from the way C passes arguments to functions. C passes arguments by value—when you call a function with arguments, the values of the arguments are copied to a special area of memory known as the *stack*, and the function uses these copies for its operation. To see the effect of *call by value*, consider the following code:

```
    void twice(int a)
    {
        a *= 2;
    }
    .
    .
    int x = 5;

// Call the "twice" function
    twice(x);

    printf("x = %d\n", x);
```

Note that this program prints 5, not 10, as the value of x, even though the twice function multiplies its argument by 2. This result (5) happens because the twice function receives a copy of x and any change it makes to that copy is lost upon return from the function.

In C, the only way you can change the value of a variable through a function is by explicitly passing the address of the variable to the function. For example, to double the value of a variable, you can write the function twice as:

```
    void twice(int *a)
    {
        *a *= 2;    // Double the value
    }
    .
    .+
    .
    int x = 5;

// Call "twice" with the address of x as argument
    twice(&x);

    printf("x = %d\n", x);
```

This time, the program prints 10 as the result. Therefore, you can pass pointers to alter variables through a function call, but the syntax is messy. In the function, you must dereference the argument with the * operator.

C++ provides a way of passing arguments by introducing a *reference*: the definition of an alias or alternative name for any instance of data. Syntactically, you append an ampersand (&) to the name of the data type. For example, if you have:

```
int i = 5;
int *p_i = &i;  // a pointer to int initialized to point to i
int &r_i = i;   // a reference to the int variable i
```

you can use r_i anywhere you would use i or *p_i. In fact, if you write:

```
r_i += 10;  // adds 10 to i
```

i changes to 15, because r_i is simply another name for i.

Using reference types, you can rewrite the function named twice to multiply an integer by 2 in a much simpler manner:

```
    void twice(int &a)
    {
        a *= 2;
    }
    .
    .
    int x = 5;
// Call "twice" Argument automatically passed by reference
    twice(x);

    printf("x = %d\n", x);
```

As expected, the program prints 10 as the result, but it looks a lot simpler than trying to accomplish the same task with pointers.

When classes are passed by value, overhead occurs through copying objects to and from the stack; this is another reason for passing arguments by reference. Passing a reference to an object avoids this unnecessary copying and enables an efficient implementation of OOP.

This brings us back to the example in the previous section. Now that you know about references, you can rewrite that small complex class as follows:

```
#include <stdio.h>

class complex
{
    float real, imag;
public:
```

```
    friend complex add(const complex &a, const complex &b);
    friend void print(const complex &a);
    complex() { real = imag = 0.0;}
    complex(float a, float b) { real = a; imag = b;}
};

complex add(const complex &a, const complex &b)
{
    complex z;
    z.real = a.real + b.real;
    z.imag = a.imag + b.imag;
    return z;
}

void print(const complex &a)
{
    printf(" (%f + i %f)\n", a.real, a.imag);
}
```

You can use the class in the same manner as its old version. If you look carefully you can see that, to pass arguments by reference, you simply add an ampersand (`&`) after the data type of the argument, thus changing all `complex` types to `complex&`. (You can add a space between the type and `&`.) I also have added a `const` prefix to the arguments to emphasize that the functions `add` and `print` must not alter their arguments.

Overloaded Operators

Just as C++ enables you to define several functions with the same name but with varying arguments, it also enables you to redefine the meaning of operators such as `+`, `-`, `*`, `/`, `%`, `+=`, and `-=` for any class. In other words, you can overload the meaning of operators. Because a class is a new abstract data type, such overloaded operators provide you with the ability to define operations on this data.

For example, instead of writing an `add` function to add two complex variables, you can define the `+` operator to perform addition for the complex class shown earlier. Using `friend` functions and `const` reference types, you might define the `+` operator as follows:

```
class complex
{
    float real, imag;
public:
    friend complex operator+(const complex &a, const complex &b);
```

```
    complex() { real = imag = 0.0;}
    complex(float a, float b) { real = a; imag = b;}
};

complex operator+(const complex &a, const complex &b)
{
    complex z;
    z.real = a.real + b.real;
    z.imag = a.imag + b.imag;
    return z;
}
```

As you can see from the example, defining the operator is just like defining a function, except for a special syntax for the name of the function. This syntax is the symbol of the operator with the `operator` keyword as a prefix.

After you define a + operator for the complex class, you can use it just as you would normally use the + operator for other data types:

```
complex a, b, c;
a = complex(1.5, 2.1);
b = complex(1.1, 1.4);

c = a+b;    // Add two complex numbers a and b
```

Data Declarations in C++

In ANSI C, you cannot mix declarations with the statements of a program. You must declare all variables at the beginning of a block. C++ does not distinguish between a declaration and other statements, and it enables you to declare variables anywhere. Thus, in C++, you can write:

```
#include <stdio.h>
#include <string.h>
.
.
void convert_string(char *s)
{
    if(str == NULL) return;
    int length = strlen(s);
    .
    .
    for(int i = 0; i <= length; i++)
```

```
    {
// Convert characters in the string...
    }
}
```

This feature of C++ is handy because you can declare a variable and initialize it immediately. The program is more readable because the variable is declared and initialized close to where it actually is used.

Another interesting feature of C++ enables you to start using the name of a struct as soon as its definition is started. In C, when you define structures containing pointers to their own type, you typically use constructs like this:

```
typedef struct node
{
    struct node *prev; /* Pointer to previous node */
    struct node *next; /* Pointer to next node     */
    void        *info; /* Other members of struct  */
} node;

node *top_node;        /* Define a node */
```

In C++, the same code becomes much simpler:

```
struct node
{
    node *prev; // Pointer to previous node
    node *next; // Pointer to next node
    void *info; // Other members of struct
} node;

node *top_node; // Define a node
```

As you can see, the name of a struct can be used inside the definition of the struct itself.

How C++ Differs from C

Although it is often casually stated that C++ is a superset of C, especially ANSI standard C, a small number of things in ANSI C do not work quite the same way in C++. Here's a summary description of the differences.

New Reserved Keywords

To support object-oriented programming, C++ introduces 15 new keywords in addition to those reserved by ANSI C. You should watch out for any existing C program that might use these reserved words and make edits to change the keywords to words that are not reserved:

`asm`	`friend`	`private`	`this`
`catch`	`inline`	`protected`	`throw`
`class`	`new`	`public`	`virtual`
`delete`	`operator`	`template`	

You'll encounter most of these keywords in the rest of this book. Some of them (such as `catch`, `template`, and `throw`) are not yet in widespread use but are reserved in anticipation of new features being added to the language. The `template` keyword will be used to allow the definition of families for types or functions. A mechanism for handling exceptions will use the `catch` and `throw` keywords.

Function Prototypes

In ANSI C, if a function does not have a prototype, the compiler assumes that the function returns an integer. C++ strictly enforces prototypes and generates an error if you use a function without first declaring it. Thus, C++ displays an error when compiling the following old-style C program:

```
main()
{
    printf("Hello, World!\n"); // Allowed in C, but not in C++
                               // C++ needs prototype before use
}
```

Of course, in ANSI C you can remedy this simply by including stdio.h, which declares the `printf` function. You also can get another type of error from old-style C code, where functions are declared only when they do not return an `int`. For example, many C programs declare and use `malloc` as follows:

```
char *malloc();
int  *raw_data;

raw_data = (int *) malloc(1024);
```

This code generates an error in C++ because C++ interprets empty argument lists differently than ANSI C. In ANSI standard C, an empty argument list in a function's declaration means that the function takes zero or more arguments, but C++ considers a function declaration with an empty argument list to be equivalent to the following:

```
char *malloc(void);
```

When C++ encounters the call `malloc(1024)`, it produces an error message because it finds an argument where it expects none.

const Variables

C++ requires you to initialize `const` variables when you declare them; ANSI C does not. Thus, you have:

```
const buflen;       // OK in ANSI C, but not in C++
const buflen = 512; // OK in C++ as well as ANSI C
```

Another interesting property of `const` variables in C++ is that `const` integers can be used as subscripts in any constant expression. This is possible because C++ requires `const` variables to be initialized during declaration. Thus, the compiler always knows the value of a `const` integer. This enables you to use the following:

```
const buflen = 512;
char  buffer[buflen];  // Allowed in C++, but not in ANSI C
```

Because `const` integers declared this way are full-fledged variables, you should use them wherever you need constants. In other words, in C++, instead of writing:

```
#define  EOF    -1
#define  maxlen 128
#define  Pi     3.14159

char one_line[maxlen];   // Define an array to hold a line
```

you should write:

```
const EOF = -1;             // This is a const int by default
const maxlen = 128;
const double Pi = 3.14159; // This is a floating-point constant


char one_line[maxlen];    // Define an array to hold a line
```

void Pointers

ANSI C permits pointers of the `void *` type to be assigned to any other pointer and vice versa: any pointer can be assigned to a pointer of the `void *` type. C++ does not permit the assignment of a pointer of the `void *` type to any other pointer without an explicit *cast*. The following example illustrates the difference:

```
void *p_void;
int  i, *p_i;

p_void = &i;          /* Allowed in both C and C++      */
p_i = p_void;         /* Allowed in C, but not in C++   */
p_i = (int *)p_void; /* Cast makes it OK to use in C++ */
```

Initialization of Character Arrays

In ANSI C, you can initialize an array of three characters with the following:

```
char name[3] = "C++"; // Allowed in ANSI C, but not in C++
```

After the initialization, the array elements `name[0]`, `name[1]`, and `name[2]` are set, respectively, to C, +, and +. However, C++ does not allow this type of initialization, because the array has no room for the terminating null character. In C++, if you need to set up the `name` array as you did in C, you must rewrite the initialization as follows:

```
char name[3] = {'C', '+', '+'}; // Allowed in both C and C++
```

Of course, the following initialization is valid in both C and C++, but this sets up a 4-byte array with the last byte set to a null character:

```
char name[] = "C++"; // Allowed in both C and C++
```

sizeof Operator

In ANSI C, the size of a character constant, such as the expression `sizeof('Q')`, evaluates to the same value as `sizeof(int)`. But C++ correctly evaluates this to `sizeof(char)`. Also, in ANSI C the size of an `enum` variable is the same as `sizeof(int)`. In C++, an `enum` variable is the size of an integral type, not necessarily `sizeof(int)`.

Scope of *enum*

In ANSI C, the list of constants appearing in an `enum` variable is known throughout the file. C++ considers the constants in an `enum` to be local to a `class` or a `struct` and known only to member and `friend` functions of the class. For example, the following code is allowed in C++, but not in ANSI C:

```
struct finite_state_machine
{
    enum state{init, reset, end};
// ...
}

int init(int state);  // Allowed in C++, but not in ANSI C
```

If a class declares an `enum` variable, functions outside the class can refer to the enumerated constants by explicitly qualifying the name with the scope resolution operator. For example, suppose you want to refer to the enumerated constant `scientific`, defined in the class named `ios`. You must use the following notation to access this constant:

```
ios::scientific
```

Restriction on *goto*

With ANSI C, you can jump into a block of code, skipping over the declarations and initializations that may appear at the beginning of the block. You cannot do this in C++. Here's an example:

```
    goto Start;    // OK in ANSI C, but not in C++
// ...
    {
        int  x = 4, y = 8;
        Node t1;           // This could be a class
        char buf[10];

    Start:
// ...
    } // Class destructors are called before leaving block
```

Although jumping into a block is merely a questionable practice in C, such jumps are almost always bound to be fatal in a C++ program. This is because C++ calls constructors for any class objects created at the beginning of a block, and calls the corresponding destructors when the block ends. Jumping into the middle of a block means that calls might go to destructors for which there are no matching calls to constructors. Typically, this produces a fatal error for the program.

Summary

C++ was created by extending C with features designed to support object-oriented programming. C++'s support for OOP comes through the `class` and `struct` constructs, the concepts of overloading functions and operators, and virtual functions.

Many features of the C++ language, such as function prototypes and the `void` and `enum` types, have been incorporated into ANSI standard C. Although C++ compilers accept most ANSI C programs, certain constructs in ANSI C behave differently in C++. You should watch out for the new reserved keywords and for the strict enforcement of the function prototypes in C++.

C++ Classes for Standard I/O

Chapter 7, "C++ and ANSI Standard C," provided you with an overview of the C++ programming language and how it relates to ANSI standard C. Before you start using C++ to define your own classes, this chapter gets you started with the `iostream` class library. The `iostream` class library comes with most C++ compilers, including Microsoft Visual C++. This library is C++'s equivalent to C's `stdio` library, which includes the `printf` and `scanf` family. This chapter explains the structure of the classes that form the basis of the `iostream` library and shows you how to use these classes for various types of I/O.

C++ I/O Library

Like C, C++ contains no built-in facilities for I/O. Instead, you must rely on a library of functions for performing I/O. In ANSI C, the I/O functions are a part of the standard library; C++ does not yet have a standard library. Of course, you can call the ANSI C library routines in C++. However, for I/O, Microsoft Visual C++ provides an alternative to `printf` and `scanf`: the `iostream` library, which handles I/O through a class of objects. The following sections describe simple usage of the `iostream` library and explain the class hierarchy that constitutes the library.

Stream I/O in C++

As a programmer learning OOP, you may want to study the details of the classes in the `iostream` library. However, you don't need to know much about these classes to use the library for simple I/O. To begin, you should be familiar with the concept of a stream and know the names of the predefined streams. The idea of a *stream*—a sequence of bytes—figures prominently in UNIX and C. As a C programmer, you've heard the term *stream* in connection with ANSI C's file I/O functions, prototyped in the STDIO.H header file. A stream serves as an abstract model of I/O devices such as a disk file, the keyboard, the video display, or even a buffer in memory. In ANSI C, each stream has an associated `FILE` structure that holds the state of the stream and such data items as the buffer used for buffered I/O.

Buffered I/O

Buffered I/O refers to the use of a block of memory as a temporary storage area for the bytes being read from or written to the stream. ANSI C's stream I/O routines and C++'s `iostream` library use a buffer to hold data in transit to and from a stream.

For example, in a buffered read operation from a disk file, a fixed-size byte chunk is read from the disk into a buffer of the same size. The routines requesting data from the file actually read from the buffer. When the buffer has no characters left, it automatically is refilled by a disk read operation. A similar sequence occurs when writing to a file.

Buffered I/O operations are efficient because they minimize time-consuming read/write operations with the disk. If needed, you can turn off the buffering.

Each ANSI C stream is identified by the pointer to its associated `FILE` structure. You get this pointer back when you open the stream by calling the `fopen` function. In OOP terminology, this is equivalent to creating the stream object. Not all streams need to be explicitly opened, however. When your C program starts up, three streams are opened for you. These streams, identified as `stdin`, `stdout`, and `stderr`, are used to get input from the keyboard, display output, and display error messages, respectively. The `scanf` function reads from `stdin`, while the `printf` function sends its output to `stdout`. The `fscanf` and `fprintf` functions can handle I/O with streams that you open.

The C++ `iostream` library is an object-oriented implementation of a stream viewed as a flow of bytes from a source (producer) to a sink (consumer). As you'll see later, the `iostream` library includes input streams (the `istream` class), output streams (the `ostream` class), and streams that can handle both input and output operations (the `iostream` class). The `istream` class provides the functionality of `scanf` and `fscanf`, while the `ostream` class has capabilities similar to those of `printf` and `fprintf`. Like the predefined C streams `stdin`, `stdout`, and `stderr`, the `iostream` library includes four predefined streams:

- `cin`, an input stream connected to the standard input (analogous to `stdin` in C)
- `cout`, an output stream connected to the standard output (analogous to `stdout` in C)
- `cerr`, an output stream set up to provide unbuffered output to the standard error device (analogous to `stderr` in C)
- `clog`, a fully buffered stream like `cin` and `cout` (similar to `cerr`)

Later you'll see how to assign other streams to these identifiers so that you can redirect I/O to a different file or device.

Using *iostream*

To use the `iostream` library, your C++ program must include the IOSTREAM.H header file. This file contains the definitions of the classes that implement the stream objects and provide the buffering. The iostream.h file is analogous to stdio.h in ANSI C.

Instead of defining member functions that perform I/O, the `iostream` library provides an operator notation for input and output. It uses C++'s capability of overloading operators and defines << and >> as the output and input operators, respectively. Figure 8.1 illustrates how these operators work with the `cin` and `cout` streams.

When you see the << and >> operators in use, you realize their appropriateness. For example, consider the following program, which prints some variables to the `cout` stream (usually connected to standard output):

```
#include <iostream.h>

void main()
{
    int    count = 2;
    double result = 5.4;
    char   *id = "Trying out iostream: ";

    cout << id;
    cout << "count = " << count << '\n';
    cout << "result = " << result << '\n';
}
```

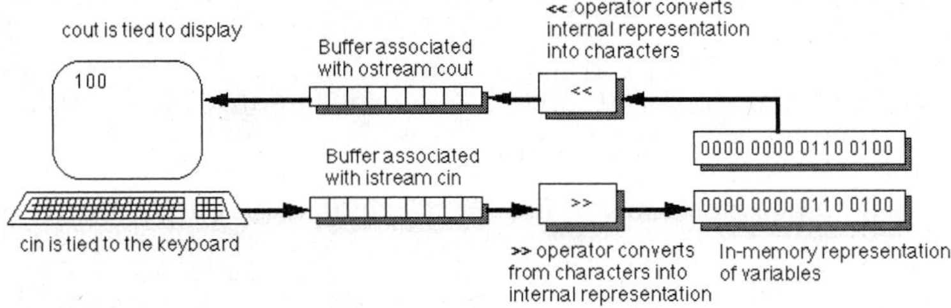

Figure 8.1. Buffered I/O with streams `cin` and `cout`.

When you run this program, it prints the following:

```
Trying out iostream: count = 2
result = 5.4
```

You can make three observations from this example:

- The << operator is a good choice to represent the output operation because it points in the direction of data movement. In this case, data movement is toward the `cout` stream.
- You can concatenate multiple << operators in a single line, all feeding the same stream.
- You can use the same syntax to print all the basic data types on a stream. The << operator automatically converts the internal representation of the variable into a textual representation. Contrast this with the need to use different format strings for printing different data types using `printf`.

Accepting input from the standard input is an easy process as well. Here's a small sample that combines both input and output:

```
#include <iostream.h>

void main()
{
    int   count;
    float price;
    char  *prompt =
          "Enter count (int) and unit price (float): ";

// Display the prompt string and flush
// to force it to be displayed
    cout << prompt << flush;

// Read from standard input
    cin >> count >> price;

// Display total cost
    cout << count << " at " << price << " will cost: ";
    cout << (price * count) << endl;
}
```

When you run the program and enter the input, the program interacts as follows:

```
Enter count (int) and unit price (float): 5 2.5
5 at 2.5 will cost: 12.5
```

Ignoring, for the moment, items that you do not recognize, notice how easy it is to read values into variables from the `cin` stream—simply send the data from `cin` to the variables using the >> operator. Just as with the << operator, you can concatenate multiple >> operators. The >> operator automatically converts the strings into the internal representations of the variables according to their types. The simple syntax of input from `cin` is in sharp contrast with ANSI C's rather complicated `scanf` function, which serves the same purpose but needs proper format strings and addresses of variables as arguments.

Using Manipulators

Among the new items in the last example, you may have noticed the identifiers `flush` (in the first `cout` statement) and `endl` (in the last `cout` statement). These are special functions known as *manipulators*. Manipulators are written so that you can alter the state of the stream by placing a manipulator in the chain of << operators. The `flush` manipulator forces cout to display its output without waiting for its buffer to fill up—the buffer is flushed. The endl manipulator sends a newline to the stream and also flushes the buffer. Table 8.1 summarizes some of the manipulators available in the iostream package. (The manipulators that take arguments are declared in the file IOMANIP.H; the rest are in IOSTREAM.H.)

Table 8.1. C++ iostream manipulators.

Manipulator	Sample Usage	Effect
dec	cout << dec << intvar; cin >> dec >> intvar;	Converts integers into decimal digits. Similar to the %d format in C.
hex	cout << hex << intvar; cin >> hex >> intvar;	Hexadecimal conversion, as in ANSI C's %x format.
oct	cout << oct << intvar; cin >> oct >> intvar;	Octal conversion (%o format in C).
ws	cin >> ws;	Discards white space characters in the input stream.
endl	cout << endl;	Sends a newline to ostream and flushes the buffer.
ends	cout << ends;	Inserts a null character into a string.
flush	cout << flush;	Flushes ostream's buffer.
resetiosflags(long)	cout << resetiosflags(ios::dec); cin >> resetiosflags(ios::hex);	Resets the format bits specified by the long integer argument.

Manipulator	Sample Usage	Effect
`setbase(int)`	`cout << setbase(10);` `cin >> setbase(8);`	Sets the base of conversion to the integer argument (must be 0, 8, 10, or 16). Zero sets the base to the default.
`setfill(int)`	`cout << setfill('.');` `cin >> setfill(' ');`	Sets the fill character used to pad fields to the specified width.

`setiosflags(long)`	`cout << setiosflags`
	`(ios::dec);`
	`cin >> setiosflags`
	`(ios::hex);`
		Sets the format bits specified by the long integer argument.

`setprecision(int)`	`cout << setprecision(6);` `cin >> setprecision(15);`	Sets the precision of floating-point conversions to the specified number of digits.

`setw(int)`	`cout << setw(6)`
	`<< var;`
	`cin >> setw(24)`
	`>> buf;`
		Sets the width of a field to the specified number of characters.

Using Manipulators for Formatted I/O

You can use manipulators for some simple formatted I/O. *Formatting* refers to the process of converting to and from the internal binary representation of a variable and its character string representation. For example, if a 16-bit integer variable holds the bit pattern `0000 0000 0110 0100`, its character string representation is `100` in the decimal number system and `64` in hexadecimal. If the base of conversion is octal, the representation is `144`. You can display all three forms on separate lines using the following output statements:

```
#include <iostream.h>

int i = 100;  // Integer initialized to 100 (decimal)

cout << dec << i << endl;  // Displays 100
cout << hex << i << endl;  // Displays 64
cout << oct << i << endl;  // Displays 144
```

This produces the output:

```
100
64
144
```

You may want to use a fixed field width of six characters to display each value. You can do this by using the `setw` manipulator as follows:

```
    #include <iostream.h>
    #include <iomanip.h>

    int i = 100;  // Integer initialized to 100 (decimal)

// Set field widths to 6
    cout << setw(6) << dec << i << endl;
    cout << setw(6) << hex << i << endl;
    cout << setw(6) << oct << i << endl;
```

This changes the output to:

```
   100
    64
   144
```

Here, each variable is displayed in a six-character field aligned to the right and padded with blanks to the left. You can change both the padding and the alignment. To change the padding character, use the `setfill` manipulator. For example, just before the `cout` statements shown above, insert the following line:

```
cout << setfill('.');
```

With that line in place, the output changes to:

```
...100
....64
...144
```

The spaces to the left are now padded with dots, the fill characters specified by the previous call to the `setfill` manipulator. One use for this feature is to prefix numeric dollar values with asterisks when printing checks. The default alignment of fixed-width output fields pads on the left, resulting in right-justified output. The justification information is stored in a bit pattern called *format bits* in a class named `ios`, which forms the basis of all stream classes (see discussion of stream classes and Figure 8.2 later in this chapter). You can set or reset specific bits with the `setiosflags` and `resetiosflags` manipulators, respectively. Here is a sample of how these manipulators work:

```
    #include <iostream.h>
    #include <iomanip.h>

    int i = 100;  // Integer initialized to 100 (decimal)

    cout << setfill('.');

// Left-justified labels followed by right-justified values...

    cout << setiosflags(ios::left);
    cout << setw(20) << "Decimal";
    cout << resetiosflags(ios::left);
    cout << setw(6) << dec << i << endl;

    cout << setiosflags(ios::left);
    cout << setw(20) << "Hexadecimal";
    cout << resetiosflags(ios::left);
    cout << setw(6) << hex << i << endl;

    cout << setiosflags(ios::left);
    cout << setw(20) << "Octal";
    cout << resetiosflags(ios::left);
    cout << setw(6) << oct << i << endl;
```

This example generates the following output:

```
Decimal.................100
Hexadecimal..............64
Octal...................144
```

This output illustrates how the `setiosflags` and `resetiosflags` manipulators work and how they should be used. All you need to know are the names of the enumerated list of formatting flags so you can use them as arguments to the `setiosflags` and `resetiosflags` manipulators. Table 8.2 lists the format bit flags and their meanings.

To use any of the format flags shown in Table 8.2, insert the manipulator `setiosflags` with the name of the flag as the argument. Use `resetiosflags` with the same argument to revert to the format state prior to your using the `setiosflags` manipulator.

Table 8.2. Names of format flags in `iostream`.

Name of Flag	Meaning When Flag is Set
`ios::skipws`	Skips white space on input
`ios::left`	Left-justifies output within the specified width of the field
`ios::right`	Right-justifies output
`ios::scientific`	Uses scientific notation for floating-point numbers (such as –1.23e+02)
`ios::fixed`	Uses decimal notation for floating-point numbers (such as –123.45)
`ios::dec`	Uses decimal notation for integers
`ios::hex`	Uses hexadecimal notation for integers
`ios::oct`	Uses octal notation for integers
`ios::uppercase`	Uses uppercase letters in output (such as F4 in hexadecimal, 1.23E+02)
`ios::showbase`	Indicates the base of the number system in the output (a `0x` prefix for hexadecimal and a `0` prefix for octal)
`ios::showpoint`	Includes a decimal point for floating-point output (for example, –123)
`ios::showpos`	Shows a positive sign when displaying positive values

> **Scope Resolution Operator (::)**
>
> The `ios::left` notation uses the scope resolution operator `::` to identify `left` as a member of the `ios` class. The names of the format flags are specified with an `ios::` prefix because they are defined in the `ios` class.

Controlling the Floating-Point Formats

You can control the floating-point format with the `setprecision` manipulator and three flags: `scientific`, `fixed`, and `showpoint`. To illustrate how these affect floating-point formatting, consider the following code, which displays a floating-point value:

```
    cout << "123.4567 in default format = ";
    cout << 123.4567 << endl;

    cout << "123.4567 in 2-digit precision = ";
    cout << setprecision(2) << 123.4567 << endl;

// Set the precision back to 6
    cout << setprecision(6);
    cout << "123.4567 in scientific notation = ";
    cout << setiosflags(ios::scientific) << 123.4567 << endl;
```

This code displays:

```
123.4567 in default format = 123.457
123.4567 in 2-digit precision = 1.2e+002
123.4567 in scientific notation = 1.234567e+002
```

The first line displays the value in the fixed format that is the default. The next line sets the precision to 2—which means you want no more than two digits after the decimal point. The floating-point number is rounded and printed. The last line shows the same number in the scientific notation. If you set the `ios::uppercase` flag, the `e` in the exponent appears in uppercase.

Overloading <<

If you define a class for complex numbers and want to use the << operator to display the objects of your class, you want code that looks like this:

```
    complex z(1.1, 1.2);
// ...
    cout << z;
```

You can do this easily by overloading the << operator. To redefine this operator, you must define the function `operator<<` for your class. Because the << operator is used with an `ostream` object on the left and a complex class object on the right, the prototype for the `operator<<` function is

```
ostream& operator<<(ostream& s, const complex& x);
```

where the arguments are passed by reference for efficiency and the `const` prefix in the second argument directs the operator not to alter the complex number. As you learn more about references, you'll see that the `operator<<` function must return a reference to the stream—this is the key to concatenating the << operators. To illustrate an actual overloading of the << operator, the following sample program uses an abbreviated definition of a complex class and follows the steps necessary to define and use the << operator:

```
#include <iostream.h>

class complex            // a simple class for complex numbers
{
    float real, imag;
public:
    complex() { real = imag = 0.0;}
    complex(float a, float b) { real = a; imag = b;}
    void print(ostream& s) const;
};

// Need this function so that operator<< can do its job
// by calling this one
void complex::print(ostream& s) const
{
    s << real << " + " << imag;
}

// Overload the operator << for use with complex class

ostream& operator<<(ostream &s, const complex& z)
{
    z.print(s);
    return s;
}
```

```
// Test the overloaded << operator...

void main()
{
    complex a(1.5, 2.1);
    cout << " a = " << a << endl;
}
```

When compiled, linked, and run, this program produces the following expected output:

```
a = 1.5 + 2.1
```

Note the following key points:

1. Define a member function that prints the class members the way you want.
2. Define the `operator<<` function with a reference to an `ostream` and a reference to your class as its first and second arguments, respectively. The function's return type should be `ostream&`. In the body of the function, call your class member function to print and to return the first argument, which happens to be the reference to the stream.

Now you can use the << operator to print objects of your class on a stream.

The *iostream* Class Hierarchy

Now that you know how to use the `iostream` library for simple I/O, take a look at Figure 8.2. This figure graphically illustrates the hierarchy of classes in a typical implementation of the `iostream` library.

As shown in the figure, the `streambuf` class provides the buffer used by the streams. All the stream classes are derived from the `ios` base class, which stores the state of the stream and handles errors. The `ios` class has an associated `streambuf` object that acts as the buffer for the stream. The `istream` and `ostream` classes, derived from `ios`, are intended for input and output, respectively. The `iostream` class uses multiple inheritance to acquire the capabilities of both `istream` and `ostream` classes and therefore, supports both input and output. The `istream_withassign`, `ostream_withassign`, and `iostream_withassign` classes are derived from `istream`, `ostream`, and `iostream`, respectively, by adding the definition of the assignment operator (=) so that you can redirect I/O by assigning one stream to another. The predefined streams `cout`, `cerr`, and `clog` are of `ostream_withassign` class, whereas `cin` is an instance of `istream_withassign` class.

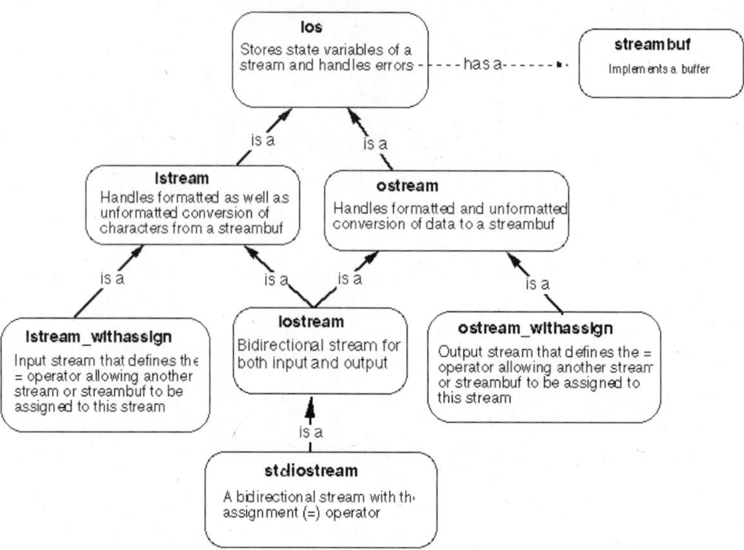

Figure 8.2. Classes in the C++ `iostream` library.

The *iostream* Classes and Multiple Inheritance

The classes declared in iostream.h use inheritance to organize the classes in the library. The `iostream` classes illustrate an interesting consequence of multiple inheritance. In C++, an instance of a derived class contains a copy of all members of its base class. Thus, a class like `iostream` that inherits from both `istream` and `ostream`, each with the same base class (`ios`), can end up with two copies of the members of `ios`. With C++, you avoid this by declaring `istream` and `ostream` with `ios` as a virtual base class, as follows:

```
class istream : virtual public ios { /* ... */ };

class ostream : virtual public ios { /* ... */ };
```

You can find further details of virtual base classes in Chapter 11, "Using Inheritance in C++," and Chapter 12, "Virtual Functions and Polymorphism."

File I/O

In ANSI C, file I/O is handled by functions such as `fopen` to open a file, `fscanf` to read from it, `fprintf` to write to it, and `fclose` to close it. In the `iostream` package, the classes intended for file I/O are defined in the FSTREAM.H header file. Thus, for file I/O, you must use:

```
#include <fstream.h>
```

There are three classes of interest in FSTREAM.H:

- The `ifstream` class, which supports input
- The `ofstream` class, which supports output
- The `fstream` class, which supports both

The following sections explain how to use the file I/O facilities in FSTREAM.H.

Simple File I/O

The easiest way to open a file for I/O is to create an instance of the `ifstream` or `ofstream` class, as follows:

```
#include <fstream.h>     // Defines classes ifstream and ofstream

// Open file named "infile" for input operations only and
// connect it to the istream "ins"
ifstream ins("infile");

// Open file named "outfile" for output operations only and
// connect it to the ostream "outs"
ofstream outs("outfile");

//...
```

As you can see, you can open a file and connect it to a stream when you create the stream. Two distinct streams exist for input and output: `ifstream` for input and `ofstream` for output. The ANSI C equivalent of connecting a file to an `ifstream` is to call `fopen` with the `r` mode; using `ofstream` with a file is similar to calling `fopen` with the `w` mode.

Before using the stream connected to a file, you should check whether the stream was successfully created. The logical NOT operator `!` is overloaded for the stream classes so that you can check a stream using a test such as this:

```
// Open stream
   ifstream ins("infile");

// Check if stream has been opened successfully...
   if(!ins)
    {
        cerr << "Cannot open: infile\n";
        exit(1);
    }
```

You need not attach an `ifstream` or `ofstream` to any file at the time of its creation. If you wish, you can create the stream first and then open the file later using the `open` member function of the stream, like this:

```
    ifstream ins;
//...
    ins.open("infile");
// Check if file opened successfully...
    if(!ins)  // Open failed...
//...
```

You can disconnect the file from the stream by closing it. To do this, call the stream's `close` member function:

```
// Close file
    ins.close();
```

This does not destroy the stream. You can reconnect it to another file by calling `open` again.

Controlling the Stream-Operating Modes

When you open a stream by supplying the name of a file to the stream's constructor, you're taking advantage of C++'s allowance for default argument values. When you call

```
ifstream ins("infile");
```

the constructor invoked is declared as follows:

```
ifstream(const char *, int = ios::in, int = filebuf::openprot);
```

The last two integer-valued arguments are used with the default values. The second argument to the constructor indicates the mode in which the stream operates. For `ifstream`, the default is `ios::in`, which means the file is open for reading. For an ofstream object, the default mode is ios::out, meaning that the file is open for writing.

What if you want to open a file for output, but you want to append data to an existing file instead of destroying its current contents? You can do this by specifying an operating mode of ios::app. Like the format flags shown in Table 8.2, the stream-operating modes also are defined in the ios class—hence, the ios:: prefix for the names. Table 8.3 summarizes these modes.

Table 8.3. Stream-operating modes.

Mode Name	Operation
ios::app	Appends data to the file
ios::ate	When first opened, positions the file at the end of the file (ate stands for "at end")
ios::in	Opens the file for reading
ios::nocreate	Fails to open the file if it does not already exist
ios::noreplace	If the file exists, open for output fails unless ios::app or ios::ate is set
ios::out	Opens the file for writing
ios::trunc	Truncates the file if it already exists

Notice that you can specify more than one mode for a file simply by using a bitwise OR of the required modes. For example, to open a file for output and to position it at the end, use the ios::out and ios::ate modes, as follows:

```
ofstream outs("outfile", ios::out | ios::ate);
```

Copying Files

As an example of file I/O in C++, consider a utility program that copies the contents of one file to another. Assume that the utility is named filecopy and that when you type the command

```
filecopy in.fil out.fil
```

filecopy copies the contents of the file named in.fil to a second file named out.fil. Implementing such a program is straightforward: open the two files (one for input, another one for output), read characters from the input file, and write them to the output file. Listing 8.1 shows a sample implementation of the `filecopy` utility program.

Listing 8.1. FILECOPY.CPP. A utility program that copies the contents of one file to another.

```
//-----------------------------------------------------------------
// FILE:  filecopy.cpp
// Copies contents of one file to another
//-----------------------------------------------------------------

#include <stdlib.h>
#include <fstream.h>

void main(int argc, char **argv)
{
// Check if there are enough arguments
    if(argc < 3)
    {
        cerr << "Usage: filecopy infile outfile\n";
        exit(0);
    }

// Open the input file and connect it to stream "ins"
    ifstream ins(argv[1]);
    if(!ins)
    {
        cerr << "Cannot open: " << argv[1];
        exit(1);
    }

// Open the output file and connect it to stream "outs"
    ofstream outs(argv[2]);
    if(!outs)
    {
        cerr << "Cannot open: " << argv[2];
        exit(1);
    }
```

```
// Read from "ins" and write to "outs"
    char c;
    while(ins.get(c) && outs) outs.put(c);
}
```

Another way to implement the last `while` loop, which does the actual copying between the files, is to read and write one line at a time. To read a line, use the same `get` function but with the address of a buffer and the buffer's size as arguments:

```
const bufsize = 128;
char buf[bufsize];
//...
ins.get(buf, bufsize);
```

This call to `get` extracts up to `bufsize-1` characters (or extracts until a newline character is encountered) from the input stream to the specified buffer. Then `get` places a terminating null character in the buffer. By default, the `get` function stops at the newline character, but you can specify another delimiter as a third argument to the `get` function. Notice that this call to `get` is similar to the `fgets` function in C except that, unlike `fgets`, `get` does not copy the newline character to the buffer, nor does `get` skip over the newline character. Therefore, to read lines repeatedly from a file, you must extract the newline separately after each line is read. Here's an example that does this:

```
#include <string.h>     // For prototype of "strlen"
#include <fstream.h>
//...
// Assume that streams "ins" and "outs" are already set up
// as shown in Listing 8.1

// Read lines from "ins" and write to "outs"

    const bufsize = 256;
    char buf[bufsize];
    char c;

    while(ins.get(buf, bufsize) && outs)
    {
// Write out buffer using the "write" function
        outs.write(buf, strlen(buf));
```

```
// Read leftover newline character and write that out also
        ins.get(c);
        outs.put(c);
    }
```

You can use this as the replacement for the last `while` loop of Listing 8.1. The actual writing of the buffer to the output file is done by the `write` function of the output stream. As shown in the listing, this function simply copies the specified number of characters from the buffer to the output stream.

Positioning in a File

Often you must read files containing binary data with a specific internal structure. For example, a 128-byte header might be followed by blocks of data. Information extracted from the header file might tell you that the data you need is at a specific location inside the file. To read this data, you must position the stream properly before reading from it. In ANSI C, you can use functions such as `fseek` and `ftell` to position streams. With the `iostream` library, you also can reposition streams. As expected, classes provide member functions that accomplish this.

You can position a stream in the `iostream` library by calling the `seekg` or `seekp` member functions of that stream. Because the same stream can be used for both input and output, stream classes work with the concept of a *get* position and a *put* position which, respectively, indicate the location from which the next read or write occurs. Set the *get* position using `seekg`; set the *put* position using `seekp`. For example, to position the stream at the 513th byte in the `ins` input stream, you can use `setg` as follows:

```
ins.seekg(512);     // next get will start at 513th byte
```

Specifying the Position: Relative Reference

You also can specify the position relative to some reference point such as the end of the file. For example, to move eight bytes backward from the end of the stream, use:

```
ins.seekg(-8, ios::end);
```

There are three reference points identified by constants defined in the `ios` class:

- `ios::beg`, representing the beginning of the stream
- `ios::end`, representing the end of the stream
- `ios::cur`, representing the current position

Getting the Current Position

You also can retrieve the current get or put position in a file. The tellg function returns the current location in an input stream, whereas the tellp function returns the corresponding item for an output stream. Both functions return a variable of the streampos type. You can save the returned value and use it with seekg or seekp to return to the old location in a file:

```
    streampos saved_pos = tellg();
// Other operations on stream...
// ...
// Get back to old location
    seekg(saved_pos);
```

Detecting Errors in File I/O

The iostream library provides several functions for checking the status of a stream. The fail function tells you if something has gone wrong. Therefore, you can check for problems by calling fail for the stream, as follows:

```
    ifstream ins("infile");
    if(ins.fail())
    {
// Stream creation has failed. Take appropriate action.
// ...
    }
```

In fact, the logical NOT operator ! has been overloaded to call fail for a stream, so the if test can be written more simply as:

```
    if(!ins)
    {
// Handle error...
    }
```

Detecting the End of the File

When reading from or writing to a file, you'll want to know if the program has reached the end of the file. The eof function returns a nonzero value if the stream is at the end of the file. Once a stream has reached the end of the file, it does not perform any I/O—this is the case even if you attempt an I/O after moving the stream away from the end by using seekg or seekp—because the stream's internal state remembers the encounter with the end of the file. You have to call clear to reset the state before any further I/O can take place. Thus, eof and clear sometimes are used as follows:

```
// "ins" is an istream. If the stream reached eof, clear the
// state before attempting to read from the stream
    if(ins.eof()) ins.clear();
// Reposition stream and read again...
    ins.seekg(-16, ios::cur); // Move back 16 bytes
    ins.get(buf, 8);          // Read 8 bytes into buffer
```

Using the *good* and *bad* Functions

Two other member functions, good and bad, indicate the general condition of a stream. As the names imply, good returns true (a nonzero value) if no error has occurred in the stream, whereas bad returns true if an invalid I/O has been attempted or if the stream has an irrecoverable failure. You can use good and bad in tests such as:

```
    if(ins.bad())
    {
// Invalid operation...
    }

    if(ins.good())
    {
// Everything ok. Continue using stream...
    }
```

String I/O

When your application uses a windowing system for I/O, you cannot readily use the cin and cout streams for I/O. With most windowing systems, you display a *string* (a null-terminated array of characters) in a window by calling a designated function from the windowing system's library. This is easy to do with plain strings, but how do you display the value of a variable?

What you need is a way to send the formatted output to a string that you then can display by using the windowing system's text output functions. In ANSI C, you can use the sprintf function to prepare a formatted string. Similarly, you can use sscanf to extract variables from a string. The C++ iostream package also includes these capabilities in the form of the istrstream and ostrstream classes for reading from and writing to a string, respectively. These classes are declared in the STRSTREA.H file.

Deviation from AT&T C++

In UNIX systems and in AT&T C++, the STRSTREA.H header file is named STRSTREAM.H. Because MS-DOS permits only eight characters to be used in a filename, this header file is named STRSTREA.H in Microsoft Visual C++.

Writing to a String

String I/O commonly is used to prepare formatted output to a string. You need an instance of an `ostrstream` class for this purpose. Typically, you have a buffer of fixed size in which to place the formatted output. To set up an `ostrstream` object connected to such a buffer, you can use the following code:

```
#include <strstrea.h>  // Defines the ostrstream class
// ...
    const buflen = 128;
    char buf[buflen];

// Set up an ostrstream connected to this buffer
    ostrstream s(buf, sizeof(buf));
```

This sets up an output stream connected to a buffer and assumes a stream operating mode of `ios::out`. As with file I/O, you can specify another mode, such as `ios::app`, to append data to an existing string. Sending output to this stream is as easy as writing to `cout`. Here's an example:

```
#include <strstrea.h>

void main()
{
    const buflen = 128;
    char buf[buflen];
    int   i = 100;
    float x = 3.1415;
// Open an output stream and connect to the buffer
    ostrstream s(buf, buflen);

// Write to the stream
    s << "i = " << i << " x = " << x << ends;
```

```
// Display the string on cout
    cout << buf << endl;
}
```

The program displays the following:

```
i = 100 x = 3.1415
```

Although here the program simply displays the buffer by sending it to cout, in practice you prepare the output in a buffer because you need it for use by a function that cannot handle formatting.

Reading from a String

String I/O also can be used to convert characters from a string to internal representation of variables. The istrstream class is designed for reading from buffers. For example, if a string holds an integer and a floating-point number, you can extract the variables using the >> operator just as you would from cin. The following program illustrates the use of an istrstream class:

```
#include <strstrea.h>

void main()
{
    const buflen = 128;
    char  buf[buflen] = "120    6.432";  // A sample buffer
    int   i;
    float x;

// Open an input stream and connect to the buffer
    istrstream s(buf, buflen);

// Read from the stream
    s >> i >> x;

// Display the result on cout
    cout << "i = " << i << " x = " << x << endl;
}
```

This program displays:

```
i = 120 x = 6.432
```

This type of conversion from a string to variables is necessary when reading data from a text file to your program.

Summary

Although you can continue to use the ANSI C I/O routines (the `printf` and `scanf` family) in C++ programs, there is a better alternative. The `iostream` I/O library included in Microsoft Visual C++ provides a cleaner, object-based mechanism for I/O. Like ANSI C's `stdin`, `stdout`, and `stderr`, the `iostream` package includes the predefined streams `cin`, `cout`, `cerr`, and `clog`, a buffered version of `cerr`.

The stream classes use a simple syntax for I/O: the << and >> operators are used for output and input, respectively. The `iostream` library includes built-in support for I/O operations involving basic data types such as `int`, `char`, `float`, and `double`. Additionally, you can overload the << and >> operators to handle I/O for your own classes. This enables you to use a consistent style for all I/O in your program.

The `iostream` package supports opening and closing files and performing I/O operations with files. The classes declared in FSTREAM.H implement file I/O capabilities similar to those provided by the C functions `fopen`, `fclose`, `fscanf`, and `fprintf`. Additionally, the I/O package includes several classes, declared in the STRSTREAM.H header file, which can read from and write to arrays of characters just like C's `sscanf` and `sprintf`.

Using the `iostream` classes is easy provided you know what classes are available and how to call their public member functions. Although you can learn some of this by browsing through the header files, to make proper use of the member functions, you need the documentation for the class. This chapter provides a reasonable amount of information about the `iostream` classes so you can begin using them for I/O in your C++ programs.

Apart from the I/O capabilities, the `iostream` package also is a good example of how C++'s support for OOP can be exploited in a class library. The classes in the library make extensive use of inheritance, including multiple inheritance and the virtual base class mechanism. Chapter 12 covers the details of these C++ language features.

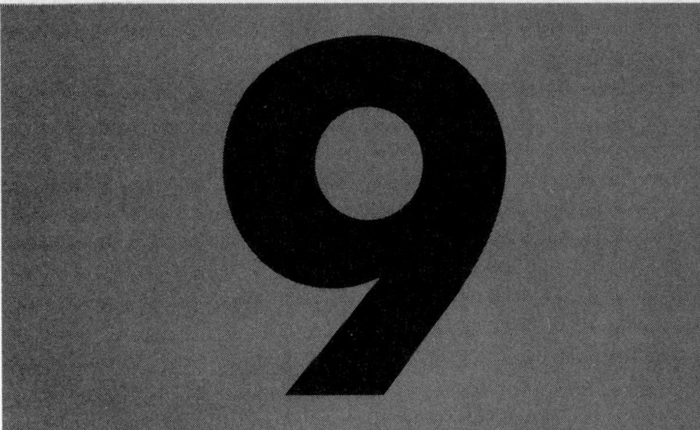

Building Objects with Classes

Beginning with this chapter, you learn the details of C++'s syntax and see how its constructs support OOP. Instead of going through a litany of seemingly unrelated features, Chapters 9 through 12 explain the syntax of most C++ features in light of some well-defined needs that arise when you use object-oriented techniques in your programs. Short examples illustrate the need for a feature and show how a particular construct fulfills that need. This chapter focuses on the `class` and `struct` constructs that enable you to define new types of objects. It also provides general guidelines for implementing and using classes.

Classes as Objects

Before you manipulate objects, you need a way to create them. Defining an object involves describing a new data type and the functions that can manipulate that data type. How do you represent a new data type? You must declare the new data type in terms of some existing type.

For instance, you can express a point in a two-dimensional plane with an x,y coordinate pair. If each coordinate is represented by an integer type, such as `int`, you can declare a point as a structure:

```
struct Point           // Declare a Point structure
{
    int x, y;
};

struct Point ul, lr;  // Define two Points
```

These are facilities already existing in C. If you prefer calling the new type `Point` (without the `struct` prefix), you can do so with the `typedef` facility:

```
typedef struct Point  // Declare a Point type
{
    int x, y;
} Point;

Point ul, lr;          // Define two Points
```

With this code segment, you can use `Point` as the name of a type, but this is not really a new data type. For example, you might want to define the addition operator (+) for `Point`. This is not possible with C's `struct`, because C enables you to group data items into a single entity but does not provide any way to declare the functions and operators inside the structure. The result is an incomplete data type with poorly-defined operations. Of course, you can write functions that manipulate `Point` structures, but you don't receive any support from the compiler to help associate these functions more closely with `Point` structures.

User-Defined Data Types

To support the definition of a full-fledged data type, C++ only needed to extend the syntax of `struct` by enabling you to include functions and operators as members of a `struct`. C++ also made the *structure tag* or *name*—the symbol following `struct`—a stand-alone name, meaning that you can use that name without the `struct` prefix. With these extensions to C's `struct`, C++ enables you to declare and use a `Point` type as follows:

```
struct Point     // Declare a Point type
{
    int x, y;
```

```
// Define operations on Point
    void operator+(const Point& p) const
    {
        return Point(x+p.x, y+p.y);
    }
//...
};

Point ul, lr;   // Define two Points
```

For now, ignore the definition of the {+} operator; it's covered in Chapter 10, "Defining Operations on Objects." Notice that you can place function definitions inside a `struct` and that the name of a `struct` serves as a data type.

As an example of another user-defined type, suppose you want to create a `String` data type that provides the functionality of C's null-terminated strings but uses an object-oriented approach. What you essentially want is a pointer to an array of characters and the ability to store C-style null-terminated strings in that array. Because the length of the string is needed often, you decide to store it as a member variable as well. Lastly, suppose you plan to use the strings to store lines of text that are being edited. Because the number of characters in each line can fluctuate as characters are added or removed, you decide to allocate a slightly larger array than necessary. To manage the string's storage properly, you also need to store the size of the allocated array. Allowing, for the moment, a lone function that returns the length of the string, you end up with this preliminary definition of `String`:

```
#include <stddef.h>   // For size_t type

struct String
{
    size_t length(void);
// Other member functions...

    char   *p_c;      // pointer to allocated space
    size_t _length;   // current length of string
    size_t _maxlen;   // number of bytes allocated
};
```

This appears clean enough, but a problem exists. By default, all members of the structure are accessible to any function that wants to use them. You don't want this because that goes against one of the basic principles of data abstraction, which advocates that you should define an abstract data type (a user-defined type) but hide the internal details of the new type. In particular, for String objects, you want to hide details, such as the way you decide to implement the string's internal storage. If programs come to rely on these details, you cannot change the implementation in the future—even if a change clearly makes manipulation of the String type more efficient.

Access Control for Class Members

For complete support of data abstraction, you need control over who can access what in a structure. C++ introduces a new keyword, class, which you can use exactly like struct. Unlike members of a struct, however, the members of a class are not accessible to outside functions. In other words, a struct is wide open, but a class is totally hidden.

Because neither of these is a good solution, C++ adds three new keywords to help specify access: private, public, and protected. You can explicitly mark sections of a class or a struct as private, public, and protected, as follows:

```
#include <stddef.h>    // For size_t type

class String           // Declare the String class
{
public:
    size_t length(void);
// Other publicly accessible member functions...

protected:
// Members accessible to derived classes only
// ...

private:
// Members accessible to other members of this class

    char   *p_c;     // pointer to allocated space
    size_t _length;  // current length of string
    size_t _maxlen;  // number of bytes allocated
};
```

The public section lists the members that are accessible to any function in the program. Only member functions of the class can access the private section. You'll learn why the protected section is needed when you read about inheritance in Chapter 11,

"Using Inheritance in C++." For now, remember that the members in the `protected` section of a class are accessible to classes derived from that class. Figure 9.1 illustrates how the access-control keywords work.

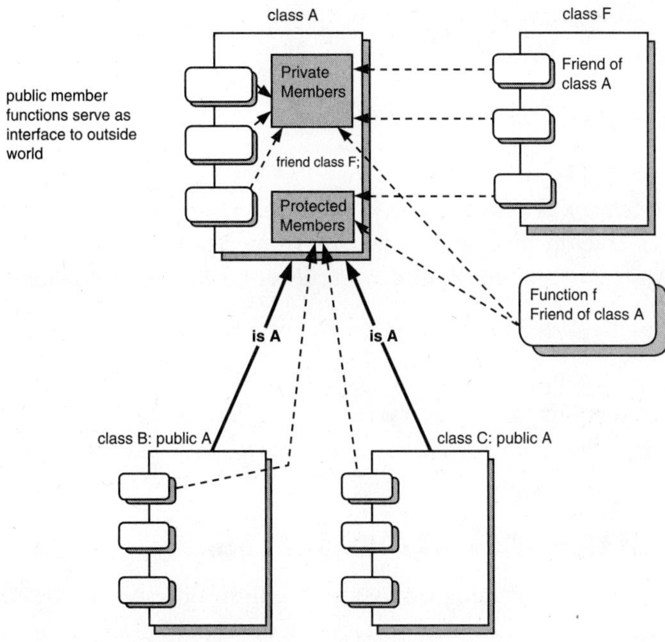

Figure 9.1. Access control in C++ classes.

Notice that you can include multiple `public`, `private`, and `protected` sections in a class. Each section label determines the access level of the members listed between that label and the next label, or between that label and the closing right brace (`}`) that marks the end of the class declaration. If you don't provide a label at the very beginning of a class, the compiler considers all members up to the next access control label as `private`. On the other hand, everything before the first access specifier is `public` in a `struct`.

How *public* Functions Can Return *private* Values

The `private` section of a class usually declares all the member functions that can be invoked from anywhere in the program. You can think of these functions as the interface to the outside world. If you need to provide the value of a `private` variable to the outside world, you can write a public member function that returns the value. A good example is the length member function of the rudimentary String class. The private variable _length holds the current length of the string. If you're working with a struct-based implementation of String without the private keyword, you might be tempted to access the length this way:

```
    String this_line;
//...
    if(this_line._length > 0)  // this refers to length of string
// ...
```

However, the principle of information hiding, enforced by the private keyword, prevents this. You can solve this problem by writing a length function that returns _length. In this case, any function can refer to the length of a string, as follows:

```
if(this_line.length() > 0)  // this refers to length of string
```

This simple example illustrates what you encounter in all class-based designs: public member functions provide access to private variables of the class. This insulates the users of the class from any changes to the class's internal variables.

Member Functions

Member functions are designed to implement the operations allowed on the data type represented by a class. To declare a member function, place its prototype in the body of the class or struct. You don't need to define the function inside the class; the definition can be outside the class or even in a separate file.

Inline Member Functions

Defining a function inside the body of a class produces a special consequence. Such definitions are considered *inline*, and the entire body of an inline function is repeated whenever that function is called. Thus, if you have an inline function in a class and if you call that function often, you can use a large amount of memory for the program. The advantage of inline functions is that you avoid the overhead of a function call when executing the body of the function.

The previous argument implies that you should make a function inline only if the overhead of calling the function is a large percentage of the time needed to execute the body of the function. When you include a simple function, such as length, in the String class, you can safely define the entire function inside the body of the class by making it inline, as follows:

```
class String
{
public:
    size_t length(void) { return _length; }
// ...

private:
// ...
    size_t _length;
};
```

You need not define a function inside a class to make it inline. C++ provides the `inline` keyword which, when placed before a function's definition, makes that function inline. Notice, however, that you can use an inline function only in the file in which it is defined. This is because the compiler needs the entire definition of an inline function so that it can insert the body of the function wherever the function is called. Therefore, you should place the definitions of inline functions in the same header file that declares a class in order to ensure that every program that uses the class also can use its inline functions.

Inline Functions and Preprocessor Macros

Inline functions are like preprocessor macros without the pitfalls. For example, the macro

```
#define  square(x)  x*x
```

provides the wrong answer when used to evaluate an expression such as `square(a+b)` because you didn't use parentheses around the macro's argument. However, if you define `square` as an inline function, like this:

```
inline double square(x) { return x*x; }
```

you can safely use `square(a+b)` to evaluate the square of `a+b`, because inline functions work just like any C++ function.

Typical *public* Member Functions

The `public` member functions of a class are important because they're the outside world's gateway to a class. For a class to be useful, it must include a complete set of public member functions. A minimal set should include the following categories of functions:

- *Class Management functions* are a standard set of functions that perform chores such as creating an instance of the class (*constructor*), destroying it (*destructor*), creating an instance and initializing it by copying from another instance (*copy constructor*), assigning one instance to another (operator= function), and converting an instance to some other type (*type conversion operator*). These functions have a standard declaration syntax. You'll encounter these functions in this and the following chapter.
- *Class Implementation functions* implement the *behavior* of the data type represented by the class. They are the workhorses of the class. For a String class, these functions might include operator+ for concatenating strings, and comparison operators such as operator==, operator>, and operator<. Chapter 10, "Defining Operations on Objects," explains how such functions are defined.
- *Class Access functions* return information about the internal variables of a class. The outside world can access the object's internal state through these functions. The length function in the String class is a good example of this type of member function.
- *Class Utility Functions*, often declared to be private, are used internally within the class for miscellaneous tasks such as error handling.

const Member Functions

If a member function alters no data in the class, you should declare that member function as a const function. For instance, the length function of the String class simply returns the value of a member variable. It's definitely a const function because it doesn't change any data of the String class. You can declare it as such by appending a const to the usual function prototype, like so:

```
size_t length(void) const;
```

This informs the compiler that the length function should not alter any variable in the class. The compiler generates an error message if the definition of the length function includes any code that inadvertently assigns a value to any variable in the String class.

Implementing Classes

The difficult part of writing object-oriented programs is deciding which classes or abstract data types you need to solve your problem. Once you know the classes, their inheritance hierarchy, and their desired behavior, implementing the classes is straightforward. The following sections offer general guidelines.

Header Files Describe the Interface

When implementing a class, think of the class as a provider of some service that other classes or functions need. In other words, the class is a server that acts upon the requests of its clients. This is the idea behind the client-server architecture, and it works well when implementing classes in object-oriented programs. The clients of a class make requests by calling the member functions of that class. The *interface* to the class refers to the information that a client must have in order to use the facilities of a class. At a minimum, the client must know:

- The names of the public member functions of the class
- The prototypes of the member functions
- The purpose of each member function

Ideally, if you want to use a class, you want a textual description of the class and how its facilities are intended for use. Without this information, you might have to manage with the header file that declares the class.

The header file describes the interface to a class. In fact, it shows you everything except the functions that are defined in another file, but your program can access only those members that appear in the `public` section. Because the public interface to the class is important to its clients, you should place these declarations at the very beginning of a class. The `protected` section can follow these declarations. The `private` members can come last because these members are visible only to the member functions of that class.

Assuming that a reasonable assortment of public member functions exists, a `String` class might include a header file STR.H, as shown in Listing 9.1.

Listing 9.1. STR.H. Header file for the `String` class.

```
//---------------------------------------------------------------
//  File:  str.h
//  Declares a "String" data type
//
//  Note: Couldn't use String.h as name because we include
//        ANSI C's string.h and some systems (such as MS-DOS)
//        do not differentiate between uppercase and lowercase
//        letters in filenames
//---------------------------------------------------------------

#if !defined(__STR_H)  // Make sure the file is included only once
#define __STR_H

// Include any other required header files...
// NOTE: The header files from the ANSI C library must enclose
//       all function declarations inside a block, like this:
//            extern "C"
//            {
//              ...
//            }
//       Microsoft Visual C++ compiler's header files do this.

#include <stddef.h>     // For "size_t" type
#include <iostream.h>   // For stream I/O
#include <string.h>     // For ANSI C string library

typedef int Boolean;    // For return type of operators

class String
{
public:
// Constructors with a variety of arguments
    String();
    String(size_t len);
    String(const char *str);
    String(const String &s);

// Destructor
    ~String();

// Overloaded operators
```

```
//    Boolean operator==(const String &s) const;
//    Boolean operator<(const String &s) const;
//    Boolean operator>(const String &s) const;
//    Boolean operator<=(const String &s) const;
//    Boolean operator>=(const String &s) const;
//    Boolean operator!=(const String &s) const;

// Assignment operator
    void operator=(const String& s);

// Type conversion operator
    operator const char*() const;

// Access operator
     char& operator[](int index);
     char& char_at_pos(int index);

// The + operator concatenates strings
    friend String operator+(const String& s1, const String& s2);

// Function giving access to internal variable
    size_t length(void) const;

// Function to print a String
    void print(ostream& os) const;

private:
// Internal data members of this class

    char   *p_c;     // pointer to allocated space
    size_t _length;  // current length of string
    size_t _maxlen;  // number of bytes allocated
};

// Stream I/O operators for String class


ostream& operator<<(ostream& os, String& s);
istream& operator>>(istream& is, String& s);

//---------------------------------------------------------------
//     I N L I N E    F U N C T I O N S
//---------------------------------------------------------------
```

continues

Listing 9.1. continued

```
//  l e n g t h
//  Returns the length of the String

inline size_t String::length(void) const
{
    return _length;
}
//------------------------------------------------------------------
//  ~ S t r i n g
//  Destroys a String

inline String::~String()
{
    delete p_c;
}
//------------------------------------------------------------------
//  o p e r a t o r   c o n s t   c h a r   *
//  Converts from String to char pointer

inline String::operator const char*() const
{
    return p_c;
}
//------------------------------------------------------------------
//  o p e r a t o r = =
//  String equality operator. Returns nonzero if strings are
//  equal

inline Boolean String::operator==(const String &s) const
{
// Use ANSI C's strcmp function to compare the strings
// Remember strcmp returns 0 if the strings match, but this
//  function has to return nonzero (true) for a match
    return(strcmp(s.p_c, p_c) == 0);
}


#endif
```

Notice that the #if !defined directive is used to ensure that the header file is included only once in any file. It's also good practice to make your header file complete by including all other header files required by your class. For example, the String class uses the size_t type, which is defined in <stddef.h>. Instead of forcing users of the String class to include <stddef.h> whenever they use the class, you should include that file in the header file for the String class. This way, a user of the String class need only remember to include STR.H, the header file that defines the interface to the String class.

C++ File-Naming Convention

The file suffix or extension—the characters following the period in a filename—used for header files and other source files varies among C++ compilers. In UNIX systems, C++ source files generally use the .C extension, while C uses the .c extension. In UNIX, header files end with .h for both C and C++ languages. Under MS-DOS, this is not possible because MS-DOS does not distinguish between lowercase and uppercase letters in filenames. C++ compilers under MS-DOS, including Microsoft Visual C++, use either .CPP or .CXX as the extension for C++ files. Header files often mirror this convention and use .HPP or .HXX as extensions instead of just .H. This book uses .H for header files and .CPP for C++ source files.

Separate Implementation from the Interface

The clients of a class do not need the definition of a class's member functions—if the member functions are adequately documented. Therefore, you can place the actual definitions of the member functions in a separate file. For a class such as String, define the interface to the class in the STR.H file, while the member functions are implemented in a second file, such as STR.CPP. The general layout of STR.CPP looks like this:

```
//-------------------------------------------------------------
//  File:  str.cpp
//  Implements the member functions of the "String" class
```

```
#include "str.h"    // For declaration of String class

// Other header files, if needed...
// Header files needed by String class should be included
// in str.h

const chunk_size = 8;  // Allocation unit for Strings

//---------------------------------------------------------------
//  S t r i n g
//  Creates a String object and initializes it from a
//  from a null-terminated C string

String::String(const char *s)
{
    _length = strlen(s);
    _maxlen = chunk_size * (_length / chunk_size + 1);
    p_c = new char[_maxlen];
    strcpy(p_c, s);
}
//---------------------------------------------------------------
//  p r i n t
//  Outputs the String on a specified output stream

void String::print(ostream& os) const
{
    os << p_c;
}
//---------------------------------------------------------------
//  o p e r a t o r < <
//  Stream insertion operator for String class

ostream& operator<<(ostream& os, String& s)
{
    s.print(os);
    return os;
}
//---------------------------------------------------------------
//  Definitions of other member functions...
//  ...
//---------------------------------------------------------------
```

When defining a member function outside the body of a class, you must associate each function with the class by explicitly using the *scope resolution operator* (`::`). For the `String` class, use a `String::` prefix with each member function, as shown in the previous example. Implementation of other parts of the `String` class is covered in Chapter 10, "Defining Operations on Objects," and the STR.CPP file is shown in its entirety in Listing 11.2.

Using Classes

A well-designed C++ class should behave like one of the basic data types, such as `int`, `char`, or `double`, except that a class is likely to permit a much larger variety of operations than those allowed for the basic types. This is because the operations defined for a class include all of the class's public member functions, which can be as diverse as the class's functionality warrants. As with the basic data types (such as `int` and `float`), you must proceed through the following steps to use a class in a program:

1. Define one or more instances of the class. These are the objects of object-oriented programming. Just as you write

   ```
   double x, y, z;  // doubles named x, y, z
   ```

   to create three instances of double variables, you can create three `String` objects with

   ```
   String s1, s2, s3; // Strings named s1, s2, s3
   ```

   For a class that provides all required interface functions, you should be able to create and initialize instances in a variety of ways:

   ```
   String s1 = "String 1";
   String s2("Testing.1..2...3");
   String s3 = s1;
   ```

   In each of these cases, the compiler calls the appropriate constructor and creates the `String`.

2. Call the member functions of the objects and use the available operators to manipulate the objects. For `String` objects, you can write code such as this:

   ```
   #include "str.h"

   void main()
   {
       String title("Object-Oriented Programming in C++");
   ```

```
    cout << "title = " << title << endl;

    String first_name("Peter"), last_name("Hipson");
    String full_name = first_name + " " + last_name;

    cout << "full_name = " << full_name << endl;

    cout << "Enter some text (end with a return):";
    String response;
    cin >> response;
    cout << "You typed: " << response << endl;
}
```

If you use the full implementation of the `String` class shown in Listing 11.2, here is what you get when you run this program (user input is in boldface):

```
title = Object-Oriented Programming in C++
full_name = Peter Hipson
Enter some text (end with a return):This is a test.
You typed: This is a test.
```

Creating Objects on the Fly

You can create instances of classes in two ways:

- Define the objects just as you define `int` or `double` variables.
- Create the objects dynamically, as needed.

When you create objects through definition, the compiler can reserve storage space for the objects during compilation. To dynamically create objects, you need a way to acquire a chunk of memory for the object. In C, you can dynamically create variables or arrays by calling the functions, such as `malloc` or `calloc`, from the C library.

While you often can create objects by defining instances of classes, dynamic allocation of objects is more interesting because, with this approach, you can use as much memory as is available in a system.

Allocating Objects in the Free Store

You may have encountered the term "heap" in reference to dynamic memory allocation in C. The *heap* is the pool of memory from which standard C functions, such as `malloc` and `calloc`, parcel out memory. C++ books and manuals refer to the heap with the term *free store.* In C++, you gain the functionality of malloc and calloc by using the new operator, which allocates enough memory to hold all members of a class or struct.

In C, if you define a structure such as

```
struct Opcode
{
    char   *name;
    void   (*action)(void);
};
```

you allocate space for an instance of this structure, like this:

```
struct Opcode *p_code;
p_code = (struct Opcode *) malloc(sizeof(struct Opcode));
```

In C++, the equivalent code to create a new Opcode reduces to this:

```
Opcode *p_code;
p_code = new Opcode;
```

Apart from the cleaner syntax, the new operator also provides another advantage. If the Opcode structure contains a constructor that takes no arguments, the new operator automatically calls that constructor to initialize the newly created instance of Opcode.

In fact, you have the option of specifying other initial values for an object allocated by new. For example, you can write:

```
String *file_name = new String("cpphelp.doc");
int    *first_byte = new int(128);
```

to allocate and initialize a String and an int object. Initialize the String to cpphelp.doc, while the int is set to 128. The String is initialized by calling the String(const char*) constructor of the String class.

Destroying Objects in the Free Store

In C, when you no longer need memory that you had previously allocated in the heap, you call the free function to release the memory. In C++, the delete operator serves the same purpose. Like free, the delete operator expects a pointer to an object as its operand. Thus, if p_code is the pointer to an instance of Opcode created by the new operator, you can destroy it with the statement:

```
delete p_code;  // Frees storage pointed to by p_code
```

In addition to freeing up storage used by the object, if that object's class has a defined destructor, `delete` calls it to ensure proper cleanup.

Allocating Arrays of Objects in the Free Store

One use of `new` is to allocate an array of objects. The syntax for this is much the same as the syntax you use to define arrays. For example, you can define an array of `String` objects by writing:

```
String edit_buf[128];
```

To create the same array on the free store, you use:

```
String *edit_buf = new String[128];
```

You can use the array of `Strings` as you would any other array. The first `String` is `edit_buf[0]`, the second one is `edit_buf[1]`, and so on.

Use the following special syntax to indicate that you're deleting an array of objects on free store:

```
delete[] edit_buf;
```

This ensures that the destructor of the `String` class is called for each element of the array. Each `String` object maintains an internal pointer to a character array that is allocated by the constructor and freed by the destructor. Therefore, a call to the destructor of each `String` in the array takes care of properly deallocating the internal `char` arrays used by the `String` objects.

Handling Errors in Memory Allocation

If you allocate many objects dynamically, chances are that sooner or later the free space will be exhausted and the `new` operator will fail. In ANSI C, when `malloc` or `calloc` fails, it returns a `NULL` pointer (a pointer set to zero). C++ provides a way to intercept allocation errors. In Microsoft Visual C++, when the `new` operator fails, it calls a function that you install by calling the `_set_new_handler` function. You can handle memory allocation errors in a central function by writing the error handler and calling `_set_new_handler` with the pointer to the error handler as an argument. The advantage of handling errors this way is that you no longer need to test each use of the `new` operator for a return value of zero.

The _set_new_handler function is declared in the new.h header file. In Microsoft Visual C++, the pointer to the error-handling function is of type _PNH, which is defined as a pointer to a function that takes a size_t argument and returns an int. The error handler tries to allocate the requested amount of memory. If it succeeds, it returns the pointer to the allocated memory; otherwise, it returns to zero. Consult the online documentation in Microsoft Visual C++ for more information on using the _set_new_handler function.

Calling Member Functions

In C++, you build object-oriented programs by creating instances of classes (the objects) as necessary. The program does its work by calling the member functions of the objects. The syntax for calling the member functions is similar to the syntax used to call any other function, except that you use the . and -> operators to identify the member function within the object. For example, to use the length function of a String object named s1, use the . operator to specify the function:

```
String s1;
size_t len;
len = s1.length();
```

Apart from the use of the . operator to identify the function, the calling syntax is like other function calls. As with any function, you must know the member function's return type, as well as the number and type of arguments that it takes. For dynamically allocated objects, use the -> operator, like this:

```
String *p_s = new String("Hello, World!");
size_t len;
len = p_s->length();
```

Using *static* Member Variables

When you define member variables for a class, each instance of that class obtains its own unique copy of the member variables. However, sometimes you want a single variable for all instances of a class. C++ makes use of the static keyword to introduce this type of member variable. Here, static member variables are introduced in the context of a rather useful class.

Most C programmers agree that at some point in time they have debugged their program by inserting calls to `printf` or `fprintf` and printing messages and values from variables of interest. These messages can help you pinpoint where a program fails. Often, programmers enclose these calls to `fprintf` in a `#if` directive, like this one:

```
#if defined(DEBUG)
    fprintf(stderr, "Loop ended. Index = %d\n", i);
#endif
```

so that such messages are printed only when the `DEBUG` preprocessor macro is defined. In C++, you can use a similar strategy for debugging, but rather than insert calls to `fprintf`, you accomplish the work with a `Debug` class. The class is designed so that whenever an instance of the `Debug` class is created, it prints a message, properly indented to make the sequence of function calls easier to follow. The `Debug` class also provides a member function called `print`, which can be used just like `printf`. Listing 9.2 shows the DEBUG.H header file, which declares the interface to the class and defines the inline functions.

Listing 9.2. DEBUG.H. Interface to the `Debug` class.

```
//--------------------------------------------------------------
//  File:  debug.h
//
//  A class for debugging C++ programs
//
//--------------------------------------------------------------
#if !defined(_ _DEBUG_H)
#define _ _DEBUG_H

#include <stdio.h>
#include <stdarg.h>

class Debug
{
public:
    Debug(const char *label = " ");
    ~Debug();
    void print(const char *format, ...);
private:
    unsigned int indent();
    void draw_separator();
```

```
    static unsigned int debug_level;
    static unsigned int debug_on;
    static unsigned int indent_by;
    static unsigned int line_size;
    enum {off = 0, on = 1};
};

//----------------------------------------------------------------
//      I N L I N E   F U N C T I O N S
//----------------------------------------------------------------
//  ~ D e b u g
//  Destructor for the Debug clss

inline Debug::~Debug()
{
    debug_level--;
    draw_separator();
}

#endif
```

At the end of the body of the `Debug` class, notice that a number of member variables are declared with the `static` keyword. These variables are static *member variables*, and the `Debug` class contains exactly one copy of them.

To understand the need for such `static` member variables, consider the `debug_level` member variable, which keeps track of how many instances of the `Debug` class have been created up to that point. As you can see from Listing 9.3, this information is used to appropriately indent the messages printed by the `print` member function. You can't use `debug_level` to keep a count of the instances of the `Debug` class if each instance has its own copy of the `debug_level` variable. The solution is to have what you might call a *class-wide global variable*, which occurs when you place the `static` keyword in front of a member variable.

Listing 9.3. DEBUG.CPP. Implementation of the `Debug` class.

```
//----------------------------------------------------------------
//  File: debug.cpp
//
```

continues

Listing 9.3. continued

```
//  Implementation of the "Debug" class
//------------------------------------------------------------------
#include "debug.h"

//------------------------------------------------------------------
//  D e b u g
//  Constructor for Debug class

Debug::Debug(const char *label)
{
    if(debug_on)
    {
        draw_separator();
        (void) indent();
        fprintf(stderr, "%s\n", label);
    }
    debug_level++;
}
//------------------------------------------------------------------
//  p r i n t
//  Uses ANSI C's vfprintf function to print debug message

void Debug::print(const char *format, ...)
{
    if(debug_on)
    {
        (void) indent();
        va_list argp;
        va_start(argp, format);
        vfprintf(stderr, format, argp);
    }
}
//------------------------------------------------------------------
//  i n d e n t
//  Indents line according to debug_level. Returns the
//  number of spaces indented

unsigned int Debug::indent()
{
    unsigned int i;
    unsigned int num_spaces = debug_level*indent_by;
```

```
    for(i = 0; i < num_spaces; i++)
        fputc(' ', stderr);
    return(num_spaces);
}
//--------------------------------------------------------------
//  d r a w _ s e p a r a t o r
//  Draws a separator using dashes (-) to identify debug levels

void Debug::draw_separator()
{
    if(debug_on)
    {
        unsigned int i;
        for(i = indent(); i < line_size; i++)
                            fputc('-', stderr);
        fputc('\n', stderr);
    }
}
//--------------------------------------------------------------
```

Initializing *static* Member Variables

Listing 9.4 shows a test program that illustrates how the `Debug` class of Listings 9.2 and 9.3 might be used. At the beginning of this program, you can see the syntax that refers to the static member variables of the `Debug` class. To refer to the static member variable of a class, use the name of the class (not the name of the instance) as the prefix, followed by the scope resolution operator (`::`). Therefore, you can set the `debug_level` member of the `Debug` class to zero by writing:

```
// Initialize static member "debug_level" of the Debug class
unsigned int Debug::debug_level = 0;
```

Except for the `Debug::` prefix, this looks like the definition of any other variable in the program.

In Listing 9.3 you'll notice that inside the member functions you can access the static member variables, such as `debug_level`, the same way you would access any other member variable of the class. Therefore, you need the scope resolution prefix (`Debug::`) for the static member variables only when referring to them outside the scope of the class.

Listing 9.4. DBGTST.CPP. Program to test the `Debug` class.

```
//--------------------------------------------------------------
//  File:  dbgtst.cpp
//
//  Test the "Debug" class
//--------------------------------------------------------------
#include "debug.h"

// Initialize the debug_level to 0 and debug_on to "on"
unsigned int Debug::debug_level = 0;
unsigned int Debug::debug_on = Debug::on;

// Set number of characters per line to 55
unsigned int Debug::line_size = 55;

// Indent by 4 spaces for each level
unsigned int Debug::indent_by = 4;
//--------------------------------------------------------------
//  f a c t o r i a l
//  Recursive function that evaluates factorial

unsigned long factorial(int n)
{
    Debug dbg("factorial");
    dbg.print("argument = %d\n", n);
    if(n == 1) return 1;
    else return n*factorial(n-1);
}
//--------------------------------------------------------------
//  m a i n
//  Main function to test 'Debug" class

void main()
{
    Debug dbg("main");
    unsigned long n = factorial(4);
    dbg.print("result = %ld\n", n);
}
```

To show the effects of `debug_level`, the sample program defines and calls a `factorial` function, a recursive function that evaluates the factorial of its integer argument. The `factorial` function creates an instance of the `Debug` class on each entry. The `Debug` class increases the indentation as the `debug_level` increases, and draws dashed lines to show increases and decreases in `debug_level`. Therefore, you'd expect to see an indented list of calls to `factorial` in the output of this program. Indeed, when you run the program built by compiling and linking the files shown in Listings 9.3 and 9.4, it displays the following output:

```
---------------------------------------------------------------
main
    -----------------------------------------------------------
    factorial
        argument = 4
        -------------------------------------------------------
        factorial
            argument = 3
            ---------------------------------------------------
            factorial
                argument = 2
                -----------------------------------------------
                factorial
                    argument = 1
                -----------------------------------------------
            ---------------------------------------------------
        -------------------------------------------------------
    -----------------------------------------------------------
    result = 24
---------------------------------------------------------------
```

Here, the indentation of the dashed lines clearly shows the sequence of function calls and returns.

Counting Class Instances

Declare a member variable as static if you want a single copy of the variable for all instances of a class. You can count the number of instances of a class by incrementing a static member variable in the constructor of the class.

Using Static Member Functions

You can work with static member functions as well as static member variables. In C programs, programmers often define static functions to confine the visibility of a function to a specific file. With the `static` keyword, you can place more than one function with the same name in different files. C++ advances one step further and enables you to place functions that are `static` within a class. You can invoke such functions without creating any instance of the class. You need only add the scope resolution operator to the class name.

As an example, suppose you want a static member function of the `Debug` class that sets `debug_on` a variable. You can declare such a function inside the body of the class as follows:

```
class Debug
{
public:
//...
static void set_debug(int on_off);    // static member function
//...
private:
//...
}
```

The function is defined just like any other member function. Notice that you don't need the `static` keyword in the definition:

```
void Debug::set_debug(int on_off)
{
    if(on_off) debug_on = on;
    else       debug_on = off;
}
```

Once defined, you can call this function just like an ordinary function, but with a `Debug::` prefix, as follows:

```
// Turn debugging off
    Debug::set_debug(0);
//...
// Turn debugging on
    Debug::set_debug(1);
```

Notice that you don't need an instance of the `Debug` class to call the `set_debug` function. The scope resolution prefix (`Debug::`) is necessary to indicate which `set_debug` function you're calling. After all, another class also might have defined a static member function named `set_debug`.

Using Pointers to Class Members

Because of encapsulation of data and functions in a class, C++ includes a pointer to a class member in addition to ordinary pointers to class and functions. A pointer *to a class member* actually is the offset of the member from the beginning of a particular instance of that class. In other words, it is a *relative address*, whereas regular pointers denote the *absolute address* of an object. The syntax for declaring a pointer to a class member is `X::*`, where `X` is the name of the class. Therefore, if you declare a class as follows:

```
class Sample
{
public:
    short step;              // Member variable
    void set_step(short s); // Member function
//...
private:
};
```

you can define and initialize a pointer to a `short` member variable of the `Sample` class, like this:

```
short Sample::*p_s;  // Pointer to short in class Sample
p_s = &Sample::step; // Initialize to member "step"
```

Notice that to define and even initialize the pointer, you do not need an instance of the `Sample` class. Contrast this with the way you initialize a regular pointer to a `short` variable. With the regular pointer you must define a `short` variable before you can assign its address to the pointer.

With pointers to class members, you need a concrete instance of the class only when using the pointers. Thus, you must define an instance of the `Sample` class before you can use the pointer `p_s`. A typical use of `p_s` might be to assign a new value to the class member through the pointer, like this:

```
Sample s1;
s1.*p_s = 5;
```

The syntax for dereferencing the pointer is of the form `x.*p`, where `x` is an instance of the class and `p` is a pointer to a class member. If, instead of a class instance, you have a pointer to an instance of a `Sample` class, the syntax for using `p_s` changes to:

```
Sample s1;
Sample *p_sample1 = &s1;
p_sample->*p_s = 5;
```

Pointers to Member Functions

The syntax for declaring a pointer to a member function of the class is similar to the syntax used for declaring a pointer to ordinary functions. The only difference is that you use the class name together with the scope resolution operator (::). Here's an example that defines a pointer to a member function of the class Sample. The definition says that the member function to which p_func points returns nothing but requires a short as argument.

```
void (Sample::*p_func)(short) = Sample::set_step;
```

The sample definition also initializes the pointer p_func to the address of the set_step function of the Sample class. You can call the function through the pointer:

```
Sample s1;
(s1.*p_func)(2);  // Call function through pointer
```

Here's another small program that illustrates how pointers to member functions are used:

```
//-----------------------------------------------------------
//  Illustrates use of pointer to member function of a class

#include <iostream.h>

class CommandSet
{
public:
    void help(){cout << "Help!" << endl;}
    void nohelp(){cout << "No Help!" << endl;}
private:
//...
};

//  Initialize pointer to member function "f_help"

void (CommandSet::*f_help)() = CommandSet::help;

main()
{
    CommandSet set1;

// Invoke a member function through the "f_help" pointer
    (set1.*f_help)();
```

```
// Redefine the "f_help" pointer and call function again
    f_help = CommandSet::nohelp;
    (set1.*f_help)();
}
```

This example program makes two calls to the function with the pointer. Between calls, it changes the pointer's value. When run, the program displays two messages:

```
Help!
No Help!
```

Pointers to Static Members

Static members of a class are not covered by the syntax used for defining and using pointers to other members of a class. A pointer to a static member is treated as a regular pointer. For example, if you declare the class

```
class Clock
{
public:
//...
    static double ticks_per_sec;
private:
//...
}z;
```

you can define a pointer to its static member variable as follows:

```
double *p_tick = &Clock::ticks_per_sec;
```

This is simply a regular pointer to `double` that has been initialized to the `ticks_per_sec` static member variable of the `Clock` class. Notice that you must use the class name with the scope resolution operator to identify the static variable `ticks_per_sec`. Use the `p_ticks` pointer like an ordinary pointer to `double`. For instance, the following statement sets the `ticks_per_sec` static variable of the `Clock` class to `18.2`:

```
*p_tick = 18.2; // Set 'ticks_per_sec' through pointer
```

Summary

C++ extends the syntax of C's `struct` and introduces the `class` construct. These enhancements enable the creation of user-defined data types that you can use the same way you use built-in types such as `int`, `char`, `float`, and `double`. In the terminology of object-oriented programming, the `class` and `struct` mechanisms support data abstraction, which is one of the basic requirements for creating objects. The class declaration indicates how the object should behave, and the instances of the class refer to the objects being manipulated by the program.

A C++ class can include both data and functions as members. Data members represent the internal state of an object of that class, while functions define the behavior of the object. By grouping the members into sections labelled `public`, `private`, and `protected`, you can control which members are accessible to the functions outside the class. The data members usually become `private`, and all interactions with the class are made through a set of `public` member functions. To implement a class, you must declare the class and define all its member functions. A good strategy for modular implementation is to declare the class in a header file and define the member functions in a separate implementation file.

Once a class is defined, you can create and use objects of that class just as you would use built-in data types such as `int`, `char`, and `double`. You can either define the objects like any other variable, or create them dynamically by calling the `new` and `delete` operators, which are analogous to the C library's `malloc` and `free` functions.

10

Defining Operations on Objects

Chapter 9, "Building Objects with Classes," focused on the use of `class` and `struct` constructs to encapsulate data with functions when defining a new data type with its own operators. That chapter explained the general strategy for implementing and using a class. The implementation includes two components:

- A header file with the declaration of the class
- A source file with the actual definition of the member functions of the class

This chapter shows you how to define the member functions and the operators for a class. While the concept of creating objects with `class` is straightforward, many small details become important when implementing classes in C++. For example, you need to know when to pass arguments by reference and how to ensure that objects are initialized properly. This chapter addresses these questions.

Arguments and Return Values

In C++, you manipulate an object, which is an instance of a class, using member functions and operators defined for that class. As a C programmer, you know that functions accept one or more arguments and return a value. C employs the *pass-by-value* mechanism for providing a function with its arguments.

In pass-by-value, functions receive their argument in a special area of memory called the *stack*, a last-in-first-out (LIFO) data structure. Before calling a function, the calling program copies each argument's value to the stack and passes control to the function. The function retrieves the arguments from the stack and uses them in the body of the function. If necessary, the function can return a single value to the calling program. The net effect of this mechanism is that the function never accesses the actual storage locations of the arguments its caller provides. Instead, it works with local copies of the arguments, and the local copies are discarded from the stack when they're returned from the function.

This pass-by-value approach is a good choice for argument passing because it guarantees that a function never alters its arguments. However, as you see next, pass-by-value is not always beneficial when you need to pass objects around.

Understanding Pointers and References

Although a function that receives its arguments by value cannot alter the arguments, what if an argument is the address of a variable or, in other words, a *pointer* to the variable? In this case, the function clearly can alter the value of the variable through that pointer. For example, if you want to swap the contents of two integer variables, one way to do this is to write a function that accepts pointers to the two `int` variables:

```
void swap_int(int *p_a, int *p_b)
{
    int temp;
    temp = *p_a;
    *p_a = *p_b;
    *p_b = temp;
}
```

You can use this function to swap integer variables as follows:

```
int x = 2, y = 3;

swap_int(&x, &y);   /* Now x = 3 and y = 2 */
```

Although you can continue to use this type of function in C++ programs, C++ introduces a reference that makes it much easier to write this type of function. A *reference* is an alternate name for an object that you can use just as you would the object itself. Think of a reference as the address of an item. Unlike a pointer, however, a reference is not a real variable. A reference is initialized when it's defined, and you cannot modify its value later. The syntax of a reference mimics that of a pointer, except that a reference requires an ampersand (&) and the pointer declaration requires an asterisk (*). Thus,

```
int *p_i;  // An unintialized pointer to integer
```

defines an `int` pointer, while

```
int &r_i = i;  // Reference to i (an int variable)
```

is a reference to an `int` variable named `i`.

As a practical example of the use of a reference, here is the `swap_int` function with arguments passed by a reference:

```
void swap_int(int &a, int &b)
{
    int temp;
    temp = a;
    a = b;
    b = temp;
}
```

Compare this version of the function with the one that uses pointers. You can see that the version that uses references looks cleaner—you no longer need to dereference pointers in each expression. The new version of the function is simpler to use because you need not provide the address of the integers being swapped as arguments. Instead, you call the function as if the arguments are being passed by value:

```
void swap_int(int&, int&);  // Prototype of function

int x = 2, y = 3;

swap_int(x, y);            // Now x = 3 and y = 2
```

The compiler knows from the function's prototype that it must pass references to the x and y variables.

As you can see from the examples in this section, you can think of a reference as a pointer with a constant value that the C++ compiler automatically dereferences whenever you use it. In other words, given the following:

```
int i;            // An integer variable
int &r_i = i;     // A reference to "i"
int *p_i = &i;    // A pointer to "i"
```

you can think of `r_i` as equivalent to `p_i` except that, wherever you use the expression `r_i`, the compiler substitutes `*p_i`. Because the value of a reference cannot change from its initial assignment, the C++ compiler need not allocate storage for a reference. The compiler only needs to implement the semantics of each reference.

Passing by Value Versus Passing by Reference

From the example of swapping integers, you might surmise that references are good for writing functions that need to alter the values of their arguments. While this is certainly one of the uses of passing arguments by reference, there's another important reason for providing the reference mechanism in C++.

Consider what happens when an object is passed to a function by value. To implement the pass-by-value semantics, the compiler must copy the object to the stack before the function is called. For large class objects, copying involves both a space penalty and a time penalty. You can avoid the overheads of copying by using a reference to the object (instead of the object itself) as an argument. If the function does not modify an argument, you can indicate this with the `const` qualifier for that reference argument. Thus, passing arguments by reference enhances the efficiency of object-based programming in C++.

Returning a Reference

Just as passing arguments by reference prevents unnecessary copying to the stack, you can avoid copying the returned object by returning an object by reference. In contrast, watch what happens when you return an object by value.

Suppose you return a `String` object from an `add_strings` function that returns the concatenation of two strings:

```
String add_strings(const String& s1, const String& s2)
{
// In function's body
    String s;
// Append s1 and s2 to s
//...
    return s;
}
```

In this case, the `return` statement must copy `String s` to an area of memory provided by the calling program. To do so properly, the `return` statement calls a special constructor, the *copy constructor*, which can create and initialize a new instance of an object from an existing one. After creating the copy, the return statement calls the destructor of the `String` class to destroy `String s` before returning to the calling program. This is a good example of the work done by the C++ compiler behind the scenes. You probably didn't realize that so much extra work was going into an innocuous `return` statement.

The example you've just seen illustrates what happens when a function returns an object. Although returning by reference would save the time spent in copying the object, you cannot return a reference to `String s` because `s` is a temporary object that exists only within the `add_strings` function; `s` is destroyed when the function returns. Therefore, be careful what you return by reference. Because a reference is like a pointer, you cannot return a reference to anything temporary.

> **The Significance of `const` Arguments**
>
> Remember that, by qualifying an argument to a function with the `const` keyword, you can inform the C++ compiler that the function should not modify the argument. The compiler generates an error message if the function inadvertently tries to alter that argument. The `const` qualifier is significant only for arguments that are pointers or that are passed by reference because changes made by a function to arguments passed by value cannot be seen in the calling program. See Chapter 7, "C++ and ANSI Standard C," for more information on the `const` keyword.

A common use of returning by reference is in an *access function*—a function that provides access to an internal element of an existing object. For example, if you want to write a member function for the String class, named char_at_pos, to provide access to the character at a specified location in an instance of String, you can safely return a reference to the character at the specified location. Thus, you might write the char_at_pos function as follows:

```
//-------------------------------------------------------------
//  c h a r _ a t _ p o s
//  Access a character in a String

char& String::char_at_pos(int index)
{
// Check if index goes beyond allocated length.
// Return last element, if it does
    if(index > _maxlen - 1) return p_c[_maxlen - 1];
    else  return p_c[index];
}
```

Here's a typical use of the function:

```
    String s1 = "Test";
// ...

// Print the second character of String s1
    cout << "3rd char = " << s1.char_at_pos(2) << endl;

// Change the first character of s1
    s1.char_at_pos(0) = 'B';  // Now s1 = "Best"
```

Although you may expect the first use of the char_at_pos function to retrieve the character at a specific position in the string, you may not realize that you can even set a character to a new value. The second use of char_at_pos is possible only because the function returns a reference to a char. Because a reference is exactly like the variable itself, you can assign a new value to the returned reference.

If you already know C++, you may realize that a better solution for accessing a character in String would be to overload the [] operator. A little later in this chapter you'll see how to define such operators for a class.

Using References: The Guidelines

You can follow several rules of thumb when deciding where to use references. You should pass arguments to a function by reference when:

- You want the function to modify the arguments.
- The function will not modify the arguments, but you want to avoid copying the objects to the stack. In this case, use the `const` qualifier to indicate that the argument being passed by reference should not be altered by the function.

As for return values, you should return a reference to an object whenever you want to use that return value as the left side of an assignment. Of course, you should return a reference to an object only when the object is guaranteed to exist after the function returns.

Creating and Destroying Objects

Because basic data types, such as `int` and `float`, are simply chunks of memory that hold a single value, a user-defined class can contain many more components—some of which may require additional work during creation besides setting aside a number of bytes of storage. Take, for instance, the `String` class. Internally, it stores a pointer to an array of characters that holds the null-terminated string. To function properly, a newly created `String` object must set this pointer to a properly allocated array of `chars` and, quite possibly, initialize that array to a specific string. After all, if you treat `String` like any other type of variable, you must be able to handle statements such as:

```
String this_os = "MS-DOS";
String new_os = this_os;
```

For proper handling of this type of initialization, C++ allows each class a special function called the *constructor*, which has the same name as the class and has no return type. Thus, the constructor for the `String` class is a function named `String`. Of course, as with other functions, you can have more than one constructor, each with a unique list of arguments and each intended for a specific type of initialization.

A constructor for a class such as `String` allocates extra memory for the null-terminated string. This means that there must be a way to release this memory when the `String` no longer is needed. C++ handles this need through a *destructor*, a function with the same name as the class but with a tilde (~) as a prefix. Thus, the destructor of the `String` class is named `~String`. Destructors do not take an argument—you cannot overload a destructor.

Constructors and Destructors for the *String* Class

Chapter 9, "Building Objects with Classes," provides you with a brief description and the declaration of a `String` class that represents a text-string data type with its own operators and string-manipulation functions. The idea is to create a pointer to an array of bytes that can hold a null-terminated array of characters, the standard way of representing strings in C and C++. The variables `_maxlen` and `_length` denote, respectively, the size of the allocated array and the length of the string stored in the array.

To allow for character insertion into the `String`, the size of the `char` array is rounded up to the next highest multiple of a specified chunk of bytes. For example, if the chunk is 8 bytes, the allocated size of the array to hold a 10-character string will be 16 bytes—the nearest multiple of 8 that exceeds 10. This idea is useful, for example, if you plan to use the `String` objects in a text editor, where you must allow for the insertion of characters into a `String`.

Listing 6.1 in Chapter 6 shows the STR.H header file, which declares the `String` class. To refresh your memory, here's a skeleton declaration of the `String` class showing the private members, the constructors, and the destructor:

```
class String
{
public:
// Constructors with a variety of arguments
    String();
    String(size_t len);
    String(const char *str);
    String(const String &s);

// Destructor
    ~String();

// ...

private:
// Internal data members of this class

    char   *p_c;      // pointer to allocated space
    size_t _length;   // current length of string
    size_t _maxlen;   // number of bytes allocated

};
```

Which Constructor Is Called?

If a class defines constructors, the C++ compiler calls an appropriate constructor to initialize each instance of a class. The way you define class instances controls which constructor is called. The constructor with no arguments is called when you define an instance but specify no initial value. For other cases, the type of initial value determines the constructor the C++ compiler calls. You can define and initialize a class instance in any of three ways:

- Use the C-style syntax as illustrated by the following example for an instance of the `String` class:

  ```
  String operating_system = "MS-DOS";
  ```

- Use a function-call syntax, such as:

  ```
  String operating_system("MS-DOS");
  ```

- Use the `new` operator to allocate on the free store:

  ```
  String *lines = new String[25];
  ```

In the first two cases, the C++ compiler calls the `String(const char*)` constructor because you're initializing the `String` object with a null-terminated character array. Thus, the compiler calls the constructor that takes as an argument the type of value you're using to initialize the class instance. In the last case, the compiler calls the constructor that takes no arguments, and calls this constructor for each of the 25 `String` objects being created.

Because the `String` class defines a constructor that accepts a string length as an argument, here's an initialization that's appropriate to use with the `String` class (even though it may look strange to C programmers):

```
String eight_blanks = 8;  // A string with 8 blanks
```

Based on the description of the `String(size_t)` constructor, this statement creates a `String` initialized with eight blank spaces.

The Default Constructor

The *default constructor* is a constructor that takes no arguments. For the `String` class, you can define the default constructor as a function that allocates a single chunk of bytes and initializes it to a zero-length string, as follows:

```
//--------------------------------------------------------------
//  S t r i n g
//  Creates a String and stores a zero-length string in it.
```

```
String::String()
{
    _maxlen = chunk_size;    // const chunk_size = 8;
    p_c = new char[_maxlen];
    _length = 0;
    p_c[0] = '\0';
}
```

In lieu of a constructor with no arguments, the upcoming ANSI standard for C++ plans to allow the compiler to use any constructor (with default values specified for all of its arguments) as a default constructor. For a `Point` class that represents a point in the x,y plane, such a default constructor might appear as follows:

```
Point::Point(int x = 0, int y = 0)
{
// Copy x and y coordinates into internal variables of Point
}
```

The default constructor is called whenever you define an instance of the class without providing an explicit initial value. Here's an example where the default constuctor is called:

```
String s1;  // s1 is initialized by calling default constructor
```

The default constructor also plays an important role when you allocate an array of class instances. Here, the C++ compiler automatically calls the default constructor for each element of the array. If you write

```
String edit_buf[24];  // Create an array of 24 Strings
```

the default constructor of `String` is called to initialize each element of the `edit_buf` array.

> **Define a Default Constructor for Each Class**
>
> If you define constructors for a class, you should always define a default constructor (a constructor that requires no arguments) as well. When you define an array of instances for a class, the C++ compiler initializes each instance in the array by calling the default constructor.

Defining Other String Constructors

The String class contains a few other constructors besides the default constructor. One of them takes a number of bytes as the argument and creates a blank string with that many bytes. Here is the definition of that constructor:

```
//--------------------------------------------------------------
//  S t r i n g
//  This version creates a blank string of size "len"

String::String(size_t len)
{
    _length = len;
// NOTE: const chunk_size = 8;
    _maxlen = chunk_size*(_length / chunk_size + 1);
    p_c = new char[_maxlen];
    int i;
    for(i = 0; i < len; i++) p_c[i] = ' ';
    p_c[i] = '\0';
}
```

First, the constructor computes _maxlen, the number of bytes to allocate. It then uses the new operator to allocate the array of chars and initialize the array to a null-terminated string that contains the specified number of space characters.

Another useful constructor for the String class is one that accepts a null-terminated character array and creates a String from it. You might define this constructor as follows:

```
//--------------------------------------------------------------
//  S t r i n g
//  Creates a String object and initializes it from a
//  null-terminated C string

String::String(const char *s)
{
    _length = strlen(s);
// NOTE: const chunk_size = 8;
    _maxlen = chunk_size*(_length / chunk_size + 1);
    p_c = new char[_maxlen];
    strcpy(p_c, s);
}
```

String Destructor

The destructor reverses anything done in the constructor. Usually, this means releasing memory that the constructor allocated when creating the object. For the `String` class, the constructor allocates the array that holds the null-terminated string. The pointer to this array is stored in the `p_c` private member variable. Thus, the `~String` destructor frees up the memory allocated for the character array:

```
//-------------------------------------------------------------
//  ~ S t r i n g
//  Destroys a String

String::~String()
{
    delete p_c;
}
```

The Copy Constructor

Another special type of constructor is the *copy constructor*, which is capable of replicating an object. To understand why a copy constructor is necessary, consider the following example.

If you decide to pass a `String` object by value to an `append_space` function, which, presumably, adds a space to the end of the string, the function would be declared and used as follows:

```
void append_space(String s);  // expects argument by value
String s1 = "Result is";
append_space(s1);             //  a sample call
```

To implement the call to `append_space`, the C++ compiler must make a copy of the `String s1` on the stack. As shown in Figure 10.1, the body of a `String` object contains a pointer to the actual null-terminated string. The constructor of the `String` class takes care of allocating and initializing this memory.

To make a copy of `String s1` on the stack, the compiler, by default, copies each member of `String s1` to the stack. This, however, results in the situation shown in Figure 10.2. Both the copy and the original `String` point to the same null-terminated string because the character pointers are identical.

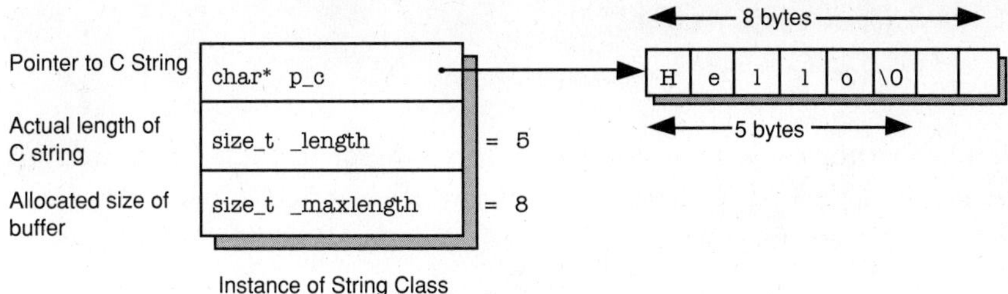

Figure 10.1. An instance of the `String` class.

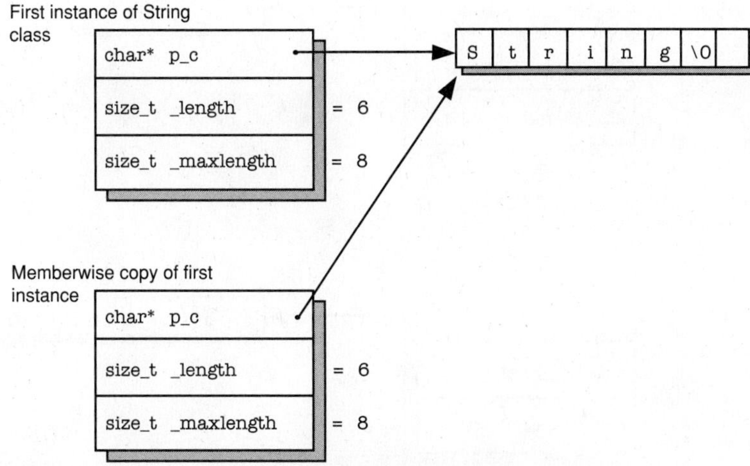

Figure 10.2. Memberwise copy of one `String` to another.

To create a complete copy, you must define a constructor for `String` that takes a `String` reference as the argument (in other words, a constructor that can create a copy of a `String`). For the `String` class, you might implement this copy constructor as follows:

```
#include "str.h"   // Header file that declares the String class

//------------------------------------------------------------
//  S t r i n g  ( c o n s t  S t r i n g & )
//  Creates a new String as a copy of another String
//  This is called the "Copy Constructor"

String::String(const String &s)
{
    _length = s._length;
    _maxlen = s._maxlen;
```

```
    p_c = new char[_maxlen];
    strcpy(p_c, s.p_c);
}
```

Notice that the copy constructor allocates room for the null-terminated string and copies into it the C string from the `String`, which was passed to it as argument. When the copy constructor is used, you receive a complete copy of the `String`, as shown in Figure 10.3.

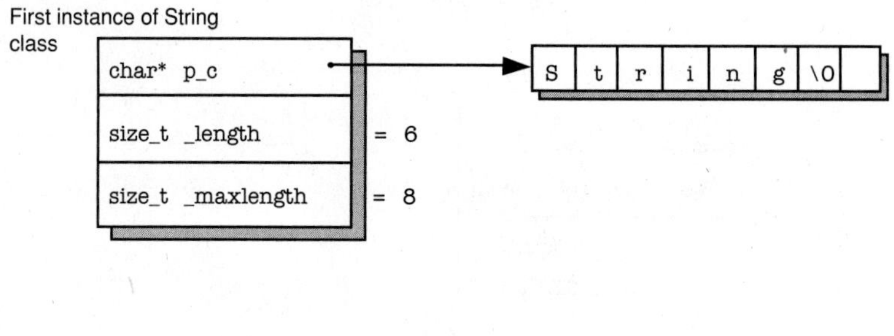

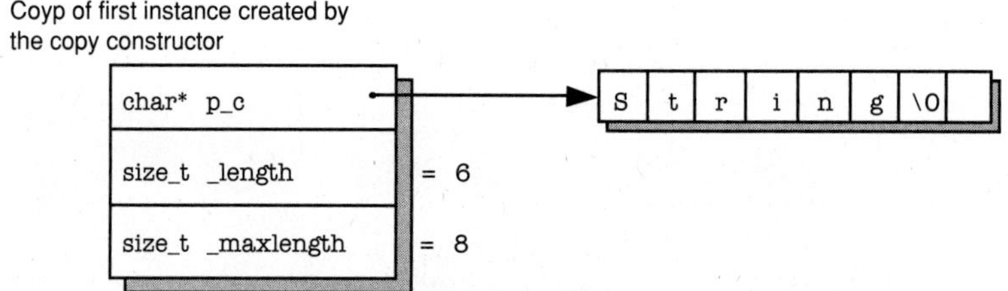

Figure 10.3. Copying with the copy constructor.

The copy constructor also comes into play when you write

```
String s1 = "Hello!";
String s2 = s1;
```

In this case, the C++ compiler must initialize `s2` with the value of another `String s1`. To do this, the compiler looks for a copy constructor for the `String` class. The copy constructor for `String` is declared as follows:

```
String(const String&);
```

Because of the form of the declaration, books and manuals on C++ often refer to this as the `X(const X&)` constructor, where `X` denotes any class.

When to Provide a Copy Constructor

If your class does not include pointers that must be properly initialized, you do not need to provide a copy constructor. The C++ compiler uses a default copy constructor that performs a memberwise copy of one class instance to another. You must provide a copy constructor only for classes with a pointer variable, such as the `String` class. If you do not, the result of copying is as shown for the `String` objects in Figure 10.2. Both copies hold pointers to a single array of characters.

Even if you can accept the memberwise copy, you run into another problem because of the destructor. If a `String` object created by a memberwise copy operation no longer is needed, the `String` destructor is called. The destructor frees the storage with the address in the character pointer of that `String`. This leaves the remaining copy of `String` with a *dangling pointer*—a pointer that does not point to any valid block of memory. When that remaining copy of `String` has to be destroyed, the `delete` operator is called with the address of memory that has already been freed. Worse yet, if that memory has been allocated to some other object, the destructor inadvertently frees memory belonging to some other object. To avoid such problems, you should always provide a copy constructor for any class that includes dynamically allocated members.

> **Copy Constructor**
>
> Provide a copy constructor of the `X::X(const X&)` form for any class that allocates memory in its constructor. The copy constructor ensures that instances of that class are copied correctly.

The Member-Initializer List

How do you initialize a class that contains an instance of another class? If you decide to implement a `Line` class, which contains two instances of the `Point` class, each representing an endpoint of the line, your class declaration might look like this:

```
class Point
{
public:
    Point(double _x=0.0, double _y=0.0)
    {
```

```
        x = _x;
        y = _y;
    }
    Point(const Point& p) { x = p.x, y = p.y;}

private:
    double x,y;      // Coordinates of point
};

class Line
{
public:
    Line(const Point& b, Point& e) : p1(b), p2(e) {}
// ...
private:
    Point p1, p2;  // End-points of line
};
```

Notice the curious way of defining the constructor for the `Line` class. The constructor takes two `Point` references as arguments. It need only copy the points to the internal points `p1` and `p2`. Of course, the obvious way is to write

```
Line::Line(const Point& b, Point& e)
{
    p1 = b;
    p2 = e;
}
```

This works, but it sets up points `p1` and `p2` using the default constructor of the `Point` class and then performs a memberwise copy of `b` to `p1` and `e` to `p2`. A more efficient approach is to initialize `p1` and `p2` with the copy constructor. However, by the time you are inside the constructor of `Line`, the `Point` instances `p1` and `p2` are already constructed. C++ solves this problem by allowing the *member-initializer list*—a list of member-variable initializations of the form

```
variable_name(value)
```

separated by commas. Here, `variable_name` refers to a member-variable of the class, and the `value` within parentheses denotes the value with which that variable is initialized. The member-initializer list appears between the function's argument list and the function's body, and is processed before the statements in the body of the function are executed.

Initializer List Versus Assignment

For another example of a member-initializer list, consider a Name class that has two String members as follows:

```
class Name
{
public:
    Name(const char *first, const char *last);
// Other public member functions...
private:
    String first_name;
    String last_name;
};
```

How do you define the constructor for this class? Most C programmers define it as follows:

```
Name::Name(const char *first, const char *last)
{
    first_name = first;
    last_name = last;
}
```

Although this looks straightforward, a lot of behind-the-scenes work is done to initialize the first_name and last_name members of the Name class. To be specific, the compiler takes the following steps:

1. The compiler calls the default constructor of the String class to create the strings first_name and last_name. Note that the default constructor allocates some space for a character array.
2. The compiler creates two temporary String objects from the first and last character arrays.
3. The compiler calls the copy constructor of the String class to initialize first_name and last_name with the temporary Strings of the preceding step. The copy constructor also allocates storage for the character array.
4. The compiler generates code that destroys the temporary Strings created in Step 2.

Consider what happens if you rewrite the Name constructor using a member-initializer list. The definition changes to

```
Name::Name(const char *first, const char *last)
          : first_name(first), last_name(last) {}
```

Now the compiler can construct an instance of Name in a single step simply by processing the initializer list. The compiler calls the String(const char*) constructor of the String class to create String first_name out of first and String last_name out of last. In this case, storage for character arrays is allocated only once for each String and no unnecessary temporary objects exist.

For reasons of efficiency, you should use initializer lists to initialize member variables. Note that you can use the initializer list syntax for built-in types such as int, double, and char*, as well.

Initialization of *const* Member Variables and References

Even if you ignore the efficiency of initializer lists, some occasions occur when you must use member-initializers to create an instance of a class. This occurs when the class in question has either:

- A const member variable
- A reference member variable

Both of these, according to the rules of C++, must be initialized when defined. In other words, these member variables must contain a constant value as soon as the class instance is created. The following fictitious class illustrates how to do this:

```
class SampleClass
{
public:
// Constructor uses member-initializer list
    SampleClass(int id) : obj_id(id), r_i(i) {}
//...
private:
    const int obj_id;
    int       i;
    int&      r_i;
};
```

Here, the integer argument to the constructor is used to initialize the const variable obj_id, while the int reference r_i is set to another integer variable within the class.

Use member-initializer lists to efficiently initialize class members that are instances of other classes. You must use member-initializers to initialize nonstatic const and reference members of a class.

Exploiting the Side Effects of Constructors and Destructors

You know that whenever an instance of a class is created, the C++ compiler automatically calls the constructor of that class. If the class instance is an automatic variable, the destructor is called when the instance goes out of scope and must be destroyed. This means that you can have classes that do all their work in the constructors and destructors.

There is nothing wrong with using classes only for the side effects of their constructors and destructors. In fact, this sometimes leads to an elegant solution of a problem. As an example, consider the dilemma of estimating the time taken to execute a block of code.

Typically, you obtain the time at the start of the computation and perform the computations many times so that you can measure the elapsed time accurately. The ANSI C library includes functions such as `time` to obtain the current time and `clock` to get the clock ticks elapsed since the program started running. (The `time` function has an accuracy of seconds, while `clock` is somewhat more accurate—each *clock tick* lasts approximately 55 milliseconds on MS-DOS systems, regardless of the CPU speed.)

A Timer Class

To perform the timing in a C++ program, write a `Timer` class with a constructor that calls `clock` to obtain the current clock ticks. In the destructor, call `clock` again and compute the difference of the starting and ending clock ticks. Report the elapsed time in seconds between construction and destruction of an instance of `Timer`. You can convert clock ticks to seconds using the preprocessor macro `CLOCKS_PER_SEC`, which supplies the number of clock ticks per second. This macro, as well as the prototype of the `clock` function, appears in the time.h ANSI C header file. Listing 10.1 shows the TIMER.H header file, which is a typical implementation of the `Timer` class.

Listing 10.1. TIMER.H. Implementation of a `Timer` class.

```
//-------------------------------------------------------------
//  File:  timer.h
//
//  Implements a timer that works solely through its
//  constructor and destructor.  Uses the "clock" function
//  of the ANSI standard C library.  The "clock" function
```

continues

Listing 10.1. continued

```
//  returns the number of clock ticks used by the current
//  process.  The preprocessor macro CLOCKS_PER_SEC tells us
//  how to convert clock ticks to seconds.
//-------------------------------------------------------------
#if !defined(_ _TIMER_H)
#define _ _TIMER_H

#include <time.h>      // For definition of the clock_t type
                       // and the CLOCKS_PER_SEC macro

#include <iostream.h> // For output to "cerr" stream

class Timer
{
public:
    Timer() { start = clock();}  // Constructor

    ~Timer()  // Destructor (compute and display elapsed time)
    {
        clock_t stop = clock();
        cerr << "Elapsed time = ";
        cerr << (stop - start)/CLOCKS_PER_SEC;
        cerr << " seconds" << endl;
    }
private:
    clock_t start;     // Store starting clock tick count
};

#endif
```

Using the *Timer* Class

Listing 10.2 shows the C++ program timertst.cpp, which uses the `Timer` class to estimate the time taken to execute a set of computations. In Listing 10.2, the `compute` function performs all the work: it defines an instance of `Timer` that starts the clock ticking, so to speak. The function then repeatedly executes the computations in a loop. When the loop ends and the function returns, the `Timer` object is destroyed. The C++ compiler automatically calls the destructor of the `Timer` class, and the destructor prints out the elapsed time.

Listing 10.2. TIMERTST.CPP. Sample use of the `Timer` class.

```
//-------------------------------------------------------------
//  File:  timertst.cpp
//
//  Use the Timer class to time a function
//-------------------------------------------------------------
#include "timer.h"

//-------------------------------------------------------------
//  c o m p u t e
//  A function that performs some computations

static void compute(unsigned long count)
{
    unsigned long i;
    double a, b, c, d;
    Timer t;                        // Create Timer to time function
    for(i = 0; i < count; i++)
    {
        a = (double)(i-1);
        b = (double)(i+1);
        c = (double)(i+i);
        d = a*b - c;
    }
}
//-------------------------------------------------------------
//  m a i n
//  Main function that times the "compute" function

void main()
{
    unsigned long count;
    cout << "How many times? ";
    cin >> count;
    compute(count);
}
```

After building the timertst.cpp program with optimizations turned off (`/Od` option for the Microsoft Visual C++ compiler), the typical output on a 50MHz Intel 80486-based PC-AT system with a floating-point coprocessor is as follows (user input is in boldface):

```
How many times? 1000000
Elapsed time = 11 seconds
```

As you can see from this example, you can have perfectly useful classes with instances used only for the side effects of their construction and destruction.

Defining Functions and Operators

Member functions and operators model the behavior of a class and define how you use the objects represented by a class. The functions of a class are defined like any other functions, except that you must indicate the association of a function with a class by using the scope-resolution operator (`::`).

You've already seen the definition of several constructors for the `String` class. The following sections present a few other functions for the `String` class and describe how to define operators for a class.

The *this* Pointer

Before describing how member functions and operators are defined, you should know about the `this` keyword. Although a unique copy of each member variable exists for each instance of a class, all instances share a single set of member functions. However, none of the member functions that you've seen so far have any way of indicating the class instance with member variables that are being used in the function. Take, for instance, the `length` function of the `String` class. If you write:

```
String s1 ("Hello"), s2("Hi");
len1 = s1.length();  // len1 = 5
len2 = s2.length();  // len2 = 2
```

each call to `length` returns a unique answer, yet the `length` function is defined as

```
inline size_t String::length(void) const
{
    return _length;
}
```

where `_length` is a member variable of the `String` class. How did the function know to return the correct length for each string? The answer is in `this`.

The C++ compiler alters each member function in a class by making two changes:

1. It passes each member function an additional argument—a `this` pointer—that points to the specific object for which the function is being invoked. Thus, the `s1.length()` call includes a `this` argument set to the address of the `String` instance `s1`.

2. It adds the `this->` prefix to all member variables and functions. Thus, the `_length` variable in the `length` function becomes `this->_length`, which refers to the copy of `_length` in the class instance with an address in `this`.

Typically, you need not use `this` explicitly in a member function, but can refer to `this` if needed. For example, if you need to return the object to a calling program, you can use the following statement to do the job:

```
return *this;
```

You can return a reference to the object with the same statement. As you'll see in the following sections, you must return references when defining certain operators, such as the assignment operator (=).

If you're still wondering about the `this` keyword and its use, you may want to revisit the example of object-oriented programming in C that appears in Chapter 5, "Basics of Object-Oriented Programming." In that chapter, you were shown that the C functions implementing the OOP techniques need a pointer to the object as an argument. That need remains in C++, but the syntax of writing member functions is made more palatable to programmers by the behind-the-scenes handling of the pointer to the object through the `this` keyword.

Operators as Functions

Defining operators for a class is easy once you know how the application of an operator is translated to a function call. For a unary operator, such as `&`, when you write

```
&X
```

where `X` is an instance of some class, the C++ compiler applies the operator by calling the function

```
X.operator&()
```

The compiler automatically passes a pointer to the class instance to binary operators such as `+`. For an expression, such as

```
X + Y
```

where X and Y are class instances, the compiler calls the function

```
X.operator+(Y)
```

As you can see, the C++ compiler reduces the application of operators to function calls. Consequently, you can overload an operator by defining a function with a name that begins with the `operator` keyword followed by the symbolic notation of that operator.

Arguments to Operator Functions

Like all member functions, operator functions receive a pointer to the class instance in the hidden argument named `this`. Because this argument is implicit, unary operator functions are defined with no arguments at all. Binary operator functions that are members of the class take a single argument that is the right side of the operator expression. However, you can define an operator function as a `friend` instead of a member function of the class. As you see next, sometimes you need to define `friend` operator functions. When declared as a `friend`, the operator function requires all arguments explicitly. This means that to declare `operator+` as a friend function of class X, you write

```
friend X operator+(X&, X&);   // Assume X is a class
```

Then, to evaluate the expression `x1 + x2` for two instances of class X, the C++ compiler will call the function operator(`x1, x2`).

Operators You Can Overload

Table 10.1 lists the C++ operators that you can overload. As you can see, you can overload almost all predefined operators in C++. The only ones you cannot overload are the following:

Member-access operator	`x.y`
Dereferencing a pointer to member	`x.*y`
Scope-resolution operator	`x::y`
Conditional operator	`x?y:z`

You cannot introduce new operator notations because the compiler is unable to parse (recognize) a new operator notation. You can only overload the predefined operators. For example, FORTRAN uses `**` to denote exponentiation. In FORTRAN, `X**Y` means X raised to the power Y. However, even with operator overloading, you cannot define a similar `**` operator in C++ because C++ lacks a predefined `**` operator.

Table 10.1. C++ operators that you can overload.

Type	Name	Notation	Comments
Unary	Preincrement	++x	Use operator++ for both
	Postincrement	x++	pre- and postincrement
	Predecrement	--x	Use operator— for both
	Postdecrement	x--	pre- and postdecrement
	Address of	&x	
	Indirection	*x	
	Plus	+x	Define as operator+()
	Minus	-x	Define as operator-()
	Bitwise NOT	~x	
	Logical NOT	!x	
	Type cast	(type)x	Define as operator type()
Arithmetic	Multiply	x*y	
	Divide	x/y	
	Remainder	x%y	
	Add	x+y	Define as operator+(y) or as friend operator+(x,y)
	Subtract	x-y	Define as operator-(y) or as friend operator -(x,y)
Shift	Left shift	x<<y	
	Right shift	x>>y	
Relational	Greater than	x>y	
	Greater than or equal	x>=y	
	Less than	x<y	
	Less than or equal	x<=y	

continues

Table 10.1. continued

Type	Name	Notation	Comments
	Equal to	x==y	
	Not equal to	x!=y	
Bitwise	Bitwise AND	x&y	
	Bitwise exclusive OR	x^y	
	Bitwise OR	x¦y	
Logical	Logical AND	x&&y	
	Logical OR	x¦¦y	
Assignment	Assignment	x=y	
	Multiply assign	x *= y	
	Divide assign	x /= y	
	Remainder assign	x %= y	
	Add assign	x += y	
	Subtract assign	x -= y	
	Left-shift assign	x <<= y	
	Right-shift assign	x >>= y	
	Bitwise AND assign	x &= y	
	Bitwise XOR assign	x ^= y	
	Bitwise OR assign	x ¦= y	

Type	Name	Notation	Comments
Data Access	Subscript	`x[y]`	
	Member selection	`x->y`	
	Dereference	`x->*y`	
	Member		
	Pointer		
Function call	Function call	`x(y)`	
Comma	Comma	`x,y`	
Storage	new	`x *p=new x`	
	delete	`delete p`	

Operator Precedence Remains Unchanged

Although C++ enables you to redefine the meaning of most built-in operator symbols for a class, you cannot change the precedence rules that dictate the order in which operators are evaluated. C++ operators follow the same precedence as those of their ANSI C counterparts as shown in Table 3.5. Even if, for some class, you were to define `+` and `*` operators as something entirely different from addition and multiplication, in an expression such as

```
a + b * c    // a, b, c are some class instances
```

the C++ compiler still would invoke the `operator*` function to evaluate `b * c` before calling `operator+`.

Defining *operator+* for the *String* Class

As an example of operator overloading, consider the `+` operator—the binary version—for the `String` class. A good interpretation of this operator for the `String` class is to concatenate two `String` objects. In other words, a typical use of the `+` operator for `String` might be:

```
String s1("This "), s2("and that"), s3;
s3 = s1+s2;  // Now s3 should contain "This and that"
```

You can get this functionality by defining the following function as a member of the `String` class:

```
//------------------------------------------------------------------
//  o p e r a t o r +
//  Member function to concatenate two String objects

String String::operator+(const String& s)
{
    size_t len = _length + s._length;
    char *t = new char[len+1];
    strcpy(t, p_c);
    strcat(t, s.p_c);
    String r(t);
    delete t;
    return (r);
}
```

Because this version of `operator+` is a member function of the `String` class, it takes only one argument: a reference to the `String` on the right side of the + operator. The function returns a new `String` object that is a concatenation of the two `Strings` being added. As you can see from the body of this `operator+` function, if you use `new` to allocate temporary storage, you are responsible for freeing the storage by using the `delete` operator.

While the `operator+` member function works fine when adding `Strings`, it cannot handle another type of use for the operator. Because a `String` is intended to model a dynamic array of characters, it's natural to allow the use of the operator in expressions such as

```
String s1 = "World!";
String s2 = "Hello," + s1; // s2 should be "Hello, World!"
```

In this case, the C++ compiler interprets the right side of the expression as

```
"Hello".operator+(s1)
```

This is an error, because `"Hello"` is not an instance of a class and, therefore, contains no member `operator+` function that can be applied to it. You might think a solution would be to convert `"Hello"` to a String and then apply the `operator+` function of the

String class. However, this doesn't happen because the C++ compiler does not automatically convert the left operand of member operator functions. On the other hand, if you define a nonmember friend operator+ function in the String class

```
friend String operator+(const String& s1, const String& s2)
```

the compiler converts the expression "Hello" + s1 to the function call

```
operator+(String("Hello"), s1)
```

which automatically converts the left side of the + operator to a String. The definition of the friend operator+ function is similar to the member function, except that it takes two String arguments, and the body of the function must refer to each argument explicitly. Here's a definition of the function

```
//-------------------------------------------------------------
//  o p e r a t o r +
//  Nonmember function that concatenates two String objects
//  (Declare as "friend" in String class)

String operator+(const String& s1, const String& s2)
{
    size_t len = s1._length + s2._length;
    char *t = new char[len+1];
    strcpy(t, s1.p_c);
    strcat(t, s2.p_c);
    String s3(t);
    delete t;
    return (s3);
}
```

The friend version of operator+ function does not require the String:: scope-resolution prefix because it's not a member function of the String class.

Testing Strings for Equality

Another interesting operator is ==. You can use this operator with the String class to compare two String instances for equality. Because the String class internally maintains a C string, the easiest way to implement this operator is to call the strcmp function from the C library, as shown here:

```
#include "str.h"  // Includes <string.h>
//...

//-------------------------------------------------------------
//  o p e r a t o r = =
//  String equality operator. Returns nonzero if strings are
//  equal

inline Boolean String::operator==(const String &s) const
{
// Use ANSI C's strcmp function to compare the strings
// Remember strcmp returns 0 if the strings match, but this
//  function has to return nonzero (true) for a match
    return(strcmp(s.p_c, p_c) == 0);
}
```

You can similarly define other relational operators, such as `operator !=`, `operator >`, and `operator <`.

Accessing and Altering Individual Characters in a String

Earlier in this chapter, you encountered a `char_at_pos` function that returned a reference to a character at a specific position in the character array inside an instance of a `String`. A better way to provide the functionality of the `char_at_pos` function is to overload the `[]` operator for the `String` class. Knowing the implementation of the `char_at_pos` function, you can define the `operator[]` function as follows:

```
//-------------------------------------------------------------
//  o p e r a t o r [ ]
//  Access a character in a String

char& String::operator[](int index)
{
// Check if index goes beyond allocated length.
// Return last element, if it does
    if(index > _maxlen-1) return p_c[_maxlen-1];
    else  return p_c[index];
}
```

With the [] operator defined in this way, you can use it in statements, such as

```
String s = "hello";
char c = s[4];      // c = 'o', the 5th character of "hello"
s[0] = 'H';         // Now String s contains "Hello"
```

Defining the Type-Conversion Operator

The String class is an abstraction of a character string and suitable for use in places where C-style, null-terminated strings are required. Suppose you want to allow String instances to be used in calls to the C library's string manipulation functions—the ones defined in the string.h header file. An example might be an expression such as

```
#include <string.h>
//...
String command;
//...
if(strcmp(command, "quit") == 0) exit(0);
```

Because the strcmp function is declared to accept two const char* arguments, the C++ compiler successfully makes this call—provided it can convert the String command to a const char*. You can help the C++ compiler do this by defining a *type-conversion operator* of the form

```
String::operator const char*()
```

Of course, for the String class, you need only return the private char pointer member p_c. Because this function is so simple, you may want to define it as inline, like this:

```
//-------------------------------------------------------------
//  o p e r a t o r   c o n s t   c h a r   *
//  Converts from String to char pointer

inline String::operator const char*() const
{
    return p_c;
}
```

Once this conversion operator is defined, calls to functions such as strcmp work even with a String as an argument.

Defining the Assignment Operator for the String Class

The = assignment operator is similar to the copy constructor, except that the copy constructor works with an uninitialized copy of an object, while the assignment operator copies an object to another that already is initialized. Thus, for a `String` object, the assignment operator must eliminate the existing character array and set up a new one with the new value. A typical implementation of this operator function looks like this:

```
//---------------------------------------------------------------
//  o p e r a t o r =
//  Assigns one String object to another

String& String::operator=(const String& s)
{
// Do nothing if left and right sides are the same
    if(this != &s)
    {
        _length = s._length;
        _maxlen = s._maxlen;
        delete p_c;
        p_c = new char[_maxlen];
        strcpy(p_c, s.p_c);
    }
    return *this;
}
```

If you compare this function with the copy constructor, you'll find the two to be very similar. One crucial difference, however, is the `if` statement at the beginning of the `operator+` function. This test ensures that the assignment operator works properly even when the left and right sides of the assignment operator are identical. When this happens, the variables `p_c` and `s.p_c` refer to the same pointer. You cannot indiscriminately delete `p_c` and expect `strcpy(p_c, s.p_c)` to work. The correctness of the assignment operation is ensured by comparing the `this` keyword with the operator's right side, which is the argument of the `operator=` function.

Why *operator=* Returns a Reference

You may have noticed that the `operator=` function for the `String` class returns `String&`, and you might have wondered why this is so. This is to allow assignments such as

```
String s1, s2, s3;
s1 = s2 = s3 = "None";
```

where the second statement initializes all three strings to the same value. This statement is possible only because the `operator=` function of the `String` class returns a reference to a `String` object and thereby can be the left side of further assignments.

> **Assignment and Initialization in C++**
>
> In C++, assignment and initialization often are denoted by very similar statements. Consider the following definitions of `String` objects:
>
> ```
> String s1 = "This is initialization";
>
> String s2;
>
> s2 = "This is assignment"
> ```
>
> This defines `String s1` and `String s2`. `String s1` is initialized by calling the `String(const char*)` constructor, while `String s2` initially is constructed by the default constructor `String()`. The third statement assigns a value to `String s2`. The definition of a class instance followed by an equal sign indicates initialization, whereas a previously defined class instance name appearing on the left side of an equal sign denotes assignment.

Overloading the Input and Output Operators

In Chapter 8, "C++ Classes for Standard I/O," you saw the `iostream` class, which defines the `>> operator` for input and the `<< operator` for output. As defined in the iostream.h header file, these operators work with all predefined types such as `int`, `long`, `double`, and `char*`. When you define your own classes, such as the `String` class, you might want to overload the definitions of the << and >> operators so that they work with your classes.

For example, once you overload the >> operator, you can read characters from an input stream to a `String` by writing

```
String user_input;
cin >> user_input;  // Accept user's input
Similarly, to display a String, you would write:

String greetings = "Hello, World!";
cout << greetings << endl;
```

The Output Operator

These operators are easy to define. To overload the output operator (<<), you need a public member function for the class that can handle the actual output. For the `String` class, you can define a `print` function to perform the output, as follows:

```
#include "str.h"   // This includes <iostream.h>
//...
//-------------------------------------------------------------
//  p r i n t
//  Outputs the String on a specified output stream

void String::print(ostream& os) const
{
    os << p_c;
}
```

Once the print function is defined, you can overload the << operator for a `String` argument as follows:

```
//-------------------------------------------------------------
//  o p e r a t o r < <
//  Stream insertion operator for String class

ostream& operator<<(ostream& os, String& s)
{
    s.print(os);
    return os;
}
```

As you can see, this operator function does its work by calling the member function named `print` from the `String` class. Note that the `ostream` class declares `operator<<` as a `friend` function.

The Input Operator

The stream extraction operator >> also is easy to implement. The following version assumes a maximum string length of 256 characters, including the null byte, and uses the `get` function of the input stream to read the characters into an internal array. It then creates a new `String` object from that character array and returns the `String`.

```
//------------------------------------------------------------
//  o p e r a t o r > >
//  Stream extraction operator for String class

istream& operator>>(istream& is, String& s)
{
    const bufsize = 256;
    char buf[bufsize];

    if(is.get(buf, bufsize)) s = String(buf);
    return is;
}
```

Overloading Operators *new* and *delete*

The dynamic storage allocation operators `new` and `delete` are two more interesting operators that you also can overload. You can overload the `new` operator to use another method for allocating storage. You might want to do this, for example, because it's inefficient to allocate many small objects on the free store using the `new` default operator. One way to improve the efficiency of memory allocation is to obtain a large chunk of memory and use that as the pool of memory from which an overloaded version of the `new` operator doles out storage for the objects.

Like other operators, overriding `new` and `delete` for any class involves defining the functions `operator new` and `operator delete`.

Some Rules for *new* and delete

Follow these rules when overriding new and delete:

- The first argument of operator new must be of the size_t type (as defined in the stddef.h ANSI C header file) and must return a void*. Consequently, a prototype for operator new is as follows:

  ```
  void* operator new(size_t numbytes);
  ```

- The first argument to operator delete must be of the void* type and must not return a value. You also can have a second argument of the size_t type. A typical prototype for operator delete is

  ```
  void operator delete(void *p);
  ```

Whenever you define the operator new and operator delete functions for a class, the C++ compiler automatically treats them as static member functions of that class. This is true even if you do not explicitly declare them as static. The C++ compiler must call new before the constructor and delete after the destructor. In other words, the compiler must be able to call these operators even when no instance of the class exists. To make this possible, the compiler treats operator new and operator delete as static.

Placement Syntax for *operator new*

There is an intriguing way of using the new operator to initialize objects in preallocated memory. This is done with the placement syntax of the new operator. The following example shows how you might initialize a buffer in-place with instances of a fictitious my_widget class:

```
//-------------------------------------------------------------
//  Illustrates placement syntax of operator "new"

#include <iostream.h>
#include <stddef.h>

class my_widget
{
public:
    my_widget(int x, int y) : _x(x), _y(y){}

// Define default new operator.
// NOTE: This simply calls global copy of "operator new"
    void* operator new(size_t sz) { return ::operator new(sz);}
```

```
// Define "new" invoked with placement syntax
    void* operator new(size_t sz, void* p)
    {
        return (my_widget*)p;
    }

// Another member function
    int& getx(){ return _x;}

private:
    int _x, _y;
};

//----------------------------------------------------------------
// Test program

main()
{
    char buf[10*sizeof(my_widget)];
    int i=1;

// Initialize chunks of buf with instances of "my_widget"
    for(char *b=buf; b < buf+10*sizeof(my_widget);
        b += sizeof(my_widget), i++)
    {
        (void) new(b) my_widget(i, i);  // placement syntax
    }

// See if it worked...
    my_widget* widget = (my_widget*) buf;

    for(i=0; i<10; i++)
        cout << widget[i].getx() << " ";

    cout << endl;
}
```

When run, this sample program generates the following output:

```
1 2 3 4 5 6 7 8 9 10
```

which is what you would expect because of the way the instances of `my_widget` are initialized.

This approach of placing a new object in a predefined area of memory has a purpose. Some environments, such as Microsoft Windows and Apple Macintosh, have their own memory-management scheme that good programs are supposed to follow. If you happen to use C++ to write application programs for such environments, you can allocate a block of memory by calling an environment-specific function, and you can use the placement syntax of `operator new` to initialize instances of objects in that block of memory.

Using *friend* Classes

Sometimes the data-hiding rules of C++ classes can be too restrictive. If, for reasons of efficiency, you want to provide an `A` class access to all members of a `B` class, you can do so by embedding the following statement in the declaration of class `B`:

```
class A;
class B
{
    friend A;  // A can access all members of this class
//...
};
```

To see how `friend` classes are used, consider the example in the next section.

Using a File as an Array

To treat a file as an array of characters, you should create a `File` class and use it as follows:

```
File f("sample.dat");  // Open a file
char c = f[10];        // Get byte at index 10
f[128] = ']';          // Store ']' into a byte in the file
```

This tells you that you need a `File` constructor that takes a file's name as an argument. In the constructor, you must open the file and include the `FILE` pointer—assuming that you use the standard C file I/O functions to the actual I/O operations with the file. Additionally, you must overload `operator[]` to read from and write to the file.

With the `File` class alone, it's difficult to define this operator. You can do so, however, by using a helper class called `FileLoc`. The idea is to define `operator[]` for the `File` class so that applying the operator to a `File` implies creation of a `FileLoc` object—as the name implies, this object keeps track of the position within the file. The FileLoc object positions the stream and defines appropriate operators to read from and write to the disk file. The File and FileLoc classes are declared as friends of each other so that the I/O operations can be as efficient as possible. Listing 10.3 shows the actual declarations of the classes, as well as a small test program.

Listing 10.3. FARRAY.CPP. Classes that treat a disk file as an array of characters.

```
//-------------------------------------------------------------------
//  File:  farray.cpp
//  Treats a file as an array of bytes
//-------------------------------------------------------------------

#include <stdio.h>
#include <iostream.h>

//-------------------------------------------------------------------
//  Declare the "FileLoc" class_the helper of File class

class File;

class FileLoc
{
public:
    friend File;

    void operator=(char c);
    void operator=(const char* str);
    operator const char();

private:
    File* p_file;
    fpos_t file_loc;
    FileLoc(File& f, fpos_t loc): p_file(&f), file_loc(loc){}
};
//-------------------------------------------------------------------
//  Now declare the "File" class

class File
```

continues

Listing 10.3. continued

```
{
public:
    friend FileLoc;

// Constructor open file for read and write operations
    File(const char* name)
    {
        fp = fopen(name, "r+");  // open for read and write
    }

// Destructor closes file
    ~File() { fclose(fp);}

// operator[] positions file and creates an instance of FileLoc
    FileLoc operator[](fpos_t loc)
    {
        fseek(fp, loc, SEEK_SET);
        return FileLoc(*this,loc);
    }

private:
    FILE* fp;  // ANSI C stream pointer
};
//---------------------------------------------------------------
//     M e m b e r   F u n c t i o n s
//---------------------------------------------------------------
//  o p e r a t o r = ( c h a r )
//  Handles assignments of the form:
//       f[n] = c, where f[n] is a FileLoc and c is a char
//  by storing the character in the file

void FileLoc::operator=(char c)
{
    if(p_file->fp != NULL)
    {
        putc(c, p_file->fp);
    }
}
//---------------------------------------------------------------
//  o p e r a t o r = ( c h a r * )
//  Handles assignments of the form:
```

```
//        f[n]="string", where f[n] is a FileLoc object
//   This stores the string into the file

void FileLoc::operator=(const char* str)
{
    if(p_file->fp != NULL)
    {
        fputs(str, p_file->fp);
    }
}
//----------------------------------------------------------------
//   o p e r a t o r   c o n s t   c h a r ( )
//   Handles assignments of the form:
//        c = f[n], where f[n] is a FileLoc and c is a char
//   This reads a character from the file.

FileLoc::operator const char()
{
    if(p_file->fp != NULL)
    {
        return getc(p_file->fp);
    }
    return EOF;
}
//----------------------------------------------------------------
//   m a i n
//   A program to test the File and FileLoc classes
//   Before running program, create a file "test.dat"
//   with the following line:
//
//       Testing: File and FileLoc classes

void main()
{
    File f("test.dat");
    int i;
    char c;
    cout << "First 14 bytes = " << endl;
    for(i=0; i<14; i++)
    {
        c = f[i];
        cout << c;
    }
```

continues

Listing 10.3. continued

```
    cout << endl;

// Change first 7 bytes to ' ' (blank space)
    for(i=0; i<7; i++) f[i] = ' ';

// Display the first 14 characters again
    cout << "Now the first 14 bytes = " << endl;
    for(i=0; i<14; i++)
    {
        c = f[i];
        cout << c;
    }
    cout << endl;

// Store a string in the file
    f[0] = "Creating";

    cout << "After string insert: the first 25 bytes = " << endl;
    for(i=0; i<25; i++)
    {
        c = f[i];
        cout << c;
    }
    cout << endl;
}
```

If you prepare a file named TEST.DAT with the following line:

```
Testing: File and FileLoc classes.
```

and run the program shown in Listing 10.3, you should see the following output:

```
First 14 bytes =
Testing: File
Now the first 14 bytes =
       : File
After string insert: the first 25 bytes =
Creating File and FileLoc
```

When you write

```
char c = f[i];  // f is a File, i an integer
```

the expression `f[i]` results in a `FileLoc` object, which positions the file to the character at location `i`. The C++ compiler then applies `FileLoc::operator const char()` to this `FileLoc` object. As you can see from the definition of `FileLoc::operator const char()`, this action reads a character from the file. On the other hand, when you write

```
f[i] = c;  // f is a File, i is an integer, c, a char
```

the expression `f[i]` again creates a `FileLoc` object that positions the file to the position `i`. The C++ compiler then invokes the function `FileLoc::operator=(char)`, which writes the character to the file. This operator is overloaded for a string argument as well, so that an entire string can be written to a file.

This is a good example of using a `friend` class as an intermediary when implementing a desired syntax of usage for a class. Here, as the sole purpose of the `FileLoc` class, you can use the `File` class not only to view a disk file as an array of characters, but you can use the array-access syntax of the file `class` to read from and write to a file.

Summary

The `class` construct forms the basis of object-oriented programming in C++. The member functions of a class control how the class can be used. To make a class as easy to use as the built-in data types, you must define a complete assortment of member functions for each class. Constructors that the C++ compiler calls to initialize a newly created instance of a class are important. At a minimum, you should provide the default constructor, which takes no arguments, and the copy constructor, which initializes a new instance of a class from an existing instance. When initializing a class that includes instances of other classes as members, use member-initializer list syntax to initialize these class instances. The initializer list is the only way to initialize constant member variables.

To make classes easy to use, C++ enables you to redefine most operators so that they can be used with instances of a class to perform meaningful operations. For example, for a `String` class, the `+` operator can be defined to concatenate two `Strings`. Overloading operators involves defining functions with names that begin with the `operator` keyword followed by the symbol used for the operator.

Although C++ supports strict data hiding, you can use the `friend` keyword to declare one class or a function as a friend of another class. A friend can access all members of a class: `public` as well as `private` and `protected`. An example illustrates how you can use a `friend` class to implement a convenient syntax of usage for a class that lets you treat a file as an array of bytes.

Using Inheritance in C++

The last two chapters focused on data abstraction. This is only one ingredient, albeit an important one, of object-oriented programming. The other two components of OOP are *inheritance* and *polymorphism.* Although data abstraction helps you define a new data type, you need inheritance to exploit the common features of related data types or to extend the functionality provided by one or more existing classes.

Inheritance enables you to:

- Classify objects. For instance, with inheritance you can categorize circles, rectangles, and triangles because different types of shapes share everything that they have in common.
- Express the differences between related classes while sharing the functions and member variables that implement the common features.
- Reuse existing code from one or more classes simply by deriving a new class from them.
- Extend an existing class by adding new members to it.

This chapter explains how to use inheritance in C++ classes.

Derived Classes

Suppose you have a C++ class that implements a specific data type, and you need another data type that's similar to the first but has some additional member variables or functions. Rather than create the new data type from scratch, OOP techniques suggest that you inherit from the existing type and add the necessary capabilities to the inherited type. In C++, you can do this by deriving the new class from the existing class. You can add capabilities to the derived class by:

- Defining new member variables
- Defining new member functions
- Overriding the definition of inherited member functions

Inheritance and the "Is a" Relationship

One common use of inheritance is to express the *is a* relationship among various types of objects. The geometric shapes discussed in Chapter 6, "C++ and Object-Oriented Programming," are based on this idea. Because a circle *is a* shape and a rectangle *is a* shape, the `circle_shape` and `rectangle_shape` classes inherit from the `shape` class. We call this attribute the "is a" relationship.

In some object-oriented languages, such as SmallTalk, `circle_shape` is called a *subclass* of `shape`, which in turn is the *superclass* of `circle_shape`. In C++, the `circle_shape` and `rectangle_shape` classes are derived from the `shape` class, which is their *base class.* Figure 11.1 illustrates this concept. Notice that you may further specialize the `rectangle_shape` class by deriving from it a `rounded_rectangle_shape` class that represents rectangles with rounded corners.

As you can see, a base class can have more than one derived class, and a derived class can serve as the base class for others. Thus, you end up with a tree-structured hierarchy of classes in which the classes near the bottom (the leaves) are more specialized versions of the classes at the top.

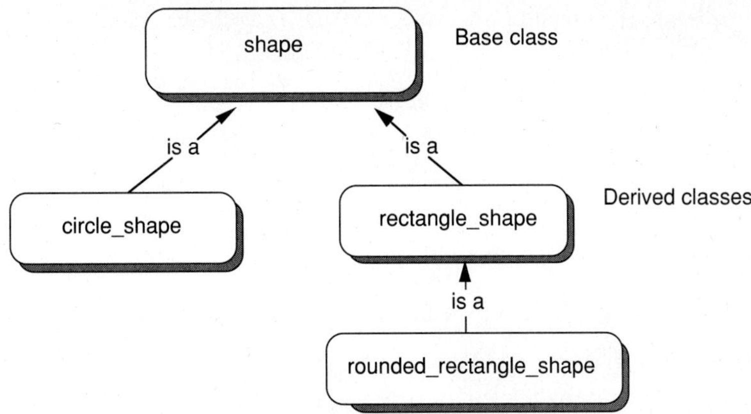

Figure 11.1. Inheritance in C++.

Inheritance and Class Extension

In addition to seeing inheritance as a mechanism for implementing the *is a* relationship among types of objects, you also can use inheritance to extend the functionality provided by one or more classes. Suppose you have a class named `single_link` that maintains a pointer to another instance of the same class. You plan to use the `single_link` objects in a linked list. You might declare the `single_link` as follows:

```
class single_link
{
public:
    single_link(): _next(0) {}

    single_link(single_link& sl) : _next(sl._next) {}

// Other member functions...

protected:
    single_link* _next;  // link to next "single_link"
};
```

Later, you might want a doubly linked list, for which you would need a `double_link` class with instances capable of holding two pointers—one to the next instance and the other to the previous one. Instead of defining the list from scratch, you can create the `double_link` class by simply deriving it from `single_link` and adding a new member variable, like this:

```
// Include declaration of "single_link" class here

class double_link: public single_link
{
public:
    double_link() : single_link(), _previous(0){}

//  Other member functions...

protected:
    single_link* _previous;  // Add another "link"
};
```

As you'll soon learn, making the `_next` data item in the `single_link` class `protected` allows derived classes, such as `double_link`, to directly access the `_next` pointer. This improves the speed with which a program can manipulate the items in linked lists that use these classes. Later in this chapter you'll see an example that uses these link classes to construct linked list data structures.

Syntax of a Derived Class

The `class` construct of C++ already includes the syntax necessary to indicate that a class is derived from another. For a base class, you declare the `class` exactly like a `struct`:

```
class shape
{
public:
// ...
};
```

For a derived class, you must list the name of its base class:

```
class circle_shape: public shape  // circle is derived from shape
{
public:
// ...
private:
    double x_center, y_center;
    double radius;
};
```

Access to the Base Class

The public keyword preceding the name of the base class indicates how circle_shape is derived from shape. In this case, circle_shape is publicly derived from shape. In other words, shape is a public base class of circle_shape. This means all public and protected members of shape are also public and protected members of circle_shape.

You also can specify a private keyword in front of the base class name. In this case, all public and protected members of the base class become private members of the derived class. As illustrated in Figure 11.2, the net effect is that if rectangle_shape is privately derived from shape, the rounded_rectangle_shape class derived from rectangle_shape no longer can access the public and protected members of shape. In effect, a privately derived class blocks any further access to members of its base class.

When you use the class keyword to define object types, the default derivation is private. In other words, if you forget the access specifier and write:

```
class rectangle_shape: shape
{
// rectangle_shape is privately derived from shape
// ...
};
```

you get a private derivation of shape. On the other hand, with the struct keyword, all derivations are public by default. Thus, the following code declares a rectangle_shape class with a public base class named shape:

```
struct rectangle_shape: shape
{
// rectangle_shape is publicly derived from shape
// ...
};
```

Using Inheritance to Build a Substring Class

Chapter 9, "Building Objects with Classes," and Chapter 10, "Defining Operations on Objects," use a String class as an example. Suppose you want to create a new class, called Substring, with which you can access a part of a String object. The following code should accomplish this:

```
String path_name(32); // 32-character string, set to all blanks
path_name(0,4) = "/bin"; // Replace substring with "/bin"
```

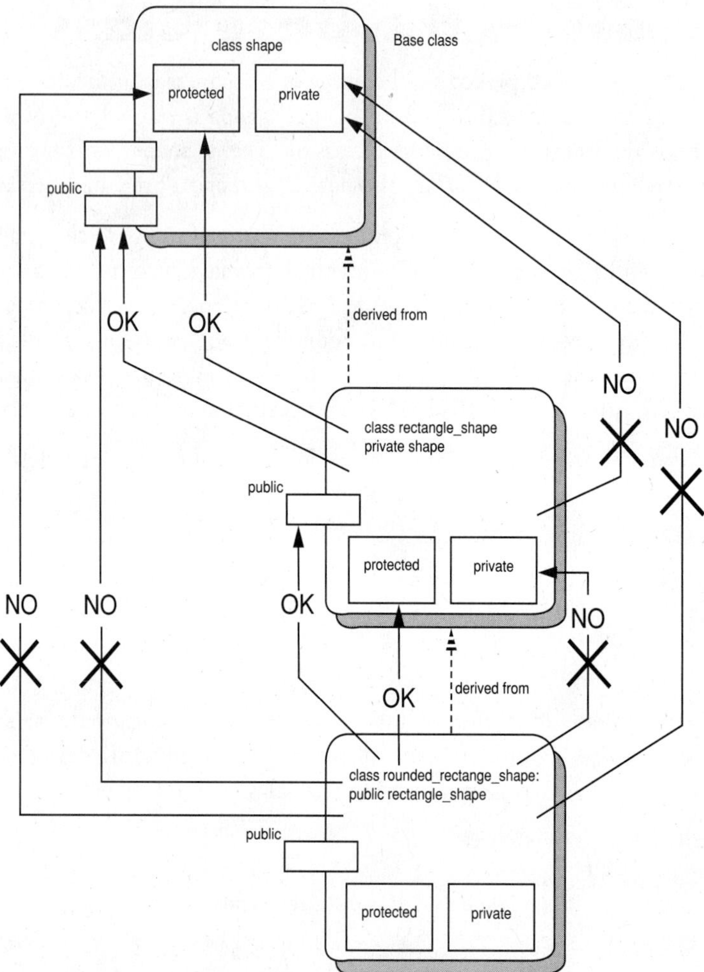

Figure 11.2. Controlling access to members of base class.

One way to make this work is to overload the `operator()` for the `String` class so that it returns a `Substring`. The C string `/bin` then is copied into the substring. The code sets the first four characters of `String path_name` to `/bin`.

Deriving *Substring* from *String*

Because a `Substring` is a `String`, an easy way to define `Substring` is to derive it from `String`. As a benefit of deriving it from the `String` class, all operations defined for the `String` class are immediately available to the `Substring` class. A `Substring` is a full-fledged String, but it holds a reference to the String from which it was derived. This is necessary so that the original String can be altered through a statement such as the following:

```
String path_name(32);
path_name(0,4) = "/bin";
```

This path_name(0,4) expression creates a Substring class and the Substring::operator=(const char*) function replaces four characters, starting at the first character of path_name with the /bin string.

Listing 11.1 shows a revised STR.H header file that declares both the String and Substring classes. Before defining the Substring class, change the private members of String to protected so that Substring objects can access the internal variables of the Strings.

Initializing the Base Class

As you can see from Listing 11.1, declaring the Substring class is a straightforward process. Notice how you initialize a base class from the constructor of the derived class. In Chapter 10, "Defining Operations on Objects," you learned how member initializer lists are used to initialize static members and member classes—that is, class instances that appear as a member of another class. You can use the same technique to initialize the base class in the constructor of a derived class. As an example, consider the following Substring constructor:

```
// Substring constructor
   Substring(String& s, const char *cs, size_t pos, size_t len) :
       String(cs, len), s_original(s), _pos(pos) { }
```

This creates a Substring by copying len characters starting at position pos of the specified String. As you can see, the body of this constructor is empty. All initializations are done through the initializer list, which invokes an appropriate String constructor and initializes the members of the newly created Substring.

Listing 11.1. Revised STR.H file with declaration of String and Substring classes.

```
//-------------------------------------------------------------
//  File:  str.h
//  Declares a "String" class and a "Substring" class derived
//  from the "String" class
//-------------------------------------------------------------
```

continues

Listing 11.1. continued

```
#if !defined(_ _STR_H)  // Be sure file is included only once
#define _ _STR_H

// Include other required header files...
// The ANSI C headers work because they are already enclosed
// in an extern "C"{...}
// Be sure your compiler does this.

#include <stddef.h>      // For "size_t" type
#include <iostream.h>    // For stream I/O
#include <string.h>      // For ANSI C string library

typedef int Boolean;     // For return type of operators

class Substring;

class String
{
public:
// Constructors with a variety of arguments
    String();
    String(size_t len);
    String(const char *str);
    String(const char *str, size_t len);
    String(const String &s);

// Destructor
    ~String() { delete p_c;}

// Overloaded operators
    Boolean operator==(const String& s) const
   {
        return(strcmp(s.p_c, p_c) == 0);
    }

// Assignment operator
    String& operator=(const String& s);

// Type conversion operator
    operator const char*() const { return p_c;}
```

```
// Access operator
    char& operator[](int index);

// Replace a portion of a string with another.
// Used to insert or delete parts of a string.
   String& replace(size_t pos, size_t len, const char* s);

//  o p e r a t o r ( )
//  Overload the function call operator to return a Substring

    Substring operator()(size_t pos, size_t len);

// The + operator concatenates strings
    friend String operator+(const String& s1, const String& s2);

// Function giving access to internal variable
    size_t length(void) const { return _length;}

// Function to print a String
    void print(ostream& os) const;

protected:   // so that derived classes can access these data

    char   *p_c;      // pointer to allocated space
    size_t _length;  // current length of string
    size_t _maxlen;  // number of bytes allocated

};

// Stream I/O for String class

#include <iostream.h>

ostream& operator<<(ostream& os, String& s);
istream& operator>>(istream& is, String& s);

//------------------------------------------------------------
//  Declare the "Substring" class

class Substring: public String
{
```

continues

Listing 11.1. continued

```
public:
    friend String;  // Give the String class access to this one

// Substring operators...
    String& operator=(const char* str)
    {
        return s_original.replace(_pos, _length, str);
    }
    String& operator=(Substring& s)
    {
        return s_original.replace(_pos, _length, s.p_c);
    }

private:
    String& s_original;  // Reference to original String
    size_t  _pos;        // Position of Substring in String

// Substring constructor
    Substring(String& s, const char *cs, size_t pos, size_t len) :
        String(cs, len), s_original(s), _pos(pos) { }

// Substring copy constructor

    Substring(const Substring& s) : String(s),
        s_original(s.s_original), _pos(s._pos) { }

};


#endif
```

Modifying the Original *String* Through a *Substring*

As mentioned earlier, one reason to introduce the `Substring` class is to use it in statements such as the following, which modifies a portion of a `String` through an intermediate `Substring` created by the `String::operator()`:

```
String hello = "Hello......";
hello(5,3) = " there";   // Now hello = "Hello there..."
```

To make this work, you must define Substring::operator=(const char*) and have a way to replace a number of characters in a String. To this end, add a String::replace function, shown toward the end of Listing 11.2. That listing shows the str.cpp file, an implementation of the String class. With the String::replace function in place, you can implement the operator= function for the Substring class simply by calling String::replace as follows:

```
String& operator=(const char* str)
{
// Invoke the original String's "replace" function
    return s_original.replace(_pos, _length, str);
}
```

The *String::operator()*

Substrings are created through the operator() function of the String class. This operator is invoked with two size_t arguments, the first denoting the starting position of the substring and the second indicating the substring's length. Once you've defined a constructor for the Substring class that can create a Substring from a String, you can define the String::operator() as follows:

```
Substring String::operator()(size_t pos, size_t len)
{
    return Substring(*this, &(p_c[pos]), pos, len);
}
```

This function simply returns a new Substring by calling the Substring constructor.

Listing 11.2. STR.CPP. Implementation of the String class.

```
//-------------------------------------------------------------
//  File:  str.cpp
//  Implements the member functions of the "String" class

#include "str.h"    // For declaration of String class

const chunk_size = 8;

//-------------------------------------------------------------
//  S t r i n g
//  Creates a String object and initializes it
//  from a null-terminated C string
```

continues

Listing 11.2. continued

```
String::String(const char *s)
{
    _length = strlen(s);
    _maxlen = chunk_size*(_length / chunk_size + 1);
    p_c = new char[_maxlen];
    strcpy(p_c, s);
}
//-------------------------------------------------------------
// S t r i n g
// Creates a String object and initializes it using a
// specified number of characters from a null-terminated
// C string

String::String(const char *s, size_t len)
{
    _length = len;
    _maxlen = chunk_size*(_length / chunk_size + 1);
    p_c = new char[_maxlen];
    p_c[len] = '\0';
    strncpy(p_c, s, len);
}
//-------------------------------------------------------------
// S t r i n g
// Creates a String and stores a zero-length string in it.

String::String()
{
    _maxlen = chunk_size;
    p_c = new char[_maxlen];
    _length = 0;
    p_c[0] = '\0';
}
//-------------------------------------------------------------
// S t r i n g
// This version creates a blank string of size "len"

String::String(size_t len)
{
    _length = len;
    _maxlen = chunk_size*(_length / chunk_size + 1);
    p_c = new char[_maxlen];
```

```
    int i;
    for(i = 0; i < len; i++) p_c[i] = ' ';
    p_c[i] = '\0';
}
//-------------------------------------------------------------
//  S t r i n g
//  Creates a new String as a copy of another String
//  This is often called the "Copy Constructor"

String::String(const String &s)
{
    _length = s._length;
    _maxlen = s._maxlen;
    p_c = new char[_maxlen];
    strcpy(p_c, s.p_c);
}
//-------------------------------------------------------------
//  o p e r a t o r +
//  Concatenates two String objects

String operator+(const String& s1, const String& s2)
{
    size_t len = s1._length + s2._length;
    char *t = new char[len+1];
    strcpy(t, s1.p_c);
    strcat(t, s2.p_c);
    String s3(t);
    delete t;
    return (s3);
}
//-------------------------------------------------------------
//  o p e r a t o r =
//  Assigns one String object to another

String& String::operator=(const String& s)
{
    if(this != &s)
    {
        _length = s._length;
        _maxlen = s._maxlen;
        delete p_c;
        p_c = new char[_maxlen];
```

continues

Listing 11.2. continued

```
        strcpy(p_c, s.p_c);
    }
    return *this;
}
//-------------------------------------------------------------
// p r i n t
// Outputs the String on a specified output stream

void String::print(ostream& os) const
{
    os << p_c;
}
//-------------------------------------------------------------
// o p e r a t o r < <
// Stream insertion operator for String class

ostream& operator<<(ostream& os, String& s)
{
    s.print(os);
    return os;
}
//-------------------------------------------------------------
// o p e r a t o r > >
// Stream extraction operator for String class

istream& operator>>(istream& is, String& s)
{
    const bufsize = 256;
    char buf[bufsize];

    if(is.get(buf, bufsize)) s = String(buf);
    return is;
}
//-------------------------------------------------------------
// o p e r a t o r [ ]
// Access a character in a String

char& String::operator[](int index)
{
// Check whether the index goes beyond the allocated length.
// Return last element , if it does
```

```
    if(index > _maxlen-1) return p_c[_maxlen-1];
    else  return p_c[index];
}
//-----------------------------------------------------------------
//  r e p l a c e
//  Replace a portion of a string with another C string.

String& String::replace(size_t pos, size_t len, const char* s)
{
    size_t new_len = strlen(s);

// Check if there is enough room
    if(_length + new_len - len < _maxlen)
    {
// Move bytes around using ANSI C function "memmove"
        memmove(&(p_c[pos+new_len]), &(p_c[pos+len]),
                _length-pos-len);
        memmove(&(p_c[pos]), s, new_len);
    }
    else
    {
// Must reallocate string
        _maxlen = chunk_size * ((_length+new_len-len) /
                                chunk_size + 1);
        char *t = new char[_maxlen];
// Copy strings over...
        memmove(t, p_c, pos);
        memmove(&(t[pos]), s, new_len);
        memmove(&(t[new_len+pos]),
                &(p_c[pos+len]), _length-pos-len);
        delete p_c;
        p_c = t;
    }
// Adjust the length of the String
    _length += new_len - len;

// Terminate the new C string
    p_c[_length] = '\0';

    return *this;
}
//-----------------------------------------------------------------
```

continues

Listing 11.2. continued

```
//  o p e r a t o r ( )
//  Overload the function call operator to return a Substring

Substring String::operator()(size_t pos, size_t len)
{
    return Substring(*this, &(p_c[pos]), pos, len);
}
```

Testing the *Substring* Class

Here's a short program that tries out the `Substring` class through `operator()` applied to a `String` variable named `hello`:

```
// Test Substring class
#include "str.h"

void main()
{
    String hello = "Hello......";
    cout << "Before: " << hello << endl;

    hello(5,3) = " there";
    cout << "After: " << hello << endl;

    hello(11,1) = " C++ Programmer";
    cout << "After another 'replace': " << hello << endl;
}
```

You must rebuild this project, which includes the STR.CPP file shown in Listing 11.2. When run, the program generates the following output:

```
Before: Hello......
After: Hello there...
After another 'replace': Hello there C++ Programmer..
```

Other Issues for Derived Classes

Now that you've seen how the `Substring` class is created by deriving from `String`, you should be aware of a few more details about derived classes that were not illustrated by the `Substring` class. The following sections briefly cover these issues.

Overriding Inherited Member Functions

Presumably, your reason for declaring a derived class is to model a new type of object in terms of one or more existing types or to extend the functionality of an existing class. This usually means that you'll be adding new member variables and member functions to complete the functionality of the derived class. Adding new members is a straightforward process: simply place any new member you want to add in the definition of the derived class. Apart from adding new members, you also can redefine member functions that already appear in a base class. Do this to improve efficiency or to alter the functionality of an existing function. Whatever the reason, you can redefine member functions of the base class freely, provided you keep in mind the following rule.

> An overloaded member function in the derived class hides all inherited member functions of the same name.

This means that, if a base class provides one or more versions of a member function, overloading that function in a derived class hides all inherited versions of the function. The following example clarifies this.

Suppose the `String` class defines two versions of a member function called `insert`, one to insert a single character at a specific position and the other to insert a C string. You could declare the functions as follows:

```
class String
{
public:
//...
    void insert(size_t pos, char c);
    void insert(size_t pos, char* str);

protected:
//...
}
```

After deriving the `Substring` class from `String`, you decide to add another version of the `insert` function, this one to insert the formatted representation of a `float` variable into a `Substring`. With this in mind, you declare the new `insert` function as follows:

```
class Substring: public String
{
public:
//...
    void insert(size_t pos, float x);
private:
//...
};
```

The rule for overriding member functions of the base class says that the function `Substring::insert` hides the functions `String::insert`. In other words, after you define the new `insert` function for `Substring`, you lose access to the `insert` function that the `Substring` class inherits from the `String` class. Keep this in mind when overloading inherited member functions in a derived class.

Order of Initialization of Classes Under Single Inheritance

Another detail worth knowing is the order in which the C++ compiler initializes the base classes of a derived class. When the C++ compiler initializes an instance of a derived class, it must initialize all the base classes first. If you're working with a hierarchy of classes, it helps to know how C++ initializes the base classes so you can track down problems that may occur due to improper initialization of a class instance. For single inheritance, the C++ compiler uses the following basic rules during initialization:

1. Initialize the base class, if any.
2. Within the base class, initialize the member variables in the order in which they are declared in the class.

The only catch is that the compiler applies these rules recursively. Also, notice that the order of member variables in the initializer list does not affect the order in which member variables of a class are initialized. The best way to see the order of initialization is to run a simple example. The following example has a class hierarchy in which class `C` is derived from `B`, and `B` in turn is derived from `A`. Another class, named `Data`, is a member of `A` and `B`. Here's a sample implementation of the classes:

```
// Illustrate order of initialization
#include <iostream.h>

class Data
{
public:
    Data(int x = 0): _x(x)
```

```
    { cout << "Data::Data(" << x << ") ";}
private:
    int _x;
};

class A
{
    Data d1;
public:
    A(int x): d1(x-1) { cout << "A::A(" << x << ") ";}
};

class B: public A
{
    Data d2;
public:
    B(int x): d2(x-1), A(x-2)
    { cout << "B::B(" << x << ") ";}
};

class C: public B
{
public:
    C(int x): B(x-1) { cout << "C::C(" << x << ") ";}
};

void main()
{
    C(5);
}
```

When run, this program generates the following output:

```
Data::Data(1) A::A(2) Data::Data(3) B::B(4) C::C(5)
```

If you trace through the program's code, you will see that the C++ compiler first initializes the `Data` member of `A` class, followed by class `A` itself. It then initializes the `Data` member of class `B`, then class `B`, and finally class `C`. All the base classes are initialized before the derived classes.

As discussed in the following sections, the order of initialization is more complicated when you use multiple inheritance.

Multiple Inheritance

The examples thus far show a derived class with a single base class. This is known as *single inheritance.* C++ also supports the notion of *multiple inheritance,* in which you can derive a class from several base classes. Support for multiple inheritance was introduced in C++ Release 2.0 to allow implementation of classes that needed to share the data and function members of several classes at once. As you'll see in the following sections, multiple inheritance is often used to reuse code from several base classes.

Of course, you can also use multiple inheritance when you feel that a particular class truly manifests the characteristics of more than one class of objects. For instance, suppose you have two classes: `CollectorsItem` and `Cars`. Perhaps the `CollectorsItem` class has member functions that can estimate the value of an object based on its age and rarity. You might decide to define a new class, `AntiqueCars`, that inherits from both `Cars` and `CollectorsItem`. In C++, you can do so by deriving `AntiqueCars` from two base classes in the following manner:

```
class Cars;
class CollectorsItem;

class AntiqueCars: public Cars, public CollectorsItem
{
//...
};
```

Now the `AntiqueCars` class can use all public members of both `Cars` and `CollectorsItem` classes. If necessary, the `AntiqueCars` class can also add new member functions and variables. Additionally, the member functions of `AntiqueCars` can access all `protected` members of its base classes.

iostream and Multiple Inheritance

The `iostream` class library, included with AT&T C++ Release 2.0, uses multiple inheritance. As discussed in Chapter 8, "C++ Classes for Standard I/O," and illustrated in Figure 8.2, the `iostream` library contains the `istream` class for input, the `ostream` class for output, and a bidirectional `iostream` class derived from both `istream` and `ostream`. Therefore, multiple inheritance allows the `iostream` class to support both input and output operations on a stream.

The Virtual Base Class

A problem with inheriting from multiple base classes is that you may end up with more than one instance of a base class. As a concrete example, consider the following hierarchy of classes:

```
// Illustrates need for "virtual base class"

#include <iostream.h>

class device
{
public:
    device()
    { cout << "device: constructor" << endl;}
};

class comm_device: public device
{
public:
    comm_device()
    { cout << "comm_device: constructor" << endl;}
};

class graphics_device: public device
{
public:
    graphics_device()
    { cout << "graphics_device: constructor" << endl;}
};

class graphics_terminal: public comm_device,
                         public graphics_device
{
public:
    graphics_terminal()
    { cout << "graphics_terminal: constructor" << endl;}
};

void main()
{
    graphics_terminal gt;
}
```

Here, the `device` class models a generic, UNIX-style device with functions to open and close the device and control it. The `comm_device` class models a communication device: it adds functions to set the communications parameters. The `graphics_device` class models a device capable of drawing graphics. Finally, the `graphics_terminal` class is derived from both `comm_device` and `graphics_device` classes. Notice what happens when an instance of the `graphics_terminal` class is created. The program prints the following:

```
device: constructor
comm_device: constructor
device: constructor
graphics_device: constructor
graphics_terminal: constructor
```

The constructor for the `device` base class is called twice because it appears twice in the inheritance hierarchy: once as base class of `comm_device` and another time as base class of `graphics_device`.

Because the `graphics_terminal` class models a physical device, you wouldn't want two instances of the `device` base class in every instance of `graphics_terminal`. You need a way to create a `graphics_terminal` class that inherits from both `comm_device` and `graphics_device` but has only one instance of the device class. You can do this with the *virtual base class*. Simply add the `virtual` keyword wherever the `device` class name appears in the inheritance list of a class. The new class definitions are as follows:

```
// Illustrates how "virtual base class" works.

#include <iostream.h>

class device
{
public:
    device()
    { cout << "device: constructor" << endl;}
};

class comm_device: public virtual device
{
public:
    comm_device()
    { cout << "comm_device: constructor" << endl;}
};
```

```
class graphics_device: public virtual device
{
public:
    graphics_device()
    { cout << "graphics_device: constructor" << endl;}
};

class graphics_terminal: public comm_device,
                         public graphics_device
{
public:
    graphics_terminal()
    { cout << "graphics_terminal: constructor" << endl;}
};

void main()
{
    graphics_terminal gt;
}
```

This version of the test program produces the following output:

```
device: constructor
comm_device: constructor
graphics_device: constructor
graphics_terminal: constructor
```

Notice that the `device` class is constructed only once.

Restrictions on Virtual Base Classes

The virtual base class mechanism fills an important need, but beware of the following restrictions when you use virtual base classes:

- You cannot initialize a virtual base class with an initializer list. For an example, look at the constructor of the `Substring` class in Listing 11.1. There, the `String` class is initialized through the initializer list. You can't do the same with a virtual base class. This implies that a class you plan to use as a virtual base class should have a *default constructor*, a constructor that takes no arguments.

- You cannot cast a virtual base class pointer as a pointer to any class that is derived from it. Therefore, in the example, you cannot cast a `device*` pointer to a `graphics_terminal*` pointer.

Order of Initialization of Classes Under Multiple Inheritance

The rules for initializing classes in the presence of multiple inheritance can seem rather complicated. Generally speaking, the C++ compiler follows this order of initialization:

1. All virtual base classes are initialized. The constructor of each virtual base class is called exactly once.
2. Nonvirtual base classes are initialized in the order in which they appear in a class declaration.
3. Member variables also are initialized in the order in which they appear in the class declaration.

The C++ compiler applies these rules recursively, just as it does under single inheritance. For further details on this topic, consult *The Annotated C++ Reference Manual*, by Margaret Ellis and Bjarne Stroustrup.

Using Inheritance

You can use inheritance to create specialized versions of a general-purpose class. Suppose you have a class named `plain_window`, which displays a rectangular area of screen wherein you can show text and graphics output. Typical members of such a class might include foreground and background colors, the font for text display, and a member function that refreshes the contents of the window.

Given the `plain_window` class, you can create a window that displays a text *label* in a window—a `static_text_window`—by deriving it from the `plain_window` class and adding a new member variable to store the text for the label. Furthermore, you can derive from `static_text_window` a `pushbutton_window` that displays a label but, unlike a `static_text_window`, it performs some action when a user selects the pushbutton with a pointing device such as a mouse. Figure 11.3 illustrates the inheritance hierarchy of these window classes. This is an example of specializing classes through inheritance.

On the other hand, inheritance can extend the functionality of a `class`. Instead of specializing, use inheritance for even broader functionality than before. You can view the `class` construct in two ways:

- As a means for defining new data types
- As a module for packaging data and functions

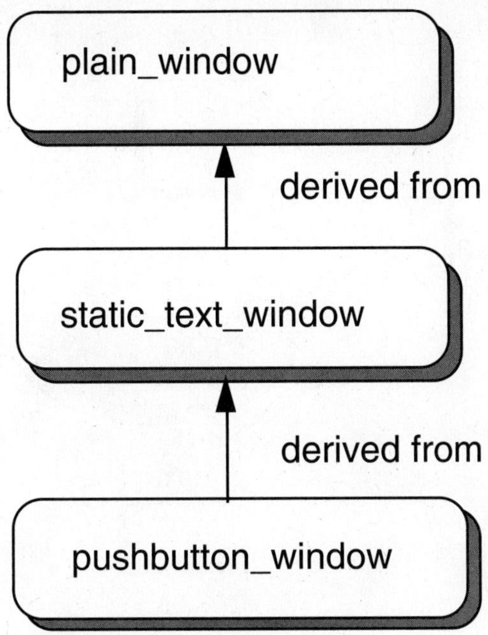

Figure 11.3. Inheritance hierarchy of window classes.

When you use `class` to define a data type, inheritance is useful in creating more specialized types. When you think of a class as a means of packaging functions, you can use inheritance to add new functions, thus extending the capabilities of the module.

Linked Lists

Basic data structures (such as linked lists, queues, stacks, and trees) are popular targets for implementation as abstract data types because they can easily be implemented in the object-oriented style. Inheritance is often useful when defining such classes. A linked list, for instance, can be the basis of several types of data structures including queues, stacks, and trees. We'll begin with an example of a singly-linked list and show how you can use inheritance to create such a data structure.

Figure 11.4 represents a singly-linked list of elements. The list consists of a number of data items, each capable of holding a pointer to another such item. In the singly-linked list, each item points to the next one in the list, so you can start at the beginning of the list and reach every element in the list by following these pointers.

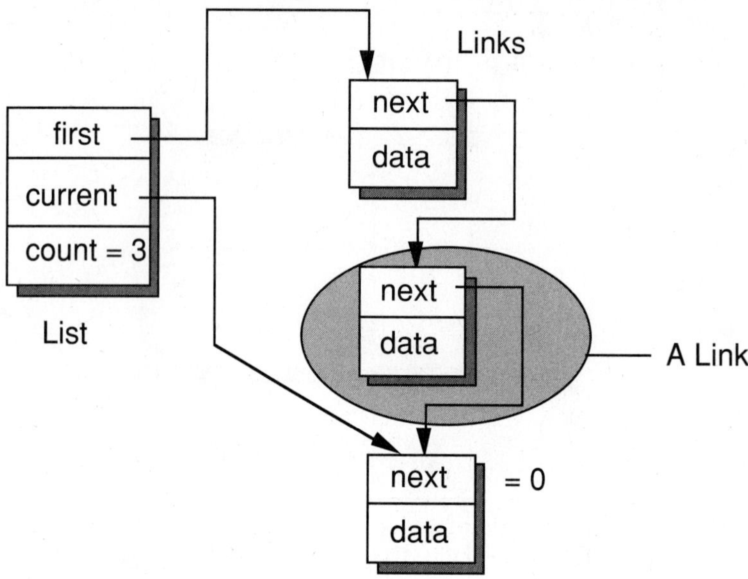

Figure 11.4. A singly-linked list data structure.

In addition to these items, the list needs a pointer to the first element so that you know where to start looking for data stored in the list. Sometimes you may also want to maintain a pointer to what you might call the current element, which is the element being accessed at that time. Another item of interest is the number of elements in the list.

As Figure 11.4 illustrates, one of the basic objects in a linked list is the *link*—an object with some data and a pointer to another link. The other object is the *list*, which holds information about the linked list, such as a pointer to the first item and the number of items. Having identified the basic objects, you can proceed to declare the C++ classes for them.

Making a Generic List

Before declaring the classes for the linked list, let's digress a bit to consider an important issue. You define data structures such as linked lists to store objects. What you really want is a linked list that can hold any type of object. If you could define a parameterized class with a parameter denoting the data type stored in each link, you could easily create linked lists capable of holding different data types by substituting an appropriate type for the parameter. As explained in Chapter 13, "Advanced Topics in C++," the `template` keyword of C++ is used to provide such a facility. However, at this point, C++ does not support parameterized classes.

All is not lost, however, because you can simulate generic lists through inheritance. The idea is to create a list that can hold links of a class named, for example, `single_link`. A `single_link` object contains no data other than a pointer to the next `single_link` object. If you want a singly-linked list of `String` objects later, you can create a new type. We'll call this new type `slink_string`, which inherits from both `single_link` and `String`. Objects of the `slink_string` class then should be able to reside in the singly-linked list you designed to hold `single_link` objects. Figure 11.5 illustrates this idea, and the following sections demonstrate how this works. The major drawback of this approach is that you cannot have a list of built-in data types such as `int`, `char`, and `double` because they are not defined as classes, and you therefore cannot create derived classes from these types.

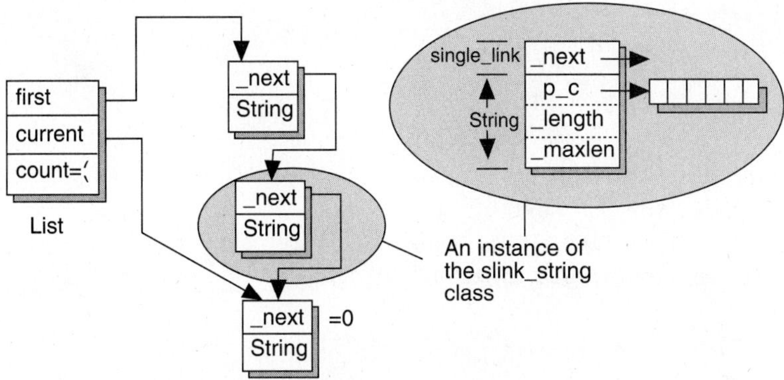

Figure 11.5. A singly-linked list capable of holding `String` objects.

The *single_link* Class

Listing 11.3 shows the slink.h header file, which declares the `single_link` class. The class has only one `protected` data member, named `_next`, which is a pointer to the next `single_link` object. You therefore can string together instances of `single_link` class through their `_next` pointers.

Apart from the constructors, the `single_link` class also provides the `next` member function, which returns its `_next` pointer, and the `set_next` function, which sets the `_next` pointer to a new value.

The class also includes two virtual functions: `clone` and `destroy`. These functions ensure that you can correctly create and destroy instances of a class derived from `single_link`. The `clone` function makes a duplicate copy of an object, while `destroy` properly deletes objects derived from `single_link`. As you will learn in Chapter 12, "Virtual Functions and Polymorphism," these functions are declared as *pure virtual.* This is what the `=0` assignment following the function's declaration does. As a side effect of this declaration, you can't create instances of the `single_link` class until you have derived another class from it and defined the functions `clone` and `destroy`.

Listing 11.3. SLINK.H. Declares the `single_link` class.

```
//------------------------------------------------------------
//  File: slink.h
//  Declares a "single link" class.

#if !defined (_ _SLINK_H)
#define _ _SLINK_H

class single_link
{
public:
    single_link(): _next(0) {}
    single_link(single_link* next) : _next(next) {}
    single_link(single_link& sl) : _next(sl._next) {}

    single_link* next() { return _next; }

    void set_next(single_link *next) { _next = next;}

    virtual single_link* clone() = 0;
    virtual void destroy() = 0;

protected:
    single_link* _next;
};

#endif
```

The *singly_linked_list* Class

Now that you have defined the links, proceed to the list itself. Listing 11.4 shows the SLLIST.H header file, which declares the `singly_linked_list` class, while Listing 11.5 has the actual implementation of some of the member functions. As expected, the

```
//----------------------------------------------------------------
//  ~ s i n g l y _ l i n k e d _ l i s t
//  Destructor for the list

singly_linked_list::~singly_linked_list()
{
    int         i;
    single_link *p_sl = _first, *t;
    if(_count > 0)
    {
        for(i = 0; i < _count; i++)
        {
            t = p_sl->next();
            p_sl->destroy();
            p_sl = t;
        }
    }
}
//----------------------------------------------------------------
//  i n s e r t
//  Insert a new item into the list

void singly_linked_list::insert(single_link& sl)
{
// Clone the element passed to the function and
// hook it up in the linked list
    single_link *t = sl.clone();
    if(_current != 0)
    {
        t->set_next(_current->next());
        _current->set_next(t);
    }
    else
    {
        _first = t;
    }

// Make this one the current item in the list
    _current = t;

// Increment of count of elements on the list
    _count++;
```

continues

Listing 11.5. continued

```
}
//------------------------------------------------------------
//  r e m o v e
//  Removes the current element from the list

void singly_linked_list::remove()
{
// Locate element that points to current
    single_link *p_sl;
    int         i;

    if(_current == 0) return;

    for(i = 0, p_sl = _first;
        p_sl->next() != _current && i < _count;
        i++, p_sl = p_sl->next()) ;

    if(i != _count)
    {
        p_sl->set_next(_current->next());
        _current->destroy();
        _current = p_sl;
        _count--;
    }
}
```

The `remove` function uses the virtual function `destroy` in a similar manner to properly delete an item from the linked list.

A Linkable *String* Class

You've already seen the `String` class in Listings 11.1 and 11.2. If you want to store `String` objects in a `singly_linked_list`, you must create a new type of `String` that might be called a *linkable* `String`. To do this, simply use multiple inheritance to derive from both `String` and `single_link`. Listings 11.6 and 11.7 show this new class, which is called `slink_string` because these are `String` objects to which a `single_link` is added.

Notice how the `clone` and `destroy` functions are defined in Listing 11.6. The `clone` function simply creates a "clone" of the current `slink_string` and returns a pointer to the new copy. The `destroy` function calls the `delete` operator for the current `slink_string`. These functions ensure that objects stored in the singly-linked list are properly initialized and destroyed.

Listing 11.6. SLSTR.H. Declares the `slink_string` class.

```
//-----------------------------------------------------------------
//  File: slstr.h
//  Singly linkable string class

#if !defined(_ _SLSTR_H)
#define _ _SLSTR_H

#include "str.h"      // String class
#include "slink.h"    // single_link class

class slink_string: public single_link, public String
{
public:
    slink_string(const char *s): String(s), single_link(0){}

    slink_string(const slink_string& s) :
        String(s.p_c), single_link(s._next) {}

    slink_string(const String& s):
        String(s), single_link() {}

    slink_string& operator=(const slink_string& s);

    void destroy() { delete this;}

    single_link* clone()
    {
        slink_string* t = new slink_string(*this);
        return t;
    }

};

#endif
```

Listing 11.7. SLSTR.CPP. Implements the assignment operator for the `slink_string` class.

```
//--------------------------------------------------------------------
// File:  slstr.cpp

#include "slstr.h"

//--------------------------------------------------------------------
// o p e r a t o r =
// Assign one "slink_string" to another

slink_string& slink_string::operator=(const slink_string& s)
{
    if(this != &s)
    {
        _next = s._next;
        _length = s._length;
        _maxlen = s._maxlen;
        delete p_c;
        p_c = new char[_maxlen];
        strcpy(p_c, s.p_c);
    }
    return *this;
}
```

A *String* List Iterator Class

Now you possess all the equipment necessary to create a linked list of `String` objects, but one problem still exists. Specifically, the `singly_linked_list` class maintains a list of `single_link` objects. It knows nothing about `slink_string` objects. So how do you traverse the list and process the `slink_string objects` in the list? You could use the `first`, `current`, and `next` member functions of the `singly_linked_list` class to traverse the list, but these return pointers to `single_link` objects. To treat them as pointers to `slink_string` objects, you must use an explicit cast. Instead of getting into details like this, it's best to create a helper class, commonly known as an *iterator* class, that provides access to the linked list of `String` objects. The class is called an iterator because it lets you *iterate*, or "loop over," the list.

Listing 11.8 shows the SLSITER.H header file, which implements the `sllist_iterator` class that acts as an iterator for the linked list of `Strings`. The `sllist_iterator` class is quite simple. It holds a reference to the list over which it iterates, and it provides the same interface to the list as does singly_linked_list. However, its member functions always return pointers to slink_string objects instead of pointers to single_link objects.

Listing 11.8. SLSITER.H. An iterator for a singly-linked list of String objects.

```
//--------------------------------------------------------------------
//  File: slsiter.h
//  Iterator for singly-linked list of strings

#if !defined(_ _SLSITER_H)
#define _ _SLSITER_H

#include "slstr.h"
#include "sllist.h"

class sllist_iterator
{
public:
    sllist_iterator(singly_linked_list& sl): sllist(sl){}

    slink_string* current()
    {
        return (slink_string*) sllist.current();
    }

    slink_string* next()
    {
        return (slink_string*) sllist.next();
    }

    slink_string* first()
    {
        return (slink_string*)sllist.first();
    }

private:
    singly_linked_list& sllist;
};

#endif
```

Trying Out a Singly-Linked Listof Strings

With all the equipment in place for working with singly-linked lists of slink_string objects, you need try out only one. Listing 11.9 shows a sample program that does this. It creates a linked list of slink_string objects and an iterator for the list. Then it inserts several slink_string objects into the list and displays what the list contains. Notice that you can display slink_string objects using the << operator because this operator is defined for the String class, and slink_string is derived from String. Finally, the program removes an item from the list and again displays the contents of the list.

Listing 11.9. A program to test a singly-linked list of Strings.

```
//---------------------------------------------------------------
// File:  tstsls.cpp
// Test a linked list of strings.

#include "slsiter.h"
//---------------------------------------------------------------
//  m a i n
//  Program that exercises a singly linked list of Strings
void main()
{
// Create a String with a single link
    slink_string s1("One");

// Create a singly linked list with s1 as first element
    singly_linked_list strlist(s1);

// Create an iterator for this linked list
    sllist_iterator si(strlist);

// Insert another copy of s1 into the list
    strlist.insert(s1);

// Change the string value of s1 and insert it again
    s1 = "Two";
    strlist.insert(s1);
    strlist.insert(s1);
    s1 = "Three";
    strlist.insert(s1);
```

```
// Display what the list contains
    cout << "------------------------------------" << endl;
    cout << "List contains:" << endl;
    slink_string* x;
    for(x = si.first(); x != 0; x = si.next())
        cout << *x << endl;

// Remove the current element from the list
// At this point, current element is the last element
    strlist.remove();

// Display the final contents of the linked list
    cout << "------------------------------------" << endl;
    cout << "Now list contains:" << endl;
    for(x = si.first(); x != 0; x = si.next())
        cout << *x << endl;
}
```

To build this program, you must compile and link the files from Listings 11.2, 11.5, 11.7, and 11.9. When run, the program displays the following output:

```
------------------------------------
List contains:
One
One
Two
Two
Three
------------------------------------
Now list contains:
One
One
Two
Two
```

A Doubly-Linked List

Now that you've created a singly-linked list, you can extend this design to create a doubly-linked list. This data type is important because you can use it as the basis of other higher-level data structures such as queues and stacks. As Figure 11.6 illustrates, a doubly-linked list is like a singly-linked list except each link can point to the previous and the next link on the list. The list also contains a pointer to the last element because you can go backward and forward on the list.

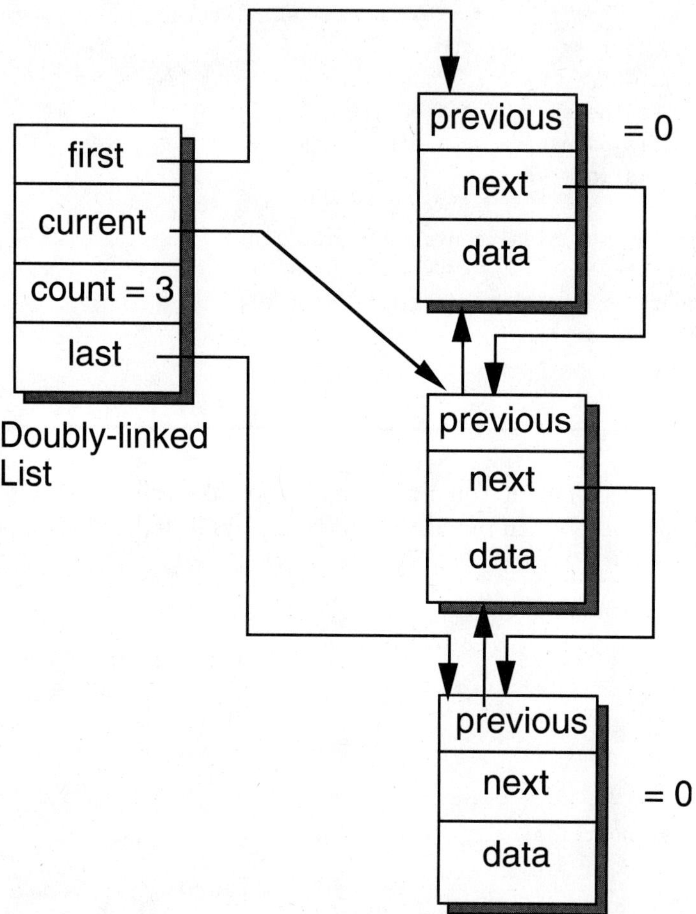

Figure 11.6. A doubly-linked list.

A *double_link* Class

You can create a class with two links by deriving it from a class with a single link. Listing 11.10 shows the DLINK.H header file, which declares the `double_link` class, derived from the `single_link` class. This serves as the base for a doubly-linked list.

The clone and destroy virtual functions still are declared as purely virtual. This means that the double_link still is an abstract class with its only purpose being to provide two links to some other data class so that the instances of the newly derived class can reside in a doubly-linked list.

Listing 11.10. DLINK.H. Declares the double_link class.

```
//------------------------------------------------------------
//  File: dlink.h
//  Declares a "double link" class

#if !defined (_ _DLINK_H)
#define _ _DLINK_H

#include "slink.h"

class double_link: public single_link
{
public:
    double_link(): single_link(0),_previous(0) {}
    double_link(double_link& dl) : single_link(dl._next),
        _previous(dl._previous) {}
    double_link(single_link* prev, single_link* next) :
       single_link(next), _previous(prev) {}

    single_link* previous() { return _previous; }

    void set_previous(single_link *previous)
    {
        _previous = previous;
    }

    virtual single_link* clone() = 0;
    virtual void destroy() = 0;

protected:
    single_link* _previous;
};

#endif
```

The *doubly_linked_list* Class

You also can exploit the existing singly_linked_list class (see Listings 11.4 and 11.5) when defining the doubly_linked_list class. As Listings 11.11 and 11.12 illustrate, you can derive the doubly_linked_list from the singly_linked_list.

The doubly_linked_list class provides the insert_last and remove_first functions for inserting and removing elements from the list. The insertion occurs at the front of the list, while the remove_last function always returns the last item in the list. I include only these two functions because I plan to use the doubly_linked_list as a queue. To use it as a stack, you must provide two more insert and remove functions, insert_first and remove_last, because a stack inserts at the top and removes from the bottom.

Listing 11.11. DLLIST.H. Declares the doubly_linked_list class.

```
//---------------------------------------------------------------
// File: dllist.h
// Declares a "doubly linked list" class.

#if !defined (_ _DLLIST_H)
#define _ _DLLIST_H

#include "dlink.h"
#include "sllist.h"

class doubly_linked_list: public singly_linked_list
{
public:
// Constructor
    doubly_linked_list(double_link& dl) : singly_linked_list(dl)
    {
        _last = (double_link*)_current;
    }

    single_link* previous()
    {
        double_link* cur = (double_link*)_current;
        single_link* t = cur->previous();
        if(t != 0) _current = t;
        return t;
```

```
    }

    double_link* last() { return _last; }

// New list insertion and deletion functions
    void insert_last(double_link& sl);
    double_link* remove_first();

protected:
    double_link *_last;
};

#endif
```

If you examine the remove_last function in Listing 11.12, you'll notice that the function "unhooks" the last element from the list and returns a pointer to that element to the calling program. Because every item in the list is created on the free store, you need to somehow destroy the item when it is no longer needed. The idea is to have a queue class that provides the final interface to the programmer. The queue class calls remove_last to get an item, copies that item into a programmer-supplied variable, and then discards the item by calling its destroy function. The get function of the string_queue class, defined in Listing 11.15, illustrates how this is done.

Listing 11.12. DLLIST.CPP. Implements the doubly_linked_list class.

```
//-------------------------------------------------------------
//  File: dllist.cpp
//  Implements "insert_last" and "remove_first" functions for a
//  doubly linked list

#include "dllist.h"

//-------------------------------------------------------------
//  i n s e r t _ l a s t
//  Insert a new item at the end of the list

void doubly_linked_list::insert_last(double_link& dl)
{
```

continues

Listing 11.12. continued

```
// Clone the element passed to the function and
// hook it up in the linked list
    double_link *t = (double_link*)dl.clone();

    if(_last != 0)
    {
        _last->set_next(t);
        t->set_previous(_last);
        t->set_next(0);
    }
    else
    {
        _first = t;
        _current = t;
    }

// Make this one the last element in the list
    _last = t;
// Increment of count of elements on the list
    _count++;
}
//------------------------------------------------------------------
//  r e m o v e _ f i r s t
//  Removes the element from the beginning of the list

double_link* doubly_linked_list::remove_first()
{
    if(_count == 0) return 0;

    double_link* cp = (double_link*)_first;
    if(_current == _first) _current = _first->next();
    _first = _first->next();

    double_link* t = (double_link*)_first;
    if(t != 0) t->set_previous(0);

    if(_last == cp) _last = 0;
    _count--;

    return cp;
}
```

A Doubly-Linkable *String*

To show a real use of the `doubly_linked_list` class, you need a data item that can be stored in the list. Like the `slink_string` class of Listings 11.6 and 11.7, you can create a `dlink_string` class that is derived from `String` and `double_link`. Instances of this class include a `String` object with two links, `_previous` and `_next`, which come from the `double_link` class. Listings 11.13 and 11.14 show the DLSTR.H and DLSTR.CPP files, which implement the `dlink_string` class.

Listing 11.13. DLSTR.H. Declares the `dlink_string` class.

```
//--------------------------------------------------------------
//  File: dlstr.h
//  Doubly linkable string class

#if !defined(_ _DLSTR_H)
#define _ _DLSTR_H

#include "str.h"        // String class
#include "dlink.h"      // double_link class

class dlink_string: public double_link, public String
{
public:
    dlink_string() : String(), double_link(0,0) {}
    dlink_string(const char *s): String(s), double_link(0,0){}

    dlink_string(const dlink_string& s) :
        String(s.p_c), double_link(s._previous, s._next) {}

    dlink_string(const String& s):
        String(s), double_link() {}

    dlink_string& operator=(const dlink_string& s);

    void destroy() { delete this;}

    single_link* clone()
    {
```

continues

Listing 11.13. continued

```
        dlink_string* t = new dlink_string(*this);
        return t;
    }
};

#endif
```

Listing 11.14. DLSTR.CPP. Implements the assignment operator for the `dlink_string` class.

```
//----------------------------------------------------------------
//  File:  dlstr.cpp

#include "dlstr.h"

//----------------------------------------------------------------
//  o p e r a t o r =
//  Assign one "dlink_string" to another

dlink_string& dlink_string::operator=(const dlink_string& s)
{
    if(this != &s)
    {
        _next = s._next;
        _previous = s._previous;
        _length = s._length;
        _maxlen = s._maxlen;
        delete p_c;
        p_c = new char[_maxlen];
        strcpy(p_c, s.p_c);
    }
    return *this;
}
```

A Queue of *String* Objects

In place of the iterator class used for the singly-linked list, I'll create a class that maintains a queue of `dlink_string` objects. This class, named `string_queue`, is defined in the SQUEUE.H file, which appears in Listing 11.15. With the `string_queue`, you can create a queue—actually a `doubly_linked_list`, for which `string_queue` provides a queue-like interface. The `get` and `put` functions, respectively, enable you to store `dlink_string` objects into the queue and retrieve them.

Think of `string_queue` as a class that knows how to use a `doubly_linked_list` class and that provides a first-in, first-out (FIFO) interface appropriate for a queue. It inserts objects at the end of the list and returns items from the front. You could similarly construct a stack class that provides a last-in, first-out (LIFO) interface to the `doubly_linked_list` class. In this case, the queue grows dynamically, but you could easily limit the size of the queue with some added code.

Listing 11.15. SQUEUE.H. Defines the `string_queue` class.

```
//-------------------------------------------------------------
//  File: squeue.h
//  Interface for a queue of doubly linkable String objects

#if !defined(_ _SQUEUE_H)
#define _ _SQUEUE_H

#include "dlstr.h"
#include "dllist.h"

class string_queue
{
public:
    string_queue(dlink_string& ds)
    {
        my_queue = new doubly_linked_list(ds);
        created_here = 1;
    }

    string_queue(doubly_linked_list& q) :
        my_queue(&q), created_here(0) {}

    ~string_queue() { if(created_here) delete my_queue;}

    int get(dlink_string& dl)
    {
     dlink_string *p;
        p = (dlink_string*)my_queue->remove_first();
```

continues

Listing 11.15. continued

```
        if(p)
        {
// Copy the item and then destroy it
            dl = *p;
            p->destroy();
            return 1;
        }
        else
            return 0;
    }

    void put(dlink_string& dl)
    {
        my_queue->insert_last(dl);
    }

private:
    doubly_linked_list* my_queue;
    int                 created_here;
};

#endif
```

Testing the Queue

Listing 11.16 shows a small program that tests the queue of `dlink_string` objects defined by the `string_queue` class. The program first creates a queue and inserts three `dlink_string` objects into it. It then retrieves the items one-by-one and displays them. Because the `dlink_string` objects are also of the `String` type, you can use the << operator with the `dlink_string` objects.

The program generates the following output:

```
------------------------------------
Queue contains:
One
Two
Three
```

Listing 11.16. Sample program to exercise the `string_queue` class.

```
//--------------------------------------------------------------
// File:  tstsq.cpp
// Test queue of strings

#include "squeue.h"
//--------------------------------------------------------------
//  m a i n
//  Program that exercises a queue of Strings

void main()
{
// Create a String with a double link
    dlink_string ds1("One");

// Create a queue with ds1 as first element
    string_queue strq(ds1);

    ds1 = "Two";
    strq.put(ds1);

    ds1 = "Three";
    strq.put(ds1);

// Get entries from the queue and display them

    cout << "Queue contains:" << endl;
    cout << "--------------" << endl;

    while(strq.get(ds1))
    {
        cout << ds1 << endl;
    }
}
```

Summary

The first major component of OOP—*data abstraction*—enables you to introduce new data types from which you can create instances of objects. The second component, *inheritance*, defines new specialized data types in terms of existing ones or for extending the functionality of an existing type. C++'s `class` construct handles both of these needs: you can encapsulate data and functions with it, and you can derive a class from one or more *base classes*. A *derived class* inherits all `public` and `protected` members of its base classes. Furthermore, you can differentiate the derived class from its base classes by one of the following methods:

- Adding new member variables
- Adding new member functions
- Overriding the definition of functions inherited from the base classes

When the `class` construct is used to define an abstract data type, inheritance enables you to create specialized subtypes. On the other hand, when a class is simply a module that encapsulates some data and functions, you can use inheritance to extend the capabilities offered by the module. When defining functions in a derived class, be aware that any overloaded function hides all inherited versions of the same name.

C++ supports single and multiple inheritance. In single inheritance, each derived class has exactly one base class; multiple inheritance enables you to derive a class from more than one base class. You can use multiple inheritance to simulate generic classes, such as linked lists and queues. This works by making the data structures capable of storing a link, for example, and then creating a linkable data type by inheriting from the link class as well as from your data type.

Another interesting feature of inheritance is that a pointer to an instance of the base class can hold the address of any of its derived class instances. The next chapter explains how this feature allows you to exploit polymorphism in C++ programs.

Virtual base classes enable you to create a class, based on several other classes, where these other classes are in turn based on a common base class. Normally the common base class's constructor would be invoked for each of the other classes. With virtual base classes, you can ensure that the common base class's constructor is only invoked a single time.

12

Virtual Functions and Polymorphism

This chapter focuses on *polymorphism*, the third basic component of object-oriented programming. Chapter 10, "Defining Operations on Objects," and Chapter 11, "Using Inheritance in C++," cover the other components of OOP—data abstraction and inheritance.

Polymorphic functions work with many different argument types. C++ supports this kind of polymorphism through function overloading. The other type of polymorphism simplifies the syntax of performing the same operation with a hierarchy of classes. This is what enables you to usc the same function name (`draw`, for example) to draw all types of `shape` objects, whether they're `circle_shapes`, `rectangle_shapes`, or `triangle_shapes`. You can therefore use polymorphism to maintain a clean interface to the classes, because you don't need to define unique function names for similar operations on each derived class. This type of polymorphism goes hand in hand with inheritance and *late* or *dynamic binding*. This chapter explains the terminology and describes how the `virtual` keyword supports polymorphism.

Dynamic Binding

The term *binding* refers to the connection between a function call and the actual code executed as a result of the call. The following sections explain how binding is determined and how it affects the style of code you write.

Static Binding

As with any new concept, the best way to explain binding is through an example. Suppose you want to process a one-character command and have defined a number of functions that perform the tasks requested by various commands. Using a `switch` statement, you might handle the commands as follows:

```
#include <ctype.h>
#include <iostream.h>
//...
static void quit(), newparams() showparams();
char ch;
//...
// Respond to user command
// Assume 'ch' holds the command character

    int code = toupper(ch);
    switch (code)
    {
        case 'Q': quit();
        case 'P': newparams();
                  break;
        case '?': showparams();
                  break;
        default:  cout << "Unknown command:" << ch << endl;
    }
```

Of course, in this case the function invoked in response to each command is known when the program is compiling because each function is explicitly called by name. This is known as *static binding*, because the compiler can figure out the function to be called before the program ever runs.

Function Call Through a Pointer

Now consider an alternate implementation of this command-processing code. Start with a table of commands that can be implemented as an array of structures, each of which holds a command character and a pointer to the function to be called when the user types that character. The processing loop simply compares the input command character with the entries in the table and, if a matching entry is found, calls the function with the pointer that appears in that slot of the table. Here's a sample implementation of this scheme.

```
#include <ctype.h>
#include <iostream.h>

// Command-processing functions...
static void quit(), newparams(), showparams();

struct command
{
    char cmdchar;      // Each command is a character
    void (*action)(); // Function called to process command
};

command cmdtable[] =  // This is the table of commands
{
    'Q',  quit,
    'q',  quit,
    'P',  newparams,
    'p',  newparams,
    '?',  showparams
};

// Number commands in the command-table
int cmdcount = sizeof(cmdtable) / sizeof(command);

char ch;
int  i;

//...
// Sample command-processing loop:
// Assume character 'ch' holds input character
// Search the command table for matching command

    for(i = 0; i < cmdcount; i++)
    {
        if(cmdtable[i].cmdchar == ch)
        {
```

```
// Found command...call the corresponding function
                (*cmdtable[i].action)();
                break;
            }
    }

    if(i == cmdcount)
        cout << "Unknown command: " << ch << endl;
```

Notice that this version of the command-processing loop differs from the previous one in two respects:

- The `switch` statement no longer is needed.
- A function call via a pointer is used to invoke the function that performs the task requested by each command. The content of the pointer determines the actual function called.

This is known as *dynamic binding*. The term *dynamic* is used because the actual function called at runtime depends on the contents of the function pointer, which in turn depends on the character in the `char` variable `ch`. Dynamic binding also is known as *late binding* because the connection between the function call and the actual code executed by the call is determined late—that is, during runtime instead of compile time.

Incidentally, the lack of a `switch` statement is a characteristic feature of dynamic binding. By using the indirection afforded by the function pointer, you can forgo the tests required in a `switch` statement. Instead, you can call a different function by simply altering the content of the function pointer.

C++ compilers usually implement dynamic binding through function pointers. Like most other features of C++, this happens behind the scenes. You need only use the `virtual` keyword, explained next.

Virtual Functions

Most of the examples you've seen thus far include classes with one or more `virtual` member functions. Consider, for example, the geometric `shape` classes introduced in Chapter 6, "C++ and Object-Oriented Programming." As you may recall, the `shape` class is the base class from which you derived several other classes, such as `rectangle_shape`, `circle_shape`, and `triangle_shape`. For a sample implementation, each shape had to be able to compute its area and draw itself. In this case, the `shape` class declares the following virtual functions:

```
class shape
{
public:
    virtual double compute_area(void) const;
    virtual void draw(void) const;

// Other member functions that define an interface to all
// types of geometric shapes
};
```

Here, the `virtual` keyword preceding a function signals the C++ compiler that, if the function is defined in a derived class, the compiler may need to call the function indirectly through a pointer. Qualify a member function of a class with the `virtual` keyword only when there is a possibility that other classes may be derived from this one.

The `shape` class is an example of an *abstract base class*—a class that embodies a standard interface to a group of classes but does not provide a concrete implementation for any of the member functions. A common use of virtual functions is in defining such an abstract base class.

Pure Virtual Functions

One problem in defining a base class with virtual functions is that you may not be able to provide appropriate implementation for all the functions. For example, you can't define a `draw` or a `compute_area` function for a generic shape. Programmers often solve this problem by providing a dummy function that prints an error message. For the `compute_area` function of the `shape` class, you might write the following:

```
virtual void draw()
{
    cerr << "Derived class must implement!" << endl;
}
```

In this case, if you forget to implement draw in a derived class such as `circle_shape` and the program calls `draw` for a `circle_chape`, it prints an error message. This isn't so bad, but the situation could be worse if you decided to call `exit` after printing the error message. A better way to handle this is to let the C++ compiler detect an unimplemented instance of a virtual class. That way, the error is detected before it's too late.

Pure virtual functions are virtual functions that the base class cannot implement. You can indicate a pure virtual function by adding the `=0` initializer following the declaration of the function. You gain two error-checking capabilities from pure virtual functions:

- The C++ compiler does not allow creation of instances of a class containing pure virtual functions. Thus, if you write

  ```
  shape s1;
  ```

  the compiler flags it as an error. This is good, because you don't want anyone to create instances of an abstract base class anyway.

- The compiler checks to be sure the pure virtual functions of a base class are implemented by one of its derived classes. If an immediate derived class cannot provide an implementation, it can simply pass the problem on to one of its derived classes by also declaring the function as pure virtual.

C++ includes the notion of pure virtual functions that you can use to indicate that certain member functions of an abstract base class are not implemented. For example, in the `shape` class you can make `draw` and `compute_area` pure virtual functions as follows:

```
class shape
{
public:
// Make these "pure virtual functions"
    virtual double compute_area(void) const = 0;
    virtual void draw(void) const = 0;

// Other member functions
};
```

Concrete Implementation of *virtual* Functions

An abstract base class uses the `virtual` keyword to qualify the member functions that constitute the interface to all the classes derived from that class. Each specific derived class must define its own concrete versions of the functions that have been declared `virtual` in the base class. Therefore, if you derive the `circle_shape` and `rectangle_shape` classes from the `shape` class, you must define the `compute_area` and `draw` member functions in each class. For instance, the definitions for the `circle_shape` class might appear like this:

```
class circle_shape: public shape
```

```
{
public:
    virtual double compute_area(void) const;
    virtual void draw(void) const;
// ...
private:
    double xc, yc;  // Coordinates of center
    double radius;  // radius of circle
};

#define M_PI 3.14159 // value of "pi"
// Implementation of "compute_area" function
circle_shape::compute_area(void) const
{
    return (M_PI * radius * radius);
}

// Implementation of "draw" function
circle_shape::draw(void) const
{
//...
}
```

When declaring the `draw` and `compute_area` functions in the derived class, you can optionally add the `virtual` keyword to emphasize that these are indeed virtual functions. The function definitions don't need the `virtual` keyword.

Dynamic Binding Through *virtual* Functions

You don't need to do anything special to use virtual functions. Treat them as you would any other member function of a class. As an example, consider the following calls to the virtual functions `draw` and `compute_area`:

```
circle_shape    c1;
rectangle_shape r1;
double area = c1.compute_area(); // Compute area of circle
r1.draw();                       // Draw a rectangle
```

When used in this manner, these functions are like any other member function. In this case, the C++ compiler can determine that you want to call the `compute_area` function of the `circle_shape` class and the `draw` function of the `rectangle_shape` class.

In fact, the compiler makes direct calls to these functions, and the function calls are bound to specific code at link time. This is static binding.

However, an interesting case occurs when you make the function calls through a pointer to a shape, like this:

```
shape*   s[10];  // Pointers to 10 shape objects
int      i, numshapes=10;
//... create shapes and store pointers in array "s"
// Draw the shapes
    for(i = 0; i < numshapes; i++) shape[i]->draw();
```

Because the individual entries in the array of shape pointers can point to any type of shape derived from the shape class, the C++ compiler cannot determine which specific implementation of the draw function to call. This is where dynamic binding and the virtual keyword come in.

> **A Pointer to a Derived Class Is also a Pointer to the Base**
>
> In C++, you can use a reference or a pointer to any derived class in place of a reference or a pointer to the base class without an explicit type cast. So, if both circle_shape and rectangle_shape are derived from the shape class, you can call a function that requires a pointer to shape with a pointer to a circle_shape or a rectangle_shape as well. The opposite is not true; you cannot use a reference or a pointer to the base class in place of a reference or a pointer to an instance of a derived class.

Virtual Function Call Mechanism

As explained previously, an indirect function call (a function call through a pointer) provides dynamic binding. C++ compilers use this idea when calling virtual functions. The virtual keyword is a signal to the compiler that the member function qualified by the keyword may need to be called through a pointer.

A typical C++ compiler constructs an array of virtual function pointers for each class. This array goes by the name of *virtual table*, or *vtable* for short. Each instance of the class has a pointer to its class-wide virtual table. Figure 12.1 illustrates the situation for the circle_shape class.

Given this arrangement, the C++ compiler can achieve dynamic binding by transforming a call to a virtual function into an indirect call through a pointer in the class virtual table. For example, if the virtual table is laid out as shown in Figure 12.1, the compiler can implement this call

```
circle_shape *c1 = new circle_shape(100.,100.,50.);
c1->draw();
```

by generating code for

```
(*(c1->vtable[1]))(c1);   // c1 is "this"
```

where the second entry in the virtual table holds the pointer to the `draw` function of the `circle_shape` class. The pointer to the object is passed as the first argument of the function just as it is done implicitly for every member function of a class. This is the `this` pointer that a member function can use to refer to the current instance of the class.

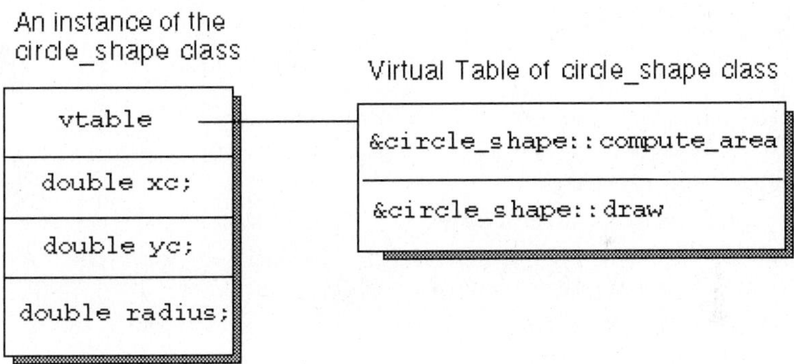

Figure 12.1. Virtual function implementation under single inheritance.

As a C++ programmer, you don't need to know how the compiler takes care of calling the correct virtual function—but you may find the knowledge helpful in understanding why a C++ program behaves the way it does. Also, C++ compilers are not required to implement the virtual function call mechanism exactly as illustrated in Figure 12.1. However, most C++ compilers do follow the same techniques, partly because these ideas are outlined in *The Annotated C++ Reference Manual*, by Margaret Ellis and Bjarne Stroustrup. This book is the basis of the ongoing standardization of C++ by the ANSI X3J16 committee. If you're curious, you may want to consult this book for further information on how various features of C++ can be implemented. For instance, with multiple inheritance, implementing a virtual function call is somewhat more complicated. For more information on this, see *The Annotated C++ Reference Manual*.

Suppressing Virtual Function Calls

The virtual-call mechanism is quite useful for implementing polymorphism, but occasions may arise when you want to call the function from the base class instead of the one from the derived class. For example, suppose you have a base class called `BaseWindow` with a virtual function called `event_handler`, which presumably processes events in a user interface. You're happy with the function, but you want a derived class called `SpecialWindow` with an `event_handler` that augments the processing done in the event-handling function of its base class. In the `event_handler` of the `SpecialWindow` class, you want to catch a special type of event and process it there. For all other types of events, you want to call the `event_handler` of the `BaseWindow` class. You can do this as follows:

```
class BaseWindow
{
public:
    virtual void event_handler(int event_id);
// Other members...
};

class SpecialWindow: public BaseWindow
{
public:
    void event_handler(int event_id)
    {
        if(event_id == SPECIAL_EVENT)
        {
// process special event...
        }
        else
        {
// Call BaseWindow's event_handler
            BaseWindow::event_handler(event_id);
        }
    }

// Other members...
};
```

You can suppress the virtual-call mechanism by explicitly qualifying a function with its class name. In this example, you can call the `event_handler` of the `BasicWindow` class by explicitly qualifying the function name with the `BasicWindow::` prefix.

Using Polymorphism

As you've seen in examples in this chapter and Chapter 6, polymorphism eliminates the `switch` statement and generally simplifies the interface to a hierarchy of classes. The geometric shapes of Chapter 5, "Basics of Object-Oriented Programming," and Chapter 6 are good examples of the use of polymorphism.

Suppose you have a collection of `shape` objects in a storage structure, such as an array or a linked list. The array simply stores pointers to `shape` objects. These pointers could point to any type of shape, provided the shape is derived from the `shape` class. When operating on these shapes, you can simply loop through the array and invoke the appropriate member function via the pointer to the instance. Of course, for this to work, the member functions must be declared as `virtual` in the `shape` class, which happens to be the base class for all geometric shapes.

As you might gather from the examples, you must do the following to use polymorphism in C++:

1. Create a class hierarchy with the important operations defined by member functions declared as virtual in the base class. If the base class is such that you cannot provide implementations for these functions, you can declare them to be purely virtual. The draw function of the `shape` class is an example.

   ```
   virtual void draw() const = 0;
   ```

2. Provide concrete implementations of the virtual classes in the derived classes. Each derived class can have its own version of the functions. For example, the implementation of the `draw` function varies from one shape to another.

3. Manipulate instances of these classes through a reference or a pointer. This is what causes the C++ compiler to use dynamic binding and call the functions using the virtual function mechanism, described earlier.

The last item—invoking member functions through a pointer—is the essence of polymorphic use in C++. This is because you get dynamic binding only when virtual member functions are invoked through a pointer to a class instance and when you need dynamic binding for polymorphism.

Implications of Polymorphic Use of Classes

Because the polymorphic use of class instances requires that you manipulate objects through pointers or references, you should be aware of certain problems that you may encounter when programming this way. The following sections briefly discuss some pitfalls.

Virtual Destructors

When you manipulate objects through pointers, you often tend to create them dynamically through the new operator and later destroy them with the `delete` operator. A typical situation might be as shown in the following example:

```
//  Illustrates why "virtual destructor" is needed

#include <iostream.h>

class Base
{
public:
    Base() { cout << "Base: constructor" << endl; }

//*** The destructor should be "virtual"
    ~Base() { cout << "Base: destructor" << endl; }
};

class Derived: public Base
{
public:
    Derived() { cout << "Derived: constructor" << endl; }
    ~Derived() { cout << "Derived: destructor" << endl; }
};

void main()
{
    Base* p_base = new Derived;

// Use the object...

// Now delete the object
    delete p_base;
}
```

This is a case where the `main` function creates a copy of a derived class using the `new` operator and later destroys that instance using `delete`. When you compile and run this program, it displays:

```
Base: constructor
Derived: constructor
Base: destructor
```

The first two lines indicate the order in which the class constructors are called: the constructor for the base class is followed by that for the derived class. This keeps the order of initialization explained in Chapter 11, "Using Inheritance in C++." The third line of output, however, seems odd. Why isn't there a call to the destructor of the derived class?

The reason is that when you called the constructor, you used the derived class name with the `new` operator and, therefore, the C++ compiler correctly created the right type of object. You saved the pointer in a `p_base` variable, which is declared as a pointer to the base class. Subsequently, when you write

```
delete p_base;
```

the compiler can't tell that you're destroying a derived class instance.

Because `delete` does its job by calling the destructor for the class, you can solve the problem by declaring the destructor of the base class `virtual`. That way, the destructor is invoked through the virtual function table and the correct destructor is called. Indeed, if you use the following for the base class destructor:

```
virtual ~Base() { cout << "Base: destructor" << endl; }
```

and rerun the program, you get the correct output, as follows:

```
Base: constructor
Derived: constructor
Derived: destructor
Base: destructor
```

Notice that the order of calls to the destructors is the opposite order in which the constructors were called. Therefore, the virtual destructor ensures that the object is properly destroyed.

How do you decide whether to declare a destructor virtual? If a class has any virtual function, chances are that instances of classes derived from this one will be manipulated through pointers to attain polymorphic behavior. In this case, you should declare a virtual destructor for the class.

Calling Virtual Functions in a Base Class Constructor

Another pitfall of using virtual functions is that certain times occur when they do not work as expected. One place where calling a virtual function may produce undesired results is in the constructor of a base class. You can see the problem from the following example program:

```
//  Illustrates what happens when a virtual function
//  is called from the constructor of a base class

#include <iostream.h>

class Base
{
public:
    Base()
    {
        cout << "Base: constructor. Calling clone()" << endl;
        clone();
    }
    virtual void clone()
    {
        cout << "Base::clone() called" << endl;
    }
};

class Derived: public Base
{
public:
    Derived()
    {
        cout << "Derived: constructor" << endl;
    }

    void clone()
    {
        cout << "Derived::clone() called" << endl;
    }
};
```

```
void main()
{
    Derived x;
    Base *p = &x;

// Call "clone" through pointer to class instance
    cout << "Calling 'clone' through instance pointer";
    cout << endl;
    p->clone();
}
```

When you run this program, you get the following output:

```
Base: constructor. Calling clone()
Base::clone() called
Derived: constructor
Calling 'clone' through instance pointer
Derived::clone() called
```

You can go over the output to see what happened. When you create an instance of the derived class, as expected, the C++ compiler first calls the constructor of the base class. At this point, the derived class instance is only partially initialized. Therefore, when the compiler encounters the call to the `clone` virtual function, it cannot bind it to the version of `clone` for the derived class. Instead, the compiler calls the version of `clone` from the base class.

The last two lines of output show that once the object is created, you can correctly invoke the `clone` function for the derived class instance through a base class pointer as is common in polymorphic use of virtual functions.

If you call a virtual function in a class constructor, the compiler invokes the base class's version of the function, not the version defined for the derived class.

Summary

The three features of object-oriented programming—*data abstraction*, *inheritance*, and *polymorphism*—go hand in hand. For realistic object-oriented programs, you need to use all these concepts together. The data and functions are encapsulated into an object by a `class` or a `struct`. Inheritance enables you to implement the *is a* relationship among objects—as in, "a circle *is a* shape." Finally, polymorphism enables you to use the same functional interface such as member functions named `draw` and `compute_area` to work with all kinds of shapes.

Several features of C++ work in concert to support polymorphism:

- You can use a pointer to a derived class anywhere a pointer to the base class is expected. The same rule applies to references.
- If a base class declares a member function with the `virtual` keyword, the compiler places the function in the class-wide virtual function table and uses the base class's implementation of the function as a default. The default is used only if a derived class does not define the function.
- If a derived class redefines a `virtual` function and you call that function through a pointer to the class instance, the compiler invokes the function through the pointer stored in the virtual table, thereby invoking the version of the function from the derived class. This is known as *dynamic binding*.

Dynamic binding makes polymorphism possible. With polymorphism, you can control a particular behavior of a whole group of objects by calling the same member function. The draw function of shape classes provides a good illustration of polymorphic usage.

When you use *virtual functions* in C++, you must watch out for some pitfalls. For example, if you call a virtual function from the constructor of a class, the compiler calls the version from itself or one of the bases, but not a version defined by derived classes. Also, you may need to declare the destructor of the base class as virtual to allow for the accurate destruction of objects.

13

Advanced Topics in C++

The previous chapters have shown you how C++ supports object-oriented programming. Despite its well-known capabilities, C++ is relatively young; it was released commercially in late 1985. In fact, features such as multiple inheritance and the `iostream` library weren't introduced until AT&T C++ Release 2.0 became available in 1989. Although the current release of AT&T C++ is 2.1, AT&T already is working on Release 3.0. Two probable new additions to that release are:

- *Templates* (also known as *parameterized types*)
- Exception handling

Another ongoing development that affects the future of C++ is the work being done by the American National Standards Institute (ANSI) C++ Technical Committee, X3J16. The X3J16 committee is developing a draft proposal to standardize the C++ programming language. The committee is starting with the following documents as the basis for its proposal:

- The ANSI C standard (ANSI X3.159-1989—Programming Language C)
- The *AT&T C++ Language System Release 2.1 Reference Manual* (also available as *The Annotated C++ Reference Manual* by Margaret A. Ellis and Bjarne Stroustrup, published by Addison-Wesley Publishing Company, 1990)

The X3J16 committee has already decided to include templates in the C++ draft standard and is considering the inclusion of exception handling as well. The templates will be based on the experimental design presented in Chapter 14 of *The Annotated C++ Reference Manual*, or *ARM*, as it is popularly known. When the X3J16 committee considers exception handling, the design will likely be derived from the material in Chapter 15 of *ARM*. This chapter gives you an overview of templates and exception handling based on information available in *ARM* and some recent articles in the *Journal of Object-Oriented Programming* (published bimonthly by SIGS Publications, New York).

Templates will enable you to define generic classes, and exception handling will provide a uniform way to cope with errors in C++ programs. Because templates and exception handling are not yet a part of the C++ language, this chapter can only show a few hypothetical examples to illustrate how you might use these features. These examples are based on the proposed syntax for templates and the proposed mechanism for exception handling, but the proposals may change in the future.

Although Microsoft Visual C++ does not support templates and exception handling, Microsoft has indicated that these features will be added soon, hopefully with the next release. When the Microsoft Visual C++ compiler begins supporting templates and exception handling, you should consult the compiler's documentation for the latest information on using these features.

Templates

When it becomes available in C++, a template will define a family of classes or functions. For example, with a class template for a `Stack` class, you can create stacks of various data types, such as `int`, `float`, and `char*`. Similarly, with a function template for a `sort` function, you can create versions of the `sort` function that will sort, for example, an array of `int`, `float`, or `char*` data. When you create a class or function template, you essentially want to define a class or a function with a *parameter*—a data type, for example, that you would specify when the class or function is being used. This is why templates are often referred to as *parameterized types*.

Stacks for *int* and *float*

As an example of a class declaration with a parameter, consider the following simple declaration of a stack class, named `intStack`, which is capable of holding `int` variables:

```
const int MAXSIZE = 128;

class intStack            // Define a stack for int variables
{
public:
    intStack() { _stackptr = 0;}
    int push(int x) {return _array[_stackptr++] = x;}
    int pop() { return _array[--stackptr];}
    int empty() const { return (_stackptr == 0);}
private:
    int _array[MAXSIZE]; // Internally, an array stores the data
    int _stackptr;
};
```

The `intStack` class uses an array of `int` variables as the internal storage for the stack. You might use the `intStack` class in this way:

```
    intStack i_stack;

// Push an integer value
    i_stack.push(301);

// Pop a number off the stack
    int last_val = i_stack.pop();
```

If you want to define a stack of `floats` (a `floatStack` class) that uses the same internal mechanism as `intStack`, simply replace every `int` in the `intStack` class declaration with `float`. This tells you that if you were able to define a single `Stack` class that accepted a data type as a parameter, and if the C++ compiler enabled you to create new class definitions by invoking `Stack`'s definition with any data type, you could use a single definition to create stacks for any type of data. In other words, what you need is a way to define parameterized classes. With the proposed templates mechanism, you'll be able to define classes and functions with parameters.

Class Templates

In C++, the reserved `template` keyword is intended to define class and function templates. (The keyword is already reserved even though templates are not yet a part of the language.) With the proposed syntax, the template for a generic `Stack` class might look like this:

```
const int MAXSIZE = 128;

template<class T> class Stack
{
public:
    Stack(T)() { _stackptr = 0;}
    T push(T x) {return _array[_stackptr++] = x;}
    T pop() { return _array[__stackptr];}
    int empty() const { return (_stackptr == 0);}
private:
    T    _array[MAXSIZE];
    int  _stackptr;
};
```

If you compare this with the approach based on the macros defined in generic.h, you'll find that the class definition is very similar. The `template<class T>` prefix in the class declaration states that you will declare a class template and that you will use `T` as a class name in the declaration. Thus, `Stack` is a parameterized class with the `T` type as its parameter. With this definition of the `Stack` class template, you can create stacks for different data types like this:

```
Stack<int>    istack;   // A stack for int variables
Stack<float>  fstack;   // A stack for float variables
```

You can similarly define a generic `Array` class as follows:

```
template<class T> class Array
{
public:
    Array(int n=16) { _pa = new T(_size = n);}
    T& operator[](int i);
//...

private:
    T*   _pa;
    int  _size;
};
```

You then can create instances of different `Array` types in the following manner:

```
Array<int>   iArray(128);  // A 128-element int array
Array<float> fArray(32);   // A 32-element float array
```

Function Templates

Like class templates, function templates define a family of functions parameterized by a data type. For example, you could define a parameterized sort function for sorting any type of array like this:

```
template<class T> void sort(Array<T>)
{
// Body of function (do the sorting)
// ...
}
```

This example essentially declares a set of overloaded sort functions, one for each type of Array. When defining the sort function, you will need a comparison operator for the class T. One restriction on using the sort function template is that the class you provide in place of T must define a comparison operator.

You can invoke the sort function as you would any ordinary function. The C++ compiler analyzes the arguments to the function and calls the proper version of the function. For example, given iArray and fArray, the arrays of int and float, you can apply the sort function to each as follows:

```
sort(iArray);   // Sort the array of int
sort(fArray);   // Sort the array of float
```

Member Function Templates

When declaring the Array class template, I left the operator[] member function undefined. Each member function in a class template is also a function template. When defined inline, no special syntax is necessary for the member functions of a template class—just use the template parameters as necessary in the function's body and in its argument list. When the member function of a class template is defined outside the body of the class, you must follow a specific syntax. For instance, you can define the operator[] function of the Array class template like this:

```
template<class T> T& Array<T>::operator[](int i)
{
    if(i < 0 || i >= _size)
    {
// Handle error condition. Assume that there is a function
// named "handle_error" available for this purpose.
        handle_error("Array: index out of range");
```

```
    }
    else
        return _pa[i];
}
```

Advantages of Templates

Templates will help you define classes that are general in nature (generic classes). Even though generic classes already can be defined, templates make the process simpler and safer.

So far, I've shown you two ways to define generic classes. Early in this chapter you saw how the macros defined in the generic.h header file can be used to declare parameterized classes. Although these macros work, they are cumbersome to define and use. The proposed syntax for templates will greatly simplify the process of defining parameterized classes.

Another approach to generic classes, explained in Chapter 11, "Using Inheritance in C++," presents a way of creating a generic `singly_linked_list` class starting with a single-linked list of a base class called `single_link`, making sure that any data type that needs to be stored in the list is also derived from the `single_link` class. The only problem with this approach is that the member functions of the `singly_linked_list` class return pointers to `single_link` but not to the type of objects actually stored in the list. Thus, you must cast each pointer returned by the `singly_linked_list` class to your data type before using it. Such type casts defeat the type-checking facilities of C++ and increase the potential for errors. With class templates, you can eliminate the need for any type casts and define parameterized classes in a safe manner.

Exception Handling

Exceptions refer to unusual conditions in a program. They can be outright errors that cause the program to fail or conditions that can lead to errors. Typically, you can always detect when certain types of errors are about to occur. For instance, when implementing the subscript function (`operator[]`) of the `Array` class, you can detect if the index is beyond the range of valid values. Such errors are called *synchronous exceptions* because they occur at a predictable time; an error caused by the array index going out of bounds occurs only after executing a statement in which that out-of-bounds index is used. Contrast this with *asynchronous exceptions*, which are caused by events (such as a keypress, a timer tick, or perhaps a hardware failure) that are beyond the control of your program; therefore, your program cannot anticipate their occurrence. The proposed exception-handling mechanism for C++ is intended to cope with synchronous exceptions only.

Benefits of Exception Handling

Although it's easy to detect synchronous exceptions such as failing to allocate memory or an array index going out of bounds, it's difficult to decide what to do when the exception occurs. Consider the `malloc` function in the ANSI C library. When you call `malloc` to allocate a block of memory, you get back a pointer to the allocated block. If `malloc` fails, it returns a NULL pointer (a zero address). The caller carries the burden of checking for this exceptional condition. As a C programmer, you're probably quite familiar with blocks of code like this:

```
#define MAXCHR 80
char *line;


if((line = (char *) malloc(MAXCHR)) == NULL)
{
/* Failed to allocate memory. Print message and exit. */
    fprintf(stderr, "Failed to allocate memory.\n");
    exit(1);
}
```

Whenever you call `malloc` in your program, you essentially repeat similar blocks of code again and again.

Now consider an alternative. Suppose `malloc` is written so that whenever it fails, it jumps (ANSI C's `setjmp` and `longjmp` functions provide the capability to jump from one function to another) to a function that you specify, perhaps with an error code—a code that indicates what went wrong—as an argument. Such a function is typically called a *handler* or an *exception handler*. If you do not provide an exception handler, `malloc` could jump to a default handler that prints a message and exits. If you do provide a handler, you could handle the error condition any way you wish. In certain applications, you may not even need to terminate the application. Best of all, with such an exception handler installed, you could call `malloc` without worrying about an error return. This is because you know that, in case of any allocation failure, `malloc` will jump to the exception handler. Thus, if you know there is an exception handler, you can eliminate all those extra lines of code that check whether `malloc` has returned a NULL pointer.

Like `malloc`, C++ class libraries have many functions that detect and handle error conditions. If exception handling is an integral part of C++, all class libraries will be able to cope with all "exceptional conditions" uniformly. Thus, the ongoing effort to provide exception handling in C++.

The Trouble with *setjmp* and *longjmp*

In ANSI C, the functions `setjmp` and `longjmp` enable you to jump back from many levels of function calls to a specific location in your program—you can abort what you were doing and return to your starting point. The `setjmp` function saves the "state" or the "context" of the process, and `longjmp` uses the saved context to revert to a previous point in the program. The terms *context* or *state* of a process refer to the information with which you can reconstruct the way the process is at a given point in its flow of execution. In ANSI C, an array data type named `jmp_buf` is available for storing information needed to restore a calling environment. This data type is defined in the setjmp.h header file.

To understand the exact mechanics of `setjmp` and `longjmp`, look at the following lines of code:

```
#include <setjmp.h>
jmp_buf saved_context;

main()
{
    if (setjmp(saved_context) == 0)
    {
// This is executed the first time set_jmp is called.
        process_commands();
    }
    else
    {
// This block is executed when longjmp is called.
        handle_error();
    }
}

process_commands()
{
    int error_flag = 0;
```

```
// When an error occurs, error_flag is set to 1
// ...
    if(error_flag) longjmp(saved_context, 1);
}
```

When you call the `setjmp` function, it will save the current context in the `jmp_buf` variable named `saved_context` and return a zero. In this case, the first `if` statement in `main` is satisfied, and the `process_commands` function is called. If an error occurs in `process_commands`, the `error_flag` will be set to a nonzero value, and you will call `longjmp` with these two arguments:

- The first argument is the `jmp_buf` variable, which contains the context to which `longjmp` should return.
- The second argument specifies the return value to be used during this return.

The `longjmp` function will revert the calling environment to this saved state. This amounts to *unrolling* or *unwinding* the stack to where it was when `setjmp` was originally called. After reverting to the saved context, `longjmp` returns. When the `return` statement in `longjmp` is executed, it will be like returning from the call to `setjmp`, which originally saved the `saved_context` buffer, except that the returned value will be provided by you as the second argument to `longjmp`. Calling `longjmp` causes the program to jump to the `else` block of the first `if` statement in `main`. In this way, `setjmp` and `longjmp` enable you to jump unconditionally from one C function to another without using conventional `return` statements. Essentially, `setjmp` marks the destination of the jump, and `longjmp` acts as a nonlocal `goto` that executes the jump.

When you first look at it, the combination of `setjmp` and `longjmp` appears to be the ideal way to handle exceptions in C++. This is indeed true, and the proposed exception-handling mechanism (to be described later) can be implemented using `setjmp` and `longjmp`—but only because the proposed design also provides a solution to another C++ problem. In C++, class instances must be initialized by calling class constructors and destroyed by calling the corresponding destructors. Because `longjmp` abruptly jumps back to a previous point in the execution of the program, situations will occur where a constructor has been called but a jump occurs before calling the destructor. In such cases, any memory allocated by a constructor will not be freed because the call to the destructor is skipped.

Other problems may also crop up because the internal state of some objects may be left in an unknown condition. Thus, if `setjmp` and `longjmp` are used to handle exceptions, there must be a way to call the destructors of all relevant objects before calling `longjmp`. Although I do not provide the details in this chapter, this is precisely what a `setjmp`/`longjmp`-based implementation of the exception-handling mechanism must do in practice.

A Proposed Exception-Handling Mechanism for C++

Andrew Koenig and Bjarne Stroustrup have proposed an exception-handling mechanism for C++ that they describe in their recent paper, "Exception Handling for C++," (*Journal of Object-Oriented Programming,* Vol.3, No.2, July/August 1990, pages 16-33). In this paper, they even outline a portable implementation of the proposed design based on C's `setjmp/longjmp` mechanism. In particular, they describe a scheme to solve the problem of ensuring that the destructors are called correctly before "unwinding" the stack. The following sections summarize how you, as a programmer, will see the proposed exception-handling features.

An Example

Consider a Forms software package that uses a `Form` class to represent a form. `Form` has a member function, `read`, to read the definition of a form from a file. Suppose you're rewriting `read` so that it uses the proposed exception-handling mechanism to cope with the exception caused by the failure to open a specified file. Here is how you would add exception handling to the `read` function of the `Form` class:

1. Define a class with a descriptive name (for example, `FormIOException`), representing the exception that can occur when trying to read or write forms. You might declare it as follows:

```
class FormIOException
{
public:
        FormIOException(char* filename) :
                _filename(filename) {}
private:
        char* _filename;
}
```

2. In the `Form::read` function, when the file cannot be opened, throw a `FormIOException` like this:

```
void Form::read(const char* filename)
{
// Open an input stream on the specified file
        ifstream fs1(filename);
        if(!fs1)
        {
```

```
// Throw exception if file could not be opened
                throw FormIOException(filename);
            }
    // Continue with normal processing
    // ...
    }
```

That's how you would throw the exception. Using the `Form` class, the programmer provides the code that catches the exception. It would look like this:

```
// Create a form and read in its definition from a file
    Form invoice;

// Be prepared to catch any exceptions
    try
    {
// If an exception is "thrown" control will transfer to the
// catch block.
        invoice.read("invoice.def");
    }
    catch(FormIOException fio)
    {
// You can display a message or display a dialog box informing
// the user that the file could not be opened.
        cout << "Error opening " << fio._filename << endl;
    }
```

This example illustrates the essential features of the proposed exception-handling mechanism. A few other important points are summarized next.

Summary of the Exception-Handling Mechanism

The general syntax of exception handling can be illustrated as follows:

```
// Exception classes
    class IOException;
    class MemAllocException;
    class MathError;

// Place inside a "try" block code that may throw exceptions
    try
    {
        process_commands();
    }
```

```
// Place the exception-handling code inside "catch" blocks_one
// for each type of exception.

    catch(IOException io)
    {
// Errors in I/O
//...
    }
    catch(MemAllocException mem)
    {
// "Out of memory" errors
//...
    }
    catch(MathError math)
    {
// Handle math errors
//...
    }
    catch(...)  // Use ... to mean any exception
    {
// Handle all other exceptions here
//...
    }
```

As you can see, each `try` block can contain several associated `catch` blocks, which establish handlers for various exceptions. The `catch` blocks are executed in the order of appearance. You should place `catch(...)` at the very end because this block is meant for any type of exception.

A function that detects errors and throws exceptions can indicate the specific exceptions that it might throw. Suppose a function named `setup_data` throws the exceptions `IOException` and `MemAllocException`. The function's declaration can indicate this as follows:

```
void setup_data() throw(IOException, MemAllocException);
```

The list of possible exceptions is called the *exception specification* of the function.

Special Functions

Two special functions are reserved for handling exceptions that occur during the exception handling itself:

- `void terminate();` is called when you do not provide an exception handler for a thrown exception, or when an error occurs during the stack unwinding. The terminate function, by default, calls the abort() function from the ANSI C library. You can, however, direct terminate to call a function that you can set up by calling the set_terminate function, which is declared as follows:

```
typedef void (*PtrFuncVoid)();
PtrFuncVoid set_terminate(PtrFuncVoid);
```

If you write a function named handle_termination to handle the termination, terminate() can call it with the following:

```
PtrFuncVoid old_term_handler; // To save old handler
void handle_termination();    // New handler
old_term_handler = set_terminate(handle_termination);
```

- void unexpected(); is called if a function throws an exception that is not in its *exception specification*—the list of exceptions that the function is supposed to throw. As the default action of unexpected(), it calls terminate(), which in turn calls abort() to exit the program. Like set_terminate, a set_unexpected function enables you to specify a function that unexpected() should call. You use set_unexpected in the same manner as set_terminate:

```
typedef void (*PtrFuncVoid)();
PtrFuncVoid old_unexpected;  // To save old handler
void handle_unexpected();    // New handler
old_unexpected = set_unexpected(handle_unexpected);
```

Summary

Even though C++ is already proving to be useful in many practical problems, it's still in its infancy and lacks certain features such as *exception handling* and *templates.* Exception handling will provide a uniform way to handle errors in C++ class libraries and programs, whereas templates will support the definition of parameterized classes and functions. The American National Standards Institute's (ANSI) X3J16 committee, which is developing a draft standard for the C++ programming language, plans to add exception handling and templates to the C++ language. The X3J16 committee will define these features using the experimental designs presented in Chapters 14 and 15 of *The Annotated C++ Reference Manual* (*ARM*) by Margaret Ellis and Bjarne Stroustrup (Addison-Wesley, 1990). This chapter provided an overview of templates and exception handling based on the designs presented in the *ARM.*

IV

Applying OOP Techniques in C++

14

Using C Libraries in C++

The first three parts of this book, Chapters 1 through 13, described the Microsoft Visual C++ Compiler, explained the terminology of object-oriented programming, and introduced you to the C++ programming language. Chapters 7 through 12, in particular, focused on the features of C++ that support data abstraction, inheritance, and polymorphism—the concepts that form the basis of object-oriented programming.

Parts IV and V, Chapters 14 through 20, focus on building and using C++ class libraries. Because there are no standard C++ libraries yet, standard C libraries still are important functionality sources for C++ programmers. This chapter describes how you can use C libraries (the standard one as well as your own) in C++ programs. It also provides a summary description of the functions in the ANSI standard C library and shows some examples of these functions in C++ programs. Chapter 15 shows you how to build (and design) C++ class libraries. Chapters 16 through 18 detail the Microsoft Foundation Class library that comes with Microsoft Visual C++ and show you how to use these classes in MS-DOS and Microsoft Windows applications.

Linkage Between C and C++

Suppose you have a library of functions that have been compiled into object code and stored in the library in object code form. When you call a function from such a library in your program, the compiler will mark the name of the function as an unresolved symbol in the object code of your program. To create an executable program, you must use a linker and make sure that the linker searches the right library for the code of that function. If the linker finds the function's object code in the library, it will combine that code with your program's object code to create an executable file. To use C functions in C++ programs, you must be able to complete this process of *linking*. The following sections explain how you can do this by using the linkage specifier syntax of C++.

Type-Safe Linkage

To understand how C++ programs link with C functions, you must know how C++ resolves the names of functions. You can overload a function name in C++ so that you can declare the same function with different sets of arguments. To help the linker, the C++ compiler uses an encoding scheme that creates a unique name for each overloaded function. The general idea of the encoding algorithm is to generate a unique signature for each function by combining the following components:

- The name of the function
- The name of the class in which the function is defined
- The list of argument types accepted by the function

You don't need to know the exact details of the encoding algorithm because they differ from one compiler to another. But knowing that a unique signature is generated for each function in a class should help you understand how the linker can determine which of the many different versions of a function to call.

Effect of Function-Name Encoding

How does function-name encoding affect C++ programs? To see one benefit of name encoding, consider the following C program:

```
//  Illustrates effect of wrong argument type

#include <stdio.h>

void print(unsigned short x)
{
    printf("x = %u", x);
}

void main(void)
{
    short x = -1;
    print(x);
}
```

The `print` function expects an `unsigned short` integer argument, but `main` calls `print` with a `signed short` integer argument. You can see the result of this type of mismatch from the output of the program:

```
x = 65535
```

Even though `print` was called with a `-1`, the printed value is `65535` because the program was run on a system that uses a 16-bit representation for `short` integers. The bit representation of the value `-1` happens to be `0xffff` (all 16 bits are `1`); when treated as an `unsigned` quantity, `0xffff` produces the value `65535`. In C++, you can avoid problems like this by defining overloaded functions—one version of `print` for `unsigned short` type and another version for `short`. With this modification, the C++ version of the C program looks like this:

```
// C++ version avoids problem by overloading function

#include <stdio.h>

void print(unsigned short x)
{
    printf("x = %u", x);
}

void print(short x)
{
    printf("x = %d", x);
}

void main(void)
{
```

```
    short x = -1;
    print(x);
}
```

When you run this C++ program, the output is

```
x = -1
```

This time, the result is correct because the C++ compiler uses function-name encoding to generate a call to the version of `print` that takes a `signed short` argument. This feature of C++—the capability to distinguish between overloaded functions based on argument types—is known as *type-safe linkage* because you cannot inadvertently call a function with the wrong types of arguments.

C Linkage Directive

Now that you know that C++ encodes all function names, you can understand the main problem with calling C functions from C++ programs. If a C++ program calls the C function `strlen` to get the length of a null-terminated string of characters

```
// C++ program

#include <stddef.h>           // for definition of "size_t"

size_t strlen(const char* s); // prototype of "strlen"

//...
char str[] = "Hello";
size_t length = strlen(str);
```

when you compile and link the program containing this C++ code with the C library, the linker will complain that the function named `strlen` is unresolved, even though you're linking with the C library that contains the code for `strlen`. This happens because the C++ compiler uses the function prototype `strlen(const char*)` to create a name that is very different from `strlen`, the name the C library uses to store the object code of the `strlen` function.

To successfully link C object code with C++ programs, you need some mechanism to prevent the C++ compiler encoding the names of C functions. The linkage directive of C++ provides this escape mechanism. You can successfully link the C++ program that uses `strlen`, for example, if you qualify `strlen` as a C function by declaring it as

```
// Specify "C" linkage for the strlen function

extern "C" size_t strlen(const char* s);
```

Other Forms of Linkage Directive

To declare a number of functions with the "C" linkage, you can use the compound form of the linkage directive.

```
// Compound form of linkage directive

extern "C"
{
    int printf(const char* format, ...);
    void exit(int status);

/* Other functions... */
}
```

Typically, header files contain such linkage directives because that's where the functions are declared.

Sharing Header Files Between C and C++ Programs

Because of the close ties between C++ and C, you often find the need to use C functions in C++ programs. In C++ programs, you must declare the C functions with an `extern "C"` linkage. You can do this easily with the compound form of the linkage directive, but that leaves the declarations unacceptable to the C compiler because the `extern "C"` directive is not a standard C construct. You can solve this problem by using a conditional compilation directive of the C preprocessor, as follows:

```
/* Header file shared between C and C++ */

#ifdef _ _cplusplus
extern "C" {      /* if it's C++, use linkage directive */
#endif

/* Declare C functions here */
void clearerr(FILE *f);
FILE* fopen(const char* name, const char* mode);
int fclose(FILE* f);

/* ... */

#ifdef _ _cplusplus
}
#endif
```

The __cplusplus macro is predefined in every C++ compiler. Compilers that can handle C and C++ programs define this symbol when compiling a C++ program. Usually, these compilers provide header files that use the #ifdef __cplusplus construct to declare the C library functions with extern "C" linkage (you need only include the header file in your C++ program). The programs in this book assume that the standard C header files, such as STDIO.H, are designed to work with C++ programs.

If you're using C header files not conditioned to work with C++ compilers, and you cannot alter the C header files, you still can specify the extern "C" linkage by surrounding the #include directive as follows:

```
extern "C"
{
#include <stdio.h>
}
```

If you must do this, the best approach is to create a new header file with an extern "C" wrapper around the #include directive, as shown in the preceding example. This enables you to avoid cluttering the C++ programs with linkage directives that rightfully belong in header files. All source files that use C functions can do so with a consistent linkage directive.

Restrictions on Linkage Directive

You can specify the linkage directive for one instance of an overloaded function. If you declare the sqrt function for the complex and binary_coded_decimal classes as follows:

```
class complex;
class binary_coded_decimal;

extern complex  sqrt(complex&);
extern binary_coded_decimal sqrt(binary_coded_decimal&);
```

you also can use the standard C sqrt function if you declare it as follows:

```
extern "C" double sqrt(double);
```

In this case, you have two instances of sqrt for C++ classes and one from the C library; however, only one version of sqrt can be defined in C.

You cannot place linkage specification restrictions because you cannot place them within a local scope—all linkage specifications must appear in the file scope. In particular, the C++ compiler flags the following as an error:

```
// This is an error: cannot have linkage specification in a
// function's scope

main()
{
extern "C" size_t strlen(const char*); // flagged as error
//...

}
```

You can correct this "error" by moving the linkage specification to the file scope as follows:

```
// This is the right place for linkage specifications, in
// file scope (outside the body of functions)

extern "C" size_t strlen(const char*);

void main()
{
//...

}
```

Linkage to Other Languages

Although you've seen only the `extern "C"` linkage directive, the appearance of `C` within quotation marks should inform you that the linkage mechanism is intended to link C++ programs with functions written in other languages as well. Indeed, the linkage specification mechanism is designed for this purpose, but C++ compilers are required to support only two linkages: `C` and `C++`. You've seen examples of C linkage; C++ is the default linkage for all C++ programs.

Using the ANSI Standard C Library

By now you know how to use C functions in C++ programs. If your C compiler's standard header files are designed to work with a C++ compiler, you can use the C functions simply by including the appropriate header files in your C++ program. If you're a C programmer, you also know that C relies on its library to provide capabilities such as I/O, memory management, and mathematical functions. Every C program of any significance uses functions—such as `printf`, `scanf`, and `gets`—that are declared in the stdio.h header file. In addition to the I/O functions, the standard C library has many more functions, such as those for string manipulation and those that return date and time in various formats. The following sections summarize the capabilities of the ANSI C library and demonstrate their use in sample C++ programs.

Overall Capabilities of the ANSI C Library

From the overview of ANSI standard C in Chapter 3, you know that the standard defines not only the C programming language, but the contents of the library as well. Even the header files and the prototypes of the functions are specified by the standard. Because most C compilers are beginning to conform to the ANSI standard for C, the standard C library is a good place to look for functions that may be useful in your C++ programs.

The ANSI standard specifies more than 140 functions for the C library, but many of these functions, not yet available in most C compliers, are for handling international character sets. Table 14.1 lists most of the functions in the standard C library, grouped according to capability. The following sections further describe each function category and how each might be used in C++ programs.

Table 14.1. Capabilities of the standard C library.

Category of Function	Function Names
Standard I/O	`clearerr, fclose, feof, ferror, fflush, fgetc, fgetpos, fgets, fopen, fprintf, fputc, fputs, fread, freopen, fscanf, fseek, fsetpos, ftell, fwrite, getc, getchar, gets, printf, putc, putchar, puts, remove, rename, rewind, scanf, setbuf, setvbuf, sprintf, sscanf, tmpfile, tmpnam, ungetc, vfprintf, vprintf, vsprintf`
Process control	`abort, assert, atexit, exit, getenv, localeconv, longjmp, perror, raise, setjmp, setlocale, signal, system`

Category of Function	Function Names
Memory allocation	calloc, free, malloc, realloc
Variable-length argument list	va_start, va_arg, va_end
Data conversions	atof, atoi, atol, strtod, strtol, strtoul
Mathematical functions	abs, acos, asin, atan, atan2, ceil, cos, cosh, div, exp, fabs, floor, fmod, frexp, labs, ldexp, ldiv, log, log10, modf, pow, rand, sin, sinh, sqrt, srand, tan, tanh
Character classification	isalnum, isalpha, iscntrl, isdigit, isgraph, islower, isprint, ispunct, isspace, isupper, isxdigit, tolower, toupper
String and buffer manipulation	memchr, memcmp, memcpy, memmove, memset, strcat, strchr, strcmp, strcoll, strcpy, strcspn, strerror, strlen, strncat, strncmp, strncpy, strpbrk, strrchr, strspn, strstr, strtok
Search and sort	bsearch, qsort
Times and date	asctime, clock, ctime, difftime, gmtime, localtime, mktime, strftime, time

Standard I/O Functions

The standard I/O functions, declared in the stdio.h header file, include some of the most commonly-used functions (such as `printf` and `scanf`) in the C library. Almost all C programs use at least one of these functions. You can continue to use these functions in C++. However, as explained in Chapter 8, "C++ Classes for Standard I/O," most C++ compilers include the `iostream` class library, which provides a cleaner, object-based mechanism for I/O in C++ programs.

Process Control Functions

This broad category of the standard C library includes

- The signal-handling functions that manage error conditions.
- Utility functions that terminate a process, communicate with the operating system, and set up numeric and currency formats, depending on the locale for which your program is customized

These functions are declared in the following header files:

- LOCALE.H declares `localeconv` and `setlocale`
- SIGNAL.H declares `raise` and `signal`
- SETJMP.H declares `longjmp` and `setjmp`
- STDLIB.H declares `abort`, `atexit`, `exit`, `getenv`, `perror`, and `system`
- ASSERT.H declares `assert`

The following sections contain a summary of these functions and their uses.

Environment Variables

The term *process* refers to an executing program—when you run a program, you create a process. The *environment* of a process includes the information necessary to execute the process. The exact interpretation of the environment differs from one operating system to another. In UNIX and MS-DOS, the environment consists of an array of null-terminated strings, with each string defining a symbol of the form

```
VARIABLE=value
```

where the symbol appearing on the left side of the equation is an environment variable. In a UNIX system, you can see the environment variables using either of the commands `printenv` or `env`. In MS-DOS, type `SET` at the DOS prompt to see a list of environment variables.

Environment variables are used to pass information to processes. For example, under UNIX, the full-screen editor `vi` uses the `TERM` environment variable to determine the type of terminal on which the text is to be displayed. You, the user, indicate the terminal type in the `TERM` environment variable, and the `vi` editor picks up this setting by determining the value of `TERM`. Your programs can exploit environment variables as well. For instance, in UNIX systems, the `TZ` environment variable indicates your time zone. You can get the value of this environment variable by calling the `getenv` function, one of the utility routines defined in the STDLIB.H header file.

Exception Handling Using *setjmp* and *longjmp*

In C, you can use `setjmp` and `longjmp` to handle exceptional conditions. You can save the state (or the context) of the process by calling `setjmp` and then calling `longjmp` with the saved context to revert to a previous point in your program. (The terms *state* and *context* have the same meaning and refer to the information needed to reconstruct the process exactly as it is at a particular point in its flow of execution.) ANSI C requires a compiler to define an array data type named `jmp_buf` that can hold the information needed to restore a calling environment. This data type is defined in the SETJMP.H header file. To understand the mechanics of `setjmp` and `longjmp`, consider the following C code:

```
/*-------------------------------------------------------------*/
/*  Illustrates use of "setjmp" and "longjmp" to
 *  handle exceptions
 */

#include <setjmp.h>
jmp_buf last_context;

void process_commands(void);
/*-------------------------------------------------------------*/
void main(void)
{
/* Establish a context to which you can return */
    if (setjmp(last_context) == 0)
    {
        process_commands();
    }
    else
    {
/* This part executed when longjmp is called.
 * Place code for handling error here...
 */

    }
}
/*-------------------------------------------------------------*/
void process_commands(void)
{
    int error_flag;
/* ... */
```

```
/* In case of error, return to last context */
    if(error_flag) longjmp(last_context, 1);
}
```

The `setjmp` function saves the current context in the `last_context` variable and returns `0`. In this case, the `if` statement in `main` is satisfied, and `process_commands()` is called. Assume that the integer `error_flag` is set to `1` when any error occurs in the `process_commands` function. You then can handle the error by testing this flag and by calling the `longjmp` function with two arguments. The first argument is the `jmp_buf` array, which contains the context to which you want to return. When the calling environment reverts to this saved state, and `longjmp` returns, it's just like returning from the call to `setjmp` (which originally saved the `last_context` buffer). The second argument to `longjmp` specifies the value to be returned by the function. It should be nonzero so that the `if` statement in `main` branches to the `else` clause when the return is induced by a `longjmp`.

You can use the combination of `setjmp` and `longjmp` to jump unconditionally from one C function to another without using the conventional `return` statement. Essentially, `setjmp` marks the destination of the jump and `longjmp` acts as a nonlocal `goto` that executes the jump.

It's tempting to use `setjmp` and `longjmp` to handle exceptions in C++, but the calls to constructors and destructors create some problems. All objects initialized up to the point of the error must be destroyed before calling `longjmp` to jump to an error handling section of the program. This can be done only if you keep track of all objects created in your program. Still, at least one major C++ class library, the *NIH Class Library* uses `setjmp` and `longjmp` to handle exceptions. (NIH stands for National Institutes of Health.) Nevertheless, you may not have to devise your own exception-handling scheme using `setjmp` and `longjmp` because the ANSI standard for C++ is expected to include a well-defined method for handling exceptions in C++ programs. Refer to Chapter 13, "Advanced Topics in C++," for further details on this topic.

Customizing Programs to a Locale

The term *locale* refers to the locality, the geographic region, for which certain aspects of your program can be customized. ANSI C groups the locale-dependent aspects of a C program into six categories, and defines macros to identify them. Table 14.2 summarizes the locale categories defined in the LOCALE.H header file. You can use the `setlocale` function to selectively set each category shown in Table 14.2 to conform to a selected locale. The locale named `C` indicates the minimal environment for C programs. Most compilers support only the locale named `C`, but future C compilers may support other locale names as well.

You can obtain the numeric- and currency-formatting style for the current locale by calling the `localeconv` function, which returns a pointer to a statically allocated `lconv` structure. You'll find the `lconv` structure declared in the LOCALE.H header file. This structure includes formatting information such as the decimal point character and the currency symbol for the current locale.

Table 14.2. Locale categories in ANSI standard C

Locale Category	Parts of Program Affected
LC_ALL	The entire program's locale-specific parts (all categories that follow)
LC_COLLATE	Behavior of the `strcoll` and `strxfrm` functions, which use the collating sequence of the character set
LC_CTYPE	Behavior of the character-classification functions
LC_MONETARY	Monetary formatting information returned by the `localeconv` function.
LC_NUMERIC	Decimal-point character for the formatted output functions (for example, `printf`) and the data conversion functions, and for the nonmonetary formatting information returned by the `localeconv` function.
LC_TIME	Behavior of the `strftime` function, which formats time.

You can use the locale mechanism to ensure that the output generated by your application program conforms to the standard representation of monetary and numeric information, as practiced in the locality where the program is being used. For instance, you may use `localeconv` to get formatting information in a C++ class designed to represent currency. Unfortunately, most C compilers (including Visual C++) still support only the `C` locale, which does not include information on formatting monetary information.

Executing Operating System Commands

Another useful function in this category is `system`, which enables you to pass a command to the command processor of the environment where your C or C++ program is running. The system function accepts the command in a null-terminated string and returns to your program after the command has been executed. You can even test whether a command processor such as MS-DOS COMMAND.COM is running by calling system with a null pointer as argument and testing for a nonzero return value. Here's a small C++ program that uses system to display a list of environment variables in an MS-DOS environment.

```
//  Demonstrate the use of "system" in a C++ program
//  Assumes an MS-DOS environment

#include <iostream.h>
#include <stdlib.h>

main()
{
    if(system(NULL))
    {
        cout << "Command Processor available" << endl;
        cout << "Current environment variables are:" << endl;
        system("SET");
    }
    else
        cout << "Sorry, no command processor!" << endl;
}
```

If you're writing a Windows application, it's not a good idea to use the system() call. Windows does, however, offer alternatives to system(), such as ShellExecute(), to provide the same functionality.

Memory Allocation

One advantage that C has over older languages such as FORTRAN is its capability to manage memory at runtime. In FORTRAN, there is no provision for requesting memory at runtime. All data items and arrays must be declared in the program. You must guess the maximum size of an array beforehand, and it is not possible to exceed the maximum without recompiling the program. This is inefficient, because you often define large arrays yet use only a small portion of each.

In C, you can request blocks of memory at runtime and release the blocks when your program no longer needs them. This allows your application to exploit all available memory in the system. Like most other capabilities in C, this comes in the form of four standard functions: calloc, malloc, realloc, and free, which are defined in the stdlib.h header file. `Calloc` and `malloc` are used for allocating memory, `realloc` for adjusting the size of a previously-allocated block, and `free` for releasing memory.

C++ not only retains C's ability to allocate memory at runtime, but also makes it a part of the language by providing two built-in operators, `new` and `delete`, to handle allocation and deallocation of objects, respectively. Of course, many C++ compilers define `new` and `delete` in terms of `malloc` and `free`. If you need to overload the `new` and `delete` operators for one of your C++ classes, you can use `malloc` and `free` to define the overloaded versions of the operators.

Variable-Length Argument Lists

In writing C programs, you have used functions (such as `printf` and `scanf`) that can take a variable number of arguments. In fact, their prototypes use an ellipsis in the argument list to reflect this:

```
int printf(const char *format_string, ...);
int scanf(const char *format_string, ...);
```

ANSI standard C includes the `va_start`, `va_arg`, and `va_end` macros, defined in the STDARG.H header file, which allow you to write functions capable of accepting a variable number of arguments. The only requirement on such functions is that they must accept at least one required argument. You can use these macros in C++ programs as well. As an example, consider a `menu_widget` class with a constructor that accepts a variable number of strings and creates a menu with those strings as labels. The following skeleton C++ program illustrates how you can use the ANSI standard approach to handle a variable number of arguments in a class member function:

```
//-------------------------------------------------------------
//  Demonstrates the use of variable-length argument lists

#include <iostream.h>
#include <stdlib.h>      // For declaration of NULL
#include <stdarg.h>

#define MENU_BAR  1
#define PULL_DOWN 2

typedef char *P_CHAR;

class menu_widget
{
```

```
public:
    menu_widget(int style, ...);
// ...
private:
// ...
};

//---------------------------------------------------------------
menu_widget::menu_widget(int style, ...)
{
// Get the first optional parameter using "va_start"
    va_list  argp;       // Used to access arguments
    va_start(argp, style);

// Get items one by one
    char     *item_text;
    int      count = 0;

    cout << "------------------------------" << endl;
    while((item_text = va_arg(argp, P_CHAR)) != NULL)
    {
        cout << "Item " << count << " = " << item_text << endl;
        count++;
    }
}
//---------------------------------------------------------------
//  Test the use of variable-length argument lists

void main()
{
    menu_widget m1(MENU_BAR, "File", "Edit", "Utilities", NULL);
    menu_widget m2(PULL_DOWN, "Open", "Close", "New", "Save",
                              "Save As...", "Quit", NULL);
//...
}
```

If you run this program, you get the following output showing that the `menu_widget` constructor is processing a variable number of arguments

```
------------------------------
Item 0 = File
Item 1 = Edit
Item 2 = Utilities
------------------------------
```

```
Item 0 = Open
Item 1 = Close
Item 2 = New
Item 3 = Save
Item 4 = Save As...
Item 5 = Quit
```

Data Conversions

The functions in this category—`atof`, `atoi`, `atol`, `strtod`, `strtol`, and `strtoul`—convert character strings into internal representations of variables. These functions are declared in the stdlib.h header file.

The conversion routines are ideal for converting command-line arguments from their string representation into the internal format. For example, in a small calculator program, you might want to process an input line of the form

```
eval 12.43 + 17.52
```

where `eval` is the name of the program that accepts a command line of the form `<value1> <operator> <value2>` and prints the result of the operation. In this example, the program should print 29.95 as the answer. When implementing this program, you can use the `atof` function to convert the second and the fourth command-line arguments to `double` variables. (The first argument is always the name of the program.) The code for the addition operator might be written as

```
#include <stdlib.h>
#include <iostream.h>

void main(int argc, char **argv)
{
    double op1, op2, result;

    op1 = atof(argv[1]);
    op2 = atof(argv[3]);

    switch(argv[2][0])
    {
// ...
        case '+':
         result = op1 + op2;
// ...
    }
```

```
    cout << result << endl;
}
```

This example assumes a decimal calculator. If you want a hexadecimal calculator so that all input and output is in hexadecimal, you can use the `strtoul` function to convert the input arguments to unsigned long integers. This is a typical use of the data-conversion functions.

Mathematical Functions

Both C and C++ support the basic floating-point data types `float` and `double` and enable you to write arithmetic expressions using these data types. Additionally, the standard C library includes a set of mathematical functions that enable you to evaluate common functions, such as *sine* and *cosine.* Most of these functions are declared in the MATH.H header file.

Basic Functions

The trigonometric functions—`cos`, `sin`, `tan`, `acos`, `asin`, `atan`, and `atan2`—evaluate the cosine, sine, and tangent of any angle in radians and compute the inverses of the cosine, sine, and tangent. These functions are useful for the transformation of rectangular to polar coordinates that often occurs in graphics programs. Other commonly used mathematical functions are

`sqrt` to compute square roots
`log` to return the natural logarithm of an argument
`log10` to return the base 10 logarithm of an argument
`exp` to compute exponentials

For example, you would call `exp(1.75)` to evaluate e1.75; `fabs` to return the absolute value of a floating-point value; `ceil` to return the nearest integer larger than a given floating-point number; and `floor` to return the nearest integer smaller than its floating-point argument.

Integer Arithmetic

Four functions, declared in STDLIB.H, handle arithmetic using integer arguments. `abs` and `labs` return, respectively, the absolute value of an integer and a long integer. `div` divides one integer by another and returns the integer quotient and an integer remainder. `ldiv` operates similarly but with long integer arguments.

Generating Random Numbers

If you need to generate random numbers (for a random screen pattern, a game, or a statistical analysis problem, for example), the ANSI C library includes a function, named `rand`, that can generate a random positive integer in the range `0` to `RAND_MAX`, a constant defined in STDLIB.H. The `rand` function generates random numbers by using a well-defined algorithm. Given the same starting number, `rand` always generates the same sequence of random numbers. In other words, instead of being truly random, the sequence generated by `rand` is a pseudorandom sequence. If the algorithm used to generate the random numbers is good, the sequence will not repeat frequently, and all numbers between `0` and `RAND_MAX` will appear with equal probability. A function named `srand` sets the starting point of the random sequence.

Sometimes you need to select a random sequence of random numbers. For example, you wouldn't want to be dealt the same hand in a card game again and again. ANSI C does not provide a routine to generate a random seed, but you can use the value returned by the `time` function as the argument to `srand` to set a new random seed for `rand`.

Character Classification

The C ctype.h header file contains several functions that are useful for classifying and converting characters. The behavior of these functions is affected by the `LC_CTYPE` category of the current locale. Table 14.3 shows a summary of ANSI C functions that can be used to classify and convert characters. These functions are useful when parsing strings. You can use the `isspace` function, for example, to locate a valid whitespace character in a string.

Table 14.3. Summary of ANSI C's character classification functions.

Name	Description
`isalnum`	Returns nonzero if character is alphanumeric
`isalpha`	Returns nonzero if character is alphabetic
`iscntrl`	Returns nonzero if character belongs to the set of control characters
`isdigit`	Returns nonzero if character is a numerical digit
`isgraph`	Returns nonzero if character is printable (excluding the space character)

continues

Table 14.3. continued

Name	Description
`islower`	Returns nonzero if character is lowercase
`isprint`	Returns nonzero if character is printable (includes space)
`ispunct`	Returns nonzero if character belongs to the set of punctuation characters
`isspace`	Returns nonzero if character belongs to the set of whitespace characters, which include space, formfeed, newline, carriage return, horizontal tab, and vertical tab
`isupper`	Returns nonzero if character is uppercase
`isxdigit`	Returns nonzero if character is a hexadecimal digit
`tolower`	Converts character to lowercase only if that character is an uppercase letter
`toupper`	Converts character to uppercase only if that character is a lowercase letter

String and Buffer Manipulation

You've already encountered some of ANSI C's string manipulation functions in the `String` class shown in Chapter 10, "Defining Operations on Objects," and Chapter 11, "Using Inheritance in C++." These functions, declared in STRING.H, primarily are for comparing two strings or buffers, copying one string or buffer into another, and searching for the occurrence of a character in a string. This section discusses the standard C library string functions.

Buffers

A *buffer* is a contiguous block of memory, and string refers to an array of characters. By convention, a string in C is marked by a null character—a byte with all zero bits. Because of this, C strings are known as *null-terminated strings*.

Strings in C and C++

Neither C nor C++ has any built-in data type for strings. Instead, strings are treated as an array of characters with a null character marking the end of the string. You can declare strings as you would any other array objects

```
char line[81], filename[]="test.1";
```

Here, `line` is a string with room for 81 characters. However, because of the terminating null character, `line` can hold no more than 80 characters. The second string, `filename`, is declared without a size, but the initial value of the string provides enough information about the size. The compiler will reserve enough storage for the string and the terminating null character. As shown in Figure 14.1, the `filename` string requires 7 bytes of storage.

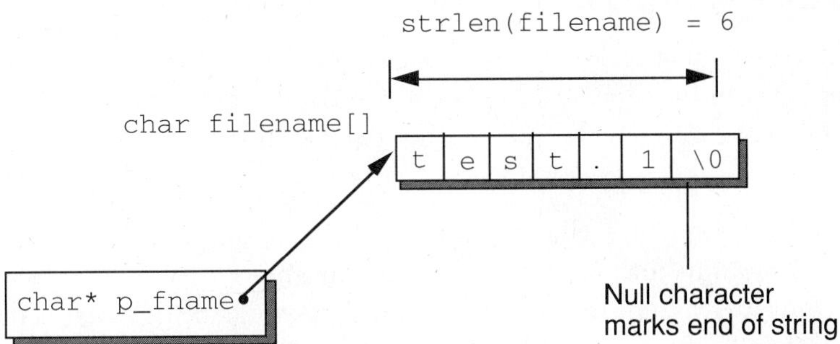

Figure 14.1. A null-terminated string in C and C++.

Because a string is an array of characters, you can also access a string through a `char*` pointer. For example, to access the `filename` string using a pointer named `p_fname`, you would write:

```
char  filename[] = "test.1";
char *p_fname = filename;
```

Once the `p_fname` pointer is initialized, you can use it to access the `filename` string as you would through the array named `filename`. Of course, as shown in Figure 14.1, the `p_fname` pointer requires some additional storage space. You also can declare and initialize a `char*` pointer to a string in a single statement. For example, you would write

```
char *p_str = "Some string";
```

to initialize the `p_str` character pointer to the string constant `Some string`. You actually have initialized `p_str` to the address of the first character of the string `Some string`.

Length of a String

The length of a C string is the number of characters in the string up to but not including the terminating null character. For example, the `filename` string in Figure 14.1 is 6 bytes long, even though 7 bytes are needed to store the string. You can use the `strlen` function to get the length of a C string.

Comparing Strings and Buffers

The string and buffer manipulation category contains five functions for comparing strings and buffers: `memcmp`, `strcmp`, `strncmp`, `strcoll`, and `strxfrm`. Each function takes two arguments and returns a zero when the arguments match. The functions return a negative value if the first argument is less than the second and a positive value if the first argument is greater than the second. This means, for strings, that the first argument will appear after the second in a dictionary of words in that character set.

The `strcmp` function is used for case-sensitive comparisons of two strings. The `memcmp` and `strncmp` functions behave like `strcmp`, but are used for comparing a specified number of characters from the beginning of each string.

The `strcoll` function is intended for use in comparing strings using a collating sequence determined by the `LC_COLLATE` category of the locale. The `strxfrm` function is a utility routine that transforms a string into a new form so that, if `strcmp` were used to compare two transformed strings, the result would be identical to that returned by `strcoll` applied to the original strings.

Concatenating and Copying Strings

The `memcpy`, `memmove`, `strcat`, `strcpy`, `strncat`, and `strncpy` functions are used for concatenating and copying strings and buffers. Each of these functions accepts two arguments. In all cases, the second argument is the source and the first is the destination. When copying or concatenating strings, you must ensure that there is enough room in the destination string to hold the source string. You can do this either by declaring an array of characters with enough room or by allocating memory at runtime.

The `memcpy` and `memmove` functions are used for copying one buffer into another. Of these two, the `memmove` function is guaranteed to work properly even if the source and destination buffers overlap. Both `memcpy` and `memmove` work with nonoverlapping source and destination buffers.

The `strcat` function appends the second string argument to the first and produces a null-terminated string as the result. The `strncat` function is similar to `strcat`, but copies only a specified number of characters from the second string to the first.

The strcpy function copies the second string argument onto the first one. While strcpy copies the entire string, strncpy copies only a specified number of characters. Because strncpy does not automatically append a null character to the destination string, you must be alert for instances where the characters being copied do not include a null character.

Search and Sort

The standard C library also includes two very useful functions: qsort (for sorting an array of objects) and bsearch (for searching for an object in a sorted array). These sort and search functions are suitable for in-memory operations when the entire array fits into memory.

Using *qsort* and *bsearch*

Figure 14.2 shows a typical sorting scenario: you have an array of pointers to String objects (see Chapter 11 for the String class), each of which contains a C string, and you want to sort the array by rearranging the pointers so that the C strings appear in ascending order. Figure 14.2 shows the original array of pointers and the array after sorting. Although the pointers have been rearranged, the String objects have remained in their original positions. Because the pointers are usually much smaller than the objects, the result is faster sorting—it's faster to shuffle the pointers than to copy the objects. However, memory usage increases because the pointers require extra storage space.

The qsort and bsearch functions are declared in stdlib.h, as follows:

```
void *bsearch(const void *key, const void *base, size_t num,
          size_t width,
          int (*compare)(const void *elem1, const void *elem2));

void qsort(const void *base, size_t num, size_t width,
          int (*compare)(const void *elem1, const void *elem2));
```

As you can see from the prototype, the qsort function expects (as argument) the starting address of the array, the number of elements in it, the size (in bytes) of each element, and a pointer to a function that performs the comparison of any two elements in the array. The bsearch function, in addition, requires a pointer to the value being sought, and the array being searched must already be sorted in ascending order.

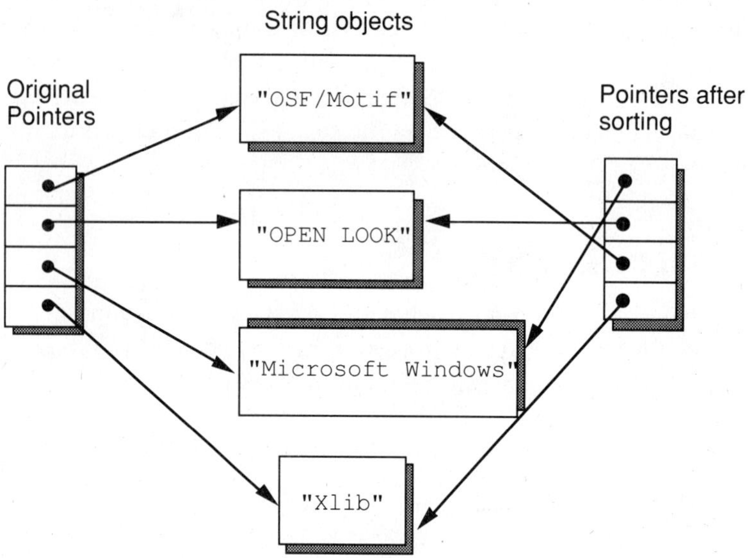

Figure 14.2. Sorting an array of `String` objects.

The key to using `qsort` and `bsearch` is to provide an appropriate comparison function, the last argument to either function. This function will receive, as argument, pointers to the two elements being compared. It must return one of the following integer values:

- A positive value if the first element is greater than the second one
- A zero if the two elements are equal
- A negative value if the first element is less than the second one

You determine the meanings of *less than*, *greater than*, and *equal*. When sorting `String` objects, for example, you compare the C string field of the two objects and return a value based on the lexicographic ordering of the strings.

Sorting an Array of String Objects

As an example of using `qsort`, consider the problem of sorting an array of `String` objects. You must first define a `StringArray` class that holds an array of pointers to instances of the `String` class. As shown in Listing 14.1, the `StringArray` class provides member functions to add new `String` objects to the array, display the current contents of the array, and sort the array. The STR.H file, which declares the `String` class, appears in Listing 11.1 in Chapter 11.

For this discussion, the interesting part of StringArray is the sort function. This function sorts by calling qsort from the ANSI C library. The final argument to qsort, the compare function, is the crucial component in making this scheme work. For the StringArray class, you can implement the compare function as a class static function that performs the comparison by calling strcmp from the ANSI C library. You can use String objects as arguments to strcmp because the String class provides a type-conversion operator that allows the C++ compiler to convert the String type to const char* type.

Listing 14.1. STRARRAY.H. Implementation of the StringArray class.

```
//--------------------------------------------------------------
//  File:  strarray.h
//  Implements an array of String objects
//
//  NOTE: The "sort" function sorts the contents of the
//        array by calling the "qsort" function from the
//        standard C library

#if !defined(_ _STRARRY_H)
#define _ _STRARRAY_H

#include <stdlib.h>
#include "str.h"

const size_t default_capacity = 16;
    typedef String* StringPtr;

class StringArray
{
public:
// Constructor
    StringArray() : _count(0), _capacity(default_capacity)
    {
        _strp = new StringPtr[default_capacity];
    }

// Destructor
    ~StringArray();
```

continues

Listing 14.1. continued

```
    void add(const char* s)
    {
// If there is no more room, you should expand the capacity
// by allocating more space.  Here, simply return.
        if(_count == _capacity) return;
        _strp[_count] = new String(s);
        _count++;
    }

// Function to be used with "qsort"
    static int compare(const void* s1, const void* s2)
    {
        return strcmp(**(String**)s1, **(String**)s2);
    }

// The "sort" function simply calls "qsort"
    void sort()
    {
        qsort(_strp, _count, sizeof(String*),
              StringArray::compare);
    }

    void show();

private:
    String** _strp;
    size_t   _count;
    size_t   _capacity;
};

//-------------------------------------------------------------
//  ~ S t r i n g A r r a y
//  Destructor for the StringArray class

StringArray::~StringArray()
{
int i;
    for(i = 0; i < _count; i++)
        delete _strp[i];
    delete _strp;
}
```

```
//-----------------------------------------------------------------
//  s h o w
//  Display the contents of the array

void StringArray::show()
{
    cout << "Contents of String array:" << endl;
    cout << "------------------------" << endl;
    int i;
    for(i = 0; i<_count; i++)
    {
        cout << *_strp[i] << endl;
    }
}

#endif
```

Listing 14.2 displays a sample program that tests the sorting operation of the `StringArray` class. The program sets up an instance of the `StringArray` class, adds some `String` objects to it, and sorts the array. After sorting the array, it displays the contents.

Listing 14.2. Sample sorting program.

```
//-----------------------------------------------------------------
//  Sample program to create an array of String objects,
//  add some Strings, and sort the array
#include "strarray.h"

void main()
{
    StringArray sa;
// Add some strings to the array
    sa.add("OSF/Motif");
    sa.add("OPEN LOOK");
    sa.add("Microsoft Windows");
    sa.add("Xlib");
// Sort the array
    sa.sort();
// Display contents
```

continues

Listing 14.2. continued

```
    sa.show();
}
```

When you run this program, it displays the following as the contents of the sorted array:

```
Contents of String array:
------------------------
Microsoft Windows
OPEN LOOK
OSF/Motif
Xlib
```

As you can see, the array is sorted in ascending order. You can reverse the order of sorting by placing a minus sign in front of the `strcmp` function call in the body of the `compare` function of the `StringArray` class.

Date and Time

The ANSI C library includes a set of functions for obtaining, displaying, and manipulating date and time information. These functions are declared in the TIME.H header file. Figure 14.3 is a pictorial representation of the different formats of date and time in ANSI C and the functions that enable you to convert from one format to another. The core of these functions is the `time` function, which returns a value of the `time_t` type (defined in the time.h header file). This `time_t` value represents the calendar time in encoded form (often called *binary time*). You can convert it to a `tm` structure with the `gmtime` and `localtime` functions. The `gmtime` function accepts a binary time and sets the fields in a `tm` structure to correspond to Greenwich Mean Time (GMT) or Universal Time Coordinated (UTC). (Universal Time Coordinated is the updated name for Greenwich Mean Time.) The `localtime` function sets the fields of the `tm` structure to local time. The `mktime` function converts time from a `tm` structure to a value of `time_t`.

Printing the Date and Time

The `asctime` function converts the value in a `tm` structure to a null-terminated C string that you can print. The `ctime` function converts the output of `time` directly to a string. Thus, you can print the current time from a C++ program as follows:

```
#include <iostream.h>
#include <time.h>
```

```
main()
{
    time_t tnow;
// Get the current time in binary form
    time(&tnow);
// Convert the time to a string and print it.
    cout << "Current time = " << ctime(&tnow) << endl;
}
```

A sample output from this program is as follows:

```
Current time = Wed Feb 19 22:16:26 1992
```

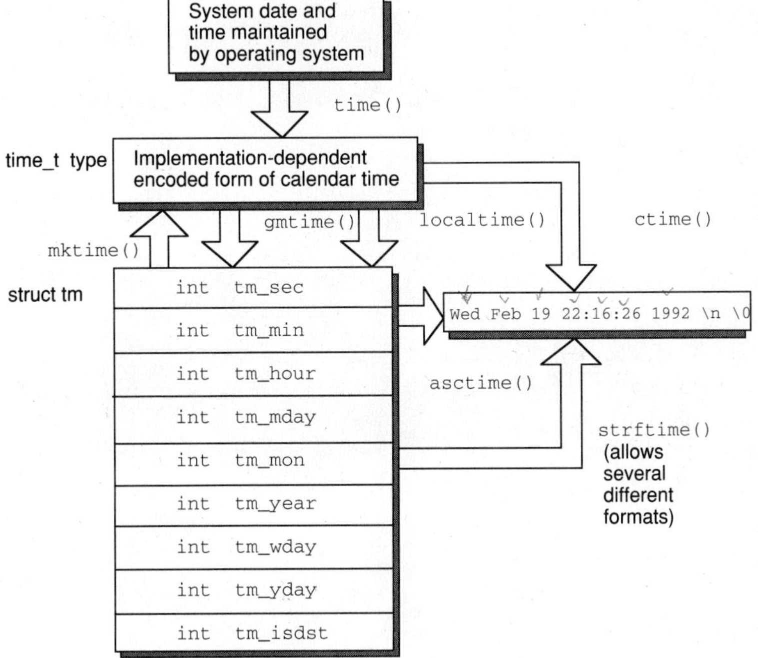

Figure 14.3. Different forms of time in ANSI C.

A *DateTime* Class

A more concrete example of the time-manipulation functions in C++ is the `DateTime` class, which represents date and time information. As shown in Listing 14.3, the `DateTime` class maintains the calendar time in binary format. Its default constructor calls the time function to get the current time. The other interesting member of this class is the addition operator that advances the date by a specified number of days. The addition operator uses the mktime function to accomplish this task. The mktime function converts calendar time from a tm structure into a time_t format. Before making this conversion, mktime also adjusts all members of the tm structure to reasonable values. As you can see from the definition of the operator+ function in Listing 14.3, you can exploit this feature of mktime to advance the DateTime values by a number of days.

The DateTime class also overloads the << operator so you can use << to print DateTime variables on an output stream. This overloading is done with the help of the print member function of the DateTime class that prints on an ostream. The print function, in turn, calls ctime from the standard C library. Note that the ctime function converts a binary time into a formatted C string.

Listing 14.3. DATETIME.H. Defines the DateTime class for manipulating calendar time.

```
//--------------------------------------------------------------
//  File:  datetime.h
//
//  A date and time class

#if !defined(__DATETIME_H)
#define __DATETIME_H

#include <time.h>      // ANSI standard "Time" functions
#include <iostream.h>  // For stream I/O

class DateTime
{
public:
DateTime() { time(&_bintime); }
    DateTime(time_t t) : _bintime(t) { }

    friend DateTime operator+(DateTime d, int n)
    {
        struct tm *ltime = localtime(&d._bintime);
        ltime->tm_mday += n;
        time_t t = mktime(ltime);
        return DateTime(t);
    }
```

```
    friend DateTime operator+(int n, DateTime d)
    {
        return d+n;
    }

    DateTime operator+=(int n)
    {
        struct tm *ltime = localtime(&_bintime);
        ltime->tm_mday += n;
        _bintime = mktime(ltime);
        return *this;
    }

    void print(ostream& os) { os << ctime(&_bintime);}

private:
    time_t     _bintime;
};

// Stream output operator for DateTime class

ostream& operator<<(ostream& os, DateTime& d)
{
    d.print(os);
    return os;
}

#end if
```

Although the `DateTime` class is far from being complete (it's intended to serve as an example that illustrates how to use ANSI C's time-manipulation functions in a C++ class), you still can use the class for some useful work. Listing 14.4 presents a small program that displays the current date and time and illustrates the use of the addition operators.

Listing 14.4. Sample program to test the `DateTime` class.

```
//-------------------------------------------------------------
//  Test the DateTime class
```

continues

Listing 14.4. continued

```
#include "datetime.h"

void main()
{
    DateTime d1;
    cout << "Current date and time = " << d1 << endl;

// Advance by 45 days
    d1 += 45;
    cout << "45 days later, it will be = " << d1 << endl;

//  Try addition operator...(add another 5 days)
    cout << "50 days later, it will be = ";
    cout << d1+5 << endl;
}
```

A sample output from this program is

```
Current date and time = Wed Feb 19 22:16:26 1992

45 days later, it will be = Sat Apr 04 22:16:26 1992

50 days later, it will be = Thu Apr 09 22:16:26 1992
```

Notice that an extra linefeed appears after each line because the `ctime` function, called by the `print` member function of `DateTime`, formats the binary time into a string with a newline character at the end. This feature of `ctime`, together with the explicit use of the `endl` manipulator, is responsible for the extra blank lines. To format the time into a string without an extra newline character, you can call the `strftime` function, which is specifically intended for formatting time information.

Compiler-Specific Libraries

Although the standard C library is a good source of portable functions, you should also examine your C++ compiler's offering of nonstandard libraries. In particular, C++ compilers for MS-DOS systems such as Microsoft Visual C++ include many additional functions in their libraries. Most notable among these functions are the ones for accessing the services of the MS-DOS operating system and those for graphics output.

If you're developing a program specifically for the MS-DOS environment and don't mind being tied to a particular compiler's library, consider making use of the compiler-specific functions. These functions are as easy to use as the standard C functions. In all likelihood, the header files are probably already conditioned to work with the C++ compiler. You need only include the header file and call the function. However, you must know the overall capabilities of the additional functions. You usually can find this information in the documentation that comes with the C++ compiler. Another possible source of information is a book that, like this one, specifically covers your C++ compiler's library.

Summary

Like C, C++ is built around a sparse core, and all major functions are delegated to support libraries. The core of the language provides a small set of built-in data types, constructs such as `class` and `struct` to define new types, operators to build expressions, and control structures to manage the flow of execution of the program. You must rely on libraries for everything from I/O to string manipulations.

Because C++ is still in a state of evolution, it does not yet have a standard library like ANSI C. Typical C++ compilers include the `complex` class for complex arithmetic and the `iostream` library for I/O. You can, however, use the functions from the standard C library in your C++ programs. To link C++ programs with the C library, you must enclose the declaration of the C functions and data inside an `extern "C" { ... }` linkage specifier. Many C++ compilers, including Microsoft Visual C++, already provide C header files with declarations enclosed in an `extern "C" { ... }` block. With such header files, using C functions is as easy as including the header files in a C++ program and making the function calls.

The standard C library includes a large assortment of functions that you are guaranteed to find in all standard-conforming C compilers. Because C++ does not yet have a standard library, the ANSI C library is a good place to look for functions that may be useful in your C++ classes. This chapter provides a summary description of the ANSI C library and shows you how to use these capabilities in C++ programs and in C++ classes.

15

Building Class Libraries in C++

In Chapter 14, "Using C Libraries in C++," you were shown how to use existing C libraries in C++ programs. This chapter examines the topics of designing, organizing, and building C++ classes that can provide specific functionality for use in C++ programs. When designing a class library, you must determine the inheritance hierarchy of the classes, the way one class uses the facilities of others, and the kinds of operations the classes will support.

Organizing C++ Classes

If a standard class library for C++ existed, deciding how to organize C++ classes would be easy—you would model your classes after the standard ones. Unfortunately, C++ does not yet have standard classes. The `iostream` class library (described in Chapter 8, "C++ Classes for Standard I/O"), which comes with AT&T's C++ 3.0, may be the only standard class library currently available. Of course, the `iostream` class library serves only I/O. You need much more than the `iostream` classes when developing complete applications in C++. Additionally, even if many standard classes for C++ were available, your particular application still would require you to write new, customized classes. The Microsoft Foundation Class library, which will be discussed in Chapter 16, "Using the Microsoft Foundation Class Library," is not a standard class library.

The point is that sooner or later you'll face the task of organizing a library of classes that will form the basis of your application. Organization of C++ classes refers to their inheritance hierarchy, as well as to the way one class can use the facilities of another. First, consider the question of inheritance hierarchy.

Inheritance Hierarchy Under Single Inheritance

Before AT&T C++ Release 2.0, a class could inherit from only one base class. As shown in Figures 15.1 and 15.2, you can organize the inheritance tree of classes under single inheritance in two distinct ways:

- A single class hierarchy with all classes in the library derived from a single root class (a base class, not derived from another class). The SmallTalk-80 programming language provides this type of class hierarchy. Therefore, this organization of C++ classes is known as the *SmallTalk model* or a *single-tree model.*
- Multiple disjoint class hierarchies with more than one root class. This has been referred to as the *forest model* because the library contains multiple trees of class hierarchies.

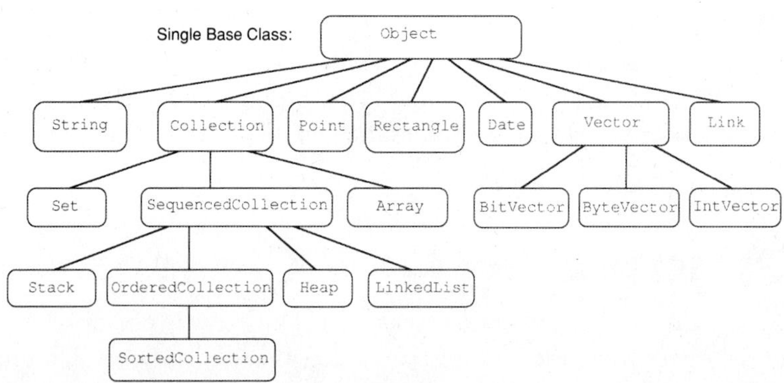

Figure 15.1. A typical single-tree organization of C++ classes patterned after SmallTalk-80.

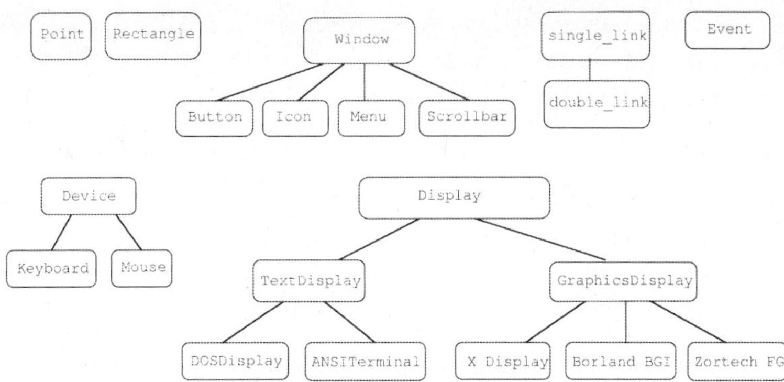

Figure 15.2. A forest of C++ classes for building user interfaces.

Single-Class Hierarchy

As Figure 15.1 shows, a library that uses a single-class hierarchy starts with a base class, usually named `Object`, which declares a host of virtual functions that apply to all other classes in the library. These virtual functions handle standard operations such as copying, printing, storing, retrieving, and comparing objects. Each derived class defines concrete versions of these functions and thereby provides a standard interface to the library. Several prominent C++ class libraries, including the NIH Class Library by Keith Gorlen, use this model of organization. (NIH stands for National Institutes of Health.) Proponents of the single-class hierarchy point out the following benefits of this approach:

- The definition of a single, root class ensures that all classes provide the same standard set of `public` interface functions. This enhances consistency and compatibility among classes.
- When all classes are guaranteed to inherit from a single base class, capabilities such as *persistence*—the capability for storing and retrieving collections of objects in a disk file—are easier to provide. The single-class hierarchy also enables you to easily provide a standard exception-handling mechanism. Again, you can achieve this by placing the exception-handling code in the `Object` class.
- Because every class in the library is an `Object`, you can easily define polymorphic data structures. For example, the following array of pointers:

```
Object *ArrayOfObjPtr[16];
```

can hold pointers to instances of any class in the library, so you can easily define data structures such as linked lists and stacks capable of holding instances of any class in the library.

However, a single-class (or *monolithic*) hierarchy has these disadvantages:

- The compiler cannot provide strict type-checking because many objects in the library are of the `Object*` type, which can point to an instance of any class in the library. Such pointers to the base class routinely are used in polymorphic container classes that are capable of storing instances of any class in the library.
- The root base class, `Object`, typically includes many virtual functions representing the union of all the virtual functions implemented by the derived classes. This is burdensome if you want to create a derived class because you must provide the definition of all the virtual functions even though many may not be relevant to that derived class.
- Although a single-root `Object` class makes it easy to create a container class capable of storing any other object from the library, you cannot use these containers to store standard C data types such as `float`, `int`, and `char`. If you want to store these types in a container, you must write your own classes that mimic the built-in types of C. For example, you could define `Float` and `Integer` classes that model, C's `float` and `int` data types.
- Because of the large size of a single-class hierarchy, compiling a single program may require processing a large number of header files. This can be a problem on MS-DOS systems, which typically have a limited amount of memory.

Multiple-Class Hierarchies

In contrast to the monolithic, single-class hierarchy of the SmallTalk-80 library, a C++ class library based on the forest model includes multiple-class trees, with each tree providing a well-defined functionality. Figure 15.2, for example, shows several class hierarchies in a C++ class library that provide the objects needed to build window-based user interfaces. Different types of windows are grouped together in the class hierarchy with the `Window` class as the root. Each window has a rectangle represented by the `Rectangle` class which, in turn, uses the `Point` class to represent the corners of the window.

The `Event` class models user inputs that come from one of the devices shown in the class hierarchy whose root is the `Device` class. The stand-alone `String` class represents text strings that might appear in windows. You can model the physical display of a class hierarchy with a generic `Display` as the base class. From this generic display, you can further specialize in text or graphics displays. You might categorize text displays in ANSI-standard terminals or IBM PC-compatible displays. Graphics displays may be based on the X Window System, Borland International's Borland Graphics Interface (BGI), or Microsoft Windows.

Here are the main advantages of the forest model of class libraries:

- Because each class hierarchy is small, you can understand and use the classes easily.
- Virtual functions declared in each root class are relevant to that class tree. It is not difficult, therefore, to implement the derived classes in each hierarchy.

On the other hand, the lack of an overall structure implies that you cannot create the elegant container classes of the SmallTalk model. Thus, the primary disadvantages of the forest model are as follows:

- Because there is no common base class, it's difficult to design container classes (such as linked lists, stacks, and queues) that can store any type of object. You must devise your own schemes for creating such data structures.
- Anything that requires a library-wide discipline becomes difficult to implement. For example, exception-handling and persistence are more difficult to support under the forest model than under a single-tree model.

Effects of Multiple Inheritance

The introduction of multiple inheritance in AT&T C++ Release 2.0 changed the implications of organizing C++ class libraries, according to either the single-tree model or the forest model. Because multiple inheritance allows a derived class to inherit from more than one base class, you can combine the capabilities of classes in unique ways to suit your needs. A good example is the single-linked list of `String` objects illustrated in Chapter 11, "Using Inheritance in C++." The linked list is constructed by linking instances of a new class, named `slink_string`, which is defined from the `String` class and the `single_link` class as follows:

```
class slink_string: public single_link, public String
{
//...
};
```

The `single_link` class is capable of holding a pointer to another instance of `single_link`. In this way, multiple inheritance enables you to combine the capabilities of two classes into a single class.

Some ways of applying multiple inheritance to extend the capabilities of C++ class libraries are:

- You can derive a class from two or more classes in a library, even if the class library follows a single-tree model of inheritance hierarchy. For example, the NIH Class Library includes a `Link` class and a `String` class. With multiple inheritance, you can combine these two classes to define a `String` with a `Link` just as you did to define the `slink_string` class in Chapter 11.

- Even with a multiple-class hierarchy, you can add a standard capability, such as persistence, by defining a new base class and deriving other classes from it. You can do this even though it takes extra work to create a new set of derived classes that incorporate the capability defined in the new base class. With single inheritance, you do not have the opportunity to combine the behavior of two or more classes packaged in a library.

Client-Server Relationship Among Classes

In addition to the inheritance relationship among classes, a class can use the facilities of another class. This is called the *client-server* relationship among classes, because the client class, in order to use the capabilities of the server class, calls the member functions of the server class. In C++, the client class needs an instance of the server class to call the member functions of the server. The client class can get this instance in one of the following ways:

- One of the member functions of the client class receives an instance of the server class as an argument.

- A member function of the client class calls a function that returns an instance of the server class.

- An instance of the server class is available as a global variable.

- The client class incorporates an instance of the server class as a member variable.

- A member variable of the client class is a pointer to an instance of the server class.

The last two cases are of interest because they constitute the most common ways of expressing a client-server relationship between two classes. This approach—using a class by incorporating an instance or a pointer to an instance—has been referred to as *composition.* The following sections briefly describe these two approaches to composition.

Class Instance as a Member

In Chapter 6, "C++ and Object-Oriented Programming," Listing 6.4 shows the declaration of several classes intended to represent geometric shapes, such as triangles and rectangles. All geometric shapes are derived from an abstract `shape` class. In particular, the `rectangle_shape` class is declared as follows:

```
class shape
{
public:
    virtual double compute_area(void) const = 0;
    virtual void draw(void) const{ } = 0;
};

// Define the "rectangle" class:

class rectangle_shape: public shape
{
private:
    double x1, y1;  // Coordinates of opposite corners
    double x2, y2;
public:
    rectangle_shape(double x1, double y1, double x2, double y2);
    double compute_area(void) const;
    void draw(void) const;
};
```

A better way to define the `rectangle_shape` class is to use the notion of a point in a plane. For instance, you can first define a `Point` class as follows:

```
//------------------------------------------------------------
//  File: point.h
//  Define a point in two-dimensional plane.

#if !defined(__POINT_H)
#define __POINT_H

#include <math.h>

typedef double Coord;
```

```
class Point
{
public:
    Point() : _x(0), _y(0) {}
    Point(Coord x, Coord y) : _x(x), _y(y) {}
    Point(const Point& p) : _x(p._x), _y(p._y) {}

    Point& operator=(const Point& p)
    {
        _x = p._x;
        _y = p._y;
         return *this;
    }

    Point operator-(const Point& p) const
    {
        return Point(_x-p._x, _y-p._y);
    }

    Coord xdistance() const { return fabs(_x);}
    Coord ydistance() const { return fabs(_y);}
private:
    Coord _x, _y;
};

#endif
```

Because a rectangle is uniquely defined by any two opposite corners, you can implement the `rectangle_shape` class using two instances of the `Point` class, as follows:

```
//------------------------------------------------------------
//  File:  rect.h
//  C++ header file with definitions of a rectangle shape


#if !defined(__RECT_H)
#define __RECT_H

#include <stdio.h>
#include <math.h>

#include "point.h"  // For definition of the Point class

class shape
```

```
{
public:
    virtual double compute_area(void) const = 0;
    virtual void draw(void) const = 0;
};

// Define the "rectangle" class:

class rectangle_shape: public shape
{
public:
    rectangle_shape(Point& c1, Point& c2) : _c1(c1), _c2(c2){}

    double compute_area(void) const
    {
        Point p = _c1 - _c2;
        return p.xdistance() * p.ydistance();
    }

    void draw(void) const { } // Not defined

private:
    Point _c1, _c2;  // Opposite corners of rectangle
};

#endif  // #if !defined(__RECT_H)
```

Points `_c1` and `_c2` denote two opposite corners of the rectangle. A sample program using the `rectangle_shape` class follows:

```
#include <iostream.h>
#include "rect.h"

int main(void)
{
    Point p1(10,10), p2(30,40);
    rectangle_shape r(p1,p2);

    cout << "Area of rectangle = " << r.compute_area();
    cout << endl;

    return 0;
}
```

When you run the program, it displays the expected output:

```
Area of rectangle = 600
```

This is an example of the `rectangle_shape` class making use of the `Point` class. Member functions of the `rectangle_shape` class access the member functions of the `Point` class through `Point` instances `_c1` and `_c2`.

Pointer to Class Instance as a Member

An alternative to incorporating `Point` instances in the `rectangle_shape` class is to define pointers to the `Point` class as members of `rectangle_shape`. Used carefully, this approach enables you to declare the `rectangle_shape` class without including the definition of the `Point` class. For instance, you can rewrite the declaration of the `rectangle_shape` class as follows:

```
//-------------------------------------------------------------
//  File:  rect_p.h
//  C++ header file with definitions of rectangle_shape class.
//  This version uses pointers to Point class.


#if !defined(__RECT_P_H)
#define __RECT_P_H

#include <stdio.h>
#include <math.h>

class Point;

class shape
{
public:
    virtual double compute_area(void) const = 0;
    virtual void draw(void) const = 0;
};

// Define the "rectangle" class:

class rectangle_shape: public shape
{
public:
    rectangle_shape() : _p1(0), _p2(0) {}
```

```
    rectangle_shape(const Point& p1, const Point& p2);
    rectangle_shape(const rectangle_shape& r);
    ~rectangle_shape();

    void operator=(const rectangle_shape& r);

    double compute_area(void) const;

    void draw(void) const { } // Not defined

private:
    Point *_p1, *_p2;    // Pointers to Points
};

#endif  // #if !defined(__RECT_P_H)
```

Notice that this declaration of the `rectangle_shape` class does not include the complete declaration of the `Point` class. This effectively hides the specification of the `Point` class from the users of the `rectangle_shape` class. The trick is to not invoke any member functions of the `Point` class within the declaration of the `rectangle_shape` class.

You can place the actual definition of the member functions of `rectangle_shape` in another file and include the declaration of the `Point` class there. For example, here's the definition of the member functions of the revised `rectangle_shape` class:

```
#include "rect_p.h"
#include "point.h"

double rectangle_shape::compute_area(void) const
{
    Point p = *_p1 - *_p2;
    return p.xdistance() * p.ydistance();
}

rectangle_shape::rectangle_shape(const Point& p1, const Point& p2)
{
    _p1 = new Point(p1);
    _p2 = new Point(p2);
}

rectangle_shape::rectangle_shape(const rectangle_shape& r)
{
    _p1 = new Point(*r._p1);
```

```
    _p2 = new Point(*r._p2);
}

void rectangle_shape::operator=(const rectangle_shape& r)
{
    if(this != &r)
    {
        if(_p1 != 0) delete _p1;
        if(_p2 != 0) delete _p2;
        _p1 = new Point(*r._p1);
        _p2 = new Point(*r._p2);
    }
}

rectangle_shape::~rectangle_shape()
{
        delete _p1;
        delete _p2;
}
```

Although `rectangle_shape` now is implemented differently, you can use it as you would use the preceding version. For example, to create a rectangle with corners at (30, 20) and (130, 60), you would write:

```
Point p1(30,20), p2(130,60); // Define the corner points
rectangle_shape r1(p1,p2);   // Create a rectangle
```

This version of the `rectangle_shape` class is much more complicated than the previous one, which uses instances of the `Point` class as member variables. The following considerations explain this complexity:

- The C++ compiler automatically creates and destroys class instances that are member variables of another class. The compiler also handles copy and assignment operations for such class-member instances.
- On the other hand, when you use pointers to class instances, you're responsible for creating and destroying these class instances. You also must define the copy constructor and the assignment operator so that these operations work correctly. Therefore, the revised version of the `rectangle_shape` class requires several additional member functions, including a destructor, a copy constructor, and an assignment operator.

As explained in Chapter 12, "Virtual Functions and Polymorphism," despite the additional work involved, managing pointers to class instances is necessary when you want to use polymorphism.

Public Interface to C++ Classes

Public interface to the classes in a library is as important as the relationships among the classes. The term *public interface* refers to the public member functions that enable you to access the capabilities of a class. Just as there is no standard C++ class library, there is no standard interface to C++ classes. If you're designing a class library, however, it's good practice to provide a minimal set of member functions. Some member functions are needed to ensure proper operations, others to provide a standard interface to the library. The following sections briefly describe some of the functions needed in each class's interface.

Default and Copy Constructors

Each class in the library should have a *default constructor*—a constructor that takes no argument. The default constructor should initialize any data members that the class contains. For example, the following is the default constructor for the `rectangle_shape` class:

```
class rectangle_shape : public shape
{
public:
    rectangle_shape() : _p1(0), _p2(0) {}
//...
private:
    Point *_p1, *_p2;
};
```

This constructor sets the data members `_p1` and `_p2` to zero.

The default constructor is important because it's called when arrays of class instances are allocated, or when a class instance is defined without an initial value. For example, the `rectangle_shape::rectangle_shape()` constructor is called to initialize the `rectangle_shape` objects in the following:

```
rectangle_shape rects[16];
rectangle_shape r;
```

Each class also should include a copy constructor of the form `X(const X&)`, in which `X` is the name of the class. The copy constructor is called in the following cases:

- When an object is initialized with another of the same type, such as:

  ```
  rectangle_shape r2 = r;// where r is a rectangle_shape
  ```

- When an object is passed by value to a function
- When an object is returned by value from a function

As explained in Chapter 10, "Defining Operations on Objects," the copy constructor is necessary for classes that contain pointers as members. If you do not define a copy constructor for a class, the C++ compiler defines one that uses memberwise copy. When a class has pointers as members, memberwise copy will cause pointers in two objects to point to identical areas of the free store.

Copying Objects

It's often necessary to make a copy of an object. For instance, Chapter 11 shows how to create a linked list capable of holding `String` objects. A new class, `slink_string`, is created by multiply-deriving from `single_link` and `String` classes. This `slink_string` class has links that enable its instances to reside in a `single_linked_list`. To insert elements into the list, you must be able to create a copy of the object. In the `slink_string` class, this is done by the virtual member function `clone` (see Listings 11.3 and 11.7 in Chapter 11). In the terminology of other C++ libraries, such as the NIH Class Library, the `clone` function is equivalent to what is known as the `deepCopy` function. This is because `clone` makes a complete copy of a `slink_string` object, including a copy of the character string allocated by the `String` class. For a class `X`, you can define the `clone` function as follows:

```
X* X::clone() { return new X(*this); }
```

As long as all classes define appropriate copy constructors, the `clone` function will make a duplicate copy of the object on the free store and return a pointer to the copy. When using functions (such as `clone`) that return a pointer to a dynamically created object, you must destroy the object by using the `delete` operator. This will delete the object, provided appropriate destructors are defined for all classes with member variables that are pointers.

Destructors

Defining a destructor is important for classes that include pointers as member variables. The destructor should reverse the effects of the constructor. If the constructor allocates memory by calling `new`, the destructor should deallocate the memory by using the `delete` operator. As explained in Chapter 12, "Virtual Functions and Polymorphism," if the class contains virtual member functions, you should declare the destructor as virtual.

Assignment Operator

You should define the assignment operator for each class, because derived classes do not inherit the assignment operator from the base class. Also, if you do not define the assignment operator, the C++ compiler provides a default one that simply copies each member of one class instance to the corresponding member of another. If a class has member variables that are pointers to other class instances, such memberwise copying will result in multiple pointers that point to a single area of the free store. When defining the assignment operator:

- Handle the special case in which an object is assigned to itself.
- Return a reference to the target of the assignment so that statements of the type `x=y=z;` work properly.

For an example, see the definition of the `String::operator=` function in Listing 11.2. in Chapter 11.

Input and Output Functions

Each class also should define two functions for I/O:

- An output function that prints a formatted text representation of each member of an object on an output stream.
- An input function that can read from an input stream the output generated by the output function and reconstruct the object.

These functions enable you to define the << and >> operators to accept instances of any class in the library as arguments. For example, you might use the names `print_out` and `read_in`, for the output and input functions. Each of these functions should take a single argument—the reference to the stream on which the I/O operation occurs. Then, for a class `X`, you would define the output `operator<<` as follows:

```
#include <iostream.h>
//...
ostream& operator<<(ostream& os, const X& x)
{
```

```
    x.print_out(os);
    return os;
}
```

Summary

Organizing a C++ class library involves deciding on the *inheritance hierarchy* of the classes, how one class uses the facilities of other classes, and what public-member functions each class supports. There are two trends in picking an inheritance hierarchy for the classes in a library: the *single-tree model*, in which all classes are ultimately derived from a single base class, and the *forest model*, in which there are multiple, disjoint hierarchies of classes. The single-tree model of inheritance hierarchy is patterned after the basic classes of the SmallTalk-80 programming language, which does not support multiple inheritance the way C++ does. With multiple inheritance, you can mix and match classes from one or more class hierarchies and create custom classes.

Inheritance is not the only relationship among classes. A class also may incorporate instances of other classes as member variables. Although inheritance models the *is a* relationship among classes, inclusion of class instances captures the *has a* relationship. The inclusion is in the form of a member variable that is either a class instance or a pointer to a class instance. Defining a class instance as a member variable is simpler than maintaining a pointer to an instance, but the pointer is necessary to exploit polymorphism.

In addition to these relationships among the classes, each class in the library should present a consistent set of member functions so that there is a standard public interface to the library. This makes the library easy to use.

16

Using the Microsoft Foundation Class Library

Developing an application in C++ can be easy—provided you can get most of the functionality of the program from existing C++ classes. Programmers embarking on large-scale C++ programming efforts typically begin by designing and developing a library of classes. Then, they build the final software products using these classes. Clearly, you can reduce the time spent on software development if an off-the-shelf class library meets the needs of a software project and if the programmers working on the project can easily use the library. This is where class libraries can be useful.

To help programmers reap the benefits of a class library, Microsoft Visual C++ comes with Version 2.0 of the Microsoft Foundation Class (MFC) library—a collection of about one hundred classes in three broad categories:

- Classes for building Microsoft Windows applications, including classes that simplify the use of the Graphics Device Interface (GDI) and support Object Linking and Embedding (OLE)

- General-purpose classes such as linked lists, dynamic arrays, files, and strings, including features to support exception handling and archiving objects in files
- Macros and Globals, which consist of a number of general-purpose macros and global objects

This chapter briefly describes the Microsoft Foundation Class library and shows how to use the library with a simple example. In Chapter 17, "Building MS-DOS Applications in C++," you will find a complete MS-DOS application that uses the Microsoft Foundation Classes extensively. Chapter 18, "Using AppWizard to Create C++ Windows Applications," shows the Microsoft Windows version of the same application. Chapter 19, "General-Purpose Microsoft Foundation Classes," and Chapter 20, "Microsoft Foundation Classes for Windows Programming," are designed for programmer's reference to the Microsoft Foundation Class library.

Microsoft Visual C++ includes the full source code for the Microsoft Foundation Classes. If you wish, you can always browse through the source code of the Microsoft Foundation Classes to see exactly how they are defined and implemented.

Microsoft Windows Programming with Microsoft Foundation Classes

Microsoft Foundation Classes primarily provide a complete application framework for building Microsoft Windows applications. When you learn more about the foundation classes, you'll notice that many functions and macros in the MFC library start with one of the following prefixes: `afx`, `Afx`, or `AFX`. Each of these stands for Application Frameworx—derived from a slight mutation of the term Application Frameworks. The collection of classes in MFC is referred to as a framework because it essentially provides all the components for skeletal programs that can easily be fleshed out into complete applications, especially Windows applications.

Model-View Controller (MVC) Architecture

Even though the Microsoft Foundation Class library includes all necessary classes to build the user interface and model various data types, you'll find it easier to build an application if you follow a well-defined architecture (structural model) for the application. The Model-View Controller (MVC) architecture, prevalent in the SmallTalk-80 programming language, is a good candidate architecture for Windows applications. Here is a brief description of the MVC model.

As Figure 16.1 shows, the MVC architecture separates the application into three separate layers:

- *Model* refers to the *application layer*, where all application-dependent objects reside. For example, in a drawing program, this is the layer that maintains the graphics objects.
- *View* refers to the *presentation layer*, which presents the application's data to the user. This layer extracts information from the Model and displays that information in windows. In a drawing program, this layer would obtain the list of graphics objects from the Model and render them in a window. Also, the View provides the windows in the application's graphical user interface (GUI).
- *Controller* refers to the *interaction layer*, which provides the interface between the input devices (such as keyboard and mouse) and the View and Model layers.

The MVC architecture does an excellent job of separating the responsibilities for the objects in the system. It insulates the application-specific details from the user interface. Also, this architecture breaks down the user interface into two parts, with the presentation handled by the View and the interaction by the Controller.

When building Windows applications using the Microsoft Foundation Classes, you don't need to follow the MVC model strictly. For instance, when you use the classes from the Microsoft Foundation Class library, you'll find it difficult to separate the View and Controller layers. As shown in Figure 16.2, your application would comprise a Model and an associated View-Controller pair. Figure 16.2 also shows the usual interactions in SmallTalk-80's MVC architecture. The Controller accepts the user's inputs and invokes the appropriate function from the Model to perform the task requested by the user. When the work is done, the function in the Model sends messages to the View and Controller. The View updates the display in response to this message, accessing the Model for further information, if necessary. Thus, the Model has a View and a Controller, but it never directly accesses either of them. The View and Controller, on the other hand, access the Model's functions and data when necessary.

The easiest way to build Windows applications is to use the AppWizard utility from the Visual Workbench's Project menu. With AppWizard, you can create a fully functional application that can then be finished off with the addition of application-specific code. For more information on AppWizard, see Chapter 18, "Using App Wizard to Create C++ Windows Applications."

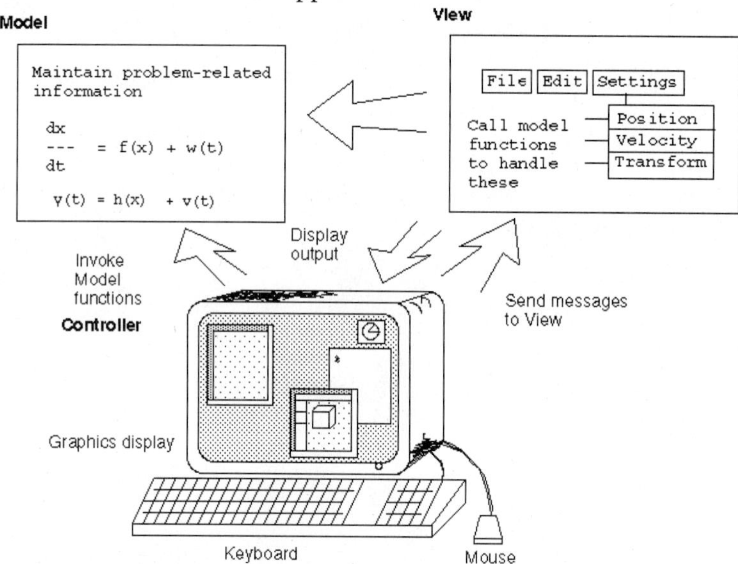

Figure 16.1. MVC architecture of SmallTalk-80.

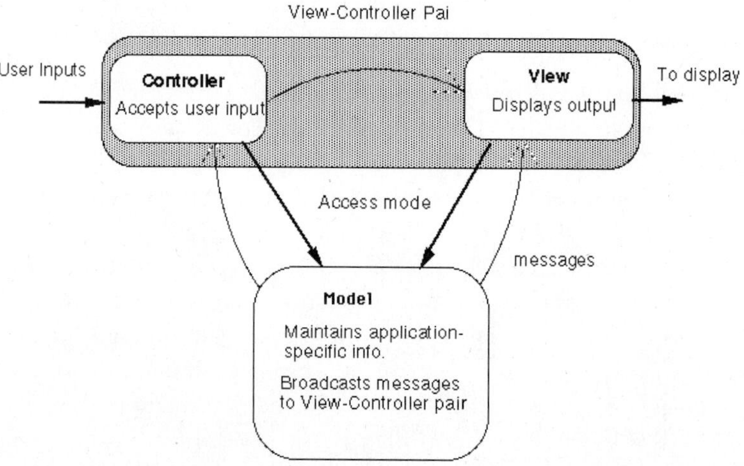

Figure 16.2. Interactions among Model, View, and Controller in the MVC model.

As you'll see in the examples that follow, most of the classes in the Microsoft Foundation Class library contribute to the View and Controller pair. You typically would use your own classes along with general-purpose classes such as strings, lists, and arrays) in the application's Model layer.

A Windows Application Using MFC

A simple example is the best way to understand the basic capabilities of the Microsoft Foundation Class library. Because MFC provides a framework for Windows applications, we'll create an application using MFC that displays `Hello, World!` in a window. Even with the Microsoft Foundation Classes, you must attend to many details when writing a Microsoft Windows application. This discussion will provide the steps.

The *HelloApp* Class

Because of the MFC application framework, all MFC-based Microsoft Windows applications rely on a class derived from the `CWinApp` class, which models the entire application.

Listing 16.1 shows the file HELLO.CPP, which implements the `HelloApp` class that models your sample application. In the `HelloApp` class you define the member function named `InitInstance`, in which all initializations are performed. If you employ the MVC architecture, the basic steps for your application are as follows:

1. Create a Model for the application. For this application, the Model is a class named `HelloModel`, defined in the HELLOMDL.H header file (Listing 16.2).
2. Create a View and store a pointer to the Model in the View. In this case, the `View` class is named `HelloView` and is declared in the HELLOVW.H header file (Listing 16.3). You'll see later that the `HelloView` class is derived from the `CFrameWnd` class of the MFC library.
3. Derive an application class from `CWinApp` and, in the `InitInstance` function of the application class, perform all necessary initializations (including the creation of the Model and the View).
4. Create a global instance of the application class. This step is enough to get the application going. Essentially, the `CWinApp` class provides the functionality of the Controller in the MVC architecture.

As you'll in see Chapter 18, "Using AppWizard to Create C++ Windows Applications," you also can use AppWizard to create your application. Using AppWizard probably is the easiest way to create a C++ Windows application. For now though, we'll continue writing the Hello program.

Listing 16.1. HELLO.CPP. The hello application.

```
//------------------------------------------------------------
//  File:  hello.cpp
//
//  A Windows application that uses the Microsoft Foundation
//  Class library

#include "hellovw.h"
#include "hellomdl.h"

class HelloApp: public CWinApp
{
public:
    BOOL InitInstance();
};

BOOL HelloApp::InitInstance()
{
    HelloModel *m = new HelloModel();
    m_pMainWnd = new HelloView(m);

// Notice that m_pMainWnd is a member variable of the CWinApp
// class (declared in the header file "afxwin.h").

    m_pMainWnd->ShowWindow(m_nCmdShow);
    m_pMainWnd->UpdateWindow();

    return TRUE;
}

// Creating an instance of the application is enough to
// get it going.

HelloApp hello_world;
```

The *Model* Class

An application's Model should store data unique to the application. In this case, the application is simple enough that you could have displayed the `Hello, World!` string directly from the `View` class. We have, however, chosen to create a `Model` class to illustrate how realistic applications are built. This application's Model, the `HelloModel` class (Listing 16.2), contains the string to be displayed in the window. The string is stored in an instance of a `CString` class (from the Microsoft Foundation Class library) created by the constructor of the `HelloModel` class. A member function named `get_string` returns a pointer to this `CString` instance. The `View` class uses this function to access the string.

Listing 16.2. HELLOMDL.H. Definition of the `HelloModel` class.

```
//-------------------------------------------------------------
//  File:  hellomdl.h
//
//  The "model" for the "hello" application. In this case,
//  the model simply stores a string to be displayed in a window.

#if !defined(__HELLOMDL_H)
#define __HELLOMDL_H

#include <afx.h>

class HelloModel
{
public:
    HelloModel() { p_str = new CString("Hello, World!");}

    ~HelloModel() { delete p_str;}

    CString* get_string() { return p_str;}

private:
    CString *p_str;
};

#endif
```

The *View* Class

The `HelloView` class, declared in the HELLOVW.H file (Listing 16.3) and implemented in hellovw.cpp (Listing 16.4), provides the View for this application. The `HelloView` class is responsible for displaying the message (stored in the `HelloModel` class) in a window. `HelloView`, derived from the `CFrameWnd` class, serves as the main window of the application. The `View` class uses the `Model` class through a pointer to the Model that it stores.

The most important function of the `HelloView` class is called `OnPaint`. The Microsoft Foundation Class library automatically calls the `OnPaint` function for a window whenever the window needs repainting. (You will soon see how the painting is done.) Notice how the `OnPaint` function is declared with an `afx_msg` prefix in Listing 16.3. This is one of the steps you need to follow to ensure that messages intended for a window get handled properly. The inclusion of the `DECLARE_MESSAGE_MAP()` macro is another required step.

Listing 16.3. HELLOVW.H. Declaration of the `HelloView` class.

```
//-----------------------------------------------------------------
//  File:  hellovw.h
//
//  The "view" for the "hello" application. In this case,
//  the view is a window where the string from the model
//  is displayed.

#if !defined(__HELLOVW_H)
#define __HELLOVW_H

// Include necessary header files:
#include <afxwin.h>
#include "hellores.h"  // Resource identifiers for application

class HelloModel;

class HelloView : public CFrameWnd
{
public:
    HelloView(HelloModel* a_model);

    void init_view();
```

```
// Declare functions for handling messages from Windows:
    afx_msg void OnPaint();
    afx_msg void OnAbout();
    DECLARE_MESSAGE_MAP()

private:
    HelloModel* model;
};

#endif
```

The `OnAbout` function also is declared as a message-handler (indicated by the `afx_msg` prefix). As you will see in Listing 16.4, this function displays a dialog box with information about the application.

Windows Message-Handling in Microsoft Foundation Classes

Microsoft Windows works by sending messages to the windows that constitute an application's user interface. The Microsoft Foundation Class library provides a unique way to map one or more of these messages to functions that you write. You declare the message-handling functions with an `afx_msg` prefix in your application's main window class—usually, a class derived from the `CFrameWnd` class. Next, you include the `DECLARE_MESSAGE_MAP()` macro in the declaration of the window class. Finally, you associate each message-handling function to a Windows message through a message map enclosed in the `BEGIN_MESSAGE_MAP()` and `END_MESSAGE_MAP()` macros.

Listing 16.4 shows the implementation of the `HelloView` class. In Listing 16.4, you see another required step of Windows programming with the Microsoft Foundation Class library: the definition of a message map—the association of a function with a Windows message so that Windows calls the specified function in response to the associated message. Because `HelloView` has two message-handlers, `OnPaint` and `OnAbout`, the message map is defined as follows:

```
// Define the "message map":
```

```
BEGIN_MESSAGE_MAP(HelloView, CFrameWnd)
    ON_WM_PAINT()
    ON_COMMAND(IDM_ABOUT, OnAbout)
END_MESSAGE_MAP()
```

You start the message map with a `BEGIN_MESSAGE_MAP` macro that takes two arguments, the name of the class for which the message map is being defined and the name of its base class. An `END_MESSAGE_MAP()` macro marks the end of the message map.

Listing 16.4. HELLOVW.CPP. Implementation of the `HelloView` class.

```
//---------------------------------------------------------------
//  File:  hellovw.cpp
//
//  The "view" layer for the "hello" application
//---------------------------------------------------------------
#include "hellovw.h"
#include " hellomdl.h

//---------------------------------------------------------------
// Define the "message map":

    BEGIN_MESSAGE_MAP(HelloView, CFrameWnd)
        ON_WM_PAINT()
        ON_COMMAND(IDM_ABOUT, OnAbout)
    END_MESSAGE_MAP()

//---------------------------------------------------------------
//  i n i t _ v i e w
//  Initialize this view.

void HelloView::init_view()
{
    VERIFY(LoadAccelTable("MainAccelTable"));
    VERIFY(Create(NULL, "Hello", WS_OVERLAPPEDWINDOW,
           rectDefault, NULL, "MainMenu"));
}
//---------------------------------------------------------------
//  H e l l o V i e w
//  Constructor for HelloView class
```

```
HelloView::HelloView(HelloModel* a_model) : model(a_model)
{
    init_view();
}
//----------------------------------------------------------------
//  O n P a i n t
//  Draw contents of window.
}
void HelloView::OnPaint()
{
// Set up the device context (DC) for drawing:
    CPaintDC dc(this);
    dc.SetTextAlign(TA_BASELINE ¦ TA_CENTER);
    dc.SetBkMode(TRANSPARENT);

// Get the message:
    CString* p_string = model->get_string();

// Get the window size:
    CRect r;
    GetClientRect(r);

    int w = r.right - r.left;
    int h = r.bottom - r.top;

// Get the number of characters in string.
    int len = p_string->GetLength();

// Display string roughly at the center of window:
    int xpos = w/2;
if(xpos < 0) xpos = 0;
    dc.TextOut(xpos, h/2, *p_string, len);
}
//----------------------------------------------------------------
//  O n A b o u t
//  Display the "About..." box.

void HelloView:: OnAbout()
{
    CModalDialog about("ABOUTHELLO", this);
    about.DoModal();
}
```

In the message map's body, you list the Windows messages for which this class provides handlers. Each message name is defined by a macro: an ON_ prefix followed by the standard Windows term for that message. Consequently, ON_WM_PAINT() indicates that this class handles WM_PAINT messages, sent by Windows when a window needs repainting. The name of the message-handling function is implicit in this case—it's OnPaint.

The next entry, ON_COMMAND(IDM_ABOUT, OnAbout), ensures that the OnAbout function is called when the menu item identified by the constant IDM_ABOUT is selected. The OnAbout message-handling function must be explicitly associated with a menu item because you, the programmer, may choose to associate any function with a message generated by a menu selection. IDM_ABOUT is a constant, defined in the hellores.h header file shown in Listing 16.7.

Because your application is supposed to display a message in its window, the code for displaying the message is embedded in the OnPaint function (Listing 16.4). In the OnPaint function, you receive the message string from the Model by calling the get_string class of the HelloModel class, as follows:

```
void HelloView::OnPaint()
{

// Get the message:
    CString* p_string = model->get_string();

// Display the message ...
}
```

The actual rendering of the string is performed by calling member functions of the CPaintDC class, which provides a device context (or, in Windows terminology, DC) for drawing in a window. The DC holds information that controls the appearance of drawings created by Windows drawing functions. With Microsoft Foundation Classes, you can obtain the DC by creating an instance of the CPaintDC class. Because a DC is created for a specific window, the constructor for CPaintDC requires the pointer to the window with which the DC is associated. In OnPaint, the DC for the window associated with the HelloView class is created and used as follows:

```
// Set up device context (DC) for drawing:
    CPaintDC dc(this);
    dc.SetTextAlign(TA_BASELINE ¦ TA_CENTER);
    dc.SetBkMode(TRANSPARENT);
//...
```

```
// Draw the string:
    dc.TextOut(xpos, h/2, *p_string, len);
```

Member functions of the `CPaintDC` object set Graphics attributes such as alignment of text and the background mode. The text string is displayed by calling the `TextOut` function. In that call to `TextOut`, `xpos` denotes the x coordinate of the location in the window where the text output originates, `h` denotes the height of the window, and `len` is the number of characters in the text string being displayed. You can obtain the size (width and height) of the window and the length of a `CString` object as follows:

```
// Get the window size:
    CRect r;
    GetClientRect(r);

    int w = r.right - r.left;
    int h = r.bottom - r.top;

// Get the number of characters in string:
    int len = p_string->GetLength();
```

If you want to draw other graphics in the window, you can call other member functions of the `CPaintDC` class. Because the `CPaintDC` class is derived from the `CDC` class (the generic `DC` class), the documentation of the `CDC` class includes information on these graphics output functions.

Building the Application

Once you ready the header files and source files, compile and link them to create a Microsoft Windows application. You can use the Visual Workbench's New Project to create the project files. The project file is a .MAK file (which is similar to the files that NMAKE uses; however, these files are not directly usable with NMAKE). For the `hello` application, the project file (named hello.mak) is shown in Listing 16.5. Given the Project in Listing 16.5, you can build the hello.exe file by selecting the Rebuild All button in the Visual Workbench's toolbar.

Notice the first line in the Visual Workbench's project file. It's always best if you don't try to directly modify the project file. Though I have modified some project files, I've found that the process can be frought with difficulties—and can lead to serious problems later when the Visual Workbench needs to modify the project itself.

Listing 16.5. Project file for creating HELLO.EXE using the Visual Workbench.

```
# Microsoft Visual C++ generated build script: Do not modify.

PROJ = HELLO
DEBUG = 1
PROGTYPE = 0
CALLER =
ARGS =
DLLS =
D_RCDEFINES = -d_DEBUG
R_RCDEFINES = -dNDEBUG
ORIGIN = MSVC
ORIGIN_VER = 1.00
PROJPATH = C:\MSVCDG\CH16\
USEMFC = 1
CC = cl
CPP = cl
CXX = cl
CCREATEPCHFLAG =
CPPCREATEPCHFLAG =
CUSEPCHFLAG =
CPPUSEPCHFLAG =
FIRSTC =
FIRSTCPP = HELLO.CPP
RC = rc
CFLAGS_D_WEXE = /nologo /G3 /FPi87 /Zp1 /W3 /Zi /AM /Od /D "_DEBUG" /FR /GA
CFLAGS_R_WEXE = /nologo /W3 /AM /O1 /D "NDEBUG" /FR /GA
LFLAGS_D_WEXE = /NOLOGO /NOD /PACKC:61440 /STACK:10240 /ALIGN:16 /
ONERROR:NOEXE /CO
LFLAGS_R_WEXE = /NOLOGO /NOD /PACKC:61440 /STACK:10240 /ALIGN:16 /
ONERROR:NOEXE
LIBS_D_WEXE = mafxcwd oldnames libw mlibcew commdlg.lib olecli.lib
olesvr.lib shell.lib
LIBS_R_WEXE = mafxcw oldnames libw mlibcew commdlg.lib olecli.lib
olesvr.lib shell.lib
RCFLAGS = /nologo
RESFLAGS = /nologo
RUNFLAGS =
DEFFILE = HELLO.DEF
OBJS_EXT =
```

```
LIBS_EXT =
!if "$(DEBUG)" == "1"
CFLAGS = $(CFLAGS_D_WEXE)
LFLAGS = $(LFLAGS_D_WEXE)
LIBS = $(LIBS_D_WEXE)
MAPFILE = nul
RCDEFINES = $(D_RCDEFINES)
!else
CFLAGS = $(CFLAGS_R_WEXE)
LFLAGS = $(LFLAGS_R_WEXE)
LIBS = $(LIBS_R_WEXE)
MAPFILE = nul
RCDEFINES = $(R_RCDEFINES)
!endif
!if [if exist MSVC.BND del MSVC.BND]
!endif
SBRS = HELLO.SBR \
          HELLOVW.SBR


HELLO_DEP = c:\msvcdg\ch16\hellovw.h \
     c:\msvcdg\ch16\hellores.h \
     c:\msvcdg\ch16\hellomdl.h


HELLOVW_DEP = c:\msvcdg\ch16\hellovw.h \
     c:\msvcdg\ch16\hellores.h \
     c:\msvcdg\ch16\hellomdl.h


HELLO_RCDEP = c:\msvcdg\ch16\hellores.h \
     c:\msvcdg\ch16\hello.ico \
     c:\msvcdg\ch16\hello.dlg


all: $(PROJ).EXE $(PROJ).BSC

HELLO.OBJ:      HELLO.CPP $(HELLO_DEP)
     $(CPP) $(CFLAGS) $(CPPCREATEPCHFLAG) /c HELLO.CPP

HELLOVW.OBJ:    HELLOVW.CPP $(HELLOVW_DEP)
     $(CPP) $(CFLAGS) $(CPPUSEPCHFLAG) /c HELLOVW.CPP
```

continues

Listing 16.5. continued

```
HELLO.RES:      HELLO.RC $(HELLO_RCDEP)
     $(RC) $(RCFLAGS) $(RCDEFINES) -r HELLO.RC


$(PROJ).EXE::  HELLO.RES

$(PROJ).EXE::  HELLO.OBJ HELLOVW.OBJ $(OBJS_EXT) $(DEFFILE)
     echo >NUL @<<$(PROJ).CRF
HELLO.OBJ +
HELLOVW.OBJ +
$(OBJS_EXT)
$(PROJ).EXE
$(MAPFILE)
c:\msvc\lib\+
c:\msvc\mfc\lib\+
$(LIBS)
$(DEFFILE);
<<
     link $(LFLAGS) @$(PROJ).CRF
     $(RC) $(RESFLAGS) HELLO.RES $@
     @copy $(PROJ).CRF MSVC.BND

$(PROJ).EXE::  HELLO.RES
     if not exist MSVC.BND    $(RC) $(RESFLAGS) HELLO.RES $@

run: $(PROJ).EXE
     $(PROJ) $(RUNFLAGS)


$(PROJ).BSC: $(SBRS)
     bscmake @<<
/o$@ $(SBRS)
<<
```

You need five more files to complete the process specified in the makefile.

1. The HELLO.DEF file (Listing 16.6) is known as the *module definition* file and is needed to build Microsoft Windows applications.
2. The HELLORES.H file (Listing 16.7) defines constants that identify resources such as menu item numbers.

3. The HELLO.RC file (Listing 16.8) is known as the resource file and is a text file that specifies the layouts and contents of menus and dialog boxes. The Microsoft resource compiler (invoked automatically by Visual Workbench when a project is built) compiles this file into binary form and appends it to the executable file.
4. The HELLO.DLG file (Listing 16.9) contains the actual layout of the "About Hello..." dialog box displayed by the HELLO application. The HELLO.RC resource file incorporates the contents of HELLO.DLG into its own list using the `RCINCLUDE` directive of the resource compiler. The dialog box is created using AppStudio, which is used to create all resources for a Windows application.
5. The HELLO.ICO file contains a small image (32 pixels by 32 pixels) that you should prepare using the AppStudio application, included with the Microsoft Visual C++ compiler. The HELLO.ICO icon file is referenced in the HELLO.RC resource file. You will find the file on the companion disk.

Listing 16.6. HELLO.DEF. Module definition file for HELLO.EXE.

```
NAME          Hello
DESCRIPTION   'Hello from Microsoft Foundation Classes'
EXETYPE       WINDOWS
STUB          'winstub.exe'

CODE          PRELOAD MOVEABLE DISCARDABLE
DATA          PRELOAD MOVEABLE MULTIPLE

HEAPSIZE      8192
```

Listing 16.7. HELLORES.H. Resource identifiers for HELLO.EXE.

```
//-------------------------------------------------------------
//  File: hellores.h
//
//  Declare the resource IDs for the Hello application.
//  In this case, we have only one.

#define IDM_ABOUT 100
```

Listing 16.8. HELLO.RC. Resource file for HELLO.EXE.

```
//--------------------------------------------------------------
//  File: hello.rc
//
//  Declare the resources for the Hello application.

#include <windows.h>
#include <afxres.h>
#include "hellores.h"

MainMenu MENU
{
    POPUP "&Help"
    {
        MENUITEM "&About Hello...\tF1", IDM_ABOUT
    }
}

MainAccelTable ACCELERATORS
{
    VK_F1,  IDM_ABOUT,  VIRTKEY
}

AFX_IDI_STD_FRAME ICON hello.ico

rcinclude hello.dlg
```

Listing 16.9. HELLO.DLG. Definition of the dialog boxes used in HELLO.EXE.

```
//--------------------------------------------------------------
//  File: hello.dlg
//
//  Define the dialog boxes used in the Hello application.
//  In this case, you have only the "About Hello..." dialog box.

ABOUTHELLO DIALOG 22, 17, 144, 75
STYLE DS_MODALFRAME | WS_CAPTION | WS_SYSMENU
CAPTION "About Hello"
BEGIN
    CTEXT "Hello, World! from", -1, 0, 2, 144, 8
```

```
    CTEXT "Microsoft Foundation Classes", -1, 0, 12, 144, 8
    CTEXT "Version 1.0", -1, 0, 22, 144, 8
    DEFPUSHBUTTON   "OK", IDOK, 56, 56, 32, 14, WS_GROUP
END
```

Testing HELLO.EXE

Once you successfully build HELLO.EXE, you can run it under the Visual Workbench either by selecting the run button or pressing F5. Additionally, outside of the Visual Workbench, you can run hello.exe from the `Run` option in the `File` menu of the Program Manager, or by creating a program icon for hello.

Figure 16.3 shows the program's output. If you resize the window, `Hello, World!` should appear centered in the window.

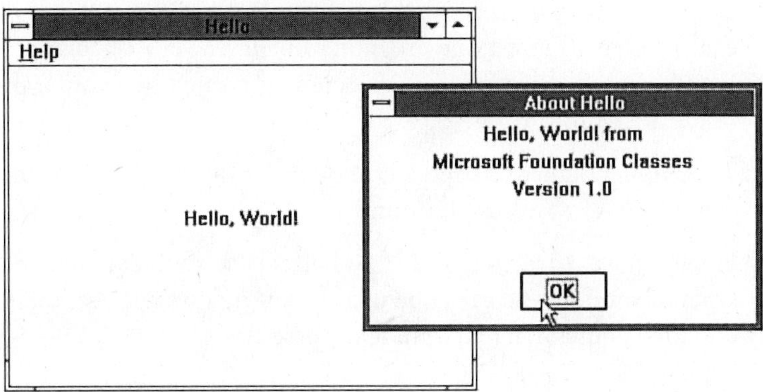

Figure 16.3. `Hello, World!` from Microsoft Foundation Class-based HELLO.EXE.

Microsoft Foundation Class Hierarchy

Now that you've seen an example of a Microsoft Windows application built using the framework provided by the Microsoft Foundation Class library, here is an overview of the entire class hierarchy. Because diagrams showing the class hierarchy can be quite helpful in forming a mental picture of how the classes fit together, Figures 16.4 and 16.5 show just that. The following discussions briefly describe the hierarchies.

Breakdown of the Classes

If you count the classes declared in the header files of the Microsoft Foundation Class library, you should find 101 classes (including three structures). Of these classes, 15 are stand-alone and 86 appear in a hierarchy derived from the `CObject` class. Here is a breakdown of the classes:

- The set of 65 classes (excluding `CObject`, but including `CException`), shown in Figure 16.4, provide support for Microsoft Windows programming.

  The `CPoint`, `CRect`, `CSize`, `CCreateContext`, `CPrintInfo`, `CMemoryState`, `CDataExchange`, and `CCmdUI` stand-alone classes are useful for representing data related to Windows.

  The other 58 classes are in seven hierarchies derived from `CObject`. Of these, `CMenu` is a single-member hierarchy representing a menu. Other hierarchies (`COleDocument`, `CDocItem`, and `COleServer`) provide support for *Object Linking and Embedding (OLE)*—a feature of Microsoft Windows that enables users to insert one program's document (a table or a chart, for instance) from directly inside a document created by another program (such as a word processor).

  The subhierarchies `CDC` and `CGdiObject` are for graphics drawing in a Microsoft Windows application.

  Finally, the `CCmdTarget`, and it's subclass `CWnd` subhierarchy embodies all types of windows that may be used in a Windows application. Chapter 20 provides a quick reference guide to these classes.

- The remaining 35 classes (Figure 16.5)—counting `CObject`, but not `CException`—are general-purpose C++ classes useful in any application, either DOS or Windows based.

  The `CString`, `CTime`, and `CTimeSpan` stand-alone classes represent dynamically allocated strings, time, and time-difference, respectively.

  Of the classes derived from `CObject`, `CFile` is for file I/O (both disk-based and in-memory files) and `CException` provides a subhierarchy of classes intended for handling exceptions.

  Sixteen other classes, derived from `CObject`, provide the facilities necessary to manage collections of objects in three different ways: indexed arrays, linked lists, or keyed maps (associative arrays or dictionaries).

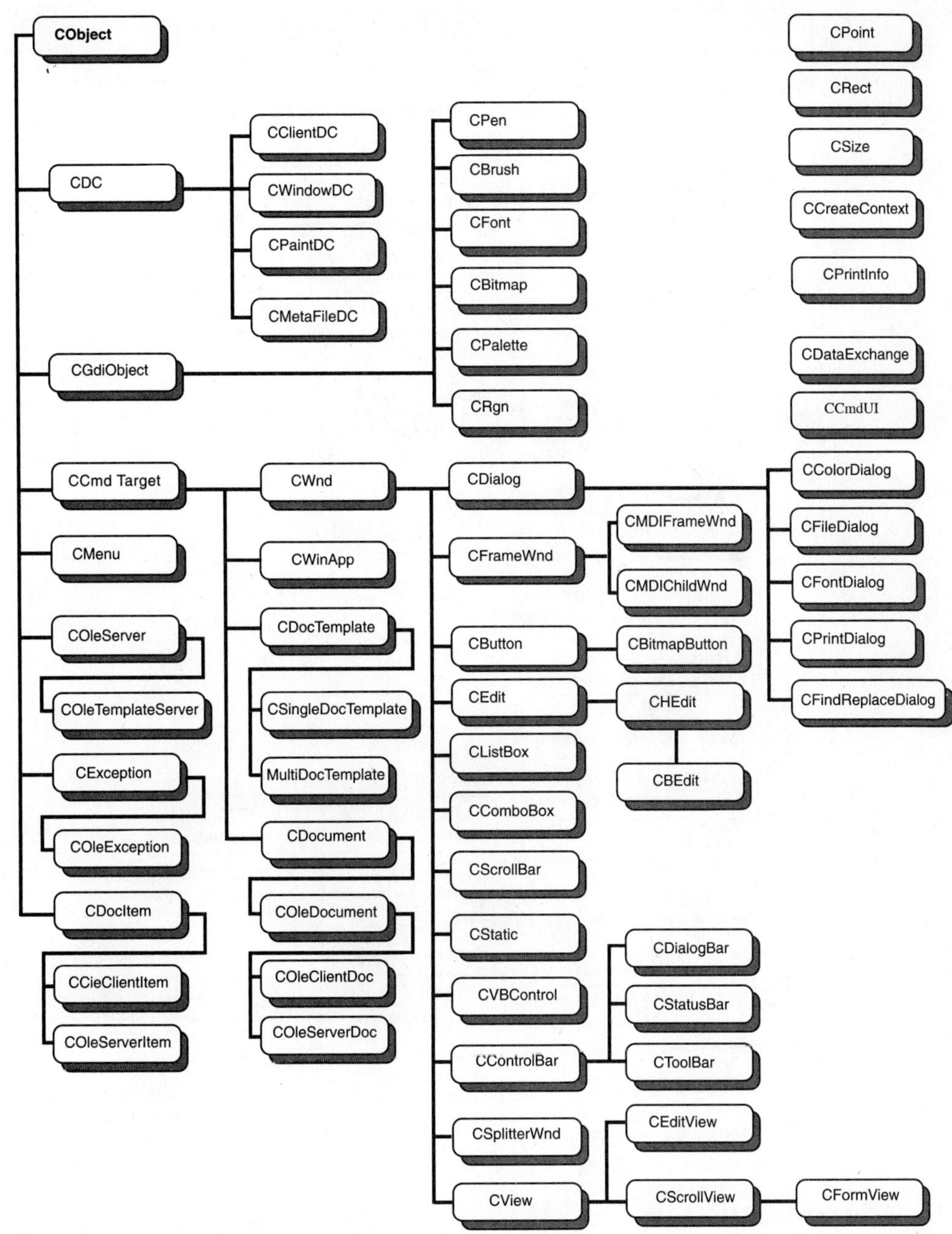

Figure 16.4. Classes for Windows programming in the Microsoft Foundation Class library.

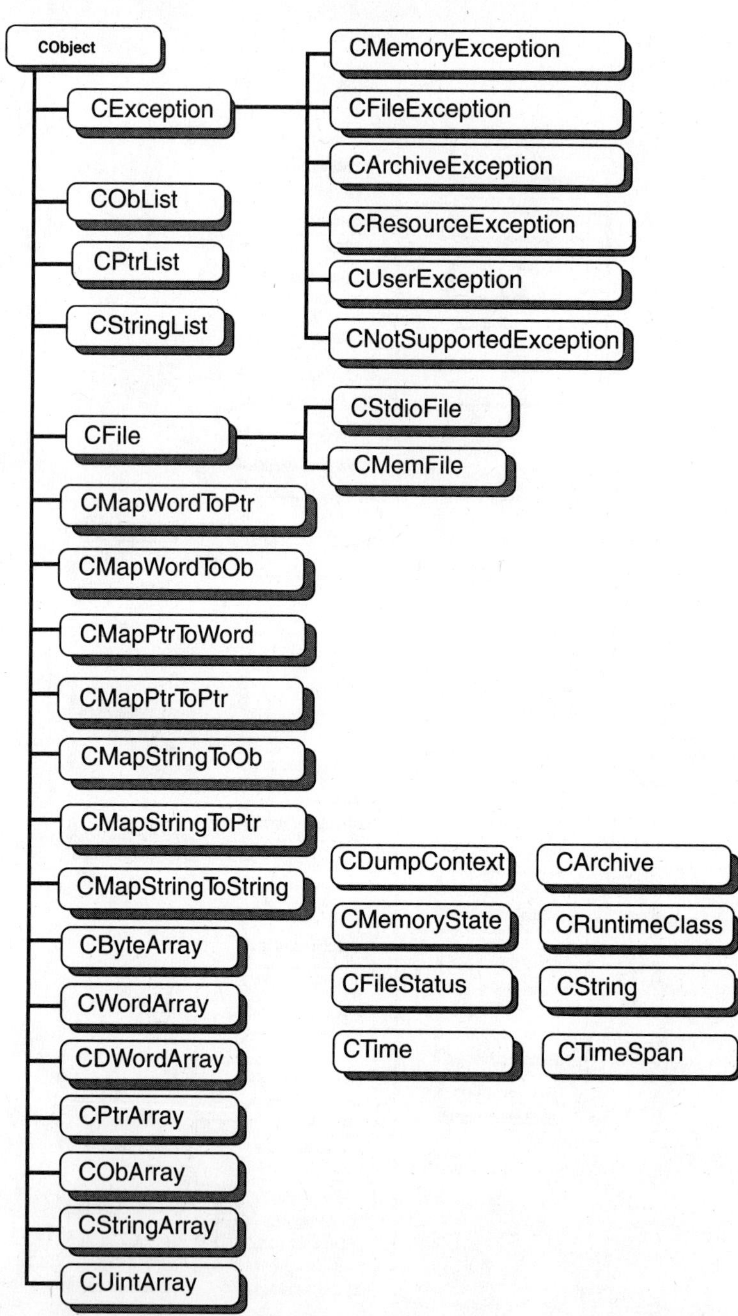

Figure 16.5. General-purpose classes in the Microsoft Foundation Class library.

Chapter 19 further describes the general-purpose classes in the Microsoft Foundation Class library and provides a quick reference guide to each class. Chapter 20 includes similar detailed information on the Microsoft Foundation Classes that support Windows programming.

Archiving and Exception-Handling in the Microsoft Foundation Class Library

The Microsoft Foundation Class library also includes support for two important features:

- The ability to archive objects in a file and retrieve them later.
- The ability to handle exceptions—error conditions—in a standard manner.

Serialization

Microsoft uses the term *serialization* to describe the property of archiving and later retrieving an object in a file. Any class derived from `CObject` can be archived or, in Microsoft's terminology, serialized. To ready a class for serialization, include the `DECLARE_SERIAL` macro in the class declaration and the `IMPLEMENT_SERIAL` macro in the file where the member functions of that class are implemented. For example, consider a class named `shape`, which you plan to serialize. You must declare the `shape` class as follows:

```
#include <afx.h>

class shape : public CObject
{
    DECLARE_SERIAL(shape)
public:
// Member functions...

// Declare the Serialize function:
    void Serialize(CArchive& archive);

private:
    CString name;   // a sample member
// Other members...
};
```

In the class body, you would include the DECLARE_SERIAL macro as shown and specify a member function named Serialize. In the file implementing the shape class, include an IMPLEMENT_SERIAL macro and define the Serialize function as shown:

```
IMPLEMENT_SERIAL(shape, CObject, 100)
void shape::Serialize(CArchive& archive)
{
// First call the "Serialize" function of the base class:
    CObject::Serialize(archive);

// Now store this object in archive (one data member
// at a time). Here you show only one member being archived.
    if(archive.IsStoring())
        archive << name;
    else
        archive >> name;
}
```

As you can see, the first two arguments to the IMPLEMENT_SERIAL macro are the names of the class being serialized and its base class. The third argument is a called a *schema number*—this serves as a version number for the object. When loading an object from an archive, the Microsoft Foundation Class library's serialization code checks this schema number against the schema number of the object in the file and throws an exception if the numbers do not match.

The actual archiving or restoration of an object requires a CArchive object. You first create a CFile object by opening a file and associating a CArchive with that CFile. For example, you would serialize a shape object as follows:

```
    shape s1;

// Archive an object. First, open a file and associate
// an archive with the file:
    cout << "Archiving..." << endl;
    CFile file("shapes.sav", CFile::modeWrite |
                             CFile::modeCreate);
    CArchive archive(&file, CArchive::store);

    archive << &s1;
    archive.Close();
```

To reload the shape from the file to an object, use the following code:

```
// Now restore a shape:
    cout << "Restoring..." << endl;
```

```
    CFile f2("shapes.sav", CFile::modeRead);
    CArchive ar(&f2, CArchive::load);

    shape *p_s = new shape;
    ar >> p_s;
```

The form fill-in software shown in Chapter 17 uses the serialization feature to archive forms in files for later retrieval. Additionally, Chapter 19 further describes the serialization feature and classes such as `CFile` and `CArchive`.

Exception Handling

As mentioned in Chapter 13, "Advanced Topics in C++," the ANSI C++ Technical Committee (X3J16) plans to include an exception-handling scheme that uses the reserved keywords `throw`, `catch`, and `try`. The Microsoft Foundation Class library uses an exception-handling scheme very similar to the one being considered by the ANSI C++ Technical Committee. The following code fragment shows an example of Microsoft Foundation Class library's exception-handling scheme based on the `TRY`, `CATCH`, `AND_CATCH`, and `END_CATCH` macros:

```
#include <iostream.h>
#include <afx.h>

//...

    TRY
    {
// In this block, place code that might cause an
// exception.

// For instance, try "archiving" an object to a file.

    }
    CATCH(CFileException, e)
    {
        cerr << "Error opening file!" << endl;
        exit(1);
    }
    AND_CATCH(CArchiveException, e)
    {
        cerr << "Error archiving!" << endl;
        exit(2);
    }
    END_CATCH
```

In this example, the operation performed in the `TRY` block is expected to cause two types of exceptions, `CFileException` and `CArchiveException`—classes derived from the `CException` base class (see Figure 16.5). If an exception occurs, the program jumps to the block that handles the appropriate exception. Each `CATCH` block should include code to handle that specific exception. The programs shown in Chapters 17 and 18 include other examples of exception handling with this scheme. Also, Chapter 19 further covers this topic.

Summary

You can reduce the time needed to develop C++ programs by using C++ class libraries if the following statements are true:

- The library includes the classes that match your needs.
- The public interface to the classes is well documented.

Microsoft Visual C++ includes the Microsoft Foundation Class library—a collection of over 100 classes that provide a framework for building Microsoft Windows applications. This chapter includes a simple example program to illustrate how you use the class library to create Windows programs.

Roughly 60 percent of the classes in the Microsoft Foundation Class library are geared toward making Windows programming easier. The remaining classes are for modeling data (such as strings and time), for organizing objects in collections, and for supporting file I/O. The library includes support for handling exceptions, and for archiving objects in files and restoring them later.

The Microsoft Foundation Class library is used extensively in the sample applications shown in Chapters 17 and 18. Also, the class library is further summarized in Chapters 19 and 20.

17

Building MS-DOS Applications in C++

The preceding chapter provided a brief overview of the Microsoft Foundation Classes that are part of Microsoft Visual C++. This chapter and the following one explain how to build complete applications in C++ using the Microsoft Foundation Class Library. To be able to successfully build DOS applications that use the Microsoft Foundation Class library, you must ensure that the necessary libraries have been built. The default installation of Visual C++ doesn't build the DOS (real-mode) MFC Libraries. Chapter 1, "The Microsoft Visual C++ Programming Environment," contains instructions on building the real-mode MFC libraries, in the subsection "Building DOS MFC Libraries."

The sample program presented in this chapter is realistic enough to show the essential features of most full-fledged applications: a user-interface and some computational modules that accomplish the tasks the application is designed to perform. This chapter presents an application for the MS-DOS environment. Chapter 18, "Using AppWizard to Create C++ Windows Applications," shows the Microsoft Windows version of a similar application.

A Forms Package

To illustrate the use of C++ and the Microsoft Foundation Class library in a realistic DOS application, consider the task of writing a Forms package with which users can create and fill in forms, save the completed forms in a file, and then retrieve them. If you keep the screen display simple for the DOS version, you can focus on creating the C++ classes necessary for representing a form in memory and devising a scheme for storing forms in a file.

Figure 17.1 shows a partially completed form as it appears to the user of the Forms software. This particular form is an invoice, but the software enables you to create and display any form. As you can see, the form shows several fields. The user fills in the form by moving the cursor to a field and typing the information for that field. Before designing the Forms software, you need a description of what you want it to do. You can start with the following requirements:

- The Forms software should enable the user to open a form, complete it, and save the form in a disk file.
- The software should support the notions of a blank form and a filled-in form. It should provide a way to store blank and completed forms in files.
- The storage scheme should be reasonably efficient. In particular, the software should maintain only one blank form but have the capacity for many instances of the filled-in data for a form.

These requirements, admittedly, are rather broad, but are sufficient as a starting point. You can start the design from this and, as you refine the design, your requirements for the software will become more clear. The following sections address the development and implementation of the C++ classes that form the basis of the Forms package.

Storage and Retrieval of Forms

Because storage and retrieval of forms is a major requirement of the software, you should start building the Forms package by considering a solution to the problem of storing a form in a file and retrieving it later. For efficient storage, you can save the blank form in one file and the filled-in data in separate files, so that a single copy of the blank form is available but multiple sets of data that fill in the form exist. These two files are called:

- The *definitions file,* which stores the definitions of a blank form
- The *data file,* which contains the filled-in data for a specific form

Figure 17.2 shows the layout of these files.

From: INVOICE No: 22750-37
Date:07/15/92

LNB Software, Inc. _
7 Welland Ct.
North Potomac, MD 20878

To:

F.O.B.	Terms	Date Shipped	Shipped Via

Ordered	Shipped	Description	Price	Per	Amount
1	1	Source code disk	29.95	ea	29.95

Figure 17.1. A sample form.

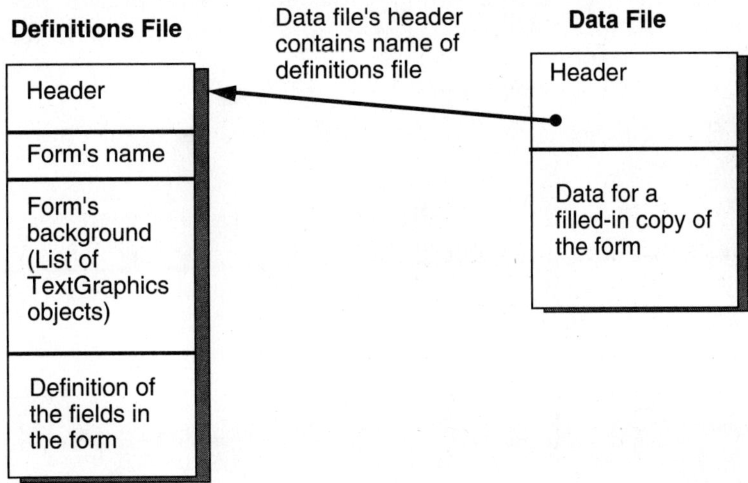

Figure 17.2. File formats for the Forms package.

Both files have a similar layout for the header—this simplifies the code that reads and interprets the header. Each file starts with a header, followed by the "data" for a form. In the definitions file, the "data" describes the layout of the form, while the entries in the data file represent the data entered by the user.

As you'll see in the following sections, you can store and retrieve a form and its data using the Microsoft Foundation Class library's built-in support for archiving objects.

The File Header

You can encapsulate the reading and writing of headers in a C++ class. The File Header class, declared in the FILEHDR.H header file (Listing 17.1), shows one possible implementation of the class. The data members of the class represent the following essential information in the header:

- A signature string (`_signature`) and a version number (`_version`). These help identify the form created by the Forms software.
- A `_filetype` string, which can take two values, interpreted as follows:

  If the filetype is `FDEF`, the file contains definitions of a form (definitions file).

  If the filetype is `FDAT`, the file is a data file with filled-in data for a form.
- A `_filename` string. For a definitions file, this is simply the name of the file itself. For a data file, this is interpreted as the name of the file containing the definitions of the form, with the filled-in data that resides in this data file. This mechanism enables you to access a form's definition given its filled-in data.
- A time stamp. This indicates when the file was last modified.
- Two static strings, `form_definition` and `form_data`. These are used to test the `_filetype` field.

Notice that the classes in this and the subsequent chapter make extensive use of classes that are part of the Microsoft Foundation Class library, such as `CString` and `CTime`. This is a good example of packaging a class once and using it everywhere, as you would a built-in C++ data type.

Leading Underscores in Names of Member Variables

You don't need the leading underscores in names of private member variables of a class; however, I have a reason for using names with leading underscores. Most private member variables require a corresponding public member function so that other classes can access the private variable. If you name the private member variable with a leading underscore, you can use the same name without the underscore for the access function. For instance, notice the private member variable named `_filetype` and the member function named `filetype` in the `FileHeader` class. By choosing the variable's name with a leading underscore (`_filetype`), you can provide an access function with a more logical name (`filetype`).

Listing 17.1. FILEHDR.H. The declaration of the `FileHeader` class, which models the file's header.

```
//------------------------------------------------------------------
//  File:  filehdr.h
//
//  Declares the FileHeader class

#if !defined(_ _FILEHDR_H)
#define _ _FILEHDR_H

#include <afx.h>

class FileHeader: public CObject
{
    DECLARE_SERIAL(FileHeader)

public:
    FileHeader() : _signature("LNBFORM"), _version(100) {}

// Override the Serialize function:
    virtual void Serialize(CArchive& archive);

    unsigned short version() { return _version;}
    void version(unsigned short vnum) {_version = vnum;}

    CString signature() { return _signature;}
    void signature(const char* sig) { _signature = sig;}
```

continues

Listing 17.1. continued

```
    CString filename() { return _filename;}
    void filename(const char* fname) { _filename = fname;}

    CString filetype() { return _filetype;}
    void filetype(const char* ftype) { _filetype = ftype;}

    CTime mod_time() { return _modtime;}
    void mod_time(CTime mt) {_modtime = mt; }

    FileHeader& operator=(const FileHeader& hdr);

    static CString  _form_definition;
    static CString  _form_data;

private:
    CString         _signature;
    unsigned short  _version;
    CString         _filetype;
    CString         _filename;
    CTime           _modtime; // Time of modification
};

#endif
```

The FILEHDR.H header file defines several inline member functions; the rest appear in the FILEHDR.CPP file, shown in Listing 17.2. This file initializes the static `CString` `form_definition` to `FDEF` and `form_data` to `FDAT`. These strings are used when testing the `_filetype` field in the header to determine whether a file has a form's definition or its data.

The `FileHeader` class is derived from the `CObject` class, the base class of most classes in the Microsoft Foundation Class library. Because it inherits from `CObject`, you can use the Microsoft Foundation Class library's built-in support for *serialization*—a term that Microsoft uses to refer to the storage and later retrieval of objects in files. As explained in Chapter 16, "Using the Microsoft Foundation Class Library," you must include the `DECLARE_SERIAL` macro in FILEHDR.H and the `IMPLEMENT_SERIAL` macro in FILEHDR.CPP to ensure that you can archive `FileHeader` objects in files. You also need to override the `Serialize` function. As shown in Listing 17.2, the `Serialize` function first calls the `Serialize` function of its base class, `CObject`, and then archives the member variables of the `FileHeader` class.

Listing 17.2. FILEHDR.CPP. The implementation of the FileHeader class.

```
//------------------------------------------------------------------
//  File:  filehdr.cpp
//  Implements the FileHeader class, which reads and interprets
//  the header block of a file

#include "filehdr.h"

CString FileHeader::_form_definition = "FDEF";
CString FileHeader::_form_data = "FDAT";

// The following is required if you want to archive objects of
// this class:

IMPLEMENT_SERIAL(FileHeader, CObject, 100)

//------------------------------------------------------------------
//  S e r i a l i z e
//  Archives and restores a file header

void FileHeader::Serialize(CArchive& archive)
{
// First, call the Serialize function of the base class:
    CObject::Serialize(archive);

// Now read/write member variables of this class:
    if (archive.IsStoring() )
    {
        archive << _signature << _version << _filetype;
        archive  << _filename << _modtime;
    }
    else
    {
        archive >> _signature;
        archive >> _version >> _filetype;
        archive >> _filename >> _modtime;
    }
}
//------------------------------------------------------------------
```

continues

Listing 17.2. continued

```
//  o p e r a t o r =
//  Assigns one FileHeader to another

FileHeader& FileHeader::operator=(const FileHeader& hdr)
{
    if(this != &hdr)
    {
        _signature = hdr._signature;
        _version = hdr._version;
        _filetype = hdr._filetype;
        _filename = hdr._filename;
        _modtime = hdr._modtime;
    }
    return *this;
}
```

Components of a Form

You can think of a form as having two major components:

- The *background*, which includes everything you see on a blank form: the lines and grid, the graphics, and the text printed on the form
- The *fields*, where you enter information when filling in a form

When you store a form in a file, both the background information and the fields information are stored in the definitions file, but the actual data for the fields resides in the data file. The following discussions describe the way you can represent the background and the fields of a form. Consult Figure 17.3 as you read the descriptions.

The *FormBackground* Class

The background of a form consists of graphics elements: lines, boxes, and text. Assuming a class named `TextGraphics` is present to provide such elements, you can create a `FormBackground` class to store such graphics objects in a double-linked list. To make `FormBackground` a double-linked list, you need only derive the `FormBackground` class from the `CObList` class in the Microsoft Foundation Class library. Because the `CObList` class is declared in the AFXCOLL.H header file, you must include this header file in FORMBG.H (see Listing 17.3).

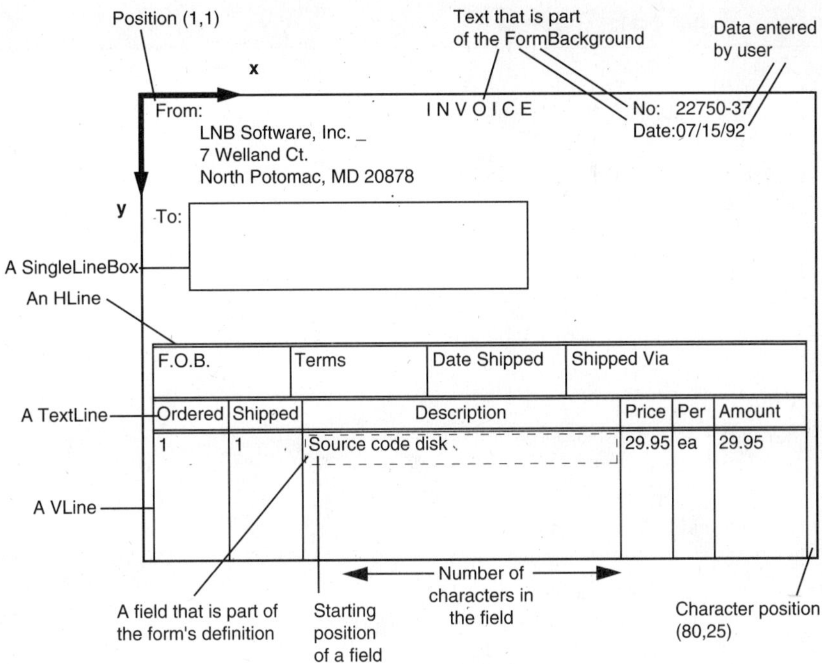

Figure 17.3. Parts of a form.

Listings 17.3 and 17.4 show the FORMBH.H and FORMBG.CPP files, which define the `FormBackground` class. `FormBackground` provides the member functions—such as `first`, `last`, `next`, and `previous`—necessary to access the `TextGraphics` objects maintained in the list. These member functions are defined in terms of member functions of the `CObList` class, from which `FormBackground` is derived.

The lone member variable in `FormBackground`, `pos`, is used to save the location of the current item in the list of `TextGraphics` objects. The variable `pos` is of the `POSITION` type—a type defined in the AFX.H header file, which is included in AFXCOLL.H.

Listing 17.3. FORMBG.H. The header file of the `FormBackground` class.

```
//--------------------------------------------------------------
//  File: formbg.h
//  Background of a form. The background is a collection of
//  graphics objects.
```

continues

Listing 17.3. continued

```
#if !defined(_ _FORMBG_H)
#define _ _FORMBG_H

#include <afxcoll.h>
#include "txtgraph.h"

class FormBackground : public CObList
{
    DECLARE_SERIAL(FormBackground)

public:
    FormBackground() {}
    ~FormBackground() { delete_all();}

    TextGraphics* first()
    {
        pos = GetHeadPosition();
        return (TextGraphics*) GetNext(pos);
    }

    TextGraphics* last()
    {
        pos = GetTailPosition();
        return (TextGraphics*) GetPrev(pos);
    }

    TextGraphics* next()
    {
        if(pos == NULL)
            return NULL;
        else
            return (TextGraphics*)GetNext(pos);
     }

    TextGraphics* previous()
    {
        if(pos == NULL)
            return NULL;
        else
            return (TextGraphics*)GetPrev(pos);
     }
```

```
    TextGraphics* current()
    {
        if(pos == NULL)
            return NULL;
        else
            return (TextGraphics*)GetAt(pos);
    }

    unsigned short count() { return GetCount();}

    void add(TextGraphics& tgr)
    {
      AddTail(tgr.clone());
    }

    void delete_all();

private:
    POSITION  pos;
};

#endif
```

Like the FileHeader class, the FormBackground class relies on the serialization capabilities of the Microsoft Foundation Class library to archive a form's background in a file and retrieve it when needed. The FormBackground class need not define the Serialize function; however, as you'll see later, each TextGraphics object must have a Serialize function to ensure that the form's background is properly archived.

Listing 17.4. FORMBG.CPP. The member functions of the FormBackground class.

```
//------------------------------------------------------------
//  File:  formbg.cpp
//  Implements the FormBackground class, which maintains the
//  background of the form

#include "formbg.h"
#include "txtgraph.h"
```

continues

Listing 17.4. continued

```
IMPLEMENT_SERIAL(FormBackground, CObList, 100);
//-----------------------------------------------------------
// d e l e t e _ a l l
// Deletes all entries in FormBackground

void FormBackground::delete_all()
{
    TextGraphics* tgr;
    for(tgr = first(); tgr != NULL; tgr = next())
        tgr->destroy();
    RemoveAll();
}
```

The *FieldList* Class

The `FormBackground` class maintains the background of a form, and the `FieldList` class, derived from `CObList`, stores all the fields of a form in a linked list. Each field is represented by an instance of the `Field` class.

Just as the `FormBackground` class does for `TextGraphics`, `FieldList` provides many functions for convenient access to the fields that `FieldList` maintains. The files shown in Listings 17.5 and 17.6 implement the `FieldList` class.

Listing 17.5. FIELDLST.H. The header file for the `FieldList` class.

```
//-----------------------------------------------------------
// File: fieldlst.h
// A double-linked list that defines the form's layout and
// contents

#if !defined(_ _FIELDLST_H)
#define _ _FIELDLST_H

#include <afxcoll.h>
#include "field.h"

class FieldList : public CObList
```

```
{
public:
    FieldList() : pos(NULL) {}

    FieldList(CArchive& archive) { read(archive);}

    ~FieldList() { delete_all();}

    Field* first()
    {
        pos = GetHeadPosition();
        return (Field*) GetNext(pos);
    }

    Field* last()
    {
        pos = GetTailPosition();
        return (Field*) GetPrev(pos);
    }

    Field* next()
    {
        if(pos == NULL)
            return NULL;
        else
            return (Field*)GetNext(pos);
     }

    Field* previous()
    {
        if(pos == NULL)
            return NULL;
        else
            return (Field*)GetPrev(pos);
     }

    Field* current()
    {
        if(pos == NULL)
            return NULL;
        else
            return (Field*)GetAt(pos);
     }
```

continues

Listing 17.5. continued

```
    void current(Field* f)
    {
        pos = Find(f, GetHeadPosition());
    }

    unsigned short count() { return GetCount();}

    Field* locate(const char* id);

    void add(Field& f)
    {
        Field *pf = new Field(f);
        AddTail(pf);
    }
    void add_data(const char* id, CArchive& archive);
    void add_data(const char* id, CString& d);
    void add_data(const char* id, const char* s);

    CString data();        // return current field's data
    void data(CString& d); // set current field's data

    void read(CArchive& archive);
    void write(CArchive& archive);

    void read_data(CArchive& archive);
    void write_data(CArchive& archive);

    void delete_all();

private:
    POSITION  pos; // Current item's position
};

#endif
```

Listing 17.6. FIELDLST.CPP. The member functions of the `FieldList` class.

```
//-----------------------------------------------------------------
//  File: fieldlst.cpp
//  Maintains a list of fields and their contents

#include "fieldlst.h"
#include <string.h>
#include <iostream.h>
//-----------------------------------------------------------------
//  r e a d
//  Reads the field definitions from an archive

void FieldList::read(CArchive& archive)
{
// How many elements to read?
    unsigned short entries;
    archive >> entries;

//  Read the field definitions one by one
    if(entries > 0)
    {
        unsigned short i;
        for(i = 0; i < entries; i++)
        {
            Field f;
            f.read(archive);
            add(f);
        }
    }
}
//-----------------------------------------------------------------
//  w r i t e
//  Writes fields to an archive.
//  This function archives everything except the data.

void FieldList::write(CArchive& archive)
{
// First, write the total number of elements:
    archive << count();
```

continues

Listing 17.6. continued

```
//  Write out fields one by one:
    if(count() > 0)
    {
        Field* p_f;
        for(p_f = first(); p_f != NULL; p_f = next())
        {
// Save the field in the archive:
            p_f->write(archive);
        }
    }
}
//------------------------------------------------------------
//  a d d _ d a t a ( c o n s t  c h a r * , C A r c h i v e & )
//  Reads data for a field from an archive

void FieldList::add_data(const char* id, CArchive& archive)
{
    Field* p_f = locate(id);
    if(p_f != NULL)
    {
        p_f->read_data(archive);
    }
}
//------------------------------------------------------------
//  a d d _ d a t a ( c o n s t  c h a r * , C S t r i n g & )
//  Sets the data for a field

void FieldList::add_data(const char* id, CString& d)
{
    Field* p_f = locate(id);
    if(p_f != NULL)
        p_f->data(d);
}
//------------------------------------------------------------
//  a d d _ d a t a ( c o n s t  c h a r * , c o n s t  c h a r *)
//  Sets the data for a field

void FieldList::add_data(const char* id, const char* s)
{
    Field* p_f = locate(id);
```

```
    if(p_f != NULL)
        p_f->data(s);
}
//------------------------------------------------------------
//  l o c a t e ( c o n s t  c h a r * )
//  Locates a specified field in the list of fields

Field* FieldList::locate(const char* id)
{
// Locate the field with specified id:
    if(count() > 0)
    {
        Field* p_f;
        for(p_f = first(); p_f != NULL; p_f = next())
        {
            if(strcmp(id, p_f->id()) == 0)
            {
                return p_f;
            }
        }
    }
    return NULL;
}
//------------------------------------------------------------
//  r e a d _ d a t a
//  Reads the field data from an archive

void FieldList::read_data(CArchive& archive)
{
// How many elements to read?
    unsigned short entries;
    archive >> entries;

//  Read the contents of each field one by one:
//  The field definitions must already exist
    if(entries > 0)
    {
        unsigned short i;
        for(i = 0; i < entries; i++)
        {
            CString field_id;
            archive >> field_id;
```

continues

Listing 17.6. continued

```
                add_data(field_id, archive);
            }
        }
}
//-------------------------------------------------------------------
//  w r i t e _ d a t a
//  Writes field data to an archive

void FieldList::write_data(CArchive& archive)
{
// First, write the total number of elements:
    archive << count();

//  Write out fields one by one:
    if(count() > 0)
    {
        Field* p_f;
        for(p_f = first(); p_f != NULL; p_f = next())
        {
// Save this field's data in the archive:
            p_f->write_data(archive);
        }
    }
}
//-------------------------------------------------------------------
//  d a t a ( )
//  Returns current field's data

CString FieldList::data()
{
    Field* p_f = current();
    return p_f->data();
}
//-------------------------------------------------------------------
//  d a t a ( C S t r i n g & )
//  Sets current field's data

void FieldList::data(CString& d)
{
    Field* p_f = current();
    p_f->data(d);
}
```

```
//-----------------------------------------------------------
// d e l e t e _ a l l
// Deletes all fields in FieldList

void FieldList::delete_all()
{
    Field* p_f;
    for(p_f = first(); p_f != NULL; p_f = next())
        delete p_f;
    RemoveAll();
}
```

Notice that most member functions of `FieldList` (see Listing 17.6) seem to appear in two forms—for instance, `read` and `read_data`, and `write` and `write_data`. This differentiation is necessary because of the requirement to keep the definition of a form separate from its data. The functions with names ending in `_data` work with the filled-in data of the form. The functions without the suffix are intended for manipulating the definition. The implementation of the `Field` class, shown in Listing 17.7, reflects this.

As a consequence of the need to store the field definitions separately from the data in the `FieldList` class, you can't exploit the serialization feature inherited from `CObList` to store or retrieve the fields of a form. Instead, the `read`, `read_data`, `write`, and `write_data` archiving functions interact directly with the archive.

The *Field* Class

A `Field` class represents each field in the form (see Listing 17.7). To keep the software simple, the Forms package assumes that each field can hold a single line of characters. Therefore, you need the following data to represent a field:

- A `CString _id` to identify the field. You use this when loading data into a form. The name of a field is used to locate the field into which the data goes.
- The `CString _data`. This denotes the actual filled-in data for the field.
- The location of the data-entry area, as given by `_dxpos` and `_dypos`. These are character locations based in the top left corner of the form with the positive x-axis pointing to the right and the positive y-axis pointing down.
- The `_numchars` variable. This denotes the maximum number of characters allowed in the data-entry area of the field.

- The _curpos variable. This is provided in case you need to track the current character position within a data-entry area.

Of these data members, _id, _dxpos, _dypos, and _numchars constitute the definition of the field, whereas _data represents the data used to fill the field. Therefore, the definitions file contains _id, _dxpos, _dypos, and _numchars, while the data file contains _id and _data for each field. The data file must store the identification (the "name") of each field so that you can load the data into the correct field.

Listing 17.7. FIELD.H. The declaration of the Field class.

```
//---------------------------------------------------------------
// File: field.h
// Declares the Field class

#if !defined(_ _FIELD_H)
#define _ _FIELD_H

#include <afx.h>

class Field : public CObject
{
public:
    Field() {};

    Field(const char* id, unsigned short xpos,
          unsigned short ypos, size_t nchar) :
          _id(id), _dxpos(xpos), _dypos(ypos),
          _numchars(nchar), _data(' ',nchar) {}

    Field(const Field& f) : _id(f._id),
        _dxpos(f._dxpos), _dypos(f._dypos),
        _numchars(f._numchars), _data(f._data) {}

    CString id() { return _id;}
    void id(const char* name) { _id = name;}
    void id(CString& s) { _id = s;}

    CString data() { return _data;}
    void data(const char* d)
    {
        _curpos = 0;
        _data = d;
```

```
}
void data(CString& s)
{
    _curpos = 0;
    _data = s;
}

void append(const char* s) { _data = _data + s;}

void delete_char(unsigned short pos)
{
    if(curwidth() > 0 && pos > 0 && pos < curwidth())
        if(curwidth()-1 == pos)
            _data = _data.Left(pos);
        else
            _data = _data.Left(pos) +
                    _data.Right(curwidth()-pos-1);
}

unsigned short xpos() { return _dxpos;}
unsigned short ypos() { return _dypos;}
unsigned short numchars() { return _numchars;}
unsigned short curpos() { return _curpos;}

void put(int c, int pos) { _data.SetAt(pos, c);}
char get(int pos) { return _data.GetAt(pos);}

unsigned short curwidth() { return _data.GetLength();}

void read(CArchive& archive)
{
    archive >> _id >> _dxpos >> _dypos >> _numchars;
}
void write(CArchive& archive)
{
    archive << _id << _dxpos << _dypos << _numchars;
}

void read_data(CArchive& archive)
{
    archive >> _data;
}
```

continues

Listing 17.7. continued

```
    void write_data(CArchive& archive)
    {
        archive << _id << _data;
    }

private:
    CString        _id;       // Field identifier
    CString        _data;     // Data for this field
    unsigned short _dxpos;    // Location of
    unsigned short _dypos;    // data-entry area
    unsigned short _numchars; // This many characters allowed
    unsigned short _curpos;   // Current character position
};

#endif
```

The `Field` class provides `write` and `read` functions to store the definition of a field in an archive and retrieve it later. The `write_data` and `read_data` functions are analogous to `write` and `read`, but they store and retrieve only the `_id` and the `_data` variables.

Several other member functions provide access to individual variables in the `Field` class.

Displaying a Form

This chapter's focus thus far has been on the storage and in-memory representation of the various elements of a form. The design of the `TextGraphics` class, mentioned in the description of the `FormBackground` class, is motivated by the need to display a form. As the name `TextGraphics` implies, this version of the Forms software will display on an MS-DOS PC's monitor in text mode.

As Listings 17.8 and 17.10 show, the `TextGraphics` class is an abstract base class derived from the `CObject` class in the Microsoft Foundation Class library. The `TextGraphics` class and all graphics classes derived from it use the serialization feature of the Microsoft Foundation Class library for storage and retrieval of `TextGraphics` objects to and from disk files. In addition to the `Serialize` function necessary for serialization, the `TextGraphics` class has two more virtual functions:

- The `draw` function, which should be defined by a derived class in such a way that you can draw the object on a device by calling this function with a pointer to the device (the `OutputDevice` class) as an argument.
- The `name` function, which returns the name of the class. This function is not necessary for the Forms package, but is useful for identifying individual graphics objects in a form's background.

TextGraphics Class Hierarchy

All useful graphics objects are derived from the `TextGraphics` abstract base class. As shown in Figure 17.4, the basic classes are:

- `TextLine` objects, for displaying a line of text at a specified location.
- `Line`, for representing lines. This class is further specialized into the `HLine` and `VLine` classes for horizontal and vertical lines.
- `Box`, for drawing rectangles. Two classes are derived from `Box`: `SingleLineBox` and `DoubleLineBox` for rectangles with single-line and double-line boundaries. Internally, a box is represented in terms of the four border lines and the corners, which are needed because of the assumption that the program will display the form in a text-mode screen.

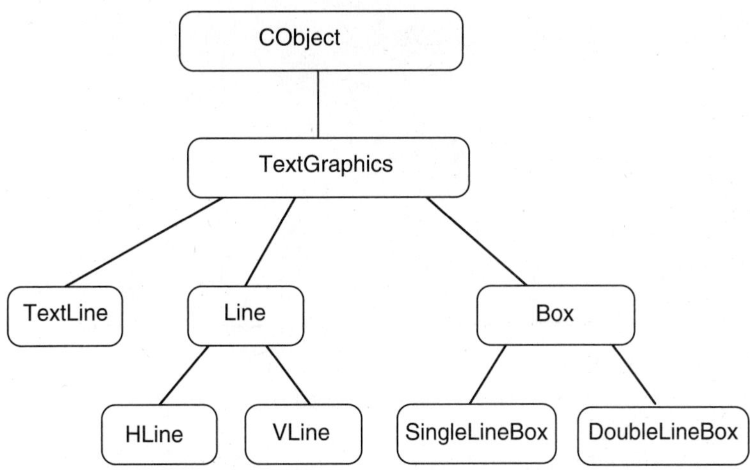

Figure 17.4. `TextGraphics` class hierarchy.

Listing 17.8. TXTGRAPH.H. The header file defining the graphics elements of a form's background.

```
//------------------------------------------------------------
//  File: txtgraph.h
//  Classes for text-mode graphics

#if !defined(_ _TXTGRAPH_H)
#define _ _TXTGRAPH_H

#include <afx.h>
#include "pcline.h"

class OutputDevice;
//------------------------------------------------------------
//  T e x t G r a p h i c s

class TextGraphics : public CObject
{
    DECLARE_SERIAL(TextGraphics)
public:
    TextGraphics() : dc(' ') {}
    TextGraphics(TextGraphics& tgr) : dc(tgr.dc) {}
    virtual void Serialize(CArchive& archive)
    {
        CObject::Serialize(archive);
        if(archive.IsStoring())
            archive << dc;
        else
            archive >> dc;
        }

    virtual void draw(OutputDevice* device) {}
    virtual char* name() { return "TextGraphics"; }

    unsigned char drawing_char() { return dc;}
    void drawing_char(unsigned char _dc) { dc = _dc; }

    virtual TextGraphics* clone()
        { return new TextGraphics(*this);}
    virtual void destroy(){ delete this;}
```

```
protected:
    unsigned char dc;          // Drawing character
};
//----------------------------------------------------------------
//  L i n e

class Line : public TextGraphics
{
    DECLARE_SERIAL(Line)
public:
    Line() : _xpos(0), _ypos(0), _length(0) { dc = ' ';}

    Line(unsigned short x, unsigned short y, unsigned short l,
         unsigned char c) : _xpos(x), _ypos(y), _length(l)
         { dc = c;}

    Line(Line& l) : _xpos(l._xpos), _ypos(l._ypos),
                    _length(l._length) { dc = l.dc;}

    virtual void draw(OutputDevice* device) {}
    virtual TextGraphics* clone() {return new Line(*this);}
    virtual void destroy() { delete this;}
    virtual char* name() { return "Line";}

    unsigned short xpos() { return _xpos;}
    unsigned short ypos() { return _ypos;}
    unsigned short length() { return _length;}

    void Serialize(CArchive& archive)
    {
        TextGraphics::Serialize(archive);
        if(archive.IsStoring())
        {
            archive << _xpos << _ypos << _length;
        }
        else
        {
            archive >> _xpos >> _ypos >> _length;
        }
    }
```

continues

Listing 17.8. continued

```
protected:
    unsigned short _xpos;
    unsigned short _ypos;
    unsigned short _length;
};
//-----------------------------------------------------------------
//  H L i n e

class HLine : public Line
{
    DECLARE_SERIAL(HLine)
public:
    HLine() : Line(0, 0, 0, HLINE_SL) {}
    HLine(unsigned short x, unsigned short y,
          unsigned short l, unsigned char c = HLINE_SL)
          : Line(x, y, l, c) {}
    HLine(const HLine& hl) :
        Line(hl._xpos, hl._ypos, hl._length, hl.dc) {}

   void draw(OutputDevice* device);
   TextGraphics* clone() { return new HLine(*this);}
    void destroy() { delete this;}
    char* name() { return "HLine";}
};

class VLine : public Line
{
    DECLARE_SERIAL(VLine)
public:
    VLine() : Line(0, 0, 0, VLINE_SL) {}
    VLine(unsigned short x, unsigned short y,
          unsigned short l, unsigned char c = VLINE_SL) :
          Line(x, y, l, c) {}
    VLine(const VLine& vl) :
        Line(vl._xpos, vl._ypos, vl._length, vl.dc) {}

    void draw(OutputDevice* device);
    TextGraphics* clone() { return new VLine(*this);}
    void destroy() { delete this;}
    char* name() { return "VLine";}
};
```

```
//----------------------------------------------------------------
//  B o x

class Box : public TextGraphics
{
    DECLARE_SERIAL(Box)
public:
    Box() : topleft(1, 1, 1), topright(1, 1, 1),
            botleft(1, 1, 1), botright(1, 1, 1),
            top(1, 1, 1), bottom(1, 1, 1),
            left(1, 1, 1), right(1, 1, 1) {}

    Box(unsigned short xul, unsigned short yul,
        unsigned short xlr, unsigned short ylr) :
        topleft(xul, yul, 1),
        topright(xlr, yul, 1),
        botleft(xul, ylr, 1),
        botright(xlr, ylr, 1),
        top(xul+1, yul, xlr-xul-1),
        bottom(xul+1, ylr, xlr-xul-1),
        left(xul, yul+1, ylr-yul-1),
        right(xlr, yul+1, ylr-yul-1) {}

    Box(Box& b) : topleft(b.topleft), topright(b.topright),
        botleft(b.botleft), botright(b.botright), top(b.top),
        bottom(b.bottom), left(b.left), right(b.right)
        { dc = b.dc;}

    virtual TextGraphics* clone() {return new Box(*this);}
    virtual void destroy() { delete this;}
    virtual char* name() {return "Box";}
    void draw(OutputDevice* device);

    void Serialize(CArchive& archive)
    {
// Call the Serialize function of the base class:
        TextGraphics::Serialize(archive);
// Now call Serialize for each member class:
        topleft.Serialize(archive);
        topright.Serialize(archive);
        botleft.Serialize(archive);
        botright.Serialize(archive);
```

continues

Listing 17.8. continued

```
            top.Serialize(archive);
            bottom.Serialize(archive);
            left.Serialize(archive);
            right.Serialize(archive);
        }

protected:
    HLine  topleft, topright;
    HLine  botleft, botright;
    HLine  top, bottom;
    VLine  left, right;
};
//--------------------------------------------------
//  S i n g l e L i n e B o x

class SingleLineBox : public Box
{
    DECLARE_SERIAL(SingleLineBox)
public:
    SingleLineBox() : Box(1, 1, 1, 1) {}
    SingleLineBox(unsigned short xul, unsigned short yul,
        unsigned short xlr, unsigned short ylr);
    SingleLineBox(SingleLineBox& slb) : Box(slb) {}

    TextGraphics* clone() { return new SingleLineBox(*this);}
    void destroy() { delete this;}
    char* name() { return "SingleLineBox";}
};
//--------------------------------------------------
//  D o u b l e L i n e B o x

class DoubleLineBox : public Box
{
    DECLARE_SERIAL(DoubleLineBox)
public:
    DoubleLineBox() : Box(1, 1, 1, 1) {}
    DoubleLineBox(unsigned short xul, unsigned short yul,
        unsigned short xlr, unsigned short ylr);
    DoubleLineBox(DoubleLineBox& dlb) : Box(dlb) {}

    TextGraphics* clone() { return new DoubleLineBox(*this);}
    void destroy() { delete this;}
```

```
    char* name() { return "DoubleLineBox";}
};
//-------------------------------------------------
//  T e x t L i n e

class TextLine : public TextGraphics
{
    DECLARE_SERIAL(TextLine)
public:
    TextLine() : text(" "), xpos(1), ypos(1) {}
    TextLine(const char* s, unsigned short x, unsigned short y) :
        text(s), xpos(x), ypos(y) {}

    TextLine(TextLine& tl) : text(tl.text), xpos(tl.xpos),
        ypos(tl.ypos) {}

    void draw(OutputDevice* device);

    TextGraphics* clone() { return new TextLine(*this);}
    void destroy() { delete this;}

    char* name() { return "TextLine";}

    virtual void Serialize(CArchive& archive)
    {
        TextGraphics::Serialize(archive);
        if(archive.IsStoring())
        {
            archive << text << xpos << ypos;
        }
        else
        {
            archive >> text >> xpos >> ypos;
        }
    }

protected:
    CString        text;
    unsigned short xpos;
    unsigned short ypos;
};

#endif
```

Character-Based Graphics

In this version of the Forms software, the `TextGraphics` objects must be displayed on an MS-DOS PC's text-mode screen. You can use the extended character set of your MS-DOS PC to draw lines and boxes. The PCLINE.H header file (see Listing 17.9) defines symbolic names for each of these drawing characters. Figure 17.5 displays several such characters, along with their symbolic names.

The `unsigned char` variable named `_dc` in the `TextGraphics` class denotes the line drawing character to be used when drawing a `TextGraphics` object.

TOPLEFT_SL	┌	TOPRIGHT_SL	┐	BOTLEFT_SL	└
BOTRIGHT_SL	┘	VLINE_SL	│	HLINE_SL	─
LEFTH_SL	├	RIGHTH_SL	┤	T_SL	┬
INVT_SL	┴	CROSS_SL	┼		
TOPLEFT_DL	╔	TOPRIGHT_DL	╗	BOTLEFT_DL	╚
BOTRIGHT_DL	╝	VLINE_DL	║	HLINE_DL	═
LEFTH_DL	╠	RIGHTH_DL	╣	T_DL	╦
INVT_DL	╩	CROSS_DL	╬		
VLINE_TK	█	HLINEB_TK	▄	VLINEL_TN	▌
VLINER_TN	▐	HLINET_TK	▀	T_HDL_VSL	╤
TL_HDL_VSL	╒	TR_HDL_VSL	╕	LH_HDL_VSL	╞
RH_HDL_VSL	╡	INVT_HDL_VSL	╧	CROSS_HDL_VSL	╪

Figure 17.5. Line drawing characters in MS-DOS PCs.

Listing 17.9. PCLINE.H. The definition of symbolic names for line drawing characters in MS-DOS PCs.

```
//--------------------------------------------------------------
//  File:  pcline.h
//  Line drawing characters for Industry Standard
//  Architecture (ISA) PCs

#if !defined(_ _PCLINE_H)
#define _ _PCLINE_H

/* Single line borders */
```

```
#define TOPLEFT_SL   0xda
#define TOPRIGHT_SL  0xbf
#define BOTLEFT_SL   0xc0
#define BOTRIGHT_SL  0xd9
#define VLINE_SL     0xb3
#define HLINE_SL     0xc4
#define LEFTH_SL     0xc3
#define RIGHTH_SL    0xb4
#define T_SL         0xc2
#define INVT_SL      0xc1
#define CROSS_SL     0xc5

/* Double Line borders */

#define TOPLEFT_DL   0xc9
#define TOPRIGHT_DL  0xbb
#define BOTLEFT_DL   0xc8
#define BOTRIGHT_DL  0xbc
#define VLINE_DL     0xba
#define HLINE_DL     0xcd
#define LEFTH_DL     0xcc
#define RIGHTH_DL    0xb9
#define T_DL         0xcb
#define INVT_DL      0xca
#define CROSS_DL     0xce

/* Thick and thin solid lines */
#define VLINE_TK     0xdb
#define HLINEB_TK    0xdc
#define VLINEL_TN    0xdd
#define VLINER_TN    0xde
#define HLINET_TK    0xdf

#define T_HDL_VSL    209
#define TL_HDL_VSL   213
#define TR_HDL_VSL   184
#define LH_HDL_VSL   198
#define RH_HDL_VSL   181
#define INVT_HDL_VSL 207
#define CROSS_HDL_VSL 216

#endif
```

Listing 17.10. TXTGRAPH.CPP. The implementation of the graphics objects used in a form's background.

```
//-----------------------------------------------
//  File: txtgraph.cpp
//  Implements classes for text-mode graphics drawing

  #include "txtgraph.h"
  #include "outdev.h"
IMPLEMENT_SERIAL(TextGraphics, CObject, 100)
IMPLEMENT_SERIAL(Line, TextGraphics, 100)
IMPLEMENT_SERIAL(HLine, Line, 100)
IMPLEMENT_SERIAL(VLine, Line, 100)
IMPLEMENT_SERIAL(Box, TextGraphics, 100)
IMPLEMENT_SERIAL(SingleLineBox, Box, 100)
IMPLEMENT_SERIAL(DoubleLineBox, Box, 100)
IMPLEMENT_SERIAL(TextLine, TextGraphics, 100)

//------------------------------------------------
//  B o x : : d r a w
//  Draws a box with single-line border

void Box::draw(OutputDevice* device)
{
// Use graphics-mode functions, if possible:
    if(!device->is_text())
    {
        device->draw_line(topleft.xpos(), topleft.ypos(),
                          topright.xpos(), topright.ypos());
        device->draw_line(topright.xpos(), topright.ypos(),
                          botright.xpos(), botright.ypos());
        device->draw_line(botright.xpos(), botright.ypos(),
                          botleft.xpos(), botleft.ypos());
        device->draw_line(botleft.xpos(), botleft.ypos(),
                          topleft.xpos(), topleft.ypos());
        return;
    }
// Otherwise, draw the lines and the corners using characters:
    topleft.draw(device);
    topright.draw(device);
    botleft.draw(device);
    botright.draw(device);
    top.draw(device);
```

```
    bottom.draw(device);
    left.draw(device);
    right.draw(device);
}
//-----------------------------------------------------------------
//  S i n g l e L i n e B o x
//  Constructs a box with single-line border

SingleLineBox::SingleLineBox(unsigned short xul,
    unsigned short yul, unsigned short xlr, unsigned short ylr) :
    Box(xul, yul, xlr, ylr)
{
    topleft.drawing_char(TOPLEFT_SL);
    topright.drawing_char(TOPRIGHT_SL);
    botleft.drawing_char(BOTLEFT_SL);
    botright.drawing_char(BOTRIGHT_SL);
    top.drawing_char(HLINE_SL);
    bottom.drawing_char(HLINE_SL);
    left.drawing_char(VLINE_SL);
    right.drawing_char(VLINE_SL);
}
//-----------------------------------------------------------------
//  D o u b l e L i n e B o x
//  Constructs a box with double-line border

DoubleLineBox::DoubleLineBox(unsigned short xul,
    unsigned short yul, unsigned short xlr, unsigned short ylr) :
    Box(xul, yul, xlr, ylr)
{
    topleft.drawing_char(TOPLEFT_DL);
    topright.drawing_char(TOPRIGHT_DL);
    botleft.drawing_char(BOTLEFT_DL);
    botright.drawing_char(BOTRIGHT_DL);
    top.drawing_char(HLINE_DL);
    bottom.drawing_char(HLINE_DL);
    left.drawing_char(VLINE_DL);
    right.drawing_char(VLINE_DL);
}
//-----------------------------------------------------------------
//  H L i n e : : d r a w
//  Draws a horizontal line
```

continues

Listing 17.10. continued

```
void HLine::draw(OutputDevice* device)
{
    if(device == NULL || _length == 0) return;

// If not "text mode" draw a line by calling draw_line:
    if(!device->is_text())
    {
        device->draw_line(_xpos, _ypos,
                          _xpos+_length, _ypos);
        return;
    }
// Create the line by writing out the "drawing character"
// repeatedly:
    char str[2];
    str[0] = dc;
    str[1] = '\0';
    int numchar = _length;
    unsigned short x = _xpos;
    while(numchar_)
    {
        device->draw_text(str, x, _ypos);
        x++;
    }
}
//-----------------------------------------------------
//  V L i n e : : d r a w
//  Draws a vertical line

void VLine::draw(OutputDevice* device)
{
    if(device == NULL || _length == 0) return;

// If not "text mode" draw a line by calling draw_line:
    if(!device->is_text())
    {
        device->draw_line(_xpos, _ypos,
                          _xpos, _ypos+_length);
        return;
    }

// Create the line by writing out the "drawing character"
// repeatedly:
```

```
    char str[2];
    str[0] = dc;
    str[1] = '\0';
    int numchar = _length;
    unsigned short y = _ypos;
    while(numchar--)
    {
        device->draw_text(str, _xpos, y);
        y++;
    }
}
//-----------------------------------------------------------------
//  T e x t L i n e : : d r a w
//  Displays a line of text

void TextLine::draw(OutputDevice* device)
{
    if(device == NULL) return;
    device->draw_text(text, xpos, ypos);
}
```

The *OutputDevice* Class

The `draw` function of the `TextGraphics` class requires a pointer to an `OutputDevice` that identifies the device where the graphics object is displayed. Like `TextGraphics`, `OutputDevice` is an abstract base class used to model any type of device capable of displaying output. In particular, an `OutputDevice` can be a text-mode display, a printer, or (as you'll see in Chapter 18) a window in Microsoft Windows. The graphics objects in the `TextGraphics` hierarchy rely on the following assumptions about the `OutputDevice` class:

- It has a `draw_line` function for drawing lines and a `draw_text` function for displaying text. These functions should be declared as follows:

```
void OutputDevice::draw_line(unsigned short x1,
                             unsigned short y1,
                             unsigned short x2,
                             unsigned short y2);
void OutputDevice::draw_text(const char* str,
                             unsigned short x,
                             unsigned short y);
```

- It has a function named `is_text()`, which returns a nonzero value if the display is text-mode.

With this information in hand, you can define the `OutputDevice` class, as shown in the outdev.h file (see Listing 17.11). For the MS-DOS version of the Forms software, you need a `TextDisplay` class that represents a text-mode screen in an MS-DOS PC. You also derive a `TextWindow` class from `TextDisplay` so that you can display the form in a text-mode window. As shown in the outdev.cpp file (see Listing 13.19), the actual `draw_line` and `draw_text` functions use the console I/O functions from the Microsoft Visual C++ library.

This approach isolates the device-dependent drawing functions in the `OutputDevice` class. As a benefit, you can easily add the code necessary to display the form on a new output device, such as a printer.

Listing 17.11. OUTDEV.H. The header file for classes representing output devices.

```
//--------------------------------------------------------------
//  File: outdev.h
//  Classes for output (text screen, printer)

#if !defined(_ _OUTDEV_H)
#define _ _OUTDEV_H

class OutputDevice
{
public:
    virtual void draw_line(unsigned short x1, unsigned short y1,
        unsigned short x2, unsigned short y2) = 0;
    virtual void draw_text(const char* str, unsigned short x,
        unsigned short y) = 0;
    virtual unsigned is_text() = 0;
};

class TextDisplay : public OutputDevice
{
public:
    TextDisplay() : left(1), top(1),
        right(80), bottom(25) {}
```

```
    TextDisplay(unsigned short l, unsigned short t,
                unsigned short r, unsigned short b) :
        left(l), top(t), right(r), bottom(b) {}

    virtual void draw_line(unsigned short x1, unsigned short y1,
        unsigned short x2, unsigned short y2) = 0;

    virtual void draw_text(const char* str, unsigned short x,
        unsigned short y) = 0;

    unsigned is_text() { return 1;}

protected:
    unsigned short left, top;
    unsigned short right, bottom;
};

class TextWindow: public TextDisplay
{
public:
    TextWindow() : TextDisplay(1, 1, 80, 25) {}
    TextWindow(unsigned short l, unsigned short t,
                unsigned short r, unsigned short b) :
        TextDisplay(l, t, r, b) {}
    void draw_line(unsigned short, unsigned short,
        unsigned short, unsigned short) {}
    void draw_text(const char* str, unsigned short x,
        unsigned short y);
};

class PostScriptPrinter : public OutputDevice
{
public:
    virtual void draw_line(unsigned short x1, unsigned short y1,
        unsigned short x2, unsigned short y2) = 0;
    virtual void draw_text(const char* str, unsigned short x,
        unsigned short y) = 0;
    unsigned is_text() { return 1;}
};

#endif
```

Listing 17.12. OUTDEV.CPP.
The implementation of the `TextWindow` output device.

```
//--------------------------------------------------------------
//  File: outdev.cpp
//  Classes for output (displaying on screen, printing, etc.)
//
//  NOTE: Uses text-mode output routines from library that comes
//        with Microsoft Visual C++ compiler.

#include <graph.h>
#include <conio.h>
#include "outdev.h"

//--------------------------------------------------------------
//  d r a w _ t e x t
//  Displays text in a window

void TextWindow::draw_text(const char* str, unsigned short x,
                           unsigned short y)
{
    _settextwindow(top, left, bottom, right);
    _settextposition(y, x);
    _cputs(str);
}
```

The *Form* Class

You now have enough information to define the `Form` class. Listing 17.13 shows the FORM.H file, which declares the `Form` class, while the FORM.CPP file in Listing 17.14 shows its implementation. The `Form` class has the following private data members:

- A `CString` called `_formname`, which holds the name of the form with the definition and data that this `Form` object holds.
- Two `FileHeaders`, `_data_filehdr` and `_defn_filehdr`, which represent the headers of the data files and the definitions file.
- A `FormBackground` object named `_form_bg`, which represents the background of the form.

- An instance of the FieldList class, _fields, which holds the fields of the form.
- A CString called _data_filename, which holds the name of a data file if one is currently open. (The filled-in data of a form is stored in the data file).
- An unsigned short variable named _is_new, which is used as a flag. (_is_new is nonzero for a blank form.)

When you use an instance of the Form class, it becomes the object through which you interact with the form. Therefore, the Form class must provide a rich set of functions so that you can access all parts of a Form, from TextGraphics background to Field. Here's a summary of some important public member functions of Form:

- read(const char* filename) opens the file specified by filename and reads the data or definition contained in the file.
- write_defn(const char* filename) writes the form's definition to a file with the specified name.
- write_data(const char* filename) writes the form's data to a file with the specified name.
- add(Field& f) adds a field to the form's definition.
- add(TextGraphics& t) adds a graphics element to the form's background.
- add_data(const char* id, const char* data) stores the string data as the data of the Field object with an ID that matches the id string.
- first_field, last_field, next_field, previous_field, and current_field are functions for accessing Fields in the form's definition maintained by the Fieldlist named _fields.
- first_bg, last_bg, next_bg, previous_bg, and current_bg are functions for accessing TextGraphics objects in the form's background maintained by the FormBackground named _form_bg.

Listing 17.13. FORM.H. The declaration of the Form class.

```
//-------------------------------------------------------------
//  File:  form.h
//
//  Describes the "Form" object
```

continues

Listing 17.13. continued

```
#if !defined(_ _FORM_H)
#define _ _FORM_H

#include <afx.h>

#include "filehdr.h"
#include "formbg.h"
#include "fieldlst.h"

class Form: public CObject
{
public:
    Form() : _formname("undefined"), _is_new(0),
             _data_filename("unknown") {}

    void add(Field& f) { _fields.add(f);}
    void add(TextGraphics& t) { _form_bg.add(t);}

    void read(const char* filename);

    void write_data(const char* filename);
    void write_defn(const char* filename);

    void setup_form(CArchive& archive);
    void setup_data(CArchive& archive);

    Field* first_field(){ return _fields.first();}
    Field* last_field(){ return _fields.last();}
    Field* next_field(){ return _fields.next();}
    Field* previous_field(){ return _fields.previous();}
    Field* current_field(){ return _fields.current();}
    void current_field(Field* f){ _fields.current(f);}

    TextGraphics* first_bg(){ return _form_bg.first();}
    TextGraphics* last_bg(){ return _form_bg.last();}
    TextGraphics* next_bg(){ return _form_bg.next();}
    TextGraphics* previous_bg(){ return _form_bg.previous();}
    TextGraphics* current_bg(){ return _form_bg.current();}

    CString name() { return _formname;}
    void name(const char* s);
```

```
    void add_data(const char* id, const char* data)
        { _fields.add_data(id, data);}

    unsigned short is_new() { return _is_new;}
    CString data_filename() { return _data_filename;}

private:
    CString        _formname;
    FileHeader     _data_filehdr;
    FileHeader     _defn_filehdr;
    FormBackground _form_bg;
    FieldList      _fields;
    CString        _data_filename;
    unsigned short _is_new;   // Nonzero if "unfilled" form
};

#endif
```

Listing 17.14. FORM.CPP.
The implementation of the `Form` class.

```
//--------------------------------------------------------------
//  File:  form.cpp
//
//  Implements the Form class

#include "form.h"
//--------------------------------------------------------------
//  r e a d
//  Loads a form from a file

void Form::read(const char* filename)
{
// Open the specified file for reading:
    TRY
    {
        CFile file(filename, CFile::modeRead);
```

continues

Listing 17.14. continued

```
// Now create an archive for storing the form's definition:
        TRY
        {
            CArchive archive(&file, CArchive::load);

// Load form from the archive.
// Start with the file header:
            FileHeader hdr;
            hdr.Serialize(archive);

// If this is a definition file, set up a blank form:
            if(hdr.filetype() == FileHeader::_form_definition)
            {
                _defn_filehdr = hdr;
                setup_form(archive);
                _is_new = 1;
            }
// If it's a data form, set up form filled with data:
            if(hdr.filetype() == FileHeader::_form_data)
            {
                _data_filename = filename;
                _data_filehdr = hdr;
                setup_data(archive);
            }
            archive.Close();
        }
        CATCH(CArchiveException, e)
        {
// Close file and throw exception to caller:
            file.Close();
            THROW_LAST();
        }
        END_CATCH
    }
    CATCH(CFileException, e)
    {
        THROW_LAST(); // Send exception to caller
    }
    END_CATCH
}
//-----------------------------------------------------------------
//  s e t u p _ f o r m
```

```
//  Creates the form (background and field definitions, not
//  "filled-in" data)

void Form::setup_form(CArchive& archive)
{
// Read the form's name from the archive:
    archive >> _formname;

// Read in the form's background:
    _form_bg.Serialize(archive);

// Read in the field definitions:
    _fields.read(archive);
}
//------------------------------------------------------------
//  s e t u p _ d a t a
//  Creates a form filled with specified data

void Form::setup_data(CArchive& archive)
{
// First, open file containing definition of form.
// Get the name from the _data_filehdr.
    TRY
    {
        CFile file(_data_filehdr.filename(), CFile::modeRead);

// Now create an archive for storing the form's definition:
        TRY
        {
            CArchive arch_def(&file, CArchive::load);

// Remember to read the header:
            _defn_filehdr.Serialize(arch_def);

// Next, load form's definition from the archive
            setup_form(arch_def);
            arch_def.Close();


// Now load form's data:
            _fields.read_data(archive);
```

continues

Listing 17.14. continued

```
        }
        CATCH(CArchiveException, e)
        {
// Close file and throw exception to caller:
            file.Close();
            THROW_LAST();
        }
        END_CATCH
    }
    CATCH(CFileException, e)
    {
        THROW_LAST(); // Send exception to caller
    }
    END_CATCH
}
//-------------------------------------------------------------
//  w r i t e _ d e f n ( c o n s t  c h a r *)
//  Saves the form's definition in the specified file (overwrites
//  contents, if file already exists)

void Form::write_defn(const char* filename)
{
// Open the specified file for writing:
    TRY
    {
        CFile file(filename, CFile::modeCreate ¦
                             CFile::modeWrite);

// Now create an archive for storing the form's definition:
        TRY
        {
            CArchive archive(&file, CArchive::store);
// At this point, you need only archive the Form's
// definition; not the filled-in data, only the definition).

// Archive form's definition as follows:
//   (1) Save the file header
//   (2) Save form's name
//   (3) Save form's background
//   (4) Save the definition of the fields
```

```
// Set up information for file header:
            _defn_filehdr.filename(filename);
            _defn_filehdr.filetype(FileHeader::_form_definition);
            _defn_filehdr.mod_time(CTime::GetCurrentTime());

            _defn_filehdr.Serialize(archive);
            archive << _formname;
            _form_bg.Serialize(archive);
            _fields.write(archive);
            archive.Close();
        }
        CATCH(CArchiveException, e)
        {
// Remove the file and throw exception to caller:
            CFile::Remove(filename);
            THROW_LAST();
        }
        END_CATCH
    }
    CATCH(CFileException, e)
    {
        THROW_LAST(); // Send exception to caller
    }
    END_CATCH

}
//------------------------------------------------------------
//  w r i t e _ d a t a ( c o n s t  c h a r *)
//  Saves the form's data in the specified file

void Form::write_data(const char* filename)
{
// Open the specified file for writing:
    TRY
    {
        CFile file(filename, CFile::modeCreate |
                             CFile::modeWrite);

// Now create an archive for storing form's data:
        TRY
        {
```

continues

Listing 17.14. continued

```
            CArchive archive(&file, CArchive::store);
// At this point, you need only archive the Form's
// data in this archive in the following order:
//   (1) Save the header.
//   (2) Save the data from all fields in the form.

// Set up information for file header.
// Data file should have name of "definition file" in header.

            _data_filehdr.filename(_defn_filehdr.filename());
            _data_filehdr.filetype(FileHeader::_form_data);

            _data_filehdr.Serialize(archive);
            _fields.write_data(archive);
            archive.Close();
        }
        CATCH(CArchiveException, e)
        {
// Remove file and throw exception to caller:
            CFile::Remove(filename);
            THROW_LAST();
        }
        END_CATCH

    }
    CATCH(CFileException, e)
    {
        THROW_LAST(); // Send exception to caller
    }
    END_CATCH

}
//-------------------------------------------------------------

void Form::name(const char* s) { _formname = s;};
```

Creating a Form

Before you can use the Forms software, you need at least one definitions file and one data file that can serve as the input for the form fill-in program (the software that enables you to display a form and enter data into the fields). You can solve this problem by writing a small program that creates a form and its data. This also is a good exercise in using the facilities offered by the C++ classes in the Forms software.

Defining a Form

The first program creates the definition of a form. The program for the invoice form shown in Figure 17.1 is in the FORMDEF.CPP file (see Listing 17.15). As shown in the file, the text items and the lines representing the form's background are prepared in an array of structures. The main program first creates a `Form`. It then creates each background element and calls the `add` function of the `Form` to add to the definition. The fields also are created and added to the form's definition. Finally, a single call to the `write_defn` function of the `Form` saves the form's definition in a file named INVOICE.DEF. The `write` operation is enclosed in an exception-handling block because the `write_defn` function might raise an exception if an error occurs when `write_defn` is saving the form's definition to the file.

Listing 17.15. FORMDEF.CPP. A program to define an invoice form.

```
//-------------------------------------------------------------
//  File: formdef.cpp
//  Creates a form and save its definition in a file

#include <iostream.h>
#include "form.h"

struct text_item
{
    char*          text;
    unsigned short xpos, ypos;
};

text_item txt_list[] =
{
```

continues

Listing 17.15. continued

```
    {"I N V O I C E", 36,  1},
    {"From:",          2,  1},
    {"No:",           60,  1},
    {"Date:",         60,  2},
    {"To:",            2,  7},
    {"F.O.B.",         2, 15},
    {"Terms",         18, 15},
    {"Date Shipped",  34, 15},
    {"Shipped Via",   50, 15},
    {"Ordered",        2, 18},
    {"Shipped",       11, 18},
    {"Description",   33 , 18},
    {"Price",         59, 18},
    {"Per",           66, 18},
    {"Amount",        70, 18}
};

int numtxt = sizeof(txt_list) / sizeof(text_item);

#define FULL_HLINE 78

struct line_item
{
    unsigned short xpos, ypos;
    unsigned short length;
    unsigned short c;
};

static line_item hlines[] =
{
    { 1, 14, 77, HLINE_DL},
    { 1, 17, 77, HLINE_DL},
    { 2, 19, 76, HLINE_DL},
    { 1, 19,  1, LH_HDL_VSL},
    {17, 17,  1, INVT_HDL_VSL},
    {33, 17,  1, INVT_HDL_VSL},
    {49, 17,  1, INVT_HDL_VSL},
};

static int numhlines = sizeof(hlines) / sizeof(line_item);
```

```
static line_item vlines[] =
{
    {17, 15,  2, VLINE_SL},
    {33, 15,  2, VLINE_SL},
    {49, 15,  2, VLINE_SL},
    {78, 15, 11, VLINE_SL},
    { 1, 15, 11, VLINE_SL},
    {10, 18,  8, VLINE_SL},
    {20, 18,  8, VLINE_SL},
    {58, 18,  8, VLINE_SL},
    {65, 18,  8, VLINE_SL},
    {69, 18,  8, VLINE_SL},
    {10, 17,  1, T_HDL_VSL},
    {20, 17,  1, T_HDL_VSL},
    {58, 17,  1, T_HDL_VSL},
    {65, 17,  1, T_HDL_VSL},
    {69, 17,  1, T_HDL_VSL},
    {10, 19,  1, CROSS_HDL_VSL},
    {20, 19,  1, CROSS_HDL_VSL},
    {58, 19,  1, CROSS_HDL_VSL},
    {65, 19,  1, CROSS_HDL_VSL},
    {69, 19,  1, CROSS_HDL_VSL},
    {17, 14,  1, T_HDL_VSL},
    {33, 14,  1, T_HDL_VSL},
    {49, 14,  1, T_HDL_VSL},
    { 1, 14,  1, TL_HDL_VSL},
    { 1, 17,  1, LH_HDL_VSL},
    {78, 14,  1, TR_HDL_VSL},
    {78, 17,  1, RH_HDL_VSL},
    {78, 19,  1, RH_HDL_VSL},
    { 1, 19,  1, LH_HDL_VSL}
};

static int numvlines = sizeof(vlines) / sizeof(line_item);

struct field_item
{
    char*          id;
    unsigned short x, y, field_width;
};
```

continues

Listing 17.15. continued

```
static field_item fields[] =
{
    {"From1",  7,  2, 39},
    {"From2",  7,  3, 39},
    {"From3",  7,  4, 39},
    {"To1",    7,  7, 39},
    {"To2",    7,  8, 39},
    {"To3",    7,  9, 39},
    {"To4",    7, 10, 39},
    {"Num",   65,  1, 10},
    {"Date",  65,  2, 10},
    {"FOB",    2, 16, 15},
    {"Terms", 18, 16, 15},
    {"Shipdate", 34, 16, 15},
    {"Shipvia",  50, 16, 20},

    {"OrdQty1",   2, 20,   8},
    {"ShpQty1",  11, 20,   8},
    {"Descr1",   21, 20,  36},
    {"Price1",   59, 20,   6},
    {"Per1",     66, 20,   3},
    {"Amt1",     70, 20,   8},

    {"OrdQty2",   2, 21,   8},
    {"ShpQty2",  11, 21,   8},
    {"Descr2",   21, 21,  36},
    {"Price2",   59, 21,   6},
    {"Per2",     66, 21,   3},
    {"Amt2",     70, 21,   8},

    {"OrdQty3",   2, 22,   8},
    {"ShpQty3",  11, 22,   8},
    {"Descr3",   21, 22,  36},
    {"Price3",   59, 22,   6},
    {"Per3",     66, 22,   3},
    {"Amt3",     70, 22,   8},
};

static int numfields = sizeof(fields) / sizeof(field_item);
//------------------------------------------------------------
//  m a i n
```

```
void main()
{
    Form inv;
// Add background items...
    SingleLineBox box1(5, 6, 46, 11);
    inv.add(box1);

// Add text items...
    int i;
    for(i = 0; i < numtxt; i++)
    {
        TextLine t(txt_list[i].text, txt_list[i].xpos,
                   txt_list[i].ypos);
        inv.add(t);
    }

// Add the horizontal lines:
    for(i = 0; i < numhlines; i++)
    {
        HLine l(hlines[i].xpos, hlines[i].ypos,
                hlines[i].length);
        l.drawing_char(hlines[i].c);
        inv.add(l);
    }

// Add the vertical lines:
    for(i = 0; i < numvlines; i++)
    {
        VLine l(vlines[i].xpos, vlines[i].ypos,
                vlines[i].length);
        l.drawing_char(vlines[i].c);
        inv.add(l);
    }

// Now add the fields...
    for(i = 0; i < numfields; i++)
    {
        Field f(fields[i].id, fields[i].x, fields[i].y,
                fields[i].field_width);
        inv.add(f);
    }
```

continues

Listing 17.15. continued

```
// Set the name of the form:
    inv.name("Invoice");

// Save the form definition in a file:
    TRY
    {
        inv.write_defn("invoice.def");
    }
    CATCH(CFileException, e)
    {
        cerr << "Error opening file!" << endl;
        exit(1);
    }
    AND_CATCH(CArchiveException, e)
    {
        cerr << "Error occurred while archiving form" << endl;
        exit(2);
    }
    END_CATCH
}
```

Building FORMDEF

Because the FORMDEF program for defining a form uses most of the classes of the Forms software, you must compile and link several files to build the executable FORMDEF.EXE. The formdef project (see the sample source files on the diskette) eases this task. With this project, you can build the FORMDEF.EXE executable file by loading the project into the Visual Workbench and selecting the Rebuild All button.

Running FORMDEF

Run the FORMDEF program with the following command at the MS-DOS prompt:

```
FORMDEF
```

This creates a file named INVOICE.DEF with the definition of an invoice form. This is a binary file, so you can't view it with an editor.

Listing 17.16. FORMDEF. Makefile for building the FORMDEF application.

```
########################################################################
#  Makefile for building the "formdef" application
##
CPPFLAGS = -D_DOS /c /AM /W3 /Zp /G2
LINKFLAGS= /NOD /ONERROR:NOEXE
LIBS=mafxcr mlibce

OBJECTS = formdef.obj form.obj  filehdr.obj \
          formbg.obj txtgraph.obj fieldlst.obj

formdef.exe:  $(OBJECTS)
        link $(LINKFLAGS) $(OBJECTS), $*, NUL, $(LIBS);

formbg.obj: formbg.cpp formbg.h txtgraph.h pcline.h

form.obj: form.cpp form.h filehdr.h  formbg.h \
          txtgraph.h field.h pcline.h

filehdr.obj: filehdr.cpp filehdr.h

txtgraph.obj: txtgraph.cpp txtgraph.h pcline.h outdev.h

fieldlst.obj: fieldlst.cpp fieldlst.h

formdef.obj: formdef.cpp form.h txtgraph.h \
             filehdr.h  formbg.h fieldlst.h \
             field.h pcline.h outdev.h
```

Creating the Form's Data

After you've created the invoice form's definitions file, you can build a data file to test the form fill-in program. Once again, you can write a small program to create the data file. Listing 17.17 shows the FORMDAT.CPP file, which prepares the data for the fields in an array, loads them into a `Form` object, and uses the `Form`'s `write_data` member function to save the data in a file named INVOICE.DAT.

Listing 17.17. FORMDAT.CPP. A program to create a form's data file.

```
//--------------------------------------------------------------
//  File: formdat.cpp
//  Fills out a form and save data in file

#include <iostream.h>
#include "form.h"

struct field_data
{
    char*  id;
    char*  data;
};

static field_data contents[] =
{
    {"From1",   "QuickC for Windows Offer"},
    {"From2",   "P.O. Box 88"},
    {"From3",   "West Peterborough, NH 03468"},
    {"Num",     "22750-37"},
    {"Date",    "12/15/92"},
    {"OrdQty1", "1"},
    {"ShpQty1", "1"},
    {"Descr1",  "Sample source code disk"},
    {"Price1",  "12.95"},
    {"Per1",    "ea"},
    {"Amt1",    "12.95"}
};

static int num_contents = sizeof(contents) / sizeof(field_data);
//--------------------------------------------------------------
//  m a i n

void main()
{
    Form inv;
// Read the form definition from a file:
    TRY
    {
        inv.read("invoice.def");
    }
```

```
    CATCH(CFileException, e)
    {
        cerr << "Error opening file!" << endl;
        exit(1);
    }
    AND_CATCH(CArchiveException, e)
    {
        cerr << "Error occurred while archiving form" << endl;
        exit(2);
    }
    END_CATCH

    int i;
// Add data for the fields...
    for(i = 0; i < num_contents; i++)
    {
        inv.add_data(contents[i].id, contents[i].data);
    }

// Save the "filled-in" form in a data file:
    inv.write_data("invoice.data");
}
```

Building FORMDAT

Use the formdat project file from the sample source disk to build the FORMDAT.EXE executable file. As you did with FORMDEF, you can build FORMDAT with Visual Workbench's Rebuild All toolbar button.

When you run FORMDAT, it creates a file named INVOICE.DAT with the data for a copy of the invoice form with a definition contained in the INVOICE.DEF file.

Filling in Forms

Now that the machinery for representing and manipulating a form is available, you can build a sample application that displays a form and enables the user to enter data. Before creating such a program, you still need to address the following questions:

- How should the form be displayed?
- How will the user interact with the software?

An easy way to answer these questions is to adopt the Model-View Controller (MVC) architecture for the application. Then, a View will handle the display and the controller will handle user interactions.

The Model-View Controller (MVC) architecture originated in SmallTalk-80. Consult Chapter 16, "Using the Microsoft Foundation Class Library," for a brief description of MVC.

The *FormView* Class

You can encapsulate the View layer of the MVC architecture in a C++ class named `FormView`, declared in formview.h (see Listing 17.18) and implemented in formview.cpp (see Listing 17.19). The `FormView` class has the following private data members:

- `Form& _form` is a reference to the `Form` of which this is a view.
- `TextWindow _w` is the text-mode window where the form is displayed.
- `Field* _curfield` is a pointer to the current `Field` object with which the user is interacting.

Listing 17.18. FORMVIEW.H. The header file for the `FormView` class.

```
//------------------------------------------------------------
//  File:  formview.h
//  Defines the classes necessary to present a view of a form

#if !defined(_ _FORMVIEW_H)
#define _ _FORMVIEW_H
#include <conio.h>
#include <graph.h>
#include "txtgraph.h"
#include "outdev.h"

#define BLACK   0
#define RED     4
#define WHITE  15

class Form;
class Field;
```

```
class FormView
{
public:
    FormView(Form& form);
    int accept_char(int c);
    void repaint();
    void save();
    void save_as();
    void backspace();
    void tab();
    int quit() { return ask_quit();}
    void putcursor();
    void gotoxy(short x, short y)
        { (void)_settextposition(y, x);}
    int ask_quit();

private:
    Form&           _form;
    TextWindow      _w;
    Field*          _curfield;
    unsigned short _has_changed;
};

#endif
```

The member functions of the `FormView` class are designed to handle single characters entered by the user. The `EventHandler` class, described next, calls an appropriate function of `FormView` when the user enters a keystroke. Characters such as Tab and Backspace require special handling; however, most characters are processed by the `accept_char` function, which simply inserts the character into the data area of the current field.

Listing 17.19. FORMVIEW.CPP. The member functions of the `FormView` class.

```
//-------------------------------------------------------------
//  File: formview.cpp
//  Displays a "view" of the form
```

continues

Listing 17.19. continued

```
#include "formview.h"
#include "field.h"
#include "form.h"

//------------------------------------------------------------
//  F o r m V i e w ( F o r m & )
//  Creates a "view" for specified form

FormView::FormView(Form& form) : _form(form), _w(1, 1, 80, 25)
{
    _curfield = _form.first_field();
    _has_changed = 0;

// Display form in the window:
    repaint();
}
//------------------------------------------------------------
//  a c c e p t _ c h a r
//  Processes a character received from the event-handler

int FormView::accept_char(int c)
{
    char s[2] = { c, '\0'};
    if(_curfield->curwidth() < _curfield->numchars())
    {
        putcursor();
        _curfield->append(s);
        _has_changed = 1;
        return 1;
    }
    else
        return 0;
}
//------------------------------------------------------------
//  t a b
//  Processes the tab character

void FormView::tab()
{
    _curfield = _form.next_field();
    if(_curfield == NULL) _curfield = _form.first_field();
    putcursor();
```

```
}
//-------------------------------------------------------------
//  r e p a i n t
//  Redraws the form's "view"

void FormView::repaint()
{
// Clear the text window (by default, a 80x25 one):
    _clearscreen(_GCLEARSCREEN);

// Draw the form's background:
    TextGraphics* p_g;
    for(p_g = _form.first_bg(); p_g != NULL;
        p_g = _form.next_bg())
    {
        p_g->draw(&_w);
    }

// Draw the contents of each field...
    Field* p_f;
    for(p_f = _form.first_field(); p_f != NULL;
        p_f = _form.next_field())
    {
// Create a TextLine graphics object with the field's data:
        TextLine* tl = new TextLine(p_f->data(),
                                    p_f->xpos(), p_f->ypos());
        tl->draw(&_w);
    }
    putcursor();
}
//-------------------------------------------------------------
//  b a c k s p a c e
//  Processes a backspace character
void FormView::backspace()
{
    _curfield->delete_char(_curfield->curwidth()-1);
    _has_changed = 1;
    putcursor();
    _putch(' ');
    putcursor();
}
//-------------------------------------------------------------
```

continues

Listing 17.19. continued

```
//  p u t c u r s o r
// Places the cursor at the end of current field

void FormView::putcursor()
{
    gotoxy(_curfield->xpos()+_curfield->curwidth(),
           _curfield->ypos());
}
//-----------------------------------------------------------------
//  s a v e
//  Saves the filled-in form in file. Prompts for filename if this
//  is a new form.

void FormView::save()
{
    if(_form.is_new() || _form.data_filename() == "unknown")
        save_as();
    else
        _form.write_data(_form.data_filename());

// Mark form "unchanged":
    _has_changed = 0;
}
//-----------------------------------------------------------------
//  s a v e _ a s
//  Prompts for a filename and save form in that file

void FormView::save_as()
{
    _settextwindow(10, 10, 16, 70);
    _setbkcolor(RED);
    _clearscreen(_GWINDOW);
    _settextposition(1,1);
    _outtext("Enter filename: ");
    _settextposition(5,1);
    _outtext("Press <Enter> to save form.");

    char filename[80];
    int c = 0, numchar = 0;
    _settextwindow(12, 15, 12, 65);
    _setbkcolor(BLACK);
```

```
    _clearscreen(_GWINDOW);
    _settextposition(1,1);

    while(c != '\r')
    {
        c = _getch();
        switch(c)
        {
            case '\r': // <Enter>
                _form.write_data(filename);
                break;
            case '\b':  // backspace
                if(numchar > 0)
                {
                    filename[_numchar] = '\0';
                }
                break;

// You should check for valid filenames, but we'll ignore
// the checks here.
            default:  // all other characters
                filename[numchar++] = c;
                filename[numchar] = '\0';
        }
// Redisplay the filename in each pass through the loop:
        _clearscreen(_GWINDOW);
        _settextposition(1, 1);
        _outtext(filename);
    }
    repaint();

    _has_changed = 0;
}
//-----------------------------------------------------------------
//  a s k _ q u i t
//  Asks the user if form should be saved

int FormView::ask_quit()
{
// Do nothing if form has not changed:
    if(!_has_changed) return 1;
```

continues

Listing 17.19. continued

```
// Ask user if form should be saved:
    _settextwindow(10, 10, 6, 70);
    _setbkcolor(RED);
    _clearscreen(_GWINDOW);
    _settextposition(5,1);
    _outtext("Press 'y' to save form or 'n' to exit "
             "without saving form.");
    _settextposition(3, 1);
    _outtext("Form changed. Save? [y/n]:");
    _setbkcolor(BLACK);

    int c = 0;
    while(1)
    {
        c = _getch();
        if(c == 'y' || c == 'Y')
        {
            repaint();
            save();
            break;
        }
        if(c == 'n' || c == 'N') break;
    }
    _setbkcolor(BLACK);
    _clearscreen(_GCLEARSCREEN);
    return 1;
}
```

The *EventHandler* Class

The remaining piece of the puzzle is the controller layer of the MVC architecture. The `EventHandler` class, declared in the EV_HNDLR.H file (see Listing 17.20) and implemented in EV_HNDLR.CPP (see Listing 17.21), maintains a reference to the `FormView` object to which it delivers the events. In this case, the events are the keystrokes from the user.

Listing 17.20. EV_HNDLR.H. The header file for the `EventHandler` class.

```
//----------------------------------------------------------------
//  File: ev_hndlr.h
//  Declares the EventHandler class

#if !defined(_ _EV_HNDLR_H)
#define _ _EV_HNDLR_H

#include <conio.h>
#include <stdlib.h>
#include "formview.h"

// This macro converts an ASCII character into a
// control character.
#define  Ctrl(X)  (X-0x40)

const int maxchars = 128;

class EventHandler
{
public:
    EventHandler(FormView& fv);
    void start();
    void send_char()
    {
        if(_formview.accept_char(_saved_char))
            _putch(_saved_char);
    }

    void quit() { if(_formview.quit())_done = 1;}
    void backspace() { _formview.backspace();}
    void tab() { _formview.tab();}
    void repaint() { _formview.repaint();}
    void save() { _formview.save();}
    void save_as() { _formview.save_as();}
    void ignore() {}

typedef void (EventHandler::*action)(void);
```

continues

Listing 17.20. continued

```
private:
    FormView&  _formview;
    action     _xlat_table[maxchars];
    int        _saved_char;
    int        _done;
};

#endif
```

One innovative feature of the `EventHandler` class is event handling through a table of commands, in which each entry has a character associated with a pointer to a member function of `EventHandler`. When the user presses that character's key, the member function is called through the associated pointer. By confining each command to a single character, you can use the character itself as the index to the table. The `xlat_table` array in the `EventHandler` class is the array of pointers to member functions that enable you to translate a character into an action. The `start` member function of the `EventHandler` class processes the keyboard events. In the `EventHandler` you can see how a character is translated to a function call.

Listing 17.21. EV_HNDLR.CPP. The member functions of the `EventHandler` class.

```
//-------------------------------------------------------------
//  File: ev_hndlr.cpp
//  Implements the event-handler class

#include "ev_hndlr.h"

struct command
{
    int    c;  // Character pressed
    EventHandler::action a;  // Function to be called
};

static command cmdtable[] =
{
    {Ctrl('X'),  EventHandler::quit},
    {Ctrl('Q'),  EventHandler::quit},
```

```
    {Ctrl('['),  EventHandler::quit},     // Ctrl-[ is Escape
    {     '\b',  EventHandler::backspace},
    {     '\t',  EventHandler::tab},
    {     '\r',  EventHandler::tab},
    {Ctrl('L'),  EventHandler::repaint},
    {Ctrl('A'),  EventHandler::save_as},
    {Ctrl('S'),  EventHandler::save}
};

static int numcmd = sizeof(cmdtable) / sizeof(command);
//-------------------------------------------------------------
//  E v e n t H a n d l e r ( F o r m V i e w & )
//  Constructor for the EventHandler class

EventHandler::EventHandler(FormView& fv) : _formview(fv),
                              _saved_char(-1), _done(0)
{
// Initialize translation table. Used to convert a keypress
// to an action.
    int i;
    for(i = 0; i < ' ';  i++)
        _xlat_table[i] = EventHandler::ignore;

    for(i = ' '; i < maxchars; i++)
        _xlat_table[i] = EventHandler::send_char;

// Add commands defined in "cmdtable":
    for(i = 0; i < numcmd; i++)
    {
        int c = cmdtable[i].c;
        _xlat_table[c] = cmdtable[i].a;
    }
}
//-------------------------------------------------------------
//  s t a r t
//  Starts processing events

void EventHandler::start()
{
    int c;
```

continues

Listing 17.21. continued

```
    while(!_done)
    {
        if(kbhit())          // Check if there is a keypress
        {
            c = _getch();      // Get character without echoing
            _saved_char = c;
            (this->*_xlat_table[c])();   // Call "action" routine
        }
        else                 // Handle other events if no keypress
        {
// You can look for mouse events in this block
            ;
        }
    }
}
```

The FORMFILL Program

You now have all the machinery needed to create a form fill-in program. Listing 17.22 shows the FORMFILL.CPP file, which constitutes the main function of the FORMFILL program. The main function is short because all the work is done by the `FormView`, `EventHandler`, and `Form` classes, which further delegate responsibilities to their component classes.

Listing 17.22. FORMFILL.CPP. The main program of a form fill-in application.

```
//-------------------------------------------------------------
//  File:  formfill.cpp
//
//  Fills out a form
//

#include <iostream.h>
#include "form.h"
#include "formview.h"
#include "ev_hndlr.h"
```

```
void main(int argc, char **argv)
{
    Form inv;
    if(argc < 2)
    {
        cout << "Use: Formfill <filename>" << endl;
        exit(0);
    }
    char* filename = argv[1];
    char* key = NULL;

// Load form...
    TRY
    {
        inv.read(filename);
    }
    CATCH(CFileException, e)
    {
        cerr << "Error opening file!" << endl;
        exit(1);
    }
    AND_CATCH(CArchiveException, e)
    {
        cerr << "Error accessing archive!" << endl;
        exit(2);
    }
    END_CATCH

cout << "Read and set up form..." << endl;

    FormView view(inv);
    EventHandler events(view);

    events.start();
}
```

Building FORMFILL

Because of the large number of header files and source modules used in the FORMFILL program, the Visual Workbench's projects are an ideal way to build this program.

Again, like the other parts of this application, load the project, and select Visual Workbench's Rebuild All toolbar button.

You can test FORMFILL with the INVOICE.DEF and INVOICE.DAT files that you created earlier. To try it, enter the following at the MS-DOS prompt:

```
formfill invoice.dat
```

The resulting screen should be the one shown in Figure 17.1. To exit the program, press either Esc, Ctrl-X, or Ctrl-Q. You can move the cursor from field to field by pressing the Tab key. After you enter data into the form, you can save it by pressing Ctrl-S, or you can save it in a new file by pressing Ctrl-A. The program prompts you for a filename when you press Ctrl-A.

Summary

This chapter develops and implements a Forms software package for creating, filling in, and storing forms. The focus is on creating the classes that are the basis of the Forms software. Each form is thought of as a collection of background graphics objects and fields. The `Form` class uses two double-linked lists, derived from the Microsoft Foundation Class `CObList`, to maintain the background objects and the fields. Each field, modeled by the `Field` class, is capable of holding a single line of data. A `CString` object in the `Field` stores the line of data for that field. To keep the design simple, forms are drawn on the screen using the extended line drawing characters available on MS-DOS PCs.

A major strength of the design is its facility for storing forms in a file and retrieving them later. A form's storage is divided into two files: one for the form's definition and the other for the data filled in by the user. Each file contains a well-defined header identifying whether a file has a form's definitions or the completed data. The Microsoft Foundation Class library's serialization capability is used to store the components of a form in a file and to retrieve the components later.

18

Using AppWizard to Create C++ Windows Applications

Microsoft Windows, *Windows* for short, is the most popular graphical operating environment for the MS-DOS operating system. Applications written for Windows always run, and have access to, the graphics screen. In addition, applications written for DOS can run under Windows. However, they run in exactly the same manner as they did under DOS, and don't have Windows to help with their graphics output.

When using Windows, you can do the following:

- Run multiple applications at once (using non-preemptive multitasking).
- Cut and paste information (including text, graphics, and more advanced items, such as cells in a spreadsheet) from one Windows application to another.

- Maintain a consistent user interface and appearance with various Windows applications. There is little risk of legal problems arising from 'look and feel.' In fact, both Microsoft and IBM recommend following a set of standards often referred to as the *Common User Access* (CUA) standards.

Windows offers a rich and full set of functions to allow programmers to interface with the computer's hardware. One of the most important aspects of Windows is that it allows the programmer to deal with a single, defined output device. This single output then is mapped to the actual output device (which could be a screen, printer, or even a pen plotter) by Windows. In addition, the programmer has a set of predefined input routines to isolate the application from the actual input hardware. For example, under Windows all mice look the same—while an individual device may be a mouse, a track-ball, or even a graphics tablet.

By isolating the application (and the programmer) from the computer's hardware, Windows enables you to concentrate on the program's functionality and not how it will interface with the hardware. With Windows, gone are the days when, if you wrote graphics software, you had to develop (or purchase) drivers for many different printers, video screens, and other I/O devices.

Unlike DOS, Windows runs in the protected mode. Under DOS your application is restricted to the memory that remains after loading DOS, device drivers, and TSR programs. Often this memory is less than 500 kilobytes. Using the protected mode of the processor, it is possible for Windows applications to use many megabytes of memory. It's not uncommon for Windows to have 5 to 10 megabytes of memory free, with some larger systems perhaps having several times that much memory free.

Because Windows runs in the protected mode, your applications will have memory protection available to them. This means that one errant application should not be able to "trash," or modify, the memory another program is using. In reality, this memory protection is not as extensive as it could be in Windows 3.x; there are some ways that one program can interfere with another program's storage. Later versions of Windows will offer much better memory protection.

There's a price to be paid for the flexibility and power that Windows offers. When Windows was first introduced, it took a competent C programmer about six months to be able to produce the basic shell Windows application (nothing fancy, mind you). With Windows 2.x, which ran only in real mode, you couldn't even compile your application while running Windows—you had to either use two computers (using a network or *sneaker-net*) or you had to shut down Windows to run the C compiler and linker. With Windows 3.x (and it's protected mode of operation) and the Microsoft

C compilers C6 and C7, you could run the compiler under Windows in a DOS window. This was a big step forward—most smaller developers just couldn't afford to have two computers that were networked, and shutting down Windows to compile and link really wasn't a feasible way of doing things—it just took too long to complete the modification, compile, link, and test cycle.

With Microsoft C/C++ Version 7.0, you still had to use a DOS box to run the development environment. This was C7's biggest flaw— it had no Windows-based development environment. To help alleviate this shortcoming, Microsoft introduced QuickC for Windows. QuickC for Windows was Microsoft's first Windows-based Integrated Development Environment (IDE). The introduction of Microsoft Visual C++, which is the successor to QuickC for Windows and C7, was a direct result of combining QuickC for Windows and C7.

With Visual C++ you now have a method of developing software under Windows. An important part of Visual C++ is a somewhat CASE-like system called AppWizard. With AppWizard, you can create the shell for a Windows application by simply selecting a few simple options. Although AppWizard isn't a true *Computer Aided Software Engineering* (CASE) system, it does save the programmer substantial development time when compared to what a programmer must do to develop an application from scratch.

Unlike a true CASE product, AppWizard doesn't allow you to do much more than create the initial application shell. With AppStudio, you can make some additions to the applications shell. However, these two products don't comprise a true CASE system.

Starting AppWizard

AppWizard is started from Visual C++'s menu, using the first selection under the Project menu. To start AppWizard, simply select it with a double-click of the left mouse button.

The first thing that you see when you start AppWizard is an initial dialog box. This dialog box, shown in Figure 18.1, enables you to select the project's name (also used as the project's directory name) and the creation options for the project. You also can set the names for many of the project's source files (those used for the definition of classes) from this dialog.

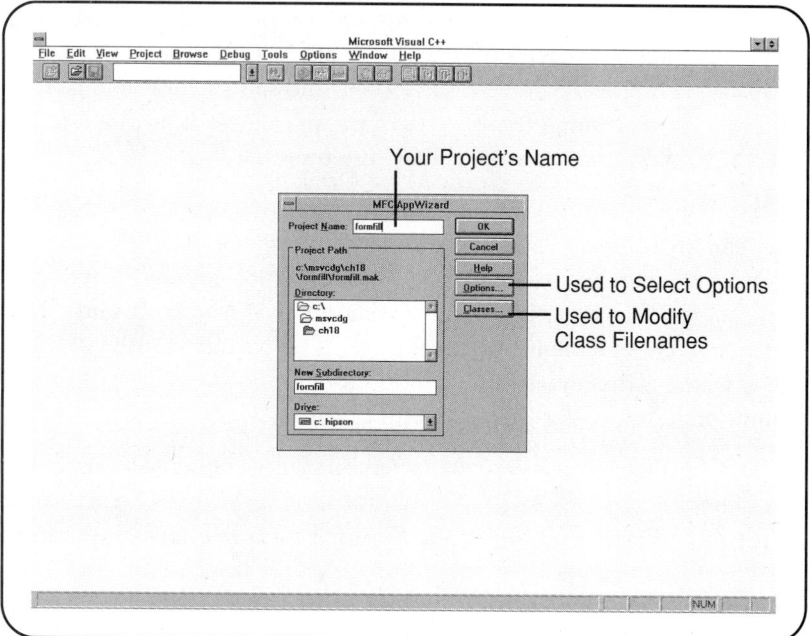

Figure 18.1. AppWizard's Initial Dialog Box.

The minimum necessary to create an application using AppWizard is to provide a (new, and unique) name for the project. Then, if the project's default options and attributes are acceptable, select OK. The project will be created for you.

For most projects, you'll need to change some of the attributes of the application. With AppWizard, these options are easy to select, and allow for the creation of applications with a strong user interface.

Setting Options for the Application

When you select the Options button in AppWizard's main dialog, you are presented with a second dialog box that enables you to customize the appearance of the application's user interface.

There are a total of eight options (see Figure 18.2, AppWizard's Options Dialog) available from which to select.

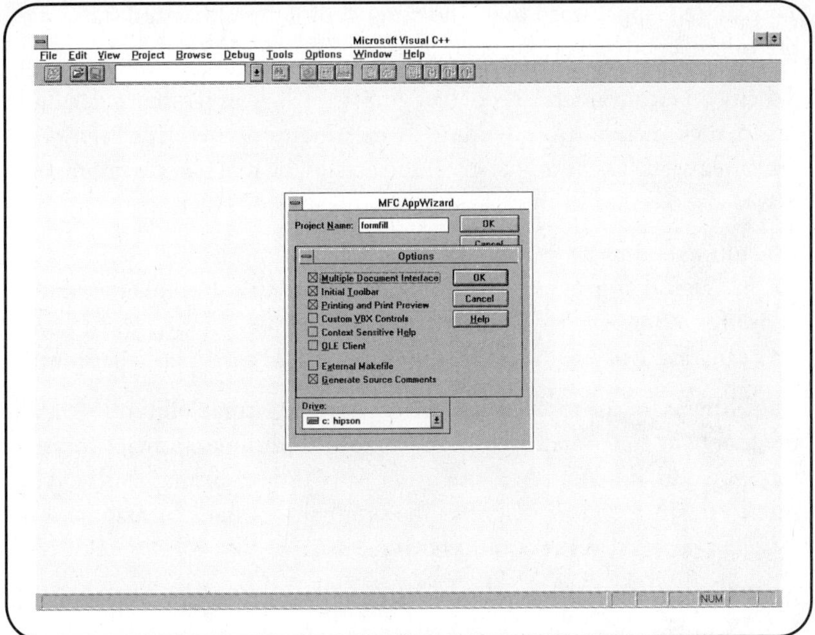

Figure 18.2 AppWizard's Options Dialog Box.

To better show the effects of selecting these options, let's take a quick look at each of them, in order.

Multiple Document Interface

A *Multiple Document Interface* (MDI) is a Windows application that can have more than one file (or document) open at a time. An example of an MDI application is the Visual Workbench. The Windows File Manager and Program Manager also are MDI applications.

If you select the Multiple Document Interface option, your application will have the necessary code to support the Windows MDI interface. If you don't select this option, the Windows' *Single Document Interface* (SDI) support is used instead. The default is to make the application an MDI program.

Initial Toolbar

If you look at the top of the Visual Workbench's main window, just below the menu, you'll see a *tool bar*. At the bottom of the main window is a *status bar*.

You can tell AppWizard to include support for a tool bar and status bar by selecting the Initial Toolbar option.

When you create a default tool bar, AppWizard gives it a set of default buttons. You can change these buttons, adding or deleting as desired. It's even possible to place other items, such as a dropdown combo box, in the tool bar. (An example of a *dropdown combo box* is found in the Visual Workbench's tool bar.)

The ultimate tool bar is one that allows the user to configure it to their desires and needs. One such program that has a fully user-customizable tool bar is Microsoft's Word for Windows. Its tool bar is fully configurable (and can be saved) so that the user can have whatever tools are useful or desired for a particular purpose.

The bitmaps for the tool bar are saved in a single bitmap object. If you want to extend the tool bar's functionality, you must create additional bitmaps for each of the buttons you add. This can be done using AppStudio's bitmap editor. You must make sure to retain the same height as the original tool bar's bitmap, and that each tool bitmap is as wide as the current button bitmaps.

AppWizard provides the code necessary to process the default tool bar buttons; you must write the code to process whatever custom controls you add to the tool bar. Often this can be as simple as having a button perform the same function as a menu item. Of course, you also could have a button that doesn't have a menu item equivalent. However, you may want to avoid duplicating functionality that's available from somewhere other than the toolbar, because it will be difficult to select the tool without using a pointing device, such as a mouse. This might make users unhappy if they're intent on using just the keyboard.

The status bar, found at the bottom of the window, displays information for the user about the status of the system and the program. In the default status bar you see a message area (showing simple help about currently selected menu items) and the status of the Caps Lock, Num Lock, and Scroll Lock keys. Each message area is called a *pane* (much like a pane of glass in a window).

You can, with a little work, add additional panes to the status bar. However, you must add code to update the pane whenever the state of whatever the pane is showing changes. As an example, a possible addition to the status bar could be a pane showing the state of the Insert key.

Printing and Print Preview

Every application (well, *almost* every application) must print hard copies of documents. There are a few exceptions—a program that plays music CDs on the CD drive, for example, or the clock program—but, generally, a program will print out things.

The idea behind Windows is that Windows applications are WYSIWYG: **W**hat **Y**ou **S**ee **I**s **W**hat **Y**ou **G**et. Well, it's not a perfect world. Few of us have screens of sufficient resolution to display a full page of printer output exactly as it's going to be on the printed page. Looking at the page by scrolling often is not satisfactory, because you may want to see the entire page's layout at one time. The solution is to show the printed page as it would look on the printout, but in a smaller (and usually unreadable) format with less resolution. This is called Print Preview.

Creating a program that has Print Preview, with the necessary code to support printing, is difficult by hand. Using AppWizard, it's possible to include both of these features by selecting a single option from AppWizard's Options Dialog box.

Custom VBX Controls

With the introduction of Microsoft Visual Basic, Microsoft created a methodology for developing and interfacing with *custom controls*. These custom controls are referred to as Visual Basic Controls or VBX controls. Generally, Visual C++ supports all features of the Visual Basic version 1.0 API. Unfortunately, Visual Basic version 2.0 API is not supported with the single exception of the `VBGetVersion()` call.

Generally, if the creator of a VBX control has followed the rules and not relied on undocumented features of Visual Basic, the control should work without problems in a Visual C++ program.

Context Sensitive Help

Your application can provide three levels of help to the users:

- *No help at all.* Perhaps very simple applications (such as Windows Clock program) have no need for help. Their operation is self-evident: no matter what the user does, either no data can be lost or, perhaps, the program simply has no options.
- *Limited help.* When help is selected by the user, the help index and search are presented. This is the most common help implementation found in existing applications. The main limitation is that the user must search for the topic or operation on which more information is needed.
- *Context sensitive help.* This mode allows the user to get help about the current operation or selection without doing a separate search. This is accomplished by calling the Windows help engine with the topic already defined.

With AppWizard you can create your application's shell, and then hook the necessary calls into the Windows help engine automatically. In addition, AppWizard both creates shell help files and the control files necessary for the help compiler to create the final .HLP files.

All source help files are in *Rich Text format* (RTF). These files can be edited with a number of advanced word processors, including Microsoft Word for Windows. When modifying source help files, be sure to save them in RTF format.

Help files are saved in a separate subdirectory, called HLP. The control (a batch) file to create the help file is in the main project directory, and is called MAKEHELP.BAT. Unfortunately, the help compiler runs under DOS and is not yet a Windows application—and therefore must be run in a DOS window.

OLE Client

Your application can support Object Linking and Embedding client documents. This support allows your application to include items that are provided by OLE servers. AppWizard doesn't provide support for OLE servers. To create an OLE server you must write the complete application yourself.

External Makefile

This option tells AppWizard to create a make file that's usable with NMAKE directly. Unlike Visual Workbench make files, this file is editable. (You should never edit or hand-modify a Visual Workbench make file.) However, when this file is used with Visual Workbench it's necessary to specify that it is an external make file.

Generally, you wouldn't select this option because applications created with AppWizard are developed with Visual Workbench and AppStudio.

Generate Source Comments

This option tells AppWizard to include comments that show you where you must add functionality to your application. These comments take the format of

```
//////////////////////////////////////////////////////////////////////////
////
// CFormfillView drawing

void CFormfillView::OnDraw(CDC* pDC)
{
    CFormfillDoc* pDoc = GetDocument();
```

```
    // TODO: add draw code here
}
```

In this example, the comment line (in bold type) tells you where to add code to draw your document. The `OnDraw()` function is called as part of the processing of the Windows `WM_PAINT` message.

Classes Created

When AppWizard runs, it creates four classes for your application. These classes are shown in Table 18.1. After these four classes are created, you can add to them as necessary to complete your application's functionality.

Three of the four created classes have names based on the application's name. The application's name is represented by `????`. The first class always has the same name, `CMainApp`.

Table 18.1. Classes Created by AppWizard for an MDI application.

Created Class	Based On	Description or function
`CMainApp`	`CMDIFrameWnd`	This class provides the necessary support for an MDI-type document window. If you've created an SDI-type application, this class would have been derived from the `CFrameWnd` class.
`C????App`	`CWinApp`	This class provides support both for initializing the application under Windows and running the application.
`C????Doc`	`CDocument`	This class provides the support for user-defined document classes. Typically, a document is what will actually be written in a file when a document is saved.
`C????View`	`CView`	The view is the part of the user's document being displayed, printed, or modified.

You can, if you wish, edit the names of the classes and their attributes. Using the Classes Dialog box (shown in Figure 18.3), you can see, and modify, each of the classes.

The most common change made to the classes created by AppWizard is to add a default file extension for files when the open and saveas file dialog boxes are presented to the user. This is done in the File Extension edit box presented when the main document class (CFormfilDoc) is edited.

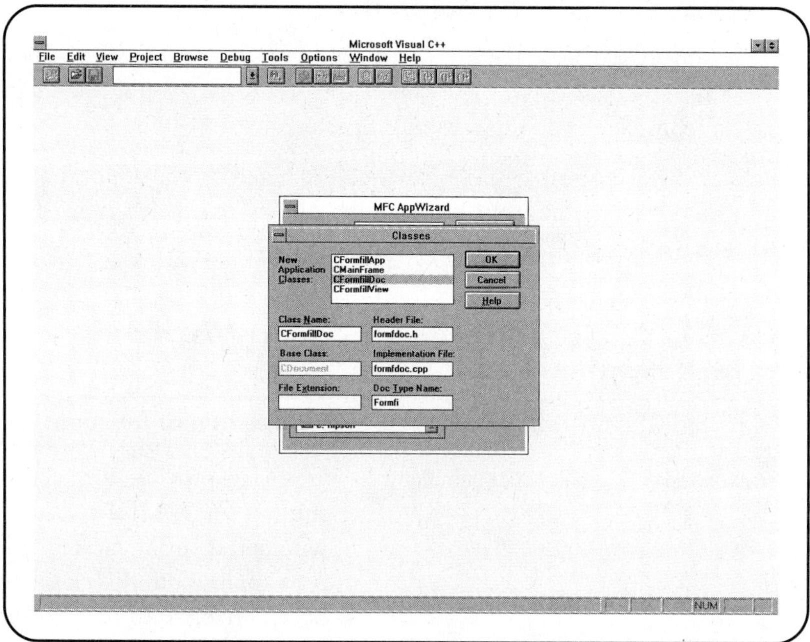

Figure 18.3. AppWizard's Classes Dialog box.

Each of the four classes is saved in separate source and header files, as discussed here.

What AppWizard Creates

Figure 18.4 shows the final dialog box presented by AppWizard. This dialog box shows the application's parameters and the names of main application files that AppWizard will create for the program.

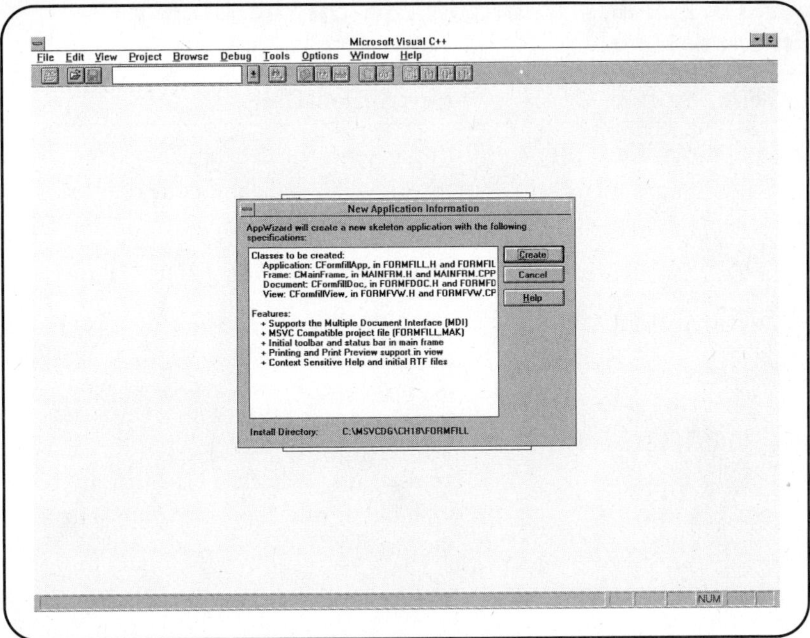

Figure 18.4. AppWizard's New Application Information Dialog box.

AppWizard makes a new directory for the project you're creating. It then places the project's files in the directory.

Other Directories Created

AppWizard also creates several subdirectories in the project's main (or *root*) directory. One subdirectory, created in a subdirectory named RES, is for the project's resources. If you've selected to have Context Sensitive Help included in your project, a subdirectory called HLP will be created for the help files.

The Main Application Directory

Table 18.2 gives descriptions of the files found in the main application directory. For the FormFill program we're creating with AppWizard, I'll describe (briefly) each of the files that are created automatically by AppWizard.

Table 18.2. Files found in the application's main directory.

File	Description/Usage
FORMFDOC.CPP	Implements the `CFormfillDoc` class. You'll add construction code and code that loads the class when a file is opened.
FORMFDOC.H	Header file for FORMFDOC.CPP
FORMFILL.CLW	The ClassWizard control file. This file contains information that ClassWizard uses to maintain the classes.
FORMFILL.CPP	This C++ source file defines the behavior of the application's classes. The source in this file covers such circumstances as program startup and shutdown.
FORMFILL.DEF	The linker definition file. This file defines the executable file's parameters, such as stack size, program executable type (such as Windows 3.0 executable, Windows 3.1 executable, or DLL), name, and description.
FORMFILL.H	The main application's header file.
FORMFILL.HPJ	This file is used by the help compiler to create the Windows help files for the application.
FORMFILL.MAK	The Visual Workbench's control file. This file is much like an NMAKE control file, but has much more in it.
FORMFILL.RC	The main resource file for the application. This file contains information for resources not found in this file.
FORMFVW.CPP	Define and implement the `CFormfillView` class, including the constructor and destructor.
FORMFVW.H	Header file for FORMFVW.CPP.

File	Description/Usage
MAINFRM.CPP	Define and implement the `CMainFrame` class, including constructor and destructor. This file defines things such as the tool bar and status bar contents and status.
MAINFRM.H	Header file for MAINFRM.CPP
MAKEHELP.BAT	The batch file used to create the application's help files. This file contains the code that invokes the help compiler passing the FORMFILL.HPJ to the help compiler.
README.TXT	A file that contains basic instructions to you, the programmer, in how to create your application. This file also tells you what each of the other files is used for.
RESOURCE.H	The header file for the application's resources.
STDAFX.CPP	Used to create the precompiled header for the standard includes.
STDAFX.H	Header file for STDAFX.CPP.

The files listed in Table 18.2 are only the ones created by AppWizard. When Visual C++ compiles and builds the project, it creates a number of additional files. These additional files include symbol files, control files, compiler output object files, linker map files, and executable files.

The Help Directory

Table 18.3 gives descriptions of the files found in the main application HLP directory. These files are part of the (context sensitive) help system created by AppWizard. If you haven't chosen to have the context sensitive help system installed, these files won't be part of your project. Unless your application is extremely simple and your uses will never need help (of course, "never" *never* happens), try to include at least a minimum level of help support. The Windows help engine is an effective way to add help to an application, but to create help files you must have an editor that will work with Rich Text Format (RTF) files. The context sensitive help system built into a project created with AppWizard is just the thing to make your new Windows application look really slick.

Table 18.3. Files found in the application's HLP directory.

File	Description/Usage
AFXCORE.RTF	The core help file. This file is standardized and must be modified to your application's actual operation and needs.
AFXPRINT.RTF	Specific help text for printing.
APPEXIT.BMP	A bitmap representation of how to use the system menu box to exit a program.
BULLET.BMP	Bitmap of a bullet character.
CURARW2.BMP	Double-sided arrow.
CURARW4.BMP	Four-headed arrow.
CURHELP.BMP	The context sensitive help tool bar button.
EDITCOPY.BMP	The Edit Copy tool bar button.
EDITCUT.BMP	The Edit Cut tool bar button.
EDITPAST.BMP	The Edit Paste tool bar button.
EDITUNDO.BMP	The Edit Undo tool bar button.
FILENEW.BMP	The File New tool bar button.
FILEOPEN.BMP	The File Open tool bar button.
FILEPRNT.BMP	The File Print tool bar button.
FILESAVE.BMP	The File Save tool bar button.
HLPSBAR.BMP	The picture of the application's status bar.
HLPTBAR.BMP	The picture of part of the application's tool bar.
SCMAX.BMP	The maximize button.
SCMENU.BMP	The system menu button.
SCMIN.BMP	The minimize button.

Each of the files used by the help compiler to create the help file may be modified as appropriate. Remember: When changing a .BMP file, you must change the application's .BMP file to match. Usually, the .BMP files used in the help system are of greater resolution than the ones the application uses. One suggestion is to first develop the application's bitmap files, then stretch them and add more detail for the help file versions.

The Resources Directory

The final directory, called RES, holds some miscellaneous resources created by AppWizard. Included in this directory are the files described in Table 18.4.

Table 18.4. Files found in the application's RES directory.

File	Description/Usage
FORMFDOC.ICO	Icon for the application's (MDI) document window when the document window is iconized. Customize these as desired.
FORMFILL.ICO	Icon for the application when it is iconized.
FORMFILL.RC2	Special resources that AppStudio won't directly manipulate have the extension of .RC2. Use the Visual Workbench's editor to change this file. Make changes to the `VERSIONINFO` block to indicate your application's information.
TOOLBAR.BMP	The main tool bar's bitmap. If you add new tools to (or remove tools from) the toolbar, you must make the necessary changes to the bitmap representation in this file.

In all, AppWizard creates almost five megabytes of files for you. The tradeoff is that you spend few minutes running AppWizard and save all the time and effort it would take to do the initial shell application development by hand.

Using a Form Document Template

With a Windows application your document can be presented either:

- As an *edit-view* based document. Think of this as a WYSIWYG view, where the document's formatting usually is defined by information contained within the document.

- As a form-based document. In this view, the document's data is formatted and displayed based on a format defined outside of the document.

Each of these is discussed in this section.

Edit-View Based Document Applications

Most Windows applications are edit-view based. A classic example is the Windows applet, Write. With Write, files are loaded, edited, and saved, with the format of the document's data defined in the .WRI file itself.

Any application that displays documents in WYSIWYG format is considered to be an edit-view based document application.

Form-Based Document Applications

Some Windows applications are form-based. A *form* usually is used when specific data, probably in a specific format, is needed from the user. Accounting programs, database systems, and information managers all are form-based document applications.

This chapter's program (based on the FormFill program from Chapter 17, "Building MS-DOS Applications in C++") is a classic example of a form-based application. The program from Chapter 17 is a DOS application, character-based, and uses the PC's line-drawing characters to create the actual input forms.

Unlike with a DOS application, when creating a Windows form-based document application, it isn't necessary to draw the forms, lines, or other text. All the form's layout and boilerplate information is stored in a standard dialog box template, which the `CFormView` class then uses to do the actual screen updating.

Most of the difficult work is in creating this dialog box. Because you only have to lay the form out—not writing a single line of code to draw it—this task isn't that difficult. We'll cover the actual technique of creating a form's dialog box template next, together with a process you can use to help convert an application from the DOS environment to a Windows application.

It's important to note that many (probably most) DOS applications can't easily be converted to Windows applications. In most cases, applications written in C don't convert very well—they're usually so overloaded with necessary housekeeping tasks that it's difficult to get at the underlying application code. With C++ applications, you may well have a better chance at converting the application to a Windows application. Most C++ applications are better written, with better separation between housekeeping code and the underlying application code.

Regardless of whether the application is written in C or C++, it's often more efficient simply to rewrite the application to take advantage of Windows features, rather than trying to bend an existing application's code to fit within the framework and standards Windows uses.

Creating FormFill's Template

We'll create our Windows version of FormFill to look and feel as much like the DOS version as possible—while making sure we don't stray far from what a typical Windows application looks and feels like. Many conversions from DOS are difficult for experienced Windows users because they retain so much of their old DOS user interface. When in doubt, follow the Windows standards, and try to eliminate those parts of your user interface that are nonstandard.

To Kludge, or Not to Kludge?

Keeping an old, nonstandard interface to make it easy for existing users to convert to Windows often is a mistake—regardless of your application, existing users are going to learn how to use Windows. In addition, a nonstandard interface is a definite turnoff to more-experienced users, who won't want to learn how to use your nonstandard Windows application.

I realize there may be demands to keep the user interface as much the same between an existing DOS application and it's new Windows version as possible. In my opinion, however, it can be extremely shortsighted to cripple a Windows application by forcing it to use some of the same kludges we've had to develop for our DOS software.

Form-based document applications aren't limited to a single form—you can have as many different forms in a single application as you want. In the case of FormFill, we have two similar forms: an order form and an invoice form. In this section we actually create the invoice form. Later in this chapter we'll cover the steps to add the order form to the program.

Microsoft has provided an example form-based document application for you to use, called CHKBOOK. This example program is found in the Visual C++ directory \MSVC\MFC\SAMPLES\CHKBOOK. If you're having problems following the material presented in this chapter, you can take a look at the CHKBOOK program. Though there is little explanation of how CHKBOOK was developed, it still serves as an excellent example of a program that uses two form documents.

Let's get started. First, you need a new program created with AppWizard.

1. Start Visual C++ and select AppWizard from the Project menu.
2. Name your project. For this chapter, I've called the program FormFill. However, any name will do as well. Choose a name that does not exist either as a directory or as a file without an extension in the directory in which the application will be located. You can use the Project Path box to select the base directory where the project will be created.
3. Select the project's options. For this example, select Context Sensitive Help to tell AppWizard to include help file support. None of the other options need be de-selected for this project. Select OK from the Options dialog box.
4. Select OK from the MFC AppWizard dialog box. You're shown the New Application Information Dialog box, which shows the parameters that have been used to create the application. If the lines in this dialog box are longer than will fit in the box, you can scroll to the right to see the end of the lines.
5. Select Create from the New Application Information Dialog box. The files are created, and the project loaded into the Visual Workbench.
6. You can test the initial application by building it. (Yes, without any changes by you, you can compile and run the application that you just created.) If you have only limited experience creating Windows applications with Visual C++, I'd suggest going ahead with the building of this program—building takes only a very short time.

Once you've built the application, try it out. Notice how you get the MDI interface; the ability to open, save, and close documents; the tool and status bars; and contextual help.

You now can complete the application's functionality. Don't forget to build the help system's files. Use MAKEHELP.BAT in a DOS window to build the initial help files. The application we've created is shown in Figure 18.5. This shows how the MDI interface is initially set up and shows the tool bar and status bar.

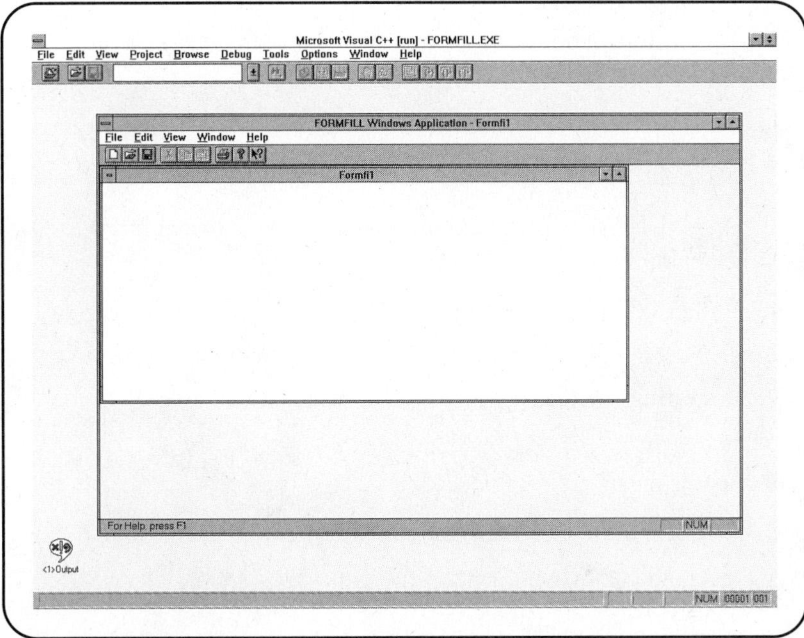

Figure 18.5. FormFill, just as AppWizard creates it.

If, for some reason, the application doesn't compile and link correctly, re-run AppWizard and determine what the problem is. One possible reason AppWizard might fail is insufficient free disk space, which you could check using the File Manager.

Creating the Form's Layout

Once the application's shell has been created, it's necessary to create the form's layout as it will be presented to the user whenever the document's data is to be edited or is displayed. This form should look similar to the invoice form found in the FormFill application in Chapter 17.

Using Application Frameworks, the easiest way to create a form document application is to use the `CFormView` class. This class takes care of the details of drawing the form in the window, filling in the form's blanks, and reading data from the filled in form. This section takes you through the steps required to create and use the CFormView class.

Create a dialog box to be used as the template for the form. For more advanced applications, you can dynamically create the dialog box template at runtime, but for this application we'll use AppStudio's dialog box editor.

Now, a few things about a form-view dialog box are special. You must create the dialog box with the following attributes:

1. Using the Style box, select the WS_CHILD style.
2. Using the Border box, select no border (The WS_BORDER style is set off).
3. Using the Visible box, turn off the visible attribute. (I know this doesn't make sense, but we have to do it this way.)
4. Using the Title bar box, turn off the title. If you selected the WS_BORDER correctly, the title should already be turned off.

When creating the dialog box, make a note of the dialog box's identifier. You can either:

- Accept the default provided.
- Provide a more informative name if desired.

The dialog box I created for the form is shown in Figure 18.6.

In the dialog box shown in Figure 18.6, there are three types of objects:

- First, we have static text, giving our company name (LNB Software, Inc.), address, and some miscellaneous title information.
- We've also added some lines and boxes (using simple rectangle dialog box controls).
- We've added 36 edit controls that will be used to accept input from the user:

  The first few edit controls (IDC_EDIT1 through IDC_EDIT4) are for the customer's name and address.

  We use IDC_EDIT5 for the invoice number (normally given by the program, but possibly it could be used to search for a specific invoice), and IDC_EDIT6 for the invoice's date (supplied by the user, or generated by the program when the invoice is created).

  Edit controls IDC_EDIT7 through IDC_EDIT11 are used to enter the number of an item that has been ordered (the number of units the customer really wants).

With `IDC_EDIT12` through `IDC_EDIT16`, we enter the actual quantity shipped for each of the items. Because we may have limited stock the number shipped may be fewer than ordered.

In `IDC_EDIT17` through `IDC_EDIT21` we enter the item's inventory number and description, while in `IDC_EDIT22` through `IDC_EDIT26` we put the item's price. In a real inventory system the price probably would be looked up in a table or database. However, in our simple program we ask the user to supply this information.

A description of how an item is priced and packaged (using words such as EACH, DOZEN, BOX, and so on) will be entered in the edit controls `IDC_EDIT27` through `IDC_EDIT31`.

The final fields, `IDC_EDIT32` through `IDC_EDIT36`, will display the amount for each item for which the customer will be billed. Because this field is computed (the number shipped times the price), we've made these fields read-only.

When the dialog box has been created, save the resource file. You now must add the necessary code to make the application use the dialog box template.

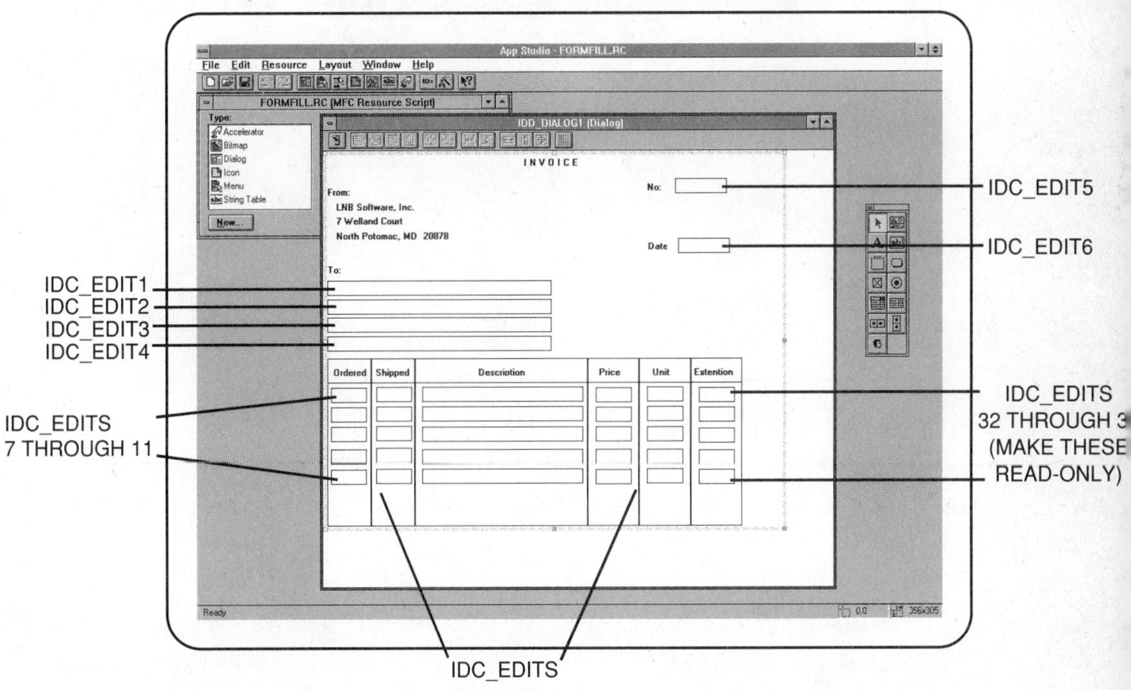

Figure 18.6. FormFill's form dialog box.

Creating the View Class

Once the dialog box template has been created, it's necessary to create a new form-view class. Use Class Wizard to create the new class. With this new class you'll have a method by which to access the invoice document's data, or fill in new data for a document, in a display window.

Select Class Wizard from the Visual Workbench's Browse menu. From the Class Wizard main dialog box, select Add Class. You'll be presented with the Add Class Dialog box, shown in Figure 18.7.

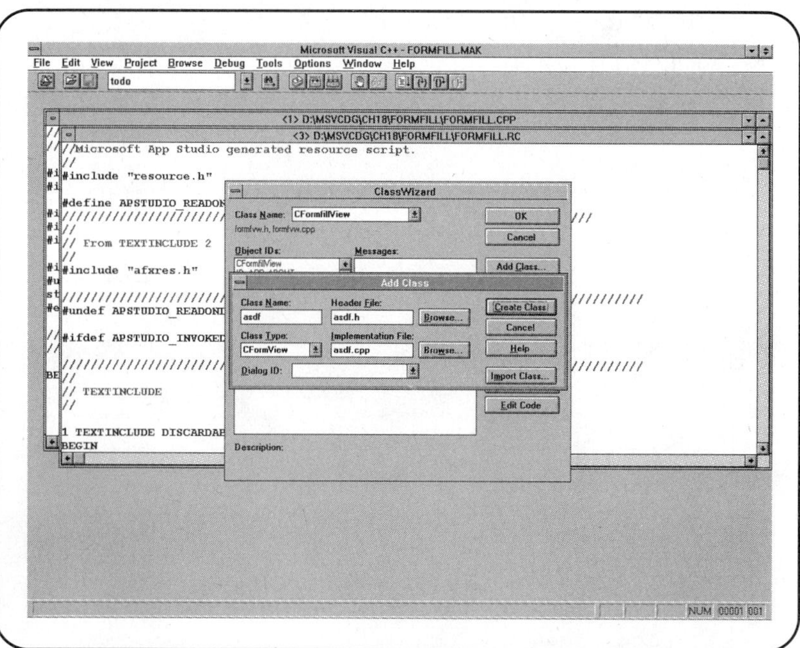

Figure 18.7. Class Wizard's Add Class dialog box.

First, you should name the new class. For our program, we'll use the name `CFrmFil`. Accept the default filenames (unless you *really* don't like them), because it will be easier to use the default names. Make sure you specify that your new class is to be based on the `CFormView` class (using the Class Type edit box).

In the Dialog ID edit box, enter the identifier for the dialog box that you've created for this form (which you noted when you created the dialog box).

The Form's Variables

You'll need several variables for each invoice. When using Class Wizard, each of these variables is logically linked to one of the dialog box's edit controls.

First, select the Edit Variables from the Class Wizard's main dialog box. You're presented with the Edit Member Variables Dialog box. The most important part of this dialog box is the Control ID list box. This list box shows each of the dialog box controls created when you designed the dialog box document template.

The easiest way to add a variable is to select a control from the Control ID list box, then select the Add Variables button in the Edit Member Variables Dialog box. This will cause the Add Member Variable Dialog box to be displayed, as shown in Figure 18.8.

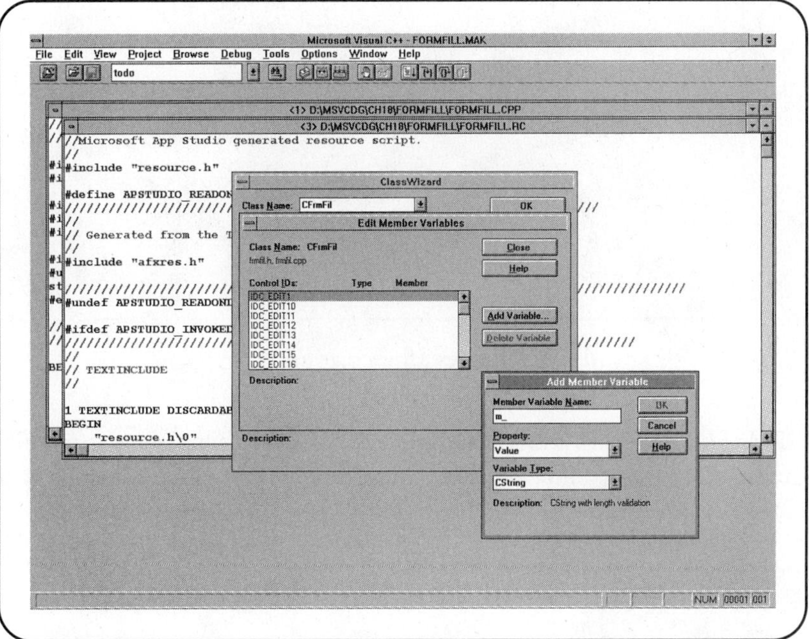

Figure 18.8. Adding variables using Class Wizard.

Assigning Computed Fields

Using the process outlined above, create a variable for each of the dialog box's edit fields with the exception of the total cost fields, as shown in Figure 18.9. The total cost fields will be computed, rather than being saved in the invoice file.

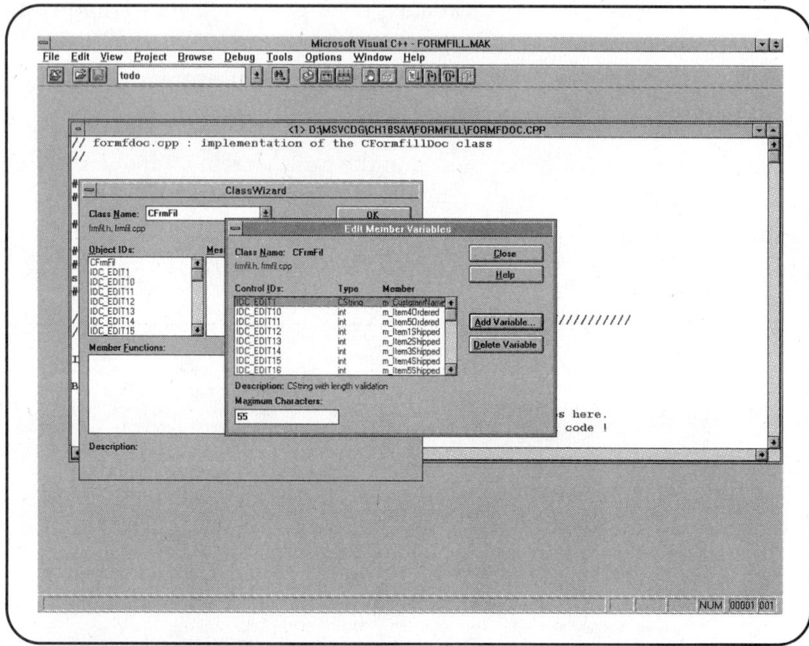

Figure 18.9. FormFill's variables after creation.

The class is saved in the source file FRMFIL.CPP. This file, shown in Listing 18.1, must be slightly modified by hand. In Listing 18.1, the lines added by hand are shown in bold. In addition to the added lines (which show the computed item totals), the file also has been modified to initialize the variables to logical initial values.

Listing 18.1. FRMFIL.CPP—The `CFrmFil` class source file.

```
// frmfil.cpp : implementation file
//

#include "stdafx.h"
#include "formfill.h"
#include "frmfil.h"
```

```
#ifdef _DEBUG
#undef THIS_FILE
static char BASED_CODE THIS_FILE[] = __FILE__;
#endif

///////////////////////////////////////////////////////////////////////////
////
// CFrmFil

IMPLEMENT_DYNCREATE(CFrmFil, CFormView)

CFrmFil::CFrmFil()
    : CFormView(CFrmFil::IDD)
{// Use initializers to ensure that all variables contain reasonable
values.
    //{{AFX_DATA_INIT(CFrmFil)
    m_CustomerName = "";
    m_CustomerAddr1 = "";
    m_CustomerAddr2 = "";
    m_CustomerCSZ = "";
    m_InvoiceNumber = 0;
    m_InvoiceDate = "03/22/93";
    m_Item1Ordered = 0;
    m_Item2Ordered = 0;
    m_Item3Ordered = 0;
    m_Item4Ordered = 0;
    m_Item5Ordered = 0;
    m_Item1Shipped = 0;
    m_Item2Shipped = 0;
    m_Item3Shipped = 0;
    m_Item4Shipped = 0;
    m_Item5Shipped = 0;
    m_Item1Description = "";
    m_Item2Description = "";
    m_Item3Description = "";
    m_Item4Description = "";
    m_Item5Description = "";
    m_Item1Price = .0;
    m_Item2Price = .0;
    m_Item3Price = .0;
    m_Item4Price = .0;
    m_Item5Price = .0;
```

continues

Listing 18.1. continued

```
    m_Item1Unit = "ea";
    m_Item2Unit = "ea";
    m_Item3Unit = "ea";
    m_Item4Unit = "ea";
    m_Item5Unit = "ea";
    //}}AFX_DATA_INIT
}

CFrmFil::~CFrmFil()
{
}

void CFrmFil::OnUpdate(CView*, LPARAM lHint, CObject* pHint)
{
        // OnUpdate() is called whenever the document has changed and,
        // therefore, the view must redisplay some or all of itself.
        // In other words, when the user selects a different invoice,
        // OnUpdate() would be called to fill in the correct values.

        // You'd get the new record, use GetDocument(), then make
        // the below two calls...

        UpdateData(FALSE);  // Copy the view form object's data to the
                            // controls (via DoDataExchange)

        Invalidate();       // Repaint the entire form view.
}


void CFrmFil::DoDataExchange(CDataExchange* pDX)
{

float    fTempTotal = (float)0.0;

    CFormView::DoDataExchange(pDX);
    //{{AFX_DATA_MAP(CFrmFil)
    DDX_Text(pDX, IDC_EDIT1, m_CustomerName);
    DDV_MaxChars(pDX, m_CustomerName, 55);
    DDX_Text(pDX, IDC_EDIT2, m_CustomerAddr1);
    DDV_MaxChars(pDX, m_CustomerAddr1, 55);
    DDX_Text(pDX, IDC_EDIT3, m_CustomerAddr2);
```

```
DDV_MaxChars(pDX, m_CustomerAddr2, 55);
DDX_Text(pDX, IDC_EDIT4, m_CustomerCSZ);
DDV_MaxChars(pDX, m_CustomerCSZ, 55);
DDX_Text(pDX, IDC_EDIT5, m_InvoiceNumber);
DDV_MinMaxInt(pDX, m_InvoiceNumber, 0, 32000);
DDX_Text(pDX, IDC_EDIT6, m_InvoiceDate);
DDX_Text(pDX, IDC_EDIT7, m_Item1Ordered);
DDV_MinMaxInt(pDX, m_Item1Ordered, 1, 32000);
DDX_Text(pDX, IDC_EDIT8, m_Item2Ordered);
DDV_MinMaxInt(pDX, m_Item2Ordered, 1, 32000);
DDX_Text(pDX, IDC_EDIT9, m_Item3Ordered);
DDV_MinMaxInt(pDX, m_Item3Ordered, 1, 32000);
DDX_Text(pDX, IDC_EDIT10, m_Item4Ordered);
DDV_MinMaxInt(pDX, m_Item4Ordered, 1, 32000);
DDX_Text(pDX, IDC_EDIT11, m_Item5Ordered);
DDV_MinMaxInt(pDX, m_Item5Ordered, 1, 32000);
DDX_Text(pDX, IDC_EDIT12, m_Item1Shipped);
DDV_MinMaxInt(pDX, m_Item1Shipped, 0, 32000);
DDX_Text(pDX, IDC_EDIT13, m_Item2Shipped);
DDV_MinMaxInt(pDX, m_Item2Shipped, 0, 32000);
DDX_Text(pDX, IDC_EDIT14, m_Item3Shipped);
DDV_MinMaxInt(pDX, m_Item3Shipped, 0, 32000);
DDX_Text(pDX, IDC_EDIT15, m_Item4Shipped);
DDV_MinMaxInt(pDX, m_Item4Shipped, 0, 32000);
DDX_Text(pDX, IDC_EDIT16, m_Item5Shipped);
DDV_MinMaxInt(pDX, m_Item5Shipped, 0, 32000);
DDX_Text(pDX, IDC_EDIT17, m_Item1Description);
DDX_Text(pDX, IDC_EDIT18, m_Item2Description);
DDX_Text(pDX, IDC_EDIT19, m_Item3Description);
DDX_Text(pDX, IDC_EDIT20, m_Item4Description);
DDX_Text(pDX, IDC_EDIT21, m_Item5Description);
DDX_Text(pDX, IDC_EDIT22, m_Item1Price);
DDV_MinMaxFloat(pDX, m_Item1Price, 0., 32000.);
DDX_Text(pDX, IDC_EDIT23, m_Item2Price);
DDV_MinMaxFloat(pDX, m_Item2Price, 0., 32000.);
DDX_Text(pDX, IDC_EDIT24, m_Item3Price);
DDV_MinMaxFloat(pDX, m_Item3Price, 0., 32000.);
DDX_Text(pDX, IDC_EDIT25, m_Item4Price);
DDV_MinMaxFloat(pDX, m_Item4Price, 0., 32000.);
DDX_Text(pDX, IDC_EDIT26, m_Item5Price);
DDV_MinMaxFloat(pDX, m_Item5Price, 0., 32000.);
DDX_Text(pDX, IDC_EDIT27, m_Item1Unit);
```

continues

Listing 18.1. continued

```
    DDX_Text(pDX, IDC_EDIT28, m_Item2Unit);
    DDX_Text(pDX, IDC_EDIT29, m_Item3Unit);
    DDX_Text(pDX, IDC_EDIT30, m_Item4Unit);
    DDX_Text(pDX, IDC_EDIT31, m_Item5Unit);
    //}}AFX_DATA_MAP

    fTempTotal = m_Item1Price * m_Item1Shipped;
    DDX_Text(pDX, IDC_EDIT32, fTempTotal);
    fTempTotal = m_Item2Price * m_Item2Shipped;
    DDX_Text(pDX, IDC_EDIT33, fTempTotal);
    fTempTotal = m_Item3Price * m_Item3Shipped;
    DDX_Text(pDX, IDC_EDIT34, fTempTotal);
    fTempTotal = m_Item4Price * m_Item4Shipped;
    DDX_Text(pDX, IDC_EDIT35, fTempTotal);
    fTempTotal = m_Item5Price * m_Item5Shipped;
    DDX_Text(pDX, IDC_EDIT36, fTempTotal);


//    DDX_Text(pDX, IDC_EDIT33, m_Item2Price * m_Item2Shipped);


}

BEGIN_MESSAGE_MAP(CFrmFil, CFormView)
    //{{AFX_MSG_MAP(CFrmFil)
        // NOTE - the ClassWizard will add and remove mapping macros
           here.
    //}}AFX_MSG_MAP
END_MESSAGE_MAP()

/////////////////////////////////////////////////////////////////////////
////
// CFrmFil message handlers
```

As shown in Listing 18.1, the program uses the `DDX_Text()` function to update each of the form's edit controls. Class Wizard adds the necessary 'glue'—the calls to `DDX_Text()`—for each of the variables you added using Class Wizard. One feature of `DDX_Text()` is that it is overloaded, allowing passing of string and numeric information to the function without having to worry whether the data is of the correct format.

For those variables not created with Class Wizard (our item totals), we must add our own calls to `DDX-Text()`. There's one hitch: `DDX_Text()` needs a pointer to a variable, so we are unable to make a call such as

```
DDX_Text(pDX, IDC_EDIT36, m_Item5Price * m_Item5Shipped); // Won't work
```

This call simply generates a compile-time message. Rather, so that we have the address of a variable to pass to `DDX_Text()`, we use a temporary variable. Notice that we've added a definition of a floating point variable, called `fTempTotal`, at the beginning of the `DoDataExchange()` function. This temporary variable is assigned the total price for an item, and then is passed to `DDX_Text()`, which then sets the edit control's text based on the variable, as in

```
fTempTotal = m_Item5Price * m_Item5Shipped;
DDX_Text(pDX, IDC_EDIT36, fTempTotal);
```

These two statements ensure that the item's total price is properly updated. Of course, when it comes time to retrieve the record's contents from the document window, you can simply ignore these fields because you'll be recomputing them whenever they're needed.

Setting Initializers for the Application

Another change I've made to the code generated by Class Wizard is to change the initializers for the variables that have been added to the class. I changed the initializers to make sure that the variables contained valid and logical values that the program then can expect.

One of the nice things about the `cString` class is that the string memory is dynamically allocated each time a (new) value is assigned to the string. This allows us to minimize the amount of storage for things such as the description field. (We don't need to have long, preallocated blocks of memory that may never be used.)

Refer to Listing 18.1 (in the constructor, `CFrmFil::CFrmFil()`) to see how the initialization was done.

Setting Up the Document Template

The final step to using a form document template is to tell the application to use the template—to tell Windows to start using the `CFrmFil` class rather than the

CFormfillView class. In the example shown in Listing 18.2, I've commented out the original AddDocTemplate() call and added a new call.

In the call to AddDocTemplate(), the only thing changed (if you don't see it right away) is the final parameter passed to CMultiDocTemplate(), which is the class for the view class. We simply use our new class rather than the one created by AppWizard (CFormfillView).

Listing 18.2. FORMFILL.CPP. The main source file for FormFill.

```
// formfill.cpp : Defines the class behaviors for the application.
//

#include "stdafx.h"
#include "formfill.h"

#include "mainfrm.h"
#include "formfdoc.h"
#include "formfvw.h"

#include "frmfil.h"

#ifdef _DEBUG
#undef THIS_FILE
static char BASED_CODE THIS_FILE[] = __FILE__;
#endif

///////////////////////////////////////////////////////////////////////////
////
// CFormfillApp

BEGIN_MESSAGE_MAP(CFormfillApp, CWinApp)
    //{{AFX_MSG_MAP(CFormfillApp)
    ON_COMMAND(ID_APP_ABOUT, OnAppAbout)
        // NOTE - the ClassWizard will add and remove mapping macros
           here.
        //    DO NOT EDIT what you see in these blocks of generated code!
    //}}AFX_MSG_MAP
    // Standard file based document commands
    ON_COMMAND(ID_FILE_NEW, CWinApp::OnFileNew)
```

```
    ON_COMMAND(ID_FILE_OPEN, CWinApp::OnFileOpen)
    // Standard print setup command
    ON_COMMAND(ID_FILE_PRINT_SETUP, CWinApp::OnFilePrintSetup)
    // Global help commands
    ON_COMMAND(ID_HELP_INDEX, CWinApp::OnHelpIndex)
    ON_COMMAND(ID_HELP_USING, CWinApp::OnHelpUsing)
    ON_COMMAND(ID_HELP, CWinApp::OnHelp)
    ON_COMMAND(ID_CONTEXT_HELP, CWinApp::OnContextHelp)
    ON_COMMAND(ID_DEFAULT_HELP, CWinApp::OnHelpIndex)
END_MESSAGE_MAP()

////////////////////////////////////////////////////////////////////////////
////
// CFormfillApp construction

CFormfillApp::CFormfillApp()
{
    // TODO: add construction code here,
    // Place all significant initialization in InitInstance
}

////////////////////////////////////////////////////////////////////////////
////
// The one and only CFormfillApp object

CFormfillApp NEAR theApp;

////////////////////////////////////////////////////////////////////////////
////
// CFormfillApp initialization

BOOL CFormfillApp::InitInstance()
{
    // Standard initialization
    // If you are not using these features and wish to reduce the size
    //  of your final executable, you should remove from the following
    //  the specific initialization routines you do not need.

    SetDialogBkColor();        // set dialog background color to gray
    LoadStdProfileSettings();  // Load standard INI file options (includ
                                  ing MRU)
```

continues

Listing 18.2. continued

```
    // Register the application's document templates.  Document templates
    //  serve as the connection between documents, frame windows and
        views.

//    AddDocTemplate(new CMultiDocTemplate(IDR_FORMFITYPE,
//            RUNTIME_CLASS(CFormfillDoc),
//            RUNTIME_CLASS(CMDIChildWnd),        // standard MDI child
                                                     frame
//            RUNTIME_CLASS(CFormfillView)));

    AddDocTemplate(new CMultiDocTemplate(IDR_FORMFITYPE,
            RUNTIME_CLASS(CFormfillDoc),
            RUNTIME_CLASS(CMDIChildWnd),        // standard MDI child
                                                   frame
            RUNTIME_CLASS(CFrmFil)));

    // create main MDI Frame window
    CMainFrame* pMainFrame = new CMainFrame;
    if (!pMainFrame->LoadFrame(IDR_MAINFRAME))
        return FALSE;
    pMainFrame->ShowWindow(m_nCmdShow);
    pMainFrame->UpdateWindow();
    m_pMainWnd = pMainFrame;

    // create a new (empty) document
    OnFileNew();

    if (m_lpCmdLine[0] != '\0')
    {
        // TODO: add command line processing here
    }

    return TRUE;
}

//////////////////////////////////////////////////////////////////////////
////
// CAboutDlg dialog used for App About

class CAboutDlg : public CDialog
{
```

```
public:
    CAboutDlg();

// Dialog Data
    //{{AFX_DATA(CAboutDlg)
    enum { IDD = IDD_ABOUTBOX };
    //}}AFX_DATA

// Implementation
protected:
    virtual void DoDataExchange(CDataExchange* pDX);    // DDX/DDV sup
                                                          port

    //{{AFX_MSG(CAboutDlg)
        // No message handlers
    //}}AFX_MSG
    DECLARE_MESSAGE_MAP()
};

CAboutDlg::CAboutDlg() : CDialog(CAboutDlg::IDD)
{
    //{{AFX_DATA_INIT(CAboutDlg)
    //}}AFX_DATA_INIT
}

void CAboutDlg::DoDataExchange(CDataExchange* pDX)
{
    CDialog::DoDataExchange(pDX);
    //{{AFX_DATA_MAP(CAboutDlg)
    //}}AFX_DATA_MAP
}

BEGIN_MESSAGE_MAP(CAboutDlg, CDialog)
    //{{AFX_MSG_MAP(CAboutDlg)
        // No message handlers
    //}}AFX_MSG_MAP
END_MESSAGE_MAP()

// App command to run the dialog
void CFormfillApp::OnAppAbout()
{
    CAboutDlg aboutDlg;
    aboutDlg.DoModal();
}
```

continues

Listing 18.2. continued

```
///////////////////////////////////////////////////////////////////////////
////
// CFormfillApp commands
```

Overriding Member Functions

It's necessary, when creating your form-view class, to override several of the base class's functions. Some of this overriding is mandatory, while other overrides are optional.

Application Foundation Class objects generally are built (that is, *derived*) one from another. For most cases, an action that is performed for a class can be passed on (*inherited*) by descendant classes. In the case of the form-view classes however, it's necessary to change a few functions.

Overriding the *OnUpdate* member

Listing 18.3 shows the `OnUpdate()` function. This function is called to update the appearance of the form's view, including updating the member variables with the current document's values.

Listing 18.3. The CFrmFil::OnUpdate() function.

```
void CFrmFil::OnUpdate(CView*, LPARAM lHint, CObject* pHint)
{
        // OnUpdate() is called whenever the document has changed and,
        // therefore, the view must redisplay some or all of itself.
        // In other words, when the user selects a different invoice,
        // OnUpdate() would be called to fill in the correct values.

        // You'd get the new record, use GetDocument(), then make
        // the below two calls...

        UpdateData(FALSE);   // Copy the view form object's data to the
                             // controls (via DoDataExchange)
```

```
        Invalidate();         // Repaint the entire form view.
}
```

Notice that the OnUpdate() function calls the DoDataExchange() function (indirectly, as UpdateData() makes the call). These calls are used to do the actual updating of the document's view in the window. The standard MFC OnUpdate() doesn't call UpdateData(), which the form-based document view requires.

To sum up the overriding of the supplied functions, we provide a new OnUpdate() function, which then calls to MFC's UpdateData() function. The MFC UpdateData() function then calls DoDataExchange(), which was created by Class Wizard, and which then does the actual updating of the classes' members.

Overriding Other Members

Generally, Class Wizard will provide the DoDataExchange() function. You provide the OnUpdate() function. There are times however, when three of the other functions that are part of the class also must be overridden. These three other functions are

- OnInitialUpdate()—Called to provide initial, one-time updating of the view.
- UpdateData()—Called by OnUpdate() to update the view's data.
- OnPrint()—Called to print the view. Because CFormView doesn't directly support printing (or Print Preview), you must provide this functionality yourself.

With each of these functions you can add new functionality to your application's implementation of the CFormView class.

Overriding *OnInitialUpdate()*

The OnInitialUpdate() function is called when the view initially is created. In the default function, the OnUpdate() function is called. You could add new functionality here for initial, one-time updating.

The following code fragment shows an implementation of OnInitialUpdate(). This function is based solely on the MFC default handler—if you're not adding to or changing the function operation, you don't need to override it.

```
void CFormView::OnInitialUpdate()
{
```

```
// Make sure that we've got a valid object
        ASSERT_VALID(this);
// Call UpdateData() to update the object's data.
// It'll return FALSE if there are problems.

        if (!UpdateData(FALSE))
                TRACE0("UpdateData failed during formview initial
update\n");
        CScrollView::OnInitialUpdate();
}
```

You need not override the `OnInitialUpdate()` function in FormFill.

Overriding *UpdateData()*

The `UpdateData()` function is supplied using a default MFC function. This function, shown in the following code fragment, basically calls `DoDataExchange()` to update the form's data.

This code fragment shows what the default processing is for a typical `UpdateData()` function. This function, based on the default MFC `UpdateData()` function, calls `DoDataExchange()` with some error-condition catching.

```
BOOL CWnd::UpdateData(BOOL bSaveAndValidate)
{
    CDataExchange dx(this, bSaveAndValidate);

    //prevent control notifications from being dispatched during
      UpdateData
    HWND hWndOldLockout = _afxLockoutNotificationWindow;
    ASSERT(hWndOldLockout != m_hWnd);   // must not recurse
    _afxLockoutNotificationWindow = m_hWnd;

    BOOL bOK = FALSE;       // assume failure
    TRY
    {
            DoDataExchange(&dx);
            bOK = TRUE;         // it worked
    }
    CATCH(CUserException, e)
    {
            // validation failed - user already alerted, fall through
            ASSERT(bOK == FALSE);
    }
```

```
    AND_CATCH_ALL(e)
    {
            // validation failed due to OOM or other resource failure
            AfxMessageBox(AFX_IDP_INTERNAL_FAILURE, MB_ICONSTOP);
            ASSERT(bOK == FALSE);
    }
    END_CATCH_ALL

    _afxLockoutNotificationWindow = hWndOldLockout;
    return bOK;
}
```

Overriding *OnPrint()*

One problem (albeit a small one) is that the `CFormView` class doesn't support printing. The main reason for this limitation is that it isn't possible to print the dialog box controls that are an integral part of a form view.

It's therefore necessary for your program to do its printing using a function to override the default `OnPrint()` function. Generally, except for special circumstances, the hard copy printout of a form document won't appear in exactly the same format as the screen window's.

An example of a hard copy of a form-view form-based document view is a simple accounting program, with checks displayed in a window formatted in an easy-to-use, generic format. The actual printing of a check, however, is based on the real check's appearance—without the need for lines, boxes, and other text used to make the window's representation of the check better.

Providing Multiple Document Templates

We used `AddDocTemplate()` to *register* (that is, to tell Windows) what our document class was. This function is used with the `CMultiDocTemplate()` function, which creates the necessary `CMultiDocTemplate` object. Looking at each of the parameters passed to `CMultiDocTemplate()`, you see how your document view class, the class's names, and so on, are related to each other:

```
CMultiDocTemplate(
    UINT nIDResource,
    CRuntimeClass* pDocClass,
```

```
    CRuntimeClass* pFrameClass,
    CRuntimeClass* pViewClass);
```

The parameters are

- *nIDResource*—Specifies the ID of the resources that describe the document type. These resources can include a menu, an icon, an accelerator table, and string-type resources. The string resource consists of up to seven substrings separated by the `\n` character. (The `\n` character is needed as a place holder if a substring is not included; however, trailing `\n` characters are not necessary.) These substrings describe the document type. For information on the substrings, see `CDocTemplate::GetDocString`. This string resource is found in the application's resource file. For example:

```
// In the file FormFill.RC

STRINGTABLE PRELOAD DISCARDABLE
BEGIN
    IDR_MAINFRAME           "FORMFILL Windows Application"
    IDR_FORMFITYPE
"\nFormfi\nFORMFI Doc\nInvoices (*.inv)\n.inv \n FormFill\nFormFill
Invoices"
END
```

  Because the first substring (the window title) is used only with SDI applications and not with MDI applications, it is not included. You can edit this string using AppStudio's string editor. Because the string is not broken into separate parts, it always appears as a single string, and not as seven separate parts.

- *pDocClass*—Points to the `CFormfillDoc` object. This class is a `CDocument`-derived class, defined by AppWizard to represent your documents.

- *pFrameClass*—Points to the `CMDIChildWnd` object, created by AppWizard. This class can be a `CMDIChildWnd`-derived class, or it can be `CMDIChildWnd` itself if you want default behavior for your document-frame windows (which is what FormFill does).

- *pViewClass*—Points to the `CFrmFil` object, which you created with Class Wizard. This is the class that you created with your dialog box.

In the FormFill program, the call to `AddDocTemplate()` looks like

```
AddDocTemplate(new CMultiDocTemplate(IDR_FORMFITYPE,
```

```
        RUNTIME_CLASS(CFormfillDoc),
        RUNTIME_CLASS(CMDIChildWnd),        // standard MDI child frame
        RUNTIME_CLASS(CFrmFil)));
```

Now suppose that you want to also have an order form as part of the application. The process isn't too difficult.

- Create a second dialog box template.
- Create a second resource string (such as `IDR_FORMFITYPE`).
- Create a new form-view document class (perhaps called `COrderFormView`).

Once you've created the dialog box template, the resource string, and the class, simply add a *second* call to `AddDocTemplate()`. The second call registers a new, second form document class. When the user selects File, New, he or she is presented with a list box from which to select the correct type of document.

Two Views of the Same Document

In the ChkBook program supplied by Microsoft in the MFC sample source files, Microsoft shows how to create two different views of the same data. In one view you see the checks as they're created (looking much like a check). In the second you see a type of ledger book listing for each check.

Of course, with such a simple application, you don't get such nice things as account codes to break down and categorize your expenses, totals, balances, or other information. You could, however, add to the example program to create a simple checkbook program that had some nice features.

Finishing FormFill: The Missing Pieces

At this stage, FormFill isn't finished. For one thing, I've included no linkage between opening a document file and saving the document file's information when the program is done. Also missing is the code to allow you to page between different invoice records in the file.

This section discusses how to include these functions. Neither is that difficult to add.

Adding the File I/O

To read a document file that has been opened by the user, you need only work with the `open` document (`OnOpenDocument`) member. The same is true for the `save/saveas` (`OnSaveDocument`) when the document is to be saved.

Selection of a Given Record

One of the best ways to select a record—and one of the easiest methods to implement—is to add a pair of buttons to the tool bar. These buttons then could be used to get either the next or the previous invoice. Simple error checking is needed to ensure the user doesn't try to move before the first invoice in the file (record number one), or past the last invoice if invoices are created automatically from orders.

Other Bells and Whistles

Some other things that FormFill could use to make it a more complete application are

- The ability to look items up in some form of an inventory database.
- Ability to print an invoice. The ability to use either a preprinted form or create the form on blank paper also would be nice.
- The ability to create order forms (and picking/packing lists).
- A more advanced system would update inventory records, and print reorder lists when stock items fall below critical limits.

And the list goes on... FormFill can be expanded in many, many different ways.

Summary

In this chapter we've used AppWizard to create an MDI Windows application. The base application was created in just a few minutes, and then necessary functionality added in step-by-step logical order.

Applications created using AppWizard are flexible and easy to build upon. They can contain such features as Context Sensitive Help, a tool bar, and a status bar simply by selecting these features from the AppWizard Options Dialog box.

AppWizard is an important tool in getting a Windows application started.

V

Microsoft Foundation Class Library

19

General-Purpose Microsoft Foundation Classes

You may recall from Chapter 16, "Using the Microsoft Foundation Class Library," that the primary purpose of the class library is to provide a framework for building Windows applications. However, Microsoft's class library includes a number of classes, such as `CString` and `CTime`, that are not specific to a Windows application. These *general-purpose classes* are useful in defining new data types. For instance, in Chapter 17, "Building MS-DOS Applications in C++" the Forms package defines classes such as `FileHeader` and `Field`, which use `CString` and `CTime` to represent strings and to store the date and time. `CString` and `CTime` are some of the general-purpose classes in the Microsoft Foundation Class library.

Part V of this book serves as a quick reference guide to the C++ classes that comprise the Microsoft Foundation Class library, version 2.0. This chapter covers the general-purpose classes such as lists, strings, and collections of objects that serve as building blocks for other classes. Chapter 20 describes the classes that serve as an object-oriented interface to the Microsoft Windows programming environment. Both chapters provide tutorial introductions to the classes followed by individual reference entries for each class.

Common Functionality from *CObject*

As you learned in Chapter 16 (see Figures 16.4 and 16.5), most of the classes in the Microsoft Foundation Class library inherit from the `CObject` base class, which you can use for the following activities:

- Identifying an object's type at runtime
- Storing objects in and retrieving them from a file
- Printing diagnostic messages at runtime

All classes derived from `CObject` inherit these capabilities. If you derive a class from `CObject`, your class also can take advantage of `CObject`'s capabilities through inheritance. As you'll see, the Microsoft Foundation Class library provides a number of macros and a step-by-step approach for using these capabilities.

Runtime Class Identification

Runtime class identification enables you to determine an object's type at runtime. For example, consider a hierarchy of classes representing graphics shapes that start with a base class shape, from which you derive classes, such as `circle` and `rectangle`, which represent specific shapes. If you derive the shape class hierarchy from `CObject` and follow a cookbook approach to enable the runtime class identification feature, you can write code like this:

```
    shape *p_s;
// ...

// Assume p_s points to a "shape" object (which
// may be any one of the shapes derived from the
// "shape" class). Assuming the shape class hierarchy
// includes support for "runtime-class identification,"
// here's how you would test the exact type of the shape
// object:

    if(p_s->IsKindOf(RUNTIME_CLASS(circle)))
    {
        // OK to cast base class pointer p_s as a pointer to a "circle."
        circle *p_c = (circle*)p_s;
        // ...
    }
```

The IsKindOf member function returns the TRUE constant if the object is of the class that its argument specifies or if the object derives from the specified class. The argument to the IsKindOf function is specified in terms of the RUNTIME_CLASS macro.

To include support for runtime class identification in a class, follow these steps:

1. Derive the class from CObject.
2. Include the DECLARE_DYNAMIC macro in the class declaration. For example, you would declare the shape and the circle classes as follows:

```
#include <afx.h>

class shape : public CObject
{
    DECLARE_DYNAMIC(shape)
public:
// Other members...
};

class circle: public shape
{
    DECLARE_DYNAMIC(circle)
public:
// Other members...
};
```

3. Include the IMPLEMENT_DYNAMIC macro for each class in the source file (the .cpp file) where you define the member functions of the class:

```
IMPLEMENT_DYNAMIC(shape, CObject)
IMPLEMENT_DYNAMIC(circle, shape)
```

Once you follow these steps, you can use the IsKindOf member function and the RUNTIME_CLASS macro to compare the class of any shape object at runtime. The IsKindOf function and the macros DECLARE_DYNAMIC, IMPLEMENT_DYNAMIC, and RUNTIME_CLASS are described in more detail in the reference section later in this chapter.

> The runtime class-identification feature of the Microsoft Foundation Class library works properly in single-inheritance hierarchies only.

Persistence

Persistence is the ability to store objects in a file and retrieve them later. You can use persistence to store complex objects in disk files with minimal effort. For instance, the Forms package in Chapter 17, "Building MS-DOS Applications in C++," uses classes derived from `CObject`, such as `FormHeader` and `TextGraphics`, so that they can be archived (stored) easily.

The Microsoft Foundation Class Library supports persistence through a process Microsoft calls *serialization*—the process by which an object writes its current state to a `CArchive` object that represents persistent (permanent) storage. When your program retrieves an object, the object also is responsible for reading its state back from the `CArchive` object. You can add the serialization functionality to any class derived from `CObject` or one of its derived classes with the following steps:

1. Include the `DECLARE_SERIAL` macro in the class declaration.
2. Provide a *default constructor*—a constructor that takes no arguments—for the class.
3. Include the `IMPLEMENT_SERIAL` macro in the C++ source file that implements the member functions of the class.
4. Define the `Serialize` member function for the class.

This chapter details the `DECLARE_SERIAL` and `IMPLEMENT_SERIAL` macros later in the list of global functions and macros.

The `FormBackground` and the `TextGraphics` class hierarchy of the Forms package shown in Chapter 17 illustrates how serialization is used in a realistic application. In the Forms package, the `FormBackground` class (see Listings 17.3 and 17.4), which is derived from `CObList`, maintains a list of `TextGraphics` objects and uses the serialization feature to permit the storage and later retrieval of `TextGraphics` objects in an archive. The `TextGraphics` hierarchy (see Figure 17.4), derived from `CObject`, represents lines, boxes, and text in the background of a form. While the `FormBackground` class provides support for serializing a list of `TextGraphics` objects, each individual `TextGraphics` object must be able to store and retrieve itself. As shown in Listings 17.9 and 17.11, each class in the `TextGraphics` hierarchy uses the `DECLARE_SERIAL` and `IMPLEMENT_SERIAL` macro and defines the `Serialize` member function to serialize itself.

Diagnostic Services

If you examine <afx.h>, the main header file of the Microsoft Foundation Class library, you'll find functions and macros defined within #ifdef _DEBUG ... #endif blocks. Additionally, most classes contain member functions and operators defined inside #ifdef _DEBUG ... #endif blocks. These functions and macros are useful for displaying the contents of objects at runtime. The idea behind these diagnostic facilities is similar to inserting calls to printf in C programs to display information that might help pinpoint errors.

Because these diagnostic operators and functions are enclosed in #ifdef _DEBUG ...#endif blocks, you can use them only if you compile your programs with the _DEBUG macro defined. A convenient way to define the _DEBUG macro is to use the /D command-line option of the Microsoft Visual C++ compiler. Just include the /D_DEBUG flag when you invoke the compiler.

Besides defining the _DEBUG macro, you must also link with the debug version of the Microsoft Foundation Class library. In Chapters 17 and 18 you used libraries such as mafxcr.lib and mafxcw.lib. These are the release versions of the Microsoft Foundation Class library for DOS and Windows. The corresponding debug versions of the libraries are mafxcrd.lib and mafxcwd.lib, —with both names ending in *d.* Do remember that you must build the DOS versions of these libraries. (See Chapter 1 for instructions on building the MFC DOS libraries.)

Dumping an Object's Contents

The Dump member function, defined when you compile your program with the /D_DEBUG flag, is useful for dumping the contents of an object—sending the textual representation of the object to an I/O stream. To use this feature, call the Dump function with a CDumpContext object as argument. The CDumpContext class serves as the I/O stream where the output of Dump appears. The Microsoft Foundation Class library includes a predefined CDumpContext object named afxDump, which you can use for diagnostic output. For example, if you derive a class named Customer from CObject, you can use its Dump function as follows:

```
// Assume that the Customer's constructor takes two string arguments:
    Customer p_cust = new Customer("Naba", "Barkakati");

// Dump the contents... only when _DEBUG is defined.

#ifdef _DEBUG
    p_cust->Dump(afxDump);
#endif
```

Although you would get a display of a limited amount of fixed information from the default Dump function inherited by the Customer class, you should override the Dump function to display useful information about the Customer class. For the Customer class, the following code fragment illustrates how to override Dump:

```
class Customer: public CObject
{
public:

    Customer(const char* first, const char* last) :
    _first_name(first), _last_name(last) {}

#ifdef _DEBUG
    virtual void Dump(CDumpContext& d) const;
#endif

private:
    CString _first_name;
    CString _last_name;
};

// Define the Dump function...only when _DEBUG is defined.

#ifdef _DEBUG
void Customer::Dump(CDumpContext& d) const
{
// Call the Dump function of the base class first.
    CObject::Dump(d);

// Now "dump" the contents of this object....
// Use the << operator.
    d << "First name: " << _first_name << "\n";
    d << "Last name:  " << _last_name  << "\n";
}
#endif
```

TRACE and ASSERT Macros

The TRACE and ASSERT macros provide yet another set of debugging tools. If you compile your program with the /D_DEBUG flag, TRACE prints its string argument to the afxDump diagnostic output. When the _DEBUG macro is not defined, TRACE does nothing. TRACE is useful for printing status messages such as:

```
    TRACE("About to load form...\n");
// Code to load form....
    TRACE("Form loaded\n");
```

The ASSERT macro is similar to the ASSERT macro in ANSI standard C. ASSERT evaluates its argument and, if that argument is zero, prints a message and terminates the program. Like TRACE, ASSERT works only when the _DEBUG macro is defined. Therefore, you can make liberal use of TRACE and ASSERT in your programs and use their diagnostic services by compiling the programs with the /D_DEBUG flag. When the programs are debugged, you can release them to the outside world by recompiling the programs without the /D_DEBUG flag.

ASSERT is useful for testing the validity of function arguments and object types. For instance, to ensure that a pointer argument to a function is not NULL, you would write the following:

```
void func(shape* s)
{
    ASSERT(s != NULL);   // Exit if s is a NULL pointer
//...
}
```

General-Purpose Classes at a Glance

The inheritance hierarchy of the general-purpose classes, shown in Figure 16.5, gives you a feel for the organization of these classes. Table 19.1 lists the general-purpose classes organized by category. The following sections summarize these classes by category.

Table 19.1. General-purpose Microsoft Foundation Classes listed by category.

Category	Classes
Strings	CString
Date and time	CTime, CTimeSpan
Arrays of objects	CByteArray, CWordArray, CDWordArray, CPtrArray, CObArray, CStringArray, CUintArray

continues

Table 19.1. continued

Category	Classes
Linked lists	CPtrList, CObList, CStringList
Mapping keys to values	CMapWordToPtr, CMapPtrToWord, CMapPtrToPtr, CMapStringToPtr, CMapStringToOb, CMapStringToString, CMapWordToOb
Exception handling	CException, CMemoryException, CArchiveException, CFileException, CResourceException, COleException, CNotSupportedException, CUserException
File I/O operations	CFile, CStdioFile, CMemFile, CFileStatus
Diagnostics support	CDumpContext, CMemoryState
Archiving objects	CArchive
Determining the class of an object at runtime	CRuntimeClass

Basic Data Types

The CString, CTime, and CTimeSpan classes represent basic data types:

- The CString class is reserved for character strings.
- CTime objects can store absolute dates and times.
- CTimeSpan represents relative time (the difference between two times).

These are stand-alone classes—unlike most other classes, they are not derived from the CObject class.

CString, CTime, and CTimeSpan classes often are used as members of other classes. For instance, you might use CStrings to store the name and address of a customer in a Customer class as follows:

```
class Customer: public CObject
{
// Various member functions...
```

```
protected:
    CString _first_name;
    CString _last_name;
    CString _title;
    CString _company;
    CString _address1;
    CString _address2;
    CString _city;
    CString _state;
    CString _postal_code;
    CString _country;
};
```

Similarly, the `FileHeader` class in Chapter 17 (see Listing 17.1) uses a `CTime` object to store the time when a file was last modified.

Collections of Objects

The Microsoft Foundation Class library provides three distinct groups of classes to organize collections of objects:

- *Arrays* (`CPtrArray`, `CObArray`, `CStringArray`, `CByteArray`, `CUintArray`, `CWordArray`, and `CDWordArray`). The array classes can store pointers to any user-defined objects as well as `void` pointers, instances of `CString`, or other fixed-size objects such as 8-, 16-, and 32-bit values. Arrays store their contents in a sequential manner, and the contents are accessed through integer indexes.
- *Linked lists* (`CPtrList`, `CObList`, and `CStringList`). The linked list classes can hold `void` pointers, pointers to `CObjects`, and pointers to `CStrings`. Linked lists provide a fast method for inserting objects into the list. In the Forms software presented in Chapter 17, the `FormBackground` and the `FieldList` classes (Listings 17.3 and 17.5) are linked lists derived from the `CObList` class. These classes provide good examples of how to create your own linked lists using the predefined linked list classes such as `CObList`.
- *Maps* with individual entries that associate a key object to a value object (`CMapWordToPtr`, `CMapPtrToWord`, `CMapPtrToPtr`, `CMapStringToPtr`, `CMapStringToOb`, `CMapStringToString`, and `CMapWordToOb`). The map classes are essentially hash tables. You can use a key to access any value, and the access is fast compared with arrays or linked lists.

Microsoft's Template Mechanism

An interesting feature of the collection classes (arrays, linked lists, and maps) in the Microsoft Foundation Class library is that they are created using a template mechanism. As explained in Chapter 13, "Advanced Topics in C++," Microsoft Visual C++ eventually will support templates that enable you to declare classes and member functions with parametric types. For instance, you can use a generic array template to define array classes for a variety of objects. You also can find more information on how to use the template mechanism in technical note #4 in the Microsoft Foundation Classes Technical Notes (MFCNOTES.HLP), which you can select with the MFC Tech Notes icon in the Program Manager's Visual C++ program group.

Exception Handling in Microsoft Foundation Classes

As explained in Chapter 13, the ANSI X3J16 Committee is working on standardizing C++. One of the Committee's additions to C++ will be a standard mechanism for exception handling (recall that exceptions refer to error conditions in your program). Chapter 13 explains the proposed syntax for exception handling. The Microsoft Foundation Class library provides support for exception handling with macros that mimic the proposed syntax.

Catching Exceptions

You've already seen examples of exception-handling macros in the Forms software presented in Chapter 17. For instance, look at Listing 17.24, which uses the `TRY`, `CATCH`, `AND_CATCH`, and `END_CATCH` macros to trap error conditions that might arise when opening a file to load a form. Additionally, the `read` member function of the `Form` class (see Listing 17.15) also uses `TRY` and `CATCH` blocks to handle errors when opening a file and reading from it.

With exception-handling macros, you can place code that might cause one or more exceptions in a `TRY` block that is enclosed in a pair of curly braces, `{...}`. Immediately following the `TRY` block, place one or more `CATCH` blocks to handle specific exceptions that are *thrown* (generated) by the code inside the `TRY` block. The following code fragment illustrates the general structure of the code:

```
TRY
{
// Code that might throw one or more exceptions.
//...
}
CATCH(CMemoryException, e)
{
// Handle "out-of-memory" conditions here.
//...
}
AND_CATCH(CResourceException, e)
{
// Handle Windows resource-allocation errors here.
//...
}
AND_CATCH(CFileException, e)
{
// Handle file errors here.
// Test e->m_cause for exact cause of error.
//...
}
AND_CATCH(CException, e)
{
// Handle any other exceptions here.
//...
}
END_CATCH
```

Each exception is represented by an object of a class derived from `CException`:

- `CArchiveException` represents errors during serialization.
- `CFileException` represents file I/O errors.
- `CMemoryException` represents memory allocation errors.
- `CNotSupportedException` represents a request made for unsupported services.
- `COleException` represents errors that occur during Object Linking and Embedding (OLE) operations under Windows.
- `CResourceException` represents Windows resource-allocation errors.

Notice that even though this chapter is supposed to describe general-purpose classes, two classes in the `CException` hierarchy, `COleException` and `CResourceException`, are specific to Microsoft Windows applications.

Local Scope of TRY and CATCH Blocks

Variables declared within a TRY block are local variables and are not accessible outside the block. Thus, the following code will fail to compile because the variable named nCount is defined within the TRY block only:

```
    TRY
    {
        int nCount;
        CFile f("test.dat", CFile::modeRead |
            CFile::typeBinary);
// Read count from file:
        (void)f.Read(&nCount, sizeof(count));

    }
    CATCH(CFileException, e)
    {
        THROW_LAST()
    }
    END_CATCH
    return nCount; // ERROR: nCount is not defined anymore
```

Determining the Cause of an Exception

The second argument in both the CATCH and AND_CATCH macros represents a pointer to an exception object. Depending on the type of the exception, you can obtain further information about it from the data members of the exception object. For example, the CFileException exception contains a member variable named m_cause, which indicates the cause of the file I/O error. To check the cause, compare the m_cause member variable with certain enumerated constants declared in the CFileException class in the following manner:

```
TRY
{
// Code that might throw a file I/O exception.
//...
}
CATCH(CFileException, e)
{
```

```
// Handle file errors here.
// Test e->m_cause for the exact cause of error.

    if(e->m_cause == CFileException::accessDenied)
        TRACE("Access denied");

    if(e->m_cause == CFileException::fileNotFound)
        TRACE("File not found");
//...
}
END_CATCH
```

Throwing Exceptions

In addition to catching exceptions with the TRY, CATCH, and AND_CATCH blocks, the Microsoft Foundation Class library provides a number of global functions with which you can throw exceptions of specific types. For instance, you can throw a file I/O error with a specific cause by calling AfxThrowFileException, as follows:

```
#include <stdio.h>

//...
{
    FILE *fp = fopen("test.dat", "r");
// Throw an exception if the file could not be opened successfully.
    if(fp == NULL)
        AfxThrowFileException(CFileException::generic);

// Okay to use fp here....

}
```

Here you throw a file I/O exception with the cause set to an unspecified (generic) error.

Other utility functions for throwing exceptions are

```
AfxThrowMemoryException()
AfxThrowNotSupportedException()
AfxThrowArchiveException()
AfxThrowOleException()
AfxThrowResourceException()
```

As you can see, a function corresponds to each type of exception. These functions are further described in the list of global functions later in this chapter.

Another useful macro for throwing exceptions is the `THROW_LAST` macro. `THROW_LAST` throws an exception to the next outer `CATCH` block. This is useful in functions where you may simply want to pass the exception along to the caller for handling. For example, the `get_count` function in the next discussion uses `THROW_LAST` to send a file exception to the caller.

Cleaning Up During Exception Handling

The exception-handling mechanism in the Microsoft Foundation Class library is based on the C library's `setjmp` and `longjmp` functions. (For Windows applications, the `Throw` and `Catch` functions of the Windows Software Development Kit are used.) The `longjmp` function reverts the stack to the state that existed when `setjmp` was called earlier, causing a return from anywhere in your program to the point of last call to `setjmp`. One flaw in handling C++ exceptions with the `setjmp`/`longjmp` functions is that memory allocated prior to the exception is not released properly. Consider the following example:

```
// Function that reads a "count" from a data file.

UINT get_count(const char* suffix)
{
    CString filename = "data_";
    CString s = suffix;
    filename = filename + s + ".dat";

    UINT count;

    TRY
    {
        CFile f(filename, CFile::modeRead | CFile::typeBinary);

// Read count from file and return....
        (void)f.Read(&count, sizeof(count));
    }
    CATCH(CFileException, e)
    {
//*** NOTE: At this point, you should release memory
//          allocated by CStrings s and filename.
//          Correct example of TRY...CATCH block follows.
```

```
// Send the exception to the caller.
        THROW_LAST()
    }
    return count;
}
//------------------------------------------------------------
// Later on in "main."
// ...
    TRY
    {
        UINT n = get_count("01");
// Other code....

    }
    CATCH(CFileException, e)
    {
        cout << "File I/O error" << endl;
//...
    }
```

Here, the `get_count` function constructs a filename in a `CString` object, opens a file through a `CFile` object, and returns a value from the file. Even though the `get_count` function appears correct at first glance, one problem exists: if an exception occurs when creating the `CFile` object, the `CATCH` block in `get_count` sends the exception to the caller, causing the `get_count` function to end prematurely. Therefore, the destructors for the `CString` objects `filename` and `s` are not called, and any memory allocated by these `CString` objects is not released properly. Knowing this, you can correct the problem by defining the `CATCH` block in `get_count` as follows:

```
    TRY
    {
// Create the CFile object....

    }
    CATCH(CFileException, e)
    {
// Empty the CStrings. This releases memory allocated by the
// CString objects:
        s.Empty();
        filename.Empty();

        THROW_LAST()
    }
    END_CATCH
```

You must be aware of problems such as this when using the exception-handling mechanism provided by the Microsoft Foundation Class Library.

Classes for File I/O

The `CFile` class is meant for use with unbuffered binary file I/O. A common use of a `CFile` object is to associate it with a `CArchive` object for use in archiving objects in a file, as illustrated by the following fragment of code:

```
// Open a file for writing. Use a TRY...CATCH block because
// file I/O exceptions may occur.

    TRY
    {
        CFile file(filename, CFile::modeCreate |
            CFile::modeWrite);

// Now create an archive for storing objects.
// Once again use a TRY...CATCH pair.

        TRY
        {
            CArchive archive(&file, CArchive::store);

// Code to store objects in the archive,
//...
            archive.Close();
        }
        CATCH(CArchiveException, e)
        {
// Handle archiving errors;
// close file and throw exception to caller:
            file.Close();
            THROW_LAST();
        }
        END_CATCH
    }
    CATCH(CFileException, e)
    {
// Handle File I/O exceptions here:
        THROW_LAST(); // Send exception to caller
    }
    END_CATCH
```

A number of other classes are derived from CFile and are useful for specialized I/O:

- CStdioFile represents a file opened for a buffered I/O using the C library function fopen.
- CMemFile provides a block of memory you can treat as a file.

Also, a CFileStatus structure stores status information about any CFile object, such as the creation date, modification date, size, attributes, and the full pathname.

Diagnostics Support

As explained earlier in this chapter, classes derived from CObject inherit the capability to dump the contents of an instance to an I/O stream. Also, macros such as TRACE and ASSERT can help debug your programs. In addition to these diagnostic capabilities, the Microsoft Foundation Class library includes the CMemoryState class to detect errors in memory allocation and deallocation. One common error with dynamic memory allocation occurs when you allocate memory (by using the new operator) and forget to delete the memory. This error commonly is referred to as a *memory leak.* You can use CMemoryState objects to detect memory leaks and obtain information about memory. The following code fragment illustrates the basic approach for using CMemoryState objects:

```
    CMemoryState first, second, diff;

// Take a "snapshot" of memory:
    first.Checkpoint();

// Code that allocates and deallocates memory goes here.
//...

// Take a second snapshot:
    second.Checkpoint();

// If there's any difference between the two snapshots,
// there must be some memory leak.

    if(diff.Difference(first, second))
    {
        TRACE("Memory leaked");
        diff.DumpStatistics();
    }
```

The `DumpStatistics` function displays useful information about blocks of memory that remain allocated and about the total memory used between the two snapshots of memory.

Global Variables, General-Purpose Macros, and Global Functions

The previous sections provided an overview of the general-purpose classes in the Microsoft Foundation Class library. The library also includes a large number of general-purpose macros and functions. These functions are not directly related to any class but are declared outside the body of all classes as global functions. This section provides reference information on the global functions, macros, and variables.

Global Variables

afxDump

```
CDumpContext& afxDump;
```

This is a globally defined instance of a `CDumpContext` that supports stream-oriented output for diagnostic messages. The `afxDump` object is available only when you compile your program with the `/D_DEBUG` flag, and is analogous to the `cerr` stream of the `iostream` library.

afxMemDF

```
int afxMemDF;
```

`afxMemDF` controls the level of diagnostic features you need for tracking down errors during memory allocation and deallocation. You can set `afxMemDF` to one of the following defined constants (and any bitwise-OR combination of these constants):

`allocMemDF`	Uses the memory allocator with debugging features. (This is the default setting in the debug library.)

`checkAlwaysMemDF`	Calls `AfxCheckMemory` every time memory is allocated or deallocated.
`delayFreeMemDF`	Delays freeing memory even when your program releases the memory.

Thus, you would set `afxMemDF` as follows to delay freeing memory and call the `AfxCheckMemory` function each time memory is allocated or deallocated:

```
afxMemDF = delayFreeMemDF | checkAlwaysMemDF;
```

afxTraceEnabled

```
BOOL afxTraceEnabled;
```

The `afxTraceEnabled` flag controls the output of `TRACE` macro. This output appears only when the flag is `TRUE`.

afxTraceFlags

```
int afxTraceFlags;
```

The bits in the `afxTraceFlags` variable are used to turn on various reporting capabilities that are built into the debug version of the Microsoft Foundation Class library. You can use the bitwise-OR combination of the following settings to enable selected features:

Flag	Meaning
0x01	Prefixes each `TRACE` output with the name of the application.
0x02	Reports Windows messages received by the application's `CWinApp` class.
0x04	Reports Windows messages dispatched in `CWnd::WindowProc`.
0x08	Reports the progress of `WM_COMMAND` messages through the classes in the application. You can use these reports in applications with MDI to determine how messages are handled by the child and the frame windows.
0x10	Reports all significant OLE notifications and requests.

General-Purpose Macros

AND_CATCH

AND_CATCH(*exception_class*, *exception_object_pointer*)

Use AND_CATCH to declare a block of code to handle additional exceptions that might be thrown by a preceding TRY block. The general structure of TRY...CATCH...AND_CATCH blocks is as follows:

```
TRY
{
// Something that causes one or more exceptions....
}
CATCH(CFileException, e)
{
// File exceptions handled here.
}
AND_CATCH(CArchiveException, e)
{
// Catch archive exception here....
}
END_CATCH
```

Notice that the variables declared within an AND_CATCH block are accessible only within that block. Also, you must use the END_CATCH macro to mark the end of the exception-handling blocks.

ASSERT

ASSERT(*expression*)

Use ASSERT to check the validity of assumptions. For example, if you're assuming that a pointer is not NULL, you can use the ASSERT macro to check this fact:

```
// Pointer p should not be null....
    ASSERT(p != NULL);
```

The ASSERT macro evaluates the expression you provide and aborts the program (by calling the global function AfxAbort) if the expression evaluates at zero. ASSERT is enabled only when the _DEBUG macro is defined.

ASSERT_VALID

```
ASSERT_VALID(pointer_to_object)
```

Use ASSERT_VALID to verify that the internal state of an object is valid. This macro calls the AssertValid member function of the specified class. Thus, you can provide the validity-checking code for your own classes by defining the AssertValid member function for each class.

CATCH

```
CATCH(exception_class, exception_object_pointer)
```

Use CATCH to define the first block of code for handling an exception of the specified class thrown in a preceding TRY block. You can use the exception_object_pointer to determine further information about the exception. Because the exception-handling code following the CATCH macro is enclosed in curly braces ({...}), any variables declared in that block are accessible only within that block.

DEBUG_NEW

```
DEBUG_NEW
```

Use DEBUG_NEW to assist in finding memory leaks. You would use DEBUG_NEW anywhere in your program you might use the new operator to allocate storage from the heap. DEBUG_NEW causes the filename and linenumber of each allocation request to be retained. You then can use CMemoryState::DumpAllObjectsSince function to view each of the objects that are currently allocated, with the filename and linenumber of the allocation request.

When the application is compiled as a release version, DEBUG_NEW resolves to the new operator.

DECLARE_DYNAMIC

```
DECLARE_DYNAMIC(class_name)
```

If you include the DECLARE_DYNAMIC macro in the declaration of a class (derived from CObject or one of its derived classes), you will be able to determine the type of objects of this class at runtime. When you include the DECLARE_DYNAMIC macro in a class declaration, you also must use the IMPLEMENT_DYNAMIC macro in the C++ source file that implements the member functions of the class. See the tutorial section, "Runtime Class Identification," earlier in this chapter for an example of how to use the IsKindOf function with the RUNTIME_CLASS macro when you're checking the type of an object at runtime.

DECLARE_DYNCREATE

`DECLARE_DYNCREATE(class_name)`

If you include the `DECLARE_DYNCREATE` macro, you'll be able to create objects of the `CObject` derived classes dynamically at runtime.

DECLARE_SERIAL

`DECLARE_SERIAL(class_name)`

Include `DECLARE_SERIAL` in the declaration of any class (derived from `CObject`) you plan to archive. The `class_name` argument is the name of the class that will have serialization capability. For example, to allow serialization for the `FileHeader` class you would declare it as:

```
#include <afx.h>

class FileHeader: public CObject
{
    DECLARE_SERIAL(FileHeader)

public:
// Other members...
}
```

Including the `DECLARE_SERIAL` macro automatically incorporates the `DECLARE_DYNAMIC` macro as well because runtime type determination is a necessary part of the scheme used by the Microsoft Foundation Class library to archive and restore objects.

If you include the `DECLARE_SERIAL` macro, you must include the `IMPLEMENT_SERIAL` macro in the C++ source file that implements the member functions of the class.

END_CATCH

`END_CATCH`

The `END_CATCH` macro marks the end of a sequence of `TRY`...`CATCH`...`AND_CATCH` blocks.

IMPLEMENT_DYNAMIC

`IMPLEMENT_DYNAMIC(class_name, base_class_name)`

The `IMPLEMENT_DYNAMIC` macro is the counterpart of the `DECLARE_DYNAMIC` macro. You must ensure that `IMPLEMENT_DYNAMIC` is included only once. One way to do this is to place the macro in the C++ source file that defines the member functions of the class.

IMPLEMENT_DYNCREATE

IMPLEMENT_DYNCREATE(*class_name, base_class_name*)

The IMPLEMENT_DYNAMIC macro is the counterpart of the DECLARE_DYNCREATE macro.

IMPLEMENT_SERIAL

IMPLEMENT_SERIAL(*class_name, base_class_name, schema_number*)

If you include DECLARE_SERIAL in the class declaration, you must include IMPLEMENT_SERIAL as well. You should include IMPLEMENT_SERIAL only once. The usual approach is to include the IMPLEMENT_SERIAL macro in the C++ source file where the member functions of the class are defined. The first two arguments to IMPLEMENT_SERIAL are the names of the class and its base class. The third argument, schema_number, is a nonzero integer value that denotes the version number that is used to identify the version of a stored object.

RUNTIME_CLASS

RUNTIME_CLASS(*class_name*)

The RUNTIME_CLASS macro returns a pointer to a CRuntimeClass object that corresponds to the specified class. Use the RUNTIME_CLASS macro together with the IsKindOf member function to check the runtime type of an object, as follows:

```
    CObject *p_obj;
//...
// Assume that the Field class is derived from CObject.
    if(p_obj->IsKindOf(RUNTIME_CLASS(Field)))
    {
// OK to cast base class pointer p_obj as a pointer to a "Field."
        Field *p_f = (Field*)p_obj;
// ...
    }
```

THROW

THROW(*exception_object_pointer*)

Use THROW to throw the exception specified by its argument. For example, to throw a CArchiveException with the cause set to CArchiveException::endOfFile (meaning that the file ended before it fully retrieved an object's data), you would write:

```
THROW(new CArchiveException(CArchiveException::endOfFile));
```

THROW_LAST

`THROW_LAST()`

Use THROW_LAST to throw the last exception to the next outer CATCH block.

TRACE

`TRACE(`*`format_string, ...`*`)`

Use TRACE to print information useful for debugging your program. TRACE accepts a variable number of arguments, just like printf in the standard C library.

TRACE0

`TRACE0(`*`output_string`*`)`

Use TRACE0 to print information useful for debugging your program. TRACE0 accepts one string (a simple text message). The string is placed in the code segment rather than the DGROUP. This action conserves memory.

TRACE1

`TRACE1(`*`format_string, single_variable`*`)`

Use TRACE1 to print information useful for debugging your program. TRACE1 accepts one string (with a single substitution), and one variable, which will be substituted. TRACE1 accepts a single argument with formatting like that of printf in the standard C library. The string is placed in the code segment rather than the DGROUP. This action conserves memory.

TRACE2

`TRACE2(`*`format_string, variable1, varible2`*`)`

Use TRACE2 to print information useful for debugging your program. TRACE2 accepts one string (with two substitutions), and two variables, which will be substituted. TRACE2 accepts two arguments with formatting like that of printf in the standard C library. The string will be placed in the code segment rather than the DGROUP. This action conserves memory.

TRACE3

TRACE3(*format_string, variable1, variable2, variable3*)

Use TRACE3 to print information useful for debugging your program. TRACE3 accepts one string (with two substitutions), and two variables, which will be substituted. TRACE3 accepts three arguments with formatting like that of printf in the standard C library. The string will be placed in the code segment rather than the DGROUP. This action conserves memory.

TRY

TRY

Use TRY with a pair of curly braces ({...}) to define a block of code that might throw one or more exceptions. The exceptions should be handled in CATCH and AND_CATCH blocks that follow the TRY block.

VERIFY

VERIFY(*expression*)

The VERIFY macro is similar to ASSERT except that, when the _DEBUG macro is not defined, VERIFY evaluates its argument but ignores the result. (ASSERT does nothing—it doesn't even evaluate its expression argument.) Use VERIFY if you're counting on the evaluation of the expression regardless of whether _DEBUG is defined or not (in other words, whether you're debugging the program or not). For instance, suppose you place the following code in a loop:

```
// WARNING: when _DEBUG is not defined, count is not updated
    ASSERT(count++ < MAX_COUNT);
```

You then can expect count to always be updated. However, this code will not work properly when you're no longer debugging—when _DEBUG is no longer defined. One way to ensure correctness is to write:

```
// With VERIFY, count is always updated.
    VERIFY(count++ < MAX_COUNT);
```

Global Functions

AfxAbort

```
void AfxAbort();
```

Use AfxAbort to terminate your program. When compiled with the _DOS macro defined, AfxAbort calls the abort function from the C library. For a Windows program, when _WINDOWS is defined, AfxAbort calls AfxWinTerm.

AfxCheckMemory

```
BOOL PASCAL AfxCheckMemory();
```

Call AfxCheckMemory to check the memory blocks that currently are allocated on the heap and to report any detected problems. AfxCheckMemory returns TRUE if it detects no problems; otherwise, it returns FALSE.

AfxDoForAllClasses

```
void PASCAL AfxDoForAllClasses(
    void (*p_fn)(const CRuntimeClass* p_class, void* p_data),
//  Function to call for each class
    void* p_data); // Data to be passed to p_fn
```

Use AfxDoForAllClasses to call the function specified by the pointer *p_fn* for all currently used classes that support runtime class identification. The *p_data* pointer is passed to the function identified by *p_fn* each time the function is called. You can use AfxDoForAllClasses only when debugging your application (when _DEBUG is defined and you link with the debug version of the Microsoft Foundation Class library). Here's a code fragment that illustrates how you might use this function:

```
void class_fn(const CRuntimeClass* p_class, void* data)
{
    cout << "Class name: " << p_class->m_pszClassName <<
        " data = " << *((int*)data) << endl;
}

// Later on in "main"...
// Call the iteration function "class_fn" for all classes.

int data = 100; // No significance, just showing how to send data
AfxDoForAllClasses(class_fn, &data);
```

AfxDoForAllObjects

```
void PASCAL AfxDoForAllObjects(
    void (*p_fn)(CObject* p_obj, void* p_data),
//  Function to call for each CObject
    void* p_data); // Data to be passed to p_fn
```

Use `AfxDoForAllObjects` to call the function specified by the pointer *p_fn* for all currently allocated instances of classes derived from `CObject`. The *p_data* pointer is passed to the function identified by *p_fn* each time the function is called. You can use `AfxDoForAllObjects` only when `_DEBUG` is defined and you link with the debug version of the Microsoft Foundation Class library. Here's how you might use this function:

```
// Count total number CObjects in the iteration function.

static int ob_count = 0;

void obj_fn(CObject* p_obj, void* data)
{
// Increment object count and display some information:
    ob_count++;
    cout << "Dumping Object: " << ob_count << endl;

    p_obj->Dump(afxDump);
    cout << "Data = " << *((int*)data) << endl;
    cout << "==================================" << endl;
}

// Later on in "main"....
// Call the iteration function "obj_fn" for all CObjects.

int data = 101; // No significance, just showing how to send data
AfxDoForAllObjects(obj_fn, &data);
```

AfxDump

```
VOID AfxDump(
    const CObject *pOjb);
```

Call `AfxDump` when in the debugger to dump the state of an object while debugging. (Also, see the global variable, `AfxDump`.) Your program should not call `AfxDump()`, but should instead call the `Dump` member function of the class.

AfxEnableMemoryTracking

```
BOOL PASCAL AfxEnableMemoryTracking(
    BOOL track_enable); // TRUE means turn on memory tracking
```

Use `AfxEnableMemoryTracking` to turn memory diagnostics on or off. The argument *`track_enable`* indicates whether you want memory tracking enabled or disabled. Memory tracking is enabled by default when the `_DEBUG` macro is defined, so you normally use `AfxEnableTrackingMemory` to temporarily disable memory tracking.

AfxFormatString1

```
BOOL PASCAL AfxFormatString1(
    CString&     rString,          // buffer to hold result
    UINT         nResID,           // Resource ID which substitution is
                                      done.
    LPCSTR       lpString);        // String that will be substituted.
```

Call `AfxFormatString1` to substitute the string *`lpString`* for the `%1` that may be found in the specified resource string. If there are multiple characters `%1` in the resource, the substitution is performed once for each occurance. For example, if the resource string is `Specified file was %1 found` and the string *`lpString`* contained `not`, the resultant string stored in *`rString`* will be `Specified file was not found.`

AfxFormatString2

```
BOOL PASCAL AfxFormatString2(
    CString&     rString,          // buffer to hold result
    UINT         nResID,           // Resource ID which substitution is
                                      done.
    LPCSTR       lpString1);       // String 1 that will be substituted.
    LPCSTR       lpString2);       // String 2 that will be substituted.
```

Call `AfxFormatString2` to substitute both strings specified by *`lpString1`* and *`lpString2`* for the `%1` and `%2` characters that may be found in the specified resource string. If there are multiple characters `%1` and `%2` in the resource, the substitution is performed once for each occurrence. For example, if the resource string is `File %1 was %2 found`, the string *`lpString1`* contains `C:\autoexec.bad`, and the string *`lpString2`* contains *not*, the resultant string stored in *`rString`* is `File C:\autoexec.bad was not found.`

The format specifiers `%1` and `%2` need not be in any specific order.

AfxIsMemoryBlock

```
BOOL PASCAL AfxIsMemoryBlock(
    const void* p,                // Identifies memory block
    UINT        numbytes,         // Size of block
    LONG*       p_sequence = NULL); // Return sequence number
```

Call `AfxIsMemoryBlock` to verify that the memory block identified by the pointer *p* is a valid memory block of size *numbytes*. The function returns `TRUE` if the block is valid and has the indicated size. Additionally, `AfxIsMemoryBlock` fills an allocation sequence number in the `LONG` variable with the address you provide in the optional argument *p_sequence*.

AfxIsValidAddress

```
BOOL FAR PASCAL AfxIsValidAddress(
    const void FAR* lp,            // Pointer to a block of memory
    UINT            numbytes,      // Size of the block
    BOOL            read_write = TRUE);// TRUE = block is for
                                       //   both reading and writing
```

`AfxIsValidAddress` returns `TRUE` if the memory block specified by the `FAR` pointer *lp* and of size *numbytes* lies entirely inside the program's memory space. A `TRUE` value for the *read_write* argument indicates whether the block is used for both reading and writing.

AfxIsValidString

```
BOOL PASCAL AfxIsValidString(
    LPCSTR    lp,              // Pointer to string to be tested
    int       nLength = -1); // Length of string
```

`AfxIsValidString` returns `TRUE` if the pointer *lp* points to a string of the specified length. If *nLength* is –1 (the default), the string is assumed to be null-terminated.

AfxSetAllocHook

```
AFX_ALLOC_HOOK AfxSetAllocHook(
    AFX_ALLOC_HOOK p_fn); // Call this function every time memory
                          //   is allocated.
```

Use `AfxSetAllocHook` to specify a function that is called each time memory is allocated. This enables you to control the allocation of memory. The function you specify with *p_fn* must have the following prototype:

```
BOOL hook_fn(
   size_t numbytes,       // About to allocate this many bytes
   BOOL IsCObjectDerived,// TRUE=This is for a CObject
   LONG sequence_number);// Allocation sequence number
```

The function should return `TRUE` to allow the allocation of the block or `FALSE` to refuse the allocation request.

AfxSetAllocStop

```
void PASCAL AfxSetAllocStop(
    LONG sequence_number); // Halt program when a memory
         // allocation request is made with this sequence number.
```

Use `AfxSetAllocStop` to specify a sequence number so that the program halts when a memory allocation request with this sequence number is made. This function is considered obsolete, and should not be used because it may not be supported in future versions of Visual C++.

AfxSetTerminate

```
AFX_TERM_PROC AfxSetTerminate(
    AFX_TERM_PROC proc); // Function to be called at termination
```

Use `AfxSetTerminate` to specify a function that will be called by `AfxTerminate` to abort your program. Listing 19.1 is a sample program that repeatedly allocates memory by calling the new operator until an exception is thrown. Because the exception is not caught, `AfxTerminate` is called. In turn, `AfxTerminate` calls the installed abort-handler function *proc*. This function is considered obsolete, and should not be used because it may not be supported in future versions of Visual C++. This function should not be used with Windows applications.

Listing 19.1. Program to illustrate the use of the AfxSetTerminate function.

```
//-----------------------------------------------------------
// File: afxterm.cpp
//
// Illustrates installing your own "abort" function.
//
// Note: Assuming you have installed the Microsoft Visual C++
// compiler in the C:\MSVC directory, the following command will
```

```
// compile and link this program (enter on a single line):
//
//     cl /AM /D_DOS /D_DEBUG /Feafxterm.exe afxterm.cpp /link
//                   c:\MSVC\mfc\lib\mafxcrd.lib
//
//-------------------------------------------------------------
#define _DOS
#include <afx.h>

unsigned long allocated = 0L;
//-------------------------------------------------------------
// a b o r t _ p r o c
//
// Our own "abort" function that will be called
// instead of AfxAbort.

void abort_proc()
{
    printf( "Out of memory after allocating %ldK!\n",
        allocated);
    exit( 1 );
}
//-------------------------------------------------------------
void main()
{
// Install our own function that gets called
// when AfxTerminate is called.

    AfxSetTerminate(abort_proc);

// Keep allocating memory until "new" fails. When this
// happens, "new" will call "AfxTerminate," which, in turn,
// calls the installed "abort" function.

    while(1)
    {
        BYTE *p = new BYTE[1024];
        allocated++;  // Count how many K allocated
    }
}
```

AfxTerminate

```
void AfxTerminate();
```

Call `AfxTerminate` to exit a program when you cannot recover from an error. Modules in the Microsoft Foundation Class library also call `AfxTerminate` when the program must be aborted because of a serious error (such as an exception that isn't caught and processed by your program). Normally, `AfxTerminate` calls `AfxAbort`. However, you can install your own abort handler by using the `AfxSetTerminate` global function. This function is considered obsolete, and should not be used because it may not be supported in future versions of Visual C++. This function should not be used with Windows applications.

AfxThrowArchiveException

```
void PASCAL AfxThrowArchiveException(
   int cause);  // Cause of exception
```

Call `AfxThrowArchiveException` to throw an archive exception. See the reference page of the `CArchiveException` class for a list of possible causes of exception.

AfxThrowFileException

```
void PASCAL AfxThrowFileException(
    int  cause,              // Cause of exception.
    LONG OSError = -1);      // Error code from operating system.
```

Call `AfxThrowFileException` to throw a file I/O exception. See the reference page of the `CFileException` class for a list of possible causes of the exception. If you have the information, you also should provide the operating system-specific reason for the I/O error.

AfxThrowMemoryException

```
void PASCAL AfxThrowMemoryException();
```

Call `AfxThrowMemoryException` to throw a `CMemoryException` object indicating a memory-allocation error.

AfxThrowNotSupportedException

```
void PASCAL AfxThrowNotSupportedException();
```

Use `AfxThrowNotSupportedException` to throw `CNotSupportedException`. This exception is thrown when a class receives a request for a service that the class does not support. For example, if you try to archive a class that does not support serialization, the `CArchive` class will call `AfxThrowNotSupportedException`.

AfxThrowOleException

```
AfxThrowOleException(
    OLESTATUS status); // Indicates the error status
```

The Microsoft Foundation Class library's OLE classes use the `AfxThrowOleException` function to a `COleException` when errors occur during OLE. OLE is a feature of Windows programs, and this function is used only by Windows programs.

AfxThrowResourceException

```
void PASCAL AfxThrowResourceException();
```

`AfxThrowResourceException` is called in a Windows program by internal Microsoft Foundation Class functions when Windows resources cannot be loaded.

AfxThrowUserException

```
void PASCAL AfxThrowUserException();
```

`AfxThrowUserException` is called when it's necessary to stop an end-user operation. Usually, `AfxThrowUserException` is called after the user responds to an unrecoverable error message (displayed by AfxMessageBox).

AfxTrace

```
void AfxTrace(const char* format_string, ...);
```

You should not directly call `AfxTrace`. Instead, use the `TRACE` macro, which calls `AfxTrace` to display formatted diagnostic messages. As a benefit of using `TRACE`, when you're debugging and the `_DEBUG` macro is defined, `TRACE` calls `AfxTrace`. However, `TRACE` does nothing when the `_DEBUG` macro is undefined. Thus, if you use `TRACE`, you can release your program by recompiling it without the `/D_DEBUG` compiler flag.

Reference

CArchive

Inheritance Hierarchy

CArchive

Summary

```
#include <afx.h>
class CArchive
{
public:
// Flags to indicate whether CArchive is open for storing or loading.
    enum Mode { store = 0, load = 1 };

// Constructor and destructor.
    CArchive(CFile* pFile, UINT nMode, int nBufSize = 512,
        void FAR* lpBuf = NULL);
    ~CArchive();

// Archive attributes.
    BOOL IsLoading() const;
    BOOL IsStoring() const;
    CFile* GetFile() const;

// Operations on the archive.
    UINT Read(void FAR* lpBuf, UINT nMax);
    void Write(const void FAR* lpBuf, UINT nMax);
    void Flush();
    void Close();

    friend CArchive& operator<<(CArchive& ar, const CObject* pOb);
    friend CArchive& operator>>(CArchive& ar, CObject*& pOb);
    friend CArchive& operator>>(CArchive& ar,
        const CObject*& pOb);

// NOTE: To enhance portability, the following operators are
//       defined only for fixed size types.
    CArchive& operator<<(BYTE by);
    CArchive& operator<<(WORD w);
    CArchive& operator<<(LONG l);
    CArchive& operator<<(DWORD dw);
```

```
    CArchive& operator>>(BYTE& by);
    CArchive& operator>>(WORD& w);
    CArchive& operator>>(DWORD& dw);
    CArchive& operator>>(LONG& l);

// Hidden implementation details....
};
```

Description

The CArchive class represents a binary stream where you can store objects for later retrieval. The storage is in a disk file. To use a CArchive class, you must first open a file through a CFile object and then create the CArchive object by invoking the constructor with that CFile object as the argument. Because CArchive can either store or load, you must create the CFile with a matching mode—to store the file, it must be opened for writing; to load from the file, it must be opened for reading.

Once CArchive is available, you can store or retrieve objects by calling the Serialize member function of the objects or by using the overloaded extraction (>>) and insertion (<<) operators. When all the input or output (I/O) operations are complete, you should call the Close member function to close the archive. This action flushes any buffered data and disconnects CArchive from CFile. After CArchive is closed, you can destroy the CFile object (this closes the file opened by CFile).

Notice that during the I/O operations, the CArchive member functions may throw exceptions of type CArchiveException and CFileException. Therefore, you should always use THROW and CATCH blocks when you work with archives.

CArchive's operators are adequately explained by the comments in the "Summary" section. The important member functions are described briefly in the next section.

Member Functions

Constructor and Destructor

```
CArchive(
    CFile* pFile,             // Pointer to initialized
                              //   CFile object.
    UINT   nMode,             // One of  CArchive::load
                              // or      CArchive::store.
    int    nBufSize = 512,    // Size of file buffer.
    void FAR* lpBuf = NULL); // Optional user-supplied buffer.
```

Constructs a CArchive object and attaches a specified CFile object to it. The CFile must be opened in the mode consistent with the selected mode for the CArchive; for example, if the CArchive is being opened in the CArchive::store mode, the CFile must be opened for writing. The `CArchive` constructor may throw one of the following exceptions: `CArchiveException`, `CFileException`, or `CMemoryException`.

```
~CArchive();
```

Closes the archive. This does not close the `CFile` and destroy it.

Archive Attributes

```
CFile* GetFile() const;
```

Returns a pointer to the `CFile` object associated with this `CArchive`. You should call the `Flush` member function before accessing the `CFile` pointer.

```
BOOL IsLoading() const;
```

Returns `TRUE` if the `CArchive` has been opened in the `CArchive::load` mode, which indicates that the archive is being used for loading objects from a disk file into memory.

```
BOOL IsStoring() const;
```

Returns `TRUE` if the `CArchive` has been opened in the `CArchive::store` mode, which indicates that the archive is being used for storing objects from memory into a disk file.

Operations

```
void Close();
```

Flushes any data remaining in the buffer and closes the archive. `void Close();` also removes any association between the `CArchive` and its `CFile` object. It may throw a `CArchiveException` or a `CFileException` in case of errors.

```
void Flush();
```

Sends data (if any) from the buffer to the file associated with the `CArchive`. `void Flush();` may throw a `CFileException`.

```
UINT Read(void FAR* lpBuf, UINT nMax);
```

Calls `Read` in the `Serialize` function of your class to read structures embedded in your class. The `Read` function reads a specified number of bytes into the buffer *`lpBuf`* and returns the number of bytes actually read. This class may throw a `CFileException` in case of an error.

```
void Write(const void FAR* lpBuf, UINT nMax);
```

Call the `Write` in the `Serialize` function of your class to store structures embedded in your class. The `Write` function writes a specified number of bytes from the buffer *`lpBuf`* into the archive. May throw a `CFileException` in case of an error.

See Also

`CArchiveException`	Exceptions that occur in `CArchive` member functions
`CFileException`	
`CFile`	You need a `CFile` before you can create a `CArchive`

CArchiveException

Inheritance Hierarchy

`CObject -> CException -> CArchiveException`

Summary

```
#include <afx.h>
class CArchiveException : public CException
{
    DECLARE_DYNAMIC(CArchiveException)
public:
    enum
    {
        none,      // No error occurred.
        generic,   // Unspecified error.
        readOnly,  // Trying to write to a read-only archive.
        endOfFile,// Reached end of file.
        writeOnly,// Cannot read from a write-only archive.
        badIndex,  // Bad file format.
        badClass,  // Reading object into an object of wrong type.
        badSchema  // Class version mismatch between stored
                   //   object and in-memory object.
    };

// Constructor.
    CArchiveException(int cause = CArchiveException::none);

// Attributes.
    int m_cause; // Cause of exception (see enum above)

// Diagnostic support.
#ifdef _DEBUG
    virtual void Dump(CDumpContext& dc) const;
#endif
};
```

Description

The `CArchiveException` class represents error conditions that may occur during I/O operations in member functions of the `CArchive` class. When the exception is thrown, the `m_cause` member variable of the `CArchiveException` object contains the cause of the error. Therefore, in the `CATCH` block, you can determine the cause by comparing `m_cause` with the enumerated list of error conditions shown in the "Summary" section.

See Also

`CFileException` `CMemoryException` `CNotSupportedException` `COleException` `CResourceException`	Other exception classes

CByteArray

Inheritance Hierarchy

`CObject -> CByteArray`

Summary

```
#include <afxcoll.h>

class CByteArray : public CObject
{
    DECLARE_SERIAL(CByteArray)
public:

// Constructor and destructor.
    CByteArray();
    ~CByteArray();

// Serializing the array.
    void    Serialize(CArchive&);

// Getting and setting attributes.
    int     GetSize() const;
    int     GetUpperBound() const;
    void    SetSize(int nNewSize, int nGrowBy = -1);

// Cleaning up.
    void    FreeExtra();
    void    RemoveAll();
```

```
// Accessing elements.
    BYTE     GetAt(int nIndex) const;
    void     SetAt(int nIndex, BYTE newElement);
    BYTE&    ElementAt(int nIndex);
    BYTE     operator[](int nIndex) const;
    BYTE&    operator[](int nIndex);

// Growing the array.
    void SetAtGrow(int nIndex, BYTE newElement);
    int  Add(BYTE newElement);

// Moving elements around.
    void InsertAt(int nIndex, BYTE newElement, int nCount = 1);
    void RemoveAt(int nIndex, int nCount = 1);
    void InsertAt(int nStartIndex, CByteArray* pNewArray);

// Debugging.
#ifdef _DEBUG
    void    Dump(CDumpContext&) const;
    void    AssertValid() const;
#endif

// Hidden implementation details....
};
```

Description

The `CByteArray` class represents an array of bytes that can grow dynamically, if necessary. `CByteArray` is part of the array classes generated from a template. Thus, all the array classes—`CByteArray`, `CDWordArray`, `CObArray`, `CPtrArray`, `CStringArray`, and `CUintArray`, *and* `CWordArray`—contain the same set of member functions. Only the data stored in the array elements varies. Because of this similarity, you can use the documentation for the `CObArray` class to see how the member functions of the `CByteArray` class work. Remember that `CObArray` stores pointers to `CObject`, but `CByteArray` stores the `BYTE` data type. So, wherever you see the `CObject*` data type in `CObArray`, replace it with `BYTE`.

See Also

`CObArray`	For more information on member functions of the array classes

CDumpContext

Inheritance Hierarchy

None.

Summary

```
#include <afx.h>
class CDumpContext
{
public:
// Constructor.
    CDumpContext(CFile* pFile); // May throw CFileException or
                                //   CMemoryException

// Attributes.
    CFile* m_pFile;         // File where the dump goes.
    int  GetDepth() const; // Return depth of dump (see SetDepth).

// Sets the "depth"--determines how objects in collections are
// dumped. If depth > 0, objects in the collection are dumped
// recursively.
    void SetDepth(int nNewDepth); // Set depth to nNewDepth

// Operations (insert variables and objects into the dump context).
    CDumpContext& operator<<(const char FAR* lpsz);
    CDumpContext& operator<<(const void FAR* lp);
    CDumpContext& operator<<(const void NEAR* np);
    CDumpContext& operator<<(const CObject* pOb);
    CDumpContext& operator<<(const CObject& ob);
    CDumpContext& operator<<(BYTE by);
    CDumpContext& operator<<(WORD w);
    CDumpContext& operator<<(UINT u);
    CDumpContext& operator<<(LONG l);
    CDumpContext& operator<<(DWORD dw);
    CDumpContext& operator<<(int n);

// Dump the pby array (of size nBytes) in a hexadecimal format
// with nWidth bytes dumped per line of output. The string
// pszLine is displayed at the beginning of each line of output.

    void HexDump(const char* pszLine, BYTE* pby,
        int nBytes, int nWidth);
```

```
// Write buffered data to the file associated with this
// CDumpContext. May throw a CFileException.

    void Flush();

// Hidden implementation details....
};
```

Description

The CDumpContext class acts as a stream to which you can direct diagnostic messages. When working with the debugging version of the Microsoft Foundation Class library, you can use a predefined CDumpContext object named afxDump to display diagnostic output. The afxDump object is similar to the cerr stream of the C++ iostream package.

You also can send diagnostic output to a specific file. To do this, you first must open the file by creating a CFile object. Then, you can invoke the CDumpContext constructor with that CFile pointer as an argument and create a dump context for use in your application. To support diagnostic dumps in your classes, you should override the Dump member function. To actually send diagnostic information to the dump context, you can either call the Dump member function of objects or use the overloaded insertion (<<) operators.

The member functions of the CDumpContext class may throw exceptions of the type CFileException and CMemoryException.

See Also

CFile	You need a CFile object to create a CDumpContext

CDWordArray

Inheritance Hierarchy

CObject -> CDWordArray

Summary

```
#include <afxcoll.h>
class CDWordArray : public CObject
{
    DECLARE_SERIAL(CDWordArray)
public:
// Constructor and destructor.
    CDWordArray();
    ~CDWordArray();
```

```
// Attributes.
    int      GetSize() const;
    int      GetUpperBound() const;
    void     SetSize(int nNewSize, int nGrowBy = -1);

// Cleaning up.
    void     FreeExtra();
    void     RemoveAll();

// Accessing elements.
    DWORD    GetAt(int nIndex) const;
    void     SetAt(int nIndex, DWORD newElement);
    DWORD&   ElementAt(int nIndex);
    DWORD    operator[](int nIndex) const;
    DWORD&   operator[](int nIndex);

// Growing the array.
    void     SetAtGrow(int nIndex, DWORD newElement);
    int      Add(DWORD newElement);

// Moving elements around.
    void     InsertAt(int nIndex, DWORD newElement,
        int nCount = 1);
    void     RemoveAt(int nIndex, int nCount = 1);
    void     InsertAt(int nStartIndex, CDWordArray* pNewArray);

// Serializing the array.
    void     Serialize(CArchive&);

// Debugging.
#ifdef _DEBUG
    void     Dump(CDumpContext&) const;
    void     AssertValid() const;
#endif

// Hidden implementation details....
};
```

Description

The `CDWordArray` class represents an array of 32-bit, double-word values that can grow dynamically, if necessary. `CDWordArray` is part of the array classes generated from a template. Thus, all the array classes—`CByteArray`, `CDWordArray`, `CObArray`, `CPtrArray`,

CStringArray, and CWordArray—contain the same set of member functions; only the data stored in the array elements varies. Because of this similarity, you can use the documentation for the CObArray class to see how the member functions of the CDWordArray class work. Remember that CObArray stores pointers to CObject, but CDWordArray stores the DWORD data type. So, wherever you see the CObject* data type in CObArray, replace it with DWORD.

See Also

CObArray	For more information on member functions of the array classes

CException

Inheritance Hierarchy

CObject -> CException

Summary

```
#include <afx.h>
class CException : public CObject
{
    DECLARE_DYNAMIC(CException)
};
```

Description

CException is the abstract base class for exceptions.

See Also

CArchiveException CFileException CMemoryException CNotSupportedException COleException CResourceException	Exception classes

CFile

Inheritance Hierarchy

CObject -> CFile

Summary

```
#include <afx.h>
class CFile : public CObject
```

```
{
    DECLARE_DYNAMIC(CFile)

public:
// Flag values.
    enum OpenFlags
    {
        modeRead =          0x0000, // Open for reading only.
        modeWrite =         0x0001, // Open for writing only.
        modeReadWrite =     0x0002, // Open for read+write.
        shareCompat =       0x0000, // Multiple open allowed.
        shareExclusive =    0x0010, // Can open only once.
        shareDenyWrite =    0x0020, // Only one process writes.
        shareDenyRead =     0x0030, // Only one process reads.
        shareDenyNone =     0x0040, // Other processes can
                                    //   read or write.
        modeNoInherit =     0x0080, // Child cannot inherit.
        modeCreate =        0x1000, // Create a new file.
                                    // (Truncate existing file.)

// typeText and typeBinary are used in derived classes only.
        typeText =          0x4000, // Open for text I/O
        typeBinary =   (int)0x8000  // Open for binary I/O
    };

    enum Attribute
    {
        normal =    0x00,
        readOnly =  0x01,
        hidden =    0x02,
        system =    0x04,
        volume =    0x08,
        directory = 0x10,
        archive =   0x20
    };

    enum SeekPosition { begin = 0x0, current = 0x1, end = 0x2 };

    enum {hFileNull = -1};

// Constructors and destructor.
    CFile();
```

```
    CFile(int hFile);
    CFile(const char* pszFileName, UINT nOpenFlags);
    virtual ~CFile();

// Attributes.
    UINT m_hFile;

    virtual DWORD GetPosition() const;
    virtual BOOL GetStatus(CFileStatus& rStatus) const;

// Operations.
    virtual BOOL Open(const char* pszFileName, UINT nOpenFlags,
        CFileException* pError = NULL);

    static void Rename(const char* pszOldName,
        const char* pszNewName);
    static void Remove(const char* pszFileName);
    static BOOL GetStatus(const char* pszFileName,
        CFileStatus& rStatus);
    static void SetStatus(const char* pszFileName,
        const CFileStatus& status);

    DWORD   SeekToEnd();
    void    SeekToBegin();

// The following functions may be overridden in derived
// classes:
    virtual CFile* Duplicate() const;

    virtual LONG Seek(LONG lOff, UINT nFrom);
    virtual void SetLength(DWORD dwNewLen);
    virtual DWORD GetLength() const;

    virtual UINT Read(void FAR* lpBuf, UINT nCount);
    virtual void Write(const void FAR* lpBuf, UINT nCount);

    virtual void LockRange(DWORD dwPos, DWORD dwCount);
    virtual void UnlockRange(DWORD dwPos, DWORD dwCount);

    virtual void Flush();
    virtual void Close();
```

```
// Diagnostic support.
#ifdef _DEBUG
    virtual void AssertValid() const;
    virtual void Dump(CDumpContext& dc) const;
#endif

// Hidden implementation details....
};
```

Description

The CFile class supports unbuffered, binary read and write operations to disk files. It also serves as the base class for CStdioFile and CMemFile classes, which offer more specialized file access and in-memory file I/O, respectively. CFile offers a number of member functions for manipulating files. It also includes several static member functions that you can use to query the status of a file or rename it without opening the file.

Use CFile to open files for binary I/O. You also need a CFile object when you create an instance of the CArchive class that can store objects for later retrieval.

Member Variables

```
UINT m_hFile;
```

This is the file handle for an open file. If m_hFile is not yet initialized, it is set to CFile::m_hFileNull. You shouldn't need to access or use this member variable directly.

Member Functions

Constructors

```
CFile();    // Default constructor. Call Open to attach file
            // Sets m_hFile to CFile::hFileNull

CFile(int hFile); // hFile = handle to file that is already open

CFile(const char* pszFileName, UINT nOpenFlags);
```

Each of these constructors creates a CFile object and associates a file with that object. You can either:

- Provide a handle (hFile) to a file that's already open.
- Specify a file by name (pszFileName).

When opening a file by name, you must specify the mode in nOpenFlags—use a bitwise-OR of enumerated constants from the enumeration nOpenFlags (see the "Summary" section). The constructor `CFile(const char*, UINT)` may throw a `CFileException` if it fails to open the specified file.

```
virtual ~CFile();
```

This closes the associated file if it's open, and destroys the `CFile` object.

Attributes

```
virtual DWORD GetPosition() const;
```

Returns the current position in the file. You can use this position in a subsequent call to `Seek` in order to reposition the file to a known location.

```
virtual BOOL GetStatus(CFileStatus& rStatus) const;
```

Copies the file's status information into a `CFileStatus` structure with an address you provide in the *rStatus* argument. See the reference entry for `CFileStatus` for more information on that structure. This segment returns `TRUE` if all goes well; otherwise, it returns `FALSE`.

Operations

```
virtual void Close();
```

Closes the file and sets `m_hFile` to the constant `CFile::hFileNull`. It may throw a `CFileException` in case of an error.

```
virtual CFile* Duplicate() const;
```

Returns a pointer to a duplicated version of this `CFile`. This is equivalent to the `dup` function of the C library. This function may throw a `CFileException` in case of an error.

```
virtual void Flush();
```

Writes any data remaining in the buffer to the file. The code may throw a `CFileException` in case of an error.

```
virtual DWORD GetLength() const;
```

Returns the current length of the file in bytes. The code may throw a `CFileException` if unsuccessful.

```
static BOOL GetStatus(const char* pszFileName,
    CFileStatus& rStatus);
```

Fills the specified `CFileStatus` structure with the status of the file named *`pszFileName`*. This segment returns `TRUE` if successful; otherwise, it returns `FALSE`.

```
virtual void LockRange(
    DWORD dwPos,     // Start locking at this position.
    DWORD dwCount); // Lock these many bytes.
```

Locks a specified range of bytes in a file to prevent access by other processes. If the region is already locked or you have not run `SHARE.EXE`, `LockRange` throws a `CFileException`.

```
virtual BOOL Open(
    const char* pszFileName, // Name of file to open.
    UINT nOpenFlags, // Open mode (see enum OpenFlags).
    CFileException* pError = NULL); // Info on error return.
```

Opens the named file using the specified open mode. You can use `Open` to associate a file with a `CFile` object that has been created with the default `CFile()` constructor. If successful, `Open` returns `TRUE`; otherwise, it returns `FALSE`. In the event of a `FALSE` return value, `Open` provides information about the cause of the error in the `CFileException` object with the address you provide in the *`pError`* argument. This function does not throw any exceptions.

```
virtual UINT Read(void FAR* lpBuf, UINT nCount);
```

Reads a specified number (*`nCount`*) of bytes from the file into the buffer *`lpBuf`* and returns the actual number of bytes read into the buffer. This segment will throw a `CFileException` in the event of an error.

```
static void Remove(const char* pszFileName);
```

Deletes the specified file. You cannot use it to delete a directory. This segment throws a `CFileException` in case of an error.

```
static void Rename(const char* pszOldName,
    const char* pszNewName);
```

Renames a file from *`pszOldName`* to *`pszNewName`*. You cannot use it to rename a directory. Throws a `CFileException` in the event of an error.

```
virtual LONG Seek(LONG lOff, UINT nFrom);
```

Sets the current position in the file to the location at an offset *`lOff`* from a specified reference point *`nFrom`*, which must be one of the following constants:

`CFile::begin`	Beginning of file
`CFile::current`	Current position
`CFile::end`	End of file

Throws a `CFileException` in the event of an error. Note that `lOff` may be positive or negative. `Seek` returns the byte offset of the new position in the file.

```
void SeekToBegin();
```

Sets the current position to the beginning of the file. Throws a `CFileException` in the event of an error.

```
DWORD SeekToEnd();
```

Sets the current position to the end of the file and returns the length of the file in bytes. This code throws a `CFileException` in the event of an error.

```
virtual void SetLength(DWORD dwNewLen);
```

Sets the desired length of the file. This code throws a `CFileException` in the event of an error.

```
static void SetStatus(const char* pszFileName,
    const CFileStatus& status);
```

Sets the status of the named file using information you provide in the `CFileStatus` structure status. This code throws a `CFileException` in the event of an error.

```
virtual void UnlockRange(
    DWORD dwPos,     // Offset of first byte.
    DWORD dwCount); // Unlock these many bytes.
```

Unlocks a specified range of bytes that previously was locked by `LockRange`. This code throws a `CFileException` in the event of an error.

```
virtual void Write(const void FAR* lpBuf, UINT nCount);
```

Writes *nCount* bytes from the buffer *lpBuf* into the file. This code throws a `CFileException` in the event of an error.

See Also

`CArchive`	`CFile` is used in `CArchive`
`CMemFile`, `CStdioFile`	Other file classes

CFileException

Inheritance Hierarchy

`CObject -> CException -> CFileException`

Summary

```
#include <afx.h>
class CFileException : public CException
{
```

```
    DECLARE_DYNAMIC(CFileException)

public:
// Enumerated constants to indicate cause of exception:
    enum
    {
        none,               // No error occurred.
        generic,            // Unspecified error.
        fileNotFound,       // No such file exists.
        badPath,            // Invalid pathname.
        tooManyOpenFiles,// Too many files open.
        accessDenied,       // Cannot access file.
        invalidFile,        // File handle is not valid.
        removeCurrentDir,// Cannot remove current working directory.
        directoryFull,      // No more directory entries.
        badSeek,            // Error setting file pointer.
        hardIO,             // Hardware error.
        sharingViolation,// Either SHARE.EXE not loaded or
                            //   shared region is locked.
        lockViolation,      // Attempting to lock a region
                            //   that is already locked.
        diskFull,           // Disk is full.
        endOfFile,          // Reached end of file.
    };

// Constructor.

    CFileException(int cause = CFileException::none,
        LONG lOsError = -1);

// Attributes.
    int  m_cause;     // Cause of error (one of the enumerated
                      //   constants shown above).
    LONG m_lOsError; // Operating system's error code for this
                      //   exception.

// Operations.
    static int OsErrorToException(LONG lOsError);
    static int ErrnoToException(int nErrno);
    static void ThrowOsError(LONG lOsError);
    static void ThrowErrno(int nErrno);

// Diagnostic support.
```

```
#ifdef _DEBUG
    virtual void Dump(CDumpContext&) const;
#endif
};
```

Description

The `CFileException` class represents file errors—exceptions that occur when you're opening or closing files and when you're reading from a file or writing to it. In the `CATCH` block for a `CFileException`, you should check the `m_cause` member variable of the `CFileException` object to determine why the exception was thrown. Another member variable, `m_IOsError`, contains an operating system-specific error code for the error that caused `CFileException` to be thrown.

Comments in the "Summary" section explain most of the variables, enumerated constants, and functions. The next section briefly describes several functions.

Member Functions

`static int ErrnoToException(int nErrno);`

Returns the enumerated constant that corresponds to an error indicated by *`nErrno`*, which is one of the error codes defined in the C library's header file errno.h.

`static int OsErrorToException(LONG lOsError);`

Returns the enumerated constant that corresponds to an operating system-dependent error code *`lOSError`*.

`static void ThrowErrno(int nErrno);`

Throws a `CFileException` object corresponding to the error code *`nErrno`*, which is one of the error codes defined in the C library's header file errno.h.

`static void ThrowOsError(LONG lOsError);`

Throws a `CFileException` object corresponding to the operating system-dependent error code *`lOSError`*.

See Also

`CFile`	Member functions of this class throw `CFileException`

`CArchiveException`
`CMemoryException`
`CNotSupportedException`
`COleException`
`CResourceException`
	Other exception classes

CFileStatus

Inheritance Hierarchy

None.

Summary

```
#include <afx.h>
struct CFileStatus
{
// Attributes.
    CTime m_ctime;        // Date/time of file creation.
    CTime m_mtime;        // Date/time of last modification.
    CTime m_atime;        // Date/time of last access.
    LONG  m_size;         // Size of file in bytes.
    BYTE  m_attribute;    // File attributes (bitwise-OR of
                          //   CFile::Attribute enum values.
    BYTE  _m_padding;     // A padding byte.
    char  m_szFullName[_MAX_PATH]; // Absolute pathname.

// Diagnostic support.
#ifdef _DEBUG
    void Dump(CDumpContext& dc) const;
#endif
};
```

Description

The `CFileStatus` structure holds information about a file. The comments in the "Summary" section explain the meaning of the member variables of `CFileStatus`.

See Also

`CFile`	`CFile` member functions use `CFileStatus` to store the file status

CMapPtrToPtr

Inheritance Hierarchy

`CObject -> CMapPtrToPtr`

Summary

```
#include <afxcoll.h>
class CMapPtrToPtr : public CObject
{
    DECLARE_DYNAMIC(CMapPtrToPtr)
```

```
public:
// Constructor and destructor.
    CMapPtrToPtr(int nBlockSize=10);
    ~CMapPtrToPtr();

// Attributes.
    int      GetCount() const;
    BOOL     IsEmpty() const;

// Operations.
    BOOL     Lookup(void* key, void*& rValue) const;
    void*&   operator[](void* key);
    void     SetAt(void* key, void* newValue);

    BOOL     RemoveKey(void* key);
    void     RemoveAll();

    POSITION GetStartPosition() const;
    void     GetNextAssoc(POSITION& rNextPosition,
        void*& rKey, void*& rValue) const;

    UINT     GetHashTableSize() const;
    void     InitHashTable(UINT hashSize);
    UINT     HashKey(void* key) const;

// Diagnostic support.
#ifdef _DEBUG
    void     Dump(CDumpContext&) const;
    void     AssertValid() const;
#endif

// Hidden implementation details....
};
```

Description

The CMapPtrToPtr class maps a void pointer to another void pointer. In other words, you can look up a void pointer using another void pointer as a key. CMapPtrToPtr is one of the map classes generated from a template. All the map classes—CMapPtrToPtr, CMapPtrToWord, CMapStringToOb, CMapStringToPtr, CMapStringToString, CMapWordToOb, and CMapWordToPtr—contain the same set of member functions; only the data types of keys and values vary. Because of this similarity, you can use the documentation for the CMapStringToOb class to observe the workings of member functions in the CMapPtrToPtr class.

Remember that `CMapStringToOb` maps `CStrings` to `CObject` pointers, but `CMapPtrToPtr` maps one void pointer to another. Therefore, wherever you see a `CObject*` return value in `CMapStringToOb`, replace it with `void*`. Similarly, any `CString` or `const char*` function arguments must be replaced by `void*`. Note that this class cannot be serialized.

See Also

`CMapStringToOb`	For more information on member functions of the map classes

CMapPtrToWord

Inheritance Hierarchy

`CObject -> CMapPtrToWord`

Summary

```
#include <afxcoll.h>
class CMapPtrToWord : public CObject
{
    DECLARE_DYNAMIC(CMapPtrToWord)
public:
// Constructor and destructor.
    CMapPtrToWord(int nBlockSize=10);
    ~CMapPtrToWord();

// Attributes.
    int     GetCount() const;
    BOOL    IsEmpty() const;

// Operations.
    BOOL   Lookup(void* key, WORD& rValue) const;
    WORD&  operator[](void* key);
    void    SetAt(void* key, WORD newValue);

    BOOL    RemoveKey(void* key);
    void    RemoveAll();

    POSITION GetStartPosition() const;
    void     GetNextAssoc(POSITION& rNextPosition,
        void*& rKey, WORD& rValue) const;

    UINT    GetHashTableSize() const;
    void    InitHashTable(UINT hashSize);
    UINT    HashKey(void* key) const;
```

```
// Diagnostic support.
#ifdef _DEBUG
    void    Dump(CDumpContext&) const;
    void    AssertValid() const;
#endif

// Hidden implementation details....
};
```

Description

The CMapPtrToWord class maps a void pointer (void*) to a 16-bit WORD. In other words, you can look up a 16-bit value using a void pointer as a key. CMapPtrToWord is one of the map classes generated from a template. All the map classes—CMapPtrToPtr, CMapPtrToWord, CMapStringToOb, CMapStringToPtr, CMapStringToString, CMapWordToOb, and CMapWordToPtr—contain the same set of member functions; only the data types of keys and values vary. Because of this similarity, you can use the documentation for the CMapStringToOb class to observe how the member functions work in the CMapPtrToWord class. Remember that CMapStringToOb maps CStrings to CObject pointers, but CMapPtrToWord maps a void pointer to a WORD. Therefore, wherever you see a CObject* return value in CMapStringToOb, replace it with WORD. Similarly, any CString or const char* function arguments must be replaced by void*.

See Also

CMapStringToOb	For more information on member functions of the map classes

CMapStringToOb

Inheritance Hierarchy

CObject -> CMapStringToOb

Summary

```
#include <afxcoll.h>

class CMapStringToOb : public CObject
{
    DECLARE_SERIAL(CMapStringToOb)
public:

// Constructor and destructor.
    CMapStringToOb(int nBlockSize=10);
    ~CMapStringToOb();
```

```
// Attributes.
    int     GetCount() const;
    BOOL    IsEmpty() const;

// Operations.
    BOOL      Lookup(const char* key, CObject*& rValue) const;
    CObject*& operator[](const char* key);

    void    SetAt(const char* key, CObject* newValue);

    BOOL    RemoveKey(const char* key);
    void    RemoveAll();

    POSITION GetStartPosition() const;
    void     GetNextAssoc(POSITION& rNextPosition, CString& rKey,
        CObject*& rValue) const;
    UINT    GetHashTableSize() const;
    void    InitHashTable(UINT hashSize);
    UINT    HashKey(const char* key) const;

// Serialization support.
    void    Serialize(CArchive&);

// Diagnostic support.
#ifdef _DEBUG
    void    Dump(CDumpContext&) const;
    void    AssertValid() const;
#endif

// Hidden implementation details....
};
```

Description

The `CMapStringToOb` class maps a `CString` to a `CObject` pointer (`CObject*`). In other words, you can look up a `CObject` pointer using a `CString` as a key. `CMapStringToOb` is one of the map classes generated from a template. All the map classes—`CMapPtrToPtr`, `CMapPtrToWord`, `CMapStringToOb`, `CMapStringToPtr`, `CMapStringToString`, `CMapWordToOb`, and `CMapWordToPtr`—contain the same set of member functions; only the data types of keys and values vary. Because of this similarity, you can use the documentation for the `CMapStringToOb` class to see how the member functions work in the other map classes. Remember that `CMapStringToOb` maps `CStrings` to `CObject` pointers, but the key and value types of the other map classes vary.

Member Functions

Constructor and Destructor

```
CMapStringToOb(int nBlockSize=10);
```

Constructs a `CMapStringToOb` collection that will grow *nBlockSize* entries at a time.

```
~CMapStringToOb();
```

Destroys the `CMapStringToOb` collection, including all `CString` objects used as keys in the map. However, the `CObject` objects are not destroyed.

Attributes

```
int GetCount() const;
```

Returns the total number of key-to-value associations in the map.

```
BOOL IsEmpty() const;
```

Returns `TRUE` if the map is empty.

Operations

```
UINT GetHashTableSize() const;
```

Returns the size of the internal hash table used to map a key to a value.

```
void GetNextAssoc(
    POSITION& rNextPosition, // Get key-value at this position
                             //   and update position afterward.
    CString& rKey,           // Retrieved key goes here.
    CObject*& rValue) const; // Retrieved value goes here.
```

Retrieves the key-value pair at the `POSITION` indicated by *rNextPosition* and updates *rNextPosition* to the next pair. The retrieved key and value are in *rKey* and *rValue*.

```
POSITION GetStartPosition() const;
```

Returns a `POSITION` value you can use with the `GetNextAssoc` function to iterate all the key-value pairs in the map.

```
UINT HashKey(const char* key) const;
```

Returns the result when applying the hash function to the key.

```
void InitHashTable(UINT hashSize);
```

Initializes a new hash table of the specified size and deletes the old hash table.

```
BOOL Lookup(const char* key, CObject*& rValue) const;
```

Retrieves the value corresponding to the specified key. The retrieved value is in *rValue*. It returns `TRUE` if the search succeeds; otherwise, it returns `FALSE`.

```
CObject*& operator[](const char* key);
```

Sets the value corresponding to a key as follows:

```
CMapStringToOb map;
// Assume Widget is a class derived from CObject
map["Item 1"] = new Widget(1);
```

Operator is a convenient substitute for the `SetAt` function.

```
void RemoveAll();
```

Removes all key-value pairs in the map and destroys the keys only.

```
BOOL RemoveKey(const char* key);
```

Removes the key-value pair corresponding to a specified key. If the entry is found and removed, `RemoveKey` returns `TRUE`; otherwise, it returns `FALSE`.

```
void SetAt(const char* key, CObject* newValue);
```

Sets the value corresponding to a key. If that key is not found, `SetAt` inserts the key-value pair as a new entry to the map.

See Also

`CMapPtrToPtr`	Other map classes
`CMapPtrToWord`	
`CMapStringToPtr`	
`CMapStringToString`	
`CMapWordToOb`	
`CMapWordToPtr`	

CMapStringToPtr

Inheritance Hierarchy

`CObject -> CMapStringToPtr`

Summary

```
#include <afxcoll.h>
class CMapStringToPtr : public CObject
{
    DECLARE_DYNAMIC(CMapStringToPtr)
public:
// Constructor and destructor.
    CMapStringToPtr(int nBlockSize=10);
    ~CMapStringToPtr();
```

```
// Attributes.
    int      GetCount() const;
    BOOL     IsEmpty() const;

// Operations.
    BOOL     Lookup(const char* key, void*& rValue) const;
    void*&   operator[](const char* key);

    void     SetAt(const char* key, void* newValue);

    BOOL     RemoveKey(const char* key);
    void     RemoveAll();

    POSITION GetStartPosition() const;
    void     GetNextAssoc(POSITION& rNextPosition,
        CString& rKey, void*& rValue) const;

    UINT     GetHashTableSize() const;
    void     InitHashTable(UINT hashSize);
    UINT     HashKey(const char* key) const;

// Diagnostic support.
#ifdef _DEBUG
    void     Dump(CDumpContext&) const;
    void     AssertValid() const;
#endif

// Hidden implementation details....
};
```

Description

The `CMapStringToPtr` class maps a `CString` to a void pointer (`void*`). In other words, you can look up a void pointer using a `CString` as a key. `CMapStringToPtr` is one of the map classes generated from a template. All the map classes—`CMapPtrToPtr`, `CMapPtrToWord`, `CMapStringToOb`, `CMapStringToPtr`, `CMapStringToString`, `CMapWordToOb`, and `CMapWordToPtr`—contain the same set of member functions; only the data types of keys and values vary. Because of this similarity, you can use the documentation for the `CMapStringToOb` class to see how the member functions work in the `CMapStringToPtr` class. Remember that `CMapStringToOb` maps `CStrings` to `CObject` pointers, but `CMapStringToPtr` maps `CString` to a void pointer. Therefore, wherever you see a `CObject*` return a value in `CMapStringToOb`, replace it with `void*`.

See Also

`CMapStringToOb`	For more information on member functions of the map classes

CMapStringToString

Inheritance Hierarchy

`CObject -> CMapStringToString`

Summary

```
#include <afxcoll.h>
class CMapStringToString : public CObject
{
    DECLARE_SERIAL(CMapStringToString)
public:
// Constructor and destructor.
    CMapStringToString(int nBlockSize=10);
    ~CMapStringToString();

// Attributes.
    int      GetCount() const;
    BOOL     IsEmpty() const;

// Operations.
    BOOL      Lookup(const char* key, CString& rValue) const;
    CString& operator[](const char* key);

    void     SetAt(const char* key, const char* newValue);

    BOOL     RemoveKey(const char* key);
    void     RemoveAll();

    POSITION GetStartPosition() const;
    void     GetNextAssoc(POSITION& rNextPosition,
        CString& rKey, CString& rValue) const;

    UINT     GetHashTableSize() const;
    void     InitHashTable(UINT hashSize);
    UINT     HashKey(const char* key) const;

// Serialization.
    void     Serialize(CArchive&);
```

```
// Diagnostic support.
#ifdef _DEBUG
    void    Dump(CDumpContext&) const;
    void    AssertValid() const;
#endif

// Hidden implementation details....
};
```

Description

The CMapStringToString class maps one CString to another CString. In other words, like a real-world dictionary, you can look up one CString using another CString as a key. CMapStringToString is one of the map classes generated from a template. All the map classes—CMapPtrToPtr, CMapPtrToWord, CMapStringToOb, CMapStringToPtr, CMapStringToString, CMapWordToOb, and CMapWordToPtr—contain the same set of member functions; only the data types of keys and values vary. Because of this similarity, you can use the documentation for the CMapStringToOb class to see how the member functions operate in the CMapStringToString class. Remember that CMapStringToOb maps CStrings to CObject pointers, but CMapStringToString maps one CString to another. Therefore, wherever you see a CObject* return value in CMapStringToOb, replace it with CString.

See Also

CMapStringToOb	For more information on member functions of the map classes

CMapWordToOb

Inheritance Hierarchy

CObject -> CMapWordToOb

Summary

```
#include <afxcoll.h>
class CMapWordToOb : public CObject
{
    DECLARE_SERIAL(CMapWordToOb)
public:
// Constructor and destructor.
    CMapWordToOb(int nBlockSize=10);
    ~CMapWordToOb();
```

```
// Attributes.
    int     GetCount() const;
    BOOL    IsEmpty() const;

// Operations.
    BOOL      Lookup(WORD key, CObject*& rValue) const;
    CObject*& operator[](WORD key);

    void    SetAt(WORD key, CObject* newValue);

    BOOL    RemoveKey(WORD key);
    void    RemoveAll();

    POSITION GetStartPosition() const;
    void     GetNextAssoc(POSITION& rNextPosition,
        WORD& rKey, CObject*& rValue) const;

    UINT    GetHashTableSize() const;
    void    InitHashTable(UINT hashSize);
    UINT    HashKey(WORD key) const;

// Serialization support.
    void    Serialize(CArchive&);

// Diagnostic support.
#ifdef _DEBUG
    void    Dump(CDumpContext&) const;
    void    AssertValid() const;
#endif

// Hidden implementation details....
};
```

Description

The `CMapWordToOb` class maps a 16-bit `WORD` to a `CObject` pointer (`CObject*`). In other words, you can look up a `CObject` pointer using a 16-bit value as a key. `CMapWordToOb` is one of the map classes generated from a template. All the map classes—`CMapPtrToPtr`, `CMapPtrToWord`, `CMapStringToOb`, `CMapStringToPtr`, `CMapStringToString`, `CMapWordToOb`, and `CMapWordToPtr`—contain the same set of member functions; only the data types of keys and values vary. Because of this similarity, you can use the documentation for the `CMapStringToOb` class to observe how the member functions operate in the

CMapWordToOb class. Remember that CMapStringToOb maps CStrings to CObject pointers, but CMapWordToOb maps a WORD to a CObject pointer. Therefore, wherever you see a CString or const char* function argument, replace it with a WORD.

See Also

CMapStringToOb	For more information on member functions of the map classes

CMapWordToPtr

Inheritance Hierarchy

CObject -> CMapWordToPtr

Summary

```
#include <afxcoll.h>
class CMapWordToPtr : public CObject
{
    DECLARE_DYNAMIC(CMapWordToPtr)
public:
// Constructor and destructor.
    CMapWordToPtr(int nBlockSize=10);
    ~CMapWordToPtr();

// Attributes.
    int      GetCount() const;
    BOOL     IsEmpty() const

// Operations.
    BOOL     Lookup(WORD key, void*& rValue) const;
    void*&   operator[](WORD key);

    void     SetAt(WORD key, void* newValue);

    BOOL     RemoveKey(WORD key);
    void     RemoveAll();

    POSITION GetStartPosition() const;
    void     GetNextAssoc(POSITION& rNextPosition,
        WORD& rKey, void*& rValue) const;

    UINT     GetHashTableSize() const;
    void     InitHashTable(UINT hashSize);
    UINT     HashKey(WORD key) const;
```

```
// Diagnostic support.
#ifdef _DEBUG
    void    Dump(CDumpContext&) const;
    void    AssertValid() const;
#endif

// Hidden implementation details....
};
```

Description

The CMapWordToPtr class maps a 16-bit WORD to a void pointer (void*). In other words, you can look up a void pointer using a 16-bit value as a key. CMapWordToPtr is one of the map classes generated from a template. All the map classes—CMapPtrToPtr, CMapPtrToWord, CMapStringToOb, CMapStringToPtr, CMapStringToString, CMapWordToOb, and CMapWordToPtr—contain the same set of member functions; only the data types of keys and values vary. Because of this similarity, you can use the documentation for the CMapStringToOb class to see how the member functions work in the CMapWordToPtr class. Remember that CMapStringToOb maps CStrings to CObject pointers, but CMapWordToPtr maps a WORD to a void pointer. Therefore, wherever you see a CObject* return value in CMapStringToOb, replace it with void*. Similarly, any CString or const char* function arguments must be replaced by WORD.

See Also

CMapStringToOb	For more information on member functions of the map classes

CMemFile

Inheritance Hierarchy

CObject -> CFile -> CMemFile

Summary

```
#include <afx.h>
class CMemFile : public CFile
{
    DECLARE_DYNAMIC(CMemFile)
public:
// Constructor and destructor.
    CMemFile(UINT nGrowBytes = 1024);
    virtual ~CMemFile();
```

```
// Attributes.
    virtual DWORD GetPosition() const;
    virtual BOOL GetStatus(CFileStatus& rStatus) const;

// Overridable operations.
    virtual LONG Seek(LONG lOff, UINT nFrom);
    virtual void SetLength(DWORD dwNewLen);
    virtual UINT Read(void FAR* lpBuf, UINT nCount);
    virtual void Write(const void FAR* lpBuf, UINT nCount);
    virtual void Flush();
    virtual void Close();

// The following are not implemented. Using them would generate
// a CNotSupportedException.
    virtual CFile* Duplicate() const;
    virtual void LockRange(DWORD dwPos, DWORD dwCount);
    virtual void UnlockRange(DWORD dwPos, DWORD dwCount);

// Diagnostic support.
#ifdef _DEBUG
    virtual void Dump(CDumpContext& dc) const;
    virtual void AssertValid() const;
#endif

// Hidden implementation details....
};
```

Description

With the `CMemFile` class, you can read from and write to a buffer in memory as if it were a file. The `CMemFile` constructor automatically allocates the memory necessary to store data; the destructor frees this memory. Because the buffer is not really a disk file, you don't need to open anything—simply creating a `CMemFile` object is enough. On the other hand, because `CMemFile` requires a buffer in memory, the constructor may throw a `CMemoryException` if any memory allocation errors occur.

`CMemFile` is derived from `CFile`. In fact, the member functions of `CMemFile` are similar to those of `CFile` except that the following member functions are not implemented in `CMemFile`:

- `Duplicate`
- `LockRange`
- `UnlockRange`

Calling any of these functions will throw a `CNotSupportedException` object to indicate that these functions are unsupported. Also, the *m_hFile* member variable has no meaning in `CMemFile` and is not used here.

See Also

`CFile` Base class of `CMemFile` (see this class for information on member functions of `CMemFile`)

CMemoryException

Inheritance Hierarchy

`CObject -> CException -> CMemoryException`

Summary

```
#include <afx.h>
class CMemoryException : public CException
{
    DECLARE_DYNAMIC(CMemoryException)
public:
    CMemoryException();
};
```

Description

The `CMemoryException` class denotes a memory-allocation error. When the C++ operator `new` runs out of memory, it throws `CMemoryExceptions`. If you use the C library functions `malloc` or `calloc` to allocate memory, you should throw a `CMemoryException` when these functions return a `NULL` pointer indicating error.

See Also

`CFileException` Other exception classes
`CArchiveException`
`CNotSupportedException`
`COleException`
`CResourceException`

CMemoryState

Inheritance Hierarchy

None.

Summary

```
#include <afx.h>
struct CMemoryState
{
```

```
// Attributes.
    enum blockUsage
    {
        freeBlock,     // Not used.
        objectBlock,   // Contains a CObject derived class object.
        bitBlock,      // Contains ::operator new data.
        nBlockUseMax,  // Total number of usages.
    };

    struct CBlockHeader* m_pBlockHeader;
    LONG m_lCounts[nBlockUseMax];
    LONG m_lSizes[nBlockUseMax];
    LONG m_lHighWaterCount;
    LONG m_lTotalCount;

// Constructor.
    CMemoryState();

// Operations.
    void Checkpoint();
    BOOL Difference(const CMemoryState& oldState,
        const CMemoryState& newState);

// Diagnostic output to afxDump.
    void DumpStatistics() const;
    void DumpAllObjectsSince() const;
};
```

Description

The `CMemoryState` structure is reserved for storing information about the heap from which memory is allocated by the `new` operator. As explained in the tutorials earlier in this chapter, you can use `CMemoryState`, and its member functions `Checkpoint` and `Difference`, to detect errors in memory allocation and deallocation. More precisely, you can detect whether your program is not freeing all the memory that it is allocating.

Member Functions

```
void Checkpoint();
```

Captures a snapshot of the heap in the `CMemoryState` object.

```
BOOL Difference(
    const CMemoryState& oldState,  // Is this memory state
    const CMemoryState& newState); //   different from this one?
```

Initializes CMemoryState with information about the difference between two specified CMemoryState objects and returns TRUE if any difference exists.

CNotSupportedException

Inheritance Hierarchy

CObject -> CException -> CNotSupportedException

Summary

```
#include <afx.h>
class CNotSupportedException : public CException
{
    DECLARE_DYNAMIC(CNotSupportedException)
public:
    CNotSupportedException();
};
```

Description

The CNotSupportedException class is used to indicate errors that occur because a requested feature is not supported by an object. For example, if you call the LockRange function for a CMemFile object, a CNotSupportedException is thrown. This indicates that although CMemFile inherits the LockRange function from its base class, CFile, CMemFile does not support the functionality offered by LockRange.

See Also

CFileException CMemoryException CArchiveException COleException CResourceException	Other exception classes

CObArray

Inheritance Hierarchy

CObject -> CObArray

Summary

```
#include <afxcoll.h>
class CObArray : public CObject
{
    DECLARE_SERIAL(CObArray)
public:
```

```
// Constructor and destructor.
    CObArray();
    ~CObArray();

// Attributes.
    int     GetSize() const;
    int     GetUpperBound() const;
    void    SetSize(int nNewSize, int nGrowBy = -1);

// Cleaning up.
    void    FreeExtra();
    void    RemoveAll();

// Accessing elements.
    CObject*    GetAt(int nIndex) const;
    void        SetAt(int nIndex, CObject* newElement);
    CObject*&   ElementAt(int nIndex);
    CObject*    operator[](int nIndex) const;
    CObject*&   operator[](int nIndex);

// Growing the array.
    void    SetAtGrow(int nIndex, CObject* newElement);
    int     Add(CObject* newElement);

// Moving elements around.
    void    InsertAt(int nIndex, CObject* newElement,
        int nCount = 1);
    void    RemoveAt(int nIndex, int nCount = 1);
    void    InsertAt(int nStartIndex, CObArray* pNewArray);

// Serializing the array.
    void    Serialize(CArchive&);

// Debugging.
#ifdef _DEBUG
    void    Dump(CDumpContext&) const;
    void    AssertValid() const;
#endif

// Hidden implementation details....
};
```

Description

The CObArray class represents an array of CObject pointers (CObject*) that can grow dynamically, if necessary. CObArray is part of the array classes generated from a template. All the array classes—CByteArray, CDWordArray, CObArray, CPtrArray, CStringArray, and CWordArray—contain the same set of member functions; only the data stored in the array elements varies. Because of this similarity, you can use the documentation for the CObArray class to see how the member functions in the other array classes work. Remember that CObArray stores pointers to CObject, but the other arrays store different data types.

Member Functions

Constructor and Destructor

```
CObArray();
```

Creates an empty array.

```
~CObArray();
```

Destroys the CObArray object. When a CobArray is destroyed, only the CObject pointers are gone. The actual CObjects still exist.

Attributes

```
int GetSize() const;
```

Returns the size—the number of elements in the array.

```
int GetUpperBound() const;
```

Returns the maximum array index (one less than the size because the first index is 0). GetUpperBounds returns –1 if the array is empty.

```
void SetSize(int nNewSize, int nGrowBy = -1);
```

Sets the new size of the array and indicates the number of elements by which the array should grow.

Cleaning Up

```
void FreeExtra();
```

Releases any extra memory that was allocated when the array had grown.

```
void RemoveAll();
```

Removes all the pointers from the array.

```
void RemoveAt(int nIndex, int nCount = 1);
```

Removes `nCount` elements starting at the index `nIndex`, which should be between 0 and the value returned by `GetUpperBound`.

Accessing Elements

```
CObject*& ElementAt(int nIndex);
```

Returns a reference to the element at `nIndex`. Also, is used internally to implement the access operators (`operator[]`).

```
CObject* GetAt(int nIndex) const;
```

Returns the `CObject` pointer at the specified index.

```
CObject* operator[](int nIndex) const;
```

Accesses the `CObject` pointer at the specified index and is a substitute for the `GetAt` function.

```
CObject*& operator[](int nIndex);
```

Gets or sets the element at a specified index.

```
void SetAt(int nIndex, CObject* newElement);
```

Sets the element at the specified index, `nIndex`, which should be between 0 and the value returned by `GetUpperBound`.

Growing the Array

```
int Add(CObject* newElement);
```

Adds the specified element to the end of the array and returns the index of the newly added element.

```
void InsertAt(int nIndex, CObject* newElement,
    int nCount = 1); // Insert nCount elements
void InsertAt(int nStartIndex, CObArray* pNewArray);
```

Inserts one or more elements into the `CObArray` starting at the specified index.

```
void SetAtGrow(int nIndex, CObject* newElement);
```

Sets the element at the specified index. Unlike `SetAt`, `SetAtGrow` grows the array automatically if necessary.

See Also

`CByteArray`
`CDWordArray`
`CPtrArray`
`CStringArray`
`CWordArray`
	Other array classes

CObject

Inheritance Hierarchy

None. `CObject` is the base class from which most other classes in the Microsoft Foundation Class Library are derived.

Summary

```
#include <afx.h>
class CObject
{
public:
// Object model (types, destruction, allocation).
    virtual CRuntimeClass* GetRuntimeClass() const;

// Virtual destructor.
    virtual ~CObject();

// Attributes.
    BOOL IsSerializable() const;

// Serialization.
    virtual void Serialize(CArchive& ar);

// Runtime type checking/construction support:
    BOOL IsKindOf(const CRuntimeClass* pClass) const;
    static void PASCAL Construct(void* pMemory);
    static CRuntimeClass NEAR classCObject;

// Diagnostic allocations:
    void* operator new(size_t, void* p);
    void* operator new(size_t nSize);
    void operator delete(void* p);

#ifdef _DEBUG
// This version of new tracks the filename and line number
// and is enabled when you
//              #define new DEBUG_NEW
    void* operator new(size_t nSize,
        const char FAR* lpszFileName, int nLine);
#endif
```

```
// Other diagnostic support:
    virtual void AssertValid() const;
    virtual void Dump(CDumpContext& dc) const;

// Hidden implementation details....
};
```

Description

The `CObject` class serves as the base class for most of the classes in the Microsoft Foundation Class library. It provides support for the following:

- *Serialization*—the ability to store objects in a file and retrieve them later
- *Runtime-Class Identification*—the ability to determine the type of an object at runtime
- *Diagnostic output*

The Microsoft Foundation Class library provides the macros `DECLARE_DYNAMIC`, `IMPLEMENT_DYNAMIC`, `DECLARE_SERIAL`, `IMPLEMENT_SERIAL`, and `RUNTIME_CLASS` to support these features. These macros are described earlier in this chapter. The next section briefly describes several functions that help implement these features.

> **`CObject` Does Not Support Multiple Inheritance**
>
> The `CObject` class does not support multiple inheritance. You can, however, use `CObject` as a base class in a class that inherits from multiple base classes as long as `CObject` appears as the leftmost base class in the declaration of that derived class.
>
> None of the other base classes can be derived from `CObject`.

Member Functions

Attributes

```
BOOL IsSerializable() const;
```

Returns `TRUE` if this class can be serialized. A class can be serialized if its declaration (the header file) contains the `DECLARE_SERIAL` macro and the implementation (the source file) includes the `IMPLEMENT_SERIAL` macro.

Serialization

```
virtual void Serialize(CArchive& ar);
```

Writes the data of this object to the archive *ar*. You must override this function in any class you want to serialize.

Runtime Class Identification

```
virtual CRuntimeClass* GetRuntimeClass() const;
```

Returns a pointer to a `CRunTimeClass` structure that corresponds to this object's class. See `CRunTimeClass` for details about the contents of that structure.

```
BOOL IsKindOf(const CRuntimeClass* pClass) const;
```

Returns `TRUE` if an object is of the specified class, or if it's an instance of a class that is derived from the specified class; otherwise, returns `FALSE`.

Diagnostic Support

```
virtual void AssertValid() const;
```

Verifies the validity of an object. You should override this function in your derived classes to provide any necessary consistency checks.

```
virtual void Dump(CDumpContext& dc) const;
```

Dumps the contents of the object to the specified `CDumpContext`. You should override this function in your derived class to dump the appropriate information in the dump context.

See Also

`CRunTimeClass`	To see what information is returned by `GetRuntimeClass`
`CDumpContext`	For information on the dump context

CObList

Inheritance Hierarchy

```
CObject -> CObList
```

Summary

```
#include <afxcoll.h>
class CObList : public CObject
{
   DECLARE_SERIAL(CObList)
public:
// Constructor and destructor.
```

```
    CObList(int nBlockSize=10);
    ~CObList();

// Attributes.
    int     GetCount() const;
    BOOL    IsEmpty() const;

// Peeking at head or tail.
    CObject*&   GetHead();
    CObject*    GetHead() const;
    CObject*&   GetTail();
    CObject*    GetTail() const;

// Adding and removing.
    CObject*    RemoveHead();
    CObject*    RemoveTail();

    POSITION AddHead(CObject* newElement);
    POSITION AddTail(CObject* newElement);

    void    AddHead(CObList* pNewList);
    void    AddTail(CObList* pNewList);

    void    RemoveAll();

// Iterating.
    POSITION GetHeadPosition() const;
    POSITION GetTailPosition() const;
    CObject*&   GetNext(POSITION& rPosition);
    CObject*    GetNext(POSITION& rPosition) const;
    CObject*&   GetPrev(POSITION& rPosition);
    CObject*    GetPrev(POSITION& rPosition) const;

// Accessing an element at a given position.
    CObject*&   GetAt(POSITION position);
    CObject*    GetAt(POSITION position) const;
    void        SetAt(POSITION pos, CObject* newElement);
    void        RemoveAt(POSITION position);

// Inserting before or after a given position.
    POSITION InsertBefore(POSITION position,
        CObject* newElement);
    POSITION InsertAfter(POSITION position,
        CObject* newElement);
```

```
// Finding an element.
    POSITION Find(CObject* searchValue,
        POSITION startAfter = NULL) const;
    POSITION FindIndex(int nIndex) const;

// Serializing.
    void    Serialize(CArchive&);

// Debugging.
#ifdef _DEBUG
    void    Dump(CDumpContext&) const;
    void    AssertValid() const;
#endif

// Hidden implementation details....
};
```

Description

The `CObList` class represents a double-linked list of `CObject` pointers (`CObject*`). `CObList` is part of the list classes generated from a template. All the linked-list classes—`CObList`, `CPtrList`, and `CStringList`—contain the same set of member functions; only the data stored in the list elements varies. Because of this similarity, you can use the documentation for the `CObList` class to see how the member functions work for all the other linked-list classes. Remember that `CObList` stores pointers to `CObject`, but the other classes store different data types.

Member Functions

Constructor and Destructor

`CObList(int nBlockSize=10);`

Creates an empty `CObList` that grows by *`nBlockSize`* elements when necessary.

`~CObList();`

Destroys the pointers in the list and the `CObList` object. Notice that this does not destroy the actual objects with addresses in the linked list.

Attributes

`int GetCount() const;`

Returns the number of elements in the list.

`BOOL IsEmpty() const;`

Returns `TRUE` if the list is empty; otherwise, it returns `FALSE`.

Peeking at Head or Tail

```
CObject*& GetHead();
CObject* GetHead() const;
```

Returns the element (or a reference to the element) at the head of the list.

```
CObject*& GetTail();
CObject* GetTail() const;
```

Returns the element at the end of the list.

Adding and Removing

```
POSITION AddHead(CObject* newElement); // Add this element.
void AddHead(CObList* pNewList); // Add all elements from.
                                 // pNewList to this list.
```

Adds one or all of the elements in another `CObList` to the head of this list. When a single element is added, `AddHead` returns the `POSITION` of that element. This may throw a `CMemoryException`.

```
POSITION AddTail(CObject* newElement);
void AddTail(CObList* pNewList);
```

Adds one or all of the elements in another `CObList` to the end of this list. When a single element is added, `AddTail` returns the `POSITION` of that element. This may throw a `CMemoryException`.

```
void RemoveAll();
```

Removes all the elements from the list and frees the associated memory. The list is empty after you call `RemoveAll`. Remember that this removes the pointers to the `CObjects` but not the `CObjects` themselves. You must delete them before you call `RemoveAll`.

```
void RemoveAt(POSITION position);
```

Removes the element from the specified position.

```
CObject* RemoveHead();
```

Removes the element at the beginning of the list and returns that element.

```
CObject* RemoveTail();
```

Removes the element at the end of the list and returns that element.

Iterating Through the List

```
POSITION GetHeadPosition() const;
```

Returns the position of the element at the beginning of the list. The function returns `NULL` if the list is empty.

```
CObject*& GetNext(POSITION& rPosition);
CObject* GetNext(POSITION& rPosition) const;
```

Returns the element (or a reference to the element) at `rPosition` and updates `rPosition` to the next element in the list.

```
CObject*& GetPrev(POSITION& rPosition);
CObject* GetPrev(POSITION& rPosition) const;
```

Returns the element (or a reference to the element) at `rPosition` and updates `rPosition` to the previous element in the list.

```
POSITION GetTailPosition() const;
```

Returns the position of the element at the end of the list. The function returns `NULL` if the list is empty.

Accessing an Element

```
CObject*& GetAt(POSITION position);
CObject* GetAt(POSITION position) const;
```

Returns the element (or a reference to the element) at the specified position.

```
void SetAt(POSITION pos, CObject* newElement);
```

Sets the element at the specified position to `newElement`.

Inserting an Element

```
POSITION InsertAfter(POSITION position,
    CObject* newElement);
```

Inserts an element after the specified position and returns the position of the newly added element.

```
POSITION InsertBefore(POSITION position,
    CObject* newElement);
```

Inserts an element before the specified position and returns the position of the newly added element.

Finding an Element

```
POSITION Find(CObject* searchValue,
    POSITION startAfter = NULL) const;
```

Searches the list to find an element matching `searchValue`, starting at the position `startAfter`. This also returns the position of the matching element, or `NULL` if no matching element exists.

```
POSITION FindIndex(int nIndex) const;
```

Returns the `POSITION` for an element at a specified index in the list.

See Also

`CPtrList`, `CStringList`	Other linked list classes

COleException

Inheritance Hierarchy

`CObject -> CException -> COleException`

Summary

```
#include <afxole.h>
class COleException : public CException
{
    DECLARE_DYNAMIC(COleException)
public:
    OLESTATUS   m_status;
    COleException(OLESTATUS status);

    static  OLESTATUS Process(CException*);
};
```

Description

The `COleException` class represents error conditions that might occur in a Microsoft Windows program with classes that support Object Linking and Embedding (OLE), which is a standard way for Windows programs to share data. (See Chapter 20, "Microsoft Foundation Classes for Windows Programming," for more information on OLE classes.) The *`m_status`* member variable of `COleException` indicates the status of the OLE operation. Consult the *Programmer's Reference to the Microsoft Windows Software Development Kit* for more information on OLE status codes.

See Also

`CFileException` `CArchiveException` `CNotSupportedException` `CMemoryException` `CResourceException`	Other exception classes
`COleServer` `COleServerDoc` `COleServerItem` `CClientDoc` `CClientItem`	Windows OLE classes (Chapter 20) that use `COleException` to indicate errors

CPtrArray

Inheritance Hierarchy

```
CObject -> CPtrArray
```

Summary

```
#include <afxcoll.h>
class CPtrArray : public CObject
{
    DECLARE_DYNAMIC(CPtrArray)
public:
// Constructor and destructor.
    CPtrArray();
    ~CPtrArray();

// Attributes.
    int     GetSize() const;
    int     GetUpperBound() const;
    void    SetSize(int nNewSize, int nGrowBy = -1);

// Removing elements.
    void    FreeExtra();
    void    RemoveAll();

// Accessing elements.
    void*   GetAt(int nIndex) const;
    void    SetAt(int nIndex, void* newElement);
    void*&  ElementAt(int nIndex);
    void*   operator[](int nIndex) const;
    void*&  operator[](int nIndex);

// Growing the array.
    void    SetAtGrow(int nIndex, void* newElement);
    int     Add(void* newElement);

// Moving elements around.
    void    InsertAt(int nIndex, void* newElement,
        int nCount = 1);
    void    RemoveAt(int nIndex, int nCount = 1);
    void    InsertAt(int nStartIndex, CPtrArray* pNewArray);

// Debugging support.
#ifdef _DEBUG
```

```
    void    Dump(CDumpContext&) const;
    void    AssertValid() const;
#endif

// Hidden implementation details....
};
```

Description

The CPtrArray class represents an array of void pointers (void*) that can grow dynamically, if necessary. CPtrArray is part of the array classes generated from a template. All the array classes—CByteArray, CDWordArray, CObArray, CPtrArray, CStringArray, and CWordArray—contain the same set of member functions; only the data stored in the array elements varies. Because of this similarity, you can use the documentation for the CObArray class to see how the member functions work in the CPtrArray class. Remember that CObArray stores pointers to CObject, but CPtrArray stores the void* data type. Therefore, wherever you see the CObject* data type in CObArray, replace it with void*.

See Also

CObArray	For more information on member functions of the array classes

CPtrList

Inheritance Hierarchy

CObject -> CPtrList

Summary

```
#include <afxcoll.h>
class CPtrList : public CObject
{
    DECLARE_DYNAMIC(CPtrList)
public:
// Constructor and destructor.
    CPtrList(int nBlockSize=10);
    ~CPtrList();

// Attributes.
    int     GetCount() const;
    BOOL    IsEmpty() const;

// Peeking at head or tail.
    void*&   GetHead();
    void*    GetHead() const;
```

```
    void*&   GetTail();
    void*    GetTail() const;

// Adding and removing.
    void*    RemoveHead();
    void*    RemoveTail();

    POSITION AddHead(void* newElement);
    POSITION AddTail(void* newElement);

    void    AddHead(CPtrList* pNewList);
    void    AddTail(CPtrList* pNewList);

    void    RemoveAll();

// Iterating.
    POSITION GetHeadPosition() const;
    POSITION GetTailPosition() const;
    void*&   GetNext(POSITION& rPosition);
    void*    GetNext(POSITION& rPosition) const;
    void*&   GetPrev(POSITION& rPosition);
    void*    GetPrev(POSITION& rPosition) const;

// Accessing an element at a given position.
    void*&   GetAt(POSITION position);
    void*    GetAt(POSITION position) const;
    void    SetAt(POSITION pos, void* newElement);
    void    RemoveAt(POSITION position);

// Inserting before or after a given position.
    POSITION InsertBefore(POSITION position,
        void* newElement);
    POSITION InsertAfter(POSITION position,
        void* newElement);

// Finding an element.
    POSITION Find(void* searchValue,
        POSITION startAfter = NULL) const;
    POSITION FindIndex(int nIndex) const;

// Debugging.
#ifdef _DEBUG
    void    Dump(CDumpContext&) const;
```

```
    void    AssertValid() const;
#endif

// Hidden implementation details.
};
```

Description

The CPtrList class represents a double-linked list of void pointers (void*). CPtrList is part of the list classes generated from a template. All the linked-list classes—CObList, CPtrList, and CStringList—contain the same set of member functions; only the data stored in the list elements varies. Because of this similarity, you can use the documentation for the CObList class to see how the member functions work in the CPtrList class. Remember that CObList stores pointers to CObject, but CPtrList stores the void* data type. Therefore, wherever you see the CObject* data type in CObList, replace it with void*.

See Also

CObList	For more information on member functions of the linked list classes

CResourceException

Inheritance Hierarchy

CObject -> CException -> CResourceException

Summary

```
#include <afxwin.h>
class CResourceException : public CException
{
    DECLARE_DYNAMIC(CResourceException)
public:
    CResourceException();
};
```

Description

The CResourceException class is used by the Windows programming classes (see Chapter 20, "Microsoft Foundation Classes for Windows Programming") to represent the error condition that occurs when Windows cannot find or allocate resources such as dialog boxes, menus, fonts, pens, and brushes.

See Also

CFileException CArchiveException CNotSupportedException CMemoryException COleException	Other exception classes

CRuntimeClass

Inheritance Hierarchy

None.

Summary

```
#include <afx.h>
struct CRuntimeClass
{
// Attributes.
    const char* m_pszClassName;  // Null-terminated class name.
    int   m_nObjectSize;         // Size of object in bytes.
    WORD  m_wSchema;             // Schema or version number.
    void (PASCAL *m_pfnConstruct)(void* p); // Pointer to default
                                            //   constructor of class.
    CRuntimeClass* m_pBaseClass; // Pointer to CRuntimeClass for
                                 //   the base class Operations.
    CObject* CreateObject();
    BOOL     ConstructObject(void* pThis);
    void     Store(CArchive& ar);
    static   CRuntimeClass* Load(CArchive& ar, WORD* pwSchema);

// Implementation details....
    static CRuntimeClass* pFirstClass; // Start of class list.
    CRuntimeClass* m_pNextClass;       // Linked list of all
                                       //   classes that support
                                       //   runtime class identification.
};
```

Description

`CRuntimeClass` provides support for runtime-type determination. You generally do not use `CRuntimeClass` directly; instead, you use the macros `DECLARE_DYNAMIC` and `IMPLEMENT_DYNAMIC` to include support for runtime-type determination in a class. Then, the macro `RUNTIME_CLASS` is used together with the `IsKindOf` member function to check an object's type at runtime.

CSharedFile

Inheritance Hierarchy

```
CObject -> CFile -> CMemFile -> CSharedFile
```

Summary

```
#include <afxole.h>
class CSharedFile : public CMemFile  // For Microsoft Windows
{
    DECLARE_DYNAMIC(CSharedFile)
public:
// Constructor and destructor.
    CSharedFile(UINT nAllocFlags = GMEM_DDESHARE,
        UINT nGrowBytes = 1024);
    ~CSharedFile();

// Attributes.
    HANDLE  Detach();
    void    SetHandle(HANDLE hGlobalMemory);

// Hidden implementation details....
};
```

Description

The `CSharedFile` class is used by the Windows OLE classes (classes with names with a `COle` prefix) to pass data between OLE client and server. OLE (Object Linking and Embedding) is a standard way to share data among Windows applications, introduced in Microsoft Windows Version 3.1. `CSharedFile` is derived from `CMemFile`. The two are similar, except that `CSharedFile` allocates the in-memory buffer using Windows memory-allocation functions and identifies the memory through a Windows handle.

See Also

`CMemFile`	Base class of `CSharedFile`

CStdioFile

Inheritance Hierarchy

```
CObject -> CFile -> CStdioFile
```

Summary

```
#include <afx.h>
class CStdioFile : public CFile
{
    DECLARE_DYNAMIC(CStdioFile)
```

```
public:
// Constructors and destructor.
    CStdioFile();
    CStdioFile(FILE* pOpenStream);
    CStdioFile(const char* pszFileName, UINT nOpenFlags);

    virtual ~CStdioFile();

// Attributes.
    FILE* m_pStream;    // Standard C FILE

// NOTE: m_hFile from base class is _fileno(m_pStream)

    virtual DWORD GetPosition() const;

// Overridable operations.
    virtual BOOL Open(const char* pszFileName, UINT nOpenFlags,
        CFileException* pError = NULL);
    virtual UINT Read(void FAR* lpBuf, UINT nCount);
    virtual void Write(const void FAR* lpBuf, UINT nCount);
    virtual LONG Seek(LONG lOff, UINT nFrom);
    virtual void Flush();
    virtual void Close();

// WriteString writes a string, like C library's fputs.
    virtual void WriteString(const char FAR* lpsz)
// ReadString reads a string, like C library's fgets.
    virtual char FAR* ReadString(char FAR* lpsz, UINT nMax);

// The next three functions are not supported by CStdioFile.
// If you call these, you will get a CNotSupportedException.
    virtual CFile* Duplicate() const;
    virtual void LockRange(DWORD dwPos, DWORD dwCount);
    virtual void UnlockRange(DWORD dwPos, DWORD dwCount);

// Diagnostic support.
#ifdef _DEBUG
    void Dump(CDumpContext& dc) const;
#endif
};
```

Description

The CStdioFile class represents a buffered stream file opened by the C library function fopen. You can open the file in text mode or binary mode.

CStdioFile is derived from CFile. In fact, most of the member functions of CStdioFile are the same as those in CFile, except that the following member functions are not implemented in CMemFile:

- Duplicate
- LockRange
- UnlockRange

Calling any of these functions causes a CNotSupportedException object to be thrown, indicating that these functions are unsupported.

The following discussions describe the member variables and functions different from those in CFile.

Member Variables

```
FILE* m_pStream;     // Standard C FILE pointer
```

This is the stream identifier of the file opened by fopen.

Member Functions

Constructors and Destructor

```
CStdioFile();
CStdioFile(FILE* pOpenStream);
CStdioFile(const char* pszFileName, // Open this file
    UINT nOpenFlags);               //   in this mode.
```

Creates a CStdioFile object, opens a file, and attaches that file to the CStdioFile object. The default constructor, CStdioFile(), does not open any file. You must call Open (inherited from CFile) to open the file. The CStdioFile(const char*, UINT) constructor may throw a CFileException if any error occurs when opening the named file.

```
virtual ~CStdioFile();
```

This closes the file and destroys the CStdioFile object.

Stream I/O

```
virtual char FAR* ReadString(char FAR* lpsz, UINT nMax);
```

Reads up to (*nMax* - 1) characters from the stream (associated with this CStdioFile object) into the character array *lpsz*. Like the C library's fgets function, reading stops if `ReadString` encounters a carriage return-linefeed pair. A null character is appended to the buffer. This also returns a pointer to the buffer and may throw a `CFileException` in the event of an error.

```
// WriteString writes a string, like C library's fputs.
virtual void WriteString(const char FAR* lpsz);
```

Writes characters from the null-terminated buffer *`lpsz`* into the stream associated with this `CStdioFile` object. Like the C library's `fgets` function, `WriteString` translates a newline (linefeed) character into a carriage return-linefeed pair. `WriteString` does not write the null character to the stream. This segment may throw a `CFileException` in the event of an error.

See Also

`CFile`	Base class of CStdioFile (see this class for information on member functions of CStdioFile)

CString

Inheritance Hierarchy

None.

Summary

```
#include <afx.h>
class CString
{
public:
// Constructors and destructor.
    CString();
    CString(const CString& stringSrc);
    CString(char ch, int nRepeat = 1);
    CString(const char* psz);
    CString(const char* pch, int nLength);
    CString(const char FAR* lpsz);
    CString(const char FAR* lpch, int nLength);

    ~CString();

// Attributes.

    int GetLength() const;
    BOOL IsEmpty() const;
    void Empty();  // Free up the data
```

```
// Operations.
    char GetAt(int nIndex) const;        // 0 = first character
    char operator[](int nIndex) const;   // same as GetAt
    void SetAt(int nIndex, char ch);
    operator const char*() const;        // as a C string

// Assignment.
    const CString& operator=(const CString& stringSrc);
    const CString& operator=(char ch);
    const CString& operator=(const char* psz);

// String concatenation.
    const CString& operator+=(const CString& string);
    const CString& operator+=(char ch);
    const CString& operator+=(const char* psz);

    friend CString operator+(const CString& string1,
        const CString& string2);
    friend CString operator+(const CString& string, char ch);
    friend CString operator+(char ch, const CString& string);
    friend CString operator+(const CString& string,
        const char* psz);
    friend CString operator+(const char* psz,
        const CString& string);

// String comparison.
    int Compare(const char* psz) const;
    int CompareNoCase(const char* psz) const;
    int Collate(const char* psz) const;

// Substring extraction.
    CString Mid(int nFirst, int nCount) const;
    CString Mid(int nFirst) const;
    CString Left(int nCount) const;
    CString Right(int nCount) const;

    CString SpanIncluding(const char* pszCharSet) const;
    CString SpanExcluding(const char* pszCharSet) const;

// Upper/lower/reverse conversion.
    void MakeUpper();
    void MakeLower();
    void MakeReverse();
```

```
// Searching (returns starting index, or -1 if not found).
// Look for a single character match.
    int Find(char ch) const;  // Like C library's strchr
    int ReverseFind(char ch) const;
    int FindOneOf(const char* pszCharSet) const;

// Look for a specific substring (like C library's strstr):
    int Find(const char* pszSub) const;

// Accessing CString as a standard C character array:
    char* GetBuffer(int nMinBufLength);
    void  ReleaseBuffer(int nNewLength = -1);
    char* GetBufferSetLength(int nNewLength);

// Serialization support:
    friend CArchive& operator<<(CArchive& ar,
        const CString& string);
    friend CArchive& operator>>(CArchive& ar,
        CString& string);

// Functions for Microsoft Windows support:
#ifdef _WINDOWS
    BOOL LoadString(UINT nID); // Load from resource
                               // 255 chars maximum
// In-place ANSI<->OEM conversions.
    void AnsiToOem();
    void OemToAnsi();
#endif // #ifdef_WINDOWS

// Diagnostic support.
#ifdef _DEBUG
    friend CDumpContext& operator<<(CDumpContext&,
        const CString& string);
#endif

// Hidden implementation details....
};
```

Description

The `CString` class represents a variable-length sequence of characters. The `CString` class essentially provides a complete replacement for C's null-terminated strings and the string manipulation functions of the standard C library. With `CString`, you need not worry about some common mistakes programmers make when they use C's string-handling functions. For instance, when you concatenate one string to another with strcat, or copy one string to another with strcpy, you must ensure that the destination string has enough room to hold the result. With CString, copying is easy: you use the assignment (=) operator. You can concatenate two CStrings by "adding" them together (adding the second to the first) as follows:

```
CString name = "formfill", ext = ".cpp";
CString filename = name + ext; // filename = "formfill.cpp"

CString new_name;              // An empty CString
new_name = filename;           // Copying...
```

With the CString class, you can manipulate arrays of characters without worrying about the capacity of the arrays.

Concerning the CString class in the Microsoft Foundation Class Library, each CString object represents a unique value. For example, when you copy one CString to another, two unique sequences of characters will exist, even though both sequences contain the same characters.

Because many functions require C-style null-terminated strings as arguments, CString maintains its string in a null-terminated format. CString provides the const char* operator, which casts a CString as a const char*—thus enabling you to use a CString where a function expects a const char* argument. At the same time, you might want to use a C-style string (const char*) where a CString is expected. To handle this conversion, the CString class includes the constructor CString(const char*).

Member Functions

Constructors and Destructor

```
CString();                              // An empty string.
CString(const CString& stringSrc);      // Copy constructor.
CString(char ch, int nRepeat = 1);      // Repeat a char, nRepeat times.
CString(const char* psz);               // Initialize using C strings.
CString(const char* pch, int nLength);
CString(const char FAR* lpsz);
CString(const char FAR* lpch, int nLength);
```

Constructs a CString and initializes it with the specified strings.

```
~CString();
```

Releases memory allocated to store this CString's sequence of characters.

Attributes

```
void Empty();
```

Empties the `CString`—it releases any memory that was allocated to hold the character data of the `CString`.

```
int GetLength() const;
```

Returns the number of characters (not counting the terminating null character) in the `CString`.

```
BOOL IsEmpty() const;
```

Returns `TRUE` if the `CString` is empty (the length is zero).

Operations

```
char GetAt(int nIndex) const;
```

Returns the character at the specified index in the string (zero being the first character).

```
char operator[](int nIndex) const;
```

Uses the subscript operator to access the character at a specified index, just like `GetAt`.

```
operator const char*() const;
```

Returns a pointer to the null-terminated string equivalent of this `CString` object.

```
void SetAt(int nIndex, char ch);
```

Sets the character at a specified index (zero being the index to the first character) to the character *ch*.

Assignment Operators

```
const CString& operator=(const CString& stringSrc);
    // Copy constructor
const CString& operator=(char ch);
const CString& operator=(const char* psz);
```

Reinitializes an existing `CString` object with new data. It may throw a `CMemoryException` because these operators allocate memory.

String Concatenation

```
const CString& operator+=(const CString& string);
const CString& operator+=(char ch);
const CString& operator+=(const char* psz);
Appends a character or a string to the end of this string.
friend CString operator+(const CString& string1,
    const CString& string2);
```

```
friend CString operator+(const CString& string, char ch);
friend CString operator+(char ch, const CString& string);
friend CString operator+(const CString& string,
    const char* psz);
friend CString operator+(const char* psz,
    const CString& string);
```

Concatenates two strings and returns the resulting `CString` object.

String Comparison

`int Collate(const char* psz) const;`

Compares this `CString` with a specified string, taking into account the collating sequence for the current locale. This uses the C library's `strcoll` function and returns 0 if the strings are identical, –1 if the `CString` is less than *psz*, and +1 if the `CString` is greater than in *psz*.

`int Compare(const char* psz) const;`

Compare this `CString` with a specified string using the C library's `strcmp` function. Returns 0 if the strings are identical, –1 if the `CString` is less than *psz*, and +1 if the `CString` is greater than in *psz*.

`int CompareNoCase(const char* psz) const;`

This code is similar to `Compare`, but performs a case-insensitive comparison. It also provides the functionality of C library's `stricmp` function.

Substring Extraction

`CString Left(int nCount) const;`

Returns a `CString` with the leftmost `nCount` characters from this `CString` object. Also throws a `CMemoryException` if an error occurs when allocating memory for a new `CString`. This function is similar to BASIC's `LEFT$` command.

```
CString Mid(int nFirst, int nCount) const;
CString Mid(int nFirst) const; // Extract rest of string
```

Returns a `CString` with the *nCount* characters from this `CString` object, starting at index *nFirst*. If you don't provide *nCount*, the rest of the string, from *nFirst* onwards, is returned. This throws a `CMemoryException` if an error occurs when allocating memory for a new `CString`. This function is similar to BASIC's `MID$` command.

`CString Right(int nCount) const;`

Returns a `CString` with the rightmost (last) *nCount* characters from this `CString` object. This also throws a `CMemoryException` if an error occurs when allocating memory for a new `CString`. This function is similar to BASIC's `RIGHT$` command.

```
CString SpanExcluding(const char* pszCharSet) const;
```

Returns a `CString` containing the largest substring (starting at the beginning of the string) that does not include any of the characters appearing in *pzCharSet*.

```
CString SpanIncluding(const char* pszCharSet) const;
```

Returns a `CString` containing the largest substring (starting at the beginning of the string) that includes only the characters appearing in *pzCharSet*.

Conversions

```
void MakeLower();
```

Converts the string to lowercase.

```
void MakeReverse();
```

Reverses the order of characters in the string.

```
void MakeUpper();
```

Converts the string to uppercase.

Searching

```
int Find(char ch) const;  // like C library's strchr
int Find(const char* pszSub) const; // like C library's strstr
```

Searches from the beginning of the `CString` for the first occurrence of a character or a string. If found, it returns the index of the first character in the `CString` that matches the specified character or substring; otherwise, it returns –1 to indicate failure.

```
int FindOneOf(const char* pszCharSet) const;
```

Searches the `CString` for the first character that matches any of the characters appearing in the string *pszCharSet*. If found, it returns the index of the first character in the `CString` that matches one of the characters in `pszCharSet`; otherwise, it returns –1 to indicate failure.

```
int ReverseFind(char ch) const; // like C library's strrchr
```

Searches backward from the end of the `CString` for the first occurrence of a specified character in the `CString`. If found, it returns the index of the first character in the `CString` that matches the specified character; otherwise, it returns –1 to indicate failure.

Accessing CString as Null-Terminated String

```
char* GetBuffer(int nMinBufLength); // Minimum size of buffer
```

Returns a pointer to the internal buffer where the character sequence of the `CString` is stored. This enables you to directly manipulate that array as a null-terminated C string. If you manipulate this buffer directly, you should call `ReleaseBuffer` before using any `CString` functions. This may throw a `CMemoryException`.

```
char* GetBufferSetLength(int nNewLength);
```

Returns a pointer to the internal buffer of the `CString` object after ensuring that the buffer size is exactly *`nNewLength`* bytes. If you manipulate the buffer directly, you should call `ReleaseBuffer` before using any `CString` functions. This may throw a `CMemoryException`.

```
void  ReleaseBuffer(int nNewLength = -1);
```

Calls to indicate that you're finished using the buffer returned by `GetBuffer`. You should provide the length of the string, not counting the terminating null character. If *`nNewLength`* is –1, `ReleaseBuffer` calls `strlen` to determine the length. (Of course, this requires that the string in the buffer is null-terminated.)

Functions for Windows Programs

```
void AnsiToOem();
```

Converts the characters in the `CString` from the ANSI character set to the OEM character set. The conversion is performed in place (that is, the characters are replaced without first creating copies of them). Consult the *Programmer's Reference to the Microsoft Windows Software Development Kit* for more information on these character sets.

```
BOOL LoadString(UINT nID); // Load from this resource
```

Loads up to a 255-character-long string from a specified resource. This may throw a `CMemoryException`. Returns `TRUE` if the string is successfully loaded into this `CString`.

```
void OemToAnsi();
```

Converts the characters in the `CString` from the OEM character set to the ANSI character set. Consult the *Programmer's Reference to the Microsoft Windows Software Development Kit* for more information on these character sets.

See Also

`CStringArray` `CStringList`	To store CStrings in arrays and linked lists

CStringArray

Inheritance Hierarchy

```
CObject -> CStringArray
```

Summary

```
#include <afxcoll.h>
class CStringArray : public CObject
{
    DECLARE_SERIAL(CStringArray)
public:
// Constructor and destructor.
    CStringArray();
    ~CStringArray();

// Attributes.
    int     GetSize() const;
    int     GetUpperBound() const;
    void    SetSize(int nNewSize, int nGrowBy = -1);

// Cleaning up.
    void    FreeExtra();
    void    RemoveAll();

// Accessing elements.
    CString    GetAt(int nIndex) const;
    void       SetAt(int nIndex, const char* newElement);
    CString&   ElementAt(int nIndex);
    CString    operator[](int nIndex) const;
    CString&   operator[](int nIndex);

// Growing the array.
    void    SetAtGrow(int nIndex, const char* newElement);
    int     Add(const char* newElement);

// Moving elements around.
    void    InsertAt(int nIndex, const char* newElement,
        int nCount = 1);
    void    RemoveAt(int nIndex, int nCount = 1);
    void    InsertAt(int nStartIndex, CStringArray* pNewArray);

// Serializing the array.
    void    Serialize(CArchive&);

// Debugging.
#ifdef _DEBUG
    void    Dump(CDumpContext&) const;
```

```
    void    AssertValid() const;
#endif

// Hidden implementation details....
};
```

Description

The CStringArray class represents an array of CString objects that can grow dynamically, if necessary. CStringArray is part of the array classes generated from a template. All the array classes—CByteArray, CDWordArray, CObArray, CPtrArray, CStringArray, and CWordArray—contain the same set of member functions; only the data stored in the array elements varies. Because of this similarity, you can use the documentation for the CObArray class to see how the member functions work in the CStringArray class. Remember that CObArray stores pointers to CObject, but CStringArray stores the CString data type. Therefore, wherever you see the CObject* data type in CObArray, replace it with CString.

See Also

CObArray	For more information on member functions of the array classes

CStringList

Inheritance Hierarchy

CObject -> CStringList

Summary

```
#include <afxcoll.h>
class CStringList : public CObject
{
    DECLARE_SERIAL(CStringList)
public:.
// Constructor and destructor.
    CStringList(int nBlockSize=10);
    ~CStringList();

// Attributes.
    int     GetCount() const;
    BOOL    IsEmpty() const;

// Peeking at head or tail.
    CString&   GetHead();
```

```
    CString    GetHead() const;
    CString&   GetTail();
    CString    GetTail() const;

// Adding or removing.
    CString    RemoveHead();
    CString    RemoveTail();

    POSITION AddHead(const char* newElement);
    POSITION AddTail(const char* newElement);

    void    AddHead(CStringList* pNewList);
    void    AddTail(CStringList* pNewList);

    void    RemoveAll();

// Iterating.
    POSITION GetHeadPosition() const;
    POSITION GetTailPosition() const;
    CString&   GetNext(POSITION& rPosition);
    CString    GetNext(POSITION& rPosition) const;
    CString&   GetPrev(POSITION& rPosition);
    CString    GetPrev(POSITION& rPosition) const;

// Accessing an element at a given position.
    CString&   GetAt(POSITION position);
    CString    GetAt(POSITION position) const;
    void    SetAt(POSITION pos, const char* newElement);
    void    RemoveAt(POSITION position);

// Inserting before or after a given position.
    POSITION InsertBefore(POSITION position,
        const char* newElement);
    POSITION InsertAfter(POSITION position,
        const char* newElement);

// Finding an element.
    POSITION Find(const char* searchValue,
        POSITION startAfter = NULL) const;
    POSITION FindIndex(int nIndex) const;

// Serializing the list.
    void    Serialize(CArchive&);
```

```
// Debugging.
#ifdef _DEBUG
    void    Dump(CDumpContext&) const;
    void    AssertValid() const;
#endif

// Hidden implementation details....
};
```

Description

The CStringList class represents a double-linked list of CString objects. CStringList is part of the list classes generated from a template. All the linked-list classes—CObList, CPtrList, and CStringList—contain the same set of member functions; only the data stored in the list elements varies. Because of this similarity, you can use the documentation for the CObList class to see how the member functions work in the CStringList class. Remember that CObList stores pointers to CObject, but CStringList stores the CString data type. Therefore, wherever you see the CObject* data type in CObList, replace it with CString.

See Also

CObList	For more information on member functions of the linked list classes

CTime

Inheritance Hierarchy

None.

Summary

```
#include <afx.h>
class CTime
{
public:
// Constructors.
    CTime();
    CTime(time_t time);
    CTime(int nYear, int nMonth, int nDay,
        int nHour, int nMin, int nSec);
    CTime(WORD wDosDate, WORD wDosTime);
    CTime(const CTime& timeSrc);

// Assignment operators.
```

```
// Copy a specified CTime object into this CTime.
    const CTime& operator=(const CTime& timeSrc);

// Copy a time_t value into this CTime.
    const CTime& operator=(time_t t);

// Attributes.
    struct tm* GetGmtTm(struct tm* ptm = NULL) const;
    struct tm* GetLocalTm(struct tm* ptm = NULL) const;

// Return a CTime representing the current date and time.
    static  CTime GetCurrentTime();

    int GetDay() const;       // Return day of month (1 to 31).

    int GetDayOfWeek() const; // Return day of the week:
                              //   1=Sun, 2=Mon, ..., 7=Sat
    int GetHour() const;      // Return hour (0 to 23).
    int GetMinute() const;    // Return minute (0 to 59).
    int GetMonth() const;     // Return month of year (1 = Jan).
    int GetSecond() const;    // Return second (0 to 59).
    time_t  GetTime() const;  // Return time_t value for this
                              //   CTime.

    int GetYear() const;      // Return year (1900 to 2036).

// Operations.

// Difference of two CTime values is a CTimeSpan.
    CTimeSpan operator-(CTime time) const;

// Add or subtract a "duration" from a CTime value:
    CTime operator+(CTimeSpan timeSpan) const;
    CTime operator-(CTimeSpan timeSpan) const;
    const CTime& operator+=(CTimeSpan timeSpan);
    const CTime& operator-=(CTimeSpan timeSpan);

// Compare two CTime objects....
    BOOL operator==(CTime time) const;
    BOOL operator!=(CTime time) const;
    BOOL operator<(CTime time) const;
    BOOL operator>(CTime time) const;
```

```
    BOOL operator<=(CTime time) const;
    BOOL operator>=(CTime time) const;

// Serialization support.
    friend CArchive& operator<<(CArchive& ar, CTime time);
    friend CArchive& operator>>(CArchive& ar, CTime& rtime);

// The following uses C library's strftime and cannot be used
// in Windows dynamic link library.
#ifndef _WINDLL
    CString Format(const char* pFormat);
    CString FormatGmt(const char* pFormat);
#endif //!_WINDLL

// Diagnostic support.
#ifdef _DEBUG
    friend CDumpContext& operator<<(CDumpContext& dc,
        CTime time);
#endif

// Hidden implementation details....
};
```

Description

The `CTime` class represents an absolute date and time. You can view it as an encapsulation of ANSI C's `time_t` data type together with the facilities offered by the C library functions `asctime`, `gmtime`, `localtime`, `strftime`, and `time`.

Some of the operators and functions of the `CTime` class are adequately explained by the comments of the "Summary" section. The rest are briefly described next.

Member Functions

Constructors

```
CTime();
CTime(time_t time);
CTime(int nYear, int nMonth, int nDay,
   int nHour, int nMin, int nSec);
CTime(WORD wDosDate, WORD wDosTime);
CTime(const CTime& timeSrc); // Copy constructor
```

Each of these five constructors creates a `CTime` object initialized with a specified date and time. The default constructor, `CTime()`, initializes the time at zero, which is not a legal value.

Attributes

```
struct tm* GetGmtTm(struct tm* ptm = NULL) const;
```

Converts the date and time represented by this `CTime` object into a broken time consisting of year, month, day, hour, minutes, seconds, and several other fields saved in a `tm` structure with an address you provide in *`ptm`*. If *`ptm`* is `NULL`, `GetGmtTm` uses a statically allocated internal `tm` structure to store the results. Returns a pointer to the `tm` structure where the results are stored. The fields set up by `GetGmtTm` correspond to the Greenwich Mean Time (GMT) as dictated by the setting of the environment variable `TZ`, which indicates the time zone and the daylight saving time zone for use in converting a local time to GMT. Consult Chapter 28, "Date and Time Management," for more information on the `TZ` environment variable and the `tm` structure.

```
struct tm* GetLocalTm(struct tm* ptm = NULL) const;
```

Converts the date and time, represented by this `CTime` object, into a broken time consisting of year, month, day, hour, minutes, seconds, and several other fields saved in a `tm` structure with an address you provide in *`ptm`*. If *`ptm`* is `NULL`, `GetLocalTm` uses a statically allocated internal `tm` structure to store the results. Returns a pointer to the `tm` structure where the results are stored. Consult Chapter 28 for more information on the `tm` structure.

Formatted Output

```
CString Format(const char* pFormat);
```

Calls the ANSI C function `strftime` to format a time according to the specified format string and to return the formatted string in a `CString` object. Consult the documentation of `strftime` (Chapter 28) for more information on the format string.

```
CString FormatGmt(const char* pFormat);
```

`FormatGmt` is like `Format`, except `FormatGmt` first converts the local time into GMT and then generates and formats the time into a string that it returns in a `CString` object. Consult the documentation of `strftime` (Chapter 28) for more information on the format string.

See Also

`CTimeSpan`	Represents time differences (such as "one hour")

CTimeSpan

Inheritance Hierarchy

None.

Summary

```
#include <afx.h>
class CTimeSpan
{
public:
// Constructors (initialize a CTimeSpan_a duration).
    CTimeSpan();
    CTimeSpan(time_t time);
    CTimeSpan(LONG lDays, int nHours, int nMins, int nSecs);
    CTimeSpan(const CTimeSpan& timeSpanSrc);

// Assignment operator (copy from a CTimeSpan into this one).
    const CTimeSpan& operator=(const CTimeSpan& timeSpanSrc);

// Attributes.
    LONG GetDays() const;          // Return total number of days.
    LONG GetTotalHours() const;    // Return total hours.
    int  GetHours() const;         // Return hours in current day.
    LONG GetTotalMinutes() const;  // Return total minutes.
    int  GetMinutes() const;       // Return minutes in current hour.
    LONG GetTotalSeconds() const;  // Return total seconds.
    int  GetSeconds() const;       // Return seconds in current minute.

// Operations.

// Add or subtract CTimeSpan values.
    CTimeSpan operator-(CTimeSpan timeSpan) const;
    CTimeSpan operator+(CTimeSpan timeSpan) const;
    const CTimeSpan& operator+=(CTimeSpan timeSpan);
    const CTimeSpan& operator-=(CTimeSpan timeSpan);

// Compare two CTimeSpan values.
    BOOL operator==(CTimeSpan timeSpan) const;
    BOOL operator!=(CTimeSpan timeSpan) const;
    BOOL operator<(CTimeSpan timeSpan) const;
    BOOL operator>(CTimeSpan timeSpan) const;
    BOOL operator<=(CTimeSpan timeSpan) const;
    BOOL operator>=(CTimeSpan timeSpan) const;

// Serialization support.
    friend CArchive& operator<<(CArchive& ar,
        CTimeSpan timeSpan);
    friend CArchive& operator>>(CArchive& ar,
        CTimeSpan& rtimeSpan);
```

```
// Diagnostic support.
#ifdef _DEBUG
    friend CDumpContext& operator<<(CDumpContext& dc,
        CTimeSpan timeSpan);
#endif

// The Format function uses C library's strftime and cannot be
// used in Windows dynamic link library.

#ifndef _WINDLL

// See ANSI C's strftime function for information on the
// format codes you can use in pFormat.

    CString Format(const char* pFormat);

#endif //!_WINDLL

// Hidden implementation details....
};
```

Description

The `CTimeSpan` class represents a duration, such as "one hour and fifteen minutes." The companion class, `CTime`, represents absolute time. `CTimeSpan` is the difference between two `CTime` values.

`CTimeSpan` stores the duration in seconds as a 32-bit signed integer value. Therefore, a `CTimeSpan` object can represent a maximum duration of 136 years. The functions and operators of the `CTimeSpan` class are adequately explained by the comments in the "Summary" section.

See Also

`CTime`	To represent an absolute date and time

CUIntArray

Inheritance Hierarchy

`CObject -> CUIntArray`

Summary

```
#include <afxcoll.h>
class CUIntArray : public CObject
```

```
{
    DECLARE_SERIAL(CUIntArray)
public:
// Constructor and destructor.
    CUIntArray();
    ~CUIntArray();

// Attributes.
    int     GetSize() const;
    int     GetUpperBound() const;
    void    SetSize(int nNewSize, int nGrowBy = -1);

// Cleaning up.
    void    FreeExtra();
    void    RemoveAll();

// Accessing elements.
    UINT    GetAt(int nIndex) const;
    void    SetAt(int nIndex, UINT newElement);
    UINT&   ElementAt(int nIndex);
    UINT    operator[](int nIndex) const;
    UINT&   operator[](int nIndex);

// Growing the array.
    void    SetAtGrow(int nIndex, UINT newElement);
    int     Add(UINT newElement);

// Moving elements around.
    void    InsertAt(int nIndex, UINT newElement,
        int nCount = 1);
    void    RemoveAt(int nIndex, int nCount = 1);
    void    InsertAt(int nStartIndex, CUIntArray* pNewArray);

// Serializing the array.
    void    Serialize(CArchive&);

// Debugging.
#ifdef _DEBUG
    void    Dump(CDumpContext&) const;
    void    AssertValid() const;
#endif
```

```
// Hidden implementation details....
};
```

Description

The CUIntArray class represents an array of unsigned integer words that can grow dynamically, if necessary. Under Windows, a 16-bit environment, each unsigned integer is 16 bits in size (therefore CUIntArray is the same as CWordArray), while under Windows NT, each element is the size of a double word (32-bits). CUIntArray is part of the array classes generated from a template. All the array classes—CByteArray, CDWordArray, CObArray, CPtrArray, CStringArray, and CUIntArray—contain the same set of member functions; only the data stored in the array elements varies. Because of this similarity, you can use the documentation for the CObArray class to see how the member functions operate in the CUIntArray class. Remember that CObArray stores pointers to CObject, but CUIntArray stores the WORD data type. Therefore, wherever you see the CObject* data type in CObArray, replace it with unsigned integer.

See Also

CObArray	For more information on member functions of the array classes

CUserException

Inheritance Hierarchy

```
CObject -> CException -> CUserException
```

Summary

```
class CUserException : public CException
{
    DECLARE_DYNAMIC(CUserException)
public:
    CUserException();
};
```

Description

The CUserException class is thrown to stop the current end-user exception. Usually thrown in response to a message displayed to the user.

Member Functions

See Also

CFile	Member functions of this class throw CFileException
CArchiveException	Other exception classes
CMemoryException	

```
CNotSupportedException
COleException
CResourceException
```

CWordArray

Inheritance Hierarchy

`CObject -> CWordArray`

Summary

```
#include <afxcoll.h>
class CWordArray : public CObject
{
    DECLARE_SERIAL(CWordArray)
public:
// Constructor and destructor.
    CWordArray();
    ~CWordArray();

// Attributes.
    int     GetSize() const;
    int     GetUpperBound() const;
    void    SetSize(int nNewSize, int nGrowBy = -1);

// Cleaning up.
    void    FreeExtra();
    void    RemoveAll();

// Accessing elements.
    WORD    GetAt(int nIndex) const;
    void    SetAt(int nIndex, WORD newElement);
    WORD&   ElementAt(int nIndex);
    WORD    operator[](int nIndex) const;
    WORD&   operator[](int nIndex);

// Growing the array.
    void    SetAtGrow(int nIndex, WORD newElement);
    int     Add(WORD newElement);

// Moving elements around.
    void    InsertAt(int nIndex, WORD newElement,
        int nCount = 1);
    void    RemoveAt(int nIndex, int nCount = 1);
    void    InsertAt(int nStartIndex, CWordArray* pNewArray);
```

```
// Serializing the array.
    void    Serialize(CArchive&);

// Debugging.
#ifdef _DEBUG
    void    Dump(CDumpContext&) const;
    void    AssertValid() const;
#endif

// Hidden implementation details....
};
```

Description

The CWordArray class represents an array of 16-bit words that can grow dynamically, if necessary. CWordArray is part of the array classes generated from a template. All the array classes—CByteArray, CDWordArray, CObArray, CPtrArray, CStringArray, CUIntArray, and CWordArray—contain the same set of member functions; only the data stored in the array elements varies. Because of this similarity, you can use the documentation for the CObArray class to see how the member functions operate in the CWordArray class. Remember that CObArray stores pointers to CObject, but CWordArray stores the WORD data type. Therefore, wherever you see the CObject* data type in CObArray, replace it with WORD.

See Also

CObArray	For more information on member functions of the array classes

Microsoft Foundation Classes for Windows Programming

In addition to the general-purpose classes described and documented in Chapter 19, "General-Purpose Microsoft Foundation Classes," the Microsoft Foundation Class Library also offers a large collection of classes that help you write applications for the Microsoft Windows environment. An example in Chapter 16, "Using the Microsoft Foundation Class Library," illustrates how to use these classes as a framework for Windows programs. The software in Chapter 18, "Using AppWizard to Create C++ Windows Applications," further demonstrates the use of the Windows programming classes in a realistic application.

This chapter provides an overview of the Windows programming classes and reference information on each class. This chapter also lists all functions, macros, and global variables in the Microsoft Foundation Class Library that are specifically designed for use in Windows programs.

What's in a Name? Windows Versus windows

This book uses the term *Windows*, with an uppercase *W*, to refer to *Microsoft Windows*, the graphical operating environment. On the other hand, the lowercase *windows* refers to the rectangular areas of the screen in which output is displayed. Like all graphical operating environments, *Windows* uses *windows* extensively.

Windows Programming Classes at a Glance

Figure 16.4 (in Chapter 16) shows the inheritance hierarchy of the Windows programming classes in the Microsoft Foundation Class Library. You should study that figure to familiarize yourself with the organization of the classes. Table 20.1 lists these classes by category, and the following sections briefly describe them.

Table 20.1. List of Windows programming classes by category.

Category	Classes
Applications	`CWinApp`
Basic Windows data types	`CPoint`, `CRect`, `CSize`
Device contexts (DCs)	`CDC`, `CClientDC`, `CWindowDC`, `CPaintDC`, `CMetafileDC`
Dialog boxes	`CDialog`, `CFindReplaceDialog`, `CFileDialog`, `CFontDialog`, `CPrintDialog`, `CColorDialog`
Graphics Device Interface (GDI) drawing tools	`CGdiObject`, `CPen`, `CBrush`, `CFont`, `CBitmap`, `CPalette`, `CRgn`
Menus	`CMenu`

Category	Classes
Object Linking and Embedding (OLE) support	`COleServer`, `COleTemplateServer`, `COleDocument`, `COleException`, `COleServerDoc`, `COleServerItem`, `COleClientDoc`, `COleClientItem`
Windows window types	`CWnd`, `CFrameWnd`, `CMDIFrameWnd`, `CMDIChildWnd`, `CStatic`, `CButton`, `CEdit`, `CListBox`, `CComboBox`, `CScrollBar`, `CBitmapButton`

Isn't Microsoft Windows Already Object-Oriented?

The Microsoft Windows environment was promoted as having an object-oriented architecture—so what do programmers gain by accessing the Windows environment through a layer of C++ classes such as those in the Microsoft Foundation Class Library?

Even though Windows supports the concept of certain objects, data encapsulation and inheritance rely on the programmer's discipline. When you write Windows programs in C, you can access and modify all parts of the structures that represent the objects. Additionally, anyone who has written a Windows program in C would know that the programmer must attend to myriad details in order for the application and its windows to look and behave properly.

An object-oriented layer in an object-oriented programming language such as C++ can help tremendously, simply by hiding many unnecessary details. Basically, that's what you get when you use C++ classes that support Windows programming. The Windows environment has an underlying, object-oriented architecture, but the Windows programming interface is procedural. Using a properly designed set of C++ classes makes the programming interface more object-oriented.

Application Class

The `CWinApp` class supplies the shell of an application that you can expand to create your own Windows application. As shown in the example in Chapter 16 and the larger application shown in Chapter 18, in order to build a Windows application you need to derive your application class from `CWinApp` and override the `InitInstance` member function.

You also would derive a window class from one of the predefined window types, such as `CFrameWnd`, and create an instance of that window in the `InitInstance` member function of the application class. Once the window is displayed, the window's message-handling mechanism takes over the interaction with the user. You must follow a cook-book approach (see Chapter 16 for an example) to handle specific Windows messages. For a complete sample application, study the listings of the application created in Chapter 18.

Prior Experience with Windows SDK is Helpful

You can follow a cookbook approach and use the Windows programming classes to develop Microsoft Windows applications. However, to fully exploit the capabilities these classes offer, you should familiarize yourself with the basics of Windows programming.

For example, experience with writing Windows programs in C with the Microsoft Windows Software Development Kit (SDK) is helpful, because the Microsoft Foundation Class Library provides classes that mimic the organization and the programming interface of the Windows SDK. This chapter does not cover the Windows SDK in detail but, rather, points out similarities between the Windows programming classes and the SDK. Consult the programmer's reference manuals that accompany the Microsoft Windows SDK for more information.

Menus

The `CMenu` class represents the menu bar in a window. `CMenu` is the class corresponding to `HMENU` in the Microsoft Windows SDK. Generally, you can define menus in resource files (for example, see the resource file on the source-code diskette for the application developed in Chapter 18), and you can initialize a `CMenu` object from the definitions in the resource file as illustrated in the application from Chapter 18.

Microsoft Windows Window Types

The CWnd class encapsulates a window handle (the HWND type from the Windows SDK) and provides the member functions necessary to manipulate the window. Additionally, and most importantly, the CWnd class defines the mechanism for processing messages that drive a Windows application. You've already seen examples of the message-processing mechanism in Chapters 16 and 18. (Message processing is further described in the reference pages on CWnd later in this chapter.)

The CWnd class serves as the base class from which a number of useful window classes are derived:

- CFrameWnd is a standard frame window. You can derive your application's main window class from CFrameWnd.
- CMDIFrameWnd is derived from CFrameWnd and is used to provide a *multiple-document interface* (MDI), wherein several child windows are managed by an outer frame window. If your application requires MDI, you can derive a class from CMDIFrameWnd and use that derived class as the work area where the multiple child windows appear.
- CMDIChildWnd is also derived from CFrameWnd. The CMDIChildWnd class represents the child windows that are managed by CMDIFrameWnd.
- CStatic provides the functionality of Windows *static controls*, which are text fields used as labels, or boxes used as decorative items.
- CButton represents a Windows button control, which is used extensively in Windows applications, especially in dialog boxes.
- CBitmapButton is derived from CButton and is used for buttons in which you can display a bitmap.
- CEdit is the C++ class corresponding to the predefined edit window type in Windows that provides a window wherein the user can enter and edit text.
- CListBox represents a Windows listbox where you can display a list of items, such as names of files. The user can view the list and select one or more items from it.
- CComboBox is equivalent to a Windows *combo box*—a combination of an edit window laid out next to a list box. Usually, the list box is hidden and a button with an arrow appears next to the edit window. The list appears when the user

selects the drop-down arrow. The edit window shows the current selection from the list.

- `CScrollBar` represents a scrollbar that you can orient horizontally or vertically.

Think of these classes in the `CWnd` hierarchy as C++ data types that represent the window types in Microsoft Windows. Consult the reference section at the end of this chapter for more information about each class.

In addition to the `CWnd` classes described so far, another subhierarchy is derived from `CWnd` that provides support for dialog boxes. These dialog classes are described next.

The `CWnd` Classes and the Windows in Microsoft Windows

The `CWnd` class and the Windows window associated with a `CWnd` object illustrate the relationship between the C++ classes and the Windows SDK. A window in Windows, represented by a window handle, `HWND`, is an internal data structure that corresponds to an area of the screen where an application's output appears. The Windows SDK provides many functions that manipulate windows and that accept a window handle as an argument. The Microsoft Foundation Class Library encapsulates a window handle, `HWND`, in the `CWnd` class and defines all necessary member functions to provide the functionality for all window-manipulation functions of the SDK.

When you define a `CWnd` object, the `CWnd` constructor does not automatically create the window. You must call the `Create` member function that produces the window and saves its handle in the `CWnd` object's public member variable, `m_hWnd`. Therefore, a `CWnd` can exist without a valid window.

The `CWnd` class contains a virtual destructor that destroys the window as well as the `CWnd` object. You can destroy just the window by calling the `DestroyWindow` member function.

Dialog Boxes

Dialog boxes are used in a *graphical user interface* (GUI) to display messages to the user and prompt for information. A simple dialog box is the window you see when you select the About... option from the Help menu in a Microsoft Windows application. Another example of a dialog box is the window that appears when you select the Open... option from the File menu in many Windows applications. The Microsoft

Foundation Class Library includes a hierarchy of C++ classes that provide several different predefined dialog boxes.

The `CDialog` class serves as the abstract base class of the dialog class hierarchy. What you use in your programs are the other dialog classes, derived from `CDialog`, which support the following types of dialog boxes:

- `CDialog` is a general-purpose class used for displaying dialog boxes in Windows. A dialog box can be either *modal* (which must be responded to prior to performing other tasks), or *modeless* (which need not be responded to prior to performing other tasks).
- `CModalDialog`, which was part of MFC 1.0, is obsolete and has been redefined as `CDialog`.
- `CFindReplaceDialog` is derived from `CDialog` and provides a modeless dialog box that prompts the user for a string and its replacement. Because this is a modeless dialog box, the user can continue to interact with other menu items in the application while `CFindReplaceDialog` is displayed.
- `CFileDialog` is derived from `CDialog` and displays a list of files and directories from which the user can select a file. This modal dialog box is based on the commdlg.dll dynamic link library.
- `CFontDialog` is derived from `CDialog` and provides a dialog box from which the user can select a font.
- `CPrintDialog` is another modal dialog box, derived from `CDialog`, that prompts the user for information and displays a message during printing.
- `CColorDialog` is derived from `CDialog`. Users employ this modal dialog box as a convenient means to pick a color.

For further information about these dialog boxes, consult the reference section pages for each individual class.

Graphics Device Interface Drawing Tools

The *graphics device interface* (GDI) refers to the device-independent set of functions that the Microsoft Windows SDK provides for graphics output. These GDI functions can use a number of drawing tools to produce different graphics outputs. The Microsoft Foundation Class Library includes a number of C++ classes that represent these drawing tools. The `CGdiObject` class serves as the base class for the following drawing-tool classes:

- `CPen` represents a GDI pen object. You can use a pen to draw the outline of graphics shapes.
- `CBrush` is the C++ class that models a GDI brush, which you can use to fill graphics shapes.
- `CFont` is an encapsulation of a font.
- `CBitmap` represents a bitmap.
- `CPalette` is a GDI color palette.
- `CRgn` represents a *region*—a combination of elliptical, rectangular, and polygonal areas that you can use for drawing or clipping.

To use the GDI drawing tools, you also need another important item: a device context, described in the next section.

Device Context Classes

In Windows, you must obtain a device context (DC) before you can use the GDI functions to display output on a device. The *device context* is an internal data structure that stores graphics attributes such as background and foreground colors, the pen, and the font. The appearance of graphics and text is controlled by these attributes. Each GDI drawing function in the Windows SDK requires a handle to a DC as an argument. In the Microsoft Foundation Class Library, the DC is encapsulated in the C++ `CDC` class, with the drawing functions defined as member functions of the `CDC` class.

For specific uses, the Microsoft Foundation Class Library includes the following classes derived from `CDC`:

- `CClientDC` represents a device context associated with the *client area* of a window (the area of a window inside the frame or the area where output appears).
- `CWindowDC` provides a device context for the entire window, including the frame.
- `CPaintDC` is a device context for use in redrawing a window's contents in response to a `WM_PAINT` message. The `CPaintDC` class encapsulates the calls to `BeginPaint` and `EndPaint` that typically enclose calls to any graphics functions in Windows programs that are developed using the SDK.
- `CMetaFileDC` provides a device context for use with a *metafile*—a file used to store GDI graphics operations in a specific format.

Classes for Object Linking and Embedding (OLE)

Object linking and embedding (OLE) was introduced in Microsoft Windows Version 3.1. OLE provides a standard way to share data among various Windows applications. Here, *sharing* is the ability to embed objects from one application into documents created in another application. Incorporating a drawing in a word-processing document is an example of this type of sharing. Although sharing was possible with cut-and-paste even before OLE arrived in Windows Version 3.1, OLE provides a more powerful and standardized way of sharing data.

With OLE, when you embed a drawing from Paintbrush, for example, into a Microsoft Word for Windows (Version 2.0) document, you can edit that drawing without leaving Word for Windows. Simply double-click the drawing to launch the Paintbrush application with that drawing loaded for editing. Of course, the applications must follow certain rules to allow this to happen. This is where OLE comes in.

OLE Terminology

OLE introduced a number of new terms to the world of Windows programming, some of which are defined here:

- An *Object* is data such as a drawing, a block of formatted text, a range of cells from a spreadsheet—anything that can be displayed and manipulated and is defined as an object in a Windows application that uses OLE. The Microsoft Foundation Class Library uses the term *item* to refer to OLE objects (to avoid confusing them with C++ objects).
- A *client application* is a Windows application that can accept, display, and store objects from servers. A *client document* is a document that displays OLE objects.
- The *server application* is a Windows application that creates and edits objects. A *server document* is the specific file from which the OLE objects are pasted into a client document.
- *Embedding* is the process of placing a complete representation of an object in the client document. You embed objects through the normal cut-and-paste operations or by selecting the Object... option from the Insert menu of the client application.

- *Linking* is the process of storing a description of the object (for instance, the file where the object resides and the name of the server) in the client document. You establish a link to an object by selecting that object in the server document and picking the Paste Special... option from the Edit menu of the client application. If you edit a linked object, the changes are automatically available in the client document.

Essentially, OLE is a protocol between two applications—a client and a server—where:

- The client can embed objects from the server inside a document being created in the client application.
- The client can request the server to manipulate that object when the user selects the embedded object.

In addition to the concept of embedding, *linking* is integral to OLE. In the process of linking, the client application remembers the full pathname of the server document from which an object is being pasted into the client. For example, if you link a range of spreadsheet cells to a word processing document, any changes to those spreadsheet cells is reflected in the information that appears in the word processing document. The disadvantage of linking is that the spreadsheet information becomes unavailable if you move or destroy the spreadsheet from which the spreadsheet cells were originally linked.

With OLE support in a Windows application, your programming project can become more involved, especially when you use the OLE library in Windows SDK. Luckily for C++ programmers, the Microsoft Foundation Class Library includes the following five classes specifically intended for incorporating OLE server and client support in a Windows application:

- `COleServer` is the OLE server application.
- `COleServerDoc` represents the document managed by the server application from which the server provides OLE objects (`COleServerItem` objects) to the client application.
- `COleServerItem` denotes an OLE object in the server's document.
- `COleClientDoc` is the client document that contains OLE objects (`COleClientItem` objects).
- `COleClientItem` represents an embedded OLE object in a client application's document.

For detailed information about these classes, please consult the reference pages for these classes.

In addition to the OLE support classes, the Microsoft Foundation Class Library includes a number of global functions that support OLE programming. These global functions have names with the prefix `AfxOle`, and are described further in the list of global functions later in this chapter.

Learning More About OLE

OLE is a significant new addition to Microsoft Windows version 3.1 and, as such, Windows lacks detailed information about programming OLE. Here are a few ways you can learn how to include OLE support in your Windows program:

- Read articles on OLE in programmers' magazines. For example, the March-April 1992 and May-June 1992 issues of the *Microsoft Systems Journal* (published bimonthly by M&T Publishing, Inc., 411 Borel Ave., Suite 100, San Mateo, CA 94402) include a two-part article about OLE programming, complete with sample code.
- Study the sample program in the directory MSVC\MFC\SAMPLES\OCLIENT. This program shows you how to use the OLE class `COleClientDoc` that is part of the Microsoft Foundation Class Library.
- Consult the *Programmer's Reference, Volume 1: Overview of the Microsoft Windows SDK* (Version 3.1) for an overview of the OLE library in the SDK.
- If you have access to the *Microsoft Developer Network CD*, check it for a number of excellent sample applications, notes, and other information about OLE.

Basic Windows Data Types

Three classes—`CPoint`, `CRect`, and `CSize`—operate as basic data types in Windows applications:

- `CPoint` represents a two-dimensional point with x,y coordinates
- `CRect` represents a rectangle.
- `CSize` represents relative coordinates.

If you have programmed with the Microsoft Windows SDK, you should recognize `CPoint`, `CRect`, and `CSize` as classes that are similar to their respective `POINT`, `RECT`, and `SIZE` structures.

Macros and Global Functions for Windows Programming

Previous sections provided an overview of the Windows programming classes. This section furnishes quick reference information about all macros and global functions in the Microsoft Foundation Class library that support Windows applications. This section also lists several global variables. You should never directly access the global variables, rather you should use the function shown to get the variable's value.

Global Variables

afxCurrentAppName

```
const char* afxCurrentAppName;
```

The `afxCurrentAppName` holds the name of the application. Use `AfxGetAppName` to access the name.

afxCurrentInstanceHandle

```
HANDLE afxCurrentInstanceHandle;
```

This is the handle to the current instance of the application. Use `AfxGetInstanceHandle` to access the handle.

afxCurrentResourceHandle

```
HANDLE afxCurrentResourceHandle;
```

You can use this handle to access the application's resources directly by using, for example, the Windows function `FindResource`. Use `AfxGetResourceHandle` to access the resource handle.

afxCurrentWinApp

```
CWinApp* afxCurrentWinApp;
```

This is a pointer to the global `CWinApp` class that represents this Windows application. Use `AfxGetApp` to access this pointer.

Macros

Macros for Windows programming primarily are intended for message handling. Use these macros in a derived window class (a class derived from `CWnd` or from a class derived from `CWnd`) to indicate the Windows messages that the window class handles. The `FormView` class in Chapter 18 illustrates the use of the message-handling macros `DECLARE_MESSAGE_MAP()`, `BEGIN_MESSAGE_MAP`, and `END_MESSAGE_MAP`, and the message-specific macros with names containing the `ON_` prefix.

BEGIN_MESSAGE_MAP

```
BEGIN_MESSAGE_MAP(class, base_class)
```

Use the `BEGIN_MESSAGE_MAP` and `END_MESSAGE_MAP()` pair to enclose one or more message-specific macros (those with names containing the `ON_` prefix) to indicate the Windows messages that a derived window class handles. Place this macro in the source file—the .cpp file where you define the member functions of the class.

The `BEGIN_MESSAGE_MAP` macro requires the name of the class and its base class as arguments. For instance, in the `CFormfillApp` class (see Chapter 18), which is derived from `CMDIChildWnd`, the message map is defined as follows:

```
BEGIN_MESSAGE_MAP(CFormfillApp, CWinApp)
        //{{AFX_MSG_MAP(CFormfillApp)
        ON_COMMAND(ID_APP_ABOUT, OnAppAbout)
             // NOTE: the ClassWizard will add and remove mapping macros
                here.
             //    DO NOT EDIT what you see in these blocks of generated
                   code !
        //}}AFX_MSG_MAP
        // Standard file-based document commands
        ON_COMMAND(ID_FILE_NEW, CWinApp::OnFileNew)
```

```
        ON_COMMAND(ID_FILE_OPEN, CWinApp::OnFileOpen)
        // Standard Print Setup command
        ON_COMMAND(ID_FILE_PRINT_SETUP, CWinApp::OnFilePrintSetup)
        // Global help commands
        ON_COMMAND(ID_HELP_INDEX, CWinApp::OnHelpIndex)
        ON_COMMAND(ID_HELP_USING, CWinApp::OnHelpUsing)
        ON_COMMAND(ID_HELP, CWinApp::OnHelp)
        ON_COMMAND(ID_CONTEXT_HELP, CWinApp::OnContextHelp)
        ON_COMMAND(ID_DEFAULT_HELP, CWinApp::OnHelpIndex)
END_MESSAGE_MAP()
```

DECLARE_MESSAGE_MAP

DECLARE_MESSAGE_MAP()

You must use the `DECLARE_MESSAGE_MAP()` macro to handle Windows messages from any derived window classes in your application. Notice that the `DECLARE_MESSAGE_MAP()` macro begins a private section of declaration followed by a protected section. Thus, declarations that follow `DECLARE_MESSAGE_MAP()` become protected by default. To avoid any problems, insert the `DECLARE_MESSAGE_MAP()` macro at the end of the class declaration.

For examples of the `DECLARE_MESSAGE_MAP()` macro, see the programs from Chapter 18. The declarations of the `FormView` and `FormWindow` classes of the Forms software are presented in that chapter.

END_MESSAGE_MAP

END_MESSAGE_MAP()

Use the `END_MESSAGE_MAP()` macro to mark the end of a message-map definition started with `BEGIN_MESSAGE_MAP`.

Notes on the Message-Map Macros

The message-map macros (with an `ON_` prefix in their names) link a Windows message to the member function of a window class (a class derived from `CWnd` or any `CWnd`-derived class). You can easily determine the Windows message a macro handles—the name of the macro is constructed by appending the standard Windows message name to the `ON_` prefix. Thus, the `WM_PAINT` message is mapped to a function by the `ON_WM_PAINT` macro.

The description of each message-map macro indicates the prototype of the member function called when the specified Windows message is sent to the window.

Many of the macros map the message to a predefined function name. For example, `ON_WM_PAINT` maps the `WM_PAINT` message to the member function `OnPaint()`. Some macros take the *`id`* and *`member_function`* arguments. *`id`* refers to a menu item ID (for menu selections) or a child window ID (for dialog boxes). *`member_function`* is the member function you want called when the specified menu or dialog box item is selected. *`member_function`* takes no arguments.

The standard message-handling functions, with names containing an `ON` prefix, are defined in the reference page of the `CWnd` class because they are member functions of that class. In your derived window class, you should override the definition of those functions that you need to handle the messages listed in the message map of the derived window.

To see a message map in action, study the Forms software example in Chapter 18. In particular, study the `FormView` class (again, see chapter 18) that handle the Windows messages in the Forms software.

ON_BN_CLICKED

`ON_BN_CLICKED``(`*`id`*`, `*`member_function`*`)`

This macro maps the `BN_CLICKED` message to *`member_function`*. This message is generated when the user clicks the button identified by *`id`*.

ON_BN_DISABLE

`ON_BN_DISABLE``(`*`id`*`, `*`member_function`*`)`

This macro maps the `BN_DISABLE` message to `member_function`. This message is generated when the button identified by *`id`* is disabled.

ON_BN_DOUBLECLICKED

`ON_BN_DOUBLECLICKED``(`*`id`*`, `*`member_function`*`)`

This macro maps the `BN_DOUBLECLICKED` message to `member_function`. This message is generated when the user double-clicks the button identified by *`id`*.

ON_BN_HILITE

`ON_BN_HILITE(id, member_function)`

This macro maps the `BN_HILITE` message to *member_function*. This message is generated when the user highlights the button identified by *id*.

ON_BN_PAINT

`ON_BN_PAINT(id, member_function)`

This macro maps the `BN_PAINT` message to *member_function*. This message is generated when the button identified by *id* needs repainting.

ON_BN_UNHILITE

`ON_BN_UNHILITE(id, member_function)`

This macro maps the `BN_UNHILITE` message to *member_function*. This message is generated when the button identified by *id* should no longer be highlighted.

ON_CBN_CLOSEUP

`ON_CBN_CLOSEUP(id, member_function)`

This macro maps the `CBN_CLOSEUP` message to *member_function*. This message is generated when the list box of the combo box identified by *id* is hidden.

ON_CBN_DBLCLK

`ON_CBN_DBLCLK(id, member_function)`

This macro maps the `CBN_DBLCLK` message to *member_function*. This message is generated when the user double-clicks a string in the list box of the combo box identified by *id*.

ON_CBN_DROPDOWN

`ON_CBN_DROPDOWN(id, member_function)`

This macro maps the `CBN_DROPDOWN` message to *member_function*. This message is generated when the list box of the combo box identified by *id* is about to be made visible (dropped down).

ON_CBN_EDITCHANGE

ON_CBN_EDITCHANGE(*id*, *member_function*)

This macro maps the CBN_EDITCHANGE message to *member_function*. This message is generated when the user edits the contents of the edit window in the combo box identified by *id*.

ON_CBN_EDITUPDATE

ON_CBN_EDITUPDATE(*id*, *member_function*)

This macro maps the CBN_EDITUPDATE message to *member_function*. This message is generated when the edit window of the combo box identified by *id* is about to be redrawn.

ON_CBN_ERRSPACE

ON_CBN_ERRSPACE(*id*, *member_function*)

This macro maps the CBN_ERRSPACE message to *member_function*. This message is generated when the combo box identified by *id* cannot allocate enough memory to process a specific request.

ON_CBN_KILLFOCUS

ON_CBN_KILLFOCUS(*id*, *member_function*)

This macro maps the CBN_KILLFOCUS message to *member_function*. This message is generated when the combo box identified by *id* loses input focus.

ON_CBN_SELCHANGE

ON_CBN_SELCHANGE(*id*, *member_function*)

This macro maps the CBN_SELCHANGE message to *member_function*. This message is generated when the selection changes in the list box of the combo box identified by *id*.

ON_CBN_SELENDCANCEL

ON_CBN_SELENDCANCEL(*id*, *member_function*)

This macro maps the CBN_SELENDCANCEL message to *member_function*. This message indicates that your application should ignore the user's selection in the list box of the combo box identified by *id*.

ON_CBN_SELENDOK

`ON_CBN_SELENDOK(id, member_function)`

This macro maps the `CBN_SELENDOK` message to *`member_function`*. This message indicates that your application should accept the user's selection from the list box of the combo box identified by *`id`*.

ON_CBN_SETFOCUS

`ON_CBN_SETFOCUS(id, member_function)`

This macro maps the `CBN_SETFOCUS` message to *`member_function`*. This message is generated when the combo box identified by *`id`* receives input focus.

ON_COMMAND

`ON_COMMAND(id, member_function)`

This macro maps the `WM_COMMAND` message to *`member_function`*. This message is generated when the user selects an item (identified by *`id`*) from a menu.

ON_CONTROL

`ON_CONTROL(notify_code, id, member_function)`

This maps any control-notification message to *`member_function`*. This message is generated when a control item such as a list box or button (identified by *`id`*) sends notification to its parent.

ON_EN_CHANGE

`ON_EN_CHANGE(id, member_function)`

This macro maps the `EN_CHANGE` message to *`member_function`*. This message is generated when the user alters the text displayed in the edit window identified by *`id`*.

ON_EN_ERRSPACE

`ON_EN_ERRSPACE(id, member_function)`

This macro maps the `EN_ERRSPACE` message to *`member_function`*. This message is generated when the edit window identified by *`id`* cannot allocate enough memory to complete its job.

ON_EN_HSCROLL

`ON_EN_HSCROLL(id, member_function)`

This macro maps the `EN_HSCROLL` message to *member_function*. This message is generated when the user clicks the horizontal scroll bar of the edit window identified by *id*.

ON_EN_KILLFOCUS

`ON_EN_KILLFOCUS(id, member_function)`

This macro maps the `EN_KILLFOCUS` message to *member_function*. This message is generated when the edit window identified by *id* loses the input focus.

ON_EN_MAXTEXT

`ON_EN_MAXTEXT(id, member_function)`

This macro maps the `EN_MAXTEXT` message to *member_function*. This message is generated when the user enters more text than the edit window (identified by *id*) can handle.

ON_EN_SETFOCUS

`ON_EN_SETFOCUS(id, member_function)`

This macro maps the `EN_SETFOCUS` message to *member_function*. This message is generated when the edit window identified by *id* receives the input focus.

ON_EN_UPDATE

`ON_EN_UPDATE(id, member_function)`

This macro maps the `EN_UPDATE` message to *member_function*. This message is generated when the text displayed in the edit window (identified by *id*) is about to be updated.

ON_EN_VSCROLL

`ON_EN_VSCROLL(id, member_function)`

This macro maps the `EN_VSCROLL` message to *member_function*. This message is generated when the user clicks the vertical scroll bar of the edit window identified by *id*.

ON_LBN_DBLCLK

ON_LBN_DBLCLK(*id*, *member_function*)

This macro maps the LBN_DBLCLK message to *member_function*. This message is generated when the user double-clicks a string in the list box identified by *id*.

ON_LBN_ERRSPACE

ON_LBN_ERRSPACE(*id*, *member_function*)

This macro maps the LBN_ERRSPACE message to *member_function*. This message is generated when the list box identified by *id* cannot allocate enough memory to store its data.

ON_LBN_KILLFOCUS

ON_LBN_KILLFOCUS(*id*, *member_function*)

This macro maps the LBN_KILLFOCUS message to *member_function*. This message is generated when the list box identified by *id* loses the input focus.

ON_LBN_SELCHANGE

ON_LBN_SELCHANGE(*id*, *member_function*)

This macro maps the LBN_SELCHANGE message to *member_function*. This message is generated when the selection in the list box identified by *id* is about to change.

ON_LBN_SETFOCUS

ON_LBN_SETFOCUS(*id*, *member_function*)

This macro maps the LBN_SETFOCUS message to *member_function*. This message is generated when the list box identified by *id* receives the input focus.

ON_MESSAGE

ON_MESSAGE(*message*, *member_function*)

This macro maps the *message* that you define to *member_function*.

ON_REGISTERED_MESSAGE

```
ON_REGISTERED_MESSAGE(message_variable, member_function)
```

This macro maps the message that you register using `RegisterWindowMessage` to *member_function*. *message_variable* is the name of the variable where you store the value returned by `RegisterWindowMessage`.

ON_UPDATE_COMMAND_UI

```
ON_UPDATE_COMMAND_UI(message_id, member_function)
```

Inserted by ClassWizard to indicate which function will handle a user-interface update command message.

ON_VBXEVENT

```
ON_VBXEVENT(notification_code, member_function)
```

Inserted by ClassWizard to indicate which function will handle a message from a Visual Basic custom control.

ON_WM_ACTIVATE

```
ON_WM_ACTIVATE()
```

This macro maps the `WM_ACTIVATE` message to a function with the following prototype:

```
afx_msg void OnActivate(UINT nState, CWnd* pWndOther,
    BOOL bMinimized);
```

The `WM_ACTIVATE` message is generated when a window is being activated or deactivated.

ON_WM_ACTIVATEAPP

```
ON_WM_ACTIVATEAPP()
```

This macro maps the `WM_ACTIVATE` message to a function with the following prototype:

```
afx_msg void OnActivateApp(BOOL bActive, HANDLE hTask);
```

The `WM_ACTIVATE` message is generated when a window belonging to a different task than the current one is being activated.

ON_WM_ASKCBFORMATNAME

ON_WM_ASKCBFORMATNAME()

This macro maps the WM_ASKCBFORMATNAME message to a function with the following prototype:

```
afx_msg void OnAskCbFormatName(UINT nMaxCount, LPSTR lpString);
```

The WM_ASKCBFORMATNAME message is sent by a Clipboard Viewer application to the Clipboard's owner when the Clipboard contains data of the CF_OWNERDISPLAY format.

ON_WM_CANCELMODE

ON_WM_CANCELMODE()

This macro maps the WM_CANCELMODE message to a function with the following prototype:

```
afx_msg void OnCancelMode();
```

The WM_CANCELMODE message is sent to a window that informs the window to cancel any internal mode.

ON_WM_CHANGECBCHAIN

ON_WM_CHANGECBCHAIN()

This macro maps the WM_CHANGECBCHAIN message to a function with the following prototype:

```
afx_msg void OnChangeCbChain(HWND hWndRemove, HWND hWndAfter);
```

The WM_CHANGECBCHAIN message is sent to the first window in the Clipboard Viewer chain, informing that window that a window is being removed from the chain.

ON_WM_CHAR

ON_WM_CHAR()

This macro maps the WM_CHAR message to a function with the following prototype:

```
afx_msg void OnChar(UINT nChar, UINT nRepCnt, UINT nFlags);
```

The WM_CHAR message is sent to a window when the user presses or releases a key.

ON_WM_CHARTOITEM

ON_WM_CHARTOITEM()

This macro maps the WM_CHARTOITEM message to a function with the following prototype:

```
afx_msg int OnCharToItem(UINT nChar, CListBox* pListBox,
    UINT nIndex);
```

The WM_CHARTOITEM message is sent to a window by a list box with the LBS_WANTKEYBOARDINPUT style when the user presses or releases a key.

ON_WM_CHILDACTIVATE

ON_WM_CHILDACTIVATE()

This macro maps the WM_CHILDACTIVATE message to a function with the following prototype:

```
afx_msg void OnChildActivate();
```

The WM_CHILDACTIVATE message is sent to an MDI child window when the user activates the child window by clicking the window's title bar.

ON_WM_CLOSE

ON_WM_CLOSE()

This macro maps the WM_CLOSE message to a function with the following prototype:

```
afx_msg void OnClose();
```

The WM_CLOSE message is sent to a window to signal that the window should be closed.

ON_WM_COMPACTING

ON_WM_COMPACTING()

This macro maps the WM_COMPACTING message to a function with the following prototype:

```
afx_msg void OnCompacting(UINT nCpuTime);
```

The WM_COMPACTING message is sent to a window to signal that system memory is low. This is detected by Windows when more than 12.5 percent of system time over a 30- to 60-second period is spent *compacting memory*—coalescing memory blocks by rearranging them in memory. In response to this message, you should free as much memory as possible.

ON_WM_COMPAREITEM

ON_WM_COMPAREITEM()

This macro maps the WM_COMPAREITEM message to a function with the following prototype:

```
afx_msg int OnCompareItem(LPCOMPAREITEMSTRUCT lpCompareItemStruct);
```

The WM_COMPAREITEM message is sent to a window in order to report the relative position of a new item in the sorted list of a list box or combo box created with the LBS_SORT or CBS_SORT style.

ON_WM_CREATE

ON_WM_CREATE()

This macro maps the WM_CREATE message to a function with the following prototype:

```
afx_msg int OnCreate(LPCREATESTRUCT lpCreateStruct);
```

The WM_CREATE message is sent to a window right after the window is created.

ON_WM_CTLCOLOR

ON_WM_CTLCOLOR()

This macro maps the WM_CTLCOLOR message to a function with the following prototype:

```
afx_msg HBRUSH OnCtlColor(CDC* pDC, CWnd* pWnd, UINT nCtlColor);
```

The WM_CTLCOLOR message is sent to a window when a control or a message box is about to be drawn. You can override this function to change the background colors of a single-line edit control.

ON_WM_DEADCHAR

ON_WM_DEADCHAR()

This macro maps the WM_DEADCHAR message to a function with the following prototype:

```
afx_msg void OnDeadChar(UINT nChar, UINT nRepCnt, UINT nFlags);
```

The WM_DEADCHAR message is sent to a window when a "dead" key is pressed and released (a *dead key* is combined with other keys to compose characters such as **ö**).

ON_WM_DELETEITEM

ON_WM_DELETEITEM()

This macro maps the WM_DELETEITEM message to a function with the following prototype:

```
afx_msg void OnDeleteItem(LPDELETEITEMSTRUCT lpDeleteItemStruct);
```

The WM_DELETEITEM message is sent to a window when items are removed from the list in a list box or a combo box.

ON_WM_DESTROY

ON_WM_DESTROY()

This macro maps the WM_DESTROY message to a function with the following prototype:

```
afx_msg void OnDestroy();
```

The WM_DESTROY message is sent to a window when it is about to be destroyed.

ON_WM_DESTROYCLIPBOARD

ON_WM_DESTROYCLIPBOARD()

This macro maps the WM_DESTROYCLIPBOARD message to a function with the following prototype:

```
afx_msg void OnDestroyClipboard();
```

The WM_DESTROYCLIPBOARD message is sent to the Clipboard owner when the contents of the Clipboard are destroyed.

ON_WM_DEVMODECHANGE

ON_WM_DEVMODECHANGE()

This macro maps the WM_DEVMODECHANGE message to a function with the following prototype:

```
afx_msg void OnDevModeChange(LPSTR lpDeviceName);
```

The WM_DEVMODECHANGE message is sent to all top-level windows after the mode settings of a device are changed.

ON_WM_DRAWCLIPBOARD

ON_WM_DRAWCLIPBOARD()

This macro maps the WM_DRAWCLIPBOARD message to a function with the following prototype:

```
afx_msg void OnDrawClipboard();
```

The WM_DRAWCLIPBOARD message is sent to the first window in the Clipboard Viewer chain when the contents of the Clipboard change.

ON_WM_DRAWITEM

ON_WM_DRAWITEM()

This macro maps the WM_DRAWITEM message to a function with the following prototype:

```
afx_msg void OnDrawItem(LPDRAWITEMSTRUCT lpDrawItemStruct);
```

The WM_DRAWITEM message is sent to the owner of an owner-drawn control (button, combo box, or list box) or menu when that item needs repainting.

ON_WM_DROPFILES

ON_WM_DROPFILES()

This macro maps the WM_DROPFILES message to a function with the following prototype:

```
afx_msg void OnDropFiles(HANDLE hDropInfo);
```

The WM_DROPFILES message is sent when the user releases the left mouse button over the window if the window accepts files dropped onto it.

ON_WM_ENABLE

ON_WM_ENABLE()

This macro maps the WM_ENABLE message to a function with the following prototype:

```
afx_msg void OnEnable(BOOL bEnable);
```

The WM_ENABLE message is sent after the window is *enabled* (made active) or *disabled* (made inactive).

ON_WM_ENDSESSION

```
ON_WM_ENDSESSION()
```

This macro maps the WM_ENDSESSION message to a function with the following prototype:

```
afx_msg void OnEndSession(BOOL bEnding);
```

The WM_ENDSESSION message is sent after the CWnd's WM_QUERYENDSESSION handler (OnQueryEndSession) returns TRUE, indicating that the session actually is ending.

ON_WM_ENTERIDLE

```
ON_WM_ENTERIDLE()
```

This macro maps the WM_ENTERIDLE message to a function with the following prototype:

```
afx_msg void OnEnterIdle(UINT nWhy, CWnd* pWho);
```

The WM_ENTERIDLE message is sent to an application's main window when a modal dialog box or a menu is in *idle state*—when no messages are waiting in the queue for that modal dialog box or menu.

ON_WM_ERASEBKGND

```
ON_WM_ERASEBKGND()
```

This macro maps the WM_ERASEBKGND message to a function with the following prototype:

```
afx_msg BOOL OnEraseBkgnd(CDC* pDC);
```

The WM_ERASEBKGND message is sent when the window's background needs erasing prior to repainting the window.

ON_WM_FONTCHANGE

```
ON_WM_FONTCHANGE()
```

This macro maps the WM_FONTCHANGE message to a function with the following prototype:

```
afx_msg void OnFontChange();
```

The WM_FONTCHANGE message is sent after fonts are added to or removed from the system.

ON_WM_GETDLGCODE

ON_WM_GETDLGCODE()

This macro maps the WM_GETDLOGCODE message to a function with the following prototype:

```
afx_msg UINT OnGetDlgCode();
```

The WM_GETDLOGCODE message is sent to a dialog box window to query which inputs the dialog box handles. Return a code that indicates the type of inputs the dialog box handles. See Table 20.2 for a list of return values.

Table 20.2. OnGetDlgCode return values.

Return value	Description
DLGC_DEFPUSHBUTTON	A default push button.
DLGC_HASSETSEL	EM_SETSEL messages.
DLGC_PUSHBUTTON	A nondefault pushbutton.
DLGC_RADIOBUTTON	A radio button.
DLGC_WANTALLKEYS	All keyboard input is wanted.
DLGC_WANTARROWS	Only the direction (arrow) keys are wanted.
DLGC_WANTCHARS	Wants all WM_CHAR messages.
DLGC_WANTMESSAGE	All keyboard input is to be processed. Passed by the application to the control.
DLGC_WANTTAB	Wants only the TAB key.

ON_WM_GETMINMAXINFO

ON_WM_GETMINMAXINFO()

This macro maps the WM_GETMINMAXINFO message to a function with the following prototype:

```
afx_msg void OnGetMinMaxInfo(LPPOINT lpPoints);
```

The WM_GETMINMAXINFO message is sent whenever Windows needs information about the following dimensions of a window:

- The position and size of the window in its maximized state
- The minimum tracking size (the smallest the user can resize the window)
- The maximum tracking size (the largest the user can resize the window)

ON_WM_HSCROLL

ON_WM_HSCROLL()

This macro maps the WM_HSCROLL message to a function with the following prototype:

```
afx_msg void OnHScroll(UINT nSBCode, UINT nPos,
    CScrollBar* pScrollBar);
```

The WM_HSCROLL message is sent to a window whenever the user clicks the horizontal scrollbar.

ON_WM_HSCROLLCLIPBOARD

ON_WM_HSCROLLCLIPBOARD()

This macro maps the WM_HSCROLLCLIPBOARD message to a function with the following prototype:

```
afx_msg void OnHScrollClipboard(CWnd* pClipAppWnd,
    UINT nSBCode, UINT nPos);
```

The WM_HSCROLLCLIPBOARD message is sent to the Clipboard owner when the Clipboard has data with the CF_OWNERDISPLAY format and the user clicks anywhere in the Clipboard Viewer's horizontal scrollbar.

ON_WM_ICONERASEBKGND

ON_WM_ICONERASEBKGND()

This macro maps the WM_ICONERASEBKGND message to a function with the following prototype:

```
afx_msg void OnIconEraseBkgnd(CDC* pDC);
```

The WM_ICONERASEBKGND message is sent to a minimized window when the background of the window's icon needs to be filled before painting.

ON_WM_INITMENU

ON_WM_INITMENU()

This macro maps the WM_INITMENU message to a function with the following prototype:

```
afx_msg void OnInitMenu(CMenu* pMenu);
```

The WM_INITMENU message is sent when the user clicks an item in the menu bar or presses a menu key.

ON_WM_INITMENUPOPUP

ON_WM_INITMENUPOPUP()

This macro maps the WM_INITMENUPOPUP message to a function with the following prototype:

```
afx_msg void OnInitMenuPopup(CMenu* pPopupMenu, UINT nIndex,
    BOOL bSysMenu);
```

The WM_INITMENUPOPUP message is sent when a pop-up menu is about to become active.

ON_WM_KEYDOWN

ON_WM_KEYDOWN()

This macro maps the WM_KEYDOWN message to a function with the following prototype:

```
afx_msg void OnKeyDown(UINT nChar, UINT nRepCnt, UINT nFlags);
```

The WM_KEYDOWN message is sent whenever the user presses a nonsystem key, which is any keypress without the Alt key held down at the same time.

ON_WM_KEYUP

ON_WM_KEYUP()

This macro maps the WM_KEYUP message to a function with the following prototype:

```
afx_msg void OnKeyUp(UINT nChar, UINT nRepCnt, UINT nFlags);
```

The WM_KEYUP message is sent whenever the user releases a nonsystem key. A *nonsystem key* refers to any keypress without the Alt key held down at the same time.

ON_WM_KILLFOCUS

ON_WM_KILLFOCUS()

This macro maps the WM_KILLFOCUS message to a function with the following prototype:

```
afx_msg void OnKillFocus(CWnd* pNewWnd);
```

The WM_KILLFOCUS message is sent to a window immediately before it loses input focus. If the window is displaying a caret (^), you must call an appropriate function to destroy the caret.

ON_WM_LBUTTONDBLCLK

ON_WM_LBUTTONDBLCLK()

This macro maps the WM_LBUTTONDBLCLK message to a function with the following prototype:

```
afx_msg void OnLButtonDblClk(UINT nFlags, CPoint point);
```

The WM_LBUTTONDBLCLK message is sent to a window if the user double-clicks the left mouse button when the cursor is located inside the window.

ON_WM_LBUTTONDOWN

ON_WM_LBUTTONDOWN()

This macro maps the WM_LBUTTONDOWN message to a function with the following prototype:

```
afx_msg void OnLButtonDown(UINT nFlags, CPoint point);
```

The WM_LBUTTONDOWN message is sent to a window if the user presses the left mouse button when the cursor is located inside the window.

ON_WM_LBUTTONUP

ON_WM_LBUTTONUP()

This macro maps the WM_LBUTTONUP message to a function with the following prototype:

```
afx_msg void OnLButtonUp(UINT nFlags, CPoint point);
```

The WM_LBUTTONUP message is sent to a window when the user releases the left mouse button with the cursor inside the window.

ON_WM_MBUTTONDBLCLK

ON_WM_MBUTTONDBLCLK()

This macro maps the WM_MBUTTONDBLCLK message to a function with the following prototype:

```
afx_msg void OnMButtonDblClk(UINT nFlags, CPoint point);
```

The WM_MBUTTONDBLCLK message is sent to a window when the user double-clicks the middle mouse button (if the system's mouse has a middle button) with the cursor inside the window.

ON_WM_MBUTTONDOWN

ON_WM_MBUTTONDOWN()

This macro maps the WM_MBUTTONDOWN message to a function with the following prototype:

```
afx_msg void OnMButtonDown(UINT nFlags, CPoint point);
```

The WM_MBUTTONDOWN message is sent to a window when the user presses the middle mouse button with the cursor inside the window.

ON_WM_MBUTTONUP

ON_WM_MBUTTONUP()

This macro maps the WM_MBUTTONUP message to a function with the following prototype:

```
afx_msg void OnMButtonUp(UINT nFlags, CPoint point);
```

The WM_MBUTTONUP message is sent to a window when the user releases the middle mouse button while the cursor is located inside the window.

ON_WM_MDIACTIVATE

ON_WM_MDIACTIVATE()

This macro maps the WM_MDIACTIVATE message to a function with the following prototype:

```
afx_msg void OnMDIActivate(BOOL bActivate, CWnd* pActivateWnd,
    CWnd* pDeactivateWnd);
```

The WM_MDIACTIVATE message is sent to a child window in an application with MDI when the child window is activated or deactivated.

ON_WM_MEASUREITEM

ON_WM_MEASUREITEM()

This macro maps the WM_MEASUREITEM message to a function with the following prototype:

```
afx_msg void OnMeasureItem(LPMEASUREITEMSTRUCT lpMeasureItemStruct);
```

The WM_MEASUREITEM message is sent to the owner of an owner-drawn button, list box, or combo box when that control window is created.

ON_WM_MENUCHAR

ON_WM_MENUCHAR()

This macro maps the WM_MENUCHAR message to a function with the following prototype:

```
afx_msg LONG OnMenuChar(UINT nChar, UINT nFlags, CMenu* pMenu);
```

The WM_MENUCHAR message is sent when the user drops down a menu and presses a character that does not match any of the predefined mnemonic characters for that menu.

ON_WM_MENUSELECT

ON_WM_MENUSELECT()

This macro maps the WM_MENUSELECT message to a function with the following prototype:

```
afx_msg void OnMenuSelect(UINT nItemID, UINT nFlags,
    HMENU hSysMenu);
```

The WM_MENUSELECT message is sent when the user selects an item from a menu.

ON_WM_MOUSEACTIVATE

ON_WM_MOUSEACTIVATE()

This macro maps the WM_MOUSEACTIVATE message to a function with the following prototype:

```
afx_msg int OnMouseActivate(CWnd* pFrameWnd, UINT nHitTest,
    UINT message);
```

The WM_MOUSEACTIVATE message is sent when the mouse cursor is on an inactive window and the user presses any mouse button.

ON_WM_MOUSEMOVE

ON_WM_MOUSEMOVE()

This macro maps the WM_MOUSEMOVE message to a function with the following prototype:

```
afx_msg void OnMouseMove(UINT nFlags, CPoint point);
```

The WM_MOUSEMOVE message is sent whenever the user moves the mouse cursor.

ON_WM_MOVE

ON_WM_MOVE()

This macro maps the WM_MOVE message to a function with the following prototype:

```
afx_msg void OnMove(int x, int y);
```

The WM_MOVE message is sent to a window after it has been moved.

ON_WM_NCACTIVATE

ON_WM_NCACTIVATE()

This macro maps the WM_NCACTIVATE message to a function with the following prototype:

```
afx_msg void BOOL OnNcActivate(BOOL bActive);
```

The WM_NCACTIVATE message is sent when the *nonclient area* of a window—the frame with the title bar and scroll bars—must change to indicate an active or inactive state.

ON_WM_NCCALCSIZE

ON_WM_NCCALCSIZE()

This macro maps the WM_NCCALCSIZE message to a function with the following prototype:

```
afx_msg void OnNcCalcSize(NCCALCSIZE_PARAMS FAR* lpncsp);
```

The WM_NCCALCSIZE message is sent when the size and position of a window's client area needs to be calculated.

ON_WM_NCCREATE

ON_WM_NCCREATE()

This macro maps the WM_NCCREATE message to a function with the following prototype:

```
afx_msg BOOL OnNcCreate(LPCREATESTRUCT lpCreateStruct);
```

The WM_NCCREATE message is sent just before the WM_CREATE message to indicate that the nonclient area of the window is being created.

ON_WM_NCDESTROY

ON_WM_NCDESTROY()

This macro maps the WM_NCDESTROY message to a function with the following prototype:

```
afx_msg void OnNcDestroy();
```

The WM_NCDESTROY message is sent to a window when that window's nonclient area—the frame—is about to be destroyed.

ON_WM_NCHITTEST

ON_WM_NCHITTEST()

This macro maps the WM_NCHITTEST message to a function with the following prototype:

```
afx_msg UINT OnNcHitTest(CPoint point);
```

The WM_NCHITTEST message is sent to a window (or the window capturing all mouse inputs by calling the SetCapture member function) whenever the user moves the mouse. The message handler should determine the part of the window where the mouse cursor is located (for example, is it in the lower border or the upper border?).

ON_WM_NCLBUTTONDBLCLK

ON_WM_NCLBUTTONDBLCLK()

This macro maps the WM_NCLBUTTONDBLCLK message to a function with the following prototype:

```
afx_msg void OnNcLButtonDblClk(UINT nHitTest, CPoint point);
```

The WM_NCLBUTTONDBLCLK message is sent to a window when the user double-clicks the left mouse button with the cursor in the window's frame (the nonclient area).

ON_WM_NCLBUTTONDOWN

ON_WM_NCLBUTTONDOWN()

This macro maps the WM_NCLBUTTONDOWN message to a function with the following prototype:

```
afx_msg void OnNcLButtonDown(UINT nHitTest, CPoint point);
```

The WM_NCLBUTTONDOWN message is sent to a window when the user presses the left mouse button with the cursor in the window's frame (the nonclient area).

ON_WM_NCLBUTTONUP

ON_WM_NCLBUTTONUP()

This macro maps the WM_NCLBUTTONUP message to a function with the following prototype:

```
afx_msg void OnNcLButtonUp(UINT nHitTest, CPoint point);
```

The WM_NCLBUTTONUP message is sent to a window when the user releases the left mouse button with the cursor in the window's frame (the nonclient area).

ON_WM_NCMBUTTONDBLCLK

ON_WM_NCMBUTTONDBLCLK()

This macro maps the WM_NCMBUTTONDBLCLK message to a function with the following prototype:

```
afx_msg void OnNcMButtonDblClk(UINT nHitTest, CPoint point);
```

The WM_NCMBUTTONDBLCLK message is sent when the user double-clicks the middle mouse button with the cursor in the nonclient area—the area outside the rectangular region where the application's output appears.

ON_WM_NCMBUTTONDOWN

ON_WM_NCMBUTTONDOWN()

This macro maps the WM_NCMBUTTONDOWN message to a function with the following prototype:

```
afx_msg void OnNcMButtonDown(UINT nHitTest, CPoint point);
```

The WM_NCMBUTTONDOWN message is sent when the user presses the middle mouse button with the cursor in the nonclient area—the area outside the rectangular region where the application's output appears.

ON_WM_NCMBUTTONUP

ON_WM_NCMBUTTONUP()

This macro maps the WM_NCMBUTTONUP message to a function with the following prototype:

```
afx_msg void OnNcMButtonUp(UINT nHitTest, CPoint point);
```

The WM_NCMBUTTONUP message is sent when the user releases the middle mouse button with the cursor in the nonclient area—the area outside the rectangular region where the application's output appears.

ON_WM_NCMOUSEMOVE

ON_WM_NCMOUSEMOVE()

This macro maps the WM_NCMOUSEMOVE message to a function with the following prototype:

```
afx_msg void OnNcMouseMove(UINT nHitTest, CPoint point);
```

The WM_NCMOUSEMOVE message is sent to a window when the user moves the mouse cursor within the nonclient area—the frame and the border of the window.

ON_WM_NCPAINT

ON_WM_NCPAINT()

This macro maps the WM_NCPAINT message to a function with the following prototype:

```
afx_msg void OnNcPaint();
```

The WM_NCPAINT message is sent to a window when its nonclient area—the frame—needs repainting.

ON_WM_NCRBUTTONDBLCLK

ON_WM_NCRBUTTONDBLCLK()

This macro maps the WM_NCRBUTTONDBLCLK message to a function with the following prototype:

```
afx_msg void OnNcRButtonDblClk(UINT nHitTest, CPoint point);
```

The WM_NCRBUTTONDBLCLK message is sent to a window when the user double-clicks the right mouse button anywhere in the nonclient area—anywhere outside the area where the application's output appears.

ON_WM_NCRBUTTONDOWN

ON_WM_NCRBUTTONDOWN()

This macro maps the WM_NCRBUTTONDOWN message to a function with the following prototype:

```
afx_msg void OnNcRButtonDown(UINT nHitTest, CPoint point);
```

The WM_NCRBUTTONDOWN message is sent to a window when the user presses the right mouse button anywhere in the nonclient area—anywhere outside the area where the application's output appears.

ON_WM_NCRBUTTONUP

ON_WM_NCRBUTTONUP()

This macro maps the WM_NCRBUTTONUP message to a function with the following prototype:

```
afx_msg void OnNcRButtonDblClk(UINT nHitTest, CPoint point);
```

The WM_NCRBUTTONUP message is sent to a window when the user releases the right mouse button anywhere in the nonclient area—anywhere outside the area where the application's output appears.

ON_WM_PAINT

ON_WM_PAINT()

This macro maps the WM_PAINT message to a function with the following prototype:

```
afx_msg void OnPaint();
```

The WM_PAINT message is sent when an area of the window needs repainting.

ON_WM_PAINTCLIPBOARD

ON_WM_PAINTCLIPBOARD()

This macro maps the WM_PAINTCLIPBOARD message to a function with the following prototype:

```
afx_msg OnPaintClipboard(CWnd* pClipAppWnd, HANDLE hPaintStruct);
```

The WM_PAINTCLIPBOARD message is sent to the Clipboard's owner when the Clipboard contains data with the CF_OWNERDISPLAY format and the Clipboard Viewer's window needs repainting.

ON_WM_PAINTICON

ON_WM_PAINTICON()

This macro maps the WM_PAINTICON message to a function. Since the WM_PAINTICON message is not usable at the application level, this macro is not supplied with Visual C++.

ON_WM_PALETTECHANGED

ON_WM_PALETTECHANGED()

This macro maps the WM_PALETTECHANGED message to a function with the following prototype:

```
afx_msg void OnPaletteChanged(CWnd* pFocusWnd);
```

The WM_PAINTICON message is sent after the system color palette has changed. You should not respond to this message if *pFocusWnd* points to your window.

ON_WM_PALETTEISCHANGING

ON_WM_PALETTEISCHANGING()

This macro maps the WM_PALETTEISCHANGING message to a function with the following prototype:

```
afx_msg void OnPaletteIsChanging(CWnd* pRealizeWnd);
```

The WM_PALETTEISCHANGING message is sent to indicate that the system color palette is about to change.

ON_WM_PARENTNOTIFY

ON_WM_PARENTNOTIFY()

This macro maps the WM_PARENTNOTIFY message to a function with the following prototype:

```
afx_msg void OnParentNotify(UINT message, LONG lParam);
```

The WM_PARENTNOTIFY message is sent to a parent window when a child window is created or destroyed, or when the user clicks the child window.

ON_WM_QUERYDRAGICON

ON_WM_QUERYDRAGICON()

This macro maps the WM_QUERYDRAGICON message to a function with the following prototype:

```
afx_msg HCURSOR OnQueryDragIcon();
```

The WM_QUERYDRAGICON message is sent when the user moves an iconized window and when an icon is not defined for the window class. You should return a cursor or an icon handle. Return NULL to use the system's default cursor.

ON_WM_QUERYENDSESSION

ON_WM_QUERYENDSESSION()

This macro maps the WM_QUERYENDSESSION message to a function with the following prototype:

```
afx_msg BOOL OnQueryEndSession();
```

The WM_QUERYENDSESSION message is sent when the user chooses to end the Windows session. You should return TRUE if your application can shut down; otherwise, return FALSE.

ON_WM_QUERYNEWPALETTE

ON_WM_QUERYNEWPALETTE()

This macro maps the WM_QUERYNEWPALETTE message to a function with the following prototype:

```
afx_msg BOOL OnQueryNewPalette();
```

The WM_QUERYNEWPALETTE message is sent when a window is about to receive the input focus, inquiring whether the window wants to use its logical palette of colors. Return TRUE if the window needs to use the palette of colors.

ON_WM_QUERYOPEN

ON_WM_QUERYOPEN()

This macro maps the WM_QUERYOPEN message to a function with the following prototype:

```
afx_msg BOOL OnQueryOpen();
```

The WM_QUERYOPEN message is sent when a minimized window is about to be opened into a full-size window. Return TRUE to indicate that the window can be maximized.

ON_WM_RBUTTONDBLCLK

ON_WM_RBUTTONDBLCLK()

This macro maps the WM_RBUTTONDBLCLK message to a function with the following prototype:

```
afx_msg void OnRButtonDblClk(UINT nFlags, CPoint point);
```

The WM_RBUTTONDBLCLK message is sent when the user double-clicks the right mouse button.

ON_WM_RBUTTONDOWN

ON_WM_RBUTTONDOWN()

This macro maps the WM_RBUTTONDOWN message to a function with the following prototype:

```
afx_msg void OnRButtonDown(UINT nFlags, CPoint point);
```

The WM_RBUTTONDOWN message is sent when the user presses the right mouse button.

ON_WM_RBUTTONUP

ON_WM_RBUTTONUP()

This macro maps the WM_RBUTTONUP message to a function with the following prototype:

```
afx_msg void OnRButtonUp(UINT nFlags, CPoint point);
```

The WM_RBUTTONUP message is sent when the user releases the right mouse button.

ON_WM_RENDERALLFORMATS

ON_WM_RENDERALLFORMATS()

This macro maps the WM_RENDERALLFORMATS message to a function with the following prototype:

```
afx_msg void OnRenderAllFormats();
```

The WM_RENDERALLFORMATS message is sent to the Clipboard's owner when the owner application is about to be destroyed. The application should provide data in all possible formats so that the Clipboard has valid data even when the application exits.

ON_WM_RENDERFORMAT

ON_WM_RENDERFORMAT()

This macro maps the WM_RENDERFORMAT message to a function with the following prototype:

```
afx_msg void OnRenderFormat(UINT nFormat);
```

The WM_RENDERFORMAT message is sent to the owner of the Clipboard when data of a specific format needs to be provided.

ON_WM_SETCURSOR

ON_WM_SETCURSOR()

This macro maps the WM_SETCURSOR message to a function with the following prototype:

```
afx_msg BOOL OnSetCursor(CWnd* pWnd, UINT nHitTest, UINT message);
```

The WM_SETCURSOR message is sent when the cursor moves within the window.

ON_WM_SETFOCUS

ON_WM_SETFOCUS()

This macro maps the WM_SETFOCUS message to a function with the following prototype:

```
afx_msg void OnSetFocus(CWnd* pOldWnd);
```

The WM_SETFOCUS message is sent after a window gains the input focus. You should call an appropriate function to display the caret.

ON_WM_SHOWWINDOW

ON_WM_SHOWWINDOW()

This macro maps the WM_SHOWWINDOW message to a function with the following prototype:

```
afx_msg void OnShowWindow(BOOL bShow, UINT nStatus);
```

The WM_SHOWWINDOW message is sent when a window is about to be hidden or made visible.

ON_WM_SIZE

ON_WM_SIZE()

This macro maps the WM_SIZE message to a function with the following prototype:

```
afx_msg void OnSize(UINT nType, int cx, int cy);
```

The WM_SIZE message is sent after a window's size has changed.

ON_WM_SIZECLIPBOARD

ON_WM_SIZECLIPBOARD()

This macro maps the WM_SIZECLIPBOARD message to a function with the following prototype:

```
afx_msg void OnSizeClipboard(CWnd* pClipAppWnd, HANDLE hRect);
```

The WM_SIZECLIPBOARD message is sent to the owner of the Clipboard if the Clipboard's data is of the CF_OWNERDISPLAY format and the user resizes the Clipboard Viewer window.

ON_WM_SPOOLERSTATUS

ON_WM_SPOOLERSTATUS()

This macro maps the WM_SPOOLERSTATUS message to a function with the following prototype:

```
afx_msg void OnSpoolerStatus(UINT nStatus, UINT nJobs);
```

The WM_SPOOLERSTATUS message is sent by the Windows Print Manager whenever a job is added or removed from the Print Manager queue.

ON_WM_SYSCHAR

ON_WM_SYSCHAR()

This macro maps the WM_SYSCHAR message to a function with the following prototype:

```
afx_msg void OnSysChar(UINT nChar, UINT nRepCnt, UINT nFlags);
```

The WM_SYSCHAR message is sent whenever a WM_SYSKEYDOWN and a WM_SYSKEYDOWN message is generated.

ON_WM_SYSCOLORCHANGE

ON_WM_SYSCOLORCHANGE()

This macro maps the WM_SYSCOLORCHANGE message to a function with the following prototype:

```
afx_msg void OnSysColorChange();
```

The WM_SYSCOLORCHANGE message is sent when the system color settings are changed.

ON_WM_SYSCOMMAND

ON_WM_SYSCOMMAND()

This macro maps the WM_SYSCOMMAND message to a function with the following prototype:

```
afx_msg void OnSysCommand(UINT nID, LONG lParam);
```

The WM_SYSCOMMAND message is sent when the user selects any item from the Control menu (the menu that appears when you click the Control menu box in the top-left corner of the window's frame).

ON_WM_SYSDEADCHAR

ON_WM_SYSDEADCHAR()

This macro maps the WM_SYSDEADCHAR message to a function with the following prototype:

```
afx_msg void OnSysDeadChar(UINT nChar, UINT nRepCnt, UINT nFlags);
```

The WM_SYSDEADCHAR message is sent if the window has the focus when a WM_SYSKEYDOWN and a WM_SYSKEYUP message is generated.

ON_WM_SYSKEYDOWN

ON_WM_SYSKEYDOWN()

This macro maps the WM_SYSKEYDOWN message to a function with the following prototype:

```
afx_msg void OnSysKeyDown(UINT nChar, UINT nRepCnt, UINT nFlags);
```

The WM_SYSKEYDOWN message is sent when the user holds down the Alt key and presses any other key.

ON_WM_SYSKEYUP

ON_WM_SYSKEYUP()

This macro maps the WM_SYSKEYUP message to a function with the following prototype:

```
afx_msg void OnSysKeyUp(UINT nChar, UINT nRepCnt, UINT nFlags);
```

The WM_SYSKEYUP message is sent when the user releases a key that was pressed with the Alt key.

ON_WM_TIMECHANGE

ON_WM_TIMECHANGE()

This macro maps the WM_TIMECHANGE message to a function with the following prototype:

```
afx_msg void OnTimeChange();
```

The WM_TIMECHANGE message is sent after the system time has changed.

ON_WM_TIMER

ON_WM_TIMER()

This macro maps the WM_TIMER message to a function with the following prototype:

```
afx_msg void OnTimer(UINT nIDEvent);
```

The WM_TIMER message is sent at regular intervals. You can set the interval by calling the SetTimer member function of the window class.

ON_WM_VKEYTOITEM

ON_WM_VKEYTOITEM()

This macro maps the WM_VKEYTOITEM message to a function with the following prototype:

```
afx_msg int OnVKeyToItem(UINT nKey, CListBox* pListBox,
    UINT nIndex);
```

The WM_VKEYTOITEM message is sent by a list box with the LBS_WANTKEYBOARDINPUT style when the list box receives a WM_KEYDOWN event.

ON_WM_VSCROLL

ON_WM_VSCROLL()

This macro maps the WM_VSCROLL message to a function with the following prototype:

```
afx_msg void OnVScroll(UINT nSBCode, UINT nPos,
    CScrollBar* pScrollBar);
```

The WM_VSCROLL message is sent when the user clicks the vertical scroll bar of the window.

ON_WM_VSCROLLCLIPBOARD

ON_WM_VSCROLLCLIPBOARD()

This macro maps the WM_VSCROLLCLIPBOARD message to a function with the following prototype:

```
afx_msg void OnVScrollClipboard(CWnd* pClipAppWnd,
    UINT nSBCode, UINT nPos);
```

The WM_VSCROLLCLIPBOARD message is sent to the owner of the Clipboard when the Clipboard's data has the CF_OWNERDISPLAY format and the user clicks anywhere on the Clipboard Viewer's vertical scroll bar.

ON_WM_WINDOWPOSCHANGED

ON_WM_WINDOWPOSCHANGED()

This macro maps the WM_WINDOWPOSCHANGED message to a function with the following prototype:

```
afx_msg void OnWindowPosChanged(WINDOWPOS FAR* lpwndpos);
```

The WM_WINDOWPOSCHANGED message is sent in Windows 3.1 or later when the window's size, position, or stacking order has changed.

ON_WM_WINDOWPOSCHANGING

ON_WM_WINDOWPOSCHANGING()

This macro maps the WM_WINDOWPOSCHANGING message to a function with the following prototype:

```
afx_msg void OnWindowPosChanging(WINDOWPOS FAR* lpwndpos);
```

The WM_WINDOWPOSCHANGING message is sent in Windows 3.1 or later when the window's size, position, and stacking order are about to change.

ON_WM_WININICHANGE

```
ON_WM_WININICHANGE()
```

This macro maps the `WM_WININICHANGE` message to a function with the following prototype:

```
afx_msg void OnWinIniChange(LPSTR lpSection);
```

The `WM_WININICHANGE` message is sent to a window after a change has been made to the Windows initialization file, win.ini.

Global Functions

AfxGetApp

```
CWinApp* AfxGetApp();
```

This function returns a pointer to the `CWinApp` object that represents the Windows application.

AfxGetAppName

```
const char* AfxGetAppName();
```

This function returns a null-terminated string that contains the name of the application.

AfxGetInstanceHandle

```
HINSTANCE AfxGetInstanceHandle();
```

This function returns a handle to the current instance of the application.

AfxGetPict

```
AFXAPI AfxGetPict(HPIC hPic, const PIC FAR * lpPicture);
```

This function is used as part of the Visual Basic custom controls support.

AfxIsMemoryBlock

```
BOOL AfxIsMemoryBlock();
```

This function tests a memory block address to ensure that the address is to a current active memory block that was allocated to this application by the debugging version of **new**.

AfxIsValidAddress

```
BOOL AfxIsValidAddress();
```

This function tests a memory address to ensure that the address is within the memory space that was allocated to this application by the debugging version of **new**.

AfxIsValidString

```
BOOL AfxIsValidString();
```

This function tests whether a pointer to a string is valid.

AfxMessageBox

```
int AfxMessageBox(LPCSTR lpszText, UINT nType = MB_OK, UINT nIDHelp = 0);
int AFXAPI AfxMessageBox(UINT nIDPrompt,
    UINT nType = MB_OK, UINT nIDHelp = (UINT) -1);
```

This function displays a message box with a defined text message. It's also possible to define the message box's style, whether there is context-sensitive help, and the help context used to locate the proper help topic.

Additional information about message box styles (the *nType* parameter) can be found in Table 20.32.

The second format of **AfxMessageBox** uses a resource id to locate a string resource, and displays the string as the message text.

AfxGetResourceHandle

```
HINSTANCE AfxGetResourceHandle();
```

This function returns a handle to the current instance of the application. You can call this function to acquire a handle that can be used in calls to the Windows SDK function FindResource, which directly accesses the application's resources.

> **Using the Global Functions for OLE Support**
>
> To use the OLE global functions (with names containing the AfxOle prefix), your application's resource (.rc) file must contain the following statements:

```
#include <afxoleui.h>
#include <afxres.h>
#include <afxolecl.rc> // For client applications
#include <afxolesv.rc> // For server applications
```

AfxOleInsertDialog

```
BOOL AfxOleInsertDialog(
    CString& name); //  A reference to a CString to store
                    //    the name the user chooses
```

Call this function to display a dialog box that enables the user to choose a server from a list of registered applications. This returns TRUE if successful.

AfxOleLinksDialog

```
BOOL AfxOleLinksDialog(
    COleClientDoc* pDoc); // A pointer to the OLE client document
                          //   that contains the links
```

Call this function to display a dialog box that enables the user to update this client's OLE links.

AfxOleRegisterServerName

```
BOOL AfxOleRegisterServerName(LPCSTR lpszTypeName, LPCSTR
lpszLocalTypeName);
```

This function registers the application as an OLE server with Windows.

AfxOleSetEditMenu

```
void AfxOleSetEditMenu(
    COleClientItem* pClient, // Pointer to the client item
    CMenu* pMenu,            // Pointer to the menu to be updated
    UINT   iMenuItem,        // Index of the menu item to be updated
    UINT   nIDVerbMin);      // Command ID corresponding to primary verb
```

Use this function to update the client document's menu with the appropriate server name and applicable verbs.

AfxRegisterWndClass

```
const char* AfxRegisterWndClass(
    UINT    nClassStyle,         // Windows class style
    HCURSOR hCursor = 0,         // Handle to cursor for the window
    HBRUSH  hbrBackground = 0,   // Handle to a brush used to paint
                                 //   the background of the windows
    HICON   hIcon = 0);          // Icon for this window class
```

Call this function to register your own window class.

AfxRegisterPict

```
BOOL AfxRegisterPict();
```

This function is used as part of the Visual Basic custom controls support.

AfxRegisterVBEvent

```
BOOL AfxRegisterVBEvent();
```

This function is used as part of the Visual Basic custom controls support and returns an atom which identifies the event.

AfxSetAllocHook

```
BOOL AfxSetAllocHook();
```

This function enables you to define a function that will be called each time, before a memory block is allocated.

AfxSetPict

```
BOOL AfxSetPict();
```

This function is used as part of the Visual Basic custom controls support.

AfxSetResourceHandle

```
BOOL AfxSetResourceHandle();
```

This function enables you to define the .exe or .dll in which an application's resources are located.

AfxThrowArchiveException

```
BOOL AfxThrowArchiveException();
```

This function enables you to throw an archive exception.

AfxThrowFileException

```
BOOL AfxThrowFileException();
```

This function enables you to throw a file exception.

AfxThrowMemoryException

```
BOOL AfxThrowMemoryException();
```

This function enables you to throw a memory exception.

AfxThrowNotSupportedException

```
BOOL AfxThrowNotSupportedException();
```

This function enables you to throw an exception for an unsupported feature.

AfxThrowOleException

```
BOOL AfxThrowOleException();
```

This function enables you to throw an OLE exception.

AfxThrowResourceException

```
BOOL AfxThrowResourceException();
```

This function enables you to throw a resource exception, such as when a resource cannot be loaded.

AfxThrowUserException

```
BOOL AfxThrowUserException();
```

This function enables you to throw an exception that will terminate the current end-user operation. Usually called after presenting a message box to the user reporting an error.

Reference

CBitmap

Inheritance Hierarchy

```
CObject -> CGdiObject -> CBitmap
```

Summary

```
#include <afxwin.h>
class CBitmap : public CGdiObject
{
    DECLARE_DYNAMIC(CBitmap)
public:
// Constructor:
    CBitmap();

// Creating and loading bitmaps:
    BOOL LoadBitmap(LPCSTR lpBitmapName);
    BOOL LoadBitmap(UINT nIDBitmap);
    BOOL LoadOEMBitmap(UINT nIDBitmap);
    BOOL CreateBitmap(int nWidth, int nHeight, BYTE nPlanes,
        BYTE nBitcount, const void FAR* lpBits);
    BOOL CreateBitmapIndirect(LPBITMAP lpBitmap);
    BOOL CreateCompatibleBitmap(CDC* pDC, int nWidth,
        int nHeight);
    BOOL CreateDiscardableBitmap(CDC* pDC, int nWidth,
        int nHeight);
    static CBitmap* FromHandle(HBITMAP hBitmap);

// Operations:

    DWORD SetBitmapBits(DWORD dwCount, const void FAR* lpBits);
    DWORD GetBitmapBits(DWORD dwCount, void FAR* lpBits) const;
    CSize SetBitmapDimension(int nWidth, int nHeight);
    CSize GetBitmapDimension() const;

};
```

Description

The `CBitmap` class represents a Windows bitmap object. `CBitmap` is derived from the `CGdiObject` class. Use `CBitmap` objects to load bitmaps from resources and manipulate them. To display a bitmap, select the `CBitmap` object in a device context (DC) and call functions such as `BitBlt` to transfer the bitmap to the display screen.

Member Functions

Constructor

```
CBitmap();
```

Constructs a CBitmap object that you must initialize with a member function.

Creating and Loading Bitmaps

```
BOOL CreateBitmap(
    int  nWidth,     // Width of bitmap in pixels
    int  nHeight,    // Height of bitmap in pixels
    BYTE nPlanes,    // Number of color planes
    BYTE nBitcount, // Bits per pixel
    const void FAR* lpBits); // Array with initial bitmap values
```

Initializes a bitmap of a specified size and bit pattern. This function returns TRUE if successful; otherwise, returns FALSE.

```
BOOL CreateBitmapIndirect(
    LPBITMAP lpBitmap); // Information to initialize bitmap
```

Initializes a bitmap using information you provide in a BITMAP structure. The BITMAP structure is declared in <windows.h> as follows:

```
typedef struct tagBITMAP
{
    int     bmType;        // Bitmap type
    int     bmWidth;       // Width of bitmap in pixels
    int     bmHeight;      // Height of bitmap in pixels
    int     bmWidthBytes; // Bytes per raster line
    BYTE    bmPlanes;      // Number of color planes
    BYTE    bmBitsPixel;   // Number of adjacent bits on each
                           //   plane needed for a pixel
    void FAR* bmBits;      // Array of bitmap values
} BITMAP;
```

Returns TRUE if successful; otherwise, returns FALSE.

```
BOOL CreateCompatibleBitmap(
    CDC* pDC,      // Create bitmap compatible with this device
    int nWidth,    // Width of bitmap in bits
    int nHeight); // Height of bitmap in bits
```

Initializes the bitmap compatible with the device specified by the *pDC* device context. Returns TRUE if successful; otherwise, returns FALSE.

```
BOOL CreateDiscardableBitmap(
    CDC* pDC,      // Create bitmap compatible with this device
    int nWidth,    // Width of bitmap in bits
    int nHeight); // Height of bitmap in bits
```

Initializes the bitmap compatible with the device specified by the `pDC` device context. The bitmap is marked as discardable so that Windows can discard it if you don't select it in a DC. Returns `TRUE` if successful; otherwise, returns `FALSE`.

```
static CBitmap* FromHandle(
    HBITMAP hBitmap); // A Windows bitmap handle
```

Returns a pointer to a `CBitmap` object after associating the bitmap identified by `hBitmap` with that `CBitmap` object. Unless `hBitmap` already is associated with a `CBitmap` object, a temporary `CBitmap` is created and the bitmap is associated with the newly created `CBitmap`. These temporary `CBitmap` objects are destroyed during the idle times in the application's event loop.

```
BOOL LoadBitmap(
    LPCSTR lpBitmapName); // The name of the bitmap resource
```

Loads the bitmap resource identified by `lpBitmapName` from the application's executable file into this `CBitmap` object. Returns `TRUE` if successful; otherwise, returns `FALSE`.

```
BOOL LoadBitmap(
    UINT nIDBitmap); // Resource ID of bitmap
```

Loads the bitmap resource identified by `nIDBitmap` from the application's executable file into this `CBitmap` object. Returns `TRUE` if successful; otherwise, returns `FALSE`.

```
BOOL LoadOEMBitmap(
    UINT nIDBitmap); // Identifier of predefined Windows bitmap
```

Loads a predefined Windows bitmap into the `CBitmap` object. Consult the Microsoft Windows SDK *Programmer's Reference, Volume 2: Functions* for detailed information on bitmap identifiers and how these predefined bitmaps look. Returns `TRUE` if successful; otherwise, returns `FALSE`.

Operations on Bitmaps

```
DWORD GetBitmapBits(
    DWORD     dwCount,        // Number of bytes to be copied
    void FAR* lpBits) const; // Buffer to receive bitmap data
```

Copies the bitmap pattern into a buffer `lpBits` with room for up to `dwCount` bytes. This also returns the actual number of bytes copied into the `lpBits` buffer, or returns zero if an error occurs.

```
CSize GetBitmapDimension() const;
```

Returns the height and width of the bitmap, measured in 0.1-millimeter units, in a `CSize` structure. Returns only the dimensions that were previously set by the `SetBitmapDimension` function.

```
DWORD SetBitmapBits(
    DWORD           dwCount, // Number of bytes in lpBits array
    const void FAR* lpBits); // Bit values for the bitmap
```

Sets the bits of the `CBitmap` object to the values that you provide in the *`lpBits`* array. Also returns the number of bytes used in setting the bitmap, or it returns zero if the function fails.

```
CSize SetBitmapDimension(
    int nWidth,   // Width of bitmap in 0.1-millimeter units
    int nHeight); // Height of bitmap in 0.1-millimeter units
```

Sets the height and width of the bitmap in 0.1-millimeter units. These values are not used by the GDI functions. Returns the previous bitmap dimensions.

See Also

`CGdiObject`	Base class of `CBitmap`

CBitmapButton

Inheritance Hierarchy

`CObject -> CCmdTarget -> CWnd -> CButton -> CBitmapButton`

Summary

```
#include <afxwin.h>
class CBitmapButton : public CButton
{
    DECLARE_DYNAMIC(CBitmapButton)
public:
// Constructors:
    CBitmapButton();
    CBitmapButton(
        LPCSTR lpBitmapResource,
        LPCSTR lpBitmapResourceSel = NULL,
        LPCSTR lpBitmapResourceFocus = NULL);

// Loading bitmaps:
    BOOL LoadBitmaps(
        LPCSTR lpBitmapResource,
```

```
        LPCSTR lpBitmapResourceSel = NULL,
        LPCSTR lpBitmapResourceFocus = NULL);
    BOOL AutoLoad(UINT nID, CWnd* pParent);

// Operations:
    void SizeToContent();

// Hidden implementation details....

};
```

Description

Sometimes you might want buttons that work like the built-in Windows button controls, except that you want to draw something other than a simple test string. One way to do this is to derive a class from the `CButton` class and override the `DrawItem` member function. Because programmers set the ability to display a bitmap in a button as a common requirement, the Microsoft Foundation Class Library includes the `CBitmapButton` class that provides this capability.

The `CBitmapButton` class, derived from `CButton`, can display up to three bitmaps in a button, each bitmap reflecting a state of the button. You can find more information on the `CBitmapButton` class from the technical note (see the on-line help item *MFC Tech Notes*, Note 14: *Custom Controls*).

Member Functions

Constructors

`CBitmapButton();`

Creates a `BitmapButton` object. You must load the bitmaps into the `BitmapButton` before you use the button.

```
CBitmapButton(
    LPCSTR lpBitmapResource,    // Name of bitmap resource for
                                //   bitmap representing the "UP"
                                //   state of the button

    LPCSTR lpBitmapResourceSel = NULL,
                                // Bitmap for "DOWN" state
    LPCSTR lpBitmapResourceFocus = NULL);
                                // Bitmap for "FOCUS" state (when
                                //   button has the input focus)
```

Creates a BitmapButton object and initializes it with the specified bitmaps. The first bitmap is required, but the other two are optional. Returns TRUE if successful; otherwise, returns FALSE.

Loading Bitmap

```
BOOL AutoLoad(
    UINT  nID,        // Resource ID of pushbutton
    CWnd* pParent); // Owner of the pushbutton
```

Loads the bitmap resources into the CBitmapButton object. AutoLoad locates the bitmaps by appending a U to the text (the caption) of CBitmapButton to create the name of the bitmap resource that defines the bitmap for the up state of the button. Similarly, AutoLoad uses a D and an F suffix to construct the names of bitmap resources for the respective down and focus states of CBitmapButton. AutoLoad returns TRUE if successful; FALSE if any errors occur.

```
BOOL LoadBitmaps(
    LPCSTR lpBitmapResource,    // Name of bitmap resource for
                                //   bitmap representing the "UP"
                                // state of the button
    LPCSTR lpBitmapResourceSel = NULL,
                                // Bitmap for "DOWN" state
    LPCSTR lpBitmapResourceFocus = NULL);
                                // Bitmap for "FOCUS" state (when
                                //   button has the input focus)
```

Loads the specified bitmap resources into the BitmapButton object. The first bitmap is required, but the other two are optional. Returns TRUE if the bitmaps have successfully loaded; otherwise, returns FALSE.

Operations

```
void SizeToContent();
```

Resizes the button to the size of the first bitmap (the bitmap used for the normal, unselected state of the button).

See Also

CButton	Base class of CBitmapButton

CBrush

Inheritance Hierarchy

```
CObject -> CGdiObject -> CBrush
```

Summary

```
#include <afxwin.h>
class CBrush : public CGdiObject
{
    DECLARE_DYNAMIC(CBrush)
public:

// Constructors:
    CBrush();
    CBrush(CBitmap* pBitmap);        //  Same as CreatePatternBrush
    CBrush(DWORD crColor);            // Same as CreateSolidBrush
    CBrush(int nIndex, DWORD crColor);// Same as CreateHatchBrush

// Initialize Brush:
    BOOL CreateBrushIndirect(LPLOGBRUSH lpLogBrush);
    BOOL CreateDIBPatternBrush(GLOBALHANDLE hPackedDIB,
        UINT nUsage);
    BOOL CreateHatchBrush(int nIndex, DWORD crColor);
    BOOL CreatePatternBrush(CBitmap* pBitmap);
    BOOL CreateSolidBrush(DWORD crColor);
    static CBrush* FromHandle(HBRUSH hBrush);

};
```

Description

`CBrush` represents a Windows *brush*—a drawing tool used to fill an area with a color. The brush is an 8x8 bitmap that is repeated horizontally and vertically to fill an area. Brushes can be solid, hatched, or patterned. You must select a brush in a DC before you can use it to fill figures such as rectangles, polygons, and ellipses.

Member Functions

Constructors

`CBrush``();`

Creates a `CBrush`, which you must initialize through other functions prior to use.

`CBrush``(CBitmap*` *`pBitmap`*`); // Pattern of the brush`

Creates a brush by calling the Windows function `CreatePatternBrush` with the specified `Cbitmap` argument. This function may throw a `CResourceException` if an error occurs when getting a Windows brush. This function also attaches the brush to the `CBrush` object.

`CBrush``(DWORD` *`crColor`*`); // Color of the brush`

Creates a brush by calling the Windows function `CreateSolidBrush` with the specified color as an argument. This may throw a `CResourceException` if an error occurs when getting a Windows brush. This function also attaches the brush to the `CBrush` object.

```
CBrush(int nIndex, DWORD crColor);// Hatch index and color
```

Creates a brush by calling the Windows function `CreateHatchBrush` with the specified hatch index and color as arguments. This may throw a `CResourceException` if an error occurs when getting a Windows brush. This function also attaches the brush to the `CBrush` object.

Initializing a *CBrush*

```
BOOL CreateBrushIndirect(
    LPLOGBRUSH lpLogBrush); // Information to initialize brush
```

Initializes a `CBrush` object using information specified in a `LOGBRUSH` structure. The `LOGBRUSH` structure is declared in `windows.h` as follows:

```
typedef struct tagLOGBRUSH
{
    UINT     lbStyle; // Style of brush
    COLORREF lbColor; // Color of brush
    int      lbHatch; // Type of hatch pattern
} LOGBRUSH;
```

Returns `TRUE` if successful; otherwise, returns `FALSE`.

```
BOOL CreateDIBPatternBrush(
    GLOBALHANDLE hPackedDIB, // A packed device-independent
                             //   bitmap (DIB)
    UINT         nUsage);    // Information about colors
```

Initializes the brush with the pattern specified by the device-independent bitmap *hPackedDIB*. Returns `TRUE` if successful; otherwise, returns `FALSE`. For more information on device-independent bitmaps and this function, please consult the Microsoft Windows SDK *Programmer's Reference, Volume 2: Functions.*

```
BOOL CreateHatchBrush(
    int   nIndex,  // Hatch type (see online documentation)
    DWORD crColor);// RGB color of brush
```

Initializes the brush with a predefined hatched pattern and a color. Returns `TRUE` if successful; otherwise, returns `FALSE`. The hatch types are `HS_DIAGONAL`, `HS_CROSS`, `HS_DIAGCROSS`, `HS_FDIAGONAL`, `HS_HORIZONTAL`, and `HS_VERTICAL`.

```
BOOL CreatePatternBrush(CBitmap* pBitmap); // Brush pattern
```

Initializes the brush using an 8x8 pattern specified by *pBitmap*. Returns TRUE if successful; otherwise, returns FALSE.

```
BOOL CreateSolidBrush(DWORD crColor); // Color of brush
```

Initializes the brush with the specified red, green, and blue (RGB) color *crColor*. Returns TRUE if successful; otherwise, returns FALSE.

```
static CBrush* FromHandle(HBRUSH hBrush);
```

Returns a pointer to a CBrush object after attaching the brush *hBrush* to that CBrush. The CBrush object may be a temporary one.

See Also

CBitmap	This specifies patterns for a brush
CDC	This selects a brush in a DC

CButton

Inheritance Hierarchy

CObject -> CCmdTarget -> CWnd -> CButton

Summary

```
#include <afxwin.h>

class CButton
{
public:
// Constructor:
    CButton();

// Create the window:
    BOOL Create(LPCSTR lpCaption, DWORD dwStyle,
        const RECT& rect, CWnd* pParentWnd, UINT nID);

// Set and get attributes:
    UINT GetState() const;
    void SetState(BOOL bHighlight);
    int  GetCheck() const;
    void SetCheck(int nCheck);
    UINT GetButtonStyle() const;
    void SetButtonStyle(UINT nStyle, BOOL bRedraw = TRUE);

// Override this if you want to draw in button:
    virtual void DrawItem(LPDRAWITEMSTRUCT lpDrawItemStruct);
```

```
// Hidden implementation details....
};
```

Description

The CButton class represents the *button control*—a predefined Windows control. The *button* is a child window that can display a label and can be clicked on or off. Windows provides many styles for buttons, and you can use them individually as well as in groups. For example, pushbuttons generally are used individually, but radio buttons and check boxes are used in groups. Buttons are used extensively in dialog boxes.

Member Functions

Constructor

CButton();

Creates a CButton without any window. You must call Create to create the window.

Creating the Window

```
BOOL Create(
LPCSTR lpCaption, // Text that appears in the button
DWORD dwStyle,    // Button's style (see online documentation)
const RECT& rect, // Button's size and position
CWnd* pParentWnd, // Button's parent window
UINT  nID);       // Button's ID
```

Creates a button window of a specified style and attaches the window to the CButton object. For a list of applicable style names (*dwStyle* argument), consult the Microsoft Visual C++ online documentation.

Set and Get Attributes

UINT **GetButtonStyle**() const;

Returns the button style. (Style names start with a BS_ prefix.)

int **GetCheck**() const;

Returns 0 if button is not checked and 1 if it is checked. This applies to a radio button or checkbox only.

UINT **GetState**() const;

Returns the state of the button. Here is how you would check the return value:

```
// Assume bstate is the button's state
    if((bstate & 0x0003) == 0) // button is not checked
// ...
    if(bstate & 0x0004) // button is highlighted
//...
```

```
    if(bstate & 0x0008) // button has the input focus
//...

void SetButtonStyle(
    UINT nStyle,  // Button style (see online documentation)
    BOOL bRedraw = TRUE); // TRUE = redraw button
```

Sets the button's style to `nStyle`.

```
void SetCheck(int nCheck); // 0 = unchecked, 1 = checked
```

Sets the check state of the button to the value specified by `nCheck`.

```
void SetState(BOOL bHighlight); // TRUE = highlight button
```

Turns the button's highlighting on or off.

See Also

`CDialog`, `CFileDialog`, `CPrintDialog`, `CColorDialog`, `CFindReplaceDialog`, `CFontDialog`	Dialog classes that use buttons
`CWnd`	Base class of `CButton`

CClientDC

Inheritance Hierarchy

`CObject -> CDC -> CClientDC`

Summary

```
#include <afxwin.h>
class CClientDC : public CDC
{
    DECLARE_DYNAMIC(CClientDC)
public:
// Constructor and destructor:
    CClientDC(CWnd* pWnd);
    virtual ~CClientDC();

// Debugging:
#ifdef _DEBUG
    virtual void AssertValid() const;
    virtual void Dump(CDumpContext& dc) const;
```

```
#endif
};
```

Description

CClientDC is derived from the CDC class and represents a DC associated with the client area of a window. You can use a CClientDC object to draw the client area of a window.

Member Functions

Constructor and Destructor

```
CClientDC(
    CWnd* pWnd); // Set up device context for this window's
                 //   client area
```

Creates a CClientDC object and sets up an associated DC for the client area of the window specified by *pWnd*. This constructor calls the Windows function GetDC to obtain a DC for the window. If it fails, it throws a CResourceException.

```
virtual ~CClientDC();
```

Destroys the CClientDC object and calls ReleaseDC to free the Windows DC that was obtained by the constructor.

See Also

CDC	Base class of CClientDC
CWindowDC	Provides a DC for both client and nonclient areas of a window

CCmdTarget

Inheritance Hierarchy

```
CObject -> CCmdTarget
```

Summary

```
class CCmdTarget : public CObject
{
    DECLARE_DYNAMIC(CCmdTarget)
// Constructor:
protected:
    CCmdTarget();

public:
// Operations:
    void BeginWaitCursor();
    void EndWaitCursor();
    void RestoreWaitCursor();
```

```
// Overrideables:
//  Control the routing and dispatching of the standard command messages
    virtual BOOL OnCmdMsg(UINT nID, int nCode, void* pExtra,
        AFX_CMDHANDLERINFO* pHandlerInfo);

// Implementation:
protected:
    CView* GetRoutingView();
// Hidden implementation details...
//...

    DECLARE_MESSAGE_MAP()
};
```

Description

CCmdTarget is derived from the CObject class and is used to create other Windows class objects, such as CWinApp, CDocTemplate, CDocument, and CWnd.

Member Functions

BeginWaitCursor();

This function causes Windows to display an hour-glass cursor.

EndWaitCursor();

This function causes Windows to restore the cursor being displayed prior to the call to BeginWaitCursor().

RestoreWaitCursor();

This function causes Windows to redisplay the hour-glass cursor after the cursor has changed.

Constructor and Destructor

See Also

CCmdUI	Used within an ON_UPDATE_COMMAND_UI handler
CDocument	A class derived from CCmdTarget
CDocTemplate	A class derived from CCmdTarget
CWinApp	A class derived from CCmdTarget
CWnd	A class derived from CCmdTarget
CView	A class derived from CWnd
CFrameWnd	A class derived from CWnd

CCmdUI

Inheritance Hierarchy

CCmdUI

Summary

```
class CCmdUI
{
public:
// Attributes:
    UINT m_nID;
    UINT m_nIndex;          // menu item index

    // if a menu item:
    CMenu* m_pMenu;         // Will be NULL if this is not a menu
    CMenu* m_pSubMenu;      // The submenu containing menu item
                            // ID for first in popup if this is a pop-up
submenu

    // if from some other window:
    CWnd* m_pOther;         // Will be NULL if not a CWnd, or is a menu

// Operations to do in ON_UPDATE_COMMAND_UI:
    virtual void Enable(BOOL bOn = TRUE);
    virtual void SetCheck(int nCheck = 1);
    virtual void SetRadio(BOOL bOn = TRUE);
    virtual void SetText(LPCSTR lpszText);

// Advanced operation:
    void ContinueRouting();

// Implementation:
    CCmdUI();
    BOOL m_bEnableChanged;
    BOOL m_bContinueRouting;
    UINT m_nIndexMax;

    void DoUpdate(CCmdTarget* pTarget, BOOL bDisableIfNoHndler);
};
```

Description

Whenever a menu is pulled down, it often is necessary to disable some items (such as the Edit menu's Paste item). Using an ON_UPDATE_COMMAND_UI handler, your application can implement the necessary interface commands.

Member Functions

`Enable(BOOL bOn = TRUE);`

Enables or disables the menu item.

`SetCheck(BOOL bCheck = 1);`

Checks, if `bCheck` is 1; unchecks, if `bCheck` is 0; or sets to indeterminate (for toolbar buttons only) if `bCheck` is 2.

`SetRadio(BOOL bCheck = 1);`

Checks, if `bCheck` is 1; unchecks, if `bCheck` is 0; or sets to indeterminate (for toolbar buttons only) if `bCheck` is 2.

`Enable(LPCSTR szString);`

Sets the text of the item to the string pointed to by `szString`.

`ContinueRouting();`

Tells the command-routing routines to route the message to the next handler in the chain. This advanced function is used only when an `ON_COMMAND_EX` handler returns `FALSE`.

Constructor and Destructor

See Also

`CCmdTarget`	Used with `CCmdUI`

CColorDialog

Inheritance Hierarchy

`CObject -> CCmdTarget -> CWnd -> CDialog -> CColorDialog`

Summary

```
#include <afxdlgs.h>
class CColorDialog : public CDialog
{
    DECLARE_DYNAMIC(CColorDialog)
public:
// Constructor:
    CColorDialog(COLORREF clrInit = 0, DWORD dwFlags = 0,
                 CWnd* pParentWnd = NULL);

// Operations:
    virtual int DoModal();
```

```
    void SetCurrentColor(COLORREF clr);
    COLORREF GetColor() const;

// Member variables

    CHOOSECOLOR m_cc;                    // color-picker parameters
    static COLORREF clrSavedCustom[16];// to save custom colors

// Diagnostic support:
#ifdef _DEBUG
    virtual void Dump(CDumpContext& dc) const;
#endif

// Hidden implementation details....
};
```

Description

`CColorDialog` is derived from the `CDialog` class and provides a standard dialog box for selecting or defining the RGB color value. The `CColorDialog` class uses the Windows 3.1 `COMMDLG` (the common dialog) functions, but doesn't require Windows 3.1 to run.

You'll find more information on the `CColorDialog` class from the technical note TN013.TXT in the DOC subdirectory of the directory in which the Microsoft Foundation Class Library is installed. (For example, if you have installed Microsoft Visual C++ in drive D:, this directory should be `D:\MSVC\MFC\DOC`.)

Member Variables

`CHOOSECOLOR m_cc;`

This is a structure that stores parameters for the color picker in `COMMDLG`.

`static COLORREF clrSavedCustom[16];`

This is an array that stores up to 16 custom colors.

Member Functions

Constructor

```
CColorDialog(
    COLORREF clrInit = 0, // Initial color selection
    DWORD dwFlags = 0,    // Flags to customize function and
                          //   appearance of dialog
    CWnd* pParentWnd = NULL); // Parent window
```

Creates and initializes a color-picker dialog box. Call `DoModal` to begin the interaction.

Operations

```
virtual int DoModal();
```

Conducts a modal interaction with the user and returns `IDOK` if the user selects the `OK` button or `IDCANCEL` to indicate user cancelled the dialog.

```
COLORREF GetColor() const;
```

Returns the current selection. Call if the value returned by `DoModal` is `IDOK`.

```
void SetCurrentColor(COLORREF clr); // New selection
```

Forces the currently selected color to the value specified by *`clr`*.

See Also

`CDialog`	Base classes of `CColorDialog`
`CFileDialog`	Other dialog classes
`CPrintDialog`	
`CFindReplaceDialog`	
`CFontDialog`	

CComboBox

Inheritance Hierarchy

`CObject -> CCmdTarget -> CWnd -> CComboBox`

Summary

```
#include <afxwin.h>
class CComboBox : public CWnd
{
    DECLARE_DYNAMIC(CComboBox)
public:
// Constructor:
    CComboBox();

// Create the window:
    BOOL Create(DWORD dwStyle, const RECT& rect,
                CWnd* pParentWnd, UINT nID);

// Attributes of entire combo box:
    int GetCount() const;
    int GetCurSel() const;
    int SetCurSel(int nSelect);
```

```
// Attributes of the edit control:
    DWORD GetEditSel() const;
    BOOL  LimitText(int nMaxChars);
    BOOL  SetEditSel(int nStartChar, int nEndChar);

// Attributes of list-box item:
    DWORD GetItemData(int nIndex) const;
    int   SetItemData(int nIndex, DWORD dwItemData);
    int   GetLBText(int nIndex, LPSTR lpText) const;
    int   GetLBTextLen(int nIndex) const;
    void  GetLBText(int nIndex, CString& rString) const;

// The following are for Windows version 3.1 or later:
#if (WINVER >= 0x030a)
    int  SetItemHeight(int nIndex, UINT cyItemHeight);
    int  GetItemHeight(int nIndex) const;
    int  FindStringExact(int nIndexStart, LPCSTR lpszFind) const;
    int  SetExtendedUI(BOOL bExtended = TRUE);
    BOOL GetExtendedUI() const;
    void GetDroppedControlRect(LPRECT lprect) const;
    BOOL GetDroppedState() const;
#endif  /* WINVER >= 0x030a */

// Showing drop-down combo boxes:
    void ShowDropDown(BOOL bShowIt = TRUE);

// Manipulating list-box items:
    int  AddString(LPCSTR lpString);
    int  DeleteString(UINT nIndex);
    int  InsertString(int nIndex, LPCSTR lpString);
    void ResetContent();
    int  Dir(UINT attr, LPCSTR lpWildCard);
    int  FindString(int nStartAfter, LPCSTR lpString) const;
    int  SelectString(int nStartAfter, LPCSTR lpString);

// Working with the clipboard:
    void Clear();
    void Copy();
    void Cut();
    void Paste();

// Overrideable functions (you must override draw, measure,
// and compare for owner-drawn combo boxes):
```

```
    virtual void DrawItem(LPDRAWITEMSTRUCT lpDrawItemStruct);
    virtual void MeasureItem(LPMEASUREITEMSTRUCT
                                        lpMeasureItemStruct);
    virtual int CompareItem(LPCOMPAREITEMSTRUCT
                                        lpCompareItemStruct);
    virtual void DeleteItem(LPDELETEITEMSTRUCT
                                         lpDeleteItemStruct);

// Hidden implementation details....
};
```

Description

The `CComboBox` class encapsulates a Windows *combo box*—an edit control joined with a list box. The list box displays a list of items, and the current selection appears in the edit box. The list box usually is hidden and may drop down when the user presses a button (one that displays an arrow) next to the edit control. The exact behavior and look of the combo box depend on its style. Combo boxes are used extensively in dialog boxes.

Member Functions

Constructor

```
CComboBox();
```

Constructs a combo box. Call `Create` to create the windows associated with the combo box.

Creating the Windows

```
BOOL Create(
    DWORD dwStyle,      // Style of the combo box
    const RECT& rect, // Position and size of combo box
    CWnd* pParentWnd, // Parent window
    UINT  nID);         // Identifier for this combo box
```

Creates a Windows combo box of a specified style and attaches it to the `CComboBox` object. See Microsoft Visual C++ online documentation for a list of style names that apply to the combo box.

Attributes of Entire Combo box

```
int GetCount() const;
```

Returns the number of items in the list or `CB_ERR` if an error occurs.

```
int GetCurSel() const;
```

Returns the index of the currently selected item in the list box, or CB_ERR if none of the items are selected.

```
int SetCurSel(int nSelect);
```

Sets the string at the *nSelect* index as the current selection. If successful, it returns the index; otherwise, returns CB_ERR. If *nSelect* is –1, the selection is cleared.

Attributes of the Edit Control

```
DWORD GetEditSel() const;
```

Returns the starting and ending character positions of the currently selected text in the edit control. In the 32-bit return value, the least-significant 16 bits contain the starting position, and the high-order 16 bits contain the first nonselected character position.

```
BOOL  LimitText(
    int nMaxChars); // User can enter nMaxChars characters at most
```

Sets the length of text that the user can enter in the edit control.

```
BOOL  SetEditSel(
    int nStartChar, // Starting position of selection
                    // -1 = remove current selection
    int nEndChar);  // Ending position of selection
                    // -1 = select all the way to end
```

Selects the specified block of characters in the edit control. Returns TRUE if successful; otherwise, returns FALSE.

Attributes of List Box Item

```
void GetDroppedControlRect( // For Windows version 3.1 or later
    LPRECT lprect) const;   // Screen coordinates of list box returned
```

Places the screen coordinates for the boundary rectangle of the list box into the RECT structure with the address that you provide in *lprect*.

```
BOOL GetDroppedState() const; // Windows version 3.1 or later
```

Returns TRUE if the drop-down list box is visible.

```
BOOL GetExtendedUI() const; // Windows version 3.1 or later
```

Returns TRUE if the combo box has the extended user interface introduced in Windows 3.1.

```
DWORD GetItemData(
    int nIndex) const; // Return data associated with this item
```

Returns the 32-bit value associated with the item identified by `nIndex`. Returns the value you have associated with an item by calling `SetItemData`.

```
int  GetItemHeight( // For Windows version 3.1 or later
    int nIndex) const;
```

Returns the height (in pixels) of the specified item in the list box.

```
int   GetLBText(int nIndex, LPSTR lpText) const;
    // Returns length of item excluding null char.
void  GetLBText(int nIndex, CString& rString) const;
```

Copies the list box item identified by `nIndex` into a string that you provide. You should use `GetLBTextLen` to ensure that the string has enough room to hold the returned item plus a terminating null character.

```
int   GetLBTextLen(int nIndex) const;
```

Returns the number of characters, excluding the terminating null, in the item at `nIndex` index in the list box.

```
int SetItemData(
    int nIndex,          // Index of item (0 = first item)
    DWORD dwItemData); // Data to associate with item
```

Associates a 32-bit value with an item in the list box and returns `CB_ERR` in case of error.

```
int  SetItemHeight( // For Windows version 3.1 or later
    int  nIndex,          // Item's index
    UINT cyItemHeight); // Item's height in pixels
```

Sets the height of an item in pixels and returns `CB_ERR` if the height or the index is invalid.

```
int  SetExtendedUI( // For Windows version 3.1 or later
    BOOL bExtended = TRUE); // TRUE = use extended user interface
```

If `bExtended` is `TRUE`, selects the extended user interface for the combo box; otherwise, it employs the default user interface. `SetExtendedUI` returns `CB_OKAY` if all goes well; otherwise, returns `CB_ERR`.

Showing Drop-Down Combo Boxes

```
void ShowDropDown(
    BOOL bShowIt = TRUE); // TRUE = show the drop-down list box
```

Shows or hides the drop-down list box.

Manipulating List Box Items

```
int  AddString(LPCSTR lpString);
```

Adds a string to the list box of the combo box.

```
int  DeleteString(UINT nIndex);
```

Deletes the string at the specified index in the list box and returns the number of items remaining in the list box.

```
int  Dir(
    UINT   attr,          // File attributes
    LPCSTR lpWildCard); // File specification (such as "*.*")
```

Displays a list of filenames in the list box and returns the index of the last filename added to the list box. If an error occurs, returns CB_ERR or CB_ERRSPACE.

```
int  FindString(
    int    nStartAfter,      // Search after item at this index
    LPCSTR lpString) const; // Look for this string
```

Searches for a string (lpString) in the list box and returns the index of the item with that string as a prefix (an index of zero represents the first item). The search is case independent.

```
int  FindStringExact( // For Windows version 3.1 or later
    int nIndexStart,  // Search after item at this index
    LPCSTR lpszFind) const; // Look for an exact match
                            //   with this string
```

Searches the list box for an item that matches a given string in its entirety. The search starts at a specified item in the list. Returns the zero-based index of the item that matches the string, or CB_ERR if the search fails. The search is case independent.

```
int  InsertString(int nIndex, LPCSTR lpString);
```

Inserts the string lpString in the list box at the position indicated by the nIndex index. If successful, this function returns the index where the string is inserted; otherwise, returns CB_ERR or CB_ERRSPACE to indicate an error.

```
void ResetContent();
```

Clears the contents of the edit control and the list box.

```
int  SelectString(int nStartAfter, LPCSTR lpString);
```

Searches for the specified string in the list box, starting with the string after the nStartAfter index. If found, that string is selected in the list box and copied to the edit control. Returns the index of the string if successful; otherwise, returns CB_ERR.

Working with the Clipboard

```
void Clear();
```

Deletes the current selection from the edit control.

```
void Copy();
```

Copies the current selection from the edit control to the clipboard.

```
void Cut();
```

Deletes the current selection from the edit control and copies the deleted text to the clipboard with a `CF_TEXT` format.

```
void Paste();
```

Copies `CF_TEXT` format data from the clipboard to the edit control at the current cursor position.

See Also

`CDialog`	Dialog boxes that use combo boxes
`CEdit, CListBox`	Edit control and list box are part of a combo box

CControlBar

Inheritance Hierarchy

`CObject -> CCmdTarget -> CWnd -> CControlBar`

Summary

```
class CControlBar : public CWnd
{
    DECLARE_DYNAMIC(CControlBar)
// Constructor:
protected:
    CControlBar();

// Attributes:
public:
    int GetCount() const;

    BOOL m_bAutoDelete;

// Implementation:
public:
    virtual ~CControlBar();
```

```
#ifdef _DEBUG
    virtual void AssertValid() const;
    virtual void Dump(CDumpContext& dc) const;
#endif

// Hidden implementation details...
//...

    DECLARE_MESSAGE_MAP()
};
```

Description

CControlBar is the base class for the CStatusBar, CToolBar, and CDialogBar classes.

Member Variables

BOOL **m_bAutoDelete**

If variable is nonzero, the CControlBar object is deleted when the control bar object is destroyed.

Member Functions

int **GetCount**()

Returns the number of non-WHND objects on the CControlBar object. If the CControlBar is a CDialogBar, this function returns zero.

Constructor and Destructor

CControlBar()

Used to construct a **CControlBar** type object.

See Also

CStatusBar, CToolBar, CDialogBar	Classes created from CControlBar

CDataExchange

Inheritance Hierarchy

CDataExchange

Summary

```
class AFX_STACK_DATA CDataExchange
{
// Attributes:
public:
```

```
    BOOL m_bSaveAndValidate;    // if TRUE, save and validate data
    CWnd* m_pDlgWnd;

// Operations:
    HWND PrepareCtrl(int nIDC);          // Control's HWND
    HWND PrepareEditCtrl(int nIDC);      // Control's HWND
    CVBControl* PrepareVBCtrl(int nIDC); // Return Visual Basic control
    void Fail();                         // Throws exception to signal
                                            failure

// Implementation:
    CDataExchange(CWnd* pDlgWnd, BOOL bSaveAndValidate);

    HWND m_hWndLastControl;  // HWND of the last control used.
    BOOL m_bEditLastControl; // TRUE if the last control was an edit
                                control
};
```

Description

`CDataExchange` is a base class used in the implementing of data exchanges between classes and dialog controls. (Chapter 18 shows a program that uses a form view which could have used custom data exchanges.)

Member Variables

`BOOL` **`m_bSaveAndValidate`**

If `TRUE`, you're setting the data in the control; if `FALSE`, retrieve the control's data and save it.

`HWND` **`m_pDlgWnd`**

Contains the handle to the window or dialog box that contains the control.

Member Functions

`VOID` **`Fail`**`();`

Signals that data input by the user is invalid. Sets focus to the prior control, and then throws an exception.

`HWND` **`PrepareCtrl`**`(int` *`nControlID`*`);`

Prepares the (non-edit) control, *`nControlID`*, for data exchange.

`HWND` **`PrepareEditCtrl`**`(int` *`nControlID`*`);`

Prepares the edit control, *`nControlID`*, for data exchange.

```
HWND PrepareVBCtrl(int nControlID);
```

Prepares the Visual Basic control, *nControlID*, for data exchange.

Constructor and Destructor

See Also

`CFormView`	Use of controls (to simulate a form) in a window

CDC

Inheritance Hierarchy

`CObject -> CDC`

Summary

```
#include <afxwin.h>
class CDC : public CObject
{
    DECLARE_DYNAMIC(CDC)
public:
// Constructor and destructor:
    CDC();
    virtual ~CDC();

// Creating and destroying a DC:
    BOOL CreateDC(LPCSTR lpDriverName, LPCSTR lpDeviceName,
            LPCSTR lpOutput, const void FAR* lpInitData);
    BOOL CreateIC(LPCSTR lpDriverName, LPCSTR lpDeviceName,
            LPCSTR lpOutput, const void FAR* lpInitData);
    BOOL CreateCompatibleDC(CDC* pDC);

    BOOL DeleteDC();

// Attributes:
    HDC m_hDC;
    HDC GetSafeHdc() const;

    static CDC* FromHandle(HDC hDC);
    static void DeleteTempMap();
    BOOL        Attach(HDC hDC);
    HDC         Detach();

// Device-context functions:
    CPoint GetDCOrg() const;
```

```
    int    SaveDC() const;
    BOOL   RestoreDC(int nSavedDC);
    int    GetDeviceCaps(int nIndex) const;

// Drawing-tool functions:
    CPoint GetBrushOrg() const;
    CPoint SetBrushOrg(int x, int y);
    CPoint SetBrushOrg(POINT point);
    int    EnumObjects(int nObjectType,
                  int (FAR PASCAL EXPORT* lpfn)(LPSTR, LPSTR),
                  LPSTR lpData);
    CGdiObject* SelectObject(CGdiObject* pObject);
    CGdiObject* SelectStockObject(int nIndex);
    CPen*    SelectObject(CPen* pPen);
    CBrush*  SelectObject(CBrush* pBrush);
    CFont*   SelectObject(CFont* pFont);
    CBitmap* SelectObject(CBitmap* pBitmap);
    int      SelectObject(CRgn* pRgn); // use this for regions

// Color and color-palette functions:
    DWORD     GetNearestColor(DWORD crColor) const;
    CPalette* SelectPalette(CPalette* pPalette,
              BOOL bForceBackground);
    UINT      RealizePalette();
    void      UpdateColors();

// Get or set drawing attributes:
    DWORD GetBkColor() const;
    DWORD SetBkColor(DWORD crColor);
    int   GetBkMode() const;
    int   SetBkMode(int nBkMode);
    int   GetPolyFillMode() const;
    int   SetPolyFillMode(int nPolyFillMode);
    int   GetROP2() const;
    int   SetROP2(int nDrawMode);
    int   GetStretchBltMode() const;
    int   SetStretchBltMode(int nStretchMode);
    DWORD GetTextColor() const;
    DWORD SetTextColor(DWORD crColor);

// Mapping (window<->viewport transformation) functions:
    int GetMapMode() const;
    int SetMapMode(int nMapMode);
```

```
// Manipulating the viewport origin:
    CPoint GetViewportOrg() const;
    CPoint SetViewportOrg(int x, int y);
    CPoint SetViewportOrg(POINT point);
    CPoint OffsetViewportOrg(int nWidth, int nHeight);

// Manipulating the viewport extent:
    CSize GetViewportExt() const;
    CSize SetViewportExt(int x, int y);
    CSize SetViewportExt(SIZE size);
    CSize ScaleViewportExt(int xNum, int xDenom,
                           int yNum, int yDenom);

// Manipulating the window origin:
    CPoint GetWindowOrg() const;
    CPoint SetWindowOrg(int x, int y);
    CPoint SetWindowOrg(POINT point);
    CPoint OffsetWindowOrg(int nWidth, int nHeight);

// Manipulating the window extent:
    CSize GetWindowExt() const;
    CSize SetWindowExt(int x, int y);
    CSize SetWindowExt(SIZE size);
    CSize ScaleWindowExt(int xNum, int xDenom,
                         int yNum, int yDenom);

// Converting coordinates:
    void DPtoLP(LPPOINT lpPoints, int nCount = 1) const;
    void DPtoLP(LPRECT lpRect) const;
    void LPtoDP(LPPOINT lpPoints, int nCount = 1) const;
    void LPtoDP(LPRECT lpRect) const;

// Working with regions:
    BOOL FillRgn(CRgn* pRgn, CBrush* pBrush);
    BOOL FrameRgn(CRgn* pRgn, CBrush* pBrush,
                  int nWidth, int nHeight);
    BOOL InvertRgn(CRgn* pRgn);
    BOOL PaintRgn(CRgn* pRgn);

// Clipping functions:
    int  GetClipBox(LPRECT lpRect) const;
    int  SelectClipRgn(CRgn* pRgn);
    int  ExcludeClipRect(int x1, int y1, int x2, int y2);
```

```
    int  ExcludeClipRect(LPRECT lpRect);
    int  ExcludeUpdateRgn(CWnd* pWnd);
    int  IntersectClipRect(int x1, int y1, int x2, int y2);
    int  IntersectClipRect(LPRECT lpRect);
    int  OffsetClipRgn(int x, int y);
    int  OffsetClipRgn(SIZE size);
    BOOL PtVisible(int x, int y) const;
    BOOL PtVisible(POINT point) const;
    BOOL RectVisible(LPRECT lpRect) const;

// Line-drawing functions:
    CPoint GetCurrentPosition() const;
    CPoint MoveTo(int x, int y);
    CPoint MoveTo(POINT point);
    BOOL   LineTo(int x, int y);
    BOOL   LineTo(POINT point);
    BOOL   Arc(int x1, int y1, int x2, int y2,
               int x3, int y3, int x4, int y4);
    BOOL   Arc(LPRECT lpRect, POINT ptStart, POINT ptEnd);
    BOOL   Polyline(LPPOINT lpPoints, int nCount);

// Simple drawing functions.
    void FillRect(LPRECT lpRect, CBrush* pBrush);
    void FrameRect(LPRECT lpRect, CBrush* pBrush);
    void InvertRect(LPRECT lpRect);
    BOOL DrawIcon(int x, int y, HICON hIcon);
    BOOL DrawIcon(POINT point, HICON hIcon);

// Drawing ellipses and polygons:
    BOOL Chord(int x1, int y1, int x2, int y2,
               int x3, int y3, int x4, int y4);
    BOOL Chord(LPRECT lpRect, POINT ptStart, POINT ptEnd);
    void DrawFocusRect(LPRECT lpRect);
    BOOL Ellipse(int x1, int y1, int x2, int y2);
    BOOL Ellipse(LPRECT lpRect);
    BOOL Pie(int x1, int y1, int x2, int y2,
             int x3, int y3, int x4, int y4);
    BOOL Pie(LPRECT lpRect, POINT ptStart, POINT ptEnd);
    BOOL Polygon(LPPOINT lpPoints, int nCount);
    BOOL PolyPolygon(LPPOINT lpPoints, LPINT lpPolyCounts,
                     int nCount);
    BOOL Rectangle(int x1, int y1, int x2, int y2);
    BOOL Rectangle(LPRECT lpRect);
```

```
    BOOL RoundRect(int x1, int y1, int x2, int y2,
                   int x3, int y3);
    BOOL RoundRect(LPRECT lpRect, POINT point);

// Working with bitmaps:
    BOOL PatBlt(int x, int y, int nWidth, int nHeight,
                DWORD dwRop);
    BOOL BitBlt(int x, int y, int nWidth, int nHeight,
                CDC* pSrcDC, int xSrc, int ySrc, DWORD dwRop);
    BOOL StretchBlt(int x, int y, int nWidth, int nHeight,
                    CDC* pSrcDC, int xSrc, int ySrc,
                    int nSrcWidth, int nSrcHeight, DWORD dwRop);
    DWORD GetPixel(int x, int y) const;
    DWORD GetPixel(POINT point) const;
    DWORD SetPixel(int x, int y, DWORD crColor);
    DWORD SetPixel(POINT point, DWORD crColor);
    BOOL  FloodFill(int x, int y, DWORD crColor);
    BOOL  ExtFloodFill(int x, int y, DWORD crColor
                       UINT nFillType);

// Displaying text:
    BOOL TextOut(int x, int y, const CString& str);
    BOOL TextOut(int x, int y, LPCSTR lpString, int nCount);
    BOOL ExtTextOut(int x, int y, UINT nOptions, LPRECT lpRect,
                LPCSTR lpString, UINT nCount, LPINT lpDxWidths);
    CSize TabbedTextOut(int x, int y, LPCSTR lpString,
                        int nCount, int nTabPositions,
                     LPINT lpnTabStopPositions, int nTabOrigin);
    int   DrawText(LPCSTR lpString, int nCount, LPRECT lpRect,
                   UINT nFormat);
    CSize GetTextExtent(LPCSTR lpString, int nCount) const;
    CSize GetTabbedTextExtent(LPCSTR lpString, int nCount,
            int nTabPositions, LPINT lpnTabStopPositions) const;

    BOOL GrayString(CBrush* pBrush,
          BOOL (FAR PASCAL EXPORT* lpfnOutput)(HDC, DWORD, int),
          DWORD lpData, int nCount,
          int x, int y, int nWidth, int nHeight);

    UINT GetTextAlign() const;
    UINT SetTextAlign(UINT nFlags);
    int  GetTextFace(int nCount, LPSTR lpFacename) const;
    BOOL GetTextMetrics(LPTEXTMETRIC lpMetrics) const;
```

```
    int  SetTextJustification(int nBreakExtra, int nBreakCount);
    int  GetTextCharacterExtra() const;
    int  SetTextCharacterExtra(int nCharExtra);

// Using fonts:
    BOOL  GetCharWidth(UINT nFirstChar, UINT nLastChar,
                       LPINT lpBuffer) const;
    DWORD SetMapperFlags(DWORD dwFlag);
    CSize GetAspectRatioFilter() const;

// Functions for printing:
    int Escape(int nEscape, int nCount, LPCSTR lpInData,
               void FAR* lpOutData);
    int StartDoc(LPCSTR pDocName);
          // In Windows 3.1 use StartDoc(LPDOCINFO lpDocInfo)
    int StartPage();
    int EndPage();
    int SetAbortProc(BOOL (FAR PASCAL EXPORT* lpfn)(HDC, int));
    int AbortDoc();
    int EndDoc();

// Scrolling:
    BOOL ScrollDC(int dx, int dy, LPRECT lpRectScroll,
                  LPRECT lpRectClip, CRgn* pRgnUpdate,
                  LPRECT lpRectUpdate);

// Displaying the metafile:
    BOOL PlayMetaFile(HANDLE hMF);

// The following GDI functions are for Windows version 3.1 or later:
#if (WINVER >= 0x030a)
    BOOL QueryAbort() const;
    UINT SetBoundsRect(const RECT FAR* lpRectBounds, UINT flags);
    UINT GetBoundsRect(LPRECT lpRectBounds, UINT flags);
    int  StartDoc(LPDOCINFO lpDocInfo);
    BOOL GetCharABCWidths(UINT nFirst, UINT nLast,
                          LPABC lpabc) const;
    DWORD GetFontData(DWORD dwTable, DWORD dwOffset,
                      LPVOID lpData, DWORD cbData) const;
    int   GetKerningPairs(int nPairs,
                          KERNINGPAIR FAR* lpkrnpair) const;
    UINT  GetOutlineTextMetrics(UINT cbData,
                      OUTLINETEXTMETRIC FAR* lpotm) const;
```

```
    DWORD GetGlyphOutline(UINT nChar, UINT nFormat,
                          GLYPHMETRICS FAR* lpgm,
                          DWORD cbBuffer, void FAR* lpBuffer,
                          const MAT2 FAR* lpmat2) const;
#endif

// Diagnostic support:
#ifdef _DEBUG
    virtual void AssertValid() const;
    virtual void Dump(CDumpContext& dc) const;
#endif

};
```

Description

The CDC class is an encapsulation of a Windows DC. You need a DC for drawing to any device, whether display screen or printer. With the member functions of the CDC class, you can access and use all the graphics drawing capabilities of Windows. In any Windows application written with the Microsoft Foundation Class Library, you must create a CDC object (or an object from one of the CDC-derived classes) for a specific device before you can generate graphics output on that device.

The Microsoft Foundation Class Library also includes many other DC classes, derived from CDC, that are intended for specific uses. For instance, to draw in a window in response to a WM_PAINT message, you would use a DC of the CPaintDC class.

Member Variables

HDC **m_hDC**;

This is the handle to the DC. Although you can access m_hDC directly, it's safer to obtain the handle by calling GetSafeHdc.

Member Functions

Constructor and Destructor

CDC();

Creates a CDC object.

virtual ~**CDC**();

Destroys the CDC object. If a Windows DC handle is associated with the CDC object, the destructor deletes the DC.

Creating and Destroying a DC

```
BOOL Attach(
    HDC hDC); // Handle of device context to be "attached" to
              // this CDC object
```

Associates the Windows DC, specified by `hDC`, with this `CDC` object.

```
BOOL CreateCompatibleDC(
    CDC* pDC); // Create an in-memory DC compatible with this one
```

Creates an in-memory DC, compatible with the `CDC` object, with the address you provide in the `pDC` argument. You can use an in-memory DC to prepare images in memory before you display them on a device. If `pDC` is `NULL`, `CreateCompatibleDC` creates a DC compatible with the system display. You must create a bitmap and select it in the in-memory `CDC` before you can draw in that DC. Returns `TRUE` if successful; otherwise, returns `FALSE`.

```
BOOL CreateDC(
    LPCSTR lpDriverName, // Name of device driver file (without
                         //   the extension)
    LPCSTR lpDeviceName, // Name of the specific device
    LPCSTR lpOutput,     // Name of output port or file
    const void FAR* lpInitData); // A DEVMODE structure with
                         //   device-specific initialization data
```

Creates a DC for the specified device. Returns `TRUE` if successful; otherwise, returns `FALSE`.

```
BOOL CreateIC(
    LPCSTR lpDriverName, // Name of device driver file (without
                         //   the extension)
    LPCSTR lpDeviceName, // Name of the specific device
    LPCSTR lpOutput,     // Name of output port or file
    const void FAR* lpInitData); // A DEVMODE structure with
                         //   device-specific initialization data
```

Creates an information context (IC) you can use to get information about a device without creating a complete DC. Returns `TRUE` if successful; otherwise, returns `FALSE`.

```
BOOL DeleteDC();
```

Deletes the windows DC attached to the `CDC` object. Use this function to delete device and information contexts created using `CreateDC`, `CreateCompatibleDC`, or `CreateIC`.

```
static void DeleteTempMap();
```

This is called during idle-time processing to delete temporary CDC objects created by FromHandle.

```
HDC Detach();
```

Disassociates the Windows DC with a handle in the m_hDC member of the CDC object and returns the handle.

```
static CDC* FromHandle(
    HDC hDC); // A Windows device-context handle
```

Returns a pointer to a CDC object with the specified DC handle, *hDC*, attached to that object. Unless the *hDC* handle already is associated with an existing CDC object, FromHandle creates a temporary CDC object and attaches *hDC* to it. These temporary CDCs are periodically destroyed.

Accessing Attributes

```
HDC GetSafeHdc() const;
```

Returns the handle to the Windows DC associated with the CDC object.

Manipulating the Device Context

```
CPoint GetDCOrg() const;
```

Returns the device coordinates for the origin of the DC's coordinate frame.

```
int GetDeviceCaps(
    int nIndex) const; // What capability to return?
```

Returns information about the device capability identified by the *nIndex* integer. Consult the online documentation in Microsoft Visual C++ compiler or the Microsoft Windows SDK *Programmer's Reference, Volume 2: Functions* for more information on the capabilities.

```
BOOL RestoreDC(
    int nSavedDC); // Restore DC to this one
```

Restores the Windows DC to the DC identified by the *nSavedDC* argument—this must be a value returned by a previous call to SaveDC. Returns TRUE if successful; otherwise, returns FALSE.

```
int SaveDC() const;
```

Saves the current Windows DC on an internal stack and returns an identifier you should use when restoring the DC.

Using the Drawing Tools

```
int EnumObjects(
    int nObjectType,  // Enumerate this type of objects (either
                      // OBJ_BRUSH or OBJ_PEN)
    int (FAR PASCAL EXPORT* lpfn)(LPSTR, LPSTR),
                      // Function called for each object in CDC
    LPSTR lpData);    // Pointer passed to the lpfn
```

This function calls the callback function specified in the `lpfn` argument for each object of the `nObjectType` type that exists in the DC. `EnumObjects` returns the last value returned by the callback function, `lpfn`.

```
CPoint GetBrushOrg() const;
```

Returns the device coordinates of the currently selected brush's origin.

```
CBitmap*    SelectObject(CBitmap* pBitmap);
CBrush*     SelectObject(CBrush* pBrush);
CFont*      SelectObject(CFont* pFont);
CGdiObject* SelectObject(CGdiObject* pObject);
CPen*       SelectObject(CPen* pPen);
```

`SelectObject` is an overloaded function that selects a specified graphics tool for this DC and returns a pointer to the previous *graphics* tool object. If any error occurs, `SelectObject` returns `NULL`.

```
int SelectObject(CRgn* pRgn); // Region to be selected
```

Use this version of `SelectObject` to select a region. In this case, `SelectObject` returns an integer value representing the complexity of the new region. The return value can be `COMPLEXREGION`, `NULLREGION`, or `SIMPLEREGION`; or `ERROR` in the case of an error.

```
CGdiObject* SelectStockObject(
    int nIndex); // Type of stock object
```

Selects a predefined stock pen, brush, or font identified by `nIndex` (see Table 20.3). Returns a pointer to the object replaced by this function. If `SelectStockObject` fails, the return value is `NULL`.

Table 20.3. Stock object types.

Value	Meaning
BLACK_BRUSH	Black brush.
DKGRAY_BRUSH	Dark gray brush.

Value	Meaning
GRAY_BRUSH	Gray brush.
HOLLOW_BRUSH	Hollow brush.
LTGRAY_BRUSH	Light gray brush.
NULL_BRUSH	Null brush.
WHITE_BRUSH	White brush.
BLACK_PEN	Black pen.
NULL_PEN	Null pen.
WHITE_PEN	White pen.
ANSI_FIXED_FONT	ANSI fixed system font.
ANSI_VAR_FONT	ANSI variable system font.
DEVICE_DEFAULT_FONT	Device-dependent font.
OEM_FIXED_FONT	OEM-dependent (OEM stands for original equipment manufacturer) fixed font. Basically, this is a vendor-specific font.
SYSTEM_FONT	System font that Windows uses to draw menus, dialog box controls, and other text.
SYSTEM_FIXED_FONT	Fixed-width system font used in Windows version 3.0 and earlier.
DEFAULT_PALETTE	The default color palette of 20 fixed colors in the system palette.

```
CPoint SetBrushOrg(int x, int y);
CPoint SetBrushOrg(POINT point);
```

Sets the `x`, `y` coordinates for the origin of a brush. These coordinates will be used for the next brush that you select. Each of the `x`, `y` coordinates must be in the range 0 through 7. Returns the old brush origin in device units.

Working with Colors and Color Palettes

```
DWORD GetNearestColor(
    DWORD crColor) const; // RGB color you want
```

Returns the 32-bit RGB color that is closest to the color specified by `crColor` and can be displayed by the device associated with this DC. Figure 20.1 shows how to interpret the 32-bit RGB color value.

```
UINT RealizePalette();
```

Takes entries from the logical palette and maps them to the system palette. This also returns the number of entries in the logical palette that were mapped to different system palette entries.

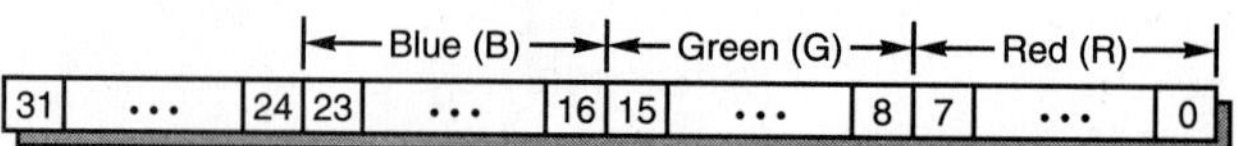

Figure 20.1. 32-bit RGB color value.

```
CPalette* SelectPalette(
    CPalette* pPalette, // Select this logical palette
    BOOL      bForceBackground); // TRUE = always use selected
                                 // palette as the background palette
```

Selects a logical palette (identified by `pPalette`) as the palette object for this DC. Use the `CreatePalette` member function of the `CPalette` class to set up the logical palette. Returns a pointer to the previous palette if successful, or it returns `NULL` if an error occurs.

```
void UpdateColors();
```

Updates the client area by matching the current color at each pixel with a color in the system palette. This occurs for all pixels in the client area.

Accessing the Drawing Attributes

```
DWORD GetBkColor() const;
```

Returns the current background color as an RGB value that occupies the low-order 24 bits of the 32-bit return value (see Figure 20.1).

```
int   GetBkMode() const;
```

Returns the background mode, which can be either:

- **OPAQUE**—Fills background color around the gaps in text and graphics.
- **TRANSPARENT**—Does not fill background around gaps when drawing text or graphics.

```
int    GetPolyFillMode() const;
```

Returns the current filling mode for polygons. The return value is either `WINDING` or `ALTERNATE`. See `CDC::SetFillPolyMode` for more information on the fill mode.

```
int    GetROP2() const;
```

Returns the current *raster-operation mode*, which controls how the pen and brush colors are combined with the colors already present on the display screen. Consult the Microsoft Windows SDK *Programmer's Reference, Volume 2: Functions* for the raster-operation modes.

```
int    GetStretchBltMode() const;
```

Returns the current bitmap stretching mode, which controls how the `StretchBlt` function works. The return value can be `BLACKONWHITE`, `WHITEONBLACK`, or `COLORONCOLOR`.

```
DWORD GetTextColor() const;
```

Returns the current text color—the foreground color to be used when you draw text. The color is returned as an RGB value.

```
DWORD SetBkColor(
    DWORD crColor); // New background color (RGB value)
```

Sets the current background color to the specified RGB value. If successful, `SetBkColor` returns the previous background color as an RGB value; otherwise, returns `0x80000000` to indicate an error.

```
int    SetBkMode(
    int nBkMode); // OPAQUE or TRANSPARENT
```

Sets the background mode to *nBkMode*, which must be either of these:

- `OPAQUE`—Fills background color around the gaps in text and graphics.
- `TRANSPARENT`—Does not fill background around gaps when drawing text or graphics.

```
int    SetPolyFillMode(
    int nPolyFillMode); // New fill mode: ALTERNATE or WINDING
```

Specifies the algorithm to be used when determining whether a point is inside a polygon. To apply the `ALTERNATE` mode to a point, imagine a line drawn from that point to a far-off point outside the polygon. The point is inside the polygon if this line crosses the edges of the polygon an odd number of times.

In the `WINDING` mode, you must use the order of the vertices. Draw an imaginary line from the test point to each vertex starting with the first one, and continue until you return to the first one again. As you do this, that imaginary line rotates. Count the number of complete clockwise and counterclockwise turns. A point is inside if the difference between these two counts is a nonzero number.

```
int    SetROP2(
    int nDrawMode); // New drawing mode (binary raster operation)
```

Sets the *drawing mode,* which determines how the pen color combines with the color that already appears on the display. Returns the previous drawing mode. Table 20.4 lists a few important drawing modes. Consult the Microsoft Windows SDK *Programmer's Reference, Volume 2: Functions* for a complete list.

Table 20.4. Binary raster operations in Windows.

Value	Meaning
R2_BLACK	Sets a pixel to black.
R2_WHITE	Sets a pixel to white.
R2_NOP	Does not change existing pixels.
R2_NOT	Inverts existing pixels.
R2_COPYPEN	Replaces existing pixels with the pen's color (this is the default).
R2_NOTCOPYPEN	Sets a pixel to the inverse of the pen's color.
R2_MERGEPEN	Sets a pixel to the bitwise-OR of the pen's color and the existing color.
R2_MASKPEN	Sets a pixel to bitwise-AND of the pen's color and the existing color.
R2_XORPEN	Sets a pixel to the bitwise exclusive-OR (XOR) of the pen's color and the existing color.

```
int    SetStretchBltMode(
    int nStretchMode); // One of BLACKONWHITE, COLORONCOLOR,
                       // or WHITEONBLACK
```

Sets a new bitmap stretching mode, which controls what information is preserved when bitmaps are compressed by the `StretchBlt` function. Returns the previous bitmap stretching mode.

```
DWORD SetTextColor(
    DWORD crColor); // RGB value to be used a color of text
```

Sets the current text color—the foreground color to be used when drawing text. The color is returned as an RGB value.

Mapping Modes

```
int GetMapMode() const;
```

Returns the current *mapping mode*—the way logical units are transformed into device coordinates. Table 20.5 lists the names of the possible mapping modes.

Table 20.5. Mapping modes in Windows.

nMapMode Values	Meaning
`MM_ANISOTROPIC`	Maps each logical unit to an arbitrary device unit with arbitrarily scaled x- and y-axes. This uses the `SetWindowExt` and `SetViewportExt` functions to specify the desired units, orientation of the axes, and scaling.
`MM_HIENGLISH`	Maps each logical unit to 0.001 inch, with the positive x-axis going right and the positive y-axis going up.
`MM_HIMETRIC`	Maps each logical unit to 0.01 millimeter, with the positive x-axis going right and the positive y-axis going up.
`MM_ISOTROPIC`	Maps each logical unit to an arbitrary device unit with equally scaled axes. This uses the `SetWindowExt` and `SetViewportExt` functions to specify the desired units and orientation of the axes.
`MM_LOENGLISH`	Maps each logical unit to 0.01 inch with the positive x-axis going right and the positive y-axis going up.
`MM_LOMETRIC`	Maps each logical unit to 0.1 millimeter with the positive x-axis going right and the positive y-axis going up.

continues

Table 20.5. continued

nMapMode Values	Meaning
MM_TEXT	Maps each logical unit to one device pixel with the positive x-axis going right and the positive y-axis going down.
MM_TWIPS	Maps each logical unit to one-twentieth of a printer's point (1/1,440 inch) with the positive x-axis going right and the positive y-axis going up.

```
int SetMapMode(
    int nMapMode); // Mapping mode
```

Sets the mapping mode to *nMapMode* (this should be one of the modes shown in Table 20.5). The mapping mode controls how a window in the logical coordinate space is transformed to a viewport in the device coordinate space. Returns the previous mapping mode.

Manipulating the Viewport Origin

```
CPoint GetViewportOrg() const;
```

Returns the origin of the viewport in device coordinates.

```
CPoint OffsetViewportOrg(
    int nXoffset,  // x-offset in device units
    int nYoffset); // y-offset in device units
```

Adds the specified *x*, *y* offsets to the *x*, *y* coordinates of the current viewport. Returns the previous coordinates of the viewport's origin.

```
CPoint SetViewportOrg(int x, int y); // Viewport's x- and y-coordinates
CPoint SetViewportOrg(POINT point);  // in device coordinates
```

Sets the location of the viewport's origin in device coordinates and returns the previous location of the viewport's origin in a `CPoint` object.

Manipulating the Viewport Extent

```
CSize GetViewportExt() const;
```

Returns the *x*,*y* extents of the viewport in device units.

```
CSize ScaleViewportExt(
    int xNum,     // Multiply x-dimension of viewport by
    int xDenom,   //   (xNum/xDenom)
```

```
    int yNum,     // Multiply y-dimension of viewport by
    int yDenom); //    (yNum/yDenom)
```

Scales the extent—the x, y measurements—of a viewport by specified amounts. Returns the previous height and width (in device units) of the viewport.

```
CSize SetViewportExt(int x, int y); // x,y extents in
CSize SetViewportExt(SIZE size);    //   device units
```

Sets the x, y extents of the viewport. You must provide these values in device units. `SetViewportExt` returns the previous extents of the viewport in a `CSize` object.

Understanding the Viewport, Window, and Mapping Mode

The terms *viewport* and *window* possess a special meaning in a DC. Here, *window* does not mean an area of the screen where an application's output appears. Rather, a window is a rectangular area in a logical coordinate space, with arbitrary units such as a hundredth of an inch. A viewport, on the other hand, is another rectangular area in the display screen. Therefore, the viewport's units are device units, such as pixels.

The term *mapping mode* refers to the way a window in logical coordinates is mapped to a viewport in the device coordinate space.

Consult Chapter 11 of Charles Petzold's *Programming Windows 3.1* (Microsoft Press, 1992) for a detailed discussion of the different coordinate systems and mapping modes in Microsoft Windows.

Manipulating the Window Origin

```
CPoint GetWindowOrg() const;
```

Returns the x,y coordinates of the window's origin in logical coordinates.

```
CPoint OffsetWindowOrg(
    int nXoffset,  // x-offset in logical units
    int nYoffset); // y-offset in logical units
```

Adds the specified x, y offsets to the x, y coordinates of the current window in the logical coordinate space. This also returns the previous coordinates of the window's origin.

```
CPoint SetWindowOrg(int x, int y); // x- and y-coordinates of window
CPoint SetWindowOrg(POINT point);  //   origin in logical units
```

Sets the location of the mapping window's origin in logical coordinates. This also returns the previous location of the window's origin in a `CPoint` object.

Manipulating the Window Extent

```
CSize GetWindowExt() const;
```

Returns the *x,y* extents of the window in logical units.

```
CSize ScaleWindowExt(
    int xNum,     // Multiply the x-dimension of window by
    int xDenom,   //    (xNum/xDenom)
    int yNum,     // Multiply the y-dimension of window by
    int yDenom);  //    (yNum/yDenom)
```

Scales the extent—the *x,y* dimensions—of the mapping window by specified amounts. Returns the previous height and width (in logical units) of the window.

```
CSize SetWindowExt(int x, int y); // x,y extents of the
CSize SetWindowExt(SIZE size);    //    window in logical units
```

Sets the *x,y* extents of the window. You must provide these values in logical units. Returns the previous extents of the window in a `CSize` object.

Converting Coordinates

```
void DPtoLP(LPPOINT lpPoints, int nCount = 1) const;
void DPtoLP(LPRECT lpRect) const;
```

Converts the coordinates of one or more points from the device coordinate system to the logical coordinate system.

```
void LPtoDP(LPPOINT lpPoints, int nCount = 1) const;
void LPtoDP(LPRECT lpRect) const;
```

Converts the coordinates of one or more points from the logical coordinate system to the device coordinate system.

Working with Regions

```
BOOL FillRgn(
    CRgn*   pRgn,     // Fill this region
    CBrush* pBrush); //    with this brush
```

Fills a region identified by `pRgn` using the brush specified by `pBrush`. Returns `TRUE` if successful.

```
BOOL FrameRgn(
    CRgn*   pRgn,     // Draw frame around this region
    CBrush* pBrush,   // Use this brush
```

```
    int     nWidth,    // Width of vertical brush strokes
    int     nHeight);  // Height of horizontal brush strokes
```

Draws a border around a region. Notice that the height and width of the border are assumed to be in logical units. Returns TRUE if successful; otherwise, returns FALSE.

```
BOOL InvertRgn(
    CRgn* pRgn); // Invert the pixels in this region
```

Inverts the pixels that lie within the specified region. InvertRgn returns TRUE if the function is successful; otherwise, returns FALSE.

```
BOOL PaintRgn(
    CRgn* pRgn); // Region to be painted
```

Fills the specified region using the currently selected brush. Returns TRUE if successful; otherwise, returns FALSE.

Clipping

```
int  ExcludeClipRect(int x1, int y1, int x2, int y2);
int  ExcludeClipRect(LPRECT lpRect);
```

Removes the specified rectangle from the current clipping region. In one form of the function, you specify the rectangle in a RECT structure; in the other, you provide the coordinates of the top left and bottom right corners of the rectangle.

```
int  ExcludeUpdateRgn(CWnd* pWnd);
```

Removes the update region of the specified window from the clipping region of the CDC object. Call this function to prevent drawing in the invalid areas of a window. Returns an integer that indicates the complexity of the region being excluded.

```
int  GetClipBox(
    LPRECT lpRect) const; // Bounding rectangle of clipping
                          //   area returned here
```

Retrieves the dimensions of the smallest rectangle that encloses the clipping region associated with this CDC object. The information is returned in a RECT structure with an address that you provide in the lpRect argument. Returns an integer denoting the type of the clipping region: COMPLEXREGION, NULLREGION, SIMPLEREGION, or ERROR.

```
int  IntersectClipRect(int x1, int y1, int x2, int y2);
int  IntersectClipRect(LPRECT lpRect);
```

Creates a new clipping region by intersecting the current region with the specified rectangle. Returns an integer code to indicate the complexity of the resulting clipping region. The return value can be COMPLEXREGION, SIMPLEREGION, NULLREGION, or ERROR.

```
int  OffsetClipRgn(int x, int y); // Amount of offset
int  OffsetClipRgn(SIZE size);    //   in logical units
```

Moves the clipping region by the specified amount of `x,y` offsets and returns the type of the new region. The type is `COMPLEXREGION`, `SIMPLEREGION`, `NULLREGION`, or `ERROR`.

```
BOOL PtVisible(int x, int y) const;
BOOL PtVisible(POINT point) const;
```

Returns `TRUE` if the specified point (in logical coordinates) lies within the clipping region of this DC; otherwise, returns `FALSE`.

```
BOOL RectVisible(
    LPRECT lpRect) const; // Does any part of this rectangle
                          //   lay in the clipping region?
```

Returns `TRUE` if any part of the specified rectangle lies within the clipping region; otherwise, returns `FALSE`.

```
int  SelectClipRgn(
    CRgn* pRgn); // Use this as the new clipping region
```

Uses the specified region as the clipping region of this DC. Returns the complexity of the region or an error indication. The return value is `COMPLEXREGION`, `SIMPLEREGION`, `NULLREGION`, or `ERROR`.

Drawing Lines

```
CPoint GetCurrentPosition() const;
```

Returns the logical coordinates of the current position.

```
BOOL LineTo(int x, int y); // Logical coordinates of endpoint
BOOL LineTo(POINT point);
```

Draws a line from the current position up to, but not including, a specified point using the currently selected pen. The line's endpoint becomes the new current position after the line is drawn. You must provide the coordinates of the point in logical units. Returns `TRUE` if it can draw the line; otherwise, returns `FALSE`.

```
CPoint MoveTo(int x, int y); // Logical coordinates of point
CPoint MoveTo(POINT point);
```

Changes the current position to a new point. Returns the logical coordinates of the previous position.

```
BOOL   Polyline(
    LPPOINT lpPoints, // Join points in this array by lines
    int     nCount);  // Number of points in array
```

Joins the points in the array by line segments using the current pen. `Polyline` does not use or alter the current position. Returns `TRUE` if successful; otherwise, returns `FALSE`.

Drawing Icons

```
BOOL DrawIcon(int x, int y, HICON hIcon);
BOOL DrawIcon(POINT point, HICON hIcon);
```

Draws the icon identified by *hIcon* with the icon's top left corner located at the specified point (in logical coordinates). Returns `TRUE` if successful.

Drawing Ellipses, Polygons, and Rectangles

```
BOOL   Arc(int x1, int y1, int x2, int y2,
           int x3, int y3, int x4, int y4);
BOOL   Arc(LPRECT lpRect, POINT ptStart, POINT ptEnd);
```

Draws an elliptical arc. Figure 20.2 illustrates how the arc is specified. Returns `TRUE` if successful.

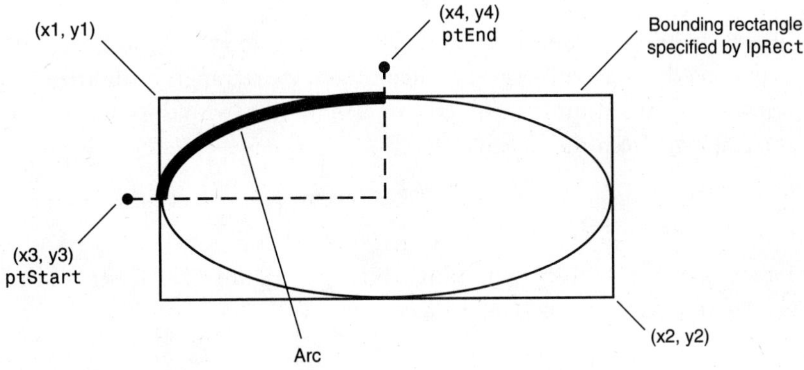

Figure 20.2. An elliptical arc drawn using `Arc`.

```
BOOL Chord(int x1, int y1, int x2, int y2,
           int x3, int y3, int x4, int y4);
BOOL Chord(LPRECT lpRect, POINT ptStart, POINT ptEnd);
```

Draws an elliptical arc and a line (the chord) joining the endpoints of the arc. Figure 20.3 illustrates the meaning of the arguments for the `Chord` function and shows what `Chord` draws. Returns `TRUE` if successful; otherwise, returns `FALSE`.

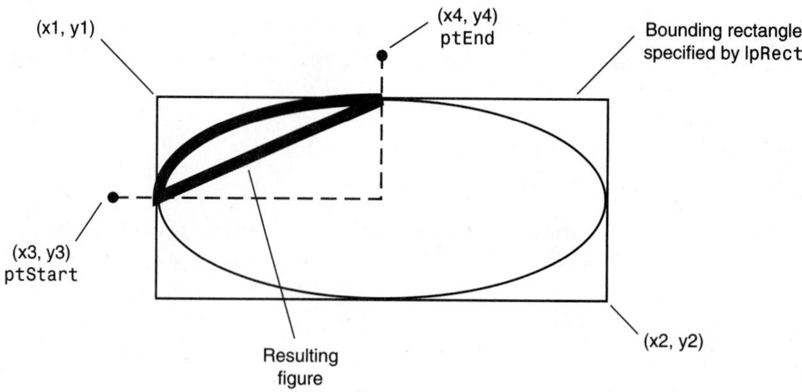

Figure 20.3. A figure drawn by `Chord`.

```
void DrawFocusRect(
    LPRECT lpRect); // Rectangle to be drawn
```

Draws the rectangle specified by the `RECT` structure with an address that you provide as the *`lpRect`* argument. `DrawFocusRect` draws the rectangle using an exclusive-**`OR`** (`XOR`) operation. Thus, calling the function a second time (with the same rectangle) removes the rectangle from the screen.

```
BOOL Ellipse(int x1, int y1, int x2, int y2);
BOOL Ellipse(LPRECT lpRect);
```

Draws an ellipse within a bounding rectangle. Figure 20.4 illustrates the meaning of the arguments. Returns `TRUE` if successful.

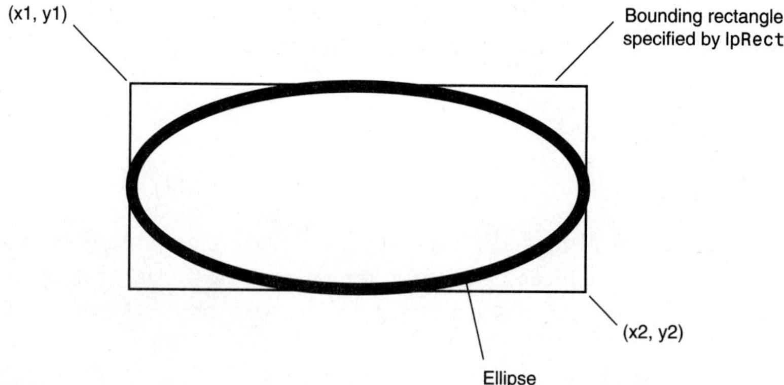

Figure 20.4. Specification of an ellipse.

```
void FillRect(
    LPRECT  lpRect, // Rectangle (logical coord) being filled
    CBrush* pBrush);// Use this brush to fill rectangle
```

Fills a rectangle using the specified brush. Notice that the right and bottom sides of the rectangle are not filled.

```
void FrameRect(
    LPRECT  lpRect, // Rectangle (logical coord) being framed
    CBrush* pBrush);// Use this brush to frame rectangle
```

Draws a border around a rectangle using the specified brush. The border is one logical unit wide.

```
void InvertRect(
    LPRECT lpRect); // Invert the contents of this rectangle
```

Inverts the contents of a rectangular area of the display. For black and white displays, this function turns black pixels into white, and white pixels into black. `InvertRect` returns `TRUE` if the function is successful; otherwise, returns `FALSE`.

```
BOOL Pie(int x1, int y1, int x2, int y2,
         int x3, int y3, int x4, int y4);
BOOL Pie(LPRECT lpRect, POINT ptStart, POINT ptEnd);
```

Draws a pie-shaped wedge. Figure 20.5 shows the meaning of the arguments that `Pie` needs. Returns `TRUE` if successful; otherwise, returns `FALSE`.

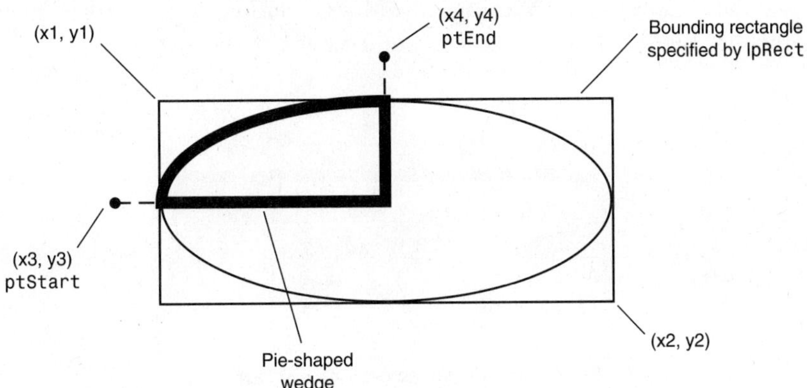

Figure 20.5. Specifying a pie-shaped wedge.

```
BOOL Polygon(
    LPPOINT lpPoints, // Array of points (vertices of polygon)
    int     nCount);  // Number of points in array
```

Draws a polygonal shape with vertices specified in an array of points (in logical coordinates). `Polygon` automatically closes the polygon by drawing a line from the last vertex to the first. Returns `TRUE` if successful; otherwise, returns `FALSE`.

```
BOOL PolyPolygon(
    LPPOINT lpPoints,      // Array of points (logical coord)
    LPINT   lpPolyCounts, // Array of integers, each entry is the
                          //   number of points in that polygon
    int     nCount);      // Number of polygons to draw (>=2)
```

Draws *nCount* (at least two) polygons using points from the *lpPoints* array as vertices. The entries in the *lpPolyCounts* array indicate how many vertices each *nCount* polygon has. Notice that, unlike `Polygon`, `PolyPolygon` does not automatically close each polygon. You must provide the appropriate vertices to close each polygon. Returns `TRUE` if successful; otherwise, returns `FALSE`.

```
BOOL Rectangle(int x1, int y1, int x2, int y2);
BOOL Rectangle(LPRECT lpRect);
```

Draws a rectangle using the current pen. Returns `TRUE` if successful; otherwise, returns `FALSE`.

```
BOOL RoundRect(int x1, int y1, int x2, int y2,
               int x3, int y3);
BOOL RoundRect(LPRECT lpRect, POINT point);
```

Draws a rectangle with rounded corners using the current pen. Figure 20.6 illustrates how the rounded corners are specified by the various arguments to the `RoundRect` function. Returns `TRUE` if successful; otherwise, returns `FALSE`.

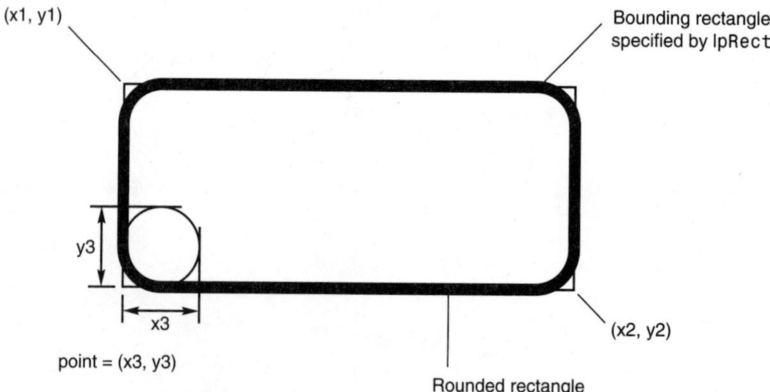

Figure 20.6. Drawing a rounded rectangle.

Working with Bitmaps

```
BOOL BitBlt(
    int    x,        // x,y coordinates of top left corner
    int    y,        //   of destination (in logical units)
    int    nWidth,   // Width of bitmap in logical coordinates
    int    nHeight,  // Height of bitmap in logical coordinates
    CDC*   pSrcDC,   // Copy bitmap from this CDC object
    int    xSrc,     // x,y coordinates of top left corner
    int    ySrc,     //   of source bitmap (in logical units).
    DWORD  dwRop);   // How to combine the source bitmap with
                     //   existing pixels in the destination.
```

Copies a bitmap from the `pSrcDC` device context to the current DC at a specified location. The `dwRop` argument specifies the *raster operation* (ROP)—how to combine the source bitmap with the destination bitmap. For the names of the raster operation codes, please consult the Microsoft Windows SDK *Programmer's Reference, Volume 2: Functions.*

```
BOOL  ExtFloodFill(
    int    x,            // The x,y coordinates of the
    int    y,            //   point where filling starts
    DWORD  crColor,      // A color used according to nFillType
    UINT   nFillType);   // One of FLOODFILLBORDER (fill area is
                         //   bordered by crColor) or FLOODFILLSURFACE
                         //   (fill area is of color crColor)
```

Fills an area with the current brush. The style of fill is specified by `nFillType`. Returns `TRUE` if successful; otherwise, returns `FALSE`.

```
BOOL  FloodFill(
    int    x,          // Start fill operation from this
    int    y,          //   logical (x,y) point.
    DWORD  crColor);   // Border color
```

Fills an area of the display screen with the current brush. The area to be filled is bounded by a border of color `crColor`. Returns `TRUE` if successful.

```
DWORD GetPixel(int x, int y) const;
DWORD GetPixel(POINT point) const;
```

Returns the RGB color value of the pixel at the specified point with coordinates that you provide in logical units.

```
BOOL PatBlt(
    int   x,      // Draw pattern into rectangle, of which the upper-left
    int   y,      //   corner is at this point in logical coordinates
```

```
    int   nWidth, // Height and width of rectangle
    int   nHeight,//   in logical units
    DWORD dwRop); // Raster-operation code
```

Fills a rectangle with a pattern using raster operations specified by the `dwRop` argument. Returns `TRUE` if the pattern is drawn; otherwise, returns `FALSE`. Consult the Microsoft Windows SDK *Programmer's Reference, Volume 2: Functions* for a complete list of raster operation codes.

```
DWORD SetPixel(int x, int y, DWORD crColor);
DWORD SetPixel(POINT point, DWORD crColor);
```

Sets the pixel at a point specified by the logical `x`,`y` coordinates to the RGB color value `crColor` (or a close approximation of that color). If successful, this returns the RGB color value actually used to paint the pixel; otherwise, returns -1 to indicate an error.

```
BOOL StretchBlt(
    int   x,           // x,y coordinates of top-left corner
    int   y,           //   of destination rectangle (logical coord)
    int   nWidth,      // Height and width of destination rectangle
    int   nHeight,     //   in logical units
    CDC*   pSrcDC,     // Source device context
    int   xSrc,        // x,y coordinates of top-left corner
    int   ySrc,        //   of source rectangle in logical units
    int   nSrcWidth,   // Height and width of source rectangle
    int   nSrcHeight,//   in logical units
    DWORD dwRop);      // Raster operation code
```

Copies a bitmap from a rectangle in a source DC to a rectangle in this `CDC` object, stretching or compressing the bitmap as necessary to fit the destination rectangle. The `dwRop` argument controls how the source bitmap is combined with the existing contents of the destination rectangle. For a complete list of the applicable raster operations, consult the Microsoft Visual C++ online documentation or the Microsoft Windows SDK *Programmer's Reference, Volume 2: Functions.* `StretchBlt` returns `TRUE` if the bitmap is successfully transferred; otherwise, returns `FALSE`.

Displaying Text

```
int   DrawText(
    LPCSTR lpString, // Text string to be drawn
    int    nCount,   // Number of characters in the string
                     // (Use -1 if lpString is null-terminated)

    LPRECT lpRect,   // Place text in this rectangle
    UINT   nFormat); // Specifies how text is positioned
```

Draws a text string inside a rectangle. You specify the positioning and format of the text in the `nFormat` argument. Consult the Microsoft Visual C++ online documentation for a list of possible values for `nFormat`. Returns the height of the line of text.

```
BOOL ExtTextOut(
    int     x,              // Logical x,y coordinate of the
    int     y,              //   first character's location
    UINT    nOptions,       // One or both of these:
                            //   ETO_CLIPPED (clip to rectangle)
                            //   ETO_OPAQUE (fill with current background)
    LPRECT lpRect,          // Rectangle where string appears
    LPCSTR lpString,        // String being displayed
    UINT    nCount,         // Number of characters
    LPINT   lpDxWidths);    // Array of separations between characters
```

Displays a string in a rectangular region using the current font. Returns `TRUE` if successful; otherwise, returns `FALSE`.

```
CSize GetTabbedTextExtent(
    LPCSTR lpString,          // Text string with tab characters
    int     nCount,           // Number of characters in lpString
    int     nTabPositions,    // Number of tab stops in next array
    LPINT   lpnTabStopPositions) const; // Tab stop positions
                                        //   in pixels
```

For a string with one or more tab characters, `GetTabbedTextExtent` returns the height and width of the string in the current font after accounting for the tab positions specified in the `lpnTabStopPositions` array.

```
UINT GetTextAlign() const;
```

Returns the current status of text alignment. The return value is a bitwise-OR combination of one or more values shown in Table 20.6.

Table 20.6. Text alignments.

Value	Meaning
TA_BASELINE	Aligns the baseline of the font with the x-axis.
TA_BOTTOM	Aligns the x-axis with the bottom of the bounding rectangle.
TA_CENTER	Aligns the y-axis with the center of the bounding rectangle.

continues

Table 20.6. continued

Value	Meaning
TA_LEFT	Aligns the y-axis with the left side of the bounding rectangle.
TA_NOUPDATE	Does not update the current position.
TA_RIGHT	Aligns the y-axis with the right side of the bounding rectangle.
TA_TOP	Aligns the x-axis with the top of the bounding rectangle.
TA_UPDATECP	Updates the current position after output.

```
int GetTextCharacterExtra() const;
```

Returns the current intercharacter spacing. (The default value is zero.)

```
CSize GetTextExtent(
    LPCSTR lpString,  // Return dimensions of this text string
    int nCount) const;// Number of characters in lpString
```

Returns the height and width of a line of text when displayed in the current font.

```
int  GetTextFace(
    int   nCount,              // Size of buffer lpFaceName
    LPSTR lpFacename) const; // Typeface name returned here
```

Fills the typeface name of the current font in a buffer with a name that you provide as the `lpFacename` argument. Returns the number of bytes copied into the buffer or 0 if an error occurs.

```
BOOL GetTextMetrics(
 LPTEXTMETRIC lpMetrics) const; // Return metrics here
```

Fills metrics for the current font in a `TEXTMETRIC` structure with an address you provide as `lpMetrics`. The `TEXTMETRIC` structure is defined in windows.h as follows:

```
typedef struct tagTEXTMETRIC
{
    int     tmHeight;          // Height of character cells
    int     tmAscent;          // Space between baseline and
                               //   top of character cell
    int     tmDescent;         // Space between bottom of character
                               //   cell and the baseline
```

```
    int     tmInternalLeading; // Difference between point size
                               //   and physical size of font
    int     tmExternalLeading; // Space between rows
    int     tmAveCharWidth;    // Average width of characters
    int     tmMaxCharWidth;    // Maximum width of widest char
    int     tmWeight;          // Font's weight (see SDK manuals)
    BYTE    tmItalic;          // Nonzero = italic font
    BYTE    tmUnderlined;      // Nonzero = underlined font
    BYTE    tmStruckOut;       // Nonzero = "struckout" font
    BYTE    tmFirstChar;       // First character defined in font
    BYTE    tmLastChar;        // Last character defined in font
    BYTE    tmDefaultChar;     // Value substituted for
                               //   characters not in font
    BYTE    tmBreakChar;       // Character used for word breaks
    BYTE    tmPitchAndFamily;  // Pitch and family of font
    BYTE    tmCharSet;         // Character set (ANSI_CHARSET,
                               // DEFAULT_CHARSET, and so on)
    int     tmOverhang;        // Extra width
    int     tmDigitizedAspectX;// Horizontal and vertical aspects
    int     tmDigitizedAspectY;//   for which the font is digitized
} TEXTMETRIC;
```

Returns TRUE if successful; otherwise, returns FALSE.

```
BOOL GrayString(
    CBrush* pBrush, // Draw text using this brush
    BOOL (FAR PASCAL EXPORT* lpfnOutput)(HDC, DWORD, int),
                    // Function that will draw the string
                    // Use NULL if you want TextOut to draw
    DWORD lpData,   // Data passed to lpfnOutput function
    int nCount,     // Number of characters to draw
    int x,          // Logical coordinates of the upper left
    int y,          //   corner of bounding rectangle
    int nWidth,     // Height and width of bounding rectangle
    int nHeight);   //   in logical coordinates
```

Draws a dimmed version of a text string. Returns TRUE if successful; otherwise, returns FALSE.

```
UINT SetTextAlign(
    UINT nFlags); // Alignment flags
```

Sets the text alignment flag that controls how text is placed within the bounding rectangle. The alignment flag *nFlags* should be the bitwise-OR combination of one or more of the values shown in Table 20.6.

```
int  SetTextCharacterExtra(
    int nCharExtra); // Extra space between characters (logical units)
```

Sets the extra space, in logical units, that is added to each character. Returns the previous value of the intercharacter spacing.

```
int  SetTextJustification(
    int nBreakExtra,  // Total space to be added to the line
    int nBreakCount); // Number of break characters in string
```

Sets the amount of space that is distributed over a specified number of break characters in a string. You would call `SetTextJustification` followed by `TextOut` to display the extra spaces around the break characters. A *break character* is a character that separates words—usually, it's the space character. `SetTextJustification` returns 1 if successful; otherwise, returns 0.

```
CSize TabbedTextOut(
    int    x,              // Logical x,y coordinates of the
    int    y,              //   starting point of string
    LPCSTR lpString,       // Display this string
    int    nCount,         // Number of characters in string
    int    nTabPositions,  // Number of tab positions
    LPINT  lpnTabStopPositions, // Array of tab positions
    int    nTabOrigin);    // Start tab expansion from this point
```

Displays a string after expanding any embedded tabs according to the array of tab positions specified in `lpnTabStopPositions`. Returns the height and width (in logical units) of the displayed string in a `CSize` object.

```
BOOL TextOut(int x, int y, const CString& str);
BOOL TextOut(int x, int y, LPCSTR lpString, int nCount);
```

Displays a string at a specified location. Returns `TRUE` if successful; otherwise, returns `FALSE`.

Using Fonts

```
CSize GetAspectRatioFilter() const;
```

Returns the current *aspect ratio*—the ratio of the device's pixel height and width. The aspect ratio filter is used to select fonts that are designed for a specific aspect ratio.

```
BOOL GetCharABCWidths(    // Windows 3.1 or later
    UINT  nFirst,         // Start with this character
    UINT  nLast,          // Up to this character
    LPABC lpabc) const;   // Return character widths here
```

Returns certain width information about several characters for the currently selected font, which must be a TrueType font for this function to work. The *lpabc* argument is an array of ABC structures that receives the width information. The ABC structure is defined in windows.h as follows:

```
typedef struct tagABC
{
    int   abcA; // The "A" spacing (added to current position
                //   before drawing character)
    UINT  abcB; // The "B" spacing (width of the character glyph)
    int   abcC; // The "C" spacing (this is added to the right
                //   of the character to provide space between charac
                     ters)
} ABC;
```

GetCharABCWidths returns TRUE if successful; otherwise, returns FALSE.

```
BOOL  GetCharWidth(
    UINT  nFirstChar,       // Return width of all characters
    UINT  nLastChar,        // between nFirstChar and nLastChar
    LPINT lpBuffer) const; // Array that receives the width information
```

Fills an array of integers with the width of each character (in the current font) in the consecutive group of characters between *nFirstChar* and *nLastChar*. GetCharWidth returns TRUE if successful; otherwise, returns FALSE.

```
DWORD GetFontData(    // Windows 3.1 or later
    DWORD  dwTable,   // Metric table ("measurement table")
                      //   to be returned
    DWORD  dwOffset, // Start at this offset in table
    LPVOID lpData,    // Return font metric here
    DWORD  cbData) const; // Return this many bytes
```

Use GetFontData in Windows version 3.1 or later to retrieve font metric information for the current font in the CDC object. The font should be a scalable, TrueType font. Returns the number of bytes of information copied to the *lpData* array.

```
DWORD GetGlyphOutline(              // Windows 3.1 or later
    UINT                nChar,      // Return this character's glyph
    UINT                nFormat,    // Format of information
    GLYPHMETRICS FAR* lpgm,         // Indicates placement of glyph
                                    //   in character cell
    DWORD               cbBuffer, // Size of buffer for return information
    void FAR*           lpBuffer, // Buffer for return information
    const MAT2 FAR*     lpmat2) const; // Transformation matrix, if
                                        //   any, to rotate glyph
```

Copies the outline of a character in the current font to the buffer specified by `lpBuffer`. Returns the number of bytes of information copied to `lpBuffer`. Consult the Microsoft Windows SDK *Programmer's Reference, Volume 2: Functions* for further information on this function.

```
int GetKerningPairs(                          // Windows 3.1 or later
    int               nPairs,                 // Number of kerning pairs
    KERNINGPAIR FAR* lpkrnpair) const; // Array for return information
```

Copies kerning pair information to the `lpkrnpair` array. A maximum of `nPairs` of kerning pairs are copied. Returns the actual number of kerning pairs for which information is being provided in the `lpkrnpair` array. Consult the Microsoft Windows SDK *Programmer's Reference, Volume 2: Functions* for further information on this function.

```
UINT GetOutlineTextMetrics( // Windows 3.1 or later
    UINT    cbData,          // Size of buffer for return info
    OUTLINETEXTMETRIC FAR* lpotm) const; // Array for return info
```

Copies certain metrics (measurements) for a TrueType font to the array of `OUTLINETEXTMETRIC` structures you provide in the `lpotm` argument. Returns a nonzero value if successful; otherwise, returns 0. Consult the Microsoft Windows *Programmer's Reference* for further information on this function.

```
DWORD SetMapperFlags(
    DWORD dwFlag); // Bit 0 = 1 means select only those fonts
                   //   that match the aspect ratio of the device
```

Controls how the font mapper maps a logical font to a physical one. Returns the previous font-mapper flag.

Printing

```
int AbortDoc();
```

Stops any printing. Returns a positive value if successful, or one of the error codes shown in Table 20.7.

Table 20.7. Errors during print spooling.

Error Code	Meaning
SP_ERROR	Indicates a general error.
SP_OUTOFDISK	Print spooling failed due to a lack of available disk space.

Error Code	Meaning
SP_OUTOFMEMORY	Print spooling failed due to a lack of available memory.
SP_USERABORT	User cancelled the print job through the Print Manager.

```
int EndDoc();
```

Marks the end of a printing job begun by `StartDoc`. Returns a positive value if successful or a negative error code if any problems occur in printing. Table 20.7 shows the possible error codes.

```
int EndPage();
```

This function calls `EndPage` to indicate that the printing device should print the current page and advance to the next page. `EndPage` returns a positive value if successful, or one of the error codes shown in Table 20.7 if an error occurs.

```
int Escape(
    int        nEscape,    // Perform this escape function
    int        nCount,     // Number of bytes in lpInData
    LPCSTR     lpInData,   // Pointer to input data for this escape
    void FAR* lpOutData);// Pointer to structure that receives
                           //   information returned by this escape
```

`Escape` is your gateway to the device-specific capabilities of printers. The *`nEscape`* argument indicates the exact function you want the device to perform. You'll find a complete list of printer escapes in the Microsoft Windows SDK *Programmer's Reference, Volume 3: Messages, Structures, and Macros.* `Escape` returns a positive value if successful; otherwise, it returns one of the error codes shown in Table 20.7.

```
BOOL QueryAbort() const;  // Windows 3.1 or later
```

This function calls the callback function that you have installed using `SetAbortProc`. Use this function to check whether the print job should be terminated. Returns `TRUE` if printing should continue (or no callback function is installed). This function passes the value returned by the callback function.

```
int StartDoc(LPCSTR pDocName);
int StartDoc(LPDOCINFO lpDocInfo) // In Windows 3.1 or later
```

Starts a new print job. The *pDocName* argument is a string (32-characters long, at most, including the null character) that is displayed in the Print Manager's window. In Windows 3.1 or later, you can provide information about the document in a `DOCINFO` structure, defined in windows.h as follows:

```
typedef struct
{
    int     cbSize;      // Size of the structure in bytes
    LPCSTR  lpszDocName; // Name of the document
    LPCSTR  lpszOutput;  // Output filename (or NULL to
                         //   send output to the device)
}   DOCINFO;
```

Returns a positive value if all goes well; otherwise, returns –1 to indicate an error.

```
int StartPage();
```

Prepares the printer to receive data for a new page. Returns a positive value if successful; otherwise, returns a negative value.

```
int SetAbortProc(
    BOOL (FAR PASCAL EXPORT* lpfn)(HDC, int)); // Abort procedure
```

Installs the abort procedure the Print Manager calls during spooling. In this way, the application may cancel the job if the user aborts the job or if an error occurs (such as lack of memory or disk space). The abort procedure should return a positive value if printing is to continue, or one of the error codes shown in Table 20.7. `SetAbortProc` returns `TRUE` if the abort procedure is successfully installed; otherwise, returns `FALSE`.

Scrolling

```
BOOL ScrollDC(
    int    dx,              // Scroll horizontally by this amount
    int    dy,              // Scroll vertically by this amount
    LPRECT lpRectScroll,    // Scroll this rectangle
    LPRECT lpRectClip,      // Clip scrolling to this rectangle
    CRgn*  pRgnUpdate,      // On return: region that needs
                            //   updating due to scrolling
    LPRECT lpRectUpdate);   // On return: largest rectangle that
                            //   needs repainting
```

Scrolls a rectangle horizontally and vertically by specified amounts. Use `ScrollDC` to scroll a portion of your application's window. To scroll the entire window, use the `ScrollWindow` member function of the window class. Returns `TRUE` if the rectangle is successfully scrolled; returns `FALSE` if an error occurs.

Displaying a Metafile

```
BOOL PlayMetaFile(HANDLE hMF);
```

Plays the contents of a metafile (thus drawing whatever picture the metafile represents) on the device associated with this `CDC` object. Returns `TRUE` if successful; otherwise, returns `FALSE`.

Manipulating Bounding Rectangles

```
UINT GetBoundsRect(        // In Windows version 3.1 or later
    LPRECT lpRectBounds,  // Information returned here
    UINT flags);          // Information to be returned
```

Copies the bounding rectangle information in the DC to the rectangle specified in `lpRectBounds`. The `flags` argument controls how the information is copied to the rectangle with an address in `lpRectBounds`. Returns the `DCB_SET` code if the bounding rectangle is not empty; otherwise, returns `DCB_RESET`.

```
UINT SetBoundsRect(                   // In Windows version 3.1 or later
    const RECT FAR* lpRectBounds,     // Pointer to new rectangle
    UINT flags);                      // How to combine new RECTs with old
                                         ones
```

Sets the bounding rectangle information in the DC using the rectangle specified in `lpRectBounds`. The `flags` argument controls how the rectangle in `lpRectBounds` is combined with the existing bounding rectangle. Returns a code to indicate the current state of the bounding rectangle.

See Also

`CClientDC`	DC for drawing in the client area of a window
`CMetaFileDC`	Used to create, save, and load a Windows metafile
`CPaintDC`	Provides a DC you can use when drawing in response to a `WM_PAINT` message
`CWindowDC`	DC for drawing in the entire window

CDialog

Inheritance Hierarchy

```
CObject -> CCmdTarget -> CWnd -> CDialog
```

Summary

```
#include <afxwin.h>
class CDialog : public CWnd
{
```

```
    DECLARE_DYNAMIC(CDialog)
public:
// Constructor, destructor, and window-creation functions are
// protected.

// Attributes:
    void MapDialogRect(LPRECT lpRect) const;

// Operations:
    BOOL IsDialogMessage(LPMSG lpMsg);

    void NextDlgCtrl() const;
    void PrevDlgCtrl() const;
    void GotoDlgCtrl(CWnd* pWndCtrl);

    void  SetDefID(UINT nID);
    DWORD GetDefID();

    BOOL  SetCtlBkColor(COLORREF clrCtlBk);

    void EndDialog(int nResult);

// Message-handling functions:
    virtual BOOL OnInitDialog();
    virtual void OnSetFont(CFont* pFont);

    afx_msg HBRUSH OnCtlColor(CDC* pDC, CWnd* pWnd,
                              UINT nCtlColor);
// Diagnostic support:
#ifdef _DEBUG
    virtual void AssertValid() const;
#endif

// Hidden implementation details....
//...

    DECLARE_MESSAGE_MAP()
};
```

Description

The `CDialog` class, derived from `CWnd`, serves as an abstract base class for displaying any type of dialog box. You can create a modeless dialog box by deriving a new class from `CDialog`. A *modeless dialog box* enables the user to continue interacting with other parts of the application even when the dialog box is on-screen. In fact, the `CFindReplaceDialog` class in the Microsoft Foundation Class Library is a modeless dialog box class derived from `CDialog`. You might want to study the source code of the `CFindReplaceDialog` class to learn how to derive a dialog box class from `CDialog`.

See Also

`CFindReplaceDialog`	Modeless dialog box class derived from `CDialog`
`CFileDialog`, `CColorDialog`, `CPrintDialog`, `CFontDialog`	Modal dialog box classes

CDialogBar

Inheritance Hierarchy

`CObject -> CCmdTarget -> CWnd -> CControlBar -> CDialogBar`

Summary

```
class CMainFrame : public CFrameWnd
{
// Constructor:
public:
    CMainFrame();

// Attributes:
public:
    BOOL m_bInsert;     // TRUE => insert mode, FALSE => overstrike mode

// Operations:
public:

// Implementation:
public:
    virtual BOOL PreCreateWindow(CREATESTRUCT& cs);
    virtual ~CMainFrame();
#ifdef _DEBUG
    virtual void AssertValid() const;
    virtual void Dump(CDumpContext& dc) const;
#endif

    BOOL CreateStyleBar();
    BOOL CreateToolBar();
```

```
    BOOL CreatePaletteBar();
    BOOL CreateStatusBar();

// Hidden implementation details...
//...

    DECLARE_MESSAGE_MAP()
};
```

Description

`CDialogBar` is derived from the `CDialog` class and represents a dialog bar object.

Member Functions

`CDialogBar``();`

Used to construct a `CDialogBar` object.

`Create``();`

Used to create the actual dialog bar window. In addition, attaches the window to the `CDialogBar` object.

Constructor and Destructor

`CDialogBar``();`

Creates a `CDialogBar` object.

See Also

`CControlBar`, `CWnd`	Base class of `CDialogBar`

CDocItem

Inheritance Hierarchy

`CObject -> CDocItem`

Summary

```
class CDocItem : public CObject
{
    DECLARE_DYNAMIC(CDocItem)

// Constructor:
protected:
    CDocItem();
```

```
// Attributes:
public:
    CDocument* GetDocument() const;

// Operations:
public:

// Overrideable:
public:
        // Functionality for data I/O in a native format:
        virtual void Serialize(CArchive& ar) = 0;

// Implementation:
public:
        virtual ~CDocItem();
#ifdef _DEBUG
        virtual void AssertValid() const;
        virtual void Dump(CDumpContext& dc) const;
#endif //_DEBUG
        friend class COleDocument;

// Hidden implementation details...
//...

};
```

Description

`CDocItem` is the base class from which the classes `COleClientItem` and `COleServerItem` are derived.

Member Functions

`CDocument*` **`GetDocument`**`() const;`

Call this function to get the document that contains the item.

Constructor and Destructor

See Also

`COleClientItem` and `COleServerItem`	Classes derived from `CDocItem`

CDocTemplate

Inheritance Hierarchy

CObject -> CCmdTarget -> CDocTemplate

Summary

```
class CDocTemplate : public CCmdTarget
{
    DECLARE_DYNAMIC(CDocTemplate)

// Constructor:
protected:
    CDocTemplate(UINT nIDResource, CRuntimeClass* pDocClass,
        CRuntimeClass* pFrameClass, CRuntimeClass* pViewClass);

// Attributes:
public:
// Iterate open documents
    virtual POSITION GetFirstDocPosition() const = 0;
    virtual CDocument* GetNextDoc(POSITION& rPos) const = 0;

// Operations:
public:
// You must override these next two functions...
    virtual void AddDocument(CDocument* pDoc);
    virtual void RemoveDocument(CDocument* pDoc);

    enum DocStringIndex
    {
        windowTitle,        // The default window title
        docName,            // The user-visible name for default document
        fileNewName,        // The user-visible name for FileNew
    //  Used for file based documents:
        filterName,         // The user-visible name for FileOpen
        filterExt,          // The user-visible extension for FileOpen
    // Used for file based documents with Shell open support:
        regFileTypeId,      // The REGEDIT-visible registered filetype ID
        regFileTypeName     // The Shell-visible registered filetype name
    };

    virtual BOOL GetDocString(CString& rString,
        enum DocStringIndex index) const;
```

```
// Overrideables:
public:
    enum Confidence
    {
        noAttempt,
        maybeAttemptForeign,
        maybeAttemptNative,
        yesAttemptForeign,
        yesAttemptNative,
        yesAlreadyOpen
    };
    virtual Confidence MatchDocType(const char* pszPathName,
        CDocument*& rpDocMatch);
    virtual CDocument* CreateNewDocument();
    virtual CFrameWnd* CreateNewFrame(CDocument* pDoc,
        CFrameWnd* pOther);
    virtual void InitialUpdateFrame(CFrameWnd* pFrame, CDocument* pDoc);
    virtual BOOL SaveAllModified();
    virtual CDocument* OpenDocumentFile(const char* pszPathName) = 0;

// Implementation:
public:
    virtual ~CDocTemplate();

    CObject* m_pAttachedServer;
            // back pointer to OLE or other server (NULL if none of
               disabled):
#ifdef _DEBUG
    virtual void Dump(CDumpContext&) const;
    virtual void AssertValid() const;
#endif //_DEBUG

// Hidden implementation details...
//...

};
```

Description

`CDocTemplate` is derived from the `CCmdTarget` class, which defines the functionality for document templates. The document template defines the relationships between the document class (`CDocument`), the view class (using one of: `CView`, `CScrollView`, `CFormView`, or `CEditView`, where `CEditView` can be directly used as well), and the frame class (`CFrameWnd` or `CMDIChildWnd`, either of which can be used directly if the default frame window is what your application requires).

Member Functions

```
virtual BOOL GetDocString(CString& csString, enum    DocStringIndex
nIndex) const;
```

In **`GetDocString`**, the returned string is placed in *`csString`*. *`nIndex`* is the index to the string to be returned. *`nIndex`* can contain any of the values from Table 20.8.

Table 20.8. `GetDocString` types

Type	Description
`CDocTemplate::windowTitle`	The application's title as it is in the main window's title bar.
`CDocTemplate::docName`	The default document's rootname. New untitled documents are built as rootname1, rootname2, etc. The default rootname is `untitled`.
`CDocTemplate::fileNewName`	This document's type. This string is displayed in the File New dialog box.
`CDocTemplate::filterName`	Document-type description, and a filename wildcard; for example, 'Star maps (*.dbc)'.
`CDocTemplate::filterExt`	The extension for the document type; for example, '*.dbc'.
`CDocTemplate::regFileTypeId`	The document's identifier, to be stored in the Windows registration database; for example, 'StarMap'.

Type	Description
`CDocTemplate::regFileTypeName`	The document's name to be stored in the Windows registration database; for example, 'Starmanager Maps'

Constructor and Destructor

See Also

`CSingleDocTemplate`, `CMultiDocTemplate`	Classes derived from `CDocTemplate`

CDocument

Inheritance Hierarchy

`CObject -> CCmdTarget -> CDocument`

Summary

```
class CDocument : public CCmdTarget
{
    DECLARE_DYNAMIC(CDocument)

public:
// Constructors:
    CDocument();

// Attributes:
public:
    const CString& GetTitle() const;
    virtual void SetTitle(const char* pszTitle);
    const CString& GetPathName() const;
    virtual void SetPathName(const char* pszPathName);

    CDocTemplate* GetDocTemplate() const;
    BOOL IsModified();
    void SetModifiedFlag(BOOL bModified = TRUE);

// Operations:
    void AddView(CView* pView);
    void RemoveView(CView* pView);
```

```
    virtual POSITION GetFirstViewPosition() const;
    virtual CView* GetNextView(POSITION& rPosition) const;

    // Perform an update of the views:
    void UpdateAllViews(CView* pSender, LPARAM lHint = 0L,
        CObject* pHint = NULL);

// Overrideables:
    virtual void OnChangedViewList();
    virtual void DeleteContents();

    // Used with files:
    virtual BOOL OnNewDocument();
    virtual BOOL OnOpenDocument(const char* pszPathName);
    virtual BOOL OnSaveDocument(const char* pszPathName);
    virtual void OnCloseDocument();
    virtual void ReportSaveLoadException(const char* pszPathName,
        CException* e, BOOL bSaving, UINT nIDPDefault);

    // Used for closing frames and documents:
    virtual BOOL CanCloseFrame(CFrameWnd* pFrame);
    virtual BOOL SaveModified();

// Implementation:
public:
    BOOL m_bAutoDelete;             // If TRUE, delete the document when
                                    //   there are no more views remaining.

#ifdef _DEBUG
    virtual void Dump(CDumpContext&) const;
    virtual void AssertValid() const;
#endif //_DEBUG
    virtual ~CDocument();
    BOOL DoSave(const char* pszPathName, BOOL bReplace = TRUE);
    void UpdateFrameCounts();

    virtual BOOL OnCmdMsg(UINT nID, int nCode, void* pExtra,
        AFX_CMDHANDLERINFO* pHandlerInfo);
    friend class CDocTemplate;

// Hidden implementation details...
//...
```

```
    DECLARE_MESSAGE_MAP()
};
```

Description

`CDocument` is the base class for most user-defined document classes.

Member Functions

`AddView(CView* pView);`

Attaches the view pointed to by *pView* to the document.

`CDocTemplate* GetDocTemplate();`

Used to get a pointer to the document template for this document.

`virtual POSITION GetFirstViewPosition() const;`

Used to get the position of the first view of the document in the list of views.

`virtual CView* GetNextView(POSITION& Position);`

Returns the view identified by *Position*, then modifies *Position* to point to the next view (or `NULL` if this is the last view).

`const CString& GetPathName() const;`

Used to get the fully qualified path of the document's file.

`const CString& GetTitle() const;`

Used to get the document's title, which usually is derived from the document's filename.

`BOOL IsModified();`

Returns `TRUE` if the document has been changed and has not been saved.

`RemoveView(CView* View);`

Used to detach the view specified by *View* from the document.

`SetModifiedFlag(BOOL bChanged = TRUE);`

Used to set the modified flag (see **`IsModified()`**, above). Call this function whenever the document has been changed.

`virtual void SetPathName(const char* szPathname);`

Used to set the document data file's (fully qualified) path name.

`virtual void SetTitle(const char* szTitle);`

Used to set the document's title, which is displayed in the frame window's title bar.

```
UpdateAllViews(CView* Sender, LPARAM lpHint = 0l, CObject* oHint = NULL);
```

Used to notify each of the views of a given document that the document has changed.

```
virtual BOOL CanCloseFrame(CFrameWnd* FrameWnd);
```

Called before a frame window displaying the document is closed. Normally, if this is the last frame window for the document, the user is prompted for a save if the document has been modified.

```
DeleteContents();
```

Used prior to reusing a document (for example, with a single document interface application prior to performing a new or open document operation). Typically clears all of the document's data, and cleans up any other information pertaining to the data that has been deleted.

```
OnChangedViewList();
```

Used whenever a view has been added to or removed from the document.

```
OnCloseDocument();
```

Called whenever a document is being closed.

```
virtual BOOL OnNewDocument();
```

Called whenever a new document is being created.

```
virtual BOOL OnOpenDocument(const char* szPathName);
```

Called whenever the user is opening a new file.

```
virtual BOOL OnSaveDocument(const char* szPathName);
```

Called whenever the user is saving a file, either to a new or existing document file.

```
virtual void ReportSaveLoadException(const char* pszPathName,
    CException* e, BOOL bSaving, UINT nIDPDefault);
```

Called whenever a save or load to a document file cannot be completed because of an error.

```
virtual BOOL SaveModified();
```

Used to prompt, asking if a document that has been modified should be saved. Typically called when the application exits, or the document is being closed.

Constructor and Destructor

CDocument();

Creates a CDocument object. You can override the the **OnNewDocument** member function to perform custom setup and initialization.

See Also

CCmdTarget, CView, and CDocTemplate

Base class of CClientDC

CDumpContext

Inheritance Hierarchy

CDumpContext

Summary

```
class CDumpContext
{
public:
    CDumpContext(CFile* pFile);

// Attributes:
    int GetDepth() const;       // If zero, dump this object
                                // If 1, dump child objects
    void SetDepth(int nNewDepth);

// Operations:
    CDumpContext& operator<<(LPCSTR lpsz);
    CDumpContext& operator<<(const void FAR* lp);
#ifdef _NEARDATA
    CDumpContext& operator<<(const void NEAR* np);
#endif
    CDumpContext& operator<<(const CObject* pOb);
    CDumpContext& operator<<(const CObject& ob);
    CDumpContext& operator<<(BYTE by);
    CDumpContext& operator<<(WORD w);
    CDumpContext& operator<<(UINT u);
    CDumpContext& operator<<(LONG l);
    CDumpContext& operator<<(DWORD dw);
    CDumpContext& operator<<(float f);
    CDumpContext& operator<<(double d);
    CDumpContext& operator<<(int n);
    void HexDump(const char* pszLine, BYTE* pby, int nBytes, int nWidth);
    void Flush();
```

```
// Implementation:
protected:
    // NOTE: you cannot copy (or assign) dump context objects.
    CDumpContext(const CDumpContext& dcSrc);
    void operator=(const CDumpContext& dcSrc);
    void OutputString(LPCSTR lpsz);

    int m_nDepth;

public:
    CFile* m_pFile;
};
```

Description

The `CDumpContext` class is used to support stream-oriented debugging output. Use `afxDump`, a class derived from `CDumpContext`, for debugging output. As with other debugging services, you can use these classes only with the debugging version of the MFC libraries.

Member Functions

`Flush``();`

Used to force whatever debugging data exists in the buffer to be written to the output file specified.

`<<`

Overloaded operator—allows objects, strings, and other variables and constants to be dumped to the debugging stream. Table 20.9 lists the types accepted.

Table 20.9. `CDumpContext <<` output types.

Type	Description
`const CObject*`	Dump of object
`const char FAR*`	Printout of the string
`const void FAR*`	Hex dump of the address
`const void NEAR*`	Hex dump of the address
`BYTE`	The byte supplied
`WORD`	The unsigned short integer supplied

Type	Description
DWORD	The unsigned long integer supplied
int	The integer supplied
LONG	The long integer supplied
UINT	The unsigned integer supplied

```
HexDump(const char* szString, BYTE* pByte, int nBytes, int nWidth);
```

With `HexDump`, you use *`szString`* to hold a string that is output at the beginning of each line. The pointer *`pByte`* points to an array of bytes that are to be output. The *`nBytes`* parameter tells how many bytes are to be dumped, and *`nWidth`* is how many bytes (not output characters) are to be dumped. Each byte dumped takes three character positions in the output stream.

```
int GetDepth();
```

Determines whether a deep dump or shallow dump is being done. See **`SetDepth`** for more information.

```
SetDepth(int nDepth);
```

Sets whether a *deep dump* (`nDepth > 0`) or *shallow dump* (`nDepth == 0`) is being done. A deep dump is defined as being recursive, so that nested objects also are dumped. Use caution, as there is no check for circular references—which can result in an infinite loop.

Constructor and Destructor

```
CDumpContext(CFile* File);
```

Use this function to specify where the dump output is to be sent. The parameter *`File`* is the destination. Don't use *`File`* for any other purpose when using `CDumpContext`. The default output is `stderr` under DOS, and `OutputDebugString` under Windows.

See Also

`afxDump`	Class derived from **`CDumpContext`**

CEdit

Inheritance Hierarchy

```
CObject -> CCmdTarget -> CWnd -> CEdit
```

Summary

```
#include <afxwin.h>

class CEdit : public CWnd
{
    DECLARE_DYNAMIC(CEdit)
public:

// Constructor:
    CEdit();

// Initializing Edit:
    BOOL Create(DWORD dwStyle, const RECT& rect,
        CWnd* pParentWnd, UINT nID);

// Attributes:
    BOOL  CanUndo() const;
    int   GetLineCount() const;
    BOOL  GetModify() const;
    void  SetModify(BOOL bModified = TRUE);
    void  GetRect(LPRECT lpRect) const;
    DWORD GetSel() const;
    HANDLE  GetHandle() const;
    void    SetHandle(HANDLE hBuffer);

// Convention: First word in lpBuffer is the size of the buffer.
    int GetLine(int nIndex, LPSTR lpBuffer) const;
    int GetLine(int nIndex, LPSTR lpBuffer, int nMaxLength) const;

// Operations:
    void EmptyUndoBuffer();
    BOOL FmtLines(BOOL bAddEOL);

    void LimitText(int nChars = 0);
    int  LineFromChar(int nIndex = -1) const;
    int  LineIndex(int nLine = -1) const;
    int  LineLength(int nLine = -1) const;
    void LineScroll(int nLines, int nChars = 0);
    void ReplaceSel(LPCSTR lpNewText);
    void SetPasswordChar(char ch);
    void SetRect(LPRECT lpRect);
    void SetRectNP(LPRECT lpRect);
    void SetSel(DWORD dwSelection);
```

```
    void SetSel(int nStartChar, int nEndChar);
    BOOL SetTabStops(int nTabStops, LPINT rgTabStops);
    void SetTabStops();
    BOOL SetTabStops(int cxEachStop);

u Working with the Clipboard
    BOOL Undo();
    void Clear();
    void Copy();
    void Cut();
    void Paste();

#if (WINVER >= 0x030a) // Windows 3.1 or later only

    BOOL SetReadOnly(BOOL bReadOnly = TRUE);
    int  GetFirstVisibleLine() const;
    char GetPasswordChar() const;

#endif

// Hidden implementation details....
};
```

Description

The **CEdit** class, derived from CWnd, encapsulates a Windows edit control—one of Microsoft Windows' built-in window types. An *edit control* is a child window in which the user can enter and edit text.

Member Functions

Constructor

CEdit();

Constructs a CEdit object, but you still must call Create to attach a window to the CEdit object.

Initializing Edit

```
BOOL Create(
    DWORD dwStyle,      // Style of edit window (see online
                        //   documentation or SDK manuals)
    const RECT& rect,   // Position and size of the edit window
    CWnd* pParentWnd,   // Pointer to the parent window
    UINT  nID);         // Edit control's ID
```

Creates the edit control's window. For a list of valid styles of edit windows, consult Microsoft Visual C++'s online documentation or the `CreateWindow` function in the Microsoft Windows SDK *Programmer's Reference, Volume 2: Functions.* **`Create`** returns `TRUE` if successful.

Attributes

```
BOOL  CanUndo() const;
```

Returns `TRUE` if calling the `Undo` member function can undo the last edit operation.

```
int  GetFirstVisibleLine() const; // Windows 3.1 or later only
```

Returns the index of the topmost visible line in the edit control. Index 0 refers to the first line.

```
HANDLE GetHandle() const;
```

Returns a handle to the memory allocated for a multiple-line edit control or 0 if any error occurs.

```
int GetLine(int nIndex, LPSTR lpBuffer) const;
int GetLine(int nIndex, LPSTR lpBuffer, int nMaxLength) const;
```

Copies a line of text from the edit control to the buffer *`lpBuffer`*. In the first form of the function, as a convention, the first word in *`lpBuffer`* is the size of the buffer. Returns the actual number of characters copied into *`lpBuffer`*. Notice that the copied text is not terminated by a null character.

```
int   GetLineCount() const;
```

Returns the number of lines in a mulitple-line edit control.

```
BOOL  GetModify() const;
```

Returns `TRUE` if the contents of the edit control have been modified.

```
char GetPasswordChar() const; // Windows 3.1 or later only
```

Returns the password character.

```
void  GetRect(LPRECT lpRect) const;
```

Returns the formatting rectangle of the edit control.

```
DWORD GetSel() const;
```

Returns the starting and ending character positions of the current selection in the edit control.

```
void SetHandle(HANDLE hBuffer);
```

After you call `SetHandle`, the multiple-line edit control uses the memory identified by the handle *hBuffer* to store the text instead of allocating its own memory.

```
void SetModify(BOOL bModified = TRUE);
```

Sets or clears the flag indicating that text in the edit control has been modified.

```
void SetPasswordChar(char ch);
```

If *ch* is a nonzero number, this function directs the single-line edit control to display the character *ch* in the edit control whenever the user enters any character from the keyboard. To revert to normal behavior, call `SetPasswordChar` again with *ch* set to zero.

```
BOOL SetReadOnly( // Windows 3.1 or later only
    BOOL bReadOnly = TRUE);
```

If *bReadOnly* is `TRUE`, this function marks the edit control as read only. The user cannot edit the contents of a read-only edit control.

```
void SetRect(LPRECT lpRect);
```

Sets the position and size of the formatting rectangle for a multiline edit control.

```
void SetRectNP(LPRECT lpRect);
```

`SetRectNP` is identical to `SetRect`, except that the edit control's window is not redrawn.

Operations

```
void EmptyUndoBuffer();
```

Resets the undo buffer so that the last operation cannot be undone.

```
BOOL FmtLines(BOOL bAddEOL); // TRUE = add line-break characters
```

If *bAddEOL* is `TRUE`, this function formats lines in a multiline edit by inserting linebreak characters between lines. The function returns `TRUE` if the lines are formatted.

```
void LimitText(int nChars = 0);
```

Sets the maximum number of characters that the user can type in the edit control.

```
int  LineFromChar(int nIndex = -1) const;
```

Returns the line number of the line that contains the specified character index (counting from the beginning of the edit control).

```
int LineIndex(int nLine = -1) const;
```

Returns the character index of a specified line number (the character index is the number of characters from the beginning of the edit control to that line). If an error occurs, the function returns a –1.

```
int LineLength(int nLine = -1) const;
```

Returns the length of a specified line in the edit control.

```
void LineScroll(int nLines, int nChars = 0);
```

Scrolls the text in a multiline edit control vertically by `nLines` and scrolls horizontally by `nChars` character positions.

```
void ReplaceSel(LPCSTR lpNewText);
```

Replaces the current selection in the edit control with text specified by `lpNewText`. If nothing is currently selected, inserts the text at the current position.

```
void SetSel(DWORD dwSelection);
void SetSel(int nStartChar, int nEndChar);
```

Selects a range of characters in the edit control.

```
void SetTabStops();
BOOL SetTabStops(int cxEachStop);
BOOL SetTabStops(int nTabStops, LPINT rgTabStops);
```

Sets the tab stops. In the third form of the function, the tab stops are in the `rgTabStops` array of integers. The tab positions are set in dialog units. *Dialog units* are set in terms of the character sizes of the system font (1 dialog unit along the x-axis equals one-fourth the average width of a character; 1 dialog unit along the y-axis equals one-eighth the height of a character). If `nTabStops` = 0, `ngTabStops` is ignored, and tabs are set every 32 dialog units.

Working with the Clipboard

```
void Clear();
```

Clears the current selection in the edit control.

```
void Copy();
```

Copies the current selection in the edit control to the Clipboard using the `CF_TEXT` format.

```
void Cut();
```

Deletes the current selection in the edit control and copies the deleted text to the Clipboard using the `CF_TEXT` format.

```
void Paste();
```

Copies data in the CF_TEXT format from the Clipboard and inserts the text in the edit control at the current cursor location.

```
BOOL Undo();
```

Undoes the last edit operation if possible and returns TRUE if successful. Returns FALSE if undo is impossible to perform.

See Also

CWnd	Base class of CEdit
CComboBox	Uses an edit control

CEditView

Inheritance Hierarchy

COject -> CCmdTarget -> Cwnd -> CView -> CEditView

Summary

```
class CEditView : public CView
{
    DECLARE_DYNCREATE(CEditView)

// Construction:
public:
    CEditView();
    static const DWORD dwStyleDefault;

// Attributes:
public:
    // CEdit control access
    CEdit& GetEditCtrl() const;

    // Presentation attributes:
    CFont* GetPrinterFont() const;
    void SetPrinterFont(CFont* pFont);
    void SetTabStops(int nTabStops);

    // Other attributes:
    void GetSelectedText(CString& strResult) const;

// Operations:
public:
```

```
    BOOL FindText(LPCSTR lpszFind, BOOL bNext = TRUE, BOOL bCase = TRUE);
    void SerializeRaw(CArchive& ar);
    UINT PrintInsideRect(CDC* pDC, RECT& rectLayout, UINT nIndexStart,
        UINT nIndexStop);

// Overrideables:
protected:
    virtual void OnFindNext(LPCSTR lpszFind, BOOL bNext, BOOL bCase);
    virtual void OnReplaceSel(LPCSTR lpszFind, BOOL bNext,
        BOOL bCase, LPCSTR lpszReplace);
    virtual void OnReplaceAll(LPCSTR lpszFind,
        LPCSTR lpszReplace, BOOL bCase);
    virtual void OnTextNotFound(LPCSTR lpszFind);

// Implementation:
public:
    virtual ~CEditView();
#ifdef _DEBUG
    virtual void AssertValid() const;
    virtual void Dump(CDumpContext& dc) const;
#endif
    virtual void OnDraw(CDC* pDC);
    virtual void Serialize(CArchive& ar);
    virtual void DeleteContents();
    void ReadFromArchive(CArchive& ar, UINT nLen);
    void WriteToArchive(CArchive& ar);

    static const UINT nMaxSize; // maximum number of characters supported

    // Construction:
    WNDPROC* GetSuperWndProcAddr();
    virtual BOOL PreCreateWindow(CREATESTRUCT& cs);
    virtual void CalcWindowRect(LPRECT lpClientRect);

    // Printer support:
    virtual BOOL OnPreparePrinting(CPrintInfo* pInfo);
    virtual void OnBeginPrinting(CDC* pDC, CPrintInfo* pInfo);
    virtual void OnPrepareDC(CDC* pDC, CPrintInfo* pInfo);
    virtual void OnPrint(CDC* pDC, CPrintInfo* pInfo);
    virtual void OnEndPrinting(CDC* pDC, CPrintInfo* pInfo = NULL);
    BOOL PaginateTo(CDC* pDC, CPrintInfo* pInfo);
```

```
    // Search/Edit support:
    void OnEditFindReplace(BOOL bFindOnly);
    BOOL InitializeReplace();
    BOOL SameAsSelected(LPCSTR lpszCompare, BOOL bCase);

    // Buffer functions:
    LPCSTR LockBuffer() const;
    void UnlockBuffer() const;
    UINT GetBufferLength() const;

    //{{AFX_MSG(CEditView)
    afx_msg int OnCreate(LPCREATESTRUCT lpCreateStruct);
    afx_msg void OnPaint();
    afx_msg LRESULT OnSetFont(WPARAM wParam, LPARAM lParam);
    afx_msg void OnUpdateNeedSel(CCmdUI* pCmdUI);
    afx_msg void OnUpdateNeedClip(CCmdUI* pCmdUI);
    afx_msg void OnUpdateNeedText(CCmdUI* pCmdUI);
    afx_msg void OnUpdateNeedFind(CCmdUI* pCmdUI);
    afx_msg void OnUpdateEditUndo(CCmdUI* pCmdUI);
    afx_msg void OnEditChange();
    afx_msg void OnEditCut();
    afx_msg void OnEditCopy();
    afx_msg void OnEditPaste();
    afx_msg void OnEditClear();
    afx_msg void OnEditUndo();
    afx_msg void OnEditSelectAll();
    afx_msg void OnEditFind();
    afx_msg void OnEditReplace();
    afx_msg void OnEditRepeat();
    afx_msg LRESULT OnFindReplaceCmd(WPARAM wParam, LPARAM lParam);
    //}}AFX_MSG

// Hidden implementation details...
//...

    DECLARE_MESSAGE_MAP()
};
```

Description

`CEditView`, like the `CEdit` class, provides much of the functionality of a Windows edit control. With `CEditView`, you get additional abilities including: Printing, Edit features (Cut, Copy, Paste, Clear and Undo), and Find and Replace.

Member Variables

```
CEditView::dwStyleDefault
```

You can pass **dwStyleDefault** to the create function as the default style for the **CEditView** object.

Member Functions

```
CEdit& GetEditCtrl() const;
```

Used to get a reference to the edit control used by **CEditView**.

```
CFont* GetPrinterFont() const;
```

Used to get information about the current printer font.

```
GetSelectedText(CString& csReturnedString)
```

Places the currently selected text (if any) in *csReturnedString*.

```
SetPrinterFont(CFont* Font)
```

Used to set the printer font. If *Font* is null, the font is set based on the current display font.

```
SetTabStops(int nTab)
```

Used to set screen display and printing tab stops, using a single width for all tab stops. The unit of measure is dialog units, which is 25 percent of the width of the average character width.

```
BOOL FindText(LPCSTR szTextToFind,
    BOOL bDirection = TRUE, BOOL bCase = TRUE)
```

Searches the text in the **CEditView** for the string in *szTextToFind*. The parameter *bDirection* determines the direction of the search (starting from the current selection). If it's TRUE, the search is to the end of the text; if it's FALSE the search is to the beginning of the text. The parameter *bCase* determines whether the case of the text and the text in *szTextToFind* must match or not. If TRUE, the case is taken into account; if FALSE, the case is not taken into consideration. Returns a nonzero value if the text is located; returns zero if the text isn't located.

```
UINT PrintInsideRect(CDC *pDC, RECT& RectToPrint,
    UINT nStart, UINT nStop)
```

Used to print the text, specified by *nStart* and *nStop*, to the printer DC contained by *pDC* within the rectangle defined within *RectToPrint*.

```
SerializeRaw(CArchive& Archive)
```

Used to serialize a **CEditView** object to a text file.

```
virtual void OnFindNext(LPCSTR szTextToFind,
    BOOL bDirection = TRUE, BOOL bCase = TRUE)
```

Searches the text in the **CEditView** for the string in *szTextToFind*. The parameter *bDirection* determines the direction of the search (starting from the current selection). If it's TRUE, the search is to the end of the text; if it's FALSE, the search is to the beginning of the text. The parameter *bCase* determines whether the case of the text and the text in *szTextToFind* must match or not. If TRUE, the case is taken into account; if FALSE, the case is not taken into consideration.

```
virtual void OnReplaceAll(LPCSTR szTextToFind, LPCSTR szTextToReplace,
    BOOL bCase = TRUE);
```

Searches the text in the **CEditView** for the string in *szTextToFind*. Each time the text is found, it's replaced with the text in *szTextToReplace*. The parameter *bCase* determines whether the case of the text and the text in *szTextToFind* must match or not. If TRUE, the case is taken into account when the search is performed; if FALSE, the case is not taken into consideration.

```
virtual void OnReplaceSel(LPCSTR szTextToFind, BOOL bDirection,
    BOOL bCase = TRUE, LPCSTR szTextToReplace);
```

Searches the text in the **CEditView** for the string that is in *szTextToFind*. Each time the text is found, it's replaced with the text in *szTextToReplace*. The parameter *bDirection* determines the direction of the search (starting from the current selection): if it's TRUE, the search is to the end of the text, while if it's FALSE the search is to the beginning of the text. The parameter *bCase* determines whether the case of the text and the text in *szTextToFind* must match or not. If TRUE, the case is taken into account when the search is performed; if FALSE, the case is not taken into consideration.

```
virtual void OnTextNotFound(LPCSTR szTextToFind);
```

This member function is called whenever a string, contained in *szTextToFind*, is not found. The default action is to call MessageBeep, which beeps the computer's speaker.

Constructor and Destructor

CEditView()

Creates a CEditView object.

See Also

CEdit	Similar class to **CEditView**
CView	Base class for **CEditView**

CException

Inheritance Hierarchy

```
CObject -> CException
```

Summary

```
class CException : public CObject
{
    // Create an abstract class to allow dynamic type checking:
    DECLARE_DYNAMIC(CException)
};
```

Description

`CException` is the base class for all MFC exceptions. Because `CException` is an abstract class, you are not able to create `CException` class objects—if you must create an exception class object, use one of the classes listed below in Table 20.10 as a model.

Table 20.10. `CException` derived classes.

Class	Description
`CMemoryException`	An out-of-memory exception.
`CNotSupportedException`	Exception for a request for an unsupported operation.
`CArchiveException`	Occurs when there is an archive-specific exception.
`CFileException`	Occurs when there is a file-specific exception.
`CResourceException`	Occurs when a Windows resource was not found or could not be created.
`COleException`	Occurs when there is an OLE exception.

Member Functions

Constructor and Destructor

See Also

`CMemoryException`, `CNotSupportedException`	Classes created from `CException`

`CArchiveException,`	
`CFileException`	
`CResourceException,`	
`COleException`	
`CObject`	Base class of `CException`

CFile

Inheritance Hierarchy

`CObject -> CFile`

Summary

```
class CFile : public CObject
{
    DECLARE_DYNAMIC(CFile)

public:
// Constructors:
    CFile();
    CFile(int hFile);
    CFile(const char* pszFileName, UINT nOpenFlags);

// Attributes:
    UINT m_hFile;

    virtual DWORD GetPosition() const;
    BOOL GetStatus(CFileStatus& rStatus) const;

// Operations:
    virtual BOOL Open(const char* pszFileName, UINT nOpenFlags,
        CFileException* pError = NULL);

    static void PASCAL Rename(const char* pszOldName,
        const char* pszNewName);
    static void PASCAL Remove(const char* pszFileName);
    static BOOL PASCAL GetStatus(const char* pszFileName,
        CFileStatus& rStatus);
    static void PASCAL SetStatus(const char* pszFileName,
        const CFileStatus& status);

    DWORD SeekToEnd();
    void SeekToBegin();
```

```
    // Used when a read or write must exceed 32K (max signed short int):
    DWORD ReadHuge(void FAR* lpBuffer, DWORD dwCount);
    void WriteHuge(const void FAR* lpBuffer, DWORD dwCount);

// Overrideables:
    virtual CFile* Duplicate() const;

    virtual LONG Seek(LONG lOff, UINT nFrom);
    virtual void SetLength(DWORD dwNewLen);
    virtual DWORD GetLength() const;

    virtual UINT Read(void FAR* lpBuf, UINT nCount);
    virtual void Write(const void FAR* lpBuf, UINT nCount);

    virtual void LockRange(DWORD dwPos, DWORD dwCount);
    virtual void UnlockRange(DWORD dwPos, DWORD dwCount);

    virtual void Abort();
    virtual void Flush();
    virtual void Close();

// Implementation:
public:
    virtual ~CFile();
#ifdef _DEBUG
    virtual void AssertValid() const;
    virtual void Dump(CDumpContext& dc) const;
#endif

// Hidden implementation details...
//...

};
```

Description

`CFile` is derived from `CObject` and is the base for the MFC file classes.

Public Variables

`m_hFile`

Contains either the operating-system file handle, or `CFILE::m_hFileNull` if no file handle has been assigned. The *`m_hFile`* variable normally should not be directly accessed, because it's meaning can vary with the derived class.

Member Functions

```
virtual CFile* Duplicate();
```

Used to construct a duplicate **CFile** object based on this file.

```
virtual BOOL Open(const char* szFileName, UINT nFlags,
    CFileException* Error = NULL);
```

Used to safely open a file (when used with the default constructor). Returns TRUE if the file was opened, and FALSE if the function failed.

```
virtual void Close();
```

Closes a file and deletes the object. If you created the object using new, you must delete it after the file has been closed.

```
virtual UINT Read(void FAR* lpBuffer, UINT nNumberBytes);
```

Used to read *nNumberBytes* from the file into the buffer pointed to by *lpBuffer*. Returns the number of bytes read, which may be less than *nNumberBytes* when a read extends past the end of the file.

```
virtual void Write(void FAR* lpBuffer, UINT nNumberBytes);
```

Used to write *nNumberBytes* to the file from the buffer pointed to by *lpBuffer*.

```
virtual void Flush();
```

Used to force a flush of the file's buffers, causing all data not yet written to be saved to the file.

```
virtual LONG Seek(LONG lOffset, UINT nOrigin);
```

Changes the current file's position to the position specified by *lOffset*, from the origin specified by *nOrigin*. Valid values for *nOrigin* include those in Table 20.11.

Table 20.11. Origin values for Seek.

Origin	Description
CFile::begin	Determine the new position by counting from the beginning of the file.
CFile::current	Determine the new position by counting from the current position.
CFile::end	Determine the new position by counting back from the end of the file.

```
SeekToBegin();
```

Used to move the file's pointer to the beginning of the file.

```
SeekToEnd();
```

Used to move the file's pointer to the end of the file.

```
virtual DWORD GetLength();
```

Returns the length, in bytes, of the file. The length returned may be less than the space allocated for the file.

```
virtual void SetLength(const DWORD dwDesiredLength);
```

Resets the length of the file to the value contained in `dwDesiredLength`. The file's size is expanded or contracted as necessary.

```
virtual void LockRange(DWORD dwPosition, DWROD dwSize);
```

Used to lock `dwSize` bytes starting from `dwPosition`

```
virtual void UnLockRange(DWORD dwPosition, DWROD dwSize);
```

Used to unlock `dwSize` bytes starting from `dwPosition`

```
virtual DWORD GetPosition();
```

Returns the current position of the file pointer.

```
virtual BOOL GetStatus(CFileStatus& Status) const;
static BOOL PASCAL GetStatus(const char* szFileName,
    CFileStatus& Status) const;
```

Used to obtain the status of the open file. In the second version you specifiy the name of a file, while in the first version the currently open file's status is returned. The members of the `CFileStatus` structure are described in Table 20.12.

Table 20.12. `CFileStatus` structure members.

Member	Description
`CTime m_ctime`	File's creation time and date.
`CTime m_Mtime`	File's last modification time and date.
`CTime m_atime`	File's last access (read) time and date.

Member	Description
`LONG m_size`	File's length in bytes (identical to the length returned by DOS's DIR command).
`BYTE m_attribute`	File's attributes as defined by DOS. Valid attribute values are defined as an MFC enum type, and can be specified symbolically as: `num attributes {` `normal = 0x00` `readOnly = 0x01` `hidden = 0x02` `system = 0x04` `volume = 0x08` `directory = 0x10`
`char m_szFullName[_MAX_PATH]`	File's absolute name.

```
static void Rename(const char* szOldName, const char* szNewName);
```

Used to rename the file specified by `szOldName` to the name contained in `szNewName`.

```
static void Remove(const char* szFileName);
```

Used to delete the file specified by `szFileName`. This function, unlike the C library function `remove()`, cannot delete a directory.

```
static void SetStatus(const char* szFileName, const CFileStatus& status);
```

Used to set the status of the open file. See **`GetStatus`**, above, for a description of the `CFileStatus` structure.

Constructor and Destructor

```
CFile();
CFile(int hFile);
CFile(const char* szFileName, UINT nOpenFlags);
```

Used to construct a **`CFile`** object from either a filename path or from a file handle. The *`nOpenFlags`* are described in Table 20.13.

Table 20.13. Open flags for `CFile`.

Flag	Description
`CFile::modeCreate`	Creates a new file, or truncates an existing file to a length of zero.
`CFile::modeRead`	Opens, read only.
`CFile::modeReadWrite`	Opens for read and write.
`CFile::modeWrite`	Opens for write only.
`CFile::modeNoInherit`	The file cannot be inherited by any child processes.
`CFile::shareDenyNone`	Opens the file; does not deny other processes read or write access to the file. Fails if the file has already been opened in compatibility mode by another process.
`CFile::shareDenyRead`	Opens the file; denies other processes read access to the file. Fails if the file has already been opened in compatibility mode, or read access, by another process.
`CFile::shareDenyWrite`	Opens the file; denies other processes write access to the file. Fails if the file has already been opened in compatibility mode, or write access, by another process.
`CFile::shareExclusive`	Opens the file; denies other processes read and write access to the file. Fails if the file has already been opened in read or write access, by another process, including the current process.
`CFile::shareCompat`	Opens the file in compatibility mode, allowing any other processes to open the file as desired. Fails if the file has been opened with any of the other sharing modes.

Flag	Description
CFile::typeText	Opens the file in text mode (for derived classes only).
CFile::typeBinary	Opens the file in binary mode (for derived classes only).

See Also

CStdioFile, CMemFile	Classes derived from CFile

CFileDialog

Inheritance Hierarchy

CObject -> CCmdTarget -> CWnd -> CDialog -> CFileDialog

Summary

```
#include <afxdlgs.h>

class CFileDialog : public CDialog
{
    DECLARE_DYNAMIC(CFileDialog)
public:
// Constructor:
    CFileDialog(BOOL bOpenFileDialog, // TRUE for FileOpen,
                                      //   FALSE for FileSaveAs
        LPCSTR lpszDefExt = NULL,
        LPCSTR lpszFileName = NULL,
        DWORD dwFlags = OFN_HIDEREADONLY ¦ OFN_OVERWRITEPROMPT,
        LPCSTR lpszFilter = NULL,
        CWnd* pParentWnd = NULL);

// Attributes:
    OPENFILENAME m_ofn;

// Operations:
    virtual int DoModal();

    CString GetPathName() const;  // Returns full pathname
    CString GetFileName() const;  // Returns only filename
    CString GetFileExt() const;   // Returns only extension
```

```
    CString GetFileTitle() const; // Returns file title
    BOOL    GetReadOnlyPref() const; // Returns TRUE if user
                              //   checks off the read-only box

// Diagnostic support
#ifdef _DEBUG
    virtual void Dump(CDumpContext& dc) const;
#endif

// Hidden implementation details....
};
```

Description

CFileDialog is a modal dialog box derived from CDialog. The CFileDialog class displays a standard dialog box that enables the user to select a file. This dialog box uses the COMMDLG functions introduced in Windows 3.1. Specifically, CFileDialog incorporates the OPENFILENAME structure and the COMMDLG functions GetOpenFileName and GetSaveFileName.

To use a CFileDialog object, you essentially construct one with its constructor and call the DoModal member function. If this function returns IDOK, you can call GetPathName or GetFileName to acquire the filename selected by the user.

You'll find more information on the CFileDialog class from the TN013.TXT technical note in the DOC subdirectory of the directory in which the Microsoft Foundation Class Library is installed. (For example, if you installed Microsoft Visual C++ in drive D:, this directory should be D:\MSVC\MFC\DOC.)

Member Variables

OPENFILENAME **m_ofn**;

Holds information needed to initialize the file selection dialog box.

Member Functions

Constructor

```
CFileDialog(
    BOOL bOpenFileDialog, // TRUE for FileOpen dialog box
                          // FALSE for FileSaveAs dialog box
    LPCSTR lpszDefExt = NULL,  // Default extension
    LPCSTR lpszFileName = NULL,// Initial filename
    DWORD dwFlags = OFN_HIDEREADONLY |    // Flags to customize
                OFN_OVERWRITEPROMPT, // the dialog box
```

```
    LPCSTR lpszFilter = NULL,  // A list of suffixes, such
            // as "Data files (*.dat)¦Defn files (*.def)¦¦"
    CWnd* pParentWnd = NULL); // Pointer to parent window
```

Creates the file-selection dialog box using the specified attributes.

Operations

```
virtual int DoModal();
```

Begins interaction with the user. Returns `IDOK` if the user selects `OK`; returns `IDCANCEL` if user cancels the dialog box.

```
CString GetFileExt() const;
```

Returns the file extension only—without the period (.).

```
CString GetFileName() const;
```

Returns only the filename.

```
CString GetFileTitle() const; // returns file title
```

Returns the title of the file, which you should use as the caption for the window.

```
CString GetPathName() const;
```

Returns the complete pathname of the file selected by the user.

```
BOOL GetReadOnlyPref() const;
```

Returns `TRUE` if the user clicks the read-only box in the dialog box. In this case, open the file for reading only.

See Also

`CDialog`	Base classes of `CFileDialog`
`CColorDialog,` `CPrintDialog,` `CFindReplaceDialog,` `CFontDialog`	Other dialog box classes

CFileException

Inheritance Hierarchy

```
CObject -> CException -> CFileException
```

Summary

```
class CFileException : public CException
{
    DECLARE_DYNAMIC(CFileException)
```

```
public:
// Constructors:

    CFileException(int cause = CFileException::none, LONG lOsError = -1);

// Attributes:
    int m_cause;
    LONG m_lOsError;

// Operations:

    // Convert DOS error codes to m_cause values
    static int PASCAL OsErrorToException(LONG lOsError);
    static int PASCAL ErrnoToException(int nErrno);

    // Functions to throw the exception after
    //    Converting error code to an m_cause value:
    static void PASCAL ThrowOsError(LONG lOsError);
    static void PASCAL ThrowErrno(int nErrno);

#ifdef _DEBUG
    virtual void Dump(CDumpContext&) const;
#endif
};
```

Description

`CFileException` is derived from the `CException` class and represents a file related exception condition.

Member Variables

`int` **`m_cause`**

Contains portable code corresponding to the exception cause. The cause values are listed in Table 20.14.

Table 20.14. `m_cause` values.

Value	Description
`CFileException::none`	There was no error.
`CFileException::generic`	The error was not specified.

Value	Description
`CFileException::fileNotFound`	The file was not found.
`CFileException::badPath`	All or part of the path was invalid.
`CFileException::tooManyOpenFiles`	There were too many files open.
`CFileException::accessDenied`	The file could not be accessed, probably due to a sharing error.
`CFileException::invalidFile`	The file handle was not valid.
`CFileException::removeCurrentDir`	Cannot remove the current directory.
`CFileException::directoryFull`	The limit on the number of root-directory entries has been reached.
`CFileException::badSeek`	The file pointer couldn't be moved to the desired position. Either the seek was before the beginning of the file, or the file had to be extended and there was insufficient disk space.
`CFileException::hardIO`	The hardware reported an error.
`CFileException::sharingViolation`	SHARE.EXE has not been run, or a shared region was locked.
`CFileException::lockViolation`	The region being locked is already locked.
`CFileException::diskFull`	The disk is full.
`CFileException::endOfFile`	The end of file has been reached.

`long` **`m_lOsError`**

Used to hold the DOS error number. It's necessary to consult the DOS technical reference to determine the values that can be stored in this variable, which can vary with different versions of DOS.

Member Functions

```
static int OsErrorToException(LONG OSError);
```

Returns an enumerator that corresponds to the DOS error number, *OSError*. It's necessary to consult the DOS technical reference to determine the values that can be stored in *OSError*, which can vary with different versions of DOS. See `CFileException::m_cause`.

```
static int ErrnoToException(int nErrorNumber);
```

Returns an enumerator that corresponds to the library error code in *nErrorNumber*. It's necessary to consult the DOS technical reference to determine the values that can be stored in *nErrorNumber*. See `CFileException::m_cause`.

```
static void PASCAL ThrowOsError(LONG OSError);
```

Throws a file exception based on *OSError*, which specifies a DOS error number.

```
static void PASCAL ThrowErrno(int nErrorNumber);
```

Throws a file exception based on an *nErrorNumber*, which specifies a library error number (defined in `ERRNO.H`).

Constructor and Destructor

```
CFileException(int nCause = CFileException::none, LONG OSError = -1);
```

Constructs a CFileException object.

Creates a `CFileException` object and stores the cause of the exception and the DOS error code in the object.

See Also

`CFile`	MFC's file-handling classes

CFindReplaceDialog

Inheritance Hierarchy

`CObject -> CCmdTarget -> CWnd -> CDialog -> CFindReplaceDialog`

Summary

```
#include <afxdlgs.h>
class CFindReplaceDialog : public CDialog
{
    DECLARE_DYNAMIC(CFindReplaceDialog)
public:
// Constructor:
// Always use as follows:
```

```
//      CFindReplaceDialog* p_frd = new CFindReplaceDialog;
//      p_frd->Create(.....)

    CFindReplaceDialog();

// Creating the window
    BOOL Create(BOOL bFindDialogOnly, // TRUE for Find,
                                      //   FALSE for FindReplace
            LPCSTR lpszFindWhat,
            LPCSTR lpszReplaceWith  = NULL,
            DWORD dwFlags = FR_DOWN,
            CWnd* pParentWnd = NULL);

// Attributes:
    FINDREPLACE m_fr;

    static CFindReplaceDialog* GetNotifier(LONG lParam);

// Operations:
    CString GetReplaceString() const;// Get replacement string
    CString GetFindString() const;   // Get find string
    BOOL SearchDown() const;         // TRUE means search down,
                                     // FALSE = search up

    BOOL FindNext() const;           // TRUE = find next
    BOOL MatchCase() const;          // TRUE = match case
    BOOL MatchWholeWord() const; // TRUE = match whole words
    BOOL ReplaceCurrent() const; // TRUE = replace current string
    BOOL ReplaceAll() const;     // TRUE = replace all occurrences
    BOOL IsTerminating() const;  // TRUE = terminate dialog box

// Diagnostic support
#ifdef _DEBUG
    virtual void Dump(CDumpContext& dc) const;
#endif

// Hidden implementation details....
};
```

Description

The `CFindReplaceDialog` class provides a modeless dialog box that you can use to ask the user for a Find/Replace string pair. This is a dual-purpose dialog box: you can use it to prompt for a string to find, and you also can use it to implement a Find/Replace dialog box. To use `CFindReplaceDialog`, you must create an uninitialized instance of the dialog box using the new operator. Then, call its `Create` member function to create the dialog box's window and make it visible.

Because `CFindReplaceDialog` is a modeless dialog box, you must register a message named `FINDMSGSTRING` and declare a handler for that message in your application's main window. You also must include an entry in the message map in order to map that registered message to the message handler. Here are some code fragments showing how this is done:

```
// In header file....

class MyWindow : public CFrameWnd
{
public:
// Various members....

protected:
// Static pointer to a CFindReplaceDialog object.
    static CFindReplace* theFRD;

// Variable to store ID returned by RegisterMessage
    static UINT frd_message;

// Handler for FINDMSGSTRING message....
    afx_msg LONG FRDMsgHandler(UINT wParam, LONG lParam);

    DECLARE_MESSAGE_MAP()
};

//-----------------------------------------------------------
// In .CPP file....

BEGIN_MESSAGE_MAP(MyWindow, CFrameWnd)
// Usual message map entries
//...
    ON_REGISTERED_MESSAGE(frd_message, FRDMsgHandler)
END_MESSAGE_MAP

// Register the FINDMSGSTRING message....
UINT MyWindow::frd_message = ::RegisterMessage(FINDMSGSTRING);

    UINT nFlags);
```

```
// Initialize the "global" CFindReplaceDialog pointer to NULL:
CFindReplace* MyWindow::theFRD = NULL;

// Create a CFindReplaceDialog and initialize....

//-------------------------------------------------------------
// The message-handler....
LONG MyWindow::FRDMsgHandler(UINT wParam, LONG lParam)
{
// First, get a pointer to the dialog box object:
    CFindReplaceDialog* p_frd = CFindReplace::GetNotifier(lParam);

// Now access member functions of CFindReplaceDialog through
// the pointer:

    if(p_frd->IsTerminating())
    {
// Dialog box is being terminated...do any necessary cleanups.
// ...
    }

// Get the "find" string....
    CString fstr = p_frd->GetFindString();

// Continue from here....

}
```

Member Variables

`FINDREPLACE m_fr;`

Contains information on customizing the appearance and behavior of the `CFindReplaceDialog` object.

Member Functions

Constructor

`CFindReplaceDialog();`

Constructs a `CFindReplaceDialog` object, but does not create the window. Call `Create` to make the dialog box visible.

Creating the Window

```
BOOL Create(
    BOOL bFindDialogOnly, // TRUE for Find dialog box
                          // FALSE for Find/Replace dialog box
```

```
LPCSTR lpszFindWhat,  // Default search string
LPCSTR lpszReplaceWith  = NULL, // Default replacement
DWORD dwFlags = FR_DOWN, // Flags to customize the dialog box
CWnd* pParentWnd = NULL);// Pointer to parent window
```

Creates the dialog box and makes it visible.

Accessing the Dialog Box in Message Handler

`static CFindReplaceDialog* GetNotifier(LONG lParam);`

Calls this function in the message handler for the `FINDMSGSTRING` message in order to get a pointer back to the `CFindReplaceDialog` object. See the "Description" section for more details.

Operations

`CString GetReplaceString() const;`

Returns the replacement string.

`CString GetFindString() const;`

Returns the string the user wants to find.

`BOOL SearchDown() const;`

Returns `TRUE` if the user wants to search down; returns `FALSE` if the user wants to search up.

`BOOL FindNext() const;`

Returns `TRUE` if the user selects the `Find Next` button from the dialog box; otherwise, the function returns `FALSE`.

`BOOL MatchCase() const;`

Returns `TRUE` if the user wants an exact match in case during the find operation.

`BOOL MatchWholeWord() const;`

Returns `TRUE` if the user wants to match whole words during the find operation.

`BOOL ReplaceCurrent() const;`

Returns `TRUE` if the user wants to replace the current occurrence of the string.

`BOOL ReplaceAll() const;`

Returns `TRUE` if the user selects the `Replace All` button.

`BOOL IsTerminating() const;`

Returns `TRUE` if the dialog box is terminating.

See Also

`CDialog`	Base class of `CFindReplaceDialog`
`CPrintDialog, CFileDialog, CFontDialog, CColorDialog`	Other dialog box classes

CFont

Inheritance Hierarchy

`CObject -> CGdiObject -> CFont`

Summary

```
#include <afxwin.h>
class CFont : public CGdiObject
{
    DECLARE_DYNAMIC(CFont)
public:
// Constructor (you must call Create to initialize):
    CFont();

// Construct a specific font:
    BOOL CreateFontIndirect(LPLOGFONT lpLogFont);
    BOOL CreateFont(
        int nHeight, int nWidth, int nEscapement,
        int nOrientation, int nWeight,
        BYTE bItalic, BYTE bUnderline,
        BYTE cStrikeOut, BYTE nCharSet,
        BYTE nOutPrecision, BYTE nClipPrecision,
        BYTE nQuality, BYTE nPitchAndFamily,
        LPCSTR lpFacename);

// Utility function:
    static CFont* FromHandle(HFONT hFont);
};
```

Description

`CFont` is the C++ class equivalent of the Windows font resource. `CFont` includes member functions for associating a specific Windows font with a `CFont` object. After creating a font, you must select it in a DC to use it for text output.

Member Functions

```
BOOL CreateFont(
    int    nHeight,          // Height of char in logical units
    int    nWidth,           // Width of characters in logical
                             //   units
    int    nEscapement,      // Orientation of line through
                             //   first and last character on a line
    int    nOrientation,     // Orientation of baseline in 0.1
                             //   degree units clockwise from x-axis
    int    nWeight,          // Weight of font (range 0 - 1000,
                             //   normal = 400, bold = 700)
    BYTE   bItalic,          // Nonzero = italic font
    BYTE   bUnderline,       // Nonzero = underlined font
    BYTE   cStrikeOut,       // Nonzero = strikeout characters
    BYTE   nCharSet,         // Character set (ANSI, OEM, SYMBOL)
    BYTE   nOutPrecision,    // Output precision
    BYTE   nClipPrecision,   // How to clip characters at the
                             //   edge of the clipping region
    BYTE   nQuality,         // Quality (default, draft, proof)
    BYTE   nPitchAndFamily,// Font's pitch and family
    LPCSTR lpFacename);      // Name of font's typeface
```

Initializes the `CFont` object using the specified characteristics for the font. Returns `TRUE` if successful.

```
BOOL CreateFontIndirect(LPLOGFONT lpLogFont);
```

Initializes the `CFont` object using the characteristics you specify in the `LOGFONT` structure. Returns `TRUE` if successful. Consult the Microsoft Windows SDK *Programmer's Reference, Volume 3: Messages, Structures, and Macros* for more information on the `LOGFONT` structure and how to initialize fonts.

```
static CFont* FromHandle(HFONT hFont);
```

Returns a pointer to a `CFont` object after attaching to it the Windows font specified by *hFont*. If *hFont* isn't already attached to a `Cfont`, `FromHandle` creates a temporary *CFont* object and attaches *hFont* to it. Temporary `CFonts` are destroyed during idle times in the application's event loop.

See Also

`CGdiObject`	Base class of `CFont`
`CDC`	To select a font in a DC

CFontDialog

Inheritance Hierarchy

```
CObject -> CCmdTarget -> CWnd -> CDialog -> CFontDialog
```

Summary

```
#include <afxdlgs.h>

class CFontDialog : public CDialog
{
    DECLARE_DYNAMIC(CFontDialog)
public:
// Constructor:
    CFontDialog(LPLOGFONT lplfInitial = NULL,
                DWORD dwFlags = CF_EFFECTS | CF_SCREENFONTS,
                CDC* pdcPrinter = NULL,
                CWnd* pParentWnd = NULL);

// Attributes:
    CHOOSEFONT m_cf;
    LOGFONT    m_lf;

// Operations:
    virtual int DoModal();

    void GetCurrentFont(LPLOGFONT lplf);

    CString GetFaceName() const; // Returns face name of font
    CString GetStyleName() const;// Returns style name of font
    int GetSize() const;         // Returns point size of font
    COLORREF GetColor() const;   // Returns color of font
    int GetWeight() const;       // Returns chosen font weight
    BOOL IsStrikeOut() const;    // Returns TRUE if strikeout
    BOOL IsUnderline() const;    // Returns TRUE if underline
    BOOL IsBold() const;         // Returns TRUE if bold font
    BOOL IsItalic() const;       // Returns TRUE if italic font

// Diagnostic support.
#ifdef _DEBUG
    virtual void Dump(CDumpContext& dc) const;
#endif

// Hidden implementation details....
};
```

Description

The CFontDialog class provides a standard modal dialog box for selecting a font. This class uses the common dialog box module, COMMDLG, available in Windows version 3.1. To use this dialog box, you need to construct an instance of CFontDialog and call its DoModal member function to begin interaction with the user. On return from the DoModal function, if the return value is IDOK, you can use the other member functions (such as GetFaceName and GetStyleName) to certify information about the font that the user has selected.

Most member functions are self-explanatory from their declarations, as shown in the "Summary" section. Therefore, they are not repeated in the following discussion.

Member Functions

Constructor

```
CFontDialog(
    LPLOGFONT lplfInitial = NULL,  // Initial settings
    DWORD dwFlags = CF_EFFECTS |   // Flags to customize
                    CF_SCREENFONTS,//   dialog box
    CDC*  pdcPrinter = NULL,    // Provide this when selecting
                                //   fonts for a printer
    CWnd* pParentWnd = NULL); // Pointer to a parent window
```

Constructs and initializes a CFontDialog object.

See Also

CDialog	Base classes of CFontDialog
CColorDialog, CPrintDialog, CFileDialog, CFindReplaceDialog	Other dialog box classes

CFormView

Inheritance Hierarchy

CObject -> CCmdTarget -> CWnd -> CView -> CScrollView -> CFormView

Summary

```
class CFormView : public CScrollView
{
    DECLARE_DYNAMIC(CFormView)
// Construction:
protected:
// You must derive your own constructor class when
```

```
//     you create a derived class.
    CFormView(LPCSTR lpszTemplateName);
    CFormView(UINT nIDTemplate);

// Implementation:
public:
#ifdef _DEBUG
    virtual void AssertValid() const;
    virtual void Dump(CDumpContext& dc) const;
#endif

protected:
    LPCSTR m_lpszTemplateName;
    CCreateContext* m_pCreateContext;

    virtual void OnDraw(CDC* pDC);
    virtual void OnInitialUpdate();
    // The special case of override a child window creation
    virtual BOOL Create(LPCSTR, LPCSTR, DWORD,
        const RECT&, CWnd*, UINT, CCreateContext*);
    virtual BOOL PreTranslateMessage(MSG* pMsg);
    virtual WNDPROC* GetSuperWndProcAddr();

    //{{AFX_MSG(CFormView)
    afx_msg int OnCreate(LPCREATESTRUCT lpcs);
    //}}AFX_MSG
    DECLARE_MESSAGE_MAP()
};
```

Description

`CFormView` is derived from the `CScrollView` class and represents a view that contains controls (much like a dialog box). The controls are laid out using a standard dialog box template resource. The window that displays the `CFormView` object can be smaller than the actual defined form because the `CScrollView` class from which it's derived provides scroll bars to allow scrolling the form.

Member Functions

Constructor and Destructor

`CFormView``(LPCSTR` *`szTemplateName`*`);`
`CFormView``(UINT` *`nTemplateResourceID`*`);`

Creates a `CFormView` object, with either *`szTemplateName`* or *`nTemplateResourceID`* identifiying the dialog box template that defines the view.

When creating derived classes, you must create your own constructor. In your constructor, call **CFormView::CFormView()**, as described in the above paragraph.

See Also

CScrollView	Base class of CFormView
CView	Class from which CScrollView is derived.

CFrameWnd

Inheritance Hierarchy

```
CObject -> CCmdTarget -> CWnd -> CFrameWnd
```

Summary

```
#include <afxwin.h>
class CFrameWnd : public CWnd
{
    DECLARE_DYNAMIC(CFrameWnd)
public:
// Constructor and destructor:
    CFrameWnd();
    virtual ~CFrameWnd();

// Create the window:
    BOOL Create(LPCSTR lpClassName,
                LPCSTR lpWindowName,
                DWORD dwStyle = WS_OVERLAPPEDWINDOW,
                const RECT& rect = rectDefault,
                const CWnd* pParentWnd = NULL,
                                          //Not NULL for pop-ups
                LPCSTR lpMenuName = NULL);

// Member variable:
    static const CRect NEAR rectDefault;

// Operations:
    BOOL LoadAccelTable(LPCSTR lpAccelTableName);
    virtual CFrameWnd* GetParentFrame();
    virtual CFrameWnd* GetChildFrame();

// Diagnostic support:
#ifdef _DEBUG
```

```
    virtual void AssertValid() const;
    virtual void Dump(CDumpContext& dc) const;
#endif

// Hidden implementation details....
};
```

Description

The `CFrameWnd` class provides the functionality of a Windows window with the overlapped or pop-up style. You usually derive your application's main window class from the `CFrameWnd` class. In the derived window class, you must provide a message map that links Windows messages to message handlers—you need to override message handlers only for those Windows messages that your application needs. You may also add member variables to store data specific to your application.

Chapter 16, "Using the Microsoft Foundation Class Library," provides a tutorial with an example that demonstrates how to derive your own window class from `CFrameWnd`.

Member Variables

`static const CRect NEAR` *`rectDefault`*`;`

This is a rectangle you pass to the `Create` function to specify the position and size of a window.

Member Functions

Constructor and Destructor

`CFrameWnd();`

Constructs a `CFrameWnd` object without any window. Call `Create` to attach a window to the `CFrameWnd` object.

`virtual ~CFrameWnd();`

Destroys a `CFrameWnd` object (including its window) and posts a `WM_QUIT` message to close the application.

Creating the Window

```
BOOL Create(
    LPCSTR lpClassName,    // Windows class name for the window
                           //   you're creating (NULL = use defaults)
    LPCSTR lpWindowName, // Name to appear in title bar
    DWORD dwStyle = WS_OVERLAPPEDWINDOW, // Window style
    const RECT& rect = rectDefault, // Position and size of window
    const CWnd* pParentWnd = NULL,  // Parent for pop-ups
    LPCSTR lpMenuName = NULL);      // Name of menu resource to
                                    //   use with the window
```

Creates a window of the specified style and attaches it to this `CFrameWnd` object. Table 20.23 (Window styles for Microsoft Windows) in the reference pages on `CWnd` class shows the names of the window styles. You can use a bitwise-OR combination of these styles as the *`dwStyle`* argument.

Operations

```
virtual CFrameWnd* GetChildFrame();
```

Returns a pointer to `CFrameWnd` (it returns `this`). Override this function in the derived class to return a pointer to the currently active child window.

```
virtual CFrameWnd* GetParentFrame();
```

Returns a pointer to `CFrameWnd` (it returns `this`). Override this function in the derived class to return a pointer to the parent window.

```
BOOL LoadAccelTable(
    LPCSTR lpAccelTableName); // Name of accelerator
                              //   table resource
```

Loads the specified accelerator table into the `CFrameWnd` object. The accelerator table is a list of shortcut keystrokes that activate menu selections. Returns `TRUE` if successful.

See Also

`CWnd`	Base class of `CFrameWnd`; lists all message handlers
`CMDIFrameWnd`, `CMDIChildWnd`	Window classes for MDI

CGdiObject

Inheritance Hierarchy

```
CObject -> CGdiObject
```

Summary

```
#include <afxwin.h>
class CGdiObject : public CObject
{
    DECLARE_DYNAMIC(CGdiObject)
public:
// Constructor and destructor:

// (You should not use CGdiObject directly. Rather, use
// classes derived from CGdiObject.)
```

```
    CGdiObject();
    virtual ~CGdiObject();
    BOOL DeleteObject();

// Attributes:
    HANDLE m_hObject;
    HANDLE GetSafeHandle() const;

    static CGdiObject* FromHandle(HANDLE hObject);
    static void DeleteTempMap();
    BOOL   Attach(HANDLE hObject);
    HANDLE Detach();

// Operations:
    int  GetObject(int nCount, void FAR* lpObject) const;
    BOOL CreateStockObject(int nIndex);
    BOOL UnrealizeObject();

// Diagnostic support:
#ifdef _DEBUG
    virtual void Dump(CDumpContext& dc) const;
#endif
};
```

Description

`CGdiObject` is the base class for all graphics device interface (GDI) drawing tools, such as fonts, bitmaps, pens, and brushes. You need not use the `CGdiObject` class directly, but you will create instances of classes derived from `CGdiObject`, such as `CPen` and `CBrush`.

See Also

`CBrush, CBitmap, CFont, CPen, CPalette, CRgn`	GDI classes derived from `CGdiObject`
`CDC`	To select GDI objects for a DC

CHEdit

Inheritance Hierarchy

`CObject -> CCmdTarget -> CWnd -> CEdit -> CHEdit`

Summary

```
#include <afxwin.h>

class CHEdit : public CWnd
{
    DECLARE_DYNAMIC(CHEdit)
public:

// Constructor:
    CHEdit();

// Initializing Edit
    BOOL Create(DWORD dwStyle, const RECT& rect,
                CWnd* pParentWnd, UINT nID);

// Attributes:
    BOOL  CanUndo() const;
    int   GetLineCount() const;
    BOOL  GetModify() const;
    void  SetModify(BOOL bModified = TRUE);
    void  GetRect(LPRECT lpRect) const;
    DWORD GetSel() const;
    HANDLE  GetHandle() const;
    void    SetHandle(HANDLE hBuffer);

// Convention: First word in lpBuffer is the size of the buffer:
    int GetLine(int nIndex, LPSTR lpBuffer) const;
    int GetLine(int nIndex, LPSTR lpBuffer, int nMaxLength) const;

// Operations:
    void EmptyUndoBuffer();
    BOOL FmtLines(BOOL bAddEOL);

    void LimitText(int nChars = 0);
    int  LineFromChar(int nIndex = -1) const;
    int  LineIndex(int nLine = -1) const;
    int  LineLength(int nLine = -1) const;
    void LineScroll(int nLines, int nChars = 0);
    void ReplaceSel(LPCSTR lpNewText);
    void SetPasswordChar(char ch);
    void SetRect(LPRECT lpRect);
    void SetRectNP(LPRECT lpRect);
    void SetSel(DWORD dwSelection);
```

```
    void SetSel(int nStartChar, int nEndChar);
    BOOL SetTabStops(int nTabStops, LPINT rgTabStops);
    void SetTabStops();
    BOOL SetTabStops(int cxEachStop);

// Working with the Clipboard:
    BOOL Undo();
    void Clear();
    void Copy();
    void Cut();
    void Paste();

#if (WINVER >= 0x030a) // Windows 3.1 or later only

    BOOL SetReadOnly(BOOL bReadOnly = TRUE);
    int  GetFirstVisibleLine() const;
    char GetPasswordChar() const;

#endif

// Hidden implementation details....

};
```

Description

`CHEdit` is derived from the `CEdit` class and represents an object used to encapsulate the functionality of handwriting in a `CEdit` object. Because **`CHEdit`** is derived from `CEdit`, all of the functionality of the **`CEdit`** object is present in the **`CHEdit`** object. (This functionality is not reviewed in this section. See `CEdit` for more details.) Note: when discussing pen computing, the term *ink* refers to the actual handwriting input by the user. For example, the function **`GetInkHandle()`** gets a handle to whatever the user has written in the `hedit` control.

Member Functions

`BOOL` **`GetInflate`**`(LPRECTOFS` *`lpRectOffset`*`);`

Gets the rectangle in which handwriting is recognized, and places the rectangle in *`lpRectOffset`*. This rectangle is called the *inflation rectangle.*

`HPENDATA` **`GetInkHandle`**`();`

Used to obtain the handle to captured ink, which may be useful after the `hedit` control has been destroyed. Returns `NULL` if the control is not in the ink mode.

```
BOOL GetRC(LPRC RecognitionContext);
```

Used to get a pointer (placed in the `RC` structure `RecognitionContext`) to the current recognition context. The `RC` structure contains the following:

```
typedef struct tagRC
   {
   HREC hrec;
   HWND hwnd;
   UINT wEventRef;
   UINT wRcPreferences;
   LONG lRcOptions;
   RCYIELDPROC lpfnYield;
   BYTE lpUser[cbRcUserMax];
   UINT wCountry;
   UINT wIntlPreferences;
   char lpLanguage[cbRcLanguageMax];
   LPDF rglpdf[MAXDICTIONARIES];
   UINT wTryDictionary;
   CL clErrorLevel;
   ALC alc;
   ALC alcPriority;
   BYTE rgbfAlc[cbRcrgbfAlcMax];
   UINT wResultMode;
   UINT wTimeOut;
   LONG lPcm;
   RECT rectBound;
   RECT rectExclude;
   GUIDE guide;
   UINT wRcOrient;
   UINT wRcDirect;
   int nInkWidth;
   COLORREF rgbInk;
   DWORD dwAppParam;
   DWORD dwDictParam;
   DWORD dwRecognizer;
   UINT rgwReserved[cwRcReservedMax];
   }
   RC, FAR *LPRC;
```

Because the `RC` default values are shared by all applications, they should be modified only by the Control Panel and not by application programs.

```
BOOL GetUnderline();
```

Returns a nonzero value if the control's underline mode is set, otherwise returns a zero value specifying that underline mode is not set.

```
BOOL SetInflate(LPRECTOFS lpRectOffset);
```

Sets the rectangle in which handwriting is recognized (the *inflation rectangle*) from the rectangle in `lpRectOffset`.

```
BOOL SetInkMode(HPENDATA hInitialPenData = NULL);
```

Starts the initial collection of inking. If `hInitialPenData` is specified, offsets are considered to be relative to the upper-left corner of the client rectangle of the `hedit` control. A `PENDATA` structure can be created using the `CreatePenData()` function, which is part of the pen-computing extensions to Windows.

```
BOOL SetRC(LPRC Rc);
```

Sets a pointer to a recognition context. For more information about recognition contexts, see **`GetRC()`**.

```
BOOL SetUnderline(BOOL bUnderline = TRUE);
```

Turns on (`bUnderline = TRUE`), or off (`bUnderline = FALSE`), the underline mode. To use the underline mode, it's necessary to have the `hedit` control's border turned off.

```
BOOL StopInkMode(UINT Action);
```

Used to stop the collection of ink. The `Action` code specifies one of the codes shown in Table 20.15.

Table 20.15. `StopInkMode` action codes.

Code	Description
HEP_RECOG	Perform a recognition of the ink, and display the text as translated.
HEP_NORECOG	Remove the ink, do not perform a recognition.
HEP_WAITFORTAP	Recognize the ink, and display the text as translated.

Constructor and Destructor

```
CHEdit();
```

Constructs a `CEdit` object. However, you must still call `Create` to attach a window to the `CEdit` object.

Initializing Edit

```
BOOL Create(
    DWORD dwStyle,      // Style of edit window (see online
                        //   documentation or SDK manuals)
    const RECT& rect,   // Position and size of the edit window
    CWnd* pParentWnd,   // Pointer to the parent window
    UINT  nID);         // Edit control's ID
```

Creates the edit control's window. For a list of valid styles of edit windows, consult Microsoft Visual C++'s online documentation or the `CreateWindow` function in the Microsoft Windows SDK *Programmer's Reference, Volume 2: Functions.* `Create` returns `TRUE` if successful.

See Also

`CEdit`	Non-pen based edit control class, from which **`CHEdit`** is derived
`CWnd`	Class from which `CEdit` is derived

CListBox

Inheritance Hierarchy

`CObject -> CCmdTarget -> CWnd -> CListBox`

Summary

```
#include <afxwin.h>
class CListBox : public CWnd
{
    DECLARE_DYNAMIC(CListBox)
public:
// Constructor:
    CListBox();

// Create the window:
    BOOL Create(DWORD dwStyle, const RECT& rect,
                CWnd* pParentWnd, UINT nID);

// Attributes of entire list box:
    int GetCount() const;
    int GetHorizontalExtent() const;
    void SetHorizontalExtent(int cxExtent);
    int GetTopIndex() const;
    int SetTopIndex(int nIndex);
```

```
    int FindString(int nStartAfter, LPCSTR lpItem) const;
    int SelectString(int nStartAfter, LPCSTR lpItem);
    int SelItemRange(BOOL bSelect, int nFirstItem,
                     int nLastItem);

// Overrideable functions (you must override draw, measure,
// and compare for owner-drawn list boxes):
    virtual void DrawItem(LPDRAWITEMSTRUCT lpDrawItemStruct);
    virtual void MeasureItem(LPMEASUREITEMSTRUCT
                                       lpMeasureItemStruct);
    virtual int CompareItem(LPCOMPAREITEMSTRUCT
                                       lpCompareItemStruct);
    virtual void DeleteItem(LPDELETEITEMSTRUCT
                                        lpDeleteItemStruct);

// Hidden implementation details....
};
```

Description

CListBox is the C++ class equivalent of the Windows list box control. In keeping with the philosophy of providing a layer of classes on the Windows Application Programming Interface (API), the Microsoft Foundation Class Library defines the **CListBox** class to include the following:

- A handle to a Windows list box as a member variable
- Member functions that mimic sending list box messages (with message names that start with the LB_ prefix) when you program with the Windows SDK

Notice that the indexes for items in the list box start at zero; thus, the first item's index is 0.

Member Functions

Constructor

CListBox();

Constructs a **CListBox** without the window. Call **Create** to set up the window.

Creating the Window

```
BOOL Create(
    DWORD dwStyle,      // Style of list box
    const RECT& rect,   // Position and size of list box
    CWnd* pParentWnd,   // Pointer to parent window
    UINT nID);          // List box identifier
```

```
// Attributes of single-selection list boxes:
    int GetCurSel() const;
    int SetCurSel(int nSelect);

// Attributes of multiple-selection list boxes:
    int GetSel(int nIndex) const;
    int SetSel(int nIndex, BOOL bSelect = TRUE);
    int GetSelCount() const;
    int GetSelItems(int nMaxItems, LPINT rgIndex) const;

// Attributes of list box items:
    DWORD GetItemData(int nIndex) const;
    int SetItemData(int nIndex, DWORD dwItemData);
    int GetItemRect(int nIndex, LPRECT lpRect) const;
    int GetText(int nIndex, LPSTR lpBuffer) const;
    int GetTextLen(int nIndex) const;
    void GetText(int nIndex, CString& rString) const;

// You can set the following attributes, but cannot get them:
    void SetColumnWidth(int cxWidth);
    BOOL SetTabStops(int nTabStops, LPINT rgTabStops);
    void SetTabStops();
    BOOL SetTabStops(int cxEachStop);

// The following functions are available only in Windows
// version 3.1 or later:

#if (WINVER >= 0x030a)
    int SetItemHeight(int nIndex, UINT cyItemHeight);
    int GetItemHeight(int nIndex) const;
    int FindStringExact(int nIndexStart, LPCSTR lpszFind) const;
    int GetCaretIndex() const;
    int SetCaretIndex(int nIndex, BOOL bScroll = TRUE);
#endif  /* WINVER >= 0x030a */

// Manipulating list box items:
    int AddString(LPCSTR lpItem);
    int DeleteString(UINT nIndex);
    int InsertString(int nIndex, LPCSTR lpItem);
    void ResetContent();
    int Dir(UINT attr, LPCSTR lpWildCard);
```

Creates a list box with the specified style and attaches it to this `CListBox` object. `Create` returns `TRUE` if successful. For a complete list of applicable list box styles (*dwStyle*), consult the `CreateWindow` function in the Microsoft Windows SDK *Programmer's Reference, Volume 2: Functions.*

List Box Attributes

```
int GetCaretIndex() const; // Windows 3.1 or later only
```

Returns the index of the list box item with the focus.

```
int GetCount() const;
```

Returns the number of items in the list box or `LB_ERR` if an error occurs.

```
int GetHorizontalExtent() const;
```

Returns the width in pixels by which the list box can be scrolled horizontally. The list box must be created with the `WS_HSCROLL` style for this function to work.

```
int GetItemHeight(int nIndex) const; // Windows 3.1 or later
```

Returns the height (in pixels) of a specified item in the list box.

```
int GetTopIndex() const;
```

Returns the index of the first visible item in a list box.

```
int SetCaretIndex( // In Windows version 3.1 or later
    int  nIndex,     // Set focus to this item
    BOOL bScroll = TRUE); // TRUE = scroll to make item visible
```

Sets the focus to the specified item and returns `LB_ERR` if an error occurs.

```
void SetHorizontalExtent(int cxExtent); // x-extent in pixels
```

Sets the number of pixels by which the list box can be scrolled horizontally.

```
int SetItemHeight(       // In Windows version 3.1 or later
    int  nIndex,         // Set height of this item
    UINT cyItemHeight); // Height in pixels
```

Sets the height of an item in pixels and returns `LB_ERR` if an error occurs.

```
int SetTopIndex(int nIndex); // Index of topmost line
```

This function positions the specified item as the first visible item in the list box and returns `LB_ERR` if an error occurs.

Single-Selection List Boxes

```
int GetCurSel() const;
```

Returns the index of the currently selected item in the list box. The return value is `LB_ERR` if nothing is selected or if the list box permits multiple selections.

```
int SetCurSel(int nSelect); // Index of item to be selected
```

Sets the specified item as the currently selected item and returns `LB_ERR` if an error occurs.

Multiple-Selection List Boxes

```
int GetSel(int nIndex) const; // Is this item selected?
```

In a multiple-selection list box, `GetSel` returns a nonzero value if the specified item is selected. A zero indicates that the item is not selected. If an error occurs, the return value is `LB_ERR`.

```
int GetSelCount() const;
```

Returns the total number of items selected in a multiple-selection list box and returns `LB_ERR` if the list box does not permit multiple selection.

```
int GetSelItems(int nMaxItems, LPINT rgIndex) const;
```

Copies the index of selected items into the integer array *`rgIndex`*. A maximum of *`nMaxItems`* indexes are copied, and **`GetSelItems`** returns the actual number of item indexes copied into *`rgIndex`*.

```
int SetSel(int nIndex, BOOL bSelect = TRUE);
```

If *`bSelect`* is `TRUE`, this function marks the item specified by *`nIndex`* as selected (the item is highlighted). The item is unselected if you call `SetSel` with `FALSE` as the *`bSelect`* argument. Returns `LB_ERR` if an error occurs. If *`nIndex`* = –1, all items in the list box are affected by `SetSel`.

Manipulating List Box Items

```
DWORD GetItemData(int nIndex) const;
```

Returns the 32-bit value associated with the item at the *`nIndex`* index. This is the same value you set previously with a call to `SetItemData`.

```
int GetItemRect(int nIndex, LPRECT lpRect) const;
```

Initializes *`lpRect`* with the coordinates of the rectangle (in the coordinate frame of the list box client area) corresponding to the specified item. Returns `LB_ERR` if an error occurs.

```
int  GetText(int nIndex, LPSTR lpBuffer) const;
void GetText(int nIndex, CString& rString) const;
```

Returns the textual content of the item at `nIndex`. The text is returned in a `CString` or a buffer you allocate. When the text is copied to a buffer, `GetText` returns the number of bytes copied to the buffer.

```
int GetTextLen(int nIndex) const;
```

Returns the length of the specified item in bytes, excluding the terminating null character. The return value is `LB_ERR` in case of an error.

```
void SetColumnWidth(int cxWidth); // Column width in pixels
```

Sets the width of each column to `cxWidth` pixels in a multiple-column list box (created with a `LB_MULTICOLUMN` style).

```
int SetItemData(int nIndex, DWORD dwItemData);
```

Associates the 32-bit `dwItemData` value with the list box item at the `nIndex` index. Returns `LB_ERR` if an error occurs.

```
void SetTabStops(); // Defaults to tab stops every 2 dialog units
BOOL SetTabStops(int nTabStops, LPINT rgTabStops);
BOOL SetTabStops(int cxEachStop);
```

Sets the tab stops as indicated by an array of stops specified in `rgTabStops` or a tab stop every `cxEachStop` units. The tab stops are set in dialog units. *Dialog units* are set in terms of the character sizes of the system font (1 dialog unit along the x-axis equals one-fourth the average width of a character; 1 dialog unit along the y-axis equals one-eighth the height of a character). Returns `TRUE` if tabs are set successfully; otherwise, returns `FALSE`.

String Operations

```
int AddString(LPCSTR lpItem); // String to add
```

Adds a string at the end of the list box. This string returns the index of the newly added item in the list, or either `LB_ERR` or `LB_ERRSPACE` to indicate an error.

```
int DeleteString(UINT nIndex); // Index of string to delete
```

Deletes the item identified by `nIndex` and returns `LB_ERR` if an error occurs.

```
int Dir(UINT attr, LPCSTR lpWildCard);
```

Inserts a list of filenames in the list box. `attr` and `lpWildCard` control the types of filenames that are listed. Consult the Microsoft Visual C++ online documentation for a list of admissible attributes that you can provide for the `attr` argument. **`Dir`** returns the index of the last filename added to the list. If an error occurs, it returns `LB_ERR` or `LB_ERRSPACE`.

```
int FindString(int nStartAfter, LPCSTR lpItem) const;
```

Searches for an item with the string `lpItem` as a prefix, starting with the item after the one at index `nStartAfter`. If a matching item is found, **`FindString`** returns the index of the matching item. Returns `LB_ERR` if no match is found. The search is not case-sensitive.

```
int FindStringExact(          // Windows 3.1 or later
    int    nIndexStart,       // Start search after this item
    LPCSTR lpszFind) const;  // Look for this string
```

`FindStringExact` is like **`FindString`**, except that **`FindStringExact`** searches for an item that matches the search string (`lpszFind`) in its entirety. The search is not case-sensitive. Returns the index of the matching item, if any. If the search fails, **`FindStringExact`** returns `LB_ERR`

```
int InsertString(int nIndex, LPCSTR lpItem);
```

Inserts the string `lpItem` at the `nIndex` index. If successful, the function returns the index of the newly added item. If an error occurs, **`InsertString`** returns `LB_ERR` or `LB_ERRSPACE`, depending on the type of error. If `nIndex` = –1, the string is inserted at the end of the list box.

```
void ResetContent();
```

Removes all the items from the list box.

```
int SelectString(int nStartAfter, LPCSTR lpItem);
```

Searches the list box for an item with the `lpItem` string as a prefix. The search starts after the `nStartAfter` index. If a matching item is found, that item becomes the current selection.

```
int SelItemRange(
    BOOL bSelect,    // TRUE = select items, FALSE = unselect
    int nFirstItem, // Apply to the range of items from this one
    int nLastItem); //   to this one
```

If `bSelect` is `TRUE`, this marks a range of items selected—the selected items are also highlighted. If `bSelect` is `FALSE`, this removes the highlight from the specified range of items. Returns `LB_ERR` if an error occurs.

See Also

`CWnd`	Base class of `CListBox`
`CComboBox`	A `ComboBox` includes a `ListBox`

CMDIChildWnd

Inheritance Hierarchy

`CObject -> CCmdTarget -> CWnd -> CFrameWnd -> CMDIChildWnd`

Summary

```
#include <afxwin.h>
class CMDIChildWnd : public CFrameWnd
{
    DECLARE_DYNAMIC(CMDIChildWnd)
public:
// Constructor:
    CMDIChildWnd();

// Create the window:
    BOOL Create(LPCSTR lpClassName,
                LPCSTR lpWindowName,
                DWORD dwStyle = 0,
                const RECT& rect = rectDefault,
                CMDIFrameWnd* pParentWnd = NULL);

// Operations:
    void MDIDestroy();
    void MDIActivate();
    void MDIMaximize();
    void MDIRestore();

    virtual BOOL DestroyWindow();
    virtual CFrameWnd* GetParentFrame();

// Diagnostic support
#ifdef _DEBUG
    virtual void AssertValid() const;
    virtual void Dump(CDumpContext& dc) const;
#endif

// Hidden implementation details....
};
```

Description

The **CMDIChildWnd** class, derived from CFrameWnd, serves as the base class for child windows you derive to display documents inside a CMDIFrameWnd (the work area of an application with MDI). Like the CFrameWnd class, you usually derive your own child window class from **CMDIChildWnd** and use it to display documents inside a frame window derived from the CMDIFrameWnd class.

Member Functions

Constructor

```
CMDIChildWnd();
```

Constructs a **CMDIChildWnd** object without any window. Call **Create** to set up the window.

Creating the Window

```
BOOL Create(
    LPCSTR lpClassName,   // Windows class name for the window
    LPCSTR lpWindowName,  // Name to appear in title bar
    DWORD dwStyle = 0,    // Window's style (see Table 20.23, Window
                             styles for Microsoft Windows)
    const RECT& rect = rectDefault,    // Position and size
    CMDIFrameWnd* pParentWnd = NULL); // Pointer to the parent
```

Creates the window for the CMDIChildWnd object. The window's style is controlled by the *dwStyle* argument. Table 20.23 (Window styles for Microsoft Windows) in the reference pages for the CWnd class shows a list of symbols that you can use to specify the style.

Operations

```
virtual BOOL DestroyWindow();
```

If a window is attached to the CMDIChildWnd object, DestroyWindow calls MDIDestroy to destroy the window. Returns TRUE if the window is destroyed, or FALSE if no window is attached to this CMDIChildWnd.

```
virtual CFrameWnd* GetParentFrame();
```

This function returns a pointer to the MDI frame window.

```
void MDIActivate();
```

This function activates this MDI child window.

```
void MDIDestroy();
```

This function destroys this MDI child window.

```
void MDIMaximize();
```

This function maximizes this MDI child window.

```
void MDIRestore();
```

This function restores this MDI child window to its normal state.

See Also

CFrameWnd, CWnd	Classes in the inheritance hierarchy of CMDIChildWnd
CMDIFrameWnd	CMDIChildWnd windows are displayed inside a CMDIFrameWnd window

CMDIFrameWnd

Inheritance Hierarchy

CObject -> CCmdTarget -> CWnd -> CFrameWnd -> CMDIFrameWnd

Summary

```
#include <afxwin.h>
class CMDIFrameWnd : public CFrameWnd
{
    DECLARE_DYNAMIC(CMDIFrameWnd)
public:
// Constructor:
    CMDIFrameWnd();

// Create the window:
    BOOL Create(LPCSTR lpClassName,
                LPCSTR lpWindowName,
                DWORD dwStyle,
                const RECT& rect,
                const CWnd* pParentWnd,
                LPCSTR lpMenuName);

    virtual BOOL CreateClient(LPCREATESTRUCT lpCreateStruct,
                              CMenu* pWindowMenu);

// Attributes:
    HWND m_hWndMDIClient;
    virtual CFrameWnd* GetChildFrame();

// Operations:
    void MDIActivate(CWnd* pWndActivate);
```

```
    CMDIChildWnd* MDIGetActive(BOOL* pbMaximized = NULL) const;
    void MDIIconArrange();
    void MDIMaximize(CWnd* pWnd);
    void MDINext();
    void MDIRestore(CWnd* pWnd);
    CMenu* MDISetMenu(CMenu* pFrameMenu, CMenu* pWindowMenu);

    void MDICascade();
    void MDITile();

// Operations specific to Windows version 3.1 or later:
#if (WINVER >= 0x030a)
    void MDITile(int nType);
    void MDICascade(int nType);
#endif

// Diagnostic support:
#ifdef _DEBUG
    virtual void AssertValid() const;
#endif

// Hidden implementation details....
};
```

Description

`CMDIFrameWnd` is a special type of `CFrameWnd` that can serve as the frame window that displays one or more child windows in an application supporting multiple document interface (MDI). Generally, you derive your own MDI frame window class from the **`CMDIFrameWnd`** class and add the necessary message handlers and message map. You derive the child windows (managed in the client area of the MDI frame) from the `CMDIChildWnd` class.

A good example of using **`CMDIFrameWnd`** is the `FormView` class in Chapter 18. The `FormView` window serves as the main window for the Form fill-in application. `FormView` provides the MDI frame window within which you can display one or more forms using the `FormWindow` objects (`FormWindow` is derived from the `CMdiChildWnd` class).

Member Variables

`HWND` **`m_hWndMDIClient`**`;`

This is the handle to the client window inside the MDI frame. The *client window* is the window that actually manages the MDI child windows.

Member Functions

Constructor

```
CMDIFrameWnd();
```

Constructs **CMDIFrameWnd** without the window. Call **Create** to set up a window and attach it to this **CMDIFrameWnd** object.

Creating the Window

```
BOOL Create(
    LPCSTR lpClassName,       // Windows class name of the window
    LPCSTR lpWindowName,      // Name to appear in title bar
    DWORD  dwStyle,           // Window style (see Table 20.23, Window
                                 styles for Microsoft Windows)
    const  RECT& rect,        // Window position and size
    const  CWnd* pParentWnd,  // Pointer to the parent window
    LPCSTR lpMenuName);       // Name of menu resource that defines
                              //   the menu for this window
```

Creates an MDI frame window with the specified style and returns TRUE if successful.

```
virtual BOOL CreateClient(
    LPCREATESTRUCT lpCreateStruct, // A CREATESTRUCT structure
    CMenu* pWindowMenu);           // Pointer to menu
```

Creates the *client window*, which is a window inside the CMDIFrameWnd window and the one that actually manages the MDI child windows. You must call **CreateClient** in the OnCreate handler if you override the OnCreate member function. **CreateClient** returns TRUE if successful; otherwise, returns FALSE.

Operations

```
virtual CFrameWnd* GetChildFrame();
```

Returns a pointer to the currently active child window.

```
void MDIActivate(CWnd* pWndActivate); // Activate this child
```

Activates the MDI child window specified by the pointer *pWndActivate*.

```
void MDICascade();
void MDICascade(int nType); // Windows version 3.1 or later
```

Arranges the MDI child windows in a *cascade* (overlapping) format.

```
CMDIChildWnd* MDIGetActive(BOOL* pbMaximized = NULL) const;
```

Returns a pointer to the currently active child window and sets the BOOL variable to the address that you provide in the **pbMaximized** argument. The variable is TRUE if the active child window is maximized.

```
void MDIIconArrange();
```

Arranges icons for the minimized MDI child windows.

```
void MDIMaximize(CWnd* pWnd); // Maximize this child
```

Maximizes the MDI child window identified by the pointer `pWnd`.

```
void MDINext();
```

Activates the next MDI child window.

```
void MDIRestore(CWnd* pWnd); // Restore this child window
```

Restores the specified MDI child window to its normal size.

```
CMenu* MDISetMenu(
    CMenu* pFrameMenu,    // New menu for the frame window
    CMenu* pWindowMenu); // New menu for the Window pop-up menu
```

Sets the menus for the frame window as well as the Windows pop-up menu. If either menu is not being altered, provide a `NULL` argument for that menu.

```
void MDITile();
void MDITile(int nType); // Windows version 3.1 or later
```

Arranges the MDI child windows in a *tiled* format, without overlaps.

See Also

`CFrameWnd`, `CWnd`	Classes in the inheritance hierarchy of `CMDIFrameWnd`
`CMDIChildWnd`	`CMDIFrameWnd` window provides the work area where one or more `CMDIChildWnd` windows appear

CMemFile

Inheritance Hierarchy

```
CObject -> CFile -> CMemFile
```

Summary

```
class CMemFile : public CFile
{
    DECLARE_DYNAMIC(CMemFile)

public:
// Constructor:
    CMemFile(UINT nGrowBytes = 1024);
```

```
// Advanced overrideables:
protected:
    virtual BYTE FAR* Alloc(UINT nBytes);
    virtual BYTE FAR* Realloc(BYTE FAR* lpMem, UINT nBytes);
    virtual BYTE FAR* Memcpy(BYTE FAR* lpMemTarget,
        const BYTE FAR* lpMemSource, UINT nBytes);
    virtual void Free(BYTE FAR* lpMem);
    virtual void GrowFile(DWORD dwNewLen);

// Implementation:
public:
    virtual ~CMemFile();
#ifdef _DEBUG
    virtual void Dump(CDumpContext& dc) const;
    virtual void AssertValid() const;
#endif
    virtual DWORD GetPosition() const;
    BOOL GetStatus(CFileStatus& rStatus) const;
    virtual LONG Seek(LONG lOff, UINT nFrom);
    virtual void SetLength(DWORD dwNewLen);
    virtual UINT Read(void FAR* lpBuf, UINT nCount);
    virtual void Write(const void FAR* lpBuf, UINT nCount);
    virtual void Abort();
    virtual void Flush();
    virtual void Close();

    // Unsupported APIs:
    virtual CFile* Duplicate() const;
    virtual void LockRange(DWORD dwPos, DWORD dwCount);
    virtual void UnlockRange(DWORD dwPos, DWORD dwCount);

// Hidden implementation details...
//...

};
```

Description

`CMemFile` is derived from the `CFile` class and represents a memory-based file. A memory-based file has the same behavior as a binary disk file, with the exception of the fact that the file's contents are stored in RAM and not on a disk. Like any other operation that can use large amounts of memory, creating a large `CMemFile` can cause problems when sufficient memory cannot be allocated.

Unlike disk files, the following functions are not supported for memory files: `Duplicate`, `LockRange`, and `UnlockRange`. Calling any of these functions results in a `CNotSupportedException` condition.

Member Variables

`CFile::m_hFile`

This variable has no meaning in a memory based file.

Member Functions

Constructor and Destructor

```
CMemFile(
    UINT nIncrement); // How many bytes to increase the file's size
```

Creates a **`CMemFile`** object and allocates the necessary memory for the file.

```
virtual ~CMemFile();
```

Destroys the **`CMemFile`** object and releases the memory that was allocated to the file.

See Also

`CFile`	Base class of `CMemFile`

CMemoryException

Inheritance Hierarchy

`CObject -> CException -> CMemoryException`

Summary

```
class CMemoryException : public CException
{
    DECLARE_DYNAMIC(CMemoryException)
public:
    CMemoryException();
};
```

Description

`CMemoryException` is derived from the `CException` class and represents an out-of-memory condition. Memory exceptions are thrown by **`new`**. Should you create your memory allocation functions, you also must include the necessary code to throw a memory exception when the memory is allocated.

Member Functions

Constructor and Destructor

```
CMemoryException();
```

Creates a `CMemoryException` object. However, never use the constructor directly—use the **`AfxThrowMemoryException()`** function instead to create a **`CMemoryException`** object.

See Also

`CException`	Base class of `CMemoryException`
`AfxThrowMemoryException`	AFX function to create a `CMemoryException` object

CMemoryState

Inheritance Hierarchy

```
CMemoryState
```

Summary

```
struct CMemoryState
{
// Attributes:
    enum blockUsage
    {
        freeBlock,    // Memory not used
        objectBlock,  // Contains a CObject derived class object
        bitBlock,     // Contains ::operator new data
        nBlockUseMax  // Total number of usages
    };

    struct CBlockHeader* m_pBlockHeader;
    LONG m_lCounts[nBlockUseMax];
    LONG m_lSizes[nBlockUseMax];
    LONG m_lHighWaterCount;
    LONG m_lTotalCount;

    CMemoryState();

// Operations:
    void Checkpoint();  // Fill with current state
    BOOL Difference(const CMemoryState& oldState,
                    const CMemoryState& newState);  // Fill with
                    difference
```

```
    // Output to afxDump:
    void DumpStatistics() const;
    void DumpAllObjectsSince() const;
};
```

Description

`CMemoryState` is used to detect memory leaks (memory that is allocated, and then never freed). This object is a structure, and is useful only when the debugging version of a program is created.

For additional debugging information, rather than using the C++ operator **`new`**, you would instead use the macro **`DEBUG_NEW`**. The dump reports contain source file/line number information. When you create the final, release version of your application this macro will be defined as the corresponding standard C++ operator, **`new`**. The code fragment below shows a usage of **`CMemoryState`**.

```
// Usage example:
int    main()
{// Create as a QuickWin project.

// Example of CMemoryState::CMemoryState:

CMemoryState msOld, msNew, msDif;
msOld.Checkpoint();

// Cause memory to be allocated...

CString   page1 = "This is the first string allocated.";
CString   page2 = "This is the second, and last string allocated.";

// Insert additional statements allocating memory here!

// Generate statistics report (goes to debugging output):

msOld.DumpAllObjectsSince();
msNew.Checkpoint();
msDif.Difference(msOld, msNew);
msDif.DumpStatistics();

return(0);
}
#ifdef DONOTCOMPILE // Program's output, with added comments:
// DumpAllObjectsSince()
```

```
Dumping objects ->
{6} strcore.cpp(80) : non-object block at $085745D2, 47 bytes long
{5} strcore.cpp(80) : non-object block at $0857458E, 36 bytes long
Object dump complete.
// DumpStatistics()
0 bytes in 0 Free Blocks
0 bytes in 0 Object Blocks
83 bytes in 2 Non-Object Blocks
Largest number used: 83 bytes
Total allocations: 83 bytes
```

To see the effect of the `DEBUG_NEW` macro, add the following lines to the example above, and rerun the program:

```
CString   *page3 = DEBUG_NEW CString(
    "This is the first string allocated.");
CString   *page4 = DEBUG_NEW CString(
    "This is the second, and last string allocated.");
```

Member Functions

`void` **`CheckPoint`**`();`

Used to save a summary of the current state of memory. The memory state is saved in the `CMemoryState` object.

`BOOL` **`Difference`**`(const CMemoryState&` *`Old`*`, const CMemoryState&` *`New`*`);`

Takes two `CMemoryState` objects (which both were created with `CheckPoint()`), and saves the difference in the `CMemoryState` object.

`void` **`DumpAllObjectsSince`**`();`

Dumps all objects allocated since the last time `CheckPoint()` was called for this `CMemoryState` object. If the `CMemoryState` object is uninitialized, the state of all objects in memory is dumped.

`void` **`DumpStatistics`**`();`

Writes a report about memory allocated, which includes the number of objects allocated, largest number of bytes allocated to objects, and the total memory allocated.

Constructor and Destructor

`CMemoryState``();`

Creates an uninitialized `CMemoryState` object that controls the management of memory checkpoints. The `CMemoryState` object must be filled in using either `CheckPoint` or `Difference`.

See Also

`new, delete`	C++ memory allocation functions
`DEBUG_NEW, DEBUG_DELETE`	Macros to provide source file/line number information in the objects dump

CMenu

Inheritance Hierarchy

`CObject -> CMenu`

Summary

```
#include <afxwin.h>
class CMenu : public CObject
{
    DECLARE_DYNAMIC(CMenu)
public:
// Constructor and destructor:
    CMenu();
    virtual ~CMenu();

// Creating and destroying the menu:
    BOOL CreateMenu();
    BOOL CreatePopupMenu();
    BOOL LoadMenu(LPCSTR lpMenuName);
    BOOL LoadMenu(UINT nIDMenu);
    BOOL LoadMenuIndirect(const void FAR* lpMenuTemplate);
    BOOL DestroyMenu();

// Utility function:
    static CMenu* FromHandle(HMENU hMenu);
    static void DeleteTempMap();

// Attributes:
    HMENU m_hMenu;
    HMENU GetSafeHmenu() const;

// Menu operations:
    BOOL Attach(HMENU hMenu);
    HMENU Detach();

    BOOL DeleteMenu(UINT nPosition, UINT nFlags);
    BOOL TrackPopupMenu(UINT nFlags, int x, int y,
```

```
                        const CWnd* pWnd,
                        const RECT FAR* lpRect = 0);

// Manipulating menu items:
    BOOL AppendMenu(UINT nFlags, UINT nIDNewItem = 0,
                    LPCSTR lpNewItem = NULL);
    BOOL AppendMenu(UINT nFlags, UINT nIDNewItem,
                    const CBitmap* pBmp);
    UINT CheckMenuItem(UINT nIDCheckItem, UINT nCheck);
    UINT EnableMenuItem(UINT nIDEnableItem, UINT nEnable);
    UINT GetMenuItemCount() const;
    UINT GetMenuItemID(int nPos) const;
    UINT GetMenuState(UINT nID, UINT nFlags) const;
    int GetMenuString(UINT nIDItem, LPSTR lpString,
                      int nMaxCount, UINT nFlags) const;
    CMenu* GetSubMenu(int nPos) const;
    BOOL InsertMenu(UINT nPosition, UINT nFlags,
                    UINT nIDNewItem = 0,
                    LPCSTR lpNewItem = NULL);
    BOOL InsertMenu(UINT nPosition, UINT nFlags,
                    UINT nIDNewItem, const CBitmap* pBmp);
    BOOL ModifyMenu(UINT nPosition, UINT nFlags,
                    UINT nIDNewItem = 0,
                    LPCSTR lpNewItem = NULL);
    BOOL ModifyMenu(UINT nPosition, UINT nFlags,
                    UINT nIDNewItem, const CBitmap* pBmp);
    BOOL RemoveMenu(UINT nPosition, UINT nFlags);
    BOOL SetMenuItemBitmaps(UINT nPosition, UINT nFlags,
                            const CBitmap* pBmpUnchecked,
                            const CBitmap* pBmpChecked);

// Overrideable functions (you must override draw and measure
// for owner-drawn menu items):
    virtual void DrawItem(LPDRAWITEMSTRUCT lpDrawItemStruct);
    virtual void MeasureItem(LPMEASUREITEMSTRUCT
                                        lpMeasureItemStruct);

// Hidden implementation details....
#ifdef _DEBUG
    virtual void AssertValid() const;
    virtual void Dump(CDumpContext& dc) const;
#endif
};
```

Description

The `CMenu` class models a Windows menu resource. It includes a menu handle (`HMENU`) as a member variable and provides several member functions to manipulate menus. To use `CMenu`, you must first define an instance of `CMenu`, and then call `LoadMenu` to initialize the `CMenu` object by loading the menu resource from the executable file of the application.

Member Variables

```
HMENU m_hMenu;
```

This is a handle to the Windows menu object attached to `CMenu`. If `m_hMenu` is `NULL`, no menu is currently attached to this `CMenu`.

Member Functions

Constructor and Destructor

```
CMenu();
```

Creates a `CMenu` object without any Windows menu attached to it. Call a function such as `LoadMenu` or `CreateMenu` to set up the menu.

```
virtual ~CMenu();
```

Destroys the `CMenu` object as well as the Windows menu attached to it.

Creating and Destroying the Menu

```
BOOL CreateMenu();
```

Creates an empty Windows menu and attaches it to the `CMenu` object. You can add items to this menu by calling `AppendMenu` or `InsertMenu`. Returns `TRUE` if successful.

```
BOOL CreatePopupMenu();
```

Creates an empty pop-up menu and attaches it to the `CMenu` object. Returns `TRUE` if successful.

```
BOOL DestroyMenu();
```

Destroys the menu. The `CMenu` destructor calls `DestroyMenu`.

```
BOOL LoadMenu(LPCSTR lpMenuName); // Name of menu resource
BOOL LoadMenu(UINT nIDMenu);      // ID of menu resource
```

Loads a menu resource from the application's executable file and attaches it to the `CMenu` object. Returns `TRUE` if successful.

```
BOOL LoadMenuIndirect(const void FAR* lpMenuTemplate);
```

Loads a menu from a template specified by *`lpMenuTemplate`*. For more information on the template, consult the Microsoft Visual C++ online documentation.

Menu Operations

```
BOOL Attach(HMENU hMenu); // Menu to be attached
```

Attaches an existing menu resource to this `CMenu` object. Returns `TRUE` if successful.

```
BOOL DeleteMenu(UINT nPosition, UINT nFlags);
```

Deletes the menu item identified by *`nPosition`*. If `nFlags` is `MF_BYPOSITION`, *`nPosition`* is the position of the item being deleted. On the other hand, if *`nFlags`* is `MF_BYCOMMAND`, *`nPosition`* is treated as the ID you assign to that menu item in the application's resource file. Also destroys any pop-up menu associated with this menu item. Returns `TRUE` if successful.

```
HMENU Detach();
```

Disassociates the Windows menu resource attached to this `CMenu` object and returns the handle to that Windows menu.

```
HMENU GetSafeHmenu() const;
```

Returns `m_hMenu`.

```
BOOL TrackPopupMenu(
    UINT nFlags,         // Flag to control position and
                         //   mouse tracking
    int x, int y,        // Location of menu (in screen coord)
    const CWnd* pWnd,    // Pointer to owner of pop-up menu
    const RECT FAR* lpRect = 0);// User can click in this
                         //   rectangle without dismissing the menu
```

Displays a floating, pop-up menu on-screen and tracks the selection of the item in the pop-up menu.

Manipulating Menu Items

```
BOOL AppendMenu(UINT nFlags, UINT nIDNewItem = 0,
                LPCSTR lpNewItem = NULL);
BOOL AppendMenu(UINT nFlags, UINT nIDNewItem,
                const CBitmap* pBmp);
```

Appends a new item at the end of the menu. The second form of **`AppendMenu`** enables you to insert a bitmap as the menu item (instead of a string). The *`nFlags`* argument controls the appearance of the new menu item. For a list of style names (with the `MF_` prefix), consult the Microsoft Visual C++ online documentation. Returns `TRUE` if successful; otherwise, returns `FALSE`.

```
UINT CheckMenuItem(UINT nIDCheckItem, UINT nCheck);
```

Adds or removes a check mark from a menu item in a pop-up menu. The `nCheck` argument should be a bitwise-OR of two flags:

- Either `MF_BYPOSITION` or `MF_BYCOMMAND` to indicate how to interpret `nIDCheckItem`
- Either `MF_CHECKED` or `MF_UNCHECKED` to specify whether you are adding or removing a check mark

Returns the previous item's check mark status.

```
UINT EnableMenuItem(UINT nIDEnableItem, UINT nEnable);
```

Enables a specified menu item. The `nEnable` item is a bitwise-OR of `MF_BYCOMMAND` or `MF_BYPOSITION`, with `MF_DISABLED`, `MF_ENABLED`, or `MF_GRAYED`.

```
UINT GetMenuItemCount() const;
```

Returns the total number of items in a top-level or pop-up menu.

```
UINT GetMenuItemID(int nPos) const;
```

Returns the identifier (used in the resource file) for a menu item at a specified position (zero being the position of the first item).

```
UINT GetMenuState(UINT nID, UINT nFlags) const;
```

Returns the status of a specified menu item to indicate whether it is enabled or disabled.

```
int GetMenuString(UINT nIDItem, LPSTR lpString,
                  int nMaxCount, UINT nFlags) const;
```

Copies the text appearing in the menu item at the specified position to the `lpString` buffer. Returns the actual number of characters copied into `lpString`.

```
CMenu* GetSubMenu(int nPos) const;
```

Returns a pointer to the pop-up menu associated with the menu item at the specified position.

```
BOOL InsertMenu(UINT nPosition, UINT nFlags,
                UINT nIDNewItem = 0,
                LPCSTR lpNewItem = NULL);
BOOL InsertMenu(UINT nPosition, UINT nFlags,
                UINT nIDNewItem, const CBitmap* pBmp);
```

Inserts a new menu item just before an existing one identified by `nPosition` and `nFlags`. Returns `TRUE` if successful and `FALSE` if unsuccessful.

```
BOOL ModifyMenu(UINT nPosition, UINT nFlags,
                UINT nIDNewItem = 0,
                LPCSTR lpNewItem = NULL);
BOOL ModifyMenu(UINT nPosition, UINT nFlags,
                UINT nIDNewItem, const CBitmap* pBmp);
```

Modifies the menu item identified by `nPosition` and `nFlags`. The modifications are controlled by the setting of `nFlags`. Returns `TRUE` if successful and `FALSE` if unsuccessful. For more information about the flag settings, consult the Microsoft Visual C++ online documentation.

```
BOOL RemoveMenu(UINT nPosition, UINT nFlags);
```

Removes the menu item identified by `nPosition` and `nFlags`. This does not destroy the pop-up menu that might be associated with this item. Therefore, you should call **`GetSubMenu`** (prior to calling **`RemoveMenu`**) to retrieve the pop-up menu so that you can either reuse it later or destroy it separately. **`RemoveMenu`** returns `TRUE` if successful and `FALSE` if unsuccessful.

```
BOOL SetMenuItemBitmaps(
    UINT nPosition, // Position or ID (depending on nFlags)
    UINT nFlags,    // One of MF_BYCOMMAND or MF_BYPOSITION
    const CBitmap* pBmpUnchecked, // Use this when unchecked
    const CBitmap* pBmpChecked);  // Bitmap when checked
```

Associates two bitmaps (one for the checked state, the other for an unchecked menu item) with a specific menu item. Windows displays the bitmap next to the menu item. Returns `TRUE` if successful and `FALSE` if unsuccessful.

CMetaFileDC

Inheritance Hierarchy

```
CObject -> CDC -> CMetaFileDC
```

Summary

```
#include <afxwin.h>
class CMetaFileDC : public CDC
{
    DECLARE_DYNAMIC(CMetaFileDC)
public:
// Constructor:
    CMetaFileDC();
```

```
// Operations:
    BOOL Create(LPCSTR lpFilename = NULL);
    HANDLE  Close();

    BOOL SelectObject(CGdiObject* pObject);
    BOOL SelectStockObject(int nIndex);
};
```

Description

The `CMetaFileDC` class provides a DC that's customized for creating as well as reading and displaying a metafile. To create a metafile, you first must define a `CMetaFileDC` object, then call the `Create` member function to attach a Windows metafile DC to the `CMetaFileDC` object.

After the `CMetaFileDC` object is initialized, you can call the drawing functions from its base class, `CDC`, to draw in the metafile. Notice that you can use only those drawing functions, such as `Ellipse` and `Rectangle`, that actually generate output. When you finish drawing, call the `Close` member function of `CMetaFileDC`. This returns a handle to a Windows metafile that you can manipulate with Windows functions such as `CopyMetaFile`. To draw the contents of the metafile on a device, call the `PlayMetaFile` member function with the metafile handle as the argument. You're responsible for deleting the metafile by calling the Windows function `DeleteMetaFile`.

Member Functions

Constructor

`CMetaFileDC``();`

Creates a `CMetaFileDC` without any Windows metafile DC. Call **`Create`** to set up the metafile DC.

Operations

`HANDLE` **`Close`**`();`

Closes the metafile DC, and returns a Windows metafile handle that you can use with the `PlayMetaFile` function from other DCs to display the metafile.

`BOOL` **`Create`**`(LPCSTR` *`lpFilename`* `= NULL); // Name of metafile on disk`

If *`lpFilename`* is not `NULL`, **`Create`** loads an existing metafile from disk into a metafile DC and attaches that DC to the `CMetaFileDC` object. If *`lpFilename`* is `NULL`, this function creates a new in-memory metafile DC. Returns `TRUE` if successful; otherwise, returns `FALSE`.

```
BOOL SelectObject(CGdiObject* pObject); // Object to select
```

Selects the specified object (a `CBitmap`, `CBrush`, `CFont`, `CPen`, `CRgn`, or `CPalette`) to the `CMetaFileDC`. Returns `TRUE` if successful; otherwise, returns `FALSE`.

```
BOOL SelectStockObject(int nIndex);
```

Selects a predefined stock pen, brush, or font into the `CMetaFileDC`. Table 20.2 lists the names of the stock objects you can select.

See Also

`CDC`	To use the `PlayMetaFile` function to display a metafile on a device

CNotSupportedException

Inheritance Hierarchy

`CObject -> CException -> CNotSupportedException`

Summary

```
class CNotSupportedException : public CException
{
    DECLARE_DYNAMIC(CNotSupportedException)
public:
    CNotSupportedException();
};
```

Description

`CNotSupportedException` is derived from the `CException` class and represents an out-of-memory condition. `CNotSupportedException` is thrown by various objects.

Member Functions

Constructor and Destructor

```
CNotSupportedException();
```

Creates a `CNotSupportedException` object. However, never use the constructor directly—use the **`AfxThrowNotSupportedException()`** function instead to create a **`CNotSupportedException`** object.

See Also

`CException`	Base class of `CNotSupportedException`
`AfxThrowNotSupportedException`	AFX function to create a `CNotSupportedException` object

CModalDialog

See CDialog, which replaces CModalDialog.

CObject

Inheritance Hierarchy

CObject

Summary

```
class CObject
{
public:

// Allocation and destructor:
    virtual CRuntimeClass* GetRuntimeClass() const;
    virtual ~CObject();  // virtual destructors are necessary

    // Diagnostic allocations:
    void* operator new(size_t, void* p);
    void* operator new(size_t nSize);
    void operator delete(void* p);

#ifdef _DEBUG
    // Used for file name/line number tracking when debugging, if using
DEBUG_NEW
    void* operator new(size_t nSize, LPCSTR lpszFileName, int nLine);
#endif

protected:
    CObject();
private:
    CObject(const CObject& objectSrc);              // not implemented
    void operator=(const CObject& objectSrc);       // not implemented

// Attributes:
public:
    BOOL IsSerializable() const;
    BOOL IsKindOf(const CRuntimeClass* pClass) const;

// Overrideables:
    virtual void Serialize(CArchive& ar);
```

```
    // Diagnostic Support:
    virtual void AssertValid() const;
    virtual void Dump(CDumpContext& dc) const;

// Implementation:
public:
    static CRuntimeClass AFXAPI_DATA classCObject;
};
```

Description

`CObject` is the base class for virtually all MFC classes. This class serves as a base for many of the classes that you would create, also.

Member Functions

`void* operator` **`new`**`(sizet` *`nSize`*`);`
`void* operator` **`new`**`(sizet` *`nSize`*`, const char FAR*` *`szFilename`*`, int` *`nLineNumber`*`);`

For the release version of your application, the memory will be optimally allocated. For debugging versions, additional filename/line number information can be included with the object to help detect memory leaks (see `CMemoryState`, above).

`void operator` **`delete`**`(void*` *`Pointer`*`);`

For the release version of your application, the memory will be freed. For the debugging version, additional processing is performed to aid in the detection of memory leaks (see `CMemoryState`, above).

`Virtual void` **`AssertValid`**`() const;`

When in the debugging mode, checks to make sure that the object is valid.

`virtual void` **`Dump`**`(CDumpContext&` *`DumpContext`*`) const;`

Dumps the object to the `CDumpContext` object. Usable only with the debugging version of the libraries, so be sure to surround calls to **`Dump()`** with `#ifdef _DEBUG/#endif` statements.

`BOOL IsSerializable();`

Returns `TRUE` if the object can be serialized. For an object to be serialized, its declaration must contain the `DECLARE_SERIAL` macro and the implementation must contain the `IMPLEMENT_SERIAL` macro.

`virtual void` **`Serialize`**`(CArchive&` *`Archive`*`);`

Used to load or store an object from or to an archive file. For more information about the `CArchive` object, see Chapter 19, "General-Purpose Microsoft Foundation Classes."

For an object to be serialized, its declaration must contain the DECLARE_SERIAL macro and the implementation must contain the IMPLEMENT_SERIAL macro.

```
virtual CRuntimeClass* GetRuntimeClass();
```

Used to return the **CRuntimeClass** structure that corresponds to the object's class. The **CRuntimeClass** structure's fields are listed in Table 20.16.

Table 20.16. CRuntimeClass members.

Member	Description
const char* m_pszClassName	The class name in a NULL terminated string.
int m_ObjectSize	The actual size of this object.
WORD m_wSchema	The schema number (or –1 for classes that are not serialized).
void (*m_pfnConstruct)(void* p)	For serializable classes, the pointer to the default constructor.
CRuntimeClass* m_pBaseClass	Pointer to the base class's CRuntimeClass structure.

```
BOOL IsKindOf(const CRuntimeClass* Class);
```

Returns TRUE if this class is an object of the specified class or this class is derived from the specified class.

Constructor and Destructor

```
CObject() //protected, default constructor
```

```
CObject(const CObject& SourceObject) //Private, copy constructor
```

Creates or copies a CObject object.

```
virtual ~CObject();
```

Destroys the CObject object.

See Also

DECLARE_SERIAL, IMPLEMENT_SERIAL	Macros to implement serialization

DECLARE_DYNAMIC, IMPLEMENT_DYNAMIC	Macros to enhance the debugging of the objects, by including the class's name and hierarchy in the object

CObList

Inheritance Hierarchy

CObject -> CObList

Summary

```
class CObList : public CObject
{

    DECLARE_SERIAL(CObList)

public:

// Construction:
    CObList(int nBlockSize=10);

// Attributes:
    // count of elements:
    int GetCount() const;
    BOOL IsEmpty() const;

    // get the head or tail:
    CObject*& GetHead();
    CObject* GetHead() const;
    CObject*& GetTail();
    CObject* GetTail() const;

// Operations:
    // remove head or tail:
    CObject* RemoveHead();
    CObject* RemoveTail();

    // Add new head or tail:
    POSITION AddHead(CObject* newElement);
    POSITION AddTail(CObject* newElement);

    // Add new head or tail:
    void AddHead(CObList* pNewList);
    void AddTail(CObList* pNewList);
```

```
    // Remove all elements:
    void RemoveAll();

    // Iterate through the list of objects:
    POSITION GetHeadPosition() const;
    POSITION GetTailPosition() const;
    CObject*& GetNext(POSITION& rPosition);       // Returns *Position++
    CObject* GetNext(POSITION& rPosition) const; // Returns *Position++
    CObject*& GetPrev(POSITION& rPosition);       // Returns *Position--
    CObject* GetPrev(POSITION& rPosition) const; // Returns *Position--

    // Get and/or modify the element at the given position:
    CObject*& GetAt(POSITION position);
    CObject* GetAt(POSITION position) const;
    void SetAt(POSITION pos, CObject* newElement);
    void RemoveAt(POSITION position);

    // Insert before or after the specified position:
    POSITION InsertBefore(POSITION position, CObject* newElement);
    POSITION InsertAfter(POSITION position, CObject* newElement);

    // Things to help things...
    POSITION Find(CObject* searchValue, POSITION startAfter = NULL)
const;
        // Starts at head if startAfter not specified, and will return
        //    NULL if not found
    POSITION FindIndex(int nIndex) const;
        // Find the element at nIndex, or return NULL if none.

// Implementation:
public:
    ~CObList();

    void Serialize(CArchive&);
#ifdef _DEBUG
    void Dump(CDumpContext&) const;
    void AssertValid() const;
#endif

// Hidden implementation details...
//...

};
```

Description

`CObList` is derived from the `CObject` class and represents an ordered list of non-unique CObject type pointers, which can be accessed either sequentially or by pointer value. `CObList` is implemented as a double-linked list. Use a variable of type `POSITION` as a key to the list. The `POSITION` pointer may be used to sequentially access the list, or as a bookmark place holder. The list is searched in a sequential fashion; therefore, for large lists, the search times can be significant.

Member Functions

```
CObject*& GetHead();
```

```
CObject* GetHead() const;
```

Returns the *head* (first) element of the list. Before calling **`GetHead`**, make sure the list is not empty.

```
CObject*& GetTail();
CObject*  GetTail() const;
```

Returns the *tail* (last) element of the list. Before calling **`GetTail`**, make sure the list is not empty.

```
Cobject* RemoveHead();
```

Used to remove the element from the head of the list. Before calling **`RemoveHead`**, make sure the list is not empty.

```
Cobject* RemoveTail();
```

Used to remove the element from the tail of the list. Before calling **`RemoveTail`**, make sure the list is not empty.

```
POSITION AddHead(CObject* NewElement);
void     AddHead(CObList* NewList);
```

Either adds a single element, or all the elements from another list to the head of the list, making a new head for the list.

```
POSITION AddTail(CObject* NewElement);
void     AddTail(CObList* NewList);
```

Either adds a single element, or all the elements from another list to the tail of the list, making a new head for the list.

```
void RemoveAll();
```

Used to remove all the elements from the list, and free the memory that the `CObList` was using. The list may be empty.

```
POSITION GetHeadPosition() const;
```

Used to return the position of the head of the list. Returns `NULL` if the list is empty.

```
POSITION GetTailPosition() const;
```

Used to return the position of the tail of the list. Returns `NULL` if the list is empty.

```
CObject*& GetNext(POSITION& Position);
CObject*  GetNext(POSITION& Position) const;
```

Gets the next element in the list, and increments *`Position`* to the next element.

```
CObject*& GetPrev(POSITION& Position);
CObject*  GetPrev(POSITION& Position) const;
```

Gets the previous element in the list, and increments *`Position`* to the previous element.

```
CObject*& GetAt(POSITION Position);
CObject*  GetAt(POSITION Position) const;
```

Used to get the element at the position specified by *`Position`*.

```
void SetAt(POSITION Position, CObject* NewElement);
```

Used to insert *`NewElement`* into the list at *`Position`*.

```
void RemoveAt(POSITION PositionToRemove);
```

Used to remove the element at *`PositionToRemove`*.

```
POSITION InsertBefore(POSITION Position, CObject* NewElement);
```

Inserts the element *`NewElement`* before *`Position`*.

```
POSITION InsertAfter(POSITION Position, CObject* NewElement);
```

Inserts the element *`NewElement`* after *`Position`*.

```
POSITION Find(CObject* SearchObject, POSITION StartAfter = NULL);
```

Used to search the list for *`SearchObject`*, starting at *`StartAfter`*.

```
POSITION FindIndex(int nIndex);
```

Used to find the `POSITION` for the specified (zero-based) index value.

```
int GetCount();
```

Returns a count of the number of elements in the list.

```
BOOL IsEmpty();
```

Used to test for an empty list. Returns `TRUE` if the list is empty; otherwise, returns `FALSE`.

Constructor and Destructor

```
CObList(int nBlockSize = 10);
```

Creates a `CObList` object and sets the incremental amount of memory allocated for the list.

See Also

`CObject`	Base class of `CObList`

COleClientDoc

Inheritance Hierarchy

`CObject -> CCmdTarget -> CDocument -> COleDocument -> COleClientDoc`

Summary

```
#include <afxole.h>
class COleClientDoc : public CObject
{
    DECLARE_DYNAMIC(COleClientDoc);
public:
// Constructor and destructor:
    COleClientDoc();
    ~COleClientDoc();

// Initialization and cleanup
    BOOL Register(LPCSTR lpszClass, LPCSTR lpszDoc);
    void Revoke();              // called by destructor

// Member variable:
    LHCLIENTDOC m_lhClientDoc;

// Attributes:
    BOOL IsOpen() const; // TRUE = successfully registered

// Operations:
    void NotifyRename(LPCSTR lpszNewName);
                           // Call after document is renamed
```

```
    void NotifyRevert(); // Call after document reverts
                         //   to original
    void NotifySaved();  // Call after document is saved

// Override and implement the following in your derived class.
    POSITION GetStartPosition() const;
    virtual COleClientItem* GetNextItem(POSITION& rPosition,
                                        BOOL* pIsSelected) = 0;
// Diagnostic support:
#ifdef _DEBUG
    virtual void AssertValid() const;
    virtual void Dump(CDumpContext& dc) const;
#endif

// Hidden implementation details....
};
```

Description

The `COleClientDoc` class models a compound document that acts as a container for data in various formats. This data comes from another document (`COleServerDoc`), created by another application. As you might guess from the name, the Microsoft Foundation Class Library provides the `COleClientDoc` class to help you write Windows applications that support OLE, which is a standard way of sharing data between applications. (See the tutorials earlier in this chapter.)

Member Variables

`LHCLIENTDOC` **`m_lhClientDoc`**`;`

Member Functions

Constructor and Destructor

`COleClientDoc``();`

Constructs a `COleClientDoc` object. You must call `Register` before placing items in the document.

`~COleClientDoc``();`

If the client document is registered, the destructor calls `Revoke`.

Initialization and Clean Up

```
BOOL Register(
    LPCSTR lpszClass, // Client document's class (usually, the
                      //   name of the client application)
    LPCSTR lpszDoc);  // Name of the document (must be a
                      //   unique name);
```

Registers the client document with `OLECLI.DLL`; returns `TRUE` if successful.

```
void Revoke();              // Called by destructor
```

Shuts down the client document. Before calling `Revoke`, you should call `Release` or `Delete` for each `COleClientItem` object in the document.

Operations

```
BOOL IsOpen() const;
```

Returns `TRUE` if the client document is successfully registered.

```
void NotifyRename(LPCSTR lpszNewName); // New name
```

Call this function with the new document filename after the user renames the document (for instance, after the user saves the document by selecting Save As... from the File menu).

```
void NotifyRevert();
```

Call this function after the document reverts to its original state.

```
void NotifySaved();
```

Call this function after the user saves the document.

See Also

`COleClientItem`, `COleServer`, `COleServerDoc`, `COleServerItem`	Other classes for OLE support

COleClientItem

Inheritance Hierarchy

`CObject -> CDocItem -> COleClientItem`

Summary

```
#include <afxole.h>
class COleClientItem : public CObject
{
    DECLARE_DYNAMIC(COleClientItem)
public:
// Constructor and destructor:
    COleClientItem(COleClientDoc* pContainerDoc);
    ~COleClientItem();
```

```
// Creating from the Clipboard:
    BOOL    CreateFromClipboard(LPCSTR lpszItemName,
                OLEOPT_RENDER renderopt = olerender_draw,
                OLECLIPFORMAT cfFormat = 0);
    BOOL    CreateStaticFromClipboard(LPCSTR lpszItemName,
                OLEOPT_RENDER renderopt = olerender_draw,
                OLECLIPFORMAT cfFormat = 0);
    BOOL    CreateLinkFromClipboard(LPCSTR lpszItemName,
                OLEOPT_RENDER renderopt = olerender_draw,
                OLECLIPFORMAT cfFormat = 0);

// Creating from a protocol name ("Insert New Object" dialog box):
    BOOL    CreateNewObject(LPCSTR lpszClass,
                LPCSTR lpszItemName,
                OLEOPT_RENDER renderopt = olerender_draw,
                OLECLIPFORMAT cfFormat = 0);

// Creating an invisible object:
    BOOL    CreateInvisibleObject(LPCSTR lpszClass,
                LPCSTR lpszItemName,
                OLEOPT_RENDER renderopt = olerender_draw,
                OLECLIPFORMAT cfFormat = 0,
                BOOL bActivate = FALSE);

// Creating a copy:
    BOOL    CreateCloneFrom(COleClientItem* pObject,
                            LPCSTR lpszItemName);

// Member variable:
    LPOLEOBJECT m_lpObject;

// Attributes:
    OLESTATUS GetLastStatus() const;
    UINT    GetType();  // OT_LINK, OT_EMBEDDED or OT_STATIC
    CString GetName();

    BOOL    GetSize(LPPOINT lpSize);     // Return FALSE if BLANK
    BOOL    GetBounds(LPRECT lpBounds); // Return FALSE if BLANK

    BOOL    IsOpen(); // TRUE = currently open on server side

// Accessing data:
    OLECLIPFORMAT EnumFormats(OLECLIPFORMAT nFormat) const;
```

```
    HANDLE  GetData(OLECLIPFORMAT nFormat, BOOL& bMustDelete);
    void    SetData(OLECLIPFORMAT nFormat, HANDLE hData);
    void    RequestData(OLECLIPFORMAT nFormat);

    BOOL    IsEqual(COleClientItem* pObject);
    HANDLE  GetLinkFormatData();        // Used internally
    COleClientDoc* GetDocument() const;

    static BOOL InWaitForRelease();

    static BOOL CanPaste(OLEOPT_RENDER
                          renderopt = olerender_draw,
                          OLECLIPFORMAT cfFormat = 0);
    static BOOL CanPasteLink(OLEOPT_RENDER
                              renderopt = olerender_draw,
                              OLECLIPFORMAT cfFormat = 0);

// Attributes that apply to Linked Objects only:
    OLEOPT_UPDATE GetLinkUpdateOptions();
    void    SetLinkUpdateOptions(OLEOPT_UPDATE updateOpt);

// Cleaning up:
    void    Release(); // Detach (close if needed)
    void    Delete();  // Get rid of it then detach

// Drawing:
    BOOL    Draw(CDC *pDC, LPRECT lpBounds, LPRECT lpWBounds,
                 CDC* pFormatDC);

// Activation:
    void    Activate(UINT nVerb, BOOL bShow = TRUE,
                     BOOL bTakeFocus = TRUE,
                     CWnd * pWndContainer = NULL,
                     LPRECT lpBounds = NULL);
// Advanced operations:
    void    Rename(LPCSTR lpszNewname);
    void    CopyToClipboard();
    void    SetTargetDevice(HANDLE hData);
                          // ^ handle to an OLETARGETDEVICE

// Operations that apply to embedded objects only:
    void    SetHostNames(LPCSTR lpszHost, LPCSTR lpszHostObj);
```

```
    void    SetBounds(LPRECT lpRect);
    void    SetColorScheme(LPLOGPALETTE lpLogPalette);

// Operations that apply to linked objects only:
    void    UpdateLink();    // Make link up-to-date
    void    CloseLink();     // Close connection

    void    ReconnectLink();// Reactivate connection

    virtual BOOL FreezeLink(LPCSTR lpszFrozenName);
                            // Convert linked object to embedded

// Error reporting:
    virtual BOOL ReportError(OLESTATUS status);

// Serialization support for storing OLE item:
    virtual void Serialize(CArchive& ar);

// Diagnostic support:
#ifdef _DEBUG
    virtual void AssertValid() const;
    virtual void Dump(CDumpContext& dc) const;
#endif

// Utility function and friends:
    static COleClientItem* FromLp(LPOLECLIENT lpClient);

    friend struct _afxOleClientItemImplementation;
    friend class COleClientDoc;

protected:
// You must override the protected function OnChange.
// OnChange is called when the server notifies of any change
// due to link update, document save, or document close.

    virtual void OnChange(OLE_NOTIFICATION wNotification) = 0;

// Other hidden implementation details....
};
```

Description

`COleClientItem` represents data embedded or linked to a `COleClientDoc` object. This class is part of a group of five classes that support OLE, which is a standard way of sharing data between applications. (See the tutorials earlier in this chapter.)

`COleClientItem` provides the client application's view of the data provided by a server. The items could appear in their own child windows or in an area of the client application's window. A `COleClientItem` may even be invisible if it cannot be displayed in the client document.

Member Functions

Constructor and Destructor

```
COleClientItem(COleClientDoc* pContainerDoc);
```

Creates a `COleClientItem` object for the specified `COleClientDoc` that contains this item. You must call one of the create functions before you can use `COleClientItem`.

```
~COleClientItem();
```

Destroys the object by deleting it for an embedded item or by releasing the link for a linked item.

Creating from the Clipboard

```
BOOL CreateFromClipboard(
    LPCSTR lpszItemName, // Name of OLE item
    OLEOPT_RENDER renderopt = olerender_draw,
    OLECLIPFORMAT cfFormat = 0);
```

Creates an OLE item from the Clipboard and returns `TRUE` if successful. For more information, consult the Microsoft Visual C++ online documentation.

```
BOOL CreateStaticFromClipboard(
    LPCSTR lpszItemName, // Name for the OLE item
    OLEOPT_RENDER renderopt = olerender_draw,
    OLECLIPFORMAT cfFormat = 0);
```

Creates a metafile-based OLE item from the contents of the Clipboard and returns `TRUE` if successful.

```
BOOL CreateLinkFromClipboard(
    LPCSTR lpszItemName, // Name of the new OLE item
    OLEOPT_RENDER renderopt = olerender_draw,
    OLECLIPFORMAT cfFormat = 0);
```

Creates a linked OLE item from the contents of the Clipboard. Call this function when the user selects the Paste Link item in the Edit menu. Returns TRUE if successful.

Creating from a Protocol Name

```
BOOL CreateNewObject(
    LPCSTR lpszClass,     // Class name of the OLE item
    LPCSTR lpszItemName, // Name of the OLE item
    OLEOPT_RENDER renderopt = olerender_draw,
    OLECLIPFORMAT cfFormat = 0);
```

Creates a new embedded OLE item with the specified class name. The item is blank. Returns TRUE if the function successfully creates the item.

```
BOOL CreateInvisibleObject(
    LPCSTR lpszClass,     // Class name for the item
    LPCSTR lpszItemName, // Name of OLE item
    OLEOPT_RENDER renderopt = olerender_draw,
    OLECLIPFORMAT cfFormat = 0,
    BOOL bActivate = FALSE);
```

Creates an OLE item without displaying it to the user. Returns TRUE if successful.

Creating a Copy

```
BOOL CreateCloneFrom(COleClientItem* pObject,
                     LPCSTR lpszItemName); // New item's name
```

Copies the existing OLE client item, *pObject*, into this COleClientItem object. Returns TRUE if successful. This is useful for implementing the Undo operation.

Attributes

```
BOOL GetBounds(LPRECT lpBounds);
```

Copies the size of the OLE item into the RECT structure with the address contained in the *lpBounds* argument. Returns FALSE if the OLE item is blank.

```
OLESTATUS GetLastStatus() const;
```

Returns the status of the last OLE operation.

```
CString GetName();
```

Returns the name of the OLE item.

```
BOOL GetSize(LPPOINT lpSize);
```

Copies the size of the client item into the POINT structure with the address contained in *lpSize*. Returns FALSE if the OLE item is blank.

```
UINT GetType();
```

Returns OT_EMBEDDED, OT_LINK, or OT_STATIC to indicate whether the OLE item is embedded, linked, or static, respectively.

```
BOOL IsOpen();
```

Returns TRUE if the item is currently open on the server side.

Accessing Data

```
OLECLIPFORMAT EnumFormats(OLECLIPFORMAT nFormat) const;
```

Call this function in a loop to list all the Clipboard formats available for this OLE client item. For the first call, the argument should be NULL. From then on, pass the return value from the previous call as the argument in the next call. The function returns NULL when no more formats are available.

```
HANDLE  GetData(OLECLIPFORMAT nFormat, BOOL& bMustDelete);
```

Returns the handle to the data for an item in the requested format. The second argument to GetData is the address of a Boolean variable that you provide. If, on return, this variable is TRUE, you are responsible for deleting the data. If the variable is FALSE, you must make a copy of the data if you want to keep it.

```
COleClientDoc* GetDocument() const;
```

Returns a pointer to the COleClientDoc object that contains this client item.

```
BOOL IsEqual(COleClientItem* pObject);
```

Returns TRUE if this OLE client item is identical to the item identified by the *pObject* pointer.

```
void RequestData(OLECLIPFORMAT nFormat);
```

Requests data from the server in the specified format and throws a COleException if the server does not accept data requests.

```
void SetData(
    OLECLIPFORMAT nFormat, // Format of data
    HANDLE hData);         // Handle of memory block with data
                           //   in specified format
```

Sends the server data for the item identified by *hData* in the specified format.

Global Status

```
static BOOL InWaitForRelease();
```

Returns TRUE if this application is waiting for the server to complete an operation; otherwise, returns FALSE.

Clipboard Query

```
static BOOL CanPaste(OLEOPT_RENDER
                     renderopt = olerender_draw,
                     OLECLIPFORMAT cfFormat = 0);
```

Returns TRUE if the Clipboard contains an embedded or static OLE item. If this function returns TRUE, you can allow the user to choose Paste from the Edit menu.

```
static BOOL CanPasteLink(OLEOPT_RENDER
                         renderopt = olerender_draw,
                         OLECLIPFORMAT cfFormat = 0);
```

Returns TRUE if the Clipboard contains a linked OLE item. If this function returns TRUE, you can allow the user to choose Paste Link from the Edit menu.

Attributes of Linked Objects

```
OLEOPT_UPDATE GetLinkUpdateOptions();
```

Returns the current link-update option for this item. For more information about the return value, consult the Microsoft Visual C++ online documentation.

```
void SetLinkUpdateOptions(OLEOPT_UPDATE updateOpt);
```

Sets the current link-update option for this client item. For more information about the update options, consult the Microsoft Visual C++ online documentation.

Cleaning Up

```
void Release();
```

Called by the destructor to close the link for a linked item.

```
void Delete();
```

Deletes this OLE client item and eliminates the link to the server. The destructor calls Delete for embedded items.

Drawing

```
BOOL Draw(
    CDC*    pDC,         // Draw item on this DC
    LPRECT  lpBounds,    // Draw item in this bounding rectangle
    LPRECT  lpWBounds,   // Bounding rectangle of metafile DC
    CDC*    pFormatDC);// Format the item for this DC
```

Draws the OLE client item on a specified DC and returns TRUE if successful; otherwise, returns FALSE.

Activation

```
void Activate(
    UINT    nVerb,    // Index indicating what server should do
    BOOL    bShow = TRUE, // TRUE = server should show item
    BOOL    bTakeFocus = TRUE, // TRUE = server gets input focus
    CWnd*   pWndContainer = NULL, // Pointer to client window that
                                  //   contains the OLE item
    LPRECT lpBounds = NULL); // Display item within this bounding
                             //   rectangle
```

Activates the server and requests an operation to be performed on the OLE client item. The meaning of the operation and how it's specified depends on the client and the server.

Advanced Operations

```
void CopyToClipboard();
```

Copies the item to the Clipboard in a format suitable for another application to embed the item in its document.

```
void Rename(LPCSTR lpszNewname);
```

Renames the OLE item. The name must be unique within the document.

```
void SetTargetDevice(HANDLE hData);
```

Sets the item's target output device through information given in an `OLETARGETDEVICE` structure with a handle you provide in *`hData`*.

Operations on Embedded Items

```
void SetBounds(LPRECT lpRect);
```

Sets the bounding rectangle within which the embedded item appears. The coordinates are from the `MM_HIMETRIC` mapping mode (one unit equals 0.01 millimeter).

```
void SetColorScheme(LPLOGPALETTE lpLogPalette);
```

Changes the color scheme to one specified by the `LOGPALETTE` structure with an address that you specify as the *`lpLogPalette`* argument. The server interprets the first palette entry as the foreground color and the second entry as the background color.

```
void SetHostNames(
    LPCSTR lpszHost,      // Name of the client application
    LPCSTR lpszHostObj);// Name of the OLE item
```

Sets the name of the client application and the name that the client application uses to identify the embedded item. The server displays this information in the window when it edits the OLE item.

Operations on Linked Items

```
void CloseLink();
```

Closes the connection to the server, but the connection can be reopened.

```
virtual BOOL FreezeLink(LPCSTR lpszFrozenName); // New name
```

Converts a linked OLE item to an embedded one with the specified name and returns `TRUE` if successful; otherwise, returns `FALSE`.

```
void ReconnectLink();
```

Reactivates a connection to the server after you have closed it by calling `CloseLink`.

```
void UpdateLink();
```

Makes an up-to-date link to the server.

Reporting Errors

```
virtual BOOL ReportError(OLESTATUS status);
```

Displays informative message about any error that might occur during an OLE operation. The status argument is the error code provided by the `COleException` object. You can call `ReportError` from exception handlers for the `COleException`.

See Also

`COleClientDoc`, `COleServer`, `COleServerDoc`, `COleServerItem`	Other classes for OLE support

COleDocument

Inheritance Hierarchy

```
CObject -> CCmdTarget -> CDocument -> COleDocument
```

Summary

```
class COleDocument : public CDocument
{
    DECLARE_DYNAMIC(COleDocument)

// Constructor:
protected:
    COleDocument();
```

```
// Attributes:
public:
    BOOL IsOpenClientDoc() const;
    BOOL IsOpenServerDoc() const;

// Operations:
    // Go through all items using iteration:
    virtual POSITION GetStartPosition() const;
    virtual CDocItem* GetNextItem(POSITION& rPosition);

    // Add new items for implementation in derived classes:
    void AddItem(CDocItem* pItem);
    void RemoveItem(CDocItem* pItem);

// Implementation:
public:
    LHCLIENTDOC m_lhClientDoc;       // The registered client handle
    LHSERVERDOC m_lhServerDoc;       // The registered server handle
    CPtrList m_docItemList;          // Points to the list of not owned
                                        items

public:
    virtual ~COleDocument();
    virtual void DeleteContents(); // Used to delete document items in
                                      list
#ifdef _DEBUG
    virtual void AssertValid() const;
    virtual void Dump(CDumpContext& dc) const;
#endif
};
```

Description

`COleDocument` is derived from the `CDocument` class and is the base class for OLE documents. Because `COleDocument` is derived from `CDocument`, you're able to use the document and view interface that are built into `CDocument`. The `COleDocument` class also includes the functionality to treat document items as collections of `CDocItem` objects. It's important to note that you will not use the `COleDocument` class directly—rather, you will be using the `COleClientDoc` class, the `COleServerDoc` class, or both.

Member Functions

`void **AddItem**(CdocItem* *Item*);`

Used to add an item to the document. Usually, **AddItem** is called by **COleClientDoc**'s and **COleServerDoc**'s constructors.

`virtual CDocItem* **GetNextItem**(POSITION& *Position*);`

Used to get the next item in the document. Usually, **GetNextItem** is called repeatedly to allow you to access each of the items in your document. Use `GetStartPosition` to get the initial value for the *`Position`* parameter.

`virtual POSITION **GetStartPosition**();`

Used to get the `POSITION` of the first item in the document. Usually called prior to the first call to `GetNextItem`.

`BOOL **IsOpenClientDoc**() const;`

Used to test whether the document is a registered client document. It's acceptable to have a document that is both a client document and a server document at the same time. Returns other than zero if the document is a registered client document.

`BOOL **IsOpenServerDoc**() const;`

Used to test to see if the document is a registered server document. It's acceptable to have a document that is both a client document and a server document at the same time. Returns other than zero if the document is a registered server document.

`void **RemoveItem**(CdocItem* *Item*);`

Used to remove an item to the document. Usually, **RemoveItem** is called by **COleClientDoc**'s and **COleServerDoc**'s destructors.

Constructor and Destructor

`COleDocument();`

Creates a `COleDocument` object.

See Also

`CDocument`	Base class of `CClientDC`
`COleClientDoc`, `COleServerDoc`	Classes derived from COleDocument

COleException

Inheritance Hierarchy

`CObject -> CException -> COleException`

Summary

```
class COleException : public CException
{
    DECLARE_DYNAMIC(COleException)
public:
    OLESTATUS m_status;

    // Helper function:
    static OLESTATUS PASCAL Process(CException*);

// Implementation; use the AfxThrowOleException()
//    function to create the object:
    COleException(OLESTATUS status);
};
```

Description

`COleException` is derived from the `CException` class and represents an error condition related to OLE.

Member Variables

`OLESTATUS` **`m_status`**

Used as a holder for a value that indicates the reason for the OLE exception.

Constructor and Destructor

`COleException``(OLESTATUS` *`Status`*`);`

Creates a `COleException` object. Do not call the constructor directly. Rather, use the `AfxThrowOleException` function. The status variable can be set to one of the enumerators listed in Table 20.17.

Table 20.17. OLESTATUS enumerator values.

Enumerator	Description
OLE_OK	No error occurred.
OLE_BUSY	Occurs when a member function is called while another operation was in progress.
OLE_ERROR_STREAM	OLESTREAM stream error.
OLE_ERROR_STATIC	A nonstatic item was expected.

continues

Table 20.17. continued

Enumerator	Description
OLE_ERROR_BLANK	Critical data missing.
OLE_ERROR_DRAW	Error while drawing the OLE object.
OLE_ERROR_METAFILE	The metafile was invalid.
OLE_ERROR_ABORT	The metafile drawing was aborted by the client.
OLE_ERROR_CLIPBOARD	Was unable to get or set Clipboard data.
OLE_ERROR_FORMAT	The requested format is not available.
OLE_ERROR_GENERIC	A general error occurred.
OLE_ERROR_DATATYPE	The requested data format not supported.
OLE_ERROR_PALETTE	An invalid color palette was specified.
OLE_ERROR_NOT_LINK	The item was not linked.
OLE_ERROR_NOT_EMPTY	The client document still contains items.
OLE_ERROR_SIZE	The size of a passed buffer was incorrect; the string does not fit in the buffer.
OLE_ERROR_DRIVE	The document's name has an invalid drive specification.
OLE_ERROR_NETWORK	Was unable to connect to the network driver that has the OLE document.
OLE_ERROR_NAME	The document has an invalid name (document name, item name, and so forth).
OLE_ERROR_TEMPLATE	The server was unable to load template.
OLE_ERROR_NEW	The server was unable to create new document.
OLE_ERROR_EDIT	The server was unable to create embedded instance.
OLE_ERROR_OPEN	The server was unable to open document; possible invalid link.

Enumerator	Description
OLE_ERROR_NOT_OPEN	The OLE item is not open for editing.
OLE_ERROR_LAUNCH	The system was unable to launch server.
OLE_ERROR_COMM	The client was unable to communicate with server.
OLE_ERROR_TERMINATE	Could not terminate.
OLE_ERROR_COMMAND	There was an error in executing an OLE command.
OLE_ERROR_SHOW	It was not possible to show the OLE document.
OLE_ERROR_DOVERB	There was an error in sending the DO verb, or invalid verb.
OLE_ERROR_ADVISE_NATIVE	It is possible that the item is missing.
OLE_ERROR_ADVISE_PICT	It is possible that the item is missing or server doesn't understand this format.
OLE_ERROR_ADVISE_RENAME	This server doesn't support the rename function.
OLE_ERROR_POKE_NATIVE	The client was unable to poke native data to server.
OLE_ERROR_REQUEST_NATIVE	The server failed to render native data.
OLE_ERROR_REQUEST_PICT	The server failed to render presentation data.
OLE_ERROR_SERVER_BLOCKED	It was not possible to block a blocked server, or to revoke a blocked server or document.
OLE_ERROR_REGISTRATION	The server is not registered in OLE registration database.
OLE_ERROR_ALREADY_REGISTERED	Cannot register the same document more than once.
OLE_ERROR_TASK	Either the server or client task invalid.

continues

Table 20.17. continued

Enumerator	Description
OLE_ERROR_OUTOFDATE	The item is out of date.
OLE_ERROR_CANT_UPDATE_CLIENT	The client of the embedded document doesn't accept updates to the document.
OLE_ERROR_UPDATE	There was an error while trying to update.
OLE_WARN_DELETE_DATA	Warn the caller that the caller must delete data when done with it.

See Also

CException	Base class of COleException
AfxThrowOleException	AFX function to create a COleException object

COleServer

Inheritance Hierarchy

CObject -> COleServer

Summary

```
#include <afxole.h>
class COleServer : public CObject
{
public:
// Constructor and destructor:
    COleServer(BOOL bLaunchEmbedded);
    ~COleServer();

    BOOL    Register(LPCSTR lpszClass, BOOL bMultiInstance);
    void    BeginRevoke();

// Attributes:
    BOOL    IsOpen() const; // TRUE = successfully registered
    BOOL    m_bLaunchEmbedded;

// Diagnostic support:
#ifdef _DEBUG
public:
```

```
    virtual void AssertValid() const;
    virtual void Dump(CDumpContext& dc) const;
#endif

protected:
// You must implement the next two protected functions.
// You may also want to override the rest of the protected
// functions.

// These are for functions supporting embedding:
    virtual COleServerDoc* OnCreateDoc(LPCSTR lpszClass,
                                       LPCSTR lpszDoc) = 0;
    virtual COleServerDoc* OnEditDoc(LPCSTR lpszClass,
                                     LPCSTR lpszDoc) = 0;

// This is for functions supporting links:
    virtual COleServerDoc* OnOpenDoc(LPCSTR lpszDoc);

// This is for functions supporting embedding from templates:
    virtual COleServerDoc* OnCreateDocFromTemplate(
                LPCSTR lpszClass,
                LPCSTR lpszDoc, LPCSTR lpszTemplate);

// This is for those supporting DDE (Dynamic Data
// Exchange) execute commands:
    virtual OLESTATUS OnExecute(LPVOID lpCommands);

// Other hidden implementation details....
};
```

Description

`COleServer` represents the application that created the document from which one or more items have been embedded or linked to a client document. The server document is represented by the `COleServerDoc` class, and the actual items are modeled by the `COleServerItem` class. These classes help you create Microsoft Windows applications that support OLE, which is a standard mechanism for sharing data among Windows applications.

`COleServer` is the base class for any OLE server. The server receives requests from the clients through OLESVR.DLL, and it responds to the requests by creating or opening documents and by displaying them inside the client application's window.

Member Variables

```
BOOL m_bLaunchEmbedded;
```

Indicates whether the server is working with an embedded item or a linked item. If this flag is `TRUE`, the server has been launched as an embedded server.

Member Functions

Constructor and Destructor

```
COleServer(BOOL bLaunchEmbedded); // TRUE = embedded server
```

Creates a `COleServer` object. You must call `Register` before the server can begin accepting requests from clients.

```
~COleServer();
```

Destroys the `COleServer` object and calls the `BeginRevoke` function to shut down the server.

Registration and Revocation

```
void BeginRevoke();
```

When called by the destructor, begins to shut down the server.

```
BOOL Register(
    LPCSTR lpszClass,      // Class name of server document
    BOOL bMultiInstance);// TRUE = can have multiple instances
                         //   of server
```

Registers the server for the specified document type and indicates that the server is ready to accept requests from clients.

Status Query

```
BOOL IsOpen() const; // TRUE = successfully registered
```

Returns `TRUE` if the server is successfully registered; otherwise, it returns `FALSE`.

See Also

`COleClientItem`, `COleClientDoc`, `COleServerDoc`, `COleServerItem`	Other classes for OLE support

COleServerDoc

Inheritance Hierarchy

```
CObject -> CCmdTarget -> CDocument -> COleDocument -> COleServerDoc
```

Summary

```
#include <afxole.h>
class COleServerDoc : public CObject
{
    DECLARE_DYNAMIC(COleServerDoc)
public:
// Constructor and destructor:
    COleServerDoc();
    ~COleServerDoc();

// Call the following if the user opens the document:
    BOOL Register(COleServer* pServer, LPCSTR lpszDoc);

    void Revoke();

// Attributes:
    COleServer* m_pServer;
    HPALETTE m_hPalette;

    BOOL IsOpen() const; // TRUE if successfully registered

// Operations:
    void NotifyRename(LPCSTR lpszNewName);
    void NotifyRevert();
    void NotifySaved();

    void NotifyAllClients(OLE_NOTIFICATION wNotification);
    void NotifyClosed();  // Call after you close document
    void NotifyChanged(); // Call after you change some global
                          //   attribute such as dimensions of
                          //   the document
// Diagnostic support.
#ifdef _DEBUG
    virtual void AssertValid() const;
    virtual void Dump(CDumpContext& dc) const;
#endif

protected:
// You must implement the next three protected functions in
// your derived class. You may also want to override the rest
// of the protected members.
```

```
// Should return new item representing entire document:
    virtual COleServerItem* OnGetDocument() = 0;

// Should return new item for the named item:
    virtual COleServerItem* OnGetItem(LPCSTR lpszItemName) = 0;

// Should return next item in iteration:
    virtual COleServerItem* GetNextItem(POSITION& rPosition) = 0;

    virtual OLESTATUS OnSave();
    virtual OLESTATUS OnClose();
    virtual OLESTATUS OnExecute(LPVOID lpCommands);
    virtual OLESTATUS OnSetDocDimensions(LPRECT lpRect);

// Other hidden implementation details....
};
```

Description

`COleServerDoc` is the base class for the server document. The server document contains the item that is embedded or linked into the client document. That item is represented by the `COleServerItem` class. These classes help you write Windows applications that support OLE, a standard way to share data among Windows applications. (See the tutorials earlier in this chapter.)

Member Variables

`COleServer* m_pServer;`

This is a pointer to the `COleServer` object that represents the OLE server application.

`HPALETTE m_hPalette;`

This is the palette containing the color scheme that is used to display the item.

Member Functions

Constructor and Destructor

`COleServerDoc();`

Creates a `COleServerDoc` object that you must register (by calling `Register`) before you can use it.

`~COleServerDoc();`

Destroys the `COleServerDoc` object and calls the `Revoke` member function.

Registration and Revocation

```
BOOL Register(
    COleServer* pServer, // Pointer to a registered server
    LPCSTR      lpszDoc);// Full name of server document
```

Registers the document. Call this function if the user opens the document by selecting **O**pen from the **F**ile menu.

```
void Revoke();
```

Shuts down the server document and waits for the shutdown to end. The destructor calls `Revoke`.

Status Query

```
BOOL IsOpen() const;
```

Returns `TRUE` if the server document is successfully registered.

Operations

```
void NotifyAllClients(OLE_NOTIFICATION wNotification);
```

Notifies all clients of the message in *wNotification*. The message must be `OLE_CHANGED`, `OLE_SAVED`, `OLE_CLOSED`, or `OLE_RENAMED` to indicate the change to the server document that has just taken place.

```
void NotifyClosed();
```

Call this function after you close the document to notify all clients about the document's closure.

```
void NotifyChanged();
```

Call this function after you change some global attribute, such as dimensions of the document, to notify all clients about the change.

```
void NotifyRename(LPCSTR lpszNewName); // New name of document
```

Call this function after renaming the server document to inform all clients about the change in the document's filename.

```
void NotifyRevert();
```

Notifies all clients that the server document has reverted to its last saved form.

```
void NotifySaved();
```

Call this function after saving the document to notify all clients that the server document has been saved.

See Also

`COleClientDoc`, `COleClientItem`, `COleServer`, `COleServerItem`	Other classes for OLE support

COleServerItem

Inheritance Hierarchy

`CObject -> CDocItem -> COleServerItem`

Summary

```
#include <afxole.h>
class COleServerItem : public CObject
{
protected:
//...
    DECLARE_DYNAMIC(COleServerItem)

// Constructor and destructor:
    COleServerItem();
    ~COleServerItem();

// Attributes:
    COleServerDoc* m_pDocument;
    HPALETTE m_hPalette;
    CRect    m_rectBounds;

    BOOL    IsConnected();  // TRUE if connected to client

public:
    COleServerDoc* GetDocument() const;

// Operations for notifying client:
    int  NotifyClient(OLE_NOTIFICATION wNotification);
    void NotifyChanged(); // Call after you change item

    void BeginRevoke();   // Revoke client connection

    virtual HANDLE GetMetafileData(); // Calls 'OnDraw(...)'
    virtual HANDLE GetNativeData();   // Calls 'Serialize(...)'
```

```
// You must implement the Serialize function:
    virtual void Serialize(CArchive& ar) = 0;

// Diagnostic support:
#ifdef _DEBUG
    virtual void AssertValid() const;
    virtual void Dump(CDumpContext& dc) const;
#endif

protected:
// You must implement the next two protected functions:
    virtual OLESTATUS OnShow(BOOL bTakeFocus) = 0;

// Drawing for metafile format (return FALSE if not supported):
    virtual BOOL OnDraw(CMetaFileDC* pDC) = 0;
            // draw within boundaries set in m_rectBounds

// You may want to implement the following functions:
    virtual OLESTATUS OnRelease(); // for extra cleanup
    virtual OLESTATUS OnExtraVerb(UINT nVerb);
                            // support extra verbs--operations
    virtual OLESTATUS OnSetTargetDevice(LPOLETARGETDEVICE
                                        lpTargetDevice);
                            // to track target device changes

    virtual OLESTATUS OnSetBounds(LPRECT lpRect);
                            // to track size changes

// To get data as text:
    virtual BOOL OnGetTextData(CString& rStringReturn);

    virtual OLESTATUS OnGetData(OLECLIPFORMAT nFormat,
                                LPHANDLE lphReturn);

// Other hidden implementation details....
};
```

Description

`COleServerItem` provides the server's view of the items embedded or linked to client documents. A `COleServerItem` resides in a server document—an instance of the `COleServerDoc` class. The `COleServer` class models the server application that updates the documents and draws the items. These classes help you write Windows applications that support OLE, a standard method that relies on a client-server model to allow cooperating applications to share data. (See the tutorials earlier in this chapter.)

Member Variables

```
COleServerDoc* m_pDocument;
```

This is a pointer to a `COleServerDoc` object that represents the server document.

```
HPALETTE m_hPalette;
```

Provides the color scheme as specified by the client.

```
CRect  m_rectBounds;
```

Provides the bounding rectangle (measured in units of 0.01 millimeter) for the item as specified by the client.

Member Functions

Constructor and Destructor

```
COleServerItem();
```

Constructs a `COleServerItem` object.

```
~COleServerItem();
```

Destroys the server item.

Status Query

```
BOOL IsConnected();
```

Returns `TRUE` if this server item is connected to a client item.

Attributes

```
COleServerDoc* GetDocument() const;
```

Returns a pointer to the server document that contains this server item.

```
virtual HANDLE GetMetafileData();
```

This function calls the `OnDraw` member function to create a Windows metafile with an image of the server item. Returns a handle to the metafile.

```
virtual HANDLE GetNativeData();
```

This function calls the `Serialize` member function to create a copy of the server item's data in a block of memory. Returns a handle to the block of memory.

Notifying the Client

```
void BeginRevoke();
```

Revokes the connection to the client.

```
void NotifyChanged();
```

Call this function to update the client item by reflecting a change to the item.

```
int NotifyClient(OLE_NOTIFICATION wNotification);
```

Notifies the client that this server item has changed as specified in the `wNotification` argument. This argument can be one of the following:

```
OLE_CHANGED, OLE_SAVED, OLE_CLOSED, OLE_RENAMED,
OLE_QUERY_PAINT, OLE_RELEASE
```

See Also

`COleClientDoc`, `COleClientItem` `COleServer`, `COleServerDoc`	Other classes for OLE support

CPaintDC

Inheritance Hierarchy

`CObject -> CDC -> CPaintDC`

Summary

```
#include <afxwin.h>
class CPaintDC : public CDC
{
    DECLARE_DYNAMIC(CPaintDC)
public:
// Constructor and destructor:
    CPaintDC(CWnd* pWnd); // Equivalent to calling BeginPaint
    virtual ~CPaintDC();  // Calls EndPaint

// Attributes:
    PAINTSTRUCT m_ps;

// Diagnostic support
#ifdef _DEBUG
    virtual void AssertValid() const;
    virtual void Dump(CDumpContext& dc) const;
#endif
```

```
// Hidden implementation details....
};
```

Description

The CPaintDC class represents a DC that is used for updating a window's client area. Specifically, it incorporates the calls to the Windows functions BeginPaint and EndPaint, which are used in traditional Windows programs when responding to the WM_PAINT message. Use CPaintDC only to set up an appropriate DC in the OnPaint message handler of your window classes.

Member Variables

`PAINTSTRUCT m_ps;`

Contains information returned by the call to the BeginPaint function of the window for which this CPaintDC object is initialized.

Member Functions

`CPaintDC(CWnd* pWnd);`

Initializes the **CPaintDC** object by creating a DC appropriate for updating the window identified by *pWnd*. Also prepares that window for drawing, and stores the information (obtained by calling BeginPaint) in **m_ps**. The constructor throws a CResourceException when it fails to obtain a DC for the window.

`virtual ~CPaintDC();`

Destroys the CPaintDC object and calls EndPaint to mark the end of updating the window.

See Also

CDC	Base class of CPaintDC; all drawing functions are described under CDC

CPalette

Inheritance Hierarchy

`CObject -> CGdiObject -> CPalette`

Summary

```
#include <afxwin.h>

class CPalette : public CGdiObject
{
    DECLARE_DYNAMIC(CPalette)
```

```
public:
// Constructor:
    CPalette();

// Initializing a palette:
    BOOL CreatePalette(LPLOGPALETTE lpLogPalette);

// Operations:
    UINT GetPaletteEntries(UINT nStartIndex, UINT nNumEntries,
            LPPALETTEENTRY lpPaletteColors) const;
    UINT SetPaletteEntries(UINT nStartIndex, UINT nNumEntries,
            LPPALETTEENTRY lpPaletteColors);
    void AnimatePalette(UINT nStartIndex, UINT nNumEntries,
            LPPALETTEENTRY lpPaletteColors);
    UINT GetNearestPaletteIndex(DWORD crColor) const;
    BOOL ResizePalette(UINT nNumEntries);

// Utility function:
    static CPalette* FromHandle(HPALETTE hPalette);
};
```

Description

The `CPalette` class represents a Windows color palette. The palette is an array of RGB color values. Applications use the index of the palette entries to refer to different colors. As palettes change, the same index may indicate different RGB colors.

Member Functions

Constructor

`CPalette``();`

Creates a **`CPalette`** object without an associated palette. Call `CreatePalette` to set up a palette.

Initializing a Palette

`BOOL` **`CreatePalette`**`(LPLOGPALETTE` *`lpLogPalette`*`);`

Creates a Windows color palette using information you provide in a `LOGPALETTE` structure, and attaches the palette to the `CPalette` object. Returns `TRUE` if successful.

`static CPalette*` **`FromHandle`**`(HPALETTE` *`hPalette`*`);`

Returns a pointer to a `CPalette` object with the specified color palette attached to it. Creates a temporary `CPalette` object if necessary.

Manipulating the Palette

```
void AnimatePalette(
    UINT            nStartIndex,      // Start from this index
    UINT            nNumEntries,      // Change this many entries
    LPPALETTEENTRY lpPaletteColors);// New palette entries
```

Changes a specified number of palette entries, starting at the `nStartIndex` index with the new entries you provide in an array of `PALETTEENTRY` structures (`lpPaletteColors`).

```
UINT GetNearestPaletteIndex(DWORD crColor) const;
```

Returns the index of the palette entry closest to the RGB color value specified by `crColor`.

```
UINT GetPaletteEntries(
    UINT nStartIndex, // Start copying from this index
    UINT nNumEntries, // Copy this many entries
    LPPALETTEENTRY lpPaletteColors) const; // Copy into this array
```

Copies a specified number (`nNumEntries`) of palette entries from the `CPalette` object to the array of `PALETTEENTRY` structures (`lpPaletteColors`). Returns the number of entries copied, or 0 if the function fails.

```
BOOL ResizePalette(UINT nNumEntries);
```

Changes the size of the palette to ensure that it contains a specified number (`nNumEntries`) of entries after resizing. Returns `TRUE` if successful; otherwise, returns `FALSE`.

```
UINT SetPaletteEntries(
    UINT nStartIndex, // Start changing from this index
    UINT nNumEntries, // Change this many entries
    LPPALETTEENTRY lpPaletteColors); // Change to these values
```

Sets a range of entries to the values you provide in an array of `PALETTEENTRY` structures (`lpPaletteColors`). Returns the number of entries set, or 0 if the function fails.

See Also

`CDC`	To select a palette using the `SelectPalette` member function; the drawing functions are part of the `CDC` class
`CGdiObject`	Base class of `CPalette`

CPen

Inheritance Hierarchy

```
CObject -> CGdiObject -> CPen
```

Summary

```
#include <afxwin.h>
class CPen : public CGdiObject
{
    DECLARE_DYNAMIC(CPen)
public:

// Constructors:
    CPen();
    CPen(int nPenStyle, int nWidth, DWORD crColor);

// Initializing a pen:
    BOOL CreatePen(int nPenStyle, int nWidth, DWORD crColor);
    BOOL CreatePenIndirect(LPLOGPEN lpLogPen);

// Utility function:
    static CPen* FromHandle(HPEN hPen);
};
```

Description

The `CPen` class represents a Windows pen resource—one of the drawing tools used by the GDI functions. *Pens* are used for drawing lines and boundaries of figures, such as rectangles and ellipses. After creating and initializing a `CPen`, you must select it into a DC before you can use it to draw figures such as lines, rectangles, polygons, and ellipses.

Member Functions

Constructors

`CPen();`

Creates a `CPen` object, which you must initialize by calling one of the initialization functions.

```
CPen(
    int   nPenStyle, // Pen's style. One of PS_SOLID, PS_DASH,
                     // PS_DOT, PS_DASHDOT, PS_DASHDOTDOT,
                     // PS_NULL, or PS_INSIDEFRAME
    int   nWidth,    // Width of pen in pixels
    DWORD crColor);  // RGB color of pen
```

Creates and initializes a `CPen` object. You can use the `CPen` object without further initialization. This constructor may throw a `CResourceException` if an error occurs while you're creating the pen.

Initializing a CPen

```
BOOL CreatePen(int nPenStyle, int nWidth, DWORD crColor);
```

Initializes a `CPen` using the specified arguments—these are identical to the arguments required by one of the `CPen` constructors. Returns `TRUE` if successful; otherwise, returns `FALSE`.

```
BOOL CreatePenIndirect(LPLOGPEN lpLogPen);
```

Initializes a `CPen` using information that you provide in a `LOGPEN` structure. Returns `TRUE` if successful.

```
static CPen* FromHandle(HPEN hPen);
```

Returns a pointer to a `CPen` object associated with the Windows pen `hPen`. If `hPen` is not attached to any `CPen` object, this function creates a temporary `CPen` object and attaches `hPen` to that object.

See Also

`CGdiObject`	Base class of `CPen`
`CBrush`	Brushes are used to fill areas
`CDC`	To select a pen using the `SelectObject` member function; the drawing functions are part of the `CDC` class

CPoint

Inheritance Hierarchy

```
tagPOINT -> CPoint

// tagPOINT is defined in <windows.h> as
typedef struct tagPOINT
{
    int x;
    int y;
} POINT;
```

Summary

```
#include <afxwin.h>
class CPoint : public tagPOINT
```

```
{
public:
// Constructors:
    CPoint();
    CPoint(int initX, int initY);
    CPoint(POINT initPt);
    CPoint(SIZE initSize);
    CPoint(DWORD dwPoint);

// Operations:

// Offset x- and y-coordinates by specified amounts:
    void Offset(int xOffset, int yOffset);
    void Offset(POINT point);
    void Offset(SIZE size);

// Return TRUE if this CPoint matches specified POINT:
    BOOL operator==(POINT point) const;

// Return TRUE if this CPoint is not equal to the specified POINT:
    BOOL operator!=(POINT point) const;

// Add or subtract specified amounts from x- and y-coordinates:
    void operator+=(SIZE size);
    void operator-=(SIZE size);

// Operators returning CPoint values

// Return new CPoint that is the current CPoint offset by
// amounts specified by a SIZE structure:
    CPoint operator+(SIZE size) const;
    CPoint operator-(SIZE size) const;

// Operators returning CSize values

// Return a CSize representing the x- and y-differences between
// this CPoint and a specified POINT:
    CSize operator-(POINT point) const;
};
```

Description

The `CPoint` class incorporates the Windows `POINT` structure by providing a number of member functions and operators that manipulate `CPoint` and `POINT` structures. You can use a CPoint wherever a POINT (or a pointer to a POINT) is expected as an argument to a function. The member functions and operators are explained adequately by the comments in the "Summary" section.

See Also

CRect, CSize	Class equivalents of RECT and SIZE structures

CPreviewView

Inheritance Hierarchy

CObject -> CCmdTarget -> CWnd -> CView -> CScrollView -> CPreviewView

Summary

```
class CPreviewView : public CScrollView
{
    DECLARE_DYNCREATE(CPreviewView)
// Constructor:
public:
    CPreviewView();
    BOOL SetPrintView(CView* pPrintView);

// Attributes:
protected:
    CView* m_pOrigView;
    CView* m_pPrintView;
    CPreviewDC* m_pPreviewDC;
    CDC m_dcPrint;

// Operations:
    void SetZoomState(UINT nNewState, UINT nPage, CPoint point);
    void SetCurrentPage(UINT nPage, BOOL bClearRatios);

    // Will Return TRUE if in a page rect.
    // Returns the page index in nPage and
    //    the point converted to 1:1 screen device coordinates:
    BOOL FindPageRect(CPoint& point, UINT& nPage);

// Overrideables:
    virtual void OnActivateView(BOOL bActivate,
            CView* pActivateView, CView* pDeactiveView);
```

```
    // Returns .cx, .cy as the numerator/denominator pair for the ratio
    // using a CSize object:
    virtual CSize CalcScaleRatio(CSize windowSize, CSize actualSize);

    virtual void PositionPage(UINT nPage);
    virtual void OnDisplayPageNumber(UINT nPage, UINT nPagesDisplayed);
    virtual void OnPrepareDC(CDC* pDC, CPrintInfo* pInfo = NULL);

// Implementation:
public:
    virtual ~CPreviewView();
#ifdef _DEBUG
    void AssertValid() const;
    void Dump(CDumpContext& dc) const;
#endif

// Hidden implementation details...
//...

    DECLARE_MESSAGE_MAP()

    friend CView;
    friend BOOL CALLBACK _AfxPreviewCloseProc(CFrameWnd* pFrameWnd);
};
```

Description

`CPreviewView` is derived from the `CScrollView` class and used in the Print Preview feature.

Member Functions

Constructor and Destructor

`CPreviewView();`

Creates a `CPreviewView` object.

See Also

`CScrollView`	Base class of `CPreviewView`

CPrintDialog

Inheritance Hierarchy

`CObject -> CCmdTarget -> CWnd -> CDialog -> CPrintDialog`

Summary

```
#include <afxdlgs.h>

class CPrintDialog : public CDialog
{
    DECLARE_DYNAMIC(CPrintDialog)
public:
// Constructor:
    CPrintDialog(BOOL bPrintSetupOnly,
                              // FALSE for print dialog box
                 DWORD dwFlags = PD_ALLPAGES ¦
                                 PD_USEDEVMODECOPIES ¦
                                 PD_NOPAGENUMS ¦
                                 PD_HIDEPRINTTOFILE ¦
                                 PD_NOSELECTION,
                 CWnd* pParentWnd = NULL);

// Attributes:
    PRINTDLG FAR& m_pd; // reference to a parameter block

// Operations:
    virtual int DoModal();

    BOOL GetDefaults();

    int GetCopies() const;          // Number of copies requested
    BOOL PrintCollate() const;      // TRUE = collate checked
    BOOL PrintSelection() const;    // TRUE = printing a selection
    BOOL PrintAll() const;          // TRUE = printing all pages

    BOOL PrintRange() const;        // TRUE = printing page range
    int GetFromPage() const;        // Starting page and ending
    int GetToPage() const;          //   page if printing page range

    LPDEVMODE GetDevMode() const;  // Returns DEVMODE
    CString GetDriverName() const; // Returns driver name
    CString GetDeviceName() const; // Returns device name
    CString GetPortName() const;   // Returns output port name

    HDC GetPrinterDC() const;       // Returns HDC you
                                    //   must delete
```

```
// Diagnostic support
#ifdef _DEBUG
public:
    virtual void Dump(CDumpContext& dc) const;
#endif

    DECLARE_MESSAGE_MAP()

// Hidden implementation details....
};
```

Description

The `CPrintDialog` class is derived from the `CDialog` class. `CPrintDialog` provides a modal dialog box that you can use to display a standard Print Setup dialog box or a Print dialog box. The exact style is controlled by the `dwFlags` argument to the constructor. After you create a `CPrintDialog` object, call the `DoModal` member function to initiate interaction with the user. The `DoModal` function returns `IDOK` if the user selects the `OK` button. In this case, you can use various member functions of the `CPrintDialog` class to discover what items the user has selected. In particular, you can call the `GetPrinterDC` function to get a handle to a Windows DC that you can associate with a `CDC` object and use for printing graphics.

Member Functions

The intent of many member functions is apparent from the comments in the "Summary" section. Therefore, those functions are not described in this section.

Constructor

```
CPrintDialog(
    BOOL bPrintSetupOnly, // TRUE = Print Setup dialog box
                          // FALSE for Print dialog box
    DWORD dwFlags = PD_ALLPAGES |          // Flags to customize
                    PD_USEDEVMODECOPIES | // the dialog box
                    PD_NOPAGENUMS |
                    PD_HIDEPRINTTOFILE |
                    PD_NOSELECTION,
    CWnd* pParentWnd = NULL);  // Pointer to parent window
```

Creates and initializes a `CPrintDialog` object as specified by the arguments to the constructor.

Operations

```
virtual int DoModal();
```

Initiates interaction with the user and returns `IDOK` if the user selects the `OK` button.

```
BOOL GetDefaults();
```

Retrieves the default settings for the printer and stores them in the public `PRINTDLG` structure `m_pd`. Returns `TRUE` if all goes well; otherwise, returns `FALSE`.

See Also

`CDialog`	Base classes of `CPrintDialog`
`CColorDialog`	Other dialog box classes
`CFileDialog`	
`CFindReplaceDialog`	
`CFontDialog`	

CRect

Inheritance Hierarchy

```
tagRECT -> CRect

// tagRECT is defined in <windows.h> as
typedef struct tagRECT
{
    int left;
    int top;
    int right;
    int bottom;
} RECT;
```

Summary

```
#include <afxwin.h>

class CRect : public tagRECT
{
public:
// Constructors:
    CRect();
    CRect(int l, int t, int r, int b);
    CRect(const RECT& srcRect);
    CRect(LPRECT lpSrcRect);
    CRect(POINT point, SIZE size);
```

```
// Attributes (in addition to RECT members):
    int Width() const;         // Return width
    int Height() const;        // Return height
    CSize Size() const;        // Return width and height
    CPoint& TopLeft();         // Return top left point
    CPoint& BottomRight();     // Return bottom right point

    BOOL IsRectEmpty() const; // Return TRUE if width/height <= 0
    BOOL IsRectNull() const;  // Return TRUE if all coordinates zero
    BOOL PtInRect(POINT point) const; // Return TRUE if point is
                                      //   inside the CRect

// Standard Windows operations

    void CopyRect(LPRECT lpSrcRect); // Copy coordinates from lpSrcRect
                                     // to this CRect

// Return TRUE if this CRect is equal to the specified rectangle:
    BOOL EqualRect(LPRECT lpRect) const;

// Inflate rectangle by increasing width by 2x, height by 2y.
// Deflate if specified amounts are negative.
    void InflateRect(int x, int y);
    void InflateRect(SIZE size);

// Move rectangle by specified amounts in x- and y-directions:
    void OffsetRect(int x, int y);
    void OffsetRect(SIZE size);
    void OffsetRect(POINT point);

    void SetRect(int x1, int y1,  // Sets the coordinates of
                 int x2, int y2); // the CRect
    void SetRectEmpty();          // Set all coordinates to 0

// Operations that fill '*this' with result

// Set current CRect to intersection of two rectangles and
// return TRUE if intersection is not empty; FALSE otherwise:
    int IntersectRect(LPRECT lpRect1, LPRECT lpRect2);

// Set current CRect to union of two rectangles and
// return TRUE if the union is not empty; FALSE otherwise:
    int UnionRect(LPRECT lpRect1, LPRECT lpRect2);
```

```
#if (WINVER >= 0x030a)  // Only in Windows 3.1 or later //
// Set current CRect to difference of two rectangles and
// return TRUE if the difference is not empty; FALSE otherwise:
    BOOL SubtractRect(LPRECT lpRectSrc1, LPRECT lpRectSrc2);

#endif

// Convert between CRect and LPRECT (no need for &):
    operator LPRECT();

// Additional operations:
    void operator=(const RECT& srcRect);
    BOOL operator==(const RECT& rect) const;
    BOOL operator!=(const RECT& rect) const;
    void operator+=(POINT point);
    void operator-=(POINT point);
    void operator&=(const RECT& rect);
    void operator|=(const RECT& rect);

// Operators that return CRect values:
    CRect operator+(POINT point) const;
    CRect operator-(POINT point) const;
    CRect operator&(const RECT& rect2) const;
    CRect operator|(const RECT& rect2) const;
};
```

Description

The `CRect` class represents a rectangle modeled after the Windows `RECT` structure, which defines a rectangle by the coordinates of its top left and bottom right corners. You can use a `CRect` wherever a `RECT` (or a pointer to a `RECT`) is expected as an argument to a function. The comments in the "Summary" section adequately explain the member functions and operators.

See Also

`CPoint, CSize`	Class equivalents of `POINT` and `SIZE` structures

CResourceException

Inheritance Hierarchy

`CObject -> CException -> CResourceException`

Summary

```
class CResourceException : public CException
// Resource not found or couldn't-be-allocated failure.
{
    DECLARE_DYNAMIC(CResourceException)
public:
    CResourceException();
};
```

Description

`CResourceException` is derived from the `CException` class and represents the condition where Windows is unable to either find or allocate a requested resource.

Member Functions

Constructor and Destructor

`CResourceException();`

Creates a `CResourceException` object. However, never use the constructor directly—use the **`AfxThrowResourceException`**`()` function instead to create a **`CResourceException`** object.

See Also

`CException`	Base class of `CMemoryException`
`AfxThrowResourceException`	AFX function to create a `CResourceException` object

CRgn

Inheritance Hierarchy

`CObject -> CGdiObject -> CRgn`

Summary

```
#include <afxwin.h>

class CRgn : public CGdiObject
{
    DECLARE_DYNAMIC(CRgn)
public:

// Constructor:
    CRgn();
```

```
// Initializing a region:
    BOOL CreateRectRgn(int x1, int y1, int x2, int y2);
    BOOL CreateRectRgnIndirect(LPRECT lpRect);
    BOOL CreateEllipticRgn(int x1, int y1, int x2, int y2);
    BOOL CreateEllipticRgnIndirect(LPRECT lpRect);
    BOOL CreatePolygonRgn(LPPOINT lpPoints, int nCount,
                          int nMode);
    BOOL CreatePolyPolygonRgn(LPPOINT lpPoints,
                              LPINT lpPolyCounts,
                              int nCount, int nPolyFillMode);
    BOOL CreateRoundRectRgn(int x1, int y1, int x2, int y2,
                            int x3, int y3);

// Operations:
    void SetRectRgn(int x1, int y1, int x2, int y2);
    void SetRectRgn(LPRECT lpRect);
    int  CombineRgn(CRgn* pRgn1, CRgn* pRgn2, int nCombineMode);
    int  CopyRgn(CRgn* pRgnSrc);
    BOOL EqualRgn(CRgn* pRgn) const;
    int  OffsetRgn(int x, int y);
    int  OffsetRgn(POINT point);
    int  GetRgnBox(LPRECT lpRect) const;
    BOOL PtInRegion(int x, int y) const;
    BOOL PtInRegion(POINT point) const;
    BOOL RectInRegion(LPRECT lpRect) const;

// Utility function:
    static CRgn* FromHandle(HRGN hRgn);
};
```

Description

The `CRgn` class is the C++ class equivalent of a Windows region—an irregularly shaped area (of a window) comprising the union and intersection of elliptical and polygonal shapes. Regions are used to control where output appears in a window. `CRgn` includes a Windows handle to the region, as well as a number of member functions that enable you to manipulate the region in various ways. To use a region in the drawing functions provided by Windows GDI, select the region into a DC object using the `SelectObject` member function of the `CDC` class.

Member Functions

Constructor

```
CRgn();
```

Creates a `CRgn` object without an associated Windows region. Call one of the initialization functions to set up the region.

Initializing a Region

```
BOOL CreateEllipticRgn(int x1, int y1, int x2, int y2);
```

Creates an ellipse-shaped region and associates that region with this `CRgn` object. The ellipse is defined by the coordinates of the top left (*x1*, *y1*) and bottom right (*x2*, *y2*) corners of its bounding rectangle. Returns `TRUE` if successful; otherwise, returns `FALSE`.

```
BOOL CreateEllipticRgnIndirect(LPRECT lpRect);
```

Creates an ellipse-shaped region and associates that region with the `CRgn` object. The ellipse is defined by the coordinates of the top left and bottom right corners of its bounding rectangle that you provide in a `RECT` structure. Returns `TRUE` if successful; otherwise, returns `FALSE`.

```
BOOL CreatePolygonRgn(
    LPPOINT lpPoints, // Vertices of the polygon
    int     nCount,   // Number of vertices
    int     nMode);   // Fill mode of region (ALTERNATE or
                      // WINDING); used to determine which points
                      //   lie inside the region
```

Creates a polygonal region and associates that region with this `CRgn` object. The polygon is defined by the coordinates of its vertices, which you provide in the *`lpPoints`* array. Returns `TRUE` if successful; otherwise, returns `FALSE`. See the `SetPolyFillMode` function of the `CDC` class for more information about the fill mode.

```
BOOL CreatePolyPolygonRgn(
    LPPOINT lpPoints,           // Array of vertices of all polygons
    LPINT   lpPolyCounts,       // Array of integers that specify
                                //   the number of vertices for the polygons
    int     nCount,             // Number of polygons
    int     nPolyFillMode);     // Fill mode (ALTERNATE or WINDING)
                                // Used to determine which points
                                //   lie inside the region
```

Creates a region consisting of several closed polygons and associates that region with this `CRgn` object. The polygons are defined by the coordinates of their vertices that you provide in the *`lpPoints`* array. Returns `TRUE` if successful; otherwise, returns `FALSE`.

See the SetPolyFillMode function of the CDC class for more information about the fill mode.

```
BOOL CreateRectRgn(int x1, int y1, int x2, int y2);
```

Creates a rectangular region and associates that region with this CRgn object. The rectangle is defined by the coordinates of its top left (*x1*,*y1*) and bottom right (*x2*,*y2*) corners. Returns TRUE if successful; otherwise, returns FALSE.

```
BOOL CreateRectRgnIndirect(LPRECT lpRect);
```

Creates a rectangular region and associates that region with the CRgn object. The rectangle is defined by the coordinates of its top left and bottom right corners that are stored in a RECT structure. Returns TRUE if successful; otherwise, returns FALSE.

```
BOOL CreateRoundRectRgn(int x1, int y1, int x2, int y2,
                        int x3, int y3);
```

Creates a rectangular region with rounded corners and associates that region with this CRgn object. Figure 20.6 illustrates how the arguments are interpreted. Returns TRUE if successful; otherwise, returns FALSE.

```
static CRgn* FromHandle(HRGN hRgn); // Handle to existing region
```

Returns a pointer to a CRgn object with *hRgn* as its region. If *hRgn* is not already associated with an existing CRgn, this function creates a temporary CRgn object, attaches *hRgn* to that object, and returns the object's address. These temporary objects are periodically destroyed.

Operations

```
int CombineRgn(CRgn* pRgn1, CRgn* pRgn2, int nCombineMode);
```

Combines two regions, *pRgn1* and *pRgn2*, using the specified mode (*nCombineMode*) and stores the resulting region handle in this CRgn object. The *nCombineMode* argument indicates how the two regions are combined and can be one of the values shown in Table 20.18.

Table 20.18. Region operations.

Operation	Description
RGN_AND	Produces a resulting region that is the intersection of the two regions.
RGN_COPY	Makes a copy of the region identified by *pRgn1*.

Operation	Description
RGN_DIFF	Subtracts the region identified by *pRgn2* from the one identified by *pRgn1*.
RGN_OR	Produces a resulting region that is the union of the two regions.
RGN_XOR	Produces a resulting region that is the exclusive-OR of two (the regions are combined, but the overlapping parts are removed).

Returns an integer indicating the type of the resulting region. The return value can be COMPLEXREGION, SIMPLEREGION, NULLREGION, or ERROR.

```
int CopyRgn(CRgn* pRgnSrc);
```

Copies a specified region to this CRgn object. Returns an integer indicating the type of the resulting region. The return value can be COMPLEXREGION, SIMPLEREGION, NULLREGION, or ERROR.

```
BOOL EqualRgn(CRgn* pRgn) const;
```

Returns TRUE if the specified region is identical to this CRgn; it returns FALSE if the two regions do not match.

```
int GetRgnBox(LPRECT lpRect) const;
```

Copies the coordinates of the region's bounding rectangle to a RECT structure—the bounding rectangle is the smallest rectangle containing the region. Returns an integer indicating the type of the resulting region. The return value can be COMPLEXREGION, SIMPLEREGION, NULLREGION, or ERROR.

```
int OffsetRgn(int x, int y);
int OffsetRgn(POINT point);
```

Moves the region by a specified amount and returns an integer indicating the type of the resulting region. The return value can be COMPLEXREGION, SIMPLEREGION, NULLREGION, or ERROR.

```
BOOL PtInRegion(int x, int y) const;
BOOL PtInRegion(POINT point) const;
```

Returns TRUE if the specified point is inside the Windows region associated with this CRgn object.

```
BOOL RectInRegion(LPRECT lpRect) const;
```

Returns TRUE if any part of the specified rectangle is inside the Windows region associated with this CRgn object.

```
void SetRectRgn(int x1, int y1, int x2, int y2);
void SetRectRgn(LPRECT lpRect);
```

Sets the region associated with the CRgn object to a rectangle identified by the coordinates of its top left and bottom right corners or by a RECT structure. To use this function, you must ensure that the CRgn object has an existing Windows region associated with it.

See Also

CBrush, CPen,	Other GDI objects
CBitmap, CFont, CPalette, CDC	To select a region using the SelectObject member function; the drawing functions FillRgn, FrameRgn, and PaintRgn are part of the CDC class
CGdiObject	Base class of CRgn

CScrollBar

Inheritance Hierarchy

```
CObject -> CCmdTarget -> CWnd -> CScrollBar
```

Summary

```
#include <afxwin.h>

class CScrollBar : public CWnd
{
    DECLARE_DYNAMIC(CScrollBar)
public:
// Constructor:
    CScrollBar();

// Initializing a scroll bar:
    BOOL Create(DWORD dwStyle, const RECT& rect,
                CWnd* pParentWnd, UINT nID);

// Manipulating scroll range and thumb position:
    int GetScrollPos() const;
    int SetScrollPos(int nPos, BOOL bRedraw = TRUE);
```

```
    void GetScrollRange(LPINT lpMinPos, LPINT lpMaxPos) const;
    void SetScrollRange(int nMinPos, int nMaxPos,
                        BOOL bRedraw = TRUE);
    void ShowScrollBar(BOOL bShow = TRUE);

#if (WINVER >= 0x030a) // Only in Windows version 3.1 or later //

    BOOL EnableScrollBar(UINT nArrowFlags = ESB_ENABLE_BOTH);

#endif  /* WINVER >= 0x030a */

// Hidden implementation details....
};
```

Description

The `CScrollBar` class represents a Windows scrollbar control. Usually, you create windows with attached scrollbars by using the `WS_HSCROLL` and `WS_VSCROLL` styles. However, you also can create stand-alone scrollbars by directly using the `CScrollBar` class. If you create a scrollbar in a dialog box, it's destroyed automatically with the dialog box.

Member Functions

Constructor

```
CScrollBar();
```

Constructs a `CScrollBar` object, which you must initialize by calling `Create`.

Initializing a CScrollBar

```
BOOL Create(
    DWORD dwStyle,     // Scrollbar's style
    const RECT& rect,// Scrollbar's position and size
    CWnd* pParentWnd,// Pointer to parent window (cannot be NULL)
    UINT  nID);        // Scrollbar ID
```

Creates a Windows scrollbar of specified style and shape and attaches it to the `CScrollBar` object. Returns `TRUE` if successful. For a list of style names (which start with the `SBS_` prefix) consult the CreateWindow function in the Microsoft Windows SDK *Programmer's Reference, Volume 2.*

Manipulating the Scroll Bar

```
BOOL EnableScrollBar( // Only in Windows version 3.1 or later
    UINT nArrowFlags = ESB_ENABLE_BOTH);
```

Enables or disables the scrollbar as specified by *`nArrowFlags`*. Returns TRUE if successful; otherwise, returns `FALSE`.

```
int GetScrollPos() const;
```

Returns the current position of the scrollbox (the *thumb*)—this value depends on the current scroll range. If the scroll range is between 50 and 100 and the scrollbox is in the middle, the return value would be 75.

```
void GetScrollRange(LPINT lpMinPos, LPINT lpMaxPos) const;
```

Copies the current minimum and maximum scroll positions to the integers specified by `lpMinPos` and `lpMaxPos`.

```
int SetScrollPos(int nPos, BOOL bRedraw = TRUE);
```

Sets the scrollbox's position to `nPos` and redraws the scrollbar if the value of `bRedraw` is `TRUE`. Returns the previous position of the scrollbox.

```
void SetScrollRange(int nMinPos, int nMaxPos,
                    BOOL bRedraw = TRUE);
```

Sets the minimum and maximum positions of the scrollbar and redraws the scrollbar if the value of `bRedraw` is `TRUE`.

```
void ShowScrollBar(BOOL bShow = TRUE);
```

Shows the scrollbar if `bShow` is `TRUE`; it hides the scrollbar if `bShow` is `FALSE`.

See Also

`CWnd`	Base class of `CScrollBar`

CScrollView

Inheritance Hierarchy

`CObject -> CCmdTarget -> CWnd -> CView -> CScrollView`

Summary

```
class CScrollView : public CView
{
    DECLARE_DYNAMIC(CScrollView)

// Constructor:
protected:
    CScrollView();

public:
    static const SIZE AFXAPI_DATA sizeDefault;
```

```
    // Sizes are in logical units.
    // Your application must call one of the following Set routines to
    //    initialize the object:
    void SetScaleToFitSize(SIZE sizeTotal);
    void SetScrollSizes(int nMapMode, SIZE sizeTotal,
                const SIZE& sizePage = sizeDefault,
                const SIZE& sizeLine = sizeDefault);

// Attributes:
public:
    CPoint GetScrollPosition() const;
    CSize GetTotalSize() const;

    CPoint GetDeviceScrollPosition() const;
    void GetDeviceScrollSizes(int& nMapMode,
        SIZE& sizeTotal, SIZE& sizePage, SIZE& sizeLine) const;

// Operations:
public:
    void ScrollToPosition(POINT pt);
    void FillOutsideRect(CDC* pDC, CBrush* pBrush);
    void ResizeParentToFit(BOOL bShrinkOnly = TRUE);

// Implementation:
public:
    virtual ~CScrollView();
#ifdef _DEBUG
    virtual void Dump(CDumpContext&) const;
    virtual void AssertValid() const;
#endif //_DEBUG

    void OnScroll(int nBar, UINT nSBCode, UINT nPos);
    //{{AFX_MSG(CScrollView)
    afx_msg void OnSize(UINT nType, int cx, int cy);
    afx_msg void OnHScroll(UINT nSBCode, UINT nPos, CScrollBar*
pScrollBar);
    afx_msg void OnVScroll(UINT nSBCode, UINT nPos, CScrollBar*
pScrollBar);
    //}}AFX_MSG
    DECLARE_MESSAGE_MAP()
```

```
// Hidden implementation details...
//...

};
```

Description

`CScrollView` is derived from the `CView` class and represents a CView object with additional scrolling capabilities.

Member Functions

```
void FillOutsideRect(CDC* DC, CBrush* Brush);
```

Used to fill the part of the view in the window that falls outside the scrolling area.

```
CPoint GetDeviceScrollPosition() const;
```

Used to get the current scroll position, in device units.

```
void GetDeviceScrollSizes(int& nMapMode,
    SIZE& TotalSize, SIZE& PageSize, SIZE LineSize);
```

Used to get the current window mapping mode, the total size, and the line and page sizes of the scroll view, in device units.

```
CPoint GetScrollPosition() const;
```

Used to get the current scroll position, in logical units.

```
CSize GetTotalSize() const;
```

Used to get the total size of the scroll view in logical units.

```
void ResizeParentToFit(BOOL bOnlyShrink = TRUE);
```

Used to cause the size of the view to dictate the size of its frame. When the parameter *bOnlyShrink* is used with a value of `FALSE`, the view resizes the frame window exactly.

```
void ScrollToPosition(POINT point);
```

Used to scroll the view to a given point, which is specified in logical units.

```
void SetScaleToFitSize(SIZE TotalSize);
```

Used to scale the viewport size to the current windows size automatically.

```
void SetScrollSizes(int nMapMode, SIZE TotalSize,
    const SIZE PageSize = sizeDefault, const SIZE& LineSize =
sizeDefault);
```

Used to set the scroll view's mapping mode, total size, and horizontal and vertical scroll amounts. The *nMapMode* parameter can be any mode from Table 20.19.

Table 20.19. Windows mapping modes for `SetScrollSizes`.

Mode	Meaning
`MM_HIENGLISH`	Maps each logical unit to 0.001 inch, with the positive x-axis going right and the positive y-axis going up.
`MM_HIMETRIC`	Maps each logical unit to 0.01 millimeter, with the positive x-axis going right and the positive y-axis going up.
`MM_LOENGLISH`	Maps each logical unit to 0.01 inch, with the positive x-axis going right and the positive y-axis going up.
`MM_LOMETRIC`	Maps each logical unit to 0.1 millimeter, with the positive x-axis going right and the positive y-axis going up.
`MM_TEXT`	Maps each logical unit to one device pixel, with the positive x-axis going right and the positive y-axis going down.
`MM_TWIPS`	Maps each logical unit to one-twentieth of a printer's point (1/1,440 inch), with the positive x-axis going right and the positive y-axis going up.

Constructor and Destructor

`CScrollView();`

Constructs a **`CScrollView`** object. Call either `SetScrollSizes()` or `SetScaleToFitSize()` before using the **`CScrollView`**.

See Also

`CView`	Base class of `CScrollView`

CSize

Inheritance Hierarchy

`tagSIZE -> CSize`

```
// tagSIZE is a structure defined as
typedef struct tagSIZE
```

```
{
    int cx;
    int cy;
} SIZE;
```

Summary

```
#include <afxwin.h>
class CSize : public tagSIZE
{
public:
// Constructors:
    CSize();
    CSize(int initCX, int initCY);
    CSize(SIZE initSize);
    CSize(POINT initPt);
    CSize(DWORD dwSize);

// Operations:

 // Return TRUE if this CSize matches the specified SIZE structure:
   BOOL operator==(SIZE size) const;

 // Return TRUE if this CSize is not equal to the specified SIZE:
    BOOL operator!=(SIZE size) const;

// Return a CSize that is the sum of this CSize and another SIZE:
    void operator+=(SIZE size);

// Return a CSize that is the difference of this CSize
// and another SIZE:
    void operator-=(SIZE size);

// Operators returning CSize values:
    CSize operator+(SIZE size) const; // Sum of two sizes
    CSize operator-(SIZE size) const; // Difference of two sizes
};
```

Description

The `CSize` class represents the Windows `SIZE` structure, which defines the x- and y-extents of a rectangle. You can use a `CSize` wherever a `SIZE` (or a pointer to a `SIZE`) is expected as an argument to a function. The member functions and operators are explained adequately by the comments in the "Summary" section.

See Also

`CPoint, CRect`	Class equivalents of `POINT` and `RECT` structures

CSplitterWnd

Inheritance Hierarchy

`CObject -> CCmdTarget -> CWnd -> CSplitterWnd`

Summary

```
class CSplitterWnd : public CWnd
{
    DECLARE_DYNAMIC(CSplitterWnd)

// Construction:
public:
    CSplitterWnd();
    BOOL Create(CWnd* pParentWnd,
        int nMaxRows, int nMaxCols, SIZE sizeMin,
        CCreateContext* pContext,
        DWORD dwStyle =
            WS_CHILD ¦ WS_VISIBLE ¦ WS_HSCROLL ¦
            WS_VSCROLL ¦ SPLS_DYNAMIC_SPLIT,
        UINT nID = AFX_IDW_PANE_FIRST);

    BOOL CreateStatic(CWnd* pParentWnd,
        int nRows, int nCols,
        DWORD dwStyle = WS_CHILD ¦ WS_VISIBLE,
        UINT nID = AFX_IDW_PANE_FIRST);

    virtual BOOL CreateView(int row, int col, CRuntimeClass* pViewClass,
        SIZE sizeInit, CCreateContext* pContext);

// Attributes:
public:
    int GetRowCount() const;
    int GetColumnCount() const;

    void GetRowInfo(int row, int& cyCur, int& cyMin) const;
    void SetRowInfo(int row, int cyIdeal, int cyMin);
    void GetColumnInfo(int col, int& cxCur, int& cxMin) const;
    void SetColumnInfo(int col, int cxIdeal, int cxMin);
```

```
    CWnd* GetPane(int row, int col) const;
    BOOL IsChildPane(CWnd* pWnd, int& row, int& col);
    int IdFromRowCol(int row, int col) const;

// Operations:
public:
    void RecalcLayout();

// Implementation overridables:
protected:
    // Used to allow you to customize the drawing of the window:
    enum ESplitType { splitBox, splitBar, splitIntersection };
    virtual void OnDrawSplitter(CDC* pDC, ESplitType nType, const CRect&
rect);
    virtual void OnInvertTracker(const CRect& rect);

    // Used to allow you to customize the scrollbar regions:
    virtual BOOL CreateScrollBarCtrl(DWORD dwStyle, UINT nID);

    // Used to allow you to customize the DYNAMIC_SPLIT behavior:
    virtual void DeleteView(int row, int col);
    virtual BOOL SplitRow(int cyBefore);
    virtual BOOL SplitColumn(int cxBefore);
    virtual void DeleteRow(int row);
    virtual void DeleteColumn(int row);

// Implementation:
public:
    virtual ~CSplitterWnd();
#ifdef _DEBUG
    virtual void AssertValid() const;
    virtual void Dump(CDumpContext& dc) const;
#endif

    virtual BOOL CanActivateNext(BOOL bPrev = FALSE);
    virtual void ActivateNext(BOOL bPrev = FALSE);
    virtual BOOL DoKeyboardSplit();

    struct CRowColInfo
    {
        int nMinSize;       // Don't show window if < nMinSize
        int nIdealSize;     // User-specified best size variable
```

```
        int nCurSize;           // If 0, it's invisible
                                // If -1, it's nonexistant
    };

// Hidden implementation details...
//...

    DECLARE_MESSAGE_MAP()
};
```

Description

`CSplitterWnd` is derived from the `CWnd` class and represents *splitter window* (a window which has more than one pane).

Member Functions

`int GetRowCount();`

Used to return the current pane row count.

`int GetColumnCount();`

Used to return the current pane column count.

`void GetRowInfo(int Row, int& ColumnHeight, int& MinimumHeight);`

Used to return information on the specified row.

`void SetRowInfo(int Row, int IdealColumnHeight, int MinimumHeight);`

Used to set the specified row information.

`void GetColumnInfo(int Column, int& CurrentWidth, int& MinimumWidth);`

Used to return information on the specified column.

`void SetColumnInfo(int Column, int IdealCurrentWidth, int MinimumWidth);`

Used to set the specified column information.

`CWnd* GetPane(int nRow, int nColumn);`

Used to get the pane at the specified row and column coordinates.

`BOOL IsChildPane(CWnd* Window, int& nRow, int& nColumn);`

Used to determine if the window is currently a child pane of the specified splitter window.

`int IdFromRowCol(int nRow, int nColumn);`

Used to return the child window ID of the pane at the specified row and column.

```
void RecalcLayout();
```

Used to redisplay the splitter window after adjusting row or column size.

Constructor and Destructor

```
CSplitterWnd();
```

Creates a **CSplitterWnd** object. First you must call the constructor, and then call **Create()**, to create the splitter window, and attach **CSplitterObject** to the window.

```
Create();
```

First you must call the constructor, and then call **Create()**, to create the splitter window, and attach **CSplitterObject** to the window.

```
BOOL CreateStatic(CWnd* ParentWnd, int nRows, int nColumns,
    DWORD dwStyle = WS_CHILD | WS_VISIBLE, UINT nID =
AFX_IDW_PANE_FIRST );
```

First you must call the constructor, and then call **CreateStatic()**, to create the static splitter window, and attach **CSplitterObject** to the window.

```
virtual BOOL CreateView(int nRow, int nColumn, CRuntimeClass* pViewClass,
    SIZE sizeInit, CCreateContext* pContext);
```

This member function is used to create a pane in a splitter window.

See Also

`CWnd`	Base class of `CSplitterWnd`

CStatic

Inheritance Hierarchy

```
CObject -> CCmdTarget -> CWnd -> CStatic
```

Summary

```
#include <afxwin.h>

class CStatic : public CWnd
{
    DECLARE_DYNAMIC(CStatic)
public:
// Constructor:
    CStatic();
```

```
// Initializing a static control:
    BOOL Create(LPCSTR lpText, DWORD dwStyle,
                const RECT& rect, CWnd* pParentWnd,
                UINT nID = 0xffff);

#if(WINVER >= 0x030a) /* Only in Windows version 3.1 or later */

    HICON SetIcon(HICON hIcon);
    HICON GetIcon() const;

#endif /* WINVER >= 0x030a */


// Hidden implementation details....
};
```

Description

The `CStatic` class represents a Windows static control, which is used in dialog boxes to display a rectangular border, a label, or an icon. A static control does not respond to mouse or keyboard inputs.

Member Functions

Constructor

`CStatic();`

Constructs a `CStatic` object, which you must initialize by calling the `Create` member function.

Initializing a Static Control

```
BOOL Create(
    LPCSTR lpText,          // Text to appear in control
                            // (NULL means doesn't show any text)
    DWORD  dwStyle,         // Static control's window style
    const  RECT& rect,      // Location and size of the control
    CWnd*  pParentWnd,      // Pointer to parent window
                            //   (cannot be NULL)
    UINT   nID = 0xffff);   // Static control's ID
```

Creates a Windows static control window and attaches it to the `CStatic` object. Returns `TRUE` if successful. The `dwStyle` argument controls the style of the static control's window. For a list of style names (with an `SS_` prefix), consult the Microsoft Visual C++ online documentation.

Attributes

```
HICON GetIcon() const;   // Windows version 3.1 or later

HICON SetIcon(HICON hIcon); // Windows version 3.1 or later
```

See Also

`CColorDialog`, `CDialog`, `CFileDialog`, `CFindReplaceDialog`, CFontDialog, `PrintDialog`	Dialog box classes that use static controls
`CWnd`	Base class of `CStatic`

CStatusBar

Inheritance Hierarchy

```
CObject -> CCmdTarget -> CWnd -> CControlBar -> CStatusBar
```

Summary

```
class CStatusBar : public CControlBar
{
    DECLARE_DYNAMIC(CStatusBar)
// Constructor:
public:
    CStatusBar();
    BOOL Create(CWnd* pParentWnd,
        DWORD dwStyle = WS_CHILD ¦ WS_VISIBLE ¦ CBRS_BOTTOM,
        UINT nID = AFX_IDW_STATUS_BAR);
    BOOL SetIndicators(const UINT FAR* lpIDArray, int nIDCount);

// Attributes:
public:
    int CommandToIndex(UINT nIDFind) const;
    UINT GetItemID(int nIndex) const;
    void GetItemRect(int nIndex, LPRECT lpRect) const;
public:
    void GetPaneText(int nIndex, CString& s) const;
    BOOL SetPaneText(int nIndex, LPCSTR lpszNewText, BOOL bUpdate =
    TRUE);
    void GetPaneInfo(int nIndex, UINT& nID, UINT& nStyle, int& cxWidth)
    const;
    void SetPaneInfo(int nIndex, UINT nID, UINT nStyle, int cxWidth);
```

```
// Implementation:
public:
    virtual ~CStatusBar();
    inline UINT _GetPaneStyle(int nIndex) const;
    void _SetPaneStyle(int nIndex, UINT nStyle);

#ifdef _DEBUG
    virtual void AssertValid() const;
    virtual void Dump(CDumpContext& dc) const;
#endif

// Hidden implementation details...
//...

    DECLARE_MESSAGE_MAP()
};
```

Description

`CStatusBar` is derived from the `CControlBar` class and represents a bar (usually at the bottom of the window) that contains several areas that hold status information, such as the state of the Caps Lock key, and a general output area, which can be used for messages to the user. Each of the output areas is referred to as a pane.

Member Functions

SetIndicators(const UINT FAR* *lpIndicators*, int *nNumberIndicators*);

Used to set the status bar's indicators to the identifiers specified in the array *lpIndicators*. Each element in the array *lpIndicators* should respresent a string resource ID, which is loaded and displayed in the indicator.

int **CommandToIndex**(UINT *nIndicatorID*);

Used to retrieve the indicator index for the button which resource ID *nIndicatorID* is displayed in.

UINT **GetItemID**(int *nIndex*);

Used to retrieve the resource ID of the indicator associated with the index in *nIndex*.

GetItemRect(int *nIndex*, LPRECT *lpRect*) const;

Used to get the coordinates of the bounding rectangle for the pane specified by *nIndex*.

GetPaneText(int *nIndex*, CString& *csString*);

Used to retrieve the current text for indicator *nIndex*, and store the text in *csString*.

SetPaneText(int *nIndex*, LPCSTR *szString*, BOOL *bUpdateNow* = TRUE);

Used to set the text for indicator *nIndex* to the text pointed to by *szString*, and if *bUpdateNow* is TRUE, then update the window.

GetPaneInfo(int *nIndex*, UINT& *nIndex*, UINT& *nStyle*, int& *nWidth*);

Used to retrieve information about a given status bar pane. Returns the pane's ID (in *nIndex*), the pane's style (in *nStyle*), and the width of the pane (in *nImage*). See **SetPaneInfo**().

SetPaneInfo(int *nIndex*, UINT *nIndex*, UINT *nStyle*, int *nWidth*);

Used to set the status of a given status bar pane. Sets the ID (in *nIndex*), the pane's style (in *nStyle*), and the width of the pane (in *nImage*). See Table 20.20.

Table 20.20. Status bar pane styles.

Style	Description
SBPS_NOBORDERS	Do not draw a 3-D border around the pane.
SBPS_POPOUT	Draw a "reverse" border. Makes the pane stand out, or appear to be higher than the status bar border.
SBPS_DISABLED	The text is not to be drawn.
SBPS_STRETCH	Make the pane fill unused space. Can be used for only one pane in a status bar.
SBPS_NORMAL	No stretch, no borders, and no popout.

Constructor and Destructor

CStatusBar();

Used to construct a CStatusBar object.

Create();

Used to create the actual status bar window.

See Also

CControlBar, CWnd Base class of CStatusBar

CToolBar

Inheritance Hierarchy

```
CObject -> CCmdTarget -> CWnd -> CControlBar -> CToolBar
```

Summary

```
class CToolBar : public CControlBar
{
    DECLARE_DYNAMIC(CToolBar)
// Constructor:
public:
    CToolBar();
    BOOL Create(CWnd* pParentWnd,
        DWORD dwStyle = WS_CHILD ¦ WS_VISIBLE ¦ CBRS_TOP,
        UINT nID = AFX_IDW_TOOLBAR);

    void SetSizes(SIZE sizeButton, SIZE sizeImage);
    void SetHeight(int cyHeight);
    BOOL LoadBitmap(LPCSTR lpszResourceName);
    BOOL LoadBitmap(UINT nIDResource);
    BOOL SetButtons(const UINT FAR* lpIDArray, int nIDCount);

// Attributes:
public:
    int CommandToIndex(UINT nIDFind) const;
    UINT GetItemID(int nIndex) const;
    virtual void GetItemRect(int nIndex, LPRECT lpRect) const;

public:
    void GetButtonInfo(int nIndex, UINT& nID, UINT& nStyle, int& iImage)
const;
    void SetButtonInfo(int nIndex, UINT nID, UINT nStyle, int iImage);

// Implementation:
public:
    virtual ~CToolBar();
    inline UINT _GetButtonStyle(int nIndex) const;
    void _SetButtonStyle(int nIndex, UINT nStyle);

#ifdef _DEBUG
    virtual void AssertValid() const;
    virtual void Dump(CDumpContext& dc) const;
#endif
```

```
// Hidden implementation details...
//...

    DECLARE_MESSAGE_MAP()
};
```

Description

`CToolBar` is derived from the `CControlBar` class and represents a toolbar window. This toolbar usually is located at the top of an application's main window.

Member Functions

`CToolBar``();`

Used to construct a `CToolBar` object.

`SetSozes``(Size `*`nSizeButton`*`, Size `*`nSizeImage`*`);`

Used to define the size (in pixels) of the toolbar's buttons, and the size of the bitmap image that is displayed in the toolbar buttons.

`SetHeight``(int `*`nHeight`*`);`

Used to set the height of the toolbar, in pixels.

`LoadBitmap``(LPCSTR `*`szResourceName`*`);`
`LoadBitmap``(int `*`nResourceID`*`);`

Used to load the bitmap that contains each of the buttons' images.

`SetButtons``(const UINT FAR* `*`lpwCommands`*`, int `*`nCommandCount`*`);`

Used to set the command for each toolbar button. If a button is assigned to the command ID of `ID_SEPARATOR`, this button position is made a separator. Separators need not be considered when creating a toolbar button bitmap.

`CommandToIndex``(UINT `*`wCommandIndex`*`);`

Used to return the index of the first button associated with the command that matches *`wCommandIndex`*. If the command index is not found, returns –1.

`GetItemID``(int `*`nIndex`*`) const;`

Used to return the command index for the button specified by *`nIndex`*. The count of buttons includes separators. If *`nIndex`* is a separator, the identifier `ID_SEPARATOR` is returned.

`GetItemRect``(int `*`nIndex`*`, LPRECT `*`lpRect`*`);`

Used to get the coordinates of the bounding rectangle for the button or separator specified by *`nIndex`*.

`GetButtonInfo(int nIndex, UINT& nIndex, UINT& nStyle, int& nImage);`

Used to retrieve information about a given toolbar button. Returns the command index (in *nIndex*), the button's style (in *nStyle*), and the index to the bitmap image used for this button (in *nImage*). See **SetButtonInfo()**.

`SetButtonInfo(int nIndex, UINT nIndex, UINT nStyle, int nImage);`

Used to set the status of a given toolbar button. Sets the command index (in *nIndex*), the button's style (in *nStyle*), and the index to the bitmap image used for this button (in *nImage*). See Table 20.21.

Table 20.21. Toolbar button styles.

Style	Description
TBBS_BUTTON	Standard button (the default value)
TBBS_SEPARATOR	Separator
TBB_CHECKBOX	An auto-checkbox button

Constructor and Destructor

`Create();`

Used to create the actual toolbar window.

See Also

CStatusBar, CDialogBar	Classes similar to CToolBar

CVBControl

Inheritance Hierarchy

CObject -> CCmdTarget -> CWnd -> CVBControl

Summary

```
class CVBControl : public CWnd
{
    DECLARE_DYNAMIC(CVBControl)
// Constructors:
public:
    CVBControl();
```

```
    BOOL Create(LPCSTR lpszWindowName, DWORD dwStyle,
        const RECT& rect, CWnd* pParentWnd, UINT nID,
        CFile* pFile = NULL, BOOL bAutoDelete = FALSE);

// Attributes:
    BOOL SetNumProperty(int nPropIndex, LONG lValue, int index = 0);
    BOOL SetNumProperty(LPCSTR lpszPropName, LONG lValue, int index = 0);
    BOOL SetFloatProperty(int nPropIndex, float value, int index = 0);
    BOOL SetFloatProperty(LPCSTR lpszPropName, float value, int index = 0);
    BOOL SetStrProperty(int nPropIndex, LPCSTR lpszValue, int index = 0);
    BOOL SetStrProperty(LPCSTR lpszPropName, LPCSTR lpszValue, int index = 0);
    BOOL SetPictureProperty(int nPropIndex, HPIC hPic, int index = 0);
    BOOL SetPictureProperty(LPCSTR lpszPropName, HPIC hPic, int index = 0);
    LONG GetNumProperty(int nPropIndex, int index = 0);
    LONG GetNumProperty(LPCSTR lpszPropName, int index = 0);
    float GetFloatProperty(int nPropIndex, int index = 0);
    float GetFloatProperty(LPCSTR lpszPropName, int index = 0);
    CString GetStrProperty(int nPropIndex, int index = 0);
    CString GetStrProperty(LPCSTR lpszPropName, int index = 0);
    HPIC GetPictureProperty(int nPropIndex, int index = 0);
    HPIC GetPictureProperty(LPCSTR lpszPropName, int index = 0);

    int GetPropIndex(LPCSTR lpszPropName) const;
    LPCSTR GetPropName(int nIndex) const;

    int GetEventIndex(LPCSTR lpszEventName) const;
    LPCSTR GetEventName(int nIndex) const;

    LPCSTR GetVBXClass() const;

    int GetNumProps() const;
    int GetNumEvents() const;
    BOOL IsPropArray(int nIndex) const;

    UINT GetPropType(int nIndex) const;
    DWORD GetPropFlags(int nIndex) const;

    int m_nError;
```

```
// Operations:

    static void PASCAL OpenChannel(CFile* pFile, WORD wChannel);
    static BOOL PASCAL CloseChannel(WORD wChannel);
    static CFile* PASCAL GetChannel(WORD wChannel);
    static void BeginNewVBHeap();

    void AddItem(LPCSTR lpszItem, LONG lIndex);
    void RemoveItem(LONG lIndex);
    void Refresh();
    void Move(RECT& rect);


// Implementation:
public:
    virtual ~CVBControl();
#ifdef _DEBUG
    virtual void AssertValid() const;
    virtual void Dump(CDumpContext& dc) const;
#endif

    DWORD GetModelFlags();
    DWORD GetModelStyles();
    void ReferenceFile(BOOL bReference);
    static void EnableVBXFloat();

    static BOOL ParseWindowText(LPCSTR lpszWindowName, CString&
strFileName,
        CString& strClassName, CString& strCaption);

    HCTL GetHCTL();

    BYTE FAR* GetUserSpace();

    struct CRecreateStruct
    {
        char* pText;
        DWORD dwStyle;
        CRect rect;
        HWND hWndParent;
        UINT nControlID;
    };
```

```
    virtual LRESULT DefControlProc(UINT message, WPARAM wParam, LPARAM
    lParam);
    void Recreate(CRecreateStruct& rs);
    CVBControlModel* GetModel();

public:
    int GetStdPropIndex(int nStdID) const;
    BOOL SetPropertyWithType(int nPropIndex, WORD wType,
        LONG lValue, int index);
    LONG GetNumPropertyWithType(int nPropIndex, UINT nType, int index);
    HSZ GetStrProperty(int nPropIndex, int index, BOOL& bTemp);
    CString m_ctlName;

    static void CDECL Trace(BOOL bFatal, UINT nFormatIndex, ...);
    void VBXAssertValid() const;

    static BOOL EnableMemoryTracking(BOOL bTracking);

    DECLARE_MESSAGE_MAP()

    /////////////////////
    // Implementation
    // (These APIs can not be referenced by applications):
public:
    DWORD Save(CFile* pFile);
    BOOL Load(CFile* pData);

// Hidden implementation details...
//...

};
```

Description

`CVBControl` is derived from the `CWnd` class, and allows you to use controls developed for Visual Basic.

Member Variables

`int m_nError`

Used to hold the Visual Basic or control-defined error value when a `CVBControl` get or set member function (such as `GetNumProperty`) generates an error. Possible error values include those listed in Table 20.22.

Table 20.22. General `CVBControl::m_nError` values.

Value	Description
7	Insufficient memory
61	Disk full error
62	Read after EOF
380	The property value is invalid
420	The object reference is invalid
422	The property item was not found
other values	Custom error values; refer to the control's documentation

Member Functions

```
float GetFloatProperty(int nPropertyIndex, int nIndex = 0);
float GetFloatProperty(LPCSTR szPropertyName, int nIndex = 0);
```

Used to return the floating-point value assigned to a floating-point property.

```
LONG GetNumProperty(int nPropertyIndex, int nIndex = 0);
LONG GetNumProperty(LPCSTR szPropertyName, int nIndex = 0);
```

Used to return the long integer value assigned to a long integer property.

```
HPIC GetPictureProperty(int nPropertyIndex, int nIndex = 0);
HPIC GetPictureProperty(LPCSTR szPropertyName, int nIndex = 0);
```

Used to return the picture handle (HPIC) to the picture assigned to a picture property.

```
HPIC GetStrProperty(int nPropertyIndex, int nIndex = 0);
HPIC GetStrProperty(LPCSTR szPropertyName, int nIndex = 0);
```

Used to return the string to the picture assigned to a string property.

```
float SetFloatProperty(int nPropertyIndex, float fValue, int nIndex = 0);
float SetFloatProperty(LPCSTR szPropertyName, float fValue, int nIndex = 0);
```

Used to set the floating-point property to the value contained in `fValue`.

```
LONG SetNumProperty(int nPropertyIndex, LONG lValue, int nIndex = 0);
LONG SetNumProperty(LPCSTR szPropertyName, LONG lValue, int nIndex = 0);
```

Used to set the long integer property to the value contained in `lValue`.

```
HPIC SetPictureProperty(int nPropertyIndex, HPIC hPicture, int nIndex = 0);
HPIC SetPictureProperty(LPCSTR szPropertyName, HPIC hPicture, int nIndex = 0);
```

Used to set a picture property to the picture pointed to by `hPicture`.

```
HPIC SetStrProperty(int nPropertyIndex, LPCSTR szString, int nIndex = 0);
HPIC SetStrProperty(LPCSTR szPropertyName, LPCSTR szString, int nIndex = 0);
```

Used to set the string property to the string specified by `szString`.

```
int GetEventIndex(LPCSTR szEventName) const;
```

Used to get the specified event's index number.

```
LPCSTR GetEventName(int nIndex) const;
```

Used to get the specified event's name for a given index number.

```
int GetNumEvents() const;
```

Used to get the number of events associated with the control.

```
int GetNumProps() const;
```

Used to get the number of properties that are associated with the Visual Basic custom control.

```
DWORD GetPropFlags(int nIndex) const;
```

Used to get a (unsigned long) value that defines the property flags for the Visual Basic custom control.

```
int GetPropIndex(LPCSTR szPropertyName) const;
```

Used to get the index number assigned to a control property.

```
LPCSTR GetPropName(int nIndex) const;
```

Used to get the name of the property associated with index `nIndex`.

```
UINT GetPropType(int nIndex) const;
```

Returns the type of the property, as defined in Table 20.23.

Table 20.23. Property values for Visual Basic custom controls.

Type	Description
DT_HSZ	GetStrProperty/SetStrProperty
DT_SHORT	GetNumProperty/SetNumProperty
DT_LONG	GetNumProperty/SetNumProperty
DT_BOOL	GetNumProperty/SetNumProperty
DT_COLOR	GetNumProperty/SetNumProperty
DT_ENUM	GetNumProperty/SetNumProperty
DT_REAL	GetFloatProperty/SetFloatProperty
DT_XPOS	GetNumProperty/SetNumProperty
DT_XSIZE	GetNumProperty/SetNumProperty
DT_YPOS	GetNumProperty/SetNumProperty
DT_YSIZE	GetNumProperty/SetNumProperty
DT_PICTURE	GetPictureProperty/SetPictureProperty

```
LPCSTR GetVBXClass() const;
```

Used to get the name of the control class.

```
BOOL IsPropArray(int nIndex) const;
```

Used to check if property `nIndex` is in fact an array. Returns a nonzero value if the property is an array.

```
void AddItem(LPCSTR szItem, LONG lIndex);
```

Used to add items to a list managed by a list-box or combo box control.

```
void Move(RECT& Rect);
```

Used to move the control to the location specified by `Rect`, and resizes the control at the same time.

```
void Refresh();
```

Used to update the control to reflect any changes that have been made.

`void **RemoveItem**(LONG *lIndex*);`

Used to remove an item from a list managed by a list-box or combo box control.

`static void **BeginNewVBHeap**();`

Forces the creation of a new Visual Basic custom control heap when the next Visual Basic custom control is created.

`static BOOL **CloseChannel**(WORD *wChannel*);`

Used to disassociate the file associated from the specified channel number.

`static CFile* **GetChannel**(WORD *wChannel*);`

Used to retrieve a pointer to a `CFile` object currently associated with file channel *wChannel*.

`static void PASCAL **OpenChannel**(CFile* *cFile*, WORD *wChannel*);`

Used to associate a file with file channel *wChannel*.

Constructor and Destructor

`CVBControl`

Constructs a `CVBControl` object.

`Create`

Called after the `CVBControl` object has been constructed.

See Also

`CWbd`	Base class of `CVBControl`

CView

Inheritance Hierarchy

`CObject -> CCmdTarget -> CWnd -> CView`

Summary

```
class CView : public CWnd
{
    DECLARE_DYNAMIC(CView)

// Constructor:
protected:
    CView();
```

```
// Attributes:
public:
    CDocument* GetDocument() const;

// Operations:
public:
    BOOL DoPreparePrinting(CPrintInfo* pInfo);

// Overrideables:
public:
    virtual BOOL IsSelected(const CObject* pDocItem) const;

protected:
    // Activation:
    virtual void OnActivateView(BOOL bActivate, CView* pActivateView,
        CView* pDeactiveView);

    // General drawing/updating:
    virtual void OnInitialUpdate();
    virtual void OnUpdate(CView* pSender, LPARAM lHint, CObject* pHint);
    virtual void OnDraw(CDC* pDC) = 0;
    virtual void OnPrepareDC(CDC* pDC, CPrintInfo* pInfo = NULL);

    // Printing support:
    virtual BOOL OnPreparePrinting(CPrintInfo* pInfo);

    virtual void OnBeginPrinting(CDC* pDC, CPrintInfo* pInfo);
    virtual void OnPrint(CDC* pDC, CPrintInfo* pInfo);
    virtual void OnEndPrinting(CDC* pDC, CPrintInfo* pInfo);

    virtual void OnEndPrintPreview(CDC* pDC, CPrintInfo* pInfo, POINT
point,
        CPreviewView* pView);

// Implementation:
public:
    virtual ~CView();
#ifdef _DEBUG
    virtual void Dump(CDumpContext&) const;
    virtual void AssertValid() const;
#endif //_DEBUG
```

```
    // Advanced: Used for implementing custom print preview (see
CPreviewView):
    BOOL DoPrintPreview(UINT nIDResource, CView* pPrintView,
            CRuntimeClass* pPreviewViewClass, CPrintPreviewState*
pState);

// Hidden implementation details...
//...

    DECLARE_MESSAGE_MAP()
};
```

Description

`CView` is derived from the `CWnd` class, and provides the basic functionality for user-defined view classes. A *view class* is a class that interfaces the document and the user—usually by displaying the document's data in a window.

Member Functions

`BOOL` **`DoPreparePrinting`**`(CPrintInfo*` *`Info`*`);`

Used to display the print dialog box, and create a printer device context.

`CDocument*` **`GetDocument`**`() const;`

Used to get a pointer to the document in the view.

`virtual BOOL` **`IsSelected`**`(const CObject*` *`DocumentObject`*`) const;`

Used to test whether the specified document item is selected. The default function returns `FALSE`.

`virtual void` **`OnActivateView`**`(BOOL` *`bActivate`*`,`
`CView*` *`ActivateView`*`, CView*` *`DeactivateView`*`);`

The framework calls this function when a view is activated. The function then sets focus to the view being activated.

`virtual void` **`OnBeginPrinting`**`(CDC*` *`DC`*`, CPrintInfo*` *`PrinterInfo`*`);`

This function is called when a print job, or a Print Preview, is begun. The default implementation is to do nothing. You can override this function to create special GDI resources the document may require.

`virtual void` **`OnDraw`**`(CDC*` *`DC`* `= 0);`

This function is used to render (display) an image of the document for screen display, printing, or Print Preview. You must provide this function.

```
virtual void OnEndPrinting(CDC* DC, CPrintInfo* PrinterInfo);
```

This function is called when a print job, or a Print Preview, has ended. The default implementation is to do nothing. You can override this function to destroy special GDI resources that were created in the `OnBeginPrinting()` call.

```
virtual void OnEndPrintPreview(CDC* DC,
    CPrintInfo* Info, POINT Points, CPreviewView* View);
```

This function is called when the user exits the preview mode.

```
virtual void OnInitialUpdate();
```

This function is called after a view is first attached to a document.

```
virtual void OnPrepareDC(CDC* DC, CPrintInfo* Info = NULL);
```

This function is called before the `OnDraw` function is called for screen display or the `OnPrint` function is called for printing or print preview.

```
virtual BOOL OnPreparePrinting(CPrintInfo* Info);
```

This function is called before the document is either printed or previewed. You might want to override this function to initialize a Print dialog box.

```
virtual void OnPrint(CDC DC, CPrintInfo* Info);
```

This function is called to print or preview a page of the document.

```
virtual void OnUpdate(CView* Sender, LPARAM lHints, CObject* pHints);
```

This function is called when it is necessary to notify a view that its document has been modified.

Constructor and Destructor

```
CView();
```

Constructs a CView object.

Creates a `CCViuew` object. Called when a new frame window is created or an existing frame window is split.

See Also

`CWnd`	Base class of `CView`
`CDocument, CDC`	Other related classes

CWinApp

Inheritance Hierarchy

```
CObject -> CCmdTarget -> CWinApp
```

Summary

```
#include <afxwin.h>
class CWinApp : public CObject
{
    DECLARE_DYNAMIC(CWinApp)
public:
// Constructor:
    CWinApp(const char* pszAppName = NULL);

// Member variables:
    const char* m_pszAppName;  // Initialized by constructor
    HINSTANCE   m_hInstance;
    HINSTANCE   m_hPrevInstance;
    LPSTR       m_lpCmdLine;
    int         m_nCmdShow;
    CWnd*       m_pMainWnd;        // Main window (optional)

// Set up global handles using information from this CWinApp:
    void SetCurrentHandles();

// Manipulating cursors:
    HCURSOR LoadCursor(LPCSTR lpCursorName);
    HCURSOR LoadCursor(UINT nIDCursor);
    HCURSOR LoadStandardCursor(LPCSTR
                             lpCursorName); // For IDC_ values
    HCURSOR LoadOEMCursor(UINT nIDCursor);    // For OCR_ values

// Manipulating icons:
    HICON LoadIcon(LPCSTR lpIconName);
    HICON LoadIcon(UINT nIDIcon);
    HICON LoadStandardIcon(LPCSTR lpIconName);// For IDI_ values
    HICON LoadOEMIcon(UINT nIDIcon);          // For OIC_ values

// Called internally to retrieve the next message and process it:
    BOOL PumpMessage();

// Override the following functions to perform initializations
// appropriate for your application:
    virtual BOOL InitApplication();
    virtual BOOL InitInstance();

// Run implements a message-processing loop:
    virtual int Run();
```

```
// The following are called by the standard 'Run' implementation:
    virtual BOOL PreTranslateMessage(MSG* pMsg);
    virtual BOOL OnIdle(LONG lCount);
    virtual int ExitInstance(); // Return an exit code

// Diagnostic support:
#ifdef _DEBUG
    virtual void AssertValid() const;
    virtual void Dump(CDumpContext& dc) const;
#endif

#ifdef _DEBUG
protected:
    int m_nDisablePumpCount;
public:
    void EnablePump(BOOL bEnable);
#endif

protected:
    MSG  m_msgCur; // Last Windows message retrieved by Run
};
```

Description

The `CWinApp` class represents an entire Microsoft Windows application. This class manages initialization of an instance for a Windows application and implementation of the message-handling loop. A Windows application that uses the Windows programming classes from the Microsoft Foundation Class Library has exactly one instance of the `CWinApp` class (or, to be precise, an instance of a class derived from `CWinApp`). In any realistic application, you would use an application class derived from `CWinApp`, instead of using `CWinApp` directly, because you must override the `InitInstance` member function to create the main window of your application. When an instance of the `CWinApp`-derived application class is created, the constructor calls `InitInstance`, which creates and displays the application's main window. After this step, the application instance begins to process Windows messages, and the application responds to the user's inputs.

Member Variables

`HINSTANCE` **`m_hInstance`**`;`

This is the handle to the current instance of the application. It corresponds to the `hInstance` argument passed by Windows to the `WinMain` function. Access this handle by calling the global function `AfxGetInstanceHandle`.

```
HINSTANCE m_hPrevInstance;
```

This is the handle to the previous instance of the application. The **m_hPrevInstance** variable is NULL if this is the first instance of the application.

```
LPSTR m_lpCmdLine;
```

This is the string containing the command-line arguments that start the application.

```
MSG m_msgCur;
```

This is a protected member variable that contains the last Windows message retrieved by the Run member function.

```
int m_nCmdShow;
```

Stores the **nCmdShow** argument that Windows passes to the WinMain function. If **m_nCmdShow** is TRUE, the first call to ShowWindow makes the application's main window visible.

```
CWnd* m_pMainWnd;        // Main window (optional);
```

This is a pointer to the main window of your application. You should initialize this variable in the InitInstance member function of your application class (derived from CWinApp).

```
const char* m_pszAppName;  // Initialized by constructor
```

This is the name of the application. You can access this handle by calling the global function AfxGetAppName.

Member Functions

Constructor

```
CWinApp(const char* pszAppName = NULL);
```

Constructs a CWinApp object. You can specify a name for the application, or the function will use the name of the .EXE file as the application's name.

Loading Cursors

```
HCURSOR LoadCursor(LPCSTR lpCursorName); // Cursor resource name
HCURSOR LoadCursor(UINT nIDCursor); // ID of cursor resource
```

Loads the cursor specified by a resource name or a resource identifier and returns a handle to the cursor. Returns NULL if an error occurs.

```
HCURSOR LoadOEMCursor(
    UINT nIDCursor); // Predefined Windows cursor (OCR_ values);
```

Loads a predefined Windows cursor. The cursor is identified by *nIDCursor*, a constant with the OCR_ prefix defined in windows.h. If successful, returns a handle to the cursor; otherwise, returns NULL.

```
HCURSOR LoadStandardCursor(
    LPCSTR lpCursorName); // Name of cursor (IDC_ values)
```

Loads a predefined Windows cursor. The cursor is identified by the string *lpCursorName*. Use a constant with the IDC_ prefix (such as IDC_ARROW and IDC_IBEAM) defined in windows.h. If successful, returns a handle to the cursor; otherwise, returns NULL.

Loading Icons

```
HICON LoadIcon(LPCSTR lpIconName); // Icon resource name
HICON LoadIcon(UINT nIDIcon);      // Resource ID of icon
```

Loads the icon specified by a resource name or a resource identifier and returns a handle to the icon. Returns NULL if an error occurs.

```
HICON LoadOEMIcon(
    UINT nIDIcon);   // ID of predefined icon (OIC_ values)
```

Loads a predefined Windows icon. The icon is identified by *nIDIcon*, a constant with the OIC_ prefix defined in windows.h. If successful, this returns a handle to the icon; otherwise, it returns NULL.

```
HICON LoadStandardIcon(
    LPCSTR lpIconName);// Name of predefined icon (IDI_ values)
```

Loads a predefined Windows icon. The icon is identified by the string *lpIconName*. Use a constant with the IDI_ prefix (such as IDI_HAND and IDI_QUESTION) defined in windows.h. If successful, returns a handle to the icon; otherwise, returns NULL.

Overridable Functions

```
virtual int ExitInstance();
```

Returns an exit code. You can override this function to clean up operations such as closing files and deallocating memory after your application terminates. This function is called by the standard Run function.

```
virtual BOOL InitApplication();
```

Performs initializations common to all instances of the application. Returns TRUE if initialization is successful; otherwise, returns FALSE.

```
virtual BOOL InitInstance();
```

Performs initializations for this instance of the application. You should override this function to perform all application-specific initializations, such as creating the main window of the application and making it visible. Returns `TRUE` if initialization is successful; otherwise, returns `FALSE`.

```
virtual BOOL OnIdle(
    LONG lCount); // Count of how many times GetMessage found the
                  //   message queue empty.
```

Called whenever the application's message queue is empty. You can override `OnIdle` to perform housecleaning chores during idle times. This should return `TRUE` to receive more calls during idle times; the function should return `FALSE` if no more idle time is needed.

```
virtual BOOL PreTranslateMessage(
    MSG* pMsg); // Message to process
```

You can override this function to filter out Windows messages before they're sent to `TranslateMessage` and `DispatchMessage`. This function is called by the standard `Run` function. This should return `TRUE` if the message should not be forwarded to `TranslateMessage` and `DispatchMessage` (in other words, returning `TRUE` blocks the message here); otherwise, it returns `FALSE` to process the message in the normal way.

```
virtual int Run();
```

`Run` implements a message-processing loop. `Run` retrieves and dispatches messages until a `WM_QUIT` message is received. Usually, you don't need to override `Run`, but you can do so to provide special behavior to the message-processing loop.

CWindowDC

Inheritance Hierarchy

`CObject -> CDC -> CWindowDC`

Summary

```
#include <afxwin.h>

class CWindowDC : public CDC
{
    DECLARE_DYNAMIC(CWindowDC)
public:
// Constructor and destructor:
```

```
    CWindowDC(CWnd* pWnd);
    virtual ~CWindowDC();

// Diagnostic support:
#ifdef _DEBUG
    virtual void AssertValid() const;
    virtual void Dump(CDumpContext& dc) const;
#endif

// Attributes:
protected:
    HWND m_hWnd;
};
```

Description

`CWindowDC` is derived from the `CDC` class and represents a DC associated with the entire screen area of a window. You can use a `CWindowDC` object to draw in both the client and nonclient areas of a window.

Member Functions

Constructor and Destructor

```
CWindowDC(
    CWnd* pWnd); // Set up DC for this window's screen area
```

Creates a `CWindowDC` object and sets up an associated DC for the screen area of the window specified by *pWnd*. This constructor calls the Windows function `GetDC` to obtain a DC for the window. If it fails, `CWindowDC` throws a `CResourceException`.

```
virtual ~CWindowDC();
```

Destroys the `CWindowDC` object and calls `ReleaseDC` to free the Windows DC that was obtained by the constructor.

See Also

`CClientDC`	Provides a DC for drawing in the client area of a window
`CDC`	The base class of `CWindowDC`

CWnd

Inheritance Hierarchy

`CObject -> CCmdTarget -> CWnd`

Summary

```
#include <afxwin.h>
```

```
class CWnd : public CObject
{
    DECLARE_DYNAMIC(CWnd)
public:
// Constructor and destructor:
    CWnd();
    virtual ~CWnd();

// Creating and destroying the window:
    static CWnd* FromHandle(HWND hWnd);
    static CWnd* FromHandlePermanent(HWND hWnd);
    static void DeleteTempMap();
    BOOL Attach(HWND hWndNew);
    HWND Detach();
    BOOL SubclassWindow(HWND hWnd);
    BOOL SubclassDlgItem(UINT nID, CWnd* pParent);
// For dynamic subclassing of Windows control:

// The next function is for child windows....
    BOOL Create(LPCSTR lpClassName,
                LPCSTR lpWindowName, DWORD dwStyle,
                const RECT& rect,
                 const CWnd* pParentWnd, UINT nID);



    virtual BOOL DestroyWindow();

// Attributes:
    HWND m_hWnd;
    static const CWnd NEAR wndTop;
    static const CWnd NEAR wndBottom;

#if (WINVER >= 0x030a) /* For Windows version 3.1 or later only */
    static const CWnd NEAR wndTopMost;
    static const CWnd NEAR wndNoTopMost;
#endif // WINVER >= 0x030a //

    HWND GetSafeHwnd() const;
    DWORD GetStyle() const;
    DWORD GetExStyle() const;
```

```
// Sending messages:
    LONG SendMessage(UINT message, UINT wParam = 0,
                     LONG lParam = 0);
    BOOL PostMessage(UINT message, UINT wParam = 0,
                     LONG lParam = 0);

// Manipulating window text (caption):
    void   SetWindowText(LPCSTR lpString);
    int    GetWindowText(LPSTR lpString, int nMaxCount) const;
    int    GetWindowTextLength() const;
    void   GetWindowText(CString& rString) const;
    void   SetFont(CFont* pFont, BOOL bRedraw = TRUE);
    CFont* GetFont();

// Functions for the CMenu derived class
// (for nonchild windows only):
    CMenu* GetMenu() const;
    BOOL   SetMenu(CMenu* pMenu);
    void   DrawMenuBar();
    CMenu* GetSystemMenu(BOOL bRevert) const;
    BOOL   HiliteMenuItem(CMenu* pMenu, UINT nIDHiliteItem,
                          UINT nHilite);

// Special attributes for child windows only:
    int GetDlgCtrlID() const;

// Moving and resizing windows:
    void CloseWindow();
    BOOL OpenIcon();
    void MoveWindow(int x, int y, int nWidth, int nHeight,
                    BOOL bRepaint = TRUE);
    void MoveWindow(LPRECT lpRect, BOOL bRepaint = TRUE);

    BOOL SetWindowPos(const CWnd* pWndInsertAfter, int x, int y,
               int cx, int cy, UINT nFlags);
    UINT ArrangeIconicWindows();
    void BringWindowToTop();
    void GetWindowRect(LPRECT lpRect) const;
    void GetClientRect(LPRECT lpRect) const;

#if (WINVER >= 0x030a) /* For Windows version 3.1 or later */
    BOOL GetWindowPlacement(WINDOWPLACEMENT FAR* lpwndpl) const;
```

```
    BOOL SetWindowPlacement(const WINDOWPLACEMENT FAR* lpwndpl);
#endif  // WINVER >= 0x030a //

// Converting coordinates:
    void ClientToScreen(LPPOINT lpPoint) const;
    void ClientToScreen(LPRECT lpRect) const;
    void ScreenToClient(LPPOINT lpPoint) const;
    void ScreenToClient(LPRECT lpRect) const;

#if (WINVER >= 0x030a) // For Windows version 3.1 or later //
    void MapWindowPoints(CWnd* pwndTo, LPPOINT lpPoint,
                         UINT nCount) const;
    void MapWindowPoints(CWnd* pwndTo, LPRECT lpRect) const;
#endif  // WINVER >= 0x030a //

// Updating and painting the window:
    CDC* BeginPaint(LPPAINTSTRUCT lpPaint);
    void EndPaint(LPPAINTSTRUCT lpPaint);
    CDC* GetDC();
    CDC* GetWindowDC();
    int  ReleaseDC(CDC* pDC);

    void UpdateWindow();
    void SetRedraw(BOOL bRedraw = TRUE);
    BOOL GetUpdateRect(LPRECT lpRect, BOOL bErase = FALSE);
    int  GetUpdateRgn(CRgn* pRgn, BOOL bErase = FALSE);
    void Invalidate(BOOL bErase = TRUE);
    void InvalidateRect(LPRECT lpRect, BOOL bErase = TRUE);
    void InvalidateRgn(CRgn* pRgn, BOOL bErase = TRUE);
    void ValidateRect(LPRECT lpRect);
    void ValidateRgn(CRgn* pRgn);
    BOOL ShowWindow(int nCmdShow);
    void ShowOwnedPopups(BOOL bShow = TRUE);

#if (WINVER >= 0x030a)  // For Windows version 3.1 or later //
    CDC* GetDCEx(CRgn* prgnClip, DWORD flags);
    BOOL LockWindowUpdate();
    BOOL RedrawWindow(const RECT FAR* lpRectUpdate = NULL,
                      CRgn* prgnUpdate = NULL,
                      UINT flags = RDW_INVALIDATE |
                               RDW_UPDATENOW | RDW_ERASE);
```

```
    BOOL EnableScrollBar(int nSBFlags,
                         UINT nArrowFlags = ESB_ENABLE_BOTH);
#endif  // WINVER >= 0x030a //

// Managing timers
    UINT SetTimer(int nIDEvent, UINT nElapse,
                  UINT (FAR PASCAL EXPORT* lpfnTimer)(HWND,
                                            UINT, int, DWORD));
    BOOL KillTimer(int nIDEvent);

// Accessing the current state of the window:
    BOOL IsIconic() const;
    BOOL IsZoomed() const;
    BOOL IsWindowEnabled() const;
    BOOL IsWindowVisible() const;
    BOOL EnableWindow(BOOL bEnable = TRUE);

    static CWnd* GetActiveWindow();
    CWnd*        SetActiveWindow();

    static CWnd* GetCapture();
    CWnd*        SetCapture();
    static CWnd* GetFocus();
    CWnd*        SetFocus();

    CWnd*        SetSysModalWindow();
    static CWnd* GetSysModalWindow();

    static CWnd* GetDesktopWindow();

// Manipulating dialog box items:
// (NOTE: Dialog box items may not be in dialog boxes!)
    void CheckDlgButton(int nIDButton, UINT nCheck);
    void CheckRadioButton(int nIDFirstButton, int nIDLastButton,
                          int nIDCheckButton);
    int  GetCheckedRadioButton(int nIDFirstButton,
                               int nIDLastButton);
    int  DlgDirList(LPSTR lpPathSpec, int nIDListBox,
                    int nIDStaticPath, UINT nFileType);
    int  DlgDirListComboBox(LPSTR lpPathSpec, int nIDComboBox,
                            int nIDStaticPath, UINT nFileType);
```

```
    BOOL DlgDirSelect(LPSTR lpString, int nIDListBox);
    BOOL DlgDirSelectComboBox(LPSTR lpString, int nIDComboBox);

    CWnd* GetDlgItem(int nID) const;
    UINT  GetDlgItemInt(int nID, BOOL* lpTrans = NULL,
                        BOOL bSigned = TRUE) const;
    int   GetDlgItemText(int nID, LPSTR lpStr,
                         int nMaxCount) const;

    CWnd* GetNextDlgGroupItem(CWnd* pWndCtl,
                              BOOL bPrevious = FALSE) const;

    CWnd* GetNextDlgTabItem(CWnd* pWndCtl,
                            BOOL bPrevious = FALSE) const;
    UINT  IsDlgButtonChecked(int nIDButton) const;
    LONG  SendDlgItemMessage(int nID, UINT message,
                             UINT wParam = 0, LONG lParam = 0);
    void  SetDlgItemInt(int nID, UINT nValue,
                        BOOL bSigned = TRUE);
    void SetDlgItemText(int nID, LPCSTR lpString);

// Scrolling the window:
    int  GetScrollPos(int nBar) const;
    void GetScrollRange(int nBar, LPINT lpMinPos,
                        LPINT lpMaxPos) const;
    void ScrollWindow(int xAmount, int yAmount,
                      const RECT FAR* lpRect = NULL,
                      const RECT FAR* lpClipRect = NULL);
    int  SetScrollPos(int nBar, int nPos, BOOL bRedraw = TRUE);
    void SetScrollRange(int nBar, int nMinPos, int nMaxPos,
                        BOOL bRedraw = TRUE);
    void ShowScrollBar(UINT nBar, BOOL bShow = TRUE);

#if (WINVER >= 0x030a) // For Windows version 3.1 or later //
    int ScrollWindowEx(int dx, int dy,
                       const RECT FAR* lpRectScroll,
                       const RECT FAR* lpRectClip,
                       CRgn* prgnUpdate, LPRECT lpRectUpdate,
                       UINT flags);
#endif  // WINVER >= 0x030a //

// Traversing the window hierarchy
    CWnd*        ChildWindowFromPoint(POINT point) const;
```

```
    static CWnd* FindWindow(LPCSTR lpClassName,
                            LPCSTR lpWindowName);
    CWnd* GetNextWindow(UINT nFlag = GW_HWNDNEXT) const;
    CWnd* GetTopWindow() const;

    CWnd* GetWindow(UINT nCmd) const;
    CWnd* GetLastActivePopup() const;

    BOOL  IsChild(CWnd* pWnd) const;
    CWnd* GetParent() const;
    CWnd* SetParent(CWnd* pWndNewParent);

    static CWnd* WindowFromPoint(POINT point);

// Handling alerts:
    BOOL FlashWindow(BOOL bInvert);
    int MessageBox(LPCSTR lpText, LPCSTR lpCaption = NULL,
                   UINT nType = MB_OK);

// Using the Clipboard:
    BOOL         ChangeClipboardChain(HWND hWndNext);
    HWND         SetClipboardViewer();
    BOOL         OpenClipboard();
    static CWnd* GetClipboardOwner();
    static CWnd* GetClipboardViewer();

#if (WINVER >= 0x030a) // For Windows version 3.1 or later //
    static CWnd* GetOpenClipboardWindow();
#endif // WINVER >= 0x030a //

// Managing carets (the blinking cursor that marks the text-
// insertion point):
    void          CreateCaret(CBitmap* pBitmap);
    void          CreateSolidCaret(int nWidth, int nHeight);
    void          CreateGrayCaret(int nWidth, int nHeight);
    static CPoint GetCaretPos();
    static void   SetCaretPos(POINT point);
    void          HideCaret();
    void          ShowCaret();

// Diagnostic support:
#ifdef _DEBUG
```

```
    virtual void AssertValid() const;
    virtual void Dump(CDumpContext& dc) const;
#endif


// Member functions for handling Windows messages:
protected:
// This function creates and attaches a window to CWnd.
    BOOL CreateEx(DWORD dwExStyle, LPCSTR lpClassName,
                  LPCSTR lpWindowName, DWORD dwStyle,
                  int x, int y, int nWidth, int nHeight,
                  HWND hwndParent, HMENU nIDorHMenu);

    virtual BOOL OnCommand(UINT wParam, LONG lParam);

    afx_msg void OnActivate(UINT nState, CWnd* pWndOther,
                            BOOL bMinimized);
    afx_msg void OnActivateApp(BOOL bActive, HANDLE hTask);
    afx_msg void OnCancelMode();
    afx_msg void OnChildActivate();
    afx_msg void OnClose();
    afx_msg int  OnCreate(LPCREATESTRUCT lpCreateStruct);

    afx_msg HBRUSH OnCtlColor(CDC* pDC, CWnd* pWnd,
                              UINT nCtlColor);
    afx_msg void OnDestroy();
    afx_msg void OnEnable(BOOL bEnable);
    afx_msg void OnEndSession(BOOL bEnding);
    afx_msg void OnEnterIdle(UINT nWhy, CWnd* pWho);
    afx_msg BOOL OnEraseBkgnd(CDC* pDC);
    afx_msg void OnGetMinMaxInfo(LPPOINT lpPoints);
    afx_msg void OnIconEraseBkgnd(CDC* pDC);
    afx_msg void OnKillFocus(CWnd* pNewWnd);
    afx_msg LONG OnMenuChar(UINT nChar, UINT nFlags,
                            CMenu* pMenu);
    afx_msg void OnMenuSelect(UINT nItemID, UINT nFlags,
                              HMENU hSysMenu);
    afx_msg void OnMove(int x, int y);
    afx_msg void OnPaint();
    afx_msg void OnParentNotify(UINT message, LONG lParam);

    afx_msg HCURSOR OnQueryDragIcon();
```

```
    afx_msg BOOL OnQueryEndSession();
    afx_msg BOOL OnQueryNewPalette();
    afx_msg BOOL OnQueryOpen();
    afx_msg void OnSetFocus(CWnd* pOldWnd);
    afx_msg void OnShowWindow(BOOL bShow, UINT nStatus);
    afx_msg void OnSize(UINT nType, int cx, int cy);

#if (WINVER >= 0x030a) // For Windows 3.1 or later //
    afx_msg void OnWindowPosChanging(WINDOWPOS FAR* lpwndpos);
    afx_msg void OnWindowPosChanged(WINDOWPOS FAR* lpwndpos);
#endif // WINVER >= 0x030a //

// Message handlers for nonclient-area messages (nonclient area
// includes the caption bar, the menu bar, and the scrollbars):
    afx_msg BOOL OnNcActivate(BOOL bActive);
    afx_msg void OnNcCalcSize(NCCALCSIZE_PARAMS FAR* lpncsp);
    afx_msg BOOL OnNcCreate(LPCREATESTRUCT lpCreateStruct);
    afx_msg void OnNcDestroy();
    afx_msg UINT OnNcHitTest(CPoint point);
    afx_msg void OnNcLButtonDblClk(UINT nHitTest, CPoint point);
    afx_msg void OnNcLButtonDown(UINT nHitTest, CPoint point);
    afx_msg void OnNcLButtonUp(UINT nHitTest, CPoint point);
    afx_msg void OnNcMButtonDblClk(UINT nHitTest, CPoint point);
    afx_msg void OnNcMButtonDown(UINT nHitTest, CPoint point);
    afx_msg void OnNcMButtonUp(UINT nHitTest, CPoint point);
    afx_msg void OnNcMouseMove(UINT nHitTest, CPoint point);
    afx_msg void OnNcPaint();
    afx_msg void OnNcRButtonDblClk(UINT nHitTest, CPoint point);
    afx_msg void OnNcRButtonDown(UINT nHitTest, CPoint point);
    afx_msg void OnNcRButtonUp(UINT nHitTest, CPoint point);

// Handling system messages:

#if (WINVER >= 0x030a) // For Windows version 3.1 or later //
    afx_msg void OnDropFiles(HANDLE hDropInfo);
    afx_msg void OnPaletteIsChanging(CWnd* pRealizeWnd);
#endif // WINVER >= 0x030a //

    afx_msg void OnSysChar(UINT nChar, UINT nRepCnt, UINT nFlags);
    afx_msg void OnSysCommand(UINT nID, LONG lParam);
    afx_msg void OnSysDeadChar(UINT nChar, UINT nRepCnt,
                               UINT nFlags);
```

```
    afx_msg void OnSysKeyDown(UINT nChar, UINT nRepCnt,
                              UINT nFlags);
    afx_msg void OnSysKeyUp(UINT nChar, UINT nRepCnt,
                            UINT nFlags);
    afx_msg void OnCompacting(UINT nCpuTime);
    afx_msg void OnDevModeChange(LPSTR lpDeviceName);
    afx_msg void OnFontChange();
    afx_msg void OnPaletteChanged(CWnd* pFocusWnd);
    afx_msg void OnSpoolerStatus(UINT nStatus, UINT nJobs);
    afx_msg void OnSysColorChange();
    afx_msg void OnTimeChange();
    afx_msg void OnWinIniChange(LPSTR lpSection);

// Handling mouse and keyboard messages:
    afx_msg void OnChar(UINT nChar, UINT nRepCnt, UINT nFlags);
    afx_msg void OnDeadChar(UINT nChar, UINT nRepCnt, UINT nFlags);
    afx_msg void OnHScroll(UINT nSBCode, UINT nPos,
                           CScrollBar* pScrollBar);
    afx_msg void OnKeyDown(UINT nChar, UINT nRepCnt, UINT nFlags);
    afx_msg void OnKeyUp(UINT nChar, UINT nRepCnt, UINT nFlags);
    afx_msg void OnLButtonDblClk(UINT nFlags, CPoint point);
    afx_msg void OnLButtonDown(UINT nFlags, CPoint point);
    afx_msg void OnLButtonUp(UINT nFlags, CPoint point);
    afx_msg void OnMButtonDblClk(UINT nFlags, CPoint point);
    afx_msg void OnMButtonDown(UINT nFlags, CPoint point);
    afx_msg void OnMButtonUp(UINT nFlags, CPoint point);
    afx_msg int  OnMouseActivate(CWnd* pFrameWnd, UINT nHitTest,
                                 UINT message);
    afx_msg void OnMouseMove(UINT nFlags, CPoint point);
    afx_msg void OnRButtonDblClk(UINT nFlags, CPoint point);
    afx_msg void OnRButtonDown(UINT nFlags, CPoint point);
    afx_msg void OnRButtonUp(UINT nFlags, CPoint point);
    afx_msg BOOL OnSetCursor(CWnd* pWnd, UINT nHitTest,
                             UINT message);
    afx_msg void OnTimer(UINT nIDEvent);
    afx_msg void OnVScroll(UINT nSBCode, UINT nPos,
                           CScrollBar* pScrollBar);

// Handling initialization messages:
    afx_msg void OnInitMenu(CMenu* pMenu);
    afx_msg void OnInitMenuPopup(CMenu* pPopupMenu,
                                 UINT nIndex, BOOL bSysMenu);
```

```
// Handling Clipboard messages:
    afx_msg void OnAskCbFormatName(UINT nMaxCount,
                                   LPSTR lpString);
    afx_msg void OnChangeCbChain(HWND hWndRemove,
                                 HWND hWndAfter);
    afx_msg void OnDestroyClipboard();
    afx_msg void OnDrawClipboard();
    afx_msg void OnHScrollClipboard(CWnd* pClipAppWnd,
                                    UINT nSBCode, UINT nPos);
    afx_msg void OnPaintClipboard(CWnd* pClipAppWnd,
                                  HANDLE hPaintStruct);
    afx_msg void OnRenderAllFormats();
    afx_msg void OnRenderFormat(UINT nFormat);
    afx_msg void OnSizeClipboard(CWnd* pClipAppWnd, HANDLE hRect);
    afx_msg void OnVScrollClipboard(CWnd* pClipAppWnd,
                                    UINT nSBCode, UINT nPos);

// Handling control messages:
    afx_msg int  OnCharToItem(UINT nChar, CListBox* pListBox, UINT
nIndex);
    afx_msg int  OnCompareItem(LPCOMPAREITEMSTRUCT lpCompareItemStruct);
    afx_msg void OnDeleteItem(LPDELETEITEMSTRUCT lpDeleteItemStruct);
    afx_msg void OnDrawItem(LPDRAWITEMSTRUCT lpDrawItemStruct);
    afx_msg UINT OnGetDlgCode();
    afx_msg void OnMeasureItem(LPMEASUREITEMSTRUCT lpMeasureItemStruct);
    afx_msg int  OnVKeyToItem(UINT nKey, CListBox* pListBox, UINT
nIndex);

// Handling MDI messages:
    afx_msg void OnMDIActivate(BOOL bActivate,
                    CWnd* pActivateWnd, CWnd* pDeactivateWnd);

// Other protected member functions that you might override
// in derived classes.
// Use the following when you are deriving from a standard control:
    virtual WNDPROC* GetSuperWndProcAddr();

// Used to translate Windows messages in CWinApp's message handler:
    virtual BOOL PreTranslateMessage(MSG* pMsg);

// To override the processing of Windows messages:
    virtual LONG WindowProc(UINT message, UINT wParam,
                            LONG lParam);
```

```
// This function processes any message not handled by the application:
    LONG        Default();

// This function calls Default to provide default processing:
    virtual LONG DefWindowProc(UINT message, UINT wParam, LONG lParam);

// Override if you need custom cleanup after WM_NCDESTROY:
    virtual void PostNcDestroy();

// Miscellaneous:
    static const MSG* GetCurrentMessage();

    friend void FAR PASCAL AFX_EXPORT _AfxSendMsgHook(int,
                                              UINT, LONG);
    friend LONG _AfxCallWndProc(CWnd*, HWND, UINT, UINT, LONG);

    friend class CWinApp; // CWinApp accesses PreTranslate

    DECLARE_MESSAGE_MAP()
};
```

Description

`CWnd` is the base class for all window classes in the Microsoft Foundation Class Library. It provides all the message-handling functions that a window class should need. Typically, you derive your application's main window class from either the `CFrameWnd` or `CMDIFrameWnd` classes (derived from `CWnd`). In your derived window class, you override and implement only the message-handling functions your application needs. You might derive other child windows in your application directly from `CWnd` or `CMDIChildWnd`.

You must learn about both the public and the protected members in `CWnd` because you usually derive your window classes from `CWnd`, and derived classes can access protected members of the base class.

Member Variables

`HWND` **`m_hWnd`**`;`

This is the handle of the window attached to this `CWnd` object.

Member Functions

Constructor and Destructor

`CWnd``();`

This constructor creates a `CWnd` object but does not create the window associated with the `CWnd`. You must explicitly call the `Create` member function to construct a window and attach it to the `CWnd` object.

```
virtual ~CWnd();
```

Destroys a `CWnd` object and its associated window. The destructor is declared as `virtual` to ensure that the correct destructor is called for derived classes.

Creating and Destroying the window

```
BOOL Attach(
    HWND hWndNew); // A Windows window handle
```

Call `Attach` to associate the specified window handle, *`hWndNew`*, with this `CWnd` object. `Attach` returns `TRUE` if successful.

```
virtual BOOL PreCreateWindow(CREATESTRUCT& cs)
```

Called prior to the creation of the window for the `CWnd` object. The `CREATESTRUCT` structure (defined in windows.h) has the following format:

```
typedef struct tagCREATESTRUCT {
   void FAR* lpCreateParams;
   HINSTANCE hInstance;
   HMENU     hMenu;
   HWND      hwndParent;
   int       cy;
   int       cx;
   int       y;
   int       x;
   LONG      style;
   LPCSTR    lpszName;
   LPCSTR    lpszClass;
   DWORD     dwExStyle;
} CREATESTRUCT;
```

```
virtual void CalcWindowRect(LPRECT ClientRect);
```

This function calculates the size of a window based on the client area. You then can use the resultant *`ClientRect`* to pass to the `Create` function.

```
BOOL SubclassWindow(HWND hWnd)
```

This function can be used to subclass a window dynamically. If done, the window's messages are routed through the `CWnd`'s message map, and `CWnd`'s message handlers are called first.

```
BOOL Create(
    LPCSTR       lpClassName,  // Name of the class
    LPCSTR       lpWindowName, // Name of the window
    DWORD        dwStyle,      // Window style; see Table 20.24,
                               //   Window styles for Microsoft Windows
    const RECT& rect,          // Size and position of window
    const CWnd* pParentWnd,    // Parent CWnd object
    UINT         nID);         // Child window's ID
```

Creates a child window and attaches it to the `CWnd`. The window style is specified by bitwise-OR from one or more individual styles selected from those shown in Table 20.24. `Create` returns `TRUE` if the window is successfully created; otherwise, it returns `FALSE`.

Table 20.24. Window styles for Microsoft Windows.

Style	Meaning
`DS_LOCALEDIT`	Directs Edit controls in dialog boxes to use memory allocated in the application's data segment.
`DS_MODALFRAME`	Creates a dialog box with a modal dialog box frame.
`DS_NOIDLEMSG`	Does not send `WM_ENTERIDLE` messages to the owner of a dialog box.
`DS_SYSMODAL`	Creates a system modal dialog box.
`WS_BORDER`	Adds a border to the window.
`WS_CAPTION`	Includes a title bar in the window. (Implies that window has a border.) Do not use this with the `WS_DLGFRAME` style.
`WS_CHILD`	Creates a child window (as opposed to a pop-up window specified by the `WS_POPUP` style).
`WS_CLIPCHILDREN`	Does not draw inside the child windows when you are drawing in the parent window's client area.

Style	Meaning
WS_CLIPSIBLINGS	When child windows overlap, does not allow drawings inside a child window to affect any of the overlapping sibling windows. Use this with the WS_CHILD style only.
WS_DISABLED	Initially disables the window.
WS_DLGFRAME	Creates a window with a dialog box frame that has a double border but no title.
WS_GROUP	In dialog boxes, indicates a group of controls. Specify the WS_GROUP style for the first control in the group (within a group of controls, the user can move from one control to another with the arrow keys).
WS_HSCROLL	Includes a horizontal scrollbar in the window.
WS_ICONIC	Displays the window in an initially minimized state (appears as an icon). Use this with the WS_OVERLAPPED style only.
WS_MAXIMIZE	Displays the initial size of the window at the maximum size allowed.
WS_MAXIMIZEBOX	Includes a maximize box in the window's frame.
WS_MINIMIZE	Displays the window in an initially minimized state (appears as an icon). Use this with the WS_OVERLAPPED style only.
WS_MINIMIZEBOX	Includes a minimize box in the window's frame.
WS_OVERLAPPED	Creates an *overlapped window*—a window with a caption and a border.
WS_OVERLAPPEDWINDOW	Creates an overlapped window with the following styles: WS_OVERLAPPED ¦ WS_CAPTION ¦ WS_SYSMENU ¦ WS_THICKFRAME ¦ WS_MINIMIZEBOX ¦ WS_MAXIMIZEBOX.
WS_POPUP	Creates a pop-up window (as opposed to a child window specified by the WS_CHILD style).

continues

Table 20.24. continued

Style	Meaning
WS_POPUPWINDOW	Creates a pop-up window with the following styles: WS_BORDER ¦ WS_POPUP ¦ WS_SYSMENU. The system menu becomes visible only when you add the WS_CAPTION style to WS_POPUPWINDOW.
WS_SYSMENU	Includes a system menu in the title bar of the window.
WS_TABSTOP	In dialog boxes, indicates that the user should be able to move from one control to another by pressing the Tab key.
WS_THICKFRAME	Adds a thick frame to the window. The user can use this frame to resize the window.
WS_VISIBLE	Displays the window as initially visible (applies to overlapped and pop-up windows).
WS_VSCROLL	Includes a vertical scrollbar in the window.

```
BOOL CreateEx(
    DWORD  dwExStyle,      // Extended window style (Table 20.25)
    LPCSTR lpClassName,    // Class name
    LPCSTR lpWindowName,   // Window name (appears as the caption)
    DWORD  dwStyle,        // Window style (see Table 20.24)
    int    x,              // (x,y) = position of window
    int    y,
    int    nWidth,         // Width and
    int    nHeight,        //   height of the window
    HWND   hwndParent,     // Handle of the parent window
    HMENU  nIDorHMenu);    // Handle of a menu or a child window ID
```

CreateEx is an extended version of Create. Call **CreateEx** to create a window with the extended style specified by *dwExStyle* and to associate that window to the CWnd object. Specify the standard window style, *dwStyle*, by bitwise-OR of symbols from Table 20.24. Similarly, the extended window style, *dwExStyle*, is specified by bitwise-OR of one or more of the symbols shown in Table 20.25. CreateEx returns TRUE if the window is successfully created; otherwise, it returns FALSE. CreateEx is a protected function that can be used only in classes derived from CWnd.

Table 20.25. Extended window styles for Microsoft Windows.

Style	Meaning
WS_EX_ACCEPTFILES	Indicates that the window accepts drag-and-drop files.
WS_EX_DLGMODALFRAME	Creates a window with a double border that can have a title bar if the WS_CAPTION style is specified in the *dwStyle* argument.
WS_EX_NOPARENTNOTIFY	Does not send a WM_PARENTNOTIFY message when the child window is created or destroyed.
WS_EX_TOPMOST	Creates a window that stays on top of all others, even when deactivated.
WS_EX_TRANSPARENT	Creates a transparent window.

```
static void DeleteTempMap();
```

This is automatically called by the *idle handler*—the message handler that's called when no Windows events are pending. It destroys any temporary CWnd objects created by FromHandle.

```
virtual BOOL DestroyWindow();
```

Call DestroyWindow to destroy the window attached to CWnd. **DestroyWindow** returns TRUE if the window is destroyed; otherwise, it returns FALSE.

```
HWND Detach();
```

Use Detach to disassociate the window handle from a CWnd. Detach returns the window handle.

```
static CWnd* FromHandle(HWND hWnd);
```

FromHandle provides an alternate way to construct a CWnd object. Call this function with a window handle as an argument. It returns a pointer to a CWnd object. If the *hWnd* window handle already is attached to a CWnd, FromHandle returns a pointer to that CWnd object. Otherwise, FromHandle creates a temporary CWnd object, attaches the window handle to that CWnd, and returns the CWnd object's address.

```
static CWnd* FromHandlePermanent(HWND hWnd);
```

Call FromHandlePermanent with a window handle to return the pointer to an existing CWnd object. This function is similar to FromHandle, but FromHandlePermanent does not create a temporary CWnd object if *hWnd* is not attached to any existing CWnd.

Accessing Attributes

```
HWND GetSafeHwnd() const;
```

Returns m_hWnd if this, the CWnd's address, is not NULL. Otherwise, GetSafeHwnd returns NULL.

```
DWORD GetStyle() const;
```

Returns the window style of the window attached to the CWnd.

```
DWORD GetExStyle() const;
```

Returns the extended window style of the window attached to the CWnd.

Sending Messages

```
BOOL PostMessage(
    UINT message,      // Message to be sent
    UINT wParam = 0,   // Additional information that
    LONG lParam = 0);  //   depends on the message being sent
```

PostMessage is like SendMessage (see the next entry) but, after placing the message in the CWnd object's message queue, PostMessage returns immediately without waiting for the message to be processed. Returns TRUE if successful; otherwise, returns FALSE.

```
LONG SendMessage(
    UINT message,      // Message to be sent
    UINT wParam = 0,   // Additional information that
    LONG lParam = 0);  //   depends on the message being sent
```

Call SendMessage to send a specified message to the CWnd object's window procedure—the function that processes all messages. Notice that SendMessage does not return until the message is processed. The return value is the same as the value returned by the window procedure that processed the message.

```
virtual BOOL PreTranslateMessage(MSG* Message);
```

You can override this function to filter messages prior to the messages being sent to TranslateMessage and DispatchMessage.

```
static const MSG* PASCAL GetCurrentMessage();
```

This protected function is used to return a pointer to the message that is being currently processed. Call this function only from an On*Message* handler.

```
LRESULT Default();
```

This protected function calls the default window procedure, and is used to ensure that every message is processed.

```
virtual WNDPROC* GetSuperWndProcAddr();
```

This protected function gets the default `WndProc` address for this `CWnd` class.

```
virtual LRESULT WindowProc(UINT Message, WPARAM wParam, LPARAM lParam);
```

This protected function is the window call back function for the `CWnd` object.

```
virtual LRESULT DefWindowProc(UINT Message, WPARAM wParam, LPARAM
lParam);
```

This protected function is used to call the default window call back function for the `CWnd` object to process any messages that the `WindowProc` doesn't handle.

```
virtual void PostNcDestroy();
```

This function calls the default `OnNcDestroy` function after the window has been destroyed. Useful when you must do cleanup.

```
virtual BOOL OnChildNotify(UINT Message, WPARAM wParam,
    LPARAM lParam, LRESULT* LResult);
```

This protected function is called by this window's parent whenever the parent receives a message that applies to this window.

Manipulating the Window Caption

```
CFont* GetFont();
```

Call `GetFont` to obtain a pointer to the current font.

```
void GetWindowText( // A const function
    CString& rString) const; // Window caption returned here
```

Call this version of `GetWindowText` with `CString` as an argument. On return, the *window caption* (window text) is in the `CString`.

```
int GetWindowText( // A const function
    LPSTR lpString,          // Buffer in which window text is returned
    int   nMaxCount) const; // Size of the buffer
```

Call this version of `GetWindowText` with a pointer to a buffer and the maximum size of the buffer as arguments. Upon return, the buffer is filled with the window caption and `GetWindowText` returns the length of the caption.

```
int GetWindowTextLength() const;
```

Returns the length of the *window text*—this is the window caption or, in case of a control (such as an edit control), the contents of the control.

```
void SetFont(
    CFont* pFont,              // New font
    BOOL   bRedraw = TRUE); // TRUE = redraw the window
```

Call `SetFont` to specify a new font for the `CWnd`. If the *bRedraw* argument is `TRUE`, the window is redrawn.

```
void SetWindowText(
    LPCSTR lpString); // New caption (null-terminated string)
```

Sets the window caption or text within a control to the specified text.

Manipulating Menus

```
void DrawMenuBar();
```

Redraws the menu bar. If you change the menu bar after the window is created, call `DrawMenubar` to update the menu bar.

```
CMenu* GetMenu() const;
```

Returns a pointer to the `CWnd` object's menu. If no menu exists, the return value is `NULL`. For child windows (with style `WS_CHILD`), the return value is undefined, because child windows do not contain menus.

```
CMenu* GetSystemMenu(     // A const function
    BOOL bRevert) const; // TRUE = reset the System menu to its
                         //   default state, FALSE = return current
                         // System menu
```

Call `GetSystemMenu` with a `FALSE` argument to return a pointer to the *system menu*—the menu that pops up when the user clicks the box at the top-left corner of the window frame. You can modify this menu if necessary. To reset the menu to the default state, call `GetSystemMenu` with a `TRUE` argument. (Do not use the return value in this case.)

```
BOOL HiliteMenuItem(
    CMenu* pMenu,          // Menu with item being highlighted
    UINT   nIDHiliteItem, // Integer identifier of menu item
    UINT   nHilite);       // Bitwise-OR of values from Table 20.26
```

Call `HiliteMenuItem` to highlight a menu item in a menu or to remove a highlight. The exact task and the meaning of the menu item's identifier, *nIDHiliteItem*, are specified by bitwise-OR from symbols in Table 20.26. `HiliteMenuItem` returns `TRUE` if the item is highlighted; otherwise, it returns `FALSE`.

Table 20.26. Highlighting menu items.

Symbol	Meaning
MF_BYCOMMAND	Interprets `nIDHiliteItem` as an integer identifier for the menu item. This is the default interpretation.
MF_BYPOSITION	Interprets `nIDHiliteItem` as the position of the menu item in the menu (zero refers to the first item).
MF_HILITE	Highlights the menu item.
MF_UNHILITE	Removes highlighting from the menu item. This is the default.

```
BOOL SetMenu(
CMenu* pMenu); // Menu to be associated with CWnd
```

Call `SetMenu` to specify a new menu for a `CWnd`. `SetMenu` returns `TRUE` if it can change the menu; otherwise, it returns `FALSE`. Notice that `SetMenu` does not destroy the previous menu; you should call the `CMenu`'s `DestroyMenu` function to destroy the old menu.

Child Window Attributes

```
int GetDlgCtrlID() const;
```

If the `CWnd` is attached to a child window (the window style is `WS_CHILD`), `GetDlgCtrlID` returns the integer identifier of the child window. If the window is not a child window, `GetDlgCtrlID` returns `NULL`.

Moving and Resizing the Window

```
UINT ArrangeIconicWindows();
```

Call this function to arrange all the minimized child windows. To arrange the icons on the desktop, first get a pointer to the desktop window by calling `GetDesktopWindow` and then call `ArrangeIconicWindows` for the desktop window object. `ArrangeIconicWindows` returns the height of a row of icons, or zero if no icons exist.

```
void BringWindowToTop();
```

Brings the current window to the top of the stack of overlapping windows.

```
void CloseWindow();
```

This function currently is obsolete, and should not be used in new code.

Reduces the window to an icon (*minimizes* it) if the window is an overlapped window created with the style WS_OVERLAPPED. CloseWindow has no effect if the window is not of the style WS_OVERLAPPED.

```
void GetClientRect(
    LPRECT lpRect) const; // Pointer to a RECT where the
                          //   client area coordinates are returned
```

Copies the coordinates of the client area from the CWnd's window to the RECT structure associated with the address you provide in the lpRect argument.

```
BOOL GetWindowPlacement( // For Windows version 3.1 or later
    WINDOWPLACEMENT FAR* lpwndpl) const; // Information returned here
```

Call GetWindowPlacement to retrieve information about the window's positions in normal, minimized, and maximized states. The information is returned in a WINDOWPLACEMENT structure with an address that you provide in the lpwndpl argument. The WINDOWPLACEMENT structure is defined in windows.h as follows:

```
typedef struct tagWINDOWPLACEMENT
{
    UINT  length;             // Length of this struct in bytes
    UINT  flags;              // Controls position when minimized
    UINT  showCmd;            // Current state of window
    POINT ptMinPosition;      // Top-left corner when minimized
    POINT ptMaxPosition;      // Top-left corner when maximized
    RECT  rcNormalPosition; // Window's coordinates when normal size
} WINDOWPLACEMENT;
```

Returns TRUE if successful; otherwise, it returns FALSE.

```
void GetWindowRect(
    LPRECT lpRect) const; // Window dimensions returned here
```

Copies the coordinates of the bounding rectangle of the CWnd object's window to the RECT structure with an address you provide in lpRect.

```
void MoveWindow(
    int  x,                  // New x-position of window
    int  y,                  // New y-position of window
    int  nWidth,             // New width of window
    int  nHeight,            // New height of window
    BOOL bRepaint = TRUE); // TRUE = window should be repainted
```

```
void MoveWindow(
    LPRECT lpRect,              // New size and position of window
    BOOL   bRepaint = TRUE);  // TRUE = window should be repainted
```

Moves and resizes the window. For top-level windows, the position is assumed to be relative to the top-left corner of the screen; for child windows, the position is relative to the upper-top-corner of the parent's client area.

```
BOOL OpenIcon();
```

This function is currently obsolete, and should not be used in new code.

Restores an iconic window to its original size and position. Returns `TRUE` if successful; otherwise, returns `FALSE`.

```
BOOL SetWindowPlacement(  // For Windows version 3.1 or later
    const WINDOWPLACEMENT FAR* lpwndpl); //
```

Sets the window's state and positions in normal, minimized, and maximized states. You must specify the information in a `WINDOWPLACEMENT` structure with an address you provide in the `lpwndpl` argument. See `GetWindowPlacement` for the definition of the `WINDOWPLACEMENT` structure.

```
BOOL SetWindowPos(
    const CWnd* pWndInsertAfter, // Insert after this window
    int         x,               // x-coordinate of top-left corner
    int         y,               // y-coordinate of top-left corner
    int         cx,              // Width of window
    int         cy,              // Height of window
    UINT        nFlags);         // Size and positioning options
```

Changes the size, position, and ordering of the window in a stack of windows. For the `nFlags` argument, provide a bitwise-OR from the values shown in Table 20.27.

Table 20.27. Flags for `SetWindowPos`.

Value	Meaning
SWP_DRAWFRAME	Draws a frame around the window.
SWP_HIDEWINDOW	Hides the window.
SWP_NOACTIVATE	Does not activate the window.
SWP_NOMOVE	Retains the current position.

continues

Table 20.27. continued

Value	Meaning
SWP_NOREDRAW	Does not redraw window after changes.
SWP_NOSIZE	Retains the current size.
SWP_NOZORDER	Retains the current ordering in the stack of windows.
SWP_SHOWWINDOW	Displays the window.

Converting Coordinates

```
void ClientToScreen(
    LPPOINT lpPoint) const; // Coordinates to be converted
```

Converts the coordinates of a point from client's coordinate frame to the screen.

```
void ClientToScreen(
    LPRECT lpRect) const; // Rectangle with coordinates to
                          //   be converted
```

Converts the coordinates of the rectangle from client's coordinate frame to the screen.

```
void MapWindowPoints(       // For Windows version 3.1 or later
    CWnd*    pwndTo,        // Convert to this window's coordinates
    LPPOINT lpPoint,        // Array of points
    UINT     nCount) const; // How many points?
```

Converts the coordinates of the points in an array from this window's coordinate frame to the coordinate frame of the window specified by *pwndTo*.

```
void MapWindowPoints(      // For Windows version 3.1 or later
    CWnd* pwndTo,          // Convert to this window's frame
    LPRECT lpRect) const;  // The points in this rectangle
```

Converts the coordinates of a rectangle from this window's coordinate frame to the coordinate frame of the window specified by *pwndTo*.

```
void ScreenToClient(
    LPPOINT lpPoint) const; // Coordinates to be converted
```

Converts the coordinates of the specified point from screen coordinates to the coordinate frame of the client area of this window.

```
void ScreenToClient(
    LPRECT lpRect) const; // Rectangle for which coordinates are
                          //   to be converted in place
```

Converts the coordinates of the specified rectangle from screen coordinates to the coordinate frame of the client area of this window.

Updating and Painting the Window

```
CDC* BeginPaint(
    LPPAINTSTRUCT lpPaint); // Pointer to structure where
                            //   information is returned
```

Prepares the window for painting and fills information about the painting in a PAINTSTRUCT structure with an address that you provide in *lpPaint*. Returns a device context for this window. The PAINTSTRUCT structure is defined in windows.h as follows:

```
typedef struct tagPAINTSTRUCT
{
    HDC  hdc;               // DC used for painting
    BOOL fErase;            // TRUE = background has to be redrawn
    RECT rcPaint;           // Top-left and bottom-right corners
                            // Window that needs painting
    BOOL fRestore;          // Used internally by Windows
    BOOL fIncUpdate;        // Used internally by Windows
    BYTE rgbReserved[16]; // Used internally by Windows
} PAINTSTRUCT;
```

There must be a corresponding call to EndPaint.

```
void EndPaint(
    LPPAINTSTRUCT lpPaint); // Pointer to PAINTSTRUCT returned
                            // BeginPaint
```

Marks the end of painting in the window.

```
CDC* GetDC();
```

Returns a pointer to the DC for the client area of the window. Remember to call ReleaseDC to release the DC after painting with it.

```
CDC* GetDCEx(          // For Windows version 3.1 or later
    CRgn* prgnClip,  // Clipping region to be combined with the
                     //   visible region of the window
    DWORD flags);    // Indicates how to create the DC
```

GetDCEx, an extended version of GetDC, provides you with more control over how the DC is created. GetDCEx returns a pointer to the CDC object representing the new DC. For more information, see the GetDCEx function in the Microsoft Windows SDK *Programmer's Reference: Volume 2.*

```
BOOL GetUpdateRect(
    LPRECT lpRect,          // "Update rectangle" returned here
    BOOL   bErase = FALSE); // TRUE = erase background of update region
```

Fills the `RECT` structure (which has its address in `lpRect`) with information about the smallest rectangle that encloses the region to be updated. If the `bErase` flag is `TRUE`, the background of the update region is erased. `GetUpdateRect` returns `TRUE` if the update region is not empty; otherwise, it returns `FALSE`.

```
int  GetUpdateRgn(
    CRgn* pRgn,             // "Update region" returned here
    BOOL  bErase = FALSE);  // TRUE = erase update region's background
```

Fills information about the update region in a `CRgn` object with an address you provide in the `pRgn` argument. `GetUpdateRgn` returns an integer to indicate the type of update region. The return value can be one of the values shown in Table 20.28.

Table 20.28. Region types.

Type	Description
`COMPLEXREGION`	The region has overlapping borders.
`ERROR`	No region is created.
`NULLREGION`	The region is empty.
`SIMPLEREGION`	The region has no overlapping borders.

```
CDC* GetWindowDC();
```

Returns a DC for the entire window, including the title bar, the menus, and the scrollbars. Using this DC, you can paint anywhere in the window. You must call `ReleaseDC` when you're done drawing in the window.

```
void Invalidate(
    BOOL bErase = TRUE); // TRUE = erase background of update region
```

Invalidates the entire client area of the window—the entire area is treated as a region to be updated.

```
void InvalidateRect(
    LPRECT lpRect,          // Rectangle to be invalidated
    BOOL   bErase = TRUE);  // TRUE = erase background
```

Adds the specified rectangle to the window's update region. If `LpRect` is `NULL`, the entire client area of the window is updated.

```
void InvalidateRgn(
    CRgn* pRgn,              // Region to be invalidated
    BOOL  bErase = TRUE);  // TRUE = erase background
```

Adds the specified region to the window's update region. If `pRgn` is `NULL`, the entire client area of the window is to be updated.

```
BOOL LockWindowUpdate(); // For Windows version 3.1 or later
```

When first called, this function disables drawing in the window. Call the function again to reenable drawing in the window. Returns `TRUE` if successful; otherwise, returns `FALSE`.

```
BOOL RedrawWindow( // For Windows version 3.1 or later
    const RECT FAR* lpRectUpdate = NULL, // Update rectangle
    CRgn* prgnUpdate = NULL,             // Update region, if any
    UINT  flags = RDW_INVALIDATE ¦       // Controls the redraw
                  RDW_UPDATENOW  ¦ RDW_ERASE); // operation
```

Updates the specified rectangle or region of the window.

```
int  ReleaseDC(
    CDC* pDC);    // DC to be released
```

Releases the specified DC.

```
void SetRedraw(
    BOOL bRedraw = TRUE); // TRUE = set the redraw flag
```

Call `SetRedraw` to `TRUE` so changes can be redrawn. By calling `SetRedraw` with a `FALSE` argument, you can prevent the changes from being redrawn.

```
void ShowOwnedPopups(
    BOOL bShow = TRUE); // TRUE = show the pop-up windows
                        // FALSE = hide the pop-up windows
                        //   owned by this window
```

Shows or hides all pop-up windows owned by this window.

```
BOOL ShowWindow(
  int nCmdShow); // Controls how window is shown (Table 20.29)
```

Shows or hides the window according to the setting of the integer flag `nCmdShow`. The flag can take any one of the values shown in Table 20.29. Returns the previous flag.

Table 20.29. Flags for `ShowWindow`.

Value	Meaning
SW_HIDE	Hides this window and activates another one.
SW_MINIMIZE	Minimizes this window and activates the next top-level window in the window manager's list.
SW_RESTORE	Activates and displays the window (same as SW_SHOWNORMAL).
SW_SHOW	Activates the window and displays it in its current size and position.
SW_SHOWMAXIMIZED	Activates the window and displays it in its maximized form.
SW_SHOWMINIMIZED	Activates the window and displays it as an icon (minimized window).
SW_SHOWMINNOACTIVE	Displays the window as an icon without changing its activation status.
SW_SHOWNA	Displays the window in its current state.
SW_SHOWNOACTIVATE	Displays the window in its most recent size and position without affecting the activation status.
SW_SHOWNORMAL	Activates and displays the window. Also, restores the window to its original size and position (same as SW_SHOWNORMAL).

```
void UpdateWindow();
```

Call `UpdateWindow` to send a `WM_PAINT` message to the window if the update region is not empty and some part of the window needs repainting.

```
void ValidateRect(
    LPRECT lpRect); // Rectangle to be validated
```

Removes the specified rectangle from the update region of the window. If *`LpRect`* is `NULL`, the entire window is validated.

```
void ValidateRgn(
    CRgn* pRgn);  // Region to be validated
```

Removes the specified region from the update region of the window. If `pRgn` is `NULL`, the entire window is validated.

Managing Timers

```
BOOL KillTimer(
    int nIDEvent); // Timer identifier that you provided
                   //   when you called SetTimer
```

Removes the specified timer. Returns `TRUE` if successful; otherwise, returns `FALSE`.

```
UINT SetTimer(
    int  nIDEvent, // Identifies the timer
    UINT nElapse,  // Time-out duration in milliseconds
    UINT (FAR PASCAL EXPORT* lpfnTimer)(HWND, UINT, int, DWORD));
                   // Callback function to be called when the
                   // WM_TIMER message is sent by Windows; if
                   //   this is NULL, CWnd handles the WM_TIMER message.
```

Installs a timer with a specified time-out value. When the specified amount of time has elapsed, Windows calls the installed callback function with a `WM_TIMER` message. The prototype of the timer callback is as follows:

```
UINT FAR PASCAL EXPORT timer_callback(
    HWND hWnd,      // Window handle of CWnd that had called SetTimer
    UINT nMsg,      // WM_TIMER
    int  nIDEvent,  // Identifies the timer
    DWORD dwTime);  // System time
```

Accessing Window States

```
BOOL EnableWindow(
    BOOL bEnable = TRUE); // TRUE = enable the window
```

Enables or disables the window as specified by the `bEnable` flag. When enabled, a window accepts mouse and keyboard inputs. Returns the state of the window before `EnableWindow` was called.

```
static CWnd* GetActiveWindow();
```

Returns a pointer to the currently active window.

> **Temporary CWnd Objects**
>
> Notice that many static member functions of the **CWnd** class return a temporary pointer to a **CWnd** object. You should not store such pointers for later use. Instead, call the static function every time you need a pointer to the object.

`static CWnd* GetCapture();`

Returns a pointer to the window that has captured the mouse inputs or NULL if no window has captured the mouse.

`static CWnd* GetDesktopWindow();`

Returns a pointer to the Windows desktop. This is the window that covers the entire screen, and on which all other windows appear.

`static CWnd* GetFocus();`

Returns a pointer to the window with the input focus—the window that receives all the keystrokes—or NULL if none of the windows has the focus.

`static CWnd* GetSysModalWindow();`

This function currently is obsolete, and should not be used in new code.

Returns a pointer to the system modal window or NULL if none of the windows are system-wide modal.

`BOOL IsIconic() const;`

Returns TRUE if the window is in an iconic (minimized) state; otherwise, returns FALSE.

`BOOL IsWindowEnabled() const;`

Returns TRUE if the window is *enabled* (accepts mouse and keyboard input). Returns FALSE if the window is disabled.

`BOOL IsWindowVisible() const;`

Returns TRUE if the window is in a visible state (even if the window is completely covered by another window). You can call the ShowWindow member function to make a window visible.

`BOOL IsZoomed() const;`

Returns TRUE if the CWnd's window is maximized; otherwise, returns FALSE.

```
CWnd* SetActiveWindow();
```

Designates this window as the active window. Normally, the user makes a window active by clicking it. Therefore, you don't need to explicitly call `SetActiveWindow`. Returns a pointer to the previously active window.

```
CWnd* SetCapture();
```

After you call this function, Windows sends all mouse events to this window regardless of the cursor's position. Returns a pointer to the previous window that had captured the mouse.

```
CWnd* SetFocus();
```

Designates this window as the *focus window*—the window that receives all keystrokes. Returns a pointer to the previous focus window.

```
CWnd* SetSysModalWindow();
```

This function currently is obsolete, and should not be used in new code.

Designates this window as the system-modal window and returns a pointer to the window that was previously system modal.

Manipulating Dialog Box Items

```
void CheckDlgButton(
    int  nIDButton, // Button control being affected
    UINT nCheck);   // 1 = place a check mark; 0 = remove check
```

If *nCheck* is 1, this function places a check mark next to the button control identified by *nIDButton*. To remove the check mark, call `CheckDlgButton` again, but set *nCheck* at zero. If *nCheck* is 2, the button is grayed.

```
void CheckRadioButton(
    int nIDFirstButton, // Identifies first radio button in group
    int nIDLastButton,  // Identifies last radio button in group
    int nIDCheckButton);// Radio button being checked
```

Turns the radio button identified by *nIDCheckButton* on and all others within the range of *nIDFirstButton* and *nIDLastButton* off.

```
int  DlgDirList(
    LPSTR lpPathSpec,     // List contents of this directory
    int   nIDListBox,     // List box in which filenames appear
    int   nIDStaticPath,  // Static control in which current drive
                          //   and directory names are displayed
    UINT  nFileType);     // Attributes of files to be listed
```

Displays the contents of the directory specified by *lpPathSpec* in the list box identified by *nIDListBox*. The nFileType argument controls the types of files and directories listed in the list box. Set *nFileType* to zero for a list of all files with read and write attributes. Returns a nonzero value if successful; otherwise, returns zero.

```
int  DlgDirListComboBox(
    LPSTR lpPathSpec,     // List contents of this directory
    int   nIDComboBox,    // Show filenames in this combo box
    int   nIDStaticPath,  // Static control in which current drive
                          //   and directory names are displayed
    UINT nFileType);      // Attributes of files to be listed
```

Displays the contents of the directory specified by *lpPathSpec* in the combo box identified by *nIDComboBox*. The *nFileType* argument controls the types of files and directories listed in the list box. Set *nFileType* to zero for a list of all files with read and write attributes. Returns a nonzero value if successful; otherwise, returns zero.

```
BOOL DlgDirSelect(
    LPSTR lpString,      // Current selection returned here
    int   nIDListBox); // List box filled by DlgDirList
```

Copies the current selection from a list box to the buffer specified by *lpString*. Assumes that the list box has been filled by a previous call to DlgDirList. DlgDirSelect returns TRUE if the current selection is a directory name; otherwise, returns FALSE.

```
BOOL DlgDirSelectComboBox(
    LPSTR lpString,      // Current selection returned here
    int   nIDComboBox); // Combo box filled by DlgDirListComboBox
```

Copies the current selection from a combo box to the buffer specified by *lpString*. Assumes that the combo box has been filled by a previous call to DlgDirListComboBox. DlgDirSelectComboBox returns TRUE if the current selection is a directory name; otherwise, returns FALSE.

```
int  GetCheckedRadioButton(
    int nIDFirstButton, // ID of first button in the group
    int nIDLastButton); // ID of last button in the group
```

Returns the ID of the checked radio button in the group specified by the range of identifiers *nIDFirstButton* and *nIDLastButton*.

```
CWnd* GetDlgItem(
    int nID) const; // Identifier of item to be retrieved
```

Returns a pointer to a CWnd object corresponding to the specified control in a dialog box. If no control with the specified ID exists, GetDlgItem returns NULL.

```
UINT  GetDlgItemInt(
    int nID,                // ID of item to be translated
    BOOL* lpTrans = NULL, // If not NULL, status returned here
    BOOL bSigned = TRUE) const; // TRUE = Retrieve values as signed
```

Converts the contents of a dialog box item to an integer value and returns that value. You can receive a status report in a `BOOL` variable with an address you provide as the second argument to `GetDlgItemInt`. If all goes well, `GetDlgItemInt` returns a nonzero value in this `BOOL` variable.

```
int   GetDlgItemText(
    int   nID,       // Dialog box item with text to be retrieved
    LPSTR lpStr,     // Buffer in which text is returned
    int   nMaxCount) const; // How many bytes to retrieve, at most
```

Copies a caption or text from a specified dialog box item to a buffer with an address you provide as the *lpStr* argument. The *nMaxCount* argument indicates the maximum number of bytes that can be copied to `lpStr`. `GetDlgItemText` returns the actual number of bytes copied to *lpStr*.

```
CWnd* GetNextDlgGroupItem(
    CWnd* pWndCtl,          // Start search at this control
    BOOL bPrevious = FALSE) const; // TRUE = search for previous
                            // control, FALSE = search for next one
```

Searches for the previous or next control in a group of controls starting with the one identified by *pWndCtl*. Returns a pointer to the control that is found.

```
CWnd* GetNextDlgTabItem(
    CWnd* pWndCtl,          // Start search at this control
    BOOL bPrevious = FALSE) const; // TRUE = search for previous
                            // control, FALSE = search for next one
```

Searches for the previous or next control that was created with the `WS_TABSTOP` style, starting with the control identified by *pWndCtl*. Returns a pointer to the control that is found.

```
UINT  IsDlgButtonChecked(
    int nIDButton) const; // Is this button checked?
```

Returns a nonzero value if the button identified by *nIDButton* is checked; otherwise, returns a zero.

```
LONG  SendDlgItemMessage(
    int  nID,          // Dialog box item that receives message
    UINT message,      // Send this message
```

```
    UINT wParam = 0,  // First message parameter
    LONG lParam = 0); // Second message parameter
```

Sends the specified message to the control, identified by `nID`, in the dialog box. Returns the result of the message being processed by the dialog item. The meaning of the return value depends on the message being sent. This function returns only after the message has been processed.

```
void  SetDlgItemInt(
    int  nID,               // Display value in this item
    UINT nValue,            // Value being set
    BOOL bSigned = TRUE); // TRUE = treat nValue as signed
```

Sets the caption of the dialog box item `nID` to the textual representation of the value specified in `nValue`.

```
BOOL SubclassDlgItem(UINT nItemID, CWnd* Parent);
```

This function can be used to subclass a dialog control dynamically. If done, the dialog control's messages are routed through `CWnd`'s message map and `CWnd`'s message handlers are called first.

```
void SetDlgItemText(
    int    nID,        // Display lpString in this item
    LPCSTR lpString); // String copied into dialog box item
```

Copies the string `lpString` to the caption (or text) of the dialog box item `nID` in a dialog box.

```
void UpdateDialogControls(CCmdTarget* Target, BOOL bDisable);
```

Used to update dialog controls and buttons that use the `ON_UPDATE_COMMAND_UI` callback mechanism.

```
BOOL UpdateData(BOOL bSaveValidate = TRUE);
```

Used to initialize a dialog box's data. A second use is to retrieve (and, optionally, validate) data.

```
virtual void DoDataExchange(CDataExchange* pDX);
```

This protected function should not be directly called—it is called by `UpdateData()`.

Scrolling the Window

```
BOOL EnableScrollBar( // For Windows version 3.1 or later
    int nSBFlags,     // Scrollbar type. One of
                      //   SB_BOTH, SB_CTL, SB_VERT, or SB_HORZ
    UINT nArrowFlags = ESB_ENABLE_BOTH); // Action to take
```

Enables or disables one or both arrows of a scrollbar. The *nArrowFlags* argument specifies the action to take. It can be one of the values shown in Table 20.30.

Table 20.30. Enable scroll-bar action flags.

Flag	Description
ESB_DISABLE_LTUP	Disables the left or up arrow.
ESB_DISABLE_RTDN	Disables the right or down arrow.
ESB_DISABLE_BOTH	Disables both arrows.
ESB_ENABLE_BOTH	Enables both arrows.

EnableScrollBar returns TRUE if successful; otherwise, returns FALSE.

```
void EnableScrollBarCtrl(int nScrollBar, BOOL bEnable = TRUE);
```

Used to enable/disable the scroll bar for this window.

```
virtual CScrollBar* GetScrollBarCtrl(int nScrollBar) const;
```

Used to get a pointer to CWnd's scroll bar. The *nScrollBar* parameter can be either SB_HORZ or SB_VERT.

```
void RepositionBars(UINT nFirstID, UINT nLastID, UINT nLeftOverID);
```

Used to reposition (and resize) the client-area scroll bars.

```
int  GetScrollPos(
    int nBar) const; // Return current position of this scrollbar
```

Returns the current position of the scrollbar identified by *nBar*, which can be SB_CTL, SB_HORZ, or SB_VERT. For example, if the scrolling range is 100 to 200 and the thumb is in the middle, GetScrollPos would return the current position as 150.

```
void GetScrollRange(
    int   nBar,            // Get range of this scrollbar
                           // SB_VERT, SB_HORZ, or SB_CTL

    LPINT lpMinPos,        // Value for minimum position and
    LPINT lpMaxPos) const; //   maximum position returned here
```

Returns the integer values corresponding to the minimum and maximum positions of the thumb that are returned in the integer variables with addresses you provide in *lpMinPos* and *lpMaxPos*, respectively.

```
void ScrollWindow(
    int xAmount, // Device units to scroll in x direction
    int yAmount, // Device units to scroll in y direction
    const RECT FAR* lpRect = NULL, // Rectangle to be scrolled
    const RECT FAR* lpClipRect = NULL); // Clip lpRect against
                 //   this rectangle (only bits inside this
                 //   rectangle are scrolled)
```

Scrolls the contents of the window's client area by specified amounts in x- and y-axes' directions.

```
int ScrollWindowEx( // For Windows version 3.1 or later
    int dx, // Amount to scroll horizontally
    int dy, // Amount to scroll vertically
    const RECT FAR* lpRectScroll, // Rectangle to scroll
    const RECT FAR* lpRectClip,    // Clipping rectangle
    CRgn*  prgnUpdate,     // On return: region invalidated
                           //   by the scrolling
    LPRECT lpRectUpdate,   // On return: rectangle invalidated
                           //   by the scrolling
    UINT   flags);         // Indicates how to scroll
```

Scrolls the contents of a window, like `ScrollWindow`, but offers some additional features: the rectangle and regions invalidated by the scrolling are returned through *`lpRectUpdate`* and *`prgnUpdate`*, respectively. `ScrollWindowEx` returns a constant indicating the type of the invalidated region. The return value can be `SIMPLEREGION`, `COMPEXREGION`, or `NULLREGION`.

```
int  SetScrollPos(
    int  nBar,             // Set position of this scrollbar
                           // SB_VERT, SB_HORZ, or SB_CTL
    int  nPos,             // New position (within scroll range)
    BOOL bRedraw = TRUE);  // TRUE = redraw the scrollbar
```

Sets the current position of the thumb within the limits of the scrollbar range. `SetScrollPos` returns the previous position of the scrollbar.

```
void SetScrollRange(
    int  nBar,             // Set scroll range of this scrollbar:
                           // SB_VERT, SB_HORZ, or SB_CTL

    int  nMinPos,          // Value corresponding to minimum
    int  nMaxPos,          //   and maximum positions of scrollbar
    BOOL bRedraw = TRUE);  // TRUE = redraw the scrollbar
```

Sets the *scroll range*—the values corresponding to the minimum and maximum positions of the thumb in the scrollbar identified by `nBar`.

```
void ShowScrollBar(
    UINT nBar,              // Show or hide this scrollbar:
                            // SB_BOTH, SB_VERT, SB_HORZ, or SB_CTL

    BOOL bShow = TRUE); // TRUE = make scrollbar visible
```

Displays or hides the specified scrollbar.

Traversing the Window Hierarchy

```
CWnd* ChildWindowFromPoint(
    POINT point) const; // Determine child window that contains
                        //   this point
```

Returns a pointer to the child window that contains the specified point, or `NULL` if the point lies outside the client area of the window.

```
static CWnd* FindWindow(
    LPCSTR lpClassName,    // Class name of window's class
    LPCSTR lpWindowName); // Name appearing in window's title bar
```

Returns a pointer to the window with the specified class name and caption, or `NULL` if no such window exists.

```
CWnd* GetLastActivePopup() const;
```

Returns a pointer to the most recently active pop-up window.

```
CWnd* GetNextWindow(
    UINT nFlag = GW_HWNDNEXT) const; // Next or previous?
```

This function calls `GetNextWindow` with `nFlag` set to `GW_HWNDNEXT` to return a pointer to the next window in window manager's list. You can get the previous window by specifying `nFlag` as `GW_HWNDPREV`.

```
CWnd* GetParent() const;
```

Returns a pointer to the parent window, or `NULL` if this window has no parent.

```
CWnd* GetTopWindow() const;
```

Returns a pointer to the top-level child window of this window, or `NULL` if this window has no child windows.

```
CWnd* GetWindow(
    UINT nCmd) const; // Which window should be retrieved?
```

Depending on the value of *nCmd*, returns a pointer to a window, or it returns NULL if the search fails. The *nCmd* argument can take one of the values shown in Table 20.31.

Table 20.31. GetWindow window types.

Type	Description
GW_CHILD	Returns the first child window.
GW_HWNDFIRST	If this is a child window, returns the first sibling; otherwise, returns the first top-level window.
GW_HWNDLAST	If this is a child window, returns the last sibling; otherwise, returns the last top-level window.
GW_HWNDNEXT	Returns the next window in window manager's list.
GW_HWNDPREV	Returns the previous window in window manager's list.
GW_OWNER	Returns the owner of this window.

```
BOOL  IsChild(
    CWnd* pWnd) const; // Is pWnd a child window of this window?
```

Returns TRUE if the specified CWnd is a child window of this window.

```
CWnd* SetParent(
    CWnd* pWndNewParent); // Make this the new parent window
```

Changes the parent of this window to the new window specified in pWndNewParent. Returns a pointer to the previous parent.

```
static CWnd* WindowFromPoint(
    POINT point); // Return window containing this point
```

Returns a pointer to a window containing the specified point (expressed in screen coordinates).

```
Cwnd* GetDescendantWindow(int nWindowID) const;
```

This function gets the descendant window based on the *nWindowID* parameter. The search is not limited to the immediate children; the entire window chain is searched.

```
void SendMessageToDescendants(UINT message,
    WPARAM wParam = 0, LPARAM lParam = 0, BOOL bDeep = TRUE);
```

Used to send the message to all descendant windows. The `bDeep` parameter specifies whether the message is sent to immediate children only (`bDeep == FALSE`), or all descendant child windows (`bDeep == TRUE`).

```
CFrameWnd* GetParentFrame() const;
```

Used to get the parent frame window. Searches the parent chain looking for a `CFrameWnd` object.

Handling Alerts

```
BOOL FlashWindow(
    BOOL bInvert); // TRUE = flash the window's title bar
```

If `bInvert` is `TRUE`, flashes the window once—toggles the window's title bar from its current state (active or inactive) to the opposite. To return the window to its original state, call `FlashWindow` with `bInvert` set to `FALSE`. Returns the state of the window before this call.

```
int MessageBox(
    LPCSTR lpText,              // Message to be displayed
    LPCSTR lpCaption = NULL,    // Caption of the message box
    UINT nType = MB_OK);        // Controls contents of message box
```

Displays a window with a specified caption and a message. The `nType` argument controls the rest of the message box's contents. Use bitwise-OR combinations of one or more values shown in Table 20.32. Returns a nonzero constant identifying the button that the user had pressed, or zero to indicate an error. Also see the `AfxMessageBox()` function, above.

Table 20.32. Values that control contents of a message box.

Value	Meaning
`MB_ABORTRETRYIGNORE`	Displays three pushbuttons labeled Abort, Retry, and Ignore.
`MB_APPLMODAL`	Requires user to respond to the message box before the user can continue with the application. The user may interact with windows of other applications. `MB_APPLMODAL` is the default setting.
`MB_DEFBUTTON1`	Sets the first button as the *default button*—the one that activates when the user presses the Enter key.

continues

Table 20.32. continued

Value	Meaning
MB_DEFBUTTON2	Sets the second button as the default.
MB_DEFBUTTON3	Sets the third button as the default.
MB_ICONEXCLAMATION	Displays an exclamation point icon in the message box.
MB_ICONINFORMATION	Displays an icon showing a lowercase *i* within a circle in the message box.
MB_ICONQUESTION	Displays a question mark icon in the message box.
MB_ICONSTOP	Displays a stopsign icon in the message box.
MB_OK	Displays one pushbutton labeled `OK`.
MB_OKCANCEL	Displays two pushbuttons, labeled `OK` and `Cancel`.
MB_RETRYCANCEL	Displays two pushbuttons, labeled `Retry` and `Cancel`.
MB_SYSTEMMODAL	Makes the dialog box system modal. Requires the user to respond to the message box before continuing any further interaction, even with other applications.
MB_YESNO	Displays two pushbuttons, labeled `Yes` and `No`.
MB_YESNOCANCEL	Displays three pushbuttons, labeled `Yes`, `No`, and `Cancel`.

Using the Clipboard

```
BOOL ChangeClipboardChain(
    HWND hWndNext); // Window that follows this one in the
                    //   Clipboard Viewer chain.
```

Removes the current window from the chain of windows registered as Clipboard Viewers. The `hWndNext` argument identifies the window that follows this window in the Clipboard Viewer chain. Returns `TRUE` if this window is removed from the linked list of Clipboard Viewers.

```
static CWnd* GetClipboardOwner();
```

Returns a pointer to the window that currently owns the Clipboard or returns NULL if none of the windows owns the Clipboard.

```
static CWnd* GetClipboardViewer();
```

Returns a pointer to the first window in the Clipboard Viewer chain or returns NULL if no windows are in the linked list of Clipboard Viewers.

```
static CWnd* GetOpenClipboardWindow(); // For Windows 3.1 or later
```

Returns a pointer to the window with the Clipboard currently open or returns NULL if the function fails.

```
BOOL OpenClipboard();
```

Opens the Clipboard for use by this window. Returns TRUE if the Clipboard is successfully opened, or FALSE if some other window already has opened the Clipboard.

```
HWND SetClipboardViewer();
```

Places this window in the linked list of Clipboard Viewers (the Clipboard Viewer chain) and returns the handle of the window that follows the current window in the Viewer chain.

Managing Carets

```
void CreateCaret(
    CBitmap* pBitmap); // Bitmap that defines the caret's shape
```

Creates a new *caret* (the blinking cursor that marks the text insertion point) using the shape specified by the bitmap object with an address that you provide in the *pBitmap* object. You must call ShowCaret to make the caret visible. Because carets are a shared resource, you should create a caret only when your application's window receives the input focus.

```
void CreateGrayCaret(
    int nWidth,    // Width of caret (in logical units)
    int nHeight); // Height of caret (in logical units)
```

Creates a gray rectangular caret.

```
void CreateSolidCaret(
    int nWidth,    // Width of caret (in logical units)
    int nHeight); // Height of caret (in logical units)
```

Creates a solid colored rectangular caret.

```
static CPoint GetCaretPos();
```

Returns the coordinates of the caret's current location in the client area's coordinate frame.

```
void HideCaret();
```

Hides the caret.

```
static void SetCaretPos(
    POINT point); // New location of the caret in logical coordinates.
```

Moves the caret to a new position specified by the `point` argument.

```
void ShowCaret();
```

Makes the caret visible.

Handling Windows Messages

```
afx_msg void OnActivate(
    UINT  nState,        // Nonzero = window is minimized
    CWnd* pWndOther,     // Window being activated or deactivated
    BOOL  bMinimized); // TRUE = window is being activated
```

Called in response to a `WM_ACTIVATE` message, which is generated when a window is being activated or deactivated.

```
afx_msg void OnActivateApp(
    BOOL   bActive, // TRUE = window is being activated
    HANDLE hTask);  // Handle to task that owns window
```

Called in response to a `WM_ACTIVATEAPP` message, which is generated when a window belonging to a different task than the current one is being activated.

```
afx_msg void OnAskCbFormatName(
    UINT  nMaxCount, // Maximum number of bytes to copy
    LPSTR lpString); // Copy format name into this buffer
```

Called to handle a `WM_ASKCBFORMATNAME` message, which is sent by a Clipboard Viewer application to the Clipboard's owner when the Clipboard contains data of `CF_OWNERDISPLAY` format. This function should copy the format's name into `lpString`.

```
afx_msg void OnCancelMode();
```

Called in response to a `WM_CANCELMODE` message, which is sent to a window when a dialog box or a message box is displayed, informing it to cancel any internal mode (such as mouse capture).

```
afx_msg void OnChangeCbChain(
    HWND hWndRemove, // Window being removed from viewer chain
    HWND hWndAfter); // Window that follows hWndRemove
```

Called in response to a WM_CHANGECBCHAIN message, which is sent to the first window in the Clipboard Viewer chain, informing it that a window is being removed from the chain.

```
afx_msg void OnChar(
    UINT nChar,    // Key code
    UINT nRepCnt, // Repeat count
    UINT nFlags); // Flag indicating scan code, key transition
                  //   code, previous state of key, and context
```

Called to handle a WM_CHAR message, which is sent to a window when the user presses or releases a key.

```
afx_msg int OnCharToItem(
    UINT      nChar,     // Key code
    CListBox* pListBox, // Pointer to list box
    UINT      nIndex);  // Item where caret lies
```

Called to process a WM_CHARTOITEM message, which is sent by a list box with the LBS_WANTKEYBOARDINPUT style to a window when the user presses or releases a key. The return value should indicate how this function handled the message. Consult the Microsoft Visual C++ *Class Libraries Reference* for further details.

```
afx_msg void OnChildActivate();
```

Called to handle a WM_CHILDACTIVATE message, which is sent to a MDI child window when the user activates the child window by clicking the window's title bar.

```
afx_msg void OnClose();
```

Called to handle a WM_CLOSE message, which is sent to a window to signal that the window should be closed.

```
virtual BOOL OnCommand(
    UINT wParam, // Identifies menu item or control
    LONG lParam);// Additional information
```

This is called to handle a WM_COMMAND message, which is sent when the user selects an item from a menu bar or selects an item from a dialog box. This function returns TRUE if the message is processed; otherwise, returns FALSE.

```
afx_msg void OnCompacting(
    UINT nCpuTime); // Ratio of CPU time spent compacting memory
                    // Note: A value of 0x8000 means 50%
```

Called to process a WM_COMPACTING message, which is sent to a window to signal that system memory is low. This is detected by Windows when more than 12.5 percent of system time over a 30- to 60-second period is spent *compacting memory*—coalescing memory blocks by rearranging them in memory.

```
afx_msg int OnCompareItem(
    LPCOMPAREITEMSTRUCT lpCompareItemStruct);
```

Called to handle a WM_COMPAREITEM message, which is sent to a window to report the relative position of a new item in the sorted list of a list box or combo box created with the LBS_SORT or CBS_SORT style. Consult the Microsoft Visual C++ *Class Libraries Reference* for further details.

```
afx_msg int OnCreate(
    LPCREATESTRUCT lpCreateStruct); // Information about window
```

Called to handle a WM_CREATE message, which is sent to a window just after it's created. This function should return zero to continue creation of the window or –1 if an error occurs.

```
afx_msg HBRUSH OnCtlColor(
    CDC* pDC,          // DC for the pWnd
    CWnd* pWnd,        // Pointer to the control's window
    UINT nCtlColor);   // Specifies type of control
```

Called to process a WM_CTLCOLOR message, which is sent to a window when a control or a message box is about to be drawn. With this, you can change the color of a control's background. If you override this function, it should return a handle to the brush that is used for painting the control's background.

```
afx_msg void OnDeadChar(
    UINT nChar,    // Key code
    UINT nRepCnt,  // Repeat count
    UINT nFlags);  // Flags (same as those for OnChar)
```

Called to handle a WM_DEADCHAR message, which is sent to a window when a dead key is pressed and released. A *dead key* is combined with other keys to compose characters such as umlaut-O (ö).

```
afx_msg void OnDeleteItem(
    LPDELETEITEMSTRUCT lpDeleteItemStruct);
```

Called to handle a WM_DELETEITEM message, which is sent to a window when items are removed from the list in a list box or a combo box.

```
afx_msg void OnDestroy();
```

Called to process a WM_DESTROY message, which is sent to a window when it is about to be destroyed.

```
afx_msg void OnDestroyClipboard();
```

Called to process a WM_DESTROYCLIPBOARD message, which is sent to the Clipboard owner when the contents of the Clipboard are destroyed.

```
afx_msg void OnDevModeChange(
    LPSTR lpDeviceName); // Device name from WIN.INI file
```

Called to handle a WM_DEVMODECHANGE message, which is sent to all top-level windows after the mode settings of a device are changed.

```
afx_msg void OnDrawClipboard();
```

Called to handle a WM_DRAWCLIPBOARD message, which is sent to the first window in the Clipboard Viewer chain when the contents of the Clipboard change. Each window should call SendMessage to send a WM_DRAWCLIPBOARD message to the next window in the Clipboard Viewer chain.

```
afx_msg void OnDrawItem(
    LPDRAWITEMSTRUCT lpDrawItemStruct); // Information on item
                                        //   being drawn
```

Called to handle a WM_DRAWITEM message, which is sent to the owner of an owner-drawn control (button, combo box, or list box) or menu when that item needs to be repainted.

```
afx_msg void OnDropFiles(HANDLE hDropInfo);
```

Called to process a WM_DROPFILES message, which is sent when the user releases the left mouse button over the window, provided that the window accepts files dropped onto it.

```
afx_msg void OnEnable(
    BOOL bEnable); // TRUE = Enable the window
```

Called to process a WM_ENABLE message, which is sent after the window is enabled.

```
afx_msg void OnEndSession(
    BOOL bEnding); // TRUE = Session is being ended
```

Called to handle a WM_ENDSESSION message, which is sent after the CWnd's WM_QUERYENDSESSION handler (OnQueryEndSession) returns TRUE, indicating that the session actually is ending.

```
afx_msg void OnEnterIdle(
    UINT  nWhy,  // Reason: MSGF_DIALOGBOX or MSGF_MENU
    CWnd* pWho); // Pointer to dialog box or menu
```

Called to process a WM_ENTERIDLE message, which is sent to an application's main window when a modal dialog box or a menu is in an *idle* state (no messages are waiting in the queue for that modal dialog box or the menu).

```
afx_msg BOOL OnEraseBkgnd(
    CDC* pDC); // DC
```

Called to handle a WM_ERASEBKGND message, which is sent when the window's background needs erasing prior to repainting the window. This function should return TRUE to erase the background.

```
afx_msg void OnFontChange();
```

This function is called in response to a WM_FONTCHANGE message, which is sent after fonts are added to or removed from the system.

```
afx_msg UINT OnGetDlgCode();
```

This function is called to handle a WM_GETDLGCODE message, which is sent to a dialog box window to query which inputs the dialog box handles. This function returns a constant indicating the types of inputs that the dialog box accepts.

```
afx_msg void OnGetMinMaxInfo(
    LPPOINT lpPoints); // Array of 5 points with information
```

This function is called to process a WM_GETMINMAXINFO message, which is sent whenever Windows needs information about the following dimensions of a window:

- The position and size of the window in its maximized state
- The minimum tracking size (the smallest the user can resize the window)
- The maximum tracking size (the largest the user can resize the window)

```
afx_msg void OnHScroll(
    UINT        nSBCode,      // What to scroll?
    UINT        nPos,         // Scroll box position
    CScrollBar* pScrollBar);  // Pointer to scrollbar control
```

This function is called to handle a WM_HSCROLL message, which is sent to a window whenever the user clicks the horizontal scrollbar.

```
afx_msg void OnHScrollClipboard(
    CWnd* pClipAppWnd, // Pointer to Clipboard Viewer window
```

```
    UINT  nSBCode,        // Scroll request identifier
    UINT  nPos);          // Scroll box position
```

This function is called to process a WM_HSCROLLCLIPBOARD message, which is sent to the Clipboard owner when the Clipboard contains data with the CF_OWNERDISPLAY format and the user clicks anywhere on the Clipboard Viewer's horizontal scrollbar.

```
afx_msg void OnIconEraseBkgnd(
    CDC* pDC); // DC to draw the icon
```

This function is called in response to a WM_ICONERASEBKGND message, which is sent to a minimized window when the background of the window's icon must be filled before Windows paints the icon.

```
afx_msg void OnInitMenu(
    CMenu* pMenu); // Pointer to menu being initialized
```

This function is called to handle a WM_INITMENU message, which is sent when the user clicks an item in the menu bar or presses a menu key.

```
afx_msg void OnInitMenuPopup(
    CMenu* pPopupMenu, // Pointer to pop-up menu
    UINT   nIndex,     // Index of the pop-up in main menu
    BOOL   bSysMenu);  // TRUE = pop-up is the system menu
```

This function is called to handle a WM_INITMENUPOPUP message, which is sent when a pop-up menu is about to become active.

```
afx_msg void OnKeyDown(UINT nChar, UINT nRepCnt, UINT nFlags);
```

This function is called to handle a WM_KEYDOWN message, which is sent whenever the user presses a *nonsystem key* (any keypress without the Alt key held down at the same time).

```
afx_msg void OnKeyUp(UINT nChar, UINT nRepCnt, UINT nFlags);
```

This function is called to handle a WM_KEYUP message, which is sent whenever the user releases a nonsystem key.

```
afx_msg void OnKillFocus(
    CWnd* pNewWnd); // Window that receives input focus
```

This function is called to process a WM_KILLFOCUS message, which is sent to a window immediately before it loses the input focus.

```
afx_msg void OnLButtonDblClk(
    UINT   nFlags, // Indicates what keys are pressed
    CPoint point); // Mouse cursor position (relative to CWnd)
```

This function is called to handle a WM_LBUTTONDBLCLK message, which is sent to a window if the user double-clicks the left mouse button when the cursor is located inside the window.

```
afx_msg void OnLButtonDown(
    UINT   nFlags, // Indicates what keys are pressed
    CPoint point); // Mouse cursor position (relative to CWnd)
```

This function is called to handle a WM_LBUTTONDOWN message, which is sent to a window if the user presses the left mouse button when the cursor is located inside the window.

```
afx_msg void OnLButtonUp(
    UINT   nFlags, // Indicates what keys are pressed
    CPoint point); // Mouse cursor position (relative to CWnd)
```

This function is called to handle a WM_LBUTTONUP message, which is sent to a window if the user releases the left mouse button when the cursor is located inside the window.

```
afx_msg void OnMButtonDblClk(
    UINT   nFlags, // Indicates what keys are pressed
    CPoint point); // Mouse cursor position (relative to CWnd)
```

This function is called to handle a WM_MBUTTONDBLCLK message, which is sent to a window if the user double-clicks the middle mouse button when the cursor is located inside the window.

```
afx_msg void OnMButtonDown(
    UINT   nFlags, // Indicates what keys are pressed
    CPoint point); // Mouse cursor position (relative to CWnd)
```

This function is called to handle a WM_MBUTTONDOWN message, which is sent to a window if the user presses the middle mouse button when the cursor is located inside the window.

```
afx_msg void OnMButtonUp(
    UINT   nFlags, // Indicates what keys are pressed
    CPoint point); // Mouse cursor position (relative to CWnd)
```

This function is called to handle a WM_MBUTTONUP message, which is sent to a window if the user releases the middle mouse button when the cursor is located inside the window.

```
afx_msg void OnMDIActivate(
    BOOL  bActivate,         // TRUE = activating child window
    CWnd* pActivateWnd,      // Activate this child window
    CWnd* pDeactivateWnd);   // Deactivate this child window
```

This function is called to process a WM_MDIACTIVATE message, which is sent to a child window in an application with MDI when the child window is activated or deactivated.

```
afx_msg void OnMeasureItem(
    LPMEASUREITEMSTRUCT lpMeasureItemStruct);
```

This function is called to handle a WM_MEASUREITEM message, which is sent to the owner of an owner-drawn button, list box, or combo box when that control window is created.

```
afx_msg LONG OnMenuChar(
    UINT   nChar,  // ASCII character that the user entered
    UINT   nFlags, // MF_POPUP is pop-up menu, MF_SYSMENU if
                   //   system menu
    CMenu* pMenu); // Pointer to selected menu
```

This function is called to process a WM_MENUCHAR message, which is sent when the user drops down a menu and enters a character that does not match any of the predefined mnemonic characters for that menu.

```
afx_msg void OnMenuSelect(
    UINT  nItemID,   // Item selected
    UINT  nFlags,    // Identifies item
    HMENU hSysMenu); // If nFlags has MF_SYSMENU, this is the
                     //   handle to the system menu
```

This function is called to process a WM_MENUSELECT message, which is sent when the user selects an item from a menu.

```
afx_msg int OnMouseActivate(
    CWnd* pFrameWnd, // Pointer to topmost parent window
    UINT  nHitTest,  // Area where cursor is located
    UINT  message);  // Message number
```

This function is called to handle a WM_MOUSEACTIVATE message, which is sent if the mouse cursor is located in an inactive window when the user presses any mouse button. This function should return a constant to indicate whether to activate the window and discard the mouse event.

```
afx_msg void OnMouseMove(
    UINT   nFlags, // Indicates what keys are pressed
    CPoint point); // Mouse cursor position (relative to CWnd)
```

This function is called to process a WM_MOUSEMOVE message, which is sent whenever the user moves the mouse cursor.

```
afx_msg void OnMove(
    int x, int y); // New position
```

This function is called to process a WM_MOVE message, which is sent to a window after it has been moved.

```
afx_msg void BOOL OnNcActivate(
    BOOL bActive); TRUE = show active caption bar or icon
```

This function is called to handle a WM_NCACTIVATE message, which is sent when the nonclient area of a window—the frame with the title bar and scrollbars—has changed to indicate an active or inactive state.

```
afx_msg void OnNcCalcSize(
    NCCALCSIZE_PARAMS FAR* lpncsp);
```

This function is called to handle a WM_NCCALCSIZE message, which is sent when the size and position of a window's client area needs to be calculated.

```
afx_msg BOOL OnNcCreate(
    LPCREATESTRUCT lpCreateStruct);
```

This function is called to handle a WM_NCCREATE message, which is sent just before the WM_CREATE message to indicate that the nonclient area of the window is being created. This function should return TRUE if the nonclient area is successfully created and FALSE otherwise.

```
afx_msg void OnNcDestroy();
```

This function is called to process a WM_NCDESTROY message, which is sent to a window when that window's nonclient area—the frame—is about to be destroyed.

```
afx_msg UINT OnNcHitTest(
    CPoint point); // x- and y-coordinates of mouse cursor
                   // These are screen coordinates
```

This function is called to handle a WM_NCHITTEST message, which is sent to a window (or the window that is capturing all mouse inputs by calling the SetCapture member function) whenever the user moves the mouse. The message handler should determine the part of the window where the mouse cursor is located (for example, is it in the lower border? the upper border?) and return a code indicating the location. Consult the WM_NCHITTEST message in the Microsoft Windows SDK *Programmer's Reference, Volume 3* for information about these codes.

```
afx_msg void OnNcLButtonDblClk(
    UINT   nHitTest,// Hit-test code indicating cursor location
    CPoint point);  // Cursor position in screen coordinates
```

This function is called to handle a WM_NCLBUTTONDBLCLK message, which is sent to a window when the user double-clicks the left mouse button with the cursor in the window's frame (the nonclient area).

```
afx_msg void OnNcLButtonDown(
    UINT   nHitTest,// Hit-test code indicating cursor location
    CPoint point);  // Cursor position in screen coordinates
```

This function is called to handle a WM_NCLBUTTONDOWN message, which is sent to a window when the user presses the left mouse button with the cursor in the window's frame (the nonclient area).

```
afx_msg void OnNcLButtonUp(
    UINT   nHitTest,// Hit-test code indicating cursor location
    CPoint point);  // Cursor position in screen coordinates
```

This function is called to process a WM_NCLBUTTONUP message, which is sent to a window when the user releases the left mouse button with the cursor in the window's frame (the nonclient area).

```
afx_msg void OnNcMButtonDblClk(
    UINT   nHitTest,// Hit-test code indicating cursor location
    CPoint point);  // Cursor position in screen coordinates
```

This function is called to process a WM_NCMBUTTONDBLCLK message, which is sent when the user double-clicks the middle mouse button with the cursor in the nonclient area (the area outside the rectangular region where the application's output appears).

```
afx_msg void OnNcMButtonDown(
    UINT   nHitTest,// Hit-test code indicating cursor location
    CPoint point);  // Cursor position in screen coordinates
```

This function is called to handle a WM_NCMBUTTONDOWN message, which is sent when the user presses the middle mouse button with the cursor in the nonclient area.

```
afx_msg void OnNcMButtonUp(
    UINT   nHitTest,// Hit-test code indicating cursor location
    CPoint point);  // Cursor position in screen coordinates
```

This function is called to process a WM_NCMBUTTONUP message, which is sent when the user releases the middle mouse button with the cursor in the nonclient area.

```
afx_msg void OnNcMouseMove(
    UINT   nHitTest,// Hit-test code indicating cursor location
    CPoint point);  // Cursor position in screen coordinates
```

This function is called to handle a WM_NCMOUSEMOVE message, which is sent to a window when the user moves the mouse cursor within the nonclient area (the frame and the border of the window).

```
afx_msg void OnNcPaint();
```

This function is called to process a WM_NCPAINT message, which is sent to a window when its nonclient area—the frame—must be repainted.

```
afx_msg void OnNcRButtonDblClk(
    UINT   nHitTest,// Hit-test code indicating cursor location
    CPoint point);  // Cursor position in screen coordinates
```

This function is called to process a WM_NCRBUTTONDBLCLK message, which is sent to a window when the user double-clicks the right mouse button anywhere in the nonclient area—anywhere outside the area where the application's output appears.

```
afx_msg void OnNcRButtonDown(
    UINT   nHitTest,// Hit-test code indicating cursor location
    CPoint point);  // Cursor position in screen coordinates
```

This function is called to handle a WM_NCRBUTTONDOWN message, which is sent to a window when the user presses the right mouse button anywhere in the nonclient area.

```
afx_msg void OnNcRButtonDblClk(
    UINT   nHitTest,// Hit-test code indicating cursor location
    CPoint point);  // Cursor position in screen coordinates
```

This function is called to handle a WM_NCRBUTTONUP message, which is sent to a window when the user releases the right mouse button anywhere in the nonclient area.

```
afx_msg void OnPaint();
```

This function is called to handle a WM_PAINT message, which is sent when an area of the window must be repainted. You should override this function to draw application-specific items in your application's windows.

```
afx_msg OnPaintClipboard(
    CWnd* pClipAppWnd,      // Pointer to Clipboard Viewer window
    HANDLE hPaintStruct); // Information on what to paint
```

This function is called to handle a WM_PAINTCLIPBOARD message, which is sent to the Clipboard's owner when the Clipboard contains data with the CF_OWNERDISPLAY format and the Clipboard Viewer's window needs repainting.

```
afx_msg void OnPaletteChanged(
    CWnd* pFocusWnd); // Window that caused the change in palette
```

This function is called to handle a WM_PALETTECHANGED message, which is sent after the system color palette has changed.

```
afx_msg void OnPaletteIsChanging(CWnd* pRealizeWnd);
```

This function is called to handle a WM_PALETTEISCHANGING message, which is sent to indicate that the system color palette is about to change.

```
afx_msg void OnParentNotify(
    UINT message, // Parent is being notified of this event
    LONG lParam); // Low word = Window handle of child window
```

This function is called to handle a WM_PARENTNOTIFY message, which is sent to a parent window when a child window is created or destroyed or when the user clicks the child window.

```
afx_msg HCURSOR OnQueryDragIcon();
```

This function is called to handle a WM_QUERYDRAGICON message, which is sent when the user moves an iconized window and the window class does not have a defined icon. This function should return a monochrome cursor or icon, which is used while the minimized window is being dragged. The function can return NULL to indicate that the default cursor should be used.

```
afx_msg BOOL OnQueryEndSession();
```

This function is called to handle a WM_QUERYENDSESSION message, which is sent when the user chooses to end the Windows session. Returns TRUE if the application can be shut down; otherwise, returns FALSE.

```
afx_msg BOOL OnQueryNewPalette();
```

This function is called to handle a WM_QUERYNEWPALETTE message, which is sent when a window is about to receive the input focus, inquiring whether the window wants to use its logical palette of colors. This function should return TRUE if the window realizes its palette; otherwise, it should return FALSE.

```
afx_msg BOOL OnQueryOpen();
```

This function is called to handle a WM_QUERYOPEN message, which is sent when an iconic window is about to be opened to a full size window.

```
afx_msg void OnRButtonDblClk(
    UINT   nFlags, // Indicates what keys are pressed
    CPoint point); // Mouse cursor position (relative to CWnd)
```

This function is called to handle a WM_RBUTTONDBLCLK message, which is sent when the user double-clicks the right mouse button.

```
afx_msg void OnRButtonDown(
    UINT   nFlags, // Indicates what keys are pressed
    CPoint point); // Mouse cursor position (relative to CWnd)
```

This function is called to handle a `WM_RBUTTONDOWN` message, which is sent when the user presses the right mouse button.

```
afx_msg void OnRButtonUp(
    UINT   nFlags, // Indicates what keys are pressed
    CPoint point); // Mouse cursor position (relative to CWnd)
```

This function is called to process a `WM_RBUTTONUP` message, which is sent when the user releases the right mouse button.

```
afx_msg void OnRenderAllFormats();
```

This function is called to handle a `WM_RENDERALLFORMATS` message, which is sent to the clipboard's owner when the owner application is about to be destroyed. This function should render the data in all formats that this application is capable of supporting, and pass a handle to the rendered data for each format to the Clipboard by calling the `SetClipboardData` function.

```
afx_msg void OnRenderFormat(
    UINT nFormat);
```

This function is called to process a `WM_RENDERFORMAT` message, which is sent to the owner of the Clipboard when data of a specific format needs to be rendered. This function should render the data in the specified format and pass the data handle to the Clipboard by calling the `SetClipboardData` function.

```
afx_msg BOOL OnSetCursor(
    CWnd* pWnd,      // Pointer to window with cursor
    UINT  nHitTest, // Hit-test code (where is cursor)
    UINT  message); // Message number
```

This function is called to handle a `WM_SETCURSOR` message, which is sent when the cursor moves within the window. This function should return `TRUE` if the message is handled and `FALSE` otherwise.

```
afx_msg void OnSetFocus(
    CWnd* pOldWnd); // Window that loses the focus
```

This function is called to handle a `WM_SETFOCUS` message, which is sent after a window gains input focus.

```
afx_msg void OnShowWindow(
    BOOL bShow,     // TRUE = show the window
    UINT nStatus); // Status of window being shown
```

This function is called to handle a `WM_SHOWWINDOW` message, which is sent when a window is about to be hidden or made visible.

```
afx_msg void OnSize(
    UINT nType, // Type of resizing (SIZEFULLSCREEN, SIZEICONIC,
                // SIZENORMAL, SIZEZOOMHIDE, or SIZEZOOMSHOW)
    int  cx,    // Width of client area
    int  cy);   // Height of client area
```

This function is called to handle a `WM_SIZE` message, which is sent after a window's size has changed.

```
afx_msg void OnSizeClipboard(
    CWnd*  pClipAppWnd, // Clipboard Viewer window
    HANDLE hRect);      // Area of clipboard to paint
```

This function is called to handle a `WM_SIZECLIPBOARD` message, which is sent to the owner of the Clipboard if the Clipboard's data is of the `CF_OWNERDISPLAY` format and if the user resizes the Clipboard Viewer window.

```
afx_msg void OnSpoolerStatus(
    UINT nStatus, // The SP_JOBSTATUS flag
    UINT nJobs);  // Number of jobs remaining in queue
```

This function is called to process a `WM_SPOOLERSTATUS` message, which is sent by the Windows Print Manager whenever a job is added or removed from the Print Manager queue.

```
afx_msg void OnSysChar(UINT nChar, UINT nRepCnt, UINT nFlags);
```

This function is called to handle a `WM_SYSCHAR` message, which is sent whenever a `WM_SYSKEYDOWN` or `WM_SYSKEYDOWN` message is generated.

```
afx_msg void OnSysColorChange();
```

This function is called to handle a `WM_SYSCOLORCHANGE` message, which is sent when the user changes the system color settings.

```
afx_msg void OnSysCommand(
    UINT nID,      // Type of system command
    LONG lParam); // Cursor position (low word = x-coordinate)
```

This function is called to process a `WM_SYSCOMMAND` message, which is sent when the user selects any item from the system menu.

```
afx_msg void OnSysDeadChar(UINT nChar, UINT nRepCnt,
    UINT nFlags);
```

This function is called to handle a WM_SYSDEADCHAR message, which is sent when the user holds down the Alt key and presses or releases a *dead key* (a key combined with other keys to compose special characters).

```
afx_msg void OnSysKeyDown(UINT nChar, UINT nRepCnt,
    UINT nFlags);
```

This function is called to process a WM_SYSKEYDOWN message, which is sent when the user holds down the Alt key and then presses any other key.

```
afx_msg void OnSysKeyUp(UINT nChar, UINT nRepCnt,
    UINT nFlags);
```

This function is called to handle a WM_SYSKEYUP message, which is sent when the user releases a key that was pressed together with the Alt key.

```
afx_msg void OnTimeChange();
```

This function is called to handle a WM_TIMECHANGE message, which is sent after the system time is changed by the user.

```
afx_msg void OnTimer(
    UINT nIDEvent); // Identifier of the time
```

This function is called to process a WM_TIMER message, which is sent at regular intervals. You can set the interval by calling the SetTimer member function of the window class.

```
afx_msg int OnVKeyToItem(
    UINT       nKey,      // Virtual key code of key pressed
    CListBox* pListBox, // Pointer to list box
    UINT       nIndex);   // Item containing the caret
```

This function is called to handle a WM_VKEYTOITEM message, which is sent by a list box with the LBS_WANTKEYBOARDINPUT style when the list box receives a WM_KEYDOWN event.

```
afx_msg void OnVScroll(
    UINT          nSBCode,      // Scroll request
    UINT          nPos,         // Scroll box position
    CScrollBar* pScrollBar); // Pointer to scrollbar control
```

This function is called to handle a WM_VSCROLL message, which is sent when the user clicks the vertical scrollbar of the window.

```
afx_msg void OnVScrollClipboard(
    CWnd* pClipAppWnd, // Pointer to Clipboard Viewer window
    UINT  nSBCode,     // What should be scrolled?
    UINT  nPos);       // Scroll box position
```

This function is called to handle a `WM_VSCROLLCLIPBOARD` message, which is sent to the owner of the Clipboard when the Clipboard's data has the `CF_OWNERDISPLAY` format and the user clicks anywhere on the vertical scrollbar of the Clipboard Viewer.

```
afx_msg void OnWindowPosChanged(WINDOWPOS FAR* lpwndpos);
```

This function is called to handle a `WM_WINDOWPOSCHANGED` message, which is sent (with Windows 3.1 and later versions) after the window's size, position, or stacking order has changed.

```
afx_msg void OnWindowPosChanging(WINDOWPOS FAR* lpwndpos);
```

This function is called to process a `WM_WINDOWPOSCHANGING` message, which is sent (in Windows 3.1 and later versions) when the window's size, position, or stacking order is about to change.

```
afx_msg void OnWinIniChange(
    LPSTR lpSection); // Name of the section that changed
                      // Does not include the square brackets
```

This function is called to handle a `WM_WININICHANGE` message, which is sent to a window after a change occurs to the Windows initialization file, WIN.INI.

Drag and Drop support

```
void DragAcceptFiles(BOOL bAcceptFiles = TRUE);
```

Used from the application's main window to tell Windows that the window accepts files (if *`bAcceptFiles`* `= TRUE`) that are dragged and dropped from the Windows File Manager.

See Also

`CDialog,` `CFindReplaceDialog,` `CFileDialog,` `CPrintDialog,` `CFontDialog,` `CColorDialog`	Use these classes for the dialog boxes in your application.
`CFrameWnd,` `CMDIChildWnd,` `CMDIFrameWnd`	Derive your application's window classes from one of these.

`CStatic`, `CButton`, `CEdit`, `CListBox`, `CComboBox`, `CScrollBar`, `CBitmapButton`	These are predefined Windows controls.
`CWinApp`	Derive your application class from this.

VI

Functions for File Handling and I/O

21

File and Directory Management

Almost all applications store data and results in files so that they can be retrieved and used later. To use files effectively, you should understand how files are organized in a hierarchy of directories and how files are viewed in C. This chapter briefly describes the MS-DOS operating system's organization of directories and files, how files and directories are named, and how the contents of a file are interpreted.

In addition, Microsoft Visual C++ includes a full complement of functions for file- and directory-management tasks such as:

- Creating and deleting directories
- Searching for a file
- Checking the status of a file

This chapter briefly describes how these functions are used, as well.

By reading this chapter, you should be better prepared to use the stream and low-level input and output (I/O) functions described in Chapter 22, "Stream I/O," and

Chapter 23, "Low-Level I/O," because file- and directory-management tasks generally precede I/O. The functions described in this chapter also handle chores such as searching for a specific file and checking whether a file exists.

The latter part of the chapter serves as a reference guide to the file- and directory-management functions.

MS-DOS File System

Like most operating systems, such as UNIX and Digital Equipment Corporation's VMS, MS-DOS organizes files and directories into a tree-like hierarchy. All files and directories on a hard disk or diskette appear under a single *root directory* (indicated by a backslash, \). You do not have to create the root directory; MS-DOS creates the root directory when you format a diskette or a *hard disk partition*—a portion of the physical medium of the hard disk. Each directory can, in turn, contain more directories and files—this is how the tree-like hierarchy is formed.

Pathnames

Because the file system can be on a diskette or a hard disk, MS-DOS requires you to specify a drive letter to completely identify a file. In fact, the complete name of a file—the full *pathname*—identifies the drive as well as all the directories, from the root directory onward. The full pathname of a file starts with a drive letter followed by a colon (`:`); after that comes a single backslash (`\`) to denote the root directory. The subsequent directory names are listed one after another with intervening backslash separators. The file's name appears at the end of the pathname.

In MS-DOS, filenames consist of up to eight characters followed by a period and then an *extension* of up to three characters. The Microsoft Visual C++ library includes functions such as `_fullpath`, `_makepath`, and `_splitpath` to manipulate pathnames.

Leading Underscore in Names of Nonstandard Functions

Microsoft Visual C++ adds an underscore prefix to many functions (such as `_access`, `_chdir`, and `_chmod`) in keeping with ANSI Standard C's naming conventions for nonstandard functions. In many other C compilers (including earlier versions of Microsoft C compilers), as well as in UNIX and POSIX, these function are available with names that do not have the leading

> underscores. Note that you can use the names without underscore prefix in Microsoft Visual C++ as well. The functions without underscore prefixes are in a library named oldnames.lib, which the linker searches by default.

Current Drive

The full pathname is necessary to identify a file anywhere in the system, but you don't have to provide a full pathname at all times. MS-DOS does have the notion of the *current drive* and the *current working directory*. If you do not specify the drive letter in a pathname, the referenced file is assumed to be on the current drive. Similarly, omitting the directory names implies that you're referring to a file in the current working directory.

Under MS-DOS, a *drive* refers to a *device*—a diskette or a hard disk drive. The usual meaning of the drive letters are as follows:

- Drives A: and B: refer to the first and second diskette drives, respectively.
- Drive letters C: through Z: identify hard disk drives, with C: denoting the first hard disk drive.

To determine the current drive from your program, or change it, use the `_getdrive` and `_chdrive` functions, respectively.

Current Working Directory

Just as MS-DOS keeps track of the current drive, it also keeps track of the current directory. In your C programs, you can get the full pathname of the current directory by calling the `_getcwd` function.

You can change the current directory with the DOS command `CHDIR`, or `CD` (change directory). To create a new directory, use the `MKDIR` or `MD` (make directory) command, whereas the `RD` (remove directory) command deletes an empty directory. Microsoft Visual C++ includes functions such as `_chdir`, `_mkdir`, and `_rmdir` to perform these chores from within your programs.

Devices as Files

Although most files refer to storage on a disk, some filenames in DOS refer to devices, such as a printer or a serial communications port. Here are some of the filenames that refer to devices:

- AUX refers to the first serial communications port.
- COM1 and COM2 are the first and second serial communications ports.
- COM3 and COM4 are the third and fourth serial communications ports. Due to shared interrupts, there can be problems with using more than two serial communications ports on a PC.
- CON refers to the *console*—the combination of the keyboard and the display screen.
- PRN refers to the first parallel printer port.
- LPT1, LPT2, and LPT3 are the first, second, and third parallel printer ports.
- NUL is the dummy device—sending output to NUL produces nothing.

You cannot use any of these names—either in lowercase or uppercase—for disk-based program or data filenames, even if you supply a file extension. They may only be used to access devices.

File Characteristics

In addition to its name, a DOS file has the following important characteristics that affect I/O operations with that file:

- *Permission setting* determines the type of file as well as its accessibility—whether the file is read-only or both read and write operations are allowed on the file. Permission setting is a part of DOS.
- *Translation mode* determines how the contents of the file are interpreted during I/O operations. Translation is a part of the C language.

Permission Setting

The permission setting of a file indicates the operations that are permitted on that file. In MS-DOS, you can have a file marked read only or read and write (MS-DOS does not support write-only files, nor does DOS support execute-only files). You can use the _chmod function to set the permission setting of a file.

The _access function enables you to determine the types of access allowed to a file. Note that when you open a file using a function such as fopen, you must specify the *access mode*—the mode in which you want to open the file. For example, you can open a file with read-and-write permission as read-only, write-only, or for both reading and writing.

Translation Mode

When you open a file using `fopen` (see Chapter 22, "Stream I/O"), in addition to the read-write access, you also can specify how the contents of the file should be interpreted. You have two options:

- Text mode
- Binary mode

In *binary mode,* every byte in the file is provided to your program without any alteration. In *text mode,* the following translations and interpretations take place when your program reads from the file or writes to the file:

- When you read from the file, a carriage return-linefeed pair is translated into a single linefeed (newline character). Also, during reading, a Ctrl+Z (0x1A) is interpreted as the end-of-file (EOF).
- When you write to the file, a newline is expanded to a carriage return-linefeed pair, and these characters are written to the file.

You can specify the translation mode when you open the file. You also can alter the translation mode of an open file by using the `_setmode` function.

File Handle

Although a file's name may be the most natural way to identify the file in DOS commands, files are identified by other means in the C I/O library. As you'll see in Chapter 22, when you open files with the `fopen` function, a pointer to a `FILE` structure is returned. This pointer identifies the file in all subsequent I/O operations. Similarly, if you create or open a file using the `_open`, `_sopen`, or `_creat` functions (see Chapter 23 for details), these functions return an integer file identifier called the *file handle.* This section describes a number of functions—such as `_chsize`, `_filelength`, `_fstat`, `_isatty`, and `_locking`—that require the file handle as an argument.

Basic File and Directory Management Tasks

Now that you've seen a brief description of the MS-DOS file system, consult Table 21.1 for an alphabetic list of the file and directory management functions. Table 21.1 gives you a quick overview of these functions, and Table 21.2 organizes the functions by the tasks they perform. For more information about a function, consult the reference page of that function in the latter part of this chapter.

Table 21.1. Alphabetic listing of file and directory management functions.

Function	Description
`_access`	Checks for the existence and read-write permission settings of a file.
`_chdir`	Changes the current working directory.
`_chdrive`	Changes the current drive.
`_chmod`	Changes the read-write permission settings of a file.
`_chsize`	Changes the size of a file.
`_filelength`	Returns the length of a file in bytes.
`_fstat`	Provides information about an open file identified by its handle.
`_fullpath`	Converts a partial pathname into a full pathname.
`_getcwd`	Returns the name of the current working directory for the current drive.
`_getdcwd`	Returns the name of the current working directory for a specified drive.
`_getdrive`	Returns an integer (1 = A, 2 = B, 3 = C) identifying the current drive.
`_isatty`	Returns nonzero if a file handle refers to a character device.
`_locking`	Locks or unlocks a specified range of bytes in a file.
`_makepath`	Builds a DOS pathname from components.

Function	Description
_mkdir	Creates a new directory.
_mktemp	Returns a unique filename.
remove	Deletes a file identified by its pathname.
rename	Renames a file.
_rmdir	Removes a directory.
_searchenv	Searches for a file in a semicolon-separated list of directories specified in an environment variable.
_setmode	Sets the translation mode of an open file.
_splitpath	Breaks down a DOS pathname into its component parts.
_stat	Provides detailed information about a file identified by name.
_umask	Sets the permission mask to be used for newly opened files.
_unlink	Deletes a file identified by its pathname.

Table 21.2. Basic file and directory management tasks.

Task	Functions
Set and verify permission settings	_access, _chmod, _umask
Get and set current drive	_chdrive, _getdrive,
Manage directories	_chdir, _getcwd, _getdcwd, _mkdir, _rmdir
Locate files	_searchenv
Get and set file characteristics	_chsize, _filelength, _fstat, _isatty, _mktemp, _setmode, _stat
Delete files	remove, _unlink
Rename a file	rename
Lock a range of bytes in a file	_locking
Manipulate MS-DOS pathnames	_fullpath, _makepath, _splitpath

Changing the Drive and Directory

Sometimes, you may need to determine the current drive and the current directory on a drive from within your program. As an example, suppose you want to write a menu-driven utility program that enables the user to change the current drive and the current directory. Listing 21.1 shows such a program: dirutil.c, which uses functions such as `_getdrive`, `_getcwd`, `_chdrive`, and `_chdir` to perform the desired tasks. For the menu-driven user interface, the program uses the text-mode output functions from graph.doc on the companion disk.

Note that, in a greatly expanded version, a program such as dirutil.c might offer many more functions such as creating a directory, removing a directory, renaming a file, or deleting a file. If you want to implement such a program, you can accomplish all of these tasks by calling one or more functions described in this chapter.

Listing 21.1. dirutil.c. A menu-driven program to change current drive and current directory.

```
//-------------------------------------------------------------
// File: dirutil.c
//
// A small utility program that lets the user change the
// current drive and the current directory
//-------------------------------------------------------------
#include <stdio.h>
#include <graph.h>
#include <direct.h>
#include <process.h>
#include <conio.h>
#include <ctype.h>

static int curdrive;
static char dirname[80], drivename[8];
//-------------------------------------------------------------
void main(void)
{
    int done = 0, c;
    char outbuf[80];

    while (!done)
    {
```

```
// Get current drive and directory for display:
       curdrive = _getdrive();
       _getcwd(dirname, 80);
       sprintf(drivename, "%c", curdrive + 'A' - 1);

        _clearscreen(_GCLEARSCREEN);
        _settextwindow(10, 10, 19, 70);
        _settextposition(1,1);

// Display drive letter:
        sprintf(outbuf, "Current Drive:     %s\n", drivename);
        _outtext(outbuf);

// Display current directory:
        sprintf(outbuf, "Current Directory: %s\n", dirname);
        _outtext(outbuf);

        _settextposition(5, 1);
        _outtext(" 1  Change Drive\n");
        _outtext(" 2  Change Directory\n");
        _outtext(" 0  Exit");

        _settextposition(9, 1);
        _outtext("Enter selection: ");

// Read keypress:
        c = _getche();

// Process command implied by keypress:

        switch(c)
        {
            case '0':
                exit(0);


            case '1':
// Change drive:
                _settextposition(9,1);
                _outtext("Enter drive letter:");
                c = _getche();
```

continues

Listing 21.1. continued

```
                _chdrive(toupper(c) - 'A' + 1);
                break;

            case '2':
// Change current working directory:
                _settextposition(9,1);
                _outtext("Enter directory name:");
                gets(dirname);
                if(_chdir(dirname) != 0)
                    _outtext("\nError changing directory!");
                break;
        }
    }
}
```

To build the dirutil program, create a project using the Visual Workbench. This project should be a DOS-executable program (there's no need to include MFC support. However, if you've built the DOS MFC libraries, no errors will occur if MFC support is included.) Include the dirutil.c program in the project. You must make this program DOS executable; if you were to make this program a QuickWin program, it would run—but you wouldn't see the results of running it.

When you run the dirutil program, it displays a screen like this:

```
Current Drive:     D
Current Directory: D:\MCPB\EX\C\CH21


1  Change Drive
2  Change Directory
0  Exit

Enter selection: 0
```

You can exit the program by pressing 0. Options 1 and 2 enable you to change the current drive and the current directory, respectively. After any of these are changed, the program updates the current drive and directory names displayed above the menu.

Changing the File Permission

As another example of using the file- and directory-management functions, consider the task of making a file read-only so that it cannot be accidentally erased or overwritten. Listing 21.2 shows the program protect.c, which makes a file read-only by using the `_chmod` function. Once you compile and build the program, PROTECT.EXE, you can make a file, in this case protect.obj, read-only with the command:

```
protect protect.obj
```

Listing 21.2. protect.c. Program to protect a file from accidental erasure by making it read-only.

```
//-------------------------------------------------------------
// File: protect.c
//
// Mark a file as read-only so that it cannot be erased or
// overwritten.
//
// Use it as: protect filename.
//-------------------------------------------------------------
#include <stdio.h>
#include <sys\types.h>
#include <sys\stat.h>
#include <io.h>
//-------------------------------------------------------------
void main(int argc, char **argv)
{
    if(argc < 2)
    {
        printf(
          "Usage: %s <pathname>\n", argv[0]);
    }
    else
    {
        if(_chmod(argv[1], S_IREAD) == -1)
            perror("Error in _chmod");
        else
            printf("%s protected\n", argv[1]);
    }
}
```

Once a file is protected by using PROTECT.EXE, if you try to erase the file, you see the following error message:

```
Access denied
```

To undo the effect of PROTECT.EXE, you need another utility program—call it unprot—that reenables read-write operations on a file. Listing 21.3 shows the program unprot.c, which accomplishes this.

Listing 21.3. unprot.c. Program that enables read-write operations on a file.

```
//-----------------------------------------------------------------
// File: unprot.c
//
// Mark a file as read-write to reverse the effects of "protect."
//
// Use it as: unprot filename.
//-----------------------------------------------------------------
#include <stdio.h>
#include <sys\types.h>
#include <sys\stat.h>
#include <io.h>
//-----------------------------------------------------------------
void main(int argc, char **argv)
{
    if(argc < 2)
    {
        printf(
          "Usage: %s <pathname>\n", argv[0]);
    }
    else
    {
        if(_chmod(argv[1], S_IREAD¦S_IWRITE) == -1)
            perror("Error in _chmod");
        else
            printf("%s unprotected\n", argv[1]);
    }
}
```

_access

MSC6	MSC7	VC++	QC2.5	QC-WIN	TC2	TC++	BC++2	BC++3	ANSI	POSIX	UNIX V	DOS	QWIN	WIN	WINDLL
X	X	X	X	X	X	X	X	X		X	X	X	X	X	X

See the note earlier in this chapter about the leading underscore in this function's name.

Summary

```
#include <io.h>

int _access(
    const char *name, // Pathname of file to be checked
    int         mode); // Can file be accessed in this mode?
```

Description

Checks whether a file (identified by `name`) exists and whether the file can be accessed in the specified access mode. The `mode` argument can be one of the following:

00	Check whether file exists
02	Check whether writing to file is allowed
04	Check whether reading from the file is allowed
06	Check whether both reading and writing are allowed

Returns

0 The requested access is allowed.

–1 Indicates an error. Sets `errno` to `EACCES` to indicate that access is denied. If the specified file does not exist, sets `errno` to `ENOENT`.

Sample Call

```
if(_access("invoice.def", 0) == 0) puts("File exists");
```

See Also

`_chmod`, `_fstat`, `_stat`

_chdir

MSC6	MSC7	VC++	QC2.5	QC-WIN	TC2	TC++	BC++2	BC++3	ANSI	POSIX	UNIX V	DOS	QWIN	WIN	WINDLL
X	X	X	X	X	X	X	X	X		X	X	X	X	X	X

See the note earlier in this chapter about the leading underscore in this function's name.

Summary

```
#include <direct.h>

int _chdir(
    const char *new_path); // Name of the new directory
```

Description

The `_chdir` function changes the current working directory for the current drive to the directory specified by *new_path*.

Sample Call

```
// Change to directory: D:\MSVC\MFC\DOC.
    if(_chdir("D:\\MSVC\\MFC\\DOC") != 0) perror("_chdir");
```

Returns

0 The current working directory was successfully changed.

–1 Indicates failure. Also sets `errno` to `ENOENT`.

See Also

`_mkdir`, `_rmdir`

_chdrive

MSC6	MSC7	VC++	QC2.5	QC-WIN	TC2	TC++	BC++2	BC++3	ANSI	POSIX	UNIX V	DOS	QWIN	WIN	WINDLL
X	X	X	X	X				X				X	X	X	X

Summary

```
#include <direct.h>

int _chdrive(
    int drive_num); // Drive, 1=A, 2=B, 3=C, 4=D, and so on
```

Description

Changes the current working drive to the drive specified by the integer argument *drive_num*.

Returns

0 The drive was successfully changed.

–1 Indicates an error.

Sample Call

```
// Change to drive E:.
    int drive_letter = 'e';
// Make sure drive_letter is uppercase.
    drive_letter = toupper(drive_letter);
    if(_chdrive(drive_letter - 'A' + 1) != 0)
    {
        fprintf(stderr,"Error changing drive!\n");
    }
```

See Also

`_dos_setdrive` (Chapter 32), `_getdrive`

_chmod

MSC6	MSC7	VC++	QC2.5	QC-WIN	TC2	TC++	BC++2	BC++3	ANSI	POSIX	UNIX V	DOS	QWIN	WIN	WINDLL
x	x	x	x	x	x	x	x	x		x	x	x	x	x	x

See the note earlier in this chapter about the leading underscore in this function's name.

Summary

```
#include <io.h>          // For function prototype
#include <sys\types.h> // The next header needs this file
#include <sys\stat.h>  // For permission settings (SI_READ, and so on)

int _chmod(
    const char *path,  // Change this file's permission setting
    int        mode);  //   to this one
```

Description

Sets the read-write permission setting of a file to a new value specified by *mode*, which can be one of the following combinations:

`_S_IWRITE`	Allow both read and write operations (because MS-DOS does not allow write-only files).
`_S_IREAD`	File is read only.
`_S_IREAD ¦ _S_IWRITE`	Allow both read and write operations.

Returns

0	The permission setting was successfully changed.
–1	Indicates an error. Sets `errno` to `ENOENT` to indicate that the specified file does not exist.

Sample Call

```
// Make the index file read only.
    _chmod("index.dat", _S_IREAD);
```

See Also

`_access`, `_fstat`, `_stat`

_chsize

MSC6	MSC7	VC++	QC2.5	QC-WIN	TC2	TC++	BC++2	BC++3	ANSI	POSIX	UNIX V	DOS	QWIN	WIN	WINDLL
X	X	X	X	X	X	X	X	X			X	X	X	X	X

See the note earlier in this chapter about the leading underscore in this function's name.

Summary

```
#include <io.h>

int _chsize(
    int  handle, // Handle to an open file being resized
    long size);  // New length of file in bytes
```

Description

Sets the new size of an open file (identified by `handle`) to `size` bytes. If the file is extended, null characters are appended to the file.

Returns

0 The size of the file was successfully reset.

–1 Indicates an error. Also sets `errno` to `EACCES`, `EBADF`, or `ENOSPC` to indicate access failure, bad file handle, or lack of disk space, respectively.

Sample Call

```
// Truncate an open file to zero length.
    if(_chsize(fhandle, 0L) == -1) perror("_chsize");
```

See Also

`_fileno` (Chapter 22), `_close` (Chapter 23), `_creat` (Chapter 23), `_open` (Chapter 23)

_filelength

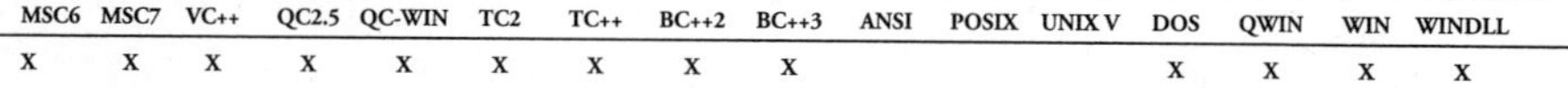

MSC6	MSC7	VC++	QC2.5	QC-WIN	TC2	TC++	BC++2	BC++3	ANSI	POSIX	UNIX V	DOS	QWIN	WIN	WINDLL
X	X	X	X	X	X	X	X	X				X	X	X	X

See the note earlier in this chapter about the leading underscore in this function's name.

Summary

```
#include <io.h>

long _filelength(int handle); // Handle to open file
```

Description

Returns the length of an open file identified by `handle`.

Returns

When the function completes successfully, the return value is a long integer containing the length of the file in bytes.

-1 Indicates an error. Sets errno to EBADF to indicate a bad file handle.

Sample Call

```
// Get the length of the file.
    if((filesize = _filelength(fhandle)) == -1)
        perror("_filelength");
```

See Also

_chsize, _fileno, _fstat, _stat

_fstat

MSC6	MSC7	VC++	QC2.5	QC-WIN	TC2	TC++	BC++2	BC++3	ANSI	POSIX	UNIX V	DOS	QWIN	WIN	WINDLL
x	x	x	x	x	x	x	x	x		x	x	x	x	x	x

See the note earlier in this chapter about the leading underscore in this function's name.

Summary

```
#include <sys\types.h> // Required by <sys\stat.h>
#include <sys\stat.h>  // Function prototype

int _fstat(
    int            handle,  // Return information about this file
    struct _stat *info);   // Information returned here
```

Description

Copies information about the file identified by *handle* into the _stat structure associated with the address you provide in the *info* argument. The _stat structure is defined in the header file sys\stat.h as follows:

```
struct _stat        // struct stat in UNIX and POSIX
{
    _dev_t          st_dev;    // Drive number or handle
    _ino_t          st_ino;    // Not used in MS-DOS
    unsigned short st_mode;   // File's mode
    short           st_nlink; // Set to 1 under MS-DOS
    short           st_uid;    // Not used in MS-DOS
    short           st_gid;    // Not used in MS-DOS
    _dev_t          st_rdev;   // Drive number or handle
    _off_t          st_size;   // Size of file in bytes
    time_t          st_atime; // Time of last access
```

```
    time_t          st_mtime; // Time of last modification
    time_t          st_ctime; // Time of creation
};
```

Note that this structure is defined as `struct stat` (without the leading underscore) in other compilers and in UNIX and POSIX.

Returns

0 The information was successfully copied.

–1 Indicates an error. Also sets `errno` to `EBADF` to indicate a bad file handle.

Sample Call

```
    struct _stat info;
// Get information about the stdout stream.
    if(_fstat(fileno(stdout), &info) != 0) perror("_fstat");
```

See Also

`_access`, `_stat`

_fullpath

MSC6	MSC7	VC++	QC2.5	QC-WIN	TC2	TC++	BC++2	BC++3	ANSI	POSIX	UNIX V	DOS	QWIN	WIN	WINDLL
X	X	X	X	X				X				X	X	X	X

Summary

```
#include <stdlib.h>
char *_fullpath(
    char        *buf,     // Buffer where full pathname is returned
    const char *path,     // Pathname to be converted into full path
    size_t      nbytes); // Size of the buffer "buf"
```

Description

Converts a relative pathname into a full pathname (including the drive letter and the full directory name) and copies the result into the specified buffer *buf*. The *nbytes* argument indicates the length of the buffer in bytes. This function can handle relative pathnames containing the fragments `.\` and `..\`, whereas `_makepath` cannot handle such paths.

If *buf* is `NULL`, `_fullpath` allocates a buffer of size `_MAX_PATH` and uses that buffer to store the pathname. You must free this buffer when you no longer need it.

Returns

When the function completes successfully, the return value is a pointer to the buffer containing the full pathname.

`NULL` Indicates an error.

Sample Call

```
    char fpname[_MAX_PATH];
// Expand ..\include into a full pathname.
    if(_fullpath(fpname, "..\\include",_MAX_PATH) != NULL)
        printf("Full pathname is: %s\n", fpname);
```

See Also

`_getcwd`, `_makepath`, `_splitpath`

_getcwd

MSC6	MSC7	VC++	QC2.5	QC-WIN	TC2	TC++	BC++2	BC++3	ANSI	POSIX	UNIX V	DOS	QWIN	WIN	WINDLL
X	X	X	X	X	X	X	X	X		X	X	X	X	X	X

See the note earlier in this chapter about the leading underscore in this function's name.

Summary

```
#include <direct.h>

char *_getcwd(
    char *pbuf,     // Return current dir name here
    int  maxchar); // Size of buffer
```

Description

Places the pathname of the current working directory in *pbuf*. If `pbuf` is `NULL`, `_getcwd` allocates *maxchar* bytes by calling `malloc` and stores the pathname in that space.

Returns

When the function completes successfully, the return value is a pointer to the buffer where the pathname is stored. If *pbuf* was `NULL`, the return value points to the buffer allocated by `_getcwd`. You should free this memory by calling `free`.

`NULL` Indicates an error. Also sets `errno` to `ENOMEM` or `ERANGE` to indicate lack of memory for buffer or too long a pathname, respectively.

Sample Call

```
    char buffer[_MAX_DIR]; // _MAX_DIR is defined in stdlib.h
//...
    if(_getcwd(buffer, _MAX_DIR) == NULL) perror("_getcwd");
```

See Also

`_dos_getdrive` (Chapter 32), `_chdir`, `_getdcwd`

_getdcwd

MSC6	MSC7	VC++	QC2.5	QC-WIN	TC2	TC++	BC++2	BC++3	ANSI	POSIX	UNIX V	DOS	QWIN	WIN	WINDLL
X	X	X	X	X				X				X	X	X	X

Summary

```
#include <direct.h>

char * _getdcwd(
    int  drive_num, // Drive: 1=A, 2=B, 3=C, and so on
    char *cwd_name, // Buffer where directory name is returned
    int  maxlen);   // Size of the cwd_name buffer
```

Description

Copies into the buffer *cwd_name* the name of the current working directory for the specified drive. If *cwd_name* is `NULL`, `_getdcwd` allocates *maxlen* bytes by calling `malloc` and stores the pathname in that space.

Returns

When the function completes successfully, the return value is a pointer to the buffer where the current directory name is returned. If *cwd_name* is `NULL`, this is a pointer to the buffer allocated by `_getdcwd`; you should release this memory by calling `free`.

`NULL` Indicates an error. Also sets `errno` to `ENOMEM` or `ERANGE` to indicate lack of memory for a new buffer or too long a pathname, respectively.

Sample Call

```
    char buffer[_MAX_PATH]; // _MAX_PATH is defined in stdlib.h

// Get current working directory of drive C (drive number 3):
    if(_getdcwd(3, buffer, _MAX_PATH) == NULL) perror("_getdcwd");
```

See Also

`_dos_getdrive` (Chapter 32), `_chdir`, `_getcwd`, `_getdrive`

_getdrive

MSC6	MSC7	VC++	QC2.5	QC-WIN	TC2	TC++	BC++2	BC++3	ANSI	POSIX	UNIX V	DOS	QWIN	WIN	WINDLL
X	X	X	X	X			X	X				X	X	X	X

Summary

```
#include <direct.h>

int _getdrive(void);
```

Description

Returns the current disk drive's identifier.

Returns

When the function completes successfully, the return value is an integer denoting the current disk drive:

1	Indicates the A: drive
2	Indicates the B: drive

and so on.

Sample Call

```
// Save the current drive before you change drives:
    saved_drive_num = _getdrive();
```

See Also

`_dos_getdrive` (Chapter 32), `_dos_setdrive` (Chapter 32), `_chdrive`, `_getcwd`, `_getdcwd`

_isatty

MSC6	MSC7	VC++	QC2.5	QC-WIN	TC2	TC++	BC++2	BC++3	ANSI	POSIX	UNIX V	DOS	QWIN	WIN	WINDLL
X	X	X	X	X	X	X	X	X		X	X	X	X	X	X

See the note earlier in this chapter about the leading underscore in this function's name.

Summary

```
#include <io.h>

int _isatty(int handle); // Is this file a character device?
```

Description

Determines whether the file specified by `handle` refers to a character device, such as the console, printer, or a serial port.

Returns

nonzero	Indicates that the handle refers to a character device.
0	Indicates that the handle is that of a regular file.

Sample Call

```
// Check that stdout is not directed to a file:
    if(_isatty(fileno(stdout)))
        puts("Interactive mode (stdout tied to console)");
```

See Also

`_fstat`, `_stat`

_locking

MSC6	MSC7	VC++	QC2.5	QC-WIN	TC2	TC++	BC++2	BC++3	ANSI	POSIX	UNIX V	DOS	QWIN	WIN	WINDLL
X	X	X	X	X				X			X	X	X	X	X

See the note earlier in this chapter about the leading underscore in this function's name.

Note: In earlier versions of Borland compilers the equivalent functions are `lock` and `unlock`.

Summary

```
#include <sys\locking.h> // Definition of _LK_ constants
#include <io.h>

int _locking(
    int  handle,   // Handle to an open file
    int  lmode,    // Locking mode
    long nbytes); // Number of bytes to lock or unlock
```

Description

Under MS-DOS versions 3.0 or later, `_locking` locks or unlocks a specified number of bytes in a file. This feature is useful when file sharing is enabled by running the SHARE program. The *`lmode`* argument indicates the operation you want to perform; this can be one of the following constants:

`_LK_LOCK`	Locks the bytes. If an attempt fails, retries up to 10 times at one-second intervals.
`_LK_NBLCK`	"Nonblocking lock" tries to lock but does not retry.
`_LK_NBRCLK`	Same as `_LK_NBLCK`.
`_LK_RCLK`	Same as `_LK_LOCK`.
`_LK_UNLCK`	Unlocks the specified bytes (must be the same bytes that you locked earlier).

Returns

0 Indicates the unlock was successful.

–1 Indicates an error. Also sets errno to EACCES, EBADF, EDEADLOCK, or EINVAL to indicate an error.

Sample Call

```
// Lock 256 bytes at current location in file:
    if(_locking(fhandle, LK_NBLCK, 256) == -1) perror("_locking");
```

See Also

_creat (Chapter 23), _open (Chapter 23), _sopen (Chapter 23)

_makepath

MSC6	MSC7	VC++	QC2.5	QC-WIN	TC2	TC++	BC++2	BC++3	ANSI	POSIX	UNIX V	DOS	QWIN	WIN	WINDLL
X	X	X	X	X				X				X	X	X	X

Note: In earlier versions of Borland compilers the equivalent function is fnmerge.

Summary

```
#include <stdlib.h>
void _makepath(
    char       *path,  // Buffer of size _MAX_PATH for
                       //   pathname being returned
    const char *drive, // Drive letter (with or without colon)
    const char *dir,   // Directory name
    const char *fname, // Filename
    const char *ext);  // File extension (with or without period)
```

Description

Combines the drive letter, directory name, filename, and extension into a full pathname, such as

```
c:\data\today\sales.tot
```

The _makepath function automatically inserts the colon following the drive letter and the period that comes between the filename and the extension.

Sample Call

```
char pname[_MAX_PATH];
_makepath(pname, "c:", "temp", "wtemp", ".doc");
// pname will contain c:\temp\wtemp.doc.
```

See Also

`_fullpath`, `_splitpath`

_mkdir

MSC6	MSC7	VC++	QC2.5	QC-WIN	TC2	TC++	BC++2	BC++3	ANSI	POSIX	UNIX V	DOS	QWIN	WIN	WINDLL
X	X	X	X	X	X	X	X	X		X		X	X	X	X

See the note earlier in this chapter about the leading underscore in this function's name.

Note: POSIX and UNIX versions have a second argument indicating the directory's access mode.

Summary

```
#include <direct.h>
int _mkdir(const char *pathname); // Name of new directory
```

Description

Creates a new directory specified by *pathname*.

Returns

0 The directory was successfully created.

–1 Indicates an error. Also sets `errno` to `ENOENT` if pathname is invalid, or to `EACCES` if the pathname refers to an existing file, directory, or drive.

Sample Call

```
// Create the directory C:\FORMS\DOC.
    if(_mkdir("C:\\FORMS\\DOC") == -1) perror("_mkdir");
```

See Also

`_chdir`, `_rmdir`

_mktemp

MSC6	MSC7	VC++	QC2.5	QC-WIN	TC2	TC++	BC++2	BC++3	ANSI	POSIX	UNIX V	DOS	QWIN	WIN	WINDLL
X	X	X	X	X	X	X	X	X			X	X	X	X	X

See the note earlier in this chapter about the leading underscore in this function's name.

Summary

```
#include <io.h>
char *_mktemp(char *template); // Pattern for name
```

Description

Constructs a unique filename by modifying a portion of the template string that must be of the form *baseXXXXXX*. The *base* is a two-character name supplied by you; `_mktemp` replaces the pattern *XXXXXX* with a single, alphanumeric character followed by a unique five-digit number derived from the process ID. You can use `_mktemp` to create names for temporary files created by your program.

Returns

When the function completes successfully, the return value is a pointer to the modified template string.

`NULL` Indicates that more unique names can be created from that template.

Sample Call

```
    char *template = "nbXXXXXX";
// Create a unique filename:
    if(_mktemp(template) == NULL)
            printf("Error creating name!\n");
```

See Also

`_tempnam` (Chapter 22), `tmpfile` (Chapter 22), `tmpnam` (Chapter 22)

remove

MSC6	MSC7	VC++	QC2.5	QC-WIN	TC2	TC++	BC++2	BC++3	ANSI	POSIX	UNIX V	DOS	QWIN	WIN	WINDLL
X	X	X	X	X	X	X	X	X	X			X	X	X	X

Summary

```
#include <stdio.h>
int remove(const char *pathname); // Name of file to remove
```

Description

Deletes the file specified by *pathname*.

Returns

0 The file was successfully deleted.

–1 Indicates an error. Also sets `errno` to `EACCES` or `ENOENT` to indicate that the specified file is read-only or the pathname is invalid, respectively.

Sample Call

```
// Delete the temporary file C:\TMP\FORM.TMP:
    if(remove("C:\\TMP\\FORM.TMP") == -1) perror("remove");
```

See Also

`_unlink`

rename

MSC6	MSC7	VC++	QC2.5	QC-WIN	TC2	TC++	BC++2	BC++3	ANSI	POSIX	UNIX V	DOS	QWIN	WIN	WINDLL
X	X	X	X	X	X	X	X	X	X	X		X	X	X	X

Summary

```
#include <stdio.h>
int rename(
    const char *old,  // Old name
    const char *new); // New name (may be in another directory
                      //   but not on a different drive)
```

Description

Changes the name of a file or a directory from *old* to *new*. You can use `rename` to move files from one directory to another in the same drive.

Returns

0	The name of the file or directory was successfully changed.
Nonzero	Indicates an error. Also sets `errno` to `EACCES`, `ENOENT`, or `EXDEV` to indicate access error, invalid name, or attempt to move file to a different device, respectively.

Sample Call

```
// Move the file \TMP\T001.DAT to \SALES\TODAY.DAT.
    if(rename("\\TMP\\T001.DAT", "\\SALES\\TODAY.DAT") != 0)
        perror("rename");
```

_rmdir

MSC6	MSC7	VC++	QC2.5	QC-WIN	TC2	TC++	BC++2	BC++3	ANSI	POSIX	UNIX V	DOS	QWIN	WIN	WINDLL
X	X	X	X	X	X	X	X	X		X		X	X	X	X

See the note earlier in this chapter about the leading underscore in this function's name.

Summary

```
#include <direct.h>
int _rmdir(const char *pathname); // Name of directory to delete
```

Description

Deletes the directory specified by *pathname*. The directory must be empty before you try to delete it and it must not be the current working directory.

Returns

0 The directory was successfully deleted.

–1 Indicates an error. Also sets `errno` to `EACCES` or `ENOENT` to indicate problem deleting the directory or a bad pathname, respectively.

Sample Call

```
// Delete C:\TMP\INSTALL.
    if(_rmdir("C:\\TMP\\INSTALL") == -1) perror("_rmdir");
```

See Also

`_chdir`, `_mkdir`

_searchenv

MSC6	MSC7	VC++	QC2.5	QC-WIN	TC2	TC++	BC++2	BC++3	ANSI	POSIX	UNIX V	DOS	QWIN	WIN	WINDLL
X	X	X	X	X	X	X	X	X				X	X	X	X

See note earlier in this chapter about the leading underscore in this function's name.

Summary

```
#include <stdlib.h>
void _searchenv(
    const char *name,    // Look for this file in the directories
                         //   listed in env_var.
    const char *env_var, // Environment variable with a semicolon-
                         //   separated list of directories.
    char       *buf);    // Return full pathname of file, if found.
```

Description

Searches the current working directory for the file specified by *name*. If file is not in the current directory, searches each directory in a semicolon-separated list of directories, defined in the environment variable *env_var*. If the file is found, `_searchenv` copies the full pathname into the buffer *buf*, which you allocate and provide.

Sample Call

```
    char pathname[_MAX_PATH];
// Search directories in PATH for the "hosts.lis" file:
    _searchenv("hosts.lis", "PATH", pathname);
```

_setmode

MSC6	MSC7	VC++	QC2.5	QC-WIN	TC2	TC++	BC++2	BC++3	ANSI	POSIX	UNIX V	DOS	QWIN	WIN	WINDLL
X	X	X	X	X	X	X	X	X				X	X	X	X

See note earlier in this chapter about the leading underscore in this function's name

Summary

```
#include <io.h>
#include <fcntl.h>
int _setmode(
    int handle, // Open file for which translation mode is being set
    int tmode); // Translation mode: _O_TEXT or _O_BINARY
```

Description

Sets the translation mode of a file to the mode specified by *tmode*. You can use `_setmode` to alter the default translation mode of the predefined streams `stdin`, `stdout`, `stderr`, `_stdaux`, and `_stdprn`.

Returns

When the function completes successfully, the previous translation mode is successfully set.

–1 Indicates an error. Also sets the global variable `errno` to `EBADF` or `EINVAL` to indicate a bad file handle or invalid mode argument, respectively.

Sample Call

```
// Change stdout's mode from the default "text" to "binary:"
    if(_setmode(fileno(stdout), _O_BINARY) == -1)
                                        perror("_setmode");
```

See Also

`fopen` (Chapter 22), `_creat` (Chapter 23), `_open` (Chapter 23)

_splitpath

MSC6	MSC7	VC++	QC2.5	QC-WIN	TC2	TC++	BC++2	BC++3	ANSI	POSIX	UNIX V	DOS	QWIN	WIN	WINDLL
X	X	X	X	X				X				X	X	X	X

See note earlier in this chapter about the leading underscore in this function's name.

Note: In earlier versions of Borland compilers the equivalent function is `fnsplit`.

Summary

```
#include <stdlib.h>
void _splitpath(
```

```
const char *pathname, // Full pathname to be split
char       *drive,    // Drive letter returned here
                      //   (includes a colon at the end)
char       *dir,      // Directory name returned here
char       *file,     // Filename returned here
char       *ext);     // File extension returned here
                      //   (includes the leading period)
```

Description

Breaks down a full pathname into four components: the drive letter, directory name, filename, and an extension.

Sample Call

```
   char drive[_MAX_DRIVE], dir[_MAX_DIR],
        fname[_MAX_FNAME], ext[_MAX_EXT]
   char *pname = "C:\\FORMS\\DEF\\1040.DEF";
// Split pathname into components....
   _splitpath(pname, drive, dir, fname, ext);
```

See Also

`_fullpath`, `_makepath`

_stat

MSC6	MSC7	VC++	QC2.5	QC-WIN	TC2	TC++	BC++2	BC++3	ANSI	POSIX	UNIX V	DOS	QWIN	WIN	WINDLL
X	X	X	X	X	X	X	X	X		X	X	X	X	X	X

See note earlier in this chapter about the leading underscore in this function's name.

Summary

```
#include <sys\types.h> // Required by <sys\stat.h>
#include <sys\stat.h>  // Function prototype

int _stat(
    const char   *pathname, // Name of existing file
    struct _stat *info);    // Information returned here
```

Description

Copies status information about a file identified by *`pathname`* into a `_stat` structure. See the reference entry of `_fstat` for the definition of the `_stat` structure.

Returns

0 The status information was successfully copied.

–1 Indicates an error. Also sets `errno` to `ENOENT` to indicate an invalid pathname.

Sample Call

```
    struct _stat info;
// Get information about C:\CONFIG.SYS:
    if(_stat("C:\\CONFIG.SYS", &info) != 0) perror("_stat");
```

See Also

_access, _fstat

_umask

MSC6	MSC7	VC++	QC2.5	QC-WIN	TC2	TC++	BC++2	BC++3	ANSI	POSIX	UNIX V	DOS	QWIN	WIN	WINDLL
X	X	X	X	X	X	X	X	X		X	X	X	X	X	X

See note earlier in this chapter about the leading underscore in this function's name.

Summary

```
#include <io.h>          // For function prototype
#include <sys\types.h> // The next header needs this file
#include <sys\stat.h>  // For permission settings (SI_READ, and so on)

int _unmask(int pmask);// Permission mask used when creating files
```

Description

Sets the permission settings mask (*pmask*) used for all subsequent file creations. You can specify one of the following for *pmask*:

`_S_IWRITE` — Disallow write operations (file is read-only).

`_S_IREAD` — Disallow write operations (this is ignored in MS-DOS).

`_S_IREAD | _S_IWRITE` — Disallow both read and write operations (in MS-DOS only reading is disallowed).

Contrast the meaning of these symbols as permission masks with their meaning when used as argument in the _chmod function. In _chmod, a permission symbol makes one or more operations allowable, but the same symbol causes _umask to disallow the same operations on the file.

Returns

When the function completes successfully, it returns the previous setting of the permission mask.

Sample Call

```
    int oldmask;
// Make all future files read only.
    oldmask = _umask(_S_IWRITE);
```

See Also

`_creat` (Chapter 23), `_open` (Chapter 23), `_chmod`

_unlink

MSC6	MSC7	VC++	QC2.5	QC-WIN	TC2	TC++	BC++2	BC++3	ANSI	POSIX	UNIX V	DOS	QWIN	WIN	WINDLL
X	X	X	X	X	X	X	X	X		X	X	X	X	X	X

See note earlier in this chapter about the leading underscore in this function's name.

Summary

```
#include <io.h>    // Or <stdio.h>

int _unlink(const char *pathname);// Name of file to delete
```

Description

Deletes the file specified by `pathname`. The ANSI Standard C version of this function is `remove`.

Returns

0 The file was successfully deleted.

–1 Indicates an error. Also sets `errno` to `EACCES` or `ENOENT` to indicate that the specified file is read-only or the pathname is invalid, respectively.

Sample Call

```
// Delete the temporary file C:\TMP\FORM.TMP.
    if(_unlink("C:\\TMP\\FORM.TMP") == -1) perror("_unlink");
```

See Also

`_remove`

22

Stream I/O

Chapter 21, "File and Directory Management," covered the C library functions that handle file- and directory-management tasks. In this chapter, you'll find information on the most widely used input and output (I/O) functions—the ones for stream I/O.

The chapter starts with a brief tutorial of all of the functions that support stream I/O. The functions are listed alphabetically, and also organized by groups of tasks. The tutorial is followed by individual reference entries for all the functions. Because of space limitations, each function does not have its own example. Instead, a number of larger examples illustrate how to use the most common stream I/O functions. Each function does show a sample call that should give you a clear idea of how to call the function from your program.

Streams

In UNIX, all I/O operations—including those with devices—are performed on files. A file is viewed as a stream of bytes. Because of its UNIX heritage, C follows a similar model for I/O. As in UNIX, a text file in C consists of lines of text with each line terminated by a newline (linefeed) character. Internally C maintains this model, even though MS-DOS stores text files in a slightly different way—in MS-DOS each line of text is terminated by a carriage return-linefeed (CR-LF). This means that when a DOS file is being interpreted as a text file by a C program, each CR-LF pair has to be translated into a single newline character. When writing the text back, the reverse process has to occur—each newline has to be expanded into a CR-LF pair. The stream I/O functions take care of these conversions when you open a file in text mode as follows:

```
    FILE *fp;
// Open a text file for reading (the t in the second
// argument to fopen indicates "text mode"):
    if((fp = fopen("c:\\autoexec.bat", "rt")) == NULL)
    {
// Error opening file.
// ...
    }
```

When you open a file as a binary stream, the C library's reading and writing functions do not interpret the characters in any way.

Buffered I/O

The stream I/O functions described in this chapter use the stream model of a file together with a *buffer*—a fixed-size storage area for the stream of bytes being read from or written to a file. In a buffered read operation from a disk file, the library functions read a fixed block of bytes with the same size as the buffer. When you call an I/O function, it gets the bytes from the buffer. When the buffer becomes empty, another read operation fills the buffer with a block of data from the disk file.

By using a buffer, the stream I/O functions work more efficiently than they would by accessing the disk directly for each I/O operation. This is because disk accesses are much slower than retrieving bytes from a buffer in memory, and it's just as fast to read a block of bytes from a disk as it is to read a single byte.

Flushing Buffers

One drawback of using buffered I/O is that, when you write to a file, the bytes don't go to the disk until the buffer is filled. The library functions automatically flush the buffer by writing it to the disk when it gets full. However, if your program exits due to a fatal error, or if you end the program by calling `_exit`, the stream buffers are not flushed, and the data remaining in the buffers is lost.

If you want to forcibly flush a stream buffer, you can call the `fflush` function to do so.

Buffering by the Operating System

Even when you flush a buffer associated with a stream, the data may not get written to the disk file; instead, the operating system (MS-DOS or Windows) may buffer the data before writing it out later. To ensure that the data is forced out to disk when a buffer is flushed, you should use the *commit to disk* feature. You can enable this feature when you open the stream by calling `_fdopen`, `fopen`, or `freopen`. See Table 22.6, later in the chapter, for the character codes that enable or disable committing to disk.

Disabling Buffering

Although streams have buffering enabled by default, you can choose to disable buffering by calling the `setvbuf` function with an appropriate argument. You also can associate with a stream your own buffer instead of using the one allocated by the C library.

The *FILE* Type

C's stream I/O functions use an internal data structure to store information about the file being accessed. The `FILE` data structure, defined in stdio.h, holds this information. Although the definition of `FILE` may vary from system to system, the details are hidden from you, the programmer, much as the implementation details of a C++ class are hidden. The only way you use `FILE` is to declare pointers to the `FILE` type and use these pointers to identify open files—streams with which your program performs I/O. In fact, the term *stream* is used by C programmers to refer to open files represented by `FILE` pointers.

Formatted and Unformatted I/O

One important aspect of the stream I/O functions is the ability to *format* a variable—convert the internal binary representation of a variable into a text string that can be displayed on the console or written to a file. For example, formatting the 8-bit binary value 0011 0000 (the binary representation of decimal value 48) as a decimal integer results in two characters: 4 and 8. Functions such as `fprintf`, `printf`, and `sprintf` provide the ability to format output.

In addition to formatting a value for output, you also may want to store binary values directly in a file. One reason is that a binary representation takes less disk space than the same value represented as formatted text. For instance, when represented as a binary value, a single byte could hold any decimal quantity between 0 and 255. In textual form, you would need up to three bytes to store this information (for example, when the value is 255, you need three characters to represent the value, with each character requiring a byte of storage). The `fread` and `fwrite` stream I/O functions are for reading and writing unformatted binary data.

Current Position in a File

The stream I/O functions rely on the notion of a current position in a file—if you think of the file as a stream of bytes, the current position is the location at which the next read or write operation starts. The current position is represented by the offset from the beginning of the file. You can use the function pairs `fgetpos` and `fsetpos` or `ftell` and `fseek` to manipulate the current position in a stream.

Predefined Streams

The five streams shown in Table 22.1 are predefined for your convenience. You can access these streams by their stream names `stdin`, `stdout`, `stderr`, `_stdaux`, and `_stdprn` (these are constant `FILE` pointers) or by their file handles. The streams `stdin`, `stdout`, and `stderr` refer to the standard input, output, and error streams. By default, `stdin` is connected to the keyboard, whereas `stdout` and `stderr` are connected to the display screen.

Leading Underscore in Names of Nonstandard Functions

Microsoft Visual C++ adds an underscore prefix to many functions (such as `_fdopen`, `_fileno`, and `_rmtmp`) in keeping with ANSI Standard C's naming conventions for nonstandard functions. In many other C compilers (including earlier versions of Microsoft C compilers), as well as in UNIX and POSIX, these functions are available with names that do not have the leading underscores. Note that you can use the names without underscore prefix in Microsoft Visual C++ as well. The functions without underscore prefixes are in a library named oldnames.lib, which the linker searches by default.

Table 22.1. Predefined streams.

Stream	Description
`stdaux`	Connected to the DOS device AUX (serial port COM1) with unbuffered read-write access and binary translation mode.
`stderr`	Standard error stream connected to the display screen (the MS-DOS device named `CON`) with unbuffered write-only access and text translation mode. This stream is unaffected by I/O redirection at the command line level.
`stdin`	Standard input stream connected to the keyboard (the MS-DOS device named `CON`) with buffered read-only access and text translation mode.
`stdout`	Standard output stream connected to the display screen (the MS-DOS device named `CON`) with buffered write-only access and text translation mode.
`stdprn`	Connected to the DOS device PRN (parallel port LPT1) with buffered write-only access and binary translation mode.

String I/O

A number of stream I/O functions perform formatted input and output with strings instead of files. You can use these functions to prepare textual representations of variables in a string and display the string with graphics output functions. For example, to construct a string that includes one or more formatted values of variables, you would write

```
    char buf[80];
    int index;
    double a[128];
//...
// Prepare a string with the formatted value of a[index]:
    sprintf(buf, "Value of a[%d] = %f\n", index, a[index]);
```

Basic Stream I/O Tasks

Table 22.2 shows an alphabetic list of the stream I/O functions and gives you a quick overview of these functions. Table 22.3 organizes these functions by the tasks they perform. Some of these functions are illustrated by several sample programs in the following sections. For more information on a function, consult the reference entry for that function in the reference section that follows.

Table 22.2. Alphabetic listing of stream I/O functions.

Function	Description
`clearerr`	Clears a stream's error indicator.
`fclose`	Closes a stream.
`fcloseall`	Closes all currently open streams.
`fdopen`	Associates a stream with a file opened by a low-level I/O function such as `_open` (see Chapter 23, "Low-Level I/O").
`feof`	Returns a nonzero value if the current position in the file is at the end of the file.
`ferror`	Returns a nonzero value if an error occurred in a previous I/O operation.
`fflush`	Flushes a buffer associated with a stream by writing the contents of the buffer to the disk.
`fgetc`	Reads a character from a stream.
`fgetchar`	Reads a character from `stdin`.
`fgetpos`	Returns the current value of the stream's position indicator.
`fgets`	Reads a line from a stream (reads up to and including a newline character).
`fileno`	Returns the file handle associated with a stream.
`flushall`	Flushes the buffers of all open streams.
`fopen`	Opens a file as a buffered stream.
`fprintf`	Writes formatted text to a stream.

Function	Description
`fputc`	Writes a character to a stream.
`fputchar`	Writes a character to `stdout`.
`fputs`	Writes a line of text to a stream.
`fread`	Reads unformatted binary data from a stream.
`freopen`	Reassigns a stream to a new file.
`fscanf`	Reads formatted input from a stream.
`fseek`	Sets the current position to a specified offset within the file.
`fsetpos`	Sets the stream's position indicator to a specified value.
`fsopen`	Opens a file as a stream with file sharing enabled.
`ftell`	Returns the current position in the file.
`fwrite`	Writes unformatted binary data to a stream.
`getc`	Reads a character from a stream.
`getchar`	Reads a character from `stdin`.
`gets`	Reads a line from `stdin` (reads up to a newline character).
`getw`	Reads a binary integer value from a stream.
`perror`	Prints an error message corresponding to the error code in the global variable `errno`.
`printf`	Writes formatted output to `stdout`.
`putc`	Writes a character to a stream.
`putchar`	Writes a character to `stdout`.
`puts`	Writes a line of text to `stdout` (automatically adds a newline).
`putw`	Writes a binary integer value to a stream.
`rewind`	Sets the current position to the beginning of the file.
`rmtmp`	Deletes any files created by `tmpfile`.
`scanf`	Reads formatted input from `stdin`.

continues

Table 22.2. continued

Function	Description
`setbuf`	Assigns a fixed-size buffer to a stream.
`setvbuf`	Assigns a variable-length buffer to a stream.
`snprintf`	Writes formatted output to a buffer, without writing more than a specified maximum number of characters.
`sprintf`	Writes formatted output to a buffer.
`sscanf`	Reads formatted input from a buffer.
`tempnam`	Generates a temporary filename for a specified directory.
`tmpfile`	Creates a temporary file and opens it for buffered stream I/O.
`tmpnam`	Generates a temporary filename.
`ungetc`	Places a character back into a stream's buffer.
`vfprintf`	Like `fprintf`, but accepts a pointer to a list of arguments.
`vprintf`	Like `printf`, but accepts a pointer to a list of arguments.
`vsnprintf`	Like `_snprintf`, but accepts a pointer to a list of arguments.
`vsprintf`	Like `sprintf`, but accepts a pointer to a list of arguments.

Table 22.3. Basic stream I/O tasks.

Task	Functions
Open and close files	`fclose`, `fcloseall`, `fopen`, `freopen`, `_fsopen`
Formatted input	`fscanf`, `scanf`, `sscanf`
Formatted output	`fprintf`, `printf`, `_snprintf`, `sprintf`, `vfprintf`, `vprintf`, `_vsnprintf`, `vsprintf`
Read a character from a stream	`fgetc`, `_fgetchar`, `getc`, `getchar`
Write a character to a stream	`fputc`, `_fputchar`, `putc`, `putchar`

Task	Functions
Read a line of text	`fgets`, `gets`
Write a line of text	`fputs`, `puts`
Read and write binary data	`fread`, `fwrite`, `_getw`, `_putw`
Get or set current position in file	`fgetpos`, `fseek`, `fsetpos`, `ftell`, `rewind`
Flush buffer associated with a stream	`fflush`, `_flushall`
Check for error or end-of-file	`clearerr`, `feof`, `ferror`
Create and delete temporary files	`rmtmp`, `_tempnam`, `tmpfile`, `tmpnam`
Set buffer associated with a stream	`setbuf`, `setvbuf`
Get the file handle of a stream	`fileno`
Associate a stream with a file handle	`fdopen`
Place a character back into a buffer	`ungetc`
Write error message to `stdout`	`perror`

Adding Line Numbers to a File

As an example of a program that manipulates a text file, consider the problem of adding line numbers to each line in a text file. Suppose you want to use the program—call it number—in the following way:

```
number infile outfile
```

where `infile` is the input text file and `outfile` is the output file—a line numbered version of the input file. Listing 22.1 shows the file number.c, which implements the line-numbering program.

Listing 22.1. number.c. A line-numbering program.

```
//---------------------------------------------------------------
//  File: number.c
//
//  A program to add a line number to each line in a text file.
//  Assumes a maximum of 9999 lines in the file and up to 256
//  characters per line.
```

continues

Listing 22.1. continued

```
//
//  Use as:    number <infile> <outfile>
//-----------------------------------------------------------------
#include <stdio.h>
#include <process.h>

#define MAXCHR  (256 + 6) /* space for the line number plus 256 charac-
ters */

void main(int argc, char **argv)
{
    char line[MAXCHR], *tline;

    FILE *infile, *outfile;
    int lineno = 0;

    tline = &line[6];

// Check to see if there are enough command-line arguments:
    if(argc < 3)
    {
        printf("Usage: %s <infile> <outfile>\n", argv[0]);
        exit(1);
    }

// Open input file in text mode for read operations:

    if ((infile = fopen(argv[1],"r")) == NULL)
    {
        printf("Error opening %s\n", argv[1]);
        exit(1);
    }

// Open output file in text mode for write operations:

    if ((outfile = fopen(argv[2],"w")) == NULL)
    {
        printf("Error opening %s\n", argv[2]);
        exit(1);
    }

// Read a line at a time from the input file, add a line
```

```
// number, and write each line out:

    while(1)
    {
        if(fgets(tline, MAXCHR, infile) == NULL)
        {
            if(ferror(infile) != 0)
                puts("Error during read");

            if(feof(infile) != 0)
                    puts("File ended");

            clearerr(infile);
            break;              // Exit the while loop
        }
        else
        {
// Add the line number, colon and a space before the line's data:
            lineno++;

            sprintf(line, "%4d", lineno);
            line[4] = ':';
            line[5] = ' ';

            fputs(line, outfile);
        }
    }
    printf("Saved %d lines in %s\n", lineno, argv[2]);

// Close both files:

    fclose(infile);
    fclose(outfile);
}
```

A Simple Address Book

As another example of the use of stream I/O functions, consider a small application that maintains an address book—a set of records containing names, addresses, and phone numbers. To build the address book application, you can start by defining a format for an address book file—a good one would be a fixed-length header followed by zero or more fixed-length address entries. Here's a C structure that you might use to define the header:

```
// Header of address book file:
typedef struct ADBOOK_HEADER
{
    char desc[40];       // Descriptive name of address book
    unsigned numrecords; // Number of entries in file
} ADBOOK_HEADER;
```

You also would need a structure for each address entry. One possible structure would be:

```
// Format of each address book entry:
typedef struct ADBOOK_ENTRY
{
    char name[40];
    char adrs1[40];
    char adrs2[40];
    char phone[20];
} ADBOOK_ENTRY;
```

Once the file format and the structures are defined, you easily can implement the address book application by using the C library's stream I/O functions. For example, you can use `fopen` to open the file, `fread` and `fwrite` to read and write the fixed-length address book entries as binary data, and `rewind` to go to the beginning of the file. Listing 22.2 shows the program adbook.c, which allows the user to add an address entry, locate a specific name, and save the addresses in an address book file.

Listing 22.2. adbook.c. An address book program.

```
//--------------------------------------------------------------
//  File: adbook.c
//
//  A simple address book
//--------------------------------------------------------------
#include <stdio.h>
#include <malloc.h>
#include <string.h>
#include <process.h>
#include <ctype.h>

// Header of address book file:
typedef struct ADBOOK_HEADER
{
```

```
    char desc[40];
    unsigned numrecords;
} ADBOOK_HEADER;

// Format of each address book entry:
typedef struct ADBOOK_ENTRY
{
    char name[40];
    char adrs1[40];
    char adrs2[40];
    char phone[20];
} ADBOOK_ENTRY;

// In-memory representation of address book entries:
typedef struct ADRS_INMEM
{
    ADBOOK_ENTRY      entry;
    unsigned          index;
    struct ADRS_INMEM *next;
    struct ADRS_INMEM *prev;
} ADRS_INMEM;


static ADBOOK_HEADER adbkhdr = { " ", 0 };
static ADRS_INMEM    *address = NULL, *current = NULL;
static FILE          *adbkfile;
static char          adbkname[80];

// Function prototypes:
static void read_adbook(void);
static void save_adbook(void);
static void readone(void);
static void disp_current(void);
static void next_entry(void);
static void prev_entry(void);
static void find_entry(void);
static void new_adrs(void);
static void add_adrs(void);
//------------------------------------------------------------
//  m a i n
//  The main function of the address book program
```

continues

Listing 22.2. continued

```
void main(void)
{
    int c, done = 0;

    printf("Address Book\n");

    printf("Enter name of address book file:");
    gets(adbkname);

// Open the address book file:

    if ((adbkfile = fopen(adbkname, "rb+")) != NULL)
    {
// File exists; read in all address entries:
        read_adbook();
    }
    else
    {
// File does not exist; create it:
        if ((adbkfile = fopen(adbkname, "wb+")) == NULL)
        {
            fprintf(stderr, "%s <- Cannot create\n",
                    adbkname);
            exit(1);
        }
// Ask user for a comment:
        printf("File created. Enter comment: ");
        fgets(adbkhdr.desc, 40, stdin);

// Write the header to the file:
        if(fwrite(&adbkhdr, sizeof(ADBOOK_HEADER), 1,
                  adbkfile) != 1)
        {
            fprintf(stderr, "Error writing to: %s\n",
                    adbkname);
            exit(2);
        }
    }

// Show addresses and let the user manipulate the address book.
// You can improve this greatly by using text and graphics
```

```
// functions from Chapter 33.

    while(!done)
    {
// Show current entry:
        disp_current();

        printf("\nEnter command\n(a = add, f = find, "
               "n = next, s = save, q = quit):");
        c = getchar();
        fflush(stdin);

        switch(toupper(c))
        {
            case 'A':  // Add a new record
                add_adrs();
                break;

            case 'F':  // Find an entry
                find_entry();
                break;

            case 'N':  // Next entry
                next_entry();
                break;

            case 'P':  // Previous entry
                prev_entry();
                break;

            case 'S':  // Save all addresses
                save_adbook();
                break;

            case 'Q':  // Exit program
                printf("Exiting...\n");
                done = 1;
        }
    }
// Close file:
    fclose(adbkfile);
}
```

continues

Listing 22.2. continued

```
//-----------------------------------------------------------------
static void read_adbook(void)
{
    unsigned int i;

// Read in header:
    if(fread(&adbkhdr, sizeof(ADBOOK_HEADER), 1, adbkfile)
       != 1)
    {
        fprintf(stderr, "Error reading from: %s\n", adbkname);
        exit(1);
    }

// Now read in each address record and store in an in-memory
// linked list:

    printf("Reading %d entries\n", adbkhdr.numrecords);
    for(i = 0; i < adbkhdr.numrecords; i++)
    {
        new_adrs();
        readone();
        printf(".");
    }
}
//-----------------------------------------------------------------
static void new_adrs(void)
{
    ADRS_INMEM *p;

// Latest entry is always the current entry:
    current = malloc(sizeof(ADRS_INMEM));

    if(current == NULL)
    {
        fprintf(stderr, "Error allocating memory\n");
        exit(1);
    }
    current->next = NULL;
```

```
// Add new ADRS_INMEM item to linked list:
    if(address == NULL)
    {
        address = current;
        current->prev = NULL;
        current->index = 1;
    }
    else
    {
        for(p = address; p->next != NULL; p = p->next)
            ; // Null statement

        p->next = current;
        current->prev = p;
     current->index = p->index + 1;
    }
}
//-------------------------------------------------------------
static void readone(void)
{
// Read an entry from the address book file:

    if(fread(&current->entry, sizeof(ADBOOK_ENTRY), 1, adbkfile)
       != 1)
    {
        fprintf(stderr, "Error reading entry from: %s\n",
                adbkname);
        exit(1);
    }
}
//-------------------------------------------------------------
static void add_adrs(void)
{
    new_adrs();

// Prompt for the fields (this part could benefit from a
// better user interface):

    fflush(stdin);
    printf("\nEnter Name:");
    fgets(current->entry.name, 40, stdin);
```

continues

Listing 22.2. continued

```
        printf("Enter Address line 1:");
        fgets(current->entry.adrs1, 40, stdin);

        printf("Enter Address line 2:");
        fgets(current->entry.adrs2, 40, stdin);

        printf("Enter Phone #:");
        fgets(current->entry.phone, 20, stdin);

        adbkhdr.numrecords++;
    }
    //------------------------------------------------------------
    static void save_adbook(void)
    {
        ADRS_INMEM *p;
        unsigned count = 0;

    // Go to the beginning of file:
        rewind(adbkfile);

    // Write the header:
        if(fwrite(&adbkhdr, sizeof(ADBOOK_HEADER), 1, adbkfile)
           != 1)
        {
            fprintf(stderr, "Error reading from: %s\n", adbkname);
            exit(1);
        }
        printf("Wrote header.\n");

    // Now write each address record:

        for(p = address; p != NULL; p = p->next)
        {
            if(fwrite(&p->entry, sizeof(ADBOOK_ENTRY), 1, adbkfile)
                != 1)
            {
                fprintf(stderr, "Error writing entry to: %s\n",
                    adbkname);
                exit(1);
            }
```

```
        printf(".");
        count++;
    }
    printf("%d entries written to %s\n", count, adbkname);
}
//-----------------------------------------------------------------
// d i s p _ e n t r y
//
// Display the current entry:

static void disp_current(void)
{
    printf("\n-------------------------------------\n");
    printf("%s\n", adbkhdr.desc);

    if(current == NULL) return;

    printf("\n---------- Entry %d of %d ------------\n",
           current->index, adbkhdr.numrecords);

    printf("\nName:       %s", current->entry.name);
    printf("Address1:  %s",    current->entry.adrs1);
    printf("Address2:  %s",    current->entry.adrs2);
    printf("Phone:     %s", current->entry.phone);
}
//-----------------------------------------------------------------
static void next_entry(void)
{
    if(current->next== NULL) return;
    current = current->next;
}
//-----------------------------------------------------------------
static void prev_entry(void)
{
    if(current->prev == NULL) return;
    current = current->prev;
}
//-----------------------------------------------------------------
static void find_entry(void)
{
    ADRS_INMEM *p;
    char name[40], len;
```

continues

Listing 22.2. continued

```
// Prompt user for the name to find:

    fflush(stdin);
    printf("\nEnter Name:");
    fgets(name, 40, stdin);

// Length of search string (excluding the newline):
    len = strlen(name) - 1;

// Now search each address record for a match:

    for(p = address; p != NULL; p = p->next)
    {
        if(_strnicmp(p->entry.name, name, len) == 0)
        {
            printf("Found...\n");
            current = p;
            return;
        }
    }
    printf("Cannot find anyone named: %s", name);
}
```

When run, the address book program adbook prompts the user for the name of a file. If the file exists, adbook reads in all the records into an in-memory linked list of address entries. If the file does not exist, adbook creates a new file with zero entries. Later, the user can add more entries to the address book and save it back to the file.

The program interacts with the user by accepting one of several one-letter commands. Here is a sample interaction with the adbook program showing how the user searches for a name in the address book:

```
XXXXXXXXXXXXXXXXXXXXXXX
Enter command:
(a = add, f = find, n = next, s = save, q = quit):f

Enter Name:PETER
Found...

--------------------------------------
Peter's address book
```

```
---------- Entry 3 of 8 ----------

Name:       Peter Hipson
Address1:   P.O. Box 88
Address2:   West Peterborough, NH 03468-0088
Phone:      1-603-555-6912

Enter command:
(a = add, f = find, n = next, s = save, q = quit):q
Exiting...
```

The user interface of the adbook program could certainly benefit from some of the text and graphics output functions that are described in the graph.doc text file on the companion disk. However, the application adequately illustrates how to use the stream I/O functions to store and retrieve binary data from a file.

A Convenient Way to Display Error Messages

As a final example of using stream I/O functions in applications, consider the task of writing a function—call it `disp_error`—that accepts a variable number of arguments and displays a formatted error message on `stderr`. Listing 22.3 shows an implementation of the `disp_error` function together with a test program. As you can see from Listing 22.3, the `disp_error` function uses `vfprintf` to do its job.

Listing 22.3. disp_err.c. Displaying error messages with vfprintf.

```
//--------------------------------------------------------------
// File: disp_err.c
// Test the function disp_error.
//--------------------------------------------------------------
#include <stdio.h>
#include <stdarg.h>

void disp_error(char *fmt, ...); // Prototype of error handler
//--------------------------------------------------------------
// main

void main(void)
{
```

continues

Listing 22.3. continued

```
    char *func_name = "search";
    int  elem_index = 100;

// An error message that's a simple string:
    disp_error("Unknown error\n");

// An error message with formatting (assume func_name and
// elem_index have appropriate values):

    disp_error("%s: Error accessing element at: %d\n",
               func_name, elem_index);
}
//-------------------------------------------------------------
// d i s p _ e r r o r
//
// Accepts a variable of number of arguments and uses
// vfprintf to display a formatted error message on the
// stderr stream.

void disp_error(char *fmt, ...)
{
    va_list argp;

// First argument is treated as a format string; the rest are
// variables to be formatted and displayed in the error message.

    va_start(argp, fmt);

// Call vfprintf to do the job:
    vfprintf(stderr, fmt, argp);

    va_end(argp);
}
```

clearerr

MSC6	MSC7	VC++	QC2.5	QC-WIN	TC2	TC++	BC++2	BC++3	ANSI	POSIX	UNIX V	DOS	QWIN	WIN	WINDLLX
X	X	X	X	X	X	X	X	X	X	X	X	X	X	X	X

Summary

```
#include <stdio.h>

void clearerr(FILE *fp); // Clear error indicator of this stream
```

Description

Clears the end-of-file and error indicators of the stream identified by *fp*.

Sample Call

```
// If there is an error, clear the error flag:
if(ferror(infile)) clearerr(infile);
```

See Also

feof, ferror

fclose

MSC6	MSC7	VC++	QC2.5	QC-WIN	TC2	TC++	BC++2	BC++3	ANSI	POSIX	UNIX V	DOS	QWIN	WIN	WINDLL
X	X	X	X	X	X	X	X	X	X	X	X	X	X	X	X

Summary

```
#include <stdio.h>

int fclose(FILE *fp); // Close this open stream
```

Description

Closes the open stream identified by *fp*.

Returns

0	The open stream was successfully closed.
EOF	Indicates failure. EOF is a constant defined in stdio.h.

Sample Call

```
FILE *inputfile;
// Open the file....
//...
// Close file.
fclose(inputfile);
```

See Also

_fcloseall, fopen

_fcloseall

MSC6	MSC7	VC++	QC2.5	QC-WIN	TC2	TC++	BC++2	BC++3	ANSI	POSIX	UNIX V	DOS	QWIN	WIN	WINDLL
X	X	X	X	X	X	X	X	X				X	X	X	X

Summary

```
#include <stdio.h>
int _fcloseall(void);
```

Description

Closes all streams that were opened with `fopen` or `tmpfile`. The predefined streams `stdin`, `stdout`, `stderr`, `_stdaux`, and `_stdprn` are not affected.

Returns

When the function completes successfully, the return value is the total number of streams closed.

`EOF` Indicates an error. `EOF` is a constant defined in stdio.h.

Sample Call

```
_fcloseall();
```

See Also

`fclose`, `fopen`, `tmpfile`

_fdopen

MSC6	MSC7	VC++	QC2.5	QC-WIN	TC2	TC++	BC++2	BC++3	ANSI	POSIX	UNIX V	DOS	QWIN	WIN	WINDLL
X	X	X	X	X	X	X	X	X		X	X	X	X	X	X

Summary

```
#include <stdio.h>
FILE *_fdopen(
    int         handle, // Handle of open file
    const char *mode); // Access mode (see Table 22.4)
```

Description

Associates a stream with a file (identified by *`handle`*) that is currently open for unbuffered, unformatted I/O. The *`mode`* argument specifies the read-write access to the stream. The *`mode`* argument can be one of the strings shown in Table 22.4.

Table 22.4. Access modes for streams.

Mode String	Description
`r`	Opens file as read only. The file must already exist.
`w`	Opens a new file for writing. The existing file is truncated to zero length.
`a`	Opens new or existing file for appending.
`r+`	Opens an existing file for both read and write operations. The file must already exist.
`w+`	Opens a new file for reading and writing. The existing file is truncated to zero length.
`a+`	Opens new or existing file for reading and appending.

In addition to the modes shown in Table 22.4, you can append one character each from the lists shown in Tables 22.5 and 22.6. These characters control the translation mode and the "commit to disk" feature (see tutorial section).

Table 22.5. Translation modes for streams.

Mode Character	Description
`b`	Opens file as a binary file. Characters read from the file are not interpreted in any way.
`t`	Opens file as a text file. When you are reading from the file, a Ctrl+Z character signifies end-of-file and each carriage return-linefeed (CR-LF) pair is replaced by a single linefeed (the "newline") character. When you are writing to the file, each newline character expands to a CR-LF pair.

Table 22.6. Disabling and enabling "commit to disk" for streams.

Mode Character	Description
c	Flushed contents of the file are committed to disk.
n	Operating system is free to cache data from flushed buffers.

Returns

When the function completes successfully, the return value is a FILE pointer.

NULL Indicates an error.

Sample Call

```
int handle;
FILE *infile;
// Open a file with low-level I/O functions (_open):
//...
// Now associate stream with the handle:
    if((infile = _fdopen(handle, "r")) == NULL)
    {
// Error opening stream....
//...
    }
```

See Also

fclose, _fcloseall, fopen

feof

MSC6	MSC7	VC++	QC2.5	QC-WIN	TC2	TC++	BC++2	BC++3	ANSI	POSIX	UNIX V	DOS	QWIN	WIN	WINDLL
X	X	X	X	X	X	X	X	X	X	X	X	X	X	X	X

Summary

```
#include <stdio.h>
int feof(FILE *fp); // Is this stream at the end-of-file?
```

Description

Checks whether the end-of-file has been reached for a stream.

Returns

The first read operation that tries to read beyond the end-of-file of the stream returns a nonzero value.

0 Indicates that the stream is not at end-of-file.

Sample Call

```
    FILE *infile;
// Assume file has been opened.
// Read until end-of-file:
    while(!feof(infile))
    {
// Read from file....
    }
```

See Also

clearerr, feof, rewind

ferror

MSC6	MSC7	VC++	QC2.5	QC-WIN	TC2	TC++	BC++2	BC++3	ANSI	POSIX	UNIX V	DOS	QWIN	WIN	WINDLL
x	x	x	x	x	x	x	x	x	x	x	x	x	x	x	x

Summary

```
#include <stdio.h>
int ferror(FILE *fp); // Is the error flag set for this stream?
```

Description

Checks whether an error had occurred during the last I/O operation performed on a stream.

Returns

When the function completes successfully, the return value is 0.

Nonzero Indicates an error.

Sample Call

```
FILE *fp;
// Assume stream has been opened and some I/O attempted:
//...
if(ferror(fp))
{
// Error detected....
//...
}
```

See Also

clearerr

fflush

MSC6	MSC7	VC++	QC2.5	QC-WIN	TC2	TC++	BC++2	BC++3	ANSI	POSIX	UNIX V	DOS	QWIN	WIN	WINDLL
X	X	X	X	X	X	X	X	X	X	X	X	X	X	X	X

Summary

```
#include <stdio.h>
int fflush(FILE *fp); // Flush this open stream's buffer
```

Description

Writes (*flushes*) the contents of the buffer associated with a specified stream to the file. If the stream is open for reading only, `fflush` clears the buffer. Note that a stream's buffer is flushed automatically when full; you should call `fflush` only when you want the data in the buffer written to the file without waiting for the buffer to become full. Because the operating system may cache data flushed from a stream's buffer, you can force writing to disk only if you open the stream with the `c` flag (see Table 22.6).

Returns

0	The buffer was successfully flushed.
`EOF`	Indicates an error. `EOF` is a constant defined in stdio.h.

Sample Call

```
    char input[81];
// Read a string from stdin using scanf:
    scanf("%s", input);
// Now flush stdin before you read anything else:
    fflush(stdin);
```

See Also

`fclose`, `_flushall`

fgetc

MSC6	MSC7	VC++	QC2.5	QC-WIN	TC2	TC++	BC++2	BC++3	ANSI	POSIX	UNIX V	DOS	QWIN	WIN	WINDLL
X	X	X	X	X	X	X	X	X	X	X	X	X	X	X	X

Summary

```
#include <stdio.h>

int fgetc(FILE *fp); // Read a character from this stream
```

Description

Reads a single character from the stream *fp*.

Returns

When the function completes successfully, the return value is the character read from the stream.

`EOF` Indicates an error. `EOF` is a constant defined in stdio.h.

Sample Call

```
    FILE *infile;
    int c;
// Assume file has been opened.
    c = fgetc(infile);
```

See Also

`_fgetchar`, `getc`

_fgetchar

MSC6	MSC7	VC++	QC2.5	QC-WIN	TC2	TC++	BC++2	BC++3	ANSI	POSIX	UNIX V	DOS	QWIN	WIN	WINDLL
X	X	X	X	X	X	X	X	X	X				X	X	

Summary

```
#include <stdio.h>
int _fgetchar(void);
```

Description

Reads a single character from `stdin`. Note that because of the buffered text-mode operation of `stdin`, the read operation ends only when a newline is encountered (that is, the user presses the Enter key). To read a single character without waiting for a newline, use the low-level function `_getch` or `_getche` (described in Chapter 23).

Returns

When the function completes successfully, the return value is the character read from `stdin`.

`EOF` Indicates an error. `EOF` is a constant defined in stdio.h.

Sample Call

```
char input[81];
int i, c;
// Read a line from stdin (up to the newline character):
c = fgetchar();
for(i=0; (i<80) && (c != '\n'); i++)
{
    buffer[i] = c;
    c = fgetchar();
}
```

See Also

fgetc, getc

fgetpos

MSC6	MSC7	VC++	QC2.5	QC-WIN	TC2	TC++	BC++2	BC++3	ANSI	POSIX	UNIX V	DOS	QWIN	WIN	WINDLL
X	X	X	X	X	X	X	X	X	X			X	X	X	X

Summary

```
#include <stdio.h>
int fgetpos(
    FILE   *fp,    // Get current position in this open stream
    fpos_t *pos); // Position returned here
```

Description

Copies the current position in the stream *fp* into the `fpos_t` variable, associated with the address you provide in the *pos* argument. The position returned by `fgetpos` is suitable only for use with `fsetpos`.

Returns

0	The current position was succesfully copied.
Nonzero	Indicates an error. Also sets `errno` to `EBADF` or `EINVAL` to indicate a bad *fp* argument.

Sample Call

```
    fpos_t curpos;
    FILE   *fp;
// Assume "fp" refers to an open stream.
// Get current position in stream:
    if(fgetpos(fp, &curpos) != 0) perror("fgetpos");
```

See Also

fsetpos

fgets

MSC6	MSC7	VC++	QC2.5	QC-WIN	TC2	TC++	BC++2	BC++3	ANSI	POSIX	UNIX V	DOS	QWIN	WIN	WINDLL
X	X	X	X	X	X	X	X	X	X	X	X	X	X	X	X

Summary

```
#include <stdio.h>
char *fgets(
    char *str,    // Read characters into this char array
    int  maxchr, // Read at most this many characters
    FILE *fp);    // Read from this stream
```

Description

Reads characters from stream *fp* into a character array *str* that has room for at least *maxchr* characters. The `fgets` function reads at most one fewer than *maxchr* characters or until a newline character (`'\n'`) is encountered. The newline character is copied into the *str* array and a null character (`'\0'`) is appended. Note that this behavior is similar to that of `gets`, except that `gets` replaces the newline (`'\n'`) with a null character.

Returns

When the function completes successfully, the return value is the `str` argument.

`NULL` Indicates an error. Use `feof` or `ferror` to determine why `fgets` failed.

Sample Call

```
    FILE *fp;
    char line[81];
// Assume fp is set up to read from a text file.
// Read and display lines of text from a file:
    while(fgets(fp(str, 81, fp) != NULL)
    {
        fputs(stdout, str);
    }
```

See Also

`fputs`, `gets`, `puts`

_fileno

MSC6	MSC7	VC++	QC2.5	QC-WIN	TC2	TC++	BC++2	BC++3	ANSI	POSIX	UNIX V	DOS	QWIN	WIN	WINDLL
X	X	X	X	X	X	X	X	X		X	X	X	X	X	X

Note: `_fileno` cannot be used with `_dup` or `_dup2` in QuickWin applications with the `stdin`, `stdout`, or `stderr` streams.

Summary

```
#include <stdio.h>
int _fileno(FILE *fp); // Return handle for this open stream
```

Description

Retrieves the integer file descriptor (handle) associated with the stream *fp*.

Returns

When the function completes successfully, the return value is the handle for the specified stream.

The return value when *fp* does not refer to an open stream is undefined.

Sample Call

```
// Get the handle of stdin (should be 0):
    printf("File handle for stdin is: %d\n", fileno(stdin));
```

See Also

fopen

_flushall

MSC6	MSC7	VC++	QC2.5	QC-WIN	TC2	TC++	BC++2	BC++3	ANSI	POSIX	UNIX V	DOS	QWIN	WIN	WINDLL
X	X	X	X	X	X	X	X	X				X	X	X	X

Summary

```
#include <stdio.h>
int _flushall(void);
```

Description

Flushes all buffers associated with the currently open streams, including stdin, stdout, stderr, _stdaux, and _stdprn.

Returns

The return value is the number of buffers flushed. (This should be the same as the number of open streams.)

Sample Call

```
int nfiles;
//...
nfiles = _flushall();
```

See Also

fflush

fopen

MSC6	MSC7	VC++	QC2.5	QC-WIN	TC2	TC++	BC++2	BC++3	ANSI	POSIX	UNIX V	DOS	QWIN	WIN	WINDLL
X	X	X	X	X	X	X	X	X	X	X	X	X	X	X	X

Summary

```
#include <stdio.h>

FILE *fopen(
    const char *name,  // Name of file to be opened
    const char *mode); // Mode in which file is opened
```

Description

Opens the file specified by the *name* argument. The *mode* argument indicates whether the file is being opened for reading, writing, or both. Table 22.4 in the reference discussion of `_fdopen` lists the strings you can use as the *mode* argument to `fopen`. Here are some important points about the *mode* argument:

- The first character of *mode* is `r`, `w`, or `a`, denoting that the file is being opened for reading, writing, or appending, respectively.
- A `+` as the second or third character of *mode* indicates that the file will be updated—both read and write operations are permitted on the file.
- If a file is opened in append mode, existing data in the file cannot be destroyed because all write operations are forced to occur at the end of the file.
- If a file is opened for updating, you must call a file-positioning function such as `fseek`, `fsetpos`, or `rewind` when you switch between read and write operations. Additionally, you can switch from writing to reading with an intervening call to the `fflush` function.
- An optional `b` or `t` (see Table 22.5) appearing in the *mode* string indicates the translation mode—how the contents of the file are translated during read and write operations. (See the tutorial for details.) If you do not specify a translation mode explicitly, the translation is determined by the global variable `_fmode`, declared in the header file stdio.h.
- An optional `c` or `n` (see Table 22.6) indicates whether you want flushed buffers committed to disk.

Returns

When the function completes successfully, the return value is a pointer to a `FILE` structure.

`NULL` Indicates an error.

Sample Call

```
    FILE *infile;

// Open the file and check for errors.
    if((infile = fopen("c:\\config.sys", "rt")) == NULL)
    {
        fprintf(stderr, "Failed to open: config.sys\n");
        exit(1);
    }
```

See Also

`fclose`, `_fdopen`, `freopen`

fprintf

MSC6	MSC7	VC++	QC2.5	QC-WIN	TC2	TC++	BC++2	BC++3	ANSI	POSIX	UNIX V	DOS	QWIN	WIN	WINDLL
X	X	X	X	X	X	X	X	X	X	X	X	X	X	X	

Summary

```
#include <stdio.h>

int fprintf(
    FILE *fp,             // Formatted output goes to this stream
    const char *format, // Format specification
    ...);                 // Variable number of arguments
```

Description

Formats a variable number of values into text form according to a specified format and sends the output to the stream *fp*. Consult the reference entry of `printf` for more information about the format string.

Returns

When the function completes successfully, the return value is the number of characters printed.

A negative value indicates an error.

Sample Call

```
int abort_code = 7;
// Display error code (assume error code is in abort_code:
fprintf(stderr, "Aborting start-up sequence. Error code: %d\n",
        abort_code);
```

See Also

`printf`, `scanf`, `sprintf`

fputc

MSC6	MSC7	VC++	QC2.5	QC-WIN	TC2	TC++	BC++2	BC++3	ANSI	POSIX	UNIX V	DOS	QWIN	WIN	WINDLL
X	X	X	X	X	X	X	X	X	X	X	X	X	X	X	X

Summary

```
#include <stdio.h>
```

```
int fputc(
    int  c,     // Write this character
    FILE *fp); //   to this stream
```

Description

Writes the character `c` to the stream `fp`.

Returns

When the function completes successfully, the return value is the character.

`EOF` Indicates an error. `EOF` is a constant defined in stdio.h.

Sample Call

```
FILE *fp;
// Assume fp is set up for write operations.
fputc('.',fp);
```

See Also

`_fputchar`, `putc`, `putchar`

_fputchar

MSC6	MSC7	VC++	QC2.5	QC-WIN	TC2	TC++	BC++2	BC++3	ANSI	POSIX	UNIX V	DOS	QWIN	WIN	WINDLL
X	X	X	X	X	X	X	X	X				X	X		

Summary

```
#include <stdio.h>

int _fputchar(int c); // Write character c to stdout
```

Description

Writes the character `c` to `stdout`.

Returns

`c` The character was successfully written to `stdout`.

`EOF` Indicates an error. `EOF` is a constant defined in stdio.h.

Sample Call

```
_fputchar('>');
```

See Also

`fputc`, `putc`, `putchar`

fputs

MSC6	MSC7	VC++	QC2.5	QC-WIN	TC2	TC++	BC++2	BC++3	ANSI	POSIX	UNIX V	DOS	QWIN	WIN	WINDLL
X	X	X	X	X	X	X	X	X	X	X	X	X	X	X	X

Summary

```
#include <stdio.h>

int fputs(
    const char *str, // Write this null-terminated string
    FILE       *fp); //   to this stream
```

Description

Writes the null-terminated string `str` to the stream `fp`.

Returns

When the function completes successfully, it returns a non-negative value.

`EOF` Indicates an error. `EOF` is a constant defined in stdio.h.

Sample Call

```
fputs("Hello\n", stdout); // same as puts("Hello");
```

See Also

`fgets`, `gets`, `puts`

fread

MSC6	MSC7	VC++	QC2.5	QC-WIN	TC2	TC++	BC++2	BC++3	ANSI	POSIX	UNIX V	DOS	QWIN	WIN	WINDLL
X	X	X	X	X	X	X	X	X	X	X	X	X	X	X	X

Summary

```
#include <stdio.h>

size_t fread(
    void   *buf,       // Read from the stream into this buffer
    size_t el_size,    // Each data item is of this size (in bytes)
    size_t el_count,   // Number of data items to be read
    FILE   *fp);       // Read from this open stream
```

Description

Reads `el_count` data items from the stream `fp` into the buffer `buf`. Each data item is `el_size` bytes long. The current position in the stream is updated after the read operation. The `fread` function is primarily used to read unformatted data from a binary stream.

Returns

When the function completes successfully, the return value is the number of data items (not bytes) actually read from the stream.

If this is less than *el_count*, call `feof` or `ferror` to check for error conditions.

Sample Call

```
    FILE *fp;
    short buf[256];
    size_t numread;
FILE *fp = fopen ("text.dat", "rb");
// Read 256 "short int" values from the file.
    numread = fread(buf, sizeof(short), 256, fp);
```

See Also

`fwrite`

freopen

MSC6	MSC7	VC++	QC2.5	QC-WIN	TC2	TC++	BC++2	BC++3	ANSI	POSIX	UNIX V	DOS	QWIN	WIN	WINDLL
X	X	X	X	X	X	X	X	X	X	X	X	X	X	X	X

Summary

```
#include <stdio.h>

FILE *freopen(
    const char *name,// New file to open
    const char *mode,// Read-write access mode of file
    FILE       *fp); // Close this stream and reopen with new file
```

Description

Closes the file associated with the stream *fp* and reopens that stream with a new file identified by a name. The *mode* argument, interpreted as in `fopen`, indicates the read-write access and the translation mode of the reopened stream. Use `freopen` to redirect `stdin` or `stdout` to a file.

Returns

If the stream is successfully reopened, the return value is the `FILE` pointer *fp*.

`NULL` Indicates an error.

Sample Call

```
// Redirect stdout to a file named "session.log:"
    if(freopen("session.log", "w", stdout) == NULL)
    {
```

```
// Error reopening stdout....
//...
    }
```

See Also

fopen

fscanf

MSC6	MSC7	VC++	QC2.5	QC-WIN	TC2	TC++	BC++2	BC++3	ANSI	POSIX	UNIX V	DOS	QWIN	WIN	WINDLL
X	X	X	X	X	X	X	X	X	X	X	X	X	X	X	

Summary

```
#include <stdio.h>

int fscanf(
    FILE       *fp,      // Read characters from this stream
    const char *format, //   and format according to this.
    ...);               // Addresses of variables that receive
                        //   values read from fp
```

Description

Reads characters from the stream *fp* and converts them to internal representations of variables according to the specified *format* string. A variable number of arguments following the format string represent the addresses of the variables where the converted values are stored. Consult the reference entry of the scanf function for information on the syntax of *format*.

Returns

When the function completes successfully, the return value is the number of input items that were successfully read, converted, and stored in specified addresses.

EOF Indicates an error. EOF is a constant defined in stdio.h.

Sample Call

```
    char code[80];
    int  month, day, year;
    double payment;
    FILE *fp = fopen("paid.dat", "rt");
// Read from a text stream fp:
    fscanf(fp, "Date: %d/%d/%d Code: %s Paid: %lf ",
               &month, &day, &year, code, &payment);
```

See Also

scanf, sscanf

fseek

MSC6	MSC7	VC++	QC2.5	QC-WIN	TC2	TC++	BC++2	BC++3	ANSI	POSIX	UNIX V	DOS	QWIN	WIN	WINDLL
X	X	X	X	X	X	X	X	X	X	X	X	X	X	X	X

Summary

```
#include <stdio.h>

int fseek(
    FILE *fp,     // Set the current position of this stream
    long offset, //   to this offset (in number of bytes)
    int  origin);//   from this reference point; should be
                 //   SEEK_SET, SEEK_CUR, or SEEK_END
```

Description

Sets the current position in the stream `fp` to a new position `offset`, expressed in terms of the number of bytes from the location specified by `origin`. The `origin` argument can `SEEK_SET`, `SEEK_END`, or `SEEK_CUR` to indicate the beginning, end, or the current position of the file, respectively.

Returns

0	The current position of the stream was successfully reset.
Nonzero	Indicates an error.

Sample Call

```
// Go to the beginning of the file (same as rewind):
    fseek(fp, 0L, SEEK_SET);
```

See Also

ftell

fsetpos

MSC6	MSC7	VC++	QC2.5	QC-WIN	TC2	TC++	BC++2	BC++3	ANSI	POSIX	UNIX V	DOS	QWIN	WIN	WINDLL
X	X	X	X	X	X	X	X	X	X		X	X	X	X	X

Summary

```
#include <stdio.h>
```

```
int fsetpos(
    FILE          *fp,   // Set current position of this stream
    const fpos_t *pos);// New position (value from previous
                       //   call to fgetpos)
```

Description

Sets the current position of the stream *fp* to the value contained in the `fpos_t` vari able associated with the address you provide in the *pos* argument. This value mus have been obtained by an earlier call to `fgetpos`.

Returns

0	The current position of the stream *fp* was successfully reset.
Nonzero	Indicates an error. Also sets `errno` to `EBADF` or `EINVAL`.

Sample Call

```
    fpos_t savepos;
// Save current position in stream:
    if(fgetpos(fp, &savepos) != 0) perror("fgetpos");
// Other operations on file....
//...
// Set position back to saved position:
    if(fsetpos(fp, &savepos) != 0) perror("fsetpos");
```

See Also

fgetpos

_fsopen

MSC6	MSC7	VC++	QC2.5	QC-WIN	TC2	TC++	BC++2	BC++3	ANSI	POSIX	UNIX V	DOS	QWIN	WIN	WINDLL
X	X	X	X	X				X				X	X	X	X

Summary

```
#include <stdio.h>
#include <share.h>    // For sharing mode constants

FILE *_fsopen(
    const char *pathname, // Open this file
    const char *mode,     //   with this read-write access
    int         shmode);  //   and in this sharing mode
```

Description

Opens a file just as `fopen` does, except that `_fsopen` also prepares the file for shared access according to the sharing mode indicated by the *shmode* argument, which can take one of the following values:

`_SH_COMPAT`	No other process can access the file. (This is called *compatibility mode*, because this is how MS-DOS normally operates.)
`_SH_DENYRW`	Only one process can read from and write to file.
`_SH_DENYWR`	Other processes can read from but cannot write to file.
`_SH_DENYRD`	Other processes can write to but cannot read from file.
`_SH_DENYNO`	Other processes can access file for both reading and writing.

The read-write access modes that you would specify through the *mode* argument are described in the reference entry for the `_fdopen` function.

The `_fsopen` function is useful in controlling access to files in a networked environment, where many systems might access files on a single file server.

Returns

When the function completes successfully, the return value is a `FILE` pointer identifying the stream.

`NULL` Indicates an error.

Sample Call

```
// Open an output for writing and don't allow any other
// process "write" access to the file:
   if((fp = _fsopen("summary.dat", "wt", _SH_DENYWR))
                                              == NULL)

   {
// Error opening file....
//...
   }
```

See Also

`fclose`, `fopen`

ftell

MSC6	MSC7	VC++	QC2.5	QC-WIN	TC2	TC++	BC++2	BC++3	ANSI	POSIX	UNIX V	DOS	QWIN	WIN	WINDLL
X	X	X	X	X	X	X	X	X	X	X	X	X	X	X	X

Summary

`#include <stdio.h>`

```
long ftell(FILE *fp); // Return current position in this stream
```

Description

Returns the current position in an open stream identified by *fp*.

Returns

When the function completes successfully, the return value is the current position as a byte offset from the beginning of the file.

–1 Indicates an error. Also sets errno to EBADF or EINVAL.

Sample Call

```
    long curpos;
// After file has been opened and some I/O operations
// performed on it....
    if((curpos = ftell(fp)) == -1) perror("ftell");
```

See Also

fseek

fwrite

MSC6	MSC7	VC++	QC2.5	QC-WIN	TC2	TC++	BC++2	BC++3	ANSI	POSIX	UNIX V	DOS	QWIN	WIN	WINDLL
X	X	X	X	X	X	X	X	X	X	X	X	X	X	X	X

Summary

```
#include <stdio.h>

size_t fwrite(
    void   *buf,      // Write from this buffer to the stream
    size_t el_size,   // Each data item is of this size (in bytes)
    size_t el_count,  // Number of data items to be written
    FILE   *fp);      // Write to this open stream
```

Description

Writes *el_count* data items from the buffer *buf* to the stream *fp*. Each data item is *el_size* bytes long. The current position in the stream is updated after the write operation. The fread function is used primarily to write unformatted data to a binary stream.

Returns

When the function completes successfully, the return value is the number of data items (not bytes) actually written to the stream.

If this is less than *el_count*, an error may have occurred.

Sample Call

```
    FILE *fp;
    short buf[256];
    size_t numwrite;
// Assume fp is set up for binary-mode write.
// Write 256 "short int" from buf to this file:
    numwrite = fwrite(buf, sizeof(short), 256, fp);
```

See Also

fread

getc

MSC6	MSC7	VC++	QC2.5	QC-WIN	TC2	TC++	BC++2	BC++3	ANSI	POSIX	UNIX V	DOS	QWIN	WIN	WINDLL
X	X	X	X	X	X	X	X	X	X	X	X	X	X	X	X

```
#include <stdio.h>

int getc(FILE *fp); // Read a single character from this stream
```

Description

Reads a character from the stream *fp*.

Returns

When the function completes successfully, the return value is the character read from the stream.

EOF — Indicates an error. When an error is returned, call feof and ferror to determine whether the file ended or some other error occurred.

Sample Call

```
    int c;
// Assume fp is set up for reading.
    c = getc(fp);
```

See Also

fgetc, _fgetchar, getchar

getchar

MSC6	MSC7	VC++	QC2.5	QC-WIN	TC2	TC++	BC++2	BC++3	ANSI	POSIX	UNIX V	DOS	QWIN	WIN	WINDLL
X	X	X	X	X	X	X	X	X	X	X	X	X	X		

Summary

```
#include <stdio.h>

int getchar(void);
```

Description

Reads a single character from `stdin`. However, even when you try to read a single character, the reading does not end until the Enter key is pressed on the keyboard.

Returns

When the function completes successfully, the return value is the character read from `stdin`.

`EOF` Indicates an error. `EOF` is a constant defined in stdio.h.

Sample Call

```
int c;

c = getchar();
```

See Also

`fgetc`, `_fgetchar`, `getc`

gets

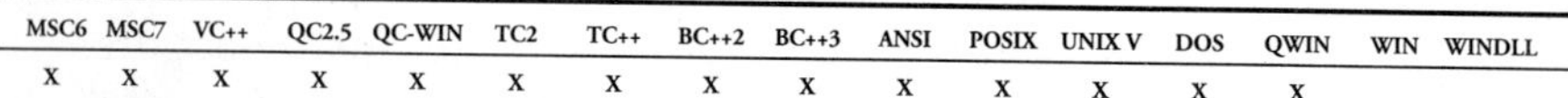

MSC6	MSC7	VC++	QC2.5	QC-WIN	TC2	TC++	BC++2	BC++3	ANSI	POSIX	UNIX V	DOS	QWIN	WIN	WINDLL
X	X	X	X	X	X	X	X	X	X	X	X	X	X		

Summary

```
#include <stdio.h>

char *gets(char *buf);// Read characters into this array
```

Description

Reads a line of text from `stdin` and stores the characters in the character array *`buf`*. You must ensure that there is enough room in *`buf`* to handle the maximum number of characters entered at the keyboard. Reading stops when `gets` reads a newline character (`'\n'`), which it replaces with a null character (`'\0'`).

Returns

When the function completes successfully, the return value is `buf`.

`NULL` Indicates an error.

Sample Call

```
char filename[81];
//...
printf("Enter name of file to open: ");
gets(filename);
```

See Also

`fgets`

_getw

MSC6	MSC7	VC++	QC2.5	QC-WIN	TC2	TC++	BC++2	BC++3	ANSI	POSIX	UNIX V	DOS	QWIN	WIN	WINDLL
X	X	X	X	X	X	X	X	X			X	X	X	X	X

Summary

```
#include <stdio.h>

int _getw(FILE *fp);// Read an integer from this stream
```

Description

Reads an integer (without any formatting) from the stream `fp`.

Returns

When the function completes successfully, the return value is the integer read from the stream `fp`.

`EOF` Indicates an error. If the return value is `EOF`, call `feof` and `ferror` to determine whether the file ended or there was some other error.

Sample Call

```
    FILE *fp;
    int  word1;
// Assume that fp is set up for binary read.
    if((word1 = _getw(fp)) == EOF)
    {
// May be an error. Call feof and ferror....
//...
    }
```

See Also

putw

perror

MSC6	MSC7	VC++	QC2.5	QC-WIN	TC2	TC++	BC++2	BC++3	ANSI	POSIX	UNIX V	DOS	QWIN	WIN	WINDLL
X	X	X	X	X	X	X	X	X	X	X	X	X	X		

Summary

```
#include <stdio.h>

void perror(const char *msg); // Your part of the error message
```

Description

Prints an error message constructed by appending a colon and a space to the message specified by the null-terminated string *msg*, and then concatenating to that a message corresponding to the current setting of the global error indicator `errno`.

Sample Call

```
// Try changing directory to a nonexistent path.
    if(_chdir("xxxx") != 0) perror("_chdir");
```

This prints the following message (notice the colon appended to the argument passed to `perror`):

```
_chdir: No such file or directory
```

See Also

`strerror` (Chapter 26)

printf

MSC6	MSC7	VC++	QC2.5	QC-WIN	TC2	TC++	BC++2	BC++3	ANSI	POSIX	UNIX V	DOS	QWIN	WIN	WINDLL
X	X	X	X	X	X	X	X	X	X	X	X	X	X		

Summary

```
#include <stdio.h>

int printf(
    const char *fmt, // Format output according to this string.
    ...);            // Variable number of arguments (items
                     //   being printed).
```

Description

Writes textual output to `stdout` according to the formatting commands specified in the null-terminated string *fmt*. The `printf` function formats the value of each argument according to the codes embedded in the string *fmt*. Each format code starts with a % character. The format specification is of the following form:

```
%[Flags][Width][.Precision][Addr_mode][Size][Type]
```

Table 22.7 summarizes each component of the format string. Tables 22.8, 22.9, and 22.10 summarize the `Type`, `Flag`, and `Precision` fields, respectively.

Returns

When the function completes successfully, the return value is the number of characters printed.

A negative value indicates an error.

Sample Call

```
float result;
// Print a float value with 2 digits following decimal point:
printf("The result is: %.2f\n", result);
```

See Also

`fprintf`, `sprintf`, `vfprintf`, `vprintf`, `_vsnprintf`, `vsprintf`

Table 22.7. The fields in the format string for `printf`.

Field	Description
`%`	A required field indicating the start of a format specification. Use `%%` to print a single percentage sign.
`Flags`	An optional field consisting of one or more of the characters `-`, `+`, `#`, `0` or a blank space (see Table 22.9 for further details).
`Width`	An optional numeric field indicating how many characters, at a minimum, must be used to print the value. An asterisk (`*`) in this field indicates that an integer variable appearing in the argument list contains the width—this integer variable precedes the actual variable being printed.
`Precision`	An optional numeric field specifying how many characters, at most, can be used in printing the value. When printing integer variables, this is the minimum number of digits to be printed. A decimal point precedes the `Precision` field and is needed only when `Precision` is specified. See Table 22.10 for further information on `Precision`.

continues

Table 22.7. continued

Field	Description
`Addr_mode`	This optional Microsoft-specific field can be one of the letters F (for *far*) or N (for *near*) that you can use to override the default addressing mode of the memory model being used.
`Size`	This optional field is a single character that modifies the Type field, which follows the Size field. You can use one of the following characters in this field: *Character* — *Meaning* `h` — Used with integer types `d`, `i`, `o`, `u`, `x`, and `X` to indicate that the variable is a `short` integer. Used with type `p` to indicate that you want to print a 16-bit address. `i` — Used with integer or unsigned integer types to indicate that the variable to be printed is a `long` integer. Also used with floating-point types to indicate that a variable is `double` rather than `float`. `l` — Used with floating-point types to indicate that the variable is a `long double`.
`Type`	This is a required field with a single character that indicates the type of variable being printed (see Table 22.8).

Table 22.8. The Type characters in the format specification for `printf`.

Type	Description
`c`	Prints a single character. For instance, `printf("%c", 'q');` prints a "q".
`d`	Prints a signed decimal integer as a sequence of digits with or without a sign depending on the `Flags` used. For example, `printf("%d", 2005);` prints "2005".

Type	Description
e	Prints a double or a float variable as a signed value in the scientific format. For example, the value -321.4567 is printed as "–3.214567e+002".
E	Prints a double or a float variable as a signed value in the scientific format; the above example prints as "–3.214567E+002" if the %E format is used.
f	Prints a double or a float variable as a signed value in the format (sign)(digits).(digits). In this format, -321.4567 prints as "–321.456700".
g	Prints a double or a float variable as a signed value, using the %e or %f format. The format that generates the most compact output for the given Precision is selected.
G	Prints a double or a float variable as a signed value, using the %g format, but with the letter E in place of "e" whenever exponents are printed.
i	Prints a signed decimal integer as a sequence of digits with or without a sign depending on the Flags field.
n	This format expects an int pointer as the argument. Before returning, the printf function places in this integer the total number of characters it has printed to the output stream.
o	Prints an unsigned integer using octal digits without any sign.
p	Prints the value of a far pointer to void as an address in hexadecimal format. The printed address is of the form *XXXX*:*YYYY*, where *XXXX* denotes the segment address and *YYYY* is the offset (each with four hexadecimal digits).
u	Prints an unsigned variable as an unsigned decimal value.
x	Prints an unsigned variable as a hexadecimal value using lowercase hexadecimal digits (abcdef).
X	Prints an unsigned variable as a hexadecimal value using uppercase hexadecimal digits (ABCDEF).

Table 22.9. The Flags field in the format specification for `printf`.

Flag	Interpretation
-	Left justify output value. The default is to right justify the output.
+	If the output value is a numerical one, print a + or a - according to the sign of the value. The default setting is to print a negative sign for negative values only.
`0`	If a zero appears as the leading numeral in the `Width` field, leading zeros are added to the output. The default is to not use any zero padding.
<space>	Add leading blank spaces to positive numerical values. The default setting does not print leading blanks.
#	When used with octal or hexadecimal types (`%o`, `%x`, or `%X`), nonzero values are prefixed with 0, 0x, or 0X. The default setting is to suppress these special prefixes.

When printing floating-point values in `%e`, `%E`, or `%f` format, this flag forces the printing of a decimal point. By default, a decimal point appears only if there are digits following the decimal point.

When used with `%g` or `%G` formats, this flag prints a decimal point and prints all trailing zeros. The default is to suppress trailing zeros and print a decimal point only when there are digits following the decimal point.

Table 22.10. Effect of `Precision` on formatting different Type.

Type	How `Precision` Is Used
`c`	`Precision` is ignored.
`d, i, o, u, x, X`	`Precision` is interpreted as the minimum number of digits that will be printed. When the value occupies fewer characters than the specified precision, the output is padded on the left with zeros. Note, however, that if the text representation of a value requires more characters

Type	How Precision Is Used
	than the precision, `printf` uses as many characters as necessary to express the value fully. The default precision is 1.
`e, E`	`Precision` is used as the number of digits to be printed after the decimal point. The last printed digit is rounded. The default precision is 6. You can suppress the decimal point by specifying a zero precision, or by placing a period after the `Width` field without providing any other numerals after that period.
`f`	`Precision` is used as the number of digits to be printed after the decimal point. The value is rounded to the specified number of digits and, when a decimal point is printed, at least one digit appears before it. The default precision is 6. You can suppress the decimal point by specifying a zero precision or by placing a period after the `Width` field without providing any other numerals after that period.
`g, G`	`Precision` specifies the maximum number of significant digits to print. The default precision is 6. Trailing zeros are discarded.
`s`	`Precision` indicates the maximum number of characters to print. In this case, `printf` truncates the string and print only the number of characters specified by the precision. With the default setting, `printf` prints the characters in the string until it encounters a null character.

putc

MSC6	MSC7	VC++	QC2.5	QC-WIN	TC2	TC++	BC++2	BC++3	ANSI	POSIX	UNIX V	DOS	QWIN	WIN	WINDLL
X	X	X	X	X	X	X	X	X	X	X	X	X	X	X	X

Summary

```
#include <stdio.h>
```

```
int putc(
   int   c,     // Write this character
    FILE *fp); //   to this stream
```

Description

Writes the single character *c* to the stream *fp*.

Returns

When the function completes successfully, the return value is the character written to the stream.

EOF Indicates an error. EOF is a constant defined in stdio.h.

Sample Call

```
// Assume stream fp is set up for writing.
    putc('*', fp);
```

See Also

fputc, _fputchar, putchar

putchar

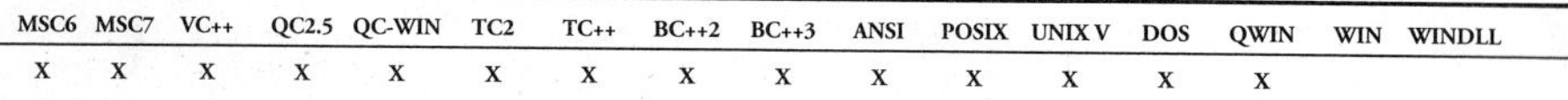

MSC6	MSC7	VC++	QC2.5	QC-WIN	TC2	TC++	BC++2	BC++3	ANSI	POSIX	UNIX V	DOS	QWIN	WIN	WINDLL
X	X	X	X	X	X	X	X	X	X	X	X	X	X		

Summary

```
#include <stdio.h>

int putchar(int c); // Write this character to stdout
```

Description

Writes the single character *c* to stdout.

Returns

When the function completes successfully, the return value is the character written to stdout.

EOF Indicates an error. EOF is a constant defined in stdio.h.

Sample Call

```
// Display the prompt character:
    putchar('>');
```

See Also

fputc, _fputchar, putc

puts

MSC6	MSC7	VC++	QC2.5	QC-WIN	TC2	TC++	BC++2	BC++3	ANSI	POSIX	UNIX V	DOS	QWIN	WIN	WINDLL
x	x	x	x	x	x	x	x	x	x	x	x	x	x		

Summary

```
#include <stdio.h>

int puts(const char *str); // Null-terminated string to be printed
```

Description

Writes the null-terminated string *str* to `stdout`. The `puts` function replaces the terminating null character (`'\0'`) with a newline (`'\n'`). That means you don't need an explicit newline character in a string being displayed using `puts`.

Returns

When the function completes successfully, the return value is nonnegative.

`EOF` Indicates an error. `EOF` is a constant defined in stdio.h.

Sample Call

```
puts("Dictionary full!");
```

See Also

`fputs`, `gets`

_putw

MSC6	MSC7	VC++	QC2.5	QC-WIN	TC2	TC++	BC++2	BC++3	ANSI	POSIX	UNIX V	DOS	QWIN	WIN	WINDLL
x	x	x	x	x	x	x	x	x			x	x	x	x	x

Summary

```
#include <stdio.h>

int _putw(
    int  iv,     // Write this integer
    FILE *fp);  //   to this stream
```

Description

Writes the binary representation of the integer value *iv* (without any formatting) to the stream *fp*.

Returns

When the function completes successfully, the return value is the value written to the stream.

`EOF` Indicates an error. Because `EOF` may be a valid integer value, you should cal `ferror` to determine whether there is really an error.

Sample Call

```
// Assume stream fp is set up for binary write operations.
    _putw(0x4949);
```

See Also

`_getw`

rewind

MSC6	MSC7	VC++	QC2.5	QC-WIN	TC2	TC++	BC++2	BC++3	ANSI	POSIX	UNIX V	DOS	QWIN	WIN	WINDLL
X	X	X	X	X	X	X	X	X	X	X	X	X	X	X	X

Summary

```
#include <stdio.h>

void rewind(FILE *fp); // Go to the beginning of this stream
```

Description

Sets the current position of the file pointer associated with the stream *fp* to the beginning of the file.

Sample Call

```
    FILE *datafile;
// Assume datafile set up for writing....
//...
// Go back to the beginning to write file header:
    rewind(datafile);
```

See Also

`fseek`

_rmtmp

MSC6	MSC7	VC++	QC2.5	QC-WIN	TC2	TC++	BC++2	BC++3	ANSI	POSIX	UNIX V	DOS	QWIN	WIN	WINDLL
X	X	X	X	X				X				X	X	X	X

Summary

```
#include <stdio.h>

int _rmtmp(void);
```

Description

Closes and deletes all temporary files created by `tmpfile` in the current working directory.

Returns

When the function completes, the return value is the number of temporary files deleted.

Sample Call

```
printf("Deleted %d temporary files\n", _rmtmp());
```

See Also

`tmpfile`

scanf

MSC6	MSC7	VC++	QC2.5	QC-WIN	TC2	TC++	BC++2	BC++3	ANSI	POSIX	UNIX V	DOS	QWIN	WIN	WINDLL
X	X	X	X	X	X	X	X	X	X	X	X	X	X		

Summary

```
#include <stdio.h>

int scanf(
    const char *fmt, // Format string
    ...);            // Addresses of variables that receive
                     //   values read from stdin
```

Description

Reads characters from `stdin` and converts them to values of C variables according to format specified in the string *`fmt`*. The format specification for each variable has the following form:

`%[*][Width][Addr_mode][Size][Type]`

Table 22.11 summarizes the purpose of each field in the format specification used by `scanf`. Table 22.12 explains the characters that can appear in the `Type` field and the type of format conversion each character implies.

Normally, `scanf` expects strings read using the `%s` format to be delimited by blank spaces. If you want `scanf` to read a string delimited by any character other than those in a specific set, you can specify the set of characters within brackets and use this in place of the letter s in the format specification. On the other hand, if the first character inside the brackets is a caret (^), `scanf` interprets the rest of the characters in the set to be characters that terminate the string. Thus, the format `%[^'\"]` causes `scanf` to read a string delimited by single or double quote characters.

If you need to read a string without the terminating null character, use the `%nc` format, where `n` is a decimal integer specifying the number of characters to be read into the string.

Returns

When the function completes successfully, the return value is the number of input items (not characters) that were successfully read, converted, and stored in variables. This does not include fields converted but not stored (for example, when you use the `*` field in the format string).

`EOF` Indicates that the stream reached end-of-file during reading.

Sample Call

```
    char name[80];
    double payment;

// Prompt for a name:
    printf("Enter name: ");

// Read all lower- and uppercase characters plus
// any space character (which is 040 in octal):
    scanf("%[a-zA-Z\040]", name);

// Flush buffer to ensure no mixup with next field:
    fflush(stdin);
    printf("Enter amount: ");
    scanf("%lf", &payment);
```

See Also

`fscanf`, `sscanf`

Table 22.11. Fields in format specification for `scanf`.

Field	Description
`%`	A required field indicating the beginning of a format specification. To read a single percentage sign from the input, use `%%` in the format specification.
`*`	An optional field indicating a value that should be read but not stored anywhere. You can use this field to skip over values of specific types from the input stream.

Field	Description
`Width`	An optional positive value specifying the maximum number of characters to be read as the value of this variable.
`Addr_mode`	An optional field that overrides the default addressing mode of the memory model being used. It can be one of the letters `F` (for *far*) or `N` (for *near*).
`Size`	An optional single character that modifies the `Type` field that follows the `Size` field. You can use one of the following characters for this field: *Character* — *Meaning* `h` — Used when you're reading integers to indicate that the variable being read is a `short` integer. `l` — Used when you're reading integers or unsigned integers to indicate that the variable to be read is a `long` integer. Also used with floating-point types to indicate that a variable being read is a `double`, rather than a `float`.
`Type`	A required single-character field that indicates the type of variable being read. Table 22.12 lists the characters that can appear in this field.

Table 22.12. `Type` field in format specification for `scanf`.

Type	Description
`c`	Reads a single character and stores the character in the `char` variable associated with the address you provide as the argument corresponding to this format.
`d`	Reads a decimal integer value and stores it in the `int` variable associated with the address you provide as the corresponding argument.

continues

Table 22.12. continued

Type	Description
`e, E, f, g, G`	Reads a signed value in the scientific format, such as –3.214567e+002 and 4.296543e–002 or in the format: `[sign][digits].[digits]` such as –3.214567 and 426.543 and stores the converted value in a `float` variable associated with the address you have to provide as an argument. Use an `l` prefix (see Table 22.11) to read the value into a double variable.
`i`	Reads a decimal, hexadecimal, or octal value and stores it in an `int` variable associated with the address you provide as an argument.
`n`	Does not read anything from the stream, but before returning, `scanf` stores (in the `int` variable associated with the address you provide as argument) the total number of characters it has read thus far in this call to `scanf`.
`o`	Reads octal digits without a sign and stores the value in the `int` variable associated with the address you provide as argument to `scanf`.
`p`	Reads hexadecimal digits of the form *XXXX:YYYY*, where *X* and *Y* are uppercase hexadecimal digits. Stores converted value in a pointer to a far pointer to `void`.
`s`	Reads a character string. (See the Description section for information on delimiting strings.) You should provide as argument a `char` pointer or the name of a `char` array with enough room to hold the characters plus a terminating null character, which `scanf` automatically appends.
`u`	Reads an unsigned decimal integer value and stores it in the `unsigned int` variable associated with the address you provide as an argument.
`U`	Reads an unsigned decimal integer value and stores it in the `unsigned long` variable associated with the address you provide as an argument.

Type	Description
`x`	Reads hexadecimal digits and stores the value in the `int` variable associated with the address you provide as argument to `scanf`. The input characters should not include a `0x` prefix.

setbuf

MSC6	MSC7	VC++	QC2.5	QC-WIN	TC2	TC++	BC++2	BC++3	ANSI	POSIX	UNIX V	DOS	QWIN	WIN	WINDLL
x	x	x	x	x	x	x	x	x	x	x	x	x	x	x	x

Summary

```
#include <stdio.h>

void setbuf(
    FILE *fp,   // Assign a buffer to this stream
    char *buf); // Use this buffer (NULL means no buffering)
```

Description

Assigns the buffer specified by the pointer *`buf`* to the stream *`fp`*. If the *`buf`* pointer is `NULL`, buffering is turned off. If *`buf`* is not `NULL`, it must point to a block of memory at least `BUFSIZ` bytes long (`BUFSIZ` is defined in stdio.h as `512`).

Sample Call

```
    char my_buffer[BUFSIZ];
// Assume fp is an open stream.
    setbuf(fp, my_buffer);
```

See Also

`setvbuf`

setvbuf

MSC6	MSC7	VC++	QC2.5	QC-WIN	TC2	TC++	BC++2	BC++3	ANSI	POSIX	UNIX V	DOS	QWIN	WIN	WINDLL
x	x	x	x	x	x	x	x	x	x		x	x	x	x	x

Summary

```
#include <stdio.h>

int setvbuf(
    FILE  *fp,        // Set up this stream's buffering
    char  *buf,       // Buffer to be assigned to stream
```

```
    int      buf_mode,  // Buffering level: One of _IOFBF (full
                        //   buffering), _IOLBF (line buffering), or
                        //   _IONBF (no buffering)
    size_t buf_size);   // Size of buffer (in bytes)
```

Description

Assigns the buffer `buf` to stream `fp` and sets the level of buffering to `buf_mode`. The buffer is `buf_size` bytes long. The level of buffering can be `_IOFBF` for full buffering, `_IOLBF` for line buffering, or `_IONBF` for no buffering. If you specify `buf_mode` as `_IONBF`, `setvbuf` ignores the other arguments. Also, for other buffering levels, if you provide a `NULL` argument for `buf`, `setvbuf` allocates a buffer of size `buf_size` and uses that buffer.

Returns

0	The buffer was assigned and the level of buffering was successfully set.
Nonzero	Indicates an error.

Sample Call

```
char buf[1024];

if(setvbuf(infile, buf, _IOFBF, 1024) != 0)
{
// Error setting buffer....
//...
}
```

See Also

setbuf

_snprintf

MSC6	MSC7	VC++	QC2.5	QC-WIN	TC2	TC++	BC++2	BC++3	ANSI	POSIX	UNIX V	DOS	QWIN	WIN	WINDLL
	X	X										X	X	X	

Summary

```
#include <stdio.h>

int _snprintf(
    char        *str,    // Array for storing formatted output
    size_t      maxchr,// At most this many characters stored
    const char *fmt,    // Format string
    ...);               // Variables being formatted for output
```

Description

Accepts a variable number of arguments, converts their values to characters, and stores these characters in the char array *str*. The specification of the format string *fmt* is explained in the reference entry for printf. The _snprintf function is a safe version of sprintf, with the restriction that no more than *maxchr* bytes of formatted text are copied into the array *str*.

Returns

When the function completes successfully, the return value is the number of characters stored in *str*, not counting the terminating null character.

–1 Indicates that the number of bytes required for output exceeds *maxchr*. In that case, _snprintf copies only *maxchr* bytes and returns.

Sample Call

```
char buf[80];
_snprintf(buf, 80, "Mouse coordinates = (%d,%d)",
        xmouse, ymouse);
```

See Also

printf, sprintf

sprintf

MSC6	MSC7	VC++	QC2.5	QC-WIN	TC2	TC++	BC++2	BC++3	ANSI	POSIX	UNIX V	DOS	QWIN	WIN	WINDLL
X	X	X	X	X	X	X	X	X	X	X	X	X	X	X	

Summary

```
#include <stdio.h>

int sprintf(
    char       *str,   // Array for storing formatted output
    const char *fmt,   // Format string
    ...);              // Variables being formatted for output
```

Description

Accepts a variable number of arguments, converts their values to characters, and stores these characters in the char array *str*. The specification of the format string *fmt* is explained in the reference entry for printf.

Returns

When the function completes successfully, the return value is the number of characters stored in *str*, not counting the terminating null character.

Sample Call

```
char buf[81];
double cost = 102.37;
//...
sprintf(buf, "Total cost is %.2f", cost);
```

See Also

printf, _snprintf

sscanf

MSC6	MSC7	VC++	QC2.5	QC-WIN	TC2	TC++	BC++2	BC++3	ANSI	POSIX	UNIX V	DOS	QWIN	WIN	WINDLL
x	x	x	x	x	x	x	x	x	x	x	x	x	x	x	

Summary

```
#include <stdio.h>

int sscanf(
    const char *buf,     // Read characters from this array
    const char *format, //   and format according to this
    ...);                // Addresses of variables that receive
                         //   values read from buf
```

Description

Reads characters from the array *buf* and converts them into internal representations of variables according to the specified format string. A variable number of arguments following the format string *fmt* represent the addresses of the variables where the converted values are stored. Consult the reference entry of the scanf function for information on the syntax of the format string.

Returns

When the function completes successfully, the return value is the number of input items (not characters) that were successfully read, converted, and stored in the specified variables.

EOF Indicates an error. EOF is a constant defined in stdio.h.

Sample Call

```
// A sample buffer to read with sscanf.
    char *buf = "Date: 6/26/92 Code: MVXPNS Paid: 2245.95";
// Variables to be read....
    char code[80];
    int  month, day, year;
    double payment;
```

```
//...
// Read from the array buf:
    sscanf(buf, "Date: %d/%d/%d Code: %s Paid: %lf ",
                &month, &day, &year, code, &payment);
```

See Also

`scanf`

_tempnam

MSC6	MSC7	VC++	QC2.5	QC-WIN	TC2	TC++	BC++2	BC++3	ANSI	POSIX	UNIX V	DOS	QWIN	WIN	WINDLL
X	X	X	X	X	X	X	X	X			X	X	X	X	X

Summary

```
#include <stdio.h>

char *_tempnam(
    char *dirname, // Directory name (to be used if environment
                   //   variable TMP is not defined
    char *fname_prefix); // Prefix characters for the filename
```

Description

Constructs a temporary filename with a specified directory name and a prefix for the filename. The directory name comes from the environment variable `TMP`, if defined. Otherwise, the name you provide in *`dirname`* is used. If *`dirname`* is `NULL` and `TMP` is undefined, the constant `P_tmpdir` (defined in stdio.h) is used as the directory name. If `P_tmpdir` does not exist, the returned filename will not have a directory name; therefore, when you create the file, it will be in the current working directory.

Returns

When the function completes successfully, the return value is a pointer to the generated name.

`NULL` Indicates that the generated filename is not unique.

Sample Call

```
char *filename;
filename = _tempnam(NULL, "mcpb");
```

See Also

`tmpfile`, `tmpnam`

tmpfile

MSC6	MSC7	VC++	QC2.5	QC-WIN	TC2	TC++	BC++2	BC++3	ANSI	POSIX	UNIX V	DOS	QWIN	WIN	WINDLL
X	X	X	X	X	X	X	X	X	X	X	X	X	X	X	X

Summary

```
#include <stdio.h>

FILE *tmpfile(void);
```

Description

Opens a temporary file in the current directory for binary read and write operations (`wb+` access mode). The temporary file is automatically deleted when the file is closed, the program terminates normally, or when `_rmtmp` is called.

Returns

When the function completes successfully, the return value is a `FILE` pointer identifying the open file.

`NULL` Indicates a failure.

Sample Call

```
FILE *ftemp;
//...
ftemp = tmpfile();
```

See Also

`rmtmp`

tmpnam

MSC6	MSC7	VC++	QC2.5	QC-WIN	TC2	TC++	BC++2	BC++3	ANSI	POSIX	UNIX V	DOS	QWIN	WIN	WINDLL
X	X	X	X	X	X	X	X	X	X	X	X	X	X	X	X

Summary

```
#include <stdio.h>

char *tmpnam(
    char *fname); // If not NULL, filename returned in this array
```

Description

Constructs a temporary filename by using the `string` constant `P_tmpdir` as the directory name and a sequence of six numerals as the filename. The filename is returned in the array identified by the *`fname`* argument provided *`fname`* is not `NULL`. If *`fname`* is `NULL`, `tmpnam` stores the name in an internal buffer.

Returns

When the function completes successfully, the return value is a pointer to the buffer in which the name is stored.

`NULL` Indicates an error in generating a unique name.

Sample Call

```
char *tfname;
// Get a unique filename for a temporary file:
tfname = tmpfile(NULL);
```

See Also

`_tempnam`, `tmpfile`

ungetc

MSC6	MSC7	VC++	QC2.5	QC-WIN	TC2	TC++	BC++2	BC++3	ANSI	POSIX	UNIX V	DOS	QWIN	WIN	WINDLL
X	X	X	X	X	X	X	X	X	X	X	X	X	X	X	X

Summary

```
#include <stdio.h>

int ungetc(
    int  c,     // Push this character back to the buffer of
    FILE *fp); //    this stream
```

Description

Places the character `c` back into the buffer associated with the stream *`fp`*. You can push back any character except the constant `EOF`.

Returns

When the function completes successfully, the return value is the character `c` that was pushed back.

`EOF` Indicates an error. `EOF` is a constant defined in stdio.h.

Sample Call

```
    int c;
// Assume c holds a character.
    if(c != EOF && !isdigit(c)) ungetc(c);
```

See Also

`getc`, `getchar`

vfprintf

MSC6	MSC7	VC++	QC2.5	QC-WIN	TC2	TC++	BC++2	BC++3	ANSI	POSIX	UNIX V	DOS	QWIN	WIN	WINDLL
X	X	X	X	X	X	X	X	X	X		X	X	X	X	

Summary

```
#include <varargs.h> // For UNIX System V compatibility
#include <stdarg.h>  // For ANSI C compatibility

#include <stdio.h>   // Function prototype

int vfprintf(
    FILE       *fp,   // Write formatted output to this file
    const char *fmt,  //   according to this format string
    va_list    argp);// Pointer to a list of argument
```

Description

Formats the values of the variables identified by *argp* according to the format specification *fmt* and writes the formatted text to the stream *fp*. The reference entry for the `printf` function describes how to specify the format string.

Returns

When the function completes successfully, the return value is the number of characters written to the stream, not counting the terminating `NULL` character.

A negative value indicates an error.

Sample Call

```
#include <stdarg.h>
//...
void save_info(FILE*, char*, ...);
//...
FILE *finfo;
char *form_name = "invoice";
int  field_no = 0;
//...
// Assume finfo is a stream opened for writing.

// Save some information to that file by calling save_info:
   save_info(finfo, "Searching for form named: %s\n", form_name);

// Another call to save some other information:
   save_info(finfo, "Now at Field %d in form: %s\n", field_no,
             form_name);
```

```
//...
//-----------------------------------------------------------
// ANSI C-compatible function that accepts variable number
// of arguments

void save_info(FILE *fp, char *fmt, ...)
{
    va_list argp;
    va_start(argp, fmt);
    vfprintf(fp, fmt, argp);
    va_end(argp);
}
```

See Also

`printf`, `vprintf`, `_vsnprintf`, `vsprintf`

vprintf

MSC6	MSC7	VC++	QC2.5	QC-WIN	TC2	TC++	BC++2	BC++3	ANSI	POSIX	UNIX V	DOS	QWIN	WIN	WINDLL
x	x	x	x	x	x	x	x	x	x		x	x	x		

Summary

```
#include <varargs.h> // For UNIX System V compatibility
#include <stdarg.h>  // For ANSI C compatibility

#include <stdio.h>   // Function prototype

int vprintf(
    const char *fmt, // Format string
    va_list    argp);// Pointer to a list of arguments
```

Description

Formats the values of the variables identified by *argp* according to the format specification *fmt* and writes the formatted text to `stdout`. Consult the reference entry for the `printf` function for information about specifying the format string.

Returns

When the function completes successfully, the return value is the number of characters written to `stdout`, not counting the terminating `NULL` character.

Sample Call

```
// See example for vfprintf. Use in a similar manner.
```

See Also

printf, vfprintf

_vsnprintf

MSC6	MSC7	VC++	QC2.5	QC-WIN	TC2	TC++	BC++2	BC++3	ANSI	POSIX	UNIX V	DOS	QWIN	WIN	WINDLL
	X	X										X	X		

Summary

```
#include <varargs.h>    // For UNIX System V compatibility
#include <stdarg.h>     // For ANSI C compatibility

#include <stdio.h>      // Function prototype

int _vsnprintf(
    char       *buf,    // Formatted output goes to this buffer
    size_t     maxchr,  // Maximum number of characters to write
    const char *fmt,    // Format string
    va_list    argp);   // Pointer to list of arguments
```

Description

Formats the values of the variables identified by *argp* according to the format specification *fmt* and stores the formatted text in the char array identified by *buf*. Writes at most *maxchr* characters to buf. Consult the reference entry for the printf function for information on specifying the format string. You can use _vsnprintf to prepare formatted text in a buffer for eventual display with some other function, perhaps a graphics text display function.

The _vsnprintf function is a safer version of vsprintf—unlike vsprintf, _vsnprintf limits the number of characters that may be written to the string designated to hold the output.

Returns

When the function completes successfully, the return value is the number of characters written to *buf*, not counting the terminating NULL character.

–1 Indicates that the output exceeds *maxchr* characters.

Sample Call

```
// See example for vfprintf. Call in a similar manner.
```

See Also

printf, vfprintf, vsprintf

vsprintf

MSC6	MSC7	VC++	QC2.5	QC-WIN	TC2	TC++	BC++2	BC++3	ANSI	POSIX	UNIX V	DOS	QWIN	WIN	WINDLL
X	X	X	X	X	X	X	X	X	X		X	X	X	X	

Summary

```
#include <varargs.h>  // For UNIX System V compatibility
#include <stdarg.h>   // For ANSI C compatibility

#include <stdio.h>    // Function prototype

int vsprintf(
    char       *buf,  // Formatted output goes to this buffer
    const char *fmt,  // Format string
    va_list    argp); // Pointer to list of arguments
```

Description

Formats the values of the variables identified by *argp* according to the format specification *fmt*, and stores the formatted text in the `char` array identified by *buf*. Consult the reference entry for the `printf` function for information on specifying the format string. You can use `_vsprintf` to prepare formatted text in a null-terminated string for eventual display with some other function, perhaps a graphics text display function.

Returns

When the function completes successfully, the return value is the number of characters written to *buf*, not counting the terminating `NULL` character.

Sample Call

```
// See example for vfprintf. Call in a similar manner.
```

See Also

`printf`, `vfprintf`, `_vsnprintf`

23

Low-Level I/O

Chapter 22, "Stream I/O," covers *buffered* stream I/O, and this chapter describes a number of functions that perform *unbuffered* and *unformatted* I/O. These low-level I/O functions originated in UNIX and primarily are offered for compatibility with UNIX. Because the ANSI Standard C library does not include these functions, Microsoft Visual C++ adds a leading underscore to each of the names; however, if you need full compatibility with the UNIX low-level I/O functions, you can continue to call these functions by their names without the underscore prefix.

Basics of Low-Level I/O

Low-level I/O refers to unformatted and unbuffered input and output (I/O) operations. Because there is no buffering, each read or write operation in low-level I/O results in disk access. Because disk accesses are time-consuming, you normally would use low-level I/O functions to read or write large blocks of data at a time.

Low-level I/O functions have no formatting capability; therefore, they are not suitable for I/O that involves reading variables from text files and converting elements from a string to an internal representation. Similarly, writing a variable to a text file requires the reverse operation of converting the binary representation into a text string.

However, the low-level I/O functions are useful for reading and writing binary data which do not require any formatting.

Text and Binary Modes

Although low-level I/O functions provide no formatting capability, they still enable you to select whether a file is treated as a text file or a binary file. As described in Chapter 22, the contents of a binary file are not interpreted in any way. However, when you open the same file as a text file, the following translations occur.

- When you're reading from the file, each carriage return-linefeed (CR-LF) pair is converted to a newline (`\n`) character (a newline character is the same as a linefeed). Also a Ctrl+Z is treated as an end-of-file marker.
- When you're writing to the file, each newline character expands to a CR-LF pair.

You can control the mode when opening a file by specifying the flags `_O_TEXT` and `_O_BINARY` in the second argument to the `_open` function. (See the reference entry for `_open` later in this chapter.)

Leading Underscore in Names of Nonstandard Functions

Microsoft Visual C++ adds an underscore prefix to many functions (such as `_open`, `_read`, `_write`) in keeping with ANSI Standard C's naming conventions for nonstandard functions. In many other C compilers (including earlier versions of Microsoft C compilers) as well as in UNIX and POSIX some of these functions are available with names that do not have the leading underscores. Note that you can use the names without an underscore prefix in Microsoft Visual C++ as well. The names without underscores are in a library named oldnames.lib, which the linker searches by default.

Buffering by the Operating System

Although the low-level I/O functions do not themselves have buffering, the operating system (MS-DOS or Windows) usually uses a buffer to avoid excessive disk accesses. This means that even with unbuffered low-level I/O, you could not write data directly to the disk. Sometimes, however, you may want the contents of a file updated as soon as you write new data to the file. In Microsoft Visual C++, you can force a write operation directly to the file by calling the `_commit` function.

File Handle

Like the stream I/O functions described in Chapter 22, low-level I/O functions maintain information on each open file in internal data structures. This information includes the read-write position in the file and the read-write operations allowed on the file. Like the FILE pointer used to identify streams, the low-level I/O functions use a unique integer, called a *file handle*, to identify each open file. The I/O library includes the `_fileno` function (described in Chapter 22), which you use to get a handle for an open stream, and the `_fdopen` function (also described in Chapter 22) to associate a stream with a file open for low-level I/O.

As explained in Chapter 22, there are five open streams (`stdin`, `stdout`, `stderr`, `_stdaux`, and `_stdprn`) that are always available to your program. Each of these streams have the following preassigned handles as well.

`stdin`	0
`stdout`	1
`stderr`	2
`_stdaux`	3
`_stdprn`	4

You can use these handles without explicitly opening any files.

Maximum Number of File Handles

The `FILES` statement in the config.sys file controls the total number of files that can be open at one time in an MS-DOS system. Even when this number is large enough, the C I/O library, by default, allows a maximum of 20 open files. This limit is large enough for most applications, but if your application needs more open files, you can change the limit by editing a line in a file named crt0dat.asm, located in the SOURCE\STARTUP\DOS subdirectory of the directory in which you have Microsoft Visual C++ installed. (For example, if you installed in C:\MSVC, the full pathname of this file is C:\MSVC\SOURCE\STARTUP\DOS\CRT0DAT.ASM.) In the crt0dat.asm file, you'll find the following line.

```
_NFILE_ =       20              ; Maximum number of file handles
```

By changing 20 to a higher value, you can alter the upper limit on the number of open files. To use the modified start-up file, you must run an MS-DOS batch file named cstartup.bat, located in the SOURCE\STARTUP subdirectory (one level above where the crt0dat.asm file is located). The readme.txt file in that same directory has further information on altering the start-up module of C programs.

Basic Low-Level I/O Tasks

Table 23.1 shows an alphabetic list of the low-level I/O functions and gives you a quick overview of these functions. Table 23.2 organizes these functions by the tasks they perform. Some of these tasks are illustrated by short sample programs in the following discussions. For more information on a function, consult the reference entry for that function in the latter part of this chapter.

Table 23.1. Alphabetic listing of stream I/O functions.

Function	Description
`_close`	Closes an open file identified by a handle.
`_commit`	Writes directly to the disk file, bypassing any buffering in the operating system.
`_creat`	Creates and opens a new file.
`_dup`	Creates a second handle for an existing one associated with a file.
`_dup2`	Assigns a specified handle to a file that's already open and has an associated handle.
`_eof`	Returns 1 if the current position in file is at end-of-file.
`_lseek`	Sets the current position of an open file to a specified offset.
`_open`	Opens a file for unbuffered, unformatted I/O.
`_read`	Reads a specified number of bytes from a file.
`_sopen`	Opens a file for shared I/O.
`_tell`	Returns the current position in an open file.
`_write`	Writes a specified number of bytes to a file.

Table 23.2. Basic low-level I/O tasks.

Task	Functions
Open, create, and close files	`_close`, `_creat`, `_open`, `_sopen`
Read and write binary data	`_read`, `_write`
Get or set current position in file	`_lseek`, `_tell`
Force writing directly to a file	`_commit`
Check for end-of-file	`_eof`
Duplicate a handle	`_dup`, `_dup2`

Copying Files

One good example of the process of opening, reading, and writing files is to copy one file to another. If all you want to do is make a copy of a file regardless of the file's contents, low-level I/O functions are ideal for this purpose.

Listing 23.1 shows the file cpfile.c, which accomplishes this task. As you can see from the listing, the program opens both the source and destination files in binary mode and with appropriate read-write access. The only flag worthy of note is the `_O_TRUNC` flag. If you do not use the `_O_TRUNC` flag, writing a small amount of data (say, 2K) into a larger-sized existing file (6K, for instance) changes only the first 2K of that file; the file will retain its original larger size (6K). However, by using the `_O_TRUNC` flag, you can ensure that the file is truncated to zero before copying data into it.

The cpfile program uses a large buffer as the intermediary in the copy operation—it uses the `read` function to copy data from the source file into the buffer and then calls the `write` function to write the buffer to the destination file. In fact, the entire copy operation is accomplished by the following `while` loop:

```
//...
// This is where all the work is done (read from source file
// and write to destination, until done).

    while (numread = _read(h_src, buf, bufsize))
        _write(h_dst, buf, numread);
```

Listing 23.1. A program that makes a copy of a file.

```
//------------------------------------------------------------
//  File: cpfile.c
//
//  Copies one file to another (opens the source file in
//  binary mode and copies it to a destination without
//  interpretation or translation).
//------------------------------------------------------------
#include <stdio.h>
#include <fcntl.h>
#include <sys\types.h>
#include <sys\stat.h>
#include <io.h>
#include <malloc.h>
#include <process.h>

// Attempt to use a buffer size of 60K:

#define NBYTES (60L * 1024L)

//------------------------------------------------------------
//  m a i n

int main(void)
{
    char *buf = NULL;
    char filename[80];
    int h_src, h_dst;
    unsigned int numread;
    size_t bufsize = NBYTES;

// Allocate the buffer. Start with a size of NBYTES.
// If allocation fails, try half the previous buffer
// size. Continue as long as bufsize exceeds 512 bytes.

    while (bufsize > 512 &&
          (buf = malloc(bufsize)) == NULL)
    {
        bufsize /= 2;
    }

// If still unable to allocate memory, exit program:
```

```
    if(buf == NULL)
    {
        printf("Failed to allocate %d bytes for buffer\n",
                bufsize);
        exit(1);
    }

    printf("bufsize used = %u\n", bufsize);

// Get name of source file from user and open it
// in binary read-only mode:

    printf("Source file:");
    gets(filename);

    if((h_src = open(filename, _O_RDONLY ¦ _O_BINARY)) == -1)
    {
        printf("Cannot open source file: %s\n", filename);
        exit(1);
    }

// Get name of source file from user and open it
// in binary write-only mode (create it, if necessary):

    printf("Destination file:");
    gets(filename);

    if((h_dst = open(filename, _O_CREAT ¦ _O_WRONLY ¦
                    _O_TRUNC ¦ _O_BINARY, S_IWRITE )) == -1)
    {
        printf("Cannot open destination file: %s\n", filename);
        exit(1);
    }

// This is where all the work is done (read from source file
// and write to destination, until done):

    while (numread = read(h_src, buf, bufsize))
        write(h_dst, buf, numread);

// Close both files
```

continues

Listing 23.1. continued

```
    close(h_src);
    close(h_dst);

    return(0);
}
```

Redirecting *stdout* Using *_dup* and *_dup2*

As another example of the low-level I/O functions, consider the use of the `_dup` and `_dup2` functions to create a duplicate handle for `stdout` and redirect the standard output stream to a file. Suppose you have a function, named `disp_result`, that displays the results of your program by writing to the `stdout` stream. Later on you decide to add a feature to enable the user to request that the output be redirected to a file instead of the console. (Yes, the user could do this from the DOS command line by using the redirection capability offered by the > operator. Ignore that mechanism for now.)

Using `_dup` and `_dup2`, you can provide the redirection capability with minimal effort by assigning a different file handle to `stdout`. The existing `disp_result` function would then write output to the file instead of the console. Listing 23.2 shows a sample program that illustrates the idea.

Listing 23.2. Redirecting `stdout` using `_dup` and `_dup2`.

```
//-------------------------------------------------------------
//  File: redirect.c
//
//  Illustrates use of _dup and _dup2 to redirect stdout to
//  another file
//-------------------------------------------------------------
#include <stdio.h>
#include <io.h>
#include <fcntl.h>
#include <process.h>

void disp_result(void);
//-------------------------------------------------------------
//  m a i n
```

```
void main(int argc, char **argv)
{
    int handle, dup_handle;

    if(argc < 2)
    {
        printf("Usage: %s <filename> (redirected output file)\n",
                   argv[0]);
        exit(1);
    }

// Call disp_result; output appears in stdout:
    disp_result();

// Open file to which stdout is redirected:
    if((handle = _open(argv[1], O_WRONLY |
                                   O_TEXT | O_CREAT)) == -1)
    {
        perror("_open");
        exit(1);
    }

// Duplicate the handle corresponding to stdout (1):
    if((dup_handle = dup(1)) == -1)
    {
        perror("_dup");
        exit(1);
    }

// Redirect stdout to file:
    if(dup2(handle, 1) == -1)
    {
        perror("_dup2");
        exit(1);
    }

// Call disp_result; output appears in file:
    disp_result();
    fflush(stdout);

// Other processing...
//...
```

continues

Listing 23.2. continued

```
    _close(handle);

// Reset stdout to console:
    dup2(dup_handle, 1);

    printf("Enter the command: TYPE %s\nto see result\n",
           argv[1]);

}
//-----------------------------------------------------------------
//  d i s p _ r e s u l t
//
//  Displays results on stdout

void disp_result(void)
{
    int i;
    double t;

    printf("=========================\n");
    printf("   R E S U L T S\n");
    printf("=========================\n");
    printf("Time\t\tPosition\n");

// Display some made-up values...
    for(i = 0; i < 5; i++)
    {
        t = (double)i / 10.0;
        printf("%.2f\t\t%.2f\n", t, 10.0*t*t);
    }
    printf("=========================\n");
}
```

_close

MSC6	MSC7	VC++	QC2.5	QC-WIN	TC2	TC++	BC++2	BC++3	ANSI	POSIX	UNIX V	DOS	QWIN	WIN	WINDLL
X	X	X	X	X	X	X	X	X		X	X	X	X	X	X

See note earlier in this chapter about the leading underscore in this function's name.

Summary

```
#include <io.h>

int _close(int handle); // Handle of file to be closed
```

Description

Closes the open file identified by `handle`.

Returns

0	The file successfully closed.
–1	In case of error. Also sets `errno` to `EBADF` indicating a bad file handle.

Sample Call

```
_close(handle);
```

See Also

`_open`

_commit

MSC6	MSC7	VC++	QC2.5	QC-WIN	TC2	TC++	BC++2	BC++3	ANSI	POSIX	UNIX V	DOS	QWIN	WIN	WINDLL
	X	X		X								X	X	X	X

See note earlier in this chapter about the leading underscore in this function's name.

Summary

```
#include <io.h>

int _commit(int handle); // File to be forcibly written to disk
```

Description

Flushes any operating system assigned buffers for the file identified by `handle` to the disk.

Returns

0	The file successfully closed.
–1	In case of error. Also sets `errno` to `EBADF` indicating a bad file handle.

Sample Call

```
// Assume fhandle is a valid file handle.
_commit(fhandle);
```

See Also

`_close`, `_open`, `_read`, `_write`

_creat

MSC6	MSC7	VC++	QC2.5	QC-WIN	TC2	TC++	BC++2	BC++3	ANSI	POSIX	UNIX V	DOS	QWIN	WIN	WINDLL
x	x	x	x	x	x	x	x	x	x	x	x	x	x	x	x

See note earlier in this chapter about the leading underscore in this function's name

Summary

```
#include <sys\types.h>     // Required by <sys\stat.h>
#include <sys\stat.h>      // Defines permission constants (_SI_...)

#include <io.h>            // For function prototype

int _creat(
    const char *pathname, // Name of file to be created
    int         rwmode);  // Read-write permission settings
```

Description

Creates a new file with specified name or truncates an existing file to zero length. The creat function opens the file for write access.

If a new file is created, the *rwmode* argument specifies the read-write permission settings associated with the file. The *rwmode* argument can be one of the following:

S_IWRITE	Allow both read and write operations (because MS-DOS does not allow write-only files).
S_IREAD	File is read only.
S_IREAD ¦ _S_IWRITE	Allow both read and write operations.

Returns

When the function completes successfully, the return value is the file handle.

–1	Indicates an error. Also sets errno to one of the following:
EACCES	Attempted to open existing directory or read-only file.
EMFILE	Too many open files.
ENOENT	Invalid pathname.

Sample Call

```
int h_catalog;
//...
h_catalog = _creat("catalog.dat", _S_IREAD ¦ _S_IWRITE);
```

See Also

_close, _open

_dup

MSC6	MSC7	VC++	QC2.5	QC-WIN	TC2	TC++	BC++2	BC++3	ANSI	POSIX	UNIX V	DOS	QWIN	WIN	WINDLL
x	x	x	x	x	x	x	x	x		x	x	x	x	x	x

See note earlier in this chapter about the leading underscore in this function's name.

Note: `_dup` and `_dup2` cannot be used with `_fileno` in QuickWin applications with the `stdin`, `stdout`, or `stderr` streams.

Summary

```
#include <io.h>

int _dup(int handle); // Return another handle for this file
```

Description

Creates a second handle for the open file identified by *handle*. In a QuickWin program (see the quick.doc text file on the companion disk), you cannot use `_dup` on `stdin`, `stdout`, and `stderr`.

Returns

When the function completes successfully, the return value is the new handle.

–1 Indicates an error. Also sets `errno` to either `EMFILE` if no more files can be opened or to `EBADF` if the handle argument is invalid.

Sample Call

```
    int new_stdout;
// Create another handle for stdout.
    if((new_stdout = _dup(1)) == -1) perror("_dup");
```

See Also

_dup2

_dup2

MSC6	MSC7	VC++	QC2.5	QC-WIN	TC2	TC++	BC++2	BC++3	ANSI	POSIX	UNIX V	DOS	QWIN	WIN	WINDLL
x	x	x	x	x	x	x	x	x		x	x	x	x	x	x

See note earlier in this chapter about the leading underscore in this function's name.

Note: `_dup` and `_dup2` cannot be used in QuickWin applications with the `stdin`, `stdout`, or `stderr` streams.

Summary

```
#include <io.h>
```

```
int _dup2(
    int handle1,   // Handle of an open file
    int handle2); // Associate this handle with same file
```

Description

Forces a second handle, `handle2`, to refer to the open file identified by `handle1`. In UNIX programs, `_dup2` is used to redirect standard input and output, `stdin` and `stdout`. Note, however, that in a QuickWin program (see the quick.doc text file on the companion disk), you cannot use `_dup2` on `stdin`, `stdout`, and `stderr`.

Returns

0	The new handle now identifies the open file.
–1	Indicates an error and sets `errno` to either `EMFILE` if no more files can be opened or to `EBADF` if *`handle1`* is invalid.

Sample Call

```
    int new_stdout;
// Assume new_stdout refers to a open file.
// Assign this handle to stdout by calling _dup2:
    if(_dup2(new_stdout,1) == -1) perror("_dup2");
```

See Also

`_dup2`

_eof

MSC6	MSC7	VC++	QC2.5	QC-WIN	TC2	TC++	BC++2	BC++3	ANSI	POSIX	UNIX V	DOS	QWIN	WIN	WINDLL
X	X	X	X	X	X	X	X	X				X	X	X	X

See note earlier in this chapter about the leading underscore in this function's name.

Summary

```
#include <io.h>

int _eof(int handle); // Is this file at end-of-file?
```

Description

Checks if the current position in the specified file is at end-of-file.

Returns

0	The current position in the file is not at end-of-file.
1	The current position in the file is at end-of-file.
–1	Indicates an error. Also sets `errno` to `EBADF` to indicate an invalid *`handle`* argument.

Sample Call

```
// Assume fhandle refers to an open file's handle.
// Read file until it ends:
    while( !eof(fhandle))
    {
// Read data from file....
//...
    }
```

_lseek

MSC6	MSC7	VC++	QC2.5	QC-WIN	TC2	TC++	BC++2	BC++3	ANSI	POSIX	UNIX V	DOS	QWIN	WIN	WINDLL
x	x	x	x	x	x	x	x	x		x	x	x	x	x	x

See note earlier in this chapter about the leading underscore in this function's name.

Summary

```
#include <stdio.h> // Definition of SEEK_ constants
#include <io.h>    // For function prototype

long _lseek(
    int  handle,   // Set current position in this file
    long offset,   //   to this offset (in number of bytes)
    int  origin);  //   from this reference position (SEEK_SET,
                   //   SEEK_CUR, or SEEK_END).
```

Description

Sets the current position in a file to a specified `offset` (in bytes) from a reference position identified by the `origin` argument, which can be one of the following:

```
SEEK_SET     Beginning of file.
SEEK_CUR     Current position in file.
SEEK_END     End of file.
```

Returns

When the function completes successfully, the return value is the offset, in bytes, of the new position from the beginning of the file.

–1 Indicates an error. Also sets `errno` to `EBADF` or `EINVAL` to indicate a bad file handle or invalid combination of offset and origin, respectively.

Sample Call

```
    int fh;
    long newpos;
// Assume fh refers to an open file.
```

```
// Skip the first 128 bytes (say, a header):
    newpos = _lseek(fh, 128L, SEEK_SET);
```

See Also

`_tell`

_open

MSC6	MSC7	VC++	QC2.5	QC-WIN	TC2	TC++	BC++2	BC++3	ANSI	POSIX	UNIX V	DOS	QWIN	WIN	WINDLL
X	X	X	X	X	X	X	X	X		X	X	X	X	X	X

See note earlier in this chapter about the leading underscore in this function's name.

Summary

```
#include <sys\types.h>    // Required by <sys\stat.h>
#include <sys\stat.h>     // Defines permission constants (_SI_...)
#include <fcntl.h>        // Defines the open modes (_O_...)

#include <io.h>           // For function prototype

int _open(
    const char *pathname,       // Name of file to be opened
    int         opmode,         // Operations allowed on the file
    ...);                       // Read-write permission
```

Description

Opens the file specified by `pathname` and prepares the file for read-write operations as indicated by the `opmode` argument, which can be bitwise-OR of the following constants:

`_O_APPEND` Always write at the end of the file.

`_O_BINARY` Open in binary or untranslated mode (see the tutorial in Chapter 22 for an explanation of *translation mode*).

`_O_CREAT` Create a new file and open it for writing.

`_O_EXCL` When specified with `_O_CREAT`, return an error value if file already exists.

`_O_RDONLY` Open for reading only.

`_O_RDWR` Open for both reading and writing.

`_O_TEXT` Open in text or translated mode. This is the same text mode used with `fopen`. (See the tutorial in Chapter 22 for an explanation of *translation mode*).

`_O_TRUNC` Open an existing file and truncate it to zero length, thus destroying the file's current contents.

`_O_WRONLY` Open for writing only.

If you're creating a new file by setting *opmode* to `_O_CREAT`, you should provide a third argument indicating the read-write permission settings associated with the file. This argument can be one of the following:

`_S_IWRITE` Allow both read and write operations (because MS-DOS does not allow write-only files).

`_S_IREAD` File is read-only.

`_S_IREAD ¦ _S_IWRITE` Allow both read and write operations.

Returns

When the function completes successfully, the return value is the file handle.

–1 Indicates an error. Also sets `errno` to one of the following:

`EACCES` Attempt to open a directory or a file in a disallowed mode.

`EEXIST` File already exists but the opmode is `_O_CREAT ¦ _O_EXCL`.

`EINVAL` Invalid argument to `_open`.

`EMFILE` Too many open files.

`ENOENT` Invalid pathname.

Sample Call

```
int h_catalog;
//...
h_catalog = _open("catalog.dat", _O_CREAT, _S_IREAD ¦ _S_IWRITE);
```

See Also

`_close`, `_creat`

_read

MSC6	MSC7	VC++	QC2.5	QC-WIN	TC2	TC++	BC++2	BC++3	ANSI	POSIX	UNIX V	DOS	QWIN	WIN	WINDLL
X	X	X	X	X	X	X	X	X		X	X	X	X	X	X

See note earlier in this chapter about the leading underscore in this function's name.

Summary

```
#include <io.h>

int _read(
    int          handle, // Read from this open file
    void         *buf,   //   into this buffer
    unsigned int nbytes);// Read this many bytes
```

Description

Reads a specified number of bytes from a file into a buffer. Reading begins at the current position within the file and the position is incremented as the bytes are read.

Returns

When the function completes successfully, the return value is the actual number of bytes read from the file.

–1 Indicates an error. Also sets `errno` to `EBADF` to indicate a bad file handle.

Sample Call

```
    char buf[1024];
    int fh;
// Assume fh is the handle of a file opened for reading.
    if(_read(fh, buf, 1024) == -1) perror("_read");
```

See Also

`_write`

_sopen

MSC6	MSC7	VC++	QC2.5	QC-WIN	TC2	TC++	BC++2	BC++3	ANSI	POSIX	UNIX V	DO	QWIN	WIN	WINDLL
X	X	X	X	X	X	X	X	X			X	X	X	X	X

See note earlier in this chapter about the leading underscore in this function's name.

Summary

```
#include <sys\types.h> // Required by <sys\stat.h>
#include <sys\stat.h>  // Defines permission constants (_SI_...)
#include <fcntl.h>     // Defines the open modes (_O_...)

#include <io.h>        // For function prototype

int _sopen(
    const char *pathname,// Name of file to be opened
    int        opmode,   // Operations allowed on the file
    int        shmode,   // Type of sharing allowed
    ...);                // Read-write permission
```

Description

Opens a file just as _open does, except that with _sopen you can specify a file-sharing mode through the *shmode* argument, which can be one of the following:

_SH_COMPAT	No other process can access the file (called *compatibility mode* because this is how MS-DOS normally operates).
_SH_DENYRW	Only one process can read from and write to file.
_SH_DENYWR	Other processes can read from but cannot write to file.
_SH_DENYRD	Other processes can write to but cannot read from file.
_SH_DENYNO	Other processes can access file for both reading and writing.

Consult the reference entry for _open for a description of the other arguments.

Note that file sharing is possible only in MS-DOS version 3.0 or higher, and only when share.exe (share.com for some versions of DOS) is installed. If SHARE is not installed, _sopen ignores the *shmode* argument.

Returns

When the function completes successfully, the return value is the file handle.

–1 Indicates an error. Also, sets errno as explained in the description of the _open function.

Sample Call

```
int fh;
if((fh = _sopen("c:\\config.sys", _O_RDONLY, _SH_DENYRW)) == -1)
    perror("_sopen");
```

See Also

_open

_tell

MSC6	MSC7	VC++	QC2.5	QC-WIN	TC2	TC++	BC++2	BC++3	ANSI	POSIX	UNIX V	DOS	QWIN	WIN	WINDLL
X	X	X	X	X	X	X	X	X				X	X	X	X

See note earlier in this chapter about the leading underscore in this function's name.

Summary

```
#include <io.h>

long _tell(int handle); // Get current position of this file
```

Description

Retrieves the current position in an open file identified by *handle*.

Returns

When the function completes successfully, the return value is the offset of the current position in number of bytes from the beginning of the file.

–1 Indicates an error. Also sets `errno` to `EBADF` to indicate an invalid file handle.

Sample Call

```
    long curpos;
// Assume fh is the handle of an open file.
    curpos = _tell(fh);
```

See Also

`_lseek`

_write

MSC6	MSC7	VC++	QC2.5	QC-WIN	TC2	TC++	BC++2	BC++3	ANSI	POSIX	UNIX V	DOS	QWIN	WIN	WINDLL
X	X	X	X	X	X	X	X	X		X	X	X	X	X	X

See note earlier in this chapter about the leading underscore in this function's name.

Summary

```
#include <io.h>

int _write(
    int          handle, // Write to this open file
    void         *buf,   //   from this buffer
    unsigned int nbytes);// Write this many bytes
```

Description

Writes a specified number of bytes from a buffer into a file.

Returns

When the function completes successfully, the return value is the actual number of bytes written to the file.

–1 Indicates an error. Also sets `errno` to `EBADF` to indicate a bad file handle or to `ENOSPC` to indicate that the disk is full.

Sample Call

```
    char buf[1024];
    int fh;
// Assume fh is the handle of a file opened for writing.
    if(_write(fh, buf, 1024) == -1) perror("_write");
```

See Also

`_read`

24

Console and Port I/O

The I/O functions described in this chapter are meant for direct access to the keyboard, the screen, and the I/O ports in an Industry Standard Architecture (ISA) PC running MS-DOS or Windows. Because these I/O functions are not a part of the ANSI Standard C library, Microsoft Visual C++ adds a leading underscore to the names—in earlier versions of Microsoft C compilers, these function names do not include the underscore prefix. Note that the old function names are still available in Microsoft Visual C++.

> Under DOS, the keyboard and the display screen (the monitor) are together called the *console*.

Basics of Console and Port I/O

Various peripheral devices (such as the keyboard, the monitor, or the serial and parallel ports) in a PC are controlled by reading from or writing to 8- and 16-bit registers known as *I/O ports.* These I/O ports are similar to memory locations, but are physically separate from conventional memory and located in a separate I/O address space. The Microsoft Visual C++ library functions `_inp` and `_outp` (and `_inpw` and `_outw`) enable you to read from and write to the I/O ports using the assembly language instructions `IN` and `OUT`.

Bang! You're dead, Jim!

You must be very, very careful when writing to output ports. The output ports are one case where it's possible to do real damage to the system, and even possibly cause hardware failure.

Always be absolutely sure of the port you're writing to, and what constitutes valid data for that port.

A number of other console I/O functions such as `_getch` and `_putch` are meant for reading keystrokes from the keyboard and sending characters to the display screen. Using these functions is equivalent to accessing the I/O capabilities of the Basic Input and Output System (BIOS) built into each PC. (BIOS functions are described in Chapter 32, "DOS and BIOS Calls.") There is no buffering of any sort, and you do not have to open or close anything before calling the console I/O functions.

Not in Windows...

Because of the way Windows interfaces with hardware, the console I/O functions don't work under Windows. Don't despair—Microsoft has provided Windows-specific functions that allow for the same functionality.

Resist the urge to 'do an end run around Windows' when it comes to interfacing with the hardware. Creating a program that does things to the system's hardware while Windows is running can create some really strange and difficult problems—which, of course, usually won't appear until the software has been released!

Console and Port I/O Tasks

Table 24.1 shows an alphabetic list of the console and port I/O functions and gives you a quick overview of these functions. Table 24.2 organizes these functions by the tasks they perform. Some of these functions are illustrated by the sample program in the following sections. For more information on any function in Table 24.2, consult the reference entry for that function in the reference section that follows.

Table 24.1. Alphabetic listing of stream I/O functions.

Function	Description
`_cgets`	Reads a line of text (up to a carriage return-linefeed) from the console.
`_cprintf`	Writes formatted output to console.
`_cputs`	Writes a text string to the console.
`_cscanf`	Reads formatted input from the console.
`_getch`	Reads a character from the console without echoing (returns as soon as a single character is entered).
`_getche`	Reads a character from the console and echoes it (displays it on the screen).
`_inp`	Reads a byte from an I/O port.
`_inpw`	Reads a word (two contiguous bytes) from an I/O port.
`_kbhit`	Returns a nonzero value if any keystroke is waiting to be read.
`_outp`	Writes a byte to an I/O port.
`_outpw`	Writes a word (two contiguous bytes) to an I/O port.
`_putch`	Writes a single character to the console.
`_ungetch`	Stores a character back in the console so that the next call to `_getch` or `_getche` reads that character.

Table 24.2. Basic console and port I/O tasks.

Task	Functions
Read and write a single character	`_getch`, `_getche`, `_putch`
Read from and write to an I/O port	`_inp`, `_inpw`, `_outp`, `_outpw`
Check if a keystroke is waiting to be read	`_kbhit`
Read and write a string	`_cgets`, `_cputs`
Formatted input and output	`_cprintf`, `_cscanf`
Push a character back to the console	`_ungetch`

Producing a Tone with *inp* and *outp*

In Intel 80x86-based Industry Standard Architecture (ISA) PCs, you can generate a tone by programming the I/O port address 0x61 and using the system timer to control the speaker. Essentially, the steps involved are as follows:

1. Set up the timer as an oscillator by sending the data byte 0xB6 to the timer at the I/O port address 0x43.
2. Compute the ratio of the timer's clock frequency (1.19 MHz) and the frequency of the tone you want.
3. Write the ratio obtained in Step 2 to I/O port address 0x42.
4. Enable the PC's speaker under the control of the timer by reading from the port 0x61 and writing the value back with the first two bits set to 1 (use a bitwise-OR with 3).

The speaker sounds the specified tone until you disable it. To disable the speaker as well as the timer, read from port 0x61 again and set the bits 0 and 1 to zero.

Listing 24.1 shows the file mktone.c, which implements the tone-generation process described in these steps. It illustrates the use of the `_inp` and `_outp` functions to read from and write to I/O ports. Also, the `_cprintf` and `_cgets` functions are used for console I/O.

Listing 24.1. mktone.c. A program that sounds a note by using port I/O functions.

```
//-----------------------------------------------------------
//  File: mktone.c
//
//  Generates a tone of specified frequency by controlling
//  the PC's speaker through a timer
//-----------------------------------------------------------
#include <conio.h>
#include <stdio.h>
#include <process.h>
#include <stdlib.h>

#define FREQUENCY  1193180L // Timer clock freq = 1.19 MHz
#define COUNT8253  0x42     // 8253 timer — count.
#define MODE_SET   0x43     // 8253 timer control port.
#define OSCILLATE  0xb6     // Make timer work as oscillator.
#define PORT8255   0x61     // 8255 PPI output port address.
#define SPKRON     3        // Bit 0 set = control speaker
                            //             through the timer.
                            // Bit 1 turns speaker on/off.
//-----------------------------------------------------------
void main(int argc, char **argv)
{
    unsigned freq, status, ratio, lobyte, hibyte;
    char     junk[10] = {8}; // Length is stored in first two bytes...

    if(argc < 2)
    {
        printf("Usage: %s <frequency> in Hz.\n", argv[0]);
        exit(1);
    }
    freq = atoi(argv[1]);

// Read and save current status of the 8255 chip. (Some
// systems do not use the 8255, but the same port number
// controls the timer and the speaker.)

    status = _inp(PORT8255);
```

continues

Listing 24.1. continued

```
// Make timer operate as an oscillator at a set frequency:
    _outp(MODE_SET, OSCILLATE);

    ratio = (unsigned)(FREQUENCY/freq);

    lobyte = ratio & 0xff;           // low byte of ratio
    _outp(COUNT8253, lobyte);

    hibyte = (ratio >> 8) & 0xff;    // high byte of ratio
    _outp(COUNT8253, hibyte);

// Now turn speaker on to generate the tone:
    _outp(PORT8255, (status | SPKRON));

// Ask user to indicate when to stop the tone:
    _cprintf("\nHit return to stop tone:");
    _cgets(junk);

// To turn speaker off, get the current status:
    status = _inp(PORT8255);

// Then reset the bits that turns speaker on/off.

// (NOTE: If you do not turn speaker off and exit
//  the program with a CTRL-C, the speaker will
//  continue generating the tone even after the
//  program exits.)

    _outp(PORT8255, (status & ~SPKRON));
}
```

Leading Underscore in Names of Nonstandard Functions

Microsoft Visual C++ adds an underscore prefix to many functions (such as `_getch`, `_kbhit`, `_inp`) in keeping with ANSI Standard C's naming conventions for nonstandard functions. In the other C compilers (including earlier versions of the Microsoft C compiler) some of these functions are available with names that do not have the leading underscores. Note that you can continue to use the names without underscore prefixes in Microsoft Visual C++ as well. The functions with names without underscore prefixes are in a library named oldnames.lib, which the linker searches by default.

_cgets

MSC6	MSC7	VC++	QC2.5	QC-WIN	TC2	TC++	BC++2	BC++3	ANSI	POSIX	UNIX V	DOS	QWIN	WIN	WINDLL
X	X	X	X	X	X	X	X	X				X			

See note earlier in this chapter about the leading underscore in this function's name.

Summary

```
#include <conio.h>

char *_cgets(char *buf); // Store characters in buf
```

Description

Reads a text string from the keyboard and stores the characters in the `char` array *`buf`* *starting at the third location*; that is, at *`buf`*`[2]`. The first character must contain the maximum number of characters to be read from the keyboard. The `_cgets` function reads up to the maximum number of characters or until a newline character is reached. When reading ends, `_cgets` terminates the string with a null character and stores the actual length of the string in the second character of the buffer (*`buf`*`[1]`).

Returns

When the function completes successfully, the return value is a pointer to the location *`buf`*`[2]`, which is the beginning of the string.

Sample Call

```
    char line[82], *input;
// Set first character to maximum number of characters that
// can be read by _cgets:
    line[0] = 80;
    input = _cgets(line);
```

See Also

`_getch`, `_getche`

_cprintf

MSC6	MSC7	VC++	QC2.5	QC-WIN	TC2	TC++	BC++2	BC++3	ANSI	POSIX	UNIX V	DOS	QWIN	WIN	WINDLL
X	X	X	X	X	X	X	X	X				X			

Summary

```
#include <conio.h>

int _cprintf(
    const char *fmt, // Format string
    ...);            // Variables being printed to console
```

Description

Formats zero or more variables according to the format specification *fmt* and writes the characters to the display screen. Consult the reference entry for the `printf` function in Chapter 22, "Stream I/O," for more information on specifying the format string.

Returns

When the function completes successfully, the return value is the number of characters written to the display screen.

Sample Call

```
char *fname = "irimage.raw";
long fsize = 122978;
cprintf("Generating file %s of size %ld bytes\n", fname, fsize);
```

See Also

`printf` (Chapter 22)

_cputs

MSC6	MSC7	VC++	QC2.5	QC-WIN	TC2	TC++	BC++2	BC++3	ANSI	POSIX	UNIX V	DOS	QWIN	WIN	WINDLL
X	X	X	X	X	X	X	X	X				X			

Summary

```
#include <conio.h>

int _cputs(const char *str); // String to display on screen
```

Description

Writes the null-terminated string *str* to the display screen. Does not write a newline character after the string.

Returns

0	The string was successfully written to the display screen.
Nonzero	Indicates an error.

Sample Call

```
_cputs("File changed. Save [Y]?");
```

See Also

_putch

_cscanf

MSC6	MSC7	VC++	QC2.5	QC-WIN	TC2	TC++	BC++2	BC++3	ANSI	POSIX	UNIX V	DOS	QWIN	WIN	WINDLL
X	X	X	X	X	X	X	X	X				X			

Summary

```
#include <conio.h>

int _cscanf(
    const char *fmt, // Read values according to this format
    ...);            // Addresses of zero or more variables
                     //   associated with values that are being read
```

Description

Reads characters directly from the keyboard and converts them into values of variables with addresses you provide in the variable-length list of arguments following the format string *fmt*. Consult the reference entry for the scanf function in Chapter 22 for more information on how the format string *fmt* controls the conversion from text into internal representations of the variables.

Returns

When the function completes successfully, the return value is the number of fields that were successfully read, converted, and stored in variables.

Sample Call

```
int hour, minute;
cscanf(" %d:%d", &hour, &minute);
```

See Also

scanf (Chapter 22)

_getch

MSC6	MSC7	VC++	QC2.5	QC-WIN	TC2	TC++	BC++2	BC++3	ANSI	POSIX	UNIX V	DOS	QWIN	WIN	WINDLL
X	X	X	X	X	X	X	X	X				X			

Summary

```
#include <conio.h>

int _getch(void);
```

Description

Reads a character from the keyboard without echoing it to the display screen. Does not read Ctrl+C. To read the function keys and arrow keys, you must call `_getch` twice. The first time it returns a zero or `0xe0`, and the second character is the actual key code.

Returns

When the function completes successfully, the return value is the character read from the keyboard.

Sample Call

```
_cputs("Press a key to continue...");
_getch(); // Ignore the character read from the keyboard
```

See Also

`_getche`

_getche

MSC6	MSC7	VC++	QC2.5	QC-WIN	TC2	TC++	BC++2	BC++3	ANSI	POSIX	UNIX V	DOS	QWIN	WIN	WINDLL
X	X	X	X	X	X	X	X	X				X			

Summary

```
#include <conio.h>

int _getche(void);
```

Description

Reads a character from the keyboard and echoes it to the display. Does not read Ctrl+C. To read the function keys and arrow keys, you have to call `_getche` twice. The first time it returns a zero or `0xe0`. The second call to `_getche` returns the actual key code.

Returns

When the function completes successfully, the return value is the character read from the keyboard.

Sample Call

```
    char buf[81];
    int i;
//...
```

```
// Read a line using _getche:
    for(i = 0; i < 80; i++)
    {
        if((buf[i] = _getche()) == '\r') break;
    }
```

See Also

_getch

_inp

MSC6	MSC7	VC++	QC2.5	QC-WIN	TC2	TC++	BC++2	BC++3	ANSI	POSIX	UNIX V	DOS	QWIN	WIN	WINDLL
X	X	X	X	X	X	X	X	X				X			

Borland compilers provide this function with the name `inportb`, but they define a macro named `inp` for compatibility with Microsoft compilers.

Summary

```
#include <conio.h>

int _inp(unsigned port); // Read byte from this I/O port
```

Description

Reads a byte from a specified I/O *port*. The port address can range from 0 to 65535, but most Industry Standard Architecture (ISA) peripherals decode only 10 bits of the I/O port address, thus limiting the port addresses from 0 to 1023. In hexadecimal notation, typical port numbers range from `0` to `0x3ff`, although there are some exceptions.

Returns

When the function completes successfully, the return value is the byte read from the specified I/O port.

Sample Call

```
int c;
c = _inp(0x3f8);
```

See Also

_inpw, _outp, _outpw

_inpw

MSC6	MSC7	VC++	QC2.5	QC-WIN	TC2	TC++	BC++2	BC++3	ANSI	POSIX	UNIX V	DOS	QWIN	WIN	WINDLL
X	X	X	X	X	X	X	X	X				X			

Borland compilers provide this function with the name inport or inportw, but the define a macro named inpw for compatibility with Microsoft compilers.

Summary

```
#include <conio.h>

unsigned _inpw(unsigned port); // Read 16-bit word from this port
```

Description

Reads a 16-bit word from the specified I/O *port* address. You can use _inpw to rea two adjacent byte-sized I/O port registers.

Returns

When the function completes successfully, the return value is the 16-bit value rea from the I/O port.

Sample Call

```
unsigned status;
status = _inpw(0x20);
```

See Also

_inp, _outp, _outpw

_kbhit

MSC6	MSC7	VC++	QC2.5	QC-WIN	TC2	TC++	BC++2	BC++3	ANSI	POSIX	UNIX V	DOS	QWIN	WIN	WINDLL
X	X	X	X	X	X	X	X	X				X			

Summary

```
#include <conio.h>

int _kbhit(void);
```

Description

Checks whether a keystroke is waiting to be read. Does not wait for a keypress. You must use _getch or _getche to read the waiting keystroke.

Returns

Nonzero	A keystroke is waiting to be read.
0	There is nothing to read.

Sample Call

```
// An event-processing loop that quits when user
// presses a key:
```

```
    while(!kbhit())
    {
// Continue processing events....
//...
    }
```

See Also

_getch, _getche

_outp

MSC6	MSC7	VC++	QC2.5	QC-WIN	TC2	TC++	BC++2	BC++3	ANSI	POSIX	UNIX V	DOS	QWIN	WIN	WINDLL
x	x	x	x	x	x	x	x	x				x			

Borland compilers provide this function with the name outportb, but they define a macro named outp for compatibility with Microsoft compilers.

Summary

```
#include <conio.h>

int _outp(
    unsigned port,    // Write to this I/O port address
    int      abyte); // Write least significant byte of this int
```

Description

Writes a byte (the least significant byte of the *abyte* argument) to the specified I/O *port* address.

Returns

When the function completes successfully, the return value is the byte sent to the I/O port.

Sample Call

```
_out(0x3f8, '!');
```

See Also

_inp, _inpw, _outpw

_outpw

MSC6	MSC7	VC++	QC2.5	QC-WIN	TC2	TC++	BC++2	BC++3	ANSI	POSIX	UNIX V	DOS	QWIN	WIN	WINDLL
x	x	x	x	x	x	x	x	x				x			

Borland compilers provide this function with the name outport or outportw, but they define a macro named outpw for compatibility with Microsoft compilers.

Summary

```
#include <conio.h>

unsigned _outpw(
    unsigned port,    // Write to this I/O port address
    unsigned aword);  // Write this 16-bit value to the port
```

Description

Writes a 16-bit value specified in *aword* to the I/O port address specified in *port*.

Returns

When the function completes successfully, the return value is the 16-bit word written to the port.

Sample Call

```
// Put EGA/VGA adapter in write mode 2.
_outpw(0x3ce, (2<<8) | 0x5);
```

See Also

_inp, _inpw, _outp

_putch

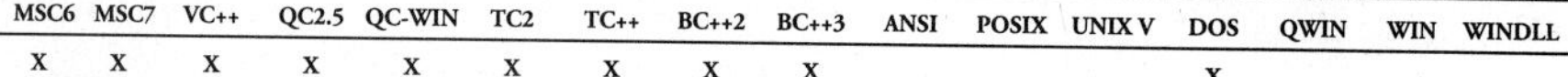

MSC6	MSC7	VC++	QC2.5	QC-WIN	TC2	TC++	BC++2	BC++3	ANSI	POSIX	UNIX V	DOS	QWIN	WIN	WINDLL
X	X	X	X	X	X	X	X	X				X			

Summary

```
#include <conio.h>

int _putch(int c); // Display this character
```

Description

Writes the character *c* to the display screen.

Returns

`c` The character is written to the display screen.

`EOF` A constant, defined in stdio.h, which indicates an error.

Sample Call

```
_putch('?');
```

See Also

_cprintf, _cputs

_ungetch

MSC6	MSC7	VC++	QC2.5	QC-WIN	TC2	TC++	BC++2	BC++3	ANSI	POSIX	UNIX V	DOS	QWIN	WIN	WINDLL
X	X	X	X	X	X	X	X	X				X			

Summary

```
#include <conio.h>

int _ungetch(int c); // Push the character back to the keyboard
```

Description

Pushes the character `c` (must not be equal to the constant `EOF`) to the keyboard's buffer so that it's the next character read by `_getch` or `_getche`. This function will fail if you call it more than once before the next read operation.

Returns

`c` The character `c` was successfully placed in the buffer.

`EOF` Indicates an error. This means you cannot push back `EOF`.

Sample Call

```
    int c;
//...
// Push back c....
    if(c != EOF) _ungetch(c);
```

See Also

`_getch`, `_getchec`

VII

Data Processing Functions

Character and Data Conversion

Character- and data-conversion functions enable you to test individual characters in various ways and convert the values of variables to and from their internal representation and human-readable text form.

You may have already seen several other data-conversion functions—the `sprintf` and `sscanf` functions (Chapter 22) can convert internal values to strings and strings back to internal values, respectively. The functions presented in this chapter are similar and, in some cases, more versatile than `sprintf` and `sscanf`. For example, `sprintf` cannot convert a string into an integer using an arbitrary radix, but `_itoa` can convert a value into various representations such as decimal, octal, and hexadecimal.

Basics of Character and Data Conversion

Of the character- and data-conversion functions, a large number (with names having an `is` prefix) are used to test *American Standard Code for Information Interchange*

(ASCII) character codes with values in the range 0 to 127. These functions determine whether a character is alphabetic, numeric, alphanumeric, or one of the other categories. Several other functions convert ASCII characters from lowercase to uppercase and vice versa.

Classifying Characters

Most C compilers, including Microsoft Visual C++, store the characteristics of each character in an array of unsigned characters that is accessed by using the character's ASCII code as an index. The characteristics indicate whether a character is uppercase, lowercase, a digit, a punctuation character, and so on. This information for each character is encoded in the bits of the array entry—each entry is a single byte—corresponding to that character. With this scheme, the character-classification functions can be implemented as simple macros that essentially involve accessing an element in an array and testing a bit or two. For instance, you could test whether a character is uppercase by writing this:

```
    if((c >= 'A') && (c <= 'Z')
    {
// Character is uppercase
    }
```

However, the `isupper` macro will be faster, because it tests a bit in a single byte.

The functions for classifying and testing characters are declared in the header file ctype.h.

Possible Side Effects of the Character Conversion Macros

Because the character-conversion functions are really macros, you have to be aware of the side effects of macros, especially when you use other function calls as an argument to a macro. Consider the `toupper` macro, defined in ctype.h as

```
#define toupper(_c) ((islower(_c)) ? _toupper(_c) : (_c))

#define _toupper(_c) ( (_c)-'a'+'A' )
```

Suppose you use the `toupper` macro to read a character from the console and convert it to uppercase, as follows:

```
int c;

c = toupper(_getch());
```

The side effects of macro substitution cause this code to behave differently than expected, because the C preprocessor substitutes the definitions of the macros and produces the following code:

```
c = ((islower(_getch())) ? ((_getch())-'a'+'A') : (_getch()));
```

If you look at this code carefully, you'll see that the `_getch()` function is called twice—in other words, you'll end up reading two characters instead of one. Microsoft Visual C++ includes nonmacro versions of `toupper` and `tolower` that do not suffer from these problems.

Converting Data

In a C program, numbers are internally represented in several forms, depending on the type of C variable in which the value is stored. When the numbers are displayed or printed, they have to be converted from the internal form into a textual representation. On the other hand, you also have to read text strings from the keyboard (or a file) and convert the string into an internal form, such as an integer or a floating-point value. The data-conversion functions, such as `atoi`, `atof`, `strtod`, `_itoa`, and `_fcvt`, provide the facilities for conversions between the internal form of a C variable and its textual representation.

But not in Windows

When writing applications that will be running under Windows, it's generally preferable to use the character-processing functions and macros provided with Windows—if Windows has an available function that performs the desired task. Some of the Windows string conversion functions include

`AnsiLower`	Converts string to lowercase
`AnsiLowerBuff`	Converts buffer string to lowercase
`AnsiNext`	Moves to the next character in a string

`AnsiPrev`	Moves to the previous character in a string
`AnsiToOem`	Translates a Windows string to an OEM string
`AnsiToOemBuff`	Translates a Windows string to an OEM buffer string
`AnsiUpper`	Converts a string to uppercase
`AnsiUpperBuff`	Converts a buffer string to uppercase
`IsCharAlpha`	Determines whether a character is alphabetic
`IsCharAlphaNumeric`	Determines whether a character is alphanumeric
`IsCharLower`	Determines whether a character is lowercase
`IsCharUpper`	Determines whether a character is uppercase
`lstrcat`	Appends one string to another
`lstrcmp`	Compares two character strings
`lstrcmpi`	Compares two character strings
`lstrcpy`	Copies a string to a buffer
`lstrcpyn`	Copies characters from a string to a buffer
`lstrlen`	Returns the length, in bytes, of a string
`OemToAnsi`	Translates an OEM string to a Windows string
`OemToAnsiBuff`	Translates an OEM string to a Windows buffer string

`ToAscii`	Translates virtual-key code to Windows character

Most of these functions are necessary because Windows doesn't use the same character set that DOS does.

Character- and Data-Conversion Tasks

Table 25.1 shows an alphabetic list of the character- and data-conversion functions and gives you a quick overview of these functions. Table 25.2 organizes these functions by the tasks they perform. Some of these tasks are illustrated by one or more sample programs in the following section. For more information on a function, consult the reference entry for that function in the reference section that follows.

Table 25.1. Alphabetic listing of character- and data-conversion functions.

Function	Description
`atof`	Converts a character string to a floating-point `double` value.
`atoi`	Converts a string to an integer.
`atol`	Converts a string to a long integer.
`_atold`	Converts a string to a `long double` value.
`_ecvt`	Converts a `double` into a string without an embedded decimal point.
`_fcvt`	Similar to `_ecvt`, but rounds the value to a specified number of digits.
`_gcvt`	Converts a `double` to a string (you provide the storage for the string).
`isalnum`	Returns a nonzero value if a character is alphanumeric.

continues

Table 25.1. continued

Function	Description
`isalpha`	Returns a nonzero value if a character is alphabetic.
`__isascii`	Returns a nonzero value if an integer is an ASCII character.
`iscntrl`	Returns a nonzero value if a character is a control character (ASCII code 0 through 0x1f and 0x7f).
`__iscsym`	Returns a nonzero value if a character is a letter, an underscore, or a digit.
`__iscsymf`	Returns a nonzero value if a character is a letter or an underscore.
`isdigit`	Returns a nonzero value if a character is a digit (0-9).
`isgraph`	Returns a nonzero value if a character is a printable character except space.
`islower`	Returns a nonzero value if a character is lowercase.
`isprint`	Returns a nonzero value if a character is a printable character, including a space.
`ispunct`	Returns a nonzero value if a character is a punctuation character.
`isspace`	Returns a nonzero value if a character is a whitespace character (ASCII codes 0x09 through 0x0d or the space character).
`isupper`	Returns a nonzero value if a character is uppercase.
`isxdigit`	Returns a nonzero value if a character is a hexadecimal digit (0-9, a-f, and A-F).
`_itoa`	Converts an `int` to a string.
`_ltoa`	Converts a `long` to a string.
`strtod`	Converts a string to a `double`.
`strtol`	Converts a string to a `long`.
`_strtold`	Converts a string to a `long double`.

strtoul	Converts a string to an unsigned long.
__toascii	Converts an int to a valid ASCII code.
tolower	If a character is uppercase, converts it to lowercase.
_tolower	Converts a character to lowercase without checking whether the conversion is necessary.
toupper	If a character is lowercase, converts it to uppercase.
_toupper	Converts a character to uppercase without checking whether the conversion is necessary.
_ultoa	Converts an unsigned long to a string.

Table 25.2. Basic character- and data-conversion tasks.

Task	Functions
Convert string to integer values	atoi, atol, strtol, strtoul
Convert integer value to string	_itoa, _ltoa, _ultoa
Convert string to floating-point values	atof, _atold, strtod, _strtold
Convert floating-point value to string	_ecvt, _fcvt, _gcvt
Test the type of a character	isalnum, isalpha, __isascii, iscntrl, __iscsym, __iscsymf, isdigit, isgraph, islower, isprint, ispunct, isspace, isupper, isxdigit
Convert case of a character	_tolower, tolower, _toupper, toupper

Converting a Text String to Lowercase

As an example of the character conversion function, consider the task of converting all the characters in a line of text. Suppose you want a program that reads lines from a text file and converts each character to lowercase. You can call the `tolower` function in a loop to convert the entire string to lowercase. (The `_strlwr` function, described in Chapter 26, can convert a string to lowercase.) Listing 25.1 shows the program lcase.c, which accepts the name of an input file and an output file as arguments, converts all lines from the input file to lowercase, and saves them in the output file.

Listing 25.1. lcase.c. A program that converts a text file to lowercase.

```
//---------------------------------------------------------------
//  File: lcase.c
//
//  Reads an input file and writes all lines into an output
// file after converting each line into lowercase.
//---------------------------------------------------------------
#include <stdio.h>
#include <ctype.h>
#include <process.h>

// Assume each line has at most 256 characters.
#define MAXCHARS  256

int main(int argc, char **argv)
{
    char line[MAXCHARS];
    FILE *infile, *outfile;
    unsigned long count = 0L;
    int i;

    if(argc < 3)
    {
        printf("Usage: lcase <infile> <outfile>\n");
        exit(1);
    }

// Open the input file for reading in text mode:
    if((infile = fopen(argv[1], "rt")) == NULL)
    {
        printf("Cannot open %s for input\n", argv[1]);
        exit(2);
    }
```

```
// Open the output file for writing in text mode:
    if((outfile = fopen(argv[2], "wt")) == NULL)
    {
        printf("Cannot open %s for input\n", argv[2]);
        exit(2);
    }

// Now read lines from input file and convert them
// to lowercase:
    while(fgets(line, MAXCHARS, infile) != NULL)
    {
        for(i = 0; line[i] != '\0'; i++)
            line[i] = tolower(line[i]);

        fputs(line, outfile);
        count++;
    }
    printf("%ld lines converted to lowercase\n", count);

    return 0;
}
```

A Simple Calculator

Data-conversion functions are ideal for converting command-line arguments from their text-string form to the internal representation of variables. For example, suppose you want to create a small calculator program to use from the DOS command line, as follows:

```
calc 24.95 * 14
```

where `calc` is the name of the executable program that accepts a command line of the form `<operand1> <operator> <operand2>`, computes the specified operation, and displays the result. Listing 25.2 shows an implementation of the calc program.

Listing 25.2. calc.c. A simple calculator program.

```
//-------------------------------------------------------------
//  File: calc.c
//
```

continues

Listing 25.2. continued

```
//  A simple calculator program
//-------------------------------------------------------------
#include <stdio.h>
#include <math.h>
#include <process.h>

int main(int argc, char **argv)
{
    double x, y, result = 0.0;
    if(argc < 4)
    {
        printf("Usage: calc <operand1> <operator> <operand2>\n");
        exit(1);
    }

// Get the operands:
    x = atof(argv[1]);
    y = atof(argv[3]);

// Perform requested computation:
    switch(argv[2][0])
    {
        case '+':
            result = x + y;
            break;

        case '-':
            result = x - y;
            break;

        case '*':
            result = x * y;
          break;

        case '/':
            if(fabs(y) > 1.e-10)
                result = x / y;
            else
                printf("Divisor too small!\n");
            break;
    }
```

```
// Display result:
    printf("%s %s %s = %f\n", argv[1], argv[2], argv[3], result);

    return 0;
}
```

> **Leading Underscore in Names of Nonstandard Functions**
>
> Microsoft Visual C++ adds an underscore prefix to many functions (such as `ecvt`, `fcvt`, `_gcvt`) in keeping with ANSI Standard C's naming conventions for nonstandard functions. In many other C compilers (including earlier versions of Microsoft C compilers) as well as UNIX, these functions are available with names that do not have the leading underscores. You can use the names without the underscore prefix in Microsoft Visual C++ as well.
>
> Some of the functions in this chapter are prefixed with two underscores. These functions include `__isascii`, `__iscsym`, `__iscsymf`, and `__toascii`.

atof

Summary

```
#include <stdlib.h>

double atof(const char *str); // String to convert to double value
```

Description

Converts the string *str* to a double value. Continues to convert characters from the string until it encounters a character (such as the null character) it cannot handle.

Returns

When the function completes successfully, the return value is the converted `double` value. Because a return of zero is also valid, it is not possible to detect errors.

Sample Call

```
double x;
x = atof("39.95 Dollars"); // x will be 39.95
```

See Also

`atoi`, `atol`, `_atold`

atoi, atol

MSC6	MSC7	VC++	QC2.5	QC-WIN	TC2	TC++	BC++2	BC++3	ANSI	POSIX	UNIX V	DOS	QWIN	WIN	WINDLL
X	X	X	X	X	X	X	X	X	X	X	X	X	X	X	X

Summary

```
#include <stdlib.h>

int atoi(const char *str);  // String to convert to int value
long atol(const char *str); // String to convert to long value
```

Description

The `atoi` and `atol` functions convert a string to `int` and `long` values, respectively. The functions convert characters from the input string until reaching a character that cannot be a part of an integer value.

Returns

When the function completes successfully, the return is the converted values. Because a return of zero is also valid, it is not possible to detect errors.

Sample Call

```
int  pagecount;
long maxsize;
//...
pagecount = atoi("1400 pages");    // Pagecount = 1400
maxsize = atol("19656000 bytes"); // Maxsize = 19656000
```

See Also

`atof`, `_atold`

_atold

MSC6	MSC7	VC++	QC2.5	QC-WIN	TC2	TC++	BC++2	BC++3	ANSI	POSIX	UNIX V	DOS	QWIN	WIN	WINDLL
X	X	X	X				X				X	X	X	X	

Summary

```
#include <stdlib.h>

long double _atold(const char *str); // String to convert
```

Description

Converts the string *`str`* to a `long double` value.

Returns

When the function completes successfully, it returns the converted `long double` value. Because a return of zero is also valid, it is not possible to detect errors.

Sample Call

```
long double x;
char *str = "1.141e4000"
//...
x = _atold(str);
```

See Also

`atof`, `atoi`, `atol`

_ecvt, _fcvt

MSC6	MSC7	VC++	QC2.5	QC-WIN	TC2	TC++	BC++2	BC++3	ANSI	POSIX	UNIX V	DOS	QWIN	WIN	WINDLL
x	x	x	x	x	x	x	x	x			x	x	x	x	x

See note earlier in this chapter about the leading underscore in this function's name.

Summary

```
#include <stdlib.h>

char *_ecvt(
    double value,    // Floating-point value to be converted
    int    ndigits,  // Number of digits to be stored
    int    *decpos,  // Address of int where decimal point's
                     //   location is returned
    int    *sign);   // Address of int where sign of the
                     //   value is returned
char *_fcvt(
    double value,    // Floating-point value to be converted
    int    ndigits,  // Number of digits to be stored
    int    *decpos,  // Address of int where decimal point's
                     //   location is returned
    int    *sign);   // Address of int where sign of the
                     //   value is returned
```

Description

Both functions convert the floating-point number value into a null-terminated string with *`ndigit`* digits. The position of the decimal point and the sign of the value are returned in the integers associated with the addresses you provide in the arguments *`decpos`* and *`sign`*. The decimal point's position is zero if the decimal point is to appear at the beginning of the string, and positive if it should be somewhere within the string. For a positive number, the returned value of *`sign`* is zero.

The difference between `_ecvt` and `_fcvt` is that `_fcvt` rounds the value to ndigit digits.

Returns

When the function completes successfully, the return value is a pointer to an internal buffer where the converted string is stored. A subsequent call to `_ecvt` or `_fcvt` destroys the contents of this buffer.

Sample Call

```
double result = 4.26e5;
int dec, sign;
//...
printf("Result = %s\n", _ecvt(result, 6, &dec, &sign));
```

See Also

`_gcvt`

_gcvt

MSC6	MSC7	VC++	QC2.5	QC-WIN	TC2	TC++	BC++2	BC++3	ANSI	POSIX	UNIX V	DOS	QWIN	WIN	WINDLL
X	X	X	X	X	X	X	X	X			X	X	X	X	X

Summary

```
#include <stdio.h>

char *_gcvt(
    double value, // Floating-point value to convert
    int    ndigit,// Number of significant digits to store
    char   *buf); // Buffer you provide where result is returned
```

Description

Like `_ecvt` and `_fcvt`, converts a floating-point value to a string. Unlike them, `_gcvt` saves the converted string in a buffer, which you provide in *`buf`*.

Returns

When the function completes successfully, the return value is the function argument *`buf`*.

Sample Call

```
char buf[81];
double x = 3.995e2;
//...
_gcvt(x, 6, buf);
```

See Also

`_ecvt`, `_fcvt`

isalnum

MSC6	MSC7	VC++	QC2.5	QC-WIN	TC2	TC++	BC++2	BC++3	ANSI	POSIX	UNIX V	DOS	QWIN	WIN	WINDLL
X	X	X	X	X	X	X	X	X	X	X	X	X	X	X	X

Summary

```
#include <ctype.h>

int isalnum(int c); // Check whether c is alphanumeric character
```

Description

Checks whether the character `c` is alphanumeric—one of the digits 0-9 or an uppercase or lowercase letter.

Returns

When the function completes successfully, the return value is nonzero if `c` is alphanumeric, or zero if otherwise.

Sample Call

```
if(isalnum(c)) printf("%c is alphanumeric\n", c);
```

See Also

`isalpha`, `__isascii`

isalpha

MSC6	MSC7	VC++	QC2.5	QC-WIN	TC2	TC++	BC++2	BC++3	ANSI	POSIX	UNIX V	DOS	QWIN	WIN	WINDLL
X	X	X	X	X	X	X	X	X	X	X	X	X	X	X	X

Summary

```
#include <ctype.h>

int isalpha(int c); // Is c an alphabetic character?
```

Description

Checks whether `c` is one of the uppercase or lowercase letters A-Z.

Returns

When the function completes successfully, the return value is nonzero if `c` is alphabetic; zero if otherwise.

Sample Call

```
if(isalpha(c)) printf("%c is a letter\n", c);
```

See Also

`isalnum`, `__isascii`

__isascii

MSC6	MSC7	VC++	QC2.5	QC-WIN	TC2	TC++	BC++2	BC++3	ANSI	POSIX	UNIX V	DOS	QWIN	WIN	WINDLL
X	X	X	X	X	X	X	X	X			X	X	X	X	X

Summary

```
#include <ctype.h>

int __isascii(int c); // Is c a valid ASCII code?
```

Description

Checks whether the integer value `c` lies in the range 0-127, which is range of values the ASCII character set occupies.

Returns

When the function completes successfully, the return value is nonzero if `c` is a valid ASCII character; zero if otherwise.

Sample Call

```
if(__isascii(c))printf("%d is a valid ASCII code\n", c);
```

See Also

`__toascii`

iscntrl, isdigit, isgraph, islower, isprint, ispunct, isspace, isupper, isxdigit

MSC6	MSC7	VC++	QC2.5	QC-WIN	TC2	TC++	BC++2	BC++3	ANSI	POSIX	UNIX V	DOS	QWIN	WIN	WINDLL
X	X	X	X	X	X	X	X	X	X	X	X	X	X	X	X

Summary

```
#include <ctype.h>

int iscntrl(int c);

int isdigit(int c);

int isgraph(int c);

int islower(int c);

int isprint(int c);

int ispunct(int c);
```

```
int isspace(int c);

int isupper(int c);

int isxdigit(int c);
```

Description

These functions check for specific properties of the character c, such as whether it's a control character, a digit, lowercase, printable, and so on. Table 25.3 shows the test performed by each of the functions. Note that you should use these functions only after ensuring that c is a valid ASCII character (use __isascii to check this).

Table 25.3. Tests performed by the character-classification functions.

Name	Tests for
iscntrl	Control character (0x7f or in the range 0-0x1f)
isdigit	Decimal digit (0-9)
isgraph	Printable character excluding the space (ASCII codes 0x21-0x7e)
islower	Lowercase letter (a-z)
isprint	Printable character including space (ASCII codes 0x20-0x7e)
ispunct	Punctuation character (0x21-0x2f, 0x3a-0x40, 0x5b-0x60, 0x7b-0x7c)
isspace	Whitespace character (space; formfeed, \f; newline, \n; carriage return, \r; horizontal tab, \t; and vertical tab, \v)
isupper	Uppercase letter (A-Z)
isxdigit	Hexadecimal digit (0-9, A-F, a-f)

Returns

When any of these functions complete successfully, the return value is nonzero value if c satisfies the test criteria for that function.

Otherwise, each functions returns 0.

Sample Call

```
// Convert character to lowercase:
if(isupper(c)) c = _tolower(c);
```

See Also

`__isascii`

__iscsym, __iscsymf

MSC6	MSC7	VC++	QC2.5	QC-WIN	TC2	TC++	BC++2	BC++3	ANSI	POSIX	UNIX V	DOS	QWIN	WIN	WINDLL
X		X	X								X	X	X	X	

Summary

```
#include <ctype.h>

int __iscsym(int c);  // Is c a letter, an underscore, or a digit?
int __iscsymf(int c); // Is c a letter or an underscore?
```

Description

The `__iscsym` function checks whether *c* can appear in a symbol in a C program. Use `__iscsymf` to determine whether *c* can be the first character of a valid symbol in C.

Returns

When either of these function completes successfully, the return value is nonzero if the test condition is satisfied; zero if otherwise.

Sample Call

```
if(__iscsymf(c))
   printf("%c can be the first character of a C symbol\n", c);
```

See Also

`isalnum`, `isalpha`

_itoa, _ltoa

MSC6	MSC7	VC++	QC2.5	QC-WIN	TC2	TC++	BC++2	BC++3	ANSI	POSIX	UNIX V	DOS	QWIN	WIN	WINDLL
X	X	X	X	X	X	X	X	X				X	X	X	X

Summary

```
#include <stdlib.h>

char *_itoa(
    int  value, // Convert this int value to a text string
    char *str,  // Return resulting characters here
    int  radix);// Express value in this radix (2_36)
```

```
char *_ltoa(
    long value, // Convert this long value to a text string
    char *str,  // Return resulting characters here
    int  radix);// Express value in this radix (2_36)
```

Description

Converts an integer or a long value into a null-terminated text string with up to 17 characters, depending on the selected radix. If *radix* is 10 and *value* is negative, the first character of the converted string is a minus sign.

Returns

When either of these functions completes successfully, the return value is the argument *str*.

Sample Call

```
char buf[17];
//...
_itoa(20, buf, 16); // buf will have "14"
_ltoa(0x10000, buf, 10) // buf = "65536"
```

See Also

`_ultoa`

strtod

MSC6	MSC7	VC++	QC2.5	QC-WIN	TC2	TC++	BC++2	BC++3	ANSI	POSIX	UNIX V	DOS	QWIN	WIN	WINDLL
X	X	X X	X	X	X	X	X	X		X	X	X	X	X	

Summary

```
#include <stdlib.h>

double strtod(
    const char *str,    // Convert this string into a double value.
    char       **endp);// Location for returning pointer to
                        //   the character that stops the conversion.
```

Description

Converts the string *str* to a `double` value. The string should be of this form:

[whitespace][sign][digits.digits][exponent_letter][sign][digits]

where *whitespace* refers to (optional) blanks and tab characters, *sign* is an addition (+) or minus (-) sign, and the digits are decimal digits. The *exponent_letter* can be any one of `d`, `D`, `e`, or `E`; no matter which exponent letter is used, the exponent always denotes a power of 10.

The `strtod` function stops the conversion process as soon as it encounters a character that does not fit the expected pattern. The function then sets a pointer to that character in a `char*` variable associated with the address you provide as the *`endp`* argument.

Returns

When the function completes successfully, it returns the converted `double` value.

If the converted value overflows a `double`, `strtod` returns plus or minus `HUGE_VAL` and sets the global variable `errno` to `ERANGE`.

0 Indicates that no conversion was performed.

Sample Call

```
    char str[80], *endp;
    double value;
// Assume str has the text form of a floating-point value.
// Convert it to a double value:
    value = strtod(str, &endp);
```

See Also

`atof`, `_strtold`

strtol

MSC6	MSC7	VC++	QC2.5	QC-WIN	TC2	TC++	BC++2	BC++3	ANSI	POSIX	UNIX V	DOS	QWIN	WIN	WINDLL
X	X	X	X	X	X	X	X	X	X		X	X	X	X	X

Summary

```
#include <stdlib.h>

long strtol(
    const char *str,    // Convert this string into a long value
    char       **endp,  // Location for returning pointer to
                        //   the character that stops the conversion
    int        radix);  // Express value in this radix
                        //   (in the range 2 through 36)
```

Description

Converts the string *`str`* to a long value. The string *`str`* is expected to be of this form:

`[`*`whitespace`*`][`*`sign`*`][0][x¦X][`*`digits`*`]`

where *`whitespace`* refers to (optional) blanks and tab characters, *`sign`* is an addition (+) or minus (-) sign, `x` or `X` can be entered (in either case), and the digits are decimal digits. The string is expected to contain a textual representation of a long integer using the specified radix as the base of the number system. However, if `radix` is zero, `strtol` uses the first character in the string to determine the radix of the value. The rules are as follows:

First character	Next character	Radix selected
0	0-7	Radix 8 is used (octal digits expected)
0	x or X	Radix 16 (hexadecimal digits expected)
1-9	...	Radix 10 (decimal digits expected)

The `strtol` function stops the conversion process as soon as it encounters a character that does not fit the expected pattern and sets up a pointer to that character in a `char*` variable associated with the address you provide as the *endp* argument.

Returns

When the function completes successfully, the return value is the converted `long` value.

If the converted value overflows a `long int`, `strtol` returns either `LONG_MIN` or `LONG_MAX` and sets `errno` to `ERANGE`.

0 Indicates that no conversion was performed.

Sample Call

```
char buf[80], *endp;
long value;
//...
value = strtol(buf, &endp, 10);
```

See Also

`atol`, `strtoul`

_strtold

MSC6	MSC7	VC++	QC2.5	QC-WIN	TC2	TC++	BC++2	BC++3	ANSI	POSIX	UNIX V	DOS	QWIN	WIN	WINDLL
X	X	X	X	X				X				X	X	X	X

Summary

```
#include <stdlib.h>

long double _strtold(
    const char *str,    // Convert this string to a long double
    char       **endp);// Location for returning pointer to
                        //   the character that stops the conversion
```

Description

Works like strtod, except that _strtold converts a string to a long double value.

Returns

When the function completes successfully, the return value is the converted long double value.

If the converted value overflows a long double, _strtold returns plus or minus HUGE_VAL and sets the global variable errno to ERANGE.

0 Indicates that no conversion was performed.

Sample Call

```
    char str[80], *endp;
    long double value;
// Assume str has the text form of a floating-point value.
// Convert it to a long double value:
    value = _strtold(str, &endp);
```

See Also

atof, strtod

strtoul

MSC6	MSC7	VC++	QC2.5	QC-WIN	TC2	TC++	BC++2	BC++3	ANSI	POSIX	UNIX V	DOS	QWIN	WIN	WINDLL
X	X	X	X	X	X	X	X	X	X			X	X	X	X

Summary

```
#include <stdlib.h>

long strtoul(
    const char *str,    // Convert this string into an
                        //   unsigned long value
    char       **endp, // Location for returning pointer to
                        //   the character that stops the conversion
    int        radix); // Express value in this radix
                        //   (in the range 2_36)
```

Description

Works like strtol, except that strtoul converts the string *str* to an unsigned long value.

Returns

When the function completes successfully, the return value is the converted unsigned long value. Because a return of zero is also valid, it is not possible to detect errors.

If the converted value overflows an unsigned long, strtoul returns ULONG_MAX and sets errno to ERANGE.

Sample Call

```
char buf[80], *endp;
long value;
//...
value = strtol(buf, &endp, 10);
```

See Also

atol, strtol

__toascii

MSC6	MSC7	VC++	QC2.5	QC-WIN	TC2	TC++	BC++2	BC++3	ANSI	POSIX	UNIX V	DOS	QWIN	WIN	WINDLL
X	X	X	X	X	X	X	X	X			X	X	X	X	X

Summary

```
#include <ctype.h>

int __toascii(int c); // Convert c to a valid ASCII code
```

Description

Converts the integer value c to a valid ASCII code by setting all but the low-order 7 bits of c to zero.

Returns

When the function completes successfully, the return value is the converted character.

Sample Call

```
// Make c ASCII....
    c = _ _toascii(c);
```

See Also

__isascii

_tolower, tolower

MSC6	MSC7	VC++	QC2.5	QC-WIN	TC2	TC++	BC++2	BC++3	ANSI	POSIX	UNIX V	DOS	QWIN	WIN	WINDLL
X	X	X	X	X	X	X	X	X	X	X	X	X	X	X	X

Note: Only the `tolower` function is part of the ANSI standard C library (`_tolower` is not in the ANSI C standard).

Summary

```
#include <ctype.h>

int tolower(int c); // If c is uppercase, convert it to lowercase
int _tolower(int c);// Convert c to lowercase without testing
```

Description

Converts the character *c* to lowercase: `tolower` converts only if *c* is uppercase, while `_tolower` applies the conversion without checking whether *c* is uppercase.

Returns

When the function completes successfully, the return value is the converted character.

Sample Call

```
// Make c lowercase....
    c = tolower(c);
```

See Also

`toupper`, `_toupper`

_toupper, toupper

MSC6	MSC7	VC++	QC2.5	QC-WIN	TC2	TC++	BC++2	BC++3	ANSI	POSIX	UNIX V	DOS	QWIN	WIN	WINDLL
X	X	X	X	X	X	X	X	X	X	X	X	X	X	X	X

Note: Only the `toupper` function is part of the ANSI standard C library (`_toupper` is not in the ANSI C standard).

Summary

```
#include <ctype.h>

int toupper(int c); // If c is lowercase, convert it to uppercase
int _toupper(int c);// Convert c to uppercase without testing
```

Description

Converts the character *c* to uppercase: `toupper` converts only if *c* is lowercase, while `_toupper` applies the case conversion without checking whether *c* needs the conversion.

Returns

When the function completes successfully, the return value is the converted character.

Sample Call

```
// Make c uppercase....
    c = toupper(c);
```

See Also

tolower, _tolower

_ultoa

MSC6	MSC7	VC++	QC2.5	QC-WIN	TC2	TC++	BC++2	BC++3	ANSI	POSIX	UNIX V	DOS	QWIN	WIN	WINDLL
X	X	X	X	X	X	X	X	X				X	X	X	X

Summary

```
#include <stdlib.h>

char *_ultoa(
    unsigned long value, // Convert this to a text string
    char          *str,  // Return string here
    int           radix);// Express value in this radix
```

Description

Creates a textual representation of an `unsigned long` integer *value* in a specified radix (between 2 and 36).

Returns

When the function completes successfully, the return value is the text representation (up to 33 characters) in *str*.

Sample Call

```
char buf[17];
//...
_ultoa(0x100000, buf, 10) // buf = "131072"
```

See Also

_itoa, _ltoa

26

String and Buffer Handling

String- and buffer-handling functions manipulate the contents of an array of bytes. Although the terms *string* and *buffer* often are used interchangeably, *string* refers to an array of `char` variables. The end of a text string is marked with a byte containing a zero, often referred to as the *terminating null character*. Most applications use and manipulate strings and buffers. For instance, an application might read a command entered by the user at the keyboard, store it as a text string, and parse the command to perform the requested task. To accomplish these steps, the application program usually would call one or more of the string- and buffer-handling functions described in this chapter. Most of the functions described here are declared in the header file string.h.

Strings and Buffers in C

C does not have a built-in data type for strings. Instead, a string is defined to be an array of `char` variables with a null character marking the end of the string. Because of this convention, C strings often are referred to as *null-terminated strings*. Most of the string-handling functions (with names that have the str prefix) rely on the presence of a terminating null character for their operation.

Buffers are more general than strings—a *buffer* is simply a block of memory with arbitrary contents. Because a string is also a block of memory (an array of char variables), a string is also a buffer—a special one that holds zero or more characters with a zero byte marking the end. You might use a buffer, for instance, to store an image or to load the contents of a file into memory.

Declaring Strings and Buffers

Because a string is simply an array of char variables, you can declare a string and initialize it with a statement such as

```
char cname[] = "Microsoft Visual C++", line[80];
```

This defines cname to be an array of characters long enough to hold the characters in Microsoft Visual C++ and the terminating null character. The line variable, on the other hand, is an 80-character string that has not been initialized.

The name of the array is equivalent to the address of the first element in the array. Thus, cname can be used wherever a char pointer is expected. On the other hand, you may also explicitly define a char pointer variable and initialize it to a string. For instance, you might write

```
    char *p_cname;
//...
    p_cname = cname;
```

Lexicographic Ordering

String- and buffer-comparison functions, such as strcmp and memcmp, compare and order strings as they would have appeared in a dictionary (a lexicon). Thus, the ordering is known as *lexicographic*. The comparison is based on the collating sequence of the characters in corresponding bytes of the two strings. For the ASCII character set, the collating sequence of the letters corresponds to their place in the lexicon.

Multibyte and Wide-Character Strings

ANSI C introduced the notion of two character sets that are relevant to a C program:

- The *source* character set in which the program is written
- The *execution* character set, understood by the program when it runs

These character sets may use multibyte encodings—the code for a single character may require more than one byte to store. ANSI C also supports a data type, `wchar_t`, for representing wide characters. A *wide character* is a single integral type whose range of values is large enough to represent all members of the largest extended character set supported by the compiler. For example, if the largest character set has more than 256 but fewer than 32,767 characters, a `short int` type could be used as `wchar_t` to hold the wide characters.

Far Buffers and Strings

In the list of string- and buffer-handling functions in Table 26.1, you'll notice a large number of functions with the `_f` prefix. These functions accept and return far pointers—pointers qualified by the `__far` keyword. Far pointers are an artifact of the memory-addressing scheme used by the Intel 80x86 family of microprocessors. Essentially, memory is broken down into segments, each up to 64K in size. This allows the processor to use a 16-bit offset from the start of the segment to address any byte within a segment. The segment is identified by a 16-bit segment address, which is the location where the segment starts. Microsoft Visual C++ accommodates the segmented addressing scheme of the Intel 80x86 microprocessors by providing a number of memory models—each memory model specifies the number of segments of code and data allowed within a program. Chapter 31, "Memory Management," further explains the tiny, small, medium, compact, large, and huge memory models supported in Microsoft Visual C++.

Normally, in small and medium memory models, the compiler sets up the segment address once and uses the offset within the segment to access variables. When you use far pointers, the compiler generates code to use the complete segment and offset address to reference a memory location. Also, when a function accepts a far pointer as argument, the compiler ensures that the full segment and offset address is passed to the function, regardless of which memory model currently is in use. The net result is that functions with the `_f` prefix in their names can be used to operate on buffers and strings in any memory model.

Basic String- and Buffer-Handling Tasks

Table 26.1 shows an alphabetic list of the console and port I/O functions and gives you a quick overview of these functions. Table 26.2 organizes these functions by the tasks they perform. Some of these tasks are illustrated by short sample programs in the following sections. For more information about a function, consult the reference entry for that function in the reference entries that follow.

Table 26.1. Alphabetic listing of string and buffer-handling functions.

Function	Description
`_fmblen`	Finds length of multibyte character stored in a far buffer.
`_fmbstowcs`	Converts a multibyte string to a wide-character string.
`_fmbtowc`	Converts a multibyte character to a wide character.
`_fmemccpy`	Copies from one far buffer to another, copying up to and including a specific character or until a specified number of characters is copied.
`_fmemchr`	Finds the first occurrence of a character in a far buffer.
`_fmemcmp`	Compares a specified number of characters from two far buffers.
`_fmemcpy`	Copies a specified number of characters from one far buffer to another.
`_fmemicmp`	Compares a specified number of characters from two far buffers without regard to case.
`_fmemmove`	Copies a specified number of bytes from one far buffer to another (source and destination buffers may overlap).
`_fmemset`	Sets a specified number of bytes in a far buffer to a given value.

Function	Description
_fstrcat	Concatenates two far strings.
_fstrchr	Finds the first occurrence of a specified character in a far string.
_fstrcmp	Compares two far strings.
_fstrcpy	Copies one far string into another.
_fstrcspn	Finds the position of the first character that belongs to a specified set of characters.
_fstrdup	Duplicates a far string and returns a far pointer to the duplicate.
_fstricmp	Compares two far strings without regard to case.
_fstrlen	Returns the number of characters in a far string.
_fstrlwr	Converts a far string to lowercase.
_fstrncat	Concatenates a specified number of characters from one far string to another.
_fstrncmp	Compares a specified number of characters of one far string to another.
_fstrncpy	Copies a specified number of characters from one far string to another.
_fstrnicmp	Compares a specified number of characters from two far strings without regard to case.
_fstrnset	Sets a specified number of characters in a far string a given value.
_fstrpbrk	Finds the first occurrence of any character from one far string in another.
_fstrrchr	Finds the last occurrence of a character in a far string.
_fstrrev	Reverses the order of characters in a far string.
_fstrset	Sets all characters in a null-terminated far string to a given value.

continues

Table 26.1. continued

Function	Description
`_fstrspn`	Finds the position in a far string of the first character that does not belong to a given set of characters.
`_fstrstr`	Locates the first occurrence of one string in another.
`_fstrtok`	Returns the next token (indicated by a set of token-delimiting characters) from a far string.
`_fstrupr`	Converts a far string to uppercase.
`_fwcstombs`	Converts a far array of wide characters into a sequence of multibyte characters.
`_fwctomb`	Converts a wide character into a multibyte character.
`mblen`	Determines the number of bytes in a multibyte character.
`mbstowcs`	Converts a sequence of multibyte characters into a sequence of wide characters.
`mbtowc`	Converts a multibyte character into a wide character.
`_memccpy`	Copies a specified number of bytes from one buffer to another (source and destination buffers cannot overlap).
`memchr`	Searches a specified number of bytes of a buffer for the first occurrence of a given character.
`memcmp`	Compares a specified number of bytes of two buffers.
`memcpy`	Copies a specified number of bytes from one buffer to another.
`_memicmp`	Compares a specified number of bytes from two buffers without regard to case.
`memmove`	Copies a specified number of bytes from one buffer to another (source and destination buffers are allowed to overlap).

Function	Description
memset	Sets a specified number of bytes in a buffer to a given value.
_movedata	Copies specified number of bytes from a buffer with specified segment and offset address to another buffer.
_nstrdup	Duplicates a string in the near heap and returns a near pointer to the duplicate copy.
strcat	Concatenates one string with another.
strchr	Finds the first occurrence of a character in a string.
strcmp	Compares two null-terminated strings.
_strcmpi	Compares two null-terminated strings without regard to case. This function has been replaced with the `_stricmp` function, and should not be used in new applications.
strcoll	Compares two null-terminated strings using the collating sequence specified by the `LC_COLLATE` category of the current locale (see Chapter 30, "Process Control").
strcpy	Copies one null-terminated string into another.
strcspn	Returns the position in a string of the first character that belongs to a specified set of characters.
_strdup	Duplicates a string and returns a pointer to the duplicate copy.
_strerror	Builds a string consisting of a user-supplied message and the error message corresponding to the last error.
strerror	Returns a string containing the error message corresponding to a specified error number.
_stricmp	Compares two null-terminated strings without regard to case.

continues

Table 26.1. continued

Function	Description
`strlen`	Returns the number of characters in a null-terminated string, not counting the terminating null character.
`_strlwr`	Converts a null-terminated string to all lowercase.
`strncat`	Concatenates a specified number of characters from one string to another.
`strncmp`	Compares a specified number of characters from two strings.
`strncpy`	Copies a specified number of characters from one string to another.
`_strnicmp`	Compares specified number of characters from two strings without regard to case.
`_strnset`	Sets a specified number of characters in a string to a given value.
`strpbrk`	Locates the first occurrence of any character from one string in another.
`strrchr`	Finds the last occurrence of a character in a string.
`_strrev`	Reverses the order of characters in a string.
`_strset`	Sets all characters in a null-terminated string to a specified value.
`strspn`	Finds the position in a string of the first character that does not belong to a given set of characters.
`strstr`	Searches for the first occurrence of one string in another.
`strtok`	Returns the next token (identified by delimiting characters in another string) from a string.
`_strupr`	Converts a null-terminated string to all uppercase.

Function	Description
strxfrm	Transforms a string to a form so that if the strcmp function is applied to two transformed strings, the returned result is the same as that returned by strcoll applied to the original string.
_swab	Swaps each pair of adjacent bytes in an array.
wcstombs	Converts an array of wide characters into a sequence of multibyte characters.
wctomb	Converts a wide character into a multibyte character.

Table 26.2. Basic string- and buffer-handling tasks.

Task	Functions
Copy buffers and strings	_memccpy, _fmemccpy, memcpy, _fmemcpy, memmove, _fmemmove, _movedata, strcpy, _fstrcpy, strncpy, _fstrncpy, strdup, _fstrdup, _nstrdup
Compare buffers and strings	memcmp, _fmemcmp, _memicmp, _fmemicmp, strcmp, _fstrcmp, _strcmpi, _stricmp, _fstricmp, strncmp, _fstrncmp, _strnicmp, _fstrnicmp, strcoll, strxfrm
Find length	mblen, strlen, _fstrlen
Locate a character or a substring	memchr, _fmemchr, strchr, _fstrchr, strcspn, _fstrcspn, strpbrk, _fstrpbrk, strrchr, _fstrrchr, strspn, _fstrspn, strstr, _fstrstr
Convert case	_strlwr, _fstrlwr, _strupr, _fstrupr

continues

Table 26.2. continued

Task	Functions
Convert between multibyte and wide-character types	`mbstowcs`, `_fmbstowcs`, `mbtowc`, `_fmbtowc`, `wcstombs`, `_fwcstombs`, `wctomb`, `_fwctomb`
Extract tokens	`strtok`, `_fstrtok`
Set string or buffer to a given value	`memset`, `_fmemset`, `_strnset`, `_fstrnset`, `_strset`, `_fstrset`
Construct error message strings	`strerror`, `_strerror`
Other transformations	`_strrev`, `_fstrrev`, `_swab`

Copying Video Memory

As an example of using buffers, consider the problem of saving the contents of the display screen (in text mode) and restoring it later. Listing 26.1 shows the program savescr.c, which saves the current contents of the text-mode screen in a buffer. It then clears the screen by copying another buffer, containing all zeros, to the video memory. The program then prompts the user for a keypress. When the user presses a key, the previous screen is restored.

Note: this program is intended to be run under DOS only, and it will not function correctly if it is created as a QuickWin program!

Listing 26.1. Program that saves and restores the text-mode video screen.

```
//-------------------------------------------------------------
// File: savescr.c
//
// Saves a text-mode screen in a buffer, clears the screen,
// and restores it after the user presses a key. Assumes
// that the text-mode video memory starts at segment 0xb800
// and offset 0x0000.
//-------------------------------------------------------------
#include <stdio.h>
#include <io.h>
```

```
#include <dos.h>
#include <memory.h>
#include <conio.h>

static short saved_buf[25][80], clr_buf[25][80];

void main(void)
{
    void __far *address;
    unsigned bufseg, bufoff;

// Save current screen in saved_buf.
// Get segment and offset address of buffer.
    address = (void __far *)saved_buf;
    bufseg = _FP_SEG(address);
    bufoff = _FP_OFF(address);

// Copy video memory into buffer:
    _movedata(0xb800, 0x0000, bufseg, bufoff,
              sizeof(saved_buf));

// To clear screen, first initialize clr_buf to zero:
    memset(clr_buf, '\0', sizeof(clr_buf));

// Get segment and offset address of buffer:
    address = (void __far *)clr_buf;
    bufseg = _FP_SEG(address);
    bufoff = _FP_OFF(address);

// Copy buffer into video memory--this clears the screen:
    _movedata(bufseg, bufoff, 0xb800, 0x0000,
              sizeof(clr_buf));

// Prompt user for a keypress:
    printf("Press any key to restore old screen...");
    getch();

// Restore saved screen.
// Get segment and offset address of buffer.
    address = (void __far *)saved_buf;
    bufseg = _FP_SEG(address);
    bufoff = _FP_OFF(address);
```

continues

Listing 26.1. continued

```
// Copy buffer into video memory to restore old screen:
    _movedata(bufseg, bufoff, 0xb800, 0x0000,
              sizeof(saved_buf));

}
```

Parsing a Line of Text

A common task in many applications is reading a line of command (from the keyboard or a file) and separating the line into tokens identified by a specified set of delimiting characters. The `strtok` function is ideal for this purpose. Listing 26.2 shows the program for a function named `cmdparse`, which parses a command-line into tokens. The tokens are returned through a static array named `argvec` of `char` pointers. Listing 26.2 includes a `main` function so that you can build an executable program and test the `cmdparse` function.

Listing 26.2. A function to parse a line of text into tokens.

```
//-------------------------------------------------------------
// File: cmdparse.c
//
// Demonstrates a function that parses a line of text into
// tokens.
//-------------------------------------------------------------
#include <stdio.h>
#include <string.h>

#define MAXCHR 256
#define MAXARG  64

// Parsed tokens and a count of tokens returned through these
// variables.

static char *argvec[MAXARG];
static int  nargs = 0;

//-------------------------------------------------------------
// c m d p a r s e
```

```
//
// Parses command-line into tokens identified by the delimiting
// characters specified in the tokensep argument. The argvec
// array points to the parsed tokens.

void cmdparse(char *line, char *tokensep)
{
    char *token;

// Set nargs to zero, indicating that no tokens have been found yet:
    nargs = 0;

// Call strtok with the line as argument to initialize it and
// get the first token:
    token = strtok(line, tokensep);

// Keep calling strtok to get all the tokens:
    while(token != NULL)
    {
        argvec[nargs++] = token;
        token = strtok(NULL, tokensep);
    }
}
//------------------------------------------------------------
// Remove next line when testing is done.

#define TEST
//------------------------------------------------------------

#ifdef TEST
//------------------------------------------------------------
// m a i n
// Tests the cmdparse function.

void main(void)
{
    int i, done = 0;
    char *delim = " \t\n,"; // Token delimiters
    char cmdline[MAXCHR];   // Command line

    while(!done)
    {
```

continues

Listing 26.2. continued

```
        printf("Command (Enter quit to stop)> ");
        gets(cmdline);

        cmdparse(cmdline, delim);
        for(i = 0; i < nargs; i++)
        {
            printf("Token %d:  %s\n", i+1, argvec[i]);
        }
// If first token is "quit", exit program.
        if(_stricmp(argvec[0], "quit") == 0) done = 1;
    }
}
#endif
```

Leading Underscore in Names of Nonstandard Functions

Microsoft Visual C++ adds an underscore prefix to many functions (such as `_movedata`, `_strdup`, and `_strlwr`) in keeping with ANSI Standard C's naming conventions for nonstandard functions. In many other C compilers (including earlier versions of Microsoft C compilers) as well as in UNIX, these functions are available with names that do not have the leading underscores. You can continue to use the names without the underscore prefix in Microsoft Visual C++ as well.

fmblen, _fmblen

MSC6	MSC7	VC++	QC2.5	QC-WIN	TC2	TC++	BC++2	BC++3	ANSI	POSIX	UNIX V	DOS	QWIN	WIN	WINDLL
	X	X		X			X	X	X			X	X	X	X

Note: `_fmblen` is available in MSC7, Visual C++, and QC-WIN only.

Summary

```
#include <stdlib.h>

int mblen(
    const char *s, // Determine length of multibyte character in
                   //   this array.
```

```
    size_t     n); // Maximum number of bytes that can be present
                   //   in a multibyte character.

int __far _fmblen(const char far *s, size_t n); // See mblen
```

Description

Examines up to *n* bytes in the array *s* and determines the number of bytes that constitute a valid multibyte character. The constant `MB_CUR_MAX`, defined in stdlib.h, denotes the maximum number of bytes that comprise a multibyte character in the current locale.

The `_fmblen` function is similar to `mblen` except that `_fmblen` can be used in any memory model to work with far arguments.

Returns

When the function completes successfully, the return value is the length of multibyte character, provided *s* is not `NULL` and a valid multibyte character is found within the first *n* bytes of *s*.

–1	Indicates that a valid character is not found.
0	Indicates that *s* is `NULL`.

Sample Call

```
    int len;
    char *p_mb;
// Assume p_mb points to a multibyte character.
    len = mblen(p_mb);
```

See Also

`mbtowc`, `mbstowcs`, `wctomb`, `wcstombs`

mbstowcs, _fmbstowcs

MSC6	MSC7	VC++	QC2.5	QC-WIN	TC2	TC++	BC++2	BC++3	ANSI	POSIX	UNIX V	DOS	QWIN	WIN	WINDLL
	X	X		X			X	X	X			X	X	X	X

Note: `_fmbstowcs` is available in MSC7, Visual C++, and QC-WIN only.

Summary

```
#include <stdlib.h>

size_t mbstowcs(
    wchar_t    *wcs, // Array where wide characters are returned.
    const char *mbs, // Convert this sequence of multibyte character.
```

```
    size_t      n);     // Maximum number of wide characters to
                        //   be stored in wcs.

size_t __far _fmbstowcs(wchar_t __far *wcs,    // See mbstowcs
                        const char __far *mbs, size_t n);
```

Description

Converts the sequence of multibyte characters in `mbs` into a sequence of wide characters and stores, at most, *n* wide characters in the array `wcs`.

The `_fmbstowcs` function is similar to `mbstowcs` except that `_fmbstowcs` can be used in any memory model to work with far arguments.

Returns

When the function completes successfully, the return value is the number of wide characters stored in `wcs`.

–1 Indicates that there is an invalid multibyte character in `mbs`.

n Indicates that the wide-character string is not null-terminated.

Sample Call

```
    wchar_t wcs[20];
    char    *mbs;
    size_t  nconv;
// Assume that mbs contains a sequence of multibyte characters.
    nconv = mbstowcs(wcs, mbs, 15];
```

See Also

`mblen`, `mbtowc`, `wctomb`, `wcstombs`

mbtowc, _fmbtowc

MSC6	MSC7	VC++	QC2.5	QC-WIN	TC2	TC++	BC++2	BC++3	ANSI	POSIX	UNIX V	DOS	QWIN	WIN	WINDLL
	X	X		X			X	X	X			X	X	X	X

Note: `_fmbtowc` is available in MSC7, Visual C++, and QC-WIN only.

Summary

```
#include <stdlib.h>

int mbtowc(
    wchar_t    *wc,   // Array where converted wide character returned.
    const char *mb,   // Convert this multibyte char to wide char.
    size_t     nmb);  // Max. number of char in each multibyte char.
```

```
int __far _fmbtowc(wchar_t __far *wc,   // See mbtowc
                   const char __far *mb, size_t nmb);
```

Description

Checks up to *nmb* bytes in the array *mb* for a valid multibyte character. If one is found, converts it to wide character (`wchar_t` type) and stores the result in the wide character *wc*.

The `_fmbtowc` function is similar to `mbtowc`, except that `_fmbtowc` can be used in any memory model to work with far arguments.

Returns

When the function completes successfully, the return value is the number of bytes composing the converted multibyte character, provided *mb* is not `NULL` and a valid multibyte character is found within *nmb* bytes.

0 Indicates that *mb* is `NULL`.

–1 Indicates an error.

Sample Call

```
    wchar_t *wc;
    char *mb;
    int  len;
// Assume mb points to a multibyte character.
    len = mbtowc(wc, mb, MB_CUR_MAX);
```

See Also

`mblen`, `mbstowcs`, `wctomb`, `wcstombs`

_memccpy, _fmemccpy

MSC6	MSC7	VC++	QC2.5	QC-WIN	TC2	TC++	BC++2	BC++3	ANSI	POSIX	UNIX V	DOS	QWIN	WIN	WINDLL
x	x	x	x	x	x	x	x	x			x	x	x	x	x

Note: `_fmemccpy` is available in MSC6, MSC7, Visual C++, QC-WIN, BC++2, and BC++3 only.

Summary

```
#include <string.h>        // Or <memory.h>

void *_memccpy(
    void          *dest,   // Copy characters to this buffer
    const void    *src,    //   from this one.
```

```
    int            c,      // Last character to be copied from src.
    unsigned int count); // Copy at most this many bytes.

void __far * __far _fmemccpy(void __far *dest,  // See _memccpy
        const void __far *src, int c, unsigned int count);
```

Description

Copies characters from the array *src* to *dest* until the character *c* is copied, or until a total of *count* characters have been copied.

The `_fmemccpy` function is similar to `_memccpy` except that `_fmemccpy` can be used to manipulate far buffers in any memory model.

Returns

When the function completes successfully, the return value is a pointer to the character following *c* in the buffer *src*, provided that the character *c* was copied.

`NULL` Indicates that *c* was not copied.

Sample Call

```
memccpy (outbuf, inbuf, '\0', 81);
```

See Also

memcpy, strcpy, strncpy

memchr, _fmemchr

MSC6	MSC7	VC++	QC2.5	QC-WIN	TC2	TC++	BC++2	BC++3	ANSI	POSIX	UNIX V	DOS	QWIN	WIN	WINDLL	
x	x	x	x	x	x	x	x	x	x	x		x	x	x	x	x

Note: `_fmemchr` is available in MSC6, MSC7, Visual C++, QC-WIN, BC++2, and BC++3 only.

Summary

```
#include <string.h>    // Or <memory.h>

void *memchr(
    const void *buf,    // Search this buffer
    int         c,      //   for this character.
    size_t      count); // Examine this many bytes at most.

void __far * __far _fmemchr(  // See memchr
    const void __far *buf, int c, size_t count);
```

Description

Searches through the first *count* bytes in the buffer *buf* to find the first occurrence of the character *c*.

The `_fmemchr` function is similar to `memchr` except that `_fmemchr` can be used to search through far buffers in any memory model.

Returns

When the function completes successfully, the return value is a pointer to the character in the buffer, if found.

`NULL` Indicates that the search was unsuccessful.

Sample Call

```
    char *buf = "Be yourself";
    char *first_y;
// Search for the first occurrence of 'y' in the buffer:
    first_y = memchr(buf, 'y', 10);
```

See Also

`memcmp`, `strchr`

memcmp, _fmemcmp

MSC6	MSC7	VC++	QC2.5	QC-WIN	TC2	TC++	BC++2	BC++3	ANSI	POSIX	UNIX V	DOS	QWIN	WIN	WINDLL	
x	x	x	x	x	x	x	x	x	x	x		x	x	x	x	x

Note: `_fmemcmp` is available in MSC6, MSC7, Visual C++, QC-WIN, BC++2, and BC++3 only.

Summary

```
#include <string.h>     // Or <memory.h>

int memcmp(
    const void *buf1,   // Compare this buffer
    const void *buf2,   //   with this one.
    size_t     count);  // Compare this many bytes.

int __far _fmemcmp(const void __far *buf1, // See memcmp
                   const void __far *buf2, size_t count);
```

Description

Compares the first *count* bytes of the buffers *buf1* and *buf2*.

The `_fmemcmp` function is similar to `memcmp` except that `_fmemcmp` can be used to compare far buffers in any memory model.

Returns

Negative Indicates that *buf1* is less than *buf2*.

Zero Indicates that the first *count* characters of *buf1* and *buf2* match.

Positive Indicates that *buf1* is greater than *buf2*.

Sample Call

```
    char *buf1, *buf2;
//...
// Check whether first 16 characters of buf1 and buf2 match:
    if(memcmp(buf1, buf2, 16) == 0)
            printf("The buffers match\n");
```

See Also

_memicmp, strcmp, strncmp

memcpy, _fmemcpy

MSC6	MSC7	VC++	QC2.5	QC-WIN	TC2	TC++	BC++2	BC++3	ANSI	POSIX	UNIX V	DOS	QWIN	WIN	WINDLL
X	X	X	X	X	X	X	X	X	X		X	X	X	X	X

Note: _fmemcpy is available in MSC6, MSC7, Visual C++, QC-WIN, BC++2, and BC++3 only.

Summary

```
#include <string.h>     // Or <memory.h>

void *memcpy(
    void        *dest,  // Copy into this buffer
    const void *src,    //    from this one.
    size_t      count); // Copy this many bytes.

void __far * __far _fmemcpy(void __far *dest,  // See memcpy
        const void __far *src, size_t count);
```

Description

Copies *count* bytes from buffer *src* to *dest*. Do not use this function for overlapping source and destination buffers; use memmove to copy between overlapping buffers.

The _fmemcpy function is similar to memcpy except that you can use _fmemcpy in any memory model to copy far buffers.

Returns

The return value is a pointer to the destination buffer (which is the argument *dest*).

Sample Call

```
    char *dest, *src;
// Assume buffers are allocated with proper size, and so on....
// Copy 80 characters from src to dest:
    memcpy(dest, src, 80);
```

See Also

`_memccpy`, `memmove`, `strcpy`, `strncpy`

_memicmp, _fmemicmp

MSC6	MSC7	VC++	QC2.5	QC-WIN	TC2	TC++	BC++2	BC++3	ANSI	POSIX	UNIX V	DOS	QWIN	WIN	WINDLL
x	x	x	x	x	x	x	x	x			x	x	x	x	x

Note: `_fmemicmp` is available in MSC6, MSC7, Visual C++, QC-WIN, BC++2, and BC++3 only.

Summary

```
#include <string.h>     // Or <memory.h>

int _memicmp(
    const void *buf1,   // Compare this buffer
    const void *buf2,   //   with this one.
    size_t     count);  // Compare this many bytes.

int __far _fmemicmp(const void __far *buf1, // See _memicmp
                    const void __far *buf2, size_t count);
```

Description

Works the same way as `memcmp` and `_fmemcmp` except that the comparison is case-insensitive.

Returns

Negative Indicates that *buf1* is less than *buf2*.

Zero Indicates that the first *count* characters of *buf1* and *buf2* match.

Positive Indicates that *buf1* is greater than *buf2*.

Sample Call

```
    char *buf1, *buf2;
//...
// Check whether first 16 characters of buf1 and buf2 match
// (ignoring case):
    if(_memicmp(buf1, buf2, 16) == 0)
            printf("The buffers match\n");
```

See Also

memcmp, strcmp, strncmp

memmove, _fmemmove

MSC6	MSC7	VC++	QC2.5	QC-WIN	TC2	TC++	BC++2	BC++3	ANSI	POSIX	UNIX V	DOS	QWIN	WIN	WINDLL
X	X	X	X	X	X	X	X	X	X			X	X	X	X

Note: _fmemmove is available in MSC6, MSC7, Visual C++, QC-WIN, BC++2, and BC++3 only.

Summary

```
#include <string.h>     // Or <memory.h>

void *memove
    void        *dest,  // Copy into this buffer
    const void *src,    //    from this buffer.
    size_t      count); // Copy this many bytes.

void __far * __far _fmemmove(void __far *dest,   // See memmove
       const void __far *src, size_t count);
```

Description

Copies *count* bytes from the buffer *src* to *dest*. Works properly even if the *src* and *dest* buffers overlap.

The _fmemmove function is similar to memmove except that you can use _fmemmove in any memory model to copy far buffers.

Returns

The return value is the pointer to the destination buffer (which is the *dest* argument).

Sample Call

```
    char str[80] = "NB-MCPB";
// Shift string to the right by 2 bytes.
    memmove(&str[2], str, strlen(str));
```

See Also

_memccpy, memcpy, strcpy, strncpy

memset, _fmemset

MSC6	MSC7	VC++	QC2.5	QC-WIN	TC2	TC++	BC++2	BC++3	ANSI	POSIX	UNIX V	DOS	QWIN	WIN	WINDLL
x	x	x	x	x	x	x	x	x	x		x	x	x	x	x

Note: _fmemset is available in MSC6, MSC7, Visual C++, QC-WIN, BC++2, and BC++3 only.

Summary

```
#include <string.h> // Or <memory.h>

void *memset(
    void   *buf,     // Set bytes in this buffer
    int    c,        // Set each byte to this character
    size_t count);   // Set this many bytes

void __far * __far _fmemset(void __far *buf,  // See memset
                            int c, size_t count);
```

Description

Sets each of the first *count* bytes of the buffer *buf* to the character *c*.

The _fmemset function works similarly to memset except that _fmemset can be used to set bytes in a far buffer in all memory models.

Returns

The return value is the argument *buf*.

Sample Call

```
    char buf[1024];
// Set buf to all zeros
    memset(buf, '\0', 1024);
```

See Also

_strset, _strnset

_movedata

MSC6	MSC7	VC++	QC2.5	QC-WIN	TC2	TC++	BC++2	BC++3	ANSI	POSIX	UNIX V	DOS	QWIN	WIN	WINDLL
x	x	x	x	x	x	x	x	x				x	x	x	x

Summary

```
#include <string.h>          // Or <memory.h>

void _movedata(
    unsigned int s_segment, // Copy from this segment and
    unsigned int s_offset,  //   offset address
    unsigned int d_segment, //   to a buffer at this segment
    unsigned int d_offset,  //   and offset.
    unsigned int count);    // Copy this many bytes
```

Description

Copies `count` bytes from a source address to a destination address. Use this function to move data between two different segments.

Returns

No return value.

Sample Call

```
    char __far *buf;
//...
    if((buf = _fmalloc(64)) != NULL)
    {
// Copy 64 bytes from F000:E000 (in the ROM BIOS) into buf.
        _movedata(0xf000, 0xe000,
                  _FP_SEG(buf), _FP_OFF(buf), 64);
    }
```

See Also

`_FP_OFF` (Chapter 32), `_FP_SEG` (Chapter 32), `memcpy`, `memmove`, `_segread` (Chapter 32)

strcat, _fstrcat

MSC6	MSC7	VC++	QC2.5	QC-WIN	TC2	TC++	BC++2	BC++3	ANSI	POSIX	UNIX V	DOS	QWIN	WIN	WINDLL
x	x	x	x	x	x	x	x	x	x	x	x	x	x	x	x

Note: `_fstrcat` is available in MSC6, MSC7, Visual C++, QC-WIN, BC++2, and BC++3 only.

Summary

```
#include <string.h>

char *strcat(
    char       *dest, // Append to this string
    const char *src); //   all the characters from this string

char __far * __far _fstrcat(char __far *dest, // See strcat
    const char __far *src);
```

Description

Appends the string *src* to *dest*. Both *src* and *dest* must be null-terminated strings. Use the `_fstrcat` function in any memory model to concatenate far strings.

Returns

The return value is the *dest* argument.

Sample Call

```
char str[80] = "C++";
//...
strcat(str, " and C"); // Now str = "C++ and C"
```

See Also

`strcpy`, `strncat`

strchr, _fstrchr

MSC6	MSC7	VC++	QC2.5	QC-WIN	TC2	TC++	BC++2	BC++3	ANSI	POSIX	UNIX V	DOS	QWIN	WIN	WINDLL
X	X	X	X	X	X	X	X	X	X	X	X	X	X	X	X

Note: `_fstrchr` is available in MSC6, MSC7, Visual C++, QC-WIN, BC++2, and BC++3 only.

Summary

```
#include <string.h>

char *strchr(
    const char *str,// Search from the beginning of this string
    int        c);  //   for the first occurrence of this character.

char __far * __far _fstrchr(         // See strchr
                    const char __far *str, int c);
```

Description

Searches the null-terminated string *str* for the first occurrence of the character c. Use the _fstrchr function to search through a far string in any memory model.

Returns

When the function completes successfully, the return value is a pointer to the first occurrence of c in *str*, if found.

NULL Indicates that c was not found in *str*.

Sample Call

```
    char result[] = "Part number: LNB-920626-01";
    char *part_no;
// Locate the part number by searching for an L:
    part_no = strchr(result, 'L');
```

See Also

strcspn, strpbrk, strstr

strcmp, _fstrcmp

MSC6	MSC7	VC++	QC2.5	QC-WIN	TC2	TC++	BC++2	BC++3	ANSI	POSIX	UNIX V	DOS	QWIN	WIN	WINDLL
X	X	X	X	X	X	X	X	X	X	X	X	X	X	X	X

Note: _fstrcmp is available in MSC6, MSC7, Visual C++, QC-WIN, BC++2, and BC++3 only.

Summary

```
#include <string.h>

int strcmp(
    const char *str1, // Compare this null-terminated string
    const char *str2);//   with this one.

int __far _fstrcmp(const char __far *str1,  // See strcmp
                   const char __far *str2);
```

Description

Compares two null-terminated strings, *str1* and *str2*. Use _fstrcmp to compare null-terminated far strings in any memory model.

Returns

Negative Indicates that *str1* is less than *str2*.

Zero Indicates that the characters in *str1* and *str2* match.

Positive Indicates that *str1* is greater than *str2*.

Sample Call

```
char *username;
//...
if(strcmp(username, "NETADMIN") != 0) exit(1);
```

See Also

memcmp, _memicmp, _stricmp

_strcmpi

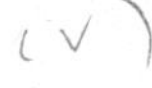

MSC6	MSC7	VC++	QC2.5	QC-WIN	TC2	TC++	BC++2	BC++3	ANSI	POSIX	UNIX V	DOS	QWIN	WIN	WINDLL
	X	X		X	X	X	X	X				X	X	X	X

Summary

```
#include <string.h>

int _strcmpi(
    const char *str1, // Compare this null-terminated string
    const char *str2);//   with this one without regard to case.
```

Description

Compares the null-terminated strings *str1* and *str2* in their lowercase form (thus making the comparison case-insenstive).

The _stricmp function is identical to _strcmpi. The strings are not altered by _stricmpi.

This function has been replaced with the _stricmp function, and should not be used in new applications.

Returns

Negative	Indicates that *str1* is less than *str2*.
Zero	Indicates that the characters in *str1* and *str2* match.
Positive	Indicates that *str1* is greater than *str2*.

Sample Call

```
int result;
result = _strcmpi("Object", "OBJECT"); // result should be zero
```

See Also

strcmp, _stricmp

strcoll

MSC6	MSC7	VC++	QC2.5	QC-WIN	TC2	TC++	BC++2	BC++3	ANSI	POSIX	UNIX V	DOS	QWIN	WIN	WINDLL
x	x	x	x	x		x	x	x	x			x	x	x	x

Summary

```
#include <string.h>

int strcoll(
    const char *str1, // Compare this null-terminated string
    const char *str2);//   with this one using the collating
                      //   sequence from the LC_COLLATE category
```

Description

Compares the null-terminated strings *str1* and *str2* after interpreting each according to the character collating sequence specified by the `LC_COLLATE` category of the current locale. Use the `setlocale` function to select a locale (see tutorial in Chapter 30 for information on locales and the `setlocale` function).

Returns

Negative	Indicates that *str1* is less than *str2*.
Zero	Indicates that the characters in *str1* and *str2* match.
Positive	Indicates that *str1* is greater than *str2*.

Sample Call

```
// Assume username and adminname are null-terminated
// strings_appropriately initialized....
if(strcoll(username, adminname) != 0) exit(1);
```

See Also

`memcmp`, `strcmp`, `strncmp`

strcpy, _fstrcpy

MSC6	MSC7	VC++	QC2.5	QC-WIN	TC2	TC++	BC++2	BC++3	ANSI	POSIX	UNIX V	DOS	QWIN	WIN	WINDLL
x	x	x	x	x	x	x	x	x	x	x	x	x	x	x	x

Note: `_fstrcpy` is available in MSC6, MSC7, Visual C++, QC-WIN, BC++2, and BC++3 only.

Summary

```
#include <string.h>

char *strcpy(
    char       *dest, // Copy into this buffer
    const char *src); //   this null-terminated string.

char __far * __far _fstrcpy(char __far *dest,  // See strcpy
                            const char __far *src);
```

Description

Copies the null-terminated string *src* (including the terminating null character) into the buffer *dest*. You must ensure that the buffer *dest* has enough room to hold the entire string *src*.

The `_fstrcpy` function is similar to `strcpy` except that `_fstrcpy` can be used to copy far strings in any memory model.

Returns

The return value is a pointer to the copied string, which is the *dest* argument.

Sample Call

```
char buf[80];
//...
strcpy(buf, "Project No.:");
```

See Also

`strdup`, `strncpy`

strcspn, _fstrcspn

MSC6	MSC7	VC++	QC2.5	QC-WIN	TC2	TC++	BC++2	BC++3	ANSI	POSIX	UNIX V	DOS	QWIN	WIN	WINDLL
x	x	x	x	x	x	x	x	x	x	x	x	x	x	x	x

Note: `_fstrcspn` is available in MSC6, MSC7, Visual C++, QC-WIN, BC++2, and BC++3 only.

Summary

```
#include <string.h>

size_t strcspn(
    const char *str,    // Search this string for the first
    const char *cset); //   occurrence of a character from this set

size_t __far _fstrcspn(const char __far *str,   // See strcspn
                       const char __far *cset);
```

Description

Searches the null-terminated string *str* for the first occurrence of any character from the second null-terminated string *cset*.

The `_fstrcspn` function is similar to `strcspn` except that you can use `_fstrcspn` in any memory model with far pointer arguments.

Returns

When the function completes successfully, the return value is the index of the first character in *str* that belongs to the set *cset*.

If *str* contains none of the characters in *cset*, the return value is the length of the string *str*. You can think of this return value as the length of the longest initial substring of *str* that does not contain any of the characters from the string *cset*.

Sample Call

```
    int i;
    char *whitespace = " \t\n";
    char cmdline[80];
// Assume cmdline contains a line of command.
// Locate the first whitespace character:
    i = strcspn (p_cmdline,whitespace);
```

See Also

strpbrk, strspn

_strdup, _fstrdup, _nstrdup

MSC6	MSC7	VC++	QC2.5	QC-WIN	TC2	TC++	BC++2	BC++3	ANSI	POSIX	UNIX V	DOS	QWIN	WIN	WINDLL
X	X	X	X	X	X	X	X	X			X	X	X	X	X

Note: `_fstrdup` is available in MSC6, MSC7, Visual C++, QC-WIN, BC++2, and BC++3 only; `_nstrdup` is available in MSC6, MSC7, Visual C++, and QC-WIN only.

Summary

```
#include <string.h>

char *_strdup(
    const char *str); // Duplicate this null-terminated string

char __far * __far _fstrdup(const char __far *str);  // See strdup
char __near * __far _nstrdup(const char __far *str); // See strdup
```

Description

Allocates enough memory to hold the null-terminated string *str* and copies the string, including the terminating null character, to the newly allocated memory. The allocated memory is in the near heap for the tiny, small, and medium model programs and in the far heap in compact, large, and huge model programs.

To always allocate memory in the far heap, use the `_fstrdup` function. Calling `_nstrdup` guarantees that the allocated memory is in the near heap.

Remember: you're responsible for freeing the memory allocated by these functions.

Returns

When the function completes successfully and memory allocation succeeds, the return value is a pointer to the duplicated string.

`NULL` Indicates that memory allocation failed.

Sample Call

```
    char cmdline[80];
    char *saved_cmd;
//...
// Make a copy of the command line:
    saved_cmd = strdup(cmdline);
```

See Also

`strcat, strcpy`

_strerror

MSC6	MSC7	VC++	QC2.5	QC-WIN	TC2	TC++	BC++2	BC++3	ANSI	POSIX	UNIX V	DOS	QWIN	WIN	WINDLL
x	x	x	x	x	x	x	x	x				x	x	x	x

Summary

```
#include <string.h>

char *_strerror(
    const char *msg); // Part of error message that you provide
```

Description

Constructs an error message by appending a colon to the null-terminated string *msg* and concatenating to it a system message corresponding to the last system error.

Returns

The return value is a pointer to the constructed error message.

Sample Call

```
char *emsg;
//...
emsg = _strerror("Error opening database");
```

See Also

perror (Chapter 22), strerror

strerror 

MSC6	MSC7	VC++	QC2.5	QC-WIN	TC2	TC++	BC++2	BC++3	ANSI	POSIX	UNIX V	DOS	QWIN	WIN	WINDLL
X	X	X	X	X	X	X	X	X	X			X	X	X	X

Summary

```
#include <string.h>

char *strerror(int errnum); // Return error message corresponding
                            //   to this error number.
```

Description

Call strerror immediately after an error return from a library function to retrieve an error message corresponding to an error number *errnum*. Use the global variable errno as the errnum argument to strerror.

Returns

The return value is a pointer to the error message. You can use this pointer to print the error message.

Sample Call

```
// Assume an error has occurred.
   fprintf(stderr, "%s\n", strerror(errno));
```

See Also

perror (Chapter 22), _strerror

_stricmp, _fstricmp

MSC6	MSC7	VC++	QC2.5	QC-WIN	TC2	TC++	BC++2	BC++3	ANSI	POSIX	UNIX V	DOS	QWIN	WIN	WINDLL
X	X	X	X	X	X	X	X	X				X	X	X	X

Note: _fstricmp is available in MSC6, MSC7, Visual C++, QC-WIN, BC++2, and BC++3 only.

Summary

```
#include <string.h>

int _stricmp(
    const char *str1,  // Compare this null-terminated string
    const char *str2); //   with this one without regard to case.

int __far _fstricmp(const char __far *str1, // See _stricmp
                    const char __far *str2);
```

Description

Compares the null-terminated strings `str1` and `str2` in their lowercase form (thus making the comparison case-insensitive).

The `_fstricmp` function is identical to `_stricmp` except that you can use `_fstricmp` to compare far strings in any memory model.

The strings being compared are not altered by these functions.

Returns

Negative	Indicates that `str1` is less than `str2`.
Zero	Indicates that the characters in `str1` and `str2` match.
Positive	Indicates that `str1` is greater than `str2`.

Sample Call

```
int result;
result = _stricmp("Usenet", "USENET"); // result should be zero
```

See Also

`strcmp`

strlen, _fstrlen

MSC6	MSC7	VC++	QC2.5	QC-WIN	TC2	TC++	BC++2	BC++3	ANSI	POSIX	UNIX V	DOS	QWIN	WIN	WINDLL
x	x	x	x	x	x	x	x	x	x	x	x	x	x	x	x

Note: `_fstrlen` is available in MSC6, MSC7, Visual C++, QC-WIN, BC++2, and BC++3 only.

Summary

```
#include <string.h>

size_t strlen(const char *str); // Get length of this string

size_t __far _fstrlen(const char __far *str); // See strlen
```

Description

Determines the length of the null-terminated *str* in bytes, not counting the terminating null character. Use `_fstrlen` to find the length of a far string in any memory model.

Returns

The return value is the number of characters in the string, excluding the null character.

Sample Call

```
size_t len;
len = strlen("Hello"); // len = 5
```

See Also

`strcspn`

_strlwr, _fstrlwr

MSC6	MSC7	VC++	QC2.5	QC-WIN	TC2	TC++	BC++2	BC++3	ANSI	POSIX	UNIX V	DOS	QWIN	WIN	WINDLL
X	X	X	X	X	X	X	X	X				X	X	X	X

Note: `_fstrlwr` is available in MSC6, MSC7, Visual C++, QC-WIN, BC++2, and BC++3 only.

Summary

```
#include <string.h>

char *_strlwr(char *str); // Convert this string to lowercase

char __far * __far _fstrlwr(char __far *str); // See _strlwr
```

Description

Converts all characters in the string *str* to lowercase.

The `_fstrlwr` function is similar to `_strlwr` except that `_fstrlwr` works with a far pointer to a string.

Returns

The return value is a pointer to the converted string (the argument *str*).

Sample Call

```
char cmdline[80] = "INIT";
//...
_strlwr(cmdline); // cmdline = "init"
```

See Also

_strupr

strncat, _fstrncat

MSC6	MSC7	VC++	QC2.5	QC-WIN	TC2	TC++	BC++2	BC++3	ANSI	POSIX	UNIX V	DOS	QWIN	WIN	WINDLL
X	X	X	X	X	X	X	X	X	X	X	X	X	X	X	X

Note: `_fstrncat` is available in MSC6, MSC7, Visual C++, QC-WIN, BC++2, and BC++3 only.

Summary

```
#include <string.h>

char *strncat(
    char       *dest,     // Append to this string
    const char *src,      //    from this string.
    size_t     count);    // Append this many characters, at most.

char __far __far _fstrncat(char __far *dest,  // See strncat
          const char __far *src, size_t count);
```

Description

Appends, at most, the first *count* characters from the null-terminated string *src* to *dest*. If the length of the string *src* is less than *count*, the entire *src* string is appended to *dest*. Terminates the concatenated string with a null character. You must ensure that the *dest* string has enough room to hold the entire concatenated string.

The `_fstrncat` function behaves similarly but works on far strings.

Returns

The return value is a pointer to the concatenated string (this is the same as the *dest* argument).

Sample Call

```
    char userid[20] = "PDH_", *firstname = "Peter";
// Append first 4 characters of firstname to userid prefix:
    strncat(userid, firstname, 4); // userid = PDH_Pete
```

See Also

strcat, strcpy, strncpy

strncmp, _fstrncmp

MSC6	MSC7	VC++	QC2.5	QC-WIN	TC2	TC++	BC++2	BC++3	ANSI	POSIX	UNIX V	DOS	QWIN	WIN	WINDLL
x	x	x	x	x	x	x	x	x	x	x	x	x	x	x	x

Note: `_fstrncmp` is available in MSC6, MSC7, Visual C++, QC-WIN, BC++2, and BC++3 only.

Summary

```
#include <string.h>

int strncmp(
    const char *str1,   // Compare this string
    const char *str2,   //   with this one.
    size_t     count);  // Compare the first count bytes.

int __far _fstrncmp(const char __far *str1,    // See strncmp
                    const char __far *str2, size_t count);
```

Description

Compares the characters of the string *str1* with the corresponding characters of *str2*. The comparison ends as soon as *count* characters are compared or the terminating null character of one of the strings is reached.

The `_fstrncmp` function is similar to `strncmp` except that `_fstrncmp` accepts far pointers as arguments.

Returns

Negative Indicates that the first *count* characters of *str1* are less than the first *count* characters of *str2*.

Zero Indicates that the first *count* characters of *str1* and *str2* match.

Positive Indicates that the first *count* characters of *str1* are greater than the first *count* characters of *str2*.

Sample Call

```
int result;
result = strncmp("LNB-1101", "LNB-ACCT", 3); // result = 0
```

See Also

`strcmp`, `strnicmp`

strncpy, _fstrncpy

MSC6	MSC7	VC++	QC2.5	QC-WIN	TC2	TC++	BC++2	BC++3	ANSI	POSIX	UNIX V	DOS	QWIN	WIN	WINDLL
x	x	x	x	x	x	x	x	x	x	x	x	x	x	x	x

Note: _fstrncpy is available in MSC6, MSC7, Visual C++, QC-WIN, BC++2, and BC++3 only.

Summary

```
#include <string.h>

char *strncpy(
    char       *dest,  // Copy into this buffer
    const char *src,   //   characters from this string.
    size_t     count); // Copy at most this many characters.

char __far * __far _fstrncpy(char __far *dest, // See strncpy
        const char __far *src, size_t count);
```

Description

Copies *count* characters (or, if *count* exceeds the length of *src*, the entire string) from the null-terminated string *src* into the char array *dest*. You must ensure that there is enough room in *dest* to hold the copied string. Use the _fstrncpy function to copy far strings in any memory model.

Note that if you copy less than the length of the string *src*, no terminating null character is appended to the copied string in *dest*.

Returns

The return value is a pointer to the copied string (which is the *dest* argument).

Sample Call

```
    char *long_fname; // A long filename
    char fname[20];
// Set filename to be first 8 characters of long filename.
    strncpy(fname, long_fname, 8);
```

See Also

strcat, strcpy, strdup, strncat

_strnicmp, _fstrnicmp

MSC6	MSC7	VC++	QC2.5	QC-WIN	TC2	TC++	BC++2	BC++3	ANSI	POSIX	UNIX V	DOS	QWIN	WIN	WINDLL
x	x	x	x	x	x	x	x	x				x	x	x	x

Note: _fstrnicmp is available in MSC6, MSC7, Visual C++, QC-WIN, BC++2, and BC++3 only.

Summary

```
#include <string.h>

int _strnicmp(
    const char *str1,  // Compare this string
    const char *str2,  //   with this one.
    size_t     count); // Compare the first count bytes.

int __far _fstrnicmp(const char __far *str1,   // See strncmp
                     const char __far *str2, size_t count);
```

Description

Compares the characters of the string *str1* with the corresponding characters of *str2*, ignoring the case of the characters. The comparison ends as soon as *count* characters are compared or the terminating null character of one of the strings is reached.

The `_fstrnicmp` function is similar to `_strnicmp` except that `_fstrnicmp` accepts far pointers as arguments.

Returns

Negative	Indicates that the first *count* characters of *str1* are less than the first *count* characters of *str2*.
Zero	Indicates that the first *count* characters of *str1* and *str2* match.
Positive	Indicates that the first *count* characters of *str1* are greater than the first *count* characters of *str2*.

Sample Call

```
    char input[20];
//...
    if(_strnicmp(input, "Y", 1) == 0) accept_input();
```

See Also

`strcmp`, `strncmp`

_strnset, _fstrnset

MSC6	MSC7	VC++	QC2.5	QC-WIN	TC2	TC++	BC++2	BC++3	ANSI	POSIX	UNIX V	DOS	QWIN	WIN	WINDLL
X	X	X	X	X	X	X	X	X				X	X	X	X

Note: `_fstrnset` is available in MSC6, MSC7, Visual C++, QC-WIN, BC++2, and BC++3 only.

Summary

```
#include <string.h>

char *_strnset(
    char   *str,     // Set characters in this string
    int    c,        // Set each character to this value
    size_t count);  // Set this many characters

char __far * __far _fstrnset(char __far *str,      // See _strnset
                             int c, size_t count);
```

Description

Sets the first *count* characters of the null-terminated string *str* to *c*. If *count* exceeds the length of the string *str*, the entire string, excluding the terminating null character, is set to *c*.

Returns

The return value is the *str* argument.

Sample Call

```
    char tmpfname = "0172005";
// Set first two characters to 'x':
    _strnset(tmpfname, 'x', 2); // tmpfname = "xx72005"
```

See Also

_strset

strpbrk, _fstrpbrk

MSC6	MSC7	VC++	QC2.5	QC-WIN	TC2	TC++	BC++2	BC++3	ANSI	POSIX	UNIX V	DOS	QWIN	WIN	WINDLL
x	x	x	x	x	x	x	x	x	x	x	x	x	x	x	x

Note: _fstrpbrk is available in MSC6, MSC7, Visual C++, QC-WIN, BC++2, and BC++3 only.

Summary

```
#include <string.h>

char *strpbrk(
    const char *str,     // Search this string and return pointer
    const char *cset);  //    to first occurrence of any character
                        //    in the string cset.

char __far * __far _fstrpbrk(          // See strpbrk
        const char __far *str, const char __far *cset);
```

Description

Locates the first occurrence in string *str* of any character from the string *cset*. Both strings must be null-terminated.

The _fstrpbrk function works just like strpbrk, except that you can use _fstrpbrk in any memory model with far pointer arguments.

Returns

When the function completes successfully, the return value is a pointer to the first occurrence of any character from string *cset* in *str*.

NULL Indicates that the string *str* has no characters in common with the string *cset*.

Sample Call

```
char report[80] = "Total Cost = $426,900.00";
char *price;
//...
price = strpbrk(report, "$"); // price = "$426,900.00"
```

See Also

strchr, strcspn, strrchr, strspn

strrchr, _fstrrchr

MSC6	MSC7	VC++	QC2.5	QC-WIN	TC2	TC++	BC++2	BC++3	ANSI	POSIX	UNIX V	DOS	QWIN	WIN	WINDLL
X	X	X	X	X	X	X	X	X	X	X	X	X	X	X	X

Note: _fstrrchr is available in MSC6, MSC7, Visual C++, QC-WIN, BC++2, and BC++3 only.

Summary

```
#include <string.h>

char *strrchr(
    const char *str, // Search from the end of this string
    int        c);   //   for the last occurrence of this character.

char __far * __far _fstrrchr(           // See strrchr
          const char __far *str, int c);
```

Description

Searches the null-terminated string *str* for the last occurrence of the character *c*. You also can search for the terminating null character.

The _fstrrchr function is similar to strrchr except that _fstrrchr works with far pointers.

Returns

When the function completes successfully, the return value is a pointer to the last occurrence of the specified character *c*, provided the character is found.

NULL   Indicates that *c* was not found.

Sample Call

```
char *a_book = "Title = Adventures in Llithings, Date: 11/1/94";
char *pub_year;
//...
pub_year = strrchr(a_book, '/');
pu_year++; // Skip over the '/'
```

See Also

strchr, strpbrk

_strrev, _fstrrev

MSC6	MSC7	VC++	QC2.5	QC-WIN	TC2	TC++	BC++2	BC++3	ANSI	POSIX	UNIX V	DOS	QWIN	WIN	WINDLL
X	X	X	X	X	X	X	X	X				X	X	X	X

Note: _fstrrev is available in MSC6, MSC7, Visual C++, QC-WIN, BC++2, and BC++3 only.

Summary

```
#include <string.h>

char *_strrev(char *str); // Reverse the order of characters in str.

char __far * __far _fstrrev(char __far *str); // See _strrev
```

Description

Reverses the order of characters in the null-terminated string *str*.

The _fstrrev function works the same as _strrev, except that you can use it in any memory model to reverse a far string.

Returns

The return value is a pointer to the reversed string, which is the same as the *str* argument.

Sample Call

```
char input[80];
//...
strrev(input); // Reverse the string
```

See Also

strcpy, strncpy

_strset, _fstrset

MSC6	MSC7	VC++	QC2.5	QC-WIN	TC2	TC++	BC++2	BC++3	ANSI	POSIX	UNIX V	DOS	QWIN	WIN	WINDLL
x	x	x	x	x	x	x	x	x				x	x	x	x

Note: _fstrset is available in MSC6, MSC7, Visual C++, QC-WIN, BC++2, and BC++3 only.

Summary

```
#include <string.h>

char *_strset(
    char *str,  // Set all characters in this string
    int  c);    //   to this value.

char __far * __far _fstrset(         // See _strset
             char __far *str, int c);
```

Description

Sets all characters of a null-terminated string *str* to the value *c*.

The _fstrset function is similar to _strset, except that you can use _fstrset in any memory model to set characters in a far string.

Returns

The return value is a pointer to the string *str*.

Sample Call

```
    char *account = "12345678";
// Set account to all blanks:
    _strset(account, ' ');
```

See Also

memset, _strnset

strspn, _fstrspn

MSC6	MSC7	VC++	QC2.5	QC-WIN	TC2	TC++	BC++2	BC++3	ANSI	POSIX	UNIX V	DOS	QWIN	WIN	WINDLL
x	x	x	x	x	x	x	x	x	x	x	x	x	x	x	x

Note: `_fstrspn` is available in MSC6, MSC7, Visual C++, QC-WIN, BC++2, and BC++3 only.

Summary

```
#include <string.h>

size_t strspn(
    const char *str,    // Locate first character in str
    const char *cset);  //   that does not match any character
                        //   in this string.

size_t __far _fstrspn(const char __far *str,      // See strspn
                      const char __far *cset);
```

Description

Locates the first character in the string *str* that does not match any of the characters in the string *cset*.

The `_fstrspn` function is similar to `strspn` except that `_fstrspn` works with far strings.

Returns

The return value is the index of the first character in *str* that does not match the characters in *cset*. This happens to be the length of the largest initial substring of *str* that is composed entirely of characters from the set in string *cset*.

Sample Call

```
    char *whitespace = " \t\n";
    char cmdline[80];
    int nw;
//...
// Skip over all whitespaces. First find the length of
// the whitespace sequence:
    nw = strspn(cmdline, whitespace);
```

See Also

`strcspn`

strstr, _fstrstr

MSC6	MSC7	VC++	QC2.5	QC-WIN	TC2	TC++	BC++2	BC++3	ANSI	POSIX	UNIX V	DOS	QWIN	WIN	WINDLL
x	x	x	x	x	x	x	x	x	x	x		x	x	x	x

Note: `_fstrstr` is available in MSC6, MSC7, Visual C++, QC-WIN, BC++2, and BC++3 only.

Summary

```
#include <string.h>

char *strstr(
    const char *str,    // Search this string for first occurrence
    const char *sub);   //   of this substring.

char __far * __far _fstrstr(const char __far *str,  // See strstr
                            const char __far *sub);
```

Description

Locates the first occurrence of the substring *sub* in the string `str`. Both strings must be null-terminated.

The `_fstrstr` function works similarly to `strstr` except that `_fstrstr` accepts far pointers.

Returns

When the function completes successfully, the return value is a pointer to the first character of the matching substring in `str`, provided a match is found.

`NULL` Indicates that the search failed.

Sample Call

```
char dbresult[80] = "Part number: LNB-MCPB-92-06";
char *part_no;
//...
part_no = strstr(dbresult, "LNB"); // part_no = "LNB-MCPB-92-06"
```

See Also

strchr, strcspn, strspn

strtok, _fstrtok

MSC6	MSC7	VC++	QC2.5	QC-WIN	TC2	TC++	BC++2	BC++3	ANSI	POSIX	UNIX V	DOS	QWIN	WIN	WINDLL
x	x	x	x	x	x	x	x	x	x	x	x	x	x	x	x

Note: `_fstrtok` is available in MSC6, MSC7, Visual C++, QC-WIN, BC++2, and BC++3 only.

Summary

```
#include <string.h>

char *strtok(
    char       *str,       // Get tokens from this string.
    const char *delim);    // Tokens are delimited by characters
                           //   in this null-terminated string.

char __far * __far _fstrtok(char __far *str,  // See strtok
                            const char __far *delim);
```

Description

Isolates a token or a substring from *str* using the characters in *delim* as token delimiters. To extract all the tokens from a string, call `strtok` for the first time with the string and the delimiters as arguments. From then on, call `strtok` with `NULL` as the first argument and the delimiting characters appropriate for the current token as the second string. You can change the set of delimiting characters in each call to `strtok`. This process of extracting tokens from *str* modifies the string—`strtok` inserts null characters in place of delimiters to convert each token into a null-terminated string.

The `_fstrtok` function behaves just like `strtok` except that `_fstrtok` works with far string arguments.

Returns

When the function completes successfully, the return value is a pointer to the next token. Each token is a null-terminated string.

`NULL` Indicates that there are no more tokens left.

Sample Call

```
char *delim = " \t", // Space- or tab-separated tokens
char buf[80], *token;
//...
// Extract all tokens from buf:
token = strtok(buf, delim);
```

```
while(token != NULL)
{
    token = strtok(NULL, delim);
// Process token appropriately....
//...
}
```

See Also

strcspn, strspn

_strupr, _fstrupr

MSC6	MSC7	VC++	QC2.5	QC-WIN	TC2	TC++	BC++2	BC++3	ANSI	POSIX	UNIX V	DOS	QWIN	WIN	WINDLL
X	X	X	X	X	X	X	X	X				X	X	X	X

Note: _fstrupr is available in MSC6, MSC7, Visual C++, QC-WIN, BC++2, and BC++3 only.

Summary

```
#include <string.h>

char *_strupr(char *str); // Convert this string to lowercase

char __far * __far _fstrupr(char __far *str); // See _strupr
```

Description

Converts all characters in the string *str* to uppercase.

The _fstrupr function is similar to _strupr except that _fstrupr works with a far pointer to a string.

Returns

When the function completes successfully, the return value is a pointer to the converted string (the argument *str*).

Sample Call

```
char cmdline[80] = "dir *.*";
//...
_strupr(cmdline); // cmdline = "DIR *.*"
```

See Also

_strlwr

strxfrm

MSC6	MSC7	VC++	QC2.5	QC-WIN	TC2	TC++	BC++2	BC++3	ANSI	POSIX	UNIX V	DOS	QWIN	WIN	WINDLL
X	X	X	X	X		X	X	X	X			X	X	X	X

Summary

```
#include <string.h>

size_t strxfrm (
    char        *dest,  // Store the transformed string here.
    const char *src,    // Transform this string using locale-
                        //   specific information.
    size_t     count); // Store at most this many characters
                        //   in dest.
```

Description

Transforms at most *count* characters (including the null character) from the string *src* to a new form in *dest*. Thus, when `strcmp` is applied to two transformed strings, the result is the same as that returned by `strcoll` applied to the original strings.

Returns

The return value is the length of the transformed string, not counting the terminating null character. Do not use the transformed string if the returned value is greater than or equal to *count*.

Sample Call

```
char xstr[81];
char istr[81];
//...
if(strxfrm(xstr, istr, 81) >= 81)
{
    fprintf(stderr, "Transformed string too long!\n");
    exit(1);
}
```

See Also

`localeconv` (Chapter 30), `setlocale` (Chapter 30), `strcmp`, `strcoll`

_swab

MSC6	MSC7	VC++	QC2.5	QC-WIN	TC2	TC++	BC++2	BC++3	ANSI	POSIX	UNIX V	DOS	QWIN	WIN	WINDLL
X	X	X	X	X	X	X	X	X			X	X	X	X	X

Summary

```
#include <stdlib.h>

void _swab(
    char *src,     // Swap adjacent bytes of this buffer
    char *dest,    //   and save swapped data here.
    int  count);   // Swap at most this many bytes (must be even).
```

Description

Copies *count* bytes from *src* to *dest*, at the same time swapping each pair of adjacent bytes.

Returns

There is no return value.

Sample Call

```
char temp[20];
_swab(temp, "ABCD", 4); // temp = "BADC"
```

wcstombs, _fwcstombs

MSC6	MSC7	VC++	QC2.5	QC-WIN	TC2	TC++	BC++2	BC++3	ANSI	POSIX	UNIX V	DOS	QWIN	WIN	WINDLL
	X	X		X			X	X	X			X	X	X	X

Note: _fwcstombs is available in MSC7, Visual C++ and QC-WIN only.

Summary

```
#include <stdlib.h>

size_t wcstombs(
char           *mbs,    // Store converted multibyte sequence here.
const wchar_t  *wcs,    // Convert this wide-character array to
                        //   multibyte sequence.
size_t         count);  // Convert at most this many wide character.

size_t __far _fwcstombs(char __far *mbs,   // See wcstombs
           const wchar_t __far *wcs, size_t count);
```

Description

Converts, at most, *count* wide characters from the array *wcs* into a multibyte sequence and stores them in the array *mbs*.

The `_fwcstombs` function is similar to `wcstombs` except that you can use `_fwcstombs` in any memory model to convert far arrays of wide characters.

Returns

When the function completes successfully, the return value is the number of wide characters converted, excluding the wide-character null (`L'\0'`).

–1 For either function , indicates an encounter with invalid wide characters in `wcs`.

Sample Call

```
char    mb_array[20*MB_LEN_MAX];
wchar_t wc_array[20];
size_t nconv;
//...
nconv = wcstombs(mb_array, wc_array, 16);
```

See Also

`mblen`, `mbstowcs`, `mbtowc`, `wctomb`

wctomb, _fwctomb

MSC6	MSC7	VC++	QC2.5	QC-WIN	TC2	TC++	BC++2	BC++3	ANSI	POSIX	UNIX V	DOS	QWIN	WIN	WINDLL
	X	X		X			X	X	X			X	X	X	X

Note: `_fwctomb` is available in MSC7, Visual C++ and QC-WIN only.

Summary

```
#include <stdlib.h>

int wctomb(
    char    *mb, // Store converted multibyte character here.
    wchar_t wc); // Convert this wide character to
                 //   multibyte form.

int __far _fwctomb(char __far *mb, wchar_t wc); // See wctomb
```

Description

Converts the wide character *wc* into a multibyte character and stores the bytes in the buffer *mb*.

The `_fwctomb` function is similar to `wctomb` except that `_fwctomb` works with a far buffer.

Returns

When the function completes successfully, the return value is the number of bytes in the converted multibyte character. (This value should not be greater than MB_CUR_MAX.)

–1 Indicates that the conversion failed.

Sample Call

```
char mb[MB_LEN_MAX];
wchar_t wc;
//...
wctomb(mb, wc);
```

See Also

mblen, mbstowcs, mbtowc, wcstombs

Search and Sort

Search and sort operations are at the heart of many data-manipulation tasks. Algorithms for searching and sorting appear in every computer science textbook on algorithms. In fact, search and sort algorithms are the focus of an entire volume by Knuth (*The Art of Computer Programming, Volume 3: Sorting and Searching*, Addison-Wesley, 1973).

Of the many different algorithms covered in textbooks such as Knuth's, the *quicksort* algorithm, invented by C. A. R. Hoare in 1962, is a popular, general-purpose sort algorithm for sorting in-memory arrays. For searching, two simple algorithms are the *linear search* and the *binary search*. The Microsoft Visual C++ library includes four functions—`bsearch`, `_lfind`, `_lsearch`, and `qsort`—that implement these simple search and sort algorithms. This chapter describes how to use these functions and provides reference information on each function.

Basic Search and Sort Tasks

Table 27.1 shows an alphabetic list of the search and sort functions and gives you a quick overview of these functions. As you can see from the table, there are three functions for searching (`bsearch`, `_lfind`, and `_lsearch`) and one for sorting (`qsort`). The use of `qsort` and `bsearch` is illustrated by a short sample program later in this section. For more information on any of these functions, consult the reference entry for that function in the reference section that follows.

Table 27.1. Alphabetic listing of search and sort functions.

Function	Description
`bsearch`	Searches for an element in a sorted array using the binary search algorithm.
`_lfind`	Searches linearly through an unsorted array for a specified element.
`_lsearch`	Searches linearly through an unsorted array for a specified element *and* appends the element to the array if it is not found.
`qsort`	Sorts an array using the quicksort algorithm.

Looking Up Environment Variables

In Microsoft Visual C++, the main function can accept up to three arguments:

- An integer containing the number of command-line arguments
- The array of strings representing the command-line arguments
- A third array of strings representing the list of environment variables—the list that you see when you enter the SET command at the MS-DOS prompt

Listing 27.1 shows the program showenv.c, which sorts this list of environment variables in alphabetic order using the `qsort` function. The program also searches the list for a specified environment variable—the user does not have to enter the complete name of the environment variable; the program can look up a partial name. The showenv program illustrates the use of the `qsort` and `bsearch` functions.

Listing 27.1. A program that displays a sorted list of environment variables and searches for a specified environment variable.

```
//-------------------------------------------------------------
// File: showenv.c
//
// Displays the sorted environment list and looks for a
// specified environment variable in the environment.
//-------------------------------------------------------------
#include <stdio.h>
#include <string.h>
#include <search.h>

// Function that compares two entries
int compare(const void *str1, const void *str2);

int main(int argc, char **argv, char **envp)
{
unsigned int i, count;

char **p_env, **result;

// Find length of environment list
    for(count = 0, p_env = envp;
        *p_env != NULL;
        p_env++, count++);   // Null statement

// Sort the environment list using "qsort"
    qsort((void *) envp, (size_t)count,
          (size_t)sizeof(char *), compare);

    if(argc < 2)
    {
// No search key specified
// Print sorted environment list
        printf("===== Current environment list =====\n");
        for(i = 0, p_env = envp; i < count; i++)
        {
            printf("%s\n", *p_env);
            p_env++;
        }
```

continues

Listing 27.1. continued

```
        }
        else
        {
    // Search for the specified variable in the environment, first in the
       user's
    //    case, then if not found, convert to uppercase. This is necessary
          since
    //    Windows stores the environment variable 'windir' in lowercase. All
    //    user environment variables are converted to uppercase by DOS when
    //    stored.

            result = (char **) bsearch((const void *)&argv[1],
                                       (const void *)envp,
                                       (size_t)count,
                                       (size_t)sizeof(char *),
                                       compare);

            if (result == NULL)
            {
                printf("\n'%s' was not found, trying to find as
    uppercase...\n",
                    argv[1]);

                _strupr((char *)argv[1]);

                result = (char **) bsearch((const void *)&argv[1],
                                       (const void *)envp,
                                       (size_t)count,
                                       (size_t)sizeof(char *),
                                       compare);
            }

            if(result != NULL)
            {
                printf("\nFound %s in\n\n    %s\n", argv[1], *result);
            }
            else
            {
                printf("\n'%s' not found.\n", argv[1]);
            }
        }
```

```
    return(0);
}
//-----------------------------------------------------------
int compare(char **str1, char **str2)
{
// Compare two strings up to the length of the string being sought
    return(strncmp(*str1, *str2, strlen(*str1)));
}
```

Leading Underscore in Names of Nonstandard Functions

Microsoft Visual C++ adds an underscore prefix to many functions (such as `_lfind` and `_lsearch`) in keeping with ANSI Standard C's naming conventions for nonstandard functions. In many other C compilers (including earlier versions of Microsoft C compilers) as well as in UNIX, these functions are available with names that do not have the leading underscores. Note that you can use the names without underscore prefix in Microsoft Visual C++ as well.

bsearch

MSC6	MSC7	VC++	QC2.5	QC-WIN	TC2	TC++	BC++2	BC++3	ANSI	POSIX	UNIX V	DOS	QWIN	WIN	WINDLL
X	X	X	X	X	X	X	X	X	X	X	X	X	X	X	X

Summary

```
#include <stdlib.h>

void *bsearch(
    const void *key,      // Search for this item
    const void *base,     // Beginning of array to search
    size_t     nelem,     // Number of elements in array
    size_t     elemsize,  // Size of each element in bytes
    int (*compare)(const void *skey,     // Function called to
                   const void *elem));   //   compare key with
                                         //   an element
```

Description

Searches a sorted array that starts at *base* and contains *nelem* elements, each of size *elemsize* bytes. The *key* is the value being sought, and compare is the function called to compare any two elements from the array. The `compare` function should compare two elements and return one of the following values:

Negative	Indicates that *elem1* is less than *elem2*
Zero	Indicates that the *elem1* and *elem2* match
Positive	Indicates that *elem1* is greater than *elem2*

Note: for strings, *greater than* and *less than* refer to alphabetic order—for instance, the string XYZ is greater than ABC.

Use `qsort` to sort the array before calling `bsearch` to search for a value.

Returns

When the function completes successfully, the return value is a pointer to an occurrence of the *key* in the array.

`NULL` Indicates that *key* was not found.

Sample Call

See the use of `bsearch` in the program shown in Listing 27.1 in the tutorial part of the chapter.

See Also

`qsort`

_lfind, _lsearch

MSC6	MSC7	VC++	QC2.5	QC-WIN	TC2	TC++	BC++2	BC++3	ANSI	POSIX	UNIX V	DOS	QWIN	WIN	WINDLL
X	X	X	X	X	X	X	X	X			X	X	X	X	X

Summary

```
#include <search.h>

void *_lfind(
    const void *key,         // Search for this element
    const void *base,        // Starting location of array
    unsigned int *count,     // Pointer to location where
                             // array's element count is stored
    unsigned int elemsize,   // Size of each element in bytes
    int (*compare)(const void *elem1,    // Function called to
                   const void *elem2));  // compare two elements

void *_lsearch(
    const void *key,         // Search for this element
```

```
    void        *base,        // Starting location of array
    unsigned int *count,      // Pointer to location where
                              // array's element count is stored
    unsigned int elemsize, // Size of each element in bytes
    int (*compare)(const void *skey,    // Function called to
                   const void *elem)); // compare key with
                                       // an element
```

Description

Searches linearly through an array that starts at *base* and contains count elements, each of size *elemsize* bytes. The *key* denotes the value to be located and the total number of elements should be in an unsigned int whose address you provide in the count argument. The compare function is called to compare the *key* with an element. The compare function accepts pointers to two elements as arguments and it should return zero if the elements are identical. Otherwise, it should return a nonzero value.

The _lfind and _lsearch functions are identical except that if *key* is not found, _lsearch appends *key* to the array and updates the count of elements in the array.

Returns

When the function completes successfully, the return value is a pointer to the first occurrence of the element that matches *key*.

If *key* is not found, _lfind returns NULL, but _lsearch appends key to the array and returns a pointer to the appended element.

Sample Call

```
//...

struct person
{
    char fname[20];
    char lname[25];
    char ssn[10];
};

struct person employees[40];
// Assume array is initialized.

//------------------------------------------
// The "comparison" function.
int cmp_person(const void *key, const void *elem)
{
```

```
    struct person  *p2 = (struct person*)elem;
    return stricmp((const char*)key, p2->lname);
}
//-----------------------------------------------------
void main(int argc, char **argv)
{
    struct person *p;
//...
    p = (struct person *) _lfind(
            argv[1],
            employees,
            &count,
            sizeof(struct person),
            cmp_person);
//...
```

See Also

bsearch

qsort

MSC6	MSC7	VC++	QC2.5	QC-WIN	TC2	TC++	BC++2	BC++3	ANSI	POSIX	UNIX V	DOS	QWIN	WIN	WINDLL
X	X	X	X	X	X	X	X	X	X	X	X	X	X	X	X

Summary

```
#include <stdlib.h>

void qsort(
    void    *base,     // Beginning of array to sort
    size_t  nelem,     // Number of elements in array
    size_t  elemsize, // Size of each element in bytes
    int (*compare)(const void *elem1,    // Function called to
                   const void *elem2)); // compare two elements
```

Description

Sorts an array that starts at *base* and contains *nelem* elements, each of size *elemsize* bytes. The compare function is called to compare any two elements from the array. The compare function should compare two elements and return one of the following values:

Negative	Indicates that *elem1* is less than *elem2*
Zero	Indicates that the *elem1* and *elem2* match
Positive	Indicates that *elem1* is greater than *elem2*

Note: for strings, *greater than* and *less than* refer to alphabetic order—for instance, the string XYZ is greater than ABC.

Returns

No return value.

Sample Call

See the use of `qsort` in the program shown in Listing 27.1.

See Also

`bsearch`

28

Date and Time Management

Date- and time-management functions help you retrieve the current date and time in various formats and convert dates and times from one form to another. The system date and time is used by the operating system to timestamp each file as it's modified. You might need to get the current date and time to display it or to use as a timestamp in data files created by your application. Most of the date and time management functions are declared in the header file time.h.

Time Formats

At the heart of the date- and time-management functions is a function named `time`, which returns the current date and time as a value of type `time_t` in an implementation-dependent encoded form. For instance, in Microsoft C, prior to Version 7.0, `time` is the number of seconds elapsed since midnight Greenwich Mean Time (GMT), January 1, 1970. In Microsoft C/C++ 7.0, the `time` encoding changed; with `time` returning the seconds elapsed since midnight GMT, December 31, 1899. This change wasn't well accepted, and with Visual C++, again the `time` function returns the number of seconds elapsed since midnight Greenwich Mean Time (GMT), January 1, 1970. Although this might be an interesting fact, you don't need to know it to use the date and time functions described in this chapter.

Local Time, GMT, and UTC

Local time refers to the date and time as reported by MS-DOS. GMT is *Greenwich Mean Time*, which is the standard reference for time. UTC is the currently accepted acronym for what used to be GMT—the acronym is derived from the French version of the full name in English: *Universal Coordinated Time.* This chapter uses the terms GMT and UTC interchangeably.

To convert local time to GMT, Microsoft Visual C++ uses an environment variable named `TZ`, which should be set to a string indicating the time zone of the geographic location of the system. For a system in the Eastern time zone with daylight saving time honored, the definition of `TZ` will be this:

```
TZ=EST5EDT
```

If `TZ` is not defined, a default setting of `TZ=PST8PDT` is assumed.

As explained in the reference entry for the `_tzset` function, the information from the `TZ` environment variable can be loaded into three global variables maintained by the library:

- `_daylight`. The `_daylight` variable is an integer that contains a one or a zero—a one indicates that daylight saving time is honored in this region.
- `_timezone`. The `long int` variable `_timezone` should contain the number of seconds to be added to the local time to convert it to GMT.
- `_tzname`. The `_tzname` is an array of two strings:

  The first holds the name of the time zone (such as EST and PST).

  The second holds the corresponding daylight saving zone (such as EDT and PDT).

Date- and time-management functions use the settings of these global variables to convert time from one form to another.

Time Conversions

In addition to the `time_t` data type used to store encoded time, a `tm` structure is used to store date and time in a broken-down format. (See the reference entry of the `asctime` function for a listing of the `tm` structure.) A third format is the `_timeb` structure, defined in sys\timeb.h and used by the `ftime` function to return the current date and time. The `time` field in the `_timeb` structure is identical to the value returned by the `time` function.

Several functions are available to convert time from one representation to another. The `gmtime` and `localtime` functions convert a `time_t` value into a `tm` structure. The `mktime` function performs the reverse operation: it constructs a `time_t` value out of the fields of a `tm` structure.

To convert a `time_t` value into a text string, use the `ctime` function. The `asctime` function, on the other hand, converts the date and time in a `tm` structure into a null-terminated string that you can print.

Basic Date- and Time-Management Tasks

Table 28.1 shows an alphabetic list of the date- and time-management functions and gives you a quick overview of these functions. Table 28.2 organizes these functions by the tasks they perform. Some of these tasks are illustrated by short sample programs in the following sections. For more information on a function, consult the reference entry for that function in the reference entries that follow.

Table 28.1. Alphabetic listing of date- and time-management functions.

Function	Description
`asctime`	Converts date and time from a `tm` structure into a null-terminated string.
`clock`	Provides the elapsed processor time in number of ticks.
`ctime`	Converts date and time from a `time_t` value into a null-terminated string.

continues

Table 28.1. continued

Function	Description
difftime	Computes the difference of two time_t values.
ftime	Returns the current time in a _timeb structure.
gmtime	Converts date and time from a time_t value into a tm structure with the values corresponding to Universal Coordinated Time (UTC).
localtime	Converts date and time from a time_t value into a tm structure with the values corresponding to local time.
mktime	Converts date and time from a tm structure into a time_t value, adjusting the fields of the tm structure to bring them into valid range.
_strdate	Returns the current system date as an eight-character string of the form MM/DD/YY.
strftime	Prepares a string with the current date and time from a tm structure, formatted according to a specified format.
_strtime	Returns the current system time as an eight-character string of the form HH:MM:SS.
time	Returns current date and time as a binary value in a time_t variable.
_tzset	Sets the values of the global variables _daylight, _timezone, and _tzname from the TZ environment variable.
_utime	Sets the time of last modification of a file.

Table 28.2. Date- and time-management tasks.

Task	Functions
Get the current date and time	_ftime, _strdate, _strtime, time
Convert the date and time into strings	asctime, ctime, strftime
Convert time from one form to another	gmtime, localtime, mktime

Task	Functions
Compute elapsed time	`clock`, `difftime`
Set time zone	`_tzset`
Set the modification time of a file	`_utime`

Accessing and Printing the Current Date and Time

One of the simplest tasks you can perform with date- and time-management functions is to retrieve the current date and time, convert it to a string, and display it. Listing 28.1 shows a program named dt.c (for date and time), which displays the current date and time. It uses the `time` function to get the current time and converts that value into a text string by calling `ctime`.

Listing 28.1. dt.c.
Program to display the current date and time.

```
//-------------------------------------------------------------
// File: dt.c
//
// Displays the current date and time.
//-------------------------------------------------------------
#include <stdio.h>
#include <time.h>

int main(void)
{
    time_t tnow;

// Get the current date and time in encoded form.
    time(&tnow);

// Convert the encoded time into a string and print it.
// No need for newline because converted string has a
// newline character at the end.
```

continues

Listing 28.1. continued

```
    printf("%s", ctime(&tnow));

    return 0;
}
```

Printing a Monthly Calendar

One good way to show the versatility of the `mktime` function is to use it in preparing a calendar for any month of any year. Although this isn't readily apparent from the description of `mktime`, you can use `mktime` to determine the day of the week for any specified day, month, and year. Essentially, all you have to do is set the relevant fields (`tm_mon`, `tm_year`, and `tm_mday`) of a `tm` structure and call the `mktime` function. The `mktime` function will first adjust the fields of the `tm` structure to bring all the fields within valid range. In the process of doing so, `mktime` will set the `tm_wday` field—the day of the week—to the proper value. Using this property of `mktime`, you can easily write a program that prints a calendar for any month of any year.

Listing 28.2 shows the program cal.c, which uses the `mktime` function to prepare the calendar. Specifically, the calendar is prepared in a five-by-seven array of integers with the columns representing the days of the week and each integer holding the day of the month. The `fill_calendar` function fills this array with the appropriate days, and `print_calendar` displays the calendar. After building the CAL.EXE file, you can run it with the name of a month and a year on the command line. For instance, to get a calendar of June 1992, you would enter the following:

```
cal jun 1992
```

The program then displays the calendar for June 1992 in the following format:

```
        June  1992
---------------------------
Sun Mon Tue Wed Thu Fri Sat
      1   2   3   4   5   6
  7   8   9  10  11  12  13
 14  15  16  17  18  19  20
 21  22  23  24  25  26  27
 28  29  30
```

Listing 28.2. cal.c. A calendar printing program.

```
//----------------------------------------------------------------
// File: cal.c
//
// Prepares a calendar for a specified month and year
// and displays it. Uses the mktime function to determine
// the weekday for each day of a month
//----------------------------------------------------------------
#include <stdio.h>
#include <string.h>
#include <time.h>
#include <process.h>
#include <stdlib.h>

static char *weekdays[] =
    {"Sun", "Mon", "Tue", "Wed", "Thu", "Fri", "Sat"};

// The calendar is prepared and stored in this array

static short calendar[5][7];

static int start_wday = -1, end_row = -1, end_wday = -1;

// Names of months

static char *months[12] =
    { "January", "February", "March",
      "April",   "May",      "June",
      "July",    "August",   "September",
      "October", "November", "December"
    };

// Function prototypes

int get_wday(struct tm *p_tm);
void fill_calendar(int month, int year);
void print_calendar(int month, int year);

//----------------------------------------------------------------
// m a i n
//
```

continues

Listing 28.2. continued

```
int main(
    int argc,
    char **argv)
{

int i = 0;
int len = 0;
int month = 0;
int year = 0;

    if(argc < 3)
    {
        printf("Usage: cal <month> <year>\n");
        exit(1);
    }

// Find month number

      month = atoi(argv[1]);

    if (month <= 0)
    {
        len = strlen(argv[1]);

        for(i = 0; i < 12; i++)
        {
            if(_strnicmp(argv[1], months[i], len) == 0)
                break;
        }

        if(i > 11)
        {
            printf("Unknown month: %s\n", argv[1]);
            exit(1);
        }

        month = i;
    }
    else
```

```
    {
        --month;
    }

      year = atoi(argv[2]);

    if (year > 1900)
    {
        year -= 1900;
    }

// Prepare the calendar

    fill_calendar(month, year);

// Display the calendar
    print_calendar(month, year);

    return 0;
}
//---------------------------------------------------------------
//  g e t _ w d a y
//
//  Call this function after setting the year, month, and
//  day of month fields of a tm structure. This function will
//  return the weekday for that day of a month, or -1 if
//  the day is invalid for that month.
//
//  Intrepret return value as follows:
//     (0 = Sunday, 1 = Monday, and so on)

int get_wday(struct tm *p_tm)
{
    time_t tbin;
    int    month, year, day_of_month;

// Save current month, year, and day of month
    month = p_tm->tm_mon;
    year = p_tm->tm_year;
    day_of_month = p_tm->tm_mday;
```

continues

Listing 28.2. continued

```
    if((tbin = mktime(p_tm)) == (time_t)-1)
        return -1;

// See if month, year, and day of month still same
    if( (year == p_tm->tm_year) &&
        (month == p_tm->tm_mon) &&
        (day_of_month == p_tm->tm_mday) &&
        (p_tm->tm_wday <= 6))
    {
// Return the day of the week
        return p_tm->tm_wday;
    }
    else
    {
        return -1;
    }
}
//------------------------------------------------------------
//  b u i l d _ c a l
//
//  Fill the calendar
void fill_calendar(int month, int year)
{
    struct tm t;
    int i, row = 0, day, old_wday = 0, firsttime = 1;


// Loop over the days of month and get the weekday
    for(i = 1; i < 32; i++)
    {
// Zero out the tm structure
    memset(&t, 0, sizeof(struct tm));

// To get weekday, first set up a tm structure. Then
// call the get_wday function

        t.tm_mon = month;
        t.tm_year = year;
        t.tm_mday = i;

        if((day = get_wday(&t)) != -1)
        {
```

```
// Adjust the row number
            row = (7*row + old_wday +1) / 7;
            if(firsttime)
            {
                start_wday = day;
                firsttime = 0;
            }
            calendar[row][day] = i;
            old_wday = day;
        }
        else
        {
            break;
        }
    }

// Save last row number and last weekday
    end_row = row;
    end_wday = old_wday;
}
//---------------------------------------------------------------
//  p r i n t _ c a l e n d a r

void print_calendar(int month, int year)
{
    int row, day;

// First the month and year
    printf("       %s  %d\n", months[month], year+1900);
    printf("----------------------------\n");

    for(day = 0; day < 7; day++)
        printf("%s ", weekdays[day]);
    printf("\n");

// Row 1 of calendar
    for(day = 0; day < 7; day++)
    {
        if(day < start_wday)
            printf("    ");
        else
```

continues

Listing 28.2. continued

```
                printf("%3d ", calendar[0][day]);
        }
        printf("\n");

// Rest of the rows...
        for(row = 1; row < end_row; row++)
        {

            for(day = 0; day < 7; day++)
            {
                printf("%3d ", calendar[row][day]);
            }
            printf("\n");
        }

// Last row...
        for(day = 0; day <= end_wday; day++)
        {
            printf("%3d ", calendar[end_row][day]);
        }
        printf("\n");

}
```

Leading Underscore in Names of Nonstandard Functions

Microsoft Visual C++ adds an underscore prefix to many functions (such as `_ftime`, `_tzset`, and `_utime`) in keeping with ANSI Standard C's naming conventions for nonstandard functions. In many other C compilers (including earlier versions of Microsoft C compilers), as well as in UNIX and POSIX, these functions are available with names that do not have the leading underscores. You can continue to use the names without underscore prefix in Microsoft Visual C++ as well.

asctime

MSC6	MSC7	VC++	QC2.5	QC-WIN	TC2	TC++	BC++2	BC++3	ANSI	POSIX	UNIX V	DOS	QWIN	WIN	WINDLL
X	X	X	X	X	X	X	X	X	X	X	X	X	X	X	X

Summary

```
#include <time.h>

char *asctime(const struct tm *t); // Convert this tm structure
                                   // to a string
```

Description

Converts the date and time stored in a `tm` structure into a string with 26 characters, counting the null character at the end. The converted string has the following form:

```
Mon Jun 08 23:31:09 1992\n\0
```

You can set up the `tm` structure by calling the `localtime` or `gmtime` function. The `tm` structure is defined in time.h as follows:

```
struct tm
{
    int tm_sec;    // Seconds after the minute - [0,61]
                   // (To allow for 2 leap seconds)
    int tm_min;    // Minutes after the hour   - [0,59]
    int tm_hour;   // Hours since midnight     - [0,23]
    int tm_mday;   // Day of the month         - [1,31]
    int tm_mon;    // Months since January     - [0,11]
    int tm_year;   // Years since 1900
    int tm_wday;   // Days since Sunday        - [0,6]
    int tm_yday;   // Days since January 1     - [0,365]
    int tm_isdst;  // Daylight saving (DST) time flag
                   //     >  0 if DST is in effect
                   //     == 0 if DST is not in effect
                   //     <  0 if DST status is unknown
};
```

Returns

The return value is a pointer to an internal data area containing the string with the date and time.

Sample Call

```
struct tm *t;
time_t bt;
//...
time(&bt);
t = localtime(&bt);
//...
printf("Current Date and Time: %s", asctime(t);
```

See Also

`ctime`, `gmtime`, `localtime`, `time`

clock

MSC6	MSC7	VC++	QC2.5	QC-WIN	TC2	TC++	BC++2	BC++3	ANSI	POSIX	UNIX V	DOS	QWIN	WIN	WINDLL
X	X	X	X	X	X	X	X	X	X			X	X	X	

Summary

```
#include <time.h>

clock_t clock(void);
```

Description

Computes the amount of processor time used by the current process.

Returns

When the function completes successfully, the return value is the number of clock ticks used by the process. Divide the returned value by the constant `CLOCKS_PER_SECOND` (defined in time.h) to get the time in seconds.

Sample Call

```
clock_t ticks1;
//...
ticks1 = clock();
```

See Also

`difftime`, `time`

ctime

MSC6	MSC7	VC++	QC2.5	QC-WIN	TC2	TC++	BC++2	BC++3	ANSI	POSIX	UNIX V	DOS	QWIN	WIN	WINDLL
X	X	X	X	X	X	X	X	X	X	X	X	X	X	X	X

Summary

```
#include <time.h>

char *ctime(const time_t *t); // Convert this time to a string
```

Description

Converts a binary time to a string.

Returns

When the function completes successfully, the return value is a pointer to an internal string containing the date and time in a format similar to that returned by `asctime`. If the date is before midnight, January 1, 1970, the return value is `NULL`.

Sample Call

```
time_t bt;
time(&bt);
//...
printf("Current Date and Time: %s", ctime(&bt));
```

See Also

`asctime`, `time`

difftime

MSC6	MSC7	VC++	QC2.5	QC-WIN	TC2	TC++	BC++2	BC++3	ANSI	POSIX	UNIX V	DOS	QWIN	WIN	WINDLL
x	x	x	x	x	x	x	x	x	x		x	x	x	x	x

Summary

```
#include <time.h>

double difftime(
    time_t start, // Compute difference between start and end times
    time_t end);  // by subtracting start from end
```

Description

Computes the difference between *start* and *end* (`end - start`).

Returns

When the function completes successfully, the return value is the elapsed time (`end - start`) in seconds as a double-precision floating-point number.

Sample Call

```
    time_t t1, t2;
    double et;
    time(&t1);
// Some computations....
    time(&t2);
// Compute elapsed time.
    et = difftime(t1, t2);
```

See Also

`time`

_ftime

MSC6	MSC7	VC++	QC2.5	QC-WIN	TC2	TC++	BC++2	BC++3	ANSI	POSIX	UNIX V	DOS	QWIN	WIN	WINDLL
X	X	X	X	X	X	X	X	X				X	X	X	X

Summary

```
#include <sys\timeb.h>

void _ftime(
    struct _timeb *p_tb); // Structure in which time is returned
```

Description

Stores the current time in a `_timeb` structure associated with the address you provide in the *p_tb* argument. The `_timeb` structure is defined in sys\timeb.h as:

```
struct _timeb
{
    time_t         time;      // Time in seconds elapsed
                              // since midnight GMT 01/01/1970
    unsigned short millitm;   // Millisecond portion of time
    short          timezone;  // Difference between GMT and
                              // local time, in minutes, moving
                              // westward
    short          dstflag;   // Nonzero = daylight saving is on
};
```

Returns

There is no return value.

Sample Call

```
struct _timeb tb;
//...
ftime(&tb);
printf("Current Date and Time is %s", ctime(&tb.time));
```

See Also

time, _tzset

gmtime, localtime

MSC6	MSC7	VC++	QC2.5	QC-WIN	TC2	TC++	BC++2	BC++3	ANSI	POSIX	UNIX V	DOS	QWIN	WIN	WINDLL
X	X	X	X	X	X	X	X	X	X	X	X	X	X	X	X

Summary

```
#include <time.h>

struct tm *gmtime(const time_t *t);    // Convert t into GMT
struct tm *localtime(const time_t *t); // Convert t into local time
```

Description

Breaks down a binary time *t* into year, month, day, hours, minutes, seconds, and several other fields that are saved in a `tm` structure, maintained internally. See the reference entry for `asctime` for a definition of the `tm` structure.

The `gmtime` function sets up the fields of the internal `tm` structure in Greenwich Mean Time (GMT)—or UTC, as this standard time is known nowadays. The `localtime` function sets up the fields of the `tm` structure in local time.

Use the `asctime` function to convert the date and time in the `tm` structure into a string that you can print.

Returns

The return value is a pointer to an internally maintained `tm` structure where the converted time is stored.

Sample Call

```
time_t bt;
struct tm *gmt;
//...
time(&bt);
gmt = gmtime(&bt);
printf("Universal Coordinated Time is %s", asctime(gmt));
```

See Also

`asctime`, `time`

mktime

MSC6	MSC7	VC++	QC2.5	QC-WIN	TC2	TC++	BC++2	BC++3	ANSI	POSIX	UNIX V	DOS	QWIN	WIN	WINDLL
X	X	X	X	X			X	X	X	X		X	X	X	X

Summary

```
#include <time.h>

time_t mktime(struct tm *t); // Convert t into a time_t value
```

Description

Converts the `localtime` in the `tm` structure at the address *t* into a binary time that has the same binary encoding as the value returned by the `time` function. During conversion, ignores the `tm_wday` (day of the week) and `tm_yday` (day of the year) fields of the `tm` structure. Sets all fields of the `tm` structure to values that are within normal ranges before returning.

Returns

When the function completes successfully, the return value is a `time_t` value corresponding the date and time in the `tm` structure.

–1	Indicates that conversion failed.

Sample Call

```
    struct tm *t;
    time_t bt;
    time(&bt);
    t = localtime(&bt);
// Add 5 days to the tm_mday field.
    t->tm_mday += 5;
// Now call mktime to bring all fields into valid ranges.
    if((bt = mktime(t)) != (time_t)-1)
    {
        printf("5 days from now it will be %s", ctime(bt));
    }
```

See Also

`asctime`, `ctime`, `time`

_strdate

MSC6	MSC7	VC++	QC2.5	QC-WIN	TC2	TC++	BC++2	BC++3	ANSI	POSIX	UNIX V	DOS	QWIN	WIN	WINDLL
X	X	X	X	X	X	X	X	X				X	X	X	X

Summary

```
#include <time.h>

char *_strdate(char *date); // Array where date is returned
```

Description

Copies the current date as a null-terminated, eight-character string into a nine-character buffer that you allocate and provide as the *date* argument. The date uses this form:

```
10/26/92\0
```

Returns

The return value is the *date* argument.

Sample Call

```
char dbuf[9];
printf("Today's date: %s\n", _strdate(dbuf));
```

See Also

strtime

strftime

MSC6	MSC7	VC++	QC2.5	QC-WIN	TC2	TC++	BC++2	BC++3	ANSI	POSIX	UNIX V	DOS	QWIN	WIN	WINDLL
X	X	X	X	X	X	X	X	X	X	X		X	X	X	

Summary

```
#include <time.h>

size_t strftime(
    char              *buf,    // Buffer in which formatted time saved
    size_t            maxchr,  // Size of buffer
    const char        *fmt,    // Format string
    const struct tm *t);       // Time to be formatted
```

Description

Formats the date and time from a `tm` structure and places the resulting string into *buf*. At most, *maxchr* characters are stored in *buf*. The format string *fmt* has a form similar to that used with `printf` and `sprintf` (see Chapter 22). The format codes for `strftime` are

%a	Current locale's abbreviated name for the weekday
%A	Current locale's full name for the weekday
%b	Current locale's abbreviated name for the month
%B	Current locale's full name for the month
%c	Date and time representation appropriate for the locale
%d	Day of the month as a decimal number (01-31)
%H	Hour in a 24-hour clock as a decimal number (00-23)
%I	Hour in a 12-hour clock as a decimal number (01-12)
%j	Day of the year as a decimal number (001-366)

`%m`	Month as a decimal number (01-12)
`%M`	Minute as a decimal number (00-59)
`%p`	Current locale's AM/PM indicator
`%S`	Second as a decimal number (00-60)
`%U`	Week of the year as a decimal number (Sunday is taken as the first day of a week) (00-53)
`%w`	Weekday as a decimal number (Sunday is 0, 0-6)
`%W`	Week of the year as a decimal number (Monday is taken as the first day of a week) (00-53)
`%x`	Date representation for current locale
`%X`	Time representation for current locale
`%y`	Year without the century as a decimal number (00-99)
`%Y`	Year with the century as a decimal number
`%z`	Name of time zone (or nothing if time zone is unknown)
`%%`	A percent sign (%)

The `LC_TIME` category of the current locale affects the formatting done by `strftime`.

Returns

When the function completes successfully, the return value is the total number of characters copied to *buf*, including the terminating null character.

0	Indicates that the number of characters exceeds *maxchr*, in which case the contents of the string are undefined.

Sample Call

```
    char tstr[80];
    time_t bt;
    struct tm *t;
    time(&bt);
    t = localtime(&bt);
// Format date and time....
    strftime(tstr, 80, "%a %b %c\n", t);
```

See Also

`asctime`, `gmtime`, `localeconv` (Chapter 30), `localtime`, `setlocale` (Chapter 30), `time`

_strtime

MSC6	MSC7	VC++	QC2.5	QC-WIN	TC2	TC++	BC++2	BC++3	ANSI	POSIX	UNIX V	DOS	QWIN	WIN	WINDLL
X	X	X	X	X	X	X	X	X				X	X	X	X

Summary

```
#include <time.h>

char *_strtime(char *time); // Array where time is returned
```

Description

Copies the current time as a null-terminated, eight-character string into a nine-character buffer that you allocate and provide as the *time* argument. The time is of this form:

```
23:55:09\0
```

Returns

The return value is the *time* argument.

Sample Call

```
char tbuf[9];
printf("Time now: %s\n", _strtime(tbuf));
```

See Also

_strdate

time

MSC6	MSC7	VC++	QC2.5	QC-WIN	TC2	TC++	BC++2	BC++3	ANSI	POSIX	UNIX V	DOS	QWIN	WIN	WINDLL
X	X	X	X	X	X	X	X	X	X	X	X	X	X	X	X

Summary

```
#include <time.h>

time_t time(
    time_t *bintime); // Store encoded time at this location
```

Description

Stores the current date and time (in encoded format) in the `time_t` variable with the address you provide in the *bintime* argument, provided that argument is not `NULL`.

Returns

When the function completes successfully, the return value is the current time in elapsed seconds from a specific reference date and time.

Note this change: in Microsoft C/C++ 7.0, this reference is midnight GMT, December 31, 1899. In Visual C++, and earlier versions of Microsoft C, the reference is midnight GMT, January 1, 1970. (This is the reference for UNIX systems.)

Sample Call

```
time_t bintime;
//...
time(&bintime);
```

See Also

ctime, gmtime, localtime, _tzset

_tzset

MSC6	MSC7	VC++	QC2.5	QC-WIN	TC2	TC++	BC++2	BC++3	ANSI	POSIX	UNIX V	DOS	QWIN	WIN	WINDLL
X	X	X	X	X	X	X	X	X		X	X	X	X	X	X

Summary

```
#include <time.h>

void _tzset(void);
```

Description

Uses the current setting of the environment variable TZ to assign appropriate values to the global variables _daylight, _timezone, and _tzname. The functions _ftime, localtime, and time use these global variables. The environment variable TZ is of this form:

```
timezone[+ or -]hh[:mm[:ss]][dstzone]
```

where timezone and dstzone are the three-letter names of the timezone (such as EST for Eastern standard time and PST for Pacific standard time) and daylight saving zone (such as EDT and PDT), respectively. The daylight saving zone is optional.

Between the names of the time zone (required) and the daylight saving zone (optional) comes the time difference between Universal Coordinated Time (called UTC from the abbreviation of its French name) and the local time. This time is specified by an optional sign and followed by the hours, minutes, and seconds, of which only the hours are required. Some sample settings of the TZ environment variable are EST5EDT and PST8PDT.

The global variables _daylight, _timezone, and _tzname, which are set by _tzset, have the following meanings:

`_daylight` An integer that has a nonzero value if `TZ` includes the name of a daylight saving zone. Otherwise, it's zero. By default this variable is nonzero.

`_timezone` A `long int` value denoting the time difference in seconds between UTC and local time. The default is 28800, which corresponds to `TZ` set to `PST8PDT` (meaning that the local time is 28,800 seconds, or eight hours, later than UTC).

`_tzname[0]` A string containing the three-letter name of time zone from `TZ`. The default is `PST`.

`_tzname[1]` A string containing the three-letter name of daylight saving time zone from `TZ`. The default is `PDT`.

Returns

There is no return value.

Sample Call

```
_tzset();
```

See Also

`_ftime`, `localtime`, `time`

_utime

MSC6	MSC7	VC++	QC2.5	QC-WIN	TC2	TC++	BC++2	BC++3	ANSI	POSIX	UNIX V	DOS	QWIN	WIN	WINDLL
x	x	x	x	x				x		x	x	x	x	x	x

Summary

```
#include <sys\utime.h>

int _utime(
    const char      *pathname, // Set this file's modification
    struct _utimbuf *t);       // time using information from t
```

Description

Sets the time of last modification of a file specified by *`pathname`*. The modification time is specified through the `modtime` field of a `_utimbuf` structure, which is defined in sys\utime.h as this:

```
struct _utimbuf
{
    time_t actime;  // Access time
    time_t modtime; // Modification time
};
```

If the second argument *t* is `NULL`, `_utime` sets the modification time to the current time.

Returns

0	Indicates that the function completed successfully.
–1	Indicates an error. Also sets `errno` to `EACCES`, `EINVAL`, `EMFILE`, or `ENOENT` to indicate the cause of the error.

Sample Call

```
    char filename[80]; // Assume the name is initialized

// Set the modification time of a file to current time.
    if(_utime(filename, NULL) == -1) perror("_utime");
```

See Also

`_fstat` (Chapter 22), `time`

29

Math Functions

The math functions in the Microsoft Visual C++ library provide computational support beyond the basic floating-point arithmetic operations supported by the C programming language. This category includes trigonometric functions such as sines and cosines, Bessel functions, logarithms, and exponentials. Most of the math functions are declared in the header file math.h, with the rest declared in float.h and stdlib.h.

Floating-Point Math

Floating-point variables such as `double`, `float`, and `long double` are used to store floating-point values, which are numbers with fractional parts. These numbers are written with a decimal point as, for example, 39.95 and 9.345e9. Internally, a floating-point value is stored by breaking it down into the form of a *mantissa* (m) and an integer exponent (n) so that the original floating-point value is approximated by $m \times 2^n$. Then, the mantissa, the exponent, and the sign of the floating-point value are stored in binary form in various parts of a `double`, `float`, or `long double` variable.

Floating-Point Storage Formats

In Microsoft Visual C++, the bit pattern representing a floating-point value is defined according to a standard developed by the Institute of Electrical and Electronics Engineers (IEEE). The IEEE standard for binary floating-point arithmetic is described in the *IEEE Standard for Binary Floating-Point Arithmetic, ANSI/IEEE Std 754-1985*, available from Global Engineering Documents, 2805 McGaw Avenue, Irvine, CA 92714.

Another floating-point format is the one used by Microsoft BASIC in versions prior to 6.0. Although the IEEE and Microsoft Binary (MSBIN) floating-point variables are of similar size, the internal bit patterns differ. The Microsoft Visual C++ math library includes functions such as `_dieeetomsbin` and `_dmsbintoieee` to convert between these two formats.

Types of Floating-Point Variables

Microsoft Visual C++ supports three types of floating-point variables:

- `float` for storing single-precision values. A `float` variable occupies 4 bytes and is accurate to up to 6 significant decimal digits. A `float` variable can represent floating-point values between the approximate limits of 1.175e–38 and 3.4e38. You can add an `F` suffix to a floating-point constant to indicate that the value should be represented in a `float` format. For instance, `39.95F` denotes a `float` value.

- `double` for storing double-precision values. A `double` variable occupies 8 bytes and provides 15 significant decimal digits. A `double` variable can represent floating-point values between approximately 2.23e–308 and 1.79e308.

- `long double` for storing long double-precision values. A `long double` variable occupies 10 bytes and provides 18 significant decimal digits. A `long double` variable can represent floating-point values between approximately 3.362e–4932 and 1.189e4932. To indicate that a floating-point constant is to be represented in a `long double` format, add an `L` suffix to the constant. For instance, `1.41e6L` denotes a `long double` value.

Floating-Point Package

Because many PCs do not have a math coprocessor, Microsoft Visual C++ uses an elaborate mechanism to ensure that floating-point operations can be used on all PCs.

The compiler includes what is known as an *alternate math library* as well as a library that emulates the floating-point operations of a math coprocessor. The following compiler options give you control over the manner in which floating-point math is supported in your program:

`/FPa`	Generates calls to an alternate math library for floating-point arithmetic. Does not require a math coprocessor, and will not use one even if the system has it.
`/FPc`	Generates calls to a floating-point emulator library for floating-point arithmetic. Does not require a math coprocessor, but will use the math coprocessor if the system has it.
`/FPc87`	Generates calls to an 80x87 library. Requires a math coprocessor at runtime.
`/FPi`	Generates inline code to use the emulator library. The code is such that the program can use an 80x87, if one is found at runtime. If a math coprocessor is not found, the math coprocessor instructions are processed by functions in the emulator library. This is the default option for floating-point math.
`/FPi87`	Generates inline 80x87 instructions that require an 80x87 math coprocessor at runtime.

Errors in Math Functions

In general, two types of errors can occur in math functions:

- *Domain errors* occur when the arguments to a function are outside the set of values for which the function is defined. When this error occurs, the global variable `errno` is set to the constant `EDOM`.
- *Range errors* occur when the result of a math function is beyond the limits of values that can be represented in a `double` variable (or `long double` for certain functions). If the result is too large (*overflow*), the function returns the constant `HUGE_VAL`. If the value is too small (*underflow*), the function returns zero. In both cases, `errno` is set to the constant `ERANGE`.

When an error occurs in a math function, that function calls the `_matherr` function (or the `_matherrl` function, when the error is in one of the functions that work with `long double` variables). Thus, you can override the default handling of an error by writing your own version of the `_matherr` function and linking that `_matherr` function with your program.

Types of Math Functions

Table 29.1 shows an alphabetic list of the math functions and gives you a quick overview of these functions. Table 29.2 organizes these functions by the tasks they perform. A few of these functions are illustrated by two short sample programs in the following sections. For more information on a function, consult the reference entry for that function in the reference section that follows.

Table 29.1. Alphabetic listing of math functions.

Function	Description
`abs`	Returns absolute value of an integer.
`acos`	Computes the arc cosine of a value between –1 and 1.
`acosl`	Similar to `acos`, but accepts and returns `long double`.
`asin`	Computes the arc sine of a value between –1 and 1.
`asinl`	Similar to `asin`, but accepts and returns `long double`.
`atan`	Computes the arc tangent of a value.
`atanl`	Similar to `atan`, but accepts and returns `long double`.
`atan2`	Computes the arc tangent of the ratio of its arguments.
`atan2l`	Similar to `atan2`, but accepts and returns `long double`.
`_cabs`	Computes the magnitude of a complex number specified by its real and imaginary parts.
`_cabsl`	Similar to `cabs`, but accepts and returns `long double`.
`ceil`	Returns the smallest integer larger than or equal to a floating-point value.
`ceill`	Similar to `ceil`, but accepts and returns `long double`.
`_clear87`	Clears the status word of the floating-point package.
`_control87`	Retrieves or sets the control word of the floating-point package.

Function	Description
cos	Computes the cosine of an angle in radians.
cosh	Computes the hyperbolic cosine of a specified value.
coshl	Similar to cosh, but accepts and returns a long double argument.
cosl	Similar to cos, but accepts and returns a long double argument.
_dieeetomsbin	Converts a double-precision, floating-point value from IEEE format to Microsoft Binary (MSBIN) format used in some versions of Microsoft BASIC.
div	Divides one integer by another, returning an integer quotient and an integer remainder.
_dmsbintoieee	Converts a double-precision, floating-point value from Microsoft Binary (MSBIN) format (used in some versions of Microsoft BASIC) to IEEE format.
exp	Computes the exponent of its argument.
expl	Same as exp, but accepts and returns a long double value.
fabs	Returns the absolute value of a floating-point argument.
fabsl	Same as fabs, but accepts and returns a long double value.
_fieeetomsbin	Converts a single-precision, floating-point value from IEEE format to Microsoft Binary (MSBIN) format used in some versions of Microsoft BASIC.
floor	Returns the largest integer smaller than or equal to a floating-point value.
floorl	Same as floor, but accepts and returns a long double value.
fmod	Returns floating-point remainder after dividing one floating-point value by another with the largest possible integral quotient.
fmodl	Same as fmod, but accepts and returns a long double value.

continues

Table 29.1. continued

Function	Description
`_fmsbintoieee`	Converts a single-precision floating-point value from Microsoft Binary (MSBIN) format (used in some versions of Microsoft BASIC) to IEEE format.
`_fpreset`	Resets the floating-point math package.
`frexp`	Breaks down a `double` value x into a mantissa m that lies between 0.5 and 1.0 and an integer exponent n such that $x = m \times 2^n$.
`frexpl`	Similar to `frexp`, but accepts a `long double` argument and returns a `long double` mantissa.
`_hypot`	Computes the length of the hypotenuse of a right triangle.
`_hypotl`	Same as `_hypot`, but accepts and returns `long double` values.
`_j0`	Evaluates the Bessel function of the first kind of order zero.
`_j0l`	Same as `_j0`, but accepts and returns a `long double` value.
`_j1`	Evaluates the Bessel function of the first kind of order one.
`_j1l`	Same as `_j1`, but accepts and returns a `long double` value.
`_jn`	Evaluates the Bessel function of the first kind of a specified integer order.
`_jnl`	Same as `_jn`, but accepts and returns a `long double` value.
`labs`	Returns the absolute value of a `long` integer value.
`ldexp`	Given a floating-point mantissa m and an integer exponent n computes and returns the value $m \times 2^n$.
`ldexpl`	Same as `ldexp`, but accepts a `long double` mantissa and returns a `long double` value.
`div`	Divides one `long` integer by another, returning a `long` integer quotient and a `long` integer remainder.
`log`	Evaluates the natural logarithm of its argument.
`log10`	Evaluates logarithm to the base 10 of its argument.

Function	Description
log10l	Same as log10, but accepts and returns a long double value.
logl	Same as log, but accepts and returns a long double value.
_lrotl	Rotates the bits in a long integer to the left by a specified number of bits.
_lrotr	Rotates the bits in a long integer to the right by a specified number of bits.
_matherr	Handles errors occurring in functions in the math package.
_matherrl	Same as _matherr, but meant for handling errors occurring in math functions that accept and return long double values.
__max	Returns the maximum of two arguments.
__min	Returns the minimum of two arguments.
modf	Breaks down a floating-point value into its integral and fractional parts.
modfl	Same as modf, but breaks down a long double argument.
pow	Raises one floating-point value to the power of another.
powl	Same as pow, but accepts long double arguments and returns a long double value.
rand	Returns a random integer between 0 and RAND_MAX (a constant defined in the header file stdlib.h).
_rotl	Rotates the bits in an integer to the left by a specified number of bits.
_rotr	Rotates the bits in a integer to the right by a specified number of bits.
sin	Computes the sine of an angle in radians.
sinh	Computes the hyperbolic sine of a specified value.
sinhl	Similar to sinh, but accepts and returns a long double argument.

continues

Table 29.1. continued

Function	Description
sinl	Similar to sin, but accepts and returns a long double argument.
sqrt	Evaluates the square root of a floating-point value.
sqrtl	Same as sqrt, but accepts and returns a long double value.
srand	Sets the seed of the random number generator.
_status87	Returns the status word of the floating-point math package.
tan	Computes the tangent of an angle in radians.
tanh	Computes the hyperbolic tangent of a specified value.
tanhl	Similar to tanh, but accepts and returns a long double argument.
tanl	Similar to tan, but accepts and returns a long double argument.
_y0	Evaluates the Bessel function of the second kind of order zero.
_y0l	Same as _y0, but accepts and returns a long double value.
_y1	Evaluates the Bessel function of the second kind of order one.
_y1l	Same as _y1, but accepts and returns a long double value.
_yn	Evaluates the Bessel function of the second kind of a specified integer order.
_ynl	Same as _yn, but accepts and returns a long double value.

Table 29.2. Categories of math functions.

Task	Functions
Evaluate trigonometric functions	acos, acosl, asin, asinl, atan, atanl, atan2, atan2l, cos, cosl, sin, sinl, tan, tanl
Evaluate hyperbolic functions	cosh, coshl, sinh, sinhl, tanh, tanhl
Evaluate Bessel functions	_j0, _j0l, _j1, _j1l, _jn, _jnl, _y0, _y0l, _y1, _y1l, _yn, _ynl
Compute logarithms and powers	exp, expl, frexp, frexpl, ldexp, ldexpl, log, log10, log10l, logl, pow, powl, sqrt, sqrtl
Compute magnitudes and absolute values	abs, _cabs, _cabsl, fabs, fabsl, _hypot, _hypotl, labs,
Find the nearest integer	ceil, ceill, floor, floorl
Perform floating-point divisions	fmod, fmodl, modf, modfl
Perform integer divisions	div, ldiv
Compare values	__max,__min
Generate pseudorandom numbers	rand, srand
Handle errors in math functions	_matherr, _matherrl
Rotate bits	_lrotl, _lrotr, _rotl, _rotr
Convert between floating-point formats	_dieeetomsbin, _dmsbintoieee, _fieeetomsbin, _fmsbintoieee
Set up and initialize floating-point package	_clear87, _control87, _fpreset, _xstatus87

Computing Monthly Payments on a Loan

Suppose you're borrowing an amount *P* at an annual interest rate of *R* percent and you want to pay back the loan in *N* monthly payments. How much would you have to pay each month? You can compute the monthly payment, *M*, using the following formula:

$$M = P\ r\ (1 + r)^N\ /\ ((1 + r)^N - 1)$$

where $r = R\ /\ (12 \times 100)$, the monthly interest rate expressed as a decimal value (instead of a percentage).

You can evaluate this formula easily using the `pow` function from the math library. Listing 29.1 shows the program payment.c, which accepts a loan amount, annual interest rate, and the number of months as command-line arguments and computes the monthly payment. For example, if you were to borrow $150,000 at 8.875 percent for 30 years (360 months), you would run the payment.c program as follows:

```
payment 150000 8.875 360
```

The program would then display the following result:

```
Loan amount  : $150000.00
Interest rate: 8.875% per annum
Pay back in  : 360 monthly installments

Monthly payment: $1193.47
Total Payments: $429648.24
```

Listing 29.1. payment.c. A program that computes the monthly payments for a loan.

```
//-------------------------------------------------------------
// File: payment.c
//
// Computes the monthly payment given the loan amount,
// the yearly interest rate, and the number months in which
// to pay back the loan. For example, to compute the monthly
// payment on a $100,000 30-year loan at 8.5% per annum,
// enter:
//           payment 100000 8.5 360
//-------------------------------------------------------------
#include <stdio.h>
#include <math.h>
```

```
#include <process.h>
#include <stdlib.h>

int main(int argc, char **argv)
{
    double P, R, r, factor, M;
    int    N;

    if(argc < 4)
    {
        printf("Usage: payment <principal> "
               "<interest_rate> <months>\n");
        exit(1);
    }

// Get principal amount, rate, and number of months
// from command line.

    P = atof(argv[1]);     // Principal amount
    R = atof(argv[2]);     // Yearly rate (%)
    r = R / 12.0 / 100.0; // Monthly rate
    N = atoi(argv[3]);     // Number of months

    factor = pow((1.0 + r), (double)N);

// Compute monthly payment:
    M = P * r * factor / (factor - 1.0);

// Display result:
    printf("Loan amount   : $%.2f\n"
           "Interest rate: %.3f%% per annum\n"
           "Pay back in   : %d monthly installments\n\n",
           P, R, N);
    printf("Monthly payment: $%.2f\n", M);
    printf("Total payments: $%.2f\n", M*N);
    return 0;
}
```

Evaluating Sines and Cosines

As an example of computing sines and cosines, Listing 29.2 shows a program, sinecos.c, which displays a table of sines and cosines of the angles from 0° to 180° in steps of

10°. Although the example is simplistic, it shows how easy it is to use the math functions in a program.

Listing 29.2. sinecos.c. Program that displays table of sines and cosines.

```
//-----------------------------------------------------------------
// File: sinecos.c
//
// Displays a table of sines and cosines of angles between
// 0 and 180 degrees in steps of 10 degrees.
//-----------------------------------------------------------------
#include <stdio.h>
#include <math.h>

// Degrees per radian.
#define DEG_PER_RAD 57.29578

void main(void)
{
    double degrees, radians, sine, cosine;

    printf("Degrees\t\tSine\t\tCosine\n");

    for(degrees = 0.0; degrees <= 180.0; degrees += 10.0)
    {
        radians = degrees / DEG_PER_RAD;
        sine = sin(radians);
        cosine = cos(radians);
        printf("%.2f\t\t%f\t\t%f\n", degrees, sine, cosine);
    }
}
```

abs

MSC6	MSC7	VC++	QC2.5	QC-WIN	TC2	TC++	BC++2	BC++3	ANSI	POSIX	UNIX V	DOS	QWIN	WIN	WINDLL
X	X	X	X	X	X	X	X	X	X	X	X	X	X	X	X

Summary

```
#include <math.h> // Or <stdlib.h>

int abs(int x); // Return the absolute value of x
```

Description
Evaluates absolute value of the integer *x*.

Returns
The return value is the absolute value of *x*.

Sample Call
```
int x = -16, y;
//...
y = abs(x); // y = 16
```

See Also
`cabs, fabs, labs`

acos, acosl

MSC6	MSC7	VC++	QC2.5	QC-WIN	TC2	TC++	BC++2	BC++3	ANSI	POSIX	UNIX V	DOS	QWIN	WIN	WINDLL
x	x	x	x	x	x	x	x	x	x	x	x	x	x	x	x

Note: `acosl` is available in MSC6, MSC7, Visual C++, QC-WIN, and BC++3 only.

Summary
```
#include <math.h>

double acos(double x); // Compute arc cosine of x
long double acosl(long double x);
```

Description
Computes the arc cosine of *x*.

The `acosl` function is similar to `acos` except that `acosl` accepts and returns a `long double` (80-bit floating-point representation) value.

Returns
When the function completes successfully, the return value is the arc cosine of *x*, provided *x* is between –1 and 1. The arc cosine lies in the range 0 to π radians.

0 Indicates that *x* is not in the range of –1 to 1. Also sets `errno` to `EDOM` and prints an error message.

Sample Call
```
double theta = acos(0.5);
```

See Also
`asin, cos`

asin, asinl

MSC6	MSC7	VC++	QC2.5	QC-WIN	TC2	TC++	BC++2	BC++3	ANSI	POSIX	UNIX V	DOS	QWIN	WIN	WINDLL
x	x	x	x	x	x	x	x	x	x	x	x	x	x	x	x

Note: `asinl` is available in MSC6, MSC7, Visual C++, QC-WIN, and BC++3 only.

Summary

```
#include <math.h>

double asin(double x); // Compute arc sine of x
long double asinl(long double x);
```

Description

Computes the arc sine of *x*.

The `asinl` function is similar to `asin` except that `asinl` accepts and returns a `long double` (80-bit floating-point representation) value.

Returns

When the function completes successfully, the return value is the arc sine of *x*, provided *x* is between –1 and 1. The arc sine lies in the range $-\pi/2$ to $\pi/2$ radians.

0 Indicates that *x* is not in the range –1 and 1. Also sets `errno` to `EDOM` and prints an error message.

Sample Call

```
double theta = asin(0.707);
```

See Also

`acos`, `sin`

atan, atanl

MSC6	MSC7	VC++	QC2.5	QC-WIN	TC2	TC++	BC++2	BC++3	ANSI	POSIX	UNIX V	DOS	QWIN	WIN	WINDLL
x	x	x	x	x	x	x	x	x	x	x	x	x	x	x	x

Note: `atanl` is available in MSC6, MSC7, Visual C++, QC-WIN, and BC++3 only.

Summary

```
#include <math.h>

double atan(double x); // Compute arc tangent of x
long double atanl(long double x);
```

Description

Computes the arc tangent of *x*.

The `atanl` function is similar to `atan` except that `atanl` accepts and returns a `long double` (80-bit floating-point representation) value.

Returns

When the function completes successfully, the return value is the arc tangent of *x* in the range –π/2 to π/2 radians.

0 If both parameters are 0.

Sample Call

```
double theta = atan(1.0);
```

See Also

atan2, tan

atan2, atan2l

MSC6	MSC7	VC++	QC2.5	QC-WIN	TC2	TC++	BC++2	BC++3	ANSI	POSIX	UNIX V	DOS	QWIN	WIN	WINDLL
X	X	X	X	X	X	X	X	X	X	X	X	X	X	X	X

Note: `atan2l` is available in MSC6, MSC7, Visual C++, QC-WIN, and BC++3 only.

Summary

```
#include <math.h>

double atan2(double y, double x); // Compute arc tangent of x/y
long double atan2l(long double y, long double x);
```

Description

Computes the arc tangent of *y/x*.

Returns

When the function completes successfully, the return value is the arc tangent of *y/x* with values in the range –π to π radians.

0 For either function, indicates that both *x* and *y* are zero. In that case, each of these functions sets `errno` to `EDOM` and prints an error message.

Sample Call

```
double theta = atan2(300.0, 8000.0);
```

See Also

atan, tan

Bessel Functions

MSC6	MSC7	VC++	QC2.5	QC-WIN	TC2	TC++	BC++2	BC++3	ANSI	POSIX	UNIX V	DOS	QWIN	WIN	WINDLL
x	x	x	x	x							x	x	x	x	x

Note: `_j0l`, `_j1l`, `_jnl`, `_y0l`, `_y1l`, `_ynl` are available in MSC6, MSC7, QC2.5, and QC-WIN only. The function names have leading underscores in MSC7 only.

Summary

```
#include <math.h>
//--------------------------------------------------------------
// Bessel functions of the first kind.

double      _j0(double x);
long double _j0l(long double x);
double      _j1(double x);
long double _j1l(long double x);
double      _jn(int n, double x);
long double _jnl(int n, long double x);

//--------------------------------------------------------------
// Bessel functions of the second kind (x should be positive).

double      _y0(double x);
long double _y0l(long double x);
double      _y1(double x);
long double _y1l(long double x);
double      _yn(int n, double x);
long double _ynl(int n, long double x);
```

Description

Evaluates first and second order Bessel functions of integer order for specified arguments. The functions with an `l` suffix accept and return `long double` values. For more information on Bessel functions, consult a reference book such as *Handbook of Mathematical Functions* by M. Abramowitz and I. A. Stegun (Dover, 1970).

Returns

When the function completes successfully, the return value is the value of the Bessel function at the specified argument *x*.

If *x* is negative, the Bessel functions of the second kind return `HUGE_VAL` and set `errno` to `EDOM` to indicate a domain error.

Sample Call

```
double z = _jn(2, 0.995);
```

See Also

```
_matherr
```

_cabs, _cabsl

MSC6	MSC7	VC++	QC2.5	QC-WIN	TC2	TC++	BC++2	BC++3	ANSI	POSIX	UNIX V	DOS	QWIN	WIN	WINDLL
x	x	x	x	x	x	x	x	x			x	x	x	x	x

Note: `cabsl` is available in MSC6, MSC7, Visual C++, QC-WIN, and BC++3 only. The function names have leading underscore in MSC7 only.

Summary

```
#include <math.h>

double _cabs(struct _complex c); // Compute magnitude of complex
                                 //   number denoted by c
long double _cabsl(struct _complexl c);
```

Description

Evaluates the magnitude of a complex number represented by the `_complex` structure, which is defined in math.h as

```
struct _complex
{
    double x; // Real part of the complex number
    double y; // Imaginary part of complex number
};
```

The `_cabsl` function expects a `_complexl` structure that represents real and imaginary parts using `long double` variables and computes the magnitude as a `long double`.

Returns

When the function completes successfully, the return value is the magnitude of the complex number represented by `c`.

Returns `_LHUGE_VAL` if the magnitude is too large and sets `errno` to `ERANGE`.

Sample Call

```
struct _complex z = { 0.6, 0.3};
double zmag = _cabs(z);
```

See Also

`fabs`, `_hypot`

ceil, ceill

MSC6	MSC7	VC++	QC2.5	QC-WIN	TC2	TC++	BC++2	BC++3	ANSI	POSIX	UNIX V	DOS	QWIN	WIN	WINDLL
x	x	x	x	x	x	x	x	x	x	x	x	x	x	x	x

Note: `ceill` is available in MSC6, MSC7, Visual C++, QC-WIN, and BC++3 only.

Summary

```
#include <math.h>

double ceil(double x); // Find smallest integral value equal
                       //   to or greater than x
long double ceill(long double x);
```

Description

Finds the *ceiling* of `x`—the smallest integral value equal to or greater than `x`.

The `ceill` function is same as `ceil` except that `ceill` accepts and returns a `long double` value.

Returns

When the function completes successfully, the return value is the ceiling of *x*.

Sample Call

```
double max_scale = ceil(24.3); // max_scale = 25.0
double lower_limit = ceil(-3.5); // lower_limit = -3.0
```

See Also

`floor`

_clear87, _control87

MSC6	MSC7	VC++	QC2.5	QC-WIN	TC2	TC++	BC++2	BC++3	ANSI	POSIX	UNIX V	DOS	QWIN	WIN	WINDLL
x	x	x	x	x	x	x	x	x				x	x	x	x

Summary

```
#include <float.h>

unsigned int _clear87(void); // Clear the status word

unsigned int _control87(
    unsigned int cwval,  // New bits for control word
    unsigned int cwmask);// Mask to control which bits change
```

Description

The _clear87 function retrieves and clears the floating-point status word, which is a combination of the 80x87 math coprocessor's status word and conditions detected by the math coprocessor's exception handler.

The _control87 function retrieves and sets the floating-point control word that controls the precision, rounding, infinity mode, and exceptions to be generated during floating-point computations. To set the control word, pick a mask from Table 29.3 and use it as the *cwmask* argument; then provide, as *cwval*, a value from Table 29.3 corresponding to that mask.

Table 29.3. Mask and values for _control87.

Mask	Value	Description
_MCW_EM		Generates floating-point exception on:
	_EM_INVALID	Invalid operation
	_EM_DENORMAL	Denormalized argument
	_EM_ZERODIVIDE	Divide by zero
	_EM_OVERFLOW	Overflow
	_EM_UNDERFLOW	Underflow
	_EM_INEXACT	Loss of precision
_MCW_IC		Interprets infinity as:
	_IC_AFFINE	Affine (positive and negative infinity are different)
	_IC_PROJECTIVE	Projective (positive and negative infinity are the same)
_MCW_RC		Rounds off results:
	_RC_CHOP	By chopping
	_RC_UP	By rounding up
	_RC_DOWN	By rounding down
	_RC_NEAR	By rounding to nearest number

continues

Table 29.3. continued

Mask	Value	Description
`_MCW_PC`		Sets level of precision to:
	`_PC_24`	24 bits
	`_PC_53`	53 bits
	`_PC_64`	64 bits

Returns

The `_clear87` function returns the previous contents of the floating-point status word. See the header file `<float.h>` for a list of constants (with names that start with `_SW_`) that indicate the meaning of specific bits in the status word.

The `_control87` function returns the current floating-point control word.

Sample Call

```
_clear87();
_control87(PC_24, MCW_PC); // Set precision to 24-bits
```

See Also

`_status87`

cos, cosl

MSC6	MSC7	VC++	QC2.5	QC-WIN	TC2	TC++	BC++2	BC++3	ANSI	POSIX	UNIX V	DOS	QWIN	WIN	WINDLL
x	x	x	x	x	x	x	x	x	x	x	x	x	x	x	x

Note: `cosl` is available in MSC6, MSC7, Visual C++, QC-WIN, and BC++3 only.

Summary

```
#include <math.h>

double cos(double x); // Compute cosine of x (in radians)
long double cosl(long double x);
```

Description

Computes the cosine of the angle *x* in radians.

The `cosl` function is similar to `cos`, except that `cosl` accepts and returns a `long double` value.

Returns

When the function completes successfully, the return value is the cosine of angle *x*.

Generates a _PLOSS error if *x* is large enough to cause a loss of precision.

0 Indicates a total loss of precision. This loss is due to the very large size of *x*. Generates a _TLOSS error. Also sets errno to ERANGE when there is loss of precision.

Sample Call

```
double cosx = cos(1.3);
```

See Also

acos, sin

cosh, coshl

MSC6	MSC7	VC++	QC2.5	QC-WIN	TC2	TC++	BC++2	BC++3	ANSI	POSIX	UNIX V	DOS	QWIN	WIN	WINDLL
X	X	X	X	X	X	X	X	X	X	X	X	X	X	X	X

Note: coshl is available in MSC6, MSC7, Visual C++, QC-WIN, and BC++3 only.

Summary

```
#include <math.h>

double cosh(double x); // Compute the hyperbolic cosine of x
long double coshl(long double x);
```

Description

Computes the hyperbolic cosine of *x*.

The coshl function is similar to cosh except that coshl accepts and returns a long double value.

Returns

When the function completes successfully, the return value is the hyperbolic cosine of *x*.

Returns _LHUGE_VAL if the result is too large and, at the same time, sets errno to ERANGE.

Sample Call

```
double y = cosh(1.337);
```

See Also

exp, sinh

_dieeetomsbin, _dmsbintoieee

MSC6	MSC7	VC++	QC2.5	QC-WIN	TC2	TC++	BC++2	BC++3	ANSI	POSIX	UNIX V	DOS	QWIN	WIN	WINDLL
X	X	X	X	X								X	X	X	X

Note: The names have a leading underscore in MSC7 and Visual C++ only.

Summary

```
#include <math.h>

int _dieeetomsbin(
    double *src,    // IEEE-format double being converted
    double *dest); //   to MS Binary format and returned here

int _dmsbintoieee(
    double *src,    // MS Binary-format double being converted
    double *dest); //   to IEEE format and returned here
```

Description

Converts a double-precision, floating-point value to and from the following representations:

- IEEE (Institute of Electrical and Electronics Engineers) format used in C programs
- Microsoft Binary (MS Binary) format used in Microsoft BASIC

Returns

0 Indicates the conversion was successful.

1 Indicates that conversion caused an overflow.

Sample Call

```
double x_ieee = 4.265e5;
double x_msbin;
//...
_dieeetomsbin(&x_ieee, &x_msbin);
```

See Also

_fieeetomsbin, _fmsbintoieee

div

MSC6	MSC7	VC++	QC2.5	QC-WIN	TC2	TC++	BC++2	BC++3	ANSI	POSIX	UNIX V	DOS	QWIN	WIN	WINDLL
X	X	X	X	X	X	X	X	X	X			X	X	X	X

Summary

```
#include <stdlib.h>

div_t div(int numer, int denom); // Divide numer by denom
```

Description

Divides the integer *numer* by *denom*.

Returns

When the function completes successfully, the return value is a `div_t` data type containing the quotient and the remainder. The `div_t` data type is defined in stdlib.h in this way:

```
typedef struct _div_t
{
    int quot;   // The quotient
    int rem;    // The remainder
} div_t;
```

If the denominator is zero, the program terminates.

Sample Call

```
div_t r = div(25, 4) // r.quot = 6, r.rem = 1
```

See Also

`ldiv`

exp, expl

MSC6	MSC7	VC++	QC2.5	QC-WIN	TC2	TC++	BC++2	BC++3	ANSI	POSIX	UNIX V	DOS	QWIN	WIN	WINDLL
X	X	X	X	X	X	X	X	X	X	X	X	X	X	X	X

Note: `expl` is available in MSC6, MSC7, Visual C++, QC-WIN, and BC++3 only.

Summary

```
#include <math.h>

double exp(double x); // Compute the exponential of x
long double expl(long double x);
```

Description

Computes the exponential of `x` (e^x, where $e = 2.71828$, the base of the natural logarithm).

The `expl` function is similar to `exp` except that `expl` accepts and returns `long double` value.

Returns

When the function completes successfully, the return value is the exponential of `x`.

Returns `_LHUGE_VAL` if the result is too large and, at the same time, sets `errno` to `ERANGE`.

Sample Call

```
double y = exp(-1.345);
```

See Also

`log`, `pow`

fabs, fabsl

MSC6	MSC7	VC++	QC2.5	QC-WIN	TC2	TC++	BC++2	BC++3	ANSI	POSIX	UNIX V	DOS	QWIN	WIN	WINDLL
X	X	X	X	X	X	X	X	X	X	X	X	X	X	X	X

Note: `fabsl` is available in MSC6, MSC7, Visual C++, QC-WIN, and BC++3 only.

Summary

```
#include <math.h>

double fabs(double x); // Compute absolute value of x
long double fabsl(long double x);
```

Description

Evaluates the absolute value of the floating-point value `x`. The `fabsl` function is for obtaining the absolute value of a `long double` value.

Returns

When the function completes successfully, the return value is the absolute value.

Sample Call

```
double x = fabs(-1.41) // x = 1.41
```

See Also

`abs`, `_cabs`, `labs`

_fieeetomsbin, _fmsbintoieee

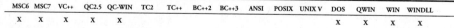

MSC6	MSC7	VC++	QC2.5	QC-WIN	TC2	TC++	BC++2	BC++3	ANSI	POSIX	UNIX V	DOS	QWIN	WIN	WINDLL
X	X	X	X	X								X	X	X	X

Note: The names have a leading underscore in MSC7 and Visual C++ only.

Summary

```
#include <math.h>
```

```
int _fieeetomsbin(
    float *src,   // IEEE-format float being converted
    float *dest); //   to MS Binary format and returned here

int _fmsbintoieee(
    float *src,   // MS-Binary format float being converted
    float *dest); //   to IEEE format and returned here
```

Description

Converts a single-precision, floating-point value to and from the following representations:

- IEEE (Institute of Electrical and Electronics Engineers) format used in C programs
- Microsoft Binary (MS Binary) format used in Microsoft BASIC

Returns

0 Indicates that the conversion was successful.

1 Indicates that conversion caused an overflow.

Sample Call

```
float x_ieee = 318.95;
float x_msbin;
//...
_fieeetomsbin(&x_ieee, &x_msbin);
```

See Also

`_dieeetomsbin`, `_dmsbintoieee`

floor, floorl

MSC6	MSC7	VC++	QC2.5	QC-WIN	TC2	TC++	BC++2	BC++3	ANSI	POSIX	UNIX V	DOS	QWIN	WIN	WINDLL
x	x	x	x	x	x	x	x	x	x	x	x	x	x	x	x

Note: `floorl` is available in MSC6, MSC7, Visual C++, QC-WIN, and BC++3 only.

Summary

```
#include <math.h>

double floor(double x); // Find largest integral value less
                        //   than or equal to x
long double floorl(long double x);
```

Description

Finds the *floor* of *x*—the largest integral value less than or equal to *x*.

The `floorl` function is same as `floor` except that `floorl` accepts and returns a `long double` value.

Returns

When the function completes successfully, the return value is the floor of *x*.

Sample Call

```
double min_scale = floor(5.7); // min_scale = 5.0
double x = floor(-3.5); // x= -4.0
```

See Also

`ceil`

fmod, fmodl

MSC6	MSC7	VC++	QC2.5	QC-WIN	TC2	TC++	BC++2	BC++3	ANSI	POSIX	UNIX V	DOS	QWIN	WIN	WINDLL
X	X	X	X	X	X	X	X	X	X	X	X	X	X	X	X

Note: `fmodl` is available in MSC6, MSC7, Visual C++, QC-WIN, and BC++3 only.

Summary

```
#include <math.h>

double fmod(double num, double denom);// Divide num by denom
long double fmodl(long double num, long double denom);
```

Description

Computes the floating-point remainder after dividing *num* by *denom* and ensuring that the quotient is the largest allowable integer quotient for the division operation.

Returns

When the function completes successfully, the return value is the remainder after the division.

0 Indicates that *denom* is zero.

Sample Call

```
double y = fmod(-13.0, 4.0); // y = -1.0
```

See Also

`floor`

_fpreset

MSC6	MSC7	VC++	QC2.5	QC-WIN	TC2	TC++	BC++2	BC++3	ANSI	POSIX	UNIX V	DOS	QWIN	WIN	WINDLL
x	x	x	x	x	x	x	x	x				x	x	x	x

Summary

```
#include <float.h>

void _fpreset(void);
```

Description

Resets the floating-point math package. Use `_fpreset` after handling floating-point exceptions (such as the `SIGFPE` signal) to start subsequent floating-point operations with a reinitialized floating-point package.

Returns

No return value.

Sample Call

```
_fpreset();
```

See Also

`signal` (see Chapter 30)

frexp, frexpl

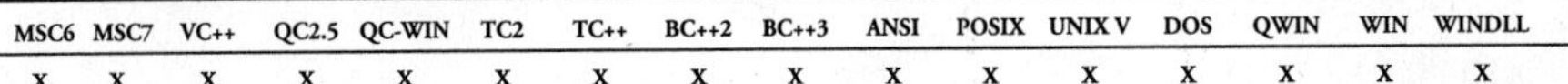

MSC6	MSC7	VC++	QC2.5	QC-WIN	TC2	TC++	BC++2	BC++3	ANSI	POSIX	UNIX V	DOS	QWIN	WIN	WINDLL
x	x	x	x	x	x	x	x	x	x	x	x	x	x	x	x

Note: `frexpl` is available in MSC6, MSC7, Visual C++, QC-WIN, and BC++3 only.

Summary

```
#include <math.h>

double frexp(
    double x,       // Decompose x into a mantissa between
    int    *pexp);  //   0.5 and 1 and return the integer exponent
                    //   in the integer whose address is in pexp

long double frexpl(long double x, int *pexp);
```

Description

Decomposes *x* into a mantissa *m* with absolute value between 0.5 and 1.0, and an integer exponent *n* such that $x = m \times 2^n$.

The `frexpl` function works similarly except that `frexpl` works with `long double` values.

Returns

When the function completes successfully, the return value is the mantissa *m*, computed as described above.

0 Indicates that *x* is zero.

Sample Call

```
int n;
double y = frexp(6.225, &n); // y = 0.778125, n = 3

// Because 6.225 = 0.778125 times 2 raised to 3
```

See Also

`ldexp`

_hypot, _hypotl

MSC6	MSC7	VC++	QC2.5	QC-WIN	TC2	TC++	BC++2	BC++3	ANSI	POSIX	UNIX V	DOS	QWIN	WIN	WINDLL
X	X	X	X	X	X	X	X	X				X	X	X	X

Note: `_hypotl` is available in MSC6, MSC7, Visual C++, QC-WIN, and BC++3 only. The function names have leading underscore in MSC7 and Visual C++ only.

Summary

```
#include <math.h>

double _hypot(
    double x,  // Compute sqrt (x*x + y*y)
    double y);

long double _hypotl(long double x, long double y);
```

Description

Computes the hypotenuse of a right triangle when the length of the sides that meet at the right angle are given in *x* and *y*.

Returns

When the function completes successfully, the return value is the value `sqrt(x*x + y*y)`.

Returns `_LHUGE_VAL` in case of overflow and sets `errno` to `ERANGE`.

Sample Call

```
double slant_range = _hypot(10000.0, 1200.0);
// slant_range =  10071.742650
```

See Also

_cabs

labs

MSC6	MSC7	VC++	QC2.5	QC-WIN	TC2	TC++	BC++2	BC++3	ANSI	POSIX	UNIX V	DOS	QWIN	WIN	WINDLL
X	X	X	X	X	X	X	X	X	X	X	X	X	X	X	X

Summary

```
#include <stdlib.h> // Or <math.h>

long labs(long x);   // Evaluate absolute value of x
```

Description

Evaluates the absolute value of the long integer *x*.

Returns

When the function completes successfully, the return value is the absolute value of *x*.

Sample Call

```
long result = labs(-123456L); // result = 123456
```

See Also

abs, _cabs, fabs

ldexp, ldexpl

MSC6	MSC7	VC++	QC2.5	QC-WIN	TC2	TC++	BC++2	BC++3	ANSI	POSIX	UNIX V	DOS	QWIN	WIN	WINDLL
X	X	X	X	X	X	X	X	X	X	X	X	X	X	X	X

Note: `ldexpl` is available in MSC6, MSC7, Visual C++, QC-WIN, and BC++3 only.

Summary

```
#include <math.h>

double ldexp(
    double x,  // Compute x times 2 raised
    int    n); //   to the power n

long double ldexpl(long double x, int n);
```

Description

Computes a floating-point value from the mantissa *x* and the integer exponent *n* by evaluating $x \times 2^n$.

Returns

When the function completes successfully, the return value is the computed $x \times 2^n$.

Returns `_LHUGE_VAL` if this value is too large. Also sets `errno` to `ERANGE` in this case.

Sample Call

```
double y = ldexp(0.778125, 3) // y = 6.225000
// Because 0.778125 times 2 raised to 3 = 6.225000
```

See Also

`frexp`

ldiv

MSC6	MSC7	VC++	QC2.5	QC-WIN	TC2	TC++	BC++2	BC++3	ANSI	POSIX	UNIX V	DOS	QWIN	WIN	WINDLL
X	X	X	X	X	X	X	X	X	X			X	X	X	X

Summary

```
#include <stdlib.h>

ldiv_t ldiv(long numer, long denom); // Divide numer by denom
```

Description

Divides the long integer *numer* by *denom*.

Returns

When the function completes successfully, the return value is an `ldiv_t` data type containing the quotient and the remainder. The `ldiv_t` data type is defined in stdlib.h as follows:

```
typedef struct _ldiv_t
{
    long quot; // The quotient
    long rem;  // The remainder
} ldiv_t;
```

Sample Call

```
ldiv_t r;
r = ldiv(122000, 1024) // r.quot = 119, r.rem = 144
```

See Also

`div`

log, log10, logl, log10l

MSC6	MSC7	VC++	QC2.5	QC-WIN	TC2	TC++	BC++2	BC++3	ANSI	POSIX	UNIX V	DOS	QWIN	WIN	WINDLL
x	x	x	x	x	x	x	x	x	x	x	x	x	x	x	x

Note: `logl` and `log10l` are available in MSC6, MSC7, Visual C++, QC-WIN, and BC++3 only.

Summary

```
#include <math.h>

double log(double x); // Compute natural logarithm of x
long double logl(long double x);

double log10(double x); // Compute logarithm to the base 10 of x
long double log10l(long double x);
```

Description

Computes the natural logarithm and logarithm to the base 10 of the positive argument *x*.

Returns

When the function completes successfully, the return value is the computed logarithm, provided *x* is positive.

Prints a `_DOMAIN` error, sets `errno` to `EDOM`, and returns `_LHUGE_VAL` if *x* is negative.

Behaves similarly when `x` is zero except that a `_SING` message is printed to indicate a *singularity* (a point where the logarithm is infinity).

Sample Call

```
double x = log10(2); // x = 0.301030
// This means 10 raised to the power 0.301030 is 2.0
```

See Also

`exp`, `pow`

_lrotl, _lrotr

MSC6	MSC7	VC++	QC2.5	QC-WIN	TC2	TC++	BC++2	BC++3	ANSI	POSIX	UNIX V	DOS	QWIN	WIN	WINDLL
x	x	x	x	x	x	x	x	x		x	x	x	x	x	x

Summary

```
#include <stdlib.h>

unsigned long _lrotl(
```

```
    unsigned long value, // Value to rotate to the left
    int           shift);//   by these many bit positions

unsigned long _lrotr(
    unsigned long value, // Value to rotate to the right
    int           shift);//   by these many bit positions
```

Description

Rotates *value* to the left or right by the specified number of bits.

Returns

When the function completes successfully, it returns the rotated value.

Sample Call

```
unsigned long x = _lrotl(0x89abcdef, 16); // x = 0xcdef89ab
// Because 0x89abcdef rotated left by 16 bits = 0xcdef89ab

unsigned long x = _lrotr(0x89abcdef, 8); // x = 0xef89abcd
```

See Also

`_rotl`, `_rotr`

_matherr, _matherrl

MSC6	MSC7	VC++	QC2.5	QC-WIN	TC2	TC++	BC++2	BC++3	ANSI	POSIX	UNIX V	DOS	QWIN	WIN	WINDLL
X	X	X	X	X	X	X	X	X			X	X	X	X	X

Note: `_matherrl` is available in MSC6, MSC7, Visual C++, QC-WIN, and BC++3 only. The `_matherr` function's name has a leading underscore in MSC7 and Visual C++ only.

Summary

```
#include <math.h>

int _matherr(
    struct _exception *e); // Structure with error information

int _matherrl(struct _exceptionl *e);
```

Description

Other math-library functions call the `_matherr` function when an error occurs. You can override the default error handling by providing your own `_matherr` function. The function will be called with a single argument, `e`, a pointer to an `_exception` structure that holds information about the most recent math error. The `_exception` structure is defined in math.h as follows:

```
struct _exception
{
    int    type;   // Type of exception type, one of:
                   //   _DOMAIN, _SING, _OVERFLOW, _PLOSS,
                   //   _TLOSS, and _UNDERFLOW
    char   *name;  // Name of function where error occurred
    double arg1;   // First argument to function
    double arg2;   // Second argument (if any) to function
    double retval;// Value to be returned by function
} ;
```

Provide the `_matherrl` function to handle errors occurring in the `long double` functions such as `cosl`, `logl`, and `sinl`. The `_matherrl` function is called with a pointer to an `_exceptionl` structure that's similar to `_exception` structure except that all floating-point fields are `long double` instead of plain `double`.

Returns

Nonzero	Indicates a successful recovery from error.
0	Indicates an error

Sample Call

You do not explicitly call `_matherr`; instead, other math functions call `_matherr` when an error occurs.

_ _max, _ _min

MSC6	MSC7	VC++	QC2.5	QC-WIN	TC2	TC++	BC++2	BC++3	ANSI	POSIX	UNIX V	DOS	QWIN	WIN	WINDLL
X	X	X	X	X	X	X	X	X				X	X	X	X

Summary

```
#include <stdlib.h>

<type> _ _max(<type> x, <type> y); // Values to compare
<type> _ _min(<type> x, <type> y);
```

Description

The `_ _max` and `_ _min` macros accept two values of any numerical type.

Returns

The `_ _max` and `_ _min` macros return the larger and smaller of the two values, respectively.

Sample Call

```
double x = 2.54, y = 3.141;
double z = _ _max(x,y); // z = 3.141
```

modf, modfl

MSC6	MSC7	VC++	QC2.5	QC-WIN	TC2	TC++	BC++2	BC++3	ANSI	POSIX	UNIX V	DOS	QWIN	WIN	WINDLL
X	X	X	X	X	X	X	X	X	X	X	X	X	X	X	X

Note: `modfl` is available in MSC6, MSC7, Visual C++, QC-WIN, and BC++3 only.

Summary

```
#include <math.h>

double modf(
    double x,          // Value to be decomposed
    double *intpart); // Integral part returned here

long double modfl(long double x, long double *intpart);
```

Description

Breaks down the floating-point value `x` into an integral part, which it stores in the floating-point variable associated with the address you provide in the *`intpart`* argument.

Returns

The return value is the signed fractional part of `x`.

Sample Call

```
double intpart, fract;
fract = modf(-5.625, &intpart); // intpart = -5.0, fract = -0.625
```

See Also

`frexp`, `ldexp`

pow, powl

MSC6	MSC7	VC++	QC2.5	QC-WIN	TC2	TC++	BC++2	BC++3	ANSI	POSIX	UNIX V	DOS	QWIN	WIN	WINDLL
X	X	X	X	X	X	X	X	X	X	X	X	X	X	X	X

Note: `powl` is available in MSC6, MSC7, Visual C++, QC-WIN, and BC++3 only.

Summary

```
#include <math.h>
```

```
double pow(double x, double y);// Compute x raised to the power of y

long double powl(long double x, long double y);
```

Description

Computes x raised to the power of y.

Returns

When the function completes successfully, it returns the value x^y, provided both x and y are nonzero positive numbers.

HUGE_VAL	Indicates that x is zero and y is negative. Also sets errno to EDOM.
1	Indicates that x is nonzero, but y is zero.
0	Indicates that both x and y are zero or if x is negative and y is not an integral value. In this case, prints a _DOMAIN error message and sets errno to EDOM.

Sample Call

```
double x = pow(10.0, 0.3); // x =  1.995262
```

See Also

exp, log, log10, sqrt

rand

MSC6	MSC7	VC++	QC2.5	QC-WIN	TC2	TC++	BC++2	BC++3	ANSI	POSIX	UNIX V	DOS	QWIN	WIN	WINDLL
X	X	X	X	X	X	X	X	X	X	X	X	X	X	X	X

Summary

```
#include <stdlib.h>

int rand(void);
```

Description

Generates a pseudorandom integer in the range 0 to RAND_MAX (which is defined to be 32,767 in Microsoft Visual C++). Use srand to set the *seed*—the starting point—of the pseudorandom integer sequence.

Returns

The return value is the pseudorandom integer value.

Sample Call

```
int scount = rand();
```

See Also

srand

_rotl, _rotr

MSC6	MSC7	VC++	QC2.5	QC-WIN	TC2	TC++	BC++2	BC++3	ANSI	POSIX	UNIX V	DOS	QWIN	WIN	WINDLL
X	X	X	X	X	X	X	X	X				X	X	X	X

Summary

```
#include <stdlib.h>

unsigned int _rotl(
    unsigned int value, // Value to rotate to the left
    int          shift);//   by these many bit positions

unsigned int _rotr(
    unsigned int value, // Value to rotate to the right
    int          shift);//   by these many bit positions
```

Description

Rotates *value* to the left or right by the specified number of bits.

Returns

The return value is the rotated value.

Sample Call

```
unsigned int x = _rotl(0x1234, 2); // x = 0x48d0
// Because 0x1234 rotated left by 2 bits = 0x48d0

unsigned long x = _rotr(0x1234, 4); // x = 0x4123
// Because 0x1234 rotated right by 4 bits = 0x4123
```

See Also

_lrotl, _lrotr

sin, sinl

MSC6	MSC7	VC++	QC2.5	QC-WIN	TC2	TC++	BC++2	BC++3	ANSI	POSIX	UNIX V	DOS	QWIN	WIN	WINDLL
X	X	X	X	X	X	X	X	X	X	X	X	X	X	X	X

Note: `sinl` is available in MSC6, MSC7, Visual C++, QC-WIN, and BC++3 only.

Summary

```
#include <math.h>
```

```
double sin(double x); // Compute the sine of x
long double sinl(long double x);
```

Description

Computes the sine of the angle `x`, in radians.

Returns

When the function completes successfully, the return value is the sine of angle `x`.

A `_PLOSS` error indicates that `x` is large enough to cause a loss of precision. Also sets `errno` to `ERANGE`.

0 Indicates a total loss of precision and generates a `_TLOSS` error. This loss is due to the very large value of *x*. Also sets `errno` to `ERANGE`.

Sample Call

```
double sinx = sin(0.345);
```

See Also

`asin`, `cos`

sinh, sinhl

MSC6	MSC7	VC++	QC2.5	QC-WIN	TC2	TC++	BC++2	BC++3	ANSI	POSIX	UNIX V	DOS	QWIN	WIN	WINDLL
x	x	x	x	x	x	x	x	x	x	x	x	x	x	x	x

Note: `sinhl` is available in MSC6, MSC7, Visual C++, QC-WIN, and BC++3 only.

Summary

```
#include <math.h>

double  sinh(double x);  // Compute hyperbolic sine of x
long double  sinhl(long double x);
```

Description

Computes the hyperbolic sine of `x`.

The `sinhl` function is similar to `sinh` except that `sinhl` accepts and returns a `long double` value.

Returns

When the function completes successfully, the return value is the hyperbolic sine of `x`.

Returns `HUGE_VAL` if the result is too large and, at the same time, sets `errno` to `ERANGE`.

Sample Call

```
double y = sinh(5.437);
```

See Also

exp, cosh

sqrt, sqrtl

MSC6	MSC7	VC++	QC2.5	QC-WIN	TC2	TC++	BC++2	BC++3	ANSI	POSIX	UNIX V	DOS	QWIN	WIN	WINDLL
X	X	X	X	X	X	X	X	X	X	X	X	X	X	X	X

Note: `sqrtl` is available in MSC6, MSC7, Visual C++, QC-WIN, and BC++3 only.

Summary

```
#include <math.h>

double  sqrt(double x); // Compute the square root of x
long double  sqrtl(long double x);
```

Description

Computes the square root of the non-negative floating-point number *x*.

Returns

When the function completes successfully, the return value is the square root of *x*.

0 Indicates *x* is negative. Also sets `errno` to `EDOM` and prints a domain error message.

Sample Call

```
double x = sqrt(2.0); // x = 1.41421
```

See Also

pow, log

srand

MSC6	MSC7	VC++	QC2.5	QC-WIN	TC2	TC++	BC++2	BC++3	ANSI	POSIX	UNIX V	DOS	QWIN	WIN	WINDLL
X	X	X	X	X	X	X	X	X	X	X	X	X	X	X	X

Summary

```
#include <stdlib.h>

void srand(unsigned int seed); // Set new seed to be used by rand
```

Description

Sets a new *seed* to be used by the `rand` function to generate sequences of pseudorandom numbers. Note that a single seed uniquely defines an entire sequence of pseudorandom numbers. If the seed is 1, the random number generator is initialized to its default starting point—the seed that `rand` uses when `rand` is called without a prior call to `srand`. The current time (the binary value returned by the `time` function) often is used as the seed.

Sample Call

```
// Set the seed of the random number generator
   srand((unsigned)time(NULL));
```

See Also

`rand`

_status87

MSC6	MSC7	VC++	QC2.5	QC-WIN	TC2	TC++	BC++2	BC++3	ANSI	POSIX	UNIX V	DOS	QWIN	WIN	WINDLL
X	X	X	X	X	X	X	X	X				X	X	X	X

Summary

```
#include <float.h>

unsigned int _status87(void);
```

Description

Provides access to the floating-point status word.

Returns

When the function completes successfully, the return value is the current floating-point status word. See the header file float.h for a list of constants (with names that start with `_SW_`) that indicate the meaning of specific bits in the status word.

Sample Call

```
unsigned fstatus;
//...
fstatus = _status87();
if(fstatus & _SW_INEXACT)
{
// Loss of precision...
//...
}
```

See Also

_clear87

tan, tanl

MSC6	MSC7	VC++	QC2.5	QC-WIN	TC2	TC++	BC++2	BC++3	ANSI	POSIX	UNIX V	DOS	QWIN	WIN	WINDLL
X	X	X	X	X	X	X	X	X	X	X	X	X	X	X	X

Note: tanl is available in MSC6, MSC7, Visual C++, QC-WIN, and BC++3 only.

Summary

```
#include <math.h>

double  tan(double x); // Compute the tangent of x radians
long double  tanl(long double x);
```

Description

Computes the tangent of the angle *x* (assumed to be in radians).

Returns

When the function completes successfully, the return value is the tangent of *x*.

Sets errno to ERANGE and generates a _PLOSS error if *x* is large enough to cause a partial loss of precision.

0 Indicates that x is so large that precision is totally lost. Generates a _TLOSS error. Also sets errno to ERANGE.

Sample Call

```
double x = tan(1.02); // x = 1.628130
```

See Also

atan, cos, sin

tanh, tanhl

MSC6	MSC7	VC++	QC2.5	QC-WIN	TC2	TC++	BC++2	BC++3	ANSI	POSIX	UNIX V	DOS	QWIN	WIN	WINDLL
X	X	X	X	X	X	X	X	X	X	X	X	X	X	X	X

Note: tanhl is available in MSC6, MSC7, Visual C++, QC-WIN, and BC++3 only.

Summary

```
#include <math.h>

double  tanh(double x); // Compute the hyperbolic tangent of x
long double  tanhl(long double x);
```

Description

Computes the hyperbolic tangent of `x`.

Returns

When the function completes successfully, the return value is the hyperbolic tangent of `x`.

There is no error return.

Sample Call

```
double a = tanh(2.45); // a = 0.985217
```

See Also

`coshl`, `sinhl`

Process Control and Memory Management Functions

Process Control

Process-control functions provide facilities to start a child process, terminate the current process, handle exceptions, pass a command to the operating system's command interpreter, and set up locale-specific numeric and currency formats. The functions described in this chapter are declared in the header files process.h, stdlib.h, signal.h, and setjmp.h. This chapter also covers a number of macros (defined in the header files stdarg.h and varargs.h) that are useful for accessing a variable number of arguments in a function.

Be careful: most of the process control functions shouldn't be used under Windows. Microsoft provides substitute functions to provide the same functionality when writing Windows applications.

Managing Processes

The term *process* refers to an executable program in memory. At any moment there are one or more processes running in a system. In an MS-DOS system, the command interpreter, COMMAND.COM, is the process that usually is running all the time. When you execute any other program (by entering the program's name at the DOS prompt), that program runs as a child of the command interpreter process. The `exec` and `spawn` functions in the process control category enable you to start child processes from your application.

Environment

The *environment* of a process is an array of null-terminated strings of the form:

```
VARIABLE=variable's definition
```

which defines an *environment variable*. On the left of the equal sign is the name of the environment variable; on the right is the definition of the variable. You can define an environment variable with the `SET` command at the DOS prompt.

Environment variables are useful for passing information to processes. For example, the Microsoft Visual C++ compiler looks for header files in the semicolon-separated list of directories specified in the `INCLUDE` environment variable. If you want the compiler to search for header files in the directories D:\MSVC\INCLUDE, D:\MSVC\MFC\INCLUDE, and the current working directory, in that order, you would define `INCLUDE` as follows:

```
INCLUDE=D:\MSVC\INCLUDE;D:\MSVC\MFC\INCLUDE;.
```

You can use environment variables in your programs as well. Use the `getenv` function to retrieve the definition of an environment variable from the environment of your process.

Signals

Signals refer to notification from the operating system to your process about exceptions and error conditions. Like the interrupt handler at the microprocessor level, you can set up a function that will be called whenever a signal is sent to your program. To set up a signal handler for a specific signal number, call the `signal` function. The `raise` function enables you to artificially send a signal to your own process, somewhat akin to generating software interrupts (see Chapter 32, "DOS and BIOS Calls").

Variable-Length Argument Lists

You may have noticed functions such as `printf` and `scanf`, which accept a variable number of arguments. You can write such functions using a set of macros (`va_start`, `va_arg`, and `va_end`) available in Microsoft Visual C++. There are two sets of identically named macros available. One set conforms to the ANSI standard for C and is defined in the header file stdarg.h. The other set is compatible with UNIX System V and is defined in varargs.h. Consult the reference entries for these macros (at the end of this chapter) for more information on accessing a variable number of arguments in a function.

Locale

The term *locale* refers to a geographic locality or a programming environment (such as the C language environment) for which certain aspects of a program can be customized. In ANSI standard C, the locale-dependent features of a program are grouped into six categories:

Category	Affects
`LC_ALL`	Entire program
`LC_COLLATE`	Collating sequence of character set (affects `strcoll` and `strxfrm` functions, described in Chapter 26)
`LC_CTYPE`	The multibyte character functions
`LC_MONETARY`	Formatting of monetary data
`LC_NUMERIC`	Formatting of numeric data (for example, output of `printf`)
`LC_TIME`	Formatting of time by `strftime` function (described in Chapter 28)

You use the `setlocale` function to set any of these locale categories to a selected locale. All ANSI standard C compilers, including Microsoft Visual C++, support the `C` locale, which refers to the C programming environment. Use the `localeconv` function to retrieve locale-specific numeric and currency formatting information in an `lconv` structure. (See reference entry of the `localeconv` function.)

Basic Process Control Tasks

Table 30.1 lists the console and port I/O functions alphabetically and gives you a quick overview of these functions. Table 30.2 organizes these functions by the tasks they perform. Some of these tasks are illustrated by a sample program in the following section. For more information on a function, consult the reference entry for that function in the reference section that follows.

Table 30.1. Alphabetic listing of process control functions.

Function	Description
abort	Exits program by raising a SIGABRT signal.
assert	Exits program if the argument evaluates to zero.
atexit	Sets up to 32 functions that are called in last-in first-out order when the program terminates.
_c_exit	Exits the C library without terminating the program (flushes all file buffers but does not call the exit handlers installed by atexit).
_cexit	Exits the C library without terminating the program (flushes all file buffers and calls the exit handlers installed by atexit).
_execl	Executes child process by overlaying the parent in memory. Accepts command-line arguments in a list.
_execle	Same as _execl, but also accepts a NULL-terminated environment list.
_execlp	Same as _execl, but searches the directories listed in the PATH environment variable to locate the child's executable file.
_execlpe	Same as _execlp, but accepts a NULL-terminated environment list.
_execv	Executes child process by overlaying the parent in memory. Accepts command-line arguments in a variable-length array with the end marked by a NULL.
_execve	Same as _execv, but also accepts a variable-length array of environment variables.
_execvp	Same as _execv, but searches the directories listed in the PATH environment variable to locate the child's executable file.
_execvpe	Same as _execvp, but accepts command-line arguments in a variable-length array with the end marked by a NULL.
exit	Terminates a process and returns to parent after flushing buffers and calling the functions installed by atexit or _onexit.

Function	Description
_exit	Terminates a process immediately without flushing buffers or calling the functions installed by atexit or _onexit.
_fatexit	Same as atexit, but installs a far function as an exit-handler.
_fonexit	Same as _onexit, but installs a far function as an exit-handler.
getenv	Retrieves the definition of an environment variable from the environment of the process.
_getpid	Returns a unique integer identifier for the process.
localeconv	Returns numeric and monetary formatting information for the current locale in an lconv structure.
longjmp	Restores the stack environment to one saved by a previous call to setjmp. The effect is an unconditional jump to the location of the previous call to setjmp.
_onexit	Sets up to 32 functions to be called in last-in, first-out manner when the program terminates.
_putenv	Adds the definition of an environment variable to the environment of the process.
raise	Sends a signal to the process.
setjmp	Saves the stack environment so the process can jump back to this location by a subsequent call to longjmp.
setlocale	Sets the locale for a specified portion of the program's locale-dependent aspects.
signal	Sets up a function to be called when a specified signal (exception) is sent to the process.
_spawnl	Executes a child process either by overlaying the parent or leaving the parent intact and returning to it after the child terminates. Accepts command-line arguments in a NULL-terminated list.
_spawnle	Same as _spawnl, but also accepts a NULL-terminated environment list.

continues

Table 30.1. continued

Function	Description
_spawnlp	Same as _spawnl, but searches the directories listed in the PATH environment variable to locate the child's executable file.
_spawnlpe	Same as _spawnlp, but accepts a NULL-terminated environment list.
_spawnv	Executes a child process either by overlaying the parent or leaving the parent intact and returning to it after the child terminates. Accepts command-line arguments in a variable length array with the end marked by a NULL.
_spawnve	Same as _spawnv, but also accepts a variable-length array of environment variables.
_spawnvp	Same as _spawnv, but searches the directories listed in the PATH environment variable to locate the child's executable file.
_spawnvpe	Same as _spawnvp, but accepts command-line arguments in a variable-length array with the end marked by a NULL.
system	Passes a command to the operating system's command interpreter for execution.
va_arg	Retrieves next argument from the stack.
va_end	Ends argument retrieval from the stack.
va_start	Starts argument retrieval from the stack.

Table 30.2. Basic process control tasks.

Task	Functions
Execute a child process	_execl, _execle, _execlp, _execlpe, _execv, _execve, _execvp, _execvpe, _spawnl, _spawnle, _spawnlp, _spawnlpe, _spawnv, _spawnve, _spawnvp, _spawnvpe

Task	Functions
Handle process termination	`abort`, `atexit`, `_c_exit`, `_cexit`, `exit`, `_exit`, `_fatexit`, `_fonexit`, `_onexit`
Access environment and process ID	`getenv`, `_getpid`, `_putenv`
Handle exceptions	`longjmp`, `raise`, `setjmp`, `signal`
Pass a command to operating system	`system`
Get or set locale-specific information	`localeconv`, `setlocale`
Access variable-length argument lists	`va_arg`, `va_end`, `va_start`

A Tiny Shell

A *shell* is a program that acts as a command interpreter that reads commands from the user and acts on the commands. The COMMAND.COM program in MS-DOS is an example of a shell. One hallmark of a shell program is its ability to start child processes. With the `spawn` functions available in Microsoft Visual C++, it's easy to write a simple shell. Listing 30.1 shows a simple-minded shell program, tshell.c, that understands four commands:

- A generic `run` command that causes `tshell` to spawn a child process using the next argument as the name of the executable file. This simple command greatly enhances the power of even this simple shell because you can execute any program with the `run` command.
- The `protect` and `unprot` commands, which execute the sample programs of same name from Chapter 21.
- The `exit` command, which causes the tiny shell to exit.

In addition to a command-processing scheme, the tshell.c program also illustrates how to handle a Ctrl+C keypress using the `setjmp` and `longjmp` functions.

Here's a sample session with tshell (note that `D:\MSVCDG\CH30\>` is the DOS prompt):

```
D:\MSVCDG\CH30>tshell
tshell> run command.com


Microsoft(R) MS-DOS(R) Version 6.00
          (C)Copyright Microsoft Corp 1981-1993.
```

```
D:\MSVCDG\CH30>exit
tshell> run mem

mem

Memory Type        Total =  Used  +  Free
----------------  ------   ------   ------
Conventional        640K     180K     460K
Upper                 0K       0K       0K
Adapter RAM/ROM     384K     384K       0K
Extended (XMS)    16384K   15360K    1024K
----------------  ------   ------   ------
Total memory      17408K   15924K    1484K

Total under 1 MB    640K     180K     460K

Total Expanded (EMS)                 1024K (1048576 bytes)
Free Expanded (EMS)                  1024K (1048576 bytes)
Largest executable program size       460K  (471056 bytes)
Largest free upper memory block         0K       (0 bytes)
MS-DOS is resident in the high memory area.

tshell> protect tshell.c
tshell.c protected
tshell> unprot tshell.c
tshell.c unprotected
tshell> exit
```

As you can see, the run command enables you to run any executable file, including COMMAND.COM to launch the default MS-DOS shell program or MEM.EXE to query the status of memory available in the system.

Listing 30.1. tshell.c. A shell program that illustrates how to run child processes.

```
//--------------------------------------------------------------
//  File: tshell.c
//
//  A tiny shell program that starts child processes by calling
//  the "spawn" functions. This shell understands four commands:
//
//  (1) run <exefile>      -- runs the specified executable file
```

```
//  (2) protect <filename> -- uses program from Chapter 21
//                            to mark a file as read-only
//  (3) unprot <filename>  -- uses program from Chapter 21
//                            to mark a file as read-write
//  (4) exit               -- exit the shell
//----------------------------------------------------------------
#include <stdio.h>
#include <ctype.h>
#include <string.h>
#include <conio.h>
#include <process.h>
#include <setjmp.h>
#include <signal.h>
#include <errno.h>

#define MAXCHR 256
#define MAXARG  64

typedef struct COMMAND
{
    char *name;
    char *exefile;
}COMMAND;

COMMAND cmdlist[] =
{
    "run",       NULL,
    "protect",   "..\\ch21\\protect.exe",
    "unprot",    "..\\ch21\\unprot.exe"
};


// Parsed tokens and count of tokens returned in these
// variables
static char *argvec[MAXARG];
static int  nargs = 0;

static jmp_buf top_of_menu;
static char *prompt = "tshell> ";
static char cmdline[MAXCHR];
```

continues

Listing 30.1. continued

```
void cmdparse(char *line, char *tokensep);
int process_cmd(void);
void handle_ctrlc(int signum);
//-------------------------------------------------------------
//  m a i n

int main(void)
{
    int done = 0;

// Install CTRL-C handler
    if(signal(SIGINT, handle_ctrlc) == SIG_ERR)
    {
        perror("signal failed");
    }

// Mark this place using setjmp so that we can get back later
// by calling longjmp
    if(setjmp(top_of_menu) != 0)
    {
// If here, it's a return from a longjmp
        printf("Resuming...\n");
        fflush(stdin);
    }

    while(!done)
    {
        printf(prompt);
        gets(cmdline);
        cmdparse(cmdline, " \t\n");
        done = process_cmd();
    }
    return 0;
}
//-------------------------------------------------------------
//  p r o c e s s _ c m d
//
//  Process a "tiny shell" command

int process_cmd(void)
{
```

```
int i;
int nReturn = 0;

    if(argvec[0] == NULL || nargs <= 0) return 0;

    if(_stricmp(argvec[0], "exit") == 0) return 1;

// Search list of commands
    for(i = 0; i < sizeof(cmdlist)/sizeof(cmdlist[0]); i++)
    {
        if(_stricmp(cmdlist[i].name, argvec[0]) == 0)
        {

// When found, excute specified executable with command-line
// arguments

            nReturn = ENOENT;

            if(cmdlist[i].exefile == NULL)
            {
                if(argvec[1] != NULL)
                {
                    nReturn = _spawnvp(_P_WAIT, argvec[1], &argvec[1]);
                }
            }
            else
            {
                argvec[0] = cmdlist[i].exefile;
                nReturn =  _spawnvp(_P_WAIT, cmdlist[i].exefile,
                    &argvec[0]);
            }

            switch(nReturn)
            {
                case E2BIG:
                    printf("argument list exceeds 128 bytes,"
                        " or environment >32K\n");
                    break;
                case EINVAL:
                    printf("The mode argument is invalid.\n");
                    break;
```

continues

Listing 30.1. continued

```
                case ENOENT:
                    printf("The file or path is not found.\n");
                    break;
                case ENOEXEC:
                    printf("The specified file not executable "
                        "or is invalid.\n");
                    break;
                case ENOMEM:
                    printf("Not enough memory is available to"
                        " execute the child process.\n");
                    break;
                default:
                    printf("done!\n");
                    break;
            }
        }
    }
    return 0;
}
//-------------------------------------------------------------
//  h a n d l e _ c t r l c
//
//  Handles CTRL-C keypress (SIGINT signal)

void handle_ctrlc(int signum)
{
    int c;

// Ignore further CTRL-C keypresses
    signal(SIGINT, SIG_IGN);

    printf("\nCTRL-C Interrupt. Press y to quit.\n");
    c = _getch();
    if(tolower(c) == 'y') exit(0);

// Reinstall this handler
    signal(SIGINT, handle_ctrlc);

// Jump back to top of main menu
    longjmp(top_of_menu, 1);
}
```

```
//------------------------------------------------------------
//  c m d p a r s e
//
//  Parses command-line into tokens identified by the delimiting
//  characters specified in the tokensep argument. The argvec
//  array points to the parsed tokens.

void cmdparse(char *line, char *tokensep)
{
    char *token;

// Set nargs to zero indicating that no tokens found yet
    nargs = 0;

// Call strtok with the line as argument to initialize it and
// get the first token
    token = strtok(line, tokensep);

// Keep calling strtok to get all the tokens
    while(token != NULL)
    {
        argvec[nargs++] = token;
        token = strtok(NULL, tokensep);
    }

// Mark end of argument list with a NULL pointer
    argvec[nargs+1] = NULL;
}
```

Leading Underscore in Names of Nonstandard Functions

Microsoft Visual C++ adds an underscore prefix to many functions (such as the _`exec` functions, _`getpid`, and _`putenv`) in keeping with ANSI Standard C's naming conventions for nonstandard functions. In many other C compilers (including earlier versions of Microsoft C compilers), as well as in UNIX and POSIX, these functions are available with names that do not have the leading underscores. Note that you can use the names without underscore prefix in Microsoft Visual C++ as well. The functions with names without underscore prefixes are in a library named oldnames .lib, which the linker searches by default.

abort

MSC6	MSC7	VC++	QC2.5	QC-WIN	TC2	TC++	BC++2	BC++3	ANSI	POSIX	UNIX V	DOS	QWIN	WIN	WINDLL
X	X	X	X	X	X	X	X	X	X	X	X	X	X	X	X

Summary

```
#include <stdlib.h>

void abort(void);
```

Description

Under DOS, prints an error message to `stderr` and exits the program abnormally by calling `raise(SIGABRT)`. The default handler for the `SIGABRT` signal terminates the program by calling `exit(3)`. Does not flush file buffers or call the functions set up by `atexit` or `_onexit`. Under Windows, `abort` terminates the program after displaying the `"Abnormal Program Termination"` message in a pop-up window.

Sample Call

```
if(argc < 3) abort();
```

See Also

`exit`, `raise`, `signal`

assert

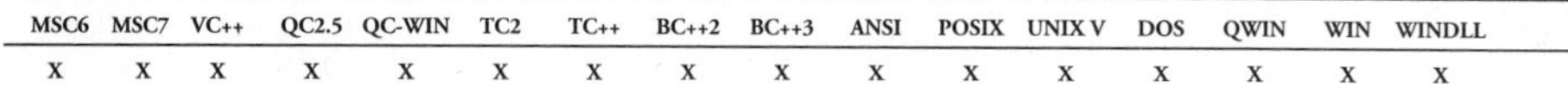

MSC6	MSC7	VC++	QC2.5	QC-WIN	TC2	TC++	BC++2	BC++3	ANSI	POSIX	UNIX V	DOS	QWIN	WIN	WINDLL
X	X	X	X	X	X	X	X	X	X	X	X	X	X	X	X

Summary

```
#include <assert.h>

void assert(int expr); // Test the integer-valued expression
```

Description

Tests the integer-valued expression `expr` and, if it's zero, prints a diagnostic message indicating the current source filename and line number, and exits the program by calling `abort`.

If the `NDEBUG` macro is defined at compile time, all calls to `assert` will be skipped. Under Windows, the message from assert appears in a window with the `"Assertion Failed"` caption.

Sample Call

```
void a_function(int an_arg)
{
```

```
    assert(an_arg > 0);  // Make sure the argument is > 0
//...
}
```

See Also

abort

atexit, _fatexit

MSC6	MSC7	VC++	QC2.5	QC-WIN	TC2	TC++	BC++2	BC++3	ANSI	POSIX	UNIX V	DOS	QWIN	WIN	WINDLL
x	x	x	x	x	x	x	x	x	x			x	x	x	x

Note: _fatexit is available in MSC7 and Visual C++ only.

Summary

```
#include <stdlib.h>

int atexit(
    void (*func)(void)); // Function to be called when program
                         // exits normally

int __far _fatexit(void (__cdecl __far *func)(void));
```

Description

Sets up a function, func, to be called when the program terminates normally. You can set up a maximum of 32 such functions, which are called in last-in, first-out order.

The _fatexit function is similar to atexit except that you can use _fatexit in any memory model to set up a far function as an "exit handler."

Returns

0	Indicates the function was successfully set up.
Nonzero	Indicates an error.

Sample Call

```
void exit_handler(void);
//...
atexit(exit_handler);
```

See Also

exit, _onexit

_cexit, _c_exit

MSC6	MSC7	VC++	QC2.5	QC-WIN	TC2	TC++	BC++2	BC++3	ANSI	POSIX	UNIX V	DOS	QWIN	WIN	WINDLL
X	X	X	X				X				X	X	X	X	

Summary

```
#include <process.h>

void _cexit(void);
void _c_exit(void);
```

Description

Flushes all file buffers. The `_cexit` function also calls the exit handlers installed by `atexit` and `_onexit`. You can think of these functions as ways of terminating the C library without exiting the process.

Sample Call

```
_cexit();
```

See Also

`abort`, `atexit`, `exit`, `_onexit`

_execl, _execle, _execlp, _execlpe, _execv, _execve, _execvp, _execvpe

MSC6	MSC7	VC++	QC2.5	QC-WIN	TC2	TC++	BC++2	BC++3	ANSI	POSIX	UNIX V	DOS	QWIN	WIN	WINDLL
X	X	X	X	X	X	X	X	X		X	X	X			

Summary

```
#include <process.h>

// path is the pathname of executable file to run as a
// child process.

int _execl(const char *path, const char *arg0, ...);
int _execle(const char *path, const char *arg0, ...);
int _execlp(const char *path, const char *arg0, ...);
int _execlpe(const char *path, const char *arg0, ...);

int _execv(const char *path, const char * const *argv);
int _execve(const char *path, const char * const *argv,
            const char * const *envp);
int _execvp(const char *path, const char * const *envp);
int _execvpe(const char *path, const char * const *argv,
             const char * const *envp);
```

Description

Loads and executes a child process by overlaying the memory currently occupied by the calling program. The path argument identifies the executable file for the child process. The eight different versions of the _exec functions are as follows:

_execl	Accepts a variable number of command-line arguments with a NULL marking the end of the list. Inherits the environment variables from the parent process.
_execle	Like _execl, except that _execle allows the environment variables for the child process to be predefined. To do this, the second-to-last argument is a NULL marking the end of a variable number of command-line arguments. The last argument is of type char**, and provides an array of null-terminated strings representing the environment variables to be used by the child process.
_execlp	Similar to _execl, with the additional property that the directories specified in the PATH environment variable are searched to locate the executable file to be loaded and run as a child process.
_execlpe	Behaves as a combination of _execlp and _execle.
_execv	Accepts an array of strings (with a NULL marking the end of the array) representing the variable number of command-line arguments. Inherits the environment variables from the parent process.
_execve	Like _execv, but accepts an additional argument that is an array of null-terminated strings, representing the environment variables to be used by the child process. The end of the array is marked by a NULL pointer.
_execvp	Similar to _execv, with the additional feature that the directories specified in the PATH environment variable are searched to locate the executable file to be loaded and run as a child process.
_execvpe	Behaves as a combination of (f)_execvp and _execve.

Use the _execl form when the command-line arguments for the child process are known in advance. The _execv form is appropriate if you have to construct an array of command-line argument strings on the fly and pass that array to the _execv functions.

Returns

If successful, overlays the parent and does not return.

–1 Indicates an error. Also sets errno to one of the following:

E2BIG	The total length of the command-line arguments exceeds 128 bytes, or memory required for the environment variables is more than 32K.
EACCES	Cannot access file specified by path (sharing violation).
EMFILE	Too many files open.
ENOENT	Executable file could not be located.
ENOEXEC	File specified by path argument is not an executable file.
ENOMEM	Not enough memory to run child process.

Sample Call

```
// Execute the program named loadfile.exe.
if(_execl("loadfile.exe", "loadfile.exe", "test.dat", NULL);
```

See Also

_spawn functions

exit

MSC6	MSC7	VC++	QC2.5	QC-WIN	TC2	TC++	BC++2	BC++3	ANSI	POSIX	UNIX V	DOS	QWIN	WIN	WINDLL
X	X	X	X	X	X	X	X	X	X	X	X	X	X	X	

Summary

```
#include <stdlib.h>

void exit(int status); // Exit status code
```

Description

Terminates the current program in a normal manner by flushing file buffers, closing files, and calling the functions set up by earlier calls to atexit and _onexit. The low-order byte of the status argument is provided to the parent process (the MS-DOS command-interpreter, for instance) as an exit code for the program. In an MS-DOS batch file, you can check this status code with the IF ERRORLEVEL command. Normally, status should be zero if the program terminates without any errors.

Sample Call

```
    FILE *fp;
// Attempt to open file....
// Exit if fp is NULL.
    if(fp == NULL) exit(1); // Exit status is 1
```

See Also

_cexit, _c_exit, _exit

_exit

MSC6	MSC7	VC++	QC2.5	QC-WIN	TC2	TC++	BC++2	BC++3	ANSI	POSIX	UNIX V	DOS	QWIN	WIN	WINDLL
X	X	X	X	X	X	X	X	X			X	X	X	X	

Summary

```
#include <.h>

void _exit(int status); // Exit status code
```

Description

Terminates the current program immediately without flushing buffers or calling the functions installed by atexit and _onexit. The low-order byte of the status argument is provided to the parent process (the MS-DOS command-interpreter, for instance) as an exit code for the program. In an MS-DOS batch file, you can check this status code with the IF ERRORLEVEL command.

Sample Call

```
    FILE *fp;
// Open file for writing text.
    fprintf(fp, "This line won't appear in the file if "
                "the program terminates by calling _exit\n");
//...
    _exit(0); // Buffers not flushed
```

See Also

_cexit, _c_exit, exit

getenv

MSC6	MSC7	VC++	QC2.5	QC-WIN	TC2	TC++	BC++2	BC++3	ANSI	POSIX	UNIX V	DOS	QWIN	WIN	WINDLL
X	X	X	X	X	X	X	X	X	X	X	X	X	X	X	X

Summary

```
#include <stdlib.h>

char *getenv(
    const char *env_var); // Look for this environment variable
```

Description

Gets the definition of the environment variable `env_var` from the list of environment variables associated with the current process.

Returns

A pointer to the null-terminated string containing the definition of the environment variable `env_var`. Thus, if the environment variable `WINDIR` is defined as `WINDIR=D:\WINDOWS`,

```
getenv("WINDIR");
```

returns a pointer to the string `D:\WINDOWS`.

`NULL` Indicates that the environment variable is not defined.

Sample Call

```
char *pathlist = getenv("PATH");
```

See Also

`_putenv`

_getpid

MSC6	MSC7	VC++	QC2.5	QC-WIN	TC2	TC++	BC++2	BC++3	ANSI	POSIX	UNIX V	DOS	QWIN	WIN	WINDLL
X	X	X	X	X			X	X		X	X	X	X	X	X

Summary

```
#include <process.h>

int _getpid(void);
```

Description

Retrieves the process ID, an integer that uniquely identifies the current process.

Returns

The return value is the process ID.

Sample Call

```
int pid = _getpid();
```

localeconv

MSC6	MSC7	VC++	QC2.5	QC-WIN	TC2	TC++	BC++2	BC++3	ANSI	POSIX	UNIX V	DOS	QWIN	WIN	WINDLL
X	X	X	X	X		X	X	X	X	X	X	X	X	X	X

Summary

```
#include <locale.h>

struct lconv *localeconv(void);
```

Description

Fills in the fields of an `lconv` structure with detailed information about formatting monetary and numeric values for the current locale, which refers to a country, a geographic region, or a programming environment. (See the beginning of this chapter for more information.)

Returns

When the function completes successfully, the return value is a pointer to a statically allocated `lconv` structure whose fields contain information that you can use to format monetary and numeric values for the current locale. The `lconv` structure is defined in locale.h as

```
struct lconv
{
    char *decimal_point;      // Decimal point character for
                              // nonmonetary quantities

    char *thousands_sep;      // Character that separates groups
                              // of digits to the left of decimal
                              // point for nonmonetary quantities

    char *grouping;           // Size of group of digits in
                              // nonmonetary quantities

    char *int_curr_symbol;    // International currency symbol
                              // for the current locale

    char *currency_symbol;    // Local currency symbol for
                              // the current locale

    char *mon_decimal_point; // Decimal  point character for
                              // monetary quantities
```

```
char *mon_thousands_sep; // Character that separates groups
                         // of digits to the left of decimal
                         // point for monetary quantities

char *mon_grouping;      // Size of group of digits in
                         // monetary quantities

char *positive_sign;     // Character denoting sign for
                         // nonnegative monetary quantities

char *negative_sign;     // Character denoting sign for
                         // negative monetary quantities

char int_frac_digits;    // Number of digits to the right of
                         // decimal point in formatted
                         // monetary in international format

char frac_digits;        // Number of digits to the right of
                         // decimal point in formatted
                         // monetary quantities

char p_cs_precedes;      // Set to 1 if currency_symbol
                         // precedes nonnegative monetary
                         // quantity. Set to 0 if symbol
                         // follows positive value

char p_sep_by_space;     // Set to 1 if there is space
                         // between the currency_symbol and
                         // positive values. Set to 0 for
                         // no space

char n_cs_precedes;      // Set to 1 if currency_symbol
                         // precedes negative monetary
                         // quantity. Set to 0 if symbol
                         // follows negative value

char n_sep_by_space;     // Set to 1 if there is space
                         // between the currency_symbol and
                         // negative values. Set to 0 for
                         // no space

char p_sign_posn;        // Position of positive sign in
                         // positive monetary quantities
```

```
    char n_sign_posn;          // Position of negative sign in
                               // negative monetary quantities

};
```

Sample Call

```
struct lconv *p_locale = localeconv();
```

See Also

setlocale

longjmp

MSC6	MSC7	VC++	QC2.5	QC-WIN	TC2	TC++	BC++2	BC++3	ANSI	POSIX	UNIX V	DOS	QWIN	WIN	WINDLL
x	x	x	x	x	x	x	x	x	x	x	x	x	x	x	x

Summary

```
#include <setjmp.h>

void longjmp(
    jmp_buf context, // Restore stack to this saved context
    int retval);     // The previous call to setjmp appears
                     // to return this value (must be nonzero)
```

Description

Restores the stack as well as certain registers to the values saved in *context*, which is a `jmp_buf` data type set up by an earlier call to `setjmp`. The restoration of the stack appears as a return from the `setjmp` function with a return value equal to *retval*.

As explained in Chapter 13 ("Advanced Topics in C++"), you should not use `longjmp` and `setjmp` in C++ programs. Also, `longjmp` may not properly restore register-based and `volatile` variables.

Sample Call

```
    jmp_buf context1;
// Call setjmp to save context.
    if(setjmp(context1) != 0)
    {
// When here, we must have called "longjmp(context1, ...)".
//...
    }
//...
// Call longjmp to jump back to old state....
    longjmp(context1, 1);
```

See Also

setjmp

_onexit, _fonexit

MSC6	MSC7	VC++	QC2.5	QC-WIN	TC2	TC++	BC++2	BC++3	ANSI	POSIX	UNIX V	DOS	QWIN	WIN	WINDLL
X	X	X	X	X							X	X	X	X	X

Note: `_fonexit` is available in MSC7 and Visual C++ only.

Summary

```
#include <stdlib.h>

_onexit_t _onexit(_onexit_t func); // Function to be called when
                                    // program exists normally
_fonexit_t _ _far _fonexit(_fonexit_t func);
```

Description

Sets up a function, *func*, to be called when the program terminates normally. You can establish up to 32 such functions, to be called in last-in, first-out order.

The `_fonexit` function is similar to `_onexit` except that you can use it in any memory model to set up a far function as an "exit handler."

Returns

When the function completes successfully, the return value is a pointer to the function *func*.

`NULL` Indicates an error.

Sample Call

```
void exit_handler(void);
//...
_onexit(exit_handler);
```

See Also

atexit, exit

_putenv

MSC6	MSC7	VC++	QC2.5	QC-WIN	TC2	TC++	BC++2	BC++3	ANSI	POSIX	UNIX V	DOS	QWIN	WIN	WINDLL
X	X	X	X	X	X	X	X	X			X	X	X	X	X

Summary

```
#include <stdlib.h>
```

```
int _putenv(const char *envdef); // Definition of an environment
                                 // variable
```

Description

Adds a new environment variable or modifies the definition of an existing environment variable. The string `envdef` is of the form

```
VARNAME=DEFINITION
```

If `VARNAME` already appears in the list of environment variables, it is redefined. Otherwise, the definition of `VARNAME` is added to the environment.

You cannot use `_putenv` to alter the environment variables of its parent process, which usually is the DOS command-interpreter. However, any alterations you make to the environment can be made available to any child process launched by your program using the `_exec` or `_spawn` functions.

Returns

0	Indicates the environment variable was successfully added or modified.
–1	Indicates an error.

Sample Call

```
// Change PATH before the spawning process....
    _putenv("PATH=c:\\windows\\system");
```

See Also

`getenv`

raise

MSC6	MSC7	VC++	QC2.5	QC-WIN	TC2	TC++	BC++2	BC++3	ANSI	POSIX	UNIX V	DOS	QWIN	WIN	WINDLL
X	X	X	X	X	X	X	X	X	X			X	X	X	X

Summary

```
#include <signal.h>

int raise(int signum); // Signal to be raised
```

Description

Generates an exception ("raises a signal") corresponding to the signal number `signum`. See the reference entry for signal for a list of constants denoting signal numbers.

Returns

0	Indicates an exception was successfully generated.
Nonzero	Indicates a failure to generate the exception.

Sample Call

```
// Abort the program.
   raise(SIGABRT);
```

See Also

signal

setjmp

MSC6	MSC7	VC++	QC2.5	QC-WIN	TC2	TC++	BC++2	BC++3	ANSI	POSIX	UNIX V	DOS	QWIN	WIN	WINDLL
x	x	x	x	x	x	x	x	x	x	x	x	x	x	x	x

Summary

```
#include <setjmp.h>

int setjmp(jmp_buf context); // Save current context here
```

Description

Saves the current stack environment in the `jmp_buf` argument *`context`*. Later on in the program, you can restore the stack to this saved context by calling `longjmp`, thus achieving the effect of a nonlocal `goto`. As explained in Chapter 13, "Advanced Topics in C++," you should not use `setjmp` in C++ programs.

Returns

0 Indicates that the current stack environment was successfully saved.

When the return is due to a call to `longjmp`, the returned value is the same as the second argument to `longjmp`. (However, if the second argument to `longjmp` is zero, it is automatically converted to 1.)

Sample Call

```
jmp_buf a_context;
//...
if(setjmp(a_context) != 0)
{
// Here when return is due to longjmp.
//...

}
```

See Also

longjmp

setlocale

MSC6	MSC7	VC++	QC2.5	QC-WIN	TC2	TC++	BC++2	BC++3	ANSI	POSIX	UNIX V	DOS	QWIN	WIN	WINDLL
X	X	X	X	X		X	X	X	X	X		X	X	X	X

Summary

```
#include <locale.h>

char *setlocale(
    int          category,// Set locale for this category of
                          // locale-dependent information. Use one
                          // of LC_ALL, LC_COLLATE, LC_CTYPE,
                          // LC_MONETARY, LC_NUMERIC, and LC_TIME
    const char *lname); // Name of locale that will control
                          // the specified category
```

Description

Sets `lname` as the name of the locale that will affect the conversion and presentation of information in the specified *category*. The category can be one of these:

Category	Affects
`LC_ALL`	Entire program (all categories listed here)
`LC_COLLATE`	Collating sequence of character set (affects `strcoll` and `strxfrm`)
`LC_CTYPE`	The multibyte character functions
`LC_MONETARY`	Formatting of monetary data
`LC_NUMERIC`	Formatting of numeric data (for example, output of printf)
`LC_TIME`	Formatting of time by `strftime` function

Returns

When the function completes successfully, the return value is a pointer to the locale name for the new locale

`NULL` Indicates that `setlocale` was unsuccessful.

Sample Call

```
// Set everything to the "C" locale (only locale supported
// in Microsoft Visual C++).
    setlocale(LC_ALL, "C");
```

See Also

`localeconv`

signal

MSC6	MSC7	VC++	QC2.5	QC-WIN	TC2	TC++	BC++2	BC++3	ANSI	POSIX	UNIX V	DOS	QWIN	WIN	WINDLL
X	X	X	X	X	X	X	X	X	X		X	X	X	X	X

Summary

```
#include <signal.h>

void (*signal(int signum, void (*func)(int signum)))(int);
```

Description

Sets up a function `func` as the handler for the exception number `signum`, which can be one of the following constants:

Signal	Description
`SIGABRT`	Abnormal termination of program. The default action terminates the program with exit code 3.
`SIGFPE`	Floating-point error, such as overflow, division by zero, or invalid operation. The default action terminates the calling program.
`SIGILL`	Illegal instruction. Not generated in MS-DOS.
`SIGINT`	Ctrl+C interrupt. The default action generates an INT 23H.
`SIGSEGV`	Illegal memory access. Not generated in MS-DOS.
`SIGTERM`	Termination request sent to the program. Not generated in MS-DOS. The default action terminates the program.

The signal-handling function `func` can be the name of a function that you provide or one of the following constants:

Name	Meaning
`SIG_DFL`	Use the default signal handler.
`SIG_IGN`	Ignore the exception condition.

Returns

When the function completes successfully, the return value is a pointer to previous signal-handling function, if successful.

Otherwise, returns the constant `SIG_ERR` and sets `errno` to `EINVAL` to indicate an invalid signal number.

Sample Call

```
// Ignore SIGINT signals.
    signal(SIGINT, SIG_IGN);
```

See Also

`_raise`

_spawnl, _spawnle, _spawnlp, _spawnlpe, _spawnv, _spawnve, _spawnvp, _spawnvpe

MSC6	MSC7	VC++	QC2.5	QC-WIN	TC2	TC++	BC++2	BC++3	ANSI	POSIX	UNIX V	DOS	QWIN	WIN	WINDLL
X	X	X	X	X	X	X	X	X				X			

Summary

```
#include <process.h>

// execmode is the mode in which the parent process operates
// while the child process is running. This can be one
// of the following:
//    P_WAIT (suspend parent process until child is done)
//    P_OVERLAY (overlay parent process with child as in _exec)

// path denotes the pathname of the executable file to be loaded
// and executed as a child process.

int _spawnl(int execmode, const char *path,
            const char *arg0, ...);
int _spawnle(int execmode, const char *path,
             const char *arg0, ...);
int _spawnlp(int execmode, const char *path,
             const char *arg0, ...);
int _spawnlpe(int execmode, const char *path,
              const char *arg0, ...);
int _spawnv(int execmode, const char *path,
            const char * const *argv);
```

```
int _spawnve(int execmode, const char *path,
            const char * const *argv, const char * const *envp);
int _spawnvp(int execmode, const char *path,
             const char * const *argv);
int _spawnvpe(int execmode, const char *path,
            const char * const *argv, const char * const *envp);
```

Description

Loads and executes the executable file specified by *path* as a child process. The *execmode* argument specifies how the calling program is treated while the child process executes. You can specify one of the following constants for the *execmode* argument:

P_OVERLAY	Child process overlays the parent (same effect as calling the corresponding _exec function).
P_WAIT	Parent process is suspended until the child terminates.

The eight different versions of the spawn functions are as follows:

_spawnl	Accepts a variable number of command-line arguments with a NULL marking the end of the list. Inherits the environment variables from the parent process.
_spawnle	Like _spawnl, except that _spawnle allows the environment variables for the child process to be specified. To do this, the second-to-last argument is a NULL marking the end of a variable number of command-line arguments. The last argument is of type char** that provides an array of null-terminated strings representing the environment variables to be used by the child process.
_spawnlp	Similar to _spawnl, with the additional property that the directories specified in the PATH environment variable are searched to locate the executable file to be loaded and run as a child process.
_spawnlpe	Behaves as a combination of _spawnlp and _spawnle.
_spawnv	Accepts an array of strings (with a NULL marking the end of the array) representing the variable number of command-line arguments. Inherits the environment variables from the parent process.

`_spawnve`	Like `_spawnv`, but accepts an additional argument that is an array of null-terminated strings representing the environment variables to be used by the child process. The end of the array is marked by a `NULL` pointer.
`_spawnvp`	Similar to `_spawnv`, with the additional feature that the directories specified in the `PATH` environment variable are searched to locate the executable file to be loaded and run as a child process.
`_spawnvpe`	Behaves as a combination of `_spawnvp` and `_spawnve`.

Use the `_spawnl` form of the functions when the command-line arguments for the child process are known in advance. The `spawnv` form is appropriate if you have to construct an array of command-line arguments on the fly and pass that array to one of the `spawnv` functions.

Returns

When the function completes successfully, the return value is the exit status of the child process if `execmode` is `P_WAIT`.

–1 Indicates an error—the child process is not started. Also sets `errno` to one of the following:

`E2BIG`	The total length of the command-line arguments exceeds 128 bytes, or memory required for the environment variables is more than 32K.
`EINVAL`	The `execmode` argument is invalid.
`ENOENT`	The executable file could not be located.
`ENOEXEC`	The file specified by `path` argument is not an executable file.
`ENOMEM`	There is not enough memory to run child process.

Sample Call

```
// Execute the program named loadfile.exe as a child process.
if(_spawnl(P_WAIT, "loadfile.exe", "loadfile.exe",
          "test.dat", NULL);
```

See Also

`_exec` functions, `system`

system

MSC6	MSC7	VC++	QC2.5	QC-WIN	TC2	TC++	BC++2	BC++3	ANSI	POSIX	UNIX V	DOS	QWIN	WIN	WINDLL
X	X	X	X	X	X	X	X	X	X		X	X			

Summary

```
#include <stdlib.h>

int system(const char *command);// Command passed to MS-DOS
                                // command interpreter
```

Description

Passes the *command* string to the MS-DOS command interpreter, which executes the string as an operating system command. You can use `system` to run DOS commands as well as any other executable programs. Use an empty *command* string to check whether the command interpreter is running.

Returns

If the *command* argument is `NULL`:

Nonzero	Indicates the existence of a command-interpreter.
0	Indicates that no command-interpreter is running.

If *command* is not `NULL`:

0	Indicates that `command` was successfully executed.
–1	Indicates an error. Also sets `errno` to one of the following:
`E2BIG`	The total length of the command-line arguments exceeds 128 bytes, or memory required for the environment variables is more than 32K.
`ENOENT`	The command interpreter cannot be found.
`ENOEXEC`	The command-interpreter file (specified by the `SHELL` directive in the `CONFIG.SYS` file) is not an executable file.
`ENOMEM`	There is not enough memory to run the command interpreter.

Sample Call

```
system("dir c:");
```

See Also

`_exec` functions, `_spawn` functions

va_arg, va_end, va_start (ANSI version)

MSC6	MSC7	VC++	QC2.5	QC-WIN	TC2	TC++	BC++2	BC++3	ANSI	POSIX	UNIX V	DOS	QWIN	WIN	WINDLL
X	X	X	X	X	X	X	X	X	X			X	X	X	X

Summary

```
#include <stdarg.h>

// argp is the pointer to the list of arguments

<type> va_arg(va_list argp, <type>);
void va_end(va_list argp);
void va_start(va_list argp, <last_reqd_arg>);
```

Description

Use these macros to access the arguments in a function that takes a fixed number of required arguments followed by a variable number of optional arguments. The steps in accessing the variable number of arguments are as follows:

1. Declare a variable named *argp* of type `va_list`.
2. Call the `va_start` macro with *argp* and the name of the last required argument. This initializes *argp* to the beginning of the list of the variable-length arguments.
3. Use the `va_arg` macro to get the next argument.
4. Repeat for each optional argument. You must know the order and the type of each argument. Also, you must decide what value marks the end of the list of arguments.
5. Use the `va_end` macro to reset the *argp* pointer.

Returns

The `va_arg` macro returns the next argument of a specified type. The `va_start` and `va_end` macros do not return anything.

Sample Call

```
// ANSI Standard C version of a function that
// finds the longest of several strings.

char *longest(char *first, ...)
{
    size_t length, maxlen = strlen(first);
    char *longest = first, *str;
```

```
    va_list argp;

// Start accessing the arguments (assume that a NULL marks
// the end of the list of optional arguments).

    va_start(argp, first);
    while((str = va_arg(argp, char*)) != NULL)
    {
        length = strlen(str);
        if(maxlen < length)
        {
            maxlen = length;
            longest = str;
        }
    }
    va_end(argp);
    return (longest);
}
```

See Also

va_arg, va_end, va_start (UNIX version)

va_arg, va_end, va_start (UNIX version)

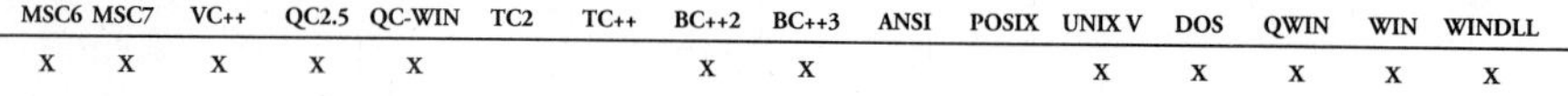

MSC6	MSC7	VC++	QC2.5	QC-WIN	TC2	TC++	BC++2	BC++3	ANSI	POSIX	UNIX V	DOS	QWIN	WIN	WINDLL
X	X	X	X	X			X	X			X	X	X	X	X

Summary

```
#include <varargs.h>

// argp is the pointer to the list of arguments

<type> va_arg(va_list argp, <type>);
void va_end(va_list argp);
void va_start(va_list argp);
```

Description

Use these macros to access the arguments in a function that accepts a variable number of optional arguments. Use the following steps to access the variable number of arguments:

1. Declare the variable-length arguments with a `va_alist` (see Sample Call).
2. Place the `va_dcl` macro (without a semicolon at the end) between the function

declaration and its body.

3. Declare a variable named *argp* of type `va_list`.
4. Call the `va_start` macro with *argp* as the argument. This initializes *argp* to the beginning of the list of the variable-length arguments.
5. Use the `va_arg` macro to get the next argument.
6. Repeat for each optional argument. You must know the order and the type of each argument. Also, you must decide what value marks the end of the list of arguments.
7. Use the `va_end` macro to reset the *argp* pointer.

Returns

The `va_arg` macro returns the next argument of a specified type. The `va_start` and `va_end` macros do not return anything.

Sample Call

```
// UNIX System V version of a function that
// finds the longest of several strings

char *longest(va_alist)    // Note declaration
va_dcl        // This macro must appear without semicolon
{
    size_t length, maxlen = 0;
    char *longest = NULL, *str;
    va_list argp;

// Start accessing the arguments (assume that a NULL marks
// the end of the list of arguments).

    va_start(argp);
    while((str = va_arg(argp, char*)) != NULL)
    {
        length = strlen(str);
        if(maxlen < length)
        {
           maxlen = length;
           longest = str;
        }
    }
```

```
    va_end(argp);
    return (longest);
}
```

See Also

va_arg, va_end, va_start (ANSI version)

31

Memory Management

Memory management functions enable you to request blocks of memory at runtime and release the blocks when your program no longer needs them. Using the memory management functions, you can ensure that your application takes advantage of all available memory in the system. Although ANSI standard C provides for only four memory management functions—`calloc`, `free`, `malloc`, and `realloc`—Microsoft Visual C++ includes a much larger repertoire of functions for managing memory, primarily to handle the variety of memory models supported by Microsoft Visual C++. Additionally, Microsoft Visual C++ includes a number of functions for allocating and managing virtual memory, where a relatively small amount of physical memory is augmented by secondary storage such as a disk (or extended memory that DOS normally cannot access), to provide a program with more memory than physically available. The functions described in this chapter are declared in the header files malloc.h and vmemory.h.

> **Memory Management in Microsoft Visual C++ Programs**
>
> For a thorough discussion of memory management techniques in C and C++ programs, consult Chapters 4 and 5 of the Programming Techniques manual that comes with the Microsoft Visual C++ compiler. Although this chapter summarizes some of the concepts and functions used for memory management, space limitations preclude coverage as thorough as that in the *Microsoft Visual C++ Programming Techniques* manual.

Basics of Memory Management

The availability of pointers—variables that can store addresses—is the key to the memory management functions in C. The basic idea behind the memory management functions is to allocate a block of memory and return a pointer to the block. The pool of available memory is called a *heap*. The heap is managed as a linked list of structures that hold information about each block in the heap. When you call a function such as `malloc` to allocate memory, the block of memory comes from the heap. There are several types of heaps—the variety can be attributed to the segmented architecture of Intel 80x86 family of processors.

Segmented Memory Addressing

The Intel 80x86 family of processors breaks memory down into segments, each up to 64K in size. This allows the processor to use a 16-bit offset from the start of the segment to address any byte within a segment. The segment is identified by a 16-bit segment address, which is the location where the segment starts. Microsoft Visual C++ accommodates the segmented-addressing scheme of the Intel 80x86 microprocessors by providing a number of memory models. Each memory model specifies the number of segments of code and data allowed within a program.

Memory Models

Each program built with the Microsoft Visual C++ compiler has at least one segment of code and a segment of data (except in the tiny model). Depending on the various combinations of allowable code and data segments, Microsoft Visual C++ supports the following six predefined memory models:

- The *tiny* model, which allows a single 64K segment for both code and data. You can generate a tiny model program by compiling with the `/AT` compiler option and by linking with the `/TINY` linker option—the executable file will have a `.COM` extension instead of `.EXE`.
- The *small* model, which limits a program to two 64K segments: one for code and the other for data. The `/AS` compiler option selects the small model.
- The *medium* model, which allows more than one code segment but only one data segment. The `/AM` compiler option selects the medium model.
- The *compact* model, which limits the code to one 64K segment but allows many data segments. The `/AC` compiler option selects the compact model.
- The *large* model, whose programs can have unlimited code and data segments, but whose data arrays must be less than 64K in size. The `/AL` compiler option selects the large memory model.
- The *huge* model, which is similar to large model except that you can have larger arrays than 64K in huge model. However, individual array elements still must be less than 64K. The `/AH` compiler option selects the huge memory model.

The data segment that contains the stack and the initialized global variables is called the *default data segment.* The segment address of the code segment is held in the CS register, and the DS register contains the segment address of the default data segment.

Near, Far, and Huge Pointers

Because of the different memory models, Microsoft Visual C++ supports three types of pointers:

- A *near pointer* refers to the 16-bit offset address within a segment.
- A *far pointer* holds the full 32-bit segment and offset address. However, address arithmetic is performed with the 16-bit offset address only. The net effect is that arrays addressed by far pointers cannot exceed a segment (64K) in size.
- A *huge pointer* is similar to a far pointer except that address arithmetic on huge pointers is performed with the full 32-bit address. Thus, arrays accessed with huge pointers can span segment boundaries and be larger than 64K in size.

The memory model determines the type of pointer used by the compiler for code and data. In the tiny and small memory models, all pointers are near pointers. In the medium memory model, data pointers are near but function pointers are far. The compact model has the reverse scenario—function addresses are near but data pointers are far. In large and huge memory models, all pointers are far pointers.

The __near, __far, and __huge Keywords

Although the predefined memory models determine the default type of pointers in a program, you can use one of the following keywords to explicitly indicate the type of address being referenced by a pointer:

- The `__near` keyword indicates that a data item or a function is to be addressed with a 16-bit offset address only. All near data resides in the default data segment and address arithmetic is performed using the 16-bit offsets only.
- The `__far` keyword indicates that the data or function it qualifies should be accessed with a full 32-bit segment and offset address. Address arithmetic still is performed with the 16-bit offset only.
- The `__huge` keyword applies to data only, and it indicates that address arithmetic should be performed using the full 32-bit address. Arrays qualified by the `__huge` keyword can be larger than 64K.

Heaps

The term *heap* refers to a pool of memory with some management scheme so that blocks of memory can be allocated from the pool. The pool of free memory available in the default data segment is known as the *near heap*; the *far heap* refers to a segment of memory beyond the default data segment. Microsoft Visual C++ includes memory management functions that are specific to a heap—near or far. The functions that work with the near heap have the `_n` prefix; the functions with the `_f` prefix manage the far heap. Those functions without an `_n`, `_b`, or `_f` prefix work on the default heap as defined in the application's memory model.

Based Heaps

In addition to the near and far heaps, Microsoft Visual C++ includes the ability to treat any segment of memory as a heap from which you can allocate blocks of memory.

Such pools of memory are referred to as *based heaps*. You can allocate a based heap with the _bheapseg function and manage the based heap with the functions with names that start with a _b prefix.

Based Pointers

Note that you need a different type of pointer to address memory allocated in a based heap—you need a *based pointer*. To declare a based pointer, you must use the __based keyword to identify the segment that acts as the base for the pointer—the based pointer will be an offset from the start of this segment. As an example, here is how you would declare a char pointer based on the default data segment (which has the name _DATA):

```
char __based(__segname("_DATA"))  *p;
```

Another keyword, __segname, identifies the base to be used for the based pointer. There are several ways to indicate the base segment, discussed in the following sections.

Base Segments of Based Pointers

There are four ways to specify the base segment for a based pointer:

- A fixed segment can be specified as the base. In this case, you can either indicate the segment by its name with the __segname keyword or use the segment keyword to specify a base segment that is the same as the segment address of another pointer. Here are some examples:

```
int __based(__segname("_DATA")) *p_i;
//...
double x;
char__based((_segment)&x) *p_c;
```

- The base can be a segment determined at runtime. Use a variable of __segment type as the base, and later initialize that __segment variable with the return value from a call to _bheapseg. Alternatively, set the __segment variable to a specific physical segment. Consider the following fragment of code:

```
_segment vmem = 0xb800;
char __based(vmem) *p_video;

int i;
for(i = 0; i < 2000; i++, p_video++, p_video++)
*p_video = 'X';
```

  This fills most of the text screen with the letter X.

- You can specify a base segment with the `__self` keyword, which refers to the segment where the based pointer itself will be located. Here is a declaration using the `__self` keyword:

```
char __based((__segment)__self) *p_buf;
```

- The fourth way is to use the `void` keyword as the base:

```
char __based(void) *p_buf;
```

Once declared this way, you can use `p_buf` with any base segment by using the `:>` operator—the so-called *base operator* unique to Microsoft Visual C++. For example, you can use the based operator to rewrite an earlier code fragment as follows:

```
char __based(void) *p_video;
int i;
for(i = 0; i < 2000; i++, p_video++, p_video++)
*(((__segment)0xb800):>p_video) = 'X';
```

Microsoft-Specific Keywords: `__based`, `__far`, `__huge`, and `__near`

In versions of Microsoft C compilers prior to Microsoft C/C++ 7.0, the keywords `__based`, `__far`, `__huge`, and `__near` were used without the leading underscores. Because the ANSI standard for C enables compiler vendors to reserve names that begin with two underscores, Microsoft has added the leading underscores to these reserved keywords. However, the older keywords still are supported for compatibility.

Virtual Memory

Starting with Microsoft C/C++ 7.0, Microsoft provides a set of functions for setting up and using virtual memory in your applications. As the name implies, virtual memory appears to be just like physical memory, but relies on secondary storage (such as disk or other types of memory—extended or expanded) to swap blocks in and out of physical memory. The appeal of virtual memory is that it allows an application to use more memory than physically available on a system. However, because any memory in actual use must reside in physical memory, each individual block must not be any larger than the largest available block of DOS memory. Additionally, because blocks are swapped in and out of physical memory as necessary, excess swapping adversely affects the program's performance.

Virtual memory management functions have names that start with a _v prefix and are declared in the header file vmemory.h. The basic steps in using virtual memory are as follows:

1. Call `_vheapinit` to initialize the virtual memory manager.
2. Call `_vmalloc` to allocate blocks of virtual memory.
3. Use `_vload` or `_vlock` to load a block of virtual memory into DOS memory and lock it so that the virtual memory manager does not swap it out while you're using that block of memory.
4. Call `_vunlock` to unlock virtual memory blocks that you do not plan to access immediately so that the virtual memory manager can move or swap these blocks as required.
5. Call `_vfree` to free virtual blocks that you no longer need.
6. When you're done using virtual memory, call `_vheapterm` to terminate the virtual memory manager.

Basic Memory Management Tasks

Table 31.1 shows an alphabetic list of the console and port I/O functions and gives you a quick overview of these functions. Table 31.2 organizes these functions by the tasks they perform. Some of these tasks are illustrated by a short sample program in the following section. For more information about a function, consult the reference entry for that function in the reference section that follows.

Table 31.1. Alphabetic listing of memory management functions.

Function	Description
`_alloca`	Allocates a number of bytes from the program's stack.
`_bcalloc`	Allocates storage for an array in a based heap.
`_bexpand`	Expands or shrinks the size of a block of memory in a based heap without moving the block in the heap.

continues

Table 31.1. continued

Function	Description
`_bfree`	Frees a block of memory allocated in a based heap.
`_bfreeseg`	Frees a based heap.
`_bheapadd`	Adds a block of memory to a based heap.
`_bheapchk`	Checks a based heap for consistency.
`_bheapmin`	Minimizes a based heap by releasing all unused memory.
`_bheapseg`	Allocates a based heap.
`_bheapset`	Fills all free locations in a based heap with a specified value.
`_bheapwalk`	Traverses the entries in a based heap and returns information on each entry.
`_bmalloc`	Allocates a specified number of bytes from a based heap.
`_bmsize`	Returns the number of bytes in an allocated block in a based heap.
`_brealloc`	Alters the size of a block of memory in a based heap, relocating the block if necessary but retaining the contents of all old locations.
`calloc`	Allocates an array of elements of specified size and initializes the array to all zeros.
`_expand`	Alters the size of a previously allocated block of memory without moving the block in the heap.
`_fcalloc`	Allocates memory for an array in the far heap and initializes each array entry to zero.
`_fexpand`	Expands or shrinks a previously allocated block of memory in the far heap without moving the block in the heap.
`_ffree`	Frees a block of memory allocated by `_fmalloc` or `_fcalloc` in the far heap.
`_fheapchk`	Checks the consistency of the far heap.
`_fheapmin`	Minimizes the size of the far heap by releasing unused blocks to the operating system.

Function	Description
_fheapset	Sets all unused entries in the far heap to a specified value.
_fheapwalk	Traverses through the entries in the far heap and returns information on each entry.
_fmalloc	Allocates an uninitialized block of memory in the far heap.
_fmsize	Returns the size of a block of memory allocated in the far heap.
_frealloc	Alters the size of a previously allocated memory in the far heap, relocating it to a new location if necessary.
free	Releases memory allocated by calloc or malloc.
_freect	Returns the approximate number of elements of a specified size that can be allocated in the near heap.
_halloc	Allocates a huge array that may exceed 64K in size.
_heapadd	Adds a block of memory to the heap.
_heapchk	Checks the consistency of the heap.
_heapmin	Reduces the size of the heap to a minimum by freeing unused blocks of memory.
_heapset	Sets all unused entries in the heap to a specified value.
_heapwalk	Traverses the entries of the heap and returns information on each entry.
_hfree	Frees a huge array allocated by _halloc.
malloc	Allocates a block of uninitialized memory in the heap.
_memavl	Returns approximate number of bytes available for allocation in the near heap.
_memmax	Returns the maximum number of contiguous bytes available for allocation in the near heap.
_msize	Returns the size of a previously allocated block of memory.
_ncalloc	Allocates memory for an array in the near heap and initializes the array to all zeros.

continues

Table 31.1. continued

Function	Description
`_nexpand`	Expands or shrinks a block of memory allocated in the near heap.
`_nfree`	Releases a previously allocated block of memory in the near heap.
`_nheapchk`	Checks the near heap for consistency.
`_nheapmin`	Reduces the size of the near heap to a minimum by freeing unused blocks.
`_nheapset`	Sets all free locations in the near heap to a specified value.
`_nheapwalk`	Traverses through all entries in the near heap, returning information on each entry.
`_nmalloc`	Allocates an uninitialized block of memory in the near heap.
`_nmsize`	Returns the size of an allocated block in near heap.
`_nrealloc`	Resizes a previously allocated block of memory in the near heap, moving the block to a new location if necessary.
`realloc`	Changes the size of a previously allocated block of memory, relocating the block if necessary but retaining the contents of all old locations.
`_stackavail`	Returns the number of bytes available in the stack for allocation by `_alloca`.
`_vfree`	Frees a previously allocated block of virtual memory.
`_vheapinit`	Initializes the virtual memory manager.
`_vheapterm`	Closes down the virtual memory manager.
`_vload`	Loads a block of virtual memory into DOS memory and returns a far pointer to the block in DOS memory.
`_vlock`	Loads a block from virtual memory into DOS memory and locks the block.
`_vlockcnt`	Returns the number of times a block of virtual memory has been locked.
`_vmalloc`	Allocates a block of virtual memory.

Function	Description
_vmsize	Returns the size of a previously allocated block of virtual memory.
_vrealloc	Resizes a previously allocated block of virtual memory, relocating the block to a new location if necessary.
_vunlock	Decrements the lock count of a block of virtual memory.

Table 31.2. Basic memory management tasks.

Task	Functions
Allocate, free, and resize blocks of memory	calloc, _expand, fcalloc, _fexpand, ffree, _fmalloc, free, hfree, malloc, _msize, ncalloc, nexpand, nfree, _nmalloc, nmsize, _ nrealloc, realloc
Manage heaps	fheapchk, fheapmin, fheapset, fheapwalk, heapadd, _heapchk, heapmin, _heapset, heapwalk, nheapchk, nheapmin, nheapset, nheapwalk,
Manage based heaps	bcalloc, _bexpand, bfree, _bfreeseg, bheapadd, _bheapchk, bheapmin, _bheapseg, bheapset, _bheapwalk, bmalloc, _bmsize, brealloc,
Allocate memory on stack	alloca, stackavail
Determine amount available in heap	freect, _memavl, memmax
Manage virtual memory	vfree, _vheapinit, vheapterm, _vload, vlock, _vlockcnt, vmalloc, _vmsize, vrealloc, _vunlock

Allocating Memory and Checking the Heap

Using memory allocation functions is straightforward, but errors related to memory allocation can be hard to locate. One way to pinpoint heap-related errors is to use functions, such as `_heapwalk`, that let you go through the heap entries and check the status of each block of memory. Listing 31.1 shows the program showheap.c that includes a function named `disp_heap` to display the contents of the heap. To illustrate the use of the `disp_heap` function, the showheap program allocates and frees some memory blocks and displays the contents of the heap after each event.

Here's a sample of what the program shows when run:

```
------------- START OF HEAP -----------------
Address: 10F6:0D3C  Status:   USED  Size:   344
Address: 10F6:0E96  Status:   USED  Size:    20
Address: 10F6:0EAC  Status:   USED  Size:   512
Address: 10F6:10AE  Status:   FREE  Size:  3920
--------------- END OF HEAP -----------------
------------- START OF HEAP -----------------
Address: 10F6:0D3C  Status:   USED  Size:   344
Address: 10F6:0E96  Status:   USED  Size:    20
Address: 10F6:0EAC  Status:   USED  Size:   512
Address: 10F6:10AE  Status:   USED  Size:    80
Address: 10F6:1100  Status:   USED  Size:   100
Address: 10F6:1166  Status:   FREE  Size:  3736
--------------- END OF HEAP -----------------
Press a key to continue
Enlarging the buffer1...
------------- START OF HEAP -----------------
Address: 10F6:0D3C  Status:   USED  Size:   344
Address: 10F6:0E96  Status:   USED  Size:    20
Address: 10F6:0EAC  Status:   USED  Size:   512
Address: 10F6:10AE  Status:   FREE  Size:    80
Address: 10F6:1100  Status:   USED  Size:   100
Address: 10F6:1166  Status:   USED  Size:   200
Address: 10F6:1230  Status:   FREE  Size:  3534
--------------- END OF HEAP -----------------
Press a key to continue
Freeing the buffer...
------------- START OF HEAP -----------------
Address: 10F6:0D3C  Status:   USED  Size:   344
Address: 10F6:0E96  Status:   USED  Size:    20
```

```
Address: 10F6:0EAC  Status:  USED  Size:   512
Address: 10F6:10AE  Status:  FREE  Size:    80
Address: 10F6:1100  Status:  USED  Size:   100
Address: 10F6:1166  Status:  FREE  Size:   200
Address: 10F6:1230  Status:  FREE  Size:  3534
---------------- END OF HEAP -----------------
```

Note that the initial display of the heap shows a number of blocks already allocated—these allocations are part of the normal program startup.

Listing 31.1. A program to display the contents of the heap.

```
//----------------------------------------------------------------
// File: showheap.c
//
// Displays the heap after allocating and freeing blocks of
// memory.
//----------------------------------------------------------------
#include <stdio.h>
#include <malloc.h>
#include <process.h>
#include <conio.h>

static void disp_heap(void);

void main(void)
{
    char *buffer1, *buffer2;

// Display the heap (empty at this point):
    disp_heap();

// Allocate a buffer:
    if((buffer1 = (char *) malloc(80)) == NULL)
    {
        printf("Error allocating memory\n");
        exit(1);
    }
// Allocate another....
    if((buffer2 = (char *) malloc(100)) == NULL)
```

continues

Listing 31.1. continued

```
    {
        printf("Error allocating memory\n");
        exit(1);
    }

// Display the heap entries now:
    disp_heap();
    printf("Press a key to continue\n");
    getch();

// Enlarge one of the buffer's size and display the heap:
    printf("Enlarging the buffer1...\n");
    if((buffer1 = realloc(buffer1, 200)) == NULL)
    {
        printf("Error reallocating memory\n");
        exit(1);
    }
    disp_heap();

    printf("Press a key to continue\n");
    getch();

// Free the memory being used by buffer and display heap:
    printf("Freeing the buffer...\n");
    free(buffer1);
    disp_heap();
}
//---------------------------------------------------------------
// d i s p _ h e a p
//
// Display the heap entries.

static void disp_heap()
{
     _HEAPINFO heapentry;
     int heapstatus;

// Set the _pentry field to NULL to begin at first entry:
     heapentry._pentry = NULL;
```

```
// Keep calling _heapwalk as long as the return value is _HEAPOK.
// Print information about entry from the heapentry structure.

    printf("------------- START OF HEAP -----------------\n");
    while ( (heapstatus = _heapwalk(&heapentry)) == _HEAPOK)
    {
        printf("Address: %Fp  Status: %6s  Size: %5u\n",
               heapentry._pentry,
               (heapentry._useflag == _FREEENTRY ? "FREE" :
                                               "USED"),
               heapentry._size);
    }

    switch (heapstatus)
    {
         case  _HEAPOK:
             printf("Heap OK\n");
             break;

         case _HEAPEMPTY:
             printf("Heap not initialized\n");
             break;

         case  _HEAPBADBEGIN:
             printf("Heap header bad\n");
             break;

         case  _HEAPBADNODE:
             printf("Heap has one or more bad nodes\n");
             break;
     }
     printf("--------------- END OF HEAP -----------------\n");
}
```

_alloca

MSC6	MSC7	VC++	QC2.5	QC-WIN	TC2	TC++	BC++2	BC++3	ANSI	POSIX	UNIX V	DOS	QWIN	WIN	WINDLL
X	X	X	X	X				X			X	X			

Note: The underscore prefix in the name `_alloca` was added in MSC7, and also is uscd in Visual C++.

Summary

```
#include <malloc.h>

void *_alloca(
    size_t n); // Number of bytes to allocate on the stack
```

Description

Allocates *n* bytes of space on the stack for temporary use that will be automatically freed as soon as the calling function returns.

Microsoft warns that when you compile with any of the optimization flags (the `/O` options), any function that calls `_alloca` must declare at least one local variable. Also, you must not call `_alloc` inside an expression that is being passed as an argument to a function.

Returns

When the function completes successfully, the return value is a the pointer to the first byte of space allocated on the stack.

`NULL` Indicates that there is not enough space on the stack.

Sample Call

```
void main()
{
    char *buf = alloca(256*sizeof(char));
//...
}
```

See Also

`calloc, malloc, _stackavail`

_bfreeseg

MSC6	MSC7	VC++	QC2.5	QC-WIN	TC2	TC++	BC++2	BC++3	ANSI	POSIX	UNIX V	DOS	QWIN	WIN	WINDLL
X	X	X	X	X								X	X	X	X

Summary

```
#include <malloc.h>

int _bfreeseg(_ _segment seg); // Segment to free
```

Description

Frees the segment of memory identified by *seg*. This must be a segment allocated for use as a based heap (see tutorial) by the `_bheapseg` function.

Returns

0 Indicates that the memory segment has successfully been freed.

–1 Indicates an error.

Sample Call

```
    _segment seg1;
// Allocate a based heap.
    if((seg1 = _bheapseg(1024*sizeof(short))) == _NULLSEG)
    {
        fprintf(stderr, "Error allocating based heap\n");
        exit(1);
    }
//...
// Free the based heap segment.
    _bfreeseg(seg1);
```

See Also

_bheapseg

_bheapseg

MSC6	MSC7	VC++	QC2.5	QC-WIN	TC2	TC++	BC++2	BC++3	ANSI	POSIX	UNIX V	DOS	QWIN	WIN	WINDLL
x	x	x	x	x								x	x	x	x

Summary

```
#include <malloc.h>

_ _segment _bheapseg(
    size_t n); // Allocate based heap of size n bytes
```

Description

Allocates an *n*-byte segment of memory for use as a based heap (see tutorial). Once the segment is allocated, you can allocate memory from the segment by calling `_bcalloc` or `_bmalloc`.

Returns

When the function completes successfully, the return value is a `_ _segment` identifier for the segment allocated by `_bheapseg`.z. Returns `_NULLSEQ` if the function fails.

Sample Call

```
    _segment seg1;
// Allocate a based heap.
    if((seg1 = _bheapseg(1024*sizeof(short))) == _NULLSEG)
    {
```

```
        fprintf(stderr, "Error allocating based heap\n");
        exit(1);
    }
// Now use _bcalloc and _bmalloc to allocate memory from
// the based heap.
```

See Also

_bfreeseg, calloc, malloc

calloc, _bcalloc, _fcalloc, _halloc, _ncalloc

MSC6	MSC7	VC++	QC2.5	QC-WIN	TC2	TC++	BC++2	BC++3	ANSI	POSIX	UNIX V	DOS	QWIN	WIN	WINDLL
X	X	X	X	X	X	X	X	X	X	X	X	X	X	X	X

Note: _fcalloc, _halloc, and _ncalloc are available in MSC6, MSC7, Visual C++, QC2.5, and QC-WIN only. The _bcalloc function is available in MSC6, MSC7, Visual C++, QC2.5, and QC-WIN. The _fcalloc and _ncalloc names also are defined in BC++2 and BC++3, with _fcalloc mapped to a function named farcalloc.

The underscore prefix to the name _halloc was added in MSC7.

Summary

```
#include <malloc.h>

void * calloc(
    size_t nelem,     // Allocate this many elements.
    size_t elemsize); // Size of each element in bytes.

void _ _based(void) * _bcalloc(
    _ _segment seg,        // Allocate from this based heap.
    size_t    nelem,       // Allocate this many elements.
    size_t    elemsize) ; // Size of each element in bytes.

void _ _far * _fcalloc(size_t nelem, size_t elemsize);

void _ _huge *_halloc(long nelem, size_t elemsize);

void _ _near * _ncalloc(size_t nelem, size_t elemsize);
```

Description

Allocates a block of memory for an array of *nelem* data elements, each of size *elemsize* bytes, and initializes all bytes to zero. In tiny, small, and medium memory models, the compiler maps calls to calloc to _ncalloc. In compact, large, and huge memory models, the `_fcalloc` function is called when you call `calloc`. You can call `_ncalloc` and `_fcalloc` explicitly to allocate near and far data items in any memory model.

Use `_bcalloc` to allocate memory from a based heap obtained by an earlier call to `_bheapseg`.

Use the `halloc` function to allocate huge arrays that can occupy more than 64K of memory. If the total size of the huge array exceeds 128K (131,072 bytes), the *`elemsize`* argument must be a power of 2.

Returns

When the function completes successfully, the return value is a pointer to the allocated block of memory.

`NULL` Indicates that there is not enough memory. The `_bcalloc` function returns `_NULLOFF` in case of error.

Sample Call

```
int *index;
//...
if((index = calloc(256, sizeof(int)) == NULL)
{
// Memory allocation error....
//...
}
```

See Also

`free`, `malloc`, `realloc`

_expand, _bexpand, _fexpand, _nexpand

MSC6	MSC7	VC++	QC2.5	QC-WIN	TC2	TC++	BC++2	BC++3	ANSI	POSIX	UNIX V	DOS	QWIN	WIN	WINDLL
X	X	X	X	X								X	X	X	X

Note: `_fexpand` and `_nexpand` are available in MSC6, MSC7, Visual C++, QC2.5, and QC-WIN only, whereas `_bexpand` is in MSC6, MSC7, Visual C++, QC2.5, and QC-WIN.

Summary

```
#include <malloc.h>

void * _expand(
    void   *ptr,      // Resize this block of memory
    size_t newsize); //   to this many bytes.
```

```
void _ _based(void) * _bexpand(
    _ _segment            seg,      // Based heap containing the
                                    //   block of memory being resized.
    void _ _based(void) *ptr,       // Resize this memory block.
    size_t               newsize); // New size in bytes.

void _ _far * _fexpand(void _ _far *, size_t);

void _ _near * _nexpand(void _ _near *, size_t);
```

Description

Resizes a previously allocated block of memory identified by `ptr` to a new size *without* moving the block in the heap.

Returns

When the function completes successfully, the return value is a pointer to the resized block, which is the same as the `ptr` argument.

`NULL` Indicates that the block cannot be resized in place. The `_bexpand` function returns `_NULLOFF` in case of failure.

Sample Call

```
    int *index;
// Assume index points to a block capable of holding
// 512 short integers. Expand it to hold 1024 elements:
    if(_expand(index, 1024*sizeof(short)) == NULL)
    {
// Failed to expand the memory block.
//...
    }
```

See Also

`realloc`

free, _bfree, _ffree, _hfree, _nfree

MSC6	MSC7	VC++	QC2.5	QC-WIN	TC2	TC++	BC++2	BC++3	ANSI	POSIX	UNIX V	DOS	QWIN	WIN	WINDLL
X	X	X	X	X	X	X	X	X	X	X	X	X	X	X	X

Note: `_ffree`, `_hfree`, and `_nfree` are available in MSC6, MSC7, Visual C++, QC2.5, and QC-WIN only. The `_bfree` function is available in MSC6, MSC7, Visual C++, QC2.5, and QC-WIN. The `_ffree` and `_nfree` names also are defined in BC++2 and BC++3, with `_ffree` mapped to a function named `farfree`.

The underscore prefix to the name _hfree was added in MSC7.

Summary

```
#include <malloc.h>

void free(void *ptr); // Block of memory to be freed

void _bfree(
    _ _segment          seg,  // Free memory from this based heap.
    void _ _based(void) *ptr);// Free this block of memory.

void _ffree(void _ _far *ptr);

void _hfree(
    void _ _huge *ptr); // Free memory allocated by halloc

void _nfree(void _ _near *ptr);
```

Description

Deallocates (returns to the pool of free memory) the block of memory identified by *ptr*. Use _bfree to release memory allocated by _bcalloc or _bmalloc, and use _hfree to free huge arrays allocated by _halloc.

Sample Call

```
    int *index;
// Assume that index points to an array allocated by calloc.
// ...
// Free the array.
    free(index);
```

See Also

calloc, malloc, realloc

_freect

MSC6	MSC7	VC++	QC2.5	QC-WIN	TC2	TC++	BC++2	BC++3	ANSI	POSIX	UNIX V	DOS	QWIN	WIN	WINDLL
X	X	X	X	X								X	X	X	X

Summary

```
#include <malloc.h>

unsigned int _freect(
    size_t elemsize); Size of each data element in bytes
```

Description

Determines how many data elements, each of size `elemsize` bytes, can be allocated in the near heap (the default data segment).

Returns

The return value is the number of elements, each of size `elemsize` bytes, that can be allocated in the near heap.

Sample Call

```
unsigned numint = _freect(sizeof(int));
```

See Also

_memavl, _memmax

_heapadd, _bheapadd

MSC6	MSC7	VC++	QC2.5	QC-WIN	TC2	TC++	BC++2	BC++3	ANSI	POSIX	UNIX V	DOS	QWIN	WIN	WINDLL
X	X	X	X	X								X	X	X	X

Note: `_heapadd` may be used in DOS only.

Summary

```
#include <malloc.h>

int _heapadd(
   void _ _far *ptr, // Block to be added to heap.
    size_t    n);    // Size of block in bytes.

int _bheapadd(
    _ _segment          seg, // Based heap.
    void _ _based(void) *ptr,// Add this block to the heap.
    size_t             n);   // Size of block in bytes.
```

Description

Adds to the heap the block of memory identified by *ptr* and of size *n* bytes. If the block is in the `DGROUP` segment, `_heapadd` adds that block to the near heap; otherwise, it adds the block to the far heap.

Returns

0 Indicates the block of memory was successfully added to the heap.

–1 Indicates an error.

Sample Call

```
    char buffer[256];
//...
// Add space used by buffer to the heap (it goes to
// the near heap):
    if(_heapadd(buffer, sizeof(buffer)) == -1)
        fprintf(stderr, "Error adding to heap\n");
```

See Also

`_heapwalk`

_heapchk, _bheapchk, _fheapchk, _nheapchk

MSC6	MSC7	VC++	QC2.5	QC-WIN	TC2	TC++	BC++2	BC++3	ANSI	POSIX	UNIX V	DOS	QWIN	WIN	WINDLL
X	X	X	X	X								X			

Note: The `_bheapchk` and `_fheapchk` functions may be used in DOS, QWIN, WIN, and WINDLL applications. Similar functions in TC2, TC++, BC++2, and BC++3 are `heapcheck` and `farheapcheck`.

Summary

```
#include <malloc.h>

int _heapchk(void);
int _bheapchk(_ _segment seg); // Identifies based heap to check.
int _fheapchk(void); // Check the consistency of the far heap.
int _nheapchk(void); // Check the consistency of the near heap.
```

Description

Checks the consistency of the appropriate heap.

Returns

When the function completes successfully, the return value is an integer denoting the status of the heap. Interpret the result by comparing with one of the following constants:

`_HEAPBADBEGIN`	Incorrect or missing initial header.
`_HEAPBADNODE`	A bad node was found in the heap.
`_HEAPEMPTY`	Uninitialized heap.
`_HEAPOK`	All entries in the heap are consistent (addresses are within limits assigned to the heap).

Sample Call

```
int heap_status;
//...
heap_status = _heapchk();
```

See Also

_heapset, _heapwalk

_heapmin, _bheapmin, _fheapmin, _nheapmin

MSC6	MSC7	VC++	QC2.5	QC-WIN	TC2	TC++	BC++2	BC++3	ANSI	POSIX	UNIX V	DOS	QWIN	WIN	WINDLL
X	X	X	X	X								X	X	X	X

Summary

```
#include <malloc.h>

int _heapmin(void);
int _bheapmin(_ _segment seg); // Identifies based heap to minimize.
int _fheapmin(void); // Minimize the far heap.
int _nheapmin(void); // Minimize the near heap.
```

Description

Minimizes the appropriate heap by releasing unused memory to the underlying operating system.

Returns

0	Indicates the unused memory was successfully released.
–1	Indicates an error.

Sample Call

```
_heapmin();
```

See Also

_heapadd

_heapset, _bheapset, _fheapset, _nheapset

MSC6	MSC7	VC++	QC2.5	QC-WIN	TC2	TC++	BC++2	BC++3	ANSI	POSIX	UNIX V	DOS	QWIN	WIN	WINDLL
X	X	X	X	X								X			

Note: The `_bheapset` and `_fheapset` functions may be used in DOS, QWIN, WIN, and WINDLL applications. Similar functions in TC2, TC++, BC++2, and BC++3 are `heapfillfree` and `farheapfillfree`.

Summary

```
#include <malloc.h>

int _heapset(
    unsigned int fillchar); // Set each byte of heap to fillchar.

int _bheapset(
    __segment    seg,       // Each byte of this based heap
    unsigned int fillchar); //   is filled with this fill character.

int _fheapset(unsigned int fillchar); // Fill far heap.
int _nheapset(unsigned int fillchar); // Fill near heap.
```

Description

Fills each byte in the unused portions of the appropriate heap with the value in *fillchar*. Also checks the consistency of the heap. You can use these functions to fill unused areas of a heap with a known value so that you can later identify any areas that may have been overwritten by erroneous code.

Returns

When the function completes successfully, the return value is an integer value denoting the status of the heap. Interpret the result by comparing the returned value with the following constants:

`_HEAPBADBEGIN`	Incorrect or missing initial header.
`_HEAPBADNODE`	A bad node was found in the heap.
`_HEAPEMPTY`	Uninitialized heap.
`_HEAPOK`	All entries in the heap are consistent (addresses are within limits assigned to the heap).

Sample Call

```
if(_heapset('X') != _HEAPOK)
    fprintf(stderr, "Heap is damaged\n");
```

See Also

`_heapchk`, `_heapwalk`

_heapwalk, _bheapwalk, _fheapwalk, _nheapwalk

MSC6	MSC7	VC++	QC2.5	QC-WIN	TC2	TC++	BC++2	BC++3	ANSI	POSIX	UNIX V	DOS	QWIN	WIN	WINDLL
X	X	X	X	X								X			

Note: The `_bheapwalk` and `_fheapwalk` functions may be used in DOS, QWIN, WIN, and WINDLL applications. Similar functions in TC2, TC++, BC++2, and BC++3 are `heapwalk` and `farheapwalk`.

Summary

```
#include <malloc.h>

int _heapwalk(
    _HEAPINFO *info); // Information returned here.

int _bheapwalk(
    _ _segment seg,     // Identifies the based heap.
    _HEAPINFO *info);   // Information returned here.

int _fheapwalk(_HEAPINFO *info); // Traverse the far heap.
int _nheapwalk(_HEAPINFO *info); // Traverse the near heap.
```

Description

Traverses the heap and returns information about the next entry in a `_HEAPINFO` structure associated with the address you provide in the *info* argument. The `_HEAPINFO` type is defined in `<malloc.h>` as

```
typedef struct _heapinfo
{
    int _ _far * _pentry; // Pointer to heap entry.
    size_t       _size;    // Size of block (in bytes).
    int          _useflag; // Set to: _USEDENTRY or _FREEENTRY.
} _HEAPINFO;
```

To traverse all entries in a heap, start by calling the function with the `_pentry` field of the *info* argument set to `NULL`. This gets you information about the first entry. From then on, keep calling the function with the same *info* argument to get information about successive entries in the heap.

Returns

When the function completes successfully, the return value is an integer value denoting the status of the heap as well as the result of the traversal through the list of entries. Interpret the result by comparing the returned value with the following constants:

_HEAPBADBEGIN	Initial header is incorrect or missing.
_HEAPBADNODE	A bad node was found in the heap.
_HEAPBADPTR	A bad _pentry field was found.
_HEAPEMPTY	The heap is uninitialized.
_HEAPEND	The end of the heap was reached.
_HEAPOK	No errors were found up to the current entry; the _HEAPINFO structure contains information about the next entry.

Sample Call

```
     _HEAPINFO heapentry;
//...
// Check the heap entries.
// Set the _pentry field to NULL to begin at first entry:

     heapentry._pentry = NULL;

// Keep calling _fheapwalk as long as return value is _HEAPOK:
     while (  _fheapwalk(&heapentry) == _HEAPOK)
     {
// Print the information from heapentry.
//...
     }
```

See Also

_heapchk, _heapset

malloc, _bmalloc, _fmalloc, _nmalloc

MSC6	MSC7	VC++	QC2.5	QC-WIN	TC2	TC++	BC++2	BC++3	ANSI	POSIX	UNIX V	DOS	QWIN	WIN	WINDLL
X	X	X	X	X	X	X	X	X	X	X	X	X	X	X	X

Note: fmalloc and nmalloc are available in MSC6, MSC7, Visual C++, QC2.5, and QC-WIN only. The _bmalloc function is available in MSC6, MSC7, Visual C++, QC2.5, and QC-WIN. A function similar to_fmalloc in TC2, TC++, BC++2, and BC++3 is farmalloc.

Summary

```
#include <malloc.h>

void * malloc(
    size_t n); // Number of bytes to allocate.
```

```
void _ _based(void) * _bmalloc(
    _ _segment seg,  // Allocate in this based heap.
    size_t    n);    // Number of bytes to allocate.

void _ _far * _fmalloc(size_t n); // Allocate in far heap.
void _ _near * _nmalloc(size_t n);// Allocate in near heap.
```

Description

Allocates a block of memory of size *n* bytes. In tiny, small, and medium memory models, the compiler maps calls to `malloc` to `_nmalloc`. In compact, large, and huge memory models, the `_fmalloc` function is called when you call `malloc`. You can call `_nmalloc` and `_fmalloc` explicitly to allocate near and far data items in any memory model.

Many Microsoft Visaul C++ library functions call `malloc` to allocate blocks of memory needed to do their work.

Returns

When the function completes successfully, the return value is a pointer to the allocated block of memory.

`NULL` Indicates that there is not enough memory. The `_bmalloc` function returns `_NULLOFF` in case of error.

Sample Call

```
int *index;
//...
if((index = malloc(256*sizeof(int)) == NULL)
{
// Memory allocation error....
//...
}
```

See Also

`calloc`, `free`, `realloc`

_memavl

MSC6	MSC7	VC++	QC2.5	QC-WIN	TC2	TC++	BC++2	BC++3	ANSI	POSIX	UNIX V	DOS	QWIN	WIN	WINDLL
X	X	X	X	X								X	X	X	X

Note: A similar function in TC2, TC++, BC++2, and BC++3 is `coreleft`.

Summary

```
#include <malloc.h>

size_t _memavl(void);
```

Description

Provides an estimate of the total number of bytes available for allocation in the near heap (default data segment).

Returns

When the function completes successfully, the return value is the total number of bytes available for allocation in the near heap.

Note that you may not be able to allocate this entire amount as a single block, because all the bytes may not be in a single block.

Sample Call

```
size_t maxmem;
//...
maxmem = _memavl(); // Total number of bytes available
```

See Also

_freect, _memmax

_memmax

MSC6	MSC7	VC++	QC2.5	QC-WIN	TC2	TC++	BC++2	BC++3	ANSI	POSIX	UNIX V	DOS	QWIN	WIN	WINDLL
X	X	X	X	X								X	X	X	X

Summary

```
#include <malloc.h>

size_t _memmax(void);
```

Description

Determines the maximum number of contiguous bytes that can be allocated from the near heap (the default data segment).

Returns

When the function completes successfully, the return value is the maximum number of contiguous bytes available in the near heap, or zero if there is no more space in the near heap.

Sample Call

```
size_t maxarray = _memmax();
```

See Also

`_freect`, `_memavl`

_msize, _bmsize, _fmsize, _nmsize

MSC6	MSC7	VC++	QC2.5	QC-WIN	TC2	TC++	BC++2	BC++3	ANSI	POSIX	UNIX V	DOS	QWIN	WIN	WINDLL
X	X	X	X	X								X	X	X	X

Summary

```
#include <malloc.h>

size_t _msize(void *ptr); // Return size of this block

size_t _bmsize(
    _ _segment          seg,  // Identifies the based heap.
    void _ _based(void) *ptr);// Return this block's size.

size_t _fmsize(void _ _far *ptr);
size_t _nmsize(void _ _near *ptr);
```

Description

Provides the size in bytes of the block of memory identified by *ptr*.

Returns

The return value is the size of the block of memory in bytes.

Sample Call

```
    char   *buf;
    size_t bsize;
// Assume buf points to an allocated block of memory.
//...
    bsize = _msize(buf);
```

See Also

`_memmax`

realloc, _brealloc, _frealloc, _nrealloc

MSC6	MSC7	VC++	QC2.5	QC-WIN	TC2	TC++	BC++2	BC++3	ANSI	POSIX	UNIX V	DOS	QWIN	WIN	WINDLL
X	X	X	X	X	X	X	X	X	X	X	X	X	X	X	X

Note: `_frealloc` and `_nrealloc` are available in MSC6, MSC7, Visual C++, QC2.5, and QC-WIN only. A function similar to `_frealloc` in TC2, TC++, BC++2, and BC++3 is `farrealloc`.

Summary

```
#include <malloc.h>

void *realloc(
    void   *ptr, // Reallocate this block of memory
    size_t n);   //   with this size (in bytes).

void __based(void) *_brealloc(
    __segment            seg, // Identifies the based heap.
    void __based(void) *ptr,// Reallocate this block
    size_t               n);  //   with this many bytes.

void __far *_frealloc(void __far *ptr, size_t n);
void __near *_nrealloc(void __near *ptr, size_t n);
```

Description

Resizes a previously allocated block of memory (identified by *ptr*) by moving it to a new location in the heap, if necessary. The argument *n* denotes the new size of the block in bytes. Allocates a block of memory of size *n* bytes if *ptr* is `NULL` (or `_NULLOFF`, in the case of `_brealloc`).

Returns

When the function completes successfully, the return value is the pointer to resized block of memory.

`NULL` Indicates that there is no room to expand the block. The `_brealloc` function returns `_NULLOFF` in case of failure.

Sample Call

```
    char *buf;
// Assume buf points to a 256-byte block of memory.
//...
// Enlarge buf to 1024 bytes:
    if((buf = realloc(buf, 1024)) == NULL)
    {
        fprintf(stderr, "Buffer could not be enlarged\n");
// buf still points to a 256-byte block....
//...
    }
```

See Also

_expand

_stackavail

MSC6	MSC7	VC++	QC2.5	QC-WIN	TC2	TC++	BC++2	BC++3	ANSI	POSIX	UNIX V	DOS	QWIN	WIN	WINDLL
X	X	X	X	X								X	X	X	X

Note: The underscore prefix to the name `_stackavail` was added in MSC7.

Summary

```
#include <malloc.h>

size_t _stackavail(void);
```

Description

Determines the approximate number of bytes available in the stack for allocation with the `_alloca` function.

Returns

When the function completes successfully, the return value is the number of bytes available in the stack.

Sample Call

```
size_t stkfree = _stackavail();
```

See Also

_alloca

_vfree

MSC6	MSC7	VC++	QC2.5	QC-WIN	TC2	TC++	BC++2	BC++3	ANSI	POSIX	UNIX V	DOS	QWIN	WIN	WINDLL
	X	X										X			

Summary

```
#include <vmemory.h>

void _ _far _ _pascal _vfree(
    _vmhnd_t hvm); // Handle of virtual memory block to free
```

Description

Releases the block of virtual memory (see tutorial) identified by the handle *hvm*. This block must have been allocated earlier by a call to `_vmalloc`. Before you call `_vfree`, call `_vlockcnt` to ensure that the lock count is zero, which indicates that the block of virtual memory is not locked.

Sample Call

```
    _vmhnd_t hvm;
// Assume hvm refers to an allocated block of virtual memory.
//...
// Free the block.
    _vfree(hvm);
```

See Also

_vlock, _vlockcnt, _vmalloc

_vheapinit

MSC6	MSC7	VC++	QC2.5	QC-WIN	TC2	TC++	BC++2	BC++3	ANSI	POSIX	UNIX V	DOS	QWIN	WIN	WINDLL
X	X	X									X				

Summary

```
#include <vmemory.h>

int __far __pascal _vheapinit(
    unsigned int min_dosmem, // Minimum amount of DOS memory
                             //   in paragraphs.
    unsigned int max_dosmem, // Maximum amount of DOS memory
                             //   in paragraphs.
    unsigned int swap_flag); // Bitwise or combination of
                             //   constants that indicate where
                             //   swapped-out blocks are held.
```

Description

Initializes the Microsoft Visual C++ virtual memory manager. You must call `_vheapinit` before you allocate any virtual memory, and call `_vheapterm` when your program is done using virtual memory.

The *min_dosmem* argument specifies the minimum amount of DOS memory that the virtual memory manager can use. The *max_dosmem*, on the other hand, indicates the maximum amount of DOS memory available to the virtual memory manager. If you want to provide all available DOS memory to the virtual memory manager, use the constant `_VM_ALLDOS` as the *max_dosmem* argument.

The *swap_flag* argument determines how the virtual memory manager handles swapping—blocks of memory that are no longer needed are saved in an auxiliary storage determined by the *swap_flag*. Use the bitwise-OR combination of one or more of the following constants as the *swap_flag* argument:

`VM_EMS`	Uses expanded memory as swap area.
`_VM_XMS`	Uses extended memory as swap area.
`_VM_DISK`	Uses disk space as swap area.
`_VM_ALLSWAP`	Uses all of above as swap area.

Returns

Nonzero	Indicates the virtual memory manager was successfully initialized.
0	Indicates a failure.

Sample Call

```
// Use all of DOS memory and all possible swap options:
    if(_vheapinit(0, _VM_ALLDOS, _VM_ALLSWAP) == 0)
    {
// Failed to initialize virtual memory manager.
// Don't use virtual memory....
//...
    }
```

See Also

`_vheapterm`

_vheapterm

MSC6	MSC7	VC++	QC2.5	QC-WIN	TC2	TC++	BC++2	BC++3	ANSI	POSIX	UNIX V	DOS	QWIN	WIN	WINDLL
	X	X										X			

Summary

```
#include <vmemory.h>

void _ _far _ _pascal _vheapterm(void);
```

Description

Closes down the virtual memory manager. If you use virtual memory, you must call `_vheapterm` before exiting your program.

Sample Call

```
//...
// Terminate virtual memory manager:
    _vheapterm();
```

See Also

`_vheapinit`

_vload

MSC6	MSC7	VC++	QC2.5	QC-WIN	TC2	TC++	BC++2	BC++3	ANSI	POSIX	UNIX V	DOS	QWIN	WIN	WINDLL
	X	X										X			

Summary

```
#include <vmemory.h>

void __far * __far __pascal _vload(
    _vmhnd_t hvm,      // Handle to a block of virtual memory.
    int      cdflag);  // Clean-dirty flag (one of: _VM_CLEAN
                       //   or _VM_DIRTY).
```

Description

Loads the block of virtual memory identified by `hvm` into DOS memory and returns a far pointer to it. The `cdflag` argument indicates whether the block of memory should be written out to the swap area or discarded when swapping occurs. Use one of the following constants as the `cdflag` argument:

`_VM_CLEAN` Block is clean; discard when swapped.

`_VM_DIRTY` Block is dirty; save when swapped.

Returns

When the function completes successfully, the return value is a far pointer to DOS memory where the block of virtual memory has been loaded.

`NULL` Indicates a failure.

Sample Call

```
    short __far *vstack;
    _vmhnd_t hvm;
// Assume hvm refers to a valid block of virtual memory.
//...
// Load the block into DOS memory:
    if((vstack = _vload(hvm, _VM_DIRTY)) == NULL)
    {
// Error loading virtual memory into DOS memory.
//...
    }
```

See Also

`_vlock`, `_vmalloc`, `_vunlock`

_vlock

MSC6	MSC7	VC++	QC2.5	QC-WIN	TC2	TC++	BC++2	BC++3	ANSI	POSIX	UNIX V	DOS	QWIN	WIN	WINDLL
	X	X										X			

Summary

```
#include <vmemory.h>

void _ _far * _ _far _ _pascal _vlock(
    _vmhnd_t hvm); // Load this block into DOS memory and lock it.
```

Description

Loads the block of virtual memory identified by *hvm* into DOS memory, locks it, and returns a far pointer to it. Because a locked block of virtual memory cannot be swapped out, you should call `_vunlock` to unlock the block when the block no longer is required to be in DOS memory.

You can call `_vlock` for the same block of virtual memory up to 255 times. Each call increments a "lock count" that you can access by calling `_vlockcnt`.

Returns

When the function completes successfully, the return value is a far pointer to DOS memory where the block of virtual memory has been loaded.

`NULL` Indicates a failure.

Sample Call

```
    short _ _far *vstack;
    _vmhnd_t hvm;
// Assume hvm refers to a valid block of virtual memory.
//...
// Load the block into DOS memory:
    if((vstack = _vlock(hvm)) == NULL)
    {
// Error loading virtual memory into DOS memory.
//...
    }
```

See Also

`_vload`, `_vlockcnt`, `_vmalloc`, `_vunlock`

_vlockcnt

MSC6	MSC7	VC++	QC2.5	QC-WIN	TC2	TC++	BC++2	BC++3	ANSI	POSIX	UNIX V	DOS	QWIN	WIN	WINDLL
	X	X										X			

Summary

```
#include <vmemory.h>

unsigned int __far __pascal _vlockcnt(
    _vmhnd_t hvm); // Return "lock count" for this block
```

Description

Provides the *lock count*—the number of times a block of virtual memory has been locked. The lock count is incremented when you call `_vlock`; it is decremented by a call to `_vunlock`.

Returns

The return value is the lock count for the block of virtual memory identified by `hvm`.

Sample Call

```
    short __far *vstack;
    _vmhnd_t hvm;
// Assume hvm refers to a valid block of virtual memory.
//...
// Check if block is locked before freeing it....
    if(_vlockcnt(hvm) == 0) _vfree(hvm);
```

See Also

`_vlock`, `_vunlock`

_vmalloc

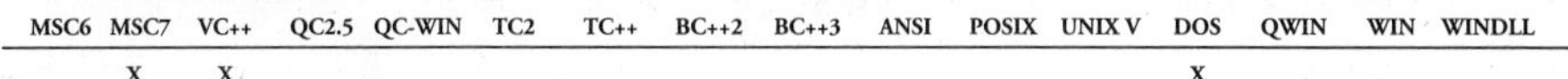

MSC6	MSC7	VC++	QC2.5	QC-WIN	TC2	TC++	BC++2	BC++3	ANSI	POSIX	UNIX V	DOS	QWIN	WIN	WINDLL
	X	X										X			

Summary

```
#include <vmemory.h>

_vmhnd_t __far __pascal _vmalloc(
    unsigned long n); // Allocate this many bytes.
```

Description

Allocates a block of virtual memory of size *n* bytes, which cannot be any larger than the maximum block that can be loaded into DOS memory.

Note that you must call `_vheapinit` before allocating any virtual memory.

Returns

When the function completes successfully, the return value is the handle to the allocated block of virtual memory.

`_VM_NULL`	Indicates that the request cannot be satisfied. (This happens if there is not enough virtual memory or if the requested block size is too large to fit into the available DOS memory.)

Sample Call

```
    _vmhnd_t hvm;
// Assume _vheapinit has been called.
//...
// Allocate a block of size 220,000 bytes:
    if((hvm = _vmalloc(220000L)) == _VM_NULL)
    {
// Allocation failure....
//...
    }
```

See Also

`_vfree`, `_vheapinit`, `_vmsize`, `_vrealloc`

_vmsize

MSC6	MSC7	VC++	QC2.5	QC-WIN	TC2	TC++	BC++2	BC++3	ANSI	POSIX	UNIX V	DOS	QWIN	WIN	WINDLL
	X	X										X			

Summary

```
#include <vmemory.h>

unsigned long __far __pascal _vmsize(
    _vmhnd_t hvm); // Return size of this block
```

Description

Determines the number of bytes in the block of virtual memory identified by the handle *hvm*.

Returns

When the function completes successfully, the return value is the size of the block of virtual memory, in bytes. Note that the returned size may be larger than the size you specified in the call to the allocation function (`_vmalloc` or `_vrealloc`) because the virtual memory manager may decide on a larger size for efficient handling of blocks.

Sample Call

```
    _vmhnd_t hvm;
    unsigned long blksize;

// Assume _vheapinit has been called.
```

```
//...
// Allocate a block of size 220,000 bytes:
    if((hvm = _vmalloc(220000L)) == _VM_NULL)
    {
// Allocation failure....
//...
    }
// Check the actual size of the allocated block:
    blksize = _vmsize(hvm);
```

See Also

_vmalloc

_vrealloc

MSC6	MSC7	VC++	QC2.5	QC-WIN	TC2	TC++	BC++2	BC++3	ANSI	POSIX	UNIX V	DOS	QWIN	WIN	WINDLL
	X	X										X			

Summary

```
#include <vmemory.h>

_vmhnd_t _ _far _ _pascal _vrealloc(
    _vmhnd_t      hvm, // Resize this block of virtual memory
    unsigned long n);  //   to this many bytes.
```

Description

Resizes a previously allocated block of virtual memory (*hvm*) to a new size (*n* bytes). The contents of the old block remain unchanged, although the block may be in a different location. Also, the old block is freed if you specify a zero as the second argument.

If *hvm* is NULL, _vrealloc behaves like _vmalloc.

Returns

When the function completes successfully, the return value is a handle to the reallocated block.

_VM_NULL	Indicates that reallocation failed. When reallocation fails, the old block remains valid.

Sample Call

```
    _vmhnd_t hvm;
    unsigned long blksize;
```

```
// Assume _vheapinit has been called.
//...
// Allocate a block of size 220,000 bytes:
    if((hvm = _vmalloc(220000L)) == _VM_NULL)
    {
// Allocation failure...
//...
    }
//...
// Resize the allocated block:
    if((hvm = _vrealloc(hvm, 240000L)) == _VM_NULL)
    {
// Reallocation failed. Old block is still valid.
//...
    }
```

See Also

_vfree, _vmalloc

_vunlock

MSC6	MSC7	VC++	QC2.5	QC-WIN	TC2	TC++	BC++2	BC++3	ANSI	POSIX	UNIX V	DOS	QWIN	WIN	WINDLL
	X	X										X			

Summary

```
#include <vmemory.h>

void _ _far _ _pascal _vunlock(
    _vmhnd_t hvm,      // Unlock this block of virtual memory.
    int      cdflag);  // Clean-dirty flag (one of _VM_CLEAN
                       //   or _VM_DIRTY.)
```

Description

Unlocks the block of virtual memory identified by `hvm` and decrements the lock count for that block. When the lock count reaches zero, the virtual memory manager may swap the block to secondary storage. The `cdflag` argument indicates whether the block of memory should be written out to the swap area or discarded when swapping occurs. Use one of the following constants as the `cdflag` argument:

`_VM_CLEAN`	Block is clean; discard when swapped.
`_VM_DIRTY`	Block is dirty; save when swapped.

Sample Call

```
    _vmhnd_t hvm;
// Assume hvm refers to a valid block of virtual memory.
// Assume that the block has been locked by _vlock.
//...
    _vunlock(hvm, _VM_DIRTY);
```

See Also

_vlock, _vlockcnt

DOS and BIOS Calls

All *Industry Standard Architecture* (ISA) and *Extended Industry Standard Architecture* (EISA) PCs come with a basic input and output system (BIOS) built into the system's read-only memory (ROM). PCs that are built with the Micro-Channel architecture also have a BIOS ROM. However, there may be some differences in Micro-Channel machines. This chapter assumes that the reader is using an ISA or EISA machine.

The BIOS provides low-level input/output (I/O) functions for accessing peripherals such as the disk drives, keyboard, printer, and the serial port. Additionally, MS-DOS provides a host of services that handle tasks such as I/O, access to the MS-DOS file system, and managing memory, among others. The Microsoft Visual C++ library includes a number of functions you can use to access most of the BIOS and DOS services. These functions have names with `_bios_` and `_dos_` prefixes and are declared in the header files bios.h and dos.h.

Because of their close connection to the PC's hardware and to MS-DOS, the DOS and BIOS functions are not portable to other operating systems, such as UNIX. In addition, many of these functions should not be called from Windows applications. Therefore, you should use these functions only if there are no equivalent ANSI standard C functions available to do the job. For instance, instead of using functions such as `_dos_open` and `_dos_read` for file I/O, you should use standard functions such as fopen and fread (described in Chapter 22, "Stream I/O"). On the other hand, to read a physical sector from a diskette, you have no other choice but to use the _bios_disk function that provides access to the BIOS disk services.

Accessing BIOS and DOS Services

The BIOS and DOS services are designed for access through the INT instruction of the Intel 80x86 processor s—this instruction generates a software interrupt. The effect is similar to that of a hardware interrupt: the processor pushes the address of the next instruction on the stack and loads an address found at a predefined location in the first 1K of memory. (The location is defined by which interrupt is being serviced.) The four bytes at that location serve as the next code segment and offset address at which the processor begins executing. This code address is referred to as an *interrupt vector.* The code at the address referenced by the interrupt vector is the *interrupt handler.* An IRET instruction marks the end of the interrupt handler. The effect of the IRET (Internet Returned) instruction is to return to the point at which the interrupt occurred.

The BIOS and DOS services are implemented as interrupt handlers corresponding to specific interrupts. All arguments needed by a service are passed and the results returned in the processor's registers. Each BIOS service is accessed through a specific interrupt, but all MS-DOS services are accessed through a single interrupt: INT 21H. (That's interrupt number 21 in hexadecimal.) A byte value in the AH register indicates the exact function to be performed by MS-DOS. The integer value generally is referred to as the *DOS function number.*

BIOS Services

The ROM-resident BIOS provides a number of services that provide access to the following peripherals:

- Keyboard (INT 16H)
- Video Monitor (INT 10H)
- Printer (INT 17H)
- System Timer (INT 1AH)

- Disk Drives (INT 13H)
- Serial Port (INT 14H)

You will find a BIOS function for each of these services except the video I/O (INT 10H). For video display, you can use the console I/O functions of Chapter 24, "Console and Port I/O" or the graphics functions in the graph.doc text file on the companion disk. You also can use the general-purpose function `int86` or `int86x` to generate an interrupt 10H and directly access the BIOS video services.

> **A Word of Caution**
>
> If you directly access the video system, be careful not to improperly program the video controller—you can cause damage to your monitor if the video controller is programmed incorrectly.

MS-DOS Functions

Compared to the BIOS services, MS-DOS offers many more functions, but all of them are accessed through a single software interrupt: INT 21H. Of the more than 100 MS-DOS functions, the Microsoft Visual C++ library provides specific access functions to 27. These functions (with the `_dos` prefix in their names) are listed in Table 32.1.

Table 32.1. Alphabetic listing of functions that support DOS and BIOS calls.

Function	Description
`_bdos`	Calls any MS-DOS function that uses the AL and DX registers only.
`_bios_disk`	Invokes interrupt 13H to access physical disk I/O services of the BIOS.
`_bios_equiplist`	Uses interrupt 11H to get a list of peripheral equipment attached to the system.
`_bios_keybrd`	Uses interrupt 16H to read characters from the keyboard.

continues

Table 32.1. continued

Function	Description
`_bios_memsize`	Uses interrupt 12H to determine the amount of memory in the system.
`_bios_printer`	Uses interrupt 17H to access the printer I/O services of the BIOS.
`_bios_serialcom`	Uses interrupt 14H to access the system's serial port.
`_bios_timeofday`	Uses interrupt 1AH to read and set the current clock tick count.
`_chain_intr`	Unconditionally jumps from one interrupt handler to another.
`_disable`	Disables all interrupts by executing a CLI instruction.
`_dos_allocmem`	Calls MS-DOS function 48H to allocate memory.
`_dos_close`	Calls MS-DOS function 3EH to close an open file.
`_dos_commit`	Calls MS-DOS function 68H (available in DOS 3.3 or later) to forcibly flush file buffers to the disk.
`_dos_creat`	Calls MS-DOS function 3CH to create a file or truncate an existing file to zero bytes. Opens the file and returns a handle.
`_dos_creatnew`	Calls MS-DOS function 5BH, which works like `_dos_creat` but fails if the named file already exists.
`_dos_findfirst`	Calls MS-DOS function 4EH to find the first occurrence of a file specified by a name that may contain wildcard characters (such as `*` or `?`).
`_dos_findnext`	Calls MS-DOS function 4FH to find the next occurrence of a file being sought by `_dos_findfirst`.
`_dos_freemem`	Calls MS-DOS function 49H to free a block of memory allocated by `_dos_allocmem`.

Function	Description
_dos_getdate	Calls MS-DOS function 2AH to get the current date.
_dos_getdiskfree	Calls MS-DOS function 36H to get information that can be used to determine the capacity of a disk and the amount available for use.
_dos_getdrive	Calls MS-DOS function 19H to get the current drive.
_dos_getfileattr	Calls MS-DOS function 43H to get the attributes of a file.
_dos_getftime	Calls MS-DOS function 57H to get the date and time of last modification of a file.
_dos_gettime	Calls MS-DOS function 2CH to get the current time.
_dos_getvect	Calls MS-DOS function 35H to get the current interrupt vector (the address to which the processor jumps when an interrupt occurs) for a specified interrupt number. This is the address to which the processor jumps when that interrupt occurs.
_dos_keep	Calls MS-DOS function 31H to make a *terminate-and-stay-resident* (TSR) program.
_dos_open	Calls MS-DOS function 3DH to open a file specified by name.
_dos_read	Calls MS-DOS function 3FH to read a specified number of bytes from a file into a buffer in memory.
_dos_setblock	Calls MS-DOS function 4AH to change the size of a previously allocated block of memory.
_dos_setdate	Calls MS-DOS function 2BH to set the system date.
_dos_setdrive	Calls MS-DOS function 0EH to set the default drive (0 = A, 1 = B, and so on).

continues

Table 32.1. continued

Function	Description
`_dos_setfileattr`	Calls MS-DOS function 43H to set the attributes of a file.
`_dos_setftime`	Calls MS-DOS function 57H to set the modification time of a file.
`_dos_settime`	Calls MS-DOS function 2DH to set the system time.
`_dos_setvect`	Calls MS-DOS function 25H to set the interrupt vector for a specified interrupt number.
`_dos_write`	Calls MS-DOS function 40H to write a specified number of bytes from a buffer to an open file.
`_dosexterr`	Calls MS-DOS function 59H to retrieve detailed information on the last error that occurred during an MS-DOS function call.
`_enable`	Enables interrupts by executing an STI instruction.
`_FP_OFF`	A macro that evaluates to the offset address of a far pointer.
`_FP_SEG`	A macro that evaluates to the segment address of a far pointer.
`_harderr`	Sets up a function as the critical error handler to be called when a critical hardware error interrupt (INT 24H) occurs.
`_hardresume`	Function called in a critical error handler to return to MS-DOS.
`_hardretn`	Function called in a critical error handler to return to the application where the hardware error occurred.
`_int86`	Generates a specified software interrupt through the INT instruction. All registers except DS and ES may be used.
`_int86x`	Similar to `_int86`, but also allows use of DS and ES registers.

Function	Description
`_intdos`	Generates an INT 21H interrupt to call the MS-DOS function specified by the AH register. All registers except DS and ES may be used.
`_intdosx`	Similar to `_intdos`, but also allows use of DS and ES registers.
`segread`	Provides the current contents of the segment registers in a structure.

Basic DOS and BIOS Tasks

Table 32.2 organizes the DOS and BIOS access functions shown in Table 32.1 by the tasks they perform. Some of these tasks are illustrated by short sample programs in the following sections. For more information about a function, consult the reference entry for that function in the reference section that follows.

Table 32.2. Tasks performed by DOS and BIOS calls.

Task	Functions
Generate any software interrupt	`int86`, `int86x`
Call any MS-DOS function	`bdos`, `intdos`, `intdosx`
Call MS-DOS file I/O functions	`dos_close`, `dos_commit`, `dos_creat`, `dos_creatnew`, `dos_open`, `dos_read`, `dos_write`
Manipulate disk and file information	`dos_findfirst`, `dos_findnext`, `dos_getdiskfree`, `dos_getdrive`, `dos_getfileattr`, `dos_getftime`, `dos_setdrive`, `dos_setfileattr`, `dos_setftime`

continues

Table 32.2. continued

Task	Functions
Manage DOS memory	`dos_allocmem`, `dos_freemem`, `dos_setblock`
Manipulate system date and time	`dos_getdate`, `dos_gettime`, `dos_setdate`, `dos_settime`
Install TSR (terminate-and-stay-resident)	`dos_keep`
Handle interrupts	`chain_intr`, `disable`, `dos_getvect`, `dos_setvect`, `enable`
Access BIOS services	`bios_disk`, `bios_equiplist`, `bios_keybrd`, `bios_memsize`, `bios_printer`, `bios_serialcom`, `bios_timeofday`
Access segment and offset addresses	`FP_OFF`, `FP_SEG`, `segread`
Handle errors	`dosexterr`, `harderr`, `hardresume`, `hardretn`

Listing Directories

The `_dos_findfirst` and `_dos_findnext` functions are useful for getting a listing of selected (or all) files in a directory. Listing 32.1 shows the program files.c, which behaves somewhat like the MS-DOS command DIR. For example, to list all files with the .com extension in the directory C:\DOS, you would run the `files` program with the following command line:

```
D:\>files c:\dos\*.com
   Files            Size (bytes)
FORMAT   COM           32911
KEYB     COM           14986
MODE     COM           23537
DOSKEY   COM            5883
MIRROR   COM           18169
SYS      COM           13440
UNFORMAT COM           18576
DOSSHELL COM            4623
```

```
EDIT     COM          413
MSHERC   COM         6934
DISKCOMP COM        10652
DISKCOPY COM        11793
MORE     COM         2618
ASSIGN   COM         6399
GRAFTABL COM        11205
GRAPHICS COM        19694
TREE     COM         6901
LOADFIX  COM         1131
COMMAND  COM        47845

19 files 257710 bytes.
```

Most of the files.c program deals with formatting and displaying the filenames. The actual work of finding the files is done by a call to `_dos_findfirst` followed by repeated calls to the `_dos_findnext` function.

Listing 32.1. A program that lists the files in a directory.

```
//------------------------------------------------------------
// File: files.c
//
// Displays a list of files using the _dos_findfirst and
// _dos_findnext functions.
//------------------------------------------------------------
#include <stdio.h>
#include <dos.h>
#include <string.h>
#include <process.h>

int main(int argc, char **argv)
{
    int           dotpos, len;
    unsigned      count;
    long          totalsize;
    struct find_t finfo;
    char          *files = "*.*"; // By default, list all files

// Use file specification from command line, if any:
    if(argc > 1) files = argv[1];
```

continues

Listing 32.1. continued

```
// Get the first matching filename:
    if (_dos_findfirst(files, _A_NORMAL, &finfo) != 0)
    {
        printf("Unsuccessful _dos_findnext call!\n");
        exit(0);
    }

    len = strlen(finfo.name);
    dotpos = strcspn(finfo.name, ".");
    finfo.name[dotpos] = '\0';
    printf("%8s        %16s\n","Files","Size (bytes)");

    if(len > dotpos)
    {
        printf("%-8s %-3s%16ld\n", finfo.name,
            &finfo.name[dotpos+1], finfo.size);
    }
    else
        printf("%-8s    %16ld\n", finfo.name,
                                   finfo.size);

    count = 1;
    totalsize = finfo.size;

// Call _dos_findfirst repeatedly until all files are found.

    while (_dos_findnext(&finfo) == 0)
    {
        count++;
        totalsize += finfo.size;
        len = strlen(finfo.name);
        dotpos = strcspn(finfo.name, ".");
        finfo.name[dotpos] = '\0';
        if(len > dotpos)
        {
            printf("%-8s %-3s%16ld\n", finfo.name,
                &finfo.name[dotpos+1], finfo.size);
        }
        else
            printf("%-8s    %16ld\n", finfo.name,
                                   finfo.size);
```

```
    }
    printf("\n%u files %ld bytes.\n", count, totalsize);
    return 0;
}
```

Viewing Physical Sectors of a Disk

You can use the BIOS disk services accessed through the `_bios_disk` function to write a utility program that allows a user to browse the physical sectors of a disk. When you call the `_bios_disk` function with the appropriate arguments, it returns the contents of a specified sector. All you have to do is display the retrieved information. Listing 32.2 shows the program seedisk.c, which implements the idea and provides a "sector-browser utility." Here is a sample screen displayed by the seedisk program:

```
Current Drive:  B
Current Head:   0
Current Track:  0
Current Sector: 1

 1  Change Drive
 2  Change Head (0 or 1)
 3  Change Track
 4  Change Sector
 0  Exit

Enter selection:


.<.MSDOS5.0........@..................)..¦.MCPB21-    FAT12   .3
.....¦...x.6.7.V.S.>¦.........E.....¦.M..G...>¦...ry3.9..¦t....¦
.. ¦..¦.&.¦...¦...¦...¦....P¦..R¦.I¦..K¦. ..&.¦...¦..H....I¦..K¦
......R¦.P¦...r......r........}..u... .....t...}._.3...^....D...
XXX...G.HH...¦2.....I¦..K¦......PRQ.:.r....T.YZXr..........¦....
.¦..$¦..I¦.K¦...p....t).........;..¦s..6.¦....0¦3..6.¦..%¦.M¦...
.....M¦.....60¦......$¦.6%¦.....Non-System disk or disk error..R
eplace and press any key when ready...IO      SYSMSDOS   SYS..U.
```

In this case, the program is displaying the contents of sector 1, track 0, and side 0 of drive B (a 3.5-inch drive). Because this is the boot sector of the disk, you can see various items of information pertaining to the MS-DOS file system. Notice the error message string (`Non-System disk...`) that usually is displayed when an attempt is made to boot from a disk that does not have certain system files.

Despite its simple appearance, the seedisk program is quite powerful. Because the program reads from an absolute physical sector of a diskette without regard to the file system, you can, for instance, read a sector from a high-density (1.44M) 3.5-inch diskette formatted on an Apple Macintosh as easily as you would read an MS-DOS diskette.

Listing 32.2. A program that displays the physical sectors of a diskette.

```
//-----------------------------------------------------------------
// File: seedisk.c
//
// A small utility program that enables the user to view the
// contents of a sector of a diskette. Uses _bios_disk to access
// the diskette. (Note: Link with GRAPHICS.LIB.)
//-----------------------------------------------------------------
#include <stdio.h>
#include <graph.h>
#include <bios.h>
#include <conio.h>
#include <ctype.h>
#include <stdlib.h>

static unsigned curdrive = 0,
                curhead = 0,
                curtrack = 0,
                cursector = 1;
static int  firsttime = 1,
            done = 0;
static char drivename[8];
static char outbuf[80];

static int retry = 3;  // Number of retries to read disk
static char _far dbuf[512];
void disp_sector(unsigned drive, unsigned head, unsigned track,
                unsigned sector, int row);

//-----------------------------------------------------------------
void main(void)
```

```
{
    int  c, num;
    char input[20];

    while (!done)
    {
        if(firsttime)
            sprintf(drivename, "NONE");
        else
            sprintf(drivename, "%c", curdrive + 'A');

         _clearscreen(_GCLEARSCREEN);
         _settextposition(1,1);

// Display drive letter:
         sprintf(outbuf, "Current Drive:  %s\n", drivename);
         _outtext(outbuf);

// Display other information:
         sprintf(outbuf, "Current Head:   %u\n", curhead);
         _outtext(outbuf);
         sprintf(outbuf, "Current Track:  %u\n", curtrack);
         _outtext(outbuf);
         sprintf(outbuf, "Current Sector: %u\n", cursector);
         _outtext(outbuf);

         _settextposition(6, 1);
         _outtext(" 1  Change Drive\n");
         _outtext(" 2  Change Head (0 or 1)\n");
         _outtext(" 3  Change Track\n");
         _outtext(" 4  Change Sector\n");
         _outtext(" 0  Exit");

// Display the contents of selected sector:
        if(!firsttime)
            disp_sector(curdrive, curhead, curtrack,
                        cursector, 15);

         _settextposition(12, 1);
         _outtext("Enter selection: ");
```

continues

Listing 32.2. continued

```
// Read keypress:
        c = _getche();

// Process command implied by keypress.

        switch(c)
        {
            case '0':
                done = 1;
                break;

            case '1':
// Change drive:
                _settextposition(12,1);
                _outtext("Enter drive letter:");
                c = _getche();
                c = toupper(c);
                if(c < 'C')    // Must be drive A or B
                    curdrive = c - 'A';
                break;

            case '2':
// Change current "head:"
                _settextposition(12,1);
                _outtext("Enter side (0 or 1):");
                c = _getche();
                num = toupper(c) - '0';
                if(num == 0 || num == 1) curhead = num;
                break;

            case '3':
// Change current track number:
                _settextposition(12,1);
                _outtext("Enter track number:");
                gets(input);
                curtrack = atoi(input);
                break;

            case '4':
// Change current sector:
                _settextposition(12,1);
                _outtext("Enter sector number:");
```

```
                gets(input);
                cursector = atoi(input);
                break;
        }
        firsttime = 0;
    }
}
//-------------------------------------------------------------
// d i s p _ s e c t o r
//
// Display the contents of a sector of a floppy disk.

void disp_sector(unsigned drive, unsigned head, unsigned track,
                 unsigned sector, int row)
{
    int i, j, n, index;
    unsigned status = 0;
    char line[66];
    struct _diskinfo_t dinfo;

// Fill in the _diskinfo_t structure:
    dinfo.drive = curdrive;
    dinfo.head = curhead;
    dinfo.track = curtrack;
    dinfo.sector = cursector;
    dinfo.nsectors = 1;
    dinfo.buffer = dbuf;

// Read selected sector from disk, making several tries to
// ensure that disk is at operational speed (3 tries should
// be enough).

    for(i = 0; i < retry; i++)
    {
        if((status = _bios_disk(_DISK_READ, &dinfo))
            == dinfo.nsectors)
        {
            _settextposition(row, 1);
            index = 0;
// Display the contents of this sector:
            for(n = 0; n < 8; n++)
```

continues

Listing 32.2. continued

```
                {
                    for(j = 0; j < 64; j++)
                    {
                        if(isascii(dbuf[index]) &&
                           isprint(dbuf[index]))
                             line[j] = dbuf[index];
                        else
                             line[j] = '.';

                        index++;
                    }
                    line[64] = '\n';
                    line[65] = '\0';
                    _outtext(line);
                }
                break;
            }
        }

// Report error message:
    status = status >> 8;
    if(status)
    {
        _settextposition(row, 1);
        sprintf(outbuf, "Error: 0x%.2x\n", status);
        _outtext(outbuf);
    }
}
```

_bdos

MSC6	MSC7	VC++	VC++	QC2.5	QC-WIN	TC2	TC++	BC++2	BC++3	ANSI	POSIX	UNIX V	DOS	QWIN	WIN	WINDLL
X	X	X	X	X	X	X	X	X	X				X	X	X	X

Note: The underscore prefix in the name `_bdos` was added in MSC7.

Summary

```
#include <dos.h>

int _bdos(
    int          dosfn,    // DOS function number.
    unsigned int dx_reg,   // Place this in the DX register.
    unsigned int al_reg);  // Place this in the AL register.
```

Description

Calls the DOS function specified by *dosfn* through an INT 21H instruction after placing the values *dx_reg* and *al_reg* into the DX and AL registers. Use `_bdos` to call those DOS functions that accept arguments in DX and AL registers only. For a more complete access to the DOS functions, use `_intdos` or `_intdosx`.

Returns

The return value is the value of the AX register at the end of the MS-DOS function call.

Sample Call

```
// Display a character using DOS function 2.
    _bdos(0x02, '>', 0);
```

See Also

`_intdos`, `_intdosx`

_bios_disk

MSC6	MSC7	VC++	VC++	QC2.5	QC-WIN	TC2	TC++	BC++2	BC++3	ANSI	POSIX	UNIX V	DOS	QWIN	WIN	WINDLL
X	X	X	X	X	X				X				X		X	X

Note: The equivalent function in TC2, TC++, BC++2, and BC++3 is `biosdisk`.

Summary

```
#include <bios.h>

unsigned _bios_disk(
    unsigned              task,     // Code for desired service.
    struct _diskinfo_t  *dinfo);  // Structure with disk parameters.
```

Description

Performs raw disk I/O by invoking INT 13H, which accesses the built-in disk I/O services of the BIOS. You can use `_bios_disk` to read and write physical sectors of a disk. You must provide information about the disk in a `_diskinfo_t` structure; provide the address for this structure in the `dinfo` argument. The `_diskinfo_t` structure is defined in bios.h as follows:

```
struct _diskinfo_t
{
    unsigned   drive;      // Drive number (0 = A, 1 = B).
    unsigned   head;       // Head number (0 or 1).
    unsigned   track;      // Track number.
    unsigned   sector;     // Starting sector number (0 being
                           //   the first sector).
    unsigned   nsectors;   // Perform requested service on
                           //   this many sectors.
    void __far *buffer;    // Buffer used in reading, writing,
                           //   or comparing.
};
```

The *task* argument is a code that indicates the service to be performed by the BIOS. Use one of the following constants as the *task* argument:

`_DISK_FORMAT`	Formats one track on one side (one *head*) of the disk. The operation is similar to that for `_DISK_WRITE`, except that the sector information is not used. To format properly, *buffer* must point to an array that contains information about the layout and size of the sectors on that track.
`_DISK_READ`	Reads one or more sectors from disk into the buffer specified in the `_diskinfo_t` structure. If successful, the high-order byte of the returned value is zero and the low-order byte has the number of sectors read. In the event of an error, an error code is returned in the high-order byte.
`_DISK_RESET`	Resets the disk controller. None of the parameters in the `_diskinfo_t` structure are used in this case.
`_DISK_STATUS`	Gets the status of the last operation. The status is returned in the low-order byte of the returned value.
`_DISK_VERIFY`	Verifies that a specified sector exists and can be read. Performs a cyclic redundancy check (CRC) on the data in the sector. If all goes well, the high-order byte of the returned value is zero and the low-order byte has the number of sectors read. In the event of error an error code is returned in the high-order byte.

`_DISK_WRITE`	Writes data from the buffer in memory (specified in the buffer field of the `_diskinfo_t` structure) to one or more disk sectors. If successful, the high-order byte of the returned value is zero and the low-order byte has the number of sectors written. In the event of an error, an error code is returned in the high-order byte.

The valid track and sector numbers depend on the type of disk. For the commonly used 5.25-inch and 3.5-inch diskettes, these ranges are as follows:

Diskette Type	Head	Valid Track Numbers	Valid Sector Numbers
5.25" DSDD (360K)	0 or 1	0 through 39	1 through 9
5.25" DSHD (1.2M)	0 or 1	0 through 79	1 through 15
3.5" DSDD (720K)	0 or 1	0 through 79	1 through 9
3.5" DSHD (1.44M)	0 or 1	0 through 79	1 through 15

Returns

When the function completes successfully, the return value is the contents of the AX register at the end of the INT 13H call. When the requested service succeeds, the meaning of the returned value depends on the exact service being performed (see the Description section). In the event of an error, the high-order byte contains an error code, which can be one of the following values:

Code (Hex)	Meaning
00	No error.
01	Unknown command.
02	Address marks missing (disk has not been formatted).
03	Disk is write-protected.
04	Sector not found.
05	Reset failed.
06	Floppy disk removed.
07	Drive parameter determination failed.

Code (Hex)	Meaning
08	Data lost during Direct Memory Access (DMA) operation.
09	DMA transfer across a 64K boundary.
0A	Detected a bad sector flag.
0B	Detected a bad track flag.
0C	Media type not found.
0D	Invalid number of sectors on format command.
10	Data read error.
11	Corrected data read error.
20	Disk controller failed.
40	Seek error (could not move to requested track).
80	Disk drive timed out (you should retry in this case).
AA	Drive not ready.
BB	Undefined error.
CC	Write fault.
E0	Status error.
FF	Failed to sense disk.

Sample Call

```
#include <bios.h>
//...
    int retry;
    unsigned status = 0;
    char buf[512];
    void far *pbuf;
    struct _diskinfo_t info;

// Set up diskette information and buffer:
    pbuf = (void _ _far *)(&buf[0]);
    info.buffer = pbuf;
    info.drive = 0;      // That's drive A
    info.head = 0;
    info.track = 0;
```

```
// First directory entry for DSDD diskettes is in sector 6:
    info.sector = 6;
    info.nsectors = 1;

// Read sector. Retry up to 3 times because errors may be
// due to the time it takes for the drive's motor to start.

    for (retry = 0; retry <= 3; retry++)
    {
        if ((status = _bios_disk(_DISK_READ, &info))
            == info.nsectors)
        {
// Contents of specified sector now in buf.
//...
        }
    }

// Read failed despite 3 retries.
//...
}
```

See Also

int86x

_bios_equiplist

MSC6	MSC7	VC++	QC2.5	QC-WIN	TC2	TC++	BC++2	BC++3	ANSI	POSIX	UNIX V	DOS	QWIN	WIN	WINDLL
X	X	X	X	X			X	X				X	X	X	X

Note: The equivalent function in TC2, TC++, BC++2, and BC++3 is `biosequip`.

Summary

```
#include <bios.h>

unsigned _bios_equiplist(void);
```

Description

Provides information about the hardware and peripherals in the PC by invoking INT 11H.

Returns

When the function completes successfully, the return value is the value of the AX register after return from the INT 11H. The meaning of the bits are as follows (bit 0 is the least-significant bit):

Bits	Meaning
0	1 = one or more disk drives present; 0 = no disk drives.
1	1 = a math coprocessor is present.
2-3	Size of system memory in 16K blocks.
4-5	Initial video mode: 00 = reserved 01 = 40 x 25 text mode with a color adapter 10 = 80 x 25 text mode with a color adapter 11 = 80 x 25 text mode on monochrome adapter
6-7	Number of floppy disk drives installed: 00 = 1 01 = 2
8	Set to 0 only if a DMA (Direct Memory Access) chip is present.
9-11	Number of RS-232 serial ports in the system.
12	1 = a game adapter is installed.
13	1 = a serial printer is attached.
14-15	Number of printers attached to system.

Sample Call

```
unsigned equip, serport;
//...
equip = _bios_equiplist();
serport = (equip & 0x0e00) >> 9;
printf("There are %d serial ports\n", serport);
```

See Also

int86, int86x

_bios_keybrd

MSC6	MSC7	VC++	QC2.5	QC-WIN	TC2	TC++	BC++2	BC++3	ANSI	POSIX	UNIX V	DOS	QWIN	WIN	WINDLL
x	x	x	x	x			x	x				x		x	x

Note: The equivalent function in TC2, TC++, BC++2, and BC++3 is `bioskey`.

Summary

```
#include <bios.h>

unsigned _bios_keybrd(unsigned task); // Task to be performed
```

Description

Performs the specified keyboard I/O task by invoking the BIOS keyboard services using INT 16H. The `task` argument can be one of the following constants:

Constant	Meaning
`KEYBRD_READ`	Waits for the next keypress and reads the character from the keyboard buffer. The low-order byte of the return value contains the ASCII code of the character, and the high-order byte has the *scan code*—a unique code that identifies each key in the keyboard.
`NKEYBRD_READ`	Same as `_KEYBRD_READ` but meant for use with enhanced keyboards to read function keys F11 and F12 and the cursor keys.
`KEYBRD_READY`	Checks the keyboard buffer for characters waiting to be read. Returns a zero if there are no characters in the buffer. If there are characters in the buffer, the next available character is returned the same way as for the `KEYBRD_READ` service except that the character is not removed from the keyboard buffer.
`NKEYBRD_READY`	Same as `_KEYBRD_READ`, but for use with enhanced keyboards.

Constant	Meaning
KEYBRD_SHIFTSTATUS	Returns current status of the Shift, Ctrl, and Alt keys, as well as the status of the Scroll Lock, Num Lock, and Caps Lock indicators. Interprets the returned status by examining the bits, which have the following meanings: 0 Rightmost Shift key pressed. 1 Leftmost Shift key pressed. 2 Ctrl key pressed. 3 Alt key pressed. 4 Scroll Lock indicator is on. 5 Num Lock indicator is on. 6 Caps Lock indicator is on. 7 In insert mode (Ins key pressed). 8 Left Ctrl key pressed. 9 Left Alt key pressed. 10 Right Ctrl key pressed. 11 Right Alt key pressed. 12 Scroll Lock key pressed. 13 Num Lock key pressed. 14 Caps Lock key pressed. 15 Sys Req key pressed.
NKEYBRD_SHIFTSTATUS	Same as _KEYBRD_SHIFTSTATUS, but for use with enhanced keyboards.

Returns

The meaning of the returned value depends on the service being requested (see the Description section).

Sample Call

```
unsigned c;
// Read a keypress
c = _bios_keybrd(_KEYBRD_READ) & 0xff;
```

See Also

`kbhit` (Chapter 24), `int86`

_bios_memsize

MSC6	MSC7	VC++	QC2.5	QC-WIN	TC2	TC++	BC++2	BC++3	ANSI	POSIX	UNIX V	DOS	QWIN	WIN	WINDLL
x	x	x	x	x			x	x				x	x	x	x

Note: The equivalent function in TC2, TC++, BC++2, and BC++3 is `biosmemory`.

Summary

```
#include <bios.h>

unsigned _bios_memsize(void);
```

Description

Provides information about the amount of memory in the PC by using the BIOS interrupt 12H.

Returns

The return value is the total memory in the system in 1K blocks. The maximum return value can be 640K representing the maximum amount of conventional memory that an Industry Standard Architecture (ISA) PC can have.

Sample Call

```
unsigned mainmem = _bios_memsize();
```

_bios_printer

MSC6	MSC7	VC++	QC2.5	QC-WIN	TC2	TC++	BC++2	BC++3	ANSI	POSIX	UNIX V	DOS	QWIN	WIN	WINDLL
x	x	x	x	x			x	x				x		x	x

Note: The equivalent function in TC2, TC++, BC++2, and BC++3 is `biosprinter`.

Summary

```
#include <bios.h>

unsigned _bios_printer(
    unsigned task,  // Print service being requested.
    unsigned pnum,  // Printer port number, 0 = LPT1, 1 = LPT2.
    unsigned data); // Character being sent to printer.
```

Description

Communicates with the printer using INT 14H. The *task* argument specifies the service being requested. Use one of the following constants:

`_PRINTER_INIT`	Initialize the printer. Ignore the *data* argument.
`_PRINTER_STATUS`	Return printer's status. Ignore the *data* argument.
`_PRINTER_WRITE`	Send the low-order byte of *data* to the specified printer.

Returns

When the function completes successfully, the return value is an integer value whose low-order byte indicates the status of the printer. The meaning of the bits are as follows:

Bit	Meaning when bit is 1
0	Printer timed out.
1	Not used.
2	Not used.
3	I/O error.
4	Printer selected for output.
5	Printer out of paper.
6	Acknowledgement from printer.
7	Printer not busy. (If this bit is 0, the printer is busy.)

Sample Call

```
_bios_printer(_PRINTER_WRITE, 0, 'X');
```

See Also

`int86`, `int86x`

_bios_serialcom

MSC6	MSC7	VC++	QC2.5	QC-WIN	TC2	TC++	BC++2	BC++3	ANSI	POSIX	UNIX V	DOS	QWIN	WIN	WINDLL
X	X	X	X	X			X	X				X		X	X

Note: The equivalent function in TC2, TC++, BC++2, and BC++3 is `bioscom`.

Summary

```
#include <bios.h>

unsigned _bios_serialcom(
    unsigned task, // Service to be performed.
    unsigned port, // Serial port number (0 = COM1, 1 = COM2).
    unsigned data);// Character sent to serial port.
```

Description

Provides access to the PC's RS-232 serial port through the communications services offered by BIOS interrupt 14H. The serial port is identified by the port argument with a zero denoting COM1 and one indicating COM2. The `task` argument indicates the service being requested. Use one of the following constants as the `task` argument:

`_COM_INIT`	Initialize serial port using parameters encoded in the `data` argument.
`_COM_RECEIVE`	Read a character from the port—the low-order byte of the return value holds the character.
`_COM_SEND`	Send the low-order byte of data to the serial port.
`_COM_STATUS`	Returns the current status of the serial port.

When you initialize the serial port with `task` set to `_COM_INIT`, specify the data argument by the bitwise-OR of one constant from each of the four categories in the following list:

Category Constant	Meaning
Baud Rate	
`COM_100`	100 baud
`COM_150`	150 baud
`COM_300`	300 baud
`COM_600`	600 baud
`COM_1200`	1200 baud
`COM_2400`	2400 baud
`COM_4800`	4800 baud
`COM_9600`	9600 baud

continues

Category Constant	Meaning
Data Bits	
COM_CHR7	7 data bits
COM_CHR8	8 data bits
Parity	
COM_NOPARITY	No parity bit
COM_EVENPARITY	Even parity (parity bit makes total number of 1s even)
COM_ODDPARITY	Odd parity (parity bit makes total number of 1s odd)
Stop Bits	
COM_STOP1	1 stop bit
COM_STOP2	2 stop bits

To set COM1 to 1200 baud, 8 data bits, no parity, and 1 stop bit (this commonly is referred to as the *1200, 8, N, 1* setting), you would use:

```
_bios_serialcom(_COM_INIT, COM1, _COM_1200 ¦ _COM_CHR8 ¦
    _COM_NOPARITY ¦ _COM_STOP1);
```

Returns

When the function completes successfully, the return value is the character read from the port when the task is _COM_RECEIVE. For _COM_RECEIVE, the high-order bits of the returned value include the status of the receive operation. The meaning of the bits (with bit 15 denoting the most-significant bit) are as follows:

Bit	Meaning When Bit Is Set
8	Received data is ready.
9	Data overrun error occurred (a character was received before the last one was read).
10	Parity error occurred.

11	Framing error occurred (the end of a character was not recognized properly).
12	"Break" signal has been detected.
13	Register holding character to be transmitted is empty.
14	Transmit shift register is empty.
15	Serial port has timed out.

For `_COM_INIT` or `_COM_STATUS`, the low-order bits of the returned value contain the status of the serial port. The meaning these 8 bits (with bit 0 denoting the least-significant bit) are as follows:

Bit	Meaning When Bit Is Set
0	Change in "Clear to Send (CTS)" signal (see bit 4) occurred.
1	Change in "Data Set Ready (DSR)" signal (see bit 5) occurred.
2	Trailing-edge ring is indicated.
3	Change detected in quality of received signal.
4	Clear to Send (means modem is ready to receive data from the serial port).
5	Data Set Ready (means modem is connected to phone line).
6	Modem is receiving a "ring" voltage (means an incoming telephone call is detected).
7	Signal detected in the receive line.

Sample Call

```
    int c;
// Assume that COM1 is properly initialized.
//...
// Read a character from COM1.
    c = 0xff & _bios_serialcom(_COM_RECEIVE, COM1, 0);
```

See Also

`int86`, `int86x`

_bios_timeofday

MSC6	MSC7	VC++	QC2.5	QC-WIN	TC2	TC++	BC++2	BC++3	ANSI	POSIX	UNIX V	DOS	QWIN	WIN	WINDLL
X	X	X	X	X				X				X	X	X	X

Note: The equivalent function in TC2, TC++, BC++2, and BC++3 is `biostime`.

Summary

```
#include <bios.h>

unsigned _bios_timeofday(
    unsigned task,    // Timekeeping task to being requested.
    long     *ticks); // Get or set clock ticks from here.
```

Description

Gets or sets the current system clock count using the time-of-day services offered by BIOS INT 1AH. The *task* argument indicates the requested service; it can be one of the following constants:

`_TIME_GETCLOCK`	Copies current clock count into the long integer whose address you provide in the *ticks* argument. The clock count is incremented 18.2 times a second, so the resolution is approximately 55 milliseconds.
`_TIME_SETCLOCK`	Sets the current system clock count to the value you provide in the long integer whose address you provide in the *ticks* argument.

Returns

When *task* is `_TIME_GETCLOCK`, the return value is 1 if midnight has passed since the last get operation. If *task* is `_TIME_SETCLOCK`, the return value has no meaning.

Sample Call

```
    long clk_count;
//...
// Get current clock count:
    if(_bios_timeofday(_TIME_GETCLOCK, &clk_count))
    {
// Midnight has passed since the last time the clock was read.
// Adjust time as needed.
//...
    }
```

See Also

`_dos_gettime`, `_dos_settime`

_chain_intr

MSC6	MSC7	VC++	QC2.5	QC-WIN	TC2	TC++	BC++2	BC++3	ANSI	POSIX	UNIX V	DOS	QWIN	WIN	WINDLL
X	X	X	X	X				X				X			

Summary

```
#include <dos.h>

void _chain_intr(
    void (_ _interrupt _ _far *func)()); // Interrupt handler
```

Description

Jumps from one interrupt handler to another (identified by the `func` argument). You should call `_chain_intr` only from within C functions that are qualified with the `interrupt` keyword.

You can use `_chain_intr` to modify the behavior of an existing interrupt handler. Get the address of the existing handler using `_dos_getvect`. Install a new interrupt handler using `_dos_setvect`. In the new handler, after performing the tasks you want done, call `_chain_intr` to jump to the old interrupt handler—the one associated with the address you obtained with `_dos_getvect`.

Sample Call

```
    void (_ _interrupt _ _far *old_handler)();
// Assume old_handler is the address of an interrupt handler.
//...
    _chain_intr(old_handler);
```

See Also

`_dos_getvect`, `_dos_setvect`

_disable

MSC6	MSC7	VC++	QC2.5	QC-WIN	TC2	TC++	BC++2	BC++3	ANSI	POSIX	UNIX V	DOS	QWIN	WIN	WINDLL
X	X	X	X	X			X	X				X	X	X	X

Note: The equivalent function in TC2 and TC++ is `disable`.

Summary

```
#include <dos.h>

void _disable(void);
```

Description

Disables interrupts by executing the CLI instruction. Call `_disable` before you modify any interrupt vectors with `_dos_setvect`.

Sample Call

```
// Turn off interrupts.
    _disable();
```

See Also

`_enable`

_dos_allocmem

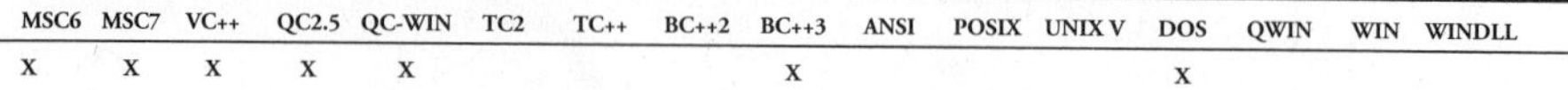

MSC6	MSC7	VC++	QC2.5	QC-WIN	TC2	TC++	BC++2	BC++3	ANSI	POSIX	UNIX V	DOS	QWIN	WIN	WINDLL
X	X	X	X	X				X				X			

Note: The equivalent function in TC2, TC++, BC++2, and BC++3 is `allocmem`.

Summary

```
#include <dos.h>

unsigned _dos_allocmem(
    unsigned numpara, // Number of paragraphs to allocate
                      //   (1 paragraph = 16 bytes).
    unsigned *seg);   // Segment address returned here.
```

Description

Allocates *numpara* paragraphs (1 paragraph = 16 bytes) of memory by calling DOS function 48H through INT 21H. The segment address of the first byte of the allocated block is returned in an unsigned integer variable. Provide the address of this variable in the *seg* argument. Note that the offset address always is zero. Call `_dos_freemem` later to release the memory.

Returns

0	Indicates that the allocation was successful.

An MS-DOS error code indicates failure. Also, sets `errno` to `ENOMEM`.

Sample Call

```
    unsigned block_seg;
// Allocate 512 bytes (= 32 paragraphs).
    _dos_allocmem(32, &block_seg);
```

See Also

`_dos_freemem`, `_dos_setblock`

_dos_close

MSC6	MSC7	VC++	QC2.5	QC-WIN	TC2	TC++	BC++2	BC++3	ANSI	POSIX	UNIX V	DOS	QWIN	WIN	WINDLL
X	X	X	X	X				X				X	X	X	X

Summary

```
#include <dos.h>

unsigned _dos_close(int handle); // Close this file
```

Description

Calls MS-DOS function 3EH to close the file, identified by `handle`, that was opened earlier by calling `_dos_creat`, `_dos_creatnew`, or `_dos_open`.

Returns

0	Indicates the file was successfully closed.

An MS-DOS error code indicates an error. In case of error, `_dos_close` also sets `errno` to `EBADF` to indicate a bad file handle.

Sample Call

```
    unsigned filehandle;
// Assume filehandle is a handle to an open file.
//...
    _dos_close(filehandle);
```

See Also

`_dos_creat`, `_dos_creatnew`, `_dos_open`

_dos_commit

MSC6	MSC7	VC++	QC2.5	QC-WIN	TC2	TC++	BC++2	BC++3	ANSI	POSIX	UNIX V	DOS	QWIN	WIN	WINDLL
	X	X		X								X	X	X	X

Summary

```
#include <dos.h>

unsigned _dos_commit(int handle);// Commit this file to disk
```

Description

Calls DOS function 68H, available in MS-DOS versions 3.3 and later, to flush to the disk the buffer associated with the file identified by `handle`.

Returns

0 Indicates that the disk was successfully flushed.

An MS-DOS error code indicates an error. In case of error, `_dos_commit` also sets `errno` to `EBADF`, indicating a bad file handle.

Sample Call

```
    unsigned filehandle;
// Assume filehandle is a handle to an open file.
//...
// Flush buffers to disk.
    _dos_commit(filehandle);
```

See Also

`_dos_close`, `_dos_creat`, `_dos_creatnew`, `_dos_open`

_dos_creat, _dos_creatnew

MSC6	MSC7	VC++	QC2.5	QC-WIN	TC2	TC++	BC++2	BC++3	ANSI	POSIX	UNIX V	DOS	QWIN	WIN	WINDLL
X	X	X	X	X				X				X	X	X	X

Summary

```
#include <dos.h>

unsigned _dos_creat(
    const char *pathname, // File to truncate or create.
    unsigned   attribute, // File's attributes.
    int        *fhandle); // Location where handle is returned.

unsigned _dos_creatnew(
    const char *pathname, // New file to create.
    unsigned   attribute, // File's attributes.
    int        *fhandle); // Location where handle is returned.
```

Description

The `_dos_creat` function calls MS-DOS function 3CH (through INT 21H) to create a new file or truncate an existing file to zero length. The `_dos_creatnew` function is similar, except that it calls MS-DOS function 5BH to create a new file—it does not truncate an existing file.

The *`pathname`* argument should be a full pathname for the file being created; the handle of the file is returned in an integer variable associated with the address you provide in the *`fhandle`* argument. The properties of the file—such as read-only or hidden—are controlled by the *`attribute`* argument. Use bitwise-OR combinations of the following constants as the *`attribute`*:

`_A_ARCH`	Mark file for archiving by MS-DOS BACKUP command.
`_A_HIDDEN`	Do not show file in the output of the DIR command.
`_A_NORMAL`	File is normal, without any read or write restrictions.
`_A_RDONLY`	File is read only.
`_A_SUBDIR`	File is a subdirectory.
`_A_SYSTEM`	Mark file as a system file (excluded from DOS DIR command).
`_A_VOLID`	Filename is a volume ID; can exist only in root directory.

Returns

0	Indicates the function successfully created or truncated the file in *pathname*.

A DOS error code indicates an error. These functions also set the global variable `errno` to one of the following error code:

`EACCES`	Access denied.
`EMFILE`	Too many files open.
`ENOENT`	Invalid `pathname`.

Additionally, `_dos_creatnew` sets `errno` to `EEXIST` if `pathname` refers to an existing file.

Sample Call

```
    int fhandle;
// Create a temporary data file.
    if(_dos_creat("c:\\tmp\\ftemp.001", _A_NORMAL, &fhandle) != 0)
    {
// Create failed.
//...
    }
```

See Also

`_dos_close`, `_dos_open`

_dos_findfirst, _dos_findnext

MSC6	MSC7	VC++	QC2.5	QC-WIN	TC2	TC++	BC++2	BC++3	ANSI	POSIX	UNIX V	DOS	QWIN	WIN	WINDLL
x	x	x	x	x			x	x				x	x	x	x

Note: The equivalent pair of functions in TC2, TC++, BC++2, and BC++3 are `findfirst` and `findnext`.

Summary

```
#include <dos.h>

unsigned _dos_findfirst(
    const char     *pathname,// Pathname of files to locate
                            //   (may contain wildcards * and ?).
    unsigned       attribute,// File attributes to match.
    struct _find_t *finfo);  // Results of search returned here.

unsigned _dos_findnext(
    struct _find_t *finfo);  // Results of search returned here.
```

Description

The `_dos_findfirst` function calls the MS-DOS function 4EH to find the first file whose name and attributes match the values specified in *`pathname`* and *`attribute`*, respectively. The specified pathname can contain wildcard characters (such as `*` and `?`) with the same meanings as in the DOS command line.

The `_dos_findnext` function follows `_dos_findfirst`. Once you have found a matching file with `_dos_findfirst`, you can call `_dos_findnext` repeatedly to invoke MS-DOS function 4FH and find any other instances of files whose names and attributes match the values used in the call to `_dos_findfirst`.

The *`attribute`* argument specifies the properties of the file—such as read-only or hidden—that you want matched. Use bitwise-OR combinations of the following constants as the *`attribute`*:

`A_ARCH`	File is marked for archiving by MS-DOS BACKUP command.
`A_HIDDEN`	File is not shown in the output of the DIR command.
`A_NORMAL`	File is normal, without any read or write restrictions.
`A_RDONLY`	File is read only.
`A_SUBDIR`	File is a subdirectory.
`A_SYSTEM`	File is a system file (excluded from DOS DIR command).
`A_VOLID`	Filename is a volume ID; can exist only in root directory.

The result of the search is returned in a `_find_t` structure associated with the address you provide in the *`finfo`* argument. The `_find_t` structure is defined in dos.h as follows:

```
struct _find_t
{
    char     reserved[21]; // Reserved.
    char     attrib;       // Attribute byte of the file.
    unsigned wr_time;      // Time of last write to file.
    unsigned wr_date;      // Date of last write to file.
    long     size;         // File's length in bytes.
    char     name[13];     // Filename (null-terminated).
};
```

Returns

0 Indicates that a match was found.

An MS-DOS error code indicates an error. In the event of an error, these functions set the global variable `errno` to `ENOENT` indicating that no matching filename was found.

Sample Call

```
    struct _find_t finfo;
// Find the volume ID of drive C:.
    if(_dos_findfirst("C:\\*.*", _A_VOLID, &finfo) == 0)
    {
        printf("Volume label of drive C: is %s\n",
               finfo.name);
    }
```

_dos_freemem

MSC6	MSC7	VC++	QC2.5	QC-WIN	TC2	TC++	BC++2	BC++3	ANSI	POSIX	UNIX V	DOS	QWIN	WIN	WINDLL
X	X	X	X	X				X				X	X	X	X

Note: The equivalent function in TC2, TC++, BC++2, and BC++3 is `freemem`.

Summary

```
#include <dos.h>

unsigned _dos_freemem(
    unsigned seg);// Segment address of block being released
```

Description

Calls MS-DOS function 49H to release a block of memory that was allocated by calling the `_dos_allocmem` function.

Returns

0	Indicates that memory was successfully freed.

An MS-DOS error code indicates an error. In the event of an error, this function sets the global variable `errno` to `ENOMEM`, indicating a bad segment address.

Sample Call

```
    unsigned seg1;
// Assume seg1 holds a segment address returned by _dos_allocmem.
//...
// Free that block of memory.
    _dos_freemem(seg1);
```

See Also

`_dos_allocmem`, `_dos_setblock`

_dos_getdate

MSC6	MSC7	VC++	QC2.5	QC-WIN	TC2	TC++	BC++2	BC++3	ANSI	POSIX	UNIX V	DOS	QWIN	WIN	WINDLL
X	X	X	X	X				X				X	X	X	X

Note: The equivalent function in TC2, TC++, BC++2, and BC++3 is `getdate`.

Summary

```
#include <dos.h>

void _dos_getdate(
    struct _dosdate_t *date);// Structure where date is returned
```

Description

Calls the MS-DOS function 2AH to get the current date. The components of the date—such as the year, month, and day—are returned in a `_dosdate_t` structure associated with the address you provide in the *date* argument. The `_dosdate_t` structure is defined in dos.h as follows:

```
struct _dosdate_t
{
    unsigned char day;        // Day of month (1-31).
    unsigned char month;      // Month (1-12).
    unsigned int  year;       // Year (1980-2099).
    unsigned char dayofweek; // Day of week (0-6, 0 = Sunday).
};
```

Sample Call

```
struct _dosdate_t date;

_dos_getdate(&date);
```

See Also

`_dos_gettime`, `_dos_setdate`

_dos_getdiskfree

MSC6	MSC7	VC++	QC2.5	QC-WIN	TC2	TC++	BC++2	BC++3	ANSI	POSIX	UNIX V	DOS	QWIN	WIN	WINDLL
x	x	x	x	x	x	x	x	x				x	x	x	x

Note: The equivalent function in TC2, TC++, BC++2, and BC++3 is `getdfree`.

Summary

```
#include <dos.h>

unsigned _dos_getdiskfree(
    unsigned            drive,   // Drive number: 0 = current
                                 //   default, 1 = A, 2 = B, and so on.
    struct _diskfree_t *dinfo);// Information returned here.
```

Description

Calls MS-DOS function 36H to obtain information about a specific disk drive. The information is stored in a `_diskfree_t` structure associated with the address you provide in the *`dinfo`* argument. The `_diskfree_t` structure is defined in dos.h as follows:

```
struct _diskfree_t
{
    unsigned total_clusters;
    unsigned avail_clusters;
    unsigned sectors_per_cluster;
    unsigned bytes_per_sector;
};
```

Returns

0	Indicates the information was obtained.
Nonzero	Indicates a failure. In the event of an error, sets `errno` to `EINVAL`, indicating that the drive number is invalid.

Sample Call

```
    unsigned long total_bytes, free_bytes, bytes_per_cluster;
    struct _diskfree_t dfinfo;

    if(_dos_getdiskfree (0, &dfinfo) !=0)
    {
        perror("_dos_getdiskfree");
        exit(0);
    }
// Compute disk spaces....
    bytes_per_cluster = dfinfo.sectors_per_cluster *
                        dfinfo.bytes_per_sector;

    total_bytes = dfinfo.total_clusters * bytes_per_cluster;

    free_bytes = dfinfo.avail_clusters * bytes_per_cluster;

    printf ("%ld bytes free out of %ld bytes of total bytes.\n",
           free_bytes, total_bytes);
```

See Also

_dos_getdrive, _dos_setdrive

_dos_getdrive

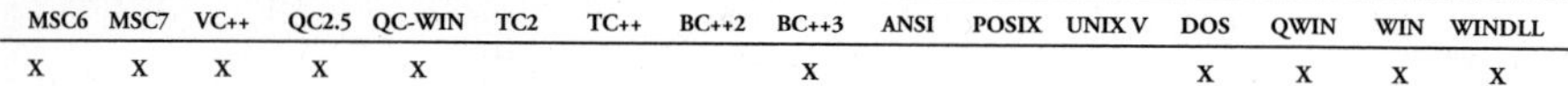

MSC6	MSC7	VC++	QC2.5	QC-WIN	TC2	TC++	BC++2	BC++3	ANSI	POSIX	UNIX V	DOS	QWIN	WIN	WINDLL
X	X	X	X	X				X				X	X	X	X

Note: The equivalent function in TC2, TC++, BC++2, and BC++3 is `getdisk`.

Summary

```
#include <dos.h>

void _dos_getdrive(
    unsigned *drive); // Drive number returned here
```

Description

Calls MS-DOS function 19H to get the current default drive number (1 = A, 2 = B, and so on). The drive number is placed in the unsigned integer whose address you provide in the *drive* argument.

Sample Call

```
    unsigned curdrive;
// Get current drive number.
    _dos_getdrive(&curdrive);
    printf("Current drive is %c\n", curdrive + 'A'- 1);
```

See Also

_dos_setdrive

_dos_getfileattr

MSC6	MSC7	VC++	QC2.5	QC-WIN	TC2	TC++	BC++2	BC++3	ANSI	POSIX	UNIX V	DOS	QWIN	WIN	WINDLL
X	X	X	X	X				X				X	X	X	X

Summary

```
#include <dos.h>

unsigned _dos_getfileattr(
    const char *pathname,    // Get this file's attributes.
    unsigned   *attribute); // Return attributes here.
```

Description

Calls MS-DOS function 43H to get the attributes of the file specified by *pathname* and store the attributes in the low-order byte of the unsigned integer associated with the address you provide in the *attribute* argument. The individual attributes are represented by the following constants defined in dos.h:

_A_ARCH	File is marked for archiving by MS-DOS BACKUP command.
_A_HIDDEN	File is not shown in the output of the DIR command.
_A_NORMAL	File is normal, without any read or write restrictions.
_A_RDONLY	File is read-only.
_A_SUBDIR	File is a subdirectory.
_A_SYSTEM	File is a system file (excluded from DOS DIR command).
_A_VOLID	Filename is a volume ID; can exist only in root directory.

Returns

0	Indicates that the file attributes of pathname were succesfully obtained and stored.

An MS-DOS error code indicates an error. Also sets the global variable `errno` to `ENOENT`, indicating that the *`pathname`* argument is invalid.

Sample Call

```
unsigned fattrib;
//...
if(_dos_getfileattr("c:\\tmp", &fattrib) == 0)
{
    if((fattrib & _A_SUBDIR) == _A_SUBDIR)
        printf("C:\\TMP is a subdirectory\n");
}
```

See Also

`_dos_setfileattr`

_dos_getftime

MSC6	MSC7	VC++	QC2.5	QC-WIN	TC2	TC++	BC++2	BC++3	ANSI	POSIX	UNIX V	DOS	QWIN	WIN	WINDLL
x	x	x	x	x				x				x	x	x	x

Note: The equivalent function in TC2, TC++, BC++2, and BC++3 is `getftime`.

Summary

```
#include <dos.h>

unsigned _dos_getftime(
    int      handle, // Handle to an open file.
    unsigned *date,  // Date in encoded form returned here.
    unsigned *time); // Time returned in encoded format.
```

Description

Calls MS-DOS function 57H to get the date and time of last modification of a file identified by *`handle`*. You must first open the file with a call to `_dos_creat`, `_dos_creatnew`, or `_dos_open`. The date and time information are returned in two unsigned integers associated with addresses you provide in the *`date`* and *`time`* arguments, respectively.

The encoding of the date is as follows:

Bits	Interpret as
0-4	Day of the month (1-31)
5-8	Month (1-12)
9-15	Years since 1980 (1992 is stored as 12)

The time is encoded as follows:

Bits	Interpret as
0-4	Number of 2 second increments (0-29)
5-10	Minutes (0-59)
11-15	Hours (0-23)

Returns

0 Indicates the function successfully obtained the date and time of the last modification of the file in *pathname*.

An MS-DOS error code indicates an error. Also, sets the global variable `errno` to `EBADF`, indicating an invalid file handle.

Sample Call

```
    int filehandle;
    unsigned date, time, day, month, year,
             hour, minute, second;
//...
// Get file's date and time stamp:
    _dos_getftime(filehandle, &date, &time);

// Decipher the returned date and time:
    second = 2 * (time & 0x1f);
    minute = (time >> 5) & 0x3f;
    hour = (time >> 11) & 0x1f;
    day = date & 0x1f;
    month = (date >> 5) & 0xf;

// NOTE: Year is relative to 1980, so we have to add 80:
    year = ((date >> 9) & 0x7f) + 80;
    printf("Last Mod Date: %d-%d-%d Time: %.2d:%.2d:%.2d\n",
            month, day, year, hour, minute, second);
```

See Also

`_dos_creat`, `_dos_creatnew`, `_dos_open`, `_dos_setftime`

_dos_gettime

MSC6	MSC7	VC++	QC2.5	QC-WIN	TC2	TC++	BC++2	BC++3	ANSI	POSIX	UNIX V	DOS	QWIN	WIN	WINDLL
X	X	X	X	X				X				X	X	X	X

Note: The equivalent function in TC2, TC++, BC++2, and BC++3 is `gettime`.

Summary

```
#include <dos.h>

void _dos_gettime(
    struct _dostime_t *time); // Structure where time is returned
```

Description

Calls the MS-DOS function 2CH to get the current time. The components of the time, such as hour, minute, and second, are returned in a `_dostime_t` structure whose address you provide in the *`time`* argument. The `_dostime_t` structure is defined in dos.h as follows:

```
struct _dostime_t
{
    unsigned char hour;     // Hour (0-23).
    unsigned char minute;   // Minutes (0-59).
    unsigned char second;   // Seconds (0-59).
    unsigned char hsecond; // Hundredth of a second (0-99).
};
```

Sample Call

```
struct _dostime_t time;

_dos_gettime(&time);
```

See Also

`_dos_getdate`, `_dos_settime`

_dos_getvect

MSC6	MSC7	VC++	QC2.5	QC-WIN	TC2	TC++	BC++2	BC++3	ANSI	POSIX	UNIX V	DOS	QWIN	WIN	WINDLL
X	X	X	X	X				X				X	X	X	X

Note: The equivalent function in TC2, TC++, BC++2, and BC++3 is `getvect`.

Summary

```
#include <dos.h>

// intnum is the interrupt number whose "vector"
// (address of interrupt-handling function) is being sought.

void (__interrupt __far *_dos_getvect(unsigned intnum))();
```

Description

Calls the MS-DOS function 35H (through an INT 21H) to get the current interrupt vector for the interrupt number *intnum*. The interrupt vector is the address of the function that is activated whenever the interrupt occurs. Use this function to retrieve and save an interrupt handler before installing a new interrupt handler with `_dos_setvect`.

Returns

The return value is a far pointer to the interrupt handler corresponding to interrupt number `intnum`.

Sample Call

```
#define TIMER_TICK_INTR 0x1c
//...
    void (interrupt far *old_handler)();

// Get and save current interrupt handler.
    old_handler = _dos_getvect(TIMER_TICK_INTR);
```

See Also

`_chain_intr`, `_dos_setvect`

_dos_keep

MSC6	MSC7	VC++	QC2.5	QC-WIN	TC2	TC++	BC++2	BC++3	ANSI	POSIX	UNIX V	DOS	QWIN	WIN	WINDLL
x	x	x	x	x				x				x			

Summary

```
#include <dos.h>

void _dos_keep(
    unsigned status, // Status code returned to parent process.
    unsigned npara); // Reserve this many paragraphs of memory.
                     //   for TSR program (1 paragraph = 16 bytes).
```

Description

Installs the current program as a terminate-and-stay-resident (TSR) program by using MS-DOS function 31H. The *npara* argument specifies the number of paragraphs of memory to be assigned to the TSR program. After making the program resident, `_dos_keep` exits the program, returning to the parent process.

Sample Call

```
    unsigned progsize;
// Assume progsize has size of program in paragraphs.
//...
// Make program TSR....

    _doskeep(0, progsize);
```

See Also

`_chain_intr`, `_dos_getvect`, `_dos_setvect`

_dos_open

MSC6	MSC7	VC++	QC2.5	QC-WIN	TC2	TC++	BC++2	BC++3	ANSI	POSIX	UNIX V	DOS	QWIN	WIN	WINDLL
X	X	X	X	X				X				X	X	X	X

Summary

```
#include <dos.h>          // For function prototype
#include <fcntl.h>
#include <share.h>

unsigned _dos_open(
    const char *pathname, // Pathname of file to be opened.
    unsigned   mode,      // Read-write and sharing flags.
    int        *handle);  // Handle returned here.
```

Description

Uses the MS-DOS function 3DH to open an existing file identified by *pathname*. The *mode* argument specifies the operations and level of sharing that are permitted for the open file. Specify the *mode* argument by bitwise-OR combination of one constant from each of the following three categories:

Category	Constant	Meaning
Read-Write	`_O_RDONLY`	File is read-only.
	`_O_WRONLY`	File is write-only.
	`_O_RDWR`	Both reading and writing are allowed.

Sharing	`_SH_COMPAT`	No other process can access the file.
	`_SH_DENYRW`	Others cannot read from or write to this file.
	`_SH_DENYWR`	Others cannot write to this file.
	`_SH_DENYRD`	Others cannot read from this file.
	`_SH_DENYNO`	File is completely shareable.
Inheritance	`_O_NOINHERIT`	File is not to be inherited by any child process.

Returns

0 Indicates the file was successfully opened.

An MS-DOS error code indicates an error. Also, sets `errno` to one of the following constants:

`EACCES`	Access denied.
`EINVAL`	Invalid sharing mode or access mode.
`EMFILE`	Too many files open.
`ENOENT`	Invalid pathname.

Sample Call

```
    unsigned filehandle;
//...
// Open the file using _dos_open:
    if (_dos_open("c:\\config.sys, _O_RDONLY, &filehandle) != 0)
    {
        perror("_dos_open");
        exit(0);
    }
```

See Also

`_dos_close`, `_dos_creat`, `_dos_creatnew`

_dos_read

MSC6	MSC7	VC++	QC2.5	QC-WIN	TC2	TC++	BC++2	BC++3	ANSI	POSIX	UNIX V	DOS	QWIN	WIN	WINDLL
x	x	x	x	x				x				x	x	x	x

Summary

```
#include <dos.h>

unsigned _dos_read(
    int          handle,     // Read from this file.
    void __far *buf,         // Read from file into this buffer.
    unsigned   readcount, // Number of bytes to read from file.
    unsigned   *numread); // Actual number of bytes read.
```

Description

Uses MS-DOS function 3FH to read `readcount` bytes from the open file identified by `handle` to the buffer `buf`. The actual number of bytes read is returned in the unsigned integer associated with the address you provide in the `numread` argument.

Returns

0 Indicates that `readcount` bytes were succesfully read.

An MS-DOS code indicates an error. Also, sets the global variable `errno` to `EBADF` or `EACCES`, indicating either a bad handle or a denied access.

Sample Call

```
    unsigned filehandle, numread;
    char buf[1024];
// Assume that filehandle contains a valid file handle.
//...
// Read 1024 bytes from the file:
    if (_dos_read(filehandle, buf, 1024, &numread) == 0)
    {
// Success....
    }
```

See Also

`_dos_close`, `_dos_open`, `_dos_write`

_dos_setblock

MSC6	MSC7	VC++	QC2.5	QC-WIN	TC2	TC++	BC++2	BC++3	ANSI	POSIX	UNIX V	DOS	QWIN	WIN	WINDLL
x	x	x	x	x				x				x			

Note: The equivalent function in TC2, TC++, BC++2, and BC++3 is `setblock`.

Summary

```
#include <dos.h>

unsigned _dos_setblock(
    unsigned newsize,     // Change size to this many paragraphs.
    unsigned seg,         // Segment address of allocated block.
    unsigned *maxavail); // Returns maximum number of
                          //   paragraphs available.
```

Description

Uses MS-DOS function 4AH to adjust the size of a block of memory previously allocated by `_dos_allocmem`. The *seg* argument is the segment address of the block of memory and *newsize* is the requested size of the block in paragraphs (1 paragraph = 16 bytes). If the function fails, it copies the maximum available number of segments into an unsigned integer variable whose address you provide in the `maxavail` argument.

Returns

0	Indicates that the size of the memory block was successfully adjusted.

An MS-DOS error code to indicates failure. Also, sets `errno` to `ENOMEM`, indicating that the segment address of the block is invalid.

Sample Call

```
    unsigned seg1, maxavail;
// Assume seg1 is the segment address of a block of memory
// allocated by _dos_allocmem.
//....
// Enlarge the block to 2,048 bytes (that's 128 paragraphs):
    if(_dos_setblock(seg1, 128, &maxavail) != 0)
    {
// Request failed. "maxavail" has maximum number of
// paragraphs available.
//...
    }
```

See Also

`_dos_allocmem`, `_dos_freemem`

_dos_setdate

MSC6	MSC7	VC++	QC2.5	QC-WIN	TC2	TC++	BC++2	BC++3	ANSI	POSIX	UNIX V	DOS	QWIN	WIN	WINDLL
X	X	X	X	X				X				X	X	X	X

Note: The equivalent function in TC2, TC++, BC++2, and BC++3 is `setdate`.

Summary

```
#include <dos.h>

unsigned _dos_setdate(
    struct _dosdate_t *date); // Structure with new date
```

Description

Calls the MS-DOS function 2BH to set the current system date. You must specify the components of the date—such as year, month, and day—in a `_dosdate_t` structure. Provide the address of the `_dosdate_t` structure in the *date* argument. The `_dosdate_t` structure is defined in dos.h as follows:

```
struct _dosdate_t
{
    unsigned char day;        // Day of month (1-31).
    unsigned char month;      // Month (1-12).
    unsigned int  year;       // Year (1980-2099).
    unsigned char dayofweek; // Day of week (0-6, 0 = Sunday).
};
```

Returns

0	Indicates that the date was successfully set.
Nonzero	Indicates an error. Also, sets the global variable `errno` to `EINVAL` to indicate an invalid date.

Sample Call

```
    struct _dosdate_t date;
// Assume that fields of date are initialized appropriately.
    _dos_setdate(&date);
```

See Also

`_dos_getdate`, `_dos_settime`

_dos_setdrive

MSC6	MSC7	VC++	QC2.5	QC-WIN	TC2	TC++	BC++2	BC++3	ANSI	POSIX	UNIX V	DOS	QWIN	WIN	WINDLL
x	x	x	x	x				x				x	x	x	x

Note: The equivalent function in TC2, TC++, BC++2, and BC++3 is `setdisk`.

Summary

```
#include <dos.h>

void _dos_setdrive(
    unsigned drive,        // Make this the new default drive
                           //   (1 = A, 2 = B, 3 = C, and so on).
    unsigned *numdrives); // Total number of drives returned here.
```

Description

Calls MS-DOS function 0EH to set the current default drive number (1 = A, 2 = B, and so on). The total number of drives in the system is placed in the unsigned integer associated with the address you provide in the *`numdrives`* argument.

Sample Call

```
    unsigned maxdrive;
// Set current drive to C: (drive number 3):
    _dos_setdrive(3, &maxdrive);
```

See Also

`_dos_getdrive`

_dos_setfileattr

MSC6	MSC7	VC++	QC2.5	QC-WIN	TC2	TC++	BC++2	BC++3	ANSI	POSIX	UNIX V	DOS	QWIN	WIN	WINDLL
x	x	x	x	x				x				x	x	x	x

Summary

```
#include <dos.h>

unsigned _dos_setfileattr(
    const char *pathname,  // Set this file's attributes.
    unsigned   attribute); // New attributes.
```

Description

Calls MS-DOS function 43H to set the attributes of the file specified by *`pathname`* to the value in the low-order byte of the unsigned *`attribute`* argument. The individual attributes are represented by the following constants defined in dos.h:

`A_ARCH`	File is marked for archiving by MS-DOS BACKUP command.
`A_HIDDEN`	File is not shown in the output of the DIR command.
`A_NORMAL`	File is normal, without any read or write restrictions.
`A_RDONLY`	File is read-only.
`A_SUBDIR`	File is a subdirectory.
`A_SYSTEM`	File is a system file (excluded from DOS DIR command).
`_A_VOLID`	Filename is a volume ID; can exist only in root directory.

Returns

0	Indicates the file attributes of the specified file were successfully set.

An MS-DOS error code indicates an error. Also, sets the global variable `errno` to `EACCES` or `ENOENT`, indicating access failure or invalid *`pathname`*, respectively.

Sample Call

```
//...
// Mark a file "hidden:"
if(_dos_getfileattr("c:\\forms.idx", _A_HIDDEN) != 0)
{
// Error setting attribute....
    perror("_dos_setfileattr");
//...
}
```

See Also

`_dos_getfileattr`

_dos_setftime

MSC6	MSC7	VC++	QC2.5	QC-WIN	TC2	TC++	BC++2	BC++3	ANSI	POSIX	UNIX V	DOS	QWIN	WIN	WINDLL
X	X	X	X	X				X				X	X	X	X

Note: The equivalent function in TC2, TC++, BC++2, and BC++3 is `setftime`.

Summary

```
#include <dos.h>

unsigned _dos_setftime(
    int      handle,// Handle to an open file.
    unsigned date,  // New date in encoded format.
    unsigned time); // New time in encoded format.
```

Description

Calls MS-DOS function 57H to set the date and time of last modification of a file identified by `handle`. You must first open the file with a call to `_dos_creat`, `_dos_creatnew`, or `_dos_open`. You must provide the date and time information in the unsigned integers *date* and *time*, respectively.

The encoding of the date is as follows:

Bits	Interpret as
0-4	Day of the month (1-31)
5-8	Month (1-12)
9-15	Years since 1980 (1992 is stored as 12)

The time is encoded as follows:

Bits	Interpret as
0-4	Number of 2 second increments (0-29)
5-10	Minutes (0-59)
11-15	Hours (0-23)

Returns

0	Indicates that the date and time of the last modification were successfully set.

An MS-DOS error code indicates an error. Also, sets the global variable `errno` to `EBADF`, indicating an invalid file handle.

Sample Call

```
    int filehandle;
    unsigned date, time;
//...
// Assume that date and time contain valid encoded
// date and time.
//...
// Set file's date and time stamp:
    _dos_setftime(filehandle, date, time);
```

See Also

_dos_creat, _dos_creatnew, _dos_getftime, _dos_open

_dos_settime

MSC6	MSC7	VC++	QC2.5	QC-WIN	TC2	TC++	BC++2	BC++3	ANSI	POSIX	UNIX V	DOS	QWIN	WIN	WINDLL
x	x	x	x	x				x				x	x	x	x

Note: The equivalent function in TC2, TC++, BC++2, and BC++3 is settime.

Summary

```
#include <dos.h>

unsigned _dos_settime(
    struct _dostime_t *time); // Structure in which time is returned
```

Description

Calls the MS-DOS function 2DH to set the current system time. You must specify the components of the time—such as hour, minute, and second—in a _dostime_t structure. Provide the address for the _dostime_t structure in the *time* argument. The _dostime_t structure is defined in dos.h as follows:

```
struct _dostime_t
{
    unsigned char hour;     // Hour (0-23).
    unsigned char minute;   // Minutes (0-59).
    unsigned char second;   // Seconds (0-59).
    unsigned char hsecond;  // Hundredth of a second (0-99).
};
```

Returns

0	Indicates the current system time was successfully set.
Nonzero	Indicates an error. Also, sets the global variable errno to EINVAL to indicate an invalid time.

Sample Call

```
    struct _dostime_t time;
// Assume that the fields of "time" are set up properly....
    _dos_settime(&time);
```

See Also

_dos_gettime, _dos_setdate

_dos_setvect

MSC6	MSC7	VC++	QC2.5	QC-WIN	TC2	TC++	BC++2	BC++3	ANSI	POSIX	UNIX V	DOS	QWIN	WIN	WINDLL
x	x	x	x	x				x				x			

Note: The equivalent function in TC2, TC++, BC++2, and BC++3 is `setvect`.

Summary

```
#include <dos.h>

void _dos_setvect(unsigned intnum,     // Set vector for this
                                       //   interrupt number.
   void (__cdecl __interrupt __far *func)()); // New interrupt
                                              //   handler.
```

Description

Uses MS-DOS function 25H to set the vector for interrupt number *`intnum`* to the function *`func`*. The interrupt vector for a specific interrupt number is the address of the function that is activated whenever the interrupt occurs. Disable all interrupt by calling `_disable` before installing a new interrupt vector using `_dos_setvect`. After you return from `_dos_setvect`, call `_enable` to reenable interrupts.

Sample Call

```
#define TIMER_TICK_INTR 0x1c
//...
void interrupt far tt_handler(void);

//...
// Install the new handler named tt_handler.
// Disable interrupts when changing handler.
// Assume old handler has been saved.

    _disable();
    _dos_setvect(TIMER_TICK_INTR, tt_handler);
    _enable();
```

See Also

`_disable`, `_dos_getvect`, `_enable`

_dos_write

MSC6	MSC7	VC++	QC2.5	QC-WIN	TC2	TC++	BC++2	BC++3	ANSI	POSIX	UNIX V	DOS	QWIN	WIN	WINDLL
X	X	X	X	X				X				X	X	X	X

Summary

```
#include <dos.h>

unsigned _dos_write(
    int          handle,          // Write to this file.
    const void __far *buf,        // Write from this buffer to file.
    unsigned     writecount,      // Number of bytes to write to file.
    unsigned     *numwrite);      // Actual number of bytes written.
```

Description

Uses MS-DOS function 40H to write `writecount` bytes from the buffer `buf` to the open file identified by `handle`. The actual number of bytes written to the file is returned in the unsigned integer associated with the address you provide in the `numwrite` argument.

Returns

0 Indicates that bytes were successfully written to the open file.

An MS-DOS code indicates an error. Also, sets the global variable `errno` to `EBADF` or `EACCES`, indicating either a bad handle or a denied access, respectively.

Sample Call

```
    int filehandle;
    unsigned numwrite;
    char buf[1024];
// Assume that filehandle contains a valid file handle.
//...
// Write buffer to file.
    if (_dos_write(filehandle, buf, 1024, &numwrite) == 0)
    {
// Success....
    }
```

See Also

`_dos_close`, `_dos_open`, `_dos_read`

_dosexterr

MSC6	MSC7	VC++	QC2.5	QC-WIN	TC2	TC++	BC++2	BC++3	ANSI	POSIX	UNIX V	DOS	QWIN	WIN	WINDLL
x	x	x	x	x	x	x	x	x				x	x	x	x

Note: The underscore prefix in the name `_dosexterr` was added in MSC7.

Summary

```
#include <dos.h>

int _dosexterr(
    struct _DOSERROR *ebuf); // Structure where information is
                             //   returned.
```

Description

Uses the MS-DOS function 59H (available in MS-DOS version 3.0 or later) to retrieve information about an error, and copies this information into the fields of a `_DOSERROR` structure whose address you provide as the *ebuf* argument. The `_DOSERROR` structure is declared in dos.h as follows:

```
struct _DOSERROR
{
    int  exterror; // Error code (contents of AX register).
    char errclass; // Error class (contents of BH).
    char action;   // Suggested action (contents of BL).
    char locus;    // Source of error (contents of CH).
};
```

Returns

When the function completes successfully, the return value is the value of the AX register after DOS function 59H is invoked—this is same as the `exterror` field of the `_DOSERROR` structure. If you call `_dosexterr` with a `NULL` argument, it simply returns the value in AX from DOS function 59H. Consult the System Call section of *The MS-DOS Encyclopedia* (Ray Duncan, Editor, Redmond, WA: Microsoft Press, 1988) for a list of the error codes.

Sample Call

```
   struct _DOSERROR err;
//...
// Assume an error has occurred. Get the detailed
// information about the cause of error.
   _dosexterr(&err);
```

_enable

MSC6	MSC7	VC++	QC2.5	QC-WIN	TC2	TC++	BC++2	BC++3	ANSI	POSIX	UNIX V	DOS	QWIN	WIN	WINDLL
x	x	x	x	x	x	x	x	x				x	x	x	x

Note: The equivalent function in TC2 and TC++ is `enable`.

Summary

```
#include <dos.h>

void _enable(void);
```

Description

Enables interrupts by executing the STI instruction.

Sample Call

```
// Turn on interrupts.
    _enable();
```

See Also

`_enable`

_FP_OFF, _FP_SEG

MSC6	MSC7	VC++	QC2.5	QC-WIN	TC2	TC++	BC++2	BC++3	ANSI	POSIX	UNIX V	DOS	QWIN	WIN	WINDLL
x	x	x	x	x	x	x	x	x				x	x	x	x

Note: The underscore prefix in the names `_FP_OFF` and `_FP_SEG` were added in MSC7.

Summary

```
#include <dos.h>

unsigned _FP_OFF(void _ _far *address);
unsigned _FP_SEG(void _ _far *address);
```

Description

Provides access to the segment and offset of a far address.

Returns

The `_FP_OFF` macro evaluates to the offset. The `_FP_SEG` macro evaluates to the segment address.

Sample Call

```
    static short dispbuf[25][80]; // Display buffer
//...
    void _ _far *address;
    unsigned bufseg, bufoff;
```

```
// Get segment and offset address of buffer:
    address = (void _ _far *)dispbuf;
    bufseg = _FP_SEG(address);
    bufoff = _FP_OFF(address);
```

See Also

_segread

_harderr, _hardresume, _hardretn

MSC6	MSC7	VC++	QC2.5	QC-WIN	TC2	TC++	BC++2	BC++3	ANSI	POSIX	UNIX V	DOS	QWIN	WIN	WINDLL
X	X	X	X	X				X				X			

Note: The equivalent functions in TC2 and TC++ are harderr, hardresume, and hardretn.

Summary

```
#include <dos.h>

// func is the critical-error handler (called on interrupt 24H).
void _harderr(void (_ _far *func)());

void _hardresume(int retcode); // Return code to DOS.

void _hardretn(int errcode);   // Error code to application.
```

Description

The _harderr function installs the function identified by *func* as the critical-error handler called by the interrupt handler for interrupt 24H. This interrupt occurs if there are hardware errors during I/O operations, such as trying to read from a floppy disk drive without any diskette in the drive. Use the _hardresume and _hardretn functions in the INT 24H handler to exit to DOS or return to the application, respectively.

The function specified by *func* should have the following prototype with three arguments:

```
void _ _far func(unsigned derror, unsigned errcode,
                 unsigned _ _far *dhdr);
```

where derror and errcode are the values of the AX and DI registers passed by MS-DOS to the INT 24H handler. The dhdr argument is a far pointer to a *device header* structure containing information about the device where the error occurred. The low-order byte of the errcode argument contains one of the following hexadecimal values:

0	Attempt to write to write-protected disk
1	Unknown source of error
2	Drive not ready
3	Unknown command
4	Data error indicated by failed Cyclic Redundancy Check (CRC)
5	Bad "drive request structure" length
6	Seek error
7	Unknown media type
8	Sector not found
9	Printer out of paper
A	Write fault
B	Read fault
C	General failure

If the error is on a disk drive, the low-order byte of `derror` has the drive number (0 = A, 1 = B, and so on), the highest order bit (bit 15) is set to zero, and the other bits have the following meanings:

Bit	Meaning
15	Disk error when bit is zero. Ignore rest of the bits if this bit is 1. When bit 15 is 1, the 16-bit word at offset 4 (`dhdr+4`) contains further information about the source of error.
14	UNUSED
13	If cleared (0), "Ignore" response is not allowed.
12	If cleared (0), "Retry" response is not allowed.
11	If cleared (0), "Fail" response is not allowed.
9-10	Indicates where error occurred: 00 MS-DOS 01 File Allocation Table (FAT)

	10 Directory
	11 Data area
8	Write error if set (1). Bit cleared if read error.

The *retcode* argument to `_hardresume` specifies what to do upon returning to DOS. Use one of the following constants, defined in dos.h, to specify an action:

`_HARDERR_ABORT`	Terminate the program by invoking INT 23H.
`_HARDERR_FAIL`	Fail the MS-DOS system call in progress (only in MS-DOS versions 3.1 and later).
`_HARDERR_IGNORE`	Ignore the error.
`_HARDERR_RETRY`	Retry the operation that caused the error.

Sample Call

```
    void __far crit_err(unsigned, unsigned, unsigned __far *);
// Set up critical-error handler:
    _harderr(crit_err);
```

See Also

`_chain_intr`, `_dos_getvect`, `_dos_setvect`

_int86, _int86x

MSC6	MSC7	VC++	QC2.5	QC-WIN	TC2	TC++	BC++2	BC++3	ANSI	POSIX	UNIX V	DOS	QWIN	WIN	WINDLL
x	x	x	x	x	x	x	x	x				x	x	x	x

Note: The underscore prefix in the names `_int86` and `_int86x` was added in MSC7.

Summary

```
#include <dos.h>

int _int86(
    int             intnum,      // Interrupt number.
    union _REGS    *inregs,      // Register values when called.
    union _REGS *outregs);       // Register values on return.

int _int86x(
    int             intnum,      // Interrupt number.
    union _REGS    *inregs,      // Register values when called.
    union _REGS    *outregs,     // Register values on return.
    struct _SREGS *segregs);     // Segment registers.
```

Description

Generates the software interrupt (using the INT instruction of the 80x86 processor) specified by interrupt number *intnum*. Before generating the software interrupt, _int86 or _int86x copies the register values from the _REGS union inregs to the corresponding processor registers. After returning from the interrupt handler, _int86 or _int86x copies the processor registers into the _REGS union identified by outregs.

Use _int86x if the interrupt handler modifies the DS register or requires input parameters in the segment registers DS and ES. The _int86x function is similar to _int86, except it also loads DS and ES from the segregs argument and restores DS before returning.

The _REGS and _SREGS unions are defined in dos.h (in terms of the _WORDREGS and _BYTEREGS structures) as follows:

```
// Word (16-bit) registers.

struct _WORDREGS
{
    unsigned int ax;
    unsigned int bx;
    unsigned int cx;
    unsigned int dx;
    unsigned int si;
    unsigned int di;
    unsigned int cflag;
};

// Byte registers.

struct _BYTEREGS
{
    unsigned char al, ah;
    unsigned char bl, bh;
    unsigned char cl, ch;
    unsigned char dl, dh;
};

union _REGS
{
    struct _WORDREGS x;
    struct _BYTEREGS h;
};
```

```
struct _SREGS
{
    unsigned int es;
    unsigned int cs;
    unsigned int ss;
    unsigned int ds;
};
```

Returns

When the function completes successfully, the return value is the contents of the AX register after the interrupt. In the event of an error, the `x.cflag` member of the returned register values (`_REGS` union) is nonzero.

Sample Call

```
#define BIOS_VIDEO 0x10
    int row, col;
    union REGS xr; // Use xr for both input/output

// Position cursor at specified row and column:
    xr.h.ah = 2;     // Function that sets cursor.
    xr.h.dh = row;   // Cursor location.
    xr.h.dl = col;
    xr.h.bh = 0;     // Assume video page 0.

// Invoke BIOS video services (interrupt 10H).
    int86(BIOS_VIDEO, &xr, &xr);
```

See Also

`_intdos`, `_intdosx`, `_segread`

_intdos, _intdosx

MSC6	MSC7	VC++	QC2.5	QC-WIN	TC2	TC++	BC++2	BC++3	ANSI	POSIX	UNIX V	DOS	QWIN	WIN	WINDLL
X	X	X	X	X	X	X	X	X				X	X	X	X

Note: The underscore prefix in the names `_intdos` and `_intdosx` were added in MSC7.

Summary

```
#include <dos.h>

int _intdos(
    union _REGS   *inregs,   // Register values when called.
    union _REGS   *outregs); // Register values on return.
```

```
int _intdosx(
    union _REGS   *inregs,   // Register values when called.
    union _REGS   *outregs,  // Register values on return.
    struct _SREGS *segregs); // Segment registers.
```

Description

The `_intdos` function copies the register values from *inregs* into the processor registers and executes an INT 21H function to access MS-DOS system functions. Before returning, `_intdos` copies the processor registers into the `_REGS` union identified by *outregs*. The task performed by MS-DOS depends on the function number you specify in the AH register (through the *inregs* argument).

The `_intdosx` function is similar to `_intdos`, except that `_intdosx` also loads DS and ES from the *segregs* argument and restores DS before returning. If you need to use the current segment register values in a call to `_intdosx`, use the `_segread` function to retrieve these values.

Consult the reference entry of `_int86` and `_int86x` for the declaration of the `_REGS` and `_SREGS` data types.

Returns

When the function completes successfully, the return value is the contents of the AX register after the INT 21H. In the event of an error, the `x.cflag` member of the returned register values (`_REGS` union) is nonzero.

Sample Call

```
#define DOS_GETDRIVE 0x19    // Get default drive number.
    union _REGS xr;
//...
// Set up input registers.
    xr.h.ah = DOS_GETDRIVE; // DOS function number.
    intdos(&xr, &xr);
    printf("Current drive: %c\n", xr.h.al+65);
```

See Also

`bdos`, `int86`, `int86x`, `_segread`

_segread

MSC6	MSC7	VC++	QC2.5	QC-WIN	TC2	TC++	BC++2	BC++3	ANSI	POSIX	UNIX V	DOS	QWIN	WIN	WINDLL
X	X	X	X	X	X	X	X	X				X	X	X	X

Note: The underscore prefix in the name `_segread` was added in MSC7.

Summary

```
#include <dos.h>

void _segread(
    struct _SREGS *sregs); // Segment registers returned here.
```

Description

Copies the current values of the segment registers into the _SREGS structure whose address you provide as the *sregs* argument. The _SREGS structure is defined in dos.h as follows:

```
struct _SREGS
{
    unsigned int es;
    unsigned int cs;
    unsigned int ss;
    unsigned int ds;
};
```

Sample Call

```
    struct _SREGS sreg;
//...
    _segread(&sreg);
```

See Also

_int86x, _intdosx

Bibliography

C++ and object-oriented programming (OOP) are steadily gaining popularity, and the number of books and articles on these topics reflect this trend. Here is a list of resources that will help you learn more about C++ and object-oriented programming. The list, organized by category, also includes a number of references for other topics such as Microsoft Windows programming and ANSI Standard C. This bibliography is by no means exhaustive; it's just a sample of the numerous books and journals that cover C++ and object-oriented programming.

C++ and Object-Oriented Programming

Most books on C++ cover object-oriented programming. One recent book, *Data Abstractions and Object-Oriented Programming in C++*, by Keith Gorlen, Sanford Orlow, and Perry Plexico, does a good job of teaching data abstraction and OOP using C++. Much of the book focuses on showing how to exploit reusable software components from class libraries such as the NIH Class Library developed by the authors.

For an official description of C++, you want a copy of *The C++ Programming Language, Second Edition,* by Bjarne Stroustrup, the inventor of C++. Another source of official description of C++ is *The Annotated C++ Reference Manual* (often referred to as the *ARM*), by Margaret Ellis and Bjarne Stroustrup. The annotations in this book can help you understand the motivation behind the choices made during the design and improvement of the C++ programming language.

The book by Mark Mullin, *Object-Oriented Program Design with Examples in C++*, is worth noting because it covers object-oriented techniques with a single, large-scale program example in C++. Jerry Smith's book, *Reusability & Software Construction: C & C++*, is another that covers the design and implementation of a single program; in this case, a window-based text editor.

There are a host of other books by authors such as Lippman, Pohl, Dewhurst, Swan, and Weiskamp that cover the C++ programming language. Some offer insights into OOP, but focus mainly on teaching the C++ language without much emphasis on object orientation.

To keep up with recent developments on how others are using C++ and how the ANSI standard for C++ is progressing, you should consult journals such as *The C++ Report*, published by SIGS Publications, New York, NY, and *The C++ Journal*, a quarterly publication of The C++ Journal, Inc. of Port Washington, NY.

Dewhurst, Stephen C. and Kathy T. Stark. *Programming in C++*, Prentice Hall, Englewood Cliffs, NJ, 1989, 239 pages.

Ellis, Margaret A. and Bjarne Stroustrup. *The Annotated C++ Reference Manual*, Addison-Wesley Publishing Company, Reading, MA, 1990, 457 pages.

Gorlen, Keith E., Sanford M. Orlow, and Perry S. Plexico. *Data Abstractions and Object-Oriented Programming in C++*, John Wiley & Sons, Ltd., Chichester, West Sussex, England, 1990, 424 pages.

Lippman, Stanley B. *C++ Primer,* Second Edition, Addison-Wesley, Reading, MA, 1991, 625 pages.

Mullin, Mark. *Object-Oriented Program Design with Examples in C++*, Addison-Wesley, Reading, MA, 1989, 329 pages.

Pohl, Ira. *C++ for C Programmers*, The Benjamin/Cummings Publishing Company, Redwood City, CA, 1989, 256 pages.

Smith, Jerry D. *Reusability & Software Construction: C & C++*, John Wiley & Sons, Inc., New York, NY, 1990, 559 pages.

Stroustrup, Bjarne. *The C++ Programming Language,* Second Edition, Addison-Wesley Publishing Company, Reading, MA, 1991, 680 pages.

Swan, Tom. *Learning C++*, Sams Publishing, Carmel, IN, 1992, 791 pages.

Weiskamp, Keith and Bryan Flamig. *The Complete C++ Primer*, Academic Press, Inc., San Diego, CA, 1990, 541 pages.

Object-Oriented Design and Programming

As a topic, object-oriented programming is still in the evolutionary stage—its very definition is a subject of debate among experts. Still, the basic concepts of OOP have been covered in many books and journal articles. Included in this section of the bibliography are articles on Microsoft Foundation Classes.

Bertrand Meyer's book, *Object-Oriented Software Construction,* has a good description of the object-oriented approach. For a high-level overview of object-oriented concepts, terminology, and software, consult the recent books by Setrag Khosafian and Razmik Abnous (*Object Orientation: Concepts, Languages, Databases, User Interfaces*) and by Ann Winblad, Samuel Edwards, and David King (*Object Orientation: Concepts, Languages, Databases, User Interfaces*).

Other good sources of information on recent developments in OOP include the proceedings of the annual *Object-Oriented Programming Systems, Languages, and Applications* (OOPSLA) conference sponsored by the Association for Computing Machinery and the *Journal of Object-Oriented Programming* published bimonthly by SIGS Publications, Inc. of New York, NY.

Object-Oriented Analysis, Design, and Programming

Object-Oriented Programming (OOP) refers to the implementation of programs using objects, preferably in an object-oriented programming language such as C++. Although this book focuses on OOP using C++, the analysis and design phases of the software development process are even more important than the language used. *Object-Oriented Analysis (OOA)* refers to methods of specifying the requirements of the software in terms of real-world objects, their behavior, and their interactions.

> Object-Oriented Design (OOD), on the other hand, turns the software requirements into specifications for objects and derives class hierarchies from which the objects can be created. OOD methods usually use a diagramming notation to represent the class hierarchy and to express the interaction among objects.

Despite a recent surge in books and articles on object-oriented design, this topic remains an elusive one to grasp. Because no single approach works for all problems, most descriptions of object-oriented design are, of necessity, a collage of case studies and extrapolations based on the experience of programmers in the field. You have to work through many examples before you can arrive at a set of guidelines for the software design approach that best suits a specific problem. Here is a selection of reading material to help you achieve that goal. Although this is a short list, each of these sources will, in turn, provide you with numerous other references on object-oriented design.

Grady Booch first described object-oriented design in his 1983 book on the Ada programming language. In his 1990 book, *Software Engineering with Ada,* he presents a more refined description of the incremental and iterative nature of object-oriented software design.

Brad Cox, the originator of the *Objective-C* language, describes his view of object-oriented programming in his 1986 book, *Object-Oriented Programming—An Evolutionary Approach.* He promotes the idea of packaging software in modular units which he calls *Software-ICs* (software integrated circuits).

Bertrand Meyer, author of an object-oriented language named *Eiffel,* describes object-oriented design as supported by the Eiffel language in his book, *Object-Oriented Software Construction.* One of his ideas is the notion of *programming by contract*—the idea that for correct operation, a software module and its consumers must, in some way, formally express the rights and obligations of each side.

The recent book by Rebecca Wirfs-Brock, Brian Wilkerson, and Lauren Wiener, *Designing Object-Oriented Software,* presents a detailed example of object-oriented design using a "responsibility-driven" approach. The idea is to identify the classes, their responsibilities, and their collaborators. In this approach, you lay out the design on a set of index cards, called CRC cards, where CRC stands for Class, Responsibility, and Collaboration. This seems to be a promising step-by-step approach to object-oriented design of software.

The September 1990 issue of *Communications of the ACM*—the flagship magazine of the Association for Computing Machinery—is a special issue on object-oriented design. Consult this issue for a good assortment of articles on the object-oriented approach. In another article in the May 1989 issue of this journal, "An Object-Oriented Requirements Specification Method," Sidney Bailin presents a method for specifying the requirements for object-oriented software.

Notational schemes are another important tool because they let you express your design in a concise, yet descriptive manner. Although Booch, Meyer, and Cox have used some form of notation in their books, there is no universally accepted convention. For a sampling of some proposed notational schemes, see the recent journal articles.

Another interesting idea is to mix conventional function-oriented design with object-oriented concepts in a hybrid design strategy. Larry Constantine, one of the pioneers of structural techniques, discusses such an approach in a *Computer Language* article called "Objects, Functions, and Program Extensibility."

For a description of SmallTalk-80's Model-View-Controller (MVC) architecture, see Adele Goldberg's recent article in *Dr. Dobb's Journal*, "Information Models, Views, and Controllers." For another good discussion of the MVC model as well as some other examples of practical applications of object-oriented methods, see the compendium of essays edited by Lewis Pinson and Richard Wiener, *Applications of Object-Oriented Programming*.

Beck and Cunningham's article in *Proceedings of OOPSLA 1989*, "A Laboratory for Teaching Object-Oriented Thinking," describes the use of index cards to record initial class designs. This tool is used by Wirfs-Brock and colleagues in their responsibility-driven design approach.

Bailin, Sidney. "An Object-Oriented Requirements Specification Method," *Communications of the ACM*, Vol. 32, No. 5, May 1989, pages 608-623.

Beck, K. and H. Cunningham. "A Laboratory for Teaching Object-Oriented Thinking," *Proceedings of OOPSLA 1989*, New Orleans, LA, October 1989, pages 1-6.

Booch, Grady. *Object-Oriented Design with Applications*, The Benjamin/Cummings Publishing Company, Redwood City, CA, 1991, 600 pages.

Booch, Grady. *Software Engineering with Ada*, The Benjamin/Cummings Publishing Company, Redwood City, CA, 1991, 600 pages.

Communications of the ACM, Special Issue on Object-Oriented Design, Volume 33, No. 9, September 1990, pages 38-159.

Constantine, Larry L. "Objects, Functions, and Program Extensibility," *Computer Language*, Vol. 7, No. 1, January 1990, pages 34-54.

Cox, Brad. *Object-Oriented Programming—An Evolutionary Approach*, Addison-Wesley Publishing Company, Reading, MA, 1986, 287 pages.

Goldberg, Adele. "Information Models, Views, and Controllers," *Dr. Dobb's Journal*, July 1990, pages 54-61.

Khosafian, Setrag and Razmik Abnous. *Object Orientation: Concepts, Languages, Databases, User Interfaces*, John Wiley & Sons, Inc., New York, NY, 1990, 448 pages.

Meyer, Bertrand. *Object-Oriented Software Construction*, Prentice Hall International (U.K.) Ltd., Hertfordshire, Great Britain, 1988, 552 pages.

Pinson, Lewis J. and Richard S. Wiener, Editors. *Applications of Object-Oriented Programming*, Addison-Wesley Publishing Company, Reading, MA, 222 pages.

Winblad, Ann L., Samuel D. Edwards, and David R. King. *Object-Oriented Software*, Addison-Wesley Publishing Company, Reading, MA, 1990, 309 pages.

Wirfs-Brock, Rebecca, Brian Wilkerson, and Lauren Wiener. *Designing Object-Oriented Software*, Prentice Hall, Englewood Cliffs, NJ, 1990, 360 pages.

Yam, Michael. "Examining MFC 2.0", *Dr. Dobb's Journal*, Volume 18, Issue 6, June 1993, Pages 114-119.

ANSI Standard C

There are many books on C and all recent books cover the ANSI standard for C. If you are familiar with C as defined in Kernighan and Ritchie's original book, *The C Programming Language, First Edition*, and want to learn about the changes wrought by the ANSI standardization of C, you can get the second edition of Kernighan and Ritchie's book. Other good references to ANSI Standard C are the books by authors such as Plauger (*Standard C*) and Kochan (*Programming in ANSI C*).

Hipson, Peter D. *Advanced C*, Sams Publishing, Carmel, IN, 1992, 777 pages.

Kernighan, Brian W. and Dennis M. Ritchie. *The C Programming Language*, First Edition, Prentice Hall, Inc., Englewood-Cliffs, NJ, 1978, 228 pages.

Kernighan , Brian W. and Dennis M. Ritchie. *The C Programming Language*, Second Edition, Prentice Hall, Inc., Englewood-Cliffs, NJ, 1988, 261 pages.

Kochan, Stephen G. *Programming in ANSI C*, Hayden Books, Carmel, IN, 1988, 450 pages.

Plauger, P.J. and Jim Brodie. *Standard C*, Microsoft Press, Redmond, WA, 1989, 217 pages.

Microsoft C/C++ and Windows Programming

Like C++, Microsoft Windows programming is a favorite topic of computer book authors. Among the available books, the books by Myers and Doner, Conger, and Schulman are very useful.

For Windows programming with the Microsoft Foundation Class library, you will find useful the recent book by Clement Shammas, *Windows Programmer's Guide to Microsoft Foundation Class Library*. Microsoft provides several volumes of detailed documentation on the Microsoft Foundation Class Library and the Microsoft Windows Software Development Kit. Because of their sheer size and detailed coverage, Microsoft's manuals remain the best source of detailed information on the Microsoft Foundation Class Library and their use in Windows application.

Conger, James L. *The Waite Group's Windows API Bible*, Waite Group Press, Mill Valley, CA, 1992, 1,030 pages.

Microsoft Corporation, *Microsoft C/C++ Class Libraries Reference*, 1991, 1,034 pages.

Microsoft Corporation, *Microsoft C/C++ Run-Time Library Reference*, 1991, 937 pages.

Microsoft Corporation, *Programmer's Reference, Volume 1: Overview*, Microsoft Windows Software Development Kit, 1992, 520 pages.

Microsoft Corporation, *Programmer's Reference, Volume 2: Functions*, Microsoft Windows Software Development Kit, 1992, 1,007 pages.

Microsoft Corporation, *Programmer's Reference, Volume 3: Message, Structures, and Macros*, Microsoft Windows Software Development Kit, 1992, 612 pages.

Myers, Brian and Chris Doner. *Programmer's Introduction to Windows 3.1*, SYBEX, Alameda, CA, 1,035 pages.

Schulman, Andrew, David Maxey, and Matt Pietrek. *Undocumented Windows*, Addison-Wesley, Reading, MA, 1992, 732 pages.

Shammas, Namir Clement. *Windows Programmer's Guide to Microsoft Foundation Class Library*, Sams Publishing, Carmel, IN, 1992, 700 pages.

INDEX

Symbols

A

C

D

E

F

G

H

I

J

K

L

M

N

O

P

Q

R

S

T

U

V

W

X-Y

Z

Book ISBN 0-672-30370-1

Installing the Floppy Disk

The disk contains complete source code and resource files from the book—more than 30 Visual C++ programs. The files on the disk must be installed to your hard drive before you use them. The installation program runs from within Windows.

To install the files on the disk, you'll need at least 4M of free space on your hard drive.

1. From File Manager or Program Manager, choose **F**ile **R**un from the menu.
2. Type ***<drive>*INSTALL** and press Enter. *<drive>* is the letter of the drive that contains the installation disk. For example, if the disk is in drive B:, type **B:INSTALL** and press Enter.

Follow the on-screen instructions in the install program. The files will be installed to a directory named \VCPPDG, unless you changed this name during the install program.

When the installation is complete, the file FILES.TXT will be displayed for you to read. This file contains information on the files and programs that were installed.